ADVERTISING
MANAGEMENT

Text and Cases

ADVERTISING
MANAGEMENT
Text and Cases

By NEIL H. BORDEN, M.B.A.

Professor of Marketing

and MARTIN V. MARSHALL, D.C.S.

Associate Professor of Business Administration

BOTH OF THE GRADUATE SCHOOL OF BUSINESS
ADMINISTRATION, HARVARD UNIVERSITY

REVISED EDITION

1959

RICHARD D. IRWIN, INC.

HOMEWOOD, ILLINOIS

REVISED EDITION

First Printing, September, 1959
Second Printing, February, 1962
Third Printing, February, 1964
Fourth Printing, May, 1965
Fifth Printing, March, 1966
Sixth Printing, January, 1967
Seventh Printing, July, 1967
Eighth Printing, August, 1969

Library of Congress Catalogue Card No. 59–13746

PRINTED IN THE UNITED STATES OF AMERICA

to
M.E.C.M. and V.D.M.

PREFACE

This book is a successor to three editions of *Problems in Advertising*[1] and one edition of *Advertising: Text and Cases*,[2] all being selections of cases taken from a larger group of cases used in the advertising courses of the Harvard Business School. The principal purpose of this book, like that of each of its predecessors, is to provide a selection of cases to those who wish to study advertising from the viewpoint of top management and by the case method, that is, by group discussion of situations which have confronted businessmen.

This book differs from *Advertising: Text and Cases* in three respects. First, all of the cases are either new or are revised, except for two (Millers' National Federation and Etna Company, Inc.). Second, substantial changes have been made in the chapters of declaratory material, particularly in the chapters dealing with the concept of the marketing mix and with the building of advertising programs. Third, a chapter of declaratory material and cases regarding the creation of advertisements have been added. Of the 80 cases in the book, 67 have been collected under the direction of Professor Marshall. He is also chiefly responsible for revisions in the declaratory material and changes in the organization of the book.

Although the structural outline of the book presents one sequential order of declaratory material and cases which we have found to be pedagogically effective, we believe that the outline can and should be rearranged to meet the specific course objectives of individual instructors and the needs of their students. As the outline stands, it provides material adequate for two semesters of advertising course work, whereas most instructors will probably desire to use the book in a one-semester course. Further, the outline employed and areas for discussion in individual cases will depend greatly upon the backgrounds which students bring to a course—upon whether they have had course work in introductory marketing, marketing management, sales management, retailing, marketing research, etc. Accordingly, a few comments about the structure of the book may be helpful to those who wish to make modifications in the outline.

Section I consists of three chapters of declaratory material regarding the use of advertising by business. These chapters stress that advertising cannot be considered as a thing apart from the rest of the business operation. They impress upon students that advertising is a selling tool whose

---

[1] Neil H. Borden, *Problems in Advertising* (New York: McGraw-Hill Book Co., Inc., 1927, 1932, 1937).

[2] Neil H. Borden, *Advertising: Text and Cases* (Homewood, Ill.: Richard D. Irwin, Inc., 1949).

effective and profitable use is inextricably intertwined with an understanding of the business and marketing operation of which it is but one
part. In having students read this introductory material, instructors may
wish also to include Chapter 6, which is an amplification of the concept
of the marketing mix discussed in Chapter 2.

In our own course work, we have always found it useful to focus the
attention of students immediately upon the principal forces in the market place which determine the basic level of demand for a class of product.
Accordingly, Section II presents cases which involve the use of advertising
by associations of manufacturers to increase the total and per capita demand for a class of product. Discussion of such cases allows students to
develop an understanding of these primary forces and preliminary views
regarding the potentialities and limitations of advertising's effectiveness in
stimulating demand.

Section III contains cases which enable students to build a familiarity
with different patterns of marketing strategy and the varying roles of
advertising therein. Whether to employ advertising, and, if so, how, are
questions which must be answered by analyzing the forces of the market
place and the specific elements of the marketing operation of the individual enterprise. The particular role of advertising in a business depends
upon many factors: the buying behavior of consumers, the importance
and influence of the trade, the activities of competitors, the product
(or service) being sold, the prices and margins obtainable, the brand
policy followed, the channels of distribution utilized, the size of the firm,
etc. In short, the use of advertising depends upon the marketing strategy
which management decides will be most profitable in the light of the
specific conditions under which it operates. Hence, the cases in this
section are designed to permit students to consider the role, if any, of
advertising in a variety of situations involving different marketing conditions.

The latter half of the book, Section IV, is designed to give students an
opportunity to consider at length the principal problems involved in the
building, implementing, and evaluating of advertising programs. Because
detailed discussion of these problem areas would require a significant addition to the number of pages in this book, we have briefly sketched a
conceptual frame of reference in Chapters 10 and 12, and have thereafter
relied upon cases and reference to lead students into more detailed consideration of copy, media, and the various means of evaluating advertising. In our own use of these cases, we have sought to make extensive use
of current literature which deals in depth with the numerous issues usually
involved in the building and evaluating of advertising programs.

In addition, we have found it highly useful to employ four types of
written assignments. First, we have asked students to become "specialists"
in an advertising medium by preparing an analysis of the uses of a given
medium together with significant facts about it. Then, in case discussions,

individual students have been expected to bring into the discussions the benefit of their "specialized" knowledge of a medium, if it is called for in the discussion. Second, we have utilized a similar assignment with respect to having students investigate methods of evaluating advertisements and advertising, such as the use of consumer juries, Starch readership data, and local area sales tests. Third, all students have been asked to prepare advertisements for a number of the cases in Chapter 12, in order that they have an appreciation of the problems of creating effective advertisements. Finally, all students have, as members of groups, undertaken semester projects involving field work with active business organizations, the objective of these projects being to prepare an annual marketing and advertising program for the organization. These projects have proved to be effective in integrating the cases included in Section IV.

The concluding section, Section V, focuses the attention of students upon management's use of and relationship with advertising agencies. It should be noted also that many of the cases throughout the book allow further consideration of agency-client relationships.

In the preparation of this book, we are greatly indebted to many people.

Hundreds of business executives have given generously of their time in order that we and our associates could obtain information for cases. They have not only given information, but have read and reread rough drafts, have offered useful suggestions regarding cases, and have taught us much about advertising. We cannot adequately express our true gratefulness for their help.

The collection of cases is an expensive business. The cases in this book were financed through the research budget of the Harvard Business School, a budget supported by far-sighted businessmen who have a real interest in the continuing education of young men and women in business administration. Although we cannot give individual credit here, we are deeply grateful to those people who have for many years supported the case collection activities of the School.

Those of us on the teaching staff of the Harvard Business School have been fortunate, too, to have cases collected at School expense made available to us for publication in case collections. For this policy, we thank our Dean, Stanley F. Teele, and the Harvard University Administration, which owns all copyrights on the cases in this book under the title of the President and Fellows of Harvard College. We are particularly grateful to Dean Teele for arranging for Professor Marshall to be relieved of advertising teaching assignments in the spring terms of 1957–58 and 1958–59, in order that he might devote full time to the development of the School's advertising courses, from which effort came many of the cases in this book; and to Professor Joseph W. Newman, who kindly took on the teaching of the advertising courses for Professor Marshall.

Acknowledgment is also due to the many young men who have, over the last few years, collected information for and prepared many of the cases in this book. Credit for authorship by these men is given as a footnote to each case.

Finally, we thank the numerous young women who have typed and retyped manuscripts for cases in this book. They are Barbara Thresher, Helen Ford, Priscilla Langley, Martha Branneman, Joan Cole, and Winifred Barnard. Particular thanks are due Miss Barnard who looked after the many details of preparing the last drafts of the cases and who typed the declaratory chapters for this book.

Neil H. Borden
Martin V. Marshall

Fryeburg, Maine
August 1959

TABLE OF CONTENTS

SECTION I

BACKGROUND MATERIAL ON THE USE OF ADVERTISING BY BUSINESS

SECTION II

THE USE OF ADVERTISING TO STIMULATE PRIMARY DEMAND

SECTION III

THE USE OF ADVERTISING TO STIMULATE SELECTIVE DEMAND

SECTION IV

THE BUILDING OF ADVERTISING PROGRAMS

Section I

BACKGROUND MATERIAL ON THE USE OF ADVERTISING BY BUSINESS

An Introductory Note

The objective of this section is to give the reader a broad perspective regarding the use of advertising by business which will be useful in the analysis of all of the cases in this book. The section consists of three chapters of declaratory material. This material does not seek to describe how or discuss why various kinds of businesses should employ different kinds and forms of advertising. Rather, its principal purposes are to indicate the factors which are involved in the use of advertising by business and to suggest the main elements which business management considers when making decisions regarding the use of advertising.

Chapter 1

∿∿∿∿∿∿∿∿∿∿∿∿∿∿∿∿∿∿∿∿∿∿∿

ADVERTISING DEFINED AND CLASSIFIED

What is advertising? Advertising consists of those activities by which visual or oral messages are addressed to selected publics for the purpose of informing and influencing them to buy products or services, or to act or to be inclined favorably toward ideas, persons, trade-marks, or institutions featured. As contrasted with publicity and other forms of propaganda, advertising messages are identified with the advertiser either by signature or oral statement. Further, advertising is a commercial transaction involving pay to publishers, broadcasters, or others whose media are employed.

Activities Included in Advertising

Just what activities shall be labeled "advertising" is often a moot question, because certain things are almost universally accepted as advertising, while arbitrary decision determines the inclusion or exclusion of other things. Clearly, advertising includes the following forms of messages: the messages carried in newspapers and magazines, on outdoor boards, on streetcar, bus, and train cards and posters, in radio and television broadcasts, and in circulars of all kinds, whether distributed by mail, by person, through tradesmen, or by inserts in packages; dealer-help materials; window display and counter display materials and efforts; store signs; house organs when directed to dealers and consumers; motion pictures used for advertising; and novelties bearing advertising messages or signature of the advertiser.

Labels, tags, and other literature accompanying merchandise are also deemed advertising, because they may reasonably be said to fall within the definition of advertising given above. Writers sometimes exclude these items.

3

Activities Excluded from Advertising

Activities sometimes referred to as advertising but which here are placed under other classifications of sales promotional effort include the offering of premiums to stimulate the sale of products; the use of exhibitions and demonstrations at fairs, shows, and conventions; the use of samples; and the so-called "publicity activities" involved in sending out news releases. Likewise, arbitrarily excluded from the category of advertising are the activities of personal selling forces, both regular and missionary salesmen; the payment of advertising allowances which are not used for advertising; the entertainment of customers; and the conducting of demonstration stores.

Often these excluded activities are embraced in advertising budgets and are directed by those in charge of advertising. On many there is room for close argument as to whether they should be called advertising or be otherwise classified. They have been excluded in our definition of advertising for one reason or another. For example, exhibitions and demonstrations at fairs and shows are thought to be more closely related to personal selling than to advertising. Publicity does not deal with messages identified with a source. But long discussion of the pros and cons regarding inclusion or exclusion of each individual item is not necessary here because in our case studies we shall give attention to many forms of *advertising, personal selling,* and *sales promotion,* and whether we call them advertising is not a matter of moment. They all have the same economic objective of stimulating sales and bringing about exchange.

Classification of Types of Advertising

Just as definitions of advertising are somewhat arbitrary, so classifications of types of advertising are established in accordance with the purposes of writers. There are many bases on which advertising may be classified: according to media, type of product, institution, type of appeal, character of action sought, and so on. A useful division is indicated in Exhibit 1.

The outline given in Exhibit 1 is not an all-inclusive classification nor are the categories set up mutually exclusive. It serves, however, to illustrate important classifications of advertising helpful in an understanding of the use of advertising by business. Attention is called to the divisions made.

1. Distinction is drawn first between manufacturers' and dealers' advertising. Manufacturers' advertising falls into two broad classes: that of consumers' goods and services, and that of industrial goods and services.

2. The advertising of both consumer and industrial goods may be divided into *product* advertising and *institutional* advertising.

3. *Product* advertising seeks to build the reputation of a manufacturer's products, usually under a brand identification, and to promote the sale of these products. A preponderant percentage of manufacturers' advertising

Exhibit 1

A CLASSIFICATION OF TYPES OF ADVERTISING

I. Manufacturers' advertising
  A. Consumers' goods advertising
    1. Advertising directed to consumers
      a) Product advertising
        (1) Direct-action brand advertising
        (2) Indirect-action brand advertising
        (3) Combination, direct-indirect action brand advertising
      b) Advertising to build institutional attitudes or patronage motives (ordinarily indirect-action advertising)
    2. Advertising directed to dealers, that is, trade advertising
      a) Product advertising
      b) Institutional or patronage motive advertising
      c) Advertising to explain policies or plans
  B. Industrial goods* advertising
    1. Advertising directed to buyers of industrial goods
      a) Product advertising
        (1) Direct-action brand advertising
        (2) Indirect-action brand advertising
        (3) Combination, direct-indirect action brand advertising
      b) Advertising to build institutional attitudes or patronage motives
    2. Advertising directed to dealers
      a) Product advertising
      b) Institutional or patronage motive advertising
      c) Advertising to explain policies or plans
II. Dealers' advertising†
  A. Advertising for immediate sale of merchandise
  B. Advertising for promotion of brands or of product lines
  C. Advertising for promotion of institution or departments

---

* Industrial goods include equipment, materials, and supplies that are used by business organizations in the conduct of their business.
  † The term "dealers' advertising" applies to both consumer and industrial goods.

is product advertising and will be the main classification studied in the cases in this book.

4. *Institutional* advertising, as contrasted to product advertising, is devoted to building consumer attitudes relating to the company or institution for the purposes of promoting patronage or building favor on the basis of these attitudes.

As noted above, manufacturers' product advertising is generally brand advertising; and brand advertisements can usually be classified as *direct-action advertisements, indirect-action advertisements,* or *combination, direct-indirect action advertisements.*[1]

---

[1] Institutional advertising is usually indirect in action, designed only to leave a message with the reader or listener rather than to stimulate any immediate response; but some institutional advertisements do seek a request for further information and may be classified as *combination, direct-indirect* action advertisements.

Direct-Action Advertising. A manufacturer's direct-action advertisement seeks as its main objective an immediate response to the advertisement in the form of the reader's sending an order for the goods advertised or a request for further information. Exhibit 2 gives an example of a manufacturer's direct-action advertisement.

Indirect-Action Advertising In contrast to the direct-action objective of the advertisement in Exhibit 2, most manufacturers' brand advertise-

Exhibit 2

EXAMPLE OF A MANUFACTURER'S DIRECT-ACTION ADVERTISEMENT

★ ★ ★ ★ ★ ★ ★ ★ ★ ★ ★ ★ ★ ★ ★ ★ ★

TOMMY DORSEY

The great Dorsey group of the late 1930s and early '40s playing their biggest hits. Featuring Frank Sinatra, Bunny Berigan, Jo Stafford with The Pied Pipers. 12 selections, including *Marie, Star Dust, I'll Never Smile Again, Song of India, Opus No. 1.*

★ ★ ★ ★ ★ ★ ★ ★ ★ ★ ★ ★ ★ ★ ★ ★ ★

GLENN MILLER

Miller's best, including *Moonlight Serenade, In the Mood, Tuxedo Junction, String of Pearls, American Patrol, Little Brown Jug, St. Louis Blues, Pennsylvania 6-5000, (I've Got a Gal in) Kalamazoo, Boulder Buff, Farewell Blues, King Porter Stomp.*

★ ★ ★ ★ ★ ★ ★ ★ ★ ★ ★ ★ ★ ★ ★ ★ ★

BENNY GOODMAN

The King, his band and Quartet, at their swinging best in 11 masterpieces; with Krupa, Hampton, etc. *Sing Sing Sing, One O'Clock Jump, And the Angels Sing, Stompin' at the Savoy, King Porter Stomp, Bugle Call Rag,* etc. The original versions.

★ ★ ★ ★ ★ ★ ★ ★ ★ ★ ★ ★ ★ ★ ★ ★ ★

DUKE ELLINGTON

Duke's all-time best band, 1940-42, with Hodges, Webster, Blanton, Stewart, Williams, Carney, Ivie Anderson, Herb Jeffries. 16 tunes, including *"A" Train, I Got It Bad, Perdido, Cotton Tail, Main Stem, Blue Serge, Flaming Sword, Rocks in My Bed.*

★ ★ ★ ★ ★ ★ ★ ★ ★ ★ ★ ★ ★ ★ ★ ★ ★

ARTIE SHAW

Shaw's two most successful big bands in 12 history-making hits recorded 1938-43. Includes *Begin the Beguine, Nightmare, Frenesi, Star Dust, Dancing in the Dark, Temptation, Indian Love Call, All the Things You Are, Serenade to a Savage,* etc.

★ ★ ★ ★ ★ ★ ★ ★ ★ ★ ★ ★ ★ ★ ★ ★ ★

Exciting offer to new members of the

RCA VICTOR POPULAR ALBUM CLUB

A 5-ALBUM SET OF SWING CLASSICS

for only **$3.98**

NATIONALLY ADVERTISED PRICES TOTAL $19.90

...if you agree to buy five albums from the Club during the next twelve months from at least 100 to be made available

THIS exciting new plan, under the direction of the Book-of-the-Month Club, enables you to have on tap a variety of popular music for family fun and happier parties . . . and at an immense saving. Moreover, once and for all, it takes bewilderment out of building such a well-balanced collection. **You pay far less for albums this way** than if you buy them haphazardly. For example, the extraordinary introductory offer described above can represent an approximate 33⅓% saving in your first year of membership. **Thereafter you can continue to save up to 33⅓%.** After buying the five albums called for in this offer, you will receive a free 12-inch 33⅓ R.P.M. album, with a nationally advertised price of at least $3.98, for every two albums purchased from the Club. **A wide choice of RCA VICTOR 12-inch long-playing albums will be described each month.** One will be singled out as the album-of-the-month. If you want it, you do nothing; it will come to you automatically. If you prefer one of the alternates—or nothing at all—you can make your wishes known on a form always provided. You pay the nationally advertised price—usually $3.98, at times $4.98 (plus a small postage and handling charge).

THE SWING CLASSICS PICTURED AT LEFT ARE 12-INCH 33⅓ R.P.M. LONG-PLAYING. THEY ARE THE ORIGINAL RECORDINGS NOW REPROCESSED TO ENHANCE THEIR SOUND

THE RCA VICTOR POPULAR ALBUM CLUB   P22-18
c/o Book-of-the-Month Club, Inc., 345 Hudson Street, New York 14, N.Y.
Please register me as a member of The RCA VICTOR Popular Album Club and send me the five-album set of Swing Classics, for which I enclose only $3.98, plus a small mailing charge. I agree to buy five other albums offered by the Club within the next twelve months, for each of which I will be billed at the nationally advertised price: usually $3.98, at times $4.98 (plus a small postage and handling charge). Thereafter, I need buy only four such albums in any twelve-month period to maintain membership. I may cancel my membership any time after buying five albums from the Club (in addition to those included in this introductory offer). After my fifth purchase, if I continue, for every two albums I buy I may choose a third album free.

Name_____

Address_____

City_____Zone____State____

NOTE: If you wish to enroll through an authorized RCA VICTOR dealer, please fill in here:

Dealer's Name_____

Address_____

PLEASE NOTE: Send no money. A bill will be sent. Albums can be shipped only to residents of the U. S., its territories and Canada. Albums for Canadian members are made in Canada and shipped duty free from Britain.

ments are *indirect-action* advertisements which seek no immediate response from the reader. Their objective, rather, is to build the reputations of the brands advertised and to enhance the wantability of the branded products offered through building mental associations relating to them. Exhibit 3 gives an example of a manufacturer's indirect-action advertisement. This "Columbia" stereophonic phonograph advertisement was not prepared with the expectation that consumers would do anything im-

Exhibit 3

AN EXAMPLE OF A MANUFACTURER'S INDIRECT-ACTION ADVERTISEMENT

Model 680: complete stereophonic twin console phonograph, six speakers: 40 watts, dual-channel amplifier. Automatic 4-speed record changer with diamond stylus. In matching mahogany, $379.95 . . . blond mahogany or walnut cabinets priced slightly higher.

Sit anywhere in the room

COLUMBIA STEREOPHONIC PHONOGRAPHS PUT YOU IN THE CENTER OF SOUND

Here is the ultimate in listening—a new Columbia stereophonic phonograph. Turn it on and you're suddenly, dramatically in the Center of Sound—the place where music takes on a third dimension. Turn the remarkable Balanced Listening Control and you shift the Center of Sound wherever you want it. This Columbia engineering exclusive, available on many models, makes it possible for you to enjoy stereophonic sound in perfect proportion —not just in one spot, but *anywhere in the room!* Superb styling and cabinetry make every Columbia Stereo-Fidelity phonograph a truly matchless instrument for your home. Prices begin at only $124.90.

STEREO-FIDELITY PHONOGRAPHS BY COLUMBIA

A division of Columbia Broadcasting System, Inc. ⑨ "Columbia" ℗ Marcas Reg.
Prices slightly higher west of the Rockies.

mediately upon reading the advertisement. Its chief objective, instead, is to associate with the trade-mark "Columbia" the idea that Columbia stereophonic hi-fidelity equipment will place the listener in the center of sound regardless of where he sits. Thus, consumers may be favorably disposed toward investigating Columbia equipment when they decide to shop for stereophonic hi-fidelity equipment.

Exhibit 4

AN EXAMPLE OF A MANUFACTURER'S COMBINATION, DIRECT-INDIRECT ACTION ADVERTISEMENT

J-M Spintex Insulation comes with aluminum or standard wrapping, in thicknesses up to 6 inches

ANNUAL SAVINGS ON HEATING BILLS

LOCATE YOUR REGION	6 INCHES OF INSULATION IN ATTIC	4 INCHES OF INSULATION IN OUTSIDE WALLS	TOTAL SAVINGS FOR YOU
REGION 1	$111	$51	$162
REGION 2	93	43	136
REGION 3	54	25	79
REGION 4	24	11	35

No matter where you live—

New Johns-Manville Home Insulation will save you money this winter

Find your savings right here. Figures above are typical savings based on the temperature zone in which you live and the specified thickness of insulation in your attic and outside walls. Figures are courtesy of Minneapolis-Honeywell Regulator Co.

Send for Free Booklet! "Comfort and its Control." Address Johns-Manville, Dept. L-5, Box 60, New York 16, N.Y. In Canada, Port Credit, Ontario.

I'm interested for new home ☐ existing home ☐

Name _____

Street _____

City _____ County _____ State _____

LOOK AT THE CHART! See the big dollar savings Johns-Manville Spintex® Insulation can give you. And you get big dividends in winter *comfort*, too. Next summer, Spintex will serve you equally well. It keeps rooms up to 15° cooler on hottest days, cuts air conditioning operating costs.

Spintex handles easily, fits snugly between joists, studs or rafters . . . you can install it yourself. If you live in a home where attic or wall space is inaccessible Spintex Insulation can be pneumatically blown in such spaces by a Johns-Manville home installation contractor.

For big savings this winter ask your J-M building materials dealer or insulation contractor about Spintex now.

JOHNS-MANVILLE

SOMEHOW, SOMEWHERE, A J-M PRODUCT SERVES YOU

Combination, Direct-Indirect Action Advertising. A great many manufacturers' advertisements are *combination, direct-indirect action* advertisements. Such advertisements have a double objective, one being to present a message which will build desired mental associations about a brand, and the second being to get immediate action of some kind, in the form of a request for a recipe booklet or perhaps the submittal of a box top and money in order to receive a premium. The forms for seeking direct action are legion. Exhibit 4 gives an example of a manufacturer's combination, direct-indirect action advertisement. In this Johns-Manville advertisement direct action is sought by offering a free booklet on temperature control; indirect action is sought in the remainder of the advertisement, the principal message being that Johns-Manville home insulation saves money.

The distinction between *direct-action* and *indirect-action* advertising is of basic importance to an understanding of advertising's use by businessmen. An appreciation of the distinction is essential, for instance, in understanding the parts played by various forms of advertising in conjunction with personal selling, sales promotion, and other elements included in sales programs designed to lead to the purchase of goods. Thus, an understanding of the distinction is essential in planning the strategy of sales campaigns. Moreover, an understanding of the distinction between direct-action and indirect-action advertising is required in building logical techniques for measuring the effects of advertising. Direct-action advertisements are measured primarily through the statistics of the direct response sought. On the other hand, measurement of indirect-action advertisements is likely to rest largely in efforts to find the degree of readership or listenership or the degree to which mental attitudes have been built by the advertising.

Dealer Advertising. Dealers' advertising, as will be seen from the classification outline given in Exhibit 1, breaks down into advertising of merchandise, on the one hand, and of the institution or of departments, on the other. If dealers have brands, there may also be some brand advertising. Dealer advertising of merchandise is for the most part direct-action advertising, in marked contrast to manufacturers' product advertising, which, as we have pointed out, is predominantly indirect-action advertising. When the retailer advertises, he generally seeks to create traffic in his store. As a rule his advertisement says: "Here is attractive merchandise at a price. Come get it." Such an advertisement is given in Exhibit 5.

While retail advertising is employed primarily to attract immediate patronage, often a minor part of a retailer's annual advertising appropriation may be devoted to featuring merchandise in ways that will build up the reputation of particular departments without featuring action-impelling price inducements. A department or specialty store, for instance, may advertise fashion merchandise with copy devoted primarily to discussion of current fashions and the success of the store or department in being

Exhibit 5

AN EXAMPLE OF A RETAILER'S DIRECT-ACTION ADVERTISEMENT

Gimbels is as close as your letter box--mail the handy coupon below

New York open 9:30 to 9 . . . Bay Shore 12 to 9
Westchester and Valley Stream 12 to 9:30

Puritron...new kind of relief for sinus and allergies

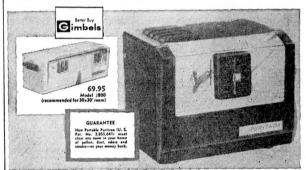

Better Buy
Gimbels

69.95
Model :800
(recommended for 30x30' room)

GUARANTEE
New Portable Puritron (U. S.
Pat. No. 2,855,641) must
clear any room in your home
of pollen, dust, odors and
smoke—or your money back.

39.95

Model F-20 (recommended for 15x15' room)

Puritron helps remove the
irritations that often cause
allergy, asthma discomfort

Puritron is a new wonder with air purifying and filtering devices
to remove dust, pollen and other irritating particles. The
resulting cleaner, purer air that Puritron produces often helps
relieve sufferers of hay fever, allergies, asthma and sinus trouble.
And Puritron's powerful fan quickly clears rooms of smoke, odors,
dust or pollen, provides a constant supply of spring-fresh, clean
air—even in unventilated rooms without the overcooling of air
conditioning. Ideal for bedrooms, kitchens, stuffy offices, conference rooms. Puritron is convenient to use, too. Light, portable, the size of a table radio, plugs into any 110 volt AC
outlet. Set on table, desk, shelf or stool. Grey finish.

Salton hotray automatically serves hot food hot

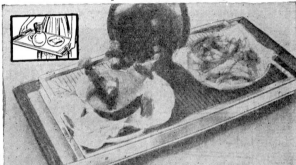

14.95

this electric hot tray serves
home meals and makes
party buffets so easy

Keep the Salton Hotray at tableside during meals to keep hot
dishes hot, save trips to kitchen for second servings . . . use
it to keep coffee and toast hot for breakfast. Or as a hot
table for parties and buffets, especially to keep hors d'oeuvres
warm. Great for outdoor parties too — wherever there's an
AC outlet. Attractively styled to fit in with your fine china
and silver. Has glass panel with heating elements sealed in and
rich walnut handles. Easy to keep clean—just wipe with damp
cloth. 10x9¼". Fully automatic. Heat is thermostatically controlled. Dine size 16x7½" . . 10.95 Patio master size . . 24.95

Protexall fire extinguisher is safety for your family

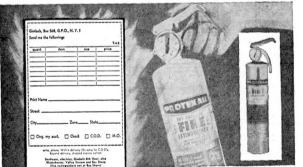

Gimbels, Box 568, G.P.O., N. Y. 1
Send me the following:
T-4-5

quant.	item	size	price

Print Name _____

Street _____

City _____ Zone ____ State ____

☐ Chrg. my acct.   ☐ Check   ☐ C.O.D.   ☐ M.O.

write, phone. With a delivery 25c extra for C.O.D's.
Beyond delivery, shipped express cost col

hardware, electrics, Gimbels 8th floor; also
Westchester, Valley Stream and Bay Shore
(fire extinguishers not at Bay Shore)

17.95

this dry chemical fire extin-
guisher protects your home by
being ready for constant use

A small fire can catch hold and destroy a large part of your
home before the fire department arrives. Here's an important
safeguard against this danger. It's made by American LaFrance,
the world's largest maker of fire-fighting equipment. Uses safe
dry chemical to smother any kind of flame from grease to electrical, with no messy foams, liquids or dangerous gases. You'll
use it against grease fires that occur frequently in the kitchen,
against electrical or appliance fires and as all important protection for your car or office. Harmless to people, pets, fabrics,
food. Rechargeable. Comes with wall bracket.

33rd & B'way, N. Y. . . . . Cross County Center, Westchester . . . Green Acres, Valley Stream . . . Bay Shore on Montauk Highway   other Gimbel news on pages 22, 23, 37, 60, 61, 94, 102, 115 and 118

FOR CASH OR FOR CREDIT—NOBODY BUT NOBODY UNDERSELLS GIMBELS   **Gimbels**

for those call your N. Y. C. needs, then PE 6-5100, Suburbanites Westchester YOrktown 3-8000, L. I.: LOcust 1-2006, Conn.: TOwnsend 9-4911.

fashion-correct. Or the wide variety of selection in particular departments may be stressed in an advertisement by the presentation of numerous items and by emphasis in the copy on the wide variety that is available.

Because this book is devoted primarily to a study of the use of advertising by manufacturers, not a great deal of attention is given to retail advertising. On the other hand, manufacturers often seek the co-operation of retailers in advertising the manufacturers' merchandise to the retailers' clientele, and, therefore, it is important that the manufacturer have a clear understanding of the usual objective of retail advertising, namely, to induce consumers to respond immediately to the retailer's advertisement.

Primary Demand and Selective Demand Advertising

Two other classifications of advertising, based upon the types of copy appeals employed, are useful when thinking about the objectives of advertising, namely, *primary demand* and *selective demand* advertising.

The objective of primary demand advertising is to induce people to buy products of the class in which the advertised article falls, that is, to increase the total demand for the product class. Such advertising employs copy appeals made to primary buying motives, for instance, the leisure that the housewife may experience from having laborsaving household equipment. An example of primary demand advertising is given in Exhibit 6. This Mobile Homes Manufacturers Association advertisement seeks to inform the public of the modernity and livability of mobile homes, thereby dispelling negative attitudes toward mobile homes or trailers held by some people and increasing the acceptance of mobile homes as an alternative form of housing.

In contrast, the objective of selective demand advertising is to induce people to buy a particular *brand* within a product class. Such advertising employs copy appeals made to selective buying motives, the appeals generally featuring superior characteristics of the brand being advertised, for instance, the advantages of swing-out shelves in a refrigerator, the special services offered passengers by an airline, the ease of application of a spray-type deodorant, or the durability of a sheet. Such appeals are designed to establish ideas regarding product quality or performance which will induce ready acceptance or even preference for the brand.

It should be recognized that most selective demand advertising is likely to have an effect upon the total demand for the product class in which the advertised brand falls. For example, although the Columbia advertisement given in Exhibit 3 emphasizes a selective appeal and was directed primarily at those consumers who were already interested in stereophonic hi-fidelity, it may have also caught the attention of consumers who were not interested in stereophonic hi-fidelity and created an interest.

Primary demand advertising is usually undertaken by industry associations or by individual manufacturers marketing new products which involve a new product class. However, in some instances, when a product

Exhibit 6

AN EXAMPLE OF PRIMARY DEMAND ADVERTISING

Has <u>your</u> home these modern conveniences?

Mobile Homes FEATURE

MORE MODERN APPLIANCES, NEW FURNISHING
IDEAS THAN MANY ORDINARY HOMES

WOULDN'T <u>YOU</u> FEEL proud to own a home that's this up-to-date? In a mobile home kitchen, for instance, you can have "waist-level" cooking, latest-model large-capacity refrigerator, formica counters, disposal, twin sinks.

Furniture is a comfortable contemporary style . . . the kind you'd pick out yourself piece by piece. You can have a complete bathroom with tub and shower. An automatic washer-dryer, automatic heat, air-conditioning, built-in TV if you like.

And your furniture, draperies, carpeting, appliances are all included in the *one* price of your home. All financed in one "package." You may pay only $75 a month, in some cases even less.

Three million people now live in mobile homes. Among them are young couples, professional men, engineers, graduate students, military men, construction and industrial workers, retired couples.

NOTE: You will find dealers in the classified ads of your newspaper and yellow pages of your telephone book under "Mobile Homes," "Trailers-House," or "Trailers-Coach."

Good neighborhoods to live in

There are many new mobile home parks with beautiful landscaping, playgrounds, swimming pools. Owners add porches and gardens to their homes, do a lot of entertaining like backyard barbecues.

SEND FOR MHMA YEARBOOK!

Mobile Homes Manufacturers Assn., Dept. L108
P.O. Box 1316, Chicago 90, Illinois

Please send MOBILE LIFE, with information on latest models of 75 manufacturers, mobile parks and living. Enclosed is 25c in coin.

Name _____

Address _____

City _____ State _____

 Mobile Homes Manufacturers Assn.

Trailer Coach Association OF THE WEST

is so highly individualized that consumers are inclined to think of it not in terms of product classifications but rather in terms of brand names, the advertiser can make effective use of primary copy appeals to secure selective results. For example, the face-cream manufacturer featuring a woman winning her man because of her beautiful skin offers not face cream in general but a specific brand as the solution to satisfy the desire for romance.

Thus, for many products for which differentiation exists or can be established in part by ideas conveyed in the advertising, advertisers use primary appeals as a basis of building a selective demand for their brands. Observation and case study indicate, however, that a preponderant share of advertising is used not so much with the thought of increasing demand for the class of product as with that of obtaining for the advertiser's brand a larger share of the existing market for the product class than would be his without such advertising. The objective of most advertisers is to affect the demand for their brands.

∿∿∿∿∿∿∿∿∿∿∿∿∿∿∿∿∿∿∿∿∿∿∿∿

Chapter 2

ADVERTISING IN A TOP-
MANAGEMENT PERSPECTIVE

From the viewpoint of the top management of a business, advertising is only one of many elements in the business operation which top management must analyze and about which it must make decisions if it is to stabilize or to increase the business' sales and profits. Accordingly, advertising is looked upon by top management not as a separate, isolated element which can be considered and acted upon independently of the other elements of the business operation. Rather, advertising is looked upon as being *inextricably intertwined* with the other elements of the business operation, particularly with the other elements of the marketing operation. Generally, advertising, if at all significant in the business operation, is analyzed and acted upon by top management more or less concurrently with analyses and decisions relative to the other major elements of the business.

The reader should keep in mind that top management's principal responsibility is to take actions which will seek to insure the future success of the firm by stabilizing or increasing sales and profits. This responsibility calls for (1) the determination of a sound *business strategy*, that is, decisions regarding the most effective utilization of the firm's human, financial, manufacturing, and marketing resources in the light of potential opportunities in the ever-changing market place; (2) the determination of a sound *merchandising strategy*, that is, decisions regarding what product (or service) to offer to what segments of the market through what channels of distribution at what margins and prices; (3) the determination of a sound *selling strategy*, that is, decisions regarding the combination of personal selling, advertising, and other sales promotional tools which promise to be most effective and economical; and (4) the determination

14

of the *type of organization* and *organization operating procedures* required to execute these strategies.

Within this complex of analyses, conclusions, and decisions regarding
all elements of the business operation, top management assesses the role of
advertising, if any, in the business operation. Clearly, whether to use advertising, how to use it, and to what extent are questions which require
top management to interrelate all elements of its marketing operation, including advertising, into a whole which promises to be successful and
economical. By and large, top management's decision making with respect to advertising is guided primarily by sales and profit considerations.

Consideration of the Probable Effect of Advertising upon Sales

When trying to determine what advertising is likely to accomplish in a
particular marketing situation, management usually begins with a careful
appraisal of the demand for its product and consideration of whether its
advertising, in association with the other selling tools, will influence demand within required cost limitations. In studying these problems, management must consider the effect of advertising not only on consumers
but also on those engaged personally in influencing and guiding consumer
buying, namely, the company's own sales organization and its channels of
distribution. The appraisal calls for estimates of the probable effects of advertising upon the prices management can ask and the numbers of units
management might sell at alternative prices. In short, it involves a realistic
study of the conditions covering demand, the competition met, the buying
habits and attitudes of consumers and of the trade, and the chances of influencing those attitudes.

Since an appraisal must be made of the effect of advertising and other
selling tools upon demand, it is desirable briefly to review some of the
economic concepts of demand.

The Demand Schedule. The demand for any product arises from the
utility[1] of that product to individuals in the market. Each consumer has
numerous wants which he desires to gratify. His separate demand for each
of many different products is determined by the character of his many
wants, his attitudes, and by his income. In purchasing to fill all these
wants, the individuals within a market create a combined demand which
we may term the "aggregate demand," as contrasted with the demand of
any individual.

Since the purchasing power of most consumers is limited, each ordinarily has to exercise choice in deciding the wants which he will satisfy
or the extent to which he will satisfy his various wants. At any given time,
the individual consumer, driven by the necessity of apportioning his income among purchases to satisfy his various wants, has for each type of

---

[1] The utility of a product is its ability to fill a want or desire of consumers.

product a demand curve. Theoretically, he has a schedule of the amounts of each which he will purchase at market prices. His demand curve for a product is affected by the utility of successive units of the product to him. It is subject, on the one hand, to the law of diminishing utility, which is a recognition of the fact that the additional benefits which he derives from a given purchase of a commodity diminish with every increase in the stock already in his possession. It is governed, on the other hand, by the strength of his desire for other products, because purchase of one thing may well mean foregoing another thing.

The Effect of Advertising upon Demand. Advertising and aggressive selling represent forces exercised by sellers chiefly to shift the demand curve, although they also may be used to change the shape of the demand curve for a product. Managements wish to move the demand curve for their product to the right, that is, to bring greater sales at a particular price or to get a higher price for a particular quantity than they would have without such selling effort. To do this they appeal to consumers' buying motives with the aim of changing the marginal utility[2] of individual consumers for the class of product featured, and, accordingly, to change its aggregate demand. For them advertising performs the economic function of leading consumers to arrive at evaluations which influence the price and volume received in such manner as may enable the enterprise to succeed.

It also may be pointed out that advertising by competing sellers, even when they employ selective appeals, under certain conditions has a primary effect; that is, it may increase total demand for any class of product or service provided this demand is expansible, as explained below.

The Concept of Expansibility of Demand. A study of demand shows that different products vary widely in the susceptibility of their primary demand to increase as a result of advertising and aggressive selling. For example, the demand for oranges has increased under aggressive selling; the demand for men's shoes has not so responded. The term frequently employed to express this susceptibility of demand for products to increase is "expansibility of demand."[3]

Expansibility of demand should be distinguished from *elasticity* of demand. Elasticity of demand is a concept relating to the shape of the de-

---

[2] The term "marginal purchase" has been used by economists to describe the unit of a commodity which the buyer "is only just induced to purchase because he is on the margin of doubt whether it is worth his while to incur the outlay necessary to obtain it. The utility of his marginal purchase may be called the marginal utility of the thing to him." Alfred Marshall, *Principles of Economics* (8th ed.; London: Macmillan & Co., Ltd., 1920), p. 93.

[3] The concept of expansibility of demand relates to change of demand, which can come about from a number of causes. For example, changes in the level of income occurring from cyclical fluctuation have the effect of shifting demand curves. In periods of depression, when buying power is low, they are shifted to the left, while in periods of high income they are shifted to the right.

mand curve, that is, to the quantities that will be taken at various prices, other things being equal, and the position of the demand curve itself being unchanged; if as prices fall the product of price times quantity increases, then the demand is elastic.[4] The concept of expansibility of demand is a part of change in demand, that is, a change in the *attitude* of the market toward a product, a change in the position of the demand curve. Such changes may come about for reasons in no way connected with the activities of businessmen—for example, rise of interest in water sports, decline in popularity of formal dress. But if a business concern or group of business concerns by various methods of sales promotion induces the market to absorb a greater quantity of a product at the same price, or even at a higher price, then the demand may be termed "expansible." A product with an expansible demand is one for which a business can increase demand readily (price being constant) through appeal to consumers' buying motives. Conversely, a product has an inexpansible demand when its sales cannot be readily increased by appeals to buying motives.

The increase in sales of a product may come (1) from individual consumers being induced to use more of it for the purposes to which they were already putting it, (2) from existing users being induced to buy more of the product for new uses featured in selling appeals, or (3) from former nonusers having their desire for the product raised to the point where they become buyers. The seller attempts to change the marginal utility of the product among individuals in the market. One of the important problems faced by management when considering the possible profitability of advertising to expand demand is that of forecasting its expansibility or its responsiveness to appeals.

Through advertising and aggressive selling, management hopes to establish a demand curve for its own brand to the right of where it would be if it did not employ advertising; that is, management hopes that at any price more units will be demanded than would be the case without advertising.

While distinction has been drawn between primary and selective advertising appeals, it is well to note that in the world of reality consumers

---

[4] Some economists have attempted to explain the responsiveness of various classes of products to advertising and selling effort in terms of elasticity of demand. A study of products will show that generally, though not always, products possessing an elastic demand are responsive to advertising and selling effort, but an explanation of responsiveness to advertising in terms of elasticity is not fully satisfactory. Any given demand schedule of the economist depicts a static situation. It shows the quantities of products which may be taken in a particular period of indefinite length at the prices named and assumes that forces other than price affecting demand are static.

Demand schedules are not static, however; they are subject to constant change. The quantities that will be taken in a period at particular prices are not in accordance with the quantities that will be taken in another period at these prices. The demand for particular products is subject to constant change; change brought about by shifts in buying power, by alteration of living habits, by shifts in buying attitudes developed by aggressive selling, and so on.

generally set values not upon classes of products, for example, shoes, but upon brands or sources of products, such as "Keds" or shoes of the Jones Shoe Store. The merchandise of different sellers in any product group is not identical. Accordingly, in place of visualizing a single demand schedule for a product class, it is more in keeping with reality in most product fields to think of each seller at any given time as having a demand curve for his brand, the quantities demanded at various prices being determined in large part by the valuations set by consumers for his brand in comparison with those set for competing brands, although, of course indirect substitutes are also a factor. The above statement gives recognition to the fact that each seller through differentiation and reputation attempts to gain for his brand a limited monopoly position. It is limited because substitution is easy.

While there may be separate demand schedules for each differentiated product and it may be, therefore, difficult to visualize a single demand schedule for all producers making a given class of products, nevertheless the student of demand can arbitrarily use product classes and through industry statistics can study the trend of demand of each class in units and dollars, relating thereto the advertising and selling efforts exerted by the industry. Such a procedure will be followed in a number of the cases in this book.

Consideration of the Probable Effect of Advertising upon Profit

As has been indicated, top management's major responsibility is to stabilize or to increase sales and profits, a profitable business operation being, of course, the predominant consideration. In considering advertising's probable effect upon profit, management must analyze its effect upon the operating statement.

Effects of Advertising upon Operating Statement. In order that the possible contribution of advertising to a business firm's sales and profits may be clearly before the reader, its effects upon a firm's operating statement are examined. From an accounting standpoint, profit is merely the residuum of sales income after all the expenses incident to the conduct of the business have been deducted. Since the use of advertising by manufacturers is in large part different from its use by distributors, the possible effects of advertising upon the items of the operating statement of a manufacturer are studied here.

A simple form of operating statement containing the essential items representative of the operations of a manufacturer is shown in Exhibit 1.

Management seeks to conduct its operations so that a profit is shown in the final item (*l*). What profit occurs is the result of the interplay among the items above (*l*). It is evident that greater or lesser use of advertising may affect both the income item and the various expense items listed.

The possible effects of advertising on the various operating items in different marketing situations are many. For clarity, only the broad effects are noted.

Questions to Consider. When a management considers use of advertising, the questions posed are as follows:

1. What will be the effect of an advertising program upon sales income (item *a*)?

Sales income is the result of the number of units sold multiplied by price per unit. Advertising is employed to increase people's desire for a product. If it accomplishes this end, it will have effect on either the number of units purchased by new and old customers or the price they pay

Exhibit 1

A SIMPLIFIED OPERATING STATEMENT

a)	Sales income (number of units sold × price per unit)..	xxxx
b)	Total manufacturing costs.........................	xxxx
c)	Gross margin available for marketing, for general administration and for profits (*a* − *b*)..............	xxxx
d)	Sales force expense..............................xxx	
e)	Sales promotion and advertising expense.............xxx	
f)	Shipping, transportation, warehouse, and delivery expense...xxx	
g)	Credit and collection expense.....................xxx	
h)	Marketing administration costs.....................xxx	
i)	Total marketing expenses (sum of *d* to *h*, inclusive)...	xxxx
j)	Balance remaining for general administration and for profit (*c* − *i*).....................................	xxxx
k)	General administrative costs.......................xxx	
l)	Balance for profit (*j* − *k*).........................	xxxx

or both. A management must ask: To what extent does advertising promise to affect sales income (*a*) through effect on units sold, and (*b*) through effect on price obtainable?

While a management can often use advertising to increase the desire of consumers for its products and thereby find it possible to increase the prices which it receives for each unit, it also can often materially affect the quantities of its products sold, and, accordingly, its sales income, by the prices it sets upon its products. It is essential, therefore, that a management properly appraise the effect of price upon the quantities of products which it may sell, if it is to get a maximum sales income. Provided a product has an elastic demand, a management may increase sales income by decreasing prices. Advertising for some products may have the effect of increasing the elasticity of demand to a point where it is good strategy for a management to decrease prices because sales income thereby may be increased. In short, if a management is to maximize its sales income, it must carefully appraise the effects both of price and of selling effort upon sales response.

2. What will be the effect of advertising upon the management's production costs?

Any advertising costs undertaken may be offset in part or in whole by reduction in unit production costs. If unit production costs are to be affected by advertising, that result must come through advertising's effect upon volume of manufacture. Provided advertising helps give a sufficient volume to make lower unit costs possible, the wider gross margin per unit and the larger number of units sold give an aggregate gross margin (item *c*), offsetting the promotional expenditure undertaken. Accordingly, an efficient management knows the effect of volume upon manufacturing costs and, consequently, upon the aggregate margin which will result.

Reduced production costs per unit may come from either (*a*) effective utilization of existing plant, which means the spreading of fixed costs over a large number of units; or (*b*) employment of increased capital in order to permit a more efficient plant and scale of operations with lower unit costs.

3. What will be the effect of advertising on the manufacturer's marketing costs?

Advertising itself (item *e*) is a cost that must be met. If the advertising outlay cannot be recouped through wider margins resulting from higher price or lower production costs or through a greater aggregate sum available from selling more units at a relatively constant margin, then possibly it may be justified from a profit standpoint, provided it represents a more economical means of obtaining sales volume than personal selling (item *d*) or other promotional methods. Or it may find its justification in making personal selling efforts more productive of sales volume than they otherwise would be, for advertising frequently has this effect.

Wide Variance in Management's Answers. Good use of advertising from a business standpoint depends upon finding answers to the questions cited above regarding advertising's effect upon units to be sold, prices received, production costs, and marketing costs, all of which combine to give a net profit result; but the answers to such questions often vary widely with different products and different operating conditions.

The answer for one type of product and for one company may not fit another product and another company. Moreover, frequently for individual companies there are several answers as to the kind and amount of advertising to combine with other operating variables to produce a profitable result. Generally, there is not just one way to produce and market a product or line of products. Any management may consider numerous alternatives for conducting its operations: alternative methods as to merchandising, pricing, channels of distribution, and selling methods. Some particular combination of methods may be most promising in a specific product field, and the firms which follow these methods may thereby become dominant in the market. But other methods can be employed and can produce a profit. The outlooks of different managements may vary widely because of differences in product lines, markets sought, size of enterprise, capital, selling channels available, and their skills of merchandising, manufacturing, promotion, and general administration. The result is a wide variety of management operating patterns with respect to the use of advertising.

Whether advertising can be profitably used depends also upon how well the various forms of advertising are fitted in with the other elements of the business and marketing operation and how well the advertising and the other operations are carried out. One of the main tasks in many of the cases in this book is to determine suitable marketing strategies for particular situations, with advertising as the focal point in the analysis. It will be found in these cases that varying decisions as to the branding policy to follow, the product characteristics or form to adopt, the prices to charge, the channels of distribution to use, and the selling methods to use, in turn have a bearing on the forms of advertising to use and the burden that will be placed on advertising.

The Objective of Longer-Term Profit. Finally, it should be noted that it has become a generally accepted principle of business strategy that immediate profit should be sacrificed whenever a practice that is dictated by immediate profit threatens to bring loss of future patronage or otherwise to harm future profitableness of an enterprise. An aphorism frequently reiterated by top management is that one-time sales are not ordinarily profitable. The low cost of making sales to constant patrons and the stability that continued patronage gives to a going concern are the best guarantees of a maximized profit over a period of time. Even when repeat sales do not occur or are very infrequent, still the policies followed by well-managed firms ordinarily stress customer satisfaction in the hope that the reputation thus gained will help them in obtaining new customers.

The long-range profit viewpoint of top management accounts for the importance attached to maintenance of quality of branded merchandise, of congenial selling contracts, of acceptable pricing, and of efficient service of one kind or another. It has a distinct bearing on advertising practices, particularly as advertising may be designed to build up ideas or attitudes regarding products or the selling institution that are conducive to continued patronage. On the negative side, it is a deterrent to adoption of advertising practices which, though possibly immediately effective, might reduce future patronage.

Customer satisfaction, upon which continued patronage depends, is not necessarily determined by management meeting the lowest prices in the market or offering products deemed good values by all potential buyers. Continued patronage generally depends rather upon the degree to which a firm can meet the desires of some segment of the market. Different buyers have different tastes and are induced to purchase by varying sets of buying motives, of which price is only one. The offering of individualized product qualities; the provision for prompt delivery, easy credit, convenience in buying, or good repair service; a reputation for fashion, dependability, generous adjustment, or courteous salespeople—all these and numerous other considerations may be relied upon by management to give buyers the satisfaction that will lead them to purchase again. This multiplicity of buying and patronage motives which appeal to various segments of the market plays a fundamental part in the development of numerous competitive business strategies with varying utilization of advertising among them.

Concluding Remarks Regarding Advertising in a Top-Management Perspective

From what has been said it should be recognized that top management cannot simply ask the question, "Shall we use or not use advertising?" and answer the question on the basis of consideration of alternative advertising proposals which have been developed by itself, its advertising department, or its advertising agency. An able management has to proceed on the basis that advertising is *inextricably intertwined* with all of the other elements of the business and marketing operation and that its decisions regarding advertising must be made in the light of a thorough understanding of those other elements and of the business, merchandising, and selling strategies to which it is committing the resources of the firm for the longer term.

Chapter 3

~~~~~~

ADVERTISING DECISION
MAKING: PRELIMINARY
CONCEPTS

The purpose of this chapter is to sketch what we have come to call "The Concept of the Marketing Mix,"[1] which essentially premises that the decision-making executive must analyze certain market forces and certain elements of marketing if he is ultimately to determine a sound "mix" of marketing elements, including advertising, which promises to be effective and profitable. The forces and elements are listed in Exhibit 1, and the concept of the marketing mix is discussed below.

Exhibit 1
THE CONCEPT OF THE MARKETING MIX

A. Market forces bearing on a manufacturer's marketing mix
  1. The behavior of consumers
  2. The behavior of the trade
  3. The behavior of competition
  4. The behavior of government agencies
B. Elements of marketing bearing on a manufacturer's marketing mix
  1. Product planning (merchandising)
  2. Packaging
  3. Pricing
  4. Branding
  5. Channels of distribution
  6. Physical handling (warehousing, transportation)
  7. Quantity and quality of personal selling

---

[1] The term "marketing mix" was originally suggested by Professor James W. Culliton, then a member of the Faculty of the Harvard Business School, now Dean, School of Commerce, University of Notre Dame.

23

Exhibit 1—Continued

   8. Servicing
   9. Quantity and quality of the other tools of sales promotion
  10. Kind and quality of marketing-research information
  11. Quantity and quality of advertising, including display

The Concept Is an Empirical Approach

Study of the marketing and advertising practices of business indicates that management has had to rely primarily upon an empirical approach, that is, experimentation, rather than primarily upon a body of knowledge, that is, principles, to guide it in making decisions regarding marketing and advertising. Management has constantly striven to devise a "mix" of marketing elements, including advertising, that is profitable; and it has constantly made changes in the mix in order to adjust to the changing circumstances of the market place. Management's success as a marketer and user of advertising has depended essentially upon its understanding of the forces that bear upon the demand for its product and its skill in devising and redevising the elements of its mix.

Study of the marketing programs or "mixes" that have been evolved by management under this empirical approach show a great variation in patterns, particularly with respect to management's use of advertising. This variation is reflected in the operating statements of manufacturers. Among such operating statements there is little uniformity, even among manufacturers in the same industry. There are no common figures of marketing expense which have much meaning as standards. Instead, the ratios of sales devoted to the various elements of marketing, including advertising, are widely diverse. For instance, the advertising expense figure, which reflects the burden placed upon advertising in the selling program, will be found to vary among all manufacturers from almost 0% to over 50%. The advertising expense figure for firms operating within the same industry also vary substantially, because the specific products sold, the volume of sales, the segments of the market covered, and the other factors that govern the operation of each company tend to be unique and not conducive to uniformity with the operation of competitors. There are some tendencies toward uniformity, of course, among companies whose product lines are subject to the same market forces.

In short, managements have combined the elements of their individual marketing operations in many ways, assigning widely varying burdens to advertising. To illustrate, some manufacturers of proprietary remedies have relied upon advertising to sell their products to consumers and literally to "pull" the products through the channels of distribution. They have often had no sales force at all. Marketers often refer to this as a *pull* strategy. In contrast, manufacturers of industrial machinery and equipment often rely primarily upon the "push" of personal selling by either a direct sales force or the sales force of distributors and put relatively little, if any, burden on advertising. Marketers often refer to this as a *push* strategy. Generally, however, manufacturers have had to utilize both personal selling and advertising in order to obtain an effective selling operation—a combination *push-pull* strategy.

In analyzing the cases in this book, the reader should keep in mind that the empirical approach calls for a broad appraisal of the market forces affecting the marketing operation and for skill in interrelating all of the elements of the operation into an effective whole, into an effective "marketing mix."

Market Forces Bearing upon the Marketing Mix

As indicated in Exhibit 1, there are four market forces which have an important effect upon the marketing mix employed by management: the behavior of consumers, of the trade, of competitors, and of government agencies. Because the consumer force—the behavior of consumers—is deemed to be the most significant force affecting the marketing mix, it will be discussed first.

The First Market Force: The Behavior of Consumers. Individuals and families constantly reshape their ways of life and consequently their demands for particular goods and services because of continuous changes in the social, economic, and technological environment in which they live. The primary demand for classes of products and services is generated by the ways in which individuals and families choose to live in the light of the opportunities and resources available to them. Accordingly, management must study the principal patterns of living in the society and the underlying forces which shape those patterns. Broad observations about fundamental social, economic, and technological forces of significance to management follow.

Social Forces. The changing number and age of the population has had a direct effect upon the demand for most products. (The growth of the population in the United States since 1800 is given in Exhibit 2, and the population by broad age groups for selected groups is given in Exhibit 3.) Many products and services have had an increase in demand, irrespective of the quantity or quality of selling effort, simply because of growth in population among certain age groups. The number and age of the population are particularly important to management in estimating potential sales and in determining the quantity, as well as the quality, of selling effort to be undertaken. The impact of gradual change in age distribution of the population upon the demand for certain products and services is apparent, such as products for babies or services for the older segment of the population.

The growth of the United States population has been accompanied, as the result of many historical developments, by fundamental changes in rural-urban patterns: consumers have moved from a highly individualized, acutely independent frontier life to highly group-oriented, extremely interdependent urban and suburban lives. As is well known, consumers

Exhibit 2

GROWTH IN THE POPULATION OF THE UNITED STATES AS INDICATED BY SIZE OF POPULATION FOR SELECTED YEARS 1800–1970

Year	Total Population	Year	Total Population
1800...........	5,308,000	1946..........	141,389,000
1810...........	7,240,000	1947..........	144,126,000
1820...........	9,638,000	1948..........	146,631,000
1830...........	12,866,000	1949..........	149,188,000
1840...........	17,069,000	1950..........	151,683,000
1850...........	23,192,000	1951..........	154,360,000
1860...........	31,443,000	1952..........	157,028,000
1870...........	39,818,000	1953..........	159,636,000
1880...........	50,156,000	1954..........	162,417,000
1890...........	62,948,000	1955..........	165,270,000
1900...........	75,995,000	1956..........	168,174,000
1910...........	91,972,000	1957..........	171,229,000
1920...........	105,711,000	1958..........	173,210,000
1930...........	122,775,000	1960 (projected)	181,154,000
1940...........	131,669,000	1965 (")	198,950,000
1945...........	139,928,000	1970 (")	219,474,000

Source: U.S. Bureau of the Census, *Statistical Abstract of the United States,* 1958, adapted from Tables 1–3, pp. 5 and 6.

Exhibit 3

U.S. POPULATION BY BROAD AGE GROUPS FOR SELECTED YEARS 1930–70
(000 Omitted)

AGE	1930	1940	1950	PROJECTED		
				1960	1965	1970
Under 5..........	11,444	10,542	16,164	21,019	23,861	26,662
5–9.............	12,608	10,685	13,200	19,159	21,861	24,259
10–14...........	12,005	11,746	11,119	17,217	19,216	21,915
15–19...........	11,552	12,334	10,617	13,406	17,267	19,262
20–24...........	10,870	11,588	11,482	11,311	13,502	17,343
25–29...........	9,834	11,097	12,242	22,824	22,527	25,222
30–34...........	9,120	10,242	11,517			
35–39...........	9,209	9,545	11,246	23,983	24,288	22,990
40–44...........	7,990	8,788	10,204			
45–49...........	7,042	8,255	9,070	20,846	22,130	23,306
50–54...........	5,976	7,257	8,272			
54–59...........	4,646	5,844	7,235	15,610	17,099	18,966
60–64...........	3,751	4,728	6,059			
65–69...........	2,771	3,807	5,003	15,779	17,638	19,966
70–74...........	1,950	2,570	3,412			
75 over.........	1,913	2,643	3,855			
	122,775	131,669	151,683	181,154	198,950	219,474

Source: U.S. Bureau of the Census, *Statistical Abstract of the United States,* 1958, adapted from Table 24, p. 27 and Table 3, p. 6.

today are primarily the product not of a rural, farming background but rather of an urban, industrial background. As a result, consumers' habits, attitudes, values, motivations, and aspirations continue to develop, to shift, and to change as they live and work and respond to a specific environment. The student of demand cannot ignore the significant, subtle characteristics of the environment in which each consumer lives, and the effect of the environmental circumstances upon demand and upon the use of advertising.

The industrialization of the United States has materially changed the character of work. People have decreased the number of hours spent in gainful employment, have consumed less physical energy in gainful employment, and consequently have substantially increased the number of hours and the amount of energy which they have for leisure-time pursuits—pursuits ordinarily involving consumption of products and services. The utilization of leisure time is again a subject for the attention of the student of demand, as an understanding of this complex area has significance to the demand for countless products and services consumed during leisure hours. The remarkable growth of the demand for products used in bowling, boating, do-it-yourself projects, and travel is due to the new leisure patterns of great numbers of Americans.

Unexplained, or rather inadequately explained, in people's ways of life are fads and fashion: fads being shorter-term, short-lived consumption patterns; fashion being more basic, longer-term consumption patterns. Whether fad or fashion, the consumption pattern induced by either can drastically affect the business operation of management and, accordingly, management must be alert to the fad and fashion trends among consumers which do affect its business operations. Fads such as the hoola hoop have little if any influence upon the operation of most business firms, but longer-term fashions, such as the use of colors other than white in kitchen appliances and paper products, do call for major changes in marketing and advertising strategy.

Finally, one other force among many significant social forces should be noted, namely, that in recent years, there has been an almost universal desire among all Americans for a high standard of living. There has been a general view that a high standard of living is obtainable by all. This mode of thinking has significantly affected the demand for many products and services; it has made the selling problem of many businesses much easier in that consumers are in many respects anxious to buy the products and services offered. And it has made the selling problem of other businesses difficult in that our economy of abundance has been characterized by a proliferation of new products which confront consumers with increasingly complex alternative choices.

Economic Forces. There are many economic forces which management must consider when it studies demand. Which forces are most important or relevant depends upon the particular product or service being considered. Generally, however, all managements are interested in study-ing the amount of total income of individual and family spending units, its distribution among spending units, and its expenditure by those units among the various classes of products and services.

The amount of income available to spending units is of basic impor-tance in estimating the potential demand for products and services. In recent decades, particularly since the end of World War II, the demand

Exhibit 4

NUMBER OF INDIVIDUAL AND FAMILY SPENDING UNITS AND THEIR INCOME BY FAMILY INCOME LEVEL, 1953–57

PERSONAL INCOME OF SPENDING UNITS BEFORE TAXES	NUMBER OF SPENDING UNITS (MILLIONS)					AGGREGATE PERSONAL INCOME (BILLIONS)				
	1953	1954	1955	1956	1957	1953	1954	1955	1956	1957
Under $2,000.....	8.5	9.0	8.2	7.6	7.3	$ 9.9	$ 10.5	$ 9.6	$ 8.9	$ 8.5
$2,000–$3,999....	13.4	13.8	13.6	12.7	12.1	40.8	42.0	41.4	38.6	36.9
$4,000–$5,999....	13.3	13.1	13.5	13.5	13.6	65.8	65.1	66.9	67.0	67.4
$6,000–$7,999....	7.8	7.7	8.5	9.2	9.6	53.5	53.2	58.5	63.5	66.3
$8,000–$9,999....	3.4	3.3	3.6	4.3	4.8	29.8	29.1	32.2	37.7	42.6
$10,000–$14,999..	2.6	2.7	3.0	3.5	3.9	31.6	31.9	36.2	42.5	46.7
Over $15,000.....	1.5	1.6	1.8	2.0	2.2	40.8	42.2	47.1	54.1	59.8
Total........	50.5	51.2	52.2	52.8	53.5	$272.2	$247.0	$291.9	$312.3	$328.2

PERCENTAGE DISTRIBUTION

PERSONAL INCOME OF SPENDING UNITS BEFORE TAXES	1953	1954	1955	1956	1957	1953	1954	1955	1956	1957
Under $2,000.....	17	18	16	14	14	4	4	3	3	3
$2,000–$3,999....	27	27	26	24	23	15	15	14	12	11
$4,000–$5,999....	26	26	26	26	25	24	24	23	22	21
$6,000–$7,999....	15	15	16	17	18	19	19	20	20	20
$8,000–$9,999....	7	6	7	8	9	11	11	11	12	13
$10,000–$14,999..	5	5	6	7	7	12	12	13	14	14
Over $15,000.....	3	3	3	4	4	15	15	16	17	18
Total........	100	100	100	100	100	100	100	100	100	100

Source: U.S. Department of Commerce, Survey of Current Business, April 1958, Table 2, p. 12.

for all goods and services has been increased substantially, not only be-cause of increases in population but because of substantial increases in total real income and of wider distribution of that income among spending units. The greater the income of a spending unit, the greater is the income available for discretionary spending, above that needed for necessities. Since the end of World War II, the demand for many products and serv-ices has been expanding because of the fact that a larger number of spend-ing units had obtained some amount of discretionary spending power. Data regarding the number of spending units and their income by selected income levels for the period 1953–57 are given in Exhibit 4.

The greatest limiting factor on the demand for many wantable products is the number of dollars which spending units have to spend. It is helpful to know not only the distribution of income among spending units but also how those spending units spend their dollars among the various classes of products and services. Study of consumer expenditures

Exhibit 5

PERSONAL CONSUMPTION EXPENDITURES BY PRODUCT AND SERVICE
CLASSES FOR SELECTED YEARS 1940–56

(In Millions)

Group	1940	1945	1950	1955	1956
Food and tobacco.............	$22,223	$ 44,573	$ 63,250	$ 81,361	$ 86,367
Clothing, accessories, and jewelry......................	8,857	19,706	22,705	25,648	27,017
Personal care................	1,036	1,982	2,355	3,182	3,581
Housing....................	9,327	12,407	21,356	31,120	32,841
Household operation..........	10,479	15,530	27,414	33,912	36,113
Medical care and death expense.	3,533	5,756	9,257	12,501	13,405
Personal business.............	3,646	4,431	8,181	12,766	13,968
Transportation...............	7,143	6,845	23,225	32,194	30,314
Recreation..................	3,761	6,139	10,768	13,020	13,844
Private education and research..	641	974	1,959	3,059	3,565
Religions and welfare activities.	1,012	1,735	2,463	3,370	3,746
Foreign travel and remittances..	223	1,621	1,093	2,288	2,399
Total...................	$71,881	$121,699	$194,026	$254,421	$267,160

PERCENTAGE DISTRIBUTION

Food and tobacco.............	30.9	36.6	32.6	32.0	32.3
Clothing, accessories, and jewelry......................	12.3	16.2	11.7	10.1	10.1
Personal care................	1.4	1.6	1.2	1.3	1.3
Housing....................	13.0	10.2	11.0	12.2	12.3
Household operation..........	14.6	12.8	14.1	13.3	13.5
Medical care and death expense.	4.9	4.7	4.8	4.9	5.0
Personal business.............	5.1	3.6	4.2	5.0	5.2
Transportation...............	9.9	5.6	12.0	12.7	11.3
Recreation..................	5.2	5.0	5.5	5.1	5.2
Private education and research..	0.9	0.8	1.0	1.2	1.3
Religions and welfare activities.	1.4	1.4	1.3	1.3	1.4
Foreign travel and remittances..	0.3	1.3	0.6	0.9	0.9
Total...................	100.0	100.0	100.0	100.0	100.0

Source: U.S. Bureau of Census, *Statistical Abtract of the United States*, 1958, Table 388, p. 308.

over time indicates trends of consumption and demand and suggests areas for inquiry regarding changes in demand. The expenditures of spending units for various classes of products and services for selected years in the period 1940–56 are given in Exhibit 5.

The reader should keep in mind, as he analyzes specific case situations, that aggregate income and expenditure data have only limited usefulness to the manufacturer. The individual manufacturer needs to obtain and analyze more detailed income and expenditure data which are relevant to his product or service. When available, such data are included in cases.

Technological Forces. The effect of invention upon the business of a manufacturer may be direct and relatively quick or it may be slow and indirect—but nevertheless powerful—through its influence upon people's living habits and wants, and consequently upon the distribution of their income among various classes of products and services. The outstanding example of the effect of invention is that of the automobile, which has affected almost every aspect of people's lives, being responsible for the growth of certain industries, such as the Portland cement industry, and being responsible for the decrease in demand for the products of other industries, such as the men's shoe industry.

In recent decades, major and minor technological developments in numerous industries have greatly affected the demand for classes of products and services; accordingly, particular attention should be given to this force in the analysis of many of the cases in this book.

Study of These Forces. By systematically studying the social, economic, and technological forces which are continually affecting demand, the business executive can develop a fairly good *approximation* of the principal determinants of the demand for the product or service class in which his merchandise falls. He can determine whether these forces are basically working to increase or decrease demand in *total* and on a *per capita* basis. This conclusion can help him to assess the probable effect of advertising upon demand. If the fashion is for men to be hatless, for instance, then the business executive will have a qualitative view of the problem confronting him if he desires to increase the demand for men's hats, a view which may suggest that advertising can be of only limited usefulness. Or, if the fashion is casual clothing for men, then the business executive may decide that advertising can be an effective means of speeding up acceptance of a fashion and hence an increasing demand for men's casual clothing.

Probably the best beginning point for study of the forces indicated above lies in study of the sales of classes of products and services over time, that is, in study of the trends in sales of new and of established products and services. Since the end of World War II, for instance, we have seen significant increases in the sales of automobiles, television and radio sets, sporting goods, electrical appliances, airline travel, power steering, plastic toys, Rock Cornish game hens, home permanents, and aluminum storm windows; and we have seen significant decreases in the per capita sales of double-breasted business suits, flour, 16-ounce woolen piece goods, wooden rowboats, laundry soap, manually operated sewing machines, and self-medication products. Recognition of these types of trends provides the basis for deeper inquiry into and better understanding of the specific forces and factors creating changes in people's living and buying behavior.

Not only must the business executive who makes decisions regarding advertising study these basic forces affecting demand but he must also study—become a student of—the behavior of individuals (psychology) and the behavior of groups (sociology), inasmuch as knowledge of individual and group behavior is important in understanding shifts in demand and consumption and in assessing the potentialities and objectives of advertising.

The Second Market Force: The Trade. In appraising and making decisions about selling strategy and the use of advertising, the business executive must also give special attention to trends in the behavior of the trade, that is, to the attitudes, motivations, reasoning, procedures, and activities of middlemen and retailers. An analysis of trade behavior with respect to the selling of a particular product is particularly helpful in formulating the objectives of advertising and in determining the advertising activities to be undertaken by management. Management must be appreciative of the viewpoint of the trade and adjust its selling and advertising program to the trade's needs, habits, and desires.

We cannot here indicate all of the trends regarding the trade which may affect the reader's thinking as he considers the case situations in this book. Several of the more significant trends are noted below, however, in order to suggest areas for discussion of cases.

1. The trend to *self-service* selling in many types of stores, such as food, variety, general-merchandise chains, discount houses, and department stores, has required the advertiser to devote more attention and promotional dollars to point-of-sale promotional effort, such as dealer display pieces, merchandise labels and tags, and product literature for prospects. As the relative effect of personal selling has lessened in stores employing more self-service selling, advertisers have been confronted with a gap in the total selling sequence which requires new types of promotional activity.

2. The trend to *scrambled retailing*, that is, the tendency of certain types of stores, such as supermarkets, to stock and sell more and more lines of merchandise not directly related to the original purpose of the business, deserves attention. There has been and is a blurring of definition of classes of retail outlets, for example, what is a supermarket? or what is a hardware store? The trend to scrambled retailing has required advertisers to adjust their selling and advertising programs to more complex channels of distribution and to a greater variety of trade requirements and desires.

3. The trend to *larger-scale retailing enterprises* has caused marked changes in trade practices which have affected the promotional activities of manufacturers. Large-scale operations, such as food chains, have been able to develop strong private labels which have competed effectively with manufacturers' brands. Because of the large volume of sales they represent to the individual manufacturer, large-scale retailers speak with much authority when they suggest or ask for changes in a manufacturer's

promotional policies. The complexities of managing a large operation has led to the development of more complicated buying procedures, such as buying committees, which in turn force manufacturers to readjust their use of salesmen and their methods of presenting the promotional and advertising plans for a brand.

4. The trend of *lower costs in operation* of many types of stores, such as chains, supermarkets, and discount houses, has forced advertisers to reconsider their pricing policies; changes in pricing policy have significantly affected the margins available for sales promotion.

5. The trend in the trade toward *better management* merits special attention. In recent years trade management has, with the aid of specialists, developed considerably more knowledge of the elements of the retail operation which affect its sales and profits. Trade management has become much more alert regarding the significance of private labels, shelf position, shelf space, pricing, packaging, and so on. It has developed a considerable knowledge not only of its own retailing operation but also of the implications of the marketing and promotion of manufacturers upon that operation. Consequently, the selling and advertising programs of manufacturers have been subject to critical appraisal. Their programs have had to be supported by good evidence regarding probable effectiveness, such as may come from successful test marketing of the product.

Over-all, with respect to the trade, the reader should bear in mind that the manufacturer's approach to the trade is determined in large part by the relative degree of control which he has over the marketing of his product. In some instances manufacturers may develop a dominant control over the entire marketing process because of the differentiating characteristics of their products and brands. In other instances the trade may play the dominant role, either because manufacturers have weak brand positions or because the trade has been effective in selling private labels. Accordingly, the manufacturer's selling and advertising approach will be determined in large part by what he has to do in his marketing effort to obtain good support from the trade at the point of purchase. In general we may state that any selling and advertising program of a manufacturer will be relatively ineffective if management ignores or miscalculates the characteristics of trade behavior which affect the selling and advertising of its product. Certainly manufacturers may expect better results from their promotional effort if they base the effort upon a realistic analysis of trade behavior and reasonably accommodate their actions to the needs and desires of the trade.

The Third Market Force: Competition. American business is characterized by fairly intense competition among manufacturers for the market or segments of a market. Trends in competition over time have a marked effect upon the selling and advertising strategy employed by competing manufacturers. Management must, accordingly, study these trends in order to devise and adjust its own strategy to the changing characteristics of competition. Several of the more significant trends regarding the force of competition are noted below:

1. The trend toward *bigness* has had many effects upon the selling and advertising strategy of competing manufacturers. The larger competitor in a given product field, for example, may find it possible to support large expenditures for nighttime network television programs, whereas the smaller competitor may find it impossible financially to consider the use of any type of nighttime or daytime network television program. Thus, the larger competitor may employ the most effective medium for the product class concerned, whereas the smaller competitor is forced to use a relatively less effective medium. Generally the larger competitor has a better opportunity to utilize all of the selling tools which he considers desirable; the smaller competitor must focus upon effective employment of one or several but not all of the selling tools which he considers desirable.

2. The trend toward *diversification* of product line or lines has intensified the advertising problem of the smaller competitor, and it has introduced new problems of co-ordination of selling and advertising effort among numerous brands for the larger, multiple-line competitor.

3. The trend to the use of *private brands*, particularly by integrated retailing operations, has already been noted, but it is emphasized here as a significant competitive force inasmuch as private-brand strategy may impose special promotional problems upon the advertiser of a manufacturer's brand. For example, in many instances, advertisers of manufacturers' brands have the very difficult problem of obtaining point-of-sale promotional effort comparable to the effort put behind competing private labels.

4. The trend toward regular programs of *new product development* and periodic, systematic *redevelopment of established products* has required the individual advertiser to reassess the position of his brand in the market place more frequently and precisely, and to reconsider of course the objectives and effectiveness of his advertising program. In product fields characterized by a constant influx of new products and modifications of established products, advertisers have had to adjust advertising activities and to seek advertising objectives relatively quickly, in order not to be executing an advertising strategy under one set of circumstances which was based upon a different set of circumstances in the past.

5. Finally, the trend toward increased use of *product, consumer, and marketing research* should be especially noted. Clearly, the probable effectiveness of any proposed advertising program will depend in large part upon the quantity and quality of information available to the decision-making executive. Increasingly, competition has been intensified by the greater use of information developed through marketing research activities. The degree to which competitors effectively develop or utilize

such information is of course an element over which the individual competitor has no control. He must seek to match or surpass competitive strategy.

The Fourth Market Force: Government Agencies. Over the last several decades, many of the advertising activities of business have been regulated or influenced by the activities of governmental agencies. Suffice it to state at this point that the advertiser must consider the effect of these activities upon his use of advertising; and, as a good citizen, he must learn to live with them.

Concluding Observations on the Market Forces Bearing upon the Marketing Mix. In the foregoing we have pointed out that management must consider the effect of four market forces upon demand if it is to begin to make a sound appraisal of the use of advertising in its business operation.

An analysis of the behavior of consumers helps management to discover the basic underlying social, economic, and technological forces which are affecting the total and per capita demand for the product or service under consideration, to conclude whether a real opportunity exists to increase total and per capita demand, to define the principal selling tasks to be undertaken if demand is to be stimulated, and to assess on a tentative basis the role to be played, if any, by advertising.

Consideration of the behavior of the trade usually provides management with a good understanding of the help which the trade can give in stimulating demand, of the limitations of the trade in undertaking certain types of selling effort, and of the problems caused by trade behavior which require the special attention of management as it devises a specific selling and advertising program. Particular tradesmen may be aggressive or unaggressive sellers, quick or slow to accept changes in retailing methods, likely or unlikely to demonstrate new products, and so on. Consideration of the specific characteristics of the behavior of particular trades is essential to the determination of the role of advertising in a given business operation.

The recognition of the impact of the behavior of competitors is generally self-evident, but special attention must be given to the position of the individual competitor relative to all other direct and pertinent indirect competitors. The larger competitor usually cannot take the risks involved in certain types of selling and advertising programs utilized by his smaller competitors; the smaller competitor usually cannot base his selling and advertising programs on as extensive market and marketing information as the larger competitor; and so on.

The over-all concept advanced above is this: as the result of analyzing the market forces bearing on the marketing mix, management has taken one step in the decision-making process regarding advertising which will allow it to determine the relative opportunity to increase demand, the marketing areas deserving special attention, and the general role, if any, which advertising might play in its business operation.

Elements of the Marketing Operation Bearing on the Marketing Mix

Although management cannot directly control the behavior of consumers, the trade, competition, and governmental agencies, it can control the elements of its own marketing operation. Management can make whatever decisions it wishes about product, packaging, branding, prices, margins and credit terms, channels of distribution, methods of physical distribution and service, quantity and quality of personal selling, quantity and quality of advertising, quantity and quality of other sales promotional tools, and so on. Thus, management, in the light of the specific circumstances confronting it in the market place, attempts to make decisions regarding the elements of its marketing operation, including decisions regarding the use of advertising, which will result in a marketing program that produces profitable sales. Decisions regarding the use of advertising call for an understanding of the specific conditions under which any business operates and of the relative contribution of each element of marketing to an effective total marketing operation.

Classification of Elements. The elements of the marketing operation of manufacturers may be classified in a variety of ways. For our purposes, we will concern ourselves with the 11 principal elements listed in Exhibit 1, as follows: (1) product planning (merchandising); (2) packaging; (3) pricing; (4) branding; (5) channels of distribution; (6) physical handling (warehousing, transportation); (7) quantity and quality of personal selling; (8) servicing; (9) quantity and quality of the other tools of sales promotion; (10) kind and quality of marketing-research information; and (11) quantity and quality of advertising, including display.

Product Planning. Clearly, the determination of the product (or service) to be offered to the market is the key marketing decision made by management. An understanding of the reasoning which leads management to the decision to market a specific product provides the executive concerned with advertising with his best basis for assessing the selling job to be done, that is, it does if management has based its decision upon good market and product information.

Of central interest are the design and qualities of the product, its potentialities and limitations in meeting a product need, and information regarding potential consumers: Who are they? Where are they? When are they in the market? And what quantities of the product are they likely to take in given periods of time? Consideration of these factors can lead the executive concerned with advertising decisions to a point where he can relate potential demand for a particular product to his analysis of the broad forces at work in the market place. He may conclude that change in product design will be required if the product is really to meet the needs of consumers; or he may conclude that the product, despite certain limitations, does fulfill a need and can be promoted effectively.

If management has conducted good product-research and consumer-research programs, good information will be available for the formulation of selling programs, perhaps even to the extent of defining the principal copy appeals to be used in advertisements. Too often, however, management lacks good product and consumer information, which makes advertising decision making a far less precise process.

In analyzing cases, the reader should sharply differentiate between situations in which he has adequate product and consumer information and situations in which he has quite inadequate information. The confidence with which he makes decisions regarding the use of advertising will be affected accordingly.

Packaging. Closely related to and often considered a part of product planning is packaging. It is separately listed here because it has become an element of importance in the marketing of most classes of consumer goods and significantly affects the advertising activities of many companies. In many instances the package itself adds to the wantability of a product—the packages used for so-called TV dinners, for example—and provides strong advertising appeals. Also, packaging has assumed greater significance at the point of sale as the amount of self-service selling has increased and the package has borne the burden of reminding prospects of a brand at the point of sale. Further, the package provides an advertising medium in that messages regarding the product may be featured on it; breakfast cereal manufacturers, for example, have utilized their packages to illustrate appetizing combinations of cereal and fruit.

With respect to advertising, management must determine the importance of packaging as it affects the opportunity to use advertising more effectively and must give proper consideration to the formulation of specific packages. Many of the cases in this book provide the basis for discussion of the importance of packaging.

Pricing. With respect to pricing and pricing policy, wide variation is to be found among businesses. In some instances management competes for sales on a price basis, that is, there is intense price competition. Accordingly, there are narrow margins available for selling effort, margins which are insufficient to support large-scale use of advertising. In other instances management competes on a nonprice basis, that is, there is less emphasis upon price and more emphasis upon product differentiation which will command a premium price. Accordingly, there are usually wide margins available for selling effort—sufficient margins to support large-scale use of advertising if advertising is deemed an effective and economical selling tool.

The degree to which price is an influence upon consumer buying behavior or to which margin is a factor in trade buying behavior is significant to the making of decisions regarding advertising. Special attention should be given to this element of the mix in the analysis of cases, because conclusions regarding the relative significance of price will influence decisions on the size of the total promotional fund and advertising budget.

Branding. Only several of many aspects of branding and branding policy will be noted here.

Generally, managements have followed one of three branding policies: developing individualized brand names, closely associating individualized brand names with the corporate or company name, or using a family brand name. In any situation attention should be given to the strengths and weaknesses of branding policy as it affects the use of advertising.

With respect to established products, the advertiser must consider, on the one hand, the brand image that he seeks to obtain as a result of his selling effort, and, on the other hand, the existing image that consumers have of his brand—the existing attitudes of prospects toward his brand. This comparison provides the advertiser with a basis for more specifically defining the advertising and selling jobs to be done. He may in certain instances find that negative attitudes or misconceptions exist which need to be corrected if his brand is to have a good image. Or he may find in other instances that positive attitudes and good conceptions exist of the brand image, and that he may then seek to refine further the image of his brand.

With respect to new products, the advertiser confronts other decisions. If he has a well-established, valuable family brand, he may wish to introduce his new product under that brand in order to obtain a ready acceptance of the new product at a low promotional cost. Or if he has followed a policy of using highly individualized brand names and desires to continue to do so with his new product, then he must take into account the relatively high costs of developing new brand names.

Whatever the circumstances, in making decisions regarding the use of advertising attention has to be given to the basis for branding, to the objectives sought in building a good brand image, to the existing conception of the brand by consumers, and to the strengths and weaknesses of the brand name as it is found in the market place. Further, attention has to be given to the basic psychological, visual, and auditory characteristics of the brand name. Some brand names evoke unpleasant mental associations, present real problems of visual presentation, or are difficult for the consumer to pronounce or spell. Other brand names have positive characteristics and associations which help make selling and advertising easier and more effective.

Channels of Distribution. Previously in this chapter observations were made regarding the influence of trade behavior upon the marketing and advertising practices of business. The essential point made was that management has to have a thorough understanding of the practices, attitudes, needs, and desires of the trade if it is to formulate effective selling and advertising programs. This element of the marketing mix has become increasingly important as the trade has gained greater influence in the total distribution process and as manufacturers have had to give increasing attention to working effectively to and through the trade.

Competitors in an industry frequently sell through different channels of distribution. For example, some manufacturers of greeting cards utilize door-to-door selling; others depend primarily upon variety and drug outlets; and still others seek sales through department stores, gift shops, and greeting-card stores. Even more often, competitors in an industry follow different selling strategies when working with the same channel of distribution. For example, in the greeting-card industry, the manufacturer of "Hallmark" greeting cards has relied heavily on brand advertising to consumers; its direct competitors have relied not upon brand advertising but rather upon personal selling and the strategy of working effectively with and through the trade.

Management's reasons for deciding to use given channels of distribution and for working with those channels in a given fashion must be taken into consideration in connection with the use of advertising, as an understanding of the reasons provides an additional basis for determining the objectives of advertising.

Physical Handling. From a marketing viewpoint, it is imperative that the manufacturer employ effective and economical systems of transportation and warehousing if he is to work successfully with the trade and consumers. In marketing industrial goods, particularly for highly standardized classes of industrial goods, these systems may provide the principal basis for advertising, such as appeals regarding well and widely located sources of supply and quick delivery. In marketing consumer goods, these systems may or may not allow certain types of promotional activities to be employed. For example, in many instances manufacturers cannot employ special promotions because their systems of physical handling will not allow proper co-ordination of advertising and physical movement of the promotion merchandise to and through the trade. Although few of the cases in this book deal with problems of physical handling, the reader should be alert to consider this element when it is an important consideration.

Personal Selling. The quantity and quality of personal selling in the marketing mixes of various businesses varies substantially. Primary dependence upon personal selling to obtain sales may be dictated over the longer run by the buying behavior of consumers and the trade and the character of competition in the industry. As has been indicated, personal selling is usually the principal selling tool for manufacturers of industrial goods. Primary dependence upon personal selling may be dictated also by the inability of management to support advertising expenditures large enough to be effective. In many instances new firms with new products will emphasize personal selling until such time as increases in sales volume will provide sufficient funds for a modest advertising program.

Advertising's relationship to personal selling must also be considered in the light of the specific objectives assigned to the sales force by management. The salesman's job may be to obtain new customers, to follow up inquiries obtained through advertising, to sell new products to existing customers, to take the orders of existing customers, to provide service to customers, to distribute dealer help materials, and so on. The role of advertising varies accordingly.

From the viewpoint of the executive who makes advertising decisions, it is essential to understand *the selling job to be done* in the marketing operation and to take into account the capacity of the sales organization to do the selling job. The quality of personal selling varies widely among businesses and over time. A new, inexperienced sales force cannot undertake as many selling jobs as a well-established, experienced sales force, nor can it do the selling job as well. The use of advertising in part depends upon the strengths and weaknesses of the existing personal selling force.

Servicing. The service provided by the manufacturer (or the service which he seeks to have the trade provide) often is an important element in the marketing operation pertinent to the use of advertising. Superior or adequate service procedures may be the chief basis for competition. Customers may be more interested in the characteristics of a manufacturer's service facilities than in the differentiating characteristics of his product. Consequently, attention should be given in analysis to the significance of service to buyers and to the opportunity to build effective advertising appeals which are based upon the service procedures of the advertiser.

Other Sales Promotional Tools. In addition to personal selling and advertising activities, as those activities are defined in Chapter 1, management frequently makes use of other tools of sales promotion to implement or to increase the effectiveness of personal selling and advertising, such as trade shows, portfolios for salesmen, and special deals for the trade and/or consumers.

Trade or consumer deals are deemed here to be essentially tactical reductions in price. Usually tactical price reductions appear in the marketing mixes of companies which compete in product fields affording limited opportunity for significant product differentiation. For example, special price deals have become an important selling element in the marketing of soap, tea, coffee, household paper products, and oleomargarine. If management decides that circumstances require regular or occasional use of price deals, then advertising's role changes. Its basic use may be to inform prospects of the special price, not to build strong attitudes toward the brand.

Marketing-Research Information. Since the end of World War I, one of the most notable advances in decision making regarding marketing and advertising has been the more factual approach employed by management in making such decisions. This approach has involved a wider awareness of the need for good information about all elements of marketing and has involved a greater use of information obtained from marketing-research activities. Although marketers and advertisers are still far from proficient in using the tools of marketing research, nonetheless they must closely examine the quality and quantity of information available to them and determine whether they are willing to make a decision based upon what is known, or whether they should postpone the decision until better information is available.

We will not here attempt even to sketch the interrelationships which may exist in actual business situations between advertising decision making, on the one hand, and the availability of good marketing information, on the other hand. Many of the cases in this book are designed to allow the reader to consider these interrelationships in some detail. Rather, let us state here that the soundness of decisions regarding advertising depends in large part upon the quantity and quality of information available to the advertising decision maker, his understanding of the potentialities and limitations of various research methods, and his use of available information.

Concluding Observations on Marketing Elements Bearing on the Marketing Mix. In the latter part of this chapter, we have pointed out that management must interrelate advertising with the other important elements of marketing. An analysis of these elements—an understanding of them—helps management to determine its selling strategy, to determine the role of advertising in the light of the strengths and weaknesses of its marketing operation, and to determine the specific objectives to be assigned to advertising. Such analysis calls for well-conceived concepts of what is involved and for skill in analysis.

A CONCLUDING NOTE TO SECTION I

The first three chapters have given a broad perspective on the use of advertising by business and of the principal factors considered by executives in top management in analyzing and making decisions regarding advertising. As was stated, in appraising the potentialities and limitations of advertising in a given situation, the individual business executive has to operate on an empirical basis. Accordingly, in analyzing the cases in this book, the reader should give particular attention to the process by which *he* analyzes and makes decisions.

The reader, like any other person coming to a situation involving advertising, undoubtedly has an inventory of ideas, theories, hypotheses, or useful working generalizations regarding marketing, selling, and advertising which determines the manner in which he considers and decides upon the use of advertising. This inventory may come from many sources: from one's own experience as a consumer and a recipient of advertising messages; from discussion with other persons of their experiences; from observation of the behavior of other people; from courses and readings in subjects relevant to advertising; from analyses of sales, market, and marketing research information; or from the appraisal of the past experience of the use of advertising by business.

Whatever the sources, everyone has such an inventory. It may be good, poor, or indifferent. It may be based upon thoughtful, systematic evaluation of good evidence or upon notions that lack a solid base of logic and evidence. Whatever the state of one's existing inventory, it is suggested that in analyzing and acting upon the cases in this book, the reader follow this procedure:

1. Identify the hypotheses which he is using to guide his analysis of case material.
2. Consider whether they are based upon good evidence and sound reasoning.
3. Recognize that hypotheses provide the bases for beginning the analytical process, not the bases for making a decision.
4. Continuously refine these hypotheses.

Section II

THE USE OF ADVERTISING TO STIMULATE PRIMARY DEMAND

An Introductory Note

This section consists of one chapter of declaratory material and eight cases which concern the use of advertising by four associations of manufacturers. As was pointed out in Chapter 2, the effective and profitable use of advertising calls for management to make a sound appraisal of whether a good opportunity exists to expand the primary demand for a class of product and then a sound appraisal of whether primary demand is likely to respond to advertising to a degree which makes the use of advertising profitable. The factors involved in appraising the expansibility of primary demand are most clearly apparent in situations wherein competing manufacturers have joined together in associations for the purpose of increasing the total demand for the class of product with which they are concerned. Accordingly, the first group of cases in this book deals with the use of advertising by associations of manufacturers.

Chapter 4

∿∿∿∿∿∿∿∿∿∿∿∿∿∿∿∿∿∿∿∿∿∿∿∿∿

THE USE OF ADVERTISING BY ASSOCIATIONS OF MANUFAC- TURERS TO STIMULATE PRIMARY DEMAND

In this century many associations of manufacturers have used advertising in their sales promotional programs in an effort to increase primary demand. In the 1950's, for example, over 50 associations were actively employing advertising as a significant element in programs directed at stimulating primary demand. Some of these associations were American Gas Association, American Petroleum Institute, American Potash Institute, American Rayon Institute, California Fruit Growers Exchange, California Raisin Advisory Board, Canvas Awning Institute, Cigar Institute of America, Douglas Fir Plywood Association, International Silk Association, Monument Association of America, National Broiler Council, National Red Cherry Association, Poultry and Egg National Board, Southern Pine Association, The Tea Council, Tile Council of America, Upholstery Leather Group, and Wine Advisory Board. Some of the other associations which have carried on co-operative advertising campaigns will be the subjects of cases in this section.

Some of these associations have been able to utilize advertising effectively and profitably for many years; others have found it unprofitable to sustain advertising campaigns even for a few years.

Study of the use of advertising by associations has led us to formulate certain generalizations regarding the effect of advertising upon primary demand and the factors which must be considered in appraising the opportunity to use advertising to affect primary demand. These generalizations are listed and discussed below.

Generalizations Regarding Advertising and Primary Demand

Reconsideration of Major Market Forces Affecting Consumers. It is clear that advertising has been effective and profitable in increasing primary demand in those instances where the social, economic, and technological forces bearing upon the demand for a particular product have been favorable to the expansion of demand. If these forces have been favorable, then intelligent use of advertising has heightened the desires already existing which favor an increase in demand and has speeded up the rate of increase in primary demand. On the other hand, if these forces have not been favorable, then the resistance which advertising has had to meet has been significant and advertising appeals have been ineffective.

As a means of affecting primary demand, advertising cannot be looked upon as so strong a force that it can counteract strong, longer-term changes in demand which are caused by longer-term, fundamental changes in social, economic, and technological circumstances. Advertising will not, if you will, induce people to replace the automobile with the horse and buggy; it will not influence homemakers to serve their families additional amounts of "fattening" foods if the weight of the prevailing medical counsel—and plain common sense—is against increased consumption of such foods.

Longer-Term versus Shorter-Term Changes. It is important to distinguish between situations in which primary demand is being affected primarily by fundamental, longer-term changes in living habits and needs and situations in which primary demand is being affected primarily by temporary, shorter-term changes in consumer attitudes and habits. In the post–World War II era the demand for many classes of products declined, not because of basic changes in living habits and needs but because of shorter-term shifts in consumer attitudes and desires. For example, the demand for jersey cloth for women's dresses declined, primarily because women, who had worn much jersey cloth during the war, desired to buy clothing which was made of fabrics that had not been generally obtainable during the war. Or to cite another example, the decision of many members of the color television set industry to discontinue the advertising of color television in the late 1950's was based not upon the conclusion that the longer-term demand outlook was poor but rather upon the conclusion that existing, unfavorable consumer attitudes regarding the quality of color television and the cost of receivers argued against profitable use of advertising at the time.

Discretionary Spending Power: A New Factor. The problem of appraising the opportunity to stimulate primary demand through the use of advertising has become increasingly difficult as more and more family buying units have obtained some amount of discretionary spending power, that is, income over and above that required to procure the necessities of life. When the majority of consumers had incomes which supported only a subsistence level of living, then the evaluation of the factors affecting their behavior and the determination of the probable effect of advertising upon behavior were relatively simple matters. But as the majority of family buying units have obtained some amount of discretionary spending power in the last several decades, their behavior has become much more complex and, accordingly, much more difficult to predict.

Consumers with discretionary spending power can consider alternative choices. They can entertain a much greater number and variety of needs, desires, attitudes, and motivations. Discretionary spending power allows a family buying unit to consider questions such as these: Will the family's *extra* dollars be spent on a motor boat for dad? summer camp for the kids? a mangle for mother? a swimming pool for the whole family? an electric organ? a second television set? a playroom in the basement? music lessons? camping equipment? membership in the local country club? or a trip to Europe? In confronting these and other questions, consumers usually can buy only several products of many that they would like to buy, and as a result, they are constantly seeking bases upon which to make reasonable value judgments about what they will buy next with their discretionary spending power. This line of thought suggests that advertising may play a far more important part in the future in shaping and reshaping the living habits, attitudes, desires, and patterns which affect the primary demand for many classes of product.

Study of Individual Consumers. Associations that have successfully employed advertising to increase primary demand have carefully studied their products in relationship to the behavior of individual consumers. They have studied the specific consumer need or needs filled by their product. More importantly, they have studied the ways in which the consumer fulfills a need by making a choice among several alternative products available to him. Ordinarily a particular need can be satisfied by at least several if not many products. A bathroom wall, for example, can be covered with ceramic tile, plastic tile, aluminum tile, wallpaper, paint, and so on. Consequently, the members of a particular industry, say the ceramics tile industry as an instance, must consider consumer attitudes regarding all types of wall coverings for the bathroom and must determine the opportunity to increase primary demand in the light of their findings regarding all types of wall coverings, not their consideration of the attributes of ceramic tile alone.

One notable aspect of the approach of associations to the problem of stimulating primary demand in recent years has been the greatly increased use of consumer research and other forms of marketing research. Without adequate marketing-research information, the appraisal of the opportunity to increase primary demand is of course difficult. Most of the cases in this section reflect the trend toward greater use of marketing-research information by associations of manufacturers.

Determination of Advertising Appeals. Closely associated with, or actually a part of, the study of the product in relationship to the behavior of consumers is the determination of appeals to buying motives for stimulating desire for the product. Study of the attitudes of consumers toward products and of the ways in which consumers use products acts as a guide to the copy appeals that can be presented to make the products wanted. The force or power of the appeals that can be associated with a product must be estimated: Are they likely to be significant with consumers? It is not enough to say that the product itself appeals to some basic want or desire of the consumer and that such appeals are "strong" ones. It is necessary always to think of appeals which are used for other products which satisfy about the same need. Thus, the advertiser must ask himself if his potential appeals are forceful or powerful enough to influence consumers to buy *his* product rather than any one of other competitive products which satisfy approximately the same want or desire.

Too often the advertising programs of associations have employed, as their principal copy appeal, an abstract idea that is not likely to induce the consumer to action. For example, years ago the retail jewelers carried on a rather extensive campaign trying to induce people to "buy gifts that last." It is questionable whether such an abstraction is likely to be effective. Certainly it lacks the force of an appeal centered on specific merchandise, the possession or use of which can be made to appear desirable. And, in the mid-1940's, the members of the men's hat industry undertook a campaign aimed essentially at influencing men to accept the notion that the fashion for men was hat wearing. This appeal was questionable because the prevailing fashion among men was "hatlessness"; that is, for many reasons, men and women either preferred or were indifferent to whether a man wore a hat or not.

Importance of a Good Merchandising Viewpoint. Study of primary demand campaigns suggests that frequently too much attention has been given to the selling of the existing product, too little attention to changing the industry's product in order that it more fully meets the needs and desires of consumers. Clearly, advertising which follows good merchandising policies achieves greater returns than does advertising which attempts to sell a product which for some reason or other fails fully to meet the needs and desires of consumers.

Building Estimates of Markets. The study of the wants which a product can fill and of the appeals which can be made to increase its use should be pursued to the desired end of building estimates of the increase in size of the market that can be developed for a product. The clearer the picture of consumer attitudes and habits of usage and buying, the better the judgments should be. At the start it is essential to determine as closely as possible the number of existing users of a product and the extent of their use of it. The quantities bought by different groups of consumers usually vary; and it is wise if possible to get some evidence regarding this variation in usage and the approximate number of people in different usage groups. Numerous questions may be raised: How frequently do members in the various usage classification buy, and in what quantity? What are the reasons for the variations in usage among groups, and to what extent can the usage be increased in the various groups? To what extent can nonusers be induced to buy, and in what quantity? Such information can be obtained in part through an analysis of existing market and sales data. Some judgments can be made on the basis of governmental statistics. Field surveys on consumer buying and usage may be desirable. Often estimates and judgments must be made on the basis of the observation of people and their habits, especially if no careful field survey of consumers' usage habits is available or possible. In the end, numerical estimates of existing and expected sales should be made, even though the latter be rough, in order to appraise the wisdom of a promotional expenditure.

The Effect of Price and Consumer Incomes. Special attention must be given to the effect of the buying power of individuals or groups of individuals in its relation to the stimulation of increased demand for a product. Unless the buying power of consumers becomes greater during a period of advertising or promotion, an inducement of increased purchases is likely to have to take place through displacement of purchases of other products. A product with high initial price will meet with relatively high resistance to purchase, especially among people with low or moderate income, unless it fills a need of some consequence and makes especially strong appeals. It is necessary always to relate price to purchasing power, importance of need, and strength of appeal. For a product of low price, even people of small means may be induced to buy if the commodity can be made attractive enough through advertising, because such a product will take relatively a small part of their incomes. Conversely, a product with high price will mean so much in the way of sacrifice of satisfactions given by other products that resistance to purchase will be great.

The Size of the Promotional Fund. As the reader will appreciate, the leaders of an industry association face several difficult problems in determining what is an adequate promotional fund and in obtaining contributions from members of their industry for the fund. The usual procedure is to determine what would be an adequate promotional fund in the light of the appraisal of the primary demand job to be done and in the light of analyses of the sizes of sales volume and gross margin before and after advertising. Then the task is to obtain contributions from industry members, who must in turn ask themselves whether the promised increases in sales and gross margins of the industry will in the longer term justify their own contributions to the promotional funds of the association.

In many instances, associations have not been able to obtain what were initially considered to be adequate promotional funds, and they then have redefined their marketing objectives and redetermined their promotional activities in the light of the size of the fund available. Too often the final promotional effort of the association has been so limited that it has been ineffective.

Practical Difficulties Met in Association Promotional Programs

It should be noted that numerous practical difficulties are met in initiating and conducting association programs, some of which are indicated in the cases contained in this book. Most of the problems to be met arise out of difficulties of obtaining wholehearted and effective co-operation from a number of firms whose managements frequently are highly individualistic and often inexperienced in sales promotion and advertising. To maintain support and interest is sometimes harder than to initiate a program; it calls for sound management and convincing leadership by association officers.

One of the greatest causes of ineffectiveness of co-operative promotional and advertising programs lies in the difficulty of obtaining effective co-ordination between the selling and advertising activities of the individual companies and the association activities. If, when an association launches an advertising program of merely an educational sort, co-operating firms sit back and expect wonders from it, they are doomed to disappointment. Such effectiveness as some association campaigns have attained seems to have come not so much from the advertising by the association as from the stimulation of more aggressive selling by all factors in the industry.

Often, when advertising is being considered by an association, other basic problems must be dealt with if advertising is to be effective. It is highly important that the over-all program be fashioned to meet the problems faced. If merchandise study is essential, the association should carry on a merchandise study. If price structures are a great hindrance to sales, an attack on the price problem should be carried on. Advertising and sales promotion are not things apart; they should not be expected to accomplish great results when conditions within the market or industry create excessive resistance.

Chapter 5

~~~~~~

CASES INVOLVING THE USE OF
ADVERTISING TO STIMULATE
PRIMARY DEMAND

This chapter consists of eight cases. The first two cases, Millers' National Federation and American Meat Institute, were selected to provide the reader with a sharp contrast in the problems facing associations of manufacturers operating in the same industry, the food industry. The third case, American Institute of Men's and Boys' Wear, Inc., deals with a number of promotional problems that involve the element of fashion. The last five cases concern Carpet Institute, Inc. They provide the reader with a more elaborate treatment of the steps undertaken by the Institute's management in appraising the desirability of employing advertising to stimulate primary demand for carpets and rugs.

Preceding each case are questions which the reader may find helpful in reading and analyzing the case. In several instances, introductory notes are also given.

~~~

CASE 1: MILLERS' NATIONAL FEDERATION[1]

QUESTIONS TO CONSIDER: (1) *Why have Americans consumed less and less wheat flour per capita, as indicated by the data in Exhibit 2? (2) Does the information presented in the study "What People Think about Bread" indicate any significant opportunities to increase the per capita consumption of wheat-flour products? (3) Was the promotional program of the Federation well planned to meet the industry's needs?*

[1] Written by Philip A. Sprague and Neil H. Borden.

The Millers' National Federation is the national association of the flour-milling industry. Its 482 members in 1949 represented over 95 per cent of the milling capacity of the United States. The Federation in 1949 was performing several functions for the industry: It served as a general center of information, holding conferences and conventions and supplying members with current bulletins on subjects of interest. It served as a clearinghouse and as a representative of the industry with regard to labor, governmental, and public relations. In addition to aiding in these functions, its 35-man staff, located in Chicago and Washington offices, worked with member companies in compiling trade statistics, in establishing trade

Exhibit 1

CONSUMPTION OF WHEAT FLOUR IN TERMS OF GRAIN IN THE UNITED STATES, 1909-39

Year	Millions of Bushels	Year	Millions of Bushels	Year	Millions of Bushels
1909........	450.7	1920.......	465.0	1931.......	491.7
1910........	467.4	1921.......	447.3	1932.......	475.2
1911........	463.2	1922.......	478.4	1933.......	464.0
1912........	480.0	1923.......	466.9	1934.......	468.7
1913........	478.9	1924.......	474.3	1935.......	465.5
1914........	489.6	1925.......	489.9	1936.......	486.3
1915........	467.7	1926.......	499.7	1937.......	476.4
1916........	498.5	1927.......	497.0	1938.......	484.2
1917........	490.6	1928.......	511.5	1939.......	485.7
1918........	402.9	1929.......	506.7		
1919........	485.4	1930.......	502.7		

Source: U.S. Department of Agriculture, Bureau of Agricultural Economics, *Agricultural Statistics, 1944* and *1946* (Washington, D.C.: Government Printing Office, 1944 and 1946).

practices and business ethics, and in setting up uniform accounting methods for the industry.

In 1939 there were approximately 2,100 establishments in the flour-milling trade, compared with over 10,000 at the start of the twentieth century. Over half of the existing mills were small, however, and served only local trade. Operations were largely automatic; only about 25,000 wage earners were employed by the industry in 1939 to turn out production valued at about $650 million. In 1948, mills located in Kansas, Minnesota, and New York (in order of importance) accounted for 40 per cent of total flour production; an additional 30 per cent came from mills in Missouri, Texas, Illinois, Washington, and Oklahoma.[2]

Statistics on wheat-flour production in 1945 revealed that the bulk of the industry's output was used for commercial baking (58.8 per cent) and home baking (24.5 per cent). The industry was characterized by overcapacity; even during the war and postwar period from 1941 to 1949,

[2] *Standard and Poor's Industry Survey B1-B,* Vol. XVII, No. 25, sec. 2, p. B1-4.

operations averaged only 71 per cent of capacity, with a high in 1947 of 84.7 per cent.

For nearly a quarter of a century prior to the end of World War II, the question of whether or not the flour-milling industry should actively advertise and promote the use of flour and wheat-flour products to consumers and special groups had been an industry issue. Discussion centered around the fact that while total consumption of wheat flour had risen slightly (see Exhibit 1), the per capita consumption of wheat flour in the United States had declined steadily since 1909. Exhibit 2 gives the per

Exhibit 2

MILLERS' NATIONAL FEDERATION

Per Capita Civilian Consumption of Wheat Flour in the
United States, 1909–47

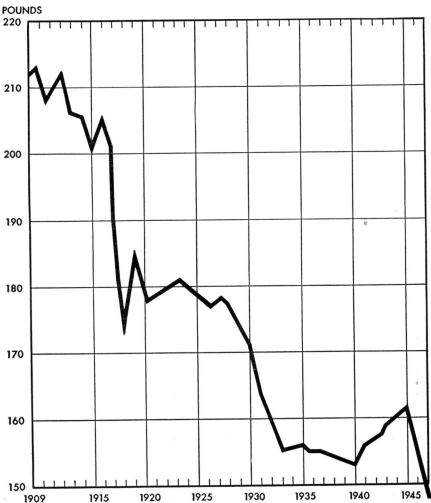

capita consumption of wheat flour in the United States from 1909 to 1947.

The first action taken by the industry through the Millers' National Federation in an attempt to alleviate this trend was the organization, in 1935, of the Wheat Flour Institute as a separate section of the Federation. The Institute worked with home economists in schools, colleges, and adult education fields; prepared recipes for use by magazine, newspaper, and food editors; wrote and distributed booklets; and photographed food subjects centered on wheat products.

As an answer to the criticism that many of the nutritive elements of wheat were removed during the milling process, the milling and baking industries in 1941 co-operated in the enrichment program inaugurated by the Foods and Nutrition Board of the National Research Council, and the Council on Foods and Nutrition and the Council on Pharmacy and Chemistry of the American Medical Association. Under this program, important B-vitamins and mineral iron were added to flour, bread, and other baked goods made from flour. The enrichment idea was publicized by the American Medical Association and was featured in the advertising of millers and bakers.

In 1946 the directors of the Millers' National Federation called in the J. Walter Thompson Company advertising agency to aid them in exploring the potentialities of a national program of consumer education to stimulate consumption of the industry's products. After thorough discussion and planning, the Federation issued a brochure to its members explaining a proposed Long-Range Program and enlisting their support. The brochure stated that the plan was based on four planks, which were described as follows:

1. *The Modern Food for Modern Living.* Paradoxically the problems which face our industry today spring largely from an assumption of long standing that our product is so essential that nothing serious could happen to it. In devoting ourselves to producing and marketing our individual brands competitively, we have neglected to fertilize the common ground which we all are cultivating. What we have really been relying on was a traditional habit of bread eating. It must now be apparent that not only is this habit on the wane, but constantly gaining momentum in the wrong direction. Thus, what we long considered an asset can, unless given a new twist, become a liability.

.   .   .   .

In other words, the popularity of our product, the desire for it, the preference for it, and the appeal it has to every person in America must be revitalized.

.   .   .   .

Times have changed since our fathers said grace for their daily bread.

.   .   .   .

And our wheat flour products are different. In their new and enriched form, they constitute an important modern food in this modern age.

.   .   .   .

Therefore, it is not necessary to embark upon the task of trying to get the public to go *back* to bread. Instead they can go *forward* to bread—to all that tempting array of wheat flour products which are now specially designed for today's faster living.

.   .   .   .

2. *The Taste Appeal.* All the vast accumulation of experience in the advertising and selling of food points to the fact that people buy one food over another because they *like* it—because *it tastes good.*

.   .   .   .

In the execution of the advertising and publicity which this plan contemplates, full use will be made of this advantage by keeping luscious pictures of bread and wheat flour products ever before the public.

3. *The Most for the Money.* The American public is canny. True, it may go on a spending orgy from time to time, and be free with its money upon occasion. But in the final analysis, it weighs values to the last penny, and the fellow with the biggest dollar's worth gets a very careful hearing from the housewife.

Here again, our industry earns first place. The advertising and publicity will make sure that every person in the country understands that nowhere but from our product can one get so much food value for so little money—so much in quantity or quality, so much in energy and in special protective nourishment for today's faster living, so much by way of variety, downright goodness, and taste satisfaction.

4. *The Great Balancer.* Running as a thread throughout every advertisement and every publicity story will be the fact that bread and wheat flour products constitute the great *balancer* of the nation's diet. This *balance* exists in all three of the fundamentals of food value.

A. Our product provides the world's most perfect *nutritional balance.*

.   .   .   .

B. Our product is almost indispensable to proper *menu balance.*

.   .   .   .

C. Our product is the housewife's foremost *budget balance.*

The brochure then proceeded to explain in general terms some of the methods which would be used in executing the plan—for example, four-color consumer magazine advertisements and special campaigns directed at food advisors, food editors, doctors, nutritionists, and educators. The brochure concluded with the following:

In entering into a long-range plan of this kind, we are not embarking in any way on new or uncharted waters. A great many industries have done it, and with extraordinarily uniform success. Just among the various food industries alone, there have been numerous promotions that are worthy of study.

Perhaps the most obvious conclusion to be drawn from the history of other industries is that if this plan fails to arrest and reverse our own downward trend, ours will be the only promotion of its kind that we know of which has so failed. If this conclusion is coupled with the fact that we have a more convincing story to tell, a better value to offer, and a wider and more constant market than any of these industries, it would seem that if we fail to change our sales curve, it could be only through inept handling of the tools at our disposal.

Regional meetings were then held throughout the country to explain the proposed Long-Range Program to Federation members. Millers were asked to accept a levy amounting to 0.8 cents per hundredweight of 1945 production for domestic consumption in order that a fund of $2.5 million to cover costs of the program for two years might be obtained. By the end of 1946, 169 members, representing 75 per cent of the milling capacity of the United States, had subscribed to assure this amount.

A Long-Range Committee, representative of the participating members, was then selected. One of its first actions was to retain the services of an experienced research organization. Subsequently, this firm presented to the committee a basic research plan (later approved by the committee) which was divided into four parts:

1. A study among the top authorities in the field of nutrition to determine where science places bread in relation to the characteristics of breadstuffs themselves and in relation to other available foods.
2. A study of consumers divided into two parts:
   a) Consumer attitudes toward wheat flour products.
   b) Consumer food habits.
3. A study of the attitudes and thinking of several professional groups, specialists in the fields of home economics, medicine, and journalism.
4. A study of wheat-flour policies and actions of restaurants, hotels, dining cars, industrial cafeterias, and school cafeterias.

While this research was being organized and undertaken, plans were formulated to begin the first consumer advertising campaign in September 1947. Unfortunately, this campaign had to be postponed because of the world-wide grain crisis and the resultant "Save Wheat" program undertaken in this country.

In the spring of 1948 the first research study, entitled "What People Think about Bread," was published and released to members. Significant findings of the study are summarized below:[3]

I. What people think about the amount of bread they eat:
   A. Types of bread consumed:

All types combined	100.0%
White bread	58.1
Biscuits	13.6
Whole wheat, cracked wheat	8.1
Rye, pumpernickel bread	4.6
Hard rolls, buns	3.1
Sweet rolls, buns	2.8
Pancakes, waffles	2.3
Corn bread	2.0
Soda crackers, tea biscuits	1.9
Muffins	1.2
All other bread types	1.7
All other bread products	0.6

[3] Generally speaking, the word "bread" as used in this study included all types of wheat breadstuffs (except sweet baked goods such as cake, pie, and cookies).

B. Quantities of bread consumed:
   The average consumption of bread products was equivalent to 6.47 slices of white bread per person per weekday.
C. Meals at which bread is eaten:

	Percentage of Respondents	Average Consumption of Bread per Meal, in Slices	Total Daily Consumption of Bread, in Slices
	100.0	2.35	6.47
Ate no bread...........	1.2	....	....
Ate at one meal only.....	6.9	1.74	1.74
Ate at two meals........	21.5	2.07	4.13
Ate at three meals.......	56.4	2.39	7.18
Ate at four meals*.......	14.0	2.52	10.09

* One or more snacks were counted as a meal.

D. Consumption by various classifications:
   1. In general, the greatest frequency of serving bread was in the South, followed by the Central, West, and finally the East.
   2. In size of community, rural farm areas led and metropolitan areas were last.
   3. Income status had little effect on consumption. The prosperous ate only slightly less than those of low income.
   4. Men ate bread more frequently than women, and children a bit more frequently than adults.
E. Attitudes about the "rightness" of the amount of bread eaten in a day:
   When asked how they considered the amount of bread eaten the previous day (see B and C), respondents answered as follows:

   "About right"...........................73.5%
   "Too much"............................. 9.9
   "Too little".............................12.2
   "Don't know"........................... 4.4

F. Lack of awareness that bread is nutritionally important:
   Most of the reasons why people felt the amount they ate was "about right" showed a lack of awareness that bread is nutritionally important. Only 16% of these respondents gave reasons based on the benefits to be derived from eating bread. Officials felt that this response indicated the small degree to which consumers associated nutritional benefits of bread with their reasoning processes concerning the amount eaten.
G. Attitudes about eating "a lot more bread":
   When asked: "How would you feel about eating a lot more bread?"
      81.2% said they would not like to eat more.
      11.9% said they would like to eat more.
       4.1% said they could eat more.
       0.9% said they should eat more.
H. Attitudes about doing without bread:
   When asked: "How would you feel about doing without bread?"
      20.4% said it would be impossible.
      26.4% said it would be difficult.
      32.4% said it would be possible but undesirable.
      19.6% said they could do so easily.

I. Attitudes of bread specified by nutritionists:
1. When asked the *maximum* proportion of the caloric intake that could come from bread and still meet nutritional standards in the United States:

40% of nutrition authorities estimated 60%–75%.

25% of nutrition authorities estimated 30%–40%.

35% of nutrition authorities felt it was impossible to make an estimate.

2. When asked the *minimum:*

48% said it would be zero.

38% said an estimate could not be made.

14% said it would be from 11% to 30%.

II. What people think about the nutritional value of bread:
A. Is bread good for people?

When asked whether eating bread is good for people:

71.4% said it was good for people.

25.4% gave qualified answers (e.g., "good to a certain extent").

2.0% said bread is not good for people.

B. Knowledge of enriched bread and appreciation of its meaning and benefits:

While about five out of six people had heard of enrichment, considerable differences existed in the various economic groups and by sex. In the prosperous classes 91.9% of the people had heard of enrichment whereas only 74.6% of the lower classes knew of it. 88.8% of the women, as against 77.3% of the men, had heard of enrichment.

C. How nutritionists define bread:

A composite majority opinion defined "bread" as a very important source of energy ("carbohydrates or calories") in the human diet.

D. Nutritionists' evaluation of enrichment:

Of the 22 nutritionists interviewed, 16 were favorable to enrichment, 5 were classified as neutral, and 1 unfavorable.

E. The place nutritionists give to bread in the diet:

Nutritionists agreed that bread was a basic food which could logically be included in the diets of young and old (even in reducing diets).

F. How consumers rate the food value of most white bread:

When asked to rate white bread in terms of what they consider its food value to be:

15.8% said "very high."

38.8% said "high."

34.1% said "fair."

5.7% said "low."

3.2% said "very low."

G. Foods selected as giving the most value:

When asked to select the foods giving the most value for the money:

16.0% named bread.

11.3% named potatoes.

31.7% named milk.

8.3% named meat and fish.

1.9% named fruit.

10.2% named eggs.

18.9% named vegetables.

III. What people think about the fattening tendency of bread:

A. Weight control and methods used:

When asked whether they had tried to gain or lose weight:

59.9% said they have not tried either.

24.0% said they have tried to lose.

1.9% said they have tried to do both.

14.2% said they have tried to gain.

B. Methods used to lose or gain weight:

People who had tried to control their weight were asked what they did to lose or gain. The consumption of bread was stated most frequently as something that was curtailed by those who tried to lose. Also, eating bread was the third most frequently mentioned method for gaining weight. In addition to those who referred to bread specifically, many others mentioned "starches" and "everything." Since these mentions could also be considered to include bread, it was concluded that bread came quite close to being almost universally considered a fattening food.

C. Nutritionists' view on the "fattening" question:

The majority of these authorities agreed that, calorie for calorie, bread and bread products were no more fattening than other food types.

D. The place of bread in reducing diets:

Most of the nutritionists who answered this question felt that bread had a definite place in reducing diets. A strong majority of these nutrition authorities were in favor of consumer education concerning weight reduction methods.

IV. What people think about bread as a product:

A. Attitudes about liking to eat bread:

When asked: "Do you like to eat bread?"

79.3% said they did.

10.0% gave qualified answers.

9.6% said they didn't.

B. Source of most loaf bread:

When asked where they obtained most of the loaf bread which they consumed, respondents replied as follows:

	Percentage of Total Respondents
Grocery or delicatessen	66.0
House-to-house delivery	10.1
Retail bakery	10.0
Baked at home	7.0
All other sources	0.4

C. Types of bread liked and disliked:

Respondents were asked to name any types of bread they liked or disliked. Almost twice as many named a type of bread they liked as named a type they did not like. There were significant differences in the extent to which people preferred or disliked different types of bread according to the various market characteristics.

PERCENTAGE OF RESPONDENTS LIKING

	East	Central	South	West
White...................	24.9	36.0	32.9	34.5
Rye or pumpernickel........	34.3	23.7	5.3	22.3
Italian, French, or Vienna...	35.4	15.9	6.4	32.6
Whole or cracked wheat....	18.0	24.2	16.6	33.2
Biscuits..................	2.8	6.2	31.7	7.2
Corn bread..............	0.5	3.1	20.3	0.3
Hot breads (unspecified)....	3.3	5.7	6.8	4.1

PERCENTAGE OF RESPONDENTS DISLIKING

	East	Central	South	West
Rye or pumpernickel........	15.9	15.5	16.4	26.6
Whole or cracked wheat...	19.3	14.8	18.3	13.5
White..................	5.7	4.6	2.7	6.3

V. What people think about bread in children's diets:
 A. Female respondents who were either mothers or members of families where there were children between the ages of 1 and 18 years were asked their opinion as to the quantity of bread and bread products a child should eat in a day in order to have a healthy and well-balanced diet. Results were as follows:

	No. of Slices per Day	
	Boys	Girls
1 year.........................	3.43	3.56
2–3 years......................	4.08	3.76
4–6 years......................	5.70	4.27
7–10 years.....................	5.37	5.05
11–14 years....................	6.60	5.88
15–18 years....................	7.44	5.56

 B. All female respondents were asked what children *should* and *do* eat when hungry between meals, with these results:

Food	Should Eat	Do Eat
Milk...........................	56.4%	13.9%
Bread..........................	50.1	35.2
Fruit..........................	44.5	14.5
Sweet baked goods...............	9.1	20.0
Candy and other sweets..........	0.7	38.3
Ice cream......................	0.5	16.2
Cake and pop...................	0.1	5.6
All other foods mentioned.........	6.3	5.2
No answer......................	2.4	16.4

With this information in front of them and with the knowledge that the grain crisis had passed, the committee and the advertising agency set out to design an advertising and promotional campaign to begin in September 1948. It was decided that the theme of the entire program would be "6-Way Nourishment," as personified by the illustration of a slice of bread with six colored flags protruding from it. This theme symbol is reproduced as Exhibit 3. Each flag bore the title and significance of one of the qualities which enriched wheat-flour products possess, as follows:

Exhibit 3

MILLERS' NATIONAL FEDERATION
Theme Symbol for Entire Long-Range Program

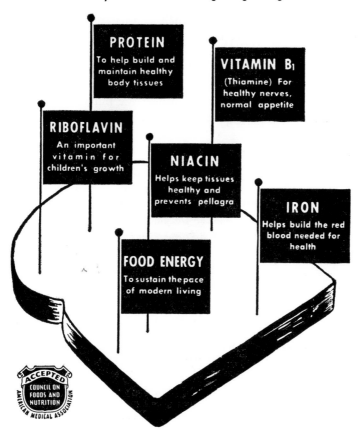

"*Protein*—to help build and maintain healthy body tissues; *Vitamin* B_1 (Thiamine)—for healthy nerves, normal appetite; *Riboflavin*—an important vitamin for children's growth; *Niacin*—helps keep tissues healthy and prevents pellagra; *Iron*—helps build the red blood needed for health; *Food Energy*—to sustain the pace of modern living." All nutritional statements were to have the acceptance of the Council on Foods and Nutrition of the American Medical Association, and all advertisements would carry the Council's "Seal of Acceptance."

Three separate campaigns were outlined, to be directed to three groups: professional people (doctors, nutritionists, and home economists); educational personnel at all levels and leaders in adult education; and the American public. The staff of the Wheat Flour Institute was expanded to enlarge its influence on the first group, professional people, as discussed earlier.

An Educational Advisory Council, a group of teachers experienced in various phases of education, was set up and was assigned the responsibility of developing and preparing the literature and other materials directed toward educational personnel and groups. Both the Wheat Flour Institute and the Educational Advisory Council worked closely with the long-range program publicity department, which prepared articles and photographs for newspapers, radio stations, and magazines.

In addition to this publicity, national magazine advertising and Sunday supplement newspaper advertising were selected as "the most powerful and direct avenue of approach, to inform the public and change what people think." The committee desired to cover all sections of the country

Exhibit 4

MILLERS' NATIONAL FEDERATION
Long-Range Program
National Advertising Schedule
(September–December 1948)
All in Four-Color. All Full Pages Except Those Starred (*)

Publication	Circulation	September†	October	November	December
Life.....................	5,200,000	out 9/10	out 10/8	out 11/19	out 12/3
The Saturday Evening Post..	3,800,000	out 9/22	out 10/20*	out 11/17	....
Better Homes & Gardens....	2,925,000	out 8/25	out 9/29*	....	out 11/24
Good Housekeeping.........	2,700,000	out 8/20	out 9/20*	out 10/20*	....
Ladies' Home Journal......	4,500,000	out 8/27	out 9/29	out 10/27*	....
McCall's.................	3,750,000	out 8/27	out 9/29*	....	out 11/26
True Story...............	2,250,000	....	out 9/15	out 10/15*	out 11/15
The Parents' Magazine......	1,150,000	out 8/20	....	out 10/20	....
Farm Journal.............	2,600,000	out 8/23	....	out 10/18*	....
Woman's Day.............	3,000,000	out 8/26	....	out 10/28*	....
Family Circle.............	1,500,000	out 8/26	out 9/30*	....	out 11/24*
American Weekly..........	9,600,000	out 9/12	....	out 11/21	....
This Week...............	8,750,000	out 9/19	....	out 11/14	....
Holland's................	500,000	out 8/15*	out 9/15*	....	out 11/15*
Progressive Farmer........	1,000,000	out 8/15*	....	out 10/15*	out 11/15*
Southern Agriculturist......	1,000,000	out 8/15*	out 9/15*	....	out 11/15*
Louisville Courier-Journal...	263,000	out 9/12*	out 10/10	....	out 12/12*
New Orleans Times-Picayune	267,000	out 9/12*	out 10/10	....	out 12/12*
Nashville Tennessean.......	130,000	out 9/12*	out 10/10*	....	out 12/12*
Total..............	54,885,000				

* Half-pages or ⅔ pages (four-color—"bleed"); all others, full pages.
† Dates shown are when publication goes into circulation.

as uniformly as possible and to influence consumers at all major economic levels.

In order to achieve these objectives, the schedules shown in Exhibits 4 and 5 were prepared. It will be noted that the newspapers specified

Exhibit 5

MILLERS' NATIONAL FEDERATION
Long-Range Program
National Advertising Schedule—as of December 22, 1948
(January–March 1949)
All Advertisements in Four Colors. All Fractional Pages, Bleed

Publication	Circulation	January†	February	March
Life....................	5,200,000	....	out 2/25	out 3/25
The Saturday Evening Post....	3,800,000	out 1/12	....	out 3/9
Better Homes & Gardens......	2,925,000	out 12/24	out 1/25*	....
Good Housekeeping...........	2,700,000	out 12/20	....	out 2/20*
Ladies' Home Journal.........	4,500,000	out 12/29	out 1/28	....
McCall's..................	3,750,000	out 12/29*	out 1/28	....
True Story.................	2,250,000	out 12/15*	out 1/15	....
The Parents' Magazine........	1,150,000	out 12/20	....	out 2/20
Farm Journal...............	2,600,000	out 12/20*	....	out 2/21*
Woman's Day...............	3,000,000	out 12/30*	....	out 2/24*
Family Circle...............	1,500,000	....	out 1/27*	....
Holland's..................	500,000	out 12/15*	....	out 2/15*
Progressive Farmer...........	1,000,000	....	out 1/15*	out 2/15*
Southern Agriculturist........	1,000,000	out 12/15*	....	out 2/15*
Louisville Courier-Journal.....	263,000	out 1/9*	....	out 3/6*
New Orleans Times-Picayune..	267,000	out 1/9*	....	out 3/6*
Nashville Tennessean.........	130,000	out 1/9*	....	out 3/6*
Atlanta Journal.............	300,000	....	out 2/6*	....
Columbia (S.C.) State........	68,000	....	out 2/6*	....
Houston Chronicle...........	177,000	....	out 2/6*	....
San Antonio Express.........	127,000	....	out 2/6*	....
Total.................	37,207,000			

* Half-pages or two columns (four-color—"bleed"); all others, full pages.
† Dates shown are when publication goes into circulation.

(with the exception of *This Week* and *American Weekly*) were exclusively southern papers. This selection was made to bolster the impact of the campaign in the South, where circulation of national magazines was lower than in other sections of the country. The large amount of baking done in the South (especially for biscuits) led to reinforcement of the campaign in this area. Exhibit 6 shows the percentage of circulation to families for the four major geographical areas of the United States.

In August 1948 the consumer campaign broke on the schedule shown in Exhibit 4. The first full-page, four-color advertisement (Exhibit 7), which typified the appeals used, was headlined "6-Way Nourishment from *Enriched* Bread and Flour."

Exhibit 6

MILLERS' NATIONAL FEDERATION

Long-Range Program Consumer Advertising Coverage:
Percentage of Circulation to Families

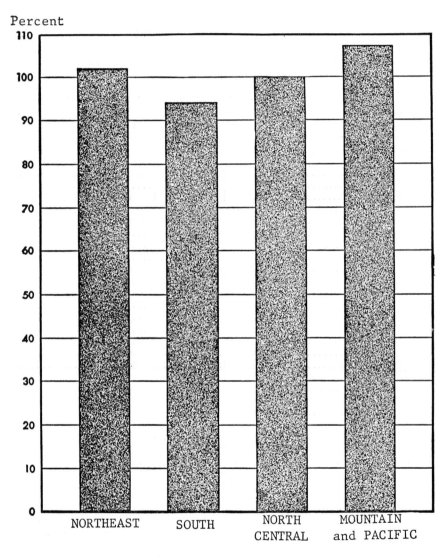

Large brochures containing advertising schedules, copies of advertisements, posters, display cards, package inserts, lapel tags, newspaper mats, radio announcements, and sales talks were sent to Federation members to be given to grocers and bakers by the millers' salesmen. Additional copies of any of these promotional pieces contained in the brochure

Exhibit 7

MILLERS' NATIONAL FEDERATION

First National Magazine Advertisement in Long-Range Program

could be obtained by the Federation members on request. They were urged to push the Long-Range Program in their advertising and to use the 6-way nourishment symbol on their stationery.

Special campaigns were also utilized. These were campaigns of short duration in which a special or timely use of wheat-flour products was accented. The first of these was the "Turkey Time" campaign run before Thanksgiving and Christmas, 1948. The following schedule of full-page, four-color advertisements was run:

Magazine	Date	Out-Date	Circulation
Life..........................	Nov. 22	Nov. 19	5,200,000
The Saturday Evening Post.......	Nov. 20	Nov. 17	3,800,000
American Weekly...............	Nov. 21	Nov. 21	9,600,000
This Week....................	Nov. 14	Nov. 14	8,750,000

The advertisement used for this campaign featured a large illustration of a turkey and hot rolls, with the headline "Turkey-time! Bread on the table . . . Bread in the bird!" Smaller illustrations showed turkey stuffing made with bread, a turkey sandwich, and a turkey casserole. Copy stressed the "holiday and everyday" deliciousness of bread, its 6-way nourishment, and the fact that it was not fattening. The 6-way symbol appeared in the right-hand corner with the Wheat Flour Institute signature.

In this campaign, also, promotional brochures explaining the advertisements and suggesting tie-ins were sent to Federation members for their salesmen's use. It was contemplated that two or three such campaigns would be run each year. A June "special event" was to feature the favorite picnic sandwiches of national celebrities.

~~~

CASE 2: AMERICAN MEAT INSTITUTE[1]

QUESTIONS TO CONSIDER: (1) *What are the principal factors which have determined the total demand for meat? (2) Has the industry's use of advertising since 1940 increased its sales and profits? (3) Was it reasonable to evaluate "meat's progress" on the basis of the percentage of consumer disposable income allotted to the purchase of meat? (4) In the light of the information given in this case, what promotional strategy do you think the Institute should pursue after 1956?*

In the period 1940–56 the American Meat Institute, the trade association of the meat-packing industry of the United States, maintained an extensive advertising and promotional program, its principal objective being to stimulate the consumption of meat by consumers. In the early part of 1957 the executives of the Institute reviewed some of the developments which had led to the decision to undertake consumer advertising and also reviewed the character of the promotional activities for the years 1940–56.

---

[1] Written by Gerald A. Simon and Martin V. Marshall.

Background of the Institute

The American Meat Institute was founded in 1919 as the Institute of American Meat Packers (the name was changed in 1940). In 1957 its membership consisted of approximately 700 companies of all sizes: about 400 members were meat packers or sausage manufacturers; about 300 "associate" members were manufacturers of products used by meat packers, such as containers and meat-cutting equipment. The total output of the meat-packer members represented the large majority of the commercial meat production in the United States. The Institute performed a number of services for its membership, as indicated by the titles of its eight operational departments: Advertising and Public Relations, Legal and Regulatory, Livestock, Marketing, Membership, Packing-House Practice and Research, Scientific Research, and Special Services.

Considerations Leading to the Promotional Program Begun in 1940

During the 1930's the meat industry, like nearly all industries in the United States, suffered from the decline in general business activity. As a result, men in all phases of the industry—from cattle growers to packers to meat retailers—gave increased attention to basic trends and characteristics of the industry in an effort not only to remedy their existing position but also to see what could be done to improve their future position.

The Trend of Per Capita Consumption. Between 1909 and 1935 the per capita consumption of meat in the United States followed a declining trend, as shown in Exhibit 1. During this period the index of meat prices was generally lower than the price index for all food prices and, in addition, was lower than the "cost-of-living" index.[2]

The principal reason for the long-continued decline in the per capita consumption of meat in the United States between 1909 and 1935 was commonly believed to be a change in the consumer diet which had been going on for several decades and which had become more noticeable in the years following 1920. Prepared cereals and foods, citrus fruits, and fresh vegetables had been assuming positions of increasing importance in the daily menu of the American people. Various dietary fads and health movements contributed to this development, and the advertising campaigns sponsored by organizations such as the California Fruit Growers Exchange apparently were influental in widening the market for and increasing the use of these products. The increase in the per capita consumption of oranges from 19 pounds in 1920 to 26 pounds in 1936 was indicative of the growing consumer interest in certain fruits and

---

[2] Also known as the consumers' price index, in which the index of food prices played a significant part.

Exhibit 1

AMERICAN MEAT INSTITUTE
Total Meat Production and Consumption in the United States, 1909–56*

Year	Beef Production Mil. Lb.	Beef Consumption Total Mil. Lb.	Beef Consumption Per Capita Lb.	Veal Production Mil. Lb.	Veal Consumption Total Mil. Lb.	Veal Consumption Per Capita Lb.	Lamb and Mutton Production Mil. Lb.	Lamb and Mutton Consumption Total Mil. Lb.	Lamb and Mutton Consumption Per Capita Lb.	Pork (Excl. Lard) Production Mil. Lb.	Pork (Excl. Lard) Consumption Total Mil. Lb.	Pork (Excl. Lard) Consumption Per Capita Lb.	All Meats Production Mil. Lb.	All Meats Consumption Total Mil. Lb.	All Meats Consumption Per Capita Lb.	Lard Production Mil. Lb.	Lard Consumption Total Mil. Lb.	Lard Consumption Per Capita Lb.	Civilian Population July 1‡ Mil.
1909	6,915	6,713	74.2	660	660	7.3	608	606	6.7	6,557	6,065	67.0	14,740	14,044	155.2	1,628	1,127	12.5	90.5
1910	6,647	6,508	70.4	667	667	7.2	597	596	6.5	6,087	5,756	62.3	13,998	13,527	146.4	1,553	1,156	12.5	92.4
1911	6,549	6,426	68.5	666	666	7.1	693	690	7.3	6,961	6,482	69.0	14,869	14,264	151.9	1,747	1,138	12.1	93.9
1912	6,234	6,153	64.6	662	662	6.9	735	729	7.7	6,822	6,357	66.7	14,453	13,901	145.9	1,658	1,102	11.6	95.3
1913	6,182	6,157	63.0	608	609	6.3	706	701	7.2	6,979	6,501	66.9	14,475	13,968	143.7	1,653	1,073	11.0	97.2
1914	6,017	6,144	62.0	569	572	5.8	693	708	7.1	6,824	6,453	65.1	14,103	13,877	140.0	1,554	1,090	11.0	99.1
1915	6,075	5,668	56.4	590	591	5.9	605	612	6.1	7,616	6,690	66.5	14,886	13,561	134.9	1,689	1,198	11.9	100.5
1916	6,460	6,003	58.9	655	656	6.4	585	595	5.8	8,207	7,037	69.0	15,907	14,291	140.1	1,706	1,228	12.0	102.0
1917	7,239	6,687	64.7	744	745	7.2	463	463	4.5	7,055	6,093	58.9	15,501	13,988	135.3	1,451	1,091	10.6	103.4
1918	7,726	7,167	68.5	760	761	7.3	506	499	4.8	8,349	6,384	61.0	17,341	14,811	141.6	1,899	1,291	12.3	104.6
1919	6,756	6,462	61.5	819	824	7.8	590	598	5.7	8,477	6,712	63.9	16,642	14,596	138.9	1,920	1,174	11.2	105.1
1920	6,306	6,293	59.1	842	852	8.0	538	578	5.4	7,648	6,766	63.5	15,334	14,489	136.0	1,958	1,319	12.4	106.5
1921	6,022	6,024	55.5	820	824	7.6	639	662	6.1	7,697	7,029	64.8	15,178	14,539	134.0	2,108	1,217	11.2	108.5
1922	6,588	6,503	59.1	852	858	7.8	553	565	5.1	8,145	7,236	65.7	16,138	15,162	137.7	2,302	1,503	13.7	110.1
1923	6,721	6,671	59.6	916	919	8.2	588	592	5.3	9,483	8,310	74.2	17,708	16,492	147.3	2,718	1,643	14.7	112.0
1924	6,877	6,786	59.5	972	977	8.6	597	596	5.2	9,149	8,451	74.0	17,595	16,810	147.3	2,660	1,663	14.6	114.1
1925	6,878	6,888	59.5	989	993	8.6	603	605	5.2	8,128	7,734	66.8	16,598	16,220	140.1	2,153	1,453	12.5	115.8
1926	7,089	7,074	60.3	955	959	8.2	639	637	5.4	7,966	7,529	64.1	16,649	16,199	138.0	2,206	1,465	12.5	117.4
1927	6,395	6,484	54.5	867	875	7.4	629	631	5.3	8,430	8,058	67.7	16,321	16,048	134.9	2,263	1,541	12.9	119.0
1928	5,771	5,872	48.7	773	781	6.5	663	662	5.5	9,041	8,545	70.9	16,248	15,860	131.6	2,458	1,626	13.5	120.5
1929	5,871	6,048	49.7	761	766	6.3	682	686	5.6	8,833	8,484	69.6	16,147	15,984	131.2	2,461	1,598	13.1	121.8
1930	5,917	6,021	48.9	792	794	6.4	825	824	6.7	8,482	8,246	67.0	16,016	15,885	129.0	2,227	1,584	12.9	123.1
1931	6,009	6,025	48.6	823	824	6.6	885	886	7.1	8,739	8,477	68.4	16,456	16,212	130.7	2,307	1,706	13.8	124.0
1932	5,789	5,830	46.7	822	822	6.6	884	882	7.1	8,923	8,825	70.7	16,418	16,359	131.1	2,380	1,814	14.5	124.8
1933§	6,440	6,469	51.5	891	891	7.1	852	849	6.8	9,234	8,885	70.7	17,417	17,094	136.1	2,475	1,772	14.1	125.6
1934§	8,345	8,066	63.8	1,246	1,182	9.4	851	798	6.3	8,397	8,141	64.4	18,839	18,187	143.9	2,091	1,648	13.0	126.4
1935§	6,608	6,770	53.2	1,023	1,087	8.5	877	923	7.3	5,919	6,155	48.4	14,427	14,935	117.4	1,276	1,226	9.6	127.2

Year																			
1936§	7,358	7,742	60.5	1,075	1,075	8.4	854	849	6.6	7,474	7,061	55.1	16,761	16,727	130.6	1,679	1,449	11.3	128.1
1937	6,798	7,107	55.2	1,108	1,108	8.6	852	857	6.6	6,951	7,185	55.8	15,709	16,257	126.2	1,431	1,361	10.6	128.8
1938	6,908	7,058	54.4	994	994	7.6	897	894	6.9	7,680	7,554	58.2	16,479	16,500	127.1	1,728	1,440	11.1	129.8
1939	7,011	7,159	54.7	991	991	7.6	872	869	6.6	8,660	8,474	64.7	17,534	17,493	133.6	2,037	1,671	12.8	130.9
1940	7,175	7,257	54.9	981	981	7.4	876	873	6.6	10,044	9,701	73.5	19,076	18,812	142.4	2,288	1,924	14.6	132.1
1941	8,082	8,021	60.9	1,036	1,005	7.6	923	901	6.8	9,528	9,007	68.4	19,569	18,934	143.7	2,228	1,879	14.3	131.8
1942	8,843	8,049	61.2	1,151	1,084	8.2	1,042	950	6.2	10,876	8,368	63.7	21,912	18,451	140.3	2,401	1,760	13.4	131.5
1943	8,571	6,860	53.3	1,167	1,059	8.2	1,104	830	5.4	13,640	10,172	78.9	24,482	18,921	146.8	2,865	1,819	14.1	128.9
1944	9,112	7,146	55.6	1,738	1,594	12.4	1,024	857	6.7	13,304	10,230	79.5	25,178	19,827	154.2	3,054	1,824	14.2	128.6
1945	10,276	7,665	59.4	1,664	1,536	11.9	1,054	943	7.3	10,697	8,598	66.6	23,691	18,742	145.2	2,066	1,622	12.6	129.1
1946	9,373	8,533	61.6	1,443	1,382	10.0	968	923	6.7	11,150	10,506	75.9	22,934	21,344	154.2	2,136	1,667	12.0	138.4
1947	10,432	9,916	69.6	1,605	1,545	10.8	799	762	5.3	10,502	9,919	69.6	23,338	22,142	155.3	2,402	1,904	13.4	142.6
1948	9,075	9,163	63.1	1,423	1,384	9.5	747	733	5.1	10,055	9,840	67.8	21,300	21,120	145.5	2,321	1,972	13.6	145.2
1949	9,439	9,439	63.9	1,334	1,310	8.9	603	609	4.1	10,286	9,991	67.7	21,662	21,349	144.6	2,534	1,892	12.8	147.6
1950	9,534	9,529	63.4	1,230	1,206	8.0	597	596	4.0	10,714	10,390	69.2	22,075	21,721	144.6	2,631	2,096	14.0	150.2
1951	8,837	8,472	56.1	1,059	1,003	6.6	521	517	3.4	11,481	10,857	71.9	21,898	20,489	138.0	2,863	2,102	13.9	151.1
1952	9,650	9,548	62.2	1,169	1,099	7.2	648	640	4.2	11,527	11,112	72.4	22,994	22,399	146.0	2,881	2,079	13.6	153.4
1953	12,407	12,113	77.6	1,546	1,485	9.5	729	735	4.7	10,006	9,900	63.5	24,688	24,233	155.3	2,355	2,010	12.9	156.0
1954	12,963	12,737	80.1	1,647	1,591	10.0	734	730	4.6	9,870	9,549	60.0	25,214	24,607	154.7	2,330	1,777	11.2	159.1
1955	13,569	13,306	82.0	1,578	1,531	9.4	758	753	4.6	10,991	10,834	66.8	26,896	26,424	162.8	2,660	1,994	12.3	162.3
1956	14,462	14,121	85.4	1,632	1,573	9.5	741	735	4.4	11,221	11,147	67.5	28,056	27,576	166.8	2,762	2,122	12.8	165.3

* Data for 1899–1908 may be found in *The Livestock and Meat Situation* for March 3, 1955, p. 20. Beginning 1940, data exclude meat produced in Hawaii and the Virgin Islands. Beginning 1941, consumption is civilian only. Units are carcass-weight equivalent; exclude edible offals.

† Computed from unrounded numbers. Includes lard entering into manufactured products.

‡ Census estimate unadjusted for underenumeration.

§ Includes production and consumption for government emergency programs.

Source: U.S. Department of Agriculture, *The Livestock and Meat Situation*, May 1957, Table No. 709–R1.

fresh vegetables. In general, after 1900 the average American consumed more fresh fruits and vegetables and more prepared foods and dairy products than ever before, all of which compared favorably in price with meat. There was one exception to the general trend of increased consumption (other than meat): the per capita consumption of grain products decreased from 300 pounds in 1910 to 200 pounds in 1935 (and to about 160 pounds in 1956).

After 1929 it became necessary for many families to economize in the purchase of food, and many observers noted that for a considerable number of families in the low-income groups, meat (even in the cheaper grades) was almost a semiluxury; the better cuts were unknown. In 1935 urban consumer groups in several cities made open and bitter protest against the high prices of meat. Strikes against the purchase of meat were carried out by militant organizations of housewives; meanwhile, dealers claimed that high prices resulted from the federal administration's program to restrict production of livestock. In reality the basic reason behind the reduced supplies and higher prices of 1935 was a serious drought which led to large-scale liquidation of livestock by the nation's farmers.

Promotion Efforts before 1940. For many years before 1940 executives of the public relations departments of a number of meat-packing companies and the American Meat Institute had tried to educate the consuming public to the virtues and problems of the industry. They had been particularly interested in explaining how retail prices were established and what were the dominant forces affecting prices. In addition, they also tried to dispel the popular belief that the profits earned by meat packers were unusually large. While there was considerable publicity on packers' problems, the amount of advertising of meat itself, sponsored either by individual packers or by trade associations, was relatively small.

Discussion of a possible co-operative advertising campaign to be sponsored by the Institute occured frequently during the 1930's. In 1935 a well-known executive in the meat-packing industry recommended that the Institute take some action immediately to promote consumption of meat. "It will take time," he declared, "to educate the housewife, and we should start now . . ."

Other industry executives, however, believed that a co-operative campaign should concern itself more with ameliorating the condition of consumer ill will toward packers. These executives were disturbed by the consumer buying strikes; they interpreted them as indicating a lack of understanding among consumers of the functions of the meat-packing industry. They concluded that an advertising campaign should try to dispel the idea among consumers that meat packers' profits were exhorbitantly high, resulting in the high prices to consumers, by explaining: (1) the economics of meat distribution, (2) the laws of supply and demand as they affect meat, (3) the low profits of packers, and (4) the extent to which the industry served as a tax collection agency for the federal government.

The attitudes toward the proposed co-operative advertising campaign of executives in the meat-packing industry were also influenced by a promotional and advertising program of another trade organization, the National Livestock and Meat Board. This organization was jointly financed by livestock growers and meat packers and was supported by the American Meat Institute.

In 1934 the National Livestock and Meat Board (NLMB) had initiated an advertising program designed (1) to emphasize the food value of meat products, and (2) to teach the housewife to cook meat properly so that, getting the most out of her meat expenditure, she would be inclined to purchase meat more often.

The NLMB Program. The NLMB program consisted of individual campaigns in three metropolitan markets—Boston, New York, and Philadelphia—and was partially supported by a large number of independent meat dealers in those cities. Each campaign was conducted as an individual unit for a one-year period. It was begun with a series of "meat for your good health" contests, in which prizes were awarded for the best recipes for preparing the particular cut of meat illustrated in a double-spread newspaper advertisement which appeared on one Sunday of each month. On each of the intervening Sundays an advertisement appeared featuring a weekly contest in which entrants were asked to supply a last line to an incomplete limerick dealing with the health benefits of meat, the winners receiving grocery prizes. The monthly contests culminated in a yearly competition, a Ford sedan being awarded for the best recipe submitted in the year's series of monthly contests.

At the close of the first full year of operation, meat dealers and the members of the Board were both pleased with the program. The Board hoped eventually to extend similar programs to every large city in the United States. This was naturally a slow process, because it was necessary to secure in advance the pledge of active participation of some 1,200 to 1,500 dealers in each market, and small independent meat dealers were said to be notoriously skeptical of the virtues of an advertising campaign.

The First Institute Campaign. Early in 1940 a portion of the membership of the American Meat Institute (representing about 70% of the meat-packing capacity of the nation) decided to underwrite a $100,000 test campaign in a national magazine to determine whether advertising could help in selling meat. Color pages in *Life* were used, featuring pork sausage links for two months and then featuring liver sausage. Some of the member packers reported a 14% rise in their sausage sales. In light of this sales evidence and the general feeling that the industry needed to advertise meat, the group decided to inaugurate an annual large-scale advertising and promotional program to increase the per capita consumption of meat. The expenses of this program were to be met by a levy of a fraction of a cent per head of dressed livestock.

Objectives of the Institute Program

The major long-run considerations behind the consumer advertising program sponsored by the American Meat Institute, as offered to the member companies in 1940 by the chairman of the Institute's Committee on Public Relations, are summarized below:

1. An advertising campaign would return more than the expense involved; a $2 million appropriation would average less than 2 cents per hundredweight.

2. In order for the meat-packing industry to produce a satisfactory return on investment, it must expand.

3. Although all meat produced was consumed with or without the use of advertising, profits of meat packers would be improved with advertising because the demand for meat would increase.

4. Essentially, meat packers have a product to offer the public which is good from any viewpoint, i.e., nutritionally, socially, and economically, and only vigorous consumer appeal was required for growth of consumer demand.

5. Advertising should be regarded as an investment which yields increases in profits.

6. The advertising expenditure of meat was less than 4% of the total annual expenditure for food advertising, while the value of meat production averaged about 17% of the total value of food produced; meat was far behind in the advertising parade.

7. Meat's percentage of the food dollar was threatened; the trend of food advertising was upward. Many food industries were just starting to advertise.

8. Meat production had not kept pace with population growth.

9. The opinions of experts, such as nutritionists, doctors, and scientists, had become more favorable to meat as compared to a few years previous. Without advertising, it would take years for these experts' favorable attitudes to become known to the public and favorably influence the public's buying behavior.

At the beginning of the program, it was recognized that adequate market data was not available for the determination of specific long-run targets for Institute advertising. As a consequence, market surveys became a regular part of the Institute's total promotional program. All of the surveys were conducted by the Elmo Roper organization. The first Roper survey, conducted in 1940, revealed that although 98.8% of the people interviewed indicated a real liking for meat, over 50% of the people interviewed believed that meats were hard to digest or otherwise not good for them. Furthermore, it was found that a large percentage of homemakers frequently bought the same 15 cuts of meat and ignored the 185 or more other cuts which were nutritions, tasty, and cheap. It was also learned that consumers were often unaware of the nutritious value of meat. (Later Roper surveys also examined consumer attitudes toward the meat-packing industry.)

The Institute's Advertising and Promotional Activities—1940–56

A summary of the advertising and promotional activities of the American Meat Institute for the period 1940–56 is given in Exhibit 2. Comments regarding various phases of these activities follow:

Except for the period 1953–54, the Institute consistently addressed three groups in its advertising: (1) consumers, (2) the medical profession, and (3) home economists and educators.

As a result of information obtained from the first Roper survey, the first major advertising campaign—the campaign of 1941—emphasized the nutritional value and digestibility of meat. In addition, homemakers were told how to get several meals from specific cuts of meat, and their attention was also directed to lesser-known cuts. These advertisements were signed by the American Meat Institute, and, in addition, they bore the seal of the Council of Foods and Nutrition of the American Medical Association.

Subsequent product advertising of the Institute essentially emphasized the nutritional values of meat and the numerous cuts which were available, as described in Exhibit 2. One example of the nutritional advertising published by the Institute is shown in Exhibit 3, an advertisement which appeared in the October 11, 1948 issue of *Life*.

As a supplement to the product advertising campaigns, the Institute maintained a public relations and publicity program. This program included a steady flow of news releases, recipes, and suggestions to food editors of magazines, newspapers, and broadcasting stations. Later, beginning in the World War II years, greater emphasis was placed on using consumer media for public relations messages. By 1949 the Institute shifted primary emphasis from product advertising to public relations advertising.

The public relations advertising program initiated in early 1949 consisted of four parts. The first part concerned the "Meat Team"—farmers, packinghouse workers, and retailers—and had as its objective the stimulation of interest by these three groups in supporting the public relations program of the meat industry. Full-page color advertisements, appearing in *Life* and *The Saturday Evening Post* in June 1949, keynoted the beginning of the campaign. These advertisements featured pictures of three men under the headline "Your Meat Team." Similar advertisements appeared in a newspaper in all participant plant cities. (Previously, a public relations promotional package, including a kit for retailers, had been distributed to participating plants.) The second phase of the public relations

Exhibit 2

AMERICAN MEAT INSTITUTE

Summary of Advertising and Promotional Activities, 1940–56

Year	Activity	Group Addressed	Themes—Appeals	Media	Expenditure	Aim
1940	Test advertising campaign.	Consuming public.	Pork sausage links, liver sausage.	*Life*—full page.	$100,000	To increase consumer use of sausage in natural casings.
	Advertising campaign.	Medical profession.	New discoveries showing that meat did not have harmful effects (e.g., high blood pressure), as previously believed.	Professional journals (e.g., *Hygeia*).		To remind medical profession of new findings regarding the value of meat in the diet and to correct misconceptions.
	First Roper survey.	Consuming public.				To determine consumer knowledge and opinion of meat.
1941	First large-scale advertising and promotional program.	1. Consuming public.	*a) Emotional Appeal:* Edgar Guest poem "Meat on the Table"; played up taste, health, thrift values of meat.	*Life, The Saturday Evening Post,* full pages, four-color.		To achieve better appreciation and greater use of meat by consumers.
			b) Educational Facts: Meat's digestibility, richness in vitamins, value as part of childrens diet.	10 general national magazines (e.g., *Collier's, Look, Redbook, Parents' Magazine, American Home*), 2 columns, black and white. 1,500-line black and white advertisements in 150 newspapers for start of campaign.		

Year	Group	Message	Media	Budget	Objectives
			Thereafter, 300-line black and white on Thursdays or Fridays.		
		c) *Service, Economy and Use:* Essentiality of meat and economy of use; specific recipes, new ideas for serving.	*Ladies' Home Journal, Good Housekeeping, McCall's, Woman's Home Companion*—1 and 2 page, full color.	$2,000,000	
		d) *Specific Products:* (e.g., sausage).	*Life, The Saturday Evening Post*—full pages, full color.		
	2. Medical profession.	Merits of meat with regard to health.	10 professional journals (e.g., *Hygeia*).		To continue educational information to medical profession regarding meat's health virtues.
	3. Home economists and educators.	Meat in diets; many uses.	4 trade papers (e.g., *Forecast for Home Economics*).		To achieve approval and understanding of meat by this group.
	4. Meat industry.	What program of American Meat Institute will do for the industry.	10 trade papers. 25 agricultural papers.		To inform industry of program and enlist its support.
	5. Institute members and their customers.		Point-of-purchase materials to be given to retailers by packer salesmen.		To tie campaign to point-of-purchase level.
1942	Continuation of program.	Same groups as in 1941 with exception of meat industry.	Generally, same as in 1941; more stress placed on unusual cuts of meat.	Generally, same as in 1941. 15% increase in newspaper appropriation. Addition of 1,700 outdoor posters, of which one half were illuminated.	$2,000,000	Same as in 1941 except for appeal to meat industry.

Exhibit 2 (Continued)

AMERICAN MEAT INSTITUTE

Summary of Advertising and Promotional Activities, 1940–56

Year	Activity	Group Addressed	Themes—Appeals	Media	Expenditure	Aim
1943 1944 1945	Continuation of program.	Same groups as in 1942.	Because of shortage of meat, appeals for greater per capita consumption were dropped. Education replaced promotion as primary theme.	Same as in 1942 with continued emphasis on newspapers for quick transmittal of OPA information to the public.	$1,500,000 to $2,000,000 per year.	To aid government in explaining shortages and rationing while still maintaining the popularity of meat in the eyes of the public.
1946	Continuation of program.	Same groups as in 1942.	Generally, the same as prewar with the following changes: 1. Promotion of a specific cut of meat each month. 2. Recipes, appetite appeals, nutrition facts. 3. Industry's position regarding controls, OPA, etc.	*Life, The Saturday Evening Post*—full pages, four-color. Radio—Fred Waring Show. 5 women's magazines (e.g., *Ladies' Home Journal*). Radio—Fred Waring Show. Newspapers. Radio—Fred Waring Show. (Tuesday and Thursday, NBC).	$2,250,000	To encourage greater public consumption of meat and explain industry's resistance to government control.
1947	Continuation of program. Second Roper survey.	Same groups as in 1942. Consuming public.	Generally, same as in 1946. Industry problems discussed in - - - - - - - →	Same as in 1946. Newspapers	$2,500,000	Same as in 1942. To determine extent of effect of program over first 7 years as well as public's opinion of and knowledge of the meat industry.

Year						
1948	Continuation of program.	Same groups as in 1942.	Some shift to public relations emphasis.	$400,000 of product copy to be replaced by pretested public relations advertising. 10 large-space advertisements in 400 newspapers, appearing monthly. 1 national weekly and 2 women's magazines dropped. Radio—Fred Waring Show.	$2,500,000	To continue to encourage greater meat consumption and educate public about meat industry (profits, etc.).
1949	Continuation of program.	Same groups as in 1942.	Increased emphasis on public relations: 1. "Your Meat Team" (what the industry does for the consumer). 2. Product advertising. 3. Service, economy, and use. 4. Both public relations and product advertising.	*Life* and *Look.* / *Life* and *Look.* *Ladies' Home Journal, Woman's Home Companion, Good Housekeeping.* Radio—Fred Waring Show, NBC, Thursday morning.	$2,500,000	Same as in 1948.
1950	Continuation of program.	Consuming public. Medical profession.	Same as in 1949.	*Life* and *Look.* 9 women's service magazines. 23 trade and influence publications, such as *Time, Atlantic.*	$2,000,000	Same as in 1948.

Exhibit 2 (Continued)

AMERICAN MEAT INSTITUTE

Summary of Advertising and Promotional Activities, 1940–56

Year	Activity	Group Addressed	Themes—Appeals	Media	Expenditure	Aim
	Third Roper survey.	Consuming public.				To determine progress made with consumers.
1951 1952	Continuation of program.	Consuming public. Medical profession.	Same as 1949.	Same as 1950.	$2,000,000 per year.	Same as 1948.
1953	Fourth Roper survey.	Selected influential leaders in government and industry.			$ 400,000	To determine attitudes toward meat packers and meat industry.
	Public relations campaign.	Thought leaders and influential figures who form public opinion.	Nutritional merits of meat, economic importance of industry, product availability, why and how industry works as it does.	17 influential magazines, such as *Atlantic, New Yorker,* plus *Life* and *The Saturday Evening Post.* Split pages, black and white.		To educate public opinion "molders" on nutrition and on services of meat packing industry.
	Continuing medical advertising.	Medical profession.	Meat is good food nutritionally.	Leading medical journals.		To keep doctors informed on latest nutritional findings on meat.

Year	Activities	Audience	Theme	Media	Budget	Objective
1954	Continuation of 1953 program.				$ 400,000	
1955	Special promotions of meat "in season."	Consuming public.	Back to original nutritional themes plus product availability "in season."	The Saturday Evening Post and store books. Periodic point-of-sale promotions.	$ 400,000	To educate on nutritional qualities of meat and to move seasonal highs in supplies into consumption.
	Continuing medical advertising.					
1956	Special Roper survey.	Consuming public.			$ 700,000	To determine consumer attitudes toward pork.
	Special pork promotion.	Consuming public.	Pork is in good supply—price is low.	Special point-of-sale promotion in 15,000 supermarkets. Network radio and television.		To move large pork supplies into consumption rapidly.
	Continuing medical advertising.					

Exhibit 3

AMERICAN MEAT INSTITUTE

An Advertisement Emphasizing the Nutritional Values of Meat

MEAT as a source of protein, B vitamins, iron

All ratings based on cooked values

KIND OF MEAT	COMPLETE PROTEIN	B VITAMINS			FOOD IRON
		THIAMINE (B₁)	RIBOFLAVIN (B₂)	NIACIN	
PORK	EXCELLENT	EXCELLENT	FAIR	EXCELLENT	EXCELLENT
BEEF	EXCELLENT	FAIR	EXCELLENT	EXCELLENT	EXCELLENT
LAMB	EXCELLENT	FAIR	GOOD	EXCELLENT	EXCELLENT
VEAL	EXCELLENT	GOOD	GOOD	EXCELLENT	EXCELLENT
VARIETY MEATS (LIVER, HEART, KIDNEY)	EXCELLENT	EXCELLENT	EXCELLENT	EXCELLENT	EXCELLENT
SAUSAGE (FRANKFURTERS, BOLOGNA)	EXCELLENT	GOOD	GOOD	GOOD	EXCELLENT

All meats also contain the minerals—copper and phosphorus—in significant quantities.

Best-Known Functions of Protein
Complete protein has all ten of the essential amino acids that the body must have to build, maintain and repair tissue. Needed by children in proportionately larger amounts than adults, for healthy growth.

Best-Known Functions of the B Vitamins
All are necessary for growth, vigor and general well-being. **Thiamine**—essential for healthy nerves, good appetite. **Riboflavin**—protects against certain eye and skin conditions. **Niacin**—for prevention of pellagra, a serious deficiency disease.

Best-Known Functions of Minerals
Iron—essential to hemoglobin, which carries oxygen in the blood. Deficiency causes anemia. **Copper**—apparently enables the body to utilize iron better. **Phosphorus**—combines with calcium in building bones and teeth.

YOU knew meat was good ... but did you know it was this good? Your instinct has always said "Yes" to meat ... now science tells why. And the chart above only begins to tell the story.

Notice that it lists *complete* protein as the kind meat has. This means meat protein has all of the ten essential "building blocks" or amino acids. This is important because these "building blocks" can work only as a team.

Laboratory research indicates that when even one of the ten is missing at a meal, the team can't go to work efficiently building muscle tissue and blood, and replacing worn-out body cells with fresh, new ones. *None of these building blocks are missing when the meal is built around meat.*

Sausage for breakfast, hamburger for lunch, roast for dinner—in any meat meal, you know that you are getting *complete* protein and all of its body-building benefits.

AMERICAN MEAT INSTITUTE
Headquarters, Chicago   •   Members throughout the U. S.

This Seal means that all nutritional statements made in this advertisement are acceptable to the Council on Foods and Nutrition of the American Medical Association.

program explained the services performed by the farmer, the processor, and the retailer in the effective distribution of meat. The third part featured an advertising program built around the theme that meat serves the consumer, the soil, and the nation. The objective of the fourth part of the 1949 public relations program was to explain how meat served everybody.

In 1953 the Institute's product advertising to consumers was discontinued altogether and the advertising budget was reduced from $2 million to $400,000. Reasons given for this move were as follows:

1. The Institute's product advertising campaigns had generally achieved their objectives in that consumers "believed in" meat.
2. Less progress had been made with consumers in their attitudes toward the meat-packing industry; public relations advertising through selected "influence" media would be less costly than product advertising.
3. While profits in the meat-packing industry were typically low, profits had been particularly low in 1952.[3] As a consequence, Institute members were agreeable to the idea of reducing the Institute's expenditure for consumer advertising.

Because of industry concern in 1953 with unfavorable consumer attitudes toward meat packers, as revealed in the Roper consumer surveys, a special Roper survey was taken of the attitudes of "thought leaders" in business and government; then, an advertising campaign was directed at this group during 1953 and 1954. An example of one of these advertisements is given in Exhibit 4.

After two years the thought-leader approach was discontinued and attention was directed back to consumers and product advertising for four reasons. First, the meat-packing industry's profits continued at a relatively low level,[4] and the Institute wanted to stimulate consumer demand for meat in the hope that meat packers' margins would increase. Second, the Institute's members were less aware of the influence campaign than they were of previous consumer campaigns. There was a consequent danger, therefore, that member companies would lose interest in the Institute's over-all program. Third, the influence advertising could not be promoted through point-of-purchase displays in retail stores where meat was sold; previously, consumer advertising had been extensively promoted through retail stores by Institute personnel. Fourth, it was difficult to measure and hard to justify the relatively "intangible" nature of the influence campaign. Institute executives concluded, as a result of their experience with the thought-leader campaign, that public relations channels should be used to sell ideas about meat and the meat industry and that advertising should be addressed to consumers, to sell meat.

National advertising to consumers, which was resumed in 1955, was significantly different from earlier consumer advertising; this advertising did not refer to the meat industry and it promoted meats "in season," while the total budget for all Institute advertising was $400,000, compared to $2 million in 1952 and $2.5 million in the late 1940's.

---

[3] Meat packers' reported earnings as a percentage of sales in 1952 was 0.5%. The average ratio of American Meat Institute member companies' earnings to net worth in 1952 was 4.4%.

[4] Earnings as percentage of sales were reported for 1953, 1954, 1955, and 1956, respectively, as follows: 0.8%; 0.4%; 0.9%; and 1.01%.

Exhibit 4

AMERICAN MEAT INSTITUTE
An Influence Advertisement

What Happened to Meat Prices?

THE year-end report of the U. S. Bureau of Labor Statistics makes mighty good reading for people who like meat, and that means about everybody.

It shows that as of December 30, average wholesale meat prices were 20% lower than the levels of August 19—the high point of the year.

While declines at retail aren't the same for all grades and cuts, by watching for specials you can get more mileage for your meat money than you could a short while back. This is especially true if you will remember that there is a lot of good meat around besides center cut pork chops ... or fancy steaks from top grades of beef.

What's the reason for lower meat prices? The answer is simple — *greater meat production* — more livestock came to market during this period.

Meat prices follow the age-old law of supply and demand ... how much meat there is, how many people want it, and how much they have to spend for it.

Did you know

... that there are more than *4,000 individual meat packing companies* in the United States ... that they compete with each other daily both for the meat animals and for customers ... that this two-way competition (plus modern, mass-production methods and full use of by-products) brings your meat to you at a *lower service cost between farm and table than almost any other food?*

AMERICAN MEAT INSTITUTE

Headquarters, Chicago • Members throughout the U. S.

Institute executives believed that they could make best use of available promotional funds by concentrating the timing of product advertising at times when supplies of specific meats were most plentiful. Therefore, pork was advertised between January and March, beef in the spring, and cold cuts and frankfurters were advertised in the summer. For example,

Exhibit 5

AMERICAN MEAT INSTITUTE

Consumer Advertisement of Pork

Why the **PORK** we like to eat does us so much good

YOU NEED BODY-BUILDING PROTEIN DAILY. The body does not store protein as readily as it does fat. It is therefore vitally necessary to health that an adequate amount of protein be included in the daily diet. Plenty of protein is helpful at all ages and particularly for growing children. Nutritionists agree that meat is one of the best ways—and one of the best tasting ways—to get protein daily.

THE PRICE OF PORK is lower in winter than in summer because the supply is greater. Pork, and all other meat, is delivered *where* you want it, *when* you want it, in all the delicious cuts and varieties you want, by the progressive meat packers who constitute the American Meat Institute ...*at the lowest cost from farm to table of almost any food.*

PORK...easily digested, deliciously tasty, highly nutritious ... is an excellent example of how meat helps maintain good nutritional health and contributes to the joy of living. Like all meat, it is rich in complete, high-quality protein, food iron and the B group of vitamins. Pork is an especially good source of B_1 (thiamine), a vitamin essential for growth, good appetite, normal digestion and healthy nerves. We really owe nature a vote of thanks...for making something that *tastes* so good *do* us so much good!

* The nutritional statements made in this advertisement have been reviewed and found consistent with current scientific opinion by the Council on Foods and Nutrition of the American Medical Association

AMERICAN **MEAT** INSTITUTE

Headquarters, Chicago ... Members throughout the U. S.

in early 1957 the advertisement shown in Exhibit 5 appeared in the January 19 issue of *The Saturday Evening Post* and in the February editions of *Everywoman's*, *Family Circle*, *Western Family*, and *Woman's Day*. A second advertisement, featuring a different cut of pork, appeared in the same publications one month later.

Regularly scheduled advertising of pork was supplemented in the fall and winter of 1955–56 by a special $700,000 promotional expenditure de-

Exhibit 6

AMERICAN MEAT INSTITUTE

Selected Data on Consumption of Beef, Pork, and All Meat

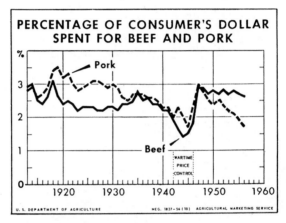

RETAIL VALUE OF MEAT CONSUMED PER PERSON, AND DISPOSABLE INCOME PER PERSON, IN THE UNITED STATES, 1915–56

Year	Retail Value of Meat Consumed			Disposable Income per Person	Retail Value— Meat Consumed as % of Disposable Income		
	Beef	Pork	All Meat		Beef	Pork	All Meat
1915–55 Avg........	$19.47	$19.93	$44.06	$ 757	2.6%	2.6%	5.8%
1947...............	33.50	35.40	76.50	1,157	2.9	3.1	6.6
1948...............	37.00	35.10	80.20	1,262	2.9	2.8	6.4
1949...............	34.10	31.40	72.80	1,244	2.7	2.5	5.9
1950...............	37.30	31.90	76.50	1,340	2.8	2.4	5.7
1951...............	38.50	35.80	81.30	1,445	2.7	2.5	5.6
1952...............	42.00	34.60	84.50	1,491	2.8	2.3	5.7
1953...............	41.70	33.40	83.90	1,545	2.7	2.2	5.4
1954...............	42.70	32.10	83.60	1,545	2.8	2.1	5.4
1955...............	43.30	30.20	81.90	1,616	2.7	1.9	5.1
1956*...............	43.90	28.90	81.20	1,681	2.6	1.7	4.8

* 1956 figures are preliminary.

Source: Agricultural Marketing Service, U.S. Department of Agriculture, Chart No. 636-R1, February 1957.

signed to move unusually large available supplies of pork quickly to market. The stated objective of this expenditure by the Institute "was to perpetuate the hog supply by helping the farmer to get a fair price for his pigs, and thereby encourage him to keep on raising a sufficient number to supply this country's ever-expanding needs."[5] Radio, television, and point of purchase was used extensively; copy emphasized low price.

In spite of the large supplies of pork which were consumed in 1955 and 1956 (the level of pork in storage remained about the same as in earlier years), the percentage of consumer disposable income spent on pork continued to drop, as shown in Exhibit 6. Because of these long-run trends unfavorable to pork, a special Roper survey was conducted in 1956, designed to throw some light on the question, "What happened to the demand for pork?"

The Roper Survey of Consumers' Attitudes towards Pork

A summary of pertinent results of the Roper survey on attitudes toward pork in 1956 follows:

1. Most people eat most kinds of pork.
2. Pork is regarded as having no strong positive virtues except for its taste.
3. Pork is considered to be fattening.
4. Pork is considered to be difficult to digest.
5. Pork is not considered to be very nourishing.
6. Pork is not considered a good value for the money.
7. Pork has considerably less "status" than beef.

As a result of these findings, Institute executives in 1957 were considering a two-year test of pork advertising. This test, in four test cities and four control cities, would cost $200,000; it would attempt to measure the results of advertising expenditures nationally at levels between $1 million and $5 million annually, in addition to media and copy approaches.

The Institute had taken additional steps within the meat-packing industry to deal with the "pork problem." The step of most immediate concern to consumers was industry-wide adoption of a closer fat trim on pork in 1956.

With regard to the effectiveness of the Institute's regular consumer advertising, additional evidence was available from Roper consumer surveys conducted in 1940, 1947, 1950, and 1953. (Two other Roper surveys have already been referred to, the survey of "thought leaders" in 1953 and the survey in 1956 of consumers' attitudes towards pork.)

The Roper Surveys of Consumer Attitudes toward Meat

Selected results of the Roper surveys of consumers' attitudes toward meat and the meat industry are given on page 86.

---

[5] From a booklet entitled *Selling Pork to America,* prepared for members of the American Meat Institute.

	1940	1947	1950	1953
MEAT				
1. Price of meat much too high..........................	......	......	51%	43%
Price of meat a little high.............................	......	......	25	30
2. Meat contains the most food value or nourishment (from				
a representative list of eight foods)...................	......	26%	25	31
Milk...	......	33	33	29
Vegetables...	......	17	21	17
3. Meat is the best source of vitamins.....................	......	8	8	8
Milk...	......	19	15	17
Vegetables...	......	47	51	50
4. Meat is the best source of protein....................	25%	36	34	41
Milk...	......	11	10	10
Eggs...	......	16	15	14
5. *Least* willing to give up meat (from a representative list				
of foods)...	32	43	......	......
6. A member of the family ate more meat than approved by				
respondent...	20	13	19	16
7. Why?				
A. Bad for health...............................			77	
Unbalanced diet...............................			37	
Bad for blood pressure.........................			8	
Too fattening.................................			7	
B. Too expensive.................................			14	
8. Would cut out meats if trying to reduce or keep weight				
down..				15
Starches...				76
Sweets...				39
Dairy products.....................................				19
9. Would eat more meat if trying to reduce or keep weight				
down..				27
Vegetables...				55
Fruits and fruit juices.............................				14
Eggs...				11
MEAT INDUSTRY				
10. Supposing there were no meat-packing companies at all,				
and retail stores got meat directly from the farmers				
who raised the cattle, hogs, and lambs.				
A. Would get better quality meat.....................	......	13	13	15
Worse..	......	42	60	51
Same...	......	23	16	23
B. The price of meat would be higher................	......	12	13	11
Lower..	......	50	57	62
Same...	......	20	16	16
C. The retail meat store would have a larger supply of				
meat to sell.................................	......	16	16	14
Smaller......................................	......	30	37	37
Same...	......	27	30	32

Results of the Review

Executives of the American Meat Institute, as a result of their review of the Institute's promotional activities in the light of supply and demand factors affecting meat, were most concerned in 1957 with the declining share of consumer disposable income allotted to the purchase of meat. They believed that the percentage of consumer disposable income allotted to the purchase of meat was the best available indicator of meat's progress for three reasons: (1) the figure "wrapped up" volume and price; (2) it was related to competition for the consumer dollar by other products and services, including food; and (3) it was related to consumer demand, as influenced by advertising.

The executives of the Institute had definitely decided to go ahead with a promotional program which would emphasize more strongly than at any time in recent years the nutritional values of meat. Medical advertising was to be doubled in volume. Furthermore, special direct-mail pieces —booklets, prepared primarily for medical doctors—were authorized for distribution to the 175,000 medical doctors in the United States. This literature would point out that meat, because of its contributions to the well-balanced diet, could be included in virtually every kind of diet, whether it was one to reduce or increase weight, or to lower or increase the calorie intake.

Consumer advertising, developed for a general audience, would feature the fact that meat if often referred to as "the good provider."

~~~

CASE 3: AMERICAN INSTITUTE OF MEN'S AND BOYS' WEAR, INC.[1]

QUESTIONS TO CONSIDER: (1) Should the members of the men's and boys' clothing industry have been disturbed by the decreasing percentage of disposable personal income and of the total consumer clothing expenditure being spent on men's and boys' clothing? (2) Men were considered to be "indifferent" to clothing. Do you agree with this conclusion? (3) Was the promotional program of the Institute well planned to meet the industry's problem? (4) Did the Institute follow a sound copy strategy? (5) In the light of your review of the Institute's promotional efforts, what recommendations would you make regarding the Institute's promotional activities in 1958?

The American Institute of Men's and Boys' Wear, Inc., was incorporated in June 1955 by men's and boys' wear retailers, textile mills, cutters, and suppliers to promote greater sales of the industry's products. In Janu-

---

[1] Written by David W. Nylen and Martin V. Marshall.

ary 1958 the executives of the Institute were evaluating the promotional efforts of the past year and one half.

Industry Conditions

In the early 1950's men's and boys' clothiers were becoming increasingly concerned over what they considered an unfavorable industry sales condition. An organizing committee, which led to the incorporation of the AIMBW, met in March 1955. Sales data prepared for the committee showed that expenditures for men's, women's, and children's clothing represented only 7.8% of disposable personal income in 1953 as contrasted to 10.1% in 1939. Between 1939 and 1953 expenditures of men's and boys' clothing had risen only 162%, whereas in the same period, total personal consumption expenditures rose 240%. Further, men's and boys' wear accounted for only 28.6% of the total consumer clothing dollar in 1953 as compared with 32.4% in 1939. (Exhibit 1 lists clothing expendi-

Exhibit 1

AMERICAN INSTITUTE OF MEN'S AND BOYS' WEAR, INC.

Selected Personal Consumption Expenditures for Clothing, 1929–56

Year	Expenditures on All Clothing and Footwear as a % of Disposable Personal Income	Personal Consumption Expenditures on All Clothing and Shoes in Billions of Dollars	Personal Consumption Expenditures on Men's and Boys' Clothing Except Footwear in Billions of Dollars	% of Men's and Boys' Expenditures to Total Clothing Expenditures
1956.....	7.6	21.8	6.4	29.4
1955.....	7.6	20.6	6.0	29.1
1954.....	7.7	19.7	5.7	28.9
1953.....	7.8	19.9	5.7	28.6
1952.....	8.4	20.1	5.9	29.4
1951.....	8.5	19.8	5.8	29.3
1950.....	8.9	18.5	5.5	29.7
1949.....	9.8	18.5	5.4	29.2
1948.....	10.4	19.6	5.7	29.1
1947.....	10.9	18.8	5.6	29.8
1946.....	11.2	18.2	5.4	29.1
1945.....	10.2	16.5	4.3	26.1
1944.....	9.2	14.6	3.8	26.7
1941.....	9.3	8.8	2.8	31.8
1940.....	9.8	7.4	2.4	32.5
1939.....	10.1	7.1	2.3	32.4
1933.....	10.1	4.6	1.5	32.6
1929.....	11.2	9.4	3.0	31.9

Source: Commerce Department, *National Income Supplement* to the *Survey of Current Business*, 1954 edition; and *Survey of Current Business*, July 1956 and July 1957.

tures for selected years 1929–56.) Women's clothing, on the other hand, was steadily increasing its share of the consumer clothing dollar from 67.6% in 1939 to 71.4% in 1953.

The executives of the Institute thought that there were two reasons for the decline in the percentage of personal income spent on men's and boys' wear. First, clothing industry promotional expenditures were relatively small as compared to other industries. Second, the executives felt that men had an indifferent attitude toward clothing in that men did not feel that particular attention to good dress was a prerequisite to success in business or social life. The executives reasoned that the solution to the problem lay in an industry-wide promotional campaign which would change purchasers' attitudes toward men's and boys' clothing and thus increase total demand.

Organization of the AIMBW

The AIMBW was formed solely as a promotional organization, seeking membership from all phases of the industry—retailers, textile mills, manufacturers, suppliers, and unions. Contributions to support the Institute were based on the sales of the member company; textile mills and manufacturers contributed one tenth of 1% of men's and boys' wear gross sales, and retailers contributed one twentieth of 1% of men's and boys' wear gross sales. All contributions were collected by a well-known public accounting firm, which kept the amount of each contribution strictly confidential so that the sales of contributors were not revealed because of their contribution to the Institute's promotional fund.

As a goal, the Institute sought $5 million a year for a campaign with a minimum duration of five years. No campaign was to be undertaken until at least $2 million in contributions had been pledged. By the spring of 1956 that target had been achieved.

General Plan of the Promotional Program

The AIMBW promotional program had four parts: (1) advertising to the trade and consumer, the latter advertising being directed to (*a*) the white-collar class, (*b*) the newly married worker, (*c*) wives and sweethearts, and (*d*) boys and men in their formative years; (2) public relations activities; (3) selling aids for retailers; and (4) marketing research. The program was formally launched in September 1956 when advertisements appeared in leading consumer magazines based upon the central campaign theme, "DRESS RIGHT, you can't afford not to."

The Advertising Program. In the period September 1956–April 1957 (fiscal year 1956), the Institute spent about $1,100,000 for consumer and trade advertising and for related promotional activities through its advertising agency, Batten, Barton, Durstine & Osborn, Inc. Consumer advertising consisted of four-color, double-page spreads in *Life, The Saturday Evening Post, Look,* and *Good Housekeeping.* The first advertisements of the 1956 campaign were built around the idea that "90% of what others see of you is your clothing, therefore you should dress right." An example of this type of advertisement is given in Exhibit 2. Later advertisements in the campaign emphasized the copy theme that "your clothes never stop talking about you," and illustrated men and boys

Exhibit 2

AMERICAN INSTITUTE OF MEN'S AND BOYS' WEAR, INC.

An Example of an AIMBW Advertisement Emphasizing the Theme: "90% of What Others See Is Your Clothing"

Exhibit 3

AMERICAN INSTITUTE OF MEN'S AND BOYS' WEAR, INC.

An Example of an AIMBW Advertisement Emphasizing the Theme:
"Your Clothes Never Stop Talking about You"

Nighttime, daytime

Swimtime, playtime

your clothes never stop talking about you

The good old summer is time for all kinds of vacation and week-end fun...
including the fun of Dressing Right for whatever under the sun (or moon) you're
doing. When you look good, you *feel* good—sure of yourself, relaxed. You're ready
to meet new people, go new places, try new things. Before you start out on vacation, stop in at men's or department stores near you that display the Dress Right
emblem. They'll give you help and advice on how to Dress Right—to be at ease!

Dress Right –
you can't afford not to!

in clothing which was considered the appropriate dress for particular occasions. An example of this type of advertisement is given in Exhibit 3. All
advertisements of the 1956 campaign carried the slogan, "DRESS RIGHT,

you can't afford not to." The media schedule and costs for the fiscal year 1956 are given in Exhibit 4.

As the result of many discussions, Institute executives decided to adopt an entirely different kind of copy approach in the fall of 1957. The executives, feeling that a new approach should more directly attack the problem of men's indifference toward clothing, decided upon a more strongly negative approach designed to shock men out of their lethargy. It was felt that effective copy appeals should stress the importance of dress

Exhibit 4

AMERICAN INSTITUTE OF MEN'S AND BOYS' WEAR, INC.
Media Schedule and Costs, Fiscal Year 1956

Date	Publication	Space	Cost
September 10.....	*Life*	Spread, 4-color	$ 63,515
22.....	*Post*	Spread, 4-color	51,936
October 2.....	*Look*	Spread, 4-color	45,280
8.....	*Life*	Spread, 4-color	63,515
27.....	*Post*	Spread, 4-color	51,936
November 5.....	*Life*	Spread, 4-color	63,515
24.....	*Post*	Spread, 4-color	51,936
December 3.....	*Life*	Spread, 4-color	63,515
	Good Housekeeping	Spread, 4-color	29,600
January 19.....	*Post*	Spread, 4-color	56,620
February 18.....	*Life*	Spread, 4-color	65,298
March 30.....	*Post*	Spread, 4-color	56,620
April 2.....	*Look*	Spread, 4-color	49,810
8.....	*Life*	Spread, 4-color	65,298
		Total Space Cost..............	$778,394
		Trade Advertising Cost........	25,415
		Total......................	$803,809*

* Production, merchandising, and local promotional costs brought total 1956 expenditures to approximately $1,100,000.

Source: AIMBW records.

(1) to impress women, (2) for business success, and (3) to impress business associates. AIMBW executives believed that men and women could be affected by copy which would point out what would happen if men did not recognize the importance of proper dress.

In addition to being a more effective copy approach, Institute executives believed that the new approach would solve the problem, inherent in the first campaign, of deciding what specific styles of clothing to illustrate in advertisements. In the past the problem of what styles to show had arisen frequently because the Institute's members were selling in different style areas of the United States and were marketing garments ranging from dungarees to dress clothing. Advertisements for the new campaign overcame this problem, since they emphasized the reasons *why* proper dress should be worn rather than displaying *what* particular styles of clothing were appropriate for particular occasions. The new advertisements continued to carry the "dress-right" slogan.

The new advertisements were pretested in order to predict their probable effectiveness. The pretests compared the advertisements used in the first campaign, the new negative-appeal advertisements, and a series of advertisements that took an approach midway between the two. The objectives of the tests were to measure all three approaches comparatively with respect to (1) the extent to which the dress-right idea was communicated, (2) the extent to which personal involvement was obtained, and (3) the extent to which the reader identified himself with the advertisement's situation. The test results convinced AIMBW executives that the negative appeal was the most effective of the three tested.

The new advertisements, which were full pages in black and white, appeared in *Life* and *The Saturday Evening Post* beginning October 7, 1957. The two advertisements that had appeared by January 1958 are shown in Exhibits 5 and 6. The media schedule and costs for the fiscal year 1957 (May 1957–April 1958) are shown in Exhibit 7.

After publication of the first two advertisements in the new series, Daniel Starch, a magazine readership measurement organization, reported that the new advertisements were 150% more effective than all comparable "institutional" advertisements appearing in the magazines carrying the AIMBW advertisements. The new advertisements also scored considerably higher over-all in terms of readership than did the previous series of advertisements.

In addition to magazine advertising, AIMBW experimented with 14 one-minute radio spots on N.B.C.'s "Monitor"[2] in the period August 17 through October 20, 1957. The time cost of these spots was $98,000. Although radio spots were considered an effective addition to the Institute's campaign during two peak promotional periods (back to school in August and the fall selling season for men), financial considerations precluded use of the medium in 1958.

In both 1956 and 1957 advertisements were placed in leading retailers' and manufacturers' trade publications which informed members and non-members of the promotional activities of the Institute.

The Public Relations Program. Since its inception the Institute and its public relations counsel, Mayer and O'Brien, had given major attention to obtaining favorable editorial comment and publicity in consumer and trade media. Frequent press releases were sent to 1,400 daily newspapers, 5,000 weekly newspapers, 1,297 radio stations, and 523 television stations. Two hundred and thirty radio stations in as many cities were programming daily public service spot announcements linked to the dress-right campaign. Press releases promoted the dress-right idea in several ways.

---

[2] "Monitor" was a week-end radio show with a magazine type format featuring news, music, sports, personalities, and features.

Exhibit 5

AMERICAN INSTITUTE OF MEN'S AND BOYS' WEAR, INC.

An Example of an AIMBW Advertisement Employing the Negative Approach

"I didn't get the promotion— Tom did"

Why was it Tom? The boss had a tough choice to make: both men were smart, good at their jobs. But Tom had something extra: better appearance. He made the right impression on the people he met — <u>and</u> on the boss. How about you — do <u>you</u> dress for success? Do your clothes help you get ahead — or do they hold you back? Remember: whatever you do, wherever you go, your clothes never stop talking about you.

Dress Right— you can't afford not to!

To Dress Right, shop at stores that display this symbol.

As seen in  LIFE and POST

Exhibit 6

AMERICAN INSTITUTE OF MEN'S AND BOYS' WEAR, INC.
An Example of an AIMBW Advertisement Employing the Negative Approach

"You can usually spot a wrong kid just by the way he looks" M-1

Call it unfair, but it's a fact: people today judge a youngster by appearance. And once they've tabbed a boy, it's tough to change their minds about him, their attitude toward him. Look at your boy. Look at him through his teacher's eyes—your neighbors' eyes. Could the way he looks, the clothes he wears, give them the wrong impression? Are you making sure he looks right, dresses right, everywhere he goes?

Dress Right—you can't afford not to!

As seen in **LIFE** and **POST**

Exhibit 7

AMERICAN INSTITUTE OF MEN'S AND BOYS' WEAR, INC.

Media Schedule and Costs, Fiscal Year 1957

Date	Publication	Space	Cost
May 4........	*Post*	Spread, 4-color	$ 56,031
13........	*Life*	Spread, 4-color	65,298
June..............	*Good Housekeeping*	Spread, 4-color	31,500
....	*Esquire*	Spread, 4-color	16,160
11........	*Look*	Spread, 4-color	49,810
24........	*Life*	Page, 4-color, bleed	33,659
July 13........	*Post*	Page, 4-color, bleed	32,217
August 24........	*Post*	Spread, 4-color	56,031
September.........	*Good Housekeeping*	Spread, 4-color	35,200
16........	*Life*	Page, 4-color	36,835
October 7........	*Life*	Page, B & W, bleed	28,194
12........	*Post*	Page, B & W, bleed	23,166
November 4........	*Life*	Page, B & W, bleed	28,194
16........	*Post*	Page, B & W, bleed	23,166
December 2........	*Life*	Page, B & W, bleed	28,194
14........	*Post*	Page, B & W, bleed	23,166
January 25........	*Post*	Page, B & W, bleed	23,166
February 24........	*Life*	Page, B & W, bleed	30,216
March 22........	*Post*	Page, B & W, bleed	23,166
April 28........	*Life*	Page, B & W, bleed	30,216
		Total Space Cost..........	$673,585
		Radio Time (Monitor).....	98,000
		Trade Advertising Cost....	20,000
		Total...................	$791,585*

* Schedule after January is predicted. Production and other costs will raise total expenditures to about $900,000.

One type of release listed suggested wardrobes for different age groups. Another release tied in the relationship of good grooming to good behavior and good scholastic progress, citing the opinions of eminent jurists and educators. Releases describing new styles in men's and boys' clothing and publicity stories on high school dress-right programs were also distributed. An example of a publicity release is given in Exhibit 8. A large amount of this publicity was published.

Additional publicity was gained through special men's and boys' clothing supplements in Sunday newspapers which contained dress-right articles submitted by local member retailers plus their advertisements. AIMBW also succeeded in placing favorable publicity in the Dick Tracy comic strip,[3] The Dorothy Dix column, and a three-page article in *Newsweek* magazine.

Another phase of the publicity program was the assistance and encouragement given to the dress-right campaign by public high schools. Based on a program developed in the Buffalo, New York, high schools under

[3] One entire Sunday strip of Dick Tracy was devoted to the importance of boys dressing right.

Exhibit 8

AMERICAN INSTITUTE OF MEN'S AND BOYS' WEAR, INC.

Example of AIMBW Publicity Release

FOR RELEASE: On Receipt

DRESS RIGHT–BEHAVE RIGHT EXHIBIT
SHOWN TO NATION'S HIGH SCHOOL HEADS

Several thousand high school principals, meeting in Indianapolis, February 15–19, at the yearly convention of the National Association of Secondary-School Principals will be shown a study of the relationship of student appearance to behavior and learning progress.

An unusual exhibit shows the connection between dress and deportment. This visual evidence is offered by the American Institute of Men's and Boys' Wear, sponsors of the exhibit and actively co-operating in the now-famed "dress-right" movement in the nation's high schools.

Credit for launching the movement goes to Dr. Joseph Manch, Superintendent of Schools of Buffalo, N.Y. Troubled as most educators have been for years over the antisocial antics of hoodlum-garbed youngsters, Dr. Manch noted that badly behaved youngsters almost always dressed the part. If tough clothes contribute to tough conduct, Dr. Manch reasoned, then neat, civilized clothes should help bring better behavior and improved attitudes.

The Buffalo Inter-High School Student Council liked this theory, too, and put it to the test. Conduct did improve; attitudes did change for the better. A study of the first year's operation of the plan in the 14 Buffalo high schools proved the point. And, learning this, hundreds of other schools—chiefly high schools—are now trying the same plan.

Such campaigns, for the most part, are initiated and run by the students themselves, through their councils or G.O.'s—general organizations.

The American Institute of Men's and Boys' Wear exhibit at the NASSP convention features an array of charts, posters, fashion show scripts, and program guides that the Institute makes available to all interested schools without charge.

Source: AIMBW records.

the guidance of Dr. Joseph Manch, Superintendent of Schools of Buffalo, New York, the program emphasized to students the relationship between good grooming and good behavior. The program, which was noncommercial in nature, was designed to combat sloppy dress and hoodlum attire. The AIMBW encouraged these dress-right programs by supplying to high school student councils the components of a program which included the following: a blue print to guide student councils in setting up dress-right programs, a "Let's DRESS RIGHT" fashion show script, illustrations of fashion show settings, a dress-right chart, and a report on the operations and progress of the Buffalo program. A poll in 1957 by *Scholastic Magazine* indicated that 65% of American public high schools had undertaken campaigns to improve student dress. Considerable publicity was developed at the local level in conjunction with these programs.

One of the achievements of the public relations campaign was a "partnership" with a television sportscaster, Jack Gregson. Mr. Gregson, impressed by the dress-right program, used it in varying ways on his program. In this way, the dress-right message reached millions of viewers without time cost to the Institute and gave Mr. Gregson's sportscast a public-service character.

Exhibit 9

AMERICAN INSTITUTE OF MEN'S AND BOYS' WEAR, INC.

An Example of a Retailer's Use of AIMBW Dealer Aid Material

In addition to consumer publicity, considerable publicity concerning activities and plans of the AIMBW was placed in trade publications. A monthly AIMBW news magazine, the *Mirror*, was also distributed to members.

In appraising the relative value of the various promotional activities undertaken since the Institute's founding, AIMBW executives believed that the public relations program was the most important phase of the Institute's activities, being the promotional element which had scored most heavily with the AIMBW members and the public. They felt the Institute's primary function was that of a public relations representative for the men's and boys' wear industry, and that advertising essentially served a public relations function.

The Program for Retailers. Display material and other selling aids were made available to member retailers. Retailer selling aids were designed to assist local retail members to tie in to the national campaign. Among the materials provided were poster blowups of magazine advertisements, advertisement mats, direct-mail pieces, banners, promotion plans, and other promotional suggestions. Most retailer aid material was provided without charge. The promotion manager of the AIMBW felt that the key to the merchandising program was display of the Institute's dress-right seal by members. Members were encouraged to display the seal both in their stores and in their advertising. Use by members of the Institute's slogan, "DRESS RIGHT, you can't afford not to," was also encouraged. As an example of retailer use of Institute dealer aid material, a picture of one retailer's window display is shown in Exhibit 9.

Local AIMBW chapters, which had been formed with the assistance of the Institute's staff, staged local promotions based on the dress-right theme.

In January 1958 the AIMBW was preparing to distribute a booklet entitled, *How to Dress Right.* The booklet contained fashion tips, color harmony charts, and a personal wardrobe check list. The booklets were to be sold for about 2 cents each to member retailers who were in turn to distribute them to customers. A sample booklet, suggestions for its distribution, and an order blank were sent to each retail member. In addition to retailer distribution, consumer advertising in 1958 was to offer the booklet to readers for 10 cents. The promotion manager stated that consumer requests for the booklet would provide additional evidence to evaluate the effectiveness of the various magazines being used by the Institute.

A U.S.O. *Dress Right* booklet for servicemen had also been prepared and was being distributed through Navy Exchanges, Post Exchanges, and other military outlets.

Marketing Research Program. The Institute's marketing research effort up to January 1958 had consisted of a study conducted by Alfred Politz, Inc. This study was designed primarily to obtain information that would assist AIMBW members to advertise and promote their products more effectively and dealt mainly with buying patterns for various types of men's and boys' wear. Survey results were given AIMBW members in monthly bulletins. A selection of survey findings is given in Exhibit 10.

The AIMBW IN January 1958

Since its founding in 1955, the membership recruitment arm of the AIMBW had been working continuously to add new members. By December 31, 1957, the membership rolls showed total members to be nearly 3,000, including 89 textile mills, 174 clothing manufacturers, 2,645 retailers, and 80 miscellaneous organizations. Although membership included many of the leading firms in the field, considerably less than a majority of

Exhibit 10

AMERICAN INSTITUTE OF MEN'S AND BOYS' WEAR, INC.

Selection of Research Findings Distributed to AIMBW Members

GENERAL

Will success in life be affected by what you wear?   All men { Yes, 34%
                                                                No, 66%

    Grouped by education: Grade school......Yes, 19.5%   No, 80.5%
                            High school.......Yes, 30.5   No, 69.5
                            College..........Yes, 58.2   No, 41.8

Whom do men dress their best for?
    For women, 36%   For business associates, 25%

SUITS

Do you tend to shop around in various stores before buying a suit?
                Yes, 25% (all men)
                Yes, 41   (student age)

Why?
    Poor selection.................35% (all men)   41% (students)
    Price wrong...................21   (all men)   18   (students)

What factors are most important in selecting a suit?

	(All Men)	(Students)
Quality............................	77%	51%
Style.............................	49	64
Fit...............................	49	46
Color.............................	44	54
Price.............................	16	13

Why do men purchase new suits?

	(All Men)	(Students)
"Old suit worn out"..................	49%	39%
"Special occasion"...................	17	44
"Good buy".........................	11	5
"Desired new suit"...................	15	6

Did wife/mother assist in suit selection?
                Yes, 36% (all men)
                Yes, 45   (students)

When was last suit purchased?
              Over one year ago.............49%
              Over two years ago.............34

SHIRTS

Who buys men's shirts?
              Men........................54%
              Wives......................29
              Sons and daughters.............12
               Don't know.................. 3
              Parents...................... 2
              Friends...................... 1

What kind of shirt was last purchased or received?
              Sport shirt......................62% (all men)
                     82   (students)
                     71   (as bought by wives)

Where was last shirt purchased?
              Department store..................43% (all men) 53% (students)
              Men's wear store.................30   (all men) 29   (students)

What factors are most important in shirt selection?
              Fabric and quality..................49%   30% (women)
              Fit and size......................51   8   (women)
              Ease of care...................... 6   31   (women)

Source: AIMBW records.

firms in the men's and boys' wear industry had contributed funds to the Institute's efforts.

The advertising budget for the first fiscal year had been about $1,100,-000 and for the second fiscal year $900,000. It was anticipated that the budget for the third fiscal year's advertising efforts would be about the same as the current year's or perhaps slightly less.

U.S. Commerce Department figures published in July 1957 indicated that the male apparel share of disposable personal income for 1956 had increased slightly over 1955. Although industry sales figures for the entire year 1957 were not available in January 1958, preliminary reports from retailers were encouraging to Institute executives.

~~~

CASE 4: CARPET INSTITUTE, INC. (A)[1]

NOTE: *For many years before 1954, the members of the United States carpet and rug industry and of the industry's trade association, Carpet Institute, Inc., had been concerned with the downward trend of per capita sales of carpets and rugs, which had decreased from slightly over one square yard per capita in 1900 to 0.56 square yards in 1950. Since the mid-1930's, industry companies, both individually and collectively through the Carpet Institute, had worked intensively to plan and execute promotional programs aimed at reversing this trend. None of the Institute programs employed advertising. Then, in early 1954, officers of the Institute decided to consider the possibilities of an Institute consumer advertising program to stimulate primary demand for carpets and rugs. In order to facilitate case analysis and discussion, the case material on the Institute has been divided arbitrarily into five cases. The first case essentially reviews the promotional efforts of the Institute before 1954.*

In considering the first case, attention might be given to the following questions: (1) How do you account for the decreasing per capita sales of carpets and rugs? (2) In the light of the information given in the Roper survey, what were the principal problems confronting the carpet and rug industry? (3) What were the principal strengths and weaknesses of the Institute's promotional approach in the period 1945–54? (4) What areas other than advertising should the Institute give special attention to after 1954? (5) Tentatively, in the light of the information given in the first case, what conclusions do you draw regarding the use of advertising to stimulate primary demand of carpets and rugs?

In early 1954, when Mr. Paul Jones, president, and other officers of Carpet Institute, Inc., decided that they should seriously consider the possibilities of employing consumer advertising as an additional association promotional activity, they first appraised the past promotional efforts of the Institute.

---

[1] Written by Donald H. Thain and Martin V. Marshall.

Background Information on the Institute

The Carpet Institute was founded in 1927. By 1954 its manufacturers membership represented about 70% of total United States carpet sales. From 1927 until the early 1940's, the primary functions of the Institute were to collect and disseminate to members information of value, to keep members informed about legislation of significance to the industry, and to present in appropriate legislative circles the industry's views on governmental policy matters, such as the tariffs on raw carpet materials and finished rugs.

In January 1952 the Institute formally adopted the following objectives which reflected its increased responsibility for industry promotional programs since earlier years:

1. To help the carpet industry to improve its service to the public.
2. To develop a wider interest in the American carpet and rug industry and to promote a greater public demand for its products.
3. To direct a market development program through the use of such merchandising procedures as market research, educational material, publicity, and public relations.
4. To foster scientific research and to disseminate technical and economic information to the industry and the public.
5. To study problems arising out of the importation of carpets, rugs, and carpet wool.
6. To co-operate with national, state, and local government agencies on all matters in which carpet and rug manufacturers have an interest.

A twelve-man board of trustees, elected by members from among the top-management executives of the industry, controlled the operations of the Institute. A full-time president and a secretary-treasurer were chosen by the board of trustees. An additional 12 full-time employees, occupied with administrative, promotional, accounting, clerical, and secretarial duties, completed the staff. The Institute staff sought to draw upon and co-ordinate the counsel and operating know-how of individual member company executives through the following advisory subcommittees which ranged in membership from 7 to 32 men each: Marketing, Market Research, Advertising, Public Relations, Sales Training, Style and Color, Traffic, Wool, Statistics, Tariff, and Technical.

Operating funds were subscribed by member companies on the basis of a per cent of sales for the year before last. The Institute's proposed budget for 1955, for example, was to be covered by an assessment of one third of 1% of members' gross sales in 1953. The assessment varied slightly from year to year, depending on the total sales of members and the total budget of the Institute.

Institute Promotional Activities: 1936–40

In 1936 the Institute undertook its first promotional program, a public relations campaign, on behalf of the entire industry. Responsibility for this activity was assigned to the Institute for two reasons: (1) there was reportedly very little brand recognition or preference in the soft floor covering field, and (2) the declining per capita sales trend had affected all manufacturers so seriously that member company executives believed that a co-ordinated industry-wide program was necessary.

The public relations program essentially involved the distribution of publicity material to consumer media and to schools and women's clubs.

Since results of the public relations activity begun in 1936 were believed to be "inadequate," the program was discontinued in 1940. Because many carpet industry companies were engaged in defense production and other wartime activities, no further promotional activities were undertaken until after World War II.

Institute Promotional and Research Activities: 1945–48

After the war, executives and members of the Institute decided to resume Institute promotional efforts; and at the same time member companies agreed that they would not reduce their own regular promotional efforts in view of those of the Institute. (Mr. Jones believed that Institute promotional expenditures in 1954 constituted about one quarter of the total promotional expenditures of the industry.)

The first promotional program, undertaken in the period 1945–47, consisted of a "Better Home Furnishings" retail-store promotion and a public relations campaign. The special retail promotion encouraged retailers to advertise, display, and attempt to sell groups of related home furnishings with a rug as the basic item. Under the plan it was expected that, whenever possible, several tastefully matched items such as a rug, furniture, drapes, and a lamp, all from different departments, would be sold to a prospect by the same salesperson. The Institute sought to gain support for the promotion by means of a direct mailing to retailers, a few direct contacts by Institute staff members, and the distribution of a special sales training movie to retail stores that requested it by mail.

The retail-store promotion plan "failed," Mr. Jones said, for four reasons: (1) it was predicated on superimposing a new type of "related-item selling" on stores which were not organized to operate in such a manner, (2) it was not supported by national advertising, (3) because of budget and staff limitations the Institute could not devote enough time to organizing and pushing the promotion, and (4) it was not adequately emphasized by member companies.

In order to gain additional insights into consumer behavior, executives at this time had the Elmo Roper research organization undertake a study, entitled "Consumer Attitudes toward Carpets and Rugs." It was completed in 1948.

1948 Elmo Roper Study

The purpose of the study of consumer attitudes toward carpets and rugs was to explore, as thoroughly as possible, consumer attitudes toward soft floor coverings. The study focused on three questions: What im-

portance do people attach to carpets and rugs? What are their preferences? How do they regard the product?

The survey was based on 6,122 interviews, 5,075 with women and
1,045 with men. The people interviewed were distributed proportionately
throughout the United States according to geographic location, age, economic level, marital status, type of dwelling, and position in family. Most
of the interviews were with women because women were assumed to be
the chief influence in home decoration. Consumers in the lowest economic levels were excluded because Institute executives believe that it
was wiser to concentrate promotional efforts on those who would clearly
be able to buy carpets and rugs if they wanted them. The distribution of
the sample used for this study is given in Exhibit 1.

Exhibit 1

CARPET INSTITUTE, INC. (A)

Distribution of the Sample Used in Roper Study

	Women	Men		Women	Men
Age:			Geographic Location:		
18–34	35.7%	40.3%	New England	7.3%	7.3%
35–49	31.4	27.3	Middle Atlantic	23.4	22.9
50 and over	32.9	32.4	East North Central	22.0	21.6
			West North Central	11.0	10.9
Economic Level*:			South Atlantic	10.1	10.4
A	9.2%	8.7%	East South Central	5.9	6.0
B	33.2	32.0	West South Central	8.3	8.6
C	57.6	59.3	Mountain	3.3	3.3
			Pacific	8.7	9.0
Marital Status:			Size of Place:		
Single	8.5%	11.4%	Over 1,000,000	13.7%	13.4%
Married	79.0	83.3	100,000 to 1,000,000	18.0	17.9
Widowed or divorced	11.7	4.9	25,000 to 100,000	12.2	11.9
No answer	0.8	0.4	2,500 to 25,000	17.1	17.4
			Under 2,500	20.2	19.9
			Rural farm	18.8	19.5
Kind of Home:					
Apartment	8.1%	8.6%			
Owned home	66.9	64.6			
Rented home	24.0	26.0			
No answer	1.0	0.8			

* Roper's definitions of economic levels are as follows:

A Level: Those who take the comforts and necessities of life for granted and are able to afford the luxuries
common to their community.

B Level: Those who take the comforts and necessities for granted except in severe depressions—but who must
decide between having one luxury as against having another.

C Level: Those who take most of the comforts and necessities of life for granted, and who reach up for and save
up for some of the *simpler* luxuries.

Source: A Summary of the Roper Survey, prepared by the Market Research Committee of the Carpet Institute,
Inc., 1948, p. 20.

A Summary of the Roper Survey

A summary of the Roper survey, as prepared by the Marketing Research Committee of the Institute, follows:

There is no question about the fact that there is a strong consumer desire for
carpets and rugs. The interviews show that 90% of the people *have* rugs or

carpets in their living rooms and 93% *want* them in the same rooms. Of those who have dining rooms, 60% *have* soft floor coverings and 79% *want* them; 79% of the respondents *have* rugs or carpets in their bedrooms and 87% *want* them. (However, it should be noted that only 33% of consumers have large-size rugs or wall-to-wall carpet and 46% have only scatter-size rugs in bedrooms.) Of more immediate interest, 43% of all women interviewed say they would like to get a large rug or carpet during the next year or so.

Soft floor covering leads as the article of furnishing considered most basic in a room. When people were presented with a list of various articles of furnishings—a rug or carpet, chairs, sofa, draperies, lamps, wallpaper—and asked to select the one they would want to decide about first if they were furnishing a living room from the beginning, 50% said they would select the rug or carpet first. This is about twice as many as would select the nearest complementary item of furnishing.

When asked to appraise the importance of rugs and carpets in a home, less than 11% of the women felt that they are unimportant. All the rest say a home *should* have good rugs or carpets in it—at least in some rooms. Proportionately, almost as many men as women share the same belief.

People value rugs and carpets because of their contribution to the appearance of a room. When asked to describe in what way good rugs and carpets add to the attractiveness of a home, most of them replied that floor coverings make a room more attractive by giving it color and tying it together. Some people expressed their feeling in terms of the atmosphere created by the presence of rugs—they make the room cozier, homier, warmer. Only a few think first of soft floor coverings as contributing to the attractiveness of a room because of practicalities of softening sound or making housework easier.

At the present time most living rooms and dining rooms contain large-size rugs. There is, however, a lively consumer interest in wall-to-wall carpets. As against 7% who now *have* wall-to-wall carpets in their living rooms, 36% would *like* them; 6% now *have* wall-to-wall carpets in their dining rooms, 29% would *like* them. People want wall-to-wall carpets mainly because they think they are more attractive, although many also regard them as more practical.

The right color in a rug or carpet is a major consideration. About 56% report that it was the *color* that particularly appealed to them in the rug or carpet they bought most recently. Almost 50% of those who want new rugs have already decided on the color they want, while only 22% have decided on what they are going to spend. Color was mentioned more than any other one thing as the problem that makes buying rugs or carpets troublesome. Further difficulties include the inability to find good quality, the right pattern or weave, and the right size. These problems of selection were undoubtedly complicated by shortages and the fact that when most women went to buy, they were looking for rugs that would "fit" the furnishings they already owned.

Perhaps the most disturbing factor developed in the survey is the tendency to procrastinate when it comes to actually buying carpets and rugs. Well over half of those who want new rugs or carpets have been thinking about getting them for over one year and 40% for over two years. It was found that this procrastination is not caused solely by financial considerations. Just about as many women in the top economic level have delayed as long in buying the rugs or carpets they want as those who are less prosperous.

The most important point brought out in the study seems to be the absence of any strong compelling urge which might cause more people who want attractive homes, and who appreciate the role carpets and rugs play in making a home attractive, to translate that want into action. This is the point at which manufacurers and retailers must concentrate their efforts. An all-out attempt must be made to bridge this gap between desire and actual purchase.

The Second Promotional Program—1948–54

The Institute's second promotional program in the post–World War II period included public relations, retail sales training, retail promotions, retailer information service, merchandising, and, later, a carpet education campaign directed to secondary schools. A summary of marketing expenditures for the period 1948–54 is given in Exhibit 2. A description of the main elements of this promotional program follows.

Public Relations. The objectives and operations of the public relations campaign were described in a report to the managements of member companies as follows.

OBJECTIVES

1. Continuing emphasis in consumer publicity on the functional benefits of carpet. This is not to say that other properties of the product—such as beauty—should be neglected; only that wherever possible we should underscore the *practical advantages* of carpet.
2. Continuing effort to show the carpet industry as *dynamic*—moving forward and creating new and interesting products.
3. Capitalize on the *success* of the industry not only in publicity addressed to consumers but also with the trade, with influence groups, and in the financial community.
4. Intensification and expansion of publicity in publications reaching *influence groups*, with emphasis on media read by builders and those reaching banks and other mortgage-writing institutions.
5. An accelerated effort to encourage the *extension of good retail practices* such as package pricing, sound credit plans, in-the-home selling, etc. A corollary of this is promotion of the Retailer Awards and the Retail Advisory Council.
6. *Co-ordination* to the greatest extent possible of the Institute's public relations with its possible advertising.
7. Development of ways and means to obtain maximum value from the Institute's *sales training program.*

BASIC PUBLIC RELATIONS PROGRAM

Newspapers

1. Releases on trends in new carpets, immediately prior to January and June markets, to newspapers, magazines, radio-TV.
2. Publicity kits of releases, photos or mats, on an "exclusive in your city" basis to 600 top daily newspapers, three times during the year: (1) following the January market, (2) late March, and (3) late August.
3. Smaller kits of a topical nature in November and June—"Carpets for Christmas," "Carpets for Relaxed Summer Living."
4. Summer push with newspaper syndicates, using material of a feature nature. Experience shows editors are more likely to use material from syndicates than direct from us during off seasons.
5. Fillers, the brief items editors find so useful, released monthly.
6. Home Furnishings Industry Committee—expanded co-operation to secure greatest emphasis on carpet in HFIC's materials.
7. National Association of Home Builders—a broadened program of co-operative publicity, based on success this year.

Exhibit 2

CARPET INSTITUTE, INC. (A)

Marketing Expenditures, 1948–54

	1948	1949	1950	1951	1952	1953	1954
Public relations	$ 94,800	$ 79,700	$ 64,900	$ 66,000	$ 65,700	$ 65,800	$ 75,100
Retail sales training	9,800	59,700	32,500	50,300	34,200	27,200	43,200
Spring carpet bazaar	6,600	47,300	56,800	43,500	49,700	49,400	28,900
Amos Parrish studies	13,000	13,900	17,200	9,100	6,900	8,000	6,800
Dun & Bradstreet studies	......	......	......	32,500	23,200	16,000	7,200
School educational program	......	......	......	......	......	......	2,500
Merchandising material	55,000	57,300	11,700	......	3,600	2,000	......
Special activities	......	......	13,400*	9,300*	......	......	......
Research	17,800†	......	15,000‡	......	......	12,800§	24,200‖
Administration	5,400	10,000	9,900	8,900	8,900	11,300	10,000
Total	$202,400	$267,900	$268,100	$248,900	$178,700	$192,500	$197,900

* "Home," *Fashion, Time*.
† Roper survey.
‡ Parrish retail study. (Subject of Case [B])
§ Vicary study. (Subject of Case [C])
‖ Advertising campaign developmental expenses.

Source: Carpet Institute, Inc., records.

8. Color photographs—stepped up promotion of new color photographs of room settings, to the growing number of major newspapers using color.
9. Creation of a better photograph file by (1) taking more shots at the markets, and (2) obtaining more prints from Institute members for exclusive use in the industry's program.

Magazines

10. Off-season stories to receive particular attention. The practice of reporting upcoming stories to members will be improved so that members can tie in more effectively.
11. Magazine evaluation reports will be made every three months, with interpretations of trends in editors' floor covering preferences.

Radio-TV

12. Radio releases—12 during the year to 1,600 stations, geared to themes of other publicity. Experience has shown releases are used on the average by better than 100 stations.
13. Industry spokesmen featured on more live shows, local and network.
14. Four TV packets of scripts and photographs to carry the story of carpet's benefits to viewers nation-wide (recent script on carpets and safety has been used by more than 50 stations).
15. Network "plugs" originating from Hollywood. To help combat the summer slump and build up interest just prior to the fall season, we will concentrate our efforts, scheduling as many as 20 plugs over a six-week period, in August and September, for example. This would in effect be a saturation job.
16. More bookings for field staff. The program to arrange appearances of field staff members on local radio and TV shows in cities where they are presenting sales training programs will be emphasized and expanded to broaden its proven impact.

Among projects designed to sway consumers which cut across the media lines established above are the following:

17. Exploitation of research. The studies initiated by the Technical Committee will be publicized to the full during the year, to the trade, to influence groups, and to consumers.
18. Co-operation with allied groups. Tie-ins with vacuum-cleaner manufacturers and other groups interested in the home, such as, for example, Operation Home Improvement (OHI).
19. Completion of encyclopedia articles. All encyclopedia articles will be updated during the year, for the use of editors when reprintings are scheduled. The *World Book Encyclopedia* article was revised and accepted by the editors.
    a) Expanded publicity on the Retail Awards contest.
    b) More publicity on the Institute's sales training program.
    c) Case history publicity of a "success story" nature.
    d) Publicity on the work of the Retail Advisory Council.
    e) More effective publicity on the advertising program.
    f) Stimulation of local newspaper supplements, or single pages, on carpets. The Institute would supply copy and photographs. Local newspapers would solicit the advertising support of retailers.
    g) An effort to revive and stimulate carpet clubs, with the Field Staff providing leadership and program ideas.

Retail Sales Training

Industry executives had agreed for many years that the inexpert handling of carpets and rugs at retail was one of their "toughest problems." As a result, the training of retail salespersons occupied a prominent place in the Institute promotional program. Such activities were carried on by a field staff of four men. With oral, slide film, and movie presentations, and special training material, they went into retail stores to help store personnel increase carpet sales through: "(1) a greater awareness of the industry's aims, (2) increasing the salesman's potential by giving him a greater knowledge of his product, and (3) sharpening a salesman's technique of handling a sale from opening to close." The field staff also carried on public relations at the local level through participation in TV and radio programs and other special appearances.

Retail Sales Promotion

In an attempt to stir up consumer interest and compensate for what was said to be a serious lack of special promotional effort at retail, the Institute in 1948 replaced the unsuccessful "Better Home Furnishings" promotion with a new retail promotion, the "Spring Carpet Bazaar." This nation-wide retail-store and consumer effort was described to the trade as "a powerful kick off for your spring selling season." The bazaar was scheduled for one week in either March or April annually from 1948 to 1954. The consumer campaign consisted of national advertising by member companies; publicity, including magazine articles, newspaper features, radio and TV program mentions; and retail advertising, displays, and sales promotion. The retailer promotion included (1) a large retail sales promotion plan book which suggested promotional planning ideas for store displays, demonstrations, newspaper and radio advertising, telephone contact sales campaigns, and special contests; (2) mats for tie-in retail newspaper advertisements; and (3) point-of-sale display kits which included a variety of window and wall posters, advertisement blowup displays, and counter cards. The operation of the promotion was carried on for the Institute by a professional promotional agency.

As far as it was possible to judge the results of such an effort, Institute executives believed it to be successful. Many stores reported increased spring sales as a result of tying in with the promotion. Retailer participation in the promotion had increased each year since its beginning. It was to be discontinued after 1954 in order to provide additional funds for other promotional activities which were believed to be more important.

Information Services for Retailers

In order "to help carpet retailers sell more carpets more profitably," the Institute had distributed to retailers various bulletins and retail operating data reports. These services began in 1948 with the distribution of a monthly bulletin entitled *Selling Facts* which was prepared for the Institute by Amos Parrish & Company, consultants on retail operations. Each of these 10- to 15-page bulletins contained what was thought to be helpful information for the retailer on a single phase of his operation, for example, the February 1953 bulletin dealt with carpet retail advertising, and contained information on why it pays a retailer to advertise, and instructions on how to plan and execute retail carpet advertising. Other issues of the bulletin discussed sales, display, layout, sales training, departmental accounting, and other related aspects of carpet department management. In 1950 the value of this bulletin was challenged, and in order to determine whether it was really useful to retailers, it was discontinued as a free service and retailers were notified that they could have it continued on a subscription basis for ten dollars per year. Since only eight retailers from a mailing list totaling several thousand ordered a subscription, the bulletin was discontinued.

In 1950 the Institute retained the Amos Parrish organization to issue a continuing series of annual reports based on a nation-wide survey of "better-than-average" examples of retail carpet sales operations. These reports described specific management, advertising, display, and sales techniques that were used by the country's most progressive and profitable retailers. The objective of the studies was to provide detailed information that would be useful to retailers in increasing their own sales and profits.

Also, in order to provide to retailers information regarding the composite operating experience of a group of stores similar to their own, the Institute in 1951 engaged Dun & Bradstreet, Inc., to make a survey of retail carpet and rug operating results. The purpose of circulating this report was to cause the managers of "lower-than-average" operations to improve their performance and thus strengthen the entire retail base of the soft floor covering industry.

In 1955 the executives of the Institute planned to reduce expenditures for retailer service information and to combine the Amos Parrish surveys of successful carpet selling and the Dun & Bradstreet surveys of operating results into a shorter survey of management information and operating results supplied by Dun & Bradstreet.

According to Mr. Jones, little information was available regarding the amount of actual study and use of such reports by retailers.

Educational Campaign

In late 1954 the Institute was to begin a secondary school home economic educational program in order to fill what executives believed to be "a long-standing need" in this area. The material prepared for this program was to be made available to home economics teachers in a comprehensive "Educational Kit," including: classroom wall charts regarding carpet values, the planning of home furnishings arrangements, and the purchase of carpets; a detailed teacher's manual; and student leaflets which covered many phases of carpet information including construction, how to buy, values to the family, and complete instructions for the care of rugs and carpets. In addition, a "swatch kit" containing 29 samples, 9 × 9 inches, of the principal types of carpets was available to teachers for classroom demonstration purposes.

Early in 1955 the Institute planned to run an advertising campaign in professional publications directed to home economics teachers, which would announce the Institute's educational program and the availability of material for classroom use. Through this program, it was expected that the study of rugs and carpets would assume a much more important place in secondary school home economics classes. Commenting on the importance of this effort, Mr. Jones said, "We should have been into this type of activity years ago, because exposing the homemaker of tomorrow to carpet values will be of inestimable value in increasing future sales."

Merchandising the Promotional Program

A substantial proportion of the total marketing budget of the Institute was spent on various merchandising activities in order to bring the promotional activities of the industry to the attention of retailers, distributors, and so-called carpet-user-influence groups, such as decorators, architects, and builders. Such activities included the preparation and distribution of material such as: (1) mailing to a list of over 13,000 retailers special promotional brochures which pointed out the importance of the consumer promotional activities of the Institute in increasing retail sales and urging retailers to tie in with special efforts of their own; (2) instructional pamphlets and brochures to be given to consumers by carpet outlets; (3) retail advertising material such as photos and mats; and (4) brochures outlining plans and ideas for retailer direct mailings.

Although hundreds of requests for such material were received and many thousands of pieces were sent out annually, it was difficult to evaluate (1) how much of the material was used, (2) how effectively it was used, and (3) if it were used, how much it contributed to the sales process. Merchandising promotional efforts was nevertheless considered to be an important activity.

Consideration of the Issue of Advertising

After reviewing the past promotional activities of the Institute, Mr. Jones and his associates began to consider the possibility of employing advertising as an additional promotional tool. They realized that members of the Institute had, for many years, spent sizable sums on consumer advertising, as indicated in Exhibit 3. They also realized that the use of consumer advertising by the Institute would require a significant increase in the Institute's budget.

Exhibit 3

CARPET INSTITUTE, INC. (A)

Advertising Expenditures of Carpet Institute Member Companies—1945–54
(In Thousands of Dollars)

	1945	1946	1947	1948	1949	1950	1951	1952	1953	1954
Artloom Carpet Co., Inc.:										
General magazines...	......	......	......	No fig-	......	$ 23	$ 113	$ 134	......	$ 63
Magazine section....	......	......	......	ures	......	30	3	......	......	......
				pub-						
Total...........	......	......	......	lished	......	$ 53	$ 116	$ 134	......	$ 63
Bigelow-Sanford:										
General magazines...	$150	$ 425	$ 480		$ 666	$ 537	$ 411	$ 598	$ 501	$ 530
Farm magazines.....	.....	22	6		27	55	53	59	26	......
Newspapers.........	....	......	32		......	......	......			
Magazine sections...	....	......	......		134	125	......			
Network television...	....	......	......		193	15	134			
Total...........	$150	$ 447	$ 518		$1,020	$ 732	$ 598	$ 657	$ 527	$ 530
Cabin Crafts, Inc.:										
General magazines...	.....	......	$ 8		$ 14	......	$ 20	$ 56	$ 136	124
Total...........			$ 8		$ 14		$ 20	$ 56	$ 136	$ 124
Downs Carpet Co., Inc.:										
General magazines...	.....	......	......		......	......	$ 30	$ 35	$ 50	$ 39
Total...........							$ 30	$ 35	$ 50	$ 39
Firth Carpet Co.:										
General magazines...	.....	......	$ 66		$ 166	$ 157	$ 219	$ 169	$ 162	99
Farm magazines.....	....	......	......		......	......	......	16	11	4
Total...........			$ 66		$ 166	$ 157	$ 219	$ 185	$ 173	$ 103
Holmes:										
General magazines...	.....	$ 37	$ 41		$ 45	$ 46	$ 32	......	......	.....
Total...........		$ 37	$ 41		$ 45	$ 46	$ 32			
A & M Karagheusian, Inc.:										
General magazines...	$ 61	$ 23	$ 119		$ 236	$ 306	$ 298	$ 169	$ 141	$ 127
Newspapers........	61	72	85		......	......	......			
Magazine sections...	....	......	......		20	......	......	35	90	.....
Farm magazines.....	....	......	......		......	......	18	9	10	.....
Total...........	$122	$ 95	$ 204		$ 256	$ 306	$ 316	$ 213	$ 241	$ 127
Loes, James & Sons Co.:										
General magazines...	.....	$ 60	$ 101		$ 272	$ 251	$ 289	$ 183	$ 235	$ 451
Farm magazines.....	....	9	18		......	......	......			
Newspapers.........	....	......	10		24	125	35	29	......	.....
Magazine sections...	....	......	......		......	......	......		60	38
Network TV........	....	......	......		......	......	......	212	314	60
Total...........		$ 69	$ 129		$ 296	$ 376	$ 324	$ 414	$ 609	$ 549
Magee:										
General magazines...	.....	$ 32	$ 49		$ 145	$ 174	$ 197	$ 173	$ 178	$ 235
Farm magazines.....	....	......	......		......	......	......		16	10
Magazine sections...	....	......	......		......	......	......		105	106
Total...........		$ 32	$ 49		$ 145	$ 174	$ 197	$ 173	$ 299	$ 351

Exhibit 3—Continued

	1945	1946	1947	1948	1949	1950	1951	1952	1953	1954
Masland:										
General magazines...	$ 8	$ 25	$ 140		$ 170	$ 145	$ 177	$ 158	....	$ 5
Farm magazines.....	14	36	49		27	4	....	....	....	.....
Newspapers........	32	96	....		....	....	....	....	....	.....
Network TV........	....	....	....		46	149	215	....	$ 276	274
Total...........	$ 54	$ 157	$ 189		$ 243	$ 298	$ 392	$ 158	$ 276	$ 279
Mohawk:										
General magazines...	.....	$ 195	$ 252		$ 253	$ 74	$ ...	$ 151	$ 269	$ 123
Farm magazines.....	....	....	....		46	24	....	27	15	.....
Magazine sections...	....	7	....		....	....	....	....	....	6
Network TV........	....	....	....		308	760	1,189	....	....	.....
Total...........		$ 202	$ 252		$ 607	$ 858	$1,189	$ 178	$ 284	$ 129
Alexander Smith, Inc.:										
General magazines...	$180	$ 311	$ 459		$ 432	$ 588	$ 503	$ 264	$ 198	$ 71
Farm magazines.....	.....	30	73		7	9	25	11	10	.....
Magazine sections...	.....	....	....		380	....	6	....	44	4
Total...........	$180	$ 341	$ 532		$ 819	$ 597	$ 533	$ 275	$ 252	$ 75
GRAND TOTAL BY CLASSIFICA-TIONS:										
General magazines...	$399	$1,108	$1,715		$2,399	$2,301	$2,289	$2,090	$1,870	$1,867
Farm magazines.....	14	97	146		107	92	96	122	88	14
Newspapers........	93	168	127		24	125	35	29	....	.....
Magazine sections...	.....	7	....		534	155	9	35	299	154
Network TV........	....	....	....		547	924	1,538	202	590	334
Total...........	$506	$1,380	$1,988		$3,611	$3,597	$3,967	$2,478	$2,847	$2,369

Source: National Advertisement Investments in magazines, Sunday supplement, magazine sections, network radio, and network TV from Publishers Information Bureau Records, 1945–54.

~~~

CASE 5: CARPET INSTITUTE, INC. (B)[1]

NOTE: *This case concerns the attitudes of retailers toward carpets and rugs. Questions to consider follow: (1) In the light of the information given in the case, what conclusions do you draw regarding the effect of retailer behavior upon sales of carpets and rugs? (2) With respect to working with and through the trade, what do you think the Institute should do after 1954? (3) Does your analysis of the information in the case change your tentative conclusions regarding the possibilities of consumer advertising for the Institute?*

In 1950 executives of the Institute became interested in learning more about "the retailer and where he fits into the promotional problems of the carpet and rug industry." Therefore, they hired Amos Parrish & Company, Inc., a consulting organization specializing in the retail field, to make a study of the activities of retailers. The purpose of the study was "to find out what successful techniques have been used by those stories

---

[1] Written by Donald H. Thain.

which do the best job in selling floor coverings." The study was conducted by means of field interviews with a representative sample of approximately 200 "better-than-average" department, furniture, and carpet specialty stores. The Parrish report, 300 pages in length, covered the following topics: (1) long-term sales trends; (2) operating results, including expenses, profits, returns, markups, and markdowns; (3) merchandising practices; (4) selling methods; (5) promotion, layout of departments, and display; and (6) management attitudes.

Of particular interest to executives of the Institute was the section of the report entitled "What are some important management attitudes expressed by floor covering dealers toward carpets?" Pertinent excerpts from this section follow.

EXCERPTS FROM THE PARRISH REPORT
REGARDING MANAGEMENT ATTITUDES

Attitudes regarding Profits

Department stores rate floor coverings profit higher than furniture, appliances, or dresses. Department stores' opinions on floor coverings net profit compared with:

	Furniture	Major Appliances	Better Dresses
Better.............	63.9%	88.5%	47.8%
Same..............	16.1	7.7	26.4
Worse............	20.0	3.8	25.8
	100.0%	100.0%	100.0%

Stores were asked how the *net profit* for their floor coverings department compared with several other operations.

In department stores, a majority rated floor coverings *stronger* in each case.

Floor coverings stood out most favorably in comparison with major appliances, 88.5% rating it better. It ranks next strongly against furniture, and then dresses. This relationship, it is interesting to note, is about the *same* as average nationwide performances for 1949.

Clearly, the facts show, department stores *recognize the profit importance* of floor coverings.

That all stores have not yet capitalized to the fullest extent on the profit potential of this operation, however, is reflected by the significant numbers who rated it "*Same*" or "*worse*" than furniture or appliances. Not until these stores have achieved the good figures previously discussed, of course, will they fully appreciate the importance of floor coverings to their own profit.

Furniture operations rank floor coverings profit higher than appliances, but below furniture. Furniture stores' opinions on floor coverings net profit compared with:

	Furniture	Major Appliances
Better................	18.2%	69.6%
Same.................	24.2	17.4
Worse................	57.6	13.0
	100.0%	100.0%

Slightly more than *two-thirds* of the furniture stores rated floor coverings net profit better than major appliances.

In comparison with furniture, the picture was less favorable, more than half rating it *below* furniture profits. By helping stores increase the efficiency of their floor coverings operation, the Carpet Institute can hope to see this relationship improved—can hope to see floor coverings *further strengthen* its standing in the minds of furniture stores.

Attitudes toward Salesmen

Top salesmen rated most important to a successful carpet operation.

	Total	Dept.	Furn.	Spec.
Dept. Layout.............	4.2%	7.2%	3.2%	1.5%
National Brands and Exclusive Lines..............	11.3	13.3	14.2	6.0
Able Salesmen............	18.3	18.1	20.6	16.5
Advertising and Display....	14.1	18.0	17.5	5.9
Price or Value............	9.9	9.6	11.1	8.9
Superior Installation Work..	8.9	6.0	6.4	14.9
Personal Attention, Service..	16.4	12.1	14.3	23.9
Balanced Stock and Assortments................	16.9	15.7	12.7	22.4
	100.0%	100.0%	100.0%	100.0%

Obviously, the opinions of retailers concerning factors most important to successful carpet operations are of vital interest to the carpet industry. By analyzing what their dealers feel about carpet selling, the industry can, of course, be in a better position to help them improve their performance.

In order to determine what the dealers themselves think is most important to a successful carpet operation, the dealers were asked to rate the various factors involved in order of importance.

Taking all stores in the survey together, "Able Salesmen" ranked *first*, receiving nearly one-fifth of the mentions. Very clearly, the caliber of *selling* in retail stores is considered of vital importance to successful operations.

"Balanced Stock and Assortments" and "Personal Attention and Service," ranked almost equally for second place.

Together, these two—plus "Able Salesmen"—account for nearly one-half of the mentions.

"Advertising and Display"—with 14.1% ranked fourth, indicating the importance which retailers place on these types of promotional media.

"National Brands" and "Exclusive Lines" rate next, pulled down substantially by the low specialty store ratings, as the breakdown figures show.

Looking at the department store column, it is evident that "Advertising and Display" rates almost a tie for first place with "Able Salesmen." Both Department and Furniture stores place *greater importance* on these factors than do specialty stores.

"Balanced Stock and Assortments" rates third on the department store list, followed closely by "National Brands and Exclusive Lines." "Personal Attention and Service" rates fifth, a sharp contrast to its specialty store standing.

To summarize, *top salesmen* are certainly ranked as one of the most important factors in operating a successful carpet operation, in the opinion of the dealers themselves. Together with "Balanced Stock and Assortments," and "Personal Attention and Service," salesmen play a vital role in making—*or breaking*—retail carpet operations.

Attitudes toward Promotion

Better promotion heads list of actions stores took to improve sales during 1949.

	Total	Department Store	Furniture Store	Specialty Store
Increased Advertising and Better Promotions........	30.9%	31.0%	28.3%	33.3%
Better Balanced Stocks.....	18.9	19.7	18.9	17.2
Stronger Sales Training....	11.6	12.7	11.5	11.1
Better Service............	10.7	8.6	11.4	13.0
Remodeled and/or Expanded	10.3	8.4	11.2	10.9
Offered Better Values......	9.9	12.9	9.6	7.5
Other Actions...........	7.7	6.7	9.1	7.0
	100.0%	100.0%	100.0%	100.0%

In each store interview, dealers were asked to describe the things which they did in 1949 which they felt helped stimulate their floor coverings volume and profit during the year.

As the figures show, *increased advertising* and *better promotions* head the list, accounting for almost one-third (30.9%) of the total mentions. This was substantially higher than the next most important factor, "Better Balanced Stocks."

"Better Service" and "Remodeled and/or Expanded Department" rank closely for fourth place, following "Stronger Sales Training."

This last, it will be noted, ranks somewhat lower than it did on the questions concerning the most important factors in operating a successful floor coverings department.

"Better Service" and "Remodeled and/or Expanded" rank next, followed by "Better Values."

A group of other factors accounted for 7.7%. Some of the actions covered in this category were: seasonal previews for special customers, adding stores' own brand of goods, closer relations with manufacturers, the addition of outside selling agents, periodic sales, centralized buying plans for all stores in a multiple unit, strengthening of store personnel, and trading up. None of these factors were mentioned by enough stores to be tabulated separately.

All in all, the factors listed by store heads represent the period of *readjustment* which characterized 1949. Competition was naturally becoming keener and keener, and stores turned to *extra promotion* and *sales training* to produce sales. Merchandise was more plentiful, and dealers were better able to offer their customers *balanced stocks.*

Attitudes toward Promotional Aids

Dealers liked promotional helps best among things resources did in 1949.

As a part of the regular questionnaire, dealers were asked to express their opinions as to the things that their favorite resource had done during 1949 to help them sell more carpeting.

Most importantly mentioned were various types of *promotional* assistance, which accounted for more than one-third of the total mentions. Most frequently mentioned subsections of this total included commendations of national advertising and special store promotions and cooperation in local dealer advertising.

	Total	Department Stores	Furniture Stores	Specialty Stores
Promotional Assistance.....	34.4%	27.4%	43.2%	34.1%
Sales Training Aids........	22.4	33.3	19.4	7.9
Resource Relations........	19.4	20.3	12.0	28.0
Merchandising Helps......	4.5	4.8	6.0	1.5
Product Improvements.....	4.0	3.5	3.0	6.5
Others.................	15.3	10.7	16.4	22.0
	100.0%	100.0%	100.0%	100.0%

Sales training ranked second in the number of mentions received, with slightly less than one-quarter (22.4%).

Very clearly, dealers welcome this kind of assistance from their resources.

Several specific factors were mentioned under the general heading of Resource Relations. Good service and delivery accounted for 14.4%. Other factors in this group which were mentioned were manufacturers' restriction of merchandise line, support of suggested resale prices, and frequent, helpful calls from manufacturers' salesmen.

Under Merchandising Helps, assistance in basic stock plans was the most commonly mentioned factor. The comments under product improvements all dealt with the development of newer and better merchandise.

The breakdown figures show that department stores gave more mentions to sales training aid than promotional assistance, although the figures were quite close. Furniture stores referred to promotional assistance—particularly in regard to local dealer advertising—as the number one category. Specialty stores put promotional assistance first, followed closely by manufacturers' relations —with special emphasis on good service and delivery.

An analysis of the comments of the best dealers shows that sales training received a somewhat *greater* number of mentions, with the top group, than with the average. Promotional assistance was also named often.

It is a fine tribute to the carpet industry as a whole that *nearly all* dealers commented favorably on one or more things their resources were doing. Out of the entire survey, *only six stores* reported that their favorite manufacturer was doing nothing to help them sell more carpeting. The facts show that floor coverings' dealers recognize and appreciate the fine assistance which their resources are giving them.

Attitudes toward Resources

[Information regarding] why stores prefer their favorite resources [is given in Exhibit 1].

Each store was asked why it preferred its favorite resources. The answers have been grouped into the categories shown.

Resource Relations—most important category in all three types of stores— included the following: Better Delivery and Service (20.8%), Friendly and Cooperative Attitude (12.1%), and Restricted Distribution of Line or Special Items (12.5%). Other factors under this heading included references to the manufacturers' willingness to police retail prices and to manufacturers' year-end allowances.

Product Qualities was second most important, accounting for one-third of the total mentions. Included in this group were Good Quality (12.9%), and Wide Assortments of Colors and Patterns (12.5%). Other dealers commended their resources' attempts to fit their pricing needs, style demands, and profit requirements, and to make up special goods to the dealer's specifications.

Exhibit 1

CARPET INSTITUTE, INC. (B)

Why Stores Prefer Their Favorite Resources

	Total	Department Stores	Furniture Stores	Specialty Stores
Resource Relations:	54.2%	50.7%	49.4%	62.8%
Better delivery and service..........	20.8%	19.5%	19.0%	24.1%
Friendly and co-operative attitude....	12.1	11.3	11.0	14.0
Restricted distribution of line or special items................	12.5	11.7	11.4	14.5
Other................	8.8	8.2	8.0	10.2
Product Qualities:	34.6	41.9	35.8	25.6
Good quality................	12.9	15.6	13.3	9.5
Wide assortment of colors and patterns...	12.5	15.1	12.9	9.2
Other................	9.2	11.2	9.6	6.9
Customer Acceptance of Brand Name........	3.3	3.7	3.7	2.6
Promotional Factors............	2.5	1.2	3.7	2.6
Others................	5.4	2.5	7.4	6.4
	100.0%	100.0%	100.0%	100.0%

Source: Carpet Institute. Inc., records.

By all odds, Resource Relations and Product Qualities were the most important reasons given by stores for liking their favorite resources. Together, the factors in these two categories accounted for *nearly 90%* of the mentions. Promotional factors—a strong category when dealers were asked what they liked about their resources' efforts to help them—shows up very low on the scale.

Inter-store comparisons indicate that specialty stores place *extra emphasis* on resource relations, paying their favorite resources particularly strong compliments for being friendly and cooperative, and for having restricted distribution on either their full line, or on special items.

Specialty Stores count more on these factors—and less on product qualities themselves—when giving their loyalties to resources.

To summarize, more than half the dealers like their favorite resources for reasons which have very *little to do* with the product they make. Primary importance, according to survey results, is placed on *delivery* and *service* factors by all three store types. The carpet industry's interest in dealer problems—and its desire to help them do an even better selling job—are certainly in line with dealers' appreciation of such activities.

The excerpts given above were taken from the section of the Parrish Report which dealt with management attitudes toward carpets. A summary of the over-all findings of the retail survey are given below.

Summary of Principal Findings

1. Good operations made full use of sound *inventory control* information.

2. Good operations concentrated their volume among relatively *few best-selling price lines.*

3. Good operations bought an above-average percentage of their goods on a *reorder basis.*

4. Good operations made fuller use of volume-increasing *selling signs* than did poorer operations.

5. Good operations took *deeper, quicker markdowns* on slow-selling goods than poorer operations.

6. Good operations kept accurate records of sales by *classification* and *price lines.*

7. Good operations carried a greater percentage of manufacturers' lines in *full stock* than did poorer operations.

8. Good operations displayed merchandise by *classification* in proportion to the sales importance of each classification.

9. Good operations concentrated a greater percentage of their selling effort on *wall-to-wall* carpeting than did poorer operations.

10. Good operations devoted a greater proportion of their selling effort to *outside selling* than did the poorer operations.

11. Good operations kept and used *basic stock* lists to a greater extent than did poorer operations.

12. Good operations paid their salespeople on a *commission basis* more consistently than did poorer operations.

13. Good operations made *six months' merchandise plans* well in advance of the season planned.

14. Good operations consistently used *dominant display features.*

15. Good operations *promoted credit terms* more frequently than poorer operations.

16. Good operations conducted *sales training programs* more consistently than did poorer operations.

17. Good operations presented *less-cluttered* and *better-lighted* appearances than did poorer operations.

18. Good operations used *roomette displays* to a greater extent than did poorer operations.

19. Good operations *had been modernized* more recently than poorer operations.

20. Good operations devoted more time and effort to *customer services* than poorer operations.

21. Good operations are those who focus their energy on serving customers in an even better, more profitable manner.

In addition to survey results, the Parrish report also presented "case studies of several of the stores that were studied during field work." Two of these case studies are given below:

Case Study A

This study was of a furniture store located on the West Coast, which was in the volume group $500,000 to $1,000,000. It was given an over-all rating of "good" by the Parrish organization. The commentary on the store follows.

This store is one of the largest furniture operations in its city. The floor coverings buyer is a man in his middle forties who has been in the floor coverings business for 17 years.

Store keeps a record of sales by classification in dollars. The buyer says he uses this to help keep his stocks more in line with sales, and to see how business appears to be shifting between different types of floor coverings. Currently, he has noticed that broadloom is becoming increasingly important in the store.

The department also keeps track of sales by price line. They do not have any records of volume by color, size, or type of weave. The buyer says he keeps these factors "in his head," but is thinking of starting such records.

Three months in advance of each new selling season, the store makes up a six months' merchandising plan for future operations. Included are projected sales by classification, purchases, markon, beginning and ending inventory by classifications, and any special promotion plan for the period.

Markdowns are not planned in advance. The buyer keeps an eye on them in relation to last year's figures. Special promotions are also planned "by type of floor covering, but I can't get the actual items so far in advance."

This store uses an inventory control system, posting stock and sales information to an index card record. Cuttings are controlled from these records, with particular attention paid to avoiding remnant sizes wherever possible.

The store does not use a basic stock list. "I know pretty well what's in stock from the inventory control records. I also stay in the floor lot, so that I know what's selling. Whenever anything gets low, the girl who keeps the inventory record lets me know about it, and I then decide whether we should get any more."

This store reported doing about 75% of its volume on reordered goods. He likes to stick to goods which do a big volume and tries to avoid fringe items. "If it's not something I can sell enough of to reorder at least once, I'd just as soon not bother with it. Having a lot of 'one-shot' patterns around just increases my remnants."

As noted, the buyer tries to keep down the number of remnants by carefully scheduling cuttings from individual rolls. However, he still has more than he would like. "I let my remnants pile up and then run special events three or four times a year. We stock them in piles on the floor by sizes and sell them at prices from 69¢ to $6.95 per square yard. I have also had some success with giving discounts to customers for multiple buying—five remnants for a certain price which is about 15% less than they would total individually."

The store operates its own workroom. The buyer said, "I think we get much better quality control. The customer likes the idea of the store doing its own installation." The workroom is laid out in a big area with plenty of room for carpet operations to be done while on the floor. This was one of the neatest workrooms we saw.

This store carries about 75% of its broadloom line in stock, and stocks about 70% of its three-quarter carpeting. The buyer believes very strongly in having heavy stocks of floor coverings.

The store concentrates its buying with few resources. The buyer felt this was important not only from a quantity discount angle, but also because it assured him better service. His main reason for liking his top resource was the consumer acceptance which the brand has achieved in this store's locality.

Markdowns are taken on slow selling goods as fast as possible. The buyer considers anything which has not shown definite sales within 30 days to be slow selling. It is his policy to get everything cleared out within 60 days of receipt (his actual stockturn was 3.7 times last year—above the furniture store average). Normally, his first markdown is about 20% of the original price. Before marking anything down, however, he gives his salesmen a special "pm" of 25 or 50¢. If the "pm" doesn't work, he then takes the markdown.

Salesmen in this store help with stockkeeping and are expert in cutting and binding although they do not regularly do this. They spend about one day a week on outside selling, mostly following up leads of people who have come into the store. Salesmen are paid on a straight salary and commission, with average earnings about $200 a week.

This store lets salesmen work out credit arrangements with each customer. The store sets only general policies and leaves it up to the salesmen to make a reasonable deal. The credit office reviews the transaction, and usually approves. This saves a lot of time, according to the buyer, and makes the salesman more interested in credit.

This store has an organized plan for trade-in allowances. The old floor covering is appraised without regard to what the customer is buying, and a valuation put on it. The store plans to make money on a trade-in reselling it through a special department handling used goods. That department, incidentally, shows a profit.

Unlike a number of furniture stores, floor covering salesmen sell only in that department, not throughout the store. The store has several decorators, however, who can sell in any department they wish. The buyer thinks this is a pretty good arrangement because it lets his men become experts in selling carpets. The decorators are a means of wrapping up coordinated sales of all types of home furnishings and help give the store an air of authority when it comes to fashion and home decoration, the buyer believes. Each week he holds a sales meeting in the department, going over all the new goods received in the stock and explaining any special promotions coming up. He places particular emphasis in telling the salesmen what to *sell*—whether it be new goods just received or merchandise with an unusually good margin. His feeling is that a good salesman can help merchandise the department by pushing what the buyer wants sold most.

Most of the store salesmen have been to one of the various manufacturer sponsored schools. The buyer thinks very highly of these organizations, and regularly sends anybody whom he feels is a potential good prospect.

This store does a big promotional job on drop patterns and seconds. They also do well on well-planned regular promotions, the buyer says.

This year, they are planning to increase their advertising expenditure, having a big space promotion at least once a week during the best selling months. The buyer would rather have a few large space ads than a series of smaller ones because, he says, "We get much better results that way."

This department was modernized in 1948, and was painted again early this Spring. There are actually two rooms to the department, roll goods being in one portion and cut rugs and samples in the other.

This department has one of the best operating figures in the survey. Markon was substantially above both average and good for furniture stores, and markdowns were less than 3%. Consequently, gross margin was above the good figure. Last year, sales volume was up 3% over the previous year—better than average.

Case Study B

This study was of a carpet specialty store located in the Middle West, which was in the volume group over $1,000,000. It was given an over-all rating of "poor" by the Parrish organization. The commentary on the store follows:

The store is in the outskirts of a large industrial city. The outside of the store needed painting—it looked dingy and dirty from the smoke and soot in the air. Inside, however, the store was clean and modern.

The owner of the store is extremely active in the business. In a sense, it is a one-man business. He is probably the only person in the company who could answer the questions on the survey.

In general, the owner of the store did not believe in keeping records. Records of sales by departments were kept by a clerk and put on the owner's desk each morning. However, no record of sales by classification, color, price lines or type of weave were kept. His comment was, "We'd spend more money on getting records of that sort together than would ever be worth to us in a year."

His merchandise planning is done six months at a time, with each merchandise plan completed about six weeks before the period which the plan covers. The plan he makes up himself—for his own purpose. It includes information primarily on sales, purchases and ending inventory.

He does all of his buying himself. His policy on buying is really controlled by the merchandising goal of the store. He buys wide assortments from many manufacturers. He estimated that about 40% of his business was on a recorder basis. It is a definite policy of this store to have salesmen sell from goods in stock rather than from sample.

Markdowns are taken about twice a year. Merchandise is usually marked into the next lowest price bracket, which usually means the merchandise is reduced by $1.

About 70% of his sales were done in broadloom; 20% in three-quarter carpeting; and the balance in cut rugs. He carried about 15 to 20 price lines in both the broadloom and 27" classifications. In cut rugs he had about 15 price lines.

He estimated that approximately a third of his total sales were in wall-to-wall carpeting. However, he felt that the limit had been reached in finding ways and means of stimulating more wall-to-wall sales.

Periodically, he has a meeting for his salespeople. The last one had been six weeks before. In general, he feels that salesmanship cannot be taught, and he pooh-poohs the manufacturers' training schools. To quote him, "You could know more about carpets than any other person in this city and still be the worst salesman. And someone who didn't know anything about carpets, but who was a born salesman, could probably sell rings around you."

Since the war, this operator has added rug cleaning, moth proofing and storage to his services. He feels that this is a profitable operation and gives him a better chance to sell new rugs to established customers.

There was no noticeable feature display. Broadloom and 27″ carpeting rolls were stacked on the floor.

Two manufacturers' cardboard displays were standing inconspicuously in the corner, but there were no merchandise display signs indicating either the price or type of merchandise visible.

The company promotes credit terms in every newspaper advertisement but there were no signs mentioning credit in the department.

Publicity money is spent largely on newspaper advertising, although the store sponsors a weekly 15-minute radio program of an institutional nature. It is usually planned two weeks in advance.

Last year, the store had high markdowns—9.7%. It also showed a slow turnover (1.6 times). The store's percentage of stock from 0–6 months old was only 62%. Last year the department showed a net profit of only .8%.

~~~

CASE 6: CARPET INSTITUTE, INC. (C)[1]

NOTE: *This case presents additional information regarding consumer attitudes toward carpets and rugs. Questions to consider follow: (1) In view of the information given in the Vicary study, what do you now see as the principal problems of the carpet and rug industry? (2) Tentatively, what conclusions do you draw regarding the use of advertising to stimulate primary demand of carpets and rugs? (3) If you think it is desirable to use consumer advertising, what should be its objectives?*

In 1953 the executives of the Carpet Institute retained the James M. Vicary Company, which did motivational research, to make a motivation survey of consumers' attitudes regarding carpets and rugs. According to Mr. Jones, the purpose of the study was to make an attempt to categorize the emotions of people toward carpet. "The study was a reflection," he said, "of the feeling at the time among industry executives that something should be done to study the consumers in depth."

In undertaking the survey, the Vicary organization first made 50 preliminary depth interviews. Experience gained from these interviews, together with experience gained from the Roper study, and questions developed by the Institute's Market Research Committee led to the construction of a final questionnaire consisting of approximately 90 questions. The questionnaire was developed to cover six areas, as follows:

---

[1] Written by Donald H. Thain.

1. Word associations to basic words related to carpets and rugs, to obtain semantic relationships and the meaning and emotional content at a symbolic level.
2. Personification questions to ascertain the respondent's self-view in buying carpets.
3. Successive word associations to CARPET to determine the kinds of associations which lie behind the first thoughts about this word and thus measure the shifting influences on this symbol at the present time.
4. Sentence completions to obtain the many rationalizations of respondents when RUGS and CARPETS are put into the context of common usage.
5. Direct questions on product usage, buying behavior, and intention to buy, as in standard marketing studies, to provide cross tabulation with motivation data.
6. Personal characteristics of the respondent for sampling purposes and cross tabulations as in No. 5 above.

Field interviews based upon the questionnaire, 911 with women and 291 with men, were conducted in 46 locations across the country in June 1953. Interviews were assigned to interviewers on a quota basis which would match the sample characteristics of the Roper survey made in 1948.

The report which was presented to Institute executives consisted of two types of material: (1) detailed tabulations of information derived from respondents' answers to questions, and (2) interpretations of the interviews.

Since the report was 150 pages in length, excerpts from it will be restricted to the interpretative material. These excerpts follow.

High Lights of the Findings of the Vicary Report

The high lights of the report were summarized by the Vicary organization in the report as follows.

In broad strokes the following high lights have been drawn from the interviews in this report. Direct quotations have been omitted here partly in the interest of brevity. It should be held in mind that these interviews are intended to be descriptive of the various ways in which people think about carpets and rugs, and cannot be used as statistical measurement of the amount of such sentiments in the population.

**** The commonest connotations of carpets are warmth, luxuriousness and a variety of expressions about how a carpet makes a house a home, pulls together a room, or creates harmony or unity in a room.

**** Color is almost always mentioned by respondents. A great deal of the testimony is concerned with design, pattern and quality.

**** Quality is almost directly related to price in respondents' minds, even when a high-price carpet fails to give good wear. The consumer in this case wonders at the reasons for failure, in view of the high price.

**** Concern over style is largely in retrospect. If their rug is rather old, they usually say styles don't change fast; if they have recently purchased a rug or are in the process of buying one, they are apt to be concerned whether the style may change. In any case, styles are said to change less rapidly in carpets than other major household items.

**** Respondents have rather distinct preferences in home furnishing trends. Largely they seem called upon to stick with whatever they have. Modern designs are sometimes criticized; traditional designs are less severely treated.

**** Aside from the warm quality of rugs and their beauty in a home, these women could not put into words specifically what a carpet does for them. Respondents predominantly *imply* the social status value of a good rug. The impression is made that the rug is a kind of vehicle by which a homemaker expresses herself of a platform on which she performs. At the same time many women have a highly emotional feeling toward their carpeting in the way it makes them feel personally . . . a kind of secure relaxation.

**** The acoustical effect of carpets is mentioned favorably in many instances. For some people noise is apparently a major irritant in the home, which carpeting alleviates.

**** There is a resistance to an easy acceptance of the opinions of others on carpets. However, respondents sometimes accept advice from their mothers or older women, and they do observe and discuss the experiences of their friends in buying and using carpets and rugs. These women especially don't like the salesman to inject his personal opinions, but at the same time complain that salesmen do not give enough information about their product. There is resistance to going into rug marts to shop, since they feel that in this one-product type of store they are more obliged to buy.

**** Most respondents select the rug or carpet to be bought without the help of any other member of the family. However, when the rug is actually purchased, the husband and wife do so together. Some men were interested enough in the subject to sit in on their wives' interview and contribute details and remarks.

**** Usually they say they know what they want before they go to the store to buy, yet they plan to shop around a good deal when they are in the market for a new carpet.

**** Although brands are often mentioned as "good names" in carpets, far more emphasis is placed on the reliability of the store from which a rug has been or will be purchased than brand names.

**** It seems surprising that even with our sample design which artificially boosts the proportion of people who plan to buy a rug or carpet, so many women want a new carpet. On the one hand women may wish to upgrade their home furnishings rather constantly, and on the other they expect a rug to have an extremely long life. Some say a good rug should last a lifetime.

**** When our respondents were approached on whether carpets should be bought first before other major items, they each apparently had a distinct point of view. One, however, would say first, another last, with several simply saying they would do it differently than last time. It would seem that a kind of mental juggle is necessary between those furnishings to be kept and new ones to add, with the carpet a kind of platform to receive the final assemblage. It is a kind of struggle to pull together a room by a process of elimination and addition. Each person creates his own kind of compromise which affects whether the rug will come first or toward the last in things to be bought.

**** Although a rug may not be bought first among a list of planned purchases, there is another kind of "firstness" which is apparent. Some respondents remarked that just a rug in a room with no other furniture gives a room a more lived-in feeling than any other item you might think of.

**** The chief planned purchase aside from carpeting was the television set. Electrical appliances and furniture were also major categories. The lists indicated a kind of maintenance basis of purchase rather than any unified plan to achieve a single purpose, except where a new house had been bought.

**** There is a great deal of confusion and misconception about the characteristics, features and terminology in carpeting. Even the terms rug vs. carpet, the type of rug construction vs. company names are confused. Many did not know the name of the company who made their rugs. It would seem at least on the surface that too wide a variety of features are pressed upon the housewife with her rather simple needs in floor covering. In any case, few women have bothered to see carpets made in factories and almost never refer to specific literature or books on the general construction and care of rugs. They say they don't even look at the full selection of merchandise, once they have made up their minds about the rug they want.

**** Our respondents were nowhere near as vague about the square yard price of carpet. When they did not have a precise notion of price, many were able to make passable guesses as to the total amount they were prepared to spend for a rug in the room in which they were being interviewed.

**** The price of rugs and carpets is always regarded as high, but at the same time respondents feel that you usually get what you pay for. Cheap rugs are avoided. Many buy wholesale, and many made a point of the fact that they don't buy at sales, since they feel that sales are run to unload leftovers.

**** The purchase of a rug is repeatedly referred to as an "investment." Other major household items may be similarly thought of, but none the less, this reflects a rather general feeling of worth and return from money spent.

**** Cotton rugs are criticized but regarded as probably good at the price, wool as far superior, and nylon as too expensive. There is some doubt about the use of synthetic materials.

**** Evenness of wear is important to many respondents. Wall-to-wall installations are especially criticized since they lead to uneven wear.

**** Wall-to-wall carpets are said to be preferred by many, but since their home is rented, or their occupation may call for a move, wall-to-wall is not actually bought.

**** There is a definite sentiment against complete carpeting in bedrooms in favor of small throw rugs.

**** These respondents rarely report a change in their living habits due to new carpets, and few special events, other than season of the year or a new home induce a sale. Many vaguely say that they buy a new carpet when they need it.

**** There is a dearth of material on the history of previous rugs, and of rugs in the parental home. What is given is mainly descriptive. More material is given on the contemporary problems of friends. Most emphasis is placed on the last carpet bought. Satisfaction with the last carpet bought ranged from very considerable dissatisfaction, some thinking that the salesman had misled them, to great satisfaction. Generally more were satisfied than not.

**** Relatively little variation is seen in this study by region of the country. In warmer areas of the country there was some indication that wool carpets tend to be too warm. A greater variance occurred between rural and urban areas, where mud became a factor in keeping the carpet clean. This does not appear to be a very serious problem.

**** There is considerable concern about wear and cleaning. There are highly varied estimates given for good wear, but it is generally compared to wear for other household items.

**** Professional cleaning of rugs is sometimes severely criticized, while others are quite happy with their experiences in this regard. There seems to be little middle ground, unless it is cleaning rugs oneself. In this case detergents and Glamorene are most frequently mentioned.

**** Olson Rugs are mentioned without criticism by a minority of respondents. It could be that these people like to throw out their old rugs and keep them too, since they evidently have the notion that their own rugs are revamped rather than merely thrown into a common pool.

**** The major story about rugs which was recalled is the Magic Carpet. This may reflect a basic fantasy among women and undoubtedly has certain sexual significance.

Discussion of Findings

The discussion of findings of the study was summarized by the Vicary organization in the report as follows.

Because our statistical results come from various techniques used in the questionnaire and often require an interplay of findings to make appropriate conclusions, the more important subject matter is brought together for discussion in this section.

IMPORTANCE OF SYMBOLS

A primary finding of this study is the change in the meaning of CARPET as a symbol. Every word or object *stands for* other ideas or objects and is associated with them. Thus a word stands for ideas about the use of the object, when it is used, how it looks, etc. These ideas and associations reflect our attitudes towards the word as a symbol. Major shifts in attitudes towards CARPET since the beginning of the century are shown in this study. Evidence is given that the greatest apparent shift in attitude came during and after World War II, although there is much reason to believe these changes were long in the making.

Previous to World War II, carpets were primarily associated with floors, and flooring. Today the chief association to CARPET IS RUG. There has been a similar change in associations to HOUSE. Early in the century the word house was associated with building and place of abode; in other words with physical aspects of a house. Today the house is more associated with home, that is, attitudes have changed from concern with the physical aspects of a house to the psychological attributes of a house.

Although CARPET has shifted away from the old associations to floor and flooring, which were similar to the associations of building to house, it has not found a satisfactory new role to play. Carpet now associates predominantly to rug, and rug associates to carpet. This means that the word carpet no longer *stands for* ideas about the use of carpet, how it looks, its advantages, and so forth. It has changed from a physical association to a purely semantic association, representing a kind of short circuiting of the symbolic process. A practical consequence of this finding suggests that almost any effort to split apart the close, circular association of CARPET to RUG is desirable.

As a result it would appear that the potential force of all communications about carpets has been considerably reduced. Rather than emphasizing advertising as an immediate method to produce sales, it would seem that for immediate purposes emphasis should be placed on the mechanics of distributing the product, the point of sale arrangements, direct service to the customer, and merchandising programs. Support of a limited nature is given for a trade-in system for merchandising carpets. There is evidence that advertising and public relations might best look to long-range objectives aimed at restoring or building the carpet symbol. In particular the younger girl, who forms her adult notions about carpets in her early adolescence, should be studied and served by advertising.

Some of the industry's terminology is confused today in adult minds. The term BROADLOOM is more frequently associated to rugs than carpets. RUG CUSHION is predominantly associated with pad and mat. Because a rather large proportion of respondents did not have associations to RUG CUSHION some variation of rug pad or rug mat might provide better terminology. BEAUTIFUL has little direct meaning of use in describing rugs and TASTEFUL almost completely associates to food and eating rather than household items. MAGIC CARPET was shown to be a very disturbing symbol in that large numbers of people either could give no association or were very hesitant in their responses. This term and ideas relating to the magic carpet motif should be very carefully tested in each new context where it is used to make sure that it contributed to the communication of an advertising message.

The word RUG is a far more common word than CARPET. RUG is given as a response in this study with great frequency to indicate that it might best be used to exclusion of CARPET except where the latter has a special and specific meaning. The use of the phrase "Rugs and carpets" should be avoided.

Although moths are not volunteered as a problem in using carpets and mothproofing is shown to relate mostly to clothing, the term MOTHPROOF is a good warning symbol. TEXTURE has connotations predominantly related to clothing but shows some signs of becoming more and more related to carpeting, being among the top four most important features of a carpet in women's minds. FLOOR COVERING. is most frequently associated with rugs and carpets, while linoleum and tile are definitely minor responses.

Almost all women when they see a bare floor feel that it looks cold, barren or unfinished in some sense. Most women, even the very few who have had little experience in buying or using rugs, feel that a floor should be covered in some way. Predominantly women feel that having a rug in a room makes it easier to keep clean or neat. Buying a rug is more often than not thought to be a pleasurable experience, although a minority criticize rug salesmen. Most women can give some idea of the price they want to pay for their next rug or carpet.

The thing a carpet does for a room is reported most frequently to be improvement in appearance and feeling of warmth.

Attitudes toward wear and expense of carpets are interrelated in an unrealistic fashion. Those who would spend least for their next carpet, expect it to last longer than those who would spend more.

The bulk of criticisms of carpets is shown to be in design and color. A test of connotations shows that STYLE is associated overwhelmingly with clothes and DECORATING connotes painting and wallpapering the interior of the house. Emphasis on style and design in carpets should be avoided, since this new role for carpets is not apparently suitable. Likewise a sizable trend influencing the carpet symbol is that of COLOR. Those people who associate color to CARPET are slightly poorer customers of carpets, indicating that the visual ornamentation features of carpets should receive far less emphasis than in the recent past.

References to period, traditional or modern designs are not prominent. Only in free associations to "FURNITURE" do as many as 11% of women make this connection. Only 4% mention specific classical designs as a most important feature of carpets.

Nothing in this study made it apparent that consumers are aware of product improvements in the industry.

Features of carpets like acoustical effects are now minor factors in consumer's attitudes, but the importance of such a feature might be built around the noise originating in the home, especially children's noisiness.

Inroads are being made by linoleum, but because this product is associated with use in the kitchen, this trend will probably continue to move slowly. Nonetheless, it should be noted that the kitchen is listed as second only to the living room as the cosiest room in the house; 12% of respondents report using rugs in the kitchen.

Surprisingly the addition of carpet to the list of major items a couple had bought in a year's time, made little difference in respondents' estimations of the kind of husband and wife these people represent. This question provides an experimental picture of a respondent's self-view, or how they would think of themselves buying a carpet. Out of seven major items the carpet was shown to be the least important in enhancing a person's self-view. Also, most of the attitudes measured in this study were found to be unrelated to buying behavior or carpet or rug usage. This weak motivational link between attitude and behavior is further underlined by the low rate of spontaneous brand association for either CARPET or RUG. By contrast the simple test word VACUUM brought more associations to vacuum cleaner brand names than did rugs or carpets.

Rather minor differences in associations occur for men as compared to women or for age groups, sections of the country and city size.

~ ~ ~

CASE 7: CARPET INSTITUTE, INC. (D)[1]

NOTE: *In order to obtain a better idea of the possibilities of a program of consumer advertising, Institute executives decided to invite one or more advertising agencies to confer with them and then to submit tentative proposals for some kind of consumer advertising effort. After investigating 26 advertising agencies, Institute executives asked two, Winston-Randall, Inc., and Wilson & Scott Advertising Agency,[2] to consider two questions: Should the Institute advertise to consumers? If so, how? The next two cases give the proposals submitted by the advertising agencies. Questions to consider in the analysis of this case follow: (1) Has Winston-Randall made a sound appraisal of the industry's problems? (2) What kind of a promotional program has Winston-Randall essentially proposed? (3) If the Winston-Randall proposal were accepted by the Institute, what do you think the proposed program would accomplish for the industry?*

WINSTON-RANDALL, INC., REPORT ON
"A GENERAL ADVERTISING PROGRAM FOR
THE CARPET INSTITUTE, INC."

May 20, 1954

In this discussion of the carpet question, we must first consider two leading questions:

---

[1] Prepared by Martin V. Marshall.

[2] Fictitious names.

1. Why have soft-surface floor covering sales remained at a stationary level during the last 30 years when the over-all United States economy has been expanding so rapidly?
2. How can an industry-wide advertising campaign provide an effective and immediate stimulus to soft-surface floor covering sales?

The answers to both of these questions are not easy ones. Many thousands of words have been written on them without supplying positive answers to either question. Several weeks ago, Winston-Randall prepared a basic report on the carpet industry in which we attempted to establish the base from which to prepare our advertising recommendations for the Carpet Institute. In this report we listed the following problems as having affected carpet sales for many years:

*1. The competition of other goods and services including hard-surface floor covering, and the fact that carpeting is an easily deferable purchase has had an adverse effect on carpeting sales.

*2. The emphasis on color and style in carpet advertising has neglected such important product advantages as ease of maintenance, safety, health, quiet, cushioning, warmth, economy, etc.

3. Consumers in general do not associate carpets with physical or emotional benefits to any satisfactory degree.

4. Consumers regard carpets as overpriced in many instances and often expect far more durability than can be reasonably expected.

5. Carpet advertising has been insufficient in volume to create the kind of consumer demand that results in a steadily increasing sales curve.

6. Present-day carpeting, though much more diversified, is not a substantially better product than was available years ago. However, it is substantially more expensive.

7. Domestic woven carpeting is faced with increasing competition from tufted carpets as well as soft-surface floor covering of foreign manufacturing.

8. An adequate supply of acceptable substitute material for wool has not yet been found for use in woven carpets.

9. The introduction of too many new patterns has not only confused the consumer and retailer but contributed to the undesirable retail price situation that currently exists.

10. Too few improvements have been made in the machinery and techniques of manufacturing carpets.

*11. Carpets have not been sufficiently exploited as a vital component of new housing. This involves development of a plan to include carpets in the mortgage as well as promotional pressure on architects, contractors, builders, and bankers.

12. While contract carpeting is an important business for many mills, the part that carpeting can play in business establishments has not been promoted hard enough.

13. More training is needed at the retail salesman's level.

*14. Price advertising at the retail level is making dangerous strides towards eliminating the qualities of value and durability from the consumer's mind.

15. Installment buying of carpets needs the stimulus of an industry-wide credit plan to spur the wider use of time buying at the consumer level.

16. The subject of "trade-ins" needs to be defined and encouraged at both retailer and consumer levels.

17. Door-to-Door selling, originally the backbone of the appliance industry, has never played a significant role in the distribution of carpeting.

Obviously, many of these problems cannot be solved with advertising, although we feel that their solution would vastly increase the selling effectiveness of any promotional program that the Carpet Institute might use. However, other problems would be helped greatly by a dynamic and aggressive industry-wide advertising campaign, and we have marked these problems with an asterisk to indicate their vulnerability to your projected program. As we outline our proposed method of preparing an advertising campaign for submission to your trustees, these will be the problems at which we will particularly aim.

In our study of the factors concerning carpet sales, two important factors emerged:

1. While people have a friendly attitude towards carpets and say that they want new ones, most of them don't get around to making the actual purchase.
2. People do not associate carpets with physical or emotional benefits.

In other words, there is no sense of urgency in the purchase of a carpet, and the American public is not sold on the over-all functional value of soft-surface floor covering. On the whole, they regard carpeting as merely a decorative accessory.

We believe that this situation exists because the carpet industry has never sold the general public on all of its inherent values. In the early days of their growth, the manufacturers of washing machines, storm windows, refrigerators, central heating, etc., sold the public on their over-all benefits before they got into the story of features and specific brands.

The carpet industry had never accomplished this basic selling job, and the competition of new and exciting products of all kinds during the last few decades has given soft-surface floor covering increasingly tough competition.

Prior to 1946, carpet advertising was limited to several of the largest manufacturers who tried to do an industry job with their relatively small budgets as well as establish brand identification.

Although the field of carpet advertisers was swelled considerably after

1946, their promotional emphasis features style and color rather than the functional values. At the same time, there was a distinct effort on the part of the aggressive manufacturers to establish "brand identification" in accordance with appliance and packaged-goods techniques. This has raised the question among some of the Institute members as to whether it is psychologically possible to build brand demand or even recognition on a product which is difficult to identify by feature or manufacturer and which is purchased on the average only twice in a lifetime. This has also raised the need for an over-all industry campaign to tell the *complete story* of soft-surface floor covering to the American public—whose discretionary spending power is at an all-time high, and whose resistance to the purchase of carpeting is almost equally high.

This brings us to a closer look at the consumer market for carpets— 165,000,000 Americans divided into approximately 45,000,000 households. Actually, this market breaks down into two types of customers:

1. The customer who has pretty well made up her mind to buy carpeting and is primarily interested in color, pattern, price, service, credit terms, and the other aspects of the purchasing transaction.
2. The customer who needs or will soon need carpeting but has no particular awareness of this need. This customer regards carpeting favorably but has no real desire for the product and unless well stimulated will make no real effort to acquire it.

We feel that the carpet industry has been competing for a share of Customer No. 1 without paying sufficient attention to Customer No. 2. Customer No. 1, actively in the market for carpeting, probably represents less than 10% of the total families in the United States. Customer No. 2 represents most of the rest of the families (minus those whose carpeting needs have been temporarily satisfied by relatively recent purchases).

For nearly ten years, both in their media and their advertising approach, most of the carpet advertisers have concentrated on Customer No. 1. Some have been more successful than others in gaining a larger share of this market, but these gains have come at the expense of other carpet manufacturers. The industry as a whole has not been successful in attracting many sales from the rank of Customer No. 2.

In other words, the soft-surface floor covering manufacturers, generally speaking, have been telling only a part of their story to a part of their market.

Consumer Program

We propose that a Carpet Institute advertising program be such that, *when superimposed on present individual manufacturer advertising*, it will tell the complete story of soft-surface floor covering to the broadest possible market.

As a consequence, we believe that the high frequency use of mass publications and spot radio in top carpet markets on a promotional basis is the best means of reaching Customer No. 2. The number of publications will depend on whether black and white or four-color space is used. A minimum of once a month should be used in the weekly publications and once every two months in the monthlies.

There are three copy approaches to be considered for this publication and radio advertising.

1. *Functional.* This approach builds consumer awareness of the basic values of carpeting such as quiet, comfort, warmth, charm, safety, and easy care. It fills in what is currently lacking in individual brand advertising.

2. *Price.* This approach establishes the fact that "carpets cost less than you think." It attempts to answer the reason most often given for not buying—"I'd like a new carpet, but it costs too much." Part of this attitude probably comes from the fact that many consumers can't figure the cost of carpeting correctly. It is surprising how badly the public needs a lesson in carpet arithmetic. This in turn leads to the possibility of getting the soft-surface floor covering industry to think and talk in terms of square feet on all occasions instead of mixing up square feet and square yards and confusing the easily confused public.

3. *Color and Style.* Although admittedly this is extremely important to a customer once she has decided to buy carpeting, we feel that the major emphasis here should be left to the manufacturers in their scramble for Customer No. 1. This main question that arises is: How much color and style must be included in our creative approach in order to avoid too radical a change from the multimillion dollar advertising investment of the carpet industry since the war?

In our discussions with your committee, we are not attempting to define specific creative doctrine or media selection. We are pointing out to you the manner in which we think and the type of program which we believe should be developed fully for you by your advertising agency.

Merchandising

We have three major merchandising ideas in connection with your consumer campaign:

1. We believe that all contributing members of the Institute should be listed in each of the advertisements. At the same time, a seal could be promoted to the public in each advertisement and then merchandised to the retail trade. This seal could be incorporated into the individual advertising and promotion of each of the contributing members to any desired degree. It may be argued that this seal, if sufficiently promoted at the consumer and retail level, might destroy the brand identification value of the larger manufacturers. Such a seal has been in use by the Gas Appliance Manufacturers for many years without causing any problem, although it

is an important factor at the consumer and retail level in many areas. This seal would be influential in bringing all members of the Institute into the program and in identifying member merchandise as something apart from much of the outside tufted carpeting now flooding the market.

2. As this general program does its job, more and more of the formerly disinterested public will become interested in soft-surface floor covering. A booklet of information on carpets should be made available to the public without charge through write-ins and pickups at the retail-store level. This booklet would be promoted in all consumer publication advertising.

3. The spot radio programs in top markets lends itself to a real push at the retail level. These programs would run one day weekly during a four- or five-week promotion with very high morning frequency (with hard-hitting, urgent messages beamed exclusively at the feminine audience which predominates on morning radio). Then newspaper mats and radio commercials would be prepared for dealers to run on the same day —utilizing the same copy theme and enabling dealers to say where after the listening audience had been told why. We believe that the accumulative effect of all this Institute and dealer advertising would create an urgency and excitement which would bring a great influx of traffic into the carpet retailers. Obviously, this approach should be tested in several markets before put into use on a broad basis.

Another merchandising activity which does not actually fall under advertising, but should be developed on a local basis, is the carpet trade-in. This is a promotional approach which might be used to combat the inertia of the millions of householders who have used carpet that needs to be replaced but who must be actively stimulated before they will buy. If a trade-in program could be worked out satisfactorily on an industry level in a local test market, this program could be expanded into other markets and might eventually become an important creative factor. However, this would have to be discussed and tested at some length before it could be integrated into the industry advertising program.

Although the consumer campaign represents the most important part of the Carpet Institute advertising program, it would be a mistake to overlook three other important markets.

1. *Builders.* There are two important reasons for telling the carpet story to the builder-contractor. First, because of the many sample homes which are erected for potential home buyers to "shop," the building industry estimates that more than 30,000,000 people go through these sample homes each year. Since only one million new homes are sold, 97% of these people are lookers. Since the features of these new houses will set future living patterns for their communities, it is important that these 30,000,000 lookers see carpeting whenever possible. Obviously, beautiful carpeting will make it easier for the builders to display and sell their

houses. As a consequence, we recommend an industry sales plan for providing builders with sample house carpeting at minimum cost backed up with a program in the builder-contractor trade magazines.

Second, with the great quantity of concrete slab houses that are being built, many aggressive builders will put in asphalt or plywood floors and then supply wall-to-wall carpeting in the pattern and color requested by the buyer. The appliance manufacturers learned to use the builder to distribute their products long ago. The carpet industry can do likewise, particularly in some states where the cost of the floor covering can be included in special mortgages. More and more builders are including appliances in their homes as permanent or optional equipment because they have learned that it helps to sell the houses. We believe that carpeting can be distributed the same way, particularly in those areas where local ordinances encourage time buying on carpets sold as part of a new house.

2. *Contract Carpeting.* There is a tremendous market for the use of soft-surface floor covering in offices and other commercial establishments, and several of the larger carpet manufacturers have done a very effective advertising job with this market. However, an industry campaign on contract carpeting should be seriously considered to supplement the advertising of the few carpet advertisers who cover this field. This program would interest the business advantages to be gained by the use of carpeting, perhaps building the campaign around a series of case history advertisements. The hard-surface floor covering and commercial air-conditioning manufacturers have done a particularly successful job in this field.

3. *Dealers.* One of the prime objectives of the Carpet Institute advertising program will be to achieve maximum dealer enthusiasm for and co-operation with the consumer effort. To a lesser degree, the same will be true of the builder and contract campaigns. Consequently, the playback of all carpet industry advertising to the dealers will be very important. A high frequency trade paper campaign will tell the dealer of the wide scope of the program and also urge him to bring the over-all carpet story into his retail selling.

If the Carpet Institute Seal is used in the consumer advertising, it should also be merchandised to the dealer in the trade papers, and to the consumer at the point of sale. The use of the seal at the point of sale might best be left up to the individual manufacturers, with the seal incorporated into the manufacturer's own display material as he saw fit.

The booklet would be merchandised to the dealer in trade advertising and direct mail, and it would be emphasized that the booklet was being featured in national advertisements and would be in demand by his customers. Supplies of the booklet would be sold to the dealer at cost.

If the radio-dealer tie-in plan was used on a wide scale, this could be promoted in the trade copy. Otherwise, it would be limited to direct mail and contact by manufacturers' salesmen in pertinent areas. This will also involve the preparation and distribution of a brochure, including newspaper mats and radio scripts, to merchandise the radio-dealer tie-in promotion.

Finally, reprints of the program would be sent to all dealers on a regular basis.

Obviously, at this time no agency could present a finished advertising program that was based on anything other than superficial thinking. That is why we have attempted to show you how we would set up a finalized program, and the general lines that such a program would follow rather than a campaign complete to media lists, comprehensive layouts, and final copy.

Once you have given us the go signal, we can rapidly develop these preliminary suggestions into a finished program. The only holdup might be two or three months of developing a thorough test on the copy theme that will be utilized this first year. Since we have already developed several promising copy approaches, we believe that a word association (Vicary type) or more standardized type of copy testing should be utilized before the final campaign is prepared.

We realize that some of the copy and merchandising ideas that we have developed may not be acceptable to an association. For this reason, we have maintained a flexibility of program that will do the job and yet be acceptable to your members. One of the hardest parts of working with an association is the fact that you are faced by many masters. For this reason, we hope to maintain a close working liaison out of both our New York and Philadelphia offices with Paul Jones and your advertising committee.

You will note that we have not established a budget. Ideally, you need between two and three million dollars a year for at least five years to accomplish a real lasting change for the better in the public desire for soft-surface floor covering. We know enough about the present profit structure of the industry to be realistic about what we can expect this first year. We know that you must be prepared to carry on the program for at least five years to gain maximum effect.

In 1953 the industry sold 66 million square yards of woven carpeting. On the basis of a levy of 2 cents a square yard against the industry, a budget of $1,300,000 would be available. Unless the industry is willing to maintain this 2 cents a square yard advertising policy for a minimum of three to five years, we believe that you would do better not to start an advertising program. The thinking that we have outlined in the preceding pages is based on a three-year appropriation of approximately $1,300,000 a year. Obviously, the program would be sufficiently flexible to grow larger or smaller in accordance with your budget without seriously affecting the over-all emphasis.

Winston-Randall has lived closely with the carpet industry during the last few months. We have learned a lot about your business—we are now ready to combine this knowledge with our marketing, merchandising, and creative know-how. The result will be an advertising campaign that will be completely in accordance with the continued dynamic growth of the American economy.

~~~

CASE 8: CARPET INSTITUTE, INC. (E)[1]

NOTE: *In concluding the analysis of the Carpet Institute situation, the reader should keep in mind that in 1954 carpet and rug manufacturers were operating at about 60% of capacity and that manufacturers' income as a percentage of sales was apparently well below their income in the pre- and immediate post–World War II periods, as indicated by the combined net profits of six primary manufacturers given below:*

NET PROFITS IN THE CARPET AND RUG INDUSTRY

(Combined Data of Six Manufacturers)*

	Net Sales	Net Income (Millions of $s)	Income as % of Sales
1939	$ 91.6	$ 8.9	9.72%
1940	98.9	7.9	7.99
1941	143.3	8.7	5.87
1942–45 avg	140.6	4.7	3.34
1946	165.8	14.0	8.44
1947	238.8	18.5	7.75
1948	319.1	24.2	7.58
1949	269.6	12.1	4.49
1950	384.3	20.6	5.36
1951	329.9	0.4	0.01
1952	283.9	1.2	0.43
1953	275.4	5.4	1.95
1954	253.7	0.1	0.39

* Taken from a report to Carpet Institute, Inc.

Questions to consider in this last Carpet Institute case follow: (1) Has Wilson & Scott made a sound appraisal of the industry's problems? How does its appraisal differ from that of Winston-Randall? (2) What kind of a promotional program has Wilson & Scott essentially proposed? How does it differ from that of Winston-Randall? (3) If you were responsible for making a decision regarding the use of consumer advertising by Carpet Institute, what decision would you make? (4) If you decide to employ consumer advertising, to which of the two advertising agencies, if either, would you give the Institute's account?

[1] Prepared by Martin V. Marshall.

One day after the executives of Carpet Institute, Inc., had reviewed the report of Winston-Randall, Inc., Wilson & Scott Advertising Agency, Inc.[2] submitted a report, entitled "An Advertising Program for the Carpet Industry." With the exception of minor deletions, the complete report of Wilson & Scott is given below:

WILSON & SCOTT REPORT ON
"AN ADVERTISING PROGRAM FOR THE CARPET INDUSTRY"

May 25, 1954

Foreword

From a high of 90,000,000 yards of woven goods produced in 1948, carpet production has fallen off to 66,837,000 yards in 1953. It is estimated that carpet mills are currently producing at only about 60% of their total production capacity.

Why?

Our study and analysis led us to isolate eight problems which we believe are contributing factors to the declining per capita consumption of carpet.

In this presentation, we are going to try to deal with these points more specifically—leading up to a comprehensive proposal of advertising, promotion, and research for the industry.

Problem I: Instability of the Wool Market

Carpet manufacturers, retailers, and consumers have all suffered from fluctuations in wool prices. For example, raw wool prices rose from about 28 cents per pound in 1947 to about $2.00 per pound four years later!

Preliminary Observations. The advent and enthusiastic consumer response to blended and tufted carpets has acted to help stabilize carpet prices. Carpet rayon and cotton have acted toward unshackling the carpet industry from the sheep. Tufted sales have grown from next to nothing in 1948 to about 15,000,000 yards produced in 1953. Blends accounted for about 36% of all woven carpet manufactured in 1953.

Suggested Approach. Let's change the consumer's belief, which high wool prices helped to bring about, that all carpet is expensive. Not only by singing the praises of lower-priced modern carpet fabrics but also by changing her *attitude* toward prices of all-wool and higher-priced lines.

The advertising plan we have prepared for your consideration stresses *economy* and tells the consumer of lasting value for money spent on carpet. Also, the consumer's misconception that all carpet is expensive is treated so that, over a period of time, homemakers will come to realize that *carpet is a necessity—not a luxury—*and *there's good carpet to fit every budget.*

---

[2] Fictitious names.

Problem II: Consumer's Attitude toward Carpet

Consumers have been slacking off from carpet buying since the early 1920's. Today, while there is more spendable income available in the hands of the consumer than at any other time in this country's history, per capita consumption of carpet is lower than ever.

Preliminary Observations. In their efforts to secure a larger share of the declining carpet market, carpet manufacturers have been emphasizing "high-style" and "pride-of-ownership" selling approaches. This seems to have caused consumers to feel that carpets are a luxury—an expensive luxury. Consumers are generally unaware of *all* the benefits of carpet. Many of them, stung by the high prices of the early 1950's, became easy targets for the "inexpensive, long-wearing, smart-modern" type copy used by the hard-surface floor people.

One survey showed that six out of seven housewives questioned felt that carpet prices were "too high" compared to other home furnishings. Few consumers plan to buy carpets now, as compared with the number who plan to buy refrigerators, TV sets, and furniture.

Today's consumer is more price conscious and demands more specific information than ever before. Uppermost in a potential carpet customer's mind are the questions: "How much does it cost?" and "How long will it last?"—not just "How beautiful is it?" and "Will it harmonize with my furnishings?"

There has also been a changing trend in buying habits. Carpets, along with automobiles and major appliances, are becoming more and more a *family* purchase; although the housewife is still a major factor.

Again, carpet has slowly fallen from a "need" in the home to a "desirable furnishing." As a consumer of other goods as well as carpet, we ask you which you would be apt to buy first: the product you *desire most* or the product you *need most?*

Suggested Approach. Perhaps the consumer's attitude toward carpet can be changed by getting her to feel that carpet is a *need* rather than a want.

The reasons why families *need* carpet as stressed in our proposed copy includes: (*a*) less noise, (*b*) easier to clean, (*c*) safer, (*d*) warmer, and (*e*) soft and friendly (psychological need).

We suggest new research to substantiate and perhaps elaborate on these definitions of carpet.

Meanwhile, a substantial advertising impact can be made using presently known needs to step up the demand for carpet.

In our suggested advertising plan for the industry, you'll recognize that the above-mentioned appeals are generally not emphasized in carpet brand advertising.

Also, we have shifted our targets to keep in step with the "family buying" trend. Although branded carpet is most economically advertised to women, and an industry effort would be mainly directed at the house-wife, it could also hit the man of the family—the one who pays the bills!

Problem III: Competition

There is always a floor to walk on, and less "luxurious" floor coverings than carpet. Compared to kitchen appliances, automobiles, TV sets, and a host of other high-priced items, carpet buying has a low "urgency" rating—it is easy to put off.

Preliminary Observations. Every high-priced piece of merchandise that competes with the carpet for the consumer's dollar must be treated as competition. However, the greatest single competitor of the carpet industry is the hard-surface floor coverings industry.

Hard-surface people have been throwing some well-loaded shots at the consumer. They have a heavily supported public relations program already under way. Hard-surface floor coverings, formerly confined to use in the kitchen, are now being advertised as the *modern* floor covering for practically every room in the house.

The floor wax industry is stressing hard-surface floors and area rugs against wall-to-wall carpet and room-size rugs.

Imported carpet, although still a relatively small factor when one considers total volume of imports versus total volume of domestic, is, nevertheless, a growing factor, especially in metropolitan areas.

Competition by other high-priced merchandise combined with the consumer's lethargy has narrowed one important part of the carpet market—the replacement market!

People "just never get around" to replacing old worn-out rugs and carpets, even though they might trade in their car every two years.

This lethargy is, we feel, a vital factor to be overcome. To our knowledge, it hasn't been strongly attacked by brand advertising. There is no "buy *now*" feeling in current carpet advertising.

Suggested Approach. First of all, it's time the carpet industry started to fight back at the hard-surface people. It's time they threw some well-loaded shots of their own at the consumer.

If the modern homeowner thinks that hard-surface floors are modern, it's only because she hasn't been told otherwise! Our advertisements tell the smart young homemaker that carpets *are* modern—and not a hangover they inherited from their parents. Our copy shots—fired from powerful media guns—will tell Young America that carpeted homes are "soft and friendly" and "a fast-growing trend in modern homes." It implies that hard-surface floor coverings make a home "cold, clammy, and *unfriendly*." The idea that carpet is old-fashioned must be erased from the consumer's mind—and we believe we can do it.

As one weapon to combat imported and off-brand carpet, we suggest a carpet institute *symbol* which will apply to all Institute-member merchandise. This symbol (we have created several tentative versions) will act to signify quality for carpets, in the same way the Good Housekeeping Seal of Approval wins their trust for other merchandise.

To help overcome the consumer's lethargy, we have prepared a hard-hitting campaign to get them to replace old and shabby carpets. This campaign aims to increase carpet's "Urgency Rating" by stirring old-carpet owners into *action*.

Problem IV: Recent Carpet Advertising

Carpet advertising by manufacturers has tended to put carpet in the *luxury class* of merchandise. Individual company advertising has stressed brand advantage and has not advertised and promoted the consumer benefits of carpet as *a basic commodity*.

Preliminary Observations. Manufacturers ask retailers to tie in with brand-name promotions, but outside of the Spring Carpet Bazaar they do little "institutional" type advertising to promote the sale of carpet as a commodity.

Brand advertising must necessarily be competitive with other brands because *it is aimed at people who are already in the market for carpet*. Most brand advertisements stress carpet trade names, or one line of carpets. This, of course, limits the scope of each advertisement.

Suggested Approach. Industry-wide advertising by the Institute as we hereby propose, emphasizing the basic *need* for carpet. It can do this because it is not restricted in scope and does not have to stress competitive claims as manufacturers do.

The consumer's attention must be gained and held not only in the face of competitive advertising, by the hard-surface people, but many others who are competing for the consumer's dollar. We do not think this can be done by advertising that is other than outstanding.

We think our ideas are outstanding because they are based on a clear definition of the targets for carpet advertising.

Problem V: Carpet Retailers

Carpet retailers have forgotten how to sell. They do not appear to be making the co-ordinated aggressive selling effort called for by current conditions.

Carpet buyers are presently buying on a cautious "hand-to-mouth" basis which seems to reflect their fear and uncertainty in the immediate future of carpets.

Preliminary Observations. Most carpet retailers are not promoters in the true sense of the word, as are, for example, most appliance dealers. The word "promotion" to nearly all carpet dealers is synonymous with the phrase "price-cut."

Who is responsible for this?

In addition to mental sluggishness and failure to keep pace with changing times on the part of the retailer, *the carpet manufacturers themselves are partly responsible for causing this attitude!*

Ask any carpet retailer when he ran his last promotion and he'll reply "My January *Sale*." He is only emulating manufacturers' methods of using promotional carpet to keep up volume. The words "promotional carpet" are the very words used by manufacturers when selling markdown or unadvertised carpet to retailers. Is it any wonder that in the retailer's vocabulary "promotion" and "sale" have become synonymous?

Another problem of the retailer is that of sales-floor personnel. Rapid turnover of sales personnel, especially in department stores, often means an inferior brand of salesmanship in showrooms.

One more headache is the influx of "cut-rate" type of carpet stores, especially in metropolitan areas, that seem to be flourishing. Despite policing efforts by some manufacturers, these operations have cut into the business of legitimate carpet outlets.

Suggested Approach. Carpet retailers should be made to pull together more often, to their mutual benefit, as they now do once a year during the Spring Carpet Bazaar.

By alerting retailers to the benefits of an all-out industry-wide effort, perhaps we can enlist their aid and *renew their faith in the future of the industry*.

A trade campaign has been prepared which aims at getting the dealers to sell through sales promotion *without cutting prices*.

This campaign would encourage them to take advantage of the many neglected tools of sales promotion that are available. Premiums, contests, visual demonstrations, product tie-ins, and unique displays can be successfully employed to promote the sale of carpet. Case histories of successful promotions, such as a "Carpet Party" or an "Old Carpet Round-up," is the theme of this campaign.

To help combat fly-by-night retailers, the Carpet Institute emblem (mentioned in problem III) could be used to identify *reliable* retailers.

The industry's Seal of Approval can be offered to qualified retailers who measure up to certain standards established by the Carpet Institute. This Seal would be presented to the public as an integrated part of the industry's advertising. The thoughts of "Buy Carpet Where You See This Sign of an Authorized Carpet Institute Dealer" and "America's leading carpet manufacturers and retailers may be recognized by this emblem" would be incorporated in consumer advertising.

The legitimate carpet retailer's main weapons for combating "price-cut" type outlets are *service* and *quality of brand names*. Both factors would be incorporated into, and associated with, this emblem.

So far as merchandising helps are concerned, we feel that retailers would be more receptive to merchandising that sells the *idea* of carpets rather than an individual brand.

This is only natural as most retailers handle several brands—and each brand is competing for his co-operation. Merchandising helps, such as mats and displays, should tie in with the industry's national theme. In addition, films and booklets on "How to select the right carpet for your home" should be provided. Sales training aids for showroom salesmen should also be available to retailers. A good sales manual on how to use modern sales techniques and perhaps even a carpet sales training course, sponsored by the Institute should be worked out.

Problem VI: "Influence Groups"

"Influence groups" such as magazine editors, decorators, and builders have advanced the cause of carpet "substitutes."

Collectively, these groups are a powerful determining force in setting interior styles across the nation.

Preliminary Observations. Area rugs, tile, linoleum, and hardwood floors are all being advocated as part of a modern trend. The California influence of "bringing the outdoors indoors" has led to wrought-iron furniture, open spaces in living rooms, gleaming floors, and an absence of carpet.

An indirect type of selling by influence groups strongly influenced the buying habits of the latest generation of housewives.

Herewith we show you the results of our interviewing ten magazine editors in the home furnishings field. All were unhappy about the carpet situation.

They agreed that carpet had for too long a time been sold as a luxury. They believe that "high-style" selling has bypassed much of the mass market. They all expressed a desire to see more consumer education in the uses and benefits of carpet. Many of them mentioned sales points such as acoustical value and warmth of carpets which are generally not stressed by manufacturers in their advertising.

Many of the "influence group," whose outlook has not been favorable toward carpet, were wooed away from carpet by hard-surface manufacturers and, in one case, by a floor wax concern.

Suggested Approach. One objective in an industry-wide campaign is to win over interior decorators, fashion editors, architects, and other "influence groups" to the ideas of using more carpet in the home. This, we realize, cannot be done in a single "blitz" type campaign, but can be accomplished through consistent hammering away on these groups—a war of attrition.

Following this direction, the wide selection of "Shelter Books" and "Influence Books" recommended in this plan will perhaps enable us to push the cause of carpets in editorial sections.

We recommend for consideration a plan to educate the newest generation of homemakers—the teen-age market.

As home economists and teachers of home economics, the firm of Harvery and Howe, Inc., had developed at our instigation a comprehensive plan for the Carpet Institute. This plan aims at girls in their late teens, who will soon become housewives. Details of this plan have been submitted to Mr. Jones.

To counteract the high-style feeling of most brand advertising, we propose campaigns which are educational and down-to-earth in copy approach and art technique. These campaigns should not emphasize luxury and beauty, but *need* and benefit.

Problem VII: Research

Preliminary Observations. Research in the carpet industry, our findings lead us to believe, has hovered all around the fringes of the target. Carpet research has come up, time and again, with the reassurance that people *want* carpet. Then, if they continue to avoid buying carpet in ever-increasing numbers, could it be that consumers fail to see any *compelling need* for carpet?

Suggested Approach. We recommend the use of research along the following lines:

1. *Basic Research* to determine buying motivations or lack of them:
   a) Why do people need rugs and carpets?
   b) Which of these needs are the most important, and which will respond most quickly to advertising impressions?
   c) Evaluation of families that rent homes or live in apartments as carpet prospects. Reasons for buying or not buying rugs or carpets.
   d) Survey to determine the ratio of replacement sales to original purchase sales. No data on this appears to be available. Reasons for replacing or not replacing rugs and carpets. Appraisal of these reasons for importance and response to advertising.
   e) Survey of "trend-setters" and home design and building fields to properly evaluate the place of rugs and carpets on an ascending or descending curve.
2. *Copy Research* to evaluate effectiveness of basic appeals:
   a) *Pre-evaluation.* This agency uses a combination of research techniques tailored to the particular situation. These are consumer jury tests of the roughs, headlines, and body text for preference measurement, eye-camera analysis, measures of visibility and readability, and test for meaning of the advertisements as shown by free and controlled association tests.
   If television is to be used, the commercials should be pretested by use of Schwerin and comprehension tests.
   b) *Post-evaluation.* This would mainly consist of Starch measurements of magazine advertisements and television commercials.
   While the Carpet Institute has no brand competition, the agency will present the Institute with a continuing analysis of how the Institute's advertising copy rates in comparison with other national advertisers.
3. *Media Research.* The series of surveys outlined under "Basic Research" will help to describe the persons to whom the Institute advertising will be addressed. Comparative measurements of various media will have to be

made using these descriptions of the Institute prospects. For print media, the Starch Consumer Report is available. For television, some information can be obtained from rating services using panels.

4. *Campaign Evaluation.* While the ultimate objective of the Institute is to increase the sales of rugs and carpets, this has to be done indirectly by changing the consumer's attitudes and buying habits. Because of the intangible nature of the task of the Carpet Institute, it is extremely important that some yardsticks be set up which will measure consumer changes from year to year.

Therefore, the agency proposes an annual survey which will ask of consumers key attitude questions about rugs and carpets. The first year, this survey will establish a bench mark. In successive years, the surveys will measure the progress from this bench mark. These surveys will demonstrate in an objective manner what has been accomplished from year to year in changing consumer's attitudes toward rugs and carpets.

Problem VIII: Carpet Manufacturers

Carpet manufacturers have necessarily emphasized competitive advantages of their brand over others in order to gain a larger share of a shrinking market. This has done nothing to arrest the over-all decline in volume.

Six publicly owned carpet companies showed a total decrease in dollar sales of 14% during 1951. If decline in per capita consumption for carpet continues, a more serious situation may develop which will effect all manufacturers.

Preliminary Observations. There is some feeling that manufacturers have recently overproduced. This is hard to believe in view of the fact that the industry has been working at an estimated rate of only 60% of their total capacity to produce. Certain mills are said to be planning to curtail production still further.

So far this year, announced price increases by some manufacturers have been postponed while others are said to be contemplating further price cuts. This would appear to be an unhealthy situation in an industry where there is already strong feeling that prices are unsatisfactory in relation to production costs.

There are many attractive carpet-brand campaigns in effect today. Some of them imply a touch of institutional-type carpet selling, benefiting all brands to a slight degree. However, it would be foolhardy to believe that any one or several manufacturers will *concentrate on selling the necessity of carpet in the home.*

Up until now, no comprehensive industry-wide effort has been made to overcome the situation outlined above.

Suggested Approach. Manufacturers will continue to gain or lose *a share of market* at the expense of their competitors. However, even though some may gain in share, all manufacturers will suffer unless the over-all volume of carpet sales can be increased.

We believe that the very best way to do this is to increase the per capita consumption of carpet.

We believe that only an industry-wide advertising effort can accomplish this needed increase.

A forceful *industry-wide* advertising campaign can accomplish more than individual manufacturers could accomplish even if each brand made an effort to sell the need for carpet.

If we may use a simple metaphor: two dozen men throwing handfuls of pebbles couldn't stop a roller skate—but if two dozen men rolled a huge rock onto the right track, it would stop a locomotive.

The impact required to halt declining carpet sales can only come about as the result of a united effort—executed in the right way.

We believe the nucleus of men at Wilson & Scott who have become deeply interested in the problems of the Carpet Industry can conceive and execute advertising which will push carpet up to the place it deserves in the home—and minds—of the American consumer.

If we are awarded the Carpet Institute account, we intend to work closely with each member company and its advertising agency.

A CONCLUDING NOTE TO SECTION II

This section has dealt exclusively with cases concerning the use of advertising by associations of manufacturers to stimulate primary demand, because the problems and factors involved in stimulating primary demand are seen most simply and clearly in such instances. As was pointed out in Chapter 1, however, individual manufacturers not infrequently must make decisions as to whether to use advertising to stimulate primary demand for their type of product, or whether to use primary appeals rather than selective appeals in their advertisements. Accordingly, in subsequent cases in this book, attention should be given to these issues, and analyses and decisions regarding them should be guided in part by the empirical generalizations that have been developed in appraising the cases of this section.

Individual manufacturers face the problem of appraising their chances of stimulating primary demand particularly when they launch products or services of an entirely new type upon the market. For example, in recent years, the manufacturers of small economy automobiles, frozen orange juice, complete home air conditioners, stereophonic hi-fidelity phonographs, color television receivers, prefabricated metal houses, mobile homes, data-processing equipment, and electronic cooking units have faced this problem. Consumers must be influenced to recognize a new want or to meet an established want in a noncustomary way. New habits must be established; prejudices against the new and unknown must be broken down. Aggressive selling is often essential in these situations if the rate of the expansion of demand is to be speeded up; but care must be exercised by the manufacturer to keep the amount of advertising geared to the actual volume of sales which may be expected for his brand, if operating losses are to be avoided; and care must be exercised in selecting the type of advertising appeal to be employed. A number of cases in this book deal with the problems of the individual manufacturer in appraising his opportunity of stimulating primary demand for new products and services. Several of these cases are Emery Air Freight Corporation, Eastman Chemical Products, Inc., and B. F. Goodrich Tubeless Tire.

Individual manufacturers must also appraise their chances of influencing primary demand whenever they consider advertising their products for new or unusual uses, such as baking soda as a dentifrice, lemons as a preventative for colds and as a beauty aid, gelatine to prevent splitting fingernails, and soup for breakfast. In many situations, management seeks to increase sales by increasing the number of uses to which its products are put. In such situations, failure to appraise properly the consumer's acceptance of and satisfaction with the product for any new uses leads to unprofitable advertising expenditure. This aspect of primary demand will be encountered particularly in the National Cranberry Association (A) and (B) cases.

Even when a manufacturer looks upon his promotional problem as one essentially of developing selective demand for his brand rather than primary demand, he may decide that it is desirable to employ primary rather than selective appeals. Numerous manufacturers have emphasized primary appeals in their advertisements, for example: "Trapéze" perfume: "danger in every drop"; "Schlitz" beer: "Know the joy of good living . . ."; "Renault" automobiles: "balancez le budget"; "Magnavox" high fidelity equipment: "a practical guide to The New World of Stereophonic Magic"; "Marchand's" hair rinse: "Lovely hair, lovely you"; and "Kress" paint: "springtime is dress-up time!" The principal question which a manufacturer faces in such a situation is whether primary appeals may stimulate a demand for his type of product but fail to direct that demand to his brand. Whenever a product is so highly individualized that consumers are inclined to think not in terms of product classifications but in terms of brands, the advertiser is safe in using primary appeals, even though he wishes to obtain a selective result.

It should be noted that all brand advertising has a primary effect in that the mere presentation and featuring of products have some effect on inducing people to buy those products. However, in most instances a sharp distinction should be made between primary appeals which seek to induce consumers to begin to be interested in a class of product, and selective appeals which seek to induce consumers who are already interested in a class of product to buy a particular brand.

Section III

THE USE OF ADVERTISING TO STIMULATE SELECTIVE DEMAND

An Introductory Note

In previous chapters, we stated that most manufacturers use advertising to stimuate demand for their brands and that their principal problem is to find a mix of marketing elements, including advertising, which is effective in stimulating selective demand. Accordingly, the next series of cases will focus upon situations wherein individual manufacturers are considering the marketing mixes which they will employ for the longer term and wherein they are particularly considering the basic role, if any, of advertising in the mix. The section consists of one chapter of declaratory material and 20 cases.

Chapter 6

~~~~~~

ADVERTISING'S ROLE IN THE
MARKETING MIX—A REVIEW
AND AMPLIFICATION

Previously we stated that decisions regarding the use of advertising are *inextricably intertwined* with decisions regarding all other aspects of the business operation. Of chief concern, however, are decisions regarding the marketing operation. In the light of the circumstances facing it in the market place, management must develop a marketing mix which promises to gain sales and profits. Whether advertising is or is not an important element in the mix depends upon the specific factors involved in any given marketing situation and upon management's judgment of those factors. The concept of the marketing mix and elements deserving special consideration were discussed in Chapter 3. Here in this chapter additional attention and amplification will be given to the concept as it applies to the determination of the role of advertising in stimulating selective demand.

The Use of the Concept of the Marketing Mix

The concept of the marketing mix calls for management (1) to appraise the strengths and weaknesses of all the elements of its marketing operation in the light of conditions in the market place; (2) to determine and to define explicitly its marketing objectives; and (3) to determine a marketing plan, including a selling plan, that promises to obtain those objectives.

Managements and individual business executives differ widely in the specific procedures which they employ to make use of the concept of the marketing mix. Some use a systematic, highly formalized procedure which has come to be known as the process of *marketing planning*, wherein analyses, objectives, and plans are in written form; others use a far less systematic approach, wherein analyses, objectives, and plans are usually handled orally. Whatever the specific procedure employed, there are several basic views regarding the use of concept of the marketing mix which should be indicated here.

Weaknesses in the Mix Deserve Special Attention

In most instances the principal problem confronting management in developing a sound marketing program is that of overcoming the weaknesses which exist in its marketing mix—overcoming the deficiencies and inefficiencies that are common to most marketing mixes. Accordingly, special attention should be given to these weaknesses in the cases in this section and in other actual business situations, as they are significant determinants of the use to which advertising is put.

An outline of the principal weaknesses commonly found in the marketing operations of manufacturers is given in Exhibit 1; the outline may be helpful in suggesting areas to be analyzed in the cases.

Exhibit 1

AN OUTLINE OF WEAKNESSES COMMONLY CONFRONTED IN THE MARKETING OPERATION

A. *Deficiencies in Product Planning (Merchandising)*
   1. Lack of facts to guide the development of new products:
      a) Lack of facts regarding the psychological and sociological forces shaping demand for classes or product. Failure to appraise trends.
      b) Lack of facts regarding the consumption behavior of consumers.
      c) Lack of facts regarding consumer wants.
   2. Lack of facts to appraise the marketing of existing products:
      a) Lack of facts regarding the consumers of the product—their number, location, buying habits, buying attitudes, buying motivations, where they buy, etc.
      b) Inability to make reliable sales forecasts.
   3. Poor analysis and use of the facts that are available.
   4. Failure to recognize the place of packaging in the marketing mix and inefficiencies resulting from poor packaging.
B. *Inefficiencies in Pricing*
   1. Failure to determine the specific role played by price in obtaining sales in situations ranging from intense price competition to nonprice competition.
   2. Lack of knowledge regarding the psychological aspects of pricing.
   3. Failure to recognize the effect of sales volume upon production and marketing costs.
   4. Failure to consider adequately the effect of pricing policy on channels of distribution.
C. *Deficiencies in Branding and Brand Policy*
   1. Failure to select good trade-marks or brands.
   2. Failure to establish and adhere to brand standards of quality.
   3. Failure to appreciate the problems of building brand reputation (or image).
   4. Failure to understand trading-up and trading-down strategy.

Exhibit 1—Continued

D. *Inefficiencies Arising in Channels of Distribution*
1. Ineffective management of the wholesaler or the retailer which affects the marketing operation of the manufacturer.
2. In manufacturer's use of channels:
    a) Failure to determine correctly the types or numbers of outlets to use.
    b) Failure to obtain adequate facts regarding trade operations.
    c) Ineffectiveness in devising marketing programs which will secure the co-operation of the trade.
    d) Inefficiencies in working with the trade—ineffective use of sales force, failure to maintain adequate inventories.
    e) Inefficiency in the servicing of channels.
    f) Inefficiencies resulting from lack of cost analysis and control of physical handling, billing, and accounting.
E. *Deficiencies in Quantity and Quality of Personal Selling*
1. Failure to study and to determine precisely the selling job to be done by salesmen.
2. Failure to manage the sales force effectively to accomplish the selling job:
    a) Inefficiencies in the selection and training of salesmen.
    b) Inefficiencies in laying out sales territories.
    c) Inefficiencies in directing and motivating salesmen.
    d) Inefficiencies in controlling and evaluating salesmen.
3. Failure to co-ordinate the activities of salesmen with the use of other selling tools.
F. *Deficiencies in Quantity and Quality of Advertising*
1. Failure to determine precisely the selling job to be done by advertising.
2. Failure to establish approximate level of advertising expenditure.
3. Employment of poor copy approaches, as the result of (*a*) a lack of information about consumers, and (*b*) poor execution of copy plans.
4. Employment of poor media, as the result of (a) a lack of knowledge of markets, and (b) a lack of knowledge of the markets reached by media.
5. Failure to use good teachniques for pre- and post-testing advertising.
6. Inefficiencies from failure to recognize the place of point-of-purchase effort in the marketing mix and deficiencies in producing point-of-purchase material.
7. Failure to establish and maintain effective working relationships with advertising agencies.
G. *Deficiencies in Quantity and Quality of Other Tools of Sales Promotion*
1. Failure to determine the need if any for implementing personal selling or advertising by the use of other tools of sales promotion.
2. Inefficiency in devising or executing promotions.
3. Failure to appraise correctly trade attitudes toward promotions.
H. *Deficiencies in Fact Finding and Analysis*
1. In product research (above).
2. In consumer research.
3. In sales and market analysis.
I. *Inefficiencies from Ineffective Marketing Organization*
1. Inefficiencies arising from internal organization which operates against attaining co-ordination and integration in planning and operation.
2. Inefficiencies arising from poor selection and development of market executives and other marketing personnel.
3. Inefficiencies from ineffective administrative practices.

It should be emphasized that the principal weakness to be taken into account is usually the lack of adequate facts regarding the product and its market. Despite the marked increase in the use of product-research and consumer-research information in the last 30 years, management still must operate in the area of product planning or merchandising with relatively inadequate knowledge regarding the specific wants of consumers, who consumers are, their number and location, their buying habits, their attitudes, motivations and beliefs, and so on. Without fairly explicit knowledge of the product relative to consumers, management necessarily incurs considerable risk in making decisions about marketing and selling.

To illustrate, in the late 1950's the manufacturers of automobiles were operating in the area of product planning with inadequate information regarding the kinds of automobiles which consumers wanted and the number of various kinds of automobiles which consumers would buy. In general it was clear that several significant market segments existed: for the so-called small, economy-type automobile as represented by numerous foreign makes; for the so-called "compact" automobile as represented by the "Rambler" or the "Lark"; for the standard-sized automobile as represented by "Chevrolet," "Ford," or "Plymouth"; for the so-called medium-priced automobile as represented by "Buick," "Mercury," or "DeSoto"; and for the high-priced, prestige automobiles as represented by "Cadillac," "Lincoln," or "Jaguar." However, the size of any given market segment and the motivations of prospects in each segment were not clear. Consequently, decisions regarding advertising were based to a large extent on *uncertainty*. The size of the advertising budget could not be determined precisely because of the uncertainty of sales forecasts; the advertising appeals could not be definitive because of the uncertainty of consumer motivations; and so on.

In almost all product fields, manufacturers operate in the area of product planning with inadequate information. Thus, in analyzing the cases in this section, the reader should take care to consider particularly the information available to him regarding the market for the product concerned and to weigh the uncertainties involved. In many instances a decision regarding advertising can be made based upon a reasonable quantity of market information with only a few areas of uncertainty; in other instances a decision may well be postponed until such time as additional information is obtained which reduces the degree of uncertainty and the element of risk.

Marketing Objectives Should Be Defined Explicitly

The job to be done by advertising obviously depends upon the marketing objectives established by management. If management has established sound, clear-cut marketing objectives, then decisions regarding advertising can be reasonably exact. But if management fails to establish marketing objectives, or defines them only in very general terms (which is often the case), then decisions regarding advertising cannot be reasonably exact. In too many instances management defines its marketing objective as that "of increasing sales at a profit." Although this is the ultimate objective of any business, in a given situation the marketing objective or objectives usually can be defined much more explicitly. To illustrate, below are the 1959 marketing objectives for Brand X, as given in the marketing plans of a large United States company:

1. To attain a sales quota of 3,350,000 cases of sizes *a* and *b* of Brand X, an objective representing a 25.5% share of market and increase in sales of 413,436 cases, or 14.1%, over 1958 sales of 2,936,564 cases.
2. To exploit fully the growth potential of Brand X in an expanding industry through product improvements, copy and media refinements, and increased advertising and promotional expenditures.
3. To introduce size *c* of Brand X successfully nationally.
4. To broaden distribution selectively in drug, variety, and department stores through the introduction of size *d* and to increase distribution in grocery outlets from the existing low level (57%).
5. To increase the number of shelf facings of Brand X relative to competitive products, and to bring about a sharp increase in the amount of in-store promotion and display activity through trade programs in conjunction with product innovation promotions.

In many of the cases of this section, one of the principal problems for the reader to contend with will be the determination of sound marketing objectives in the light of the total marketing situation confronting the company. Having defined marketing objectives, the reader can then effectively consider the part if any that advertising can play in obtaining those objectives.

The Determination of Selling Strategy

Once management has made basic merchandising decisions and has defined its marketing objectives, it then must determine the selling strategy which will be employed to obtain those objectives. By "selling strategy" we mean the determination of the combination of personal selling, advertising, and the other tools of sales promotion which will be most effective in securing sales and profits. Generally, management has alternative choices in selling strategies. In other words, there is usually more than one sound way to combine the various selling tools so that sales can be obtained at a profit.

In considering alternative means of promoting sales, management usually seeks to establish as much control over the demand for its brand as it can. The degree to which such control can be established depends primarily upon the behavior of consumers and the trade, and the skill of the manufacturer in affecting their behavior in his favor. In some instances the manufacturer can differentiate his brand so effectively that he can depend upon the consumer to insist upon it at the point of sale. Accordingly, in such a situation the manufacturer can command the margins necessary to support advertising to the consumer which will "pull" his brand through the channels and which will allow him a great deal of control over the entire marketing process. He may in such instances make relatively little if any use of personal selling or other promotional tools. In most instances, however, manufacturers cannot differentiate their products to the extent that consumers will insist upon their brands at the point of sale. Generally, manufacturers must work to and through the trade in order to sell their products, because the trade in controlling what is done at the retail level exercises a significant degree of control over the sales of any product. Thus, in determining his selling strategy, the manufacturer must consider the behavior of the trade, what they can and cannot do for him, and what they probably will and will not do.

Varying Importance of Brand for Different Merchandise

Even though brands are important as guides to consumer buying, it will be recognized immediately that their value for this purpose varies widely with different types of products. For some products the consumer is largely indifferent as to whether he buys the product of one producer or that of another; for other types of products he puts great stress on getting a particular brand or one of several brands which he considers acceptable.

Often a consumer's brand preferences are determined by objective differences in products which he can know from inspection, or the preferences may depend upon performance which can be observed and appraised. Thus "Ivory" soap may be preferred by some because if floats or because it is a mild cleanser. Association of such product characteristics or performance facts with a brand name provides a basis for brand preference, irrespective of whether aggressive advertising and selling are devoted to the brand. Advertising and selling, however, may be used to heighten the significance of these ideas in the minds of consumers. To wit, the advertising of Ivory soap over many years has been employed to enhance the desirability of floating and mildness as characteristics of soap and to associate these ideas with Ivory. In some instances the ideas which underlie consumers' brand preference may be almost entirely implanted by advertising and selling. Such is true, for example, of some proprietary remedies whose ingredients are unknown to the purchaser and whose efficacy depends largely on a mental state. In short, consumers' brand discriminations depend upon their subjective valuations, as determined by objective product characteristics, observable performance, or implanted ideas.

Where product differentiations are considered of no great consequence by consumers or are readily appraisable from inspection, brand means little. Much of the merchandise displayed on open counters in hardware stores and variety stores is of this character—screws, bolts, nails, cheap electrical fixtures, small tools not submitted to any difficult strain, kitchen spoons and gadgets, clothespins, ribbons, string, shoelaces, inexpensive toys, games, needles, pins, and many other notions. Sometimes trade-marks are affixed to such articles; in other instances they are not.

Certain products, such as granulated sugar and inexpensive sheeting, whose total demand is sufficient to warrant the sellers' desire for brand discrimination, nevertheless do not enjoy strong brand preference, be-cause consumers do not deem product differentiations of enough conse-quence to lead them to pay much attention to the brand or retail source of the product. Other products to whose brands the buyer tends to be rela-tively indifferent are those for which design or style is the important de-terminant of the consumer's purchase. In such instances a consumer can observe the designs and determine whether the products are to his liking. A clear-cut example is found in greeting cards.

The selection of merchandise on the basis of observable design, which is clearly illustrated in the case of greeting cards, applies with greater or lesser degree to a wide range of merchandise, such as textiles, fashion clothing, neckties, and furniture. In many of these products, how-ever, hidden quality characteristics are of some consequence in guiding consumer selection. For example, durability and color fastness of textiles are fixed characteristics which may be associated with brand. Hence, on many of these products, effort is made by sellers to have brands known to consumers as guides to these hidden characteristics. In some instances, expert designers have tried with some success to identify with fashion-rightness. But no designer can invariably be fashion-right. The consumer is always the judge as to the acceptability of a style.

In contrast to the examples cited above, brands tend to be important for any class of product for which sellers offer varying qualities and forms that purchasers ordinarily are not able to appraise adequately at the time of purchase. In such cases consumers rely upon brands to assure themselves of getting products they know through use or reputation. Clear examples are drugs and medicines, for which brand may be impor-tant as an assurance of expected efficacy in the cure or alleviation of ills or of purity and care in compounding. In cosmetics, brands may be im-portant because of their promised ability to give personal beauty or charm. In foods, they may be important to assure a particular flavor or form that has been found satisfying. In mechanical goods, particularly those involving large expenditure, such as automobiles, electrical appli-ances, and watches, brand is relied upon for assurance of satisfactory operation.

The varying importance of brands for different types of merchandise and for different articles within any class of merchandise has resulted in a wide variation in the importance of brands to sellers as a means of attract-ing and holding patronage. But, for almost all products, brands have had enough goodwill value and have offered sufficient advantages in influenc-ing consumer selection to lead those engaged in commerce to desire ownership or control over them. Not only have managements wished to sell their products under their own brands but the trade also has desired either to own or to exercise control over the brands it sells. The resulting struggle for brand control—and thus for control over trade—has tended to be heightened as United States industry has expanded.

The Struggle for Brand Control

While some manufacturers in the United States placed their own brands on their merchandise before 1880, the practice of aggressive promotion of manufacturers' brands to consumers as a means of controlling trade did not attain great momentum until the 1880's and 1890's. After 1880, manufacturers increasingly sought to make their brands well known to consumers, thereby hoping to gain control over ultimate demand and to decrease their dependence upon the trade. This drive by manufacturers for brand dominance has continued unabated up to the present time. But, as manufacturers have sought to gain control of ultimate demand, wholesalers and retailers have not been passive. They have resisted manufacturers' brands because experience has shown them that the handling of well-known manufacturers' brands has obten led to keen price competition among these brands within the trade, with resultant reduction of trade margins. To improve their profit outlook, wholesalers and retailers have taken measures either to establish their own brands or to get some control over manufacturers' brands which would permit them to secure desired margins from their selling operations. Consequently, there has been a continuous struggle for control of brand demand, not only between competing manufacturers but also between the trade and manufacturers. This struggle for brand control has entailed heavy selling costs and has also played an important part in shaping the forms of competition governing costs and prices of merchandise.

While the competitive struggle often centers about brands and is frequently referred to as the "battle of the brands," it should be recognized that the conflict goes beyond mere questions of brands to questions of control over demand and of control over the marketing process. In cases of competing manufacturers, the battle is for control over demand, with each manufacturer using such tools as product quality, price, service, aggressive advertising and promotion, and personal selling efforts to secure public acceptance and dealer selling support.

When manufacturers and the trade compete, however, the competition is essentially to gain control over the merchandising and promotional functions of marketing. It is a question of whether the manufacturer not only will control the merchandising function (that is, the function of determining product form) but will also reach forward and take over the promotional function (that is, the function of stimulating and fashioning consumers' desire for his products); or whether the retailer, because of his strategic position in influencing consumers, not only will guide consumers' buying (that is, will assume the promotional function) but also may even go so far as to reach back and control the merchandising function. In the latter case, he furnishes specifications to the manufacturer.

An understanding of the character of the competition growing out of this struggle for control between manufacturers and distributors is essential to an understanding of the place of advertising in the economic system. It is advisable, therefore, to inquire further why manufacturers and distributors have sought control over brands.

Reasons Why Manufacturers Seek Brand Control. The outstanding reason why manufacturers wish to put their brands on products has already been stated—namely, the desire to secure the benefit of any consumer goodwill that may attach to the products they manufacture. When products go through the channels of trade unmarked or with the mark of a distributor upon them, any consumer preference for or satisfaction with the products does not redound to the benefit of the manufacturer but rests with the distributors who sell the merchandise. When the manufacturer is successful in establishing a consumer preference for his brand, he may have a more stable business than if he were to depend upon trade patronage alone. The shifting of patronage of a few large wholesalers or retailers might mean the loss of a large volume of business, whereas the loss of individual customers does not materially affect total sales.

Manufacturers also wish to sell under their own brands because they desire to gain better direction and control of the marketing of their products. Greatest enthusiasm and interest for new products or for new developments in existing products are generally found among those who have invented and fostered the new developments. They are often more inclined to take the risks involved in advertising and promoting new or different products to consumers than are retailers or wholesalers, who may want the assurance of established demand before stocking and selling such merchandise. Often a manufacturer has an intense interest in his single article or line of merchandise, whereas retailers or wholesalers with their hundreds or thousands of items do not take particular interest in any one item. The manufacuturer, therefore, is often forced to take the risk of convincing consumers of the desirability of his new or differentiated product; and when he must take on this risk, he naturally wishes to attach his own brand to the product in order to profit from its promotion. Once the manufacturer's brand is established on a product, his self-interest leads him to try to keep the demand active.

Manufacturers also generally want to sell under their own brands because of their desire to influence the prices which they may receive, as a means to the end of maximizing net profits. They recognize that advertising and promotion of their brands may affect the valuations consumers place on their products. Although advertising and selling efforts may possibly though not necessarily increase unit costs, to the businessmen these increases may appear justified if the advertising promises to yield a larger net income (volume times price less cost) for a differentiated product than he would obtain under alternative plans of selling unbranded goods or providing private-label goods to the trade.

In brief, the manufacturer who sells through distributors would like to be in a position to have consumers' preference which would make it at least desirable if not essential for retailers and wholesalers to stock and sell his brands, taking them irrespective of the prices he sets. Insofar as advertising helps him to attain this objective, he is inclined to employ it.

The extent to which this ideal of complete control by the manufacturer can be attained varies, however, because the opportunities of influencing consumers' brand choices also vary widely. For some products, as we have indicated, a manufacturer can build a "pull" which makes it essential for retailers to handle his brand, especially when he can differentiate his product in some way that is particularly appealing to a large number of consumers. For other products, however, the maker can exert so little pull that the dealer may be relatively free to select merchandise without particular regard to brand. In between the extremes are many degrees of consumer acceptance or preference to which tradesmen may give greater or lesser heed. Hence, manufacturers' opportunities to influence the merchandise which tradesmen carry will be found to vary widely and their marketing programs to vary accordingly.

Reasons Why Some Manufacturers Do Not Seek to Establish Brands. While emphasis has been given above to the desire of manufacturers to establish their own brands, it is equally important to recognize that manufacturers do not always strive to sell under their own brands. Many gladly produce products for sale either under distributors' brands or unbranded. They are in business to make a profit and are willing to work for profit where they see it. Of these manufacturers, some produce largely for sale under the brands of others; others merely accept such business as an adjunct to sales under their own brands. In the latter cases, private brand contracts generally are taken on in order to employ plant capacity that is not taken up by sales of the manufacturers' own brands. Thus the willingness of manufactures to provide the trade with private-label merchandise permits competition which includes dealers' brands as well as manufacturers' brands.

Reasons Why Many Distributors Have Sought Brand Control. Wholesalers and retailers, like manufacturers, have sought to gain stability in their operations by obtaining consumer goodwill and patronage—by obtaining a hold on customers. One means the distributor has of gaining a hold on customers is by becoming recognized as the source of satisfactory private-label merchandise. Another means is by establishing a reputation as a source of good values in unbranded products. And another means is by becoming an exclusive representative for manufacturers' brands in a trading area. This method, however, may involve uncertainty and risk regarding the tenure of the exclusive agency.

Distributors are actuated also by a desire to be free from the intense price competition which often exists among sellers of manufacturers' brands. The prices charged to wholesalers and retailers for manufacturers' brands ordinarily are based upon retail list prices which will provide adequate margins to the trade for their services. But competing retailers, seeking to gain business, reduce prices to attract patronage and thus narrow trade margins and profits. For this reason, distributors—particularly large-scale distributors such as food chains and department stores—may attempt to build business for their own brands or for unbranded products in order to obtain adequate margins and profits, as well as to build their own reputations as sources of good merchandise.

A further reason which sometimes leads distributors to establish their own brands is their desire to offer product values that compare favorably with or excel those offered by competing merchants. By using private brands, distributors frequently can give value as good or better than competitors and can obtain freedom in selecting and pricing merchandise to meet competitors' offerings.

Reasons Why Some Distributors Do Not Seek Brand Control. Although the trade often desires to own or control the brands it sells, it is of course evident that not all wholesalers and retailers seek to establish their own brands. Distributors are often not only willing to handle manufacturers' brands but may even prefer to do so. The reasons for such a preference are many and varied. So long as the selling of manufacturers' branded products is profitable, many distributors are glad to handle them. Private branding varies widely among different product fields. In some instances it has been relatively easy for distributors to establish brands; in others, they have neither the desire nor the opportunity to do so. Often the costs of selling under their own brands are greater than the costs of selling manufacturers' advertised brands. Moreover, the ability of distributors to sell under their own brands has been governed to considerable extent by the size of their businesses.

The development of distributors' brands has been associated primarily with large-scale retail or wholesale operations. The small independent retailer, even though he might like his own brands, usually has not been in a position by himself to contract with a manufacturer for enough merchandise under his own brand to make it worthwhile for the manufacturer. The costs of special labeling and packaging for the small volume he would take have precluded private branding. In addition, the small retailer has not been in a position either to check adequately the uniformity of quality in the merchandise bought or to investigate the manufacturing sources available to him. Moreover, his reputation as a merchant often has not been such that his sponsorship would induce ready acceptance of his brands.

Leading Considerations Determining Opportunity to Stimulate Selective Demand

In this section of the book, attention in each case is centered on advertising as a tool to stimulate a profitable demand for a manufacturer's brand. In all instances, advertising is a marketing element to be combined with other marketing elements to find a *profitable* marketing mix. From a study of the individual cases and from comparison and contrast of cases, it is hoped that the reader will get a fuller appreciation of the part that advertising may play under different sets of circumstances.

The cases will serve to bring out that numerous conditions bear upon the effectiveness of advertising and that it is necessary for management to appraise carefully its opportunity for using advertising for each of its products in the light of the conditions under which it operates. It must consider conditions affecting both primary demand and selective demand. In appraising its advertising, management is interested in expanding its own demand, whether the expansion comes from attracting new users to the product field or from weaning consumers from competitors. The advertising of individual concerns, accordingly, may affect both primary and selective demand schedules. As has already been pointed out, aside from the relatively infrequent instances in which competitors band together to carry on co-operative campaigns in order to shift the demand curve of an industry, advertising's effect upon industry or primary demand comes from the aggregate effect of individual company campaigns.

It must always be kept in mind that the individual company management finds it advisable to use advertising and other selling methods to increase sales only when these selling methods serve to stimulate a volume of sales at prices which cover all costs, including the selling and advertising. While the cases will show that numerous conditions affect the opportunity to employ advertising profitably to shift the demand curves of products, five conditions stand out.

The Five Conditions. First, advertising is likely to be more effective if a company is operating with a *favorable primary demand* trend than if it is operating with an adverse trend. When an industry's sales are expanding, each concern can strive for part of an increasing whole. Thus, in the tobacco industry, most companies in recent decades have put much of their advertising and promotional effort on cigarettes because the demand for cigarettes has been expanding and promotional effort given to them has been particularly promising of bringing an increased volume of sales. In contrast, in advertising smoking tobacco and chewing tobacco, tobacco companies have operated with adverse trends, and each company has been seeking to get a share of a contracting total demand.

The second condition governing a concern's opportunity to influence its demand is the presence of a *large chance for product* differentiation. When products can be significantly differentiated, advertising is likely to be effective. Conversely, advertising is of smaller help when there is a marked tendency for the products of various producers to be closely similar. In product differentiation rests the opportunity for influencing consumers to prefer one brand to another. Moreover, product differentiations have an important bearing on the gross margins which the seller can obtain. The width of the margins, in turn, determines the availability of funds with which to support advertising and selling.

With respect to product differentiation, it should be noted that most classes of products undergo a natural evolution which has come to be called the "life cycle of a product." Generally, when a new product is introduced to the market by a manufacturer, it has many characteristics which significantly differentiate it from other products fulfilling essentially the same consumer need. Subsequently, as other manufacturers bring out directly competitive products, the characteristics of the original product afford much less opportunity for marked product differentiation. Over time, as competing manufacturers continue to redevelop their products, all brands tend to become similar in attributes and their differentiating characteristics tend to be minor rather than major in character. Eventually, there may be few if any differentiating characteristics; the competing products may be identical.

Study of the evolution of products and of accompanying promotional efforts indicates that advertising plays an important role in informing and educating consumers about new products which have significant differentiating characteristics. Later, when there are many competing products with relatively little difference in characteristics, competition tends to turn from product differentiation to price differentiation: competitors tend to compete on a basis of price, lowering price through lowered production costs, lowered marketing costs, or both. As manufacturers turn to price as a means of competition, margins available for advertising are usually reduced. Further, lacking significant differentiating features for his brand, the advertiser finds it difficult if not impossible to develop effective advertising appeals.

A third condition bearing upon the advertising opportunity for any product is the relative importance to the consumer of the *hidden qualities of the product* as contrasted with the external qualities which can be seen and appreciated. When these hidden qualities are present, consumers tend to rely upon the brand, and advertising can be used to associate the presence of the qualities with the brand. Conversely, when the characteristics of a product which are significant to a consumer can be judged at time of purchase, brand tends to lose some of its significance and advertising is less useful in building mental associations regarding these characteristics.

A fourth condition having a highly important bearing upon the opportunity for use of advertising to increase demand is the *presence of powerful emotional buying motives* which can be employed in advertising appeals to consumers. Conversely, if such strong appeals cannot be used effectively, then the advertising opportunity is not so great. In the case of oranges, effective appeals to the maintenance of health helped to build the demand for the products of the California Fruit Growers Exchange, for appeals to health and personal well-being are potent. Similarly, manufacturers of cosmetics, drugs, and food specialties have found in their products bases for appeal to strong consumer buying motives. Food and drug products give promise of health, which those who are ailing or who think they are ailing urgently desire. Cosmetics give promise of personal beauty and romance. Generally, such emotional appeals, when relevant to a product, have material effect on consumers' valuations, a fact clearly illustrated in the prices obtained for advertised drug and cosmetic products. In contrast to the above, walnut growers, sheeting manufacturers, and numerous other sellers have found their products less adapted to the use of strong emotional appeals.

A fifth condition of importance in determining the employment of advertising to increase the demand of the individual concern is whether the concern's operations provide *substantial sums with which to advertise and promote* its products in the markets it seeks to reach. Advertising must be done on a scale large enough to make an effective impression upon the market. Consequently, the size of the advertising fund is an important consideration in an appraisal of advertising's opportunity. The matter of an advertising fund for any period depends upon the number of units of the product which can be sold in the period and upon the margin available for advertising. The size of the margin depends very largely upon the effectiveness of advertising in influencing consumer valuations of a product. This influence of advertising in turn is dependent upon the extent and significance of product differentiation and upon the strength of appeals which may be employed to present the differentiated qualities. The amount of margin available for aggressive selling work depends also upon conditions of competition in an industry, that is, whether competition is carried on in price or in nonprice forms. Cigarettes and dentifrices are illustrative of products which are purchased by large numbers of consumers at relatively frequent intervals and on which the margins available for advertising have been substantial proportions of selling prices. As a result of the combination of the large number of units sold and the relatively wide promotional margins, many sellers in these fields have been able to make large advertising appropriations, in spite of the fact that the unit sale is small. In contrast, although sugar has had large sales volume, its price has provided very narrow margins which might be devoted to advertising. Again, the number of units of electric refrigerators sold is not large as compared with the above products, but the size of unit sale has been large enough to provide a relatively large margin per unit for advertising and, consequently, large total advertising appropriations for individual companies. On the other hand, manufacturers of products of high price which have a thin demand, such as electric organs for the home, have been small advertisers because they have not sold enough units to support extensive advertising programs.

In addition to the foregoing important conditions, other conditions which affect the use of advertising in individual cases might be cited. For example, the percentage of gross margin which a concern is able to secure for its product and the consequent margin available for promotion often appear to be affected by the importance of the item in the consumer's budget. When an item has an important place in the consumer's budget— that is, where usage is frequent or price is high—consumers apparently weigh price differences more carefully than they do where price is relatively low or usage is infrequent. So long as buyers behave in this way, an advertiser may be able to continue to secure a substantial volume of sales at a good margin, and consequently can continue to advertise. For instance, manufacturers of certain brands of confections and soft drinks sold at 5 or 10 cents have continued over long periods of time to secure wide percentage gross margins which support substantial advertising programs, because for such products the price appeal of competing products is not particularly effective with many consumers. Five or ten cents gives these consumers a satisfying amount of a drink or a candy or a gum, and they continue to buy a brand which they know and like even though other brands might give them a larger quantity for 5 or 10 cents or an equal quantity for less money.

Other conditions which may bear upon the opportunity of individual concerns to make effective use of advertising in influencing the demand for their brands need not be enumerated, for the five conditions mentioned above are most universal and are of first importance. It should be stressed, however, that the opportunity to use advertising effectively generally depends not on the presence of one of these conditions alone but upon the combination of conditions which exists.

The possible combinations in which these conditions are present in greater or lesser degree are almost innumerable; and each demand situation as it relates to advertising use must be considered unique, although there may be similarities in some respects with other demand situations. It is this wide variation in the demand conditions of individual concerns and the uncertainty regarding advertising's influence upon sales under the conditions met which entails much of the risk involved in advertising expenditure. On the other hand, the presence or absence of some one condition or of a favorable combination of conditions serves to explain the varying extent to which advertising has been used to influence the demand of individual concerns in different industries.

Determination of the Marketing Mix

To repeat, appraisal of the opportunity to stimulate a demand for a product rests in a *study of the marketing operation as a whole.* The place of advertising in any marketing operation depends upon management's judgment regarding a suitable marketing mix, all things considered. Accordingly in the cases ahead, constant attention must be devoted to the part that advertising is assigned and to how the elements fit together to bring actual sales. As has been stressed, any one of several marketing mixes may succeed for a company. The student of business must try to design that mix which for him promises the most profitable result over the long run.

Some of the ways in which advertising's part will vary in a program, depending on management's judgment, are indicated below:

1. *Variation in brand policy.* If a company decides to sell its merchandise under private brands or without brand, advertising will play but a small part, as will other types of promotional effort. Decision to sell under one's own brand will, in contrast, probably lead to a decision to use advertising.

2. *Variation in reliance placed on alternative selling methods.* Among the more important selling methods involved in bringing about actual purchase by consumers, the following may be listed:

Advertising to consumers in consumer media
Advertising to the trade in trade papers or by mail
Personal selling by the company's salesmen
Personal selling by wholesalers' salesmen
Personal selling by retailers' salesmen
Advertising through point-of-purchase material
Advertising by retailers
Sampling
Demonstration of the product
Sales-promotion plans, such as one-cent sales, combination deals, premium offers, etc.

Management has to determine which of these it will use at any time and what burden it will put on each. Different types of products will tend to have different sales promotional mixes. For instance, for products such as proprietary remedies, manufacturers will rely largely on advertising pull and will use little personal selling. For other products, such as high-price industrial machines, producers will rely mostly on personal selling and will place little burden on advertising. But companies with similar products will often arrive at different combinations or mixes of selling elements.

In the cases ahead, the question should also constantly be raised as to whether the combination of selling methods employed is good, considering the product, the size of the company, the competition, the character of the trade channels, and so on.

3. *Variation in channels used.* Variation in the channels of distribution used have a bearing on the part which advertising is called upon to play and on the character of the advertising. Companies selling direct to consumers generally assign advertising a different place than do companies selling similar products through the trade.

4. *Variation in merchandising policies.* Basic merchandising policies usually determine a management's use of advertising. These merchandis-

ing policies govern matters of product form, quality, packaging, pricing, and related details that affect the segment of the market to which appeal may be made. A management must decide what market it wishes to reach, the sort of product needed to satisfy this market, and the kind of promo-ional policy that is essential to establish the product in that market.

Chapter 7

∿∿∿∿∿∿∿∿∿∿∿∿∿∿∿∿∿∿∿∿∿∿∿∿

CASES INVOLVING THE

MARKETING MIX FOR

CONSUMER PRODUCTS

The cases in this chapter have been selected to allow analyses to be made of the role of advertising in the marketing mixes of manufacturers of consumer products operating under significantly different marketing conditions. As the reader analyzes successive cases, he may find it of value to contrast and compare the principal considerations governing the use of advertising by different types of business.

~~~

CASE 1: REVERE SUGAR REFINERY[1]

QUESTIONS TO CONSIDER: *(1) If Revere is to maintain a profitable operation, what elements of the marketing mix require the special attention of management? What does management have to do and do well to stabilize or increase sales and profits? (2) What kind of selling strategy has Revere employed? (3) Should Revere have adopted a program of consumer advertising? If so, why? If not, why not? (4) Should Revere continue its consumer advertising after mid-1958? If so, what should be the objectives of the consumer advertising?*

In mid-1958 executives of Revere Sugar Refinery, Boston, Massachusetts, were reviewing the promotional program for "Revere" sugar. The program had begun in April 1957 with a new package design, and since

---

[1] Written by David W. Nylen and Martin V. Marshall.

168

then a relatively large expenditure had been made for newspaper advertising and other media in an attempt to build greater consumer awareness and acceptance of Revere Sugar.

Industry Background

The sugar industry consisted of two major groups of sugar refiners, cane-suger refiners and beet-sugar refiners, having in 1957 combined sales of approximately $1,081 million—$818 million of cane and $262 million of beet. The cane-sugar refiners were located principally in the port areas of New York, Boston, Philadelphia, Baltimore, Savannah, New Orleans, Galveston, and San Francisco, and the beet-sugar refiners in several central and western states.

The bulk of the cane-sugar refining was carried on by 14 companies which handled about two thirds of the finished sugar sold. The American Sugar Refining Company, with five plants, had 22% of the total United States productive capacity; National Sugar Refining Company, with three plants, had 16% of the total productive capacity; California & Hawaiian Sugar Refining Corporation, Ltd., with one plant, had 7%; and the remaining 20% of the 66% was distributed among the remaining eleven companies.

The sugar industry was regulated by the federal government under various Sugar Acts administered by the Secretary of Agriculture. The Sugar Acts established quotas that apportioned imports to the various sugar-producing countries and adjusted total imports to total estimated consumption. Domestic growers of cane and beet sugar were also subject to production quotas. Domestic sugar producers were subsidized to allow them to maintain prices competitive with imported sugar, payments being financed by an excise tax of one-half cent per pound of raw sugar on the manufacture or importation of refined sugar.

Marketing of Sugar

The sugar industry sold to two markets: the consumer and the industrial buyer. In 1957 the industry delivered approximately half of its production to the retail trade, 5.6 billion pounds through wholesalers and 2.3 billion pounds direct to the large food chains. The remaining 8.9 billion pounds of sugar was delivered to industrial buyers, large tonnages being used by manufacturers of bakery products, confections, beverages, and canned and bottled foods. From a geographical standpoint, in 1956, the New England states used 821 million pounds of sugar; the middle atlantic states, 3.71 billion pounds; the north central states, 5.02 billion pounds; the southern states, 4.77 billion pounds; and the western states, 2.41 billion pounds.

In the 20-year period preceding 1957, total sugar consumption had increased almost proportionally to population: sugar consumption increased from 6.7 million tons in 1936 to 8.9 million tons in 1956, while population increased from 128 million to 168 million, per capita consumption changing from 97.89 pounds to 99.02 pounds.

One of the major problems of the sugar industry was excess capacity, refiners typically operating at 60% of capacity. As a result there was intense price competition.

Sugar was priced under the basing point system, under which all markets regardless of their location were quoted prices F.O.B. the seaboard refinery city from which rail or water freight rates were lowest. Refiners located in other cities from which freight rates to the place of delivery were greater than rates from the basing point absorbed the excess transportation costs. Within seaboard refinery cities such as Boston, New York, and Philadelphia, outside refineries usually found it impossible to sell profitably because of the necessity of absorbing freight costs.

The base employed for all sugar prices was the price of a 100-pound bag of extra-fine granulated sugar, which in the winter of 1957 was $9.15. Other items in a refiner's line were priced by the addition or subtraction of standard differentials reflecting the costs of packaging, labor, and refining. The most profitable items were one- and two-pound packages of granulated sugar and one-pound packages of specialty sugars, such as confectionery, brown, and cube sugars.

Some refiners guaranteed customers against sudden declines in price, rebating any reduction in sugar prices for 30 days after goods were billed to the customer.

Since there was relatively little opportunity to compete on the basis of price, competition among refiners took other forms. Although most refiners sold through sugar brokers, they usually employed a missionary sales force, which sought to develop favorable personal relationships with customers and to give service. Insofar as possible refiners attempted to develop new merchandising ideas. For example, the Revere company had developed a system of delivering bulk granulated sugar and sugar liquor by truck, either dumping or pumping sugar much in the same manner as coal or oil. Being the innovator of the system, Revere obtained and held a large share of the market for this type of delivery.

Through alteration of refining methods a refinery could make its sugar whiter or more readily soluble. The California & Hawaiian Sugar Refining Corporation, for example, in one of its attempts to enter eastern markets, set up sales offices in a number of cities east of the Mississippi and based a sales campaign on the assertion that its sugar was whiter than competing brands. Some refiners claimed that retailers and housewives attached significance to differences in degree of whiteness, solubility, and evenness of grain among various brands of sugar, but refiners claiming these advantages commanded no price differential over competing sugars. Revere executives, from their experience, believed that differences in the degree of whiteness were so slight as to be indiscernible to the ordinary housewife and thus was a sales claim of questionable validity. In general, sugar was such a highly standardized product that refiners had been able to introduce practically no significant new developments or improvements.

Because of the freight rate situation and the competition of small inland cane- and beet-sugar refineries, no brand of sugar had attained complete national distribution. The American Sugar Refining Company, by far the largest in the industry, came closest to distributing nationally, reportedly selling its sugar in all states east of and in five states west of the Mississippi.

Advertising in the Sugar Industry

Sugar was generally regarded by buyers and consumers as a highly standardized product with practically no discernible differences between the various brands. This fact combined with the narrowness of margins had resulted in little emphasis on advertising in the marketing mix of most refiners. However, the two largest companies (American and National) had for many years conducted advertising programs, and more recently other large refiners had begun to undertake some form of sales promotion.

Advertising by Refiners

With its introduction of packaged sugar in 1912, the American Sugar Refining Company initiated a campaign of magazine advertising to develop consumer demand for its "Domino" brand of packaged sugar, but had discontinued this medium in the middle twenties and had subsequently confined its principal promotion efforts to newspapers. In 1953, however, with the growing concern in American families over the high caloric value in sugar as contributing to obesity, American once again used magazines in addition to its normal newspaper schedule. American's advertising budget increased to $576,000 in 1953 as against $344,000 in 1952. American advertising was directed toward telling the consumer that the caloric value of sugar was "less than that of many other fine foods recommended in nonfattening diets." In 1956, with an expenditure of $470,000, American advertising emphasized (1) that a teaspoon of sugar contained only 18 calories—"less fattening than many . . . diet foods," (2) sugar had a quick energy value, and (3) sugar had an important nutritional value. This advertising budget was largely for newspapers and magazines, although small amounts were allocated for trade papers, dealer aids, and spot radio.

The National Sugar Refining Company likewise had sponsored continued newspaper campaigns for its "Jack Frost" brand, which was sold in a distinctive blue carton. Although a smaller company than American, National had spent more than American for advertising during the decade 1929–39; its average annual expenditure for that period was reported as $254,000 a year as against an average of $117,000 for American. After World War I, however, National's expenditures were generally less than those of American. In 1956 National spent $142,000 in newspaper advertising in addition to an unpublished amount in magazine advertising, car cards, trade papers, dealer aids, window displays, outdoor signs, counter displays, and premiums. In 1950 National's newspaper expenditure was greater than American's but was trimmed sharply in 1951 because it was considered too costly, according to the company's annual statement. In the following few years, National's management spent most of its advertising appropriation on car cards and outdoor displays, the expenditures for which were not reported. In 1955 National reported that it was going to place more emphasis on industrial sales since the trend was toward

Exhibit 1

REVERE SUGAR REFINERY

Advertising Expenditures of Selected Sugar Manufacturers
(In Thousands of Dollars)

	AMERICAN			NATIONAL	C & H, NEWSPAPER	SAVANNAH ADVERTISING†	IMPERIAL
	Magazine*	Newspaper†	Total				
1956........	$106	$364	$470	$142	$159	$75	$37
1955........	122	418	540	131	193	50	39
1954........	122	346	468	100	153	47	32
1953........	115	461	576	116	157	40	46
1952........	....	344	344	132	133	42	61
1951........	37	353	390	149	90	34	56
1950........	31	297	328	313	111	31	36
1949........	37	314	351	265	47	35	0
1948........	....	131	131	147	50	32	0

* National Advertising Investments, Leading National Advertisers, Inc.
† Expenditures of National Advertisers in Newspapers, American Newspaper Assn., Inc.

more prepared or ready-to-eat foods. In 1955 and 1956, its newspaper advertising continued to tell the housewife how to make food taste better with sugar.

The Imperial Sugar Company of Sugarland, Texas, was reported to have conducted a program of effective consumer advertising. Imperial operated one refinery in Texas and distributed its cane sugar almost exclusively within the state, where it met the aggressive competition of large distributors of all other types of sugar, including beet-sugar processors, distributors of offshore refined cane, the California & Hawaiian Sugar Refining Company, the American Sugar Refining Company, and from time to time the Louisiana refineries. The Imperial Sugar Company commenced a promotional campaign during the 1930's, reportedly setting aside 2 cents per 100 pounds of sugar to provide an annual budget of about $80,000 for newspaper advertising of its packaged sugar. The underlying theme of the campaign was, "What Texas makes, makes Texas." This exploitation of "Imperial" sugar as a local product was said to have given it an edge over competitive brands of sugar in Texas. The executives of the Revere company, however, felt that in appealing to local pride the Imperial Sugar Company was not actually selling its product on its own merits and that any success the campaign attained was chiefly because of Imperial's unusual local situation.

Exhibit 1 indicates advertising expenditures for selected sugar refiners.

Industry Advertising

Advertising had been used in 1930 and 1931 by the sugar industry in a co-operative campaign in an attempt to counteract a declining trend in sugar consumption. In the two years the Sugar Institute spent between one-quarter and one-half million dollars annually in national magazines to try to stimulate an increased use of sugar by consumers. Another co-operative campaign, that of the United States Cane Sugar Refiners' Association, attempted through the medium of four advertisements in *The Saturday Evening Post* to persuade the American people and their representatives to support the home cane-sugar refining industry in its fight against offshore tropical refined sugar. Both of these industry campaigns were considered to have been ineffective in stimulating a demand for sugar, principally because both were of brief duration in relation to their objectives and were not effectively co-ordinated with refiners' sales efforts.

In the middle 1950's, however, the sugar industry, through the Sugar Information Agency, conducted what was generally regarded as a successful advertising campaign combating the idea that sugar was to be avoided as a fattening food. This campaign was of sustained duration and was directed toward educating the public about the place of sugar in human nutrition, emphasizing that many other fine foods recommended in non-fattening diets contained more caloric value than sugar. During this period per capita consumption, which had dropped several pounds, rose again to its earlier level.

Revere Marketing Program

Revere Sugar Refinery, a subsidiary of United Fruit Company, was a medium-sized refiner. It produced a full line of bulk and packaged sugar for industrial and home use, 40% being sold to industrial users such as confectioners, bakers, ice cream manufacturers, and soft-drink manufacturers, the balance being sold through wholesalers and chain stores to the retail trade. Exhibit 2 shows the percentage distribution of 1957 total Revere production of sugar by types of containers. Revere's market was limited by freight costs to New England, excluding southwestern Connecticut, and a portion of northern New York state. Revere had roughly a 50% share of the New England market, although the share varied by region, and American Sugar's Domino brand held about a 50% share. There was no other significant competition in the area.

Revere's sales organization consisted of a vice president in charge of sales, Mr. Vincent Larkin, four assistant sales managers and nine salesmen.

Each salesman had a territory in which he was assigned wholesaler and industrial accounts. The sales manager together with his assistant serviced the food-chain accounts in addition to many other large customers. Typically, a salesman had 50 accounts: 20 of which might be industrial users; 30 wholesalers, jobbers, corporate, and voluntary chain buyers.

Salesmen normally spent two days out of each week visiting customers. These visits usually were to the larger customers and were of a missionary type to strengthen or develop the relationship. Salesmen tried to visit all customers every other week whose orders averaged between 300/500 100-pound bags. Although some orders were received in the field, buyers normally ordered by telephone, telegraph, or letter. When buyers required special services, such as help with a technical problem or sugar ground to

Exhibit 2

REVERE SUGAR REFINERY

Percentage Distribution of 1957 Total Production of Sugar by
Types of Container

Granulated:			
Cotton bags—100 lbs......................		4.0%	
Cartons — 5 lbs. and 2 lbs.............		1.0	
Paper bags —100 lbs......................29.7%			
10 lbs..................... 6.0			
5 lbs.....................21.0			
2 oz..................... 1.0	57.7		
Total Granulated......................			62.7%
Sugar syrup and bulk......................		18.0%	
Yellow......................................		9.0	
Confectioners' 1-lb. cartons..................		4.5	
Cubes and tablets..........................		2.3	
Powdered and confectioners' in 100-lb. bags....		3.5	37.3
			100.0%

specifications, salesmen arranged for company specialists to visit customers to resolve the particular problems at hand. The manager and assistant manager performed a similar kind of function with the food chains and the larger customers who were located at greater distances from the refinery.

Since most orders were received at the office, salesmen spent a major part of their time in their offices. In addition to placing orders, customers would call to get information about probable changes in prices, and occasionally customers came into the sales office to see their salesman when visiting the company's engineering department or laboratory. At the same time, many salesmen made an effort to win the favor of their customers by informing them continually of anticipated price changes and changes in market conditions.

Revere Advertising Program

Before 1957 Revere had had no major experience with consumer advertising. However, as a test of the effectiveness of consumer advertising, the company conducted a single sustained campaign over a two-year period commencing about 1936 in a representative small city near its refinery. Newspaper copy stated that Revere sugar was a local product and pointed out the advantages of a new type of package. Revere also sponsored food fairs in the same city, in which demonstrators stressed the merits of the Revere line of packaged sugar. Sales of Revere sugar increased approximately 10% in the test market over the two-year period, but the results were not felt to justify the company's expenditure of $6,000 for the advertising campaign.

Since the test advertising campaign, Revere executives had periodically reconsidered the advisability of undertaking a major advertising program to build brand recognition for Revere products. While it was difficult to evaluate accurately the effectiveness of the Domino and Jack Frost advertising campaigns, Revere executives assumed that the continued use of advertising by these refiners implied some confidence on their managements' part in the effectiveness of their promotional methods. Revere executives were convinced that through its advertising Domino had succeeded in creating some degree of brand preference in the New England area. There was sales evidence that in some areas of New England Domino was gaining business, most noticeably in the higher margin one-pound package and novelty sugars. Revere salesmen also reported spotty sales resistance toward Revere sugar by the trade, and some retailer and jobber pressure to undertake an advertising campaign. During the three years before 1957 Domino had stepped up its advertising effort to include radio and television spots in addition to national magazines.

Mr. Larkin estimated that between 75 and 90% of all retail outlets carried two brands of sugar. Only 5 to 10% of all stores *insisted* on carrying only one brand. Chain stores that stocked only one brand of sugar per store typically purchased both Revere and Domino sugar, but stocked their stores with whichever brand could be transported to the store with minimum cartage expense. According to Mr. Larkin, chain and wholesale buyers were very realistic about the homogeneous nature of sugar.

In 1957 Revere executives, impressed by the example of Domino advertising and its apparent success in gaining business, decided to undertake a consumer promotion campaign. Although they thought that "sugar is sugar," executives believed that they could develop consumer recognition and acceptance for Revere so that a consumer, when faced with the choice of Revere or Domino, would be motivated to select Revere. As a related benefit, it was believed that the campaign would have favorable effects on the trade.

After consultation with their advertising agency, Revere executives decided that the most beneficial first step would be to redesign the Revere one-pound cardboard packages. As finally developed through the joint efforts of the advertising agency and the sales staff, the new package design contained color illustrations of food associated with the kind of sugar con-

Exhibit 3

REVERE SUGAR REFINERY

Comparison of Old and New Revere Sugar Package Designs

Exhibit 4

REVERE SUGAR REFINERY

Introductory Newspaper Advertisement

The hats (left to right) are by Mr. John, John Frederics, Sally Victor and Adolpho & Emme. The packages (in the same order) are by REVERE, REVERE, REVERE and **REVERE**

THE SWEETEST THINGS IN TOWN ARE NOW IN GAY NEW DRESS

If you have always thought all sugars are alike, just try these specially-processed, special purpose delights. At your grocers now.

Revere Sugar Refinery   Boston, Mass.

tained in the carton. Exhibit 3 shows three of these new packages and one old-style package.

The new packages were introduced to consumers during the Easter season in 1957 with a six-week newspaper advertising campaign. Exhibit 4 is a newspaper advertisement of this series. In addition Revere partic-

Exhibit 5

REVERE SUGAR REFINERY

Three Newspaper Advertisements of the 1958 Campaign

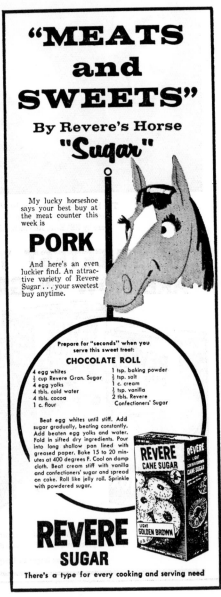

Exhibit 5—Continued

ipated for 13 weeks in the spring on the "Marjorie Mills" program, a New England homemaker's radio show.

At the conclusion of the six-week introductory campaign, Revere started a sustaining newspaper advertising campaign that was still in effect in mid-1958. Because it was difficult to find anything to say about sugar, the advertising agency determined that an unusual approach was necessary to attract reader attention on a continued basis. The agency therefore created the Revere horse, "Sugar," who appeared in Revere advertisements giving hints to housewives on good food buys and giving recipes. Exhibit 5 shows advertisements of this series.

The Revere advertisements were usually three columns by seven inches or two columns by ten inches and appeared in morning and evening newspapers in 28 New England and northern New York cities. The advertisements appeared weekly in the larger cities and two or three times a month in the smaller cities. Exhibit 6 is a list of newspapers used in the campaign.

Revere's advertising agency presented the promotional campaign to the Revere salesmen, giving them instruction on how to promote the campaign to jobbers and retailers. Salesmen were given a 13-page presentation booklet to use when explaining the new advertising program to the trade. The booklet contained copies of advertisements, a media sched-

Exhibit 6

REVERE SUGAR REFINERY

Newspapers Used in Revere Advertising Campaign, 1957–58

Massachusetts:
  *Boston Globe
  *Boston Herald-Traveler
  *Springfield Union News
  *Worcester Telegram Gazette
  Fall River Herald-News
  Lawrence Eagle-Tribune
  Lowell Sun
  New Bedford Standard-Mercury

  Maine:
  *Bangor News
  *Portland Press Herald-Express
  Augusta Kennebec-Journal
  Lewiston Sun-Journal

New Hampshire:
  *Manchester Union-Leader
  Concord Monitor-Patriot
  Keene Sentinel
  Nashua Telegraph
  Portsmouth Herald

Vermont:
  *Burlington Free Press
  Barre Times
  Rutland Herald

Connecticut:
  New London Day
  *Bridgeport Post-Telegram
  *Hartford Courant
  *Hartford Times
  *New Haven Register
  Waterbury Republican-American

Rhode Island:
  *Providence Bulletin-Journal

New York:
  *Albany Times-Union
  Schenectady Gazette
  Troy Record

---

  * Advertisements appeared once a week in these papers.
  Source: Company records.

ule, and some information on what the campaign was designed to do. No point-of-purchase material was used, because executives believed that, because of the nature of the product, stores would not accept display material on sugar.

Evaluation of 1957–1958 Revere Advertising

Both Mr. Larkin and the agency executive for the Revere account realized that short-term evaluation of the effectiveness of the Revere campaign was difficult. However, they believed that there were indications that the campaign was succeeding. Revere salesmen indicated that the trade reacted favorably to the campaign. Mr. Larkin had noted that since the beginning of the campaign, the Revere sales decline had been reduced.

He cited the example of two wholesale distributors who were convinced in 1957 for the first time, as a result of the advertising campaign, to stock Revere one-pound packages. In mid-1958 they were continuing to order the small packages in sizable quantities. The advertising account executives reported that the company had received considerable appreciative mail sent to "Sugar." He also reported that several newspaper food editors had used the Revere recipes in their columns.

~~~

CASE 2: MORTON SALT COMPANY[1]

QUESTIONS TO CONSIDER: (*1*) *One might argue that "salt is salt" as "sugar is sugar." How do you account, therefore, for the ability of the Morton company to command a premium price for its brand since 1913? (2) Has the Morton company made good use of advertising over the years? (3) What contributions has advertising made to the marketing success of the company? (4) In the light of the price competition met in 1958, what action, if any, should the company take?*

In the summer of 1958, immediately following the Morton Salt Company's introduction of a new shaker-top package, a lesser-known competitor in one region of the country reduced his price to the direct buying trade from $2.30 per case of 24 containers of free-running table salt to $1.50. As a result of this reduction retailers were able to feature the competing brand of salt at a price 3 or 4 cents, or even more, a package below Morton's published price.

The company was considering what steps, if any, it should take to meet this and similar price competition. Up to this time the company had relied on its brand reputation to maintain sales volume. One alternative being considered was to maintain Morton table salt at the same wholesale and retail price level as in other markets but to offer the direct buying wholesaler and chain at the end of 1958 a cash bonus of 50 cents for each case sold in excess of 75% of the number of cases sold by each direct buying wholesaler or chain in 1957.

Morton, an old-established name in salt, produced salt for a variety of uses, as did all its major competitors. In addition to producing a table salt it also produced a high-grade salt for food processing, farming, and industrial uses. Its production of table salt constituted only 10% of its total production, approximately 90% of which was sold in the 26-ounce container, while the remaining 10% was sold in other packs.

Morton, with production facilities in a number of areas, had national distribution for all its salt products, which it marketed through 500 company salesmen located in 18 branch offices. Its competitors sold only in

---

[1] Written by Salvatore F. Davita and Neil H. Borden.

regions where their production permitted them to be competitive, since freight was an important consideration.

The company's sales force assumed a variety of functions. The core of this group, 400 in number, called principally on grocery wholesalers, chain-store buying offices, industrial and farm supply houses, and jobbers. In a few cities, where the company had warehouses, some salesmen called directly on manufacturing companies in addition to the normal channels of distribution. All these men, however, sold the complete line of Morton products, consumer as well as industrial salt. The company also employed a few specialty salesmen in certain territories such as Battle Creek, Michigan, where one salesman called on the food manufacturers of that city, and the state of Wisconsin where a salesman specialized in sales to creameries.

The company's sales force also contained two groups of men who did not directly generate sales for the company. One group of about 50 men were sales engineers who worked on technical problems primarily in the industrial field. Another smaller group of men performed a missionary job at the retail level. These men fixed store displays and arranged for special sales promotions. In the warm seasons, joint sales promotions were pushed, such as "Morton Salt and popcorn—just naturally go together."

Morton, in business since 1848, had gained an advantage over its competition when in 1913 it introduced a new salt in the form of cubicle crystals dusted with bicarbonate of soda which would not cake or harden in damp weather. In later years the company developed more effective means than soda to make the salt free running. To further individualize its new table salt, Morton introduced it in a two-pound packaged container which was fitted with a patented aluminum spout for pouring, and on its label were printed the slogans, "Never Cakes or Hardens" and "It Pours." Later these were developed into "When it Rains it Pours."

The advertising gradually stimulated the sales of Morton packaged salt. During the early years of the advertising campaign, the task was primarily to induce purchase by brand of a product that had been standardized and sold in bulk without brand identification or in bags with little emphasis on brand.

The Morton 2-pound package encountered some sales resistance in the early years partly because of its price differential. The Morton container was priced at 10 cents in contrast to 5 cents for a 2-pound cotton bag and 1 cent per pound in bulk. The public, however, began to recognize the advantages of packaged free-running salt and slowly began to show a preference for Morton salt.

At first, many people doubted that the consumer would pay the 5 cents differential over the bagged salt for the Morton packaged container and competing companies were slow to adopt the package idea. However, as Morton's sales continued to improve, the acceptance of packaged salt became more apparent. By 1918, five years after Morton introduced the first packaged salt, the major competitors introduced packaged salt, copying the Morton 2-pound container and selling at a similar price. One company, the Myles Salt Company even adopted a slogan similar to Morton's: "It Runs for Myles." By the early twenties, most of the table salt sold was sold in packaged form.

In the 20-year period following, 1925–45, the salt industry was characterized by both price changes and stepped-up advertising. Although Morton had been looked up to as a price leader, the smaller companies began to cut their prices as a means of widening their market areas or getting deeper market penetration. The wholesale price of salt which had been $1.57/case of two dozen was dropped by 25 cents or more by most companies. To meet these competitive tactics some companies distributed premiums such as potato peelers, brushes, doll cutouts, etc. Morton, on the other hand, chose to maintain its price level and to continue to advertise as it had before. Morton was the only nationally advertised brand of salt. The Morton management found that retailers generally maintained a retail price based on normal retail markup of Morton's price at wholesale, and attributed this firm price to the effects of the company's brand advertising.

Traditionally, Morton salt was priced higher than most competing brands, both at the direct and retail buying and selling levels. However, in some areas of the country Morton's prices to the wholesalers tended to be identical to those of its competitors.

Through the A. C. Nielsen Company service Morton kept abreast of the fluctuations of prices at the retail level. Normally, Morton salt was priced higher in retail stores than competing brands, although the prices of the major competing brands were often the same as the Morton price. Salt packaged under private label brands, however, normally was priced 2 cents below Morton's price. In spite of this differential, Morton executives indicated that in stores handling private brands approximately six packages of Morton salt were sold to each package of the private brands. They attributed the consumer preference for Morton salt to Morton's national advertising and the willingness of the public to pay a little more for a product whose quality they had come to believe to be high as against a product whose quality was not so well known.

In 1923 Morton had introduced "Iodized" salt as did its competitors, at the suggestion of health authorities and medical organizations who had discovered that an insufficient amount of iodine in the body was cause of goiter. Here again, Morton's advertising was directed toward educating the public to the use of iodine as an aid to health. The company published booklets describing the cause of goiter, the results of medical investigations, and the remedy found in the judicious use of iodine. The magazine advertising, which was 60% of the total advertising appropriation that year, was over $100,000; part of this advertising carried the message about Iodized salt.

The Iodized salt advertising was reported as very successful; the new product was accepted almost immediately. By 1926 the sales of Iodized salt had passed those of the plain table salt. The company believed that the success of Iodized salt could be attributed to the high regard that had been established by the previous advertising of free-running salt. The management thought that as a result of the widespread publicity and advertising given to the dictum of medical researchers regarding the need of iodine in the diet, the public quickly accepted the use of iodine as food but apparently would accept the salt with iodine from a well-known brand in preference to brands either unknown or not well known. Fears of improper mixing and proportioning apparently were not held against Morton Iodized salt because of a tendency of the public to believe that this well-known company would not permit its reputation to be injured by advertising a product that was in any degree imperfect or harmful.

As a matter of policy, Morton's advertising expenditures were geared directly to sales. As sales increased, the advertising budget was increased proportionally. The company had not increased its advertising when it introduced new products, rather it had allocated a proportion of its normal advertising budget for this purpose.

Traditionally, Morton's advertising was directed toward presenting the message in a manner that provided quick, clear brand identification in a prestige atmosphere to denote Morton salt as top quality. The poster and magazine copy usually contained a few pointed words together with a picture of the distinctive blue-and-yellow Morton container.

During the thirties and up to the World War II, Morton expanded its operations geographically and in sales volume. It concurrently built a distribution system capable of supplying salt to any location in the United States. Then, having become a producer on a national scale, Morton expanded its national magazine and poster advertising.

As the company placed more emphasis on advertising and product recognition in its marketing strategy, Morton spent increasing efforts on modernizing its package and its advertising copy. Between the years 1913 and 1949, Morton had revised its package label seven times. Although retaining the distinctive blue label with the slogan and the trade-mark, the umbrella girl, the revisions sought to bring the style of lettering and the umbrella girl up to date as well as to improve the quality of the package and label.

While Morton was concerning itself with modernizing its package, the Leslie Company, a producer on the West Coast, introduced a new idea in packaged salt, a package containing three miniature salt containers each containing 0.4 ounces of salt. To meet the Leslie Company's innovation, Morton introduced a package of six miniatures a year later in 1950 and adopted a price of 19 cents for the package.

Later, in 1953, Morton introduced its package of Salters which contained three 4-ounce containers for a price of 29 cents. For the introduction of the Salters, Morton ventured into television for the first time, taking time on the Today Show, Home Show, and the Tonight Show, which were participating TV shows. The company's products were mentioned at least twice each week on each show, and each mention was no less than 60 seconds long. Company executives felt a visual demonstration was needed to get across to the public the usefulness and convenience of the new Salters.

In 1956 the company once again was forced to introduce another new package idea since the Leslie Company had already done so the year before. Leslie had incorporated a shaker to the normal 26-ounce container so that salt could be shaken, as well as poured, from the container. Morton introduced its new package in the western states where it competed with Leslie, since it chose to experiment further with the shaker device before using it in the national market. Then, by 1957, having perfected a shaker device which the company thought to be more sanitary and easier to use than the one produced by Leslie, Morton was ready to introduce the newer shaker to the national market.

To usher the new package into the national market in 1958, Morton sought principally television and newspaper advertising. The television promotion consisted of spot animated commercials in the principal cities at a cost of $98,000 for the year. The newspaper message, emphasizing the new shaker top, was largely full-page color advertisements, and they were placed in almost every Sunday newspaper in the country for the first several months of the campaign. Later, the company turned to smaller black-and-white advertisements placed in either the comic or women's section focusing on brand identification. The total newspaper appropriation for 1958 was $200,000.

In addition to the advertising focused on the new shaker top, Morton used general advertising to build brand identification. This advertising was done principally through the use of outdoor billboards on a budget of approximately one million dollars. This advertising consisted of 24,000 poster diaplays in 400 markets for six full months: January through March, April through May, June through August, and October through November. In addition on a budget of $100,000, Morton sponsored Alex Dreir on the NBC Network every other Saturday. Mr. Dreir presented an analysis of the news in a five-minute show.

Also, on a budget of $500,000 Morton used magazine and point-of-purchase advertising to help stimulate the sale of Morton salt by associating it with other foods which normally require salt such as tomatoes, popcorn, eggs, etc. The magazine message was contained in a full-page color advertisement in six leading magazines: *Reader's Digest, Ladies' Home Journal, Good Housekeeping, True Story, Better Homes & Gardens,* and *Progressive Farmer.* The point-of-purchase advertising frequently was a combined promotion with the other product that was featured.

On top of this advertising Morton appropriated $106,000 in 1958 for corporate advertising. This advertising focused on the facilities and the capabilities of Morton. Advertisements were placed in leading magazines such as *Business Week, U.S. News & World Report, Fortune, Chemical Week & Chemical,* and *Engineering News.* This advertising was intended to help the larger industrial buyer learn more about Morton, thus serving as an aid to the Morton salesman in selling industrial salt. The company executives, further, indicated that the consumer advertising continued to be, as it had been for years, a large help to the salesman. They indicated that since the Morton name had been nationally advertised for many years, it had become synonymous with salt; and as a result of this, Morton salesmen had found it easier to establish rapport with industrial buyers.

The price competition met in 1958 in one region brought into focus the question of whether the Morton reputation was adequate to meet the deep price cut made by competition, or whether Morton needed to take additional marketing measures.

~~~

CASE 3: LYDIA E. PINKHAM MEDICINE COMPANY[1]

QUESTIONS TO CONSIDER: (1) *What elements of the marketing mix has the Pinkham company emphasized over the years?* (2) *Did management follow sound strategy in not employing personal selling and work with the trade as basic parts of its selling program?* (3) *How do you account for the company's ability to command margins for its products which would support sizable advertising expenditures?* (4) *What changes, if any, should the company make in its marketing mix in 1957?* (5) *Should prices be increased in order to obtain a larger fund for advertising?*

In June 1956 executives of the Lydia E. Pinkham Medicine Company began to plan their marketing strategy for the year 1957. Under consideration was the whole marketing mix. Giving particular significance to this planning was the fact that company sales, which had moved up gradually from $2,600,000 in 1947 to $3,000,000 in 1953, had dropped to $2,500,000 in 1954 and to $2,250,000 during 1955. Sales to date in 1956 had shown little gain over 1955. In May 1956 the sales manager began his preparations for the June planning meetings by reviewing the company's marketing activities.

Since 1876 the principal product of the Lydia E. Pinkham Medicine Company of Lynn, Massachusetts, had been a proprietary medicine for the relief of feminine malaises, which it sold under the name "Lydia E. Pinkham's Vegetable Compound." The company had always relied on its extensive newspaper advertising to create a consumer demand for its prod-

---

[1] Written by Salvatore F. Davita and Neil H. Borden.

ucts which was translated into mail orders from the trade channels. Family owned and managed throughout its history, the company had prospered until the middle 1920's, when sales started to decline after two factions within the company began to disagree on questions of advertising strategy. In 1930 the company for the first time lost money, when the management reportedly had to assent to advertising expenditures which reached 80% of gross sales. In 1933 and 1934 operations continued to be unprofitable, with advertising expenses amounting to 79% and 82%, re-

Exhibit 1

LYDIA E. PINKHAM MEDICINE COMPANY

Operating Statistics for Selected Years, 1908–35

Year	Gross Sales	Newspaper Advertising	General Advertising*	Profit before Income Taxes
1908	$1,100,085	$ 408,579	$104,107	$169,735
1913	1,459,836	470,552	140,524	383,389
1918	2,233,048	486,143	207,495	679,902
1923	3,549,221	1,348,050	375,434	834,544
1926	3,360,268	1,721,900	421,052	287,717
1929	2,754,758	1,375,769	395,390	233,184
				33,599†
1930	2,046,039	1,389,600	341,947	240,557‡
				169,519†
1932	1,844,855	855,150	255,370	237,856
				69,102†
1934	1,987,625	1,213,420	429,719	149,578‡
				128,447†
1935	1,705,723	564,101	315,949	349,512
				35,317†

* General advertising as used here included premiums, pamphlets, etc: It did not include newspaper or magazine advertising.

† Profit of Northeastern Advertising Agency, owned by Pinkham-Gove interests.

‡ Loss.

Source: Report of Charles S. Lovejoy, Master in case of Lydia E. Pinkham Medicine Company vs. Caroline P. Gove and Lydia P. Gove et al. Published in Printers' Ink, December 10, 1936, p. 72.

spectively, of gross sales. In 1936 the management petitioned the courts to restrain the co-owners from interfering in the conduct of the business, and in July 1937 the Massachusetts Supreme Court handed down a decision favoring the management's petition. The story of the company's rise and decline up to this point is shown in Exhibit 1, which gives operating data for selected years in this period.

For the period 1908–35 for which sales and profits were revealed by the court records the total gross sales were $60,222,880 and the profits before taxes $10,233,844. During this period total advertising expenditures were $32,104,526, of which 76% was for the company's so-called "News" advertising and 24% was for their "General" advertising. (See note of Exhibit 1, regarding this classification of advertising.)

In 1956 about 60% of the company's sales represented mail orders from wholesalers, and the remaining 40% of sales were mail orders received from retailers who ordered direct from the factory. Except for a short period at the inception of the business, the company had not employed salesmen to carry a share of the work of marketing the compound. The company followed the policy of selling its compound to anyone in the trade who placed an order for five dozen or more packages. The compound could be purchased by the consumer in almost any drugstore in the United States.

In the late thirties, having had some advertising copy banned by the Federal Trade Commission, the company undertook clinical test to prove its product claims. After 12 years of research and the expenditure of considerable money, the company completely substantiated its contentions; it did, however, modify its advertising copy.

The company had achieved international fame through the popularity of its original product, Lydia E. Pinkham's Vegetable Compound. The success of this liquid tonic led to the development of the compound in tablet form. The balance of the line of products included an herb medicine, an antiseptic solution, laxative pills, both coated and uncoated, and analgesic tablets. None of these lesser items approached the popularity of the liquid vegetable compound, which, even after the expansion of the line, continued to account for most of the sales volume. In recent years, however, the tablets assumed an increasing share of compound sales.

Late in 1952 the company took several steps to modernize the merchandising of its principal product. Both the bottle and its package were redesigned to give the product more up-to-date appearance. To create more confidence and interest in the product among the younger generation, the company adopted a new advertising personality, Ann Pinkham. Ann was presented in newspaper and magazine advertisements, and over radio, as a woman who was mature enough to speak with authority and yet was young enough to be able to understand the problems of younger women.

Customers were allowed no trade discounts, quantity discounts, or cash discounts in accordance with a policy instituted by former president William H. Gove in 1917. Sales were made directly to any wholesaler or retailer at a price of $144 a gross in any quantity above the minimum. The only requirement for buying directly from the company was that the total value of an order for a single delivery of either individual items or assorted merchandise be not less than $50.

The net amount invoiced was due in 20 days without discount. The company followed a strict credit policy; it required cash with each order of all new, unrated accounts, and refused to sell to customers whose accounts were past due. The management attributed full credit to these policies for its extremely small bad debt loss, which had normally averaged no more than $500 to $1,000 a year, and in 1945 amounted to only $100 on sales of almost $3,000,000.

Before 1947 the price of the compound for many years had been $10 a dozen. Wholesalers who purchased the vegetable compound were then expected to charge retailers $1.00 a bottle, and it was assumed that retailers in turn would sell it to consumers for $1.50. In practice, however, wholesalers found it necessary to offer their customers a discount of 10% or of 10% and 2% from a wholesale price of $12 a dozen in order to enable their customers to compete with retailers who bought directly from the company.

The product, which had never been placed under price maintenance contracts, became the subject of so much deep price cutting during its

Exhibit 2

LYDIA E. PINKHAM MEDICINE COMPANY

Reports of Retail Selling Price of Vegetable Compound for 1939
(Based on Returns of 44,521 Questionnaires)

Retail Price Range	% of Sales Transactions
$0.59–$0.81	6.14%
$0.82–$0.89	28.33
$0.90–$0.96	6.88
$0.97–$1.00	38.82
$1.01–$1.08	3.17
$1.09–$1.19	12.34
$1.20–$1.39	4.18
$1.40–$1.49	0.02
$1.50	0.12
	100.00%

history that by 1939, the management undertook to study the extent to which its product was being undersold. On the basis of 44,521 package insert questionnaire returns of the retail prices at which the vegetable compound was being sold, the management found that not only were 99.88% of sales made at prices below $1.50, but 80% of retail sales were at or below the compound's normal wholesale price of $1.00. Exhibit 2 summarizes the results of this study.

The company's executives readily admitted that the vegetable compound had never enjoyed the goodwill of the trade. In general, neither wholesalers nor retailers handled the product profitably, because of the severe price cutting to which it had been almost universally subjected.

Despite the company's strong position, the management was interested in taking any measures consistent with the company's established policies which would improve the trade attitude toward the Pinkham line. Executives believed that relaxation of the Pinkham policies on terms of sale, discounts, free deals, or credit requirements might have won temporary goodwill at the expense of heavier bad debt losses and slower retail stock turnover. On the other hand, the management also concluded that the company should adopt resale price maintenance without altering its other policies. Proponents of fair trading asserted that it would not only entirely eliminate the ill will of wholesalers and retailers toward the Pinkham products but would even win the active promotional support of the trade for them.

In 1947 the company had found it necessary to increase the price of its compound from the long-established figure of $120 per gross, net, to $144 net because of increasing costs of raw materials, freight rates, and labor. In the years preceding 1947, the company had covered its rising costs by reducing the advertising appropriation and by accepting a reduced net profit.

To make the price increase more acceptable to its retailers and to stabilize the retail price, the company fair traded the retail price of the compound at $1.39 in the 45 states which had fair-trade laws. At this retail price, a druggist who bought direct from the company received a margin of 28% on each sale. This margin was considerably higher than the less than 16⅔% margin he had generally been getting previously. Even after fair trading the company received occasional complaints that retailers were selling the product as a price leader.

The management did not consider the various analgesic preparations, both proprietary and prescription tablets intended for the relief of pain, as directly competitive products, but felt that direct competition was provided by medicinal preparations of the tonic type, designed to remedy the basic causes of functional disorders. In this catagory there were two important nationally distributed, competitive products as well as various dealer brands.

In 1929 sales of one competitive produce were believed to have been equal to those of Lydia E. Pinkham's Vegetable Compound at $3,000,000, but the manufacturer did not maintain this rate and got into a more diversified line. This competitor at that time was reported to employ a sales force of 30 men and to carry on moderate advertising of its various products chiefly in daily and weekly newspapers, spot radio, farm magazines, and through its own publication.

The other leading Pinkham competitor likewise distributed its medicines through the medium of personal selling and was reported to employ aggressive promotional methods with extensive use of counter cards and point-of-purchase display supported by limited spot radio and newspaper advertising. After 1925 this competitor had not maintained its previous position in the field.

The management estimated that these two manufacturers spent 30% of their sales revenue for advertising and 20% for personal selling expense and bad debt losses. These competitors' bad debt losses were believed to have been somewhat higher than the Pinkham company's as a result of the personal selling methods which they employed.

In keeping with its no-discount policy, the company likewise had only twice in its history offered special deals involving free merchandise. The management felt it desirable not to encourage any of its customers to overstock; it preferred instead to follow a policy of selling small lots frequently in order to keep dealers' stock fresh.

For a long period of years, the management had considered 50% of its gross sales revenue as a desirable figure for advertising. During the 1944 to 1946 period, however, as shown in Exhibit 3, the company found it necessary to reduce the ratio of advertising expense to 43% and 44% of gross sales in order to absorb the sharp advances in manufacturing costs which occurred while government regulations prevented price increases. Advertising expenditures had been in excess of $1,000,000 every year since 1920 with the exception of the periods of litigation.

Exhibit 3

LYDIA E. PINKHAM MEDICINE COMPANY

Percentage Breakdown of Gross Sales, 1944, 1945, and 1946

	1944	1945	1946 (9 Mos.)
Manufacturing cost..........	27 %	30 %	29¼%
Advertising and selling expense.	43½	43¼	44½
Total selling and administrative (including advertising)......	57	58	60½
Net profit before taxes........	16	12	10¼

The management placed practically its entire marketing appropriation in consumer advertising media, with the exception of a relatively small proportion spent for sales-tracing premiums (see Exhibit 4).

The company consistently spent more than half its advertising budget in local newspapers, which, it believed, were best suited to the highly personal messages and frank, forceful style of testimonial copy which proved most effective in selling Pinkham products. In addition, the company executives viewed newspapers as the one flexible medium in which to advertise the form of the tonic (liquid or tablet) for which the locality displayed a preference.

Dealer displays and other promotional material were available to the dealers on request; however, the company did not push their use and these accounted for a small part of the promotional budget.

Exhibit 5 illustrates selected advertising copy which the company had used over a period of time.

Much experimentation had been carried on for many years in varying degree, but newspapers had generally proved to be the most productive medium. In 1955 the company made a major shift in its use of media as reflected in Exhibit 4. As before the advertising budget followed the fluctuation in sales, but in addition the company executives had faced a 25% increase in the cost of advertising space and time since 1950 and a changing effectiveness of the various advertising media in reaching the mass

Exhibit 4
LYDIA E. PINKHAM MEDICINE COMPANY
Advertising Budget for Selected Years
(In Thousands)

	1947		1948		1949		1950		1955	
Newspapers	$1,150	88%	$ 850	76%	$ 600	54%	$ 600	54%	$550	61%
Radio	100	8	150	14	350	32	450	41	160	18
Magazines			50	5	100	9			60	7
Miscellaneous	25	2	20	2	50	5	50	5		
Farm newspapers	25	2	25	2						
Trade journals			5	1						
Television									130	14
Total	$1,300	100%	$1,100	100%	$1,100	100%	$1,100	100%	$900	100%

Note: No substantial change between 1950–54 except that company experimented with the use of television spot advertising.

Exhibit 5

LYDIA E. PINKHAM MEDICINE COMPANY

"**I Wish I Could Broadcast Over the Radio How Good this Medicine Is**"

Writes Mrs. Austin Maddox, Route 2, Box 174, Oxford, Ala.

More than half the women who take Lydia E. Pinkham's Vegetable Compound bought the first bottle because some friend or neighbor recommended it. Right in your own town . . . your own neighborhood . . . there must be at least ONE woman who WANTS to tell you how good this medicine is. Ask her. Then try it for yourself. All druggists sell it. Liquid and Tablet form.

"**I Was So Sick and Nervous...**

"I had a dull headache and felt dizzy and I also had pains in my right side. Nearly every afternoon I had to lie down. My mother told me about your medicine and I took the Tablet form. It did away with the dizzy spells and built up my system. It kept me going during pregnancy. Today I have good health which I feel I would not have except for your medicine. If I could not get it I would be in bed half the time."

Mrs. Austin Maddox

that I could not do my work at home nor hold any other employment. Lydia E. Pinkham's Vegetable Compound put me on my feet. It relieved dizziness and nervousness. I am now doing my own work and working out in another home and I feel better than I have for five years. I recommend this medicine to girls and women."

Jenieve Harper,
2115 Hancock St., Louisville, Ky.

*98 out of 100 Women
Report Benefit*

LYDIA E. PINKHAM'S VEGETABLE COMPOUND

NEWSPAPER ADVERTISEMENT, 1935

"**Hot flashes" of change of life stopped**

or strikingly relieved in 63-80% of the cases in doctors' tests!

• Those suffocating "heat waves"—alternating with nervous, clammy feelings — and accompanied often by restless irritability and nervousness— are well-known to women suffering the functionally-caused distress of middle life "change"!

You want relief from such suffering. And—chances are— you can get it. Thrilling relief! *Thanks to two famous Lydia Pinkham medicines!*

In doctors' tests, Lydia Pinkham's Compound and Tablets brought such relief in 63 and 80% (respectively) of the cases tested. Complete or striking relief!

Amazing, you say? Not to the thousands of women who know from their experience what these Lydia Pinkham medicines can do!

Their action—actually—is very modern. They exert a scientifically calming, soothing effect!

Try Lydia Pinkham's on the basis of medical evidence! See if you, too, don't gain blessed relief from those terrible "hot flashes" and weakness so common in "change of life."

How Lydia Pinkham's works
It acts through a woman's sympathetic nervous system to give relief from the "hot flashes" and other functionally-caused distresses of "change of life."

Don't put it off! Get Lydia Pinkham's Vegetable Compound or new, improved Tablets with added iron (trial size only 59¢)

Wonderful—too—for the functional pains, cramps, "draggedout" feelings and other discomfort of monthly menstrual periods!

NEWSPAPER ADVERTISEMENT, 1955

consumer. The change in the use of media therefore represented management's search for a more efficient use of the advertising dollars available to them.

~~~

CASE 4: ELECTROLUX CORPORATION[1]

QUESTIONS TO CONSIDER: *(1) If you were the president of the Electrolux Corporation, what changes, if any, would you make in the company's marketing and selling strategy? (2) Would you recommend that the company make greater use of advertising? If so, how?*

In 1956 the president of the Electrolux Corporation, Mr. Walter Dietz, reviewed the marketing policies of the company in the light of increasing competition in the vacuum-cleaner industry. Since first marketing the "Electrolux" vacuum cleaner in 1924, the company had adhered to four basic marketing policies: the manufacture of a cleaner which fulfilled the needs of housewives without constant change in cleaner design; the

---

[1] Written by Martin V. Marshall and Gerald A. Simon.

utilization of house-to-house selling as the most efficient and profitable channel of distribution for the company; the use of aggressive selling techniques to create consumer demand; and the maintenance of listed prices to all buyers. After World War II Electrolux made two changes in its marketing operation: the company, in 1946, added a line of home maintenance products and, in 1952, began modest use of consumer advertising.

Pertinent Industry Background

The first practical home electric vacuum cleaner, an "upright carpet sweeper," was marketed by the Hoover Company in 1908 through selected retailers. Soon thereafter other companies entered the field, the important ones being Eureka Vacuum Cleaner Company, Inc., and Air-Way Appliance Corporation, both of which also marketed upright cleaners. Eureka and Air-Way sold house to house. Throughout the 1920's these three companies competed for the number-one sales position of the industry. Hoover, as a means of maintaining its leading position, developed a "resale plan" which provided retailers in medium- and large-sized cities with Hoover-employed salesmen who demonstrated and sold Hoover cleaners in retailers' stores. Retailers received 15% of sales for providing selling space and auxiliary services. In addition, Hoover developed two house-to-house sales forces: one to sell cleaners; the other to sell Hoover's repair service. This plan helped Hoover maintain the industry's number-one sales position in the early 1920's.

The introduction of the Electrolux vacuum cleaner in 1924 marked the first significant product innovation in the industry since 1908. The Electrolux Model V, which was initially imported into the United States from Sweden, was a cylinder-type cleaner rather than an upright type, that is, a horizontal cylinder with a metal hose-and-sweeper nozzle attachment. The cylinder-type cleaner offered housewives the advantage of using their cleaners not only to clean rugs and carpets but other household furnishings; extra attachments were available for general cleaning jobs. Also, the Model V was the first cleaner with an enclosed dust bag.

In order to take advantage of in-home demonstration, Electrolux sold house to house. Within a few years the company had built a large national sales force and had crystallized the main elements of its marketing approach. By 1934, according to Electrolux executives, the company had become the industry's sales leader, a position which was not seriously challenged until the mid-1950's.

Throughout the 1930's the industry grew slowly, because of depressed economic conditions. The most significant move made by any industry leader was that of the Eureka company, which changed its method of distribution, replacing 8,000 house-to-house salesmen with 5,500 retailers. In commenting upon this change, the company's executive vice president said in 1940: "Door-to-door selling is all right, even essential, to introduce and demonstrate an entirely new idea and product. But it is too costly a method to use for selling a product recognized as a necessity. Two hundred sixty thousand [Eureka] cleaners were sold by house-to-house salesmen—25% of the total sold in this country. Salesmen were paid $22 commission on an $80 machine. Our new method is far less costly since the firm can now control the method of transaction better, although training dealers is more difficult than direct salesmen."[2]

The end of World War II saw the resumption of consumer vacuum-cleaner production and the successful introduction of the canister or squat-tub type of cleaner by the Lewyt Corporation.

The Lewyt Corporation's entree into the industry is best summarized by its president, Alex Lewyt, who said: "it struck me that the industry was still in its infancy even though the vacuum cleaner itself has been around a long time. For one thing, only about 47% of the wired homes in the country had vacuum cleaners, whereas saturation was up to about 90% for electric refrigerators. And then there was the fact that 75% of them were still being sold by the home-demonstration method. It's all very well to sell a new appliance that way, but the vacuum cleaner had long since been accepted as a household necessity. It was high time that they were sold on a mass distribution basis. I revived the canister-type cleaner—mainly because I wanted to hit the market with something different—and put it through the normal channels of the appliance trade. Then I backed it with a strong advertising campaign. . . ."[3]

In the post–World War II period 1946–56, the industry's sales, according to the Vacuum Cleaner Manufacturers Association, were as follows:

Year	Vacuum Cleaners Sold (Units)
1946	2,289,000
1947	3,801,000
1948	3,361,000
1949	2,890,000
1950	3,529,000
1951	2,729,000
1952	2,842,000
1953	2,778,000
1954	2,658,000
1955	3,270,000
1956	3,722,000

In 1956 it was estimated that cylinder or "tank" cleaners accounted for 40% of vacuum-cleaner sales, upright cleaners for 15%, and canister cleaners for 45%.

With regard to the industry's penetration of market during the postwar period, the January 1, 1948, issue of Electrical Merchandising reported

[2] Earl Lifshey, Door-to-Door Selling (New York: Fairchild Publications, Inc., 1948). Reproduced by permission.

[3] "Whirring Vacuums," Barron's, December 19, 1955, pp. 3 ff.

that 49.5% of wired homes had vacuum cleaners, and the January 1, 1954, 1955, and 1956, issues reported 60.5, 62.2, and 64.3 per cent, respectively, of wired homes had vacuum cleaners.

In 1956 some 25 manufacturers or private-brand marketers were actively in the vacuum-cleaner market. Companies and brands are given below:

Company	Brand	Canister	Cylinder	Upright
	DOOR-TO-DOOR			
Electrolux Corporation.....	Electrolux		x	
Filtex Corporation.........	Filtex		x	
Health-Mor, Inc...........	Filter Queen	x		
Hoover Company.........	Hoover Constellation	x		
Hoover Company.........	Hoover Citation			x
Hoover Company.........	Hoover Lark			x
Landers, Frary & Clark Company..............	Universal	x		x
Landers, Frary & Clark Company..............	Universal Turbojet	x		
Scott & Fetzer Company...	Kirby			x
	RETAIL			
Apex Electrical Mfg. Co....	Apex Strato	x		
Apex Electrical Mfg. Co....	Apex Aero	x		
Eureka-Williams Company .	Eureka Roto-Matic	x		
(Formerly Eureka Vacuum Cleaner Co., Inc.).......	Eureka Automatic			x
General Electric Company..	GE Roll-Easy	x		
General Electric Company..	GE	x		
Hamilton-Beach Company..	Deap-Clean		x	
Hoover Company.........	(as above)			
Lewyt Corporation........	Lewyt	x		
Westinghouse Electric Corp.	Westinghouse			x
Westinghouse Electric Corp.	Westinghouse Carousel	x		
	PRIVATE BRANDS			
Montgomery Ward Co......	Ward's Deluxe	x		
	Ward's		x	
	Ward's Supreme			x
Sears, Roebuck & Co.......	Kenmore	x	x	
Singer Sewing Machine Co..	Singer	x		x
Western Auto Supply Co...	Wizard Deluxe	x		
	Wizard Imperial	x		

Two consumer report services gave ratings to the various brands. *Consumer Reports*[4] of August 1954 had recommended "Ward's Supreme" as the best buy among the upright cleaners and the "Eureka Roto-Matic" 800A and the "Wizard" 830 canisters as the best buys among the cylinder- and canister-type cleaners. All other models tested including Electrolux Models XXX and LX were rated as Acceptable. In January 1957 *Consumer Reports* rated the Hoover Citation 64 as the best in order of estimated over-all quality among the upright cleaners and the Electrolux Automatic E cylinder as the best in order of estimated over-all quality among

---

[4] Reproduced by permission.

cylinder- and canister-type cleaners. The Electrolux Model E was rated as Acceptable, while Models LX and XXX were not rated (Model XXX having been on the market since 1937, but discontinued at the end of 1955). The *Consumers' Research Bulletin*[5] of January 1955 recommended Hoover and Kirby among the uprights and the Hoover cylinder model; the only Electrolux cleaner to be rated was the Model XXX, listed as "not recommended." *Consumers' Research Bulletin* planned to issue a new vacuum-cleaner report in February 1957.

Traceable national advertising expenditures of vacuum-cleaner manufacturers for the period 1946–56 are given in Exhibit 1.

Electrolux's Marketing Mix

As has been stated Electrolux Corporation had adhered to approximately the same marketing approach sinch 1924. The following material describes the principal elements of the company's marketing mix for the period 1924–56.

Product Policy. Throughout these years Electrolux marketed cylinder vacuum cleaners exclusively. Although upright vacuum cleaners with their rotating brushes generally cleaned carpets and rugs more efficiently than cylinder vacuum cleaners which relied solely on suction, they were not as useful for general cleaning; general cleaning attachments for upright cleaners were not as convenient to use as attachments for cylinder cleaners. Hence, the selling of cylinder-type vacuum cleaners afforded Electrolux a broader market because housewives preferred a cleaner which would be used for general cleaning as well as carpet cleaning. (With its reintroduction by Lewyt in 1947, the canister-type cleaner had gradually grown in popularity for general cleaning use. It generally was quiet in operation, easy to store, and easy to empty. The operating characteristics of canister-type cleaners were typically similar to those of cylinder models.)

Electrolux made relatively few changes in cleaner design, in contrast to some vacuum-cleaner manufacturers who often made minor design changes in order to give their salesmen new selling points. In the 32-year period 1924–56, Electrolux had marketed only seven basic models: models V, XI, XII, XXX, LX, E, and Automatic E. Model changes had been made essentially to give housewives (*a*) more cleaning power, and (*b*) greater convenience of use. For example, Model V in 1924 had a 230-watt motor; Model XII in 1930 had a 350-watt motor; and Model XXX in 1937 had a 475-watt motor. All models manufactured after World War II employed 550-watt motors. Model V was somewhat inconvenient to use because the unit had to be held off the floor when the housewife operated the sweeper nozzle and it had an inflexible metal wand or connecting hose. Model XI in 1927 incorporated a flexible hose. Since 1930 many improve-

---

[5] Reproduced by permission.

Exhibit 1

ELECTROLUX CORPORATION

Traceable National Advertising Expenditures of Vacuum-Cleaner Manufacturers, 1946–56

	1946	1947	1948	1949	1950	1951	1952	1953	1954	1955	1956*	Total
Hoover Company:												
Hoover Electric	$210,437	$389,126	$411,591	$351,584	$479,079	$437,904	$369,925	$373,471†	$397,034	$642,044†	$524,578†	$4,586,773
Lewyt Corp.:												
Lewyt Vacuum Cleaner		87,405	212,970	198,003	310,905‡	410,601	520,216	578,526	588,600	972,320	474,585	4,354,131
General Electric Company:												
G.E. Vacuum Cleaner	96,710	190,935	136,960	3,840		205,436	370,432	432,652	322,034	316,109	140,310	2,215,418
Premier Vacuum Cleaner	96,480	191,975	116,010									404,465
Henry Motors Co., Inc.:												
Eureka Vacuum Cleaner	158,140	228,113	57,541	5,000		49,795	190,576	513,128	300,974	360,559	200,902	2,064,728
Electrolux Corp.:												
Electrolux Vacuum Cleaner						(Radio	241,089.95 163,120.00	27,438.63)† 234,960.00	192,343.30	210,608	152,657	953,681
Landers, Frary & Clark:												
Universal Vacuum Cleaner		8,710	24,930	26,655		35,610	213,410	191,550	123,255	59,530	64,225	747,875
Atlas Vacuum Cleaner											2,520	2,520
Health-Mor., Inc.:												
Filter Queen Vacuum Cleaner		57,494	67,804	34,919	8,520	28,228	173,843	48,446	23,885	26,820	10,972	480,931
Air-Way Industries, Inc.:												
Air-Way Sanitizor Vacuum Cleaner			39,600	50,390	55,117	49,181	48,446	63,382	61,382	68,681	15,025	451,817
Westinghouse Electric Corp.:												
Westinghouse Vacuum Cleaner		39,300	39,770	52,138			54,950	66,512	119,370			372,040
Royal Appliance Manufacturing Co.:												
Royal Vacuum Cleaner		67,659	113,331	48,244	38,214	32,865		22,935		20,501	10,930	354,115
Apex Electrical Manufacturing Co.:												
Apex Vacuum Cleaner		127,992	83,640				18,630	17,245		13,300	14,419	275,226
Clements Manufacturing Co.:												
Cadillac Vacuum Cleaner		3,024	32,257	58,452	53,559	45,236	36,252	23,856		19,614		272,250

* 1956—January through August.
† Television—Hoover:
1953—"Today Show"—$17,345.
1954—"Garry Moore Show"—$301,109.
1955—"Famous Film Festival," "Morning Show," "Home Show," and "Today Show"—$76,310.
‡ Television—Lewyt:
1950—"Homemakers Exchange"—$10,200.

Source: Prepared by Batten, Barton, Durstine & Osborne, Inc., for the Electrolux Corporation.

ments were made in Electrolux cleaners which gave housewives greater convenience of use, such as automatically cutting off suction when the dust bag was full. Model Automatic E, marketed in mid-1956, among other features, provided a "brain" which, as controlled by a numbered dial, automatically adjusted the cleaner to specific cleaning conditions and requirements.

In addition to the basic cleaning unit, Electrolux had always sold general cleaning attachments, such as wall brushes, upholstery nozzles, crevice tools and a floor scrubbing and polishing device, and replacement paper dust bags. After World War II a line of home maintenance products was introduced, including a floor wax, a rug shampoo, moth crystals, a moth proofer attachment, and a garment bag with a special valve attachment permitted the vacuum cleaner to force in air which had been circulated through moth crystals. Company executives stated that sales income of home maintenance products in 1956 exceeded the sales income of the vacuum-cleaner line before World War II.

Pricing. Electrolux consistently followed a policy of selling cleaners at list price. Discounts were never given any buyer, including institutions and governments. Even during World War II, the company gave the U.S. Army vacuum cleaners rather than selling cleaners at less than list price. Less-than-list-price sale to the government was then required by federal law.

In 1956 Electrolux was selling three models: Model LX at $109.97, Model E at $77.50, and Model Automatic E, introduced during the year at $89.75. These prices included a set of general cleaning attachments.

The company's management took pride in the fact that relatively few price changes were made once a model was established on the market. For example, Model XXX had been introduced in 1937 at $78; in 1939 the price was reduced to $69.75; in November 1950 it was increased to $77.50, where it was maintained until the model was discontinued at the end of 1955. Model LX had been introduced in July 1952 at $97.50; the price was raised in November 1952 to $109.97.

A selected list of competitors' list prices as of 1956 follows:

A. Canister and cylinder vacuum cleaners sold house to house: Filtex, $148.50; Filter-Queen, $149.50; Hoover's canister model, $97.50; and Universal, $49.95 and $69.95.

B. Canister and cylinder cleaners sold through retail outlets: Eureka canisters, $49.95 and $69.95; Wizard, similarly priced; Westinghouse, $69.95; Ward's, canister at $47.95 and cylinder at $58.95; Sear's Kenmore, canisters at $44.95 and $99.95 and cylinder at $54.95; General Electric, $49.95 and $69.95; and Lewyt, $59.95 and $89.95.

C. Upright cleaners sold through retail outlets: Eureka, $89.95; Hoover's Citation, $124.95, and Lark, $69.95; Singer, $99.75; Universal, $79.95; Sear's Kenmore, $74.95; and Westinghouse, $69.95.

Direct Selling. Company executives, since 1924, had believed that sales were primarily obtained as the result of aggressively creating demand for vacuum cleaners among American housewives. Therefore they made such selling the key element in their marketing operation. As one executive said, "We don't wait for the cow to be backed up to be milked." However, Electrolux's management did not believe that aggressive direct selling would result from routine sales management; they believed in a method which would result in "creative selling in its purest form," as distinguished from use of high-pressure tactics. Over the years they had, they believed, achieved this result through aggressive sales management, giving salesmen considerable freedom of action, constantly recognizing individual sales achievements, and offering high incentive compensation.

In 1956 the Electrolux sales operation was organized as follows: top marketing management was handled by Mr. Elon V. Ekman, chairman of the board; Mr. Dietz; Mr. Harry A. Strong, vice president of western operations; and Mr. Paul R. Boggs, vice president of sales. Reporting to Mr. Boggs were 30 division managers, who with the assistance of divisional sales managers, supervised 300 branch managers. Branch managers, in turn, with the assistance of "multiple" managers, were responsible for the activities of a reported 7,000 Electrolux sales representatives. All Electrolux marketing personnel sold cleaners, at least occasionally, in order to maintain a good "feel" of the selling operation.

Sales representatives were considered to be in business for themselves. The company would employ "anyone who was honest." Although various aptitude and intelligence tests had been used to screen applicants, Mr. Dietz did not believe that tests were particularly helpful. New salesmen were trained simply by accompanying successful salesmen and multiple managers on sales calls. Although many new men left the company within three months, those who stayed usually remained for a long time.

Salesmen generally operated in given areas, but they could make sales calls wherever they wished. Salesmen kept no sales records and made no sales reports, except for the number of sales made. "Thus," Mr. Dietz said, "salesmen are not faced with any disappointing record; they see only a record of accomplishment." Salesmen were responsible for unpaid credit-plan balances. They were not provided with sales leads or standardized sales procedures. Sales experience over the years, however, indicated that certain sales approaches were more effective than others.

Mr. Dietz commented on the successful sales approach as follows: "The first thing a successful salesman does is to ring the door bell, and when the door is opened, he takes off his hat, says 'good morning,' and *takes two steps backward.* More salesmen have failed to take those two steps backward! That, more than anything else, proves to the housewife you're not trying to crash the gate or force your way in. After getting in the house, it's particularly essential for the salesman to listen carefully to everything the housewife says and to watch carefully every move she makes, because that is an indication of how she is thinking. The smart, successful salesman seizes upon every indication of interest to follow through in closing the sale. For example, if the salesman happens to be demonstrating the cleaner on the rug and the housewife asks, 'Will it clean upholstered furniture?,' the right answer is not, 'We'll come to that later,' but, 'Will it! Watch this!' And then proceed to show what can be done with the cleaner on upholstered furniture."

The most important part of the sales approach was known as "the close," i.e., the time during the demonstration when the Electrolux salesman tried to make the sale. Various types of closes were used, depending upon what happened during the demonstration:

As the salesman demonstrated the vacuum cleaner, he might try the so-called "operations close": "Mrs. Smith, if we find as much dirt in your davenport as we found in your rugs, floors, and in this other furniture, you want your Electrolux today, don't you?" If the salesman noted that the prospect was starting to think about costs and terms, he might turn to the "standard close": "Most of our good customers, Mrs. Smith, give us $20 or $25 down. If you will give me $20 today, that will leave a balance of $——. Would you rather have your first payment fall due on the 18th or 19th?" If there was no answer, the salesman would go on to say: "Will the 18th be okay?" If a positive answer, the salesman said: "That's fine, just okay this order." If a negative answer, the salesman might turn to other closes. For example, if the housewife had said that she could not afford a new cleaner because she "was paying for so many things now," the salesman (still demonstrating the cleaner) would stress "the overwhelming importance of a clean home." If she asked him to come back later, he might try a "contest close": the salesman would ask for the housewife's help so that he might win a current sales contest. If that close failed, he might ask: "What is your hardest cleaning problem?" Having successfully done that job, the salesman would then hand the prospect his order book. Another common close concerned the trade-in of the prospect's old cleaner. When asked what would be given for the old cleaner, the salesman would grasp the cleaner and say: "Mrs. Smith, if I came here to sell you this machine and went over your rug with it many times, and then you got out your Electrolux cleaner and went over your rug and got out all these dirt piles . . . you wouldn't honestly pay me $5.00 for this machine. Would you?" At this time the salesman would push the old cleaner away. If he were pressed by the prospect, however, he would quote a trade-in allowance from his allowance book.

A combination of high incentive compensation, appropriate and frequent recognition of performance, and sales contests were used to maintain aggressive sales effort. In addition, in 1946 the company had instituted a jointly contributory pension plan for its sales force.

Electrolux sales representatives were paid a commission of 35% of list price on all sales, one of the highest commissions in the direct-selling field. Although total company commission payments were not made available, numerous examples of individual earnings were cited: Mr. Lau rier B. Bazinet, a sales representative operating out of Portland, Maine, received in excess of $30,000 in 1955; Mr. Victor Polity, a multiple manager operating out of Union City, New Jersey, had made $40,000 in his best year; Mr. Frank Briggs had earned in excess of $60,000 a year as assistant branch manager of the Pittsfield, Massachusetts, office and, since 1938, even more as manager of the Portland, Maine, office; and in his best year, Mr. Hillary J. McCrossin, New England division manager, had made in excess of $140,000.

Frequent use was made of sales contests. Each month salesmen were awarded lapel silver elephants if they sold 50 vacuum cleaners in the month, diamond-gold elephants if they sold 100. (Salesman Bazinet was given a platinum elephant for selling 300 cleaners in October 1955.) Assistant branch managers were awarded silver bowls and trays; company branches completed for a Sales Cup, a Supply Cup, and a Service Award. Salesmen could also win free vacation trips or take the equivalent cash.

These awards and other forms of recognition of sales performance were given at various company meetings. For example, an annual spring meeting for the Eastern Division was held in New York and for the Western Division in Phoenix, Arizona, or Palm Springs, California. Diamond-gold elephant salesmen were expected to bring their wives in addition to their branch and division managers and their wives. Varying with sales records, the couples stayed from three to five days. All expenses were paid; theater tickets were provided; wives could select their own gowns at special fashion shows; and so on. An average of about 3,800 people had attended these two meetings in recent years. Divisions and branches also held their own award meetings when appropriate.

Electrolux's sales management also used written communications to the sales force to maintain and increase sales effort. Daily, sales bulletins were sent out from New York through the Electrolux Press Service, giving sales news, praise, and advice. Weekly, a 12-page bulletin, the *Electrolux News*, was sent to all members of the sales organization. It contained slogans, such as "Timid heart ne'er won fair lady's name on the contract book," contest results, pictures of award winners and meetings, letters from satisfied customers, general sales news, and a cartoon concerning "Elux."

Credit. As true of the appliance field in general, Electrolux sold a high proportion of its cleaners on a time-payment plan. For many years two prices were quoted for each model: cash and credit price. In recent years, however, one price was quoted for each model—the cash price—and the time payment provided interest of 10% of the unpaid balance. On December 31, 1955, the company's balance sheet showed accounts receivable of $26 million, which presumably were credit extensions to customers.

Service. Repair service was a fundamental part of the marketing operation. The company had manufactured nearly all the parts for its cleaners since the early 1930's and assumed full responsibility for their effective operation. All 300 Electrolux branches maintained service departments. On special problems the company would send plant engineers into the field.

Service calls occasionally created problems. "Some customers complain," Mr. Dietz said, "that they do not like to call Electrolux for service because the service man tries to sell them a new Electrolux. We tell our men to make an honest estimate of the cost of putting the old cleaner in first-class condition. Then the customer is in a position to decide whether she wants a new machine or not."

Electrolux did not charge for service calls but did charge for parts and labor when cleaners were repaired.

Advertising. Electrolux did not advertise to consumers until 1952. At that time company executives decided to undertake a modest program of national consumer advertising for five reasons: They thought that much advertising would help to presell the superior advantages of Electrolux cleaners to new customers. They believed existing Electrolux owners would be informed of product improvements, thereby providing greater assurance of maintaining the company's customers' high degree of brand loyalty. They thought that consumer advertising probably would provide the Electrolux salesman with additional prestige when he called upon consumers. They felt the program would inform consumers that the Electrolux cleaner was available only through authorized Electrolux sales representatives. Finally, they believed a national advertising program would aid in the recruitment of new sales personnel. Because of general prosperity the company had experienced increasing difficulty in attracting sufficient numbers of new salesmen.

At first Electrolux salesmen were concerned that advertisements picturing the product would affect their demonstrations, that is, housewives would have seen and known some features of the Electrolux cleaner. Consequently, the company ran a test in one metropolitan market, using large-space newspaper advertisements with detailed illustrations of cleaners. Because sales in the market did not decrease, company executives decided to use illustrations of cleaners in the company's national advertising.

During the period 1952–56 the company spent approximately $200,-000 a year for one- and two-page, four-color advertisements in consumer magazines, such as *Good Housekeeping, Better Homes & Gardens, Ladies' Home Journal, McCall's,* and *Parents'.* Advertisements were often repeated a number of times. For example, throughout 1952 and 1953 a full-page advertisement of the Model LX was used, with the headline: "Only Electrolux sells the cleaner you *never* have to empty"; and throughout 1954 a two-page advertisement of the Model LX remained unchanged, with the headline: "Don't buy *any* cleaner until you see *the new automatic* Electrolux—the *only* cleaner you *never* have to empty. Out pops the dirt! Wrapped, sealed, and sanitary."

Reprints of Electrolux advertisements were given to salesmen who wished to use them. Salesmen often handed a reprint to a prospect, asking the prospect to "read the advertisement while I go out to my car to get a wonderful new cleaner to show you." Also, salesmen occasionally left reprints with prospects with a note, such as "Please read this: An important message about a wonderful Christmas present. Inspiring to give. Thrilling to receive. I will be back on————."

See Exhibit 1 for a comparison of Electrolux and competitive advertising expenditures for the years 1946 to 1956.

Consideration of the Future

By and large Mr. Dietz and other Electrolux executives were reasonably satisfied with past sales progress and were fairly optimistic concerning the future. Although the company did not publish sales information, the December 7, 1956, issue of *Sales Management* gave information concerning Electrolux's growth: it was estimated that sales were $78 million in 1947, $100 million in 1956, and the floor space of the company's factory had been expanded by eight times since 1934. The company's after-tax profits for the period 1946–56 were:

1946	$3,167,000
1947	4,086,000
1948	4,174,000
1949	3,372,000
1950	4,124,000
1951	3,652,000
1952	1,823,000
1953	1,885,000
1954	2,838,000
1955	2,878,000
1956	1,700,000*

* Third-quarter figure.

Mr. Dietz believed that there was a substantial future market for vacuum cleaners which held great promise for Electrolux. He said, "During the next decade there will be 10.2 million additional family units in this country whose personal income will exceed $7,500 per family per year. The total increase in personal income in that group will be $140 billion. We think that looks like a wonderful market and a great opportunity. Every housewife needs an Electrolux cleaner. It's just a question of getting around to telling them so. Ninety-five per cent of the people who will become the proud owners of a new Electrolux today had absolutely no idea of buying a new vacuum cleaner when they got up this morning."

Mr. Dietz thought that the Electrolux concept of direct selling would continue to be effective in the future. "Only a generation ago," he said, "direct selling was looked down on. When I left college and began to sell vacuum cleaners, my mother wrote to me as 'Dear Vacuum Cleaner Peddler' rather than 'Dear Son.' Today, ours is a highly dignified business. Our company was founded definitely, solidly, and permanently on the philosophy that the success of our company comes out of the success of our men. We hold to the belief that no direct-to-the consumer business can be a success unless the understandings, the human interests, and the human relationships are satisfactory. The opportunities for earning in Electrolux are limited only by the individuals themselves. We take great pride in saying of our big earners that they are the highest paid specialty salesmen in the world. They own fine homes, fine cars, and fine bank accounts. They send their children to fine colleges; they take part in civic and local affairs; and they are highly respected and dignified people."

No plans were contemplated which would materially change Electrolux's heretofore successful marketing approach. As in the past, Mr. Dietz said, the company in the future planned to improve its products constantly, to maintain a direct sales setup in which each salesman was in business for himself, and to operate under an enlightened concept of salesmanship and service.

Mr. Dietz had kept a close watch on the competitive situation. He believed that Electrolux had still retained the number-one sales position in the industry in 1956, although its share-of-industry position was below that of previous years. One industry source contended that General Electric Company had moved into the number-one position in 1956 as the result of a new marketing program begun by General Electric in 1952–53. Another industry source ranked Electrolux, Hoover, General Electric, Westinghouse, and Lewyt as the sales leaders, in that order in 1956.

General Electric had put out numerous models of vacuum cleaners under the G.E. brand for some years, but had not had a strong market position. In 1952 General Electric management set out to seek an important sales position in the vacuum-cleaner market as well as other appliance markets. Reports from the trade showed that the G.E. cleaner line was simplified by dropping upright and cylinder models with concentration on the canister-type cleaner. Reportedly a major effort was made for increased retail distribution. At the same time advertising expenditures were materially increased as reported in *National Advertising Investments* (see Exhibit 1). In 1953 advertised list prices were reduced to $89.95. In 1954 prices were again lowered to a fair-traded price of $79.95, and later in the year to $69.95, although advertisements still carried the list price as $89.95. In 1955 the advertised list price was made $69.95 and retailer margins were reduced from somewhat over 40% to about 32%. Distributor margins were also reduced somewhat.

In 1956 the price of the G.E. cleaner was listed at $49.95. As reported in *Tide*,[6] General Electric "chopped list prices on every single portable appliance the division produced, including vacuum cleaners; [the] idea: to bet for profit on volume sales rather than the industry's traditional high markup profit concept." While trade reports did not give any profit estimates of this new General Electric program, *Tide* reported that

---

[6] "G.E.'s New Appliance Marketing Strategy," *Tide*, November 9, 1956, pp. 13 ff.

General Electric's new strategy was apparently gaining sales, that sales of the Housewares Division, of which the Vacuum Cleaner Department was a member, "had doubled between 1951 and 1955 to $150 million, while 1956 sales were reported 30% ahead of 1955 sales, compared with an industry average of 20%."

As a result of General Electric's price cut, Electrolux executives studied the situation and, then in early 1956, they reacted: in January the price of Model E was increased from $69.75 to $77.50, and starting in April advertisements of Model E emphasized monthly payments as low as $5.00 rather than Model E's price of $77.50. They gave no reasons for these moves.

~~~

CASE 5: RUST CRAFT PUBLISHERS, INC.[1]

QUESTIONS TO CONSIDER: (*1*) *What elements of the marketing mix has Rust Craft's management emphasized?* (*2*) *What has the company had to do in order to obtain the help of the trade?* (*3*) *What marketing and selling problems do you foresee facing Rust Craft in the future?* (*4*) *Should Rust Craft undertake a program of consumer advertising?* (*5*) *If not, what selling strategy should the company employ?*

Early in 1956 Mr. Jonathan Wolcott, advertising manager of Rust Craft Publishers, Inc., reviewed the company's advertising and sales promotional plans in the light of principal trends in the greeting-card industry and with a view to determining the extent to which advertising should be used in marketing the company's line of greeting cards in 1956 and 1957.

The Greeting-Card Industry

The greeting-card industry had its inception around the turn of the century when several publishers began to specialize in the manufacture and marketing of greeting cards. Until the 1920's the industry grew slowly. In the 1920's the industry's trade association, to which all the principal publishers belonged, undertook a co-operative program of advertising. This program consisted of full-page advertisements in women's and general-circulation magazines which were aimed at educating the public to a more extensive use of greeting cards. Whether the program was particularly effective was not known, but greeting cards did begin to catch on with the public. By 1939 industry sales at retail were $80 million.

At the beginning of World War II a new trade association was organized to take the place of the old, which had become extinct, and it devoted itself to the stimulation of demand for greeting cards through various public relations activities. Its directors believed that consumer advertising

---

[1] Written by Gerald A. Simon and Martin V. Marshall.

was the responsibility of member companies. By 1947 industry sales at retail were estimated to be $200 million, and by 1955, $375 million. Sales of $400 million were forecast for 1956, the industry looking forward to a continued increase in demand for greeting cards.

The Greeting-Card Market. In 1956 only a limited amount of information was publicly available concerning the nature and size of the greeting-card market. One of Rust Craft's principal competitors, Norcross, Inc., sponsored a study of greeting-card shopping patterns among a group of 1,264 women in 1956.[2] This study indicated usage of various types of greeting cards as follows:

Card Type	Per Cent of All Women Sending Card Type	Average Number of Cards Sent per Year
Christmas	90%	67 cards
Valentines	49	8
Easter	35	7
Mother's Day	52	2
Father's Day	44	2
Birthdays	79	13
Illness	55	9
Sympathy	47	5
Anniversaries	40	4
Congratulations	37	5

The study indicated that 98% of all women used cards for some purpose. Usage tended to be relatively high among women with high incomes, good educations, and urban homes. The urban buyer tended to spend more per card than the rural buyer.

In getting at the question of where do women purchase cards, the study divided the sample into two groups: heavy and light buyers. "Heavy" card users included 35% of the sample, which accounted for 56% of the sample's total expenditure for cards. "Light" card users included 65% of the sample, which accounted for 44% of the sample's total expenditure. A summary of sources of purchase follows:

Where Bought	1955 Christmas Cards*	Usually Buy Other Kinds of Cards
Door-to-door, church, school, friends	33%	11%
Five- and ten-cent stores	21	28
Department stores	13	10
Drugstores	10	20
Others (including bookstores and gift shops)	10	9
Stationery stores	8	14
By mail	7	2
Greeting-card stores	5	9

(Percentages of all women not of sales volume.)
* Percentages add up to more than 100% as a result of duplication in shopping habits.

[2] Adapted by permission of the Norcross Company.

In answer to the question of why do women buy at one store rather than another, the study stated that women shopped for greeting cards in department, stationery, and greeting-card stores because they expected a wider selection of better-quality cards in those stores, and for convenience, price not being a major factor. Women shopped for greeting cards in drugstores primarily because of the neighborhood convenience and, secondarily, for a wider selection; price again was not a major factor. Women shopped for greeting cards in 5- and 10-cent stores in the hope of finding cheaper cards.

Manufacturers' Distribution Policies and Sales. Throughout the period between the two World Wars, there had been three distinct types of greeting-card manufacturers, as categorized by their method of distribution: (1) those selling boxed assortments of cards to consumers through door-to-door canvassers or agents; (2) those selling to 5- and 10-cent stores, variety chains, and jobbers; and (3) those selling to independent retailers. The third group had included Rust Craft Publishers and its major competitors and comprised most of the large companies in the field. After World War II, however, a number of publishers which had previously sold only to independent retailers began to regard other types of retailers as potential outlets. By 1956 their cards had appeared in variety and drugstores and in supermarkets, of which 59% were reported to have greeting-card departments.

In 1955, according to an industry source, ten companies out of a total of about 400 produced over 50% of the industry's sales, whereas in 1938 the top ten had accounted for 75%.[3] Although it was difficult to obtain sales figures of the major greeting-card publishers, industry executives believed that Hall Brothers and American Greetings competed for the industry's sales leadership with sales in the range of $21 million to $25 million a year.

Hall Brothers sold direct to retailers only, while American Greetings sold only through jobbers who served about 49,000 dealers, many of which were of the corner drug and candy store variety. It was reported that American Greetings' 1956 sales per account were running 47% ahead of the 1952 rate and that sales per thousand population were $168 as compared to $22 in 1944. Norcross, Inc., Gibson Art Company, and Rust Craft Publishers, Inc., all of which sold direct to retailers, were the next largest publishers, with reported sales of about $11 million each in 1955. Of these five publishers, reliable greeting-card sales figures and other financial information was available only for American Greetings and Gibson Art Company, as given in Exhibit 1.

According to the industry source referred to above the remaining five of the top ten manufacturers distributed their cards by means of canvassers or agents; these companies were Harry Doehla and Company,

---

[3] *Barron's*, December 19, 1938.

Cheerful Card Company, Artistic Card Publishing Corporation, Chilton Greetings Company, and Wallace Brown, Inc.

Advertising of Cards. As stated above, the trade association of the industry had taken the position that the advertising of greeting cards, if any, was the responsibility of association members. Between the two World Wars, there was little consumer advertising. After World War II many manufacturers began to advertise to consumers, some heavily as

Exhibit 1

SELECTED FINANCIAL DATA, AMERICAN GREETINGS AND GIBSON ART COMPANY, 1946–55
(In Thousands of Dollars)

	AMERICAN GREETINGS*			GIBSON ART COMPANY		
	Sales	Net Income after Tax	Net Worth	Sales	Net Income after Tax	Net Worth
1955.........	$21,454	$1,600	$9,249	$11,152	$ 707	$6,692
1954.........	18,149	964	8,148	10,630	761	6,489
1953.........	16,222	941	....	10,214	821	....
1952.........	14,426	901	....	9,455	814	....
1951.........	12,844	984	....	8,858	811	....
1950.........	11,145	1,130	....	8,630	1,024	....
1949.........	10,151	717	....	8,773	1,236	....
1948.........	7,068†	863†	....	8,185	1,027	....
1947.........	5,837‡	482‡	....	6,211	707	....
1946.........	9,104‡	988‡	....	7,417	1,099	....

* Includes American Color Process Division which made printing plates.
† Eight months to February 28.
‡ Years to June 30.
Source: John Moody's *Industrial Manual,* 1956.

shown in Exhibit 2. Hall Brothers, Inc., publishers of the "Hallmark" brand of greeting cards, decorated note papers, and gift wrappings, had consistently spent more on consumer advertising than had any other company. Hall Brothers' annual expenditure typically accounted for between one half and two thirds of the industry total.

In 1946 Hall Brothers began sponsoring a Sunday afternoon national network radio program featuring stage and screen stars in *Reader's Digest* dramatizations. Hall Brothers used network radio as its major medium of advertising until 1952 when the "Hallmark Hall of Fame" television program became the company's major advertising vehicle. This national network one-hour program featured well-known players, such as Sarah Churchill and Mary Martin, in live plays of high quality. In 1956 it became known that Hall Brothers would probably produce the program in color, but with a reduction in frequency because of the expense of color.

"When you care enough to send the very best" was the Hallmark slogan during the postwar years and was expressed in all the company's advertising. Magazine and newspaper advertisements also helped to remind

Exhibit 2

NATIONAL ADVERTISING EXPENDITURES, GREETING-CARD COMPANIES SPENDING $25,000 OR MORE ANNUALLY, 1946, 1950–55

	1946	1950	1951	1952	1953	1954	1955
American Greeting Publishers, Inc.	$ 76,820	$ 92,200	$ 25,875	$ (215,892)	$ (285,384)	$ 58,061	$ ......
Artistic Card Publishing, Inc.	27,436	(94,530)	(108,224)	108,446	70,838	(336,582)	$ (332,417)
Copy: Artistic cards	......	46,881	52,578	107,446	214,546	249,581	288,085
Friendship cards	......	47,649	55,646	......	......	2,875	......
Hycrest cards	......	......	......	......	......	40,400	25,304
Stylart cards	......	......	......	......	......	15,224	18,025
Syracuse cards	......	......	......	......	......	28,502	1,003
Brown, Wallace, Inc.	28,586	154,600	82,333	88,806	147,523	191,151	183,741
Cheerful Card Company	......	67,856	140,553	210,239	170,393	219,219	218,476
Chilton Greetings Company	......	89,509	88,634	104,057	95,928	147,299	121,174
Doehla, Harry, Company	34,657	239,213	219,656	127,803	131,903	179,718	206,380
Empire Card Company, Inc.	......	......	......	......	......	......	27,088
Gibson Art Company	61,000	231,366	277,855	270,935	262,270	275,935	121,129
Hall Brothers, Inc.	(598,981)	(781,773)	(954,377)	(2,044,350)	(1,849,106)	(2,641,382)	(1,558,938)
Copy: Contest	......	......	......	......	2,030	11,325	80,950
T.V. program	......	......	......	......	......	4,200	......
Greeting cards	598,981	781,773	713,886	2,044,350	1,847,076	2,549,554	1,477,988*
All products	......	......	94,770	......	......	......	......
Retail	......	......	......	......	......	10,250	......
Copy breakdown not given (in newspaper and supplement media only)	......	......	145,721	......	......	......	......
Merit Greeting Card Company	......	29,289	......	......	......	66,053	62,514
Messenger Corporation	......	......	......	......	29,476	25,777	37,842
Munson, Inc.	......	......	......	......	......	120,564	......
Norcross, Inc.	152,487	184,129	83,420	52,082	84,833	223,438	306,672
Phillips Card Company, Inc.	......	25,803	66,308	100,850	121,954	25,935	88,861
Rust Craft Publishers, Inc.	......	55,951	......	......	......	......	......
Total	$979,967	$2,046,219	$2,047,215	$3,215,014	$3,387,437	$4,324,497	$3,365,232

* Includes $174,486 for network radio measured from January to July 1955 only.

Source: *National Advertising Investments*, 1946, 1950–55; *Expenditures of National Advertisers in Newspapers*, 1950–54; *Printers' Ink*, May 25, 1956.

consumers to tune in Hallmark broadcasts. Trade publication advertising was also built around the programs and urged dealers to identify their stores as headquarters for Hallmark cards, offering them in-store advertising materials for this purpose. Dealer co-ordination with Hallmark advertising was further encouraged by the offer of free newspaper mats. Members of the industry considered that Hall Brothers had done an outstanding job in their consumer advertising and in their promotion of this advertising to dealers.

From 1943 to 1951 the Norcross company had made widespread and consistent use of small-space newspaper advertising, usually picturing one of several distinctive characters, such as "Lanky Lil," found only on Norcross cards. In 1952 and 1953 Norcross discontinued consumer advertising and devoted its efforts to trade papers and to providing dealers with large lithographed window centerpieces free of charge. For a short while in 1954 and 1955 Norcross participated as one of three sponsors of the "Omnibus" television program, but this sponsorship was discontinued in 1955.

Although Norcross produced quality greeting cards, this fact was not especially emphasized in Norcross copy. Norcross' main copy theme was the high acceptability of Norcross greetings cards on the part of recipients.

The Gibson Art Company between 1951 and 1954 employed monthly four-color, full-page insertions in *Life* magazine, but the company's expenditure was considerably reduced in 1955 when the company's management underwent a change. For Gibson's *Life* campaign, top-flight artists were employed to portray sophisticated and appealing men and women examining newly received Gibson cards. In 1955 Gibson used television for the first time, spending about $50,000 in the medium.

In 1954 the Munson Company embarked upon a national advertising program, budgeting $1,098,000 for general circulation and women's service magazines, food and drug trade papers, local radio and television spot commercials, and locally originated 15-minute filmed television programs featuring The Continental, a suave charmer of the feminine audience. In addition, the Munson Company hired a dealer sales force and built a carousel-type revolving display for its cards, all of which were priced at 15 cents, and achieved significant distribution by means of a dealer consignment plan. As of early 1956, however, industry executives were no longer aware of Munson brand advertising or retail distribution.

A dollar and percentage analysis of the industry's use of national media for 1946 and 1950–55 is given in Exhibit 3, and media usage of individual companies in 1955 is given in Exhibit 4.

The Rust Craft Company

Rust Craft Publishers was one of the first companies to undertake the large-scale manufacture of greeting cards, starting in Kansas City in

Exhibit 3

DOLLAR AND PERCENTAGE ANALYSIS OF GREETING-CARD INDUSTRY NATIONAL ADVERTISING MEDIA USAGE, 1946, 1950–55*

DOLLARS

Media	1946	1950	1951	1952	1953	1954	1955
Magazines..........	$(204,609)	$(849,240)	$(909,567)	$(1,059,486)	$(1,083,287)	$(1,114,540)	$(859,304)
General...........	200,680	811,590	875,942	1,045,619	1,078,587	1,103,256	833,716
Farm.............	3,929	37,650	33,625	13,867	4,700	11,284	25,588
Newspapers and supplements.....	230,365	514,025	349,587	417,713	614,572	593,240	804,821
Network radio.....	544,993	682,954	664,011	642,675	637,048	556,598	174,486†
Network television.....	....	....	124,070	1,095,140	1,052,530	2,060,119	1,526,621
Total.........	$ 979,967	$2,046,219	$2,047,235	$ 3,215,014	$ 3,387,437	$ 4,324,497	$3,365,232

PERCENTAGES

Media	1946	1950	1951	1952	1953	1954	1955
Magazines..........	(20.9)%	(41.5)%	(44.4)%	(32.9)%	(32.0)%	(25.8)%	(25.5)%
General...........	20.5	39.7	42.8	32.5	31.8	25.5	24.8
Farm.............	0.4	1.8	1.6	0.4	0.2	0.3	0.7
Newspapers and supplements.....	23.5	25.1	17.1	13.0	18.1	13.7	23.9
Network radio.....	55.6	33.4	32.4	20.0	18.8	12.9	5.2†
Network television.....	....	....	6.1	34.1	31.1	47.6	45.4
Total.........	100.0%	100.0%	100.0%	100.0%	100.0%	100.0%	100.0%

* Space and time expenditures only of companies spending $25,000 or more annually.
† Measured only from January to July 1955.

Sources: National Advertising Investments, 1946, 1950–55; Expenditures of National Advertisers in Newspapers, 1950–54; Printers' Ink, May 25, 1956.

Exhibit 4

SPACE AND TIME EXPENDITURES IN NATIONAL MEDIA OF GREETING-CARD ADVERTISERS SPENDING OVER $25,000, 1955

Agents Wanted Copy		Magazines			Newspapers and Supplements	Network* Radio	Network Television	Total
		Total	General	Farm				
x	*Artistic Card Publishing Corporation*	$(94,054)	$(94,054)	....	$(238,363)	....	....	$ (332,417)
x	Artistic cards	94,054	94,054	....	194,031	....	....	288,085
x	Hycrest cards	....	....	....	25,304	....	....	25,304
x	Stylart cards	....	....	....	18,025	....	....	18,025
x	Syracuse cards	....	....	....	1,003	....	....	1,003
x	Brown, Wallace, Inc.	153,673	146,509	$ 7,164	30,068	....	....	183,741
x	Cheerful Card Company	110,678	105,224	5,454	207,798	....	....	318,476
x	Chilton Greetings Company	58,404	58,404	....	62,770	....	....	121,174
x	Doehla, Harry & Company	126,300	118,440	7,860	80,080	....	....	206,380
x	Empire Card Company	23,736	23,736	....	3,352	....	....	27,088
	Gibson Art Company	73,580	73,580	....	....	....	$ 47,549	121,129
	Hallmark Cards, Inc.	(128,299)	(128,299)	....	(83,753)	$(174,486)	(1,172,400)	(1,558,938)
	Hallmark cards—TV program	80,950	80,950	....	....	....	....	80,950
	Hallmark greeting cards	47,349	47,349	....	83,753	174,486	1,172,400	1,477,988
x	Merit Greeting Card Company	19,524	19,524	....	42,990	....	....	62,514
	Messenger Corporation	(36,442)	(33,692)	(2,750)	(1,400)	....	....	(37,842)
	Maria Studios cards	500	500	....	....	....	....	500
	Messenger calendar and greeting cards	702	702	....	....	....	....	702
x	General cards	34,990	32,240	2,750	1,400	....	....	36,390
x	Maria Studios	250	250	....	....	....	....	250
	Norcross, Inc.	....	....	....	....	....	306,672	306,672
x	Phillips Card Company	34,614	32,254	2,360	54,247	....	....	88,861
	Total	$859,304	$833,716	$25,588	$ 804,821	$174,486	$1,526,621	$3,365,232

* Measured only from January to July 1955.

Sources: National Advertising Investments, 1955; Printers' Ink, May 25, 1956.

1906 with the designing and publishing, by Fred W. Rust, of a Christmas card, which the company believed was the first modern twice-folded greeting card. Valentine and Easter cards were added in 1908; and later, with the publication of birthday congratulations, the so-called "everyday" or nonseasonal line was begun. This move was followed by the development of numerous lines of special-purpose greeting cards for year-round sale; and in this field the company was the first to issue cards for graduation, illness, and bon voyage.

The company moved to Boston in 1913, and as a result of expansion, occupied several buildings by 1955. In that year the company moved into the world's largest single-floor greeting-card plant, known as Rust Craft Park. The projected manufacturing capacity of Rust Craft Park was reported to be about 50% greater than the company's 1954 level of production.

In its early years the company had obtained 40% of its volume from a line of gifts, such as letter openers, lemon forks, and card cases in decorated boxes, each with a verse on the cover. The company had not manufactured these articles but merely packaged them. In the 1920's the company found its greeting-card business so much more profitable that the gift line was discontinued, and in 1956 its facilities primarily were devoted to the creation, manufacture, and sale of a complete line of greeting cards plus a small line of decorated note paper.

About 75 million Rust Craft cards were sold during 1955, sales of which represented a 12% increase over 1954 dollar volume.

Rust Craft's Product Line and Sales Policies. Rust Craft management, believing that it was essentially engaged in a fashion business, took pains to produce greeting cards which they believed to be of outstanding style and quality; a full-time staff of competent artists and verse writers were kept busy creating the thousands of new designs and verses continually required for the company's everyday and seasonal card lines. About one half of Rust Craft's sales volume came from the seasonal lines; the major ones were Christmas, Valentine, Easter, Mother's Day, Father's Day, and graduation cards, in that order, Christmas cards accounting for almost one half of the seasonal sales total. The remaining half of the company's sales were accounted for by sales of its everyday line, which included classifications such as birthday, wedding, friendship, and invitation cards. There were at least 3,000 different numbers in Rust Craft's greeting-card lines.

Rust Craft card lines were divided into counter cards (those sold individually) and packaged cards. There were seven packaged lines: boxed Christmas assortments; boxed Christmas single-design packs; boxed Valentine and Easter children's cards; cellophane-wrapped packs of Christmas, Valentine, and Easter cards. In addition, the decorated note paper line also was packaged in boxes. Boxed assortments typically gave consumers better value than did counter cards of the same quality bought separately, since production efficiencies resulting from longer press runs permitted giving such values. Although seasonal and everyday counter cards accounted for the major share of Rust Craft's sales, Mr. Wolcott believed that packaged card sales could be increased without seriously affecting counter card sales if supported by sufficient company and dealer promotion, although the rate of profits on packaged card sales was lower than the rate for counter cards.

Although Mr. Wolcott was convinced that good relations existed between Rust Craft and the other publishers selling to retailers, he recognized that competition had steadily increased in the postwar period. The two major steps to meet this competition had consisted of a reorganization of the Rust Craft sales force and a modification of the company's policy with regard to desired retail outlets.

The sales force had increased in size from 80 men in 1946 to 150 men in 1956, while the number of dealers had increased from 5,000 to 8,000. Salesmen were compensated on a straight commission basis with adjustments made for varying territorial account densities and for seniority. Whereas previously all salesmen had reported to the general sales manager in Rust Craft's Boston office, in 1954, 11 United States sales divisions were created, each in charge of a divisional sales manager supervising as few as six and as many as 20 salesmen. The hiring, training, and supervision of salesmen became the responsibility of the divisional sales managers. In addition, divisional sales managers assumed responsibility for develop-

Exhibit 5

RUST CRAFT PUBLISHERS, INC.

Percentage of Company Dollar Sales Represented by Dealer Classifications, 1947–54

Dealer Classification	1947	1948	1949	1950	1951	1952	1953	1954
Department	18.7%	18.5%	18.5%	18.0%	17.5%	16.6%	15.3%	15.6%
Variety	9.8	11.2	12.0	13.4	16.0	19.5	21.2	21.8
Gift	23.5	23.0	22.5	22.8	22.7	21.9	22.1	21.9
Stationery	18.2	18.3	18.5	18.1	17.3	16.0	15.6	15.2
Book	4.3	4.6	4.5	4.0	3.6	3.4	3.2	3.1
Drug	5.4	5.3	5.4	5.6	5.6	5.5	5.8	6.1
Camera	3.6	3.4	3.1	3.1	3.0	2.9	2.7	2.4
Jewelry	1.6	1.4	1.3	1.2	1.0	1.0	1.0	1.0
Florist	0.8	0.9	0.8	0.7	0.7	0.7	0.6	0.6
News	3.6	3.6	3.5	3.9	4.0	3.8	3.8	3.6
Candy	2.2	2.0	2.0	1.9	1.6	1.5	1.6	1.5
Music	1.3	1.2	1.2	1.0	0.8	1.0	1.0	0.9
Appliance	0.5	0.4	0.4	0.4	0.3	0.3	0.4	0.3
Religious	1.4	1.5	1.6	1.7	1.7	1.5	1.7	1.7
Miscellaneous	5.1	4.7	4.7	4.2	4.2	4.4	4.0	4.3
Total Dollar Sales	100.0%	100.0%	100.0%	100.0%	100.0%	100.0%	100.0%	100.0%

Source: Company records.

Exhibit 6

RUST CRAFT PUBLISHERS, INC.

Percentage of All Dealers Represented by Dealer Classifications, 1947–54

Dealer Classification	1947	1948	1949	1950	1951	1952	1953	1954
Department..........	10.0%	9.9%	9.3%	8.9%	8.5%	8.2%	7.9%	7.7%
Variety..............	10.4	12.3	13.5	15.7	18.6	21.0	22.8	24.7
Gift.................	22.6	23.2	23.3	23.0	22.8	22.1	21.8	21.3
Stationery...........	17.2	17.4	17.5	17.4	16.8	16.2	15.6	14.8
Book................	5.9	5.7	5.5	5.0	4.3	4.1	3.9	3.7
Drug................	7.9	7.9	8.0	8.0	7.7	7.5	7.4	7.7
Camera.............	3.3	3.1	3.0	2.8	2.8	2.9	3.0	2.9
Jewelry.............	4.7	2.7	2.6	2.1	2.0	1.9	1.9	1.8
Florist..............	1.3	1.4	1.3	1.3	1.2	1.2	1.2	1.1
News...............	3.8	3.9	3.6	4.0	4.1	4.1	3.9	3.8
Candy..............	2.9	2.7	2.6	2.4	2.1	1.9	2.0	2.0
Music..............	1.2	1.3	1.3	1.1	1.0	1.0	0.8	0.9
Appliance...........	0.4	0.4	0.3	0.3	0.3	0.3	0.3	0.3
Religious...........	2.2	2.2	2.2	2.4	2.5	2.5	2.6	2.4
Miscellaneous........	6.2	5.9	6.0	5.6	5.3	5.1	4.9	4.9
Total Dealers.....	100.0%	100.0%	100.0%	100.0%	100.0%	100.0%	100.0%	100.0%

Source: Company records.

ing new customers and cultivating dealer goodwill, formerly the job of several missionary salesmen. Although the sales reorganization increased company selling expenses, Rust Craft management believed that in the long run increased sales resulting from the reorganization would more than offset the increase in cost.

Rust Craft made every effort to adhere to a policy of distributing only to "quality" retail outlets. But the types of stores employed had changed somewhat. Whereas up to the post–World War II era, distribution had been limited to department stores, stationery stores, and greeting-card and specialty shops, the company by 1956 also sold to first-class variety and drugstores because of their high in-store traffic. For an analysis of Rust Craft dollar sales and customers, see Exhibits 5 and 6.

Despite these changes Mr. Wolcott considered that the company's primary sales mission had remained unchanged; the installation and maintenance of its retail stock control system by means of which Rust Craft's share of dealers' display space, and thus sales, could be maintained or increased.

Rust Craft's Stock Control System. Rust Craft, sharing the expense with dealers, for many years had installed and serviced a system of stock control which enabled retailers to plan a balanced display of cards in their display racks so as to maximize sales, and provided an orderly method of inventory filing and simplified reordering system in order to minimize inventory, thus having the over-all effect of increasing dealers' stockturn. Rust Craft executives were convinced that the system had enabled dealers to handle greeting-card lines more profitably and, as a consequence, had improved the credit standing of many of their smaller retail customers. While the Rust Craft company was the first to offer this system, all major publishers selling through retailers later adopted similar plans.

It was possible for dealers to have one publisher's stock control system installed and by means of that system purchase cards from other publishers. As a matter of industry practice, however, the installing publisher took the largest share of space in the display racks, hence explaining Rust Craft's and other publishers' interest in stock control installations. For example, Norcross in 1950 embarked on a program of supplying the greeting-card departments of department stores and other large retailers with one or two young men in Norcross' employ who helped to move stock and keep displays in order. As a result, Norcross succeeded in obtaining the greeting-card stock controls in most department stores with resultant increase in their share of each store's business. Personal in-store assistance by other publishers' salesmen, including Rust Craft's, usually occurred only during the busy holiday seasons.

In 1956 about 85% of Rust Craft's sales volume was obtained from stores employing some type of stock control system, and Mr. Wolcott thought that the proportion would approach 100% in a few years.

The company maintained perpetual inventory controls in over 100 retail stores from which, in addition to its national sales experience, it was able to compute optimum methods of display of the various everyday card classifications and price lines, e.g., Humorous First Anniversary— 15 cents, in order to try to match displays to consumer demand. During the installation of a control system each space in the dealer's display rack was numbered and reserved for a card classification and price, such as above, as agreed upon by the dealer and the salesman. The dealer would decide what proportion of his rack space was to be devoted to the individual publishers with whom he did business, and it was up to the installing publisher to carry out these instructions by allotting the rack spaces (and card classifications and price lines) to the publishers in the agreed-upon proportions. In operation each publisher chose the designs and verses to be offered in the rack spaces for which he was responsible, the dealer relying upon the publishers' self-interest to use the most salable designs and verses, both of which continually changed as the publishers vied for product leadership.

Although seasonal cards were not controlled, rack spaces were reserved for them and Rust Craft salesmen were able to recommend an assortment of classifications and price lines for each holiday season on the basis of past experience, retailers making their selections after reviewing samples of the lines from competing publishers. Mr. Wolcott had found that each dealer tended to allot his purchases of seasonal cards between competing publishers in the same proportion as those publishers were represented in his everyday stock control system.

Because of the expense of installation and the time consumed in setting up a new control system, dealers were not interested in changing their stock controls very frequently. The average life of dealer stock control installations, Mr. Wolcott believed, was three to six years. Therefore, Rust Craft salesmen in addition to selling new Rust Craft installations also attempted to increase the company's share of display space in existing installations, whether Rust Craft's or not. Otherwise, dealers tended to reorder greeting cards on the basis established at the time of installation. As a consequence, until a dealer had allotted to Rust Craft the rack space reserved for, for example, Humorous First Anniversary—15 cents, no amount of advertising would have any effect on Rust Craft's sales of the card to that dealer.

Despite the efficiency of publishers' stock control systems, not all everyday cards were sold to dealers "on control." Several publishers had found it desirable to increase their display space through the promotion of small groups of everyday cards of different classifications and price lines quickly identifiable by type of illustration, shape, and so forth. For example, Hallmark salesmen had installed small wire card-and-envelope holders in conspicuous positions on many of their customers' display racks and provided dealers with a monthly change in design and verse. Because of these cards' shape they were known as the "Slim-Jim" line; however, they were soon copied by the other major publishers and incorporated into their lines sold on control. As of early 1956 Rust Craft was not selling everyday cards off control in order to gain additional display space, as above, but was attempting to increase dealer stocks of a number of the company's fastest selling everyday cards so as to prevent dealers from running out of these items.

Rust Craft's Promotional Policy. Between 1947 and 1953 Rust Craft advertised to consumers by means of magazines in order to gain the advantage of full-color advertisements. The annual expenditure increased from $44,000 in 1947 to $122,000 in 1954. Copy performed a reminder function and when seasonal cards were featured expressed a seasonal theme. The slogan "Rust Craft greeting cards most truly express your sentiments" was regularly used. (See Exhibit 7 for a summary of the company's media and copy usage for the years 1946 to 1955.)

In order to consolidate the gains expected from the 1954 sales reorganization, Rust Craft management discontinued national consumer advertising in 1954 and stepped up its dealer promotion program. The discontinuance of consumer advertising was not a major change in the company's basic promotional policy, however. Emphasis had always been placed on working to and through dealers. Even the advertising undertaken between 1947 and 1954 had been initiated in the light of its probable effect on dealers rather than consumers.

The major elements of Rust Craft's promotional budgets for the years 1953, 1954, and 1955 are given in percentage form in Exhibit 8. Mr. Wol-

Exhibit 7

RUST CRAFT PUBLISHERS, INC.
Media and Copy Schedule, 1946–55

Year	Media	Insertions	Size	Number of Colors	Copy Everyday	Copy Seasonal
1946....	(No national advertising)					
1947....	Life	2	Page	4	x	
1948....	Life	1	Page	4	x	
	Ladies' Home Journal	2	Page	4	x	
1949....	Ladies' Home Journal	3	Two ½-page facing	4	x	x
1950....	Ladies' Home Journal	1	½ page	2	x	
	Woman's Home Companion	1	½ page	2	x	
	Woman's Home Companion / The Saturday Evening Post	1	Two ½-page facing	4		x
	Ladies' Home Journal	1	½ page	4		x
	Ladies' Home Journal	1	Two ½-page facing	4		x
1951....	Ladies' Home Journal	1	½ page	4		x
	Colliers	2	Page	4		x
	The Saturday Evening Post	1	½ page	4	N.A.	N.A.
		1	½ page	4		x
1952....	The Saturday Evening Post	2	½ page	4		x
	The Saturday Evening Post	1	Double-spread	4		x
	Ladies' Home Journal	1	½ page	4		x
	Ladies' Home Journal	1	Page	4		x
1953....	McCall's	12 ⎫				
	Today's Woman	12 ⎬ Small space		N.A.	N.A.	N.A.
	Good Housekeeping	12 ⎪				
	McCall's	6 ⎭				
	Life	2	Junior center spread	4		x
	Ladies' Home Journal	1	Page	4		x
	Nancy Sasser	1	Page	4		x
	"Buy Lines" in Ladies' Home Journal	2				N.A.
	Department Store Economist	6	Page	1 ⎫	Illness booklets 9-tier rack; service; New York Stationery Show	
	Modern Stationer	3	Page	1 ⎬		
	Modern Retailing	1	Page	1 ⎪		
	NRDGA Stores	1	Page	1 ⎭		
	Photographic Trade News	1	Cover and inside page	N.A.		

Exhibit 7—Continued

Year	Media	In-sertions	Size	Number of Colors	Copy	
					Everyday	Seasonal
1954....	Pacific Stationer	4				Monthly birthday; Christmas; Institute; 9-tier rack; New York Stationery Show; coupon ads
	Department Store Economist	5				
	Gift and Art Buyer	2	Four Christmas double-spreads in two colors and 28 pages in one color			
	Giftwares	2				
	Modern Stationer	3				
	Modern Retailing	2				
	Photographic Trade News	2				
	Southern Stationer	4				
	National Stationer	1				
	NRDGA Stores	1				
	Photo Dealer	2				
	Drug Topics	2	½ page			
	American Druggist	2	½ page			
1955....	Modern Stationer	4			N.A.	N.A.
	Department Store Economist	8				
	Pacific Stationer	2				
	Southern Stationer	1	Three full-color page inserts and 22 one-color pages			
	New Outlook Magazine	1				
	National Stationer	1				
	American Druggist	3				
	NRDGA Stores	2				
	Rust Craft Rustler	2				
	New England Purchasing Agents Association	1				

N.A.—Not available.
Source: Company records.

cott believed that Rust Craft's promotional budget, not including direct sales expense, tended to be fixed at about 3% of sales and that Norcross and Gibson followed the same practice while Hall used a higher percentage.

One of Rust Craft's principal dealer promotion activities was publication of an external house organ, *The Rustler*, which had been mailed to customers monthly for 30 years.

Other dealer promotion included the Rust Craft Institute, display mobiles, and "Rustie."

The Rust Craft Institute was started in 1954 and had as its objective the development of effective sales practices in greeting-card and stationery departments of Rust Craft's department store customers. About 100 co-operating department stores reported operating figures to an independent research company retained by the institute which were then summarized, analyzed, and returned to the co-operating stores by the institute. It was hoped that all 500 of Rust Craft's department store customers would eventually be institute members.

Three car-drawn trailers, known as display mobiles, had toured Rust Craft dealers throughout the United States, illustrating recommended methods of displaying and merchandising Rust Craft cards during 1954 and 1955.

In 1955 Rust Craft hired an attractive woman airplane pilot who had considerable public relations experience. Named "Rustie" by the company, she flew all over the country visiting dealers, opening new stores, attending trade shows, conventions, fairs, stock car races, and other pub-

Exhibit 8

RUST CRAFT PUBLISHERS, INC.

Percentage Breakdown of Promotional Budgets 1953–55

Item	1953	1954	1955
Free dealer helps................	16.9%	17.1%	19.3%
Charged dealer helps.............	5.3	6.7	6.5
"Rustler"......................	6.5	6.1	6.8
"Rustie".......................	....	....	0.1
Rust Craft Institute.............	....	....	8.0
Display mobiles.................	....	10.3	11.2
Sales contest...................	....	....	6.2
Miscellaneous promotions.........	3.4	2.1	4.4
Merchandising assistance.........	1.4	2.7	....
Trade and consumer advertising....	40.8	30.9	8.4
Publicity......................	3.6	3.0	4.5
General:			
Advertising payroll.............	20.2	19.2	22.4
Travel......................	0.3	0.4	0.7
Supplies and postage...........	1.6	1.5	1.5
	100.0%	100.0%	100.0%

Source: Company records.

lic events. The company planned to establish "Rustie" as the symbol of Rust Craft to dealers and to the public. *Sentiment*, known as "Rustie's magazine," was to be sent to Rust Craft dealers' salesclerks starting in 1956.

By the end of 1955 Rust Craft management decided that the reorganization of the sales force had proceeded to the point where the promotional dollars previously diverted from consumer advertising to the sales reorganization could be used elsewhere. As a result Mr. Wolcott reviewed the place of consumer advertising in the company's selling program.

If consumer advertising were to be used once again, Mr. Wolcott considered that it would be on a one- or two-year trial basis. If dealers stocked and featured advertised items, he would conclude that the campaign was generally successful. Consumers could not be expected, he believed, to be immediately influenced to go to a store and purchase greeting cards.

Any consumer advertising program, Mr. Wolcott believed, would also have to satisfy the long-range objectives of making it easier for Rust Craft salesmen to sell present dealers more of the line and having more worthwhile new outlets seek the company as a resource.

If Mr. Wolcott recommended the use of consumer advertising to Rust Craft's top management, he needed to suggest a budget and media. If he decided not to recommend consumer advertising, he needed to outline an alternative promotional program.

~~~

CASE 6: BAUMRITTER CORPORATION[1]

NOTE: *This case gives a detailed description of the marketing mix of a manufacturer of furniture. In analyzing the case, it is suggested that consideration be given, first, to the longer-term marketing strategy of the company and, then, to the shorter-term selling strategy. Questions to consider with respect to marketing strategy: (1) Has the company followed a sound product policy? (2) Has the company been successful in its attempt to change trade practices in the selling of furniture? (3) Do you think that Baumritter's management should make significant changes in its existing marketing mix? If so, what changes? Questions to consider with respect to selling strategy: (1) What relative emphasis has the company given to personal selling, advertising, and other promotional tools? (2) Has its selling strategy been sound? (3) What selling strategy should the company pursue in the immediate future?*

In April 1958 Mr. Daniel C. Brown, advertising and sales promotion manager of Baumritter Corporation, New York City, was reviewing the company's marketing and promotional strategies since 1951 preliminary to planning the company's 1959 advertising and promotional program. Mr. Brown had become advertising and sales promotion manager of Baumritter company, a manufacturer of home, hotel, and motel furniture, shortly after graduation from the Harvard Business School.

As a result of the review and preliminary consideration of alternative 1959 promotional programs, Mr. Brown raised the following questions: (1) Had the promotional strategy employed in the years 1951–57 been reasonably effective in implementing the company's marketing objectives? (2) The company's promotional strategy had focused on working to and through retailers: was this effort with retailers now adequate so that greater attention could be devoted to consumer advertising? (3) Was the company's consumer advertising program being properly

---

[1] Written by David W. Nylen and Martin V. Marshall.

handled, especially with respect to advertising Baumritter products jointly with manufacturers of noncompetitive products and with respect to the distinctiveness of Baumritter advertisements? (4) What should Baumritter do about the increasing desire of dealers for co-operative advertising allowances? (5) To what extent should the company attempt to place its products on television "giveaway" shows?

Background on the Furniture Industry—Manufacturers

In 1957 the wood, upholstered, and metal segment of the furniture industry[2] consisted of about 4,000 manufacturers, a majority of which had less than 20 employees. In 1954 these manufacturers had sales of approximately $2.1 billion (wood furniture not upholstered, $1.1 billion; upholstered furniture $633 million; and metal furniture $403 million). Manufacturers were concentrated in and around High Point, North Carolina; New York state; Chicago; and Grand Rapids. The industry was cyclical, and manufacturers' margins were usually low, particularly for the smaller firms. Pricing by manufacturers was highly competitive, and price concessions and special deals to individual retailers were not unusual.

Most furniture manufacturers did not produce a full line either in kinds or styles of furniture. Almost all manufacturers specialized in either upholstered (couches, chairs) or case goods (bedroom and dining room) furniture. Case-goods manufacturers, especially the smaller ones, often specialized in short-line groupings called "suites." Furniture manufacturers specialized also in terms of styles of furniture, usually producing either modern, traditional, or provincial. In recent years a few manufacturers had departed from a policy of specialization and had begun to produce more complete lines.

Most manufacturers made an effort to redesign some items in their lines at least twice a year. Some made only minor modifications of the occasional pieces in the line rather than the main items in the line; many made very extensive changes in an attempt to create obsolescence. Really significant design changes did take place in the furniture field periodically, however, as evidenced by the increased utilization of plastics and metals in furniture construction and the increasing popularity of modern-styled furniture.

Almost all furniture manufacturers sold through independent sales representatives who sold several competitive lines on a commission basis. (No manufacturer as of 1958 had established his own retail stores except for a few manufacturers of high-priced lines that had their own showrooms in major markets, and only a few manufacturers had their own sales force or franchised dealers.) As their principal selling tool, the in-

---

[2] The Commerce Department classified the furniture industry into household, office, public and professional, screens, shades and blinds, and miscellaneous. Wood and upholstered and metal furniture was included in the household classification which also included mattresses and bedsprings.

dependent sales representatives usually showed retailers glossy print photographs of each item in a line and then took orders. In addition to the use of independent sales representatives, most manufacturers displayed their lines at major furniture trade shows which were held two to four times a year in Chicago (the principal show), High Point, Grand Rapids, New York City, Los Angeles, Boston, San Francisco, and Jamestown, New York. These shows were attended by retailers from all over the United States who came in order to purchase merchandise, to get new

Exhibit 1

TRACEABLE ADVERTISING EXPENDITURES OF FURNITURE COMPANIES FOR 1957*

Company	Expenditure
Baker Furniture	$ 78,154
T. Baumritter	82,280
Cavalier Corporation	33,525
Craddak Furniture Company	62,890
Cushman Company	38,582
Drexel Furniture Company	394,094
Dunbar Furniture Corporation	73,083
Futorian Manufacturing Company	150,895
Henredon Furniture Industry, Incorporated	160,305
Herman Miller Furniture	45,875
Heywood-Wakefield Company	89,925
Kling Factories	120,290
Kroehler Manufacturing Company	892,282
Lane Company	644,743
La-Z-Boy Chair Company	36,175
Lewisburg Chair and Furniture Company	59,770
Mersman Brothers Corporation	56,190
Simmons (Hide-A-Bed)	396,916
Unique Furniture	31,895
White Furniture Company	59,218
Widdicomb Furniture Company	59,578
Willett	283,559
Woodard & Sons	85,434

* Includes general and farm magazines, Sunday magazine sections, and network television only.

Source: National Advertising Investments 1957.

ideas, to see new styles, and to plan their retail offerings for the coming season. Furniture shows had influence not only in terms of a retailer's initial purchases but also in terms of establishing his general pattern of re-orders for the rest of the season. Manufacturers generally agreed that there were far too many shows to participate in; on the other hand, they felt compelled to participate in a large number of shows because competition forced it and because inspection of photographs was not an entirely adequate basis for presenting items of furniture to retailers.

Furniture manufacturers were relatively unaggressive promoters as compared to manufacturers in many other industries. The branding of furniture had usually been resisted by retailers who wished to control consumer buying by keeping the influence of brands at a minimum. Retailers often removed manufacturers' brands from furniture, substituting their own retail trade-mark. Thus it was not always easy for manufacturers to obtain identification of their brands at the retail level by consumers. Most manufacturers were so small that they could not support promotional campaigns large enough to be effective. New furniture designs were copied quickly so that manufacturers found it difficult to differentiate their products. Most manufacturers had spotty distributions; thus it was difficult to promote except on a local basis. Few manufacturers advertised their brands to consumers. The traceable consumer advertising expenditures of furniture manufacturers for 1957 are given in Exhibit 1.

It has been estimated that in the 1950's the average promotional expense for the furniture industry was 8–10% of sales volume, of which 6–7% was for personal selling expense and about 1% was for advertising.[3] It must be remembered, however, that the marketing mix pattern was not uniform for all companies. The larger companies did more than a proportionate share of the industry's advertising.

Background on the Furniture Industry—Retailers

Retail marketing practices in the furniture industry had not changed significantly in decades. According to trade reports, furniture retailers had and did dominate the industry's selling practices. Generally speaking, retailers purchased their stocks on an individual item basis from many sources. Sources of supply were often played against each other on price. Items were displayed to consumers by retailers in a fairly haphazard manner, e.g., all tables were grouped together in the retail showroom, all sofas were grouped together, etc. Relatively few retailers displayed furniture in a room setting, as it would appear in the home; thus consumers were forced to imagine how the furniture would appear in use. Most items were not available on an open-stock basis, i.e., consumers could not buy furniture with the expectation that additional items of the same line or design could be purchased at a later date if desired. Most items were not available as a part of "correlated" line, i.e., the consumer could not buy pieces of furniture of the same design from one manufacturer for each room in the house.

In addition, many furniture retailers tended to price furniture on the basis of "what the traffic would bear," partially because the quality of furniture (and a reasonable price) was difficult to determine, even by an expert. Furniture was sometimes sold at prices that were out of relationship to its costs; price comparisons were frequently exaggerated when retailers undertook special sales, fire sales, trade-in sales, and so on. Finally,

---

[3] Kenneth R. Davis, *Furniture Marketing* (Chapel Hill: University of North Carolina Press, 1957).

many retailers operated as so-called "Borax" operations, essentially providing the public with furniture of poor design and quality, promoting credit as their principal appeal. Borax operations had gradually played less of a part in the industry, however, after World War II.

Evolution of Baumritter's Marketing Strategy

The Baumritter company was founded in 1932 as a furniture jobber, that is, a selling agent for manufacturers of furniture. As Mr. Nathan S. Ancell, president and cofounder, gained experience in the furniture field (he had been a practicing attorney before entering the furniture industry), he came to the conclusion that existing furniture industry marketing practices were unsatisfactory because they were not oriented toward the satisfaction of customer wants. Mr. Ancell thought that customer wants should be the starting point for the company's marketing program, that the company's entire organization should be designed to respond to what the consumer wanted, and that all business decisions, including such things as plant location, capital investment, and product planning, should be analyzed in terms of the consumer wants.

The furniture consumer, Mr. Ancell believed, was becoming smart, sophisticated, choosy, and culture-hungry. A woman knew what she wanted when she shopped for furniture, but because of industry marketing practices, she could not find furniture so displayed and promoted that it matched her concept. Mr. Ancell believed that furniture buying could be significantly increased if the furniture were promoted and displayed as a charming, beautiful home interior that showed a woman how furniture could be used in her home. Retailers had to be convinced to sell home decoration rather than a "bunch of sticks."

It became quite evident to Mr. Ancell in the early 1930's that this type of selling job could not be accomplished unless the company had complete control of its own integrated manufacturing operations and gained some control over the marketing of its products at the retail level. To gain this control, the company decided to take four steps that were significant departures from industry practice: (1) to buy and operate its own factories; (2) to design and manufacture correlated groups of furniture, i.e., a complete line of furniture of the same design for each room in a house, which would afford to retailers a furniture package which had excellent in-store promotion possibilities; (3) to market its products through a limited number of selected outlets; and (4) to develop the company's own sales force that would devote exclusive attention to Baumritter products and Baumritter retailers.

Marketing Strategy—Product Line

Baumritter's first step in implementing its consumer-oriented marketing strategy was to begin manufacture of its own furniture, thereby gaining control over product design, quality, and price. In 1935 the company purchased its first furniture factory in Beecher Falls, Vermont, and by 1937 the company had developed a correlated group of colonial furniture which was sold under the trade name "Ethan Allen." (This line through 1957 represented the important segment of the company's sales.) The Ethan Allen line started as an open-stock group of approximately 50 pieces, including upholstered and case goods and living-room, bedroom, and dining-room furniture. Throughout the next 20 years the basic design of the Ethan Allen line was maintained, only minor changes being made in the designs of individual pieces. Additions to the Ethan Allen line were made periodically, the most important being a modular group of items introduced in the mid-1950's. By 1957 the line had 250 pieces. No attempt was made to create artificial style obsolescence. New styles were introduced to reflect architectural changes and to satisfy changing consumer needs. Six pieces of the line are shown in Exhibit 2.

By offering a long-line correlated group, Baumritter gave its retailers the opportunity to become more specialized operators rather than to continue the practice of presenting consumers a few pieces of furniture from many unco-ordinated lines. A correlated group enabled the retailer to display what the consumer probably wanted to see: a co-ordinated decoration scheme for every room in the house, as it would appear in a home.

By 1948 sales of the Ethan Allen line had increased to a substantial level and the company decided that it should discontinue distribution of other manufacturers' furniture and base its business on its own products over which it had sufficient control to apply its marketing concept. In 1948 the company discontinued the selling of the "Daystrom" dinette furniture line, which it had helped to start in 1933, and whose merchandising and sales it had controlled until that time. When this line was dropped, it was the leading brand of dinette furniture and accounted for about 50% of Baumritter's total sales.

Also in 1948 the company introduced its second correlated line, "Birchcraft," a modern design. In 1954 the "Viko" line, a lower-priced metal furniture with plastic upholstery, was introduced. In 1955 the "Roommate" line was added—a transitional design. In 1957 the company introduced the "Waldorf" line, a line of furniture especially designed for use in hotels and motels. Pieces of each of these four lines of furniture are shown in Exhibit 3.

Because of the wide range of furniture offered by Baumritter, the company's lines of furniture sold pricewise from the low to the upper middle price ranges.[4] By 1957 the company had ten plants, all in small communities, which specialized in the manufacture of various pieces of furniture, thereby obtaining what management considered to be very efficient operations which allowed the company to be quite competitive in price.

[4] Medium-priced furniture was thought of as being in the following approximate price classes: bedroom sets (double dresser, mirror, bed, and mattress), $300; dining-room set (buffet, six chairs, table), $300; living-room set (sofa, two chairs), $300.

Exhibit 2

BAUMRITTER CORPORATION

3665

No. 3665 Plastic Top 4 Drawer Dresser Desk
Top 48" x 18½"–ht. 30"–wt. 129 lbs.

No. 3661 Plastic Top Three Drawer Chest
Top 30" x 18½", ht. 30"–wt. 102 lbs.
Three drawers carved to simulate eight.

the georgetown group

This Ethan Allen dormitory room in the Brown Nutmeg finish has perfectly matching Natcolite Nevamar plastic tops on the night table, chest, bookcase desk. Included are: No. 591 3/3 bed, No. 3670 night table, No. 3668 4 drawer chest, No. 3666 book case desk, No. 420 desk chair, No. 664 book case, No. 1644 Wall Saver chair.

No. 2848 Sofa
(No. 3848 in foam rubber)
Seat depth: 21½"–width 77½"–ht. 36"–wt. 185 lbs.

418

432

No. 432 Plastic Top Center Extension Table
Top 32" x 42"; opens with one 10" leaf to 32" x 52";
wt. 60 lbs.; seats 8. Shown with No. 425 Hitchcock Chairs.
Available only with wood top.

No. 418 Plastic Top Round Extension Table
Top 42" diameter; opens with one 10" leaf to
42" x 52"; wt. 62 lbs.; seats 6. Shown with
No. 447 Captains Chairs.
Available with wood top
as No. 408 Table.

Ethan Allen

the providence group

Maximum storage at minimum cost, is featured in this Ethan Allen hotel or institutional group which includes the No. 584 Bed (3/3 or 4/6), No. 3515 combination luggage rack-coffee table-bench, No. 3670 Nite table, No. 3660 Double Dresser with No. 549 Mirror (plate 44 x 28), 2801 Arm Chair, No. 3666 Bookshelf Desk and 448 Desk chair. Natcolite plastic tops in Brown Nutmeg finish on the 3515, 3670, 3660, and 3666.

Exhibit 3

BAUMRITTER CORPORATION

Selected Pieces of the Birchcraft, Viko, Roommate, and Waldorf Lines

Marketing Strategy—Retail Outlets

As a second step in implementing its consumer-oriented marketing strategy, the company, starting with the Ethan Allen line, began to develop franchised dealerships. By offering selected furniture retailers a valuable exclusive franchise in a local market on a given line, Baumritter gained a measure of control over retail practices which allowed the company to encourage retailers to accept its display, promotional, and selling techniques. Baumritter management believed that this strategy was effective in that it resulted in significantly better display in terms of exposing furniture to consumers as it would appear in the home, in better sales techniques on the part of retailers, and in better acceptance, execution, and follow-through of the Baumritter marketing strategy by management.

As the result of intensively soliciting dealers, by 1957 the company had 6,000 dealers, about one third of which were franchised dealers for one or more of the company's correlated lines. In addition Mr. Ancell had undertaken an experiment whereby a number of young men had been encouraged to establish medium-sized furniture stores based upon floor plans, selling techniques, and display methods developed by the company. These operations had been very successful, and Mr. Ancell was of the opinion that the company might advantageously expand this approach in the future.

Marketing Strategy—Personal Selling

As has been stated, furniture manufacturers traditionally had employed independent sales representatives to sell their products to retailers. Because the Baumritter company wanted to obtain specific kinds of display, promotion, and selling effort at the retail level, management decided to depart from traditional industry practice and developed its own sales force in the 1930's. Management tried to select capable men of proven ability who would be capable of operating on a fairly independent basis. A large percentage of these men came from industries other than the furniture industry and were selected primarily for their understanding of the over-all marketing approach and for a proven selling record in their former positions. In this way, management believed that helpful new ideas would be injected into the organization.

Salesmen were assigned geographical territories and were paid a straight commission—and they paid their own expenses. In 1957 the total annual compensation of the company's 40 salesmen averaged $22,000, the highest paid salesman receiving slightly in excess of $40,000 in commissions. Expenses of salesmen ranged from $4,000 to $5,000 a year.

Management directed the sales force primarily by educating its men to sell according to a planned sales technique, through use of sales supervision, through quotas which set up yardsticks for performance, and through supplying selling aids which helped salesmen sell along lines desired by the company.

Baumritter's Promotional Activities—1951–58

In 1951 when Mr. Brown became advertising and sales promotion manager, Baumritter did not have an explicit advertising and promotional program. Management strongly believed, however, that a well-devised sales promotional program could be a highly important element in furthering its marketing objectives and therefore gave Mr. Brown the task of building an effective program, recognizing that his job would be difficult because only limited funds could be made available for promotion.

Because of the prospect of limited budgets, executives made it a basic policy that promotional efforts were to be concentrated at first in only one medium or promotional device. Only when sufficient continuity and impact were achieved in the leading medium in a field would a second medium or promotional device be added. Thus, funds were to be concentrated with media and markets being added one by one rather than spreading the budget "buckshot" fashion.

As Mr. Brown initially appraised Baumritter's marketing strategy and the promotional program which would best implement it, he decided that the program should concentrate on making the Baumritter franchise more valuable to retailers: (1) by presenting a unified picture of Baumritter to the trade as a manufacturer of furniture rather than as a distributor of furniture, and (2) by assisting retailers in their selling effort by developing the company's brand names among consumers and by providing effective selling aids, promotional ideas, and publicity ideas. The intended results were to draw the dealer closer to the company and to make him more receptive to the company's marketing program.

In order to develop Baumritter's reputation as a manufacturing resource, the company began in 1952 to use one-third page advertisements every other week in *Retailing Daily*, a trade paper widely read by furniture retailers. This program was expanded so that by 1957 it consisted of 52 full-page advertisements a year in *Retailing Daily*. Then, in 1957, when management felt that it had established Baumritter's reputation as a manufacturing source rather than as a sales agency representing other manufacturers, management changed the copy theme to one which stressed the value of the Baumritter franchise to retailers. An example of a trade advertisement of the new campaign is given in Exhibit 4. Also in 1957, the company began to use additional trade media, the total trade program budget for the year being approximately $50,000.

Promotional Activities—Selling Aids

Throughout the years 1948–57, major attention was given to the job of providing the company's sales representatives and retailers with useful selling aids.

Exhibit 4

BAUMRITTER CORPORATION

An Example of a Trade Advertisement of the New Campaign to Furniture Retailers

---

Your business is selling, not buying

...but how do you sell most profitably?

Some retailers sell only by offering wood and fabric at a dollar or two cheaper than their competitors. Their result is usually a very low profit margin—and no consumer *loyalty*.

However, alert retailers are no longer in the business of selling items at low profit—they've switched to the far more profitable method of selling *ideas*. These retailers sell home beauty . . . offer a real decorator service to their customers . . . display so that women can visualize the beauty and charm of home furnishings in their own homes. These dealers don't worry about price cutting competition—their customers are married to them—are proud of the furniture they've bought. This technique of service, of real home assistance is the most profitable way you can sell. Once a retailer has established himself as the store that *must* be shopped for ideas and help, he can ignore the tumult and frustration of trying to fight unfair competition.

When such a retailer builds on the firm foundation of customer service—and backs it with the power and protection of a promoted Baumritter franchised line, his operation is inevitably a profitable one. He benefits exclusively in his area from the impact of consistent national advertising and promotion . . . his profits never are drained away by price-cutting on his franchised line!

Baumritter's entire program of franchises, merchandising, national advertising and dealer aids is geared to solidly support those retailers, who like ourselves, believe in selling home-comfort and beauty—not in selling an item. It is a continuing program on our part to help you move furniture off your floor—not just on it.

There are a limited number of Baumritter franchises available in some areas only. Get the facts.

Baumritter

171 Madison Avenue, New York 16, New York

Manufacturers of: Birchcraft Casual Modern • Ethan Allen Early American • Restocrat • Roomates • Valley Forge Colonial • Viko

This advertisement appears in Home Furnishings Daily, March 3, 1958
Prepared by Alfred Auerbach Associates.   #1-18-12

In 1951, since promotional funds were limited, Mr. Brown's initial project was to develop new retailer selling aids and a catalogue. He also devised a standard company logo to help present a unified picture of the company to the trade and consumers. Gradually, Mr. Brown developed a number of additional selling aids, including the following:

—Brochures on the company's lines of furniture for retailer distribution to consumers. For example, a 24-page, four-color brochure was available on the Ethan Allen and Birchcraft lines, showing various combinations of bedroom, living-, and dining-room furniture in proper settings and providing the consumer with floor plan layouts and furniture cutout pieces scaled to size so that the prospect could plan a room in Baumritter furniture.

—Envelope stuffers and four-color post cards for retailers to mail to their customers. These aids showed selected pieces of Baumritter furniture in proper settings.

—Newspaper mats for retailer local advertising.

—Catalogues. For example, the 1957 Ethan Allen catalogue had 97 pages, with line sketches, four-color photographs or black-and-white photographs of all items and pictures of effective retailer showroom and window displays, as well as miscellaneous general information of interest to retailers and consumers.

—Swatch books of upholstery materials.

—Selling tags, counter and hanging signs, and reprints of trade and consumer advertisements for in-store use.

Promotional Activities—Special Promotions

Several special promotions had been sponsored by the company to develop publicity and dealer participation, because such promotions appeared to be effective selling devices and could be undertaken at very modest cost. Dealer contests for the best store displays of Baumritter were used several times and resulted in a considerable number of special displays and advertisements. Baumritter convinced the National Homes Company, a manufacturer of prefabricated houses, to purchase Baumritter products to furnish model homes, thereby gaining sizable sales, a five-page joint-advertisement section with several other home furnishings manufacturers in *Living for Young Homemakers*, and two editorial features.

The most successful promotion used by the company was an "Ethan Allen Festival," which had originated in the spring of 1956 when the merchandising manager of Joske's, a Houston, Texas, department store suggested that he needed some type of special promotion that would capture the interest of consumers. Baumritter then conceived a display of early American weapons, costumes, flags, and a model of Fort Ticonderoga that would provide the basis for floor and window display, publicity in local media, and numerous other promotional pieces.

The Ethan Allen Festival was so successful when used by Joske's that Mr. Brown decided to build a series of Festival kits and make the Festival a major promotional activity of the company. Subsequently, eight kits were developed and a booklet was prepared to assist dealers in presenting the Festival. In addition, other selling aids for the Festival were developed, including:

—Life-size Ethan Allen figures which stores could use to direct store traffic to the Festival location.

—Decorator booklets for retailer distribution to consumers. With imprint, booklets were available for $40 a thousand; without, $38 a thousand.

—Color post cards for retailer mailing to consumers, at a cost of $10 a thousand with imprint.

—Newspaper mats.

—Catalogue signs for floor display, showing the complete Ethan Allen line.

—TV slides.

—Pig-in-the-Poke signs—a blown-up reprint of a magazine article on the construction of Ethan Allen furniture.

—Wood signs to identify displays of Ethan Allen furniture.

—Counter cards.

—Suggested publicity releases.

—Ethan Allen Vermont Maple Syrup, which stores gave out to the first 100 customers to visit the Festival. Retailers were charged $6.00 a dozen for eight-ounce cans and $12.50 for 72 two-ounce cans.

—A 26-minute film entitled "Journey of a Tree" for retailer use at sales meetings, women's club meetings, and so on.

By the end of 1957 about 100 stores had used the Ethan Allen Festival promotion including Joske's San Antonio store; B. Altman of New York; Titche Goettinger, Dallas; Bon Marche, Seattle; Scruggs, Vandervoort, and Barney, St. Louis; and J. W. Robinson, Los Angeles. In early 1958 all available Festival kits were scheduled for use by stores through the remainder of the year and a number of stores had requested the opportunity to use the Festival promotion a second time. The Festival was inexpensive to run, the major expense being the original purchase of items for the kits. Retailers paid most of the other expenses.

Each of the selling aids mentioned above and all promotion and publicity ideas were promoted in every way that Mr. Brown could think of, to sales representatives and retailers. He kept up a continuous flow of direct mail to representatives and retailers regarding each selling device.

It should be noted that until 1952 all of the company's promotion budget had been devoted to the various dealer aids and catalogues described in this section of the case.

Promotional Activities—Consumer Advertising

As additional promotional funds became available in 1952, Mr. Brown began to employ advertising in consumer media. The objective of this type of advertising was primarily to provide sales representatives and retailers with an additional selling tool and to provide a basis for encouraging retailers to run advertisements of their own in local media. The first advertisement was inserted in *Living for Young Homemakers* at the cost of about $2,000. Mr. Brown selected this publication because he believed that the company would gain more from frequent insertions in a lower circulation magazine like *Living for Young Homemakers* than less frequent insertions in larger circulation magazines such as *Better Homes & Gardens,* and because an advertisement in *Living for Young Homemakers* could be promoted to the trade just as effectively as one in *Better Homes & Gardens,* although the latter cost much more. He also felt that dealers were generally unaware of circulation figures and that

Exhibit 5

BAUMRITTER CORPORATION

An Example of a Consumer Advertisement Which Listed Baumritter Dealers—1956

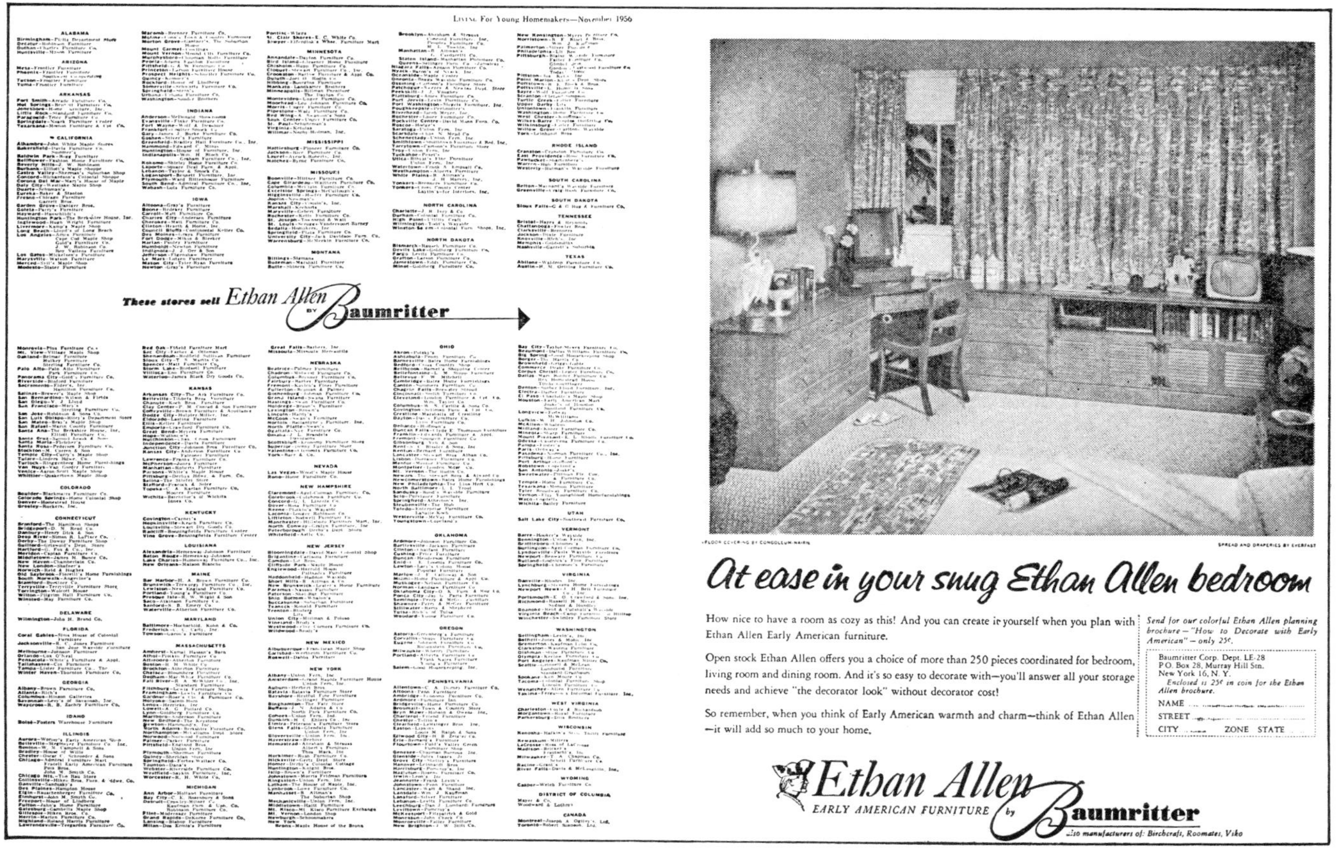

frequent pages in *Living for Young Homemakers* would be more impressive to them than fewer advertisements in a larger circulation magazine.

In 1953 the company decided to use a type of advertisement in *Living for Young Homemakers* which would include a listing of franchised Baumritter dealers on the opposite page. One of these advertisements is shown in Exhibit 5. The objective was to induce greater dealer promotional effort—a dealer's name would be listed only if he contractually agreed (1) to run an advertisement of his own in local media, and (2) to use a window display of Baumritter furniture. About 300 of the company's 1,500 dealers agreed to participate in the plan, and about 75% lived up to the agreement. In the following two years, however, the effectiveness of the plan decreased and the percentage living up to the contract dwindled to about 40%, at which time it was decided to discontinue the plan.

Starting in September 1953, Mr. Brown experimented with another type of advertising in consumer media which essentially consisted of co-operating with manufacturers of "Artloom" carpets, "Cameo" curtains, and "Devoe" paints. The basic advantage of this type of advertisement was that for the cost of one full page, the company's product appeared on four consecutive pages, thus making the most of a limited consumer advertising budget. However, since each manufacturer wanted a type of illustration which would feature his product in a particular way, it was necessary to compromise on illustrations so that they were not always as effective as Mr. Brown desired. In spite of these difficulties, he believed that the joint advertisements were very worthwhile, especially since he was attempting to stretch the advertising budget to the maximum. Subsequently, he experimented with joint one-page advertisements, wherein Baumritter advertised jointly with two other noncompetitive manufacturers. An example of a joint one-page advertisement is given in Exhibit 6.

Most of the company's consumer advertisements included coupons by which a booklet on Baumritter furniture could be ordered for 25 cents. Advertisements and media were evaluated in terms of inquiries, and the leads developed were turned over to dealers to follow up.

In 1953 and 1954 the company spent about 25% of its total promotion budget on advertising in consumer media, and in 1955–57 about 33%.

According to Mr. Brown, a consumer advertisement was the basis upon which an extensive promotion program was built. The promotion program had two purposes: to make dealers aware of the consumer advertising program and its potential value, and to encourage dealers to tie in with the national advertising by running advertisements of their own at the local level. For each national advertisement that was run, at least two or three mailings were made to dealers calling their attention to the advertisements, urging them to tie in with advertisements of their

Exhibit 6

BAUMRITTER CORPORATION

An Example of a "Joint Ad"

Proud of its heritage, and so practical too!

Warmth and a mood of relaxation make this enchanting bedroom a
haven of welcome at day's end. It's so comfortable to live with charming Early American.
And so easy to create yourself. The lovely Jean McLain wallpaper by
Imperial and the rich simplicity of the Ethan Allen furniture by Baumritter
together capture colonial charm for modern living.

Ethan Allen
Baumritter

Add new comfort, new charm and warmth to your home with Ethan Allen Early American furniture by Baumritter. This open stock collection offers more than 250 pieces for bedroom, living room and dining room—so you can make your starter purchase now, fill in later. Ethan Allen is so rewarding to plan with, too—your home will have the decorator look without decorator cost! Remember—when you think of Early American, think of Ethan Allen.

IMPERIAL
Washable
WALLPAPERS ®

How shall I do my walls? With Imperial you can decorate to mirror your taste best. Wonderful textures and designs are yours to use for delightfully different effects. Call on them rather than color alone. And, in return, they will refresh you—never bore you. It's so easy to create real charm and to bring real warmth to your home with the wizardry of Imperial. Let your Imperial dealer show you a few exciting possibilities. See opposite page for more facts on Imperial Wallpapers. Pattern illustrated is #877271.

MORE HELP FOR THE HOME DECORATOR!

For full color decorating booklet, "How Wallpaper Works Wonders In Your Home," send 10¢ to Imperial Paper and Color Corp., Dept. E-20, Glens Falls, N. Y.

For colorful Ethan Allen decorating brochure, "Planning Your Home With Early American," send 25¢ to: Baumritter Corp., Dept. LE-38, P. O. Box 28, Murray Hill Station, New York 16, N. Y.

Ethan Allen featured on cover of

LIVING
FOR YOUNG HOMEMAKERS

WESTERN UNION
SENDING BLANK

DEAR ETHAN ALLEN DEALER:

ETHAN ALLEN TO APPEAR ON "END OF THE RAINBOW T.V. PROGRAM
FEBRUARY 15TH FEATURING LIVING ROOM, BEDROOM AND DINING ROOM
FOR FULL MINUTE EXPOSURE. PROGRAM OVER COMPLETE NBC-TV
NETWORK. WONDERFUL OPPORTUNITY TO TIE-IN WITH AD AND WINDOW
DISPLAY ON YOUR OWN.

DAN BROWN
BAUMRITTER CORPORATION

Baumritter *Manufacturers of bedroom dining room living room furniture*

BAUMRITTER CORPORATION
171 MADISON AVENUE
NEW YORK 16, NEW YORK

PLEASE ADDRESS YOUR REPLY TO THE WRITER

October
10th
1957

Dear ETHAN ALLEN Dealer:

Over a million and a half people will see the beautiful exhibit
of ETHAN ALLEN Furniture on the Pier where MAYFLOWER II is
anchored in New York City.

This reconstruction of the original Pilgrim ship is drawing
tremendous crowds and every person who visits the ship must
pass our display which features an attractive living-dining
room and child's room.

The attached folder is being given to all visitors to our
display mentioning your name as a source for ETHAN ALLEN.
To get still more benefit, however, we are sending you under
separate cover, 40 discount tickets which you can offer to
your customers. A fine new window and a newspaper ad will
bring you a great deal of additional traffic and an opportunity
to expose your ETHAN ALLEN display to many more prospects.

If you want any other tickets, please let us know. Please
send us a copy of your ad. We are interested to see how
you have capitalized on this opportunity.

Lots of luck!

Sincerely,

BAUMRITTER CORPORATION

DANIEL C. BROWN
Advertising & Sales Promotion Mgr.

BAUMRITTER FAMOUS BRANDS
Barkcraft · Ethan Allen · Facsimodes · Valley Forge · Viko

PLEASE TYPE OR WRITE PLAINLY WITHIN BORDER—DO NOT FOLD

own, and offering dealer aids and display pieces. Exhibit 7 shows typical promotional mailings. In addition, the Baumritter salesmen promoted the company's advertising program to dealers, using a presentation kit showing consumer advertising insertion schedules, copies of advertisements, and dealer aids then available.

The promotion of consumer advertisements was designed to achieve the maximum results from the limited budget. Mr. Brown felt that one measure of success was the degree of which retailers had tied in with advertisements in local media. Results since 1952 were as follows:

	Baumritter Consumer Advertising	Retailer-Paid Local Advertising
1952..........	$ 2,000	$ 88,600
1953..........	42,000	152,000
1954..........	44,000	195,000
1955..........	94,000	237,000
1956..........	110,000	280,000
1957..........	126,000	361,000

In 1958 for the first time the company gave each salesman a quota of local advertising to be placed by dealers. Simultaneously the company's most aggressive merchandising campaign was launched, 45 to 50 mailings being sent to dealers during the spring. The mailings promoted a "mat of the month" and specific advertisements in different magazines. In addition, the company had promotional letters and direct-mail pieces written by the various magazines in which it advertised.

A salesmen's contest based on their advertising quotas and a dealer advertising contest were co-ordinated with this program. Salesmen received monthly reports on all advertisements run in their territories by brand and their performance percentage against their quota. They also received copies of all advertisements from their territories and frequent personal memorandums, bulletins, and copies of all direct-mail literature that went to their accounts. By receiving copies of advertisements from their areas, they were able to know which specific dealers were or were not running advertisements and thus were able to concentrate their efforts to obtain more local advertising.

The results of the increased campaign for the first four months of 1958 were as follows:

	JANUARY THROUGH APRIL		
	1957	1958	
Retailer linage..............	805,632	1,034,429	+29%
Number of ads run..........	2,736	3,933	+44%
Cost to retailer..............	135,480	186,057	+38%

In 1953–54, Baumritter launched a new group of furniture for its newly established contract department. A dealer-listing advertisement was run in *Tourist Court Dealer* to introduce the line. (The advertisement is given in Exhibit 8.) Dealers were listed in the advertisement if they agreed to buy a given number of furniture sets and some four-color post cards. Over 1,800 groups of furniture were sold in this manner. In 1957, joint advertisements were run in the contract field with Devoe paint and "Masland Vinyl" upholstery. The advertisements were extensively promoted by direct mail and through the contract line sales force.

The 1957 advertising budget for the contract field was $32,000 with the following schedule:

Tourist Court Journal	6 insertions
American Motel	6 insertions
College and University Business	6 insertions
Hotel Management	6 insertions

Because advertising funds were always limited, Mr. Brown constantly sought new budget-stretching ideas. Joint advertising was one budget-saving idea that had been used. In addition, when photographs were made for national advertisements, the same picture was also used for catalogues, consumer booklets, and promotional pieces such as color post cards, thus spreading the photographic and engraving expense over several times. The company also built its own photo studio and made its own sets, thereby saving the expense of a commercial studio.

Promotional Activities—Publicity

Mr. Brown co-operated very closely with trade and consumer magazine editors and with manufacturers of related products to develop publicity for Baumritter furniture. The company made its photographic studio and sets available to editors and "bent over backwards" to procure furniture for photographs, realizing that magazine editors worked on extremely close deadlines. Whenever an editor came to visit the company to see new lines of furniture, Mr. Brown personally escorted the editor during his visit. The result of these activities was a feeling of mutual co-operation that helped the company to place considerable publicity. Mr. Brown estimated that the company received three or four times as much publicity space as it used advertising space and for a fraction of the cost. Mr. Brown considered publicity space even more valuable than advertising space and promoted it in the same way.

Planning the 1959 Promotion Program

For 1958 Baumritter's management had given Mr. Brown a promotion budget of approximately $470,000 which included allocations for such selling devices as salesmen's kits, swatches, and catalogues. Although the 1958 advertising campaign was just starting, Mr. Brown had given con-

Exhibit 8

BAUMRITTER CORPORATION

An Advertisement Run Introducing the Company's Contract Department

wonderfully inviting room by BAUMRITTER

...and all 7 pieces for only $159.95

Now—an exciting, friendly room that means come-again business—and for amazingly little cost! Wonderfully simple to maintain, too—wear-proof wrought iron, Naxolite Nevamar plastic-top night table, dresser desk and luggage rack, plastic covered wall-saver club chair—laugh at scuffs and hard wear. No worries about alcohol or cigarette damage, either . . . this room will keep its fresh appeal and beauty indefinitely!

All pieces are of solid rock maple and birch woods finished in handsome light beige butternut tone.

You'll receive a roomy 48" 4 drawer dresser-desk, a continuous back post sturdy desk chair, night table, 4/6 headboard plus a pre-bored metal frame, comfortable wall-saver club chair, and a luggage rack which doubles as a coffee table—all 7 pieces for an almost unbelievable $159.95. This furniture available through your contract dealer.

Special 9 piece room with twin headboards and extra bedframe for $182.95.

All prices F.O.B. Factories.

Remember, no matter how difficult the problem, whether you plan redecoration or a complete new installation look to Baumritter first. Write for free contract booklet to Dept. TC-4

contract division T. BAUMRITTER CO., INC.

171 Madison Avenue, New York 16, New York

siderable thought to what changes should be made in the 1959 program, tentatively coming to the following conclusions:

1. The company was giving proper weight to promotional devices which would be useful to sales representatives and retailers; he had allocated about $265,000 for this purpose in 1958. As a result of a field trip in early 1958, Mr. Brown decided that in the area of promotional devices he should concentrate on making the company's catalogues a more effective selling tool on the sales floor, finding a better method of handling swatches, and reducing the weight of the salesmen's presentation kit.

2. The company's advertising in trade papers should be continued in 1959 approximately as in 1957 and 1958, in which years $32,000 had been allocated for the advertising of hotel and motel furniture and $18,000 had been allocated for trade advertising featuring Baumritter as a valuable franchise to retailers.

3. Mr. Brown was undecided whether or not he was gaining maximum advantage from his 1958 consumer advertising budget of $155,000. He wondered if in the future he should continue the program of co-operating with other manufacturers in joint advertisements and if he should participate to a greater extent in television giveaway shows.

Baumritter had used television giveaway shows in 1957 and 1958 to a limited extent, participating in "Bride and Groom" and "The Price Is Right" (at a cost of $200 a week in furniture) for about six months and a "Strike It Rich" contest for one month. In 1958 the company began to participate in a new television program called "Dotto" on which the company gave away $1,700 worth of furniture at cost in exchange for a minimum of 59 seconds commercial time for at least six consecutive days over the complete CBS network. Each of these commercials was worth approximately $9,000 in paid commercial time.

Giveaway shows worked as follows: Products such as Baumritter furniture were placed on the programs as quiz prizes by promoters, the product being donated by the manufacturer. Although promoters frequently received a fee for placing products on programs, Baumritter would not participate if it had to pay such a fee. The time devoted to "plugging" the product varied from a short mention to a 20- or 25-second message depending upon the program. In 1957 Baumritter had participated only in programs that promised the longer announcements on a continuous weekly basis. All programs on which Baumritter products appeared were audited by Mr. Brown, and the programs were heavily promoted to dealers. The furniture that was awarded to contestants was given through local dealers who received publicity in local media and an opportunity for follow-up sales. Dealers were encouraged to run local tie-in advertisements to take maximum advantage of the programs.

Mr. Brown believed that there were numerous opportunities to participate in such programs, and he felt that he could afford to spend up to $30,000 on them if they were effective. But since his over-all budget was limited, he was anxious to get the maximum value for his money. Mr. Brown also wondered if such promotional ventures as giveaway programs would really advance the company in achieving its over-all marketing objectives. As an alternative, he wondered if he should devote the money to another form of consumer advertising or to increase expenditures for dealer aids.

4. Mr. Brown was beginning to investigate the question of co-operative advertising which apparently was becoming more common in the furniture industry. He considered co-operative advertising as a last resort, to be used only if his promotional objectives could not be achieved in other ways and if competitive conditions forced it.

∿∿∿

CASE 7: STANDARD-TRIUMPH MOTOR COMPANY, INC.[1]

QUESTIONS TO CONSIDER: (1) *Would it be desirable to try to employ for the Triumph sedan and estate wagon the promotional strategy employed for the Triumph TR-3 sports car? (2) What should be the initial marketing mix for the sedan and estate wagon? (3) In the promotional program, how much emphasis should be placed upon working to and through the trade? (4) How much emphasis should be placed upon advertising? (5) If advertising to consumers is employed, what should be its objectives?*

In the latter part of 1957, Mr. Alan F. Bethell, president of Standard-Triumph Motor Company, Inc., New York City (which had been created in October 1953 as the United States sales and service subsidiary of the Standard Motor Company Limited, Coventry, England), was in the process of developing a sales promotional strategy for the "Triumph" sedan and estate wagon, a new line of "economy" cars that were to be sold in the United States beginning about January 1958. Mr. Bethell was particularly concerned with determining the role which advertising could play in the introductory program for the new Triumph cars.

Background Information on Standard's Marketing of Automobiles in the United States

Before World War II the Standard Motor Car Company manufactured and marketed a line of European-type motorcars under the trade name "Standard." In addition the company produced the chassis used by William Lyons to make "Jaguar" cars, an activity that helped to develop the interest of the Standard company in sports-type cars. After World War II, Standard resumed manufacture of Standard cars and began the manufacture of Triumph cars, that trade name having been acquired with the

---

[1] Written by Martin V. Marshall.

purchase of the Triumph Motor Company in 1945. The company's post-war cars were designed to be sold in the British and world markets which desired good quality and economical transportation. Until the early 1950's, no attempt was made by the company to sell cars in the United States be-cause Standard had adequate markets for its production in Great Britain and the world market.

Because approximately one half of Standard's sales were in overseas markets, Standard's management continuously studied automobile trends in each world market, including the United States, and in the early 1950's became convinced that the sports car market in the United States would shortly become a significant one. After World War II, many American servicemen and travelers to Europe had brought back European sports cars, primarily because of the appeal of a car which was designed for performance rather than comfort. Then, a few British motorcar manu-facturers, primarily Jaguar in the higher-priced field, and the British Motor Corporation with its "MG" in the lower-priced field, began to es-tablish United States sales outlets for sports cars, making sports cars more readily available to the American market. Within a few years after the war, by the early 1950's, there was general agreement among the trade that European sports cars were building an "imported car" market in the United States.

In order to gain experience in the United States market, Standard exec-utives decided in early 1952 to sell the "Triumph Mayflower," a two-door, four-seater sedan, in the United States on an experimental basis. At the time Standard did not attempt to build a special distribution organ-ization; the Triumph Mayflower was simply made available to United States foreign car dealers through an importing distributor. Because the Triumph Mayflower did not fit the needs of the market at the time (Americans were not yet interested in economy-type cars to any great extent), the company discontinued its experiment in 1953 and set out to design a sports car especially for the United States market. In October 1953 the Standard-Triumph Motor Company, Inc., was established in order that the company could build a good United States distribution setup, and in January 1954 the new sports car, the "Triumph TR-2," was introduced. It was priced initially at $2,499, F.O.B. East and Gulf Ports, and later as the Triumph TR-3, at $2,675.

Promotion of the Sports Car. In developing sales of the sports car, the company relied initially upon local promotion by Triumph distributors and dealers, word-of-mouth advertising of owners, and publicity. The company urged distributors and dealers to sponsor sports car road races in their individual markets, since these races attracted considerable con-sumer interest and created excellent publicity. Mr. Bethell believed that road races had been the most important promotional tool used by the company's dealers in 1954 and 1955, since the viewing of sports cars in action led many persons to begin to consider the possibilities of buying a sports car. The loyalty of Triumph owners was developed by establishing the Triumph Sports Car Owners Association, which released pertinent operating information on the car, helped to arrange sports car activities, and provided other information of interest to owners. Additional publicity was obtained by entering the Triumph in many sports car rallies throughout the world, such as, in 1954, the El Autodromo de Maracay in Venezuela, the Alpine Rally in Europe, and the Le Mans 24-hour race in France, and by frequent news releases to the press.

As sales and available promotional monies increased, greater use of consumer advertising and dealer selling aids was made. Consumer advertising was undertaken first in publications read by sports car enthusiasts such as *Sports Car Illustrated* and *Road and Track*, and later in publications read by a broader market, such as the *New Yorker*, *Holiday*, and *Time*. Consumer advertising was also undertaken in local media in as many as 25 of those markets which appeared to have high potential sales. Dealers were provided complete kits of selling aids, the kits including suggested radio commercials and newspaper mats, window streamers, showroom banners, display cards to sit or hang on cars, dealer salesmen's buttons, large posters emphasizing the features of the Triumph, and rally emblems. Because few foreign car manufacturers provided dealers with selling aids, Triumph's selling aids had been well received and widely used.

In the summer of 1957 Standard-Triumph employed a new sales promotional device, namely, a Triumph Rally of Europe. Under the sponsorship of the Triumph Sports Car Owners Association, arrangements were made to offer Americans a packaged tour of Europe in a new Triumph TR-3. Participants were provided a round-trip passage on a chartered airliner for $307 a person, a new Triumph TR-3 at London Airport for $600 less than the United States delivered price, and a guided three-week motor tour of Belgium, Germany, Austria, Switzerland, and France for $250 a person, the latter charge covering hotel accommodations, breakfast, and dinner. At the end of the tour, the cars were returning to the United States for a charge of about $150, including insurance. Eighty Americans participated in the tour, and they purchased 40 new Triumphs.

The tour received fairly extensive publicity, including a seven-page article in *Sports Car* magazine, the official publication of the Sports Car Club of America. As a result of the tour's success, Standard-Triumph's management decided to sponsor two tours in 1958 and prepared an eight-page, four-color brochure entitled "Tour de Force" to promote the tours. In late 1957 it appeared that the tours would be oversubscribed.

In the last few years, the company in practice spent about 50% of its promotional budget on national magazine advertisements and about 50% on local advertising, publicity, and dealer aids. The traceable advertising expenditures of the company for the period 1954–57 follow: 1954, $0;

1955, $77,845; 1956, $66,895; and 1957, $68,414. For the first six months of 1958, the company planned to increase its schedule of advertising for the Triumph TR-3. This schedule is given in Exhibit 1.

Exhibit 1

STANDARD-TRIUMPH MOTOR COMPANY, INC.

Schedule of Advertising for Triumph TR-3 for First Six Months of 1958

Medium	Jan.	Feb.	March	April	May	June
The New Yorker (National Edition)		1 p.	1 p.	1 p.	1 p.	1 p.
The New Yorker (City Edition)	1 p.	1 p.	1 p.			
Holiday			1 p.		1 p.	
Time	⅓ p.	⅓ p.	⅓ p.	⅓ p.	⅓ p.	⅓ p.
Sports Illustrated	1 p.	1 p.	1 p.	1 p.	1 p.	
Road and Track	1 p.	1 p.		1 p.		1 p.
Sports Car Illustrated	1 p.		1 p.		1 p.	1 p.
Motor Trend	1 p.		1 p.			1 p.
Sports Car	1 p.		1 p.		1 p.	

Source: Company records.

According to Mr. Chester Gore, president of the company's advertising agency, Gore, Greenland, Smith, Inc., the primary objective of Triumph TR-3 advertising was to invoke additional consumer interest in sports cars in order to broaden the market. Recent advertising had been designed to maintain the Triumph's racing image and to attract women by showing that the TR-3 fitted into her and her husband's way of life. Advertising was prepared with the Triumph dominating the layout, against background illustration which sought to associate the car with settings that suggested smart urban or suburban living. Exhibit 2 shows an advertisement which was run in the spring of 1958.

Triumph sports car sales had increased steadily after the car's introduction, as follows: 900 in 1954, 1,300 in 1955, and 2,350 in 1956. For the first ten months of 1957, sales were 5,300 cars, which represented the number-two share of market, 19.2%. The positions of principal competitors for the same period were: "MG," 11,615 cars, 44.6%; "Jaguar," 3,391 cars, 12.2%; "Austin Healey," 2,668 cars, 9.6%; "Mercedes-Benz," 2,587 cars, 9.3%; and "Porsche," 2,339 cars, 8.4%.

By the latter part of 1957, the Triumph TR-3 was marketed nationally through six distributors and about 450 dealers, with distribution being excellent except in the middlewestern states where all foreign car marketers had relatively limited distribution. Many trade papers referred to the Triumph TR-3 as "the hottest selling sports car in the market" in late 1957. Management was convinced that the car would hold the number-one sales position among sports cars by early 1958.

Exhibit 2

STANDARD-TRIUMPH MOTOR COMPANY, INC.

Example of an Advertisement of the Triumph TR-3 to Be Run in the Spring of
1958

The grandest thing about this new 1958 detachable Hard Top model is its remarkable, long-distance touring performance. More than a safe, economical driving pleasure . . . it's a true gentlemen's sport to let her out on the open road.

Traveling with plenty of trunk space behind, this weather-tight beauty is British-constructed for merciless hard driving. And you can "feel" every inch of it. Approaching a curve, you know when to let up on the progressive action of your disc brakes† . . . intuitively you snap the stubby gear-lever for a down-shift . . . your wheel-hand "feels" the turn as you start around . . . foot on pedal, you accelerate out of the curve with a roll-free security. Yet, for all this, the TR-3 is a straightforward car to service.

Once back in town, this tiger is as docile or spirited as traffic suggests. But if the gentleman in a TR-3 hangs back at a traffic light...forgive him ...it's only human to enjoy the admiring glances of passing pedestrians.

Soft top model $2675. plus tax and license at U. S. ports of entry. (Slightly higher West Coast ports.) Wire wheels, rear seat, white wall tires and overdrive, etc. optional extra
SPECIFICATIONS:
BRAKES: *Disc brakes on front wheels*†
TOP SPEED: *110 MPH* MILEAGE: *up to 35 MPG*
ENGINE: *4 cyl. (OHV) 1991 cc* OUTPUT: *100 BHP*
ACCELERATION: *0-50 in 8 sec.*
MAINTENANCE:
Parts and service available coast to coast! Free Brochure and dealer list on request. Write now—for fun!
†*A Triumph-plus . . . as standard equipment.*

STANDARD-TRIUMPH MOTOR COMPANY, INC., Dept. F 3, 1745 Broadway, (at 56th St.), New York 19, N.Y.

Exhibit 3

STANDARD-TRIUMPH MOTOR COMPANY, INC.

Information on Triumph Sedan and Estate Wagon

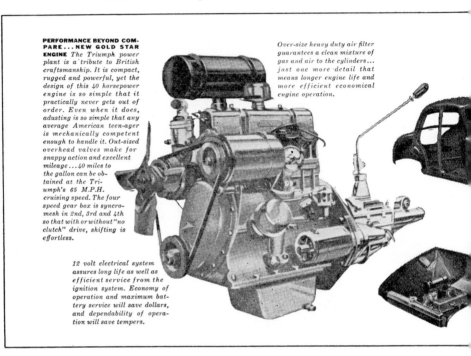

PERFORMANCE BEYOND COMPARE... NEW GOLD STAR ENGINE *The Triumph power plant is a tribute to British craftsmanship. It is compact, rugged and powerful, yet the design of this 40 horsepower engine is so simple that it practically never gets out of order. Even when it does, adjusting is so simple that any average American teen-ager is mechanically competent enough to handle it. Out-sized overhead valves make for snappy action and excellent mileage...40 miles to the gallon can be obtained at the Triumph's 65 M.P.H. cruising speed. The four speed gear box is syncromesh in 2nd, 3rd and 4th so that with or without "no clutch" drive, shifting is effortless.*

Over-size heavy duty air filter guarantees a clean mixture of gas and air to the cylinders... just one more detail that means longer engine life and more efficient economical engine operation.

12 volt electrical system assures long life as well as efficient service from the ignition system. Economy of operation and maximum battery service will save dollars, and dependability of operation will save tempers.

Decision to Market Economy Cars. While the Standard company was building its position in the sports car market, the so-called "economy," "utility," or "foreign" car market expanded suddenly in the United States. Before 1955 sports cars had outsold economy cars. Then in 1955 sales of economy cars increased to about 57,000 versus sales of about 13,000 sports cars. In 1956 sales of economy cars exceeded 100,000, and in 1957 promised to be well above 200,000 by the end of the year. The trade estimated that sales would be about 300,000 in 1958. At the same time, in 1957 particularly, many new foreign cars were being introduced to the United States market. Hence, Standard executives decided that if they were to enter the economy market, they had to do so immediately before competitors gained too strong a market position. They also felt that the company's strength among its existing dealers would be increased if dealers were provided with a full line of foreign cars. Otherwise Triumph sports car dealers would be forced to seek economy cars made by other manufacturers if they were to continue to cater to the changing needs of their markets.

In entering into the United States economy car market, the Standard company decided to modify its "Standard Super Ten" line of sedans and

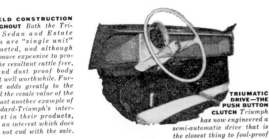

UNIWELD CONSTRUCTION THROUGHOUT *Both the Triumph Sedan and Estate Wagon are "single unit" constructed, and although this is more expensive to produce, the resultant rattle free, rust and dust proof body make it well worthwhile. Further, it adds greatly to the life and the resale value of the car...just another example of Standard-Triumph's interest in their products, an interest which does not end with the sale.*

only is the Triumph ne easy to work on...it's to get at. Positive latch lifts completely to allow access to the motor, and ere's plenty of room to reach to any part for cleaning or adjusting. This engine, normally runs 50 to 60 ousand miles without any or overhaul.

INDIVIDUAL SUSPENSION *Individual front suspension with heavy duty, low periocidy coil springs gives an exceptionally comfortable ride, plus the advantages of excellent handling on curves and around corners. There is hardly a sway or roll because the direct acting dampers control the "give" and level the ride. You'll feel the sports car engineering when you take a turn in the Triumph Sedan or Wagon.*

TRIUMATIC DRIVE—THE PUSH BUTTON CLUTCH *Triumph has now engineered a semi-automatic drive that is the closest thing to fool-proof that is to be found in any modern car. Put your thumb on the button in the top of the gear lever and shift...that's all there is to it. It works smoothly, efficiently and is amazingly simple...therefore, trouble free too. Reduces fatigue — especially in town driving, increases the safety factor, obviates faulty gear changes, makes engine stalling impossible, prevents transmission judder when starting or changing gear, simplifies learning to drive.*

GENERAL DIMENSIONS
Sedan and Estate Wagon
Wheel Base 7′ 0″
Track (front & rear) 4′ 0½″
Ground clearance 6½″
Turning Circle 32′ 0″
Overall length 12′ 1″
(Estate Wagon 12′)
Width 4′ 10″
Height 5′ 0″
Weight 1680 lbs.
(Estate – 1780 lbs.)
(complete with tools,
gas and oil, etc.)
Gas tank 8.5 gals.

ENGINE SPECIFICATIONS
40 H.P. Overhead valve engine (948 c.c.)
8.5 gallon fuel tank
8.5 pint oil reservoir
10 pint cooling system
40 plus miles per gallon
78 M.P.H. top speed
4 speed syncromesh gear box
0-50 M.P.H. in 18 secs.

PERFORMANCE
Engine– 4 cylinders O/H Valve 948 c.c.
Horse power 40 at 5,000 R.P.M.
Compression Ratio 8.00
Bore 2.48 in. Stroke 2.992 in.
Gas Consumption 40 M.P.G.
Oil Consumption 3,000 M.P.G.
Road Speed 78 M.P.H.

OPTIONAL EXTRAS
Leather upholstery or Lurex
White wall tires,
Heavy duty heater
Push-button clutch (no clutch pedal)
Chrome wheel rings
Windshield washer, Radio

STANDARD EQUIPMENT
Tubeless tires, Twin sun visors
Automatic turn indicators, Ash trays
Spare wheel, Controlled air ventilation

SEDAN COLORS
Black, Medici blue, Mandarin red,
Lichfield green, Beach white,
Silver grey, Shoal green

ESTATE WAGON
Same colors as above with duotone
white top as standard

The company reserves the right to modify the specifications contained herein without notice.

estate wagons,[2] principal modifications being slightly more engine horsepower, heavier bumpers, heavier tires, and a change in shock absorber settings. To trade on the established reputation of the Triumph TR-3, the modified versions of the standard Super Ten and "The Ten Companion" were given the trade names "Triumph Sedan" and "Triumph Estate Wagon." Pertinent information on the Triumph Sedan and the Triumph Estate Wagon is given in Exhibit 3. Pictures of the cars are given in Exhibit 4. Prices are given in Exhibit 5. While management appreciated that the company would be entering the economy car market with models which had been available to the world market for several years, it decided to do so with the general understanding that the Triumph sedan and estate wagon would be the forerunners of a new line especially designed for the United States market. Thus, potential dealers were to be assured that the company would maintain a long-run competitive position in the United States.

---

[2] In 1957 the Standard company manufactured three lines in addition to the Triumph TR-3 and Super Ten: "The Standard Vanguard III," "The Standard Sportsman," and "The Standard Eight." In the postwar period up to May 30, 1957, the Standard company had manufactured 583,204 automobiles.

Exhibit 4

STANDARD-TRIUMPH MOTOR COMPANY, INC.

The Triumph Sedan and Estate Wagon

Exhibit 5

STANDARD-TRIUMPH MOTOR COMPANY, INC.

Price Information on the 1958 Triumph Sedan and Estate Wagon

Sedan (East Coast and Gulf Ports) $1,699.00
 (West Coast) 1,749.00
Estate Wagon (East Coast and Gulf Ports) 1,899.00
 (West Coast) 1,979.00

SEDAN AND ESTATE WAGON
STANDARD EQUIPMENT

Tubeless tires
Twin sun visors
Automatic turn indicators
Ash trays
Spare wheel
Controlled air ventilation

ACCESSORIES AS ORIGINAL EQUIPMENT*

White wall tires $17.00
Rimbellishers 15.00
Heater 49.00
Windshield washer 5.00
Dual tone paint 28.00
Leather or lurex trim 38.00
Radio 72.00

 * These prices applicable only when accessories are ordered as original equipment to be fitted to car in production.

 Source: Company records.

The Economy Car Market

At the time that the introduction of the economy line was being planned, very little information was publicly available regarding who was buying economy cars or why; the economy car market had grown so rapidly that it was not possible for any manufacturer to develop definitive data regarding consumer buying behavior.

Standard-Triumph had studied ownership of Triumph sports cars in early 1957 and had found that 50.1% of the owners covered in the study owned one other car, and that 18.1% of owners had incomes of less than $5,000, 32.8% had incomes of $5,000 to $7,500, and that 49.1% had incomes over $7,500.

The August 1957 issue of *Fortune*[3] reported the results of a *Fortune* telephone survey of 153 owners of foreign cars in eight states as follows:

Do you own any other car? Yes, 58%. No, 42%.
What was your primary reason for buying a small car?

Economy of operation 49%
Ease of handling 20
Low initial cost 19
"Different" from U.S. cars 3
Other 9

[3] Robert Sheehan, "A Big Year for Small Cars," *Fortune*, August 1957, p. 196. Reprinted by permission.

Would you buy a small car again? Yes, 94%. No, 1%. Not stated, 5%.
What would you like changed?

Nothing	38%
Less noise	17
Better service facilities	14
More power	12
More space	9

What is your age?

29 and under	27%
30–39	31
40–49	25
50–59	11
60 and over	3
Not stated	3

What is your family income?

Under $5,000	25%
$5,000–$10,000	45
Over $10,000	24
Not stated	6

The growth of the imported car market, including the growth of competitors, for the period 1953–57 is indicated below:

	1953	1954	1955	1956	1957 (Est.)
Total U.S. cars	5,710,028	5,503,061	7,111,443	5,857,061	5,750,000
Total foreign cars	28,961	32,403	58,465	98,187	200,000
Percentage of U.S. cars	0.50%	0.59%	0.82%	1.65%	3.4%+
Austin	3,087	1,528	1,596	1,125	3,000
Ford	3,644	1,622	2,189	4,230	17,000
Hillman	4,506	2,430	2,778	3,415	11,000
Jaguar	3,914	3,365	3,573	3,685	4,000
Metropolitan		7,018	6,807	7,145	12,000
MG	6,606	3,454	3,001	6,094	13,500
Renault					23,000
Volkswagen		6,343	28,907	50,001	64,000
Other	7,204	6,643	9,614	22,492	67,000

In considering competition, Mr. Bethell felt that the Triumph sedans and station wagons would be in competition primarily with those cars that sold for $2,000 or less. Information on the cars of principal competitors is given in Exhibit 6.

Marketing the Triumph Line

In developing a sales promotional strategy for the new Triumph sedans and estate wagons, Mr. Bethell had several questions to resolve.

First, should the new line be introduced nationally or regionally? In the past, most foreign cars had been introduced rather consistently on a regional basis, usually first in key West Coast markets where foreign cars,

Exhibit 6

STANDARD-TRIUMPH MOTOR COMPANY, INC.

Information on Selected Foreign Cars Available in the United States in Late 1957 or Early 1958

Trade Name	Models	East Coast, POE Price	Wheel Base (Inches)	Weight (Pounds)	Engine (No. Cylinders)	Horsepower	Reported Top Speed	Reported M.P.G.
Austin A-35	2D Sedan	$1,553	79.5	N.A.	4	34	....	....
Austin A-55	4D Sedan	2,214	99.3	N.A.	4	51	60.0	30
Berkeley	2D Coupe	1,600	70.0	784	3	30	....	....
BM W Isetta 300	1D Sedan	1,048	59.0	770	1	16	....	....
BM W Isetta 600	2D Sedan	1,398	66.9	1,130	2	23	68	60
Borgward Isabella	2D Sedan	2,495	101.5	2,205	4	60	90	34
Borgward Isabella	2D Sta. Wagon	2,685						
Borgward Isabella	2D Coupe	2,845						
Citroen 2CV	2D Sedan	1,300	93.5	....	2	12	....	....
Citroen 1D 19	4D Sedan	2,995	123.0	2,464	4	75	....	....
Citroen DS 19	4D Sedan	3,595						
DK W	2D Sedan	1,995	92.0	2,000	3	40	85	40
DK W	2D Coupe	2,195						
DK W	4D Sedan	2,395						
DK W	2D Sta. Wagon	2,530						

Exhibit 6—Continued

Trade Name	Models	East Coast, POE Price	Wheel Base (Inches)	Weight (Pounds)	Engine (No. Cylinders)	Horsepower	Reported Top Speed	Reported M.P.G.
Fiat 600	2D Sedan	$1,298	72.7	1,535	2	15	....	53
Fiat 600	4D Sedan	1,598						
Fiat 600	2D Conv.	1,360						
Fiat 1100	4D Sedan	1,683	91.5	2,680	4	43	....	....
Fiat 1100	4D Sta. Wag.	2,069						
Fiat 1200	4D Sedan	2,278	91.3	2,782	4	55	87	....
Fiat 1200	2D Coupe	2,498						
Ford Anglica	2D Sedan	1,539	87.0	1,631	4	36	....	35
Prefect	4D Sedan	1,639		1,697				
Escort	2D Sta. Wagon	1,629		1,781				35
Squire	2D Sta. Wagon	1,739		1,816				
Consul	4D Sedan	2,012	104.5	2,401	4	61	....	
Consul	2D Conv.	2,351						
Zephyr	4D Sedan	2,193	107.0	2,580	6	90	....	
Zephyr	2D Conv.	2,552						
Zodiac	4D Sedan	2,365	107.0	2,627	6	90	....	
Zodiac	2D Conv.	2,910						

Exhibit 6—Continued

Trade Name	Models	East Coast, POE Price	Wheel Base (Inches)	Weight (Pounds)	Engine (No. Cylinders)	Horsepower	Reported Top Speed	Reported M.P.G.
Thamus 12M	2D Sedan	. . . .	102.5	1,810	4	67	. . . .	. . . .
Goliath 1100	2D Sedan	$1,995	89.4	1,896	4	46	. . . .	30
Goliath 1100	2D Conv.	2,395						
	2D Sta. Wagon	2,289						
	2D Coupe	2,835						
Hillman Special	4D Sedan	1,699	96.0	2,092	4	51	. . . .	. . . .
Hillman Deluxe	4D Sedan	1,844		2,135				
Hillman	2D Conv.	2,099		2,135				
Hillman Huasky	2D Sta. Wagon	1,639	84.0	1,904		38		
Hillman Minx	4D Sta. Wagon	2,299	93.0	2,259		47		
Jaguar 3.4	4D Sedan	4,460	107.5	3,024	6	210	. . . .	. . . .
Jaguar XK-150	2D Coupe	4,475	102.0	2,950		190		
XK-150	2D Conv.	4,595						
Jaguar Mark VIII	4D Sedan	5,605	120.0	3,024		210		

Exhibit 6—Continued

Trade Name	Models	East Coast, POE Price	Wheel Base (Inches)	Weight (Pounds)	Engine (No. Cylinders)	Horsepower	Reported Top Speed	Reported M.P.G.
Lloyd	Sedan	$1,295	78.8	1,193	2	24	....	....
	Conv.	1,395						
	Sta. Wagon	1,345						
	Sta. Wagon	1,545						
	Sta. Wagon	1,645						
Mercedes-Benz 180	4D Sedan	3,240	104.3	2,390	4	74		
180-D	4D Sedan	3,517		2,470	(Diesel)	46		
190-D	4D Sedan	3,341		2,450		84		
190-SL	2D Roadster	3,431	94.5	2,340		120		
190-SL	2D Coupe	5,232						
219	4D Sedan	3,823	108.3	2,580	6	100		
220S 220S	4D Sedan 2D Conv.	4,283 7,641	111.0	2,730		120		
300C	4D Sedan	7,559	124.0	4,160		180		
30C-SL	2D Coupe	8,905	94.5	2,730		240		
Metropolitan	2D Coupe	1,626	85.0	1,875	4	55	....	....
	2D Conv.	1,650						

Exhibit 6—Continued

Trade Name	Models	East Coast, POE Price	Wheel Base (Inches)	Weight (Pounds)	Engine (No. Cylinders)	Horsepower	Reported Top Speed	Reported M.P.G.
MG A	2D Conv.	$2,462	94.0	1,960	4	72	....	....
	2D Coupe	2,695						
Magnette	4D Sedan	2,740	102.0	2,400		68		40
Morris Minor 1000	2D Sedan	1,705	86.0	1,706	4	37	....	....
	2D Conv.	1,745						
	2D Sta. Wagon	1,912						
Opel Record (GM)	2D Sedan	1,955	100.0	1,911	4	56	....	....
Caravan	2D Sta. Wagon	2,370						
Penhard Dyna 58	4D Sedan	1,995	101.4	N.A.	2	42	....	....
Deluxe	4D Sedan	2,195						
Pengeot 403	4D Sedan	2,175	105.0	1,775	4	58	80	30
Porsche	2D Conv.	3,915	82.7	1,874	4	75	.	
	2D Coupe	3,665						
Renault 4CV	4D Sedan	1,345	82.7	1,150	4	28	....	....
Dauphine	4D Sedan	1,645	89.0	1,340		32		43
Riley 1.5	4D Sedan	2,316	86.0	1,974	4	68		
Rover 90	4D Sedan	3,295	111.0	3,203	6	93	....	
105S	4D Sedan	3,765		3,318		108		

Exhibit 6—Continued

Trade Name	Models	East Coast, POE Price	Wheel Base (Inches)	Weight (Pounds)	Engine (No. Cylinders)	Horsepower	Reported Top Speed	Reported M.P.G.
Saab	2D Sedan	$1,895	98.4	1,734	3	38	. . . .	. . . .
Grantnismo	2D Sedan	2,568						
Simca Ariane	4D Sedan		105.0	2,350	4	48	. . . .	42.6
Simca Oceane	2D Conv.						87	
Sunbeam Rapies	2D Coupe	2,499	96.0	2,280	4	67	. . . .	. . . .
	2D Conv.	2,649						
Vauxhall Victor	4D Sedan	1,958	98.0	2,125	4	52		35
	4D Sta. Wagon							
Volkswagen	2D Sedan	1,545	72.7	1,530	4	32		
	2D Sunroof	1,625						
	2D Conv.	2,045						
	3D Sta. Wagon	2,020		2,370				
VW Karmaun-Ghia	2D Coupe	2,445		1,650				
	2D Conv.	2,725						
Volvo	2D Sedan	2,239	102.3	2,100	4	60		
	2D Sta. Wagon	2,490		2,170				

Source: Manufacturers' published information.

both sports and utility cars, enjoyed the greatest popularity. The Triumph TR-2, for example, had originally been introduced on the West Coast and then subsequently on the East Coast. The Swedish "Volvo," a utility car, had followed the same strategy in 1956 and 1957. Generally speaking, foreign cars still enjoyed their greatest sales in 1957 in the East and West Coast markets; New England, the South, and the Middle West being distinctly smaller, although growing markets. Since the parent company desired to send about 1,000 sedans and estate wagons to the United States market each month, there was a strong argument for introducing the cars nationally because of the need of large initial sales volume. On the other hand, under any circumstances, Standard-Triumph would have a relatively limited promotional budget which might be most effectively used on a regional basis.

Second, what policy should be followed in obtaining dealers for the economy line?

Tentatively, Mr. Bethell thought that distribution should be sought among existing Triumph sports car dealers. The company had built an excellent reputation among these dealers for making highly salable products, for efficient servicing of dealer needs, and for effective promotional and advertising programs. This kind of reputation was considered to be important since many foreign car dealers had been disappointed with some foreign cars which they had handled, and many dealers, particularly the better dealers, were becoming increasingly particular about the lines they stocked. In addition, Mr. Bethell felt that some attempt should be made to obtain non-Triumph dealers, since the company's longer-run goal was 600 dealers nationally.

All manufacturers had been aggressively developing dealers in 1957, with the result that the total number of dealers selling imported cars had risen from a total of 11,088 as of January 1, 1957, to an estimated total of about 16,000 to 16,500 as of the latter part of the year. The increase in the total number of dealers had been caused primarily by General Motors Corporation's decision to market its German "Opel Record" through 3,000 Buick Dealers and its English "Vauxhall" through 2,500 Pontiac dealers. Other manufacturers had increased distribution during the year, however. By late 1957 the number of dealers for foreign cars was estimated by the trade to be approximately as follows:

Austin and Austin Healey..	480	Metropolitan	1,200
Berkeley	20	Mercedes-Benz	340
BMW-Isetta	500	Morris Minor	475
Citroen	100	MG	475
DKW	100–110	Opel Record	3,000
Fiat	225	Packard Dyna	100
Ford	400	Porsche	175
Goliath	150	Riley	475
Hillman	670	Rover	75
Jaguar	350–375	Renault	475
Lloyd	400	Saab	75–80

Simca................... 450	Volkswagen............... 350
Sunbeam................. 400	Volvo................... 300
Vauxhall.................. 2,500	

Because of the immediate need for gaining acceptance of the Triumph economy cars by dealers, Mr. Bethell wanted to develop a sales promotional program which would be highly effective in getting potential dealers to stock and to promote the new cars aggressively. Tentatively, as one part of the program, he and the company's advertising agency had decided to hold sales meetings in late 1957 with distributors and potential dealers on the East Coast and then the West and Gulf Coasts so that dealers could see the new cars; and to prepare a special kit of dealer selling aids which would be outstanding. It was the opinion of Mr. Bethell and Mr. Gore that Standard-Triumph's reputation among dealers as one of the few foreign car marketers providing worthwhile point-of-purchase selling aids would help gain dealer interest and would help to get dealers to stock the new cars.

Third, how much money should be spent advertising the new cars?

In the past most of foreign car marketers had spent relatively little on advertising or other promotional tools. The December 6, 1957 issue of *Printers' Ink* reported the dollars spent in magazine advertising per car sold in 1956 for principal competitors as follows: Volkswagen, 49 cents; Simca, 55 cents; Borgward, 76 cents; English Ford, $1.85; Mercedes-Benz, $2.46; M.G. and Morris Minor, $3.15; Hillman-Minx, $4.89; Austin and Austin-Healey, $7.89; Porsche, $9.38; Renault, $11.43; Jaguar, $22.73; Triumph, $28.50; Sunbeam, $35.88; Citroen, $64.80; and Fiat, $76.69. Trade reports indicated that total advertising expenditures would be somewhat up in 1957 over 1956 and probably in 1958, too. Volkswagen was known to have selected an advertising agency in preparation for beginning its first real advertising effort in the United States sometime in

Exhibit 7

STANDARD-TRIUMPH MOTOR COMPANY, INC.

Traceable Consumer Advertising Expenditures of Foreign or Small Car Manufacturers and Importers, 1957

Manufacturer or Importer	Trade Name	Expenditure
American Motors Corp..........	Rambler	$845,091
Ford Motor Co...............	Anglica-Prefect-Consul	8,605
Humbro Automotive Corp.......	Austin-Healey	7,843
	MG	14,640
	Morris	40,065
Jaguar Cars, Ltd..............	Jaguar	72,776
Renault Selling Branch, Inc.......	Renault	204,124
Rootes Motors, Inc............	Hillman	40,710
Standard-Triumph Motor Co.....	Triumph	68,414
Studebaker Packard Corp........	Mercedes-Benz	47,950
Volkswagenwerk..............	Volkswagen	56,230
Citroen Cars Corp.............	Citroen	51,222

1958. The traceable advertising expenditures of principal competitors for 1957 are given in Exhibit 7.

As the basis for discussion, Mr. Bethell had had the advertising agency develop an advertising schedule for the first six months of 1958 based upon an advertising budget of approximately $200,000 for the first six months. Tentatively, Mr. Bethell thought that $100,000 of the advertising budget might be allocated to national media and $100,000 to local media, the latter to be spent in those markets which responded well saleswise. The proposed national media schedule follows:

Publication	Jan.	Feb.	March	April	May	June
The New Yorker	⅓ p.		⅓ p.		⅓ p.	
Sports Illustrated	⅓ p.	⅓ p.			⅓ p.	
Holiday		¼ p.		¼ p.		¼ p.
The Saturday Evening Post	¼ p.	¼ p.	¼ p.	¼ p.	¼ p.	¼ p.
Sunset	⅓ p.	⅓ p.		⅓ p.		⅓ p.
Road and Track		1 p.	1 p.		1 p.	
Sports Car Illustrated		1 p.		1 p.		1 p.
Motor Trend		⅓ p.		⅓ p.	⅓ p.	

Fourth, what type of advertising copy should the company employ in addressing consumers?

In considering the advertising of the Triumph sedan and estate wagon, Mr. Bethell felt that its principal effect would be to stimulate general consumer interest in economy-type cars. Insofar as possible, however, he wished to employ advertising copy which would, in addition to stimulating general consumer interest, develop strong and positive consumer attitudes regarding Triumph's brand name and which would motivate prospects to visit Triumph dealers. Tentatively, Mr. Bethell and Mr. Gore had decided that the Triumph sports and economy cars would not be advertised together in the same advertisement, because the cars appealed to different markets. They were willing, however, to associate the economy cars with Triumph's reputation in the sports car field.

Relatively little was known at the time regarding the advertising copy approaches of competitors, because few manufacturers of economy cars had as yet undertaken sizable consumer advertising campaigns. Advertisements of selected competitors which were being published in late 1957 are reproduced in Exhibit 8, page 262.

~ ~ ~

CASE 8: PALM BEACH COMPANY[1]

NOTE: *This and the next case concern manufacturers who have offered advertising allowances to dealers, that is, so-called manufacturer's co-operative advertising programs.*

[1] Written by David W. Nylen.

Exhibit 8

STANDARD-TRIUMPH MOTOR COMPANY, INC.

Samples of Competitive Advertising

Many arguments are advanced regarding the advantages and disadvantages of such programs. The advantages usually advanced are: (1) Manufacturers obtain the benefit of the lower-cost local advertising rates that are secured by retailers. (2) Such allowances increase the effort of the retailer as he is spending some of his own money. (3) Because retailers share the cost of advertising, manufacturers obtain more advertising for each dollar they spend than they would otherwise. (4) Co-operative advertising programs keep advertising expenditures in line with sales results. (5) Manufacturers can trade upon the reputations of retailers. Disadvantages frequently advanced are: (1) Co-operative programs require expensive accounting and follow-up procedures. (2) They are difficult to administer. (3) Retailers often do not follow instructions. (4) Retailers sometimes cheat by sending in padded bills or bills for advertisements which were never run.

Questions to consider in the Palm Beach case: (1) What are the principal features of Palm Beach's marketing mix? (2) What role does brand play in the selling of men's suits? (3) How much control does the dealer exercise in the selling of men's suits? (4) Do you think that modifications are called for in Palm Beach's co-operative advertising plan? If so, what modifications?

In 1958 Mr. Elmer L. Ward, Jr., executive vice president of the Palm Beach Company, reviewed the company's co-operative advertising plan for retail dealers to determine if the plan could be modified so as to increase its effectiveness. The Palm Beach Company tailored and marketed several brands of lightweight men's, students', and boys' lightweight clothing, the best known of which was "Palm Beach."

The Palm Beach Company originated as the Goodall Worsted Company, a subsidiary of Goodall-Sanford, Inc., a manufacturer of various fabrics. Until 1931 the parent company had sold the Palm Beach material to cutters-up. From 1917 to 1930 the company had advertised the Palm Beach fabric, spending annually until 1930 about $400,000–$500,000, primarily in consumer magazines. In 1931 the company discontinued selling to cutters-up and formed a wholly owned subsidiary, the Goodall Company, to tailor Palm Beach suits and market them through retail dealers.

The decision to undertake manufacture and sale of Palm Beach suits came as a result of the failure of cutters-up to maintain properly the quality and prices of suits made of Palm Beach cloth. Trading upon the brand name which the Goodall Worsted Company had built up at large cost, certain suit manufacturers cut prices and the quality of their Palm Beach suits. In turn retailers often used Palm Beach suits as loss leaders in their store promotions. The results were, first, a confusion among consumers with regard to the price and quality of tailoring to be expected in suits made of Palm Beach material and, second, an avoidance of the fabric by stores which did not want to meet loss leader competition. Goodall's sales thus were adversely affected. Because of the difficulties of maintaining control over the quality standards and the market practices of cutters-up, the management decided to go into the cutting-up business, whereby it could control quality of suits, prices charged, and retail distribution.

The aggressive advertising and promotion which until 1931 had been devoted to Palm Beach fabric were thereafter directed to Palm Beach suits, which were distributed to the trade to be sold at a maintained price.

In the distribution of Palm Beach suits, the company followed a distribution plan different from that of most manufacturers of branded men's clothing, such as Hart, Schaffner & Marx and B. Kuppenheimer Company, Inc. Whereas these and other suit manufacturers selling under their own brands had a highly selected retail distribution with exclusive agents, except in large cities, the Goodall company made its products available to all reputable retailers who would maintain the resale price.

The company avoided selling to stores only when they were not good credit risks or when they would not maintain resale price.

In 1954 Burlington Industries, Inc., purchased Goodall-Sanford and with it, the Goodall company, the tailoring subsidiary. In that same year Burlington Industries sold the tailoring business to Mr. Elmer Ward, Sr., and his associates who formed the Palm Beach Company. In 1958 the Palm Beach Company was an independent tailoring company buying fabrics from many sources, foreign and domestic.

By 1958 Palm Beach Company had considerably enlarged its product line by adding new branded lines. Lines offered in 1958 included the following: "Springweave," a medium-weight wool and mohair suit retailing for $55, designed for wear during ten months of the year; "Palm Lite," a super lightweight dacron and worsted blend for $29.95; "Sunfrost," a medium-weight dacron and worsted summer suit selling for $49.95; "Palm Beach Wash'n Wear," an exclusive multifiber blend retailing for $39.95; and "Resortweave," a nine-ounce worsted-shetland sport coat retailing for $35.00. In addition the company marketed various other branded products including formal wear, sports coats, slacks, and walking shorts, plus boys' and students' lines. These lines were sold through about 3,000 retail outlets.

Advertising Strategy 1931–58

With the integration of the weaving and cutting-up business in 1931, a new approach in advertising was adopted. Goodall's management saw the need not only to build up a reputation for its Palm Beach suits but also to make certain that consumers were directed to the selected local retailers. As a result, a substantial part of the advertising appropriation was diverted from magazines to newspaper advertising carried on co-operatively with dealers.

While the co-operative advertising with dealers accounted for an important share of the company's total advertising expenditure after 1931, a still larger part of the company's appropriation was used for company advertising designed to build the reputation of Palm Beach suits and later of the various other lines such as Sunfrost and Springweave. Before 1941 this product advertising was placed primarily in national magazines.

In 1941, concurrent with a change of advertising agencies, the company shifted most of its general advertising from magazines to newspapers for two chief reasons: first, the management felt that it needed a medium permitting more flexibility of insertion than magazines allowed. The advertising for summer suits could be released in newspapers in various sections of the country in accordance with the summer suit seasons of those places, whereas advertisements in magazines reached all places on the same date. In the second place, the newspapers permitted a geographical selection in accordance with market opportunities. Summer suits had a better market in large cities and metropolitan areas than in

Exhibit 1

PALM BEACH COMPANY

1958 National Magazine Advertisement

PALM BEACH*

gives you the look you like ... in miracle wash-and-wear Travel Weave†

There's a miracle summer ahead for you with the new Travel Weave suits and separates by "Palm Beach." Tailored exclusively by "Palm Beach," this superlative blend of 75% Dacron and 25% fine cotton rarely needs pressing . . . goes direct from tub to you after a quick drip-dry. Perfect for trouble-free travelling . . . for a trouble-free summer! And throughout, the distinctive "Palm Beach" styling that provides the ultimate in luxury and fashion,

the famous-fit tailoring that assures a precise drape and all-summer-long comfort. The all-new Travel Weave collection includes handsome new suiting patterns: miniature glens, fine-line cords and colorful sportswear. See them today at your favorite store. Suits, slacks, walk-shorts, sport coats and sport shirts. Travel Weave suits are priced at $39.95. The sportswear separates are comparably low in price.

*REG. T.M. GOODALL-SANFORD, INC. † REG. APP. FOR PALM BEACH CO., 75% DACRON, 25% COTTON IN MOST STYLES. PRICES REFER TO AREAS WHERE FAIR TRADE ACTS ARE VALID AND IN EFFECT. PRICES SLIGHTLY HIGHER IN FAR WEST.

Exhibit 2

PALM BEACH COMPANY

1959 Newspaper Advertisement

NOW! A GENUINE PALM BEACH*

SUIT YOU WEAR YEAR-ROUND

COOL-DAY, WARM-DAY VERSATILITY. Springweave has sufficient "body" to be perfect for wear on cool days ... has the lightness and comfort to take you from *now* right through summer. "All-days" comfort and particularly suited to today's over-heated rooms in winter and air-conditioned places in summer.

COSTLY TAILORING DETAILS. Perfect-fit tailoring—the exclusive contour-cut collar, for example, gives an unmatched hug-fit in the neck-and-shoulder area. Amazing wrinkle-resistance and shape-holding qualities make this suit ideal for salesmen and travelers.

AMAZING "SPRING-BACK" WRINKLE RESISTANCE. The next time you shop, make this test: knot the sleeve of any Springweave suit as tight as you can, when you untie it, watch the wrinkles disappear as the fabric "springs back" into perfect, wrinkle-free shape.

COMPLETE SATISFACTION: Every feature of Springweave will please you, just as over a million owners of Springweave suits have been pleased. Slim, trim lines; new 1959 colors, patterns; the luxury look; absolutely no cool-weather static "cling" so annoying in other suits.

SPRINGWEAVE† BY PALM BEACH CO.

HERE IS WHY SPRINGWEAVE IS SUCH A PERFECT YEAR-ROUND SUIT: 1. The exclusive fabric. Woven with baby-kid mohair—one of the finest, most costly wool fibers available—and fine worsted, it has a natural springy resiliency that sheds wrinkles almost as you watch. Provides true, lightweight, all-weather comfort in all four seasons. **2. The tailoring.** Exclusive Palm Beach techniques developed in over a quarter century of fine tailoring assure the utmost in fit and comfort. The perfect fit lasts for the life of the garment. **3. The price.** You'd expect to pay much more for suits as luxurious and as versatile as these. Yet the price tag is wonderfully low. And when you actually compare Springweave with any other suit, feature for feature, you'll see Springweave can't be matched. Insist on genuine Springweave by Palm Beach. At your favorite fine store.

$55.00

*REG. T.M. GOODALL-SANFORD, INC.

†REG. T.M. PALM BEACH COMPANY

Exhibit 3

PALM BEACH COMPANY

1958 Trade Advertisement

Engineered Wash 'n Wear by PALM BEACH* defies all COMPARISON with competitive makes according to these independent laboratory TESTS

IF YOU THINK ALL WASH 'N WEAR SUITS ARE THE SAME, READ THIS: Palm Beach does not wait for wash 'n wear standards to be set. We set standards no other manufacturer equals. Wash 'n wear tailored by Palm Beach was tested and tested by us before we were finally satisfied. Then we asked an independent testing laboratory to compare our finished garments with six other leading makes ... not for just one washing, but for repeated washings ... we invite you to read these facts that even amazed us ... facts that you can prove too by actually washing our suits automatically or drip dry with any others you carry ... then have your bushelman open up the coats and linings and compare results.

Exclusive tailoring standards developed by PALM BEACH

① Collar-tailoring method exclusive with Palm Beach Company retains folded position permanently. No amount of washing can distort or destroy it.

② The topcollar stand insert forms the collar to the neck contour with no extra fullness or puckering.

③ Nylon and dacron tapes are used at the lapel, gorge, arm holes and shoulder.

④ The felt chest piece of nylon batting is over the chest and shoulder area for pliability and permanency.

⑤ The nylon batting shoulder pads and sleeve head provide a quick drying effect.

⑥ Sewings of dacron thread are used for sturdiness and a minimum of breakage on all seams and stitching . . . prevents puckering.

⑦ The front dart is tacked to the interlining with a regular sewing machine stitch for strength and permanency.

⑧ The tacking of pockets to the interlining is done throughout the entire length of the pocket solidly.

⑨ The interedges of all pocket lining seams, body linings, sleeve linings and the raw edge of the outer fabric of the sleeve seams are all permanently protected from fraying by serging and safety stitching.

⑩ The vent lining is serged directly to the fabric and regular stitching is also used to prevent fraying.

⑪ The lining at the bottom of the coat is anchored to the edge of the bottom turnup. Then it is felled to the hem (actually sewn twice to prevent fraying).

Be sure to have a wash 'n wear resource that's reliable. The latest Du Pont surveys show that over 50% of wash 'n wear suit customers are actually washing their garments. But, garments not properly constructed will develop puckering, lumpiness and raveling of fibers that come right through the fabric.

IMPORTANT TEST FINDINGS

OF THE SIX OTHER LEADING MANUFACTURERS SELLING AT THE $29.95 & $39.75 PRICE LEVELS: Only three serge and safety-stitch lower coat pockets to prevent fraying during the washing cycle. Only two serge and safety stitch inside facing pockets. Only Palm Beach among the leading manufacturers serges and safety stitches completely around all coat pockets and across the tops of the pockets.

Only one other manufacturer serges both the top and bottom sleeves to prevent fraying and raveling during the washing cycle. Only three manufacturers follow Palm Beach's lead in serging and safety stitching the sleeve lining seams.

Only two other of the leading manufacturers serge the vent lining to the fabric to prevent raveling.

No other manufacturer guards against fraying of the body lining by a double felling application of the lining turn up. This is another exclusive Palm Beach Wash 'n Wear safety precaution.

Only one other leading manufacturer uses nylon felt in the construction of the canvas, so necessary for pliability and permanency.

Only one other maker lacks the coat pocketing to the interlining, and lacks the interlining to the front dart stay for strength and permanency.

Most important of all, only Palm Beach offers a collar that retains its folded position permanently, and which hugs the neck. No amount of washing can distort it or destroy it. Originated exclusively for Palm Beach by America's top clothing designer, Jerome Giasoff.

OF THE SIX OTHER LEADING MANUFACTURERS OFFERING WASH 'N WEAR FROM $45.00 to $59.50: Only two other manufacturers used nearly as much care as Palm Beach in serging and safety stitching pockets and linings. Other than Palm Beach only one maker serged across the tops of all coat pockets.

One manufacturer in this price bracket actually failed to serge any pockets or linings, yet the product was labeled to be machine washable.

Only one other maker failed down the waistband lining to prevent curling after the drying cycle.

Only three of six competitive manufacturers serged the trouser pocketing closed prior to stitching the pockets.

*Reg. T.M. Goodall-Sanford, Inc.

WAIT FOR YOUR PALM BEACH SALESMAN TO SHOW YOU THE FINEST WASH 'N WEAR GARMENTS EVER MANUFACTURED

small city areas. Cities with warm climates were generally better markets than cities in cooler climates. Newspapers permitted an adjustment of expenditure in accordance with market potentials. While most of the general advertising was in newspapers, one- or two-color advertisements were usually run early in the summer in a magazine of wide circulation, such as the *Saturday Evening Post*.

In 1958 the Palm Beach Company's total advertising space expenditure of about $1 million was divided 60% for company advertising and 40% for co-operative advertising. In turn 80% of the 60% for company advertising was devoted to newspapers, the remaining 20% to national magazines. The newspaper advertising was full-page, ROP color or 1,500-line, black-and-white advertisements appearing in 90 markets. National magazine advertisements appeared in four colors during 1958 in *Sports Illustrated, Esquire, Newsweek, Life,* and *New Yorker*. Exhibit 1 is a national magazine advertisement run in 1958. Exhibit 2 is an advertisement scheduled for use in newspapers in 1959.

Although not a large expenditure in terms of dollars, Palm Beach did utilize trade advertising primarily to bring timely messages to retailers regarding Palm Beach products and promotional plans. The *Daily News Record*, an apparel trade paper, was the trade medium most extensively used by Palm Beach. Direct mail was also utilized. Exhibit 3 is a 1958 trade advertisement run in the *Daily News Record*.

Palm Beach Co-operative Advertising

Co-operative advertising carried on with dealers was a highly important part of the Palm Beach advertising program, and over the years management had devoted considerable time to the administration of the plan and to efforts for improvement of the plan.

Palm Beach Company, under the 1957–58 co-operative plan, paid 50% of a dealer's cost for newspaper space, radio and TV commercial time only, and billboard and car card space only. The dealer could spend up to 4% of the net wholesale price of Palm Beach merchandise shipped, and Palm Beach would reimburse the dealer for one half of this expenditure up to a maximum of 2% of the net wholesale price of merchandise purchased from Palm Beach Company. Examples of how the plan worked are given below:

	Net Wholesale Price of Purchases	Total Co-operative Allowance	Actual Expenditure	Palm Beach Share	Dealer's Share
If exactly total allowance spent....	$1,000	$40	$40	$20	$20
If less than total allowance spent....	1,000	40	26	13	13
If more than total allowance spent....	1,000	40	80	20	60

In order to be reimbursed, the dealer was required to fill out and sign a co-operative advertising billing form by the 15th of each month for reimbursement for advertising during the previous month. Exhibit 4 is a copy of the 1957–58 co-operative advertising form. Billing forms were to be accompanied by tear sheets of the newspaper advertisements run, station affidavits for time used on radio or television, and, if possible, duplicate bills.

The co-operative advertising plan did not provide reimbursement for the cost of mechanical production, artwork, programming, talent cost, or other incidentals. Dealers were to bill at the store's local advertising rate after deducting all discounts, allowances, and rebates. If a dealer had his own television or radio program, Palm Beach would include under the co-operative advertising plan the cost of up to five minutes of time for each 15 minutes' segment providing the entire 2½-minute commercial time was devoted to Palm Beach brands.

To be eligible for reimbursement under the co-operative plan, Palm

Exhibit 4

PALM BEACH COMPANY
Co-operative Advertising Form

☛ SEE REVERSE SIDE FOR EXPLANATION OF COOPERATIVE ADVERTISING PROGRAM ☚

1957-58 COOPERATIVE ADVERTISING FORM
Effective August 1, 1957 through July 31, 1958

1. This co-op form MUST be used in submitting claims and must bear LEGIBLE NAME and SIGNATURE of individual submitting claim.

2. This form must be accompanied by verification (newspaper tear sheets, radio station affidavit and scripts, billboard and car card receipts). If possible, also attach duplicate of local advertising invoice.

3. Type or print clearly all details as indicated by column headings.

4. Complete forms using exact NET LOCAL RATES.

5. BILLS MUST BE SUBMITTED MONTHLY — by the 15th of the month—for reimbursement for advertising during the previous month.

6. IMPORTANT! DO NOT DEDUCT CO-OP ADVERTISING CREDITS FROM REMITTANCES FOR MERCHANDISE BILLS.

Mail To:

Advertising Checking Bureau, Inc.
P. O. Box 1019 G. P. O.
New York 1, N. Y.

FROM_____
(Store Name)

ADDRESS_____

CITY_____ STATE_____

FOR ADVERTISING OF ALL PALM BEACH CO. LINES; REMEMBER: PALM BEACH OFFERS YOU 2% AGAINST NET PURCHASES.

MEDIA: List each newspaper, radio or TV station, car card or billboard showing, etc. separately. If newspaper copy in color, list color premium charge separately.	(1) DATES OF ADVERTISING	(2) SPACE OR TIME (In lines, inches or minutes)	(3) YOUR EXACT NET LOCAL RATE	(4) COLUMN 2 times COLUMN 3	(5) PALM BEACH COMPANY'S CO-OP COST

☐ Check here if additional forms are required. They will be sent immediately.

I certify that the above is billed at my exact LOWEST NET LOCAL RATE, computed after all normally earned discounts and expected rebates — and that the amount billed does not include (1) production costs, (2) special or preferred position premiums. If any further discounts or rebates, other than those already computed, are earned by us for space used, your share will be promptly refunded.

NAME_____ SIGNATURE_____

Exhibit 4—Continued

THE 1957-58 PALM BEACH®
CO-OP PLAN

EFFECTIVE AUGUST 1, 1957 THROUGH JULY 31, 1958

1. *The Cooperative Allowance for Advertising Space and Time.* In addition to our own national advertising program, Palm Beach makes available to you a liberal cooperative allowance whereby Palm Beach bears a part of your cost for newspaper space, radio and TV commercial time only and billboard and car card space only. In addition, Palm Beach offers you free copy suggestions, artwork and mats (as incorporated in the current year's Palm Beach Ad and Mat Book only).

2. *Palm Beach Pays HALF, Within This Allowance.* Palm Beach credits you with a co-op advertising allowance based on your net wholesale purchases of <u>all</u> Palm Beach merchandise, including sportswear. You can spend up to 4% of the net wholesale price of Palm Beach merchandise shipped to you, and Palm Beach will reimburse you for one-half of such expenditures. You can thus receive a net reimbursement of an amount up to 2% of the net wholesale price of merchandise purchased from Palm Beach Company. The allowance terms are the same for all retailers.

Net Whole-sale Price	Total Co-op Allowance	Our Share	Your Share
$1,000.00	$40.00	$20.00	$20.00

If you spend less than the total cooperative allowance, Palm Beach still shares one-half of your expenditure.

Net Whole-sale Price	Total Co-op Allowance	Expenditure	Our Share	Your Share
$1,000.00	$40.00	$25.00	$12.50	$12.50

If you spend more than the total cooperative allowance, Palm Beach will reimburse you to the extent of one-half of the cooperative credit.

Net Whole-sale Price	Total Co-op Allowance	Expenditure	Our Share	Your Share
$1,000.00	$40.00	$80.00	$20.00	$60.00

3. *How to Compute Your Allowance and Collect Your Reimbursement.* Take the net purchase price you pay for merchandise shipped to you (less credits, etc.) during the period August 1, 1957 through July 31, 1958. Multiply this by .04. This is your co-op allowance at any time. Prior to the 15th day of each month compute your co-op allowance through the end of the previous month. You are entitled to reimbursement for authorized advertising expenditures during the previous month up to one-half of this allowance, less reimbursements already made to you. If there is any question as to the net purchase price paid by you, the books of Palm Beach shall be conclusive. No reimbursement is made for co-op allowance not used.

Reimbursement will be made only on the receipt of a signed co-op billing form printed on the reverse side of this sheet (additional forms on request). Forms should be rendered by the 15th of each month for reimbursement for advertising during the previous month. Billing forms must be accompanied by tear sheets, station affidavits, and, if possible, duplicate bills.

Forms are to be mailed to: Advertising Checking Bureau, Inc.
P. O. Box 1019 G. P. O.
New York 1, N. Y.

DO NOT DEDUCT CO-OP ADVERTISING CREDITS FROM REMITTANCES TO PALM BEACH COMPANY.

4. *Advertising for Which Reimbursement is Made.* Palm Beach will recognize for reimbursement purposes only advertising of branded Palm Beach Company merchandise in the following media: (1) newspapers, (2) radio (commercial time only), (3) television (commercial time only), (4) billboard and car card (space only). Recognition is not given to the cost of mechanical production, artwork, programing, talent cost, and other incidentals, nor to non-commercial radio or TV time.

Bill only for space and commercial time purchased at your store's regular local rates, after deducting all discounts, allowances, and rebates whenever available to you. If you have your own TV or radio program, Palm Beach will recognize under and subject to the Co-op Plan the cost of up to five minutes of time for each fifteen minute segment — providing the entire 2½ minute commercial time is devoted exclusively to Palm Beach brands.

5. To be eligible for co-op reimbursement, (1) your advertisements must include proper product labels; the applicable Palm Beach Company trademark registration, and a fiber content statement; (2) advertisements and commercials must be devoted exclusively to Palm Beach products and such products must not be advertised in combination with other manufacturers' products.

6. *Local Rates.* Recognition for reimbursement purposes will be given only to the net cost of space and commercial time based on local rates after deducting all discounts, allowances and rebates whenever available to you.

7. *Period for Which This Offer is Open.* This offer applies to recognized advertising during the period from August 1, 1957 through July 31, 1958. This offer may be amended or recalled at any time by notice sent to you by regular mail provided that recognition will be given by Palm Beach to purchases by you and advertising expenditures prior to the sending of the notice. If any retailer subject to valid fair trade laws breaks a valid fair trade price of Palm Beach for any of its merchandise, Palm Beach reserves the right to refuse to make any reimbursement to such retailer for the season in which the violation occurs.

Beach Company required that the advertisements (1) include proper products labels, the applicable Palm Beach Company trade-mark registration, and a fiber content statement; and (2) be devoted exclusively to Palm Beach products and not advertised in combination with products of other manufacturers. Palm Beach reserved the right to refuse reimbursement to any retailer, subject to fair-trade laws, who broke a valid fair-trade price set by Palm Beach.

The company followed the policy of adhering strictly to the details of the plan as presented to dealers. No special deals were made with any retailer.

Promotion of the Co-operative Plan to Dealers

Because the company's sales depended in large measure on the selling and promotional efforts of its retailers, Palm Beach Company devoted considerable efforts to inducing the retailers to plan a well-balanced promotional plan and to utilize fully the co-operative fund available. As one measure of the company's success in this effort, Mr. Ward pointed out that 65% of the available co-operative funds had been utilized by retailers in 1957.

In the early spring before the opening of the lightweight clothing season, Palm Beach Company sent its retail dealers a magazine-size booklet introducing the Palm Beach lines for the coming season. The booklet included full-page color illustrations of each line (the artwork being taken from advertisements to appear during the season) with a description of the product and its features. The booklet also gave an outline of Palm Beach promotional efforts scheduled for the year.

The retailer also received a 17-inch by 25-inch co-operative advertising service book. This book contained descriptive material on the co-operative advertising, reproductions of the many newspaper mats offered by the company, and suggested radio advertising scripts. In addition to black-and-white advertising mats, Palm Beach offered to its retailers four-color plastic plates for ROP color newspaper advertisements. The plates, which were made from the illustrations used in the company newspaper advertisements, were sold at cost ($20–$35) to retailers.

Palm Beach Company's 50-man sales force devoted a major portion of its time to talking with retailers about the company's advertising and the dealer's local promotion. Early in the calendar year the salesmen gave to retailers a presentation of the Palm Beach advertising program for the year, with particular emphasis upon the newspaper campaign in the retailers' local market. The salesmen emphasized to retailers the importance of maintaining an adequate stock of Palm Beach lines that were to be featured in company advertisements in order that the retailer could take advantage of the demand created by the advertising. The salesmen also devoted considerable time, especially with the larger stores, to helping the dealer prepare his Palm Beach promotional program for the year. They urged a balanced promotional plan to include direct mail, window display, and advertisements to tie into the Palm Beach Company advertising. Since a store in the normal course of business spent 3%–4% on advertising a line such as Palm Beach, the salesmen urged the stores to spend in excess of their co-operative allowance, thus gaining above average effort for Palm Beach lines.

As the season progressed, salesmen followed the promotional programs of their dealers, following up frequently during the year to urge continued advertising effort. As noted previously, the retailer, in order to be reimbursed for advertisements, had to submit a co-operative form with a tear sheet or station affidavit. These forms were sent by the retailer to the Advertising Checking Bureau, Inc., which made up a three-part form that gave the name of the retailer, the linage or time of the advertisement, and the type of the advertisement. These forms were sent to Palm Beach Company which recorded the information in the company books and immediately mailed the form to the salesman who handled that particular account. The entire process was very quick so that the salesman received the information only a short time after submission by the retailer.

With the information provided by the checking bureau, the salesman was able to maintain a record of the promotional activity of each dealer. With this specific information, the salesman actively followed up his dealers assisting their promotional plans and maintaining their efforts.

This plan had been found to work well. The effect was good not only upon the salesman who was kept alert regarding his dealer's co-operative advertising and promotion but also upon dealers, for each dealer could observe that the salesman was definitely interested in and was following what the dealer was doing.

At the end of each selling season, each salesman was provided with an annual report of the advertising done by his dealers. This report gave in much detail the information about the advertising plans the following year. The reports in turn gave the management a chance to study the promotional efforts of its salesmen and to guide and counsel them.

Over the years the company had found that the salesmen's attention to advertising and the discussion of advertising problems with merchants were of great value in getting dealer support of the Goodall line. Talking advertising helps and advertising plans enabled the salesmen to reach top management. For instance, in his talking with the men's clothing buyer in a large midwestern department store, the salesman might say regarding a certain period, "Your store used only 784 lines of advertising on Palm Beach during this period. I can't understand why you used so little. In Pittsburgh the leading department store during this period used 6,450 lines, and in Detroit a store used 3,680 lines. How can you make people here summer clothing conscious and how can you hope to build your summer clothing sales with such inadequate advertising? (Figures fictitious.) Such an approach often led the buyer to ask the salesman to talk the problem over with the publicity director, who might then call in the merchandise manager to discuss the problem of the amount of advertising necessary to create interest in men's summer clothing and develop store traffic. The work of the salesmen was taken away from talking about the details of merchandise to discussion of retail-store management, promotional methods, markets, alteration costs, net profits, and creation of customer traffic.

The executives had weekly linage reports of Palm Beach co-operative advertising. These weekly reports gave not only the details of the advertising placed during that week but also cumulative advertising up to that date with comparative figures for the year previous. Supplementary reports gave a breakdown, showing the extent to which the company's material was used, the various copy themes that were used, the relative linage given to the various features of product, store, and the like.

Other reports were drawn up periodically with breakdown by territories, size of city, and other classifications helpful in analysis and guidance of co-operative advertising efforts.

As a result of their study of the co-operative advertising of individual customers it was not unusual for top executives of the Palm Beach Company to visit key stores whose advertising was far below the potential permitted by their volume in order to discuss with them the desirability of full use of the co-operative allowance. For instance, a leading clothing store in an eastern metropolitan area was found to have used only 15% of its allowance. A top executive of the Palm Beach Company held a meeting with the top executives of the store, at which the advantages from utilization of the full allowance were stressed. As a result of this effort, the store used its full allowance the following year.

~ ~ ~

CASE 9: GENERAL HOSIERY COMPANY[1]

QUESTIONS TO CONSIDER: (1) What factors have been most important in making General Hosiery Company one of the largest manufacturers of ladies' hosiery in the United States? (2) What have been the principal elements of General Hosiery's marketing mix? (3) Should changes be made which would develop a new "image" for the "Wear-proof" brand? (4) Should changes be made in the promotional program for the brand? (5) Should the company's management make any changes in the elements of its marketing mix?

In the fall of 1958, executives of the General Hosiery Company (Genhoco) were concerned about what moves they should take to insure the continued success of the company's Wear-proof line of women's hosiery

---

[1] Written by Salvatore F. Dauita and Neil H. Borden.

and, at the same time, to expand the sales of the company's other branded lines. In the postwar period they had been able materially to increase the company's share of the market for the brand, which was a more durable hose than competing brands because of its special weave. On the other hand, an analysis of sales data indicated that Wear-proof customers were usually middle-aged and older women. The executives attributed their sales to this segment of the market to the image the brand name had created. Wear-proof carried the connotation that the brand was designed for women whose main desire was for durability in hose. In view of the hosiery industry's focus on fashion and women's apparent desire for hose so sheer that it could hardly be seen, there was a question as to how consumers would regard Wear-proof amidst a maze of fashion centered advertising.

The Hosiery Industry

During the period between 1952 and 1958, the hosiery industry had found itself in a state of overcapacity. Returning veterans had rushed to get into the hosiery industry in the late 1940's, lured by apparent opportunity in a burgeoning postwar market for nylon hose. The demand for nylon hose at that time had been great. The larger mills had been able to sell as much hosiery as they could produce. Many mills did not even bother to brand their hose. Furthermore, many mills felt it unnecessary to have a well-organized distribution setup; wholesalers and large-scale buyers went to the mills for whatever supplies they could get. Retailers drew on any distribution service available which would keep their shelves filled. In contrast to prewar practice when even large stores restricted themselves to one or two brands, now retailers stocked a large number of brands.

In time, capacity expanding until supply caught up with demand, the sellers' market disappeared. Mills began to feel the need for more adequate marketing methods. At the same time, mill customers began to voice a preference for one type of hose or another, as a result of which competition among different types of hosiery steadily intensified. Two main trends emerged: (1) customers wanted sheerer and finer knit stockings, and (2) a significant number of customers preferred the seamless variety of hose. To satisfy either of these new wants, a considerable investment in new machinery was required of many mills.

The installation of new equipment to meet these demands increased the industry's capacity. At the same time many firms while seeking a return on their investment in full-fashion machines sold at lower prices in an attempt to generate volume. The consequence was a price-cutting free-for-all in unbranded lines. Some manufacturers sold unbranded or distributor branded stockings for as little as $3.75 a dozen, as compared with around $7.50 for their own unadvertised mill brands and around $10.50 for their nationally advertised mill brands. Thus they competed disastrously with themselves. On top of the strains to move stockings at depressed prices the industry experienced a decrease in the per capita use of stockings (by females of 15 or over) from 14.7 pairs in 1952 to 13.8 pairs in 1957. In the struggle for survival the number of hosiery mills diminished to approximately 375 in 1958 from well over 800 in 1952.

In early 1958 the mood of the entire industry was one of restrained optimism. One fact contributing to this hope for more sales was a change in women's fashions. The industry hailed the return of the sack and the chemise fashion since they de-emphasized the feminine torso and promised that the appearance of women's legs would take on increased fashion significance. Even more important, however, was the trend to colored stockings. The industry had gotten behind an industry-wide promotion on color which was backed by the two main yarn suppliers, DuPont and Chemstrand. Advertising of tinted stockings had jumped from 5% of the newspaper linage for women's hosiery in September 1956 to 19% a year later, and to 33% in March 1958. Retailers were reported equally enthusiastic about the outlook for hose.

The manufacturers felt that a variety of colors was good because consumers ultimately would require an increased wardrobe of stockings to match various colors in dress and accessories. At the same time, they thought color would help them by giving the higher-priced outlets an advantage over the supermarkets, which did not have space to stock a large variety of colors. The deeper tints were expected to give a more positive emphasis to stockings as attire than did the neutral shades. Thus the appeal of bareleggedness which had prevailed during hot weather would be reduced. All in all, however, new colors were expected to play an important role in creating new fashions for hosiery.

Background Information on the Company

In 1958 Genhoco was one of the largest women's hosiery manufacturers in the United States with an annual sales volume of about $12,000,-000. In its earlier years, the company had specialized in the manufacture of what now would be called heavy seamless hose. It had been one of the first mills to introduce seamless silk and wool hosiery to the American market. Since it was formed in 1919, the company had grown steadily and had enjoyed 39 years of profitable operations. In the period between 1947 and 1958, the company's production and shipments had increased by 500%. By 1958 the company employed 1,200 people and had grown until it had eight plants: five full-fashion hosiery plants, two seamless hosiery plants, and one finishing plant.

Late in 1946 the company management came to the conclusion that although it was one of the largest firms in the business, few people realized this fact; too few people even knew the company existed. Of those in the trade that knew of the company, the company was regarded as a very competitive, unbranded mill. Many people thought the leading brand manufacturers were much larger firms than Genhoco. Bothered by this situation, the company executives felt that consumers ought to know the company as the producer of the hose they were buying and the trade ought to know the company for what it was. Hence the company sought to develop a reputation for itself.

The Wear-proof Line. At about the same time, the company had completed a market test in an apparel chain of 85 stores, on a new reinforced hose which it had produced. The management had reinforced the upper construction of the stocking which they thought would give extra strength to help support the pull of the garter. The new stocking had appeared to be so promising that as a warranty the company had offered consumers at its introduction a new pair of hose if a stocking ran in the first two weeks of wear. The returns were negligible. In light of the small returns and the promotional value of the guarantee, the same offer was continued in years to come.

Because the new stocking offered such remarkable wearing qualities, the company decided to distribute it solely as a national brand of the mill. The company's management reasoned that under this approach the company could go after a sector of the market consisting of women who had grown unhappy with the wear qualities of other brands of hose. Hence, the company could begin to develop a name for itself in the hosiery field. In consonance with the special feature of the new hose, and to convey to the consumer the idea that this hose was more durable than other lines of hose, the company selected the name "Wear-proof" as its trade name.

The Wear-proof line, with its special reinforced construction, was a stronger, although slightly heavier, hose than most of the competing brands. It was made in six shades and two degrees of sheerness, a 60-gauge, 17-denier, and a 51-gauge, 30-denier, as were most of the competing brands. The sheerer stocking, the 60-gauge, 17-denier, was priced to retail for $1.59 a pair, while the other was priced to retail for $1.39 a pair. In addition there were two seamless styles and one full-fashion stretch style, all retailing for $1.59 a pair. As previously noted, Wear-proof was sold with the same guarantee feature as was used in the introductory period; the hose was guaranteed not to tear in the first two weeks of wear. In the event the stocking tore, for any reason, a new pair was furnished upon receipt of the torn pair and guarantee slip. The company controlled the guarantee by printing a serial number on each pair of hose. When a pair was sold, the customer received from the retailer a written guarantee which listed the serial number of the hose and the date it was purchased.

Upon establishing a distribution network for the new branded line the management found it necessary to pursue an exclusive distribution policy among retailers. It found that most dealers did not care to handle a new brand which did not already have consumer acceptance. The company reasoned that although it could develop some consumer acceptance through a large advertising outlay as a means of getting distribution, it felt that selected stores would stock the hose without a large brand advertising program. In place of seeking mass distribution, the company chose to pursue an exclusive distribution policy in which the dealer would actively participate in the promotion of the new hose.

Development of Other Lines. In addition to developing its new national branded line of hose, the company concurrently sought to become a leader in the industry. During the period 1947–58, the company took out over 20 patents on hose construction. It also became a leader in packaging. Among some of its firsts was the packaging of hose in stiff cellophane envelopes for self-service distribution. In the manufacturing end, also, the company led the trade. In 1958, as in years previous, the company executives thought they were the industry's lowest-cost producer. They had been the only firm which had been successful in putting the finishing operation on an assembly-line basis, and they believed their mills had made more headway than competitors in reducing the costs of pairing stockings.[2]

In 1958, in addition to the Wear-proof line, the company produced four other lines of hosiery. Three of these lines bore mill brands. The other was distributed under private brands or was sold unbranded. The company packaged this latter line for the distributor under the distributor's mark. For those stores which were too small to afford the cost of a private mark, the company had ten separate marks which it made available for this use. In total Genhoco produced 51 different styles of full-fashion[3] and seamless-type hose in a variety of colors. See Exhibit 1. All the styles were produced in a complete range of sizes from 8½ to 11 and in a complete range of lengths. Most of the leading competitors produced two lines of branded hose in addition to a line for private brands. In contrast to Genhoco a few of the competitors with long-established brand names did the major share of their business in their national brand merchandise. As a result of concentrating on fewer lines, most competitors did not produce as many styles and packings as did Genhoco, although some offered a wider range of colors.

The company's other mill brands consisted of "Fashion Tone," "Princess," and "Trimfit." The hose packaged under these three labels were essentially the same, although there were some minor differences. Fashion Tone, which had been introduced in 1957 in anticipation of the focus on fashion, was produced in ten different shades and was priced at 89 cents per pair. The Fashion Tone package was unique in that it suggested to

---

[2] Hosiery was made on automatic machines. Since no two machines worked exactly alike, the hose from different machines varied in over-all length and heel length. Even hose made from the same machine tended to vary, mainly due to variations in the uniformity of the yarn. To utilize all the production as pairs the hosiery mills employed a hand sorting system to pair stockings of similar dimensions.

[3] See Appendix A.

the customer desirable color combinations for the hose and other clothing. The Princess brand and the Trimfit brand differed primarily in packaging. The Princess brand was packaged in a box to be dispensed by a clerk behind a counter. Normally, this brand was sold by small specialty stores and basement department stores. This brand was produced in 12 styles and was available in as many as five shades. The Trimfit brand was also produced in 12 styles, although it did not offer a wide variety of colors. This brand was packaged in clear cellophane envelopes with a stiffener suitable for distribution at self-service counters. It was sold primarily in 5- and 10-cent variety stores, discount stores, and department-store basements. Both the Princess and Trimfit brands were priced to retail for 69 cents, 79 cents, 89 cents, and 99 cents. None of these brands, Princess, Trimfit, and Fashion Tone, had even been advertised by the company or the dealers. Information regarding the company's product lines is given in Exhibit 1.

Sales and Distribution. The company's sales of nationally advertised and unadvertised mill-branded hosiery accounted for about 20% of the company's total sales, with Wear-proof accounting for half of this. The remaining 80% was generated by hose sold under distributors' labels or unbranded. About 45% of this volume, or about 35% of the company's total volume, was sold below total cost, although a contribution to overhead was made by these sales. These sales were made to utilize mill capacity as far as possible. Almost every manufacturer in the industry had much the same pattern of sales of mill brands, distributors' brands, and unbranded merchandise though the percentage of each differed.

Nonmill brand merchandise was sold principally to supermarket chains, a channel of distribution which Genhoco had pioneered in 1947. Under private brands, this hose was sold in about 6,000 supermarkets. In 1958 the company sold to a majority of the supermarket chains in the country and had generated more volume in supermarkets than had any other competitor. The management attributed this position to having been the first firm to seek this market. Supermarket sales accounted for 40% of the company's total sales.

The sales to department stores, specialty stores, apparel stores, etc., accounted for about 30% of the company's sales, two thirds of which bore the company's brands. The discount type of department store accounted for about 10% of the company's volume, and wholesalers and jobbers accounted for about 5%. The company also merchandised its private brand hose under several different marks in 600 leased hosiery departments in a variety of stores, which when totaled generated an additional 15% of the company's total sales.

In expanding its operations in leased departments the management reasoned that this arrangement not only assured a steady market at small cost to the company but also was an attractive deal for the retailers. In return for his investment in shelf space and sales expense the dealer was

Exhibit 1

GENERAL HOSIERY COMPANY
Information Regarding Product Lines

Brand	No. of Styles	No. of Colors	Factory Price per Dozen	Retail Price per Dozen	Retailers' Gross Profit per Dozen	Retail Price per Pair
Wear-proof*........	4	6	$11.25	$19.08	$7.93	$1.59
	1	3	10.00	16.68	6.68	1.39
Fashion Tone†......	1	6	5.75	10.68	4.93	0.89
	1	2	6.50	10.68	4.68	0.89
	1	10	6.75	10.68	3.93	0.89
	1	2	6.75	10.68	3.93	0.89
Princess†..........	1	3	5.00	8.28	3.28	0.69
	1	6	5.00	8.28	3.28	0.69
	1	3	5.50	9.48	3.98	0.79
	1	4	5.50	9.48	3.98	0.79
	1	4	6.50	10.68	4.18	0.89
	1	1	6.50	10.68	4.18	0.89
	1	2	6.50	10.68	4.18	0.89
	1	4	6.50	10.68	4.18	0.89
	1	5	6.50	10.68	4.18	0.89
	1	2	7.25	11.88	4.63	0.99
	1	1	7.00	11.88	4.63	0.99
	1	1	7.25	11.88	4.63	0.99
Trimfit†..........	2	2	5.75	9.48	3.73	0.79
	1	2	5.25	8.28	3.03	0.69
	1	3	5.25	8.28	3.03	0.69
	1	1	6.25	10.68	4.43	0.89
	2	1	6.00	10.68	4.68	0.89
	1	1	6.75	11.88	5.13	0.99
	1	2	6.75	11.88	5.13	0.99
	1	1	7.25	11.88	4.63	0.99
	1	1	7.50	11.88	4.38	0.99
	1	1	7.50	11.88	4.35	0.99
Private brands	2	Varied by	5.00			0.59
and unbranded†....	1	styles	5.25			
	2	from 2	5.50			
	3	to 14	5.75			to
	2	colors	6.00			
	3		6.50			
	2		7.00			1.09
	3		7.25			

* Brand name printed on hose and on the package.
† Brand name on the package only. The hose did not have any name on it.

given a percentage of the gross sales and was relieved of the merchandising task. The company placed an inventory on consignment in the store. As sales were made the dealer deposited the receipts in the company's account in the local bank and sent the box stubs to the company for replacement of inventory. The whole leased department operation including the seeking of new accounts, promotion, inventory control, etc., was conducted by a divisional manager with the help of several clerical assistants at the company's headquarters office. Two smaller competitors controlled some leased departments but on a much smaller scale.

The company's sales organization reflected the two main channels of distribution: supermarkets and department, apparel, and variety stores. The company employed a director of sales who supervised two sales managers. One sales manager directed 12 salesmen, who were located throughout the country to sell to supermarket chains. The other sales manager directed 16 men in sales to department stores and apparel stores. This sales force covered the nation. In both cases the sales managers worked with the men and aided them in planning the development of specific markets.

The salesmen were assigned territories, and they were held responsible for their development. They were given objectives to meet by the sales managers, the accomplishment of which was their responsibility. The salesman selected which stores he wanted to carry particular lines of hose and he had the authority to negotiate a dealership. At the same time, he also had the authority to terminate a dealership. The salesmen arranged sales promotions with store officials and aided the store in maintaining a balanced inventory.

Promotion of Wear-Proof

While trying to sell the unadvertised mill brands and unbranded lines to as many outlets as possible, the company sought a more selective distribution for its own nationally advertised brand. In most cities the Wear-proof brand had been awarded exclusively to one store. In some very large cities, the company had deviated from this policy and had awarded the brand to several stores, for example: New York City had five accounts; Chicago, two; Cincinnati, two; and Philadelphia, two. The company's unadvertised brands were also awarded to selected stores, but distribution was more extensive than for Wear-proof. In this instance the company avoided placing the same brand in two stores which were in the same immediate shopping area. Retailers preferred to carry brands which were not carried by neighboring retailers, thereby to give store individuality and to avoid price wars. However, since these brands were never advertised, two stores in adjacent shopping areas frequently carried the same brand. In most of the larger metropolitan areas the company serviced about 200 small accounts.

In developing an area for the Wear-proof line, the company sought to locate retail agencies which would generate the largest sale of volume for the brand. The company's experience indicated that the stores sought were not necessarily the best stores in the trading area. They had found that to generate volume they needed: (a) a store management which would co-operate in company initiated promotions, and (b) a store which did not carry an excessive number of branded lines and therefore could focus their attention on Genhoco's brand. They had found that the larger, better stores usually resisted company promotions and that the brand was just one among several brands in the store's hosiery operation.

In 1957 and 1958, however, the company had been approached by some of the leading department stores seeking to take on the Wear-proof line in areas where lesser stores had generated a considerable volume. In one city on the West Coast where the company's third largest Wear-proof dealer had built up a consumer demand for the line in five years of vigorous advertising and promotion, the company awarded the brand to the larger store also. To compensate the original dealer for possible loss of business, the company negotiated a more liberal advertising allowance for him. The company reasoned that the two stores catered to different groups of people and that the move would not materially affect the original dealer's sales volume. After six months of operation, the original dealer's sales were about the same, while the new dealer had generated a sales volume which was about 85% of the original dealer's volume.

From the above it may be seen that the company's distribution policy for the Wear-proof brand was not consistent. Whereas in some markets the company followed its usual exclusive distribution policy, in other areas it deviated from this exclusiveness. The management hoped that ultimately the company would have the Wear-proof brand in every better store. However, they doubted whether the company could afford the large advertising expense it would have to assume if it sought true mass distribution. Also, it was concerned about the fate of Wear-proof sales if Wear-proof dealers were no longer enthusiastic about their exclusive rights. The company management was looking forward to learning more about this problem from the move made in the city on the West Coast.

The company focused its selling attention right down to the retail level. Convinced that few women had a brand loyalty for hosiery, the company sought to gain the customer through point-of-purchase displays and through the selling efforts of the salesgirl. The company salesmen supplied the retailers with a variety of point-of-purchase display materials. Some were for use on the counter, while other materials were for wall and window displays. The company officials believed that attractive displays were valuable in influencing women to buy the Wear-proof brand. In addition, the company had found that fashion shows in the larger stores proved to be sales stimulants, and as a consequence it periodically engaged models and other people to put on fashion shows or other demonstrations. These shows were offered free of charge to dealers who participated in company initiated promotions. Lastly, the company made available to its dealers, at a nominal charge, a supply of bill enclosures and direct mailers. These were printed up to coincide with the seasons and were usually used at Easter time, in the fall, and for Christmas. In the opinion of the company officials, these had proved more effective in some stores than others.

The management undertook a program to capture the salesgirls' enthusiasm for selling Wear-proof. The management wanted to impress upon the salesgirls that it needed them to sell hosiery, that they were an important element in this business. To gain their confidence and their enthusiasm, the company asked the salesgirls and the store manager to a breakfast in the nearby hotel at periodic intervals around the year. When possible the company's top management attended these breakfasts. In the relaxed atmosphere of these breakfast parties, the company tried to bring the guests up to date on the company's program and discussed new products soon to emerge. The meetings were also used to exchange ideas between the company personnel and the salespeople and thereby served to keep sales force and management informed of customer attitudes.

Twice each year the company ran a contest for salespeople. The contest was adjusted to the size of the store's operation; for example, in smaller stores in smaller cities, the sales volume required of a girl to win a prize was lower than that which was required of a girl in one of the larger department stores. In this way each girl selling Wear-proof hose had a fair chance to win a prize. In the final analysis, the company management regarded the salesgirl as the most important link in selling hosiery.

Because of the nature of the distribution setup in which relatively few stores in any given area carried the Wear-proof brand, the company found it more desirable to advertise in conjunction with the retailers rather than to do general company advertising in blanket media. The company had, some time before, undertaken a limited advertising program in selected women's and fashion magazines such as *Good Housekeeping* and *Vogue*, but judged the results not worth the expense. The company came to feel that advertising ought to tell the customer not only about the hose but also the place where she could buy it. As this conviction grew the company slowly entered into a co-operative advertising program with its retailers and was spending between $200,000 and $330,000 a year for advertising and promotion in the years between 1955 and 1958. These figures are in sharp contrast to the insignificant sums expended for advertising just ten years before. This money was spent as follows: 40% for newspaper advertising, 40% for spot TV advertising, 5% for point-of-purchase display materials, and 15% for fashion shows and incentive contests for salesgirls and salesmen.

Under the co-operative advertising plan, the company offered to reimburse the dealer for 50% of the cost of newspaper or TV advertising of Wear-proof hosiery. Participation in the plan was open to any Wear-proof dealer on a voluntary basis. As part of the plan, the company furnished the dealer, without charges, newspaper mats (see Exhibit 2) and materials and scripts for TV. In addition the company assisted the dealers in preparing and writing local advertising when requested to do so. The only requirements the company imposed on the dealer was that he had to use the Wear-proof trade-mark in the advertising. The company

Exhibit 2

GENERAL HOSIERY COMPANY

Example of Newspaper Mat

WEAR-PROOF NYLONS

First For Fit
First For Comfort
First For Wear

There must be a good reason why *WEAR-PROOF*
Nylons have been the *first choice* of
millions of fashion-wise thrifty women all over
America for many years. Your *first* pair will
show you why such popularity is so well deserved.

guaranteed against runs for any cause

All-Purpose Sheer $**1 39** *pr.*
51-Gauge WEAR-PROOF

Luxury Sheer $**1 59** *pr.*
60-Gauge WEAR-PROOF

store name

Mat No. 908

placed no requirements on advertising budget, character of copy, size of space, or frequency of insertion. The company paid its portion of the advertising cost upon receipt of the dealer's tear sheets showing the advertisements run, together with bills from the newspapers or TV companies indicating the rates actually paid.

Although the company had not placed a formal limit on how much advertising it would be willing to share, it watched the retailers' advertising activities very closely. The company executives indicated they regarded a total co-operative expenditure of $1.50 per dozen of hose sold as a desirable goal figure for co-operative advertising expenditure. The dealer was expected to pay for half of this amount. Their experience, however, indicated that the total retailers' advertising figure approached $2.00 per dozen over-all because certain retailers occasionally reached an expenditure of $3.00 per dozen. When the advertising ratio seemed to be rising among any retailers, the company salesmen moved in to talk to the dealers in an effort to bring their outlays back into line. In certain instances, however, the company encouraged a higher ratio, particularly when a store was introducing Wear-proof. In this case the company even assumed a greater share of the advertising cost than 50%. However, as the Wear-proof brand became established in the store, the company moved to the normal 50% reimbursement plan.

Out of the 1,500 Wear-proof dealers about 500 took advantage of the company's co-operative advertising plan. The remaining firms did not use the plan principally because there was no medium which they could use effectively. This was the case for those stores which were located in small towns adjacent to larger cities or stores located in outlying shopping centers serving a small segment of the city's population. Although most stores which used the plan did newspaper advertising, the company officials were of the opinion that newspapers had lost their effectiveness for advertising hosiery except for the annual 20% off sales on nationally advertised brands. The company officials thought that TV was a better medium for its agents but conceded it was a very costly medium in the larger metropolitan areas, unless many accounts were within the TV coverage area.

The company had used the co-operative advertising plan to build initial consumer acceptance. It was happy with the results. It was uncertain, however, whether its continuance would be desirable if it embarked upon an expansion of its Wear-proof distribution.

From a wear standpoint, the company executives were confident that once a woman used a pair of Wear-proof, she would buy them again if it were convenient for her to do so. From a fashion standpoint, they were less confident of the brand's appeal. They had added three additional shades to the line bringing the total number up to six. There was some question about whether this number was adequate. Also, some concern stemmed from the fact that Wear-proof was a slightly heavier hose, although this was not too noticeable. Largely, the concern stemmed from the image the brand name had created, namely, that Wear-proof hose carried the connotation of being suited for people whose primary interest was durability. In view of the heavy emphasis that was being placed on fashion by the entire industry, the company executives were reviewing the situation to determine what changes, if any, ought to be made in its branding as well as in the other elements of its marketing plans.

Information regarding the retailing of hosiery is given in Appendix B.

TERMS AND DEFINITIONS ABOUT WOMEN'S HOSIERY

Full-Fashioned

Full-fashioned stockings are knit on long machines of 30 to 32 sections which produce 30 or 32 stockings at a time. Each section is 14 inches or 14½ inches wide. The stockings are fashioned to shape by narrowing or widening the fabric, using more or less needles, according to the contour of the leg. They are knit flat from the top down to the toe. Full-fashioned stockings are identified by the seam which joins the two edges of the fabric and by the presence of fashion marks used in narrowing the fabric. There is also a small opening on the inside of the welt (or top) near the seam, called the seaming hole which denotes full-fashioned construction.

Seamless or Circular Hosiery

Seamless or circular hoisery is knit in a tubular manner on machinery containing a round dial of needles. Shaping during knitting is accomplished by tightening or loosening the stitches. This hosiery does not have a seam. One stocking at a time is knit per machine during the production cycle.

Gauge

Gauge refers to full-fashioned hosiery and represents the number of needles used per inch and a half in the horizontal dimension. A 51-gauge stocking has 34 needles to the inch or 51 needles to the inch and a half. A 60-gauge stocking has 40 needles to the inch, etc. The fineness of the fabric depends upon gauge and the looseness or tightness of knitting (as in fine against coarse stitch needlepoint work). All other things being equal a *higher-gauged* stocking is usually *finer* in appearance (i.e., more closely knit) and will wear better than looser knit lower-gauge stockings.

Needle Count

Needle count refers to seamless hosiery and denotes the number of needles around the dial (which is 3¾ inches in diameter). Popular types are 400 needles or 474 needles.

Denier

Denier indicates the circumference of the yarn used in making the stocking. The lower the denier, the thinner the yarn. A 30-denier yarn is double the thickness of a 15-denier yarn.

Sheerness

The sheerness of the hosiery is due to the denier or diameter of the yarn rather than the fineness of the gauge (closeness of the needles). The weight desired should be chosen primarily by denier. Briefly, the higher the denier, the heavier the hose; the higher the gauge, the finer the quality and stitch count of the hose. The 15-denier is ultra-sheer; 30-denier is business sheer; 70-denier is heavy service weight.

Appendix B

SOME OBSERVATIONS ON THE RETAILING OF HOSIERY

The following paragraphs are the product of the observations made and the interviews conducted by one researcher while examining the retailing aspects of the hosiery business. This examination covered several department stores, several large specialty stores and apparel chain, several shoe stores, and several smaller independent specialty stores. In addition, one wholesaler was interviewed. The reader, therefore, is cautioned to accept the generalizations contained herein as judgments which were formulated on the basis of the data which were immediately available rather than on the basis of statistical reliability. In several instances generalizations are extracted from published reports. In these cases they are so indicated.

Ladies' hosiery was sold in a variety of outlets in 1958. The major outlets included department stores, specialty stores, discount stores, and supermarkets. The discount store and the supermarket had become major outlets in the last five years with the growing trend upward self-service and lower prices. In addition to these major outlets, ladies' hosiery was sold in lesser quantities in drugstores, variety stores, garages, beauty parlors, newsstands, and vending machines.

Clearly, the department store was the largest hosiery retailer. Although figures were not available, some estimates indicated the department-store hosiery sales accounted for between 50% and 60% of the total volume of hosiery sold. Next in size was the supermarket which was credited with having sold between 30% and 40% of the total volume of hosiery sold. The remainder of the hosiery sold was distributed principally through the specialty store and the discount store. The hosiery sold by the balance of the outlets was considered to be inconsequential.

According to two surveys conducted in 1950 and in 1951 by *Hosiery Merchandising*, the department and specialty stores did at least 50% of their hose volume in nationally branded merchandise. Of this group, the independent specialty stores and the independent department stores sold between 75% and 90% of their volume in national brands while the larger chain specialty stores and the chain department stores were not so heavily entrenched in national brands. The observations made in 1958 indicated there was more private label hose sold than in 1950–51. The supermarkets did 100% of their hosiery volume in private branded merchandise.

In 1958, principally as a result of the overcapacity in the hosiery industry, more and more stores were turning to private label hosiery and unbranded hosiery. This hosiery, in addition to just being lower priced, offered most stores the opportunity to compete with the supermarkets and the discount stores. One specialty store which had adopted a "will not be undersold" policy used four separate private brands of its own to cover the complete range of prices beginning at 44 cents a pair.

The number of brands carried by any one store varied between one and ten in the stores interviewed. The relationship observed between the number of brands carried and number of stores carrying that many brands, closely approximated the results of the 1950 survey shown below:

SURVEY OF NUMBER OF BRANDS CARRIED IN 360 STORES
CARRYING NATIONAL BRANDS

Number of National Brands	% of Stores Carrying That Many Brands
1	7.5
2	5.5
3	9.0
4	17.5
5	21.0
6	13.5
7	10.0
8	6.0
9	4.5
10	5.5

Most of the larger specialty stores interviewed in 1958 carried two national brands of hose in reasonably complete lines. In addition these stores carried one or two other brands in selected styles or shades. These other brands were either the stores' own mark or the mill's unadvertised brand. In some cases the specialty store sold an unbranded line of hose. Most of these stores interviewed, however, did not regard the additional brands as part of their regular product mix, rather they were temporary additions that would probably be replaced by other temporary additions.

The stores carrying only one brand were usually either of two types: (a) a small specialty shop which carried a line of hose to capture any impulse purchases, or (b) a hosiery store which carried all its merchandise under its own brand. At the opposite end of the spectrum was the large department store which offered a very complete line in many brands of its customers.

Most of the buyers interviewed indicated they had not added nor dropped a nationally advertised brand of hose in many years. In most cases, the brands carried were taken on by the buyers before the present ones. The feeling was expressed that it was risky to drop a line of hose which had become established in the store, particularly if it was the store's only national brand. The basis for this feeling was the fear that customers might transfer their purchases to other stores if it were convenient for them to do so. The buyer of a department store which carried ten national brands of hose hesitated to eliminate some brands, although he felt sure he was carrying too many brands.

From the buyer's point of view, there was little difference between the various brands of hose. The feeling was expressed that Brand A was as good as Brand B, etc. One buyer referred to hosiery as a staple product with little differentiation and compared it to salt. There was a popular belief among buyers that although the newer styles came off new, more advanced machinery, the hosiery produced on the older machinery gave just as good wear. Because of the little differentiation between brands and the uniform markup allowed between the different manufacturers, the decision to carry one brand as against another reduced itself down to a function of the store's former relationships with the salesman, the manufacturer, or the wholesaler as the case might be.

The retail price of hosiery ranged from about 40 cents per pair for unbranded hose to about $5.00 per pair for a special ultra-sheer stocking. Actually, there were two intermediary price categories which were prevalent: from 89 cents to $1.00 for private unadvertised brands, and from $1.25 to $1.70 for nationally advertised brands. Hose priced from $2.00 to $5.00 were special very sheer dress hose. The $5.00 hose, for example, was a 99-gauge, 10-denier import from Germany. It was advertised as the "sheerest stocking in the world."

The lower-priced hose was usually found in the discount store, the basement department store, the supermarket, and the variety store. This hose was usually individually packed and sold at a self-service bar. In contrast, the higher-priced hose was sold in department specialty stores by a salesgirl over the counter where the customer could examine a variety of shades or styles before she made her selection.

According to the salespeople interviewed, few customers knew precisely what style, shade, or weight they wanted when they approached the hosiery counter. In fact, most women had difficulty in understanding the characteristics of hosiery such as denier and gauge. Normally women asked to see a pair of nylons. At that point the salesgirl attempted first to find out what kind of stockings the customer wanted, and next to suggest a pair of hose which was of a fitting weight and shade. For example, if the customer wanted a pair of hose for evening wear, the girl suggested a very sheer hose; on the other hand, if they were to be used for work, then the girl would suggest a less sheer hose which would in turn be somewhat stronger. It was the experience of the people interviewed that although the customer desired a stronger hose, when it came down to a choice, she invariably selected the sheerer pair.

Usually the customer asked for two pairs of hose so that if one stocking tore she might still get some use out of the other one. Using the same argument, the salesgirls were usually successful in pushing the purchase of a box of hose, which contained three pairs.

Hosiery buyers unanimously agreed that women, as a rule, did not plan their hosiery purchases. They tended, however, to limit their hosiery purchases to the same store. They seemed to have a greater loyalty to the store they shopped in than the brands of hose they purchased. Some buyers indicated they had been able to take advantage of this kind of loyalty by special newspaper and direct-mailer promotions. On the other hand, some other buyers felt direct mailers and newspaper advertising were not very effective means of promoting hosiery.

All the larger hosiery retailers interviewed used the newspaper as their principal advertising medium. For some, this was a more effective device than for others. One buyer indicated that newspaper advertising proved useful only when nationally advertised merchandise was to be sold at a reduced price (20%-off sale). This occurred once each year for each national brand. The smaller shops indicated they found bill stuffers to their charge customers a more effective medium than newspapers. The local small specialty stores, on the other hand, did not advertise at all since they did not have a suitable medium in which to advertise.

It was common practice for the retailer to receive an advertising allowance from the manufacturer or the wholesaler on those brands which were either nationally or regionally advertised. This allowance usually covered half of the actual advertising cost. It was, however, insufficient as an inducement to advertise aggressively in the case of the mass-distributed brand. The retailers handling brands which had mass distribution were reluctant to advertise them aggressively, since they felt the demand their advertising might stimulate, might be satisfied by some other retailer carrying the same brand. On the other hand, one retailer who had an exclusive on a national brand was excited about how he had been able to multiply his sales of that particular brand through newspaper advertising.

One thing all the buyers interviewed agreed upon was the necessity for well-trained salesgirls. Since personal selling played a major role in selling hosiery, the buyers depended on the salesgirls to create an atmosphere in which the customer would feel comfortable. Some stores went so far as to keep a record of the customer's purchases in the department for the customer's later reference.

In some cases a personal relationship evolved between certain salesgirls and certain customers. In some of these cases the salesgirls wrote post cards or made telephone calls to their customers reminding them personally that a sale was coming soon or that they were about due for replenishing their hosiery stock.

In view of the customer's need for help in selecting hosiery, the store also sought to take advantage of this opportunity to increase sales. Since customers did not have a strong loyalty to a particular brand, salesgirls were frequently successful in selling (a) a higher-priced hose than the customer asked for, and (b) an extra pair or two.

One very successful hosiery buyer of a large specialty store attributed his success to good merchandising and never-ending promotions. His total inventory consisted of fashion-centered hosiery. He took the point of view of giving the customer "what she really wants—sheer hosiery which helps her look more attractive to men." He pointed out that he brought every new style and shade into the department at least for a trial period. He worked to build the idea in the customer's mind, that if there was anything new in hosiery, his store had it first. He was an aggressive advertiser.

This same buyer took an opposite point of view than did some of his competitors on another issue. While almost all of the buyers interviewed indicated they preferred to deal direct with the manufacturer, this buyer preferred to work with a wholesaler. The preference for the manufacturer was based on two reasons: first, because the manufacturer offered a larger advertising allowance and, second, because they felt they would be better informed about new developments in the company's product line. The preference for the wholesaler, however, was based on his ability to offer better delivery service. This service was particularly important during a promotion in which a particular number was selling fast and needed to be immediately replenished. The buyer pointed out that under this arrangement, in which stocks could be replenished within an hour or so, the store had never run out of any size. In addition, he was able to keep his inventory at a low, more economical level. He pointed out further that the wholesaler carried as many styles, shades, and sizes as did the manufacturer and that he was at least as co-operative as any manufacturer, so that the scales were unbalanced by the delivery factor.

In 1958, hosiery manufacturers tended to sell their production direct to the retailer via their own sales forces. In the several years preceding 1958, a number of manufacturers assumed their own sales force as they felt the need to push the sale of their production more aggressively. This more reflected the industry's need to move its overcapacity. Hosiery wholesalers, however, continued to exist although they were not the principal method of distribution in 1958.

On the other hand, although wholesalers were not the principal means of distribution, they held a strong place in this market. Generally, they handled the distribution for smaller manufacturers who could not afford their own sales force—although some of the better-known national brands were also sold through wholesalers. One wholesaler claimed that wholesalers offered a credit line to the store that manufacturers refused to do and from this standpoint they filled a need, especially for the smaller store. As pointed out above, the wholesaler was in a better position, also, to make a delivery on shorter notice.

Regardless of who sold the store, the wholesaler's salesman or the manufacturer's salesman, the store generally received the same kind of help from either salesman. Both offered to help train the salesgirls—each instructed the girls about their own product, both aided the buyer in reordering, both offered the store mail stuffers, display materials, and advertising allowances. The wholesaler, however, did offer a lower advertising allowance than did the manufacturer. In addition, all of these salesmen acted as the communication channel between the various stores.

Buyers gave conflicting evidence of brand preferences of consumers: on one hand, they said hose was standard and had little consumer brand specified; yet buyers held on to brands for fear of losing patronage.

~ ~ ~

CASE 10: ADVERTISING TO AND THROUGH THE TRADE

Examine and compare the part played or which should have been played by (1) trade paper and direct-mail advertising to the trade, and (2) point-of-purchase advertising in the cases listed below. Prepare a list of useful generalizations regarding the use of such advertising in the advertising and promotional programs of manufacturers.

Chapter 8

~~~~~~~~~~~~~~~~~~~~~~~~~~~~~~~~~~~

CASES INVOLVING THE

MARKETING MIX FOR

INDUSTRIAL PRODUCTS

~~~

This chapter consists of six cases which concern the role of advertising in the marketing mixes of manufacturers of industrial products (including one case which concerns a business service). Particular emphasis has been given to problems that are involved in the promotion of branded parts.

~~~

CASE 1: BUCKNER TEXTILE MACHINERY COMPANY[1]

QUESTIONS TO CONSIDER: (1) *What are the principal elements of Buckner's marketing mix?* (2) *What role has advertising played in the mix?* (3) *Has the company employed a good combination of various types of advertising?* (4) *What recommendations would you make to the advertising manager as of January 1958?*

In January 1958 the advertising manager of the Buckner Textile Machinery Company, was considering whether any change in the advertising and sales promotion policies of the company were warranted in view of the market situation which had developed in the preceding year. In 1957 the company had experienced serious difficulties in making textile machinery sales and had often considered a reduction in its work force. This situation, however, was common to the industry and had been developing

---

[1] The name of the company is disguised. Written by Salvatore F. Davita and Neil H. Borden.

since 1952 when the market changed from a sellers' market to a buyers' market. Buckner increased its advertising budget threefold during this five-year period in order to hold its competitive position in light of the active promotional programs of its competitors. The advertising manager was convinced the company had to continue an aggressive advertising program and was further exploring the usefulness of a public relations department to help establish a favorable environment for the introduction of new products.

The Buckner Textile Machinery Company manufactured, sold, installed, and provided repair service for an extensive line of preparatory textile machinery. The company produced a full line of cotton machinery, which comprised 60% of its output, and a complete line of wool machinery and selected synthetic fiber machines, which made up the remaining 40%. The Buckner company did not make looms or finishing equipment but concentrated on preparatory machinery, that is, machines such as spinning frames, cards, twisters, and winders, designed for bringing the fibers up to the point at which they are ready for weaving or knitting.

Buckner was the largest manufacturer in its field, producing an estimated 50% of all textile machinery of the preparatory type. The company competed with two other large companies which also had a fairly extensive line of machines, one specializing in cotton, the other in wool. No other manufacturer had so complete a line of cotton, wool, and synthetic fiber machinery as Buckner's. In addition, in the cotton field principally, Buckner, in the preceding decade, had come to compete with a number of small specialists in the South which assumed manufacturing operations as an outgrowth of the back-yard repair shops which they had started. These small firms competed vigorously with the larger firms by offering better delivery and cutthroat prices made possible by sacrifice in quality and their lower overhead. In cotton machinery these small firms accounted for about 10% of the market, whereas Buckner had about 45%, as did Buckner's leading competitor. In wool machinery, however, Buckner had 60% of the market in contrast to the 40% held by the leading competitor, and in the synthetic fiber field Buckner held approximately 80% of the market.

In marketing its repair service for textile machinery, Buckner encountered vigorous competition from many sources, especially from small firms in the proximity of the mills. These shops, usually run by former textile mill mechanics, reportedly often did poor work and competed with the Buckner company and other textile machine manufacturers primarily on the basis of the savings they could offer their customers in delivery time and in transportation costs.

To offset the advantages of position enjoyed by these local repair shops, the Buckner company had built a new plant and sales office in High Point, North Carolina, in the heart of the southern cotton mill territory. This branch plant had originally been designed to provide efficient repair service on cotton machinery and had recently been expanded to incorporate a manufacturing facility for replacement parts and subassemblies.

Textile machines in general had an extremely long useful life. Examples were cited of 90-year-old cards still in active service. Repairs, therefore, were frequent in comparison with new installations, which ordinarily involved a major capital outlay. Accordingly, repair service was a substantial source of revenue for the Buckner company.

Moreover, through its repair service the company greatly expanded the number of people it might serve. Because of the long life of the machines, there was normally a good market for secondhand equipment, and thus in many instances where the Buckner company had not made the original installations, mills became customers for its repair service on their used Buckner machines.

The number of domestic prospects for Buckner textile machinery was relatively limited, amounting to approximately 2,000, most of whom were located on the East Coast. Of this total about 1,200 were prospects for cotton machinery, located principally in the southeastern segment of the United States. The prospects for woolen machinery, on the other hand, were located in the North Atlantic and New England states, whereas the prospects for synthetic fiber machinery were scattered throughout this entire area. In addition to these domestic mills, the company had a very large number of potential customers throughout the rest of the world, to which it expected to ship 15% of its volume in 1958.

The company's sales force consisted of 30 men, each a specialist in one kind of machine category. The cotton machine salesmen, 20 in number, were located at the High Point office and typically serviced from 50–75 small accounts each. The six wool salesmen, as did the four synthetic fiber salesmen, operated out of the home office in Boston, each servicing a very few much larger accounts. All these salesmen were technically trained, and most of them had been promoted out of some other department such as manufacturing, engineering, or service. The company, however, did employ as salesmen a limited number of graduates from technical textile schools who were put through a company product training program.

Typically, the salesmen operating out of the home office spent half of their time visiting clients, a large proportion of which was spent in travel. The salesmen operating out of the branch offices, on the other hand, spent most of their time out of the office visiting their assigned mills. Buckner salesmen called on customers and prospects two or three times a year in the case of mills located near the company's sales offices and usually once a year to those mills located in Ohio, Michigan, Minnesota, and Oregon. The company reached these more distant mills chiefly through correspondence, but this did not result in any competitive disadvantage since Buckner was well known to these mills and since Buckner's competitors used essentially the same practice.

Normally, Buckner salesmen called on their customers to keep them abreast of the changes in the Buckner line and to nurture the relationships they had developed over the years. The specific people they called on varied; whereas in some cases they called on top executives, in others, on engineers, and in still others on mill superintendents. In any case, the original call was made on the president or vice president and the following calls were made to whomever the executive recommended. During these calls, salesmen often obtained leads on mills believed to be contemplating expansion, overhaul, or the introduction of additional lines of products.

The Buckner salesmen were required to be familiar with the terminology involved in textile machines and their use and to know the construction, features, and advantages of the machinery which they were selling. Normally salesmen sent job specifications to the company's engineering department, which figured such details as the floor plan, the gearing, and the motor shaft specifications. On highly technical matters the salesmen often called on the design engineers or research personnel to make field trips with them.

In many cases, customers submitted their own specifications for specialized nonstandard equipment. Although the Buckner management did not encourage the sales of specially adapted machinery, since the manufacture of nonstandard items defeated the advantages of mass production, it was happy to take any order in 1958. Almost all the company's machinery had, in earlier years, been completely standardized, but as mill executives became more machine conscious, they began to demonstrate an increasing tendency to have their own engineers specify more precise and high-speed equipment. Approximately 60% of the parts constituting a spinning frame were standard items, but the departures from standard were numerous enough to create serious scheduling problems for the Buckner management in trying to fill the requests of individual customers.

The company was not in a position to ignore the requests of its customers for specialized adaptations of its standard machinery, for the cost of the average installation was very high, ranging from a single unit cost of from $5,000 to $6,500 to a complete mill installation cost of from $500,000 to $1,000,000. Orders for complete new mill installations had been rare following the early period of growth of the domestic textile industry but were still received occasionally from the export market. It was unusual for customers to place orders calling for some items of each type of machinery, since most sales resulted from expansion and revamping programs, and typical orders were for a number of new spinning frames or for a series of new picking room machines.

In recent years there was a tendency for mill customers to seek more and more proposals from different textile manufacturers before placing their orders. In earlier generations Buckner customers had often ordered from Buckner because they were familiar with and were impressed by the reliability of its machinery; they had built up a strong loyalty for Buckner machinery. In the last decade, however, this loyalty to a particular brand name appeared to diminish along with the identity such brands had enjoyed in the industry for so many years. This situation was indicative of the change in the buying patterns of the mills and applied not only to the textile machinery suppliers but also to all other suppliers of the textile industry.

Although not a part of the sales organization, Buckner's service men were often helpful in making sales. The service department, although headquartered in Boston, was decentralized in its operations. The headquarters sales office provided the service men with up-to-date literature on specifications and repair procedure. Each service man was assigned to work with a salesman, servicing the same accounts the salesmen serviced. Consequently the service men did not work out of the headquarters office. Although the service man did not work for the salesman, he worked very closely with him. Normally, like the salesman, the service man called on the assigned accounts on his own initiative and at no cost to the mill. The men he contacted in the mill were at a much lower echelon than the executives whom the salesman called on. During his calls, the service man was primarily interested in keeping Buckner machines adjusted for the fibers they were processing. On his call he often learned of anticipated changes in products to be manufactured that might involve changes in machines. These he quickly passed on to the salesman to whom he was assigned.

The Buckner management had felt that the company's advertising could be of limited value in inducing prospects to install its textile machinery. Publication advertising, in particular, had been deemed to play a minor role in the Buckner marketing program. The management had never undertaken an aggressive industrial paper and mail advertising campaign in its recent history except in 1930 and 1940, when it had introduced new products and felt that it had a special message to bring to the attention of the public. The advertising budget, typically in the neighborhood of $20,000, had only in the last decade increased to $60,000 in order to meet rising advertising costs and to provide additional linage to maintain the company's competitive position. Even this larger amount, however, represented less than 0.25% of the anticipated 1958 sales of $25 million.

The advertising manager believed that there were few effective types of advertising media available for selling Buckner prospects and that the best advertising policy the company could follow was to make such use of these media as appeared necessary from time to time. An exception to this policy of using media only as needed was found in the case of trade journal advertising. Here the management regularly purchased space, both as a matter of goodwill to the journals and to lend support to the salesmen's communication. The management had little expectation that the trade paper advertising itself would do more than arouse interest and produce inquiries.

While the Buckner management did not expect its advertising to actually produce sales, it was strongly opposed to using a mere business card style of advertising in trade papers and made every effort to present effective selling copy and layout. The advertisements often depicted actual installations, and the text was made fairly long to present convincing sales arguments. In 1957 the company had begun to use this medium to introduce new machines and to emphasize their outstanding characteristics. Exhibits 1 and 2 contain copy of two advertisements which are illustrative of messages presented in 1957.

In 1957 the company had taken full-page advertising space in every issue of all the leading journals of the textile industry in the United States and Canada and in one South American publication. The trade journals reciprocated by giving the Buckner company favorable publicity in their editorial columns, publishing the prepared papers which were delivered by the company's executives at conventions and business meetings.

The rough layouts and copy for the advertisements were prepared by the company's advertising manager and submitted to its advertising agency to be produced and submitted to the publications. The company advertised in the leading journals of the textile industry of the United States and Canada such as: *Canadian Textile Journal, America's Textile Reporter, Fiber & Fabric, Textile Bulletin, Textile World, Textile Industries,* and *Modern Textiles,* and in one South American publication, *Textils Pan Americanos.* In the *America's Textile Reporter,* a weekly, the company ran 24 full-page advertisements a year; in its other publications, all monthlies, the schedule called for 12 full-page insertions annually. This required the preparation of from 20 to 24 different advertisements each year, since the same copy was often not suitable for the cotton, wool, and synthetic industries.

According to the advertising manager, few sales inquiries had ever been traced to the company's trade publication advertisements. He, nevertheless, felt that in the long run it would be inadvisable to withdraw completely from the trade publications. From the short-term viewpoint it was thought that if the company discontinued its advertising in trade journals it could, without suffering competitive disadvantage, coast along on the momentum of the reputation which it had already established among currently active mill executives; but that cessation of publication advertising might eventually be misunderstood and react unfavorably to the company's prestige.

There were special occasions, however, in which management felt trade paper advertising was of vital importance. Whenever an industry trade show was held, machinery exhibited were always widely advertised in this fashion. Also when new or widely different products were introduced to the market, trade paper campaigns were frequently utilized.

Exhibit 1

BUCKNER TEXTILE MACHINERY COMPANY

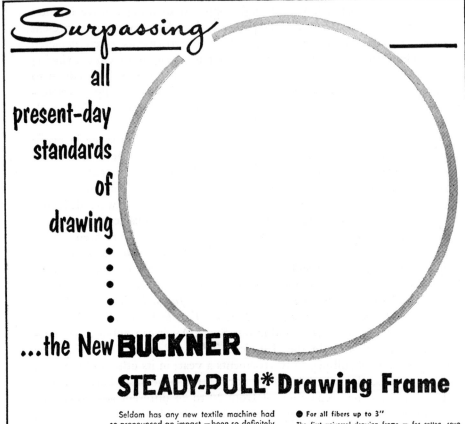

Surpassing
all present-day standards of drawing • • • • •
...the New **BUCKNER** STEADY-PULL* Drawing Frame

Seldom has any new textile machine had so pronounced an impact,—been so definitely successful — as the new BucKner Steady-Pull Drawing Frame. In many large installations (up to 80 deliveries), mills report production doubled or tripled, sliver quality reaching levels formerly unattainable, and costs slashed to new lows. In short, all current standards for drawing have been completely surpassed by this new BucKner high production, precision-made textile machine.

● **From 250-300 feet per minute Front Roll Delivery**

Production two to three times more than conventional machines, depending upon mill conditions and production needs.

● **For all fibers up to 3″**
The first universal drawing frame — for cotton, spun synthetics and blends.

● **Outstanding Sliver Quality**
Improved uniformity in both carded and combed sliver — 6 or 8 ends up.

● **Pneumafil Clearer Units**
A brand new way of removing waste fibers Developed for, and an integral part of, this machine.

● **Entirely New Design**
Two independent four-delivery heads, vibration proof construction; precision tolerances; anti-friction bearings; unique four over five roll drafting; new overarm weighting; no-twist can table; electronic stop motions and signal lights; 14″ — 15″ — 16″ cans, 36″ or 42″ high.

°TRADE MARK

BUCKNER TEXTILE MACHINERY CO.
BOSTON, MASS.   HIGHPOINT, N.C.

Exhibit 2

BUCKNER TEXTILE MACHINERY COMPANY

This installation of *NATIONAL* Roving and Spinning frames at J.B. Doe Inc. Manchester, N.H. has resulted in savings in floor space, labor costs and power consumption.

BUCKNER 10" x 5" Roving frames at J.B. Doe Inc.

Spinning frames at J.B. Doe Inc.

Are you keeping machinery *that can't earn its "Keep"?*

...then you're losing the **Profit Potential** of BUCKNER **NATIONAL SYSTEM EQUIPMENT**

The policy of harboring old out-dated equipment on the premise that it has a "few good years left in it" is dangerous! Regardless of how it may be *hidden* in the cost sheets, machinery that is not competitive is a liability!

Leaders in the industry — world-famous mills like J.B. Doe are quick to realize this. In the keenly competitive task of processing fibers for profit, they seek out the latest, most modern and most competitive equipment.

For production, quality, ease of maintenance and simplicity of operation. **BUCKNER-NATIONAL** System machinery ———— the DRAFTER, the Roving frame and the Spinning frame — offers unusual competitive advantages in the processing of worsted, synthetic and blended fibers.

To make your operation more profitable — make it **BUCKNER!**

For complete information, ask your Buckner representative — or write direct to us.

BUCKNER

TEXTILE MACHINERY CO.

BOSTON, MASS.

HIGHPOINT, N.C.

New inventions in the textile machinery industry had typically been infrequent, although changes and refinements had been more frequent. However, with the change in market conditions, the company had opened a research-engineering division in 1951 to place special emphasis on designing improvements on the existing machines and to develop entirely new machines. In 1957 the impact of this program had been felt through the introduction of a number of new machines. The advertising manager indicated, however, that the company was preparing to introduce many more efficient machines in the years following.

The Buckner catalogues were an important factor in the company's promotional program. Instead of a single general catalogue, individual pamphlets containing descriptive literature were prepared to describe each principal type of machinery, such as spinning frames and card-room machinery. These pamphlets were mailed to Buckner's customers and were used by the salesmen in illustrating the company's new machinery. The company had found that this approach was superior to a general catalogue since revision was simplified and permitted the company to gain some advertising value each time a new pamphlet was issued.

Floor plans, tables, formulas, and data of a more technical nature on gearings and motors, not suitable for inclusion in its pamphlets, were contained in various technical manuals which, like the pamphlets, were published individually for spinning frames, cards, and other of the company's major machines. These technical manuals were not sent to a mailing list but were distributed on the basis of requests resulting from offers made in the company's advertisements in the trade journals or in announcements made in the company's house organ, the *Buckner News.*

This house organ, an illustrated magazine published quarterly by the company, contained information of a semitechnical and technical nature. The management felt that the publication was a valuable promotional device despite its conservative tone. The editorial content of the *News* included articles by executives, engineers, and research personnel on plant developments, technical improvements in the field of textile machinery, and descriptions of special installations of Buckner equipment in designated textile mills. Readership of the house organ was checked by means of free offers of bulletins on technical subjects prominently featured on the inside back cover. The management had recently expanded and improved the *News* since one of the company's competitors published a house organ similar in make-up and editorial content but somewhat larger and more lavish than the *News.*

The house organ was sent to a mailing list of 9,000, which included mill executives and supervisory personnel down to the level of overseers, as well as senior textile students, teachers, and research workers. Persons on this mailing list, as well as the company's 4,500 employees, also received copies of its attractive 12-sheet calendar, which was illustrated with color photographs of New England scenes.

To supplement its advertising, Buckner participated in a number of textile machinery shows. The company had participated in a southern show and in a foreign show, both of which took place every two years. In addition, the company participated in the major industry show sponsored by the American Textile Machinery Association which was held at irregular intervals: 1950, 1954, and 1960. The company spent anywhere from $5,000 to $100,000 per show, depending on the size and location of the show. This expenditure, set up under a separate budget, normally was as large as or even larger than the advertising budget, for the management felt this medium was effective for displaying and demonstrating the company's machine products.

~~~

CASE 2: EASTMAN CHEMICAL PRODUCTS, INC.[1]

QUESTIONS TO CONSIDER: (1) *What selling jobs has Eastman Chemical attempted to undertake since 1934? (2) The company employed advertising primarily for the purpose of stimulating primary demand. Was this a sound strategy? (3) What selling jobs face the company in the future, after 1956? (4) As a member of Eastman Chemical's management, would you approve Mr. Guthrie's proposed advertising program for 1957, or would you suggest changes? If so, what changes?*

In the latter part of 1956, Mr. Dennis C. Guthrie, advertising manager for plastics for Eastman Chemical Products, Inc., was in the process of determining the 1957 advertising program for the company's various plastic materials, "Tenite Acetate," "Tenite Butyrate," and "Tenite Polyethylene."

Company Background

Eastman Chemical Products, Inc., was the wholly owned subsidiary of Eastman Kodak Company, being responsible for the marketing of all products manufactured by two divisions of Eastman Kodak Company, Tennessee Eastman Company and Texas Eastman Company. Tennessee Eastman was established in 1920 for the purpose of making wood alcohol, a solvent then used in the manufacture of nitrocellulose film base, but which is now obsolete. In the late 1920's the production of cellulose acetate was transferred from the Eastman Kodak plant at Rochester to the Tennessee Eastman plant at Kingsport, Tennessee. Cellulose acetate was used in making the base for safety film as well as acetate yarn which the company began to produce in 1931 and the cellulose plastic, Tenite Acetate, in 1932. This was followed in 1938 by the production of Tenite Butyrate, another cellulose plastic made from cellulose acetate butyrate. In 1950 Texas Eastman Company was organized to produce, from propane

---

[1] Written by Gerald A. Simon and Martin V. Marshall.

and natural gas, chemicals such as butyraldehyde and ethyl alcohol used in the production of cellulose esters. In 1954 Texas Eastman began production of Tenite Polyethylene. Thus, in 1956 Eastman Chemical Products, Inc., was selling cellulose acetate fibers, industrial chemicals, and three plastics—namely, Tenite Acetate, Tenite Butyrate, and Tenite Polyethylene.

Industry Background

Plastics were discovered in 1869, but it was not until the end of World War I that anyone in the United States did any substantial work with these materials. Subsequent growth was rapid, however; in the 1920's and 1930's the industry approximately doubled in size every three to five years. By the mid-1940's, the plastics industry was the fastest-growing industry in the United States. The end of World War II marked the beginning of extensive plant expansion, aggressive promotion, and increased competition in the industry, particularly as companies in the rubber and petroleum industries entered into the production of synthetic plastics materials.

The growth of the market for plastics was characterized historically by plastics fabricators (1) being able to substitute plastics for other materials in existing products, and (2) being able to develop new products which could be made only with plastics. Although special characteristics of certain ones of the many different kinds of plastics fitted them to some uses better than others, any one of several different types often could be used fot the same purpose; therefore, they all more or less competed for the same markets. Consequently, price was a very important factor in the marketing of plastics, and a substantial differential in cost was often enough to convince certain manufacturers to select one type of plastic in preference to another.

The expansion of demand for polystyrene, a synthetic plastic which was competitively priced with cellulose plastics, illustrated the interchangeability of one plastic material for another. Production of polystyrene had expanded about ten times faster than production of cellulose plastics between 1946 and 1955. In 1955 production of polystyrene exceeded production of cellulose plastics—515 million pounds as compared to 145 million pounds, which was about 3% of the total production of all plastics.

In late 1956 the cheapest of the plastics was the thermosetting plastics, such as "Bakelite," which sold at about 20 cents a pound.[2] The thermoplastics, characterized by the polystyrenes, such as "Styron" and "Lustrex," sold at 30 to 40 cents a pound; the celluloics, such as Tenite Acetate and Tenite Butyrate, at 38 to 50 cents a pound; the polyethylene plastics, such as Tenite Polyethylene, at 39 to 50 cents a pound; the acrylics plas-

---

[2] The prices of plastics are best compared by taking into consideration specific gravity and the resultant price per unit of bulk. The prices given here are based on the weight of a unit of bulk equal to a pound of cellulose acetate plastic.

tics, such as "Lucite" and "Plexiglas," at 55 cents a pound; and the polyamides plastics, such as "Nylon," at $1.35 a pound.

As has been stated, there were many special characteristics among the different kinds of plastics materials. Although it is not worthwhile here to list all of the special characteristics of each type of plastic material, it should be pointed out that the cellulose plastics, such as those which were sold by Eastman Chemical, were adaptable to many different uses.

The salient characteristics of cellulose plastics were toughness, high impact strength, uniform texture, permanent luster, pleasant-to-touch surface, dielectric strength, lightweight, and an unlimited range of transparent, translucent, and variegated colors. Furthermore, cellulose plastics had a high degree of dimensional stability and could be molded and extruded to close tolerances. They could be punched, stamped, drilled, riveted, crimped, and sewed. These characteristics of cellulose plastics were somewhat different than the characteristics of other plastics, such as polystyrene. As a result, polystyrene had limited the growth of cellulose plastics but had not replaced them. Specifically, polystyrene was more brittle than Tenite Acetate; however, it was also more rigid and dimensionally stable.

The polyethylene plastics were also available in a wide variety of formulations suitable for numerous applications. The molded polyethylene plastics could be made flexible or semirigid. They were chemically inert and resistant to breakage, acid, high voltage, and moisture vapor transmission.

The processing characteristics of polyethylene plastics made them suitable for numerous applications. Since they were priced competitively with a number of other plastics, such as the cellulose acetates and polystyrene, the sales of polyethylene plastics had increased substantially in the period 1953–56: from 137 million pounds to 507 million pounds. Industry executives predicted sales of one billion pounds in 1960.

Before World War II, there had been only two producers of polyethylene plastics; in 1954 Texas Eastman became the third producer. By 1956 a dozen firms were producing polyethylene plastics.

The Market for Plastics

The principal customers of the manufacturers of plastics materials were approximately 750 molders and extruders who were classified as "custom" or "proprietary." The custom firms extruded or molded plastics for approximately 2,000 fabricators, who in turn tooled the plastics or combined them with other materials to make fabricated parts primarily for the electrical radio-television, airplane, household equipment, packaging, architectural, building, and novelty industries. Often, custom molders and extruders maintained sales forces and advertising programs to promote new business and, therefore, were consulted by the users of fabricated parts, thereby affecting the type of plastic ultimately used by a fabricator in manufacturing a particular fabricated part.

There were two types of proprietary molders and extruders: the first type completed the manufacture of consumer products and sold them to retailers; the second type, the so-called "captive shops," were essentially manufacturers of fabricated parts for their own use; for instance, automobile companies which maintained fabricating departments to make automobile interior appointments or telephone manufacturers which molded their own telephone bases and handsets.

The molding and extruding phase of the industry was extremely competitive because it took only a modest capital investment for anyone to enter the business, and price usually was the newcomer's chief competitive tool. Hence, it was not at all unusual for a custom molder or extruder to develop a new application or a new account after much work and then lose it to a competitor.

Applications of Tenite Plastics

Typical uses of Tenite cellulose plastics were as rollers for lawn mowers, chessmen, both black and colored telephones, shoe heels, handles for tools, oil field and industrial pipe, steering wheels, toys, appliance housings and parts, sunglass frames, gunstocks, football helmets, outdoor signs, fishing line, and other sporting goods. A significant new application—women's shoe heels—had been discovered for acetate and butyrate in late 1955. By the end of 1956 industry consumption of acetate and butyrate for heels was at an estimated 500,000 pounds per month; without this new application, 1956 industry sales of cellulose acetates would have been less than that for 1955. About the same or a slightly higher level of consumption of acetate and butyrate for women's shoe heels was anticipated in 1957. Other comparatively recent applications of butyrate (which was tougher than acetate) were in electrical conduit for use by utilities, in pipe for transmitting natural gas and sour crude oil, and in salt water disposal.

Tenite Polyethylene had been found to be particularly suitable for use in the familiar squeeze bottles for cosmetics and foods, as extruded film for packaging, for molded household items, for extruded pipe in irrigation and other water-piping uses, and as coatings for electrical wire and cable, as indicated in the following industry sales figures for 1956:

	Per Cent of Total Sales (507 Million Pounds)
Film and sheeting	29.6%
Bottles, jars, and tubes	2.4
Molding (general)	14.8
Wire and cable insulation	11.8
Pipe	5.9
Coatings	6.9
Exports	27.6
Miscellaneous	1.0
Total	100.0%

Eastman Chemical executives believed that Tenite Polyethylene enjoyed an advantage over competitive polyethylene materials in that it was supplied in the form of spherical pellets rather than the usual odd-shaped pieces, which speeded up the flow of materials, reduced storage space, and helped to keep molding compounds dirt-free. These features were advertised from time to time, along with Eastman Chemical's "complete color service" for polyethylene formulations.

Although various properties made Tenite Acetate, Tenite Butyrate, and Tenite Polyethylene suitable for different applications, generally speaking, each of the plastics marketed by Eastman Chemical competed with other producers' plastic materials for the same or similar uses.

Eastman Chemical's Marketing Objectives

Eastman Chemical had four marketing objectives for plastic: (1) to develop end-markets for specific applications of plastics materials through stimulation of trade and consumer demand; (2) to stimulate trade and consumer demand for plastic materials, regardless of specific application; (3) to provide service and counsel to molders, extruders, and fabricators, which would help them overcome their design, production, and promotional problems; and (4) to make available to molders and extruders a wide variety of formulations, many specifically developed to meet customer requirements.

Tenite Marketing Program

Eastman Chemical sought to accomplish these sales objectives by a four-part marketing program, as follows:

1. Constant research to produce new formulations and experiment with new applications.
2. Regular publicity to the trade press of new and interesting developments.
3. Trade advertising and promotion to encourage new applications for Tenite plastics, to gain greater acceptance for existing applications, and to generate leads for the sales force.
4. Sales and service by experienced, technically trained men strategically located in Eastman Chemical branch offices throughout the United States.

The Company's Sales Force

Eastman Chemical's sales force was typical of the sales forces of the leading companies in the industry. The company maintained a staff of from one to four men in each of its sixteen regional offices: Atlanta, Chicago, Cleveland, Dayton, Detroit, Houston, Kansas City, Leominster (Mass.), Los Angeles, New York, Portland (Oregon), Rochester, St. Louis, San Francisco, Seattle, and Toronto. These men were technical salesmen and service men, generally with mechanical or chemical engineering backgrounds; all had been trained in the company's technical departments.

The Tenite representatives made frequent calls on all molders and extruders in the country. They also followed up inquiries produced by Tenite advertising; these inquiries were from molders and extruders, in addition to potential fabricators. When possible, Tenite representatives referred these fabricators to the molders and extruders who, they believed, could best handle the job. On inquiries which Tenite representatives believed held a large potential for Tenite plastics, they would frequently work in the potential fabricator's laboratory along with that company's research staff. If necessary, a manufacturer's problem would be taken to the Tenite laboratory in Kingsport, Tennessee.

Because Tenite representatives frequently discovered new customers for new and existing applications as a result of inquiries produced by Tenite advertising, advertising played a significant part in the promotional program for Tenite plastics.

The Promotion of Tenite Plastics, 1934–54

When the executives of Tennessee Eastman Corporation first marketed Tenite Acetate in 1932, they based their marketing strategy on the premise that the principal objective of the corporation's sales promotional efforts should be to develop new markets for plastics materials rather than to compete for a large share of the then small existing market. Although Tenite's sales representatives during the 1930's made frequent calls on molders, they were primarily interested in working with fabricators or manufacturers who had indicated an interest in the potential uses of plastics. Although Tenite's initial advertisements were placed in media which covered molders and fabricators, the advertisements were directed primarily to the top executives of manufacturing companies—top executives who would have to make the major policy decision to substitute plastics for a well-established material in an existing product or to enter a new product field through the use of plastics.

Eastman's first plastics advertising in 1934 and 1935 was placed in *Modern Plastics* and *Product Engineering*, on the basis that top executives who were becoming interested in the use of plastics would turn to those publications for information. In 1936 the company dropped *Product Engineering* and entered into other plastic trade papers, including—over the next ten years—the following: *Industrial Plastics*, *Plastics*, *Plastics and Resins*, *Plastics Buyer*, *Plastics World*, and *Pacific Plastics*. One of the primary reasons for the use of all of these trade papers was to lend advertising support to worthy trade publications in the plastics field; these publications carried product news which Tennessee Eastman executives believed frequently awakened more trade interest than the same information would if it were to appear in paid advertising space. The company systematically tried to capitalize on this fact by maintaining its own photographic studio in which it photographed every new application of Tenite. These pictures and the facts about each picture were subsequently released to all trade publications in the plastics field. The editorial mentions which Tenite received annually greatly exceeded the circulation attained through its paid advertising.

The theme of the advertisements used in trade papers was the same in all cases. The advertisements consisted of a photograph of a product made of Tenite and copy explaining the properties of the plastic that fitted it for such a use and similar uses. An offer to supply additional information upon request was included.

In 1938 Tennessee Eastman is said to have been the first plastics producer to advertise in *Fortune*. Full-color, photographically illustrated pages were used on a quarterly or five-times-a-year schedule, with "reason-why" copy similar to that of Tenite advertisements running in the plastics industry papers. In 1941–42 *Time* and *Business Week* were added to the advertising schedule. These three publications were used as horizontal media to reach business executives in all industries, whether or not they used plastics. The management believed that at that time potential users of Tenite were not concentrated enough in particular industries for the company to rely on selected vertical media,[3] that is, the cost of reaching individuals in the hundreds of industries which used plastics seemed prohibitive.

For a brief period in 1940–41, insertions in Sunday supplements were employed in newspapers in New York, Chicago, Detroit, Cleveland, and Boston. Although inquiries came from product manufacturers in many hitherto unexplored fields as a result of these advertisements, the newspaper schedule was discontinued with the advent of World War II, as was advertising in all but the trade papers of the plastics industry. Tenite and its ingredients had become allocated to essential wartime uses.

In 1947 Tennessee Eastman instituted a newspaper advertising campaign in the 12 cities in which it then had sales offices; these advertisements, which appeared once a week on the financial page of 19 newspapers, were 630 lines in size and were of the same type as those which continued to run in the trade magazines of the plastics industry. The main difference between advertisements in the two media was that the newspaper advertisements listed the name, address, and telephone number of the local Tenite representative.

Newspapers were used because they provided a quick and effective, although expensive, method of reaching businessmen. Toward the end of 1948, when company executives thought that they had accomplished their objective in newspapers, they discontinued their use except for the *New York Times*. Throughout the postwar years, including 1956, the business section of the *New York Times* carried regular scheduled Tenite advertisements, consisting of 24, 630-line insertions a year. The *New*

---

[3] Vertical media are those which deal with the interests of a particular industry and which accordingly are subscribed to by companies or individuals within a particular industry, that is, *Textile World Magazine, Paper Mill News, Railway Age*. Horizontal media make their appeal to the interests of functional groups and are subscribed to by the companies or industries in numerous industries, that is, *Factory Management and Maintenance, Purchasing*, and *Sales Management*.

York Times was regarded by Mr. Guthrie as a "national medium" since it developed inquiries from all sections of the United States. These advertisements listed Eastman Chemical's 16 sales offices instead of individual Tenite representatives. Photographically illustrated advertisements, such as those run by the company, were unusual for the business section and, Mr. Guthrie believed, achieved high readership.

In the years 1948–54 the company spent about $100,000 a year for advertising space in plastics trade journals and the *New York Times*. Not until late 1954, when Tenite Polyethylene was introduced, did the company regularly use media other than plastic trade journals.

Tenite Promotional Program after Introduction of Tenite Polyethylene in 1954

In 1954, with the availability of Tenite Polyethylene, Mr. Guthrie recommended the use of additional business publications. He wished to capitalize on the fact that a new supplier was entering the market for the first time in ten years. He also wanted to establish quickly the Tenite name in polyethylene since he knew that several other companies planned to produce polyethylene within the next two years.

As a first step, in late 1954 a schedule of advertisements was begun in *Newsweek, Business Week, Scientific American* (to reach technical management), and the *Wall Street Journal*. Each advertisement in these magazines featured an illustration of a successful application of Tenite Polyethylene, Tenite Acetate, or Tenite Butyrate; Tenite Polyethylene applications were shown most frequently. At the bottom of each advertisement all three Tenite plastics were listed, with the phrase "plastics by Eastman."

In 1955 Mr. Guthrie established two objectives for Tenite Polyethylene advertising: (1) to find as many new applications as possible, and (2) to publicize these applications as rapidly as possible.

Because of the growing interest by molders in applications of polyethylene for housewares, Mr. Guthrie recommended in 1955 a "saturation" schedule in publications reaching manufacturers and trade buyers of housewares products: *Housewares Review, Hardware Age*, and *Chain Store Age*. This saturation campaign, consisting of two- or three-full pages and double spreads in full color each issue, lasted four months. Afterwards, the campaign in housewares publications continued but at a more moderate rate. The company's expenditure for advertising space in 1955 was about $150,000.

Tenite sales representatives reported that molders whose housewares products were featured in Tenite advertisements were particularly pleased; these molders believed that the advertisements were read by trade buyers. Polyethylene achieved rapid acceptance in housewares in 1955; typical applications were dish pans, tumblers, laundry baskets, and waste baskets, usually in bright colors.

Exhibit 1

EASTMAN CHEMICAL PRODUCTS, INC.

Media Schedules, 1956 and 1957
(Proposed)

	Circulation (Nearest 1,000)	Products Featured	1956		1957 (Proposed)	
			Insertions	Total Space Cost	Insertions	Total Space Cost
Agriculture:						
Better Farming Methods	30,000	Polyethylene pipe	1	$ 570	6	$ 3,420
County Agent and Vo-Ag Teacher	30,000	"	1	616	6	3,696
Farm Implement News	24,000	"	......	......	6	2,100
Farm Journal	3,624,000	"	......	......	4	47,800
Implement and Tractor	24,000	"	......	......	6	2,220
Western Farm Equipment	6,000	"	......	......	3	1,944
				$ 1,186		$ 61,180
Design:						
Industrial Design	9,000	All	6	$ 3,765	6	$ 4,666
Materials and Methods	30,000	"	6	4,122	6	4,122
				$ 7,887		$ 8,788
Electrical:						
Electrical Engineering	......	Polyethylene and butyrate housings	6	$ 3,888	......	......
Electrical Manufacturing	23,000		6	3,924	6	$ 4,416
				$ 7,812		$ 4,416
Executive:						
Business Week	283,000	All	10	$ 38,778	10	$ 40,933
Journal of Commerce	39,000	"	......	......	254	3,543
Newsweek	1,063,000	"	10	75,296	10	72,358
New York Times	571,000	"	10	11,640	10	11,040
Scientific American	151,000	"	10	22,298	10	25,714
Wall Street Journal	395,000	"	10	14,520	10	16,200
				$162,532		$169,788

Exhibit 1—Continued

	Circulation (Nearest 1,000)	Products Featured	1956		1957 (Proposed)	
			Insertions	Total Space Cost	Insertions	Total Space Cost
Gas and Oil:						
Gas..........	10,000	Butyrate pipe	6	$ 2,460	6	$ 2,610
Gas Age......	7,000	" "	6	2,490	6	2,490
Oil and Gas Journal......	35,000	" "	6	3,030	6	3,570
				$ 7,980		$ 8,670
Housewares:						
Chain Store Age......	38,000	Polyethylene pipe	6	$ 4,656	....	....
Hardware Age......		"	6	3,390	6	$ 3,180
Housewares Review......		"	6	3,342	....	....
				$ 11,388		$ 3,180
Packaging:						
Modern Packaging.........	22,000	All	6	$ 3,120	6	$ 3,420
Packagine Parade.........	21,000	"	6	3,308	6	3,507
Paper, Film and Foil Converter......	6000	"	6	1,770	6	2,303
				$ 8,198		$ 9,230
Plastics:						
Canadian Plastics.........	5,000	All	12	$ 2,436	12	$ 2,940
Modern Plastics.........	26,000	"	12	6,900	12	7,980
Modern Plastics Encyclopedia.........	26,000	"	1	630	2*	1,340
Plastics Technology.........	11,000	"	....	....	6	3,030
Plastics World.........	32,000	"	12	9,000	12	8,700
SPE Journal.........	5,000	"	....	....	6	1,800
Western Plastics.........	5,000	"	....	....	6	2,280
				$ 18,966		$ 28,070
Plumbing:						
Plumbing and Heating Business......	28,000	Polyethylene pipe	....	....	6	$ 3,504

* Two advertisements in one, annual, issue.

Exhibit 1—Continued

	CIRCULATION (NEAREST 1,000)	PRODUCTS FEATURED	1956		1957 (PROPOSED)	
			Insertions	Total Space Cost	Insertions	Total Space Cost
Shoe:						
American Shoemaking	4,000	Acetate and Butyrate Women's heels	. . . . . .	. . . . . .	6	$ 1,002
Footwear News	18,000	" "	. . . . . .	. . . . . .	12	1,560
Leather and Shoes	5,000	" "	. . . . . .	. . . . . .	6	1,344
						$ 3,906
Sign:						
Screen Process	8,000	Butyrate			6	$ 1,761
Signs of the Times	15,000	"	6	$ 1,899	6	2,067
						$ 3,828
Utilities:						
Electrical World	26,000	Polyethylene and Butyrate insulation and pipe	6	$ 4,260	6	$ 4,260
Telephony	11,000		6	1,361	6	1,474
				$ 5,621		$ 5,734
Miscellaneous:						
Thomas' Register	24,000	All	1	$ 380	1	$ 500
				$233,849		$310,794

Note: Costs per insertion are not necessarily comparable due to variations in size of insertions.

In 1956 Mr. Guthrie expanded the Tenite advertising program to include additional industries served by molders and extruders of Tenite plastics, as shown in Exhibit 1, spending about $234,000.

In addition to advertising in publications, Tenite promotional activities in late 1956 included: periodic direct mailings to about 5,000 direct and indirect users of Tenite; publicity releases to the trade press; exhibits at trade shows; and Tenite tags and labels for use by fabricators. Two motion pictures were available for free showings to interested groups; one film, "Story of Tenite," was aimed at any potential customer for Tenite, while another, "Plastic Pipelines," was designed to interest executives in the natural gas and petroleum industries in the use of Tenite Butyrate pipe.

Tenite Advertising Plans for 1957

In late 1956 Mr. Guthrie was considering a proposal for the 1957 advertising program for Tenite. The advertising budget was to be increased from $234,000—the 1956 expenditure—to about $310,000. Increased emphasis was to be given to new applications of Tenite plastics, particularly of Tenite Polyethylene and Tenite Butyrate. Specifically, polyethylene, which had become well established in housewares, was now to be emphasized for agricultural pipe; therefore, two of the three housewares publications would be dropped and about $61,000 would be spent in agricultural media. (Polyethylene pipe was sold by all farm supply houses and was gaining rapid acceptance by farmers for carrying water; polyethylene pipe was easy to install, light in weight, and expanded when frozen.)

About $4,000 was to be spent in three publications serving the shoe industry; the company had never before advertised to this industry.

In considering the Tenite advertising program for 1957, Mr. Guthrie knew that Eastman Chemical's management would accept his recommendation, provided that the program performed two major functions: (1) if it helped the company to learn about new and unknown markets and applications of Tenite through production of inquiries; and (2) if it helped Tenite salesmen to close sales. In general, although formal means of evaluating advertising effectiveness were not available to him, Mr. Guthrie believed that previous Tenite advertising had been successful in achieving these objectives.

~~~

CASE 3: CRYOVAC COMPANY[1]

QUESTIONS TO CONSIDER: (1) *What are the attitudes of consumers toward food packaging? Does Cryovac's packaging process have characteristics which would be of significant interest to housewives?* (2) *What ele-*

---

[1] Written by David W. Nylen and Martin V. Marshall.

ments in the mix should Cryovac emphasize? (3) Should advertising to consumers be continued? If so, what should be the objectives of the advertising program? Can the program be effectively promoted to and through the trade?

In early September 1957 the management of the Cryovac Company, Cambridge, Massachusetts, a division of W. R. Grace and Company, was faced with the issue: Should it discontinue the company's consumer advertising campaign?

Company Background

The Cryovac Company manufactured and marketed plastic materials which allowed manufacturers of food and other products to package their products in vacuum-sealed bags. In using the Cryovac process, a product was placed in a package made of plastic material based upon a Saran formulation. Through use of special equipment, the package was then subjected to dry vacuuming so that all the air was withdrawn from the package. The Vacuum was maintained by twisting the end of the bag and clamping it with a metal clip. The final step was to immerse the bag in hot water so that it shrank to fit the contours of the product like a "second skin." Cryovac bags were sold either plain or printed with the packer's label.

Since its introduction in 1947 the Cryovac vacuum packaging process had enjoyed great success, particularly in the packaging of meat, poultry, and cheese. By 1956 sales were well over $25,000,000.

Meat packers or grocery chains cutting and packing their own smoked and processed meats found that a vacuum package offered many advantages, such as significantly reducing the spoilage of meat products, retaining the original texture and flavor, increasing the storage and shelf life, withstanding rough handling, providing good display, and extending the distances that meat could be shipped. By 1957 the Cryovac process was widely used in the packaging of frozen poultry of all sizes, cheese, hams, corned beef, luncheon meats, frankfurters, and other sausage items. The company had among its accounts all of the better-known meat packers and grocery chains in the United States, including A & P, Armour, Food Fair, Hormel, Hygrade, Oscar Mayer, Rath, Safeway, Swift, and Wilson.

Compared with competitive packaging material, Cryovac was a premium-priced product. Therefore, Cryovac had a potential market only in packaging those products for which it presented substantial benefits. To be desirable as a packaging material for a given product, Cryovac's protective features either had to lower the product's distribution costs (through lower spoilage, handling expenses, repackaging, etc.) or to permit a premium price for the product because of benefits of the packaging to consumers (e.g., it allowed housewives to store foods in freezers without rewrapping them).

Cryovac executives believed that by the end of 1957 the company would hold over 20% of the total package market for smoked meats, frozen poultry, and cheese. Shares of other individual product markets varied substantially, ranging from less than 5% for frankfurters to over 86% for frozen turkeys.

Specialized packaging machinery designed for use with Cryovac plastic materials was manufactured under contract and sold by the Cryovac Company. Users of the Cryovac process could purchase a complete, manually operated packaging system for as little as $800. A variety of semiautomatic systems tailored to the needs of users was available at costs higher than $800. Cryovac equipment prices were competitive with those of other types of packaging equipment.

After the company had built up a large sales volume for its vacuum-type bags, it developed two other types of packaging materials that allowed it to enter into more competitive packaging markets. The first type was vacuum packages developed for the sliced luncheon meat segment of the meat packaging industry. The second type was low-priced, heat shrinkable, self-sealing roll film developed to compete in the cheese and bacon market. Combined sales of these two lines were expected to exceed 7% of total sales of the company in 1957.

Cryovac's Competition

Although the Cryovac film and packaging process was patented, substantial competition was present from cellophane, Saran sheets, and other bag and pouch makers. It was the opinion of management that the company could not rely on patent protection to hold its existing markets, but had to rely instead on continued improvement of products and selling methods. No competitor had a vacuum packaging process, but the Du-Pont Company had in development a film called "Mylar" that had properties similar to Cryovac. If successful, Mylar would provide the most direct competition to Cryovac. The estimated sales of leading competitive materials in 1956 are given below:

ESTIMATED SALES OF COMPETITIVE PLASTIC
PACKAGING FILM FOR ALL TYPES OF
FOOD PACKAGING

	1956 Dollar Sales (Millions)
Cellophane	$235
Polyethylene	78
Saran	25
Pliofilm	13
Cellulose acetate	12
Vinyl	6
Mylar	3
Others	2

Marketing of Cryovac

From 1947 to 1957, the company's sales efforts had been devoted to a series of sales programs directed at various segments of the market—

turkey, ham, cheese, institutional, etc. These programs coupled direct selling with barrages of trade advertising and direct mail. The programs had been very successful in opening new markets for Cryovac. Since the company's beginning in 1947, sales had increased at the rate of about 30% a year.

Cryovac was sold nationally by 145 salesmen and supervisors organized into three sales territories—Eastern, Western, and Southern.

Cryovac salesmen sold directly to meat and poultry packers, cheese packers, and institutional meat purveyors.[2] Salesmen often worked directly with the packers' salesmen to stimulate their sales of Cryovac packaged meats. An annual sales contest for packers' salesmen was conducted by the Cryovac sales force. The contest, which was considered highly successful, offered prizes to packers' salesmen based on their sales of Cryovac meats. The tendency toward seasonality in sales (due to meat and poultry packing seasonality) was largely overcome by a discount plan that encouraged advance purchasing of Cryovac bags.

Salesmen were provided with detailed sales programs for each end-product market. For example, Cryovac salesmen were given a 43-page, single-spaced promotional portfolio for use in working with meat packers on half-hams. This portfolio included:

—Detailed instructions on how to work with packers' salesmen so that they promoted Cryovac-wrapped half-hams effectively with grocery stores. Cryovac salesmen were given ideas as to how to hold packers' salesmen meetings; an 11-minute motion picture entitled "More Profits from Ham"; sales kits for packers' salesmen; sales letters; suggested sales contests for packers' salesmen; follow-up letters for use with packers' salesmen; and a suggested letter to be sent packers' salesmen's wives.

—A detailed outline of advertising materials which was to be sent the packers' customers, including direct mail, trade paper advertisements, and suggested letters for Cryovac salesmen to send.

—A suggested promotional program for packers' use with retailers and consumers, which included commercials for use in newspapers, television, and radio; point-of-sale displays; and publicity releases.

Similar detailed sales programs and portfolios were given Cryovac salesmen for other end-product markets.

Continuous trade advertising had been used since the company's founding. In the first two years, advertising was directed at locker plants and freezer provisioners when the company was attempting to develop those markets. In 1949 and 1950 the company developed the turkey market and spent about $40,000 a year on trade advertising directed at that market. In 1951 the company started advertising to meat packers and sausage makers, markets which company executives felt would become very good. By 1953 the total trade advertising budget was about $100,000 and was spent on trade media reaching the turkey, meat, cheese, and

_____
[2] Purveyors cut and package meats for institutions, such as restaurants, hotels, and college dining services.

poultry packers. In 1954 Cryovac added a strong retailer campaign to retailers and chain-store management designed to gain acceptance of Cryovac at the retail level. By 1955 the trade advertising budget had reached $140,000; in 1956 it was reduced to $100,000 as it was thought that this budget would do an adequate job.

Background on 1957 Consumer Advertising

In the fall of 1956 Cryovac's advertising agency suggested that Cryovac conduct a consumer advertising campaign in 1957 as well as the usual trade advertising program. The company's advertising manager reacted favorably to the proposed campaign. He believed that Cryovac had educated the trade to the point where it was well aware of the benefits of Cryovac's vacuum packaging process and that additional promotional work probably was required to increase the use of Cryovac. He thought that a consumer advertising campaign would develop consumer recognition and acceptance of Cryovac-packed products and would gradually build both retailer and consumer preference. This preference, he believed, would help to hold packers to Cryovac packaging against competition because packers would hesitate to switch if Cryovac was known, accepted, and preferred by all buying factors. Furthermore, the advertising manager felt that more packers would use the Cryovac seal on their packages and use it more conspicuously in an effort to tie in to the consumer campaign. Finally, he felt that a national campaign in media would give greater prestige to the company and to the company's salesmen.

The company's sales promotion manager also favored a consumer advertising campaign, but not the campaign proposed by the agency. He did not feel that an indirect-action brand campaign would create any significant consumer preference, and that, even if it did, its value would be considerably lessened because of three factors. First, few packers used the Cryovac label on their packages. Second, the label was so small—less than one inch in diameter—that it probably would not be readily noted by consumers in stores. Third, Cryovac-packed items usually were displayed in only a small part of the meat department of stores and that part was usually a relatively low traffic area.

As an alternative, the sales promotion manager suggested that a consumer advertising campaign be used to promote a premium directed at housewives. He believed that housewives should be offered an attractive premium in return for cutting out and mailing in a given number of Cryovac labels from products packaged in Cryovac. He reasoned that his approach would provide a direct stimulus to sales, which would be appealing to packers. In addition, the consumer, through use of the product, would become familiar with the Cryovac label and would learn to differentiate the Cryovac package.

After considering the merits of consumer advertising per se, and the merits of the alternative proposals, management decided to employ the

Exhibit 1

CRYOVAC COMPANY

1957 Cryovac Consumer Advertisement

It's frozen holiday turkey... with a tender, new farm-freshness...because it's vacuum-sealed in CRYOVAC

Traditional turkey tastes better than ever in new, scientific vacuum package

It's probably been years since you've enjoyed the wonderful flavor of farm-fresh turkey. But now you can recapture that tender, fresh-dressed taste in *frozen* turkey — thanks to a new protective vacuum package called CRYOVAC. This airtight, moisture-proof "second skin" has made a revolutionary improvement in poultry flavor . . . by sealing *out* air, sealing *in* natural juices. CRYOVAC stops drying out and "freezer burn" — keeps turkey fresh and tender until the bird is on your table!

Here's how CRYOVAC packaging is done: first, the bird is placed in a special, airtight, moisture-proof bag. Then — all flavor-stealing air is vacuumed out, the bag is sealed and shrunk to fit like a transparent "second skin". It protects the contents until you break the seal.

CRYOVAC also protects the goodness of many other fine foods—hams, frozen, smoked, and processed meats, corned beef and natural cheeses. CRYOVAC is also available in Canada.

LOOK FOR THE CRYOVAC MARK OF FLAVOR PROTECTION AT YOUR FAVORITE STORE

THE CRYOVAC COMPANY
Division of W. R. Grace & Co.
Cambridge 41, Mass.

advertising manager's approach in 1957. Management made this decision with the expectation that results would be obtained only after consistent effort over a fairly long time period, perhaps three to five years.

Magazines were chosen as the most desirable medium for the 1957 consumer advertising campaign because excellent color presentation was pos-

Exhibit 2

CRYOVAC COMPANY

1957 Cryovac Consumer Advertisement

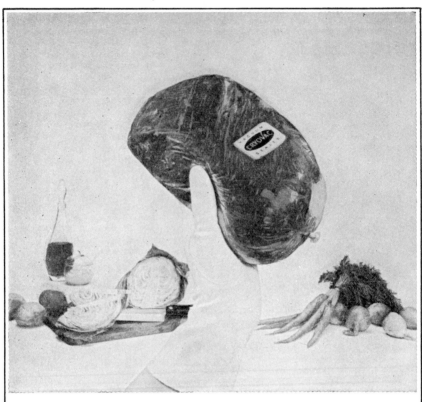

New protective CRYOVAC package locks in flavor... for keeps

Now buy meats in airtight, transparent vacuum packages that let you see the freshness!

Here's an old-fashioned favorite—brought up to date by CRYOVAC! Now you can enjoy hearty corned-beef flavor as never before—because of a special new vacuum package. Only CRYOVAC *locks in* flavorful juices and nutrition at the moment of perfection—*keeps* them there until you break the seal!

Here's how CRYOVAC packaging is done: the meat is placed in a special, airtight, moistureproof bag. Then—all flavor-stealing air is vacuumed out, the bag is sealed and shrunk so it fits like a transparent "second skin".

Look for the CRYOVAC seal of flavor protection on corned beef and other fine foods—frozen turkey and other poultry, frozen, smoked and processed meats, and cheese—at your favorite store.

THE CRYOVAC COMPANY
Division of W. R. Grace & Co.
Cambridge 40, Mass.

sible. Four-color full pages were used in *Life,* and four-color partial pages were used in *Good Housekeeping, Better Homes & Gardens,* and *Sunset.* The advertisements were designed to tell the basic Cryovac product story and to explain consumer benefits. Exhibits 1 and 2 show two advertisements used in the 1957 campaign.

The campaign had three promotion peaks: Easter, summer, and Thanksgiving. Hams were emphasized in the spring, luncheon and other meats in summer, and turkeys in the fall.

Exhibit 3 gives the consumer advertising schedule and costs.

Exhibit 3

CRYOVAC COMPANY

Consumer Advertising Schedule and Cost, 1957

Publication	Space	Dates	Cost
Good Housekeeping........	⅔ page, 4-color, bleed	April, June, July Sept., Oct., Nov......	$ 70,950
Life...................	Page, 4-color	April, May, June July, Aug., Nov......	208,200
Better Homes and Gardens..	½ page, 4-color	April, May, Aug., Sept., Oct., Nov......	69,840
Sunset................	Page, 4-color, bleed	April, May, July Aug., Sept., Nov.....	28,980
		Total Cost Space.......	$377,970
		Estimated Production Cost..............	37,000
		Total............	$414,970

The 1957 Trade Advertising Program

The 1957 trade advertising campaign had two parts. One part was designed to inform the trade of the consumer advertising campaign and sell the trade on its benefits. The other part of the trade campaign continued the program of informing the trade of the Cryovac packaging process and its advantages. Exhibit 4 gives an example of an advertisement employed in the trade advertising program, and Exhibit 5 gives the trade advertising media schedule and costs.

Promoting the 1957 Consumer Campaign

Upon adoption of the 1957 campaign, a presentation was made to the Cryovac sales force to explain the program and to develop enthusiasm for it. The sales force, in turn, promoted the consumer campaign to their customers, the packers. The salesmen promoted the program as "a second brand" for the packers' product and encouraged them to use the Cryovac label. Salesmen gave large amounts of Cryovac point-of-purchase display material to packer salesmen and encouraged them to place this material in retail stores. In some areas the Cryovac Company hired men to try to place Cryovac display material directly in stores. The Cryovac sales contest for packers' salesmen in 1957 was tied into the program by offering prizes based on the amount of display material placed.

Exhibit 4

CRYOVAC COMPANY

1957 Cryovac Trade Advertisement

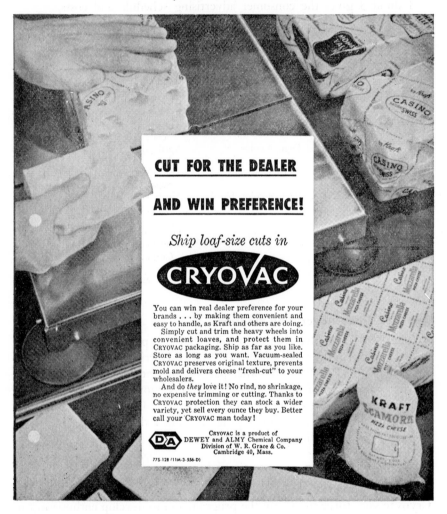

Advertising for 1958?

In early September 1957 members of Cryovac's management met on several occasions with representatives of the agency to discuss 1958 advertising plans. The agency's plan was based upon the assumption that consumer advertising would be continued in 1958. Its presentation essentially concerned a shift in media, the principal thought being that greater frequency of advertising in fewer media would increase its effectiveness.

The agency proposed a consumer-advertising budget of $510,000 for eight four-color pages in *Life* and ten four-color pages in *Better Homes*

Exhibit 5
CRYOVAC COMPANY
Trade Advertising Schedule and Costs, 1957

Publication	Space	No. of Insertions	Cost
CONSUMER MERCHANDISING CAMPAIGN			
Meat..........................	2 pages, 2-color	5	$ 3,550
National Provisioner.............	2 pages, 2-color	5	3,550
Western Meat Industry...........	2 pages, 2-color	5	2,250
Poultry Processing..............	2 pages, 2-color	3	1,590
Turkey World..................	2 pages, 2-color	3	2,910
Chain Store Age...............	2 pages, 2-color	5	9,850
Progressive Grocer.............	2 pages, 2-color	5	12,600
		Total Space Cost.....	$36,300
		Production...........	4,500
		Total...............	$40,800
BAG AND POUCH CAMPAIGN			
Meat..........................	Page, bleed.......	8	$ 2,068
National Provisioner............	Page, bleed	9	2,430
Western Meat Industry..........	Page, bleed	8	1,600
Milk Products Journal..........	Page	6	1,695
Cheese Reporter................	3 col. × 10″, page	6	509
Progressive Grocer.............	Page	6	6,060
Meat and Food Merchandising....	Page	6	5,004
		Total Space Cost......	$19,366
		Production...........	7,700
		Total...............	$27,066
		Total Trade Advertising.............	$67,866

& Gardens and $55,000 for trade publication advertising. In addition, the agency proposed that advertising copy be strengthened by placing greater emphasis on consumer benefits, particularly the flavor, taste, and freshness of Cryovac-packed products.

Several members of management raised the question as to whether the company's consumer advertising was really justified, and the ensuing discussion completely reopened the subject.

Those executives who were opposed to consumer advertising felt that the campaign, although artistically attractive, could not create any consumer demand for Cryovac. They believed that the Cryovac brand could not compete with the packers' brand names that were far more extensively promoted. It was further argued that the campaign had no appeal to the packers who would prefer a reduction in price to consumer advertising. The campaign from the viewpoint of the packers was too small to impress consumers, because it had to compete with the very large advertising expenditures of many food manufacturers.

The sales management people present expressed their opinion that the promotion of the 1957 campaign probably took too much salesman time which could have been better spent opening new markets and further developing the potential of established markets. They said that the attempt to promote the consumer campaign through point-of-purchase display had met limited success. Retailers were not enthusiastic about the display material because they desired to sell products, not packaging. It was estimated that less than 300 of Cryovac's 5,400 customers tied in with the consumer advertising at the retail level.

The advertising manager then pointed out that the consumer advertising campaign was originally conceived as a long-term project with the expectation that results would be slow. Stopping the campaign at the end of 1957, he said, would result perhaps in a loss of the $400,000 already invested in it.

Further, in support of the consumer advertising program, the advertising manager said that a recent study of consumers by the agency showed that only 3% of consumers were aware of Cryovac as compared with 87% for cellophane and 73% for "Saran." Although a slow process, he thought that consumer advertising of Cryovac would develop worthwhile consumer recognition and preference. Consumer preference in turn would induce retailer preference. The advertising manager reasoned that building a consumer and retailer preference would have considerable influence upon packers. He saw the following benefits developing:

1. Consumer preference would protect Cryovac's present accounts from the inroads of competition.
2. Consumer preference would make easier the introduction of Cryovac products in new markets.
3. Consumer preference would speed up the acceptance of Cryovac in present markets.
4. Consumer preference would allow packers to recover the higher cost of Cryovac through premium pricing.

Management believed that the company had already obtained much of the potential market for premium packaging material. Accordingly, there was need to develop cheaper new packaging materials, new materials that would solve a specific packing problem, and, if economically feasible, consumer preference that would allow packers to recover the costs of a premium package by raising retail prices. For the most part, packers were already using Cryovac where the process gave unquestionable advantages. In markets where Cryovac's advantages were economically less clear cut, there still remained some developable potential. In other markets, e.g., bacon, Cryovac bags would probably never develop large sales because the bags' premium price could not compete with lower-priced competitive products such as cellophane and Saran. It was for these markets that the Cryovac film and pouches had been developed. As opposed to the meat packer market, management believed that considerable potential for Cryovac could be developed in the packing operation of food retailers and purveyors, but there was still a substantial educational job to be accomplished with retailers and purveyors, many of whom did not yet know the specific values of Cryovac to many of their packaging operations. Management wondered if consumer knowledge of Cryovac might help sell these retailers and purveyors.

Finally, it was not at all clear whether Cryovac's benefits to consumers could be effectively communicated because of the tremendous amount of advertising in the food field. Management was quite willing to continue the company's consumer advertising if, in the long run, it would increase the company's sales and profits.

~~~

CASE 4: EMERY AIR FREIGHT CORPORATION[1]

QUESTIONS TO CONSIDER: *(1) What kind of service is Emery trying to sell: airfreight for emergency uses or airfreight for planned uses? (2) If Emery is to continue to be successful, what selling jobs have to be done? (3) What are the responsibilities of the Emery sales force? (4) For what purposes has advertising been employed? (5) What recommendations would you make to Emery's management regarding its 1958 promotion campaign?*

In late 1957, executives of Emery Air Freight Corporation were reviewing the company's advertising strategy with a view to planning the campaign for 1958. Historically, the company's advertising had evolved from a straight sale of Emery service (1949) directed at purchasing and traffic executives to a primary demand campaign (1957) directed not only to purchasing and traffic executives but also to top-management people. At the close of 1957, increasing competition, the general business recession, and the results of a customer survey led the company to reevaluate its basic strategy.

Background of Emery

Emery Air Freight Corporation, founded in 1946, was a commercial application of the U.S. Navy's World War II airfreight forwarding service. Mr. John C. Emery, whose business background was in railroading and work with the Railway Express Agency, was commanding officer of the U.S. Navy's freight forwarding service. At the end of the war, Mr. Emery and some associates raised $285,000 by public stock issue to form

---

[1] Written by David W. Nylen and Martin V. Marshall.

Exhibit 1

EMERY AIR FREIGHT CORPORATION
Operating Statistics

	1946	1947	1948	1949	1950	1951	1952	1953	1954	1955	1956	1957
Revenues ($000)	$ 30	$456	$ 709	$1,105	$2,044	$3,451	$4,665	$ 5,379	$5,384	$ 7,442	$ 9,302	$10,959
Expenses ($000)	124	426	727	1,773	1,773	3,388	4,290	4,972	5,104	6,669	8,022	9,425
Earnings before taxes ($000)	(94)	(70)	(18)	26	271	63	375	407	280	773	1,184	1,406
Net income ($000)	(94)	(70)	(18)	26	181	39	121	122	142	371	567	670
Earnings per share	(.034)	(0.21)	(0.05)	0.08	0.55	0.12	0.37	0.37	0.44	1.11	0.82	0.95
Dividends per share							0.10	0.20	0.20	0.40	0.35	0.50
Shipments (000)	1	16	41	69	90	136	177	204	205	257	306	419
Tonnage (tons)	50	700	1,350	2,050	3,650	6,700	8,800	10,300	9,650	14,000	17,200	16,971
Number of full-time employees	31	54	90	117	186	282	298	265	257	286	308	356
Number of offices	9	10	11	13	14	27	27	28	29	30	34	37

Source: Company records.

the company. Then the company waited two years for certification by the Civil Aeronautics Board so that it could operate as a common carrier. Meanwhile, the company survived as a contract carrier with limited operations.

The company incurred heavy losses in its first two years of contract operations, but by the end of 1948, when it received its certificate as a common carrier, it had established an organization of offices capable of providing nation-wide services. Revenues and profits grew substantially after 1948, and by the end of 1957, the company had offices in 37 cities, special agents in 80 additional traffic centers, and representation through Western Union in other markets. Exhibit 1 gives selected operating statistics which indicate Emery's growth from 1946–57.

Emery was an airfreight forwarder; i.e., although it was a common carrier like a railroad or airline, it did not operate the airplanes on which the freight moved. An an airfreight forwarder Emery picked up freight with its own trucks from a client, placed the freight with the most advantageous air carrier, and picked up the freight at the other end of the flight to deliver it to its final destination. Emery was able to consolidate air shipments to take advantage of lower rates on bulk shipments, but did so only when speed of delivery was not sacrificed.

Emery's competition came from three sources: other freight forwarders, airline airfreight and air express, and other forms of transportation such as trucks and railroads. In 1957 there was no other freight forwarder comparable to Emery in size or in terms of a flexible nation-wide service. Most other forwarders specialized in particular geographical areas or specific commodities. Emery was a high-rate carrier compared with other airfreight forwarders who offered a low rate hoping to attract volume. Emery charged higher rates in return for superior service. Airlines, although they carried Emery freight, provided the most direct competition to Emery in airfreight. If a shipper used regular airline airfreight, he had to designate which airline was to ship the material, and could only ship it to points that the particular airline served. Air Express, a division of the Railway Express Agency, provided a more flexible door-to-door service, allocating its shipments to airlines for which it was agent. However, the greatest competition to Emery was that of other forms of transportation. Since its inception, airfreight, and in particular Emery, had attempted to increase its share of the total transportation dollar.

Background on the Airfreight Industry[2]

The prominent characteristic of airfreight service was faster transportation at higher cost. While cost comparisons between different types of

---

[2] Information presented in this section was developed from Howard T. Lewis and James W. Culliton, *The Role of Air Freight in Physical Distribution*, Part I, Division of Research, Graduate School of Business Administration (Boston: Harvard University, 1956).

transportation were rough, a "rule-of-thumb" comparison could be made as follows:

Airfreight.......................17–22 cents per ton mile
Railway express....................13–16 cents per ton mile
Truck..............................5–18 cents per ton mile
Rail...............................3–6 cents per ton mile

The statistics available on airfreight were not adequate for a complete analysis of the industry, but certain characteristics were apparent. The industry had grown substantially since the war, tons carried increasing from 74,566 in 1946 to 325,666 in 1954, an increase of 336%. Airfreight, in terms of ton miles, represented in 1954 only an estimated four hundredths of 1% of all intercity freight traffic. Between 1947 and 1954, approximately 63% of all cargo ton miles flown were carried by domestic trunk lines in scheduled operations, presumably most of the cargo being carried on combination passengers and cargo flights. Only limited data were available on freight forwarders, but in 1954, there were 53 holding letters of registration. Emery was apparently the largest forwarder, purchasing almost as much transportation from airlines as the next eight largest companies.[3]

Lewis and Culliton in their study characterized users of airfreight as constituting a spectrum ranging from emergency users to planned users with many intermediate combinations of the two. Pure emergency shipments, resulting from floods, fires, and assembly-line shutdowns due to lack of a repair part, occurred irregularly and did not form the basis for supporting the growth that airfreight companies desired. At the other end of the spectrum were industries that used airfreight as a major means of transportation, generally industries marketing products of high density, fragility, perishability, or high value. Cut flowers, films, and certain drugs were illustrative of this type of user. Between these two extremes of users were those who used airfreight for consciously anticipated emergencies. These users operated on a reduced inventory reserve with the realization that certain emergencies would occur, but with a preplanned method of meeting the emergency—through airfreight. Management thus had to balance lower inventory costs against higher procurement costs. A similar use of airfreight was the distribution of finished products to customers, the cost of airfreight being balanced against possible savings in warehousing.

In terms of specific industries served, Lewis and Culliton listed commodities most frequently shipped in 1955 as: auto parts, machinery, electrical equipment, cut flowers, wearing apparel, machine parts, printed matter, films, aircraft parts, and drugs and biologicals.

---

[3] From statistics compiled by the CAB as quoted in company records.

Emery Marketing Strategy

The market for Emery Air Freight's services was generally the same as the one just described for the industry as a whole: general manufacturing, graphic arts, film, and the government. Exhibit 2 gives Emery's reve-

Exhibit 2

EMERY AIR FREIGHT CORPORATION

Revenue Breakdown by Market in Per Cent of Total Revenue

	1950	1951	1952	1953	1954	1956	1957
Film	10.3	7.0	6.0	7.0	8.7	5.3	6.8
Financial	7.5	4.4	3.5	2.8	2.9	3.0	2.9
Graphic arts	38.4	25.7	24.4	24.1	22.5	16.2	17.3
Labs, institutions		8.7	2.3	1.6	1.3	1.1	1.1
Manufacturers—automotive						7.1	5.5
—aviation						4.0	4.2
—electrical equipment						15.6	14.2
—machinery						14.9	14.5
—radio, TV						2.6	3.0
—other						19.6	20.6
—Total	30.9	49.0	58.8	59.4	59.1	(63.8)	(62.0)
Government		2.4	2.1	0.8	0.8	6.1	3.3
Miscellaneous	12.9	2.8	2.9	4.3	4.7	4.1	4.5
International						0.4	2.1
Total	100.0	100.0	100.0	100.0	100.0	100.0	100.0

Source: Company records.

nue breakdown by markets served. Emery management believed that the potential growth of airfreight lay in selling planned usage of airfreight on a more regular basis.

Emery's marketing strategy, which had evolved with the growth of the company, made use of both a sizable personal selling force and advertising. Executives believed that advertising was necessary to help the company become nationally known since the sales force could not possibly call on all potential shippers or consignees. Analysis of the airfreight market led management to believe that there were two important types of executives that Emery should reach in marketing its service.

When a company made the basic decision to use airfreight, especially on a regular basis, the decision usually rested with top management. Emery utilized primary demand advertising of airfreight in management magazines to influence this group, since the sales force was generally unable to call on these executives.

The other types of executives that Emery attempted to reach were the purchasing agent and traffic manager who usually decided which airfreight service to use once the basic decision to use airfreight had been made by top management. This executive group was reached by Emery's sales force which sold the Emery service on the basis of its specific advantages over competitive services. In addition, advertising in trade magazines was directed at these executives.

Personal Selling

The Emery 70-man sales force was made up of young men, averaging 27 years old, most of whom had some operational experience. Salaries of sales employees totaled $433,000 in 1957. The sales force in 1957 averaged 7,000–8,000 calls a month on established customers and prospective new business. Leads for new business, developed from direct mail and other sources, were sometimes supplied to salesmen, especially the newer ones, while other salesmen developed their own prospects.

The usual function of the salesmen was to sell the Emery service to existing users of airfreight by giving a presentation of the principal features and selling points of the Emery service to purchasing agents and traffic managers. The salesmen were not trained operational analysts, however, and were not generally called upon to make cost analyses in their selling.

Emery salesmen had several specific Emery service advantages to present to prospective customers in addition to the general advantage common to all airfreight, high-speed transportation. Because of its method of operations, Emery was able to offer clients a more flexible, nation-wide, individualized service than were competitors. Emery service was highly flexible because it could ship by any air or surface line or any combination to transport freight to the desired place as quickly as possible. Through its nation-wide offices and the use of many transportation lines, Emery was able to offer service anywhere in the country. Through its international service, first developed in 1956, Emery was rapidly becoming world-wide in its services. Unlike most competitors, Emery would pick up and deliver shipments any time of day or night. Emery service was highly individualized. A private wire communication system was used to alert agents, transmit information on services needed, and report deliveries. Through Emery's "Time of Delivery" service, customers were apprised of the progress of their shipment and the time of arrival at its destination. An "Air Procurement Service" was available whereby a customer could purchase urgently needed material at a distant point and have the material air shipped through Emery.

Advertising Program 1949–57

In early 1949, shortly after receiving its registration as a common carrier, Emery, despite its rather precarious financial position, started an advertising campaign with an investment of $14,000. Emery's attitude toward the use of advertising is reflected by a statement made by President J. C. Emery in early 1958. "We believe our advertising has benefited us in a most significant fashion, and our belief in the paramount importance of advertising to us is illustrated by two incidents in the past; in our early days when we earned $20,000 in an especially good month—I believe this was the first occasion when we used black ink on our books—we put this money instantly into advertising. Again, a couple of years later, our advertising budget in one year required our entire net income for the previous year. While perhaps imprudent for other companies, I believe these actions paid off for us."

Throughout its history, Emery had a relatively small advertising budget (about 1% of revenues) with which to do a rather complex selling job. In relation to other freight advertising, Emery's advertising expenditures were large. Of the 65 or more airlines and airfreight forwarders in business in 1957, only one spent over $200,000 in a single year, only two over $100,000, and the majority virtually nothing.

The company's first advertising program in 1949, designed with its advertising agency J. M. Mathes, Inc., consisted of publicity and a small amount of direct mail in the form of personalized letters. The advertising expenditure the first year was $14,000.

In 1950 the advertising budget was nearly doubled over 1949, permitting a small-space campaign and expanded publicity. The 1950 campaign was designed to establish Emery's identity in the business community as an airfreight forwarder. The advertisements featured the company's hourglass symbol that through the years was to be developed into a part of Emery's Corporate signature. The copy told how the Emery service worked, and a coupon offered a booklet telling the complete story of the company's services. Exhibit 3A is an advertisement of the 1950 series.

In 1951, with a budget of $121,000, the advertising was addressed to specific problems that airfreight could solve for purchasing agents and traffic managers such as fast delivery of a replacement part to keep a production line in operation. The advertisements were two-thirds pages in trade and general magazines such as *Printers' Ink, Purchasing News, Traffic World, Time, Newsweek, Business Week*, and *U.S. News and World Report*. The hourglass symbol of the previous year became the company's signature, and the copy, as in the previous year, told how Emery service worked. The heavily increased advertising expenditure in 1951 was incurred because in that year a question arose about the willingness of the airlines to renew their contract with the Air Express Division of the Railway Express Agency with the possibility that Emery would be asked to replace Air Express. Exhibit 3B is an advertisement of the 1951 series.

In 1952, with a budget slightly increased over 1951, space was increased to a full page, and a cartoon illustration was used to gain reader attention. Copy, although slightly shorter, retained the same theme. Exhibit 3C is an advertisement from the 1952 series.

A SYMBOL THAT MEANS

"The World's Fastest Transportation Service"

This is the symbol of Emery Air Freight . . . everywhere acknowledged as the "World's Fastest Transportation Service."

Today . . . and *every day* . . . Emery is serving America's leading agencies, advertisers and printers . . . making deadlines they once believed impossible.

Emery coordinates and combines the facilities of *many* different carriers . . . selects the fastest and most dependable, both ground and air, for each individual shipment. And *every* shipment, whether a national distribution or a single mailing piece, gets *personalized* handling . . . *all the way* . . . from point of origin to destination.

Emery is today answering America's advertising requirements and new defense demands with maximum speed plus *absolute control* . . . control maintained through a nationwide network of offices and agents in over 200 cities.

A call to your local Emery office or agent will bring instant action. **The shipment you hope will arrive tomorrow may yet reach you today!**

● **Get the complete story of this nation-wide, PERSONALIZED, high speed air forwarding service—call your nearest Emery office or mail this coupon today!**

EMERY AIR FREIGHT CORPORATION, Dept. PI-3
314 E. 39th St., New York 16, N.Y.
Telephone: ORegon 9-1020

Please send me, without charge, a copy of your new folder, "THE WORLD'S FASTEST TRANSPORTATION SERVICE."

*Name*_____

*Address*_____

*City*_____*State*_____

EMERY AIR FREIGHT CORPORATION

"THE WORLD'S FASTEST TRANSPORTATION SERVICE"

General Office: 314 East 39th Street, New York 16, ORegon 9-1020

Offices in Boston, Buffalo, Chicago, Cincinnati, Cleveland, Detroit, Newark, Los Angeles, Milwaukee, Philadelphia, Pittsburgh, St. Louis, San Francisco, Washington, D. C.
Agents in all other major cities and towns in the U.S.A.

A. An Advertisement from the 1950 Series

Exhibit 3—Continued

The *MOST EXPENSIVE*
SHIPMENT in the U.S.A.!

Radium? Diamonds? Uranium? Not at all . . . just a small but vital replacement part . . . *that arrived too late!* And *because* it arrived too late, a whole production line was halted for precious hours, hundreds of workers were idle and national defense suffered.

Now, more than ever, Purchasing Agents and Traffic Managers need high speed and dependability in air transportation. Yet stepped-up defense demands have greatly reduced air lift capacity and will reduce it even more. That's why the kind of air transportation Emery Air Freight provides—instant, flexible access to *every* channel of transportation . . . hundreds of trained Expediters strategically scattered throughout the country —can mean so much to you today! Emery's service works this way:

A call to your *local* Emery office starts your purchase order number and instructions speeding by direct wire to your supplier's city. There, an Emery Expediter picks up your shipment . . . gets it on the *fastest* available plane. Everywhere enroute Emery *acts as your own personal expediter*...circumvents transfer delays... wires reports on your shipment's progress . . . personally delivers it *directly* to your receiving room.

Get the complete story on this unique advance in transportation service *today!* Emery is on the job 24 hours a day, *every* day of the year. REMEMBER . . . *the most expensive shipment is the one that arrives too late!*

EMERY AIR FREIGHT CORPORATION

General Office: 801 Second Avenue, New York 17, ORegon 9-1020

Offices in Boston, Buffalo, Chicago, Cincinnati, Cleveland, Dallas, Detroit, Newark, Los Angeles, Milwaukee, Philadelphia, Pittsburgh, St. Louis, San Francisco, Syracuse, Washington, D. C.

Agents in all other major cities and towns in the U.S.A.

B. An Advertisement from the 1951 Series

Exhibit 3—Continued

EMERY—
Nation's Choice

Again Emery Air Freight is the overwhelming choice of the leading sales, advertising and promotion executives in making "timed" deliveries to any point in the Nation in the *fastest possible way.*

When you, too, have inbound or outbound shipments that *must* get delivered by deadline time, you can rely on Emery to make delivery faster and more dependably ... day or night, rain or shine.

That's because Emery is the ONLY Transportation System in the World that uses *all* airlines, *all* surface transportation, passenger or cargo, express or freight ... has access to everything that moves, in the air and on the ground ... is on the job 24 hours a day! No wonder Emery beats any ordinary air shipping service by many precious hours, even days!

On *your* next deadline shipment, call your nearest Emery office and make your own test of "The World's Fastest Transportation System." You'll discover why those who want to ship the *fastest possible way* always specify "Ship Emery."

 **EMERY AIR FREIGHT CORPORATION**

General Office: 801 Second Avenue, New York 17, ORegon 9-1020

Offices in: Atlanta, Baltimore, Boston, Buffalo, Chicago, Cincinnati, Cleveland, Dallas, Dayton, Detroit, Hartford, Houston, Indianapolis, Kansas City, Los Angeles, Milwaukee, Minneapolis-St. Paul, Newark, Philadelphia, Pittsburgh, Rochester, St. Louis, San Francisco, Seattle, Syracuse, Washington, D.C. *Agents in all other major cities and towns in the U.S.A.*

C. An Advertisement from the 1952 Series

Exhibit 3—Continued

Ever need to know where your shipment is?

Many times, probably. But all *you* could do was sit—and wait it out. What would you give for a shipping service that can tell you just where your shipment is just when you want to know— with just a simple 'phone call?

- *The use of all airlines, all surface transportation—passenger or cargo, freight or express—the best of everything that moves in the air or on the ground.*
- *Absolute control of your shipment all along the way through its own private wire system and a nationwide standby staff ready to assist your own expediting departments.*
- *Continuous contact with your shipment so it can be instantly routed around trouble-spots.*
- *Immediate confirmation of delivery—or of unavoidable delay so plans can be adjusted efficiently.*

This is what we mean by "absolute control" of shipments—new in American transportation—but it is only one of the many features that Emery Air Freight provides American industry.

Emery's new system of "door-to-door" shipping succeeds because it is organized on this basis:

This kind of operation is unique in transportation history. It's the reason why Emery is the answer to your problem: "What transportation service can I really depend upon to ship in the *fastest possible way?*"

Inbound or outbound, Emery provides "The World's Fastest Transportation System."

PRINTERS, ENGRAVERS, ELECTROTYPERS . . . SALES, ADVERTISING AND PROMOTION EXECUTIVES! Emery's Timed Delivery Service is designed to make *simultaneous* deliveries to any number of points throughout the Country. Ask us about this—and other special Emery services you can use profitably.

EMERY AIR FREIGHT CORPORATION

New York 17; Offices or agents in all major cities and towns in the United States

D. An Advertisement from the 1953 Series

By 1953 management decided that although traffic managers and purchasing agents were influential in deciding which airfreight service to use, the basic decision to use airfreight, especially on a regular basis, was a top-management decision. For this reason, the advertising program in 1953 was divided into two parts: advertisements directed to top management in general business magazines and advertisements directed to specific industries, traffic managers, and purchasing agents through trade magazines. In both cases, copy told the basic story of how Emery service works. In 1953 the cartoon illustration was dropped in favor of photographs. Exhibit 3D is an advertisement from the 1953 series. Although 1953 advertisements had a primary demand message, the Emery story was closely tied in.

By 1954 Emery had assembled a group of case histories which were used in its advertising. Because of the 1954 recession, the size of the advertisement was cut from a full page to two-thirds page. Both general and trade media were continued except that, because of their high space cost, *Time* and *Newsweek* were dropped and only *Business Week* and *U.S. News and World Report* were used for the general business media. The 1955 campaign was basically the same as 1954, except that since Starch readership studies indicated two-thirds pages to be more expensive than full pages, page space was increased again to full pages. Exhibit 4A shows an advertisement from the 1955 campaign. Case histories illustrating Emery service were retained, but emphasis was placed on what Emery could do for the user rather than how the service worked.

In 1956, after receiving an exceptionally high Starch readership rating on a human interest advertisement describing Emery's distribution of Salk vaccine, the company embarked upon an advertisement series based upon human-interest photographs with pertinent case histories. The advertisements, which were run in both trade and general magazines, were the company's principal attempt to that date to sell not only Emery but also to increase the primary demand for airfreight. However, readership ratings of the human-interest series fell off sharply and it was discontinued. The company's advertising agency believed that the Salk vaccine advertisement was successful because it was a natural and timely situation, but the later advertisements failed because the situations featured were artificial, not real, news events. Exhibit 4B is the Salk vaccine advertisement.

Also in 1956, the Harvard Business School published *The Role of Air Freight in Physical Distribution*, a study initiated and in greater part financed by Emery Air Freight. The company sponsored the study with the hope that research would uncover facts which would point the way to new uses of airfreight, thus expanding the entire industry. The study substantiated the premise that in certain instances airfreight when properly used on a planned day-to-day basis could help to lower distribution costs. Emery, in the 1956 campaign, tried to bring this concept to man-

A nose for spreading the news

How Emery

Air Freight

helps you

beat deadlines!

A Texas client of ours publishes a magazine. He had to get copies of a special issue to 206 final destinations by a deadline of Wednesday, January 26th. First shipment from the printer arrived at Emery's Dallas office on Monday, January 24th in the afternoon. From there Emery took over. Shipments had to be delivered by Emery to 25 focal points throughout the nation, and from these points distributed to the 206 destinations. Emery's nationwide team worked so efficiently that not *one* inquiry was received from these distributors concerning their shipments.

Only Emery can do this kind of nationwide job . . . for you too. Write or call today for all the facts about Emery "Consolidated Air Parcel Service."

"Air Freight Makes Better Business"

EMERY AIR FREIGHT CORPORATION

General Offices: 801 Second Avenue, New York 17, N. Y.

Other offices or agents in all major cities and towns in the United States. Emery also serves Alaska and Canada.

A. An Advertisement from the 1955 Series

Exhibit 4—Continued

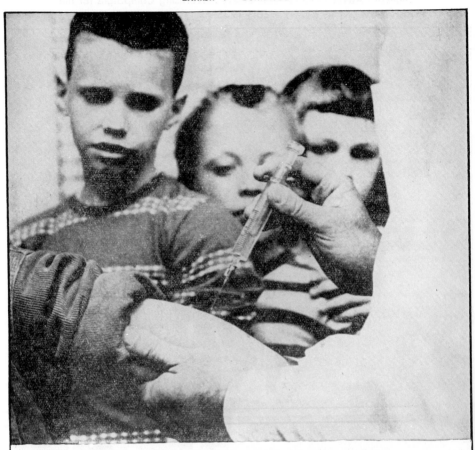

Prescription: Salk vaccine

How Emery helped speed delivery of the vaccine

Parke-Davis and Company, in Detroit, started shipments, via Emery Air Freight, at 6:35 P.M., twenty-five minutes after being granted License No. 1. The first shipment was in the air by 8:00 P.M. In just 21 hours Emery completed deliveries in 19 major cities from coast to coast.

Emery carried for another pharmaceutical house ninety per cent of its vaccine shipped for The National Foundation for Infantile Paralysis. Under the direction of The Foundation, Emery delivered to the State Health officers in 16 key cities their allotment of the vaccine within 24 hours from the pick-up time.

Distribution of allocated first orders to druggists in large and small communities across the country for Pitman-Moore Co., in Indianapolis, was a more difficult problem because many communities did not have airport facilities. But Emery Consolidated Air Parcel Service made deliveries to the General Post Office in the nearest airport city within 12 hours. As a result every vaccine order this producer could ship initially was available to physicians within 36 hours after being picked up at the Pitman-Moore Co.

High-speed air shipment via Emery has become routine throughout American business. So when high-speed distribution of the Salk polio vaccine was essential, Emery's unique system was the choice to serve the public best.

EMERY AIR FREIGHT CORPORATION

General Offices: 801 Second Avenue, New York 17, N. Y.
Other offices or agents in all major cities and towns in the United States. Emery also serves Alaska and Canada.

B. The Salk Vaccine Advertisement—1956

agement with case histories on the planned use of airfreight. Once again, in 1956, greater emphasis was placed on increasing primary demand for airfreight.

The 1957 advertising was a refinement of the 1956 campaign, using a dominant photograph with a case history illustrating the basic advantages of the planned use of airfreight. Executives believed that if this primary demand campaign succeeded in enlarging the basic market for airfreight, Emery would benefit. Exhibit 4C is an advertisement from the 1957 series.

The introduction of the Emery International Service was supported in 1956 and 1957 by an informative advertising campaign placed in trade publications: *Air Transportation, Export Trade and Shipper, Exporters' Digest,* and *International Trade Review.*

Sales Promotion, Direct Mail, and Publicity

Throughout its history, Emery had supplemented its publication advertising with sales promotion, direct mail, and publicity. In 1957 the company mailed 28,000 copies of the "Newsletter," a monthly direct-mail pamphlet with information on airfreight and the Emery service, to existing and prospective customers. A review of the Harvard study on airfreight was also promoted through direct mail.

Sales aids presenting the Emery service story were available to assist salesmen, the latest one being a large presentation folder explaining the Emery International Service. In addition, presentations for industry, based on the results of the Harvard study, were made by Emery top management.

Emery's public relations program started in 1949 and had been continued with two basic objectives: to promote the use of airfreight and to make the name "Emery" known. Releases were regularly sent to newspapers, trade magazines, and consumer magazines. In 1955 a full-length article on Emery Air Freight appeared in *The Saturday Evening Post.*

Planning for the 1958 Campaign

In planning the 1958 advertising campaign, Emery executives were aware of the need to increase the effectiveness of their sales promotional efforts although the advertising budget would be about the same as 1957 —$123,000. Not only was there a recession but more importantly there was increasing competition from other airfreight services. In addition, management was concerned with the results of a survey conducted in 1957 among persons on its "active" mailing list. Of 669 replies to the questionnaire, 278 indicated that they were not familiar with Emery's "Time of Delivery" service and 261 indicated that they were not familiar with Emery's "Air Procurement Service." These two features were basic to Emery's service, and although they had been emphasized over the years in Emery advertising and personal selling, the survey indicated to

Exhibit 4—Continued

Perfect place to start promotion planning

How Emery

Air Freight

helps strengthen

promotion plans

Management is rapidly discovering that planes and promotion *belong* together.

Through Emery, for example, an advertiser recently delivered promotion material to 1200 addresses in 400 cities in only 24 hours—enormously increasing the effectiveness of his *national* program.

Fast, dependable Emery Air Freight improves *your* promotion operations.

It enables you to plan your efforts on a nationwide scale with "split-second" timing for maximum sales impact.

And with Emery, you can expect *savings* up to 33% (depending on distance and weight) compared with the only other air express service. Of course, any emergency shipment moves better by air. But find out how Emery's nationwide door-to-door service can fit into your everyday promotion planning.

EMERY AIR FREIGHT CORPORATION

General Offices: 801 Second Avenue, New York 17. Serving the United States, Alaska, Canada . . . and Europe, Asia, Africa.

C. An Advertisement from the 1957 Series

Exhibit 5

EMERY AIR FREIGHT CORPORATION

Space Rates for *Wall Street Journal, Printers' Ink,*
Traffic World, and *Purchasing News,* 1957

	13 Times	26 Times	52 Times
Wall Street Journal			
National Edition (Circ., 481, 275):			
Full page......................	$93,506	$178,701	$357,402
½.........................	48,600	93,506	178,701
¼.........................	25,339	48,600	93,506
⅛.........................	13,708	25,339	48,600
Eastern Edition (Circ., 152,826):			
Full........................	37,402	72,034	144,069
½.........................	19,394	37,402	72,034
¼.........................	10,043	19,394	37,402
⅛.........................	5,483	10,043	19,394
Midwest Edition (Circ., 208,290):			
Full........................	30,014	57,720	115,440
½.........................	15,584	30,014	57,720
¼.........................	8,081	15,584	30,014
⅛.........................	4,329	8,081	15,584
Pacific Coast Edition (Circ., 73,156):			
Full........................	16,623	31,400	62,799
½.........................	8,658	16,623	31,400
¼.........................	4,618	8,658	16,623
⅛.........................	2,453	4,618	8,658
Southwest Edition (Circ., 47,003):			
Full........................	12,237	23,088	46,176
½.........................	6,349	12,237	23,088
¼.........................	3,290	6,349	12,237
⅛.........................	1,789	3,290	6,349
Printers' Ink			
1 page.......................	$ 660	$ 630	$ 600
⅔.........................	465	445	425
½.........................	360	345	330
⅙.........................	125	120	115
Traffic World			
1 page.......................	$ 475	$ 430	$ 380
⅔.........................	345	320	265
½.........................	270	255	225
⅙.........................	100	95	87
Purchasing News			
1 page.......................	$ 485	$ 465	$ 455
⅔.........................	350	335	325
½.........................	260	250	240
¼.........................	155	150	140

Source: Standard Rate and Data Service.

management that a large number of customers were unaware of or had forgotten these points.

Emery management believed that it should continue the case-history campaign in general magazines, a campaign designed to convince top management that airfreight could be profitably used on a day-to-day basis, thereby increasing primary demand for airfreight. In addition, executives believed that, within the limited budget, renewed emphasis had

Exhibit 6

EMERY AIR FREIGHT CORPORATION
Analysis of Circulation, March 31, 1956, *Wall Street Journal*
(National Edition)

Nature of Business:	*Per Cent*	*Circulation*
Industry and commerce:		
Manufacturing	26.48	109,530
Mining—raw materials	0.61	2,535
Oil production and refining	1.48	6,110
Construction	2.61	10,801
Public utilities	1.28	5,274
Transportation	1.81	7,480
Farming, ranching, nurseries, etc.	2.19	9,051
Wholesalers	8.03	33,189
Retailers	10.44	43,178
Service industries	4.52	18,711
Insurance	2.58	10,649
Real estate	2.26	9,356
Finance:		
Banks and trust companies	4.73	19,548
Investment bankers and dealers, stock and commodity brokers	3.87	15,998
Savings banks, savings and loan companies	0.59	2,459
Financial, miscellaneous	1.18	4,893
Professional	8.43	34,862
Government	1.84	7,606
Education	1.43	5,908
Armed forces	0.81	3,347
Housewives	1.18	4,893
Living from investments and retired	7.76	32,098
No industry given	1.62	6,694
Students	2.27	9,406
Total	100.00	413,576
Title or Position:		
Chairmen	0.55	2,257
Presidents	14.41	59,607
Owners	13.34	55,171
Partners	7.16	29,614
Publishers	0.04	178
Directors	0.58	2,409
Vice presidents	8.07	33,366
Secretaries and secretary treasurers	2.97	12,297
Treasurers	1.83	7,581
Comptrollers	0.60	2,485
Officers and assistant officers	2.26	9,330

Exhibit 6—Continued

Title or Position:	Per Cent	Circulation
Trustees	0.06	228
General managers	1.48	6,136
Department managers and assistants	11.65	48,173
Superintendents, supervisors, foremen and assistants	2.05	8,468
Editors	0.26	1,065
Engineers	2.58	10,674
Chemists	0.21	862
Purchasing agents and buyers	0.88	3,651
Cashiers and assistant cashiers	0.68	2,814
Agents, brokers, salesmen	3,52	14,553
Employees, miscellaneous	3.94	16,303
Professional	7.71	31,895
Government	0.41	1,673
Housewives	1.18	4,893
Living from investments and retired	7.76	32,098
No position given	1.55	6,389
Students	2.27	9,406
Total	100.00	413,576

Source: The Wall Street Journal Index to Subscriber Buying Power.

Exhibit 7

EMERY AIR FREIGHT CORPORATION

Analysis of Circulation, November 2, 1957, Traffic World

	Circulated
Shippers:	
Manufacturers	5,082
Shippers of raw material	116
Wholesalers, mail-order houses, retailers	302
Chambers of commerce, government depots, traffic associations	682
Carriers:	
Railroads	1,699
Motor freight lines	1,370
Steamship and barge lines	104
Airlines, pipelines, express companies, freight forwarders, and brokers	186
Traffic bureaus and associates	165
Related Groups:	
Regulatory agencies	355
Warehouses, terminals, ports, and local cartage	154
Transportation attorneys and councilors	167
Schools, students, and libraries	417
Miscellaneous	135
Average total paid circulation (6 months)	10,876

Source: Publisher's statement.

to be placed on carrying the basic Emery sales features to traffic managers and purchasing agents in order to convince them to specify Emery when procuring airfreight.

Initial discussions on how these objectives could be realized focused on the possibilities of using a campaign in newspapers in key cities of the

Exhibit 8

EMERY AIR FREIGHT CORPORATION

Analysis of Circulation, November 1, 1957, *Printers' Ink*

1. Manufacturers:
   a) Heads of business—chairmen and vice chairmen, presidents, partners, and owners 855
   b) Vice presidents 853
   c) Secretaries and treasurers 194
   d) General managers 189
   e) Sales managers 1,003
   f) Advertising managers (including sales promotion managers, directors of publicity, directors of public relations) 3,113
   g) Territorial, division, and branch subscriptions (including 747 subscriptions with title of manager, sales manager, advertising manager or above) 1,318
   h) Miscellaneous executives and all other home office employees 1,796
   i) Subscriptions in company name 847

Total of Classification 1	10,168	34.08%
2. Wholesalers, distributors, and jobbers; including their personnel	1,004	3.36
3. Public utilities (electric, gas, telephone, etc.); also local transportation companies; including their personnel	299	1.00
4. Banks, financial underwriters, and investment houses; including their personnel	277	0.93
5. Trade associations and promotional groups, including chambers of commerce; including their personnel	564	1.89
6. Retail establishments (including chain stores and mail-order houses), local service companies; including their personnel . . .	1,597	5.35
7. Advertising agencies; including their personnel		
Total of Classification 7	5,988	20.07
8. Graphic arts and other advertising services; including their personnel	2,537	8.50

9. Media including their personnel and their representatives:
   a) Newspapers 1,463
   b) Magazines, farm publications, and business publications . . .2,281
   c) Radio and television 485
   d) All other 308

Total of Classification 9	4,537	15.20
10. Schools and colleges—professors, students	1,150	3.85

11. Miscellaneous:
    a) Public libraries 215
    b) Miscellaneous 795

Total of Classification 11	1,010	3.39
12. Awaiting classification by business and industry	709	2.38
Total Paid Subscription Circulation for the November 1, 1957, issue	29,840	100.00%

Source: Publisher's statement.

United States to bolster the efforts of salesmen in selling the specific benefits of the Emery service. However, calculation of the cost of such a campaign quickly indicated to the executives that the expenditure would be far more than the company could afford. In searching for a suitable medium, executives discussed the *Wall Street Journal*, which they believed had many characteristics of a regular newspaper, yet had a more

Exhibit 9

EMERY AIR FREIGHT CORPORATION
Analysis of Circulation, December 1957—Purchasing News

Classification by Title and Occupation

Sic	Classification by Business and Industry	Total Copies	Per Cent	Copies in Co. Name	Corp. Officers, General Managers	Plant Production	Engineer and Design	Purchasing — Dept. Heads	Purchasing — Buyers and Other Pur. Personnel	All Other Employees	Unclassified by Occupation
19	Ordnance and accessories	105	0.58		6	7		50	42		
25	Furniture and fixtures	190	1.05		36	15	1	105	33		
33	Primary metal products	330	1.82	3	28	4	1	221	73		
34	Fabricated metal products (except ordnance, machinery, and transportation equipment)	2,436	13.40	1	505	113	18	1,515	281	3	
35	Machinery (except electrical)	6,099	33.54	1	970	257	68	3,396	1,399	4	4
36	Electrical machinery, equipment and supplies	4,179	22.98	14	424	155	66	2,017	1,501	2	
37	Transportation equipment	3,175	17.46	7	158	99	22	1,076	1,810	3	
38	Professional, scientific, and controlling instruments; photographic and optical goods; watches and clocks	879	4.84	2	118	27	13	457	259	1	2
39	Miscellaneous manufacturing industries	334	1.84		50	21	1	200	61	1	
89	Miscellaneous services (including consulting engineering and engineering research laboratories)	125	0.69	2	25	1	7	57	33		
90	Government	154	0.85	7	4	1	8	86	46		2
	Other SIC groups: each group amounting to less than 1% of total (10)1, (13)3, (15)1, (17)1, (20)3, (22)4, (24)5, (26)6, (27)2, (28)32, (29)17, (30)29, (31)3, (32)60, (44)1, (47)1, (82)4	173	0.95		9	6	4	106	48		
	Total Copies	18,179		37	2,333	706	209	9,286	5,586	14	8
	Per Cent		100.00	0.20	12.83	3.88	1.16	51.08	30.73	0.08	0.04
	Average Copies for Period	17,070									

Source: Publisher's statement.

selective audience in terms of Emery's market. Because of budget restrictions, executives felt that if a *Wall Street Journal* campaign were used, it might be necessary to drop the trade magazines *Purchasing News*, *Traffic World*, and *Printers' Ink* which had been used in previous years. Executives planned to limit advertising space costs to $100,000 in 1958. Exhibit 5 gives space rates, and Exhibits 6 through 9 give circulation analyses for the *Wall Street Journal*, *Purchasing News*, *Traffic World*, and *Printers' Ink*.

~~~

CASE 5: MASONITE CORPORATION[1]

QUESTIONS TO CONSIDER: *(1) What is your appraisal of Masonite's development of a marketing program for its exterior siding? (2) Was sound use made of advertising in the period 1953–57? (3) What promotional strategy would you recommend for 1958? Would you employ advertising to consumers? If so, for what purposes?*

During the period from 1953 to 1957, Masonite Corporation had introduced five new exterior home-siding products utilizing advertising programs devoted primarily to educational campaigns directed at lumber dealers, contractors, and architects. By the end of 1957, with Masonite home sidings well established, the advertising manager was attempting to decide whether or not to devote a major portion of the 1958 advertising to a consumer campaign.

Masonite Corporation—Background

In the early 1920's, Mr. William H. Mason, while working on a process of extracting turpentine and other oils from wood, developed a method for reducing the waste wood into its component fibers that could be used to make a strong tough sheet product. Mr. Mason called the material "Presdwood," and in 1929 the Masonite Corporation was formed to produce and market "Presdwood."

During the 1930's the company enjoyed steady growth by selling Presdwood primarily as a paneling and decorative product for home interiors. Only limited sales were made to industry for fabrication into new products. After the war the product was promoted and sold through lumber and building materials dealers, primarily on the basis of its interior and "handyman" uses.

In 1947 an industrial department was formed with a separate sales force and sales manager to sell Presdwood direct to industry for use in fabricating such products as trailers, furniture, and games. An aggressive sales

---
[1] Written by David W. Nylen.

and advertising program resulted in considerable growth for this department, and by the end of 1947 industrial sales had grown to 50% of the company's volume.

By 1957, 60 distinct types and thicknesses of Presdwood had been developed and the company's sales reached $58 million.

Development of Exterior Uses

Little use had been made of Presdwood for exteriors until 1939, when, through discovery of a tempering process, the company was able to produce harder varieties of Presdwood. The United States government became interested in possible exterior applications of the new harder material and built several Presdwood-sided experimental Quonset-type huts in Alaska and the Aleutians. The success of these buildings in the Alaskan temperature and humidity extremes led the government during World War II to build thousands of these huts of Presdwood in areas where other materials deteriorated under the extremes of climate. During the war, Presdwood was also used for PT boat decks, shell casings, and as a substitute for steel in refrigerators.

After the government's successful exterior application of Masonite Presdwood during the war, some Masonite dealers experimented with exterior uses of the material, primarily in applications where attractiveness was not as important as ease of application and durability, such as on barns, hog pens, and machinery sheds. The Presdwood in these cases was usually applied in the full 4-foot by 8-foot sheets with battens on the seams.

In 1951 several dealers in the central states began ripping 4-foot by 8-foot sheets into siding-width strips for sale to contractors and individuals building their own homes. Limited exterior use began to take place, promoted by word of mouth and the activities of a few dealers and salesmen. After inquiry by the sales manager in this area, the company conducted research which indicated a good market for a siding product if an exterior panel specifically designed for homes were marketed.

The first product designed was a lap siding made of tempered Presdwood ripped to 12-inch, 16-inch, and 24-inch widths with a special "Shadowline" wood strip. The new product, called "Masonite Siding," was ready for introduction to the market in January 1953.

Marketing the New Siding Products, 1953–57

Masonite siding was introduced in January 1953 through lumber and building supply dealers, the established channels for Masonite's other products. The product was sold by the existing Masonite sales force that not only called on dealers but also did considerable work acquainting home contractors with the benefits of the new siding in an attempt to build a market for Masonite dealers. In selling the new product, which competed with plywood, asbestos, wood shingles, and other siding products, salesmen could point out that it was economical both in price and in cost of application. Masonite salesmen could also point to the extreme durability of Masonite in the government's war applications. The company provided salesmen with product samples, photographs of applications, and technical booklets showing methods of application. The industrial sales force also started in 1953 to sell the siding to prefabricated house builders.

Advertising for the new siding started in January 1953 to dealers through the trade magazines *American Lumberman* and *Building Supply News*, plus several regional lumber dealer magazines, the theme being "Boost dealer profits by handling Masonite siding." Advertising to home builders started in the fall 1953 with advertisements in *American Builder*, *House and Home*, and *Practical Builder*. In addition to trade advertisements, one full-page, two-color advertisement was run in *Better Homes & Gardens* and in *American Home* plus a one-half, black-and-white advertisement in *Living for Young Homemakers*. The consumer advertisements were run primarily for their value as merchandising tools with dealers. Mounted consumer advertisement reprints and direct-mail pieces were sent to dealers. The 1953 advertising budget was about $52,000. Exhibit 1 shows selected 1953 trade and consumer advertisements, an application instruction, and the first dealer siding display piece.

By the winter of 1953 the new siding product had caught on well, but both builders and prefab manufacturers indicated the need for more than one product. By November 1954 the company had developed "Ridgeline," a 4-foot by 8-foot, striated, panel siding. Ridgeline was first introduced on the West Coast by the sales force and shortly later on a national scale. Trade advertisements to dealers and builders introduced the product in November. In addition a half-page, black-and-white advertisement announcing Ridgeline was run in *Better Homes & Gardens*, *Living for Young Homemakers*, *American Home*, and *Sunset*, and a two-color page in the *Small Homes Guide*. The consumer advertisements in 1954, as in 1953, were run primarily for their value as promotional material to dealers. The advertising budget for 1954 increased to $75,000, most of the increase being devoted to an increase in samples, mail pieces, and promotional pieces to dealers and builders. Exhibit 2 shows selected 1954 advertisements.

In 1955 two new siding products were introduced: "Shadowvent," a lap siding with aluminum mounting strips, and "Panelgroove," a 4-foot by 8-foot panel with a groove every 4 inches. The two new products were introduced together in three-page spreads in the April issues of *American Lumberman* and *Building Supply News* plus numerous regional trade magazines. Direct mail was also sent to dealers describing the new products, and extensive new dealer displays were distributed featuring the new products. The Masonite sales force introduced the new products to builders and contractors using newly designed displays

Exhibit 1

MASONITE CORPORATION

Selected 1953 Masonite Advertisements and Technical Bulletin

A Consumer Ad

Exhibit 1—Continued

Coming your way...

MASONITE SIDING
—a Presdwood Product

You'll be playing a new hit tune on your cash register!

It'll come from sales of Masonite Siding—the newest member of the famous Presdwood® family.

Masonite Corporation is launching a vigorous, all-out promotion campaign—addressed to your customers —telling how and why this new siding material will make their homes look better and last longer!

Man, what an opportunity!

Here's a superior product, tested and *not* found wanting. A famous brand name, actually a household word. A full-fledged announcement program to introduce, educate and sell! And, to cap it all, a market potential as long and broad as your entire trading area.

Your Masonite representative has the story. It's a short one, but it speaks volumes—plus profits!

BETTER HARDBOARDS FOR BETTER PROFITS

FEATURES IN A FLASH!

Deeper shadow! Shadowline wood strips, specially designed for use with Masonite Siding, produce a deep shadow. Permit smaller overlap—put more of the width to work.

Durability! Won't rust, rot or corrode. Out-weathers the weather! Tough—resists surface injuries.

Stability! Knotless, grainless. Keeps its shape. Won't split, splinter or crack. Won't push nails out.

Paint-ability! Super-smooth, even surface that won't check and crack the finish. Takes less paint, less painting time. *Extra* years between paint jobs.

Economy! No short lengths. Packaged in convenient 8', 10' and 12' lengths in conventional 12", wide 16" and extra-wide 24" widths. ¼" and 5⁄16" thicknesses.

MASONITE®
CORPORATION

"Masonite" signifies that Masonite Corporation is the source of the product
Dept. MVL-1, Box 777, Chicago 90, Illinois

A Dealer Ad

Exhibit 1—Continued

A Dealer Ad

Exhibit 1—Continued

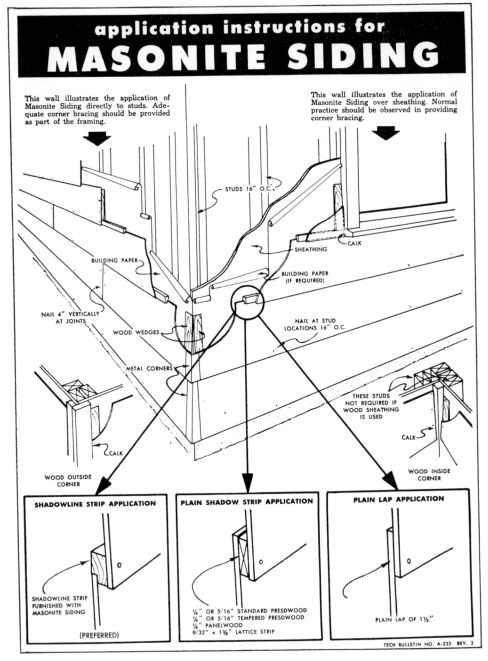

Builder Technical Bulletin

Exhibit 2
MASONITE CORPORATION
Selected 1954 Masonite Advertisements

It's new! It's textured! It's a business-builder!
MASONITE RIDGEWOOD

Here's a wide-open selling opportunity for you! It's Masonite Ridgewood, the all wood tempered hardboard with a combed effect, textured surface. This new member of the famous Presdwood® family offers all the advantages of Masonite ¼" Siding...plus a handsome ridge pattern that more and more architects, builders and home buyers are looking for. Thoroughly tested in actual use. Comes in convenient sizes for lap siding, panel siding and shingles.

Ridgewood can be used inside the home, too. In sliding doors, built-ins, cabinets, wall paneling, and in hobby work. Can be given decorative tone-on-tone finishes.

Your Masonite man has the details. Or write us for prices and sizes.

**Recommend
MASONITE RIDGEWOOD for:**

- Lap siding
- Panel siding
- Shingle siding
- Interior paneling
- Built-ins

NATURALLY STRONGER WITH LIGNIN

PRESDWOOD
WOOD MADE BETTER

MASONITE®
CORPORATION
Dept. AL-1115, Box 777, Chicago 90, Ill.
"Masonite" signifies that Masonite Corporation is the source of the product

A Dealer Ad

Exhibit 2—Continued

Best-looking house on the street... yet we saved 25% when we chose MASONITE SIDING

Save 3 Ways! Masonite Siding costs less to buy, less to apply and less to paint!

- We got the wide siding we wanted
- No waste from knots or splits
- The full-sized panels went up fast
- Easier to paint...holds paint longer

Yes! You can save up to 25% of the cost of outside material alone, by selecting Masonite Siding, pre-packaged panels of the same dense Tempered Presdwood® so well known for its resistance to the weather... its ability to take a lot of punishment without showing it.

Never before have you been able to choose siding in 12", 16" or 24" widths at the same basic price. Convenient lengths up to 16' mean fewer joints, easier application. Thicknesses of 5/16" or 1/4" for a lifetime of protection for your home.

Get an attractive, modern-styled, wide siding effect you'll be proud of, with both present and future economies from Masonite Siding.

NATURALLY STRONGER WITH LIGNIN

PRESDWOOD WOOD MADE BETTER

MASONITE® CORPORATION Dept. LFH-4, Box 777, Chicago 90, Illinois

"Masonite" signifies that Masonite Corporation is the source of the product

Please send me, without obligation:

☐ Colorful idea book on building and remodeling with Masonite Presdwood Products.

Name...

Address ....

Post Office................................Zone..........

County.......................State....................

A Consumer Ad

and presentations. There was no advertising of exterior products in builders' trade magazines in 1955, although, as in other years, the Masonite name was brought before builders through advertisements for Masonite interior products. Consumer advertising in 1955 consisted of a full-page, black-and-white advertisement in *Living for Young Homemakers* featuring Shadowvent, and a half-page, black-and-white advertisement in *Sunset* featuring Ridgewood. As in previous years, these advertisements were run primarily for their promotional value with dealers. In October 1955 advertising was directed to architects with a full-page, black-and-white advertisement in *Architectural Record* and *Progressive Architecture* featuring the four Masonite sidings. In May 1955 the first advertisement to prefabricated home builders was run in the *Magazine* of *Prefabrication*. The 1955 budget was $110,-000, with about 40% of this budget being spent for promotional and display pieces. Exhibit 3 gives selected advertisements and display material used in 1955.

Considerable work had been done in 1955 gathering pictures and case his-

Exhibit 3

MASONITE CORPORATION

Selected 1955 Masonite Advertisements and Display Material

NEWS! MASONITE PRESENTS

"PROFIT BOOSTER NO. 1"

You've Never Seen Siding Like This!

MASONITE
SHADOWVENT SIDING

New in design!   New in application!   New in profit possibilities!

- Here's a siding with Primecote...a strong, smooth film equal to several coats of hand-applied primer...perfect base for long-lasting finish coat.

- Here's a siding with no visible nails...the new patented aluminum shadow strip takes the nails, holds the panels securely. And the strip is vented...reduces moisture and condensation problems in any weather.

- Here's a siding with all the advantages of Masonite Tempered Presdwood®, that tough, grainless hardboard panel that's so popular everywhere.

- Homeowners like the long-lived protection they get, the handsome beauty of these clean-cut panels. Builders like the economy, the speed of application... now an even more attractive buy with the new application method and with Primecote. And you'll like the profits that come with promoting, displaying and selling new Masonite Shadowvent Siding.

Not immediately available west of the Rockies

Exhibit 3—Continued

"PROFIT BOOSTER NO. 2"
TURN BACK FOR "PROFIT-BOOSTER NO. 1"

Ideal for the gameroom, recreation room, den, study or modern living room. New Masonite Panelgroove brings the rustic atmosphere that people like. Sell Panelgroove to the "do-it-yourself" trade.

When Individuality Counts!

NEW MASONITE PANELGROOVE

Different—desirable—and profitable! Offers the vertical accent for exterior designs that architects, builders and homeowners like. Creates a refreshing contrast to other design treatments. Makes good-looking gables—fast! Perfect for use between windows, on short runs, and featured areas.

Masonite Panelgroove needs no joint treatment...edges are ship-lapped to create a distinctive and continuous pattern. Square-cut grooves are $\frac{3}{8}''$ wide and 4" on centers. Panels are 4' wide, $\frac{5}{16}''$ thick and up to 16' long.

When you sell Panelgroove, you sell all the weather-fighting, time-defying advantages of Masonite Tempered Presdwood—plus a high-styled design with great popular appeal—and profit! Ask your Masonite representative for complete information or write Masonite Corporation, Dept. AL-4, Box 777, Chicago 90, Illinois.

Sell This Man—He Makes The Difference

MASONITE PANELGROOVE

TEMPERED PRODUCT OF MASONITE® CORPORATION

Not immediately available west of the Rockies

tories of successful applications of Masonite siding. With this material, extensive improvements were made in promotional literature and display material. New presentation material was also provided for salesmen. Masonite had long participated in trade shows such as those of the National Association of Home Builders, the National Retail Lumber Dealers Association, and several regional shows, but in 1956 emphasis for the first

Exhibit 3—Continued

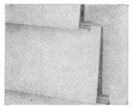

time was placed on displaying exterior sidings. Masonite also displayed sidings in the Producer's Council "Caravan" (jointly sponsored by the American Institute of Architects), a display of co-operating building materials manufacturers that toured key cities, the display being open to architects and their guests.

In 1956 for the first time a trade advertising program for Masonite sidings was begun on a continuous, regular basis. A fifth siding product,

Exhibit 3—Continued

Both contemporary and conventional styles are featured in Ashlan Park, the new George Workmon development in Fresno, Cal. Ranging from $10,500 to $15,600, these homes are imaginatively built for quality and beauty. That is the reason they selected Masonite Ridgewood for the exteriors.

For that look of distinction...

use textured MASONITE RIDGEWOOD

You'll find it better 3 ways!

1. **Lends a luxury look!** No ordinary paneling, this! Ridgewood displays an interesting combed effect on its surface that adds character to any home. You can use this distinctive texture on board and batten siding (as above), on lap siding with a deep Shadowline strip, or in shingles.
2. **Lifelong protection!** Ridgewood is a new Presdwood® product with all the strength, stability and resistance to weather that dense, rugged Masonite hardboards are noted for. Will not split, splinter or crack.
3. **Doubly economical!** With no knots or grain, every square inch of Ridgewood is usable. Goes up fast. Takes and holds paint beautifully. More years between paint jobs.
   Talk to your architect or contractor about Masonite Ridgewood. *Your building materials dealer has it!* Send coupon for more information. Masonite Corporation, Dept. SU-5, 111 Sutter Street, San Francisco 4, Calif.

Look For This Man—He Makes The Difference

MASONITE RIDGEWOOD

PANEL PRODUCT OF MASONITE® CORPORATION

Consumer Ad

Exhibit 3—Continued

MASONITE SIDING

Delivers Value Extras on National Homes

One of the busiest, best known and most successful manufacturers of homes in the country, National Homes Corporation, offers exteriors of Masonite Siding on all its models. For these logical reasons:

1. Sale-ability. Precision-cut panels of Masonite Siding enhance the appearance of any home...offer a deep shadowline that lends character and dignity.

2. Durability. Out-weathers the weather. Resists bumps, scrapes and other surface hazards.

3. Paint-ability. Smooth surface of these dense, grainless panels is easier to paint.

4. Variety. Choice of wide and extra-wide...accentuating the beauty of contemporary styling.

5. Save-ability. Sturdy all wood hardboard is economical to buy and to use. Reduces dimension, lap and cutting losses.

Wouldn't you like to know more about this increasingly popular siding? We'll be glad to give you all the details. Write Masonite Corporation, Dept. PF-5, Box 777, Chicago 90, Ill.

Look For This Man 〔🔺〕 He Makes The Difference

MASONITE SIDING

A PANEL PRODUCT OF MASONITE® CORPORATION

Prefabricator Ad

"Ridgegroove," was added without fanfare during the year. No consumer magazines were used in 1956 because executives of the company believed that with distribution and product acceptance achieved, it was not necessary to use consumer advertising. However, three consumer home annuals were used as an inexpensive way to reach consumers, and the ad-

Exhibit 3—Continued

For modern exteriors, choose modern materials—Masonite Corporation offers <u>four</u>!

Now it's easier to get the eye-pleasing, modern effects you want. Choose one or more of these sturdy, grainless Presdwood® panel products.

They have all the rugged strength, weather-resistance and durability you demand, plus welcome economies in both application and painting.

Masonite Shadowvent (A) is the improved lap siding with the revolutionary vented aluminum shadow strip that permits invisible nailing. Panels are primed; one additional coat covers.

Tempered Presdwood (B) panels with batten strips cover big areas fast, fit many architectural styles.

Masonite Ridgewood (C) presents a distinctive combed surface texture. Sizes for lap siding, panel siding or shingles.

Masonite Panelgroove (D) is a brand new Tempered Presdwood product, ¾₆″ thick, with grooves every 4″. Continuous vertical design is completed with shiplapped edges. For gables, end walls, sill courses, and accent areas.

For complete specifications on these and other famous Presdwood products, write now to Masonite® Corporation, Dept. AR-10, Box 777, Chicago 90, Ill. In Canada, address Masonite Corporation, Gatineau, Que.

Look for this man   He makes the difference

MASONITE CORPORATION
MANUFACTURER OF PRESDWOOD PANEL PRODUCTS

Architectural Ad

Exhibit 3—Continued

Dealer Counter Displays

vertisements in these annuals were promoted to dealers and builders by direct mail. The advertising budget for siding materials was $140,000 in 1956. Exhibit 4 gives selected advertisements and promotional pieces employed in 1956. The 1956 insertion schedule is given below:

Architectural Record . . . . 6 pages, B & W
Progressive Architecture . . . . 6 pages, B & W
American Lumberman . . . . 2 spreads (2 pages), B & W
4 pages, B & W
Building Supply News . . . . 2 spreads (2 pages), B & W
4 pages, B & W
House and Home . . . . 2 spreads (2 pages), B & W
4 pages, B & W
Regional lumber dealer books . . . . 6 pages, B & W
New Homes Guide . . . . 1 page, B & W
House & Garden Book of Building . . . . 1 page, B & W
House Beautiful Building Manual . . . . . 1 page, B & W

In 1957 the company's advertising program was about the same as the previous years. Advertisements stressed Masonite as a *modern* building material. Frank Lloyd Wright, a prominent architect, had designed his first prefabricated home in 1956 using Masonite Ridgeline. Advertisements were run featuring this home, and considerable publicity was generated. The 1957 advertising budget was about the same as the 1956

Exhibit 4

MASONITE CORPORATION

Selected 1956 Masonite Advertisements and Promotional Pieces

a textured surface...
Masonite Ridgegroove

Doubly appealing . . . with an interesting combed textured surface between vertical grooves for added accent. Square-cut grooves are ⅜" wide and spaced 4" or 8" on center or in random pattern. Ridgegroove's combed surface takes stains exceptionally well – producing striking, long-lasting finishes.

Masonite Ridgeline
for new design interest

Masonite Ridgeline, the versatile panel with a combed textured surface can be applied with or without battens, as horizontal siding or as shingles. Ridgeline accepts all types of finishes well, including stains – a handsome finish, whether used on the entire house or in featured areas.

for vertical accents...
Masonite Panelgroove

Different – distinctive – and most desirable! Offers the vertical accent to exteriors of contemporary homes. Creates a refreshing contrast to masonry or horizontal sidings. Panelgroove is applied without troublesome joint treatments – edges are shiplapped for a continuous design. Grooves are spaced 4" or 8" on center or in random pattern.

**Masonite
Tempered Presdwood**
where individuality counts...

For modern-minded homeowners seeking an exterior that's truly smart-looking . . . here's Masonite Tempered Presdwood with batten strips. Tempering gives these panels extra hardness, extra strength, extra resistance to moisture, impact and surface hazards.

**combinations
accents
protected exteriors**

Masonite Panelwood is an ideal material for protected exterior applications on soffits, breezeways, porches and carports. The large, smooth surfaced panels accept and hold many finishes, permitting a wide choice of attractive colors. Other Masonite products used for these applications are Tempered Presdwood® and Peg-Board,® all available with Primecote,® a factory applied primer, for quicker, longer-lasting finishes.

A Consumer Pamphlet (Color)

budget. Exhibit 5 shows advertisements run in 1957. The 1957 insertion schedule is given below:

Exhibit 4—Continued

An Architectural Ad

Exhibit 4—Continued

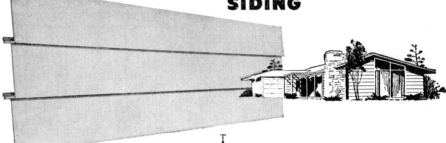

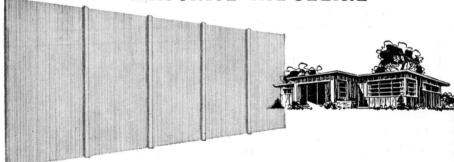

Exhibit 4—Continued

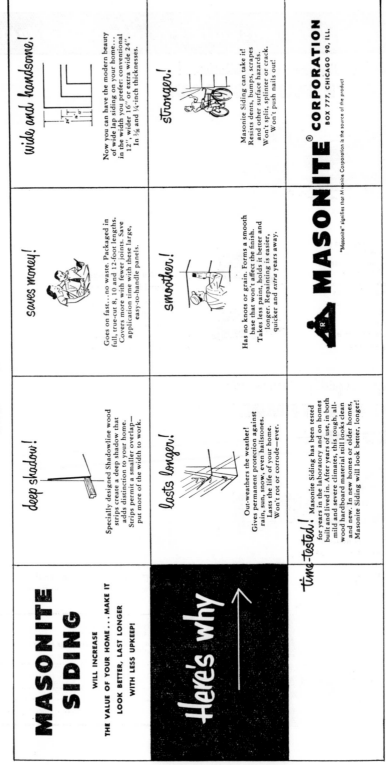

MASONITE SIDING

WILL INCREASE
THE VALUE OF YOUR HOME...MAKE IT
LOOK BETTER, LAST LONGER
WITH LESS UPKEEP!

Here's why →

deep shadow!

Specially designed Shadowline wood strips create a deep shadow that adds distinction to your home. Strips permit a smaller overlap—put more of the width to work.

lasts longer!

Out-weathers the weather! Gives permanent protection against rain, sun, snow, even hailstones. Lasts the life of your home. Won't rot or corrode—ever.

time-tested! Masonite Siding has been tested for years in the laboratory and on homes built and lived in. After years of use, in both mild and severe climates, this tough, all-wood hardboard material still looks clean and new. In new homes or older homes, Masonite Siding will look better, longer!

saves money!

Goes on fast...no waste. Packaged in full, true-cut 8, 10 and 12-foot lengths. Covers more with fewer joints. Save application time with these large, easy-to-handle panels.

smoother!

Has no knots or grain. Forms a smooth base that won't affect the finish. Takes less paint, holds it better and longer. Repainting is easier, quicker and *extra* years away.

wide and handsome!

Now you can have the modern beauty of wide lap siding on your home...in the width you prefer: conventional 12", wider 16" or extra wide 24". In ⁷⁄₁₆ and ¼-inch thicknesses.

stronger!

Masonite Siding can take it! Resists dents, bumps, scrapes and other surface hazards. Won't split, splinter or crack. Won't push nails out!

▲ **MASONITE**® **CORPORATION**
BOX 777, CHICAGO 90, ILL.

"Masonite" signifies that Masonite Corporation is the source of the product

A Consumer Pamphlet

Exhibit 4—Continued

A Trade Show Display

In 1957 the sales force increased its emphasis on selling the use of Masonite sidings to builders and architects, the company requiring that at least 45% of all sales calls be made on builders or architects. The company had found that dealers were not aggressive in selling the Masonite sidings, and Masonite executives believed that they had to build the market for dealers. In both 1956 and 1957 executives of the company did considerable work with builders' and architects' trade associations to gain acceptance and greater use of Masonite building materials.

Planning the 1958 Campaign

In late 1957, Mr. James Hurley, advertising manager, was reviewing the status of the new Masonite siding products preparatory to developing the 1958 advertising campaign. Distribution of the products was firmly established with about 20,000 dealers handling them, and substantial sales were being made to the prefabricated home market. Sales of siding by 1957 had reached $7 million, about 12% of total company sales. The few product design difficulties that had occurred had been overcome by 1957, and application of the product had proven easy and economical.

It was difficult to generalize about the cost of Masonite siding as compared with the cost of other siding products because several factors had to be considered: cost per square foot or other measure, application cost, wastage, and painting or other finishing cost. In addition, with Masonite siding, like other building products, the manufacturer could not set retail

Exhibit 5

MASONITE CORPORATION

Selected 1957 Masonite Advertisements

THE HOUSE

A new look in home manufacturing has come to Madison, Wis. Designed for upper-middle income families, this three-bedroom, two-bath house offers the economy of stock sizes plus such flexibility of room arrangement that it is certain to be the forerunner of many others.

THE DESIGNER

Frank Lloyd Wright

Whether designing a ground-hugging dwelling or proposing a mile-high skyscraper, Frank Lloyd Wright applies his deep understanding of construction materials. Whether these materials be new or old, natural or man-made, he uses them imaginatively, courageously, honestly.

THE BUILDER

Marshall ⊜ Erdman & Associates, Inc.

Giving home owners more value for their money has long been a hallmark for this established Madison firm. Its experience with home manufacturing and its insistence on quality construction are well evidenced in Mr. Wright's first efforts in this field.

THE SIDING

Masonite Ridgeline

For the exterior, Mr. Wright chose Masonite® Ridgeline in 16-inch width, with beveled wooden separators to emphasize the sweeping horizontal lines. Masonite weather-defiant panels, such as Ridgeline, reflect the natural advantages of wood, none of its deficiencies. Send the coupon for more information.

*Masonite Corporation—manufacturer of quality panel products.

MASONITE CORPORATION
Dept. HH-12, Box 777, Chicago 90, Ill.

Please send me your full-color book illustrating homes with all types of applications of Masonite exterior products.

Name...

Firm...

Address...

City.........................State.........................

Zone   County   ....

A Builder Ad

Exhibit 5—Continued

A Builder Ad

Exhibit 5—Continued

CENTEX CHOOSES

MASONITE

EXTERIOR PRODUCTS

NATION'S LARGEST HOME BUILDER
PLANS 6000 HOMES NEAR CHICAGO

When Elk Grove Village is completed, it will have a total of 6000 medium-priced ranch homes, according to the present plans of Centex Construction Company.

For each of five models being exhibited to prospective home owners, Centex has selected Masonite® Siding, Tempered Presdwood® and Panelgroove. These popular Masonite Exterior Products add appeal and durability to the well-designed Centex homes.

Here is more evidence of the high regard builders hold for Masonite Exterior Products. Not only do these tough, grainless panels provide superior construction, but they also present unlimited variations for refreshing, unusual design treatments. May we give you more particulars? Just send the coupon.

®Masonite Corporation—manufacturer of quality panel products.

MASONITE CORPORATION
Dept. HH-5, Box 777, Chicago 90, Ill.

Please send me your colorful illustrated brochure on Masonite panels for exterior applications.

Name...

Firm...

Address..

City.............................State................

Zone.............County....

A Builder Ad

prices. Therefore, Masonite was sold at different prices in different sections of the country, at different discounts to the various trade factors, and with a scale of discounts for quantity purchases. The costs were different for each of the five Masonite siding products. The following comparison, however, was generally true:

1. Masonite sidings were more expensive than the lowest-priced siding on the market such as asbestos and insulating siding.

Exhibit 5—Continued

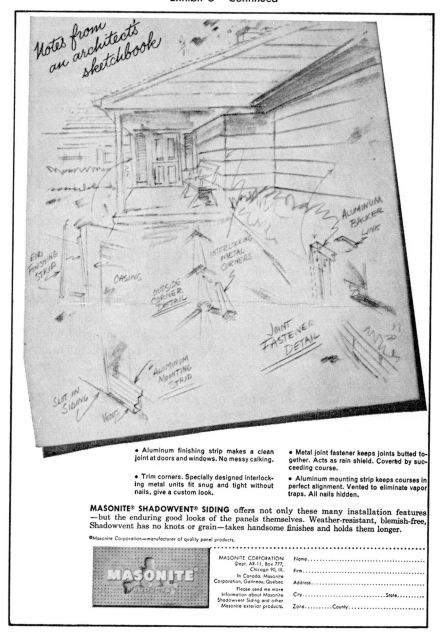

- Aluminum finishing strip makes a clean joint at doors and windows. No messy calking.

- Metal joint fastener keeps joints butted together. Acts as rain shield. Covered by succeeding course.

- Trim corners. Specially designed interlocking metal units fit snug and tight without nails, give a custom look.

- Aluminum mounting strip keeps courses in perfect alignment. Vented to eliminate vapor traps. All nails hidden.

MASONITE® SHADOWVENT® SIDING offers not only these many installation features —but the enduring good looks of the panels themselves. Weather-resistant, blemish-free, Shadowvent has no knots or grain—takes handsome finishes and holds them longer.

®Masonite Corporation—manufacturer of quality panel products.

MASONITE CORPORATION
Dept. AR-11, Box 777,
Chicago 90, Ill.
In Canada: Masonite
Corporation, Gatineau, Quebec
Please send me more
Information about Masonite
Shadowvent Siding and other
Masonite exterior products.

Name.....................................

Firm......................................

Address...................................

City..............................State..........

Zone..........County......................

An Architectural Ad

2. The Masonite products were about equal in price to the better grades of siding such as redwood.

3. Masonite sidings were considerably less expensive than prefinished aluminum.

4. Application costs for Masonite lap sidings were usually less than that of other lap siding treatments. Panel sidings were considerably less costly to apply because of their large size (4 × 8, 4 × 12, and 4 × 16).
5. There was less waste with Masonite siding than with other products.
6. Painting costs for Masonite sidings were usually low because most of the Masonite sidings were preprimed.

The specific problem faced by Mr. Hurley in planning the 1958 advertising campaign was to assist the company to build greater sales volume for its siding products in the face of increasing competition. Since 1956 several new exterior siding products of a directly competitive nature had been placed on the market. In 1959 new plant facilities would increase capacity for Masonite siding by 20%.

Since the introduction of the first siding product, advertising efforts had been devoted almost entirely to dealers, builders, and architects. The small amount of advertising in consumer magazines had been placed primarily for its value as a promotional device directed at dealers. However, for the 1958 campaign, in addition to advertising to the trade, Mr. Hurley was considering the desirability of placing advertisements in consumer magazines in order to influence prospective home purchasers.

In considering the various buying influences in the building materials market, Mr. Hurley thought that about 12% to 18% of all new homes were designed by architects, in which case the siding material would be specified by the architect concerned. Mr. Hurley believed, however, that the influence of the architect spread beyond the specific houses that he designed because the architects were, in effect, style leaders in the building industry. Builders or contractors were a very important influence since they presumably specified the siding to be used in most of the houses that they built. Mr. Hurley estimated that 20% of all new homes were built for specific owners, the remainder being built on speculation.

Although Mr. Hurley had never heard of any specific consumer resistance to Masonite as a siding material, he realized that Masonite was a new product in a field of traditional materials. He wondered if there was a need to explain to prospective home buyers the facts about Masonite Products. He reasoned that a builder, if he used a Masonite siding instead of one of the traditional materials, had to do a selling job with purchasers to convince them that Masonite was a desirable siding product. Mr. Hurley wondered if a consumer advertising campaign by Masonite would assist the builder in influencing potential customers, thus making Masonite siding more acceptable to the builder.

The 1958 advertising budget for the entire Masonite Corporation was $1.2 million. Mr. Hurley was responsible for allocating this budget to the various products of the company. He had tentatively determined that about a million dollars was needed for products other than siding and that he would consider $200,000 as being available for advertising and promotion of exterior sidings. If the trade campaign and the various promotional devices were maintained at about the 1957 rate, about one third of the budget, or $70,000, would be available for advertising in consumer media. Exhibit 6 gives the rates of selected consumer media which might be used.

Exhibit 6

MASONITE CORPORATION

Selected Consumer Magazine Space Costs
(Black and White, One-Time Rates)

	Full Page	½ Page	¼ Page
Better Homes & Gardens........	$17,235.00	$ 8,865.00	$4,475.00
House Beautiful...............	4,450.00	2,225.00	1,112.50
House & Garden...............	3,950.00	1,975.00	987.50
Living for Young Homemakers...	4,100.00	2,050.00	1,025.00
Life........................	26,275.00	14,200.00	7,350.00
The Saturday Evening Post......	23,475.00	12,580.00	6,470.00
Esquire.....................	2,300.00	1,200.00	610.00
Time.......................	11,560.00	8,265.00*	4,220.00†
Sports Illustrated..............	5,355.00	3,825.00*	1,935.00†
Ladies Home Journal..........	20,800.00	10,850.00	5,575.00

* 2 columns.
† 1 column.

Source: *Standard Rate & Data Service: Consumer Magazine and Farm Publication Rates and Data*, July 27, 1958.

~~~

CASE 6: A. M. SNEIDER COMPANY[1]

QUESTIONS TO CONSIDER: *(1) What promotional strategy would you ordinarily expect in the promotion of a product like "Incabloc"? (2) What strategy was employed? (3) Should advertising have been employed to build a reputation for "Incabloc" with the trade? With consumers? (4) Assuming that "Incabloc" is sold for 25 cents to manufacturers and a 10% gross margin is available, what is the size of the promotional fund available? (5) What recommendations would you make for promotion of "Incabloc" in 1951 and later?*

In 1948 the executives of Universal Escapement, Ltd., La Chaux-de-Fonds, Switzerland, a manufacturer of watch parts, decided to undertake a promotional campaign in the United States for one of the company's trade-marked products, "Incabloc," a shock-resisting device for watches. Universal Escapement executives selected the A. M. Sneider Company of New York as their advertising agency. The agency then organized a subsidiary, the American Incabloc Company, as the sales agency, and put Mr. Edward A. Ochs in charge of the new company. Mr. Ochs had had some years of experience in the jewelry trade, both in Boston and New

---

[1] Written by Martin V. Marshall.

York. His job was to call upon American watch manufacturers and the larger retailers of watches to promote the adoption of the Incabloc shock absorber.

The Incabloc shock absorber was a patented device, consisting of a conical brass bushing, a hole jewel, a cap jewel, and a lyre-shaped spring. An assembly was about the size of the blunt end of the lead of a pencil.

Exhibit 1

A. M. SNEIDER COMPANY
Diagram of the Incabloc Assembly

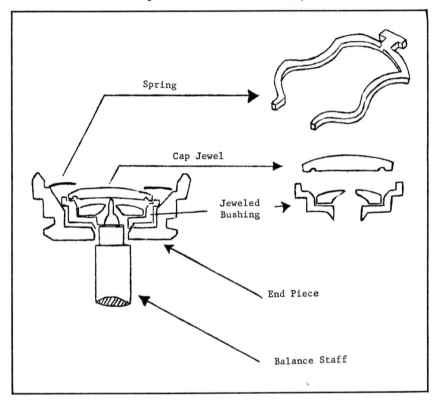

An assembly was located at each end of the balance staff of the watch. First designed in 1933, the Incabloc assembly had been improved in 1938 and was known as Model 1938. Exhibit 1 shows a diagram of the Incabloc assembly.

The Incabloc device worked under shock conditions as follows: When a watch is dropped or hit on the dial or back side, the balance staff of the watch moves according to the law of inertia, forcing out the bushing and its enclosed hole and cap jewels against the pressure of the lyre-shaped spring. The shock is partially absorbed by the lyre-shaped spring and is eventually stopped by the shoulder of the staff coming into contact with the end piece. The lyre-shaped spring then returns the bushing to its normal position and, because of the conical shape of the bushing, keeps the balance staff perfectly centered.

When the watch is dropped or hit on its side, resulting in horizontal rather than vertical shock, the bushing moves up and sideways in its conical fitting under the pressure of the balance staff pivot. This movement is also absorbed by the pressure of the lyre-shaped spring and is stopped by the end piece. The spring then returns the bushing, jewels, and balance staff to their normal positions.

Upon assuming responsibility for the account in 1948, Mr. A. M. Sneider, president, and Mrs. Casey Isaacs Herrick, executive vice president of the A. M. Sneider Company, held several conferences with Universal Escapement officials. Since these officials were ordinarily not in the United States, the agency was given full authority by them to plan and to execute the United States advertising and promotional plan for the Incabloc shock absorber. After the original conference, discussion of the Incabloc advertising program was conducted solely through correspondence. Universal Escapement officials laid down only one restriction, an initial budget for 1948 of approximately $15,000.

The agency's investigation of the watch shock-absorber market indicated that the Incabloc shock absorber was probably unique in its field. Mr. Sneider and Mrs. Herrick believed that although there were a number of other balance-staff shock devices available to watch manufacturers, none of them differed significantly from the usual method by which the ends of the balance staff were held secure against fixed jewels.

In talking with seven watch repair men, the writer found that these men believed the Incabloc shock absorber to be the best method available for absorbing balance-staff shock. This was also the opinion of the head of the quality control department of one of the largest United States watch companies. One repair man stated that the Incabloc device was the only real shock absorber manufactured. He also stated that since 50% of his watch repair business consisted of difficulties with the balance staff resulting from shock, any device that would lessen shock would materially decrease the amount of repair required to keep a watch in good mechanical condition.

The price of the Incabloc shock-absorber assembly to the watch manufacturer was not known to the agency. The price quoted to watch repair men was $2.50 for a kit, which included:

6 Incabloc springs
2 brass mounted balance jewels hole 10
1 brass mounted balance jewel hole 9
1 lyre-shaped holding spring
1 upper cap jewel
1 lower cap jewel

Also available to repair men were Universal Escapement balance staffs for shock proof watches, which were sold in kits of 24 staffs, three each of eight models, for $5.00.

The initial strategy of the Incabloc campaign, as outlined by Mrs. Herrick, was to concentrate promotion on the manufacturers and, to a secondary extent, on larger watch retailers. Space was purchased only in trade papers during 1948 and 1949. The campaign strategy used with manufacturers is indicated in two advertisements used during the summer of 1948, shown in Exhibits 2 and 3.

The agency personnel did not feel that Universal Escapement was quite ready, during 1948, to take full advantage of its advertising expenditures; consequently, only $12,000 of the $15,000 budget was spent the first year. During 1948 a small exhibit, supervised by Mr. Ochs, was used at the annual show of the American National Retail Jewelers Association. Also, several pieces of counter literature were prepared for distribution through watch retailers. The theme of the first threefold booklet was "*You* can take it, but can your watch?" The inside of the booklet contained an explanation of the Incabloc assembly. The second booklet, prepared later, presented "conclusive proof of Incabloc's superiority," an explanation of the Incabloc assembly, and pointed out that 25 million watches were equipped with the Incabloc device.

As the account executive gained more experience with Incabloc promotion, the promotional strategy was made more explicit. There was continued emphasis on getting American watch manufacturers and assemblers to use the Incabloc shock absorber in their watches. Further effort was made to get manufacturers to include the word "Incabloc" on the face of the dial, underneath the brand name, and to advertise the use of this shock-resistant device by the manufacturer in his watch advertising. Several watch manufacturers began to note or to feature the use of the Incabloc assembly in their watches during 1949. At the same time the Incabloc trade advertising was built on a series of endorsement advertisements featuring the watch manufacturers who used Incabloc. These advertisements gave the name of the manufacturer almost as much prominence as was given to "Incabloc," and were paid for by Incabloc. (One of these advertisements is reproduced in Exhibit 4.) Furthermore, free reprints were given to the endorsers for distribution to their own retailers. The agency executives believed that this strategy was enormously successful because most manufacturers were pleased to get the free advertising and co-operated in distributing these advertisements as widely as possible, at no cost to themselves. These watch companies were Harvel, Croton, Alpina, Invicta-Seeland, Ulysse Nardin, Banner, Jules Borel, and Canterbury.

During 1949 the advertising budget was increased to $23,000, most of which was spent in trade papers. Also, a large operating model of the Incabloc assembly was constructed for the 1949 A.N.R.A.J. show.

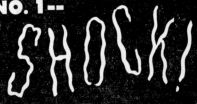
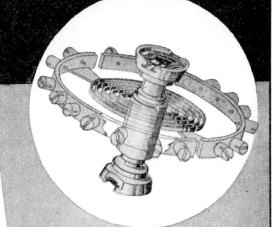

INCABLOC

THE WATCHMAKERS' CHOICE!

What leading watchmakers say
in statements about Incabloc:

"the best"
Isador Wasserman
Technical Development,
CROTON Watch Co., Inc.
New York, New York

*"the perfect
shock-resistant device"*
M. Hoffman
President of **INVICTA-SEELAND** Watches

*"the plus feature
that decides the selection"*
Rudolf S. Kelbert
President, **KELBERT** Watch Co., Inc.

*"the finest
shock-resistor made"*
Aladar Roth
President of **ULYSSE NARDIN**
Watch and Chronometer Corp. of America,

*"the finest shock-resistant
device made"*
Schwarcz
President of **DOXA** Watches

Watchmakers agree that Incabloc is the
ideal shock-resistor because it's fool-proof...
complete...adjustable to any watch...
made with standard, interchangeable parts.

Consumers too, are growing increasingly
Incabloc-conscious. They're asking for
Incabloc by name . . . because they know
that in this fast-moving, fun-loving day and
age no watch is really complete unless
it is protected against shock by Incabloc—
the "fool-proof" shock-absorber.

*"the best shock-resistant
device on the market"*
Michael Denes
Production Chief of
ALPINA Watch Corp. of America

Write today for
literature, tags and other
valuable promotional aids.

INCABLOC

CUSHION THE SHOCK WITH INCABLOC

THE AMERICAN INCABLOC COMPANY   366 Fifth Avenue, New York • FACTORIES LA CHAUX-DE-FONDS, SWITZERLAND

Exhibit 4

A. M. SNEIDER COMPANY
One of Incabloc Advertisements in Endorsement Series,
National Jeweler, February 1949
(Full Page)

The HARVEL
Sea Horse

Incabloc-projected
moisture-repellant
dust-proof
anti-magnetic
radium dial
unbreakable crystal
sweep second hand
all steel case
17 jewels

Statement by
**Mr. Henry H. Harteveldt,
Pres. of Harvel Watch Company:**

" 'Incabloc' on a watch is like
'Sanforized' on a dress or shirt.
We find that equipping our
watches with Incabloc
considerably increases
their sales appeal."

CUSTOMERS
are as sensitive
as WATCHES
when it comes to
INCABLOC

Incabloc not only protects
your watches against shock
—it substantially increases their salability too!
More and more customers are learning that watches
equipped with Incabloc are safer . . . surer
. . . stronger . . . more satisfying in the long run!
They realize that watches equipped with Incabloc
have an infinitely better chance of *staying* accurate
. . . and so they insist on INCABLOC
—the only shock resistor of its kind.
Write today for literature, tags, labels and other important dealer aids.

INCABLOC

CUSHION THE SHOCK WITH INCABLOC

THE AMERICAN INCABLOC COMPANY, 366 Fifth Avenue, New York • FACTORIES LA CHAUX DE FONDS, SWITZERLAND

Exhibit 5

A. M. SNEIDER COMPANY

Advertisement in *Fortune*, March 1950

(Full Page)

Late in 1949 agency executives decided that it was then advisable to go directly to the consumer. Although they considered the 1950 budget of $30,000 as insufficient to allow the use of mass-audience magazines, they did believe it sufficient to use *Fortune* with a limited schedule. The chief

Exhibit 6

A. M. SNEIDER COMPANY

Advertisement in *Jewelers' Circular-Keystone*, April 1950

(Full Page)

objective in using *Fortune,* according to Mrs. Herrick, was to obtain point-of-purchase display for Incabloc in retail stores selling watches. She believed that jewelers generally were extremely reluctant to use display material furnished by manufacturers but that they would take a *Fortune* counter advertisement display because of the prestige of that publication.

The first full-page advertisement which appeared in the March 1950 issue of *Fortune* is reproduced in Exhibit 5.

A tie-in advertisement appearing in the April 1950 issue of the *Jewelers' Circular-Keystone* is reproduced in Exhibit 6.

Counter displays, featuring the *Fortune* advertisement, were made available to jewelers and other retail stores selling watches. Although no exact data were available, Mrs. Herrick believed that the response had been good, as reports from manufacturers and retailers indicated that there had been considerable consumer inquiry as to the Incabloc device; some consumers even thought that Incabloc was a brand name for a watch. Mrs. Herrick mentioned one response in particular as indicative of the

Exhibit 7

A. M. SNEIDER COMPANY

Advertising Schedule of the American Incabloc Company, 1950

Publication	Circulation	Size of Advertisement	Frequency	Approximate Cost of Space
National Jeweler.	Jewelry retailers, 33,799 Wholesalers, 2,186 Manufacturers, 1,275 Miscellaneous, 572 Total, 37,133	Full page	Six times a year*	$ 978
Jewelers' Circular-Keystone..	Jewelry retailers, 15,677 Wholesalers, 1,589 Manufacturers, 1,983 Miscellaneous, 619 Total, 19,929	Full page	Six times a year	1,260
Jewelry........	Jewelry retailers, 10,288 Wholesalers, 1,182 Manufacturers, 1,424 Miscellaneous, 181 Total, 13,236	Full page	12 times a year	5,800
Total Trade Publications				$ 8,038
Fortune........ 253,432		Full page	March and December	$5,800
		One-half page	June and September	3,010
Total Consumer Publications.....				8,810
Total All Publications				$16,848†

* Alternate months with *Jewelers' Circular-Keystone.*

† This figure represents only the cost of the space used; hence, it differs from the total figure given on page 378 of the case.

success of the Incabloc campaign: "One response, from the Kelbert Watch Company, was amusing as well as informative. *Fortune* counter displays were on Mr. Rudolf Kelbert's desk, and when he was asked what he thought of the Incabloc advertising program, he indignantly—and not entirely seriously—said that it was entirely too good. He said that he would have preferred using a different shock absorber, but had been forced, through dealer and consumer demand, to use the Incabloc."

By July 1950 the following domestic watch importers or assemblers, among others, were using the Incabloc device: Gruen, Harman Watch Company, Vulcain Watch Company, Ulysse Nardin, Tissot Watch Company, Crosby, Gotham Watch Company, Ollendorf Watch Company, Kelbert Watch Company, Universal-Geneve, Bouet, Invicta-Seeland, Croton Watch Company, Helbros Watch Company, Le Mania, Eska, and Colomby. Most of these companies were assemblers of high-price Swiss watch movements and usually sold their watches through the better jewelry stores.

The advertising schedule for the American Incabloc Company for 1950 is shown in Exhibit 7. The 1950 Incabloc promotional budget was broken down into four major classifications, as follows:

1. Consumer advertising............................$13,000
2. Point-of-sale material, such as price and descriptive
   tags, counter displays, and counter literature..........   5,000
3. Trade advertising...............................   8,500
4. Trade material, such as advertisement reprints,
   broadsides, and repair instructions..................   3,500
   Total.......................................$30,000

In 1950 there were only three domestic manufacturers of watch movements, Hamilton, Elgin, and Waltham, producing approximately $3\frac{1}{4}$ million units a year. There were a number of domestic importers and assemblers, the principal such companies being Bulova, Gruen, Benrus, and Longines-Wittnauer. The following table gives imports of Swiss watches and watch movements for 1946–50:

IMPORTS OF SWISS WATCHES AND WATCH MOVEMENTS

Year	Number	Dollars
1946	9,649,023	$51,808,118
1947	7,749,819	42,866,477
1948	9,045,142	47,152,785
1949	8,096,451	39,670,079
1950	9,315,243	45,299,634

Source: National Jeweler, April 1951, p. 166.

The Elgin Watch Company was the only leading American domestic manufacturer using the Incabloc device to any great extent. Elgin had been using the Incabloc for some years for its automatic watches—the first time that an American watch manufacturer had used a wholly Swiss mechanism for its watches. Because of the eminently satisfactory results, Mrs. Herrick said, Elgin was using the Incabloc more and more in other watches in its line.

In a series of three articles about shock-protective devices for watches in the *Jewelers' Circular-Keystone* during November and December 1950 and January 1951, it became apparent that shock devices were becoming of some interest to the trade, although no specific market information was given. The November 1950 article pointed out the following:

Since the development of the shock-resistant device for watches, the generally serious results caused by sudden shock to a watch have become more or less minimized. The use of these devices for watches has grown rapidly, receiving a big impetus during the past war when this shock-protecting feature coupled with water-resistant cases and antimagnetic movements found immediate favor and ready saleability in the so-called service watches.

These three articles described three different shock-protective devices from a technical viewpoint. The devices were the frictioned KIF 370 shock protector, manufactured by Parechoc S.A. of LeSentier, Switzerland; the "Shock-Resist" and "Super Shock-Resists," manufactured by Fabrique Erismann-Schinz S.A. of La Neuveville, Switzerland; and Incabloc.

In a discussion about Incabloc, an executive of one of the largest American watch companies said the following:

From the viewpoint of my company, Incabloc does have real significance in a self-winding movement, and it is the best shock-absorber system on the market today in the opinion of the head of our quality control department. Specifically it has the following advantages in offering an improvement and in cutting down on watch repairs, but again primarily for automatic movements:
  a) It protects all four balance wheels from breaking.
  b) It protects the balance pivots from bending or breaking.
  c) It protects the oil from dust and keeps it in good condition.
  d) It allows cleaning and oiling of the balance jewels without dismantling the balance assembly.
  e) It has complete interchangeability.
Any of our watch movements that was to use the Incabloc feature would have to be designed especially to take the Incabloc. The labor cost of assembling the watch with the Incabloc would be very little more than if there were no Incabloc feature.
The American Incabloc representative has never called on us but that is understandable. Until about two years ago, all of our movements were made in our Swiss subsidiary. It was only recently that we have made movements in this country, and to date we have made only one caliber of movement here into which we would put the Incabloc feature. The Swiss representatives of Incabloc have, however, undoubtedly called on our Swiss plant executives a number of times.
We have not only considered using Incabloc but ever since 1948 when we brought out our first automatic watch, we have had the Incabloc feature in

this watch. We put Incabloc in this automatic watch and not in our nonautomatic watches because the weight of the rotator and the operation of the self-winding operation call for some sort of shock-absorbing device. The rotator in our automatic watch is one that swings back and forth and hits up against a spring. It is the shock of this hit that necessitates the Incabloc. If our rotator was the type that continued to swing completely around the watch and did not come up against any stops, there would then be considerably less shock and an Incabloc device would probably not be necessary.

There is another possible reason for the use by a watch company of Incabloc or other shock-absorbing devices. The public has become very shock-absorbing conscious because of small watch companies who put devices such as this into their watches in order to sell them. In many cases Incabloc is put into a watch primarily as a sales or advertising gimmick. I do not mean by this that the insertion of the Incabloc does not improve the ability of the watch to withstand shock. It certainly does. What I am saying is that most watches subject to normal everyday use do not get the kind of wear that makes a shock-absorbing device necessary.

The actual cost of putting in the Incabloc feature, as near as we can tell from what our Swiss people tell us, would be a total of 50 to 65 cents. This breaks down as 20 to 25 cents for the units and 30 to 35 cents additional assemblying and labor costs.

Although there are no specific figures to quote on the growth of Incabloc, Mrs. Herrick gave the following summary of the promotion of Incabloc up to the early part of 1951:

Many top watch companies that had to be sold on equipping their watches with Incabloc are now refusing substitutes even if a wait for Incabloc is involved.

Many manufacturers who did not want to associate their product with Incabloc's advertising (because too many less expensive watches were equipped with the device) are now specifying Incabloc in their own advertising, the reasoning apparently being that this is now a device common to the *entire industry*, and obviously an improvement over a watch without an Incabloc.

That practically no ladies' watches were shock protected in 1948, and yet today at least 30% of 5-inch Swiss watches are Incabloc protected.

That although about 50% of all watches have no shock protection, about 40% are Incabloc protected.

In short, the Incabloc seems to have added a new part to the fundamental makings of a watch, and through its now generally accepted excellence, it seems well on the way to being the sole mechanism used for shock protection.

The agency executives planned that the 1951 budget would be spent in approximately the same proportion as the 1950 budget, with slightly more emphasis on mass consumer publications in the fall of 1951. This stronger emphasis would be possible because the budget was increased to $40,000.

Chapter 9

∿∿∿∿∿∿∿∿∿∿∿∿∿∿∿∿∿∿∿∿∿∿∿∿∿∿∿∿∿∿∿∿

CASES INVOLVING THE USE OF
INSTITUTIONAL ADVERTISING

So far in this section attention has been focused on the part that advertising can or cannot play in a business's marketing mix when the businessman seeks to build strong associations about his brand. Often a businessman seeks not to build mental associations about the specific products he sells but rather he seeks to establish attitudes regarding his organization or institution, so-called institutional advertising.

As is brought out in the cases of this chapter, institutional advertising is broken down into several classes in accordance with the objective of the advertising and, consequently, the type of message carried. A helpful classification, although the divisions are not mutually exclusive, breaks institutional advertising into *patronage* institutional, *public relations* institutional, and *public service* institutional.

Patronage Institutional Advertising

Patronage institutional advertising has as its main objective the establishing of associations or ideas in consumers' minds about an institution, its services, or its policies which will be inducive to patronage. Ordinarily the ideas presented are appeals to patronage motives.

A patronage motive is the reason or incentive impelling a buyer to trade with a particular firm in preference to patronizing other firms which offer similar commodities. Developed in institutional advertisements are ideas relating to the extensive research conducted by a company, which connote dependability of product; the consumer research undertaken, which promises wantable merchandise; the long life and reputation for integrity, which lead one to expect honesty in the product and fair dealing; the variety of merchandise offered for selection; and the ability of the advertiser to give prompt delivery, to provide dependable repair service, to offer courteous, friendly employees, and so on.

The specialized patronage institutional campaign is used most frequently by large organizations rather than by small ones; by service organizations, such as railroads, public utilities, and hotels, to a greater extent than by product manufacturing organizations; and among product manufacturing organizations, largely by those whose products require technical skill and extensive research to keep in front in a fast-moving technological world. Among the more extensive institutional campaigns of manufacturers have been those of General Motors Corporation; General Electric Company; Westinghouse Electric and Manufacturing Company; Parke, Davis & Company; and F. R. Squibb & Sons. Among service organizations, institutional advertisers have included railroads, hotels, insurance companies, and public utilities.

Whereas specialized institutional campaigns are relatively infrequent among product manufacturers, such advertisers often weave patronage appeals into their product advertising. Thus institutional attitudes akin to those arising from specialized campaigns may be established over a period of time.

Public Relations Institutional Advertising

Public relations institutional advertising is undertaken to help a company solve public relations problems through messages which may lead to a friendly attitude toward a company and its management on the part of the public addressed. Thus, General Motors has sought to convey to the public at large the idea that the big scale of its operations has enabled it to make significant contributions to economic and social welfare. Again, many companies in recent years have carried on campaigns in plant cities to develop a friendly community attitude toward the respective companies, among other things to aid in employee relations problems.

As brought out in the cases of this section, public relations institutional advertising is but one of a number of methods or vehicles by which a management may communicate with the numerous publics whose attitudes have an important bearing on its operations. In any situation, the method or methods of communication to be used—among which are personal contact, news stories, booklets, teaching helps, moving pictures, exhibitions and shows, and advertising—must be chosen with an eye to effectiveness and cost.

Among the important groups or *publics* included in public relations programs are the consuming group, employees, stockholders, suppliers, dealers, local plant communities, and government officials. Each of these groups may present particular problems to a company and may be made the audience of a specific program.

In order that the reader may get a better perspective of the place of institutional advertising in the broad area of public relations programs, the first case in this section presents the public relations program of General Motors Corporation. This case shows that the public relations institutional advertising campaigns are just one part of a much broader program.

It is not within the scope of this book to delve far into the complex and important area of public relations. Let it suffice to say that public relations involve more than using various techniques of communication to tell specific publics about a company, its policies, procedures, or viewpoints. Sound public relations begin with company character and behavior toward its publics and may be likened to a product, which must be good if it is to provide a basis for lasting friendships with those publics. Just as a company's product must be good to secure lasting consumer goodwill, so must a company and its management be sound and proper in its policies and behavior, if it is to have a basis for lasting friendliness from various groups. Public relations imply proper management attitudes toward its publics—a right way of life.

Given sound management attitudes and policies, then advertising or other vehicles of communication may often be employed to advantage to inform the public about the company, its policies, its procedures, and its accomplishments.

Public Service Institutional Advertising

It should be noted in conjunction with this discussion of institutional advertising that during the past two decades there has been a growing conviction among businessmen that business should assume increasing responsibility for the social welfare and should exert strong leadership in public affairs. This viewpoint has been reflected in a large volume of advertising devoted by business organizations to a wide variety of public matters. These advertising campaigns have varied from those which during the war sought to aid the government in the sale of bonds, the salvage of scrap metal, and the saving of fats to those which since the war have urged upon the public adequate salaries for teachers, have fought tuberculosis, and have tried to educate the public regarding the American economic system.

~~~

CASE 1: GENERAL MOTORS CORPORATION[1]

QUESTIONS TO CONSIDER: (1) *Has General Motors management been wise in spending such large sums for institutional advertising since 1923?* (a) *For product institutional advertising?* (b) *For public relations institutional advertising?* (2) *How important a part do you feel patronage motives play in consumer buying of automobiles?* (3) *Do you think that other automobile manufacturers should undertake extensive institutional advertising programs?*

General Motors Corporation has advertised ever since it started business as the General Motors Company in New Jersey in September 1908.

---

[1] Prepared by Martin V. Marshall.

Its advertising has been of two kinds: product advertising and institutional advertising.

Product Advertising

In General Motors Corporation, product advertising has been the responsibility of the various operating divisions of the company which, as the result of GM's decentralized organization structure, have had the responsibility for the design, manufacture, and sale of their products. Of the total money expended on advertising by General Motors, an over-

Exhibit 1
GENERAL MOTORS CORPORATION
Traceable Product-Advertising Expenditures of General Motors Corporation, 1949–56

Year	Newspaper	Network Radio	Television	Magazines	Outdoor	Total
1949...	$24,419,843	$ 476,280	$ 662,381	$ 9,328,276	$ 5,618,677	$ 40,505,457
1950...	27,340,327	44,378	1,063,324	10,023,013	6,944,260	45,415,302
1951...	23,740,124	196,216	1,772,490	8,270,486	6,664,482	40,643,798
1952...	19,725,513	734,859	3,840,590	9,845,193	6,288,145	40,434,300
1953...	32,315,663	1,906,959	5,794,019	14,207,808	6,963,924	61,188,373
1954...	36,861,887	2,160,450	10,104,679	16,776,532	7,871,748	73,774,996
1955...	60,830,159	N.A.	14,029,804	21,528,061	10,223,507	104,259,772
1956...	52,272,855	N.A.	18,967,518	22,378,849	10,929,255	104,548,477

N. A. Not Available.

Sources: Publishers Information Bureau; Bureau of Advertising, American Newspaper Publishers' Association; and Outdoor Advertising, Inc.

whelming percentage has been spent on product advertising (see Exhibits 1 and 2).

Institutional Advertising

The institutional advertising activity of the corporation has been the responsibility of the central organization and has come under the supervision of the GM Public Relations Staff. Institutional advertising was begun in 1923 to inform the public about the institution behind GM products. It has been a regular part of the corporation promotional program ever since. The emphasis and type of program have varied with the particular needs of the corporation as they existed at various times. In general there have been three different types of institutional advertising in the program:

1. *Product institutional advertising* which has lent support to the divisional advertising campaigns by informing the public about General Motors' ability to build quality products as a result of its competence in such centralized activities as research, engineering, styling, and production engineering.

2. *Public relations institutional advertising* which has interpreted the General Motors position and viewpoint in relation to current external

Exhibit 2

GENERAL MOTORS CORPORATION

Traceable Institutional-Advertising Expenditures of the General
Motors Corporation, 1923–56

Year	General Magazines	Network Radio	Newspapers	National Farm	Network Television	Outdoor	Total
1923...	$ 311,320						$ 311,320
1924...	356,693						356,693
1925...	348,695		$ 300,000				648,695
1926...	272,605		350,000				622,605
1927...	227,340	$ 48,000	1,000,000				1,275,340
1928...	492,284	313,834	1,990,000				2,796,118
1929...	413,160	377,125	1,250,000				2,040,285
1930...	327,125	303,267	43,000				673,392
1931...	678,220	281,042	97,000				1,056,262
1932...	74,850	226,745	286,000				587,595
1933...	85,190		444,000			$127,932	657,122
1934...	265,440	67,584	1,128,000			27,307	1,488,331
1935...	388,065	279,734	449,000			50,894	1,167,693
1936...	615,970	625,500	751,000			172,811	2,165,281
1937...	723,672	446,026		$ 43,096		107,730	1,320,524
1938...	2,079		82,106			35,100	119,285
1939...	294,420		368,071			62,100	724,591
1940...	232,531		970,660	32,190		36,200	1,271,581
1941...	644,727		521,415	82,800		51,900	1,300,842
1942...	196,635	433,741	473,853	5,100		15,700	1,125,029
1943...	654,726	385,030	885,806	69,700		15,700	2,010,962
1944...	1,032,722	999,219	328,507	320,900			2,681,348
1945...	1,050,232	1,033,042	514,556	254,324			2,852,154
1946...	295,686	1,472,656	255,181				2,023,523
1947...	485,788	974,387	192,291			41,300	1,693,766
1948...	411,835	1,044,366	170,120	92,848			1,719,169
1949...	1,840,881	603,292	449,229	203,490	$ 2,130		3,099,022
1950...	1,677,742	616,510	253,744	225,060			2,773,056
1951...	1,277,682	502,510	54,216	135,420		286	1,970,114
1952...	1,541,496	486,430	526,038	121,850	1,168,213		3,844,027
1953...	2,490,000	684,554	628,585	122,630	2,073,609	226	5,999,604
1954...	2,128,745	620,517	529,528	120,540	199,563		3,598,893
1955...	2,390,496	600,000*	2,128,970	96,190	47,769	24,879	5,288,304
1956...	1,910,884	600,000*	2,520,274	80,000	119,128		5,230,286

* Approximate figures.

Sources: General Motors Corporation; Publishers' Information Bureau; Bureau of Advertising, American Newspaper Publisher's Association; and Outdoor Advertising, Inc.

problems of an economic, financial, sales, or social nature on which management believed its position should be made clear to the public. Institutional advertising presented ideas, viewpoints, opinions, or facts about General Motors that were not related to a specific division product.

3. *Institutional activities.* In the concept of institutional advertising at General Motors, advertising has not been restricted to the use of the conventional media—print, radio, and television. From time to time during the past 30 years General Motors has undertaken the promotion of a number of educational and public relations projects which, because they have

been noncommercial in character, are properly classified as institutional activities. Their objective has been to convey to the public via direct contacts a series of messages of great importance. Their effect is similar to that produced by institutional advertising. Examples of such activities have been the Futurama Exhibit at the New York World's Fair; sponsorship of the National 4-H Club Farm Safety Contest; the General Motors Motoramas; the GM Powerama; Previews of Progress; the GM Parade of Progress; the All-American Soap Box Derby, conducted annually by the Chevrolet Motor Division; and the Fisher Body Craftsman's Guild, sponsored each year by the Fisher Body Division.

Brief Description of General Motors and Its Operating Policies

In 1957 General Motors was primarily an operating concern with a number of decentralized manufacturing divisions. In the United States it was composed of 35 divisions with 126 plants in 70 communities in 19 states. In Canada, GM had four subsidiaries operating six plants. GM also had manufacturing and assembly operations in 16 additional foreign countries. In 1956 total employment averaged 599,243; the business was owned by more than 656,000 shareholders.

In addition there were two large groups of enterprises which, although not directly a part of the General Motors Corporation, were highly essential and directly related to the successful functioning of General Motors. First, there were the independent car and truck dealers who sold GM automotive products. There were more than 18,000 such dealers representing the five car divisions—Cadillac, Buick, Oldsmobile, Pontiac, and Chevrolet—and the two truck divisions—Chevrolet and GMC Coach and Truck. They employed about 200,000 sales and service personnel in the United States and Canada. Second, there were approximately 26,000 suppliers in the United States alone who provided tools, materials, and services. These suppliers received almost 50 cents out of every dollar General Motors received from the sale of its products in 1956, a ratio which was typical of most years.

In addition to the five makes of automobiles and two lines of trucks, General Motors manufactured in the United States the following major products: buses, Diesel engines, Diesel locomotives, off-the-highway earth moving equipment, "Frigidaire" refrigerators and other household appliances, aircraft turbo engines, and fractional horsepower motors. General Motors also made new and replacement automotive parts for its own divisions and for other manufacturers. Included were such items as bearings, batteries, electrical components, hard and soft trim parts, radiators, and engine auxiliaries.

General Motors' defense assignments over the years had included, in addition to military wheeled vehicles of various kinds, a wide variety of highly technical and complex equipment such as: "Allison" turbo-prop and turbo-jet engines, "Sapphire" jet engines, light and medium tanks, fighter aircraft, transmissions for tanks, aircraft navigational instruments and bomb sights, and Aero-products propellers. Defense sales represented only 7% of total GM sales in 1955, and 5% in 1956, having shown a continuing decline from the postwar peak of 19% of total sales in 1953.

The Organization of General Motors. General Motors' operating policy, developed in the early 1920's, is based on the concept of the importance of people. Expressed in formal terms, the philosophy is based on *decentralized operations and responsibilities with co-ordinated control.* Under this philosophy, the over-all objectives and principles or policies are determined at the top-management level, based on information flowing up from all levels of the organization. The task of reaching the objectives and embodying the principles in product and organization is the responsibility of the divisions.

The operating divisions which manufacture related products are grouped together organizationally for better co-ordination. There are six such groups: Car Division Group; Accessory Group; Engine Group; Dayton, Household Appliance and GMC Truck Group; and Overseas and Canadian Group.

Available to the executives of the corporation and to the divisions are the services of various staff activities of the central organization. Included are research, engineering, styling, manufacturing, process development, distribution, public relations, personnel, and business research. These staffs also help in formulating policies.

The assets of the Divisions of General Motors are consolidated on the balance sheet of the corporation and make up the greater part of the total assets. In 1956 total assets were $6,569,400,736, of which $2,967,812,359 represented the net amount invested in real estate, plants, and equipment after deducting for accumulated depreciation and obsolescence. In 1956 the net sales of the corporation were $10,796,442,575.

Published Expenditure for Advertising in Various Media

The total combined advertising expenditures of the Divisions of General Motors in 1956 make GM one of the largest advertisers in the United States (see Exhibit 3). In considering and comparing the figures in Exhibit 3, the following facts should be considered. All of these costs represent media costs for space or time and do not include any creative, talent, or production costs. Nor do these figures include spot television expenditures, cost of producing radio or TV commercials, or local dealer advertising expenditures. Also missing under magazine expenditures are state farm papers, and business and trade papers. And of course point-of-sale and direct-mail activities are not included.

Themes, Background, and Objectives of General Motors Institutional Advertising in Magazines and Newspapers

On the following pages in chronological order appear descriptions of the various institutional advertising programs that have been conducted

Exhibit 3

GENERAL MOTORS CORPORATION

Traceable Expenditures of Ten Leading United States Advertisers, 1949–56

Expenditures and Rank

Advertiser	1949	1950	1951	1952	1953	1954	1955	1956
Procter & Gamble	$30,705,018 (2)	$33,627,327 (2)	$47,173,616 (1)	$45,517,856 (1)	$44,016,318 (2)	$49,836,201 (2)	$49,002,374 (4)	$61,452,742 (2)
General Motors	44,402,969 (1)	49,674,745 (1)	43,592,832 (2)	45,465,663 (2)	68,841,082 (1)	79,908,575 (1)	112,907,265 (1)	109,480,189 (1)
General Foods	20,054,658 (4)	23,185,111 (3)	28,731,078 (3)	30,579,624 (3)	33,079,691 (4)	33,324,084 (4)	36,367,325 (5)	32,044,673 (7)
Lever Brothers	19,010,614 (5)	19,904,962 (4)	22,888,739 (5)	26,986,643 (5)	24,772,153 (6)	21,050,751 (7)	....	37,151,289 (5)
Colgate-Palmolive Peet	20,185,649 (3)	17,399,290 (5)	24,162,830 (4)	29,561,307 (4)	33,759,691 (3)	33,607,968 (3)	32,061,703 (6)	20,201,658 (9)
General Mills	12,447,881 (7)	13,903,228 (6)	13,965,846 (8)	16,893,528 (7)	16,079,831 (10)	18,117,526 (10)	....	....
Sterling Drug	12,702,194 (6)	11,412,484 (8)	....	....	....	....	....	....
Campbell Soup	9,395,694 (9)	9,834,351 (10)	11,203,298 (10)	13,021,592 (10)	18,358,585 (9)	....	....	....
Liggett & Myers	8,836,751 (10)	....	12,783,367 (9)	15,058,925 (9)	18,695,694 (8)	21,427,606 (6)	19,981,652 (9)	32,304,694 (6)
American Tobacco	11,476,345 (8)	11,015,077 (9)	18,383,431 (6)	15,159,135 (8)	18,852,851 (7)	19,500,175 (9)	26,494,589 (7)	....
General Electric	....	13,500,125 (7)	14,639,541 (7)	17,185,694 (6)	....	....	19,047,603 (10)	....
R. J. Reynolds	....	....	....	....	....	....	....	....
Gillette	....	....	....	....	....	20,744,721 (8)	20,426,702 (8)	19,272,219 (10)
Chrysler	....	....	....	....	28,518,886 (5)	31,991,248 (5)	52,261,863 (3)	45,495,208 (4)
Ford	....	....	....	....	....	....	53,805,371 (2)	52,376,875 (3)
American Home Products	....	....	....	....	....	....	....	20,322,540 (8)

Sources: Publishers' Information Bureau; Bureau of Advertising, American Newspaper Publishers' Association, and Outdoor Advertising, Inc.

by General Motors since 1923. Included with each campaign is a brief discussion of the conditions which existed at the time the campaign ran and which influenced GM management in its decision to select the featured theme.

The Situation in 1923. In the beginning, GM institutional advertising had two objectives: (1) to bring about a unification of spirit and interest among GM's manufacturing and distributing units, which had recently been brought together under one ownership and management; and (2) to inform the public about the real nature of the corporation in regard to its ability to add extra value to the products of the divisions through extensive research and stable management.

The situation in 1923 was described by Pierre S. du Pont, president, in a letter to the shareholders:

Two years ago (1921) General Motors began a systematic effort to give publicity to its affairs through a series of regular communications to its stockholders.

Today (1923) there are 66,000 stockholders and each one of them is in possession of facts which enable him to speak with authority about General Motors, its manufacturing facilities, its products, its finances, and its place in industry.

We feel that we are now ready to reach out to another audience—the employees of General Motors, and its dealers, the companies from which its supplies are purchased, and the more than two million families (in 1923) who own one or more of its products.

The effective means of reaching this audience, and the general public of which it is a part, is through national advertising.

The manufacturing divisions of the corporation are already advertising for the sale of their individual products. But General Motors is something more than the sum of its parts, just as the family is something more than the sum of its separate members.

General Motors gathers together the experience and engineering skill, the equipment and financial strength of all of its parts, and by an interchange of men and resources, makes possible economies in direction and production which are manifest in added value to the purchaser. Each General Motors product is a better product because General Motors also makes the others.

It is important that the public should understand this, and to this end we are beginning in the national magazines a series of advertisements designed to answer the questions: "What is General Motors?" and "Why is General Motors?" The first six advertisements will seek to establish definitely in the public mind the names and records of the passenger cars and trucks which General Motors makes, just as a family might seek to introduce itself by capitalizing the goodwill of its well-known members.

Believing that this campaign of institutional advertising would have a very large influence both on our own people and the public, we have entered into it only after very careful study and preparation. We know you will be interested in following its development in the national magazines from month to month.

Like every other important force, advertising works slowly; goodwill and public understanding are not won in a day. But as the months go on, and the story unfolds itself chapter by chapter, the average man and woman is going to have a very much clearer understanding of the scope of General Motors activities, and the larger service which large resources make possible.

Theme of the First Institutional Magazine Campaign. In 1923 the first
General Motors institutional advertising was divided into two series. The
double-page advertisement entitled "What Cadillac Brought to General
Motors" (Exhibit 4) was the first in a series of six which appeared
monthly in magazines having a nation-wide circulation. This series answered the question "Why is General Motors?" The single-page advertisement shown in Exhibit 5 was the first in a series which appeared
monthly in business and financial publications and answered the question,
"What is General Motors?"

A description of the advertising for 1924 is contained in the following
excerpt.

> . . . the advertising of the second year attempted to give a picture of the
> services rendered by General Motors and of the value which the corporation
> contributed to the products of its divisions through its research, engineering
> and styling facilities, etc. A "goodwill" series sought to attach merit to Gen-
> eral Motors itself by the indirect but graceful procedure of praising the services
> rendered by doctors and others through the use of the automobile. The second
> series, known as the "fact series," employed the news approach and gave perti-
> nent facts concerning General Motors and its units. In addition, a financial
> series, seeking to develop a market for the corporation's securities, appeared in
> business, general, and financial papers; also a foreign series, patterned after
> the domestic advertisements, appeared in 56 magazines and newspapers in 16
> foreign countries.[2]

"A Car for Every Purse and Purpose." In 1925–26 and a part of 1927,
General Motors institutional advertising talked about "A Car for Every
Purse and Purpose." Quite obviously, this campaign made a point of the
fact that one or another of the General Motors Divisions manufactured an
automobile to sell in every popular price range.

"GM and the Open Mind." In 1928 the institutional theme was
changed to "GM and the Open Mind." The slogan, "A Car for Every
Purse and Purpose," was continued in advertisements under this new
theme, but copy emphasized the fact that General Motors' "eyes" were
on the future, that the source of new ideas for further development of automobiles had not dried up, and that the public could continue to look for
many improvements and innovations in General Motors products.

"Two Cars in Every Garage." The institutional theme for 1929 and
1930 was "Two Cars in Every Garage," which grew out of the feeling,
current at the time, that a saturation point in car ownership had been
reached. It also was a further development of another phase of the 1928
theme.

Reappraisal of Institutional Advertising—1932. General Motors did
not schedule any institutional magazine advertising in 1932 and 1933
which, it should be remembered, were the worst years of the depression.
However, in 1932 the corporation engaged J. David Houser, the head

---

[2] *First Five Years Harvard Advertising Awards,* 1924–28, p. 75.

Exhibit 4

ADVERTISEMENT FROM THE 1923 SERIES WHICH ANSWERED
THE QUESTION: "WHY IS GENERAL MOTORS?"

What Cadillac brought to General Motors

SAID the Royal Automobile Club of London: "We will award the Dewar Trophy each year to the motor car demonstrating the greatest advance in the industry."

In 1909, three Cadillacs were taken from the dealer's storehouse in London to compete against the best that Europe could produce.

They were torn apart; the parts were tossed into a heap; it was impossible to tell from which of the cars any given part had come. Then an amazing thing occurred. Mechanics, with only the most ordinary tools, stepped up to the pile, reassembled the three Cadillacs and sent them whirring around the track.

No other competing car could be rebuilt without filing and hand fitting. Cadillac had revealed to the world an unsuspected American achievement—perfect interchangeability of parts.

So the Dewar Trophy was won for American industry.

The three Cadillacs at the Brooklands track. Cadillac was awarded the Dewar Trophy by London's Automobile Association of the perfect interchangeability of their parts.

The Dewar Trophy which Cadillac won.

In 1912, Cadillac built the first car ever equipped with a complete electrical system of starting, lighting and ignition, and so won the Trophy a second time.

By a long succession of similar triumphs the leadership of Cadillac was gained. That leadership it kept and brought to General Motors.

. . . . . .

General Motors has built for Cadillac a wonderful new plant. It has contributed the united experience of its seventy-one divisions and subsidiaries to Cadillac craftsmanship; it has put its Research Laboratories at the service of Cadillac engineers.

Thus, giving and receiving, the two have reinforced each other. From the strength of the parent company Cadillac draws increased strength. From twenty years of Cadillac fidelity General Motors inherits a splendid tradition and an enduring ideal.

GENERAL MOTORS

Maker of PASSENGER CARS AND TRUCKS

BUICK · CADILLAC · CHEVROLET · OAKLAND · OLDSMOBILE · GMC TRUCKS

Its Divisions and Subsidiaries make their ACCESSORIES, PARTS AND EQUIPMENT which contribute to the merit of many other trustworthy cars

This double-page advertisement is the first of a series of six to appear monthly in magazines having a nation-wide circulation. This series will seek to establish definitely in the minds of the public the names and the records of General Motors passenger cars and trucks—just as a family might seek to introduce itself by capitalizing the goodwill of its well-known members.

Exhibit 5

ADVERTISEMENT FROM THE 1923 SERIES WHICH ANSWERED THE QUESTION: "WHAT IS GENERAL MOTORS?"

What is General Motors?

GENERAL MOTORS is an operating corporation owning the plants, properties and other assets of its manufacturing divisions. It also owns part or all of the stock of other companies connected with its activities.

There are 33 manufacturing organizations, 28 sales companies and 10 miscellaneous companies, a total of 71 units in the General Motors family which has pioneered in the automotive industry, helping to produce more economical automobile transportation for people and goods.

In addition, General Motors has large investments in factory branches, service stations, and retail stores in the principal cities of this country and Canada.

Its overseas selling organizations cover every part of the globe where motor cars are used

Besides the Buick, Cadillac, Chevrolet, Oakland, Oldsmobile and GMC Truck, General Motors units make:

Fisher Bodies
Delco Light and Power Plants
Frigidaire Electric Refrigerators
Hyatt Roller Bearings
New Departure Ball Bearings
Klaxon Warning Signals
Harrison Radiators
Delco Starting Systems
Remy Starting Systems
Jaxon Rims and Wheels
Dayton Wright Special Bodies
AC Spark Plugs and Speedometers

Materials for these automobiles and accessories are purchased from more than 3,000 different business firms—an impressive reminder of the way in which the prosperity of the whole nation is bound up with the prosperity of the motor industry

A booklet entitled, "PLANTS AND PRODUCTS," giving detailed information will be mailed if a request is directed to the Department of Financial Publicity, General Motors Corporation, New York.

GENERAL MOTORS

Maker of PASSENGER CARS AND TRUCKS

BUICK   CADILLAC   CHEVROLET   OAKLAND   OLDSMOBILE   GMC TRUCKS

Its Divisions and Subsidiaries make these ACCESSORIES, PARTS AND EQUIPMENT which contribute to the merit of many trustworthy cars

Fisher Bodies   Remy Starting Systems   Delco Starting Systems   Delco Light and Power Plants
Harrison Radiators · Jaxon Rims   Klaxon Horns   Hyatt Roller Bearings
Frigidaire   New Departure Ball Bearings   AC Spark Plugs

General Motors Acceptance Corporation which finances General Motors products

This single-page advertisement is the first of a series to appear monthly in business and financial publications during 1923.

of a market research organization that specialized in the "measurement of attitudes," to define the institutional advertising problem of the corporation. The survey had the following purposes: (1) to find out what people wanted in automobiles and how well General Motors was satisfying these wants; (2) to determine the competitive position of each car in consumers' minds; and (3) to determine the relative influence of each important "consumer attitude" on the purchase of GM cars.

This survey produced the following evidence with respect to the company's institutional advertising: "General Motors' reputation in general far outdistances its competitors . . . This standing is so high as to require only enough effort to maintain it . . . This survey reveals no hostile public attitude requiring an institutional defense."

The remainder of the survey dealt with three significant points: (1) the influence of "institutional" attitudes in the buying of cars; (2) an estimate of the effectiveness of the institutional approach of the past which had emphasized "What is General Motors?" and "Why is General Motors?" and (3) the definition of the job to be done in the future through institutional advertising in view of the influence of different consumer attitudes upon buying.

With respect to the importance of institutional attitudes in the buying of cars, an interesting conclusion of the survey was that *some of these "institutional" attitudes had more influence in the buying of cars than did specific attitudes toward specific cars themselves.* As a matter of fact, certain attitudes toward the company as a whole—"institutional" attitudes —made up from one third to one half of all the buying influences at work in the public mind. There was, it is true, a great range in the influence of these attitudes. "Some had little or no importance in sales, others a moderate influence, and some were very powerful indeed . . ." A natural conclusion would seem to be that "it is a serious mistake to shelve all "institutional" emphasis just because its objective heretofore has been so vague.

The Houser report made the following recommendations: "The emphasis, in maintaining and improving General Motors' competitive position with the public, therefore, should be definitely placed *not* on what General Motors is (as a social and economic institution) but on what General Motors does for the public (in connection with its product)."

The survey was useful to the management in shaping the subsequent approaches to institutional advertising along two lines: one, a building of product attitudes; the other, a building of attitudes important in GM's public relations program.

Although the public opinion survey conducted in 1932 showed "no trend of hostile public attitude requiring an institutional defense," within the next four years—1932 to 1936—conditions changed. The change came about as a result of the depression following the stock-market crash in 1929 and created a situation which required a revision of the fundamental policy regarding institutional advertising at General Motors. Public relations had become one of the corporation's most pressing and important

problems. The following excerpt from the 1932 Annual Report is typical.

It is recognized that the corporation's most vital relationship is with the public. Its success depends on a correct interpretation of the public's needs and
viewpoints as well as on the public's understanding of the motives that actuate
the corporation in everything it does. In order to formulate its policies in harmony with this basic principle, no effort is being spared to analyze and evaluate
the public forming the corporation's actual and potential customers, in its
thinking with respect to all things in which the corporation plays a part. This
represents, however, but one phase of the corporation's public relations policy,
for, while it is essential that the corporation understand the public, it is equally
essential that the public understand the corporation. Goodwill is established and
maintained not alone by excellence of product and service, but by a combination of this with public knowledge and acceptance of the policies of the corporation.

And so it followed that the objectives of the GM public relations institutional advertising were changed. The new goal of this activity was to
acquaint the public with the general economic philosophy and principles
behind the free enterprise system and to convince the public of its social
and economic soundness. A second objective was to identify General
Motors with social progress made possible by a free competitive system
and to win the confidence of the public in its ability to further this progress. Concurrently, the entire concept of public relations was re-exam-
ined.

General Motors executives were eager to know what people were
thinking about "big business," what the corporation could do to please
the public, and how it could shape its policies, products, and services to
meet the desires of the public and obtain for itself the greatest amount of
respect. In its effort to understand the public, the corporation organized
a customer research staff. The group worked to discover the public's
attitude on questions of vital concern to the corporation. Such information was used to supplement managerial thinking both in the manufacture
of products and in the formulation of company policies.

It should be pointed out that General Motors deals with a number of
"publics": its stockholders, its employees, its dealers, its suppliers, governmental officials and employees, those people living in cities where a General Motors plant is located, and its customers. The company realized the
importance of dealing with these various groups in such a way as to create
friendly relations. It therefore developed a definite public relations program for each of them. A description of some of the efforts of this program will be found under the subsection captioned, "Public Relations Activities of an Institutional Advertising Nature."

Resumption of Institutional Advertising

"*Eye to the Future, Ear to the Ground.*" In 1934 a campaign was
launched with the theme, "Eye to the Future, Ear to the Ground." This
theme and the copy approach was designed to meet what was thought

at the time to be the competitive threat of the so-called Airflow design of automobiles produced by one of the other manufacturers.

"*. . . Great Engineering.*" In 1935 General Motors institutional advertising continued the "Eye to the Future, Ear to the Ground" theme with advertisement which featured the excellence of General Motors engineering.

"*Test the Value.*" The year 1936 saw General Motors conduct a "product institutional" campaign which stressed the "extra value" in GM products. A "Test the Value" campaign stressed: (1) GM research, which sought to improve automobile design and operation; (2) the maintenance of a proving ground where finished automobiles were tested to avoid unproved features and, at the same time, to provide products of advanced design; and (3) large financial resources which made it possible for GM Divisions to make frequent improvements in their products, improvements necessitating expenditures of large sums for plant modernization, new tools, dies, and machinery.

"*General Motors Means Good Measure.*" A second group of advertisements that appeared in 1937 stressed the theme: "General Motors Means Good Measure." The advertisements in this campaign illustrated the idea of value in terms of good measure. Good measure was visualized as a heaping bushel of grain, a heaping measure of flour, a baker's dozen. To show that General Motors gave good measure, six of their distinctive features were listed: unisteel body, knee action, hydraulic brakes, turret top, no draft ventilation, and streamline styling.

First Public Relations Institutional Campaign. The first public relations institutional advertising, which also started in 1936 and continued into 1937, appeared under the headline: "Who Serves Progress Serves America!" All advertisements in this campaign sought to teach fundamental economic truths in terms of specific examples chosen from General Motors experience. Choice of the theme was related to what was felt to be widespread misunderstanding of the basic economic reasons which caused the depression through which the country was passing at the time. The illustration in each of these advertisements pictured an historical event which typified progress. Copy explained how General Motors had served progress. For example, the following subjects were typical: the service to progress which resulted from General Motors Corporation's industrial research; the customer research activities through which General Motors was safeguarding its employees, its stockholders, its dealers, and the buyers of its cars against errors of guesswork; the development of Diesel engines by General Motors engineers, which had created new jobs and led to progress in transportation; the way in which the General Motors Proving Ground was developing and testing each advance in safety, reliability, comfort, or operating economy in automobiles. Thus by featuring the progressive developments which General Motors had made, the advertisements sought to identify General Motors with progress. The main body of the copy did not refer directly to General Motors but rather to business in general. This part of the advertisement represented a new development in the use of advertising, namely, to explain the economic philosophy behind large-scale industrial operations. The following excerpt from a typical advertisement indicates how this job was done:

How Is Progress Best Served?

Every thoughtful American realizes that the advance of this nation must come from finding more jobs for more people. How can this be best brought about? Surely not by forcing prices higher, so that fewer people can buy less wealth in factory or on farm. The whole history of the nation denies such doctrine. The sound way to make jobs more plentiful is to make goods more plentiful, increasing markets by giving more for the same money, or the same for less money . . . This is how progress can best be served—and he who serves progress serves America.[3]

In each such advertisement the selling message was contained in a single sentence which appeared in capital letters at the bottom of the page: "Your money goes farther in a General Motors Product."

"Comfort that Rests on Value." In 1939 emphasis on the extra value in GM products was continued in institutional advertising, showing that General Motors cars gave more value in styling, economy, performance, and comfort—under such typical headlines as: "Comfort that Rests on VALUE" and "Style Supported by VALUE."

"Plainview Pricing." Also in 1939 the subject of "Price Packing" was in the minds of all car buyers, and General Motors started a magazine campaign which stated very plainly the policy of the corporation and its dealers on delivered prices. A "Plainview Price Tag" was developed on which GM dealers listed factory prices, federal taxes, charges for transportation and accessories, etc., which showed the customer exactly what items made up the total delivered price of the car. This tag, which hung on all cars in dealers' showrooms, was featured prominently in all the advertisements. The "Plainview Pricing" campaign, while it dealt with products, had an important public relations purpose. It was designed to dispel misunderstanding by the public of the pricing policies of General Motors and its dealers. It was continued in 1940.

"Partners in Progress through Service." In 1941 General Motors continued to back up its dealers through an institutional campaign which presented the dealer as a fine businessman and a leader in his local community. The campaign tied the local dealer in with General Motors through the theme "Partners in Progress through Service" and featured such headlines as: "A Good Life Work for Any Man;" "General Motors? —Right Here on Main Street."

The Period of World War II. Beginning in 1942, and continuing through the war, General Motors had but one customer—Uncle Sam. The

---

[3] From an advertisement in *The Saturday Evening Post*, February 13, 1937.

broad theme of General Motors' institutional magazine campaign was "Victory Is Our Business."

In the early part of the war, the public was extremely concerned about the country's capacity and ability to build the volume of war goods needed to defeat the enemy. Consequently, GM institutional advertising dealt strictly with the production job which General Motors was doing to send war materials to the fighting fronts. Later an interesting series of advertisements was prepared, each showing how experience gained on a peacetime project was used in producing effective wartime equipment. For example, one such advertisement dealt with the subject of "marrying" rubber and metal, as applied to the production of motorcar running boards, and told how this same process was applied to the production of rubber treads for tanks.

Wartime Newspaper Advertising. Since the government was GM's sole customer during the war, it was thought proper and desirable to report to the nation, through a series of more or less regular newspaper advertisements, on GM's progress in war production and various practices designed to assist the war effort.

The first advertisement of this kind appeared April 1942, under the heading "Good News from the Production Front." This phrase was maintained as a continuing, over-all caption throughout the series, which consisted of advertisements such as the following: "Good News from the Production Front," "Announcing the First Billion of War Products," "Know-how Saves Manpower, Materials, Money," and "Production, Production—and More Production."

Farm Paper Series. During the war General Motors also initiated a series of advertisements to farmers. These advertisements were designed to present agriculture as "partners in production" who shared the slogan, "Victory Is Our Business"; to point out that the farmer's and the manufacturer's methods, problems, and aims are very similar; and to promote, thereby, a better attitude toward industry on the part of farm people. This campaign ran for about two years in national farm papers.

General Motors Postwar Institutional Advertising

With the war over, General Motors again returned to peacetime themes for its institutional advertising. Although the war had ended, reconversion from production of peacetime production took many months, and with the pent-up demand for new automobiles, there was no immediate need for institutional advertising to stimulate the sale of products. However, almost a whole new generation of potential car buyers had come into the market since General Motors last advertised its facilities and "know-how" as a builder of fine automobiles. Hence, GM's product divisions resumed direct product advertising shortly after the war although they knew the demand for new automobiles would greatly exceed the supply for several years.

General Motors' first postwar institutional advertising did not deal with a subject related to products. Rather, it selected another public relations institutional theme which dealt with the social benefits of General Motors progress and industrial progress as a whole: "The People Profit When a Business Prospers." In many ways, this campaign was an explanation and defense of the profit system of American competitive enterprise. Advertisements in this campaign told how the development of the modern motorcar enabled "Aunt Hannah to Get Around"—how "Grandma could handle a car instead of being relegated to the back seat"—how the development of good roads which came in the wake of the motorcar cut great distances to a minimum (see Exhibit 6).

Return to Selling Campaign. In the fall of 1948, after a lapse of nine years, General Motors institutional advertising again presented the merits of General Motors as a builder of fine automobiles. The "key" to this campaign was, in fact, the key to a General Motors car. A series of advertisements was prepared showing this little piece of metal as the owner's key to better research, better styling, better engineering, better production, all totaling up to greater *value* (see Exhibit 7).

The campaign was built around the key because of the elementary advertising fact that the customer should be able to identify the product. It was felt that there was further value in the "key" idea because of the symbolism that has grown up around keys throughout history, e.g., "the key to the city" . . . "the keys of the kingdom of heaven" . . . "the keys of knowledge." In addition to its symbolic meaning, the word provided a convenient means of grouping together five lines of cars, and it was a simple and natural association to link the letters GM on the key of every General Motors car with such ideas as: "The Key to Better Engineering," "The Key to Better Production," and "The Key to Peak Performance."

To capitalize further on the value of this campaign, the stamping on all actual keys for General Motors cars was changed. In addition to the letters "GM" the words "Your Key to Greater Value" were also stamped conspicuously into each key.

In most magazines, the advertisements were two-page spreads in full color. The main copy was unusually short and to the point, and, in addition to a large main illustration, each advertisement contained two or three small illustrations with explanatory cutlines on some phase of General Motors activities that resulted in better engineering, better research, better production. For example, in an advertisement on research the illustrations showed equipment used in the Research Laboratory, the Proving Ground, etc. The campaign started with advertisements for October, November, and December 1948, in *The Saturday Evening Post, Collier's, Look, American Weekly, Time, Newsweek, American Magazine, Better Homes & Gardens, Country Gentleman, Farm Journal,* and seven automotive trade papers.

Exhibit 6

ADVERTISEMENT OF FIRST POSTWAR SERIES ON THEME "THE PEOPLE PROFIT WHEN A BUSINESS PROSPERS"

Product Institutional Advertising Continued in 1952–53. The product institutional campaign bearing the "Key to Greater Value" theme continued in 1952 and 1953. The new car announcement advertisements in the fall of each year, carried in support of the car divisions introductory campaigns, bore the headlines, "These Keys Unlock Greater Values for You in 1952" and "General Motors Presents the Key Values for 1953—

Handsome examples of the engineering progress that makes the key to a General Motors car your key to greater value." Succeeding advertisements in each year's campaign featured the work of the Research Staff, Proving Ground, and Engineering Staff which enabled General Motors Divisions to build superior products. The technique of getting this story across varied. One type of advertisement carried headlines such as "Key to Carefree Driving" and featured the automatic controls that make driving simpler and safer. Supporting these statements were three examples of how GM engineers bring about such improvements as measuring "steering effort" in a research laboratory; engineering push-button windows; and applying powder metallurgy to transmission parts. A second type of advertisement carried such headings as, "What happens at our Proving Grounds?" and explained how GM engineers used a Proving Ground to accelerate and standardize test results on GM and competitive products. A third type of advertisement in the same series dramatized the work of the research scientist and the proving ground engineer. A typical headline was: "This engine kills itself off to make yours live longer."

Re-emphasizing the importance of research and advanced engineering as a source of new ideas and improvements to old ideas came at a time when the American public was becoming increasingly aware of the importance of research not only in the improvement of products but as a factor in national leadership and economic health of the United States. Among the automobile manufacturers, General Motors had for years been a leader in fundamental and applied research. Out of these programs, conducted for many years under the leadership of C. F. Kettering, had come such important developments as the modern high-compression engine, Ethyl gasoline, the high-speed, lightweight Diesel engine, and fast-drying durable automotive paints and thinners. In stressing its interest in research and engineering, General Motors sought to convey to the public the importance of such work in the manufacture of an automobile.

General Motors Features Its Styling Leadership in Product Institutional Advertising. Following World War II the demand for automobiles was such that maximum production was the goal of the entire industry. The public was not critical of automobile appearance. The custom was to make only minor changes yearly and to extend the major body change to four years or more.

In 1954 General Motors took the entire industry by surprise when it introduced some of the most advanced styling ideas ever presented on production automobiles. Panoramic windshields, textured grille surfaces, sweep spear side molding, and a new low silhouette that had great visual appeal were featured.

The decision was made to adopt these new ideas and introduce them a year earlier than was then normal. It was also decided that GM product institutional advertising was to feature the styling leadership of the corporation. To do this a campaign in *Life, The Saturday Evening Post, Look, Colliers, U.S. News and World Report, Time, Newsweek, Better Homes & Gardens, Farm Journal,* and *Country Gentleman* was launched. The introductory advertisement in the fall of 1954 carried the headline "Car of the Future styling comes true in five General Motors cars you can buy today!" This referred to the experimental dream cars featured in past General Motors Motoramas and made the point that many of the dream-car features had arrived already.

The early advertisements in the series featured automobile styling and headlines such as these: "Way, Way Ahead," "Anyway You Look at It," and "See for Yourself." All ended with the theme "General Motors Leads the Way." Each of these drew attention to the visual appeal of the GM automobiles by the first phrase of the heading and by the illustration which was a close-up of some visual feature of a new GM automobile, usually the Panoramic windshield. In the body copy, an additional message was included pointing out that GM products also had outstanding performance, smooth transmissions, many safety features, etc.

In 1955 the "General Motors Leads the Way" theme was continued. Two introductory advertisements were used, one for Chevrolet and Pontiac and one for Buick, Oldsmobile, and Cadillac. The headlines read, "Two 1955 Ways to Say General Motors Leads the Way" and "Again for '55 General Motors Leads the Way." These two advertisements were followed by a second introductory advertisement which featured all five cars by stating, "General Motors Leads the Way with the High Fashion Five for Fifty-Five." One advertisement used in this campaign is given in Exhibit 8.

During the remaining months of 1955, the emphasis continued on the styling leadership of GM automobiles. Various headlines were featured along with the theme "GM Leads the Way," such as: "From Every Viewpoint," "Four Doors to New Style Horizons" (featuring the industry's first four-door hardtops by Buick and Oldsmobile), "Something Completely New—'Four doors' with no door posts to block your view," and "With This New Kind of Car" (featuring the industry's first station wagon with a sports car appearance—the Chevrolet Nomad and the Pontiac Safari).

In 1956 the campaign was brought to its climax continuing the same theme, "GM Leads the Way," accompanied by such headline messages as: "With 4-door hardtop styling across the board" (now all divisions had this body style, another industry first), "With 4-door hardtops in all five," and "At Working Wonders with the Family Workwagon."

Later in the year the message was changed slightly to bring in one of the other sales features of GM automobiles. For example, one advertisement stated "In 4-door hardtops and Safer Stops—General Motors leads the way"; another advertisement carried this caption, "From High Com-

Exhibit 8

ADVERTISEMENT FROM 1955 "GM LEADS THE WAY" CAMPAIGN

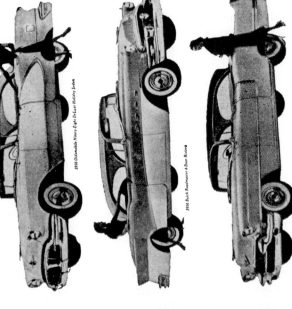

with 4-door hardtops
in all five

This newest and most popular of motor fashions is now offered by General Motors in '56 cars of every price class. And their dashing beauty is matched by equally thrilling advances in high-compression power in all five—coupled with even smoother, still more responsive Powerglide, Hydra-Matic and Dynaflow automatic drives. Plus extra-safety improvements like Power Brakes, Power Steering, Unisteel Bodies with double-locking door latches, safety-aim headlights and seat belts (optional) on every GM car. So in 1956, more than ever, your key to greater value is the key to a General Motors car.

1956 Oldsmobile Ninety-Eight De Luxe Holiday Sedan

1956 Buick Roadmaster 4-Door Riviera

1956 Cadillac Sedan de Ville

1956 Chevrolet Bel Air 4-Door Sports Sedan

1956 Pontiac Star Chief 4-Door Catalina

GENERAL MOTORS *leads the way*

CHEVROLET · PONTIAC · OLDSMOBILE · BUICK · CADILLAC · *All with Body by Fisher* · GMC TRUCK & COACH pression to High Style—General Motors leads the way"; a third advertisement said "And in smoother transmissions, too, General Motors leads the way."

New Public Relations Advertising Program Features Interdependence of Big and Little Business. General Motors in all of its public relations efforts over these years sought to show that bigness in itself is not bad; that some jobs are of a size and complexity that require bigness in the organization that is doing the job. Beyond that the executives of the corporation believed quite strongly that the American public did not understand fully how the economy worked. One of the most important and least understood factors, in their opinion, was the relationship between those who supply tools, materials, and parts and those concerns who make the finished products and take them to the market place—the relationship between the small supplier and the big contractor. In the case of General Motors, in 1957 there were more than 26,000 such suppliers of tools, materials, and services, and they received about 50 cents out of every dollar that General Motors took in. Of these 26,000 suppliers, 22,500 were small businesses, employing fewer than 500 employees and most of them employed less than 100 persons.

In January 1957 General Motors developed and presented a national advertising campaign to promote a better understanding of this relationship. The technique was to present a case history of a GM supplier and the town in which it is doing business. Photographs of the people, their homes, their social and public spirit activities as well as the background of their relationship with General Motors were used. A wide variety of businesses were chosen—for their interest to the reader and for the facts about the GM-supplier relationship that they revealed. A machine tool builder, a foundry, metal fabricators, a screw machine products manufacturer, a tool and die manufacturer, and a pallet maker to name a few. A typical advertisement is given in Exhibit 9.

Many of these advertisements carried the phrase "General Motors—Good people to work for—Good people to deal with." Factual information about the number of suppliers, location, and size was included under such subheadings as: "Small Business and General Motors," and "GM Purchases from Many, Many Small Businesses."

A complete example of the message accompanying these phrases follows:

"Small Business and General Motors
A Growing Relationship"

"Most of the business firms supplying General Motors with goods and services are small businesses with less than 500 employees. The number of firms supplying GM has been growing steadily—from 12,000 before World War II to 19,000 during the war to 26,000 today."

Special Public Relations Institutional Advertising Campaigns. In addition to the basic institutional advertising campaigns described above,

How an old New England family with young ideas furthered their town's future with some help from General Motors

PROUD MAYOR OF A PROSPEROUS CITY — Mayor J. Alfred Dennis of Keene, New Hampshire. As the Mayor confirms, busy Keene owes much of its success to the town's top employer, Kingsbury Machine Tool Corporation, a General Motors supplier since 1925.

TRADITION OF CRAFTSMANSHIP — Carefully crafted toy customers like the one held by H. T. Kingsbury, company's founder, faithfully followed auto designs.

FORD MAKER — Company Director and Public Relations head Chester L. Kingsbury ran drive to build new wing of Keene's Elliot Community Hospital.

BLUEPRINTING THE FUTURE — President Gardner Steinberg and Board Chairman Ed Kingsbury think plans for a new Kingsbury machine tool for GM.

WHETHER your business is in Detroit, Los Angeles, Kalamazoo or Keene, New Hampshire—the old saying holds. Keep up with the times and the times will be kind to you.

Take the Kingsbury family of Keene. For generations they'd applied their Yankee ingenuity to a succession of enterprises. In 1919 they were employing the native mechanical skill of Keene fathers and sons to the crafting of a famous line of mechanical and cast iron toys.

Small Business With Big Ideas

THEN—in the Twenties—young Ed Kingsbury came back to the family business with his engineering diploma from M.I.T. and a whole pack of new ideas in production.

Right off he stepped up toy production by inventing a new sensitive-feed drilling machine which bored smoothly through cast iron—kept drills from breaking when they hit a hard spot. Got so interested in drill building—he set up a machine shop in the toy factory and began turning out a drilling unit utilizing his new ideas.

Two years—the big idea—one new known to mechanical engineering students and heavy industry production engineers as the Kingsbury Method. Very simply it combines several automatic drill units into one machine—automatically moves the metal from one unit to another—progressively performs the required operations.

An Old Business Becomes A New Business

SINCE 1925, when the first Kingsbury automatic drilling and tapping machine was delivered to what is now the Delco-Remy Division of General Motors—GM has been a steady customer of the toy factory which Ed Kingsbury's idea turned into the Kingsbury Machine Tool Corporation. Right now, in fact, 29 GM divisions and plants continuously purchase the latest developments of Ed Kingsbury's brain child.

Thanks to GM and the other companies which deal with Kingsbury, the Keene outfit now employs more than 800 folks (including ½ father and son teams) all living within ten miles of the hugely expanded plant.

What has happened in Keene, New Hampshire, has happened in hundreds of towns and cities all over the United States. Local manufacturers have found that—if they meet delivery dates with their products, that GM needs, competitive prices — General Motors is interested in doing business with them. New money has flowed into these local communities—and as a result these communities in every state share in GM's success.

How much they share is shown by the first that outside sources of materials and services for GM receive, in total, close to 50¢ out of every dollar that General Motors takes in.

An idea this good never takes long to find a market. Especially at General Motors.

General Motors—Good people to work for—Good people to deal with

ONE OF 8 FATHER AND SON TEAMS — Milling Department Foreman, Earl Riley checks accuracy of machined hole on drill body indexed for GM's Cadillac Division. Young Jim Riley working drill on Delco-Remy job.

TOMORROW'S IDEA MEN — Keene High School Mechanical Arts Course is considered one of the best in the State. Machines donated by Kingsbury Machine Tool Corporation equip shop, give money for town, help school give boys actual experience.

HOMECOMING — New Hampshire Technical Institute student Blair Brown who is getting help for his education by $300 scholarship given him by Kingsbury Machine Tool Corp. Keene High School Principal Harold F. Drew welcomes him on holiday visit.

Small Business and General Motors: an Enduring Relationship

Most of the 26,000 business firms supplying GM divisions with goods and services are small businesses with less than 500 employees. About a third of these small businesses—7500 in fact—have been working with GM 11 years or more—two thousand from 21 to 30 years—and several hundred even 31 years and more.

General Motors from time to time has developed special-purpose campaigns to do particular jobs.

Youth and Teacher Program. For several years before 1950, GM undertook a special institutional advertising campaign tailored for youth and teacher publications which was designed to show the ingenuity and competence with which GM experts utilize and harness Mother Nature's principles. Each advertisement took one well-known scientific fact and, in simple layman's language, showed how General Motors researchers and engineers adapted and developed the fact for use in more and better automobiles and other things for more people.

At the bottom of each advertisement in this campaign was printed a "Note to Teachers" in which reprints of the advertisement were offered free of charge. From the time the first advertisement in this program was published in October 1946 through 1950, teachers and students had requested more than 800,000 copies of the advertisements for classroom or other reference use. The great majority of reprints were requested in bulk supply by teachers.

Campaign to Science Students. In 1953 GM inaugurated a purely institutional campaign aimed at reminding high school students of mathematics and science that the school book formulas they struggle with in class today are extremely important and have a direct tie-in with research and engineering in industry. This campaign was started because of the acute shortage of scientifically and technically trained people in the nation. GM management undertook a number of projects aimed at telling the public of the importance of training in the sciences.

In 1953 and 1954 a series of messages dramatizing this situation were featured in advertisements in *School Science and Mathematics,* the *Science Teacher, American Farm Youth, Grade Teacher, Instructor, NEA Junior, Boys Life, Scholastic Magazine,* and *Scholastic Teacher* bearing headlines such as: "This school rule helps America rule the skies," and "This schoolroom study of the spectrum throws new light on paint decay."

Driving Tips for Teen-agers. In the postwar years interest in highway safety came to be of paramount importance to the United States. Like many others, GM has always had concern and interest in traffic and highway safety. This interest has found many expressions, one example of which was found in the institutional advertising campaign, "Driving Tips for Teen-agers" carried in a number of the scholastic journals in 1954, 1955, and 1956.

The campaign was based on these concepts. First, it would show the right and wrong way to handle a given situation, and one that was fraught with danger. Second, it would quote one of the experienced GM test drivers, a man with hundreds of thousands of miles of safe driving behind him. It was the opinion of GM management that teen-agers would respect the opinion of such men because of their professional proficiency.

Every advertisement carried the admonition, "Be a *Skill*—not a *Thrill* Driver!" and the note, "This series of driver-training hints is presented in the interest of national highway safety by General Motors and its divisions." Reprints were offered without charge. A typical and self-explanatory headline was: "Keep a weather eye on conditions!"

In 1957 another campaign encouraging teen-agers to drive carefully was begun. In these advertisements, which carried such headlines as "I take the wheel and take the family to church," young people were pictured performing useful jobs in an automobile. They were shown as safe and responsible drivers.

Advertising in Connection with Public Relations Institutional Activities. Many of the public relations institutional projects such as the GM Train of Tomorrow, Powerama, Motorama, GM 50 Millionth Car Celebration, GM Parade of Progress, and GM Technical Center Dedication had in themselves high advertising value. In connection with each of these activities actual newspaper and magazine advertising played an incidental though important part. In all cases the announcement of the event was made beforehand through the medium of advertising to stir up local interest and to invite attendance. Follow-up advertisements in many cases, run after the event was completed, explained the institutional story behind the project and thanked the community for their interest.

GM Plant City Campaign. General Motors management always has considered it wise to have its factory organizations prominently identified with the interests of the communities in which they operate. For years many divisions of General Motors have told the communities in which they operate of the division's interest in community affairs—usually in outdoor billboard messages. For example, Chevrolet and Fisher Body Divisions did it this way in Oakland, California, on outdoor billboards:

> Oakland—the home of three GENERAL MOTORS PLANTS
> Chevrolet and Fisher Body Divisions
> Serving the Community
> GM—General Motors
> As Well as the Nation

Following World War II, General Motors felt that the institutional identity of the corporation, as such, should get special emphasis in cities where plants of GM Divisions operated. Consequently, an experimental series of public relations institutional advertisements was scheduled during 1947 in the local newspapers of selected GM plant cities. Copy complimented the plant city and expressed GM's gratitude at being one of its industrial citizens. Copy also mentioned specifically some of the things which GM believed the plant organization was contributing to the economic and social progress of the community. These advertisements, localized for each community, sought to (*a*) identify the community as the "home of GM plants," (*b*) develop local pride in GM plants, (*c*) identify the plants as part of the community, and (d) express seasonal messages and support of local community charity drives, etc.

This experimental series was well received by plant management in cities where the advertisements ran. Also, proofs of the advertisements were mailed to hundreds of leading citizens in each town and their comments invited. The response was deemed overwhelmingly favorable. The management felt that the advertisements contributed constructively to strengthening the understanding between the community and General Motors.

Institutional Advertising in Radio and Television. General Motors has frequently made use of radio and television to communicate its institutional messages. Several instances are described below.

GM-NBC Symphony of the Air. In August 1943 General Motors and the National Broadcasting Company jointly announced the sponsorship by General Motors of "The Symphony of the Air" under the leadership of Arturo Toscanini, Leopold Stokowski, and Frank Black. In announcing its sponsorship, General Motors issued the following statement:

General Motors is happy to sponsor the NBC Symphony Orchestra. The American people have a growing appreciation of fine music, and there is more reason now than ever before to make it available to them in their homes. In the emergency of war, with its pressing demands upon everyone, it is important that we retain insofar as possible those educational and cultural activities which have so enriched Americans in all walks of life.

A number of institutional messages were given in person in the course of the presentation of these programs between September 1943 and July 1945 by C. F. Kettering, vice president of General Motors and directing head of the General Motors Research Laboratories. Mr. Kettering gave a series of five-minute talks on various aspects of invention, science, and research. Each informal talk attempted to show how progress stems from invention and research and to draw parallels that listeners could understand. Mr. Kettering spoke on subjects such as "The Intangible in Human Progress," "They Just Wanted to Fly," and "The Birth of an Idea." Sponsorship of this program continued through July 1946.

"Your Land and Mine"—Henry J. Taylor. Beginning in December 1945 and continuing through December 1956, General Motors sponsored a series of 725 radio talks by Henry J. Taylor. The format of the program —it was called "Your Land and Mine"—was purely institutional and not an up-to-the-minute news program as such. Mr. Taylor spoke on such subjects as inflation, thrift, production, national debt, profits, prices, property and wealth, freedom, national and international problems, and on countless other social, economic, and political problems. During the years of his association with General Motors, Mr. Taylor traveled into many lands, met and talked with statesmen in almost every country on the globe, lectured in every state in the union, and brought to the public a fresh and invigorating appreciation of the American way of life. The Henry J.

Taylor talks were reprinted regularly and mailed to a large list of interested people—as many as 75,000 persons who specifically requested that their names be placed on a mailing list.

Number One Yuletide Square. An hour-long television Christmas fantasy, "Number One Yuletide Square," was sponsored by General Motors on Christmas Day, 1952. The fantasy was conceived by Leon Leonidoff, executive producer of New York's Radio City Music Hall, and starred Arthur Godfrey, Thomas Mitchell, and various members of the New York City Center Ballet Company. Harlow H. Curtice, then acting president of General Motors, delivered a special Christmas message during the program.

General Motors TV Football Game of the Week. In 1952 and 1953 General Motors undertook the sponsorship of a series of interregional college football games under the direction of the National Collegiate Athletic Association (NCAA). The schedule, arranged in co-operation with the NCAA, covered 12 week ends. In making the selection, every effort was made to pick games holding the greatest amount of promise of public interest, and each of the eight national NCAA regions was represented. Some of the teams that played to the national telecast were Texas-Oklahoma, Alabama-Tennessee, Michigan State–Michigan, USC-UCLA, Army-Navy, and Notre Dame–SMU. The commercial messages given in conjunction with the telecasts stressed the product advantages of the five lines of GM cars and the used cars handled by each division.

1953 Presidential Inauguration. On January 20, 1953, General Motors sponsored as a public service a combined television-radio coverage of the inauguration of Dwight D. Eisenhower as President of the United States. The ceremonies, which were covered in a four-hour telecast and a two-hour radio broadcast, included the Presidential procession from the White House to the Capitol; the actual swearing in ceremony of both the President and Vice-President; the President's speech at the east portico of the Capitol building; and the return parade from Capitol Hill to the White House.

June 2, 1953, Coronation of Queen Elizabeth II. General Motors sponsored the radio and television coverage of the coronation of Queen Elizabeth II in London on June 2, 1953. The technical difficulties were tremendous. Only part of the radio coverage could be live—part had to be tape-recorded beforehand. Movie and television cameras recorded the visual happenings, and the film thus produced was rushed to America via fast planes in which film processing and editing laboratories had been set up. Within 18 hours after the actual coronation proceedings had taken place, the American public was watching a filmed report on the national television network.

Technical Center Dedication Television Program—May 1956. On the occasion of the dedication of the GM Technical Center at Detroit, a special presentation TV program, "Wide Wide World," was developed.

The program, which employed live cameras at a variety of locations around the country, had been sponsored by the accessory divisions of the corporation, except for this special program in which the corporation assumed sponsorship. The program was built around a number of stories which began in some part of the Technical Center where live cameras would witness a scientist, engineer, or stylist at work on some new development. Then employing a nation-wide television hookup the scene of action was changed to see application of the principal in the field. Examples of this are: flame studies at the GM Research Laboratory to Los Angeles for discussion of the smog problem, and new turbine blade materials in an experimental foundry to an engine-removal demonstration at an Air Force field in Florida.

Information for GM Employees. General Motors executives believed that sound public relations should start with its own employees; that employees who were well-informed and who understood the plans and purposes of the company which employed them would be a valuable public or community relations asset. Here are some of the media General Motors has used from time to time to keep its employees informed: (1) *GM Folks Magazine.* An employee magazine distributed monthly to GM employees, GM dealers and their employees, and to newspapers, libraries, and other interested persons from May 1938 to June 1956. (2) *Executive Bulletin.* Distributed monthly to GM management employees from April 1944 to May 1956. (3) Divisional and plant employee publications. Monthly and semimonthly publications with circulation among employees, GM dealers, and community leaders.

Field Relations Programs. General Motors had understood for many years the great importance of localizing and personalizing public relations efforts. For this reason and because it was believed to be an important phase of good management, General Motors developed a decentralized field relations program. Its purpose was to keep in touch with the people in communities where General Motors did business and to keep them informed on the many aspects of the business which affect their standing in the community.

General Motors Management Clubs. In 1937 the first General Motors Management Clubs under the sponsorship of the central Public Relations Staff were organized. At the end of 1956 there were 33 such clubs which met at regular intervals in key cities. Each club has had its own officers; membership included divisional and plant executives in the area. Programs took the form of GM institutional motion pictures, slide film presentations, or an executive speaker on subjects pertinent to current operations. These programs frequently have been of a community relations nature and special groups of community leaders often have been invited to attend the meetings as guests.

General Motors Management Dealer Clubs. Another group called the General Motors Management Dealer Clubs—207 in number—were located in smaller cities with a large concentration of GM personnel. Nucleus of the membership in those clubs has been GM employees with headquarters in the area, plus many GM dealers in the club city and within a radius of about 35 miles. A local GM executive served as permanent chairman of each club. These clubs met on call for programs which usually were of sufficient community or national interest to include a select group of local people as guests. These programs were supplied by the central Public Relations Staff.

Community Relations Chairmen in the Dealer Organization. In 1943 GM opened another channel for direct contact with the public. It began the appointment of community relations chairmen among its dealers in towns of 10,000 population or less. GM dealers in a given town have elected one of their number to serve for a year. He served as the GM public relations contact man in the community and has rendered such public relations services as may have been requested, utilizing information and educational material developed by GM's Public Relations Staff. In 1956 there were 2,425 such community relations chairmen.

Public Relations Regional Offices. Still another channel for direct contact with the public were 12 Public Relations Regional Offices located in as many cities throughout the country. Each was in charge of a public relations regional manager, who reported to the department's central office in Detroit. They concerned themselves primarily with internal and external aspects of community relations problems throughout their regions, and they sought to co-ordinate the activities of the plant city committees, General Motors clubs, and the community relations chairmen.

Channels of Communication Other than Advertising. In addition to advertising programs and special institutional events, there have been a number of other means of getting information about General Motors into the hands of the public. Frequently the information has been brought directly to its audience at the community level through one or another of GM field relations groups—plant city committees, General Motors clubs, community relations chairmen, or the public relations regional managers. On other occasions, the information has reached a national audience through press and radio releases at Detroit. Again, direct distribution of special messages have been made from Detroit (1) as a result of individual requests or, (2) as broadside mailings to particular groups. When there was a desire to localize and personalize distribution of printed material, local mailing lists have been used.

Press Relations Activities. One of the most important functions of the Public Relations Staff was providing corporation news to the news-dispensing agencies of the country—newspapers, magazines, radio, and television. Many aspects of the corporation's activities were of great interest to the public, and these were frequently the subject of news and editorial articles. In conjunction with many special public relations programs, subjects, and newsworthy events, the Press Relations Section provided ready-made background material for the reporters in attendance. This service was rendered at the Powerama, the Motoramas, the Technical Center dedication as well as at government hearings, labor negotiations, and other newsworthy events. Each year the Press Relations Section also printed a booklet filled with vital statistics about General Motors and its divisions.

GM Educational Booklets. In 1934 General Motors issued the first book in its educational series. This booklet discussed automobile engines in simple, nontechnical language. Since the response was encouraging, the program was expanded and in 1957 there were 17 books in the series. Typical titles are: *A Power Primer, American Battle for Abundance,* and *Chemistry and Wheels.*

There were two objectives in starting this activity. First, offering these booklets was deemed a gesture of goodwill; it rendered a service to people which was appreciated. Second, the booklets were designed to help establish General Motors' reputation as a leader in the field of engineering and research. There was no advertising of any sort in them, but they did pertain in general to the corporation's products and thus were meant to do a job of low-pressure selling.

While it was not possible to evaluate this activity in terms of sales, the management believed there was no question of the goodwill obtained. Letters from all classes of people and continual requests for additional quantities were believed to indicate that these booklets were used and welcomed. In 1956, a fairly representative year, a total of 1,386,093 books in this series were distributed. Approximately 45% went to teachers and students.

GM Film Library. The production and distribution of motion pictures by GM's Public Relations Staff was begun in a small way in 1937. Films were loaned to organizations requesting them. No charge was made, except for the cost of shipping the film back to the GM Film Libraries, which were located in New York, Detroit, and San Francisco. The only other requirement has been that a report be furnished on the type of organization to which the picture has been shown, the attendance, and so on. The Film Library in 1956 had 60 institutional, educational, and safety film subjects with a total of 7,300 prints in circulation with an additional 4,100 prints on deposit or sold outright. Typical titles were: "Doctor in Industry," "To New Horizons," and "Frontiers of the Future."

In 1956 there were 315,000 showings to a total of 15,900,000 people. About 80% of these showings were to school groups. By the end of 1956, 258,000,000 people had seen these films.

During the forties General Motors began to produce newsreels for television and motion-picture consumption. In 1956 a total of 25 newsreels were produced. Included were subjects such as: "T-100 Self-Propelled Gun," "Motorama Fashions," and "Appraising the Business Outlook." Depending on the subject matter, GM newsreels and short subjects were used by: theatrical newsreels, national and regional television networks, local TV stations, GM plant city theaters, General Motors clubs, and the United States State Department and Armed Services.

Special Projects of a Public Relations Institutional Nature. In its effort to have the public understand the corporation better, General Motors undertook a series of contests, sponsorships, stage presentations, and portable, traveling, or permanent exhibits and displays to dramatize and simplify its interest in and contribution to the social, scientific, and economic progress of the country. Among these were:

The Parade of Progress. A motor caravan called the Parade of Progress began a tour of the country in 1936, presenting a tent show which dramatized the beginning of various businesses and industries such as the telegraph, the electric light, and the radio industry. GM attempted no direct selling in connection with the Parade of Progress. The object was to demonstrate the progress that had been made in industry and the part General Motors played in bringing about this progress. It was a low-pressure type of promotional activity to build attitudes among the public that General Motors was a forward-looking organization that makes excellent products. When the first Parade of Progress went off the road in 1938, it was estimated that it had been shown to more than 3,000,000 people, and that an additional 20,000,000 people had seen the caravan as it passed through their towns.

In 1952 it was decided to build a new and larger Parade of Progress to tell the new story of scientific achievement in a world recently introduced to jet propulsion, radar, atomic power, and television. One institutional purpose of the new Parade of Progress was to show how science and industry combine to contribute to the high American standard of living. Another purpose was to inspire young people with an enthusiasm for science and engineering as an avocation at a time when an alarming number of young people were shunning the basic sciences in high school and college.

The second Parade of Progress was a traveling show manned by 60 young men who operated 49 vehicles including 12 Futurliners, the specially designed trucks which became a Parade trade-mark. Under a uniquely constructed Aerodome tent visitors saw a stage show featuring dramatic presentations of the marvels of a science such as: a jet plane demonstration; making synthetic rubber in a pop bottle; a tiny motor that runs on sunshine; and the transmission of sound by microwaves. During its four-year tour the second Parade of Progress traveled 18,950 miles and played before 8,000,000 people in 148 communities. The attendance figures represented approximately 29 per cent of the total population in each community.

"My Job" Contest. A contest, "My Job and Why I Like It," was conducted in 1947 exclusively as an internal, employee relations activity. However, as with most employer activities, GM found that it had important external, community relations aspects. It was a letter-writing contest

for GM employees. As the GM vice president in charge of employee relations described it, "We invited employees 'to accentuate the positive' —to look at the doughnut instead of the hole." Of 297,000 eligible employees, 174,854, or more than 58%, entered the contest with letters about why they liked their jobs. More than 5,000 awards were made to winners. The activity brought a great deal of press, radio, and magazine comment that it was a constructive, positive approach to employee relations.

4-H Club Sponsorship. In 1945 sponsorship of the National 4-H Club Farm Safety Program was accepted by General Motors, and renewed annually through 1957. GM management thus gained association with 2,200,000 of America's farm boys and girls. Because General Motors for years had stressed safety in a thorough and successful industrial safety program in its plants and offices and in building safety into its automobiles and other products; and because of the automobile industry's interest in the street and highway traffic safety problem, General Motors believed sponsorship of the 4-H farm safety activity to be an appropriate extension of its basic interest in reducing accidents of all kinds. Beyond the humanitarian aspects of its interest in safety, General Motors executives felt that a real return in goodwill was earned through the 4-H sponsorship—not only among 4-H boys and girls but among their families and among local, county, state, and federal agencies interested in the farm safety field, as well.

Previews of Progress. Previews of Progress was a highly entertaining and educational stage presentation type of activity which was revived in 1946. The properties for the acts were portable, and the show was presented by a team of two young men to a unit. By the end of 1956 eight such units were on the road, with headquarters in cities which permitted good geographical coverage of the country. The show demonstrated how scientists and research workers unlocked nature's secrets and converted them to useful purposes for all people.

By the end of 1956, more than 14 million children and adults had seen the postwar Previews of Progress. Approximately 80% of them were school and college groups. Other audiences included convention groups, state and county fair groups, meetings of Chambers of Commerce, civic clubs, etc.

Open-House Activities. Open-house activities in General Motors plants have been an important part of GM and divisional public and community relations for many years.

Special Group Visits. The experience of GM plants with open-house activities led directly to a program of plant visits for special community groups and these have produced very favorable results.

Train of Tomorrow. The General Motors Train of Tomorrow was considered by the management to be one of the most effective and successful public relations institutional advertising projects ever undertaken by GM. Designed by General Motors as a contribution to the advancement of transportation, the Train of Tomorrow was launched on a nation-wide tour of public exhibitions in May 1947. By the end of 1948 it had been exhibited in 126 cities and 3,863,562 people had walked through it and inspected its many new and revolutionary features. During the summer of 1948 it was on exhibit at the Railroad Fair in Chicago and outdrew all other exhibits. Approximately one million people inspected it during its stay at the Fair.

The GM Aerotrain. In 1955 General Motors undertook another major railroad project as a public service. This was the GM Aerotrain, a brand new train in concept, design, and construction. The GM Aerotrain was light in weight and low in manufactured cost. As a result of these two characteristics it was hoped by General Motors executives that the Aerotrain would help reduce the cost of transporting passengers, a critical item in the operation of most United States railroads. General Motors built two Aerotrains and completed one in time for display at the GM Powerama and for a trial run between Detroit and Chicago carrying a full complement of representatives of the press.

The General Motors Better Highways Awards Contest—How to Plan and Pay for Better Highways. An important step in the continuing campaign to overcome highway and traffic problems was taken in 1952 when GM announced its "Better Highways Awards Contest." In the contest, entrants were asked to write an essay of no specified length on the subject "How to Plan and Pay for the Safe and Adequate Highways We Need." Anyone could enter. Five judges, nationally known in fields relating to the highways problem, selected the winners. Approximately 44,000 people submitted entries in the contest. The authors of the three national winning essays won $25,000 each and the privilege of having their essays reprinted in booklet form. In all, the prizes totaled $194,000. While it was difficult to accurately measure the effectiveness of such a program, GM executives believed that the program was definitely worthwhile in helping millions of Americans to understand better the problem and in winning their support to the idea that constructive action should be taken.

The GM Motorama Automobile Spectaculars. The automobile industry, as a part of its joint promotional activities, sponsored an annual National Automobile Show in New York City and Chicago during most years between 1900 and 1940. The National Automobile Show always was sponsored by the Automobile Manufacturers' Association until it was taken over by a dealer organization in Chicago in 1935 and it was discontinued in New York in 1940.

General Motors, believing in bringing its products and institutional messages into direct contact with the public, conceived the idea of sponsoring its own automobile show and in the postwar years developed the GM Motorama, which was an automobile extravaganza in every sense. Motorama, when fully developed, presented the new model GM automobiles in an attractive setting along with a specially produced musical variety show featuring Broadway talent. It was a free exhibit that went beyond the usual concept of an auto show. It had the additional features of dozens of scientific and engineering exhibits and presented a number of years ahead dream cars which incorporated advanced styling concepts of the future. Also shown were yearly versions of the "Kitchens of To-morrow," which, like the dream cars, tested new design approaches and mechanical features with appeal for homemakers.

GM Motorama began as "Transportation Unlimited" in 1949 and was shown in New York and Detroit only. In 1950, it was called the "Mid-Century Motorama" and was presented in New York only. In the years 1953, 1954, 1955, and 1956 the Motorama was shown in New York, Mi-ami, Los Angeles, and San Francisco every year as well as Dallas, Kansas City, Chicago, and Boston at certain times.

The popularity of GM Motoramas was impressive. Limited to a run of one week in each of five cities in the years 1953–56, total audiences of as many as 2,500,000 people a year came to see and enjoy the spectacle of automotive progress. The announcement of Motorama in each city was made by institutional and divisional advertisements used in conjunction with special newspaper sections which described the features of Motor-ama and invited the public to attend.

The purpose of the GM Motoramas was to promote the sale of GM products, both directly and indirectly. Salesmen in attendance at the divisional exhibits sought to convert prospects and to build prospect lists for use by local dealers. In addition to sales, the institutional effects of Motorama were far-reaching. One effect undoubtedly was to build pres-tige for GM as a leading exponent of styling, research, and engineering in automotive products. Motorama also gave the Customer Research Staff an opportunity to sample public reaction to new production cars and to advanced dream car designs. Visitors to Motorama also asked for and re-ceived many copies of GM public relations booklets.

One of the most important by-products of the Motorama was the ex-tensive amount of publicity given in the local newspapers and in the na-tional magazines. Literally thousands of pages of free and favorable pub-licity were the result. The GM Motoramas were a highly effective means of reaching large numbers of people either directly or indirectly with both product and public relations institutional messages.

Twice the Corporation sponsored national television programs in con-nection with Motoramas. The first, an hour-long program in 1955, fea-tured interviews with Harlow H. Curtice, president, and the five vice presidents of the GM car divisions. The second in 1956 featured television stars John Daley, Arlene Francis, and Jayne Meadows. Both programs were promotional in nature, giving a glimpse of the various phases of the current Motorama.

Celebration of the General Motors 50 Millionth Car. On November 23, 1954, General Motors celebrated the production of its 50 millionth automobile. As the 50 millionth car rolled off the assembly line, it touched off a public relations effort which received the broadest possible coverage in all news media. For example, 106 newspapers with a circulation of over 45,000,000 put out special commemorative sections on General Motors with more than 1,500 full pages of copy and advertising devoted exclusively to the 50 millionth car celebration. Sixty-five radio and TV stations aired special broadcasts and telecasts devoted exclusively to some phase of the celebration. And these programs were in addition to thousands of newscasts mentions. Also, 120 newspapers printed favorable editorials and thousands of papers carried spot news items.

GM Powerama. This event in the fall of 1955 was to commemorate the production of the 100 millionth diesel horsepower by the Divisions of General Motors. The institutional device was Powerama, the "World's Fair of Power" and the largest outdoor industrial exposition ever staged. The million-square-foot site was at the Chicago lakefront where $2\frac{1}{4}$ million visitors came to learn of the tremendous strides in Diesel power applications since the introduction by GM of the modern two-cycle Diesel engine in 1933.

All of the facilities of the Technical Center were opened to the 5,000 famous guests and to the families of the GM employees during the week. The climax of the Dedication Celebration was the hour-and-one-half "Wide Wide World" television program presented over NBC-TV explaining via live camera hookup the significance of the Technical Center and some of the interesting work in progress there.

The Technical Center Dedication event was one of the most widely reported and featured ever attempted. A total of 78 multiple-page newspaper sections, plus countless spot news stories, magazine articles, and radio and TV news items whetted America's interest in technological progress at General Motors.

~~~

CASE 2: JOHNS-MANVILLE CORPORATION[1]

QUESTIONS TO CONSIDER: (*1*) *Should the two objectives stated on page one of the case be treated as mutually exclusive objectives?* (*2*) *Should Johns-Manville consider some type of patronage institutional program to accomplished objective number two? If so, what kind of program?* (*3*) *Is the advertising agency proposal sound? What is it likely to accomplish for Johns-Manville?*

In May 1957 Mr. Reginald L. Johnson, vice president and director of advertising, and other top executives of Johns-Manville Corporation were faced with the question of whether or not to undertake an expanded ad-

---

[1] Written by Martin V. Marshall.

vertising program in mass-consumer publications. The expanded program being considered had two primary objectives: (1) to help to promote the sale of selected major product lines, and (2) to develop a greater awareness among various segments of the market that Johns-Manville was not exclusively a producer and marketer of asbestos roofing and insulation materials but was a highly diversified business producing and marketing over 400 products, ranging from thermal insulations for industry to brake linings for automobiles, from pipe for municipal water systems to building materials for houses, made not only of asbestos but of many other raw materials. Since the program would cost $900,000 in the last six months of 1957 and $1,300,000 in 1958, Mr. Johnson and other executives, including representatives of the corporation's advertising agency, spent considerable time evaluating the merits of the proposed program.

Corporation Background

In 1858 H. W. Johns, a pioneer in the roofing and insulation business, founded the H. W. Johns Manufacturing Company to develop new uses for asbestos, a mineral of the hornblende family which was not affected by heat. At the time asbestos was used primarily to line fireproof safes and to filter chemicals. Because of the heat-resistant qualities of asbestos and its abundance, Mr. Johns believed that he could build a sizable industry by developing new end uses. Throughout the next 40 years, the Johns company developed the asbestos market, primarily in roofing and insulation, the latter market principally in conjunction with the Manville Covering Company of Milwaukee, which produced pipe coverings and insulations for plumbing and heating systems. These companies merged in 1901.

For the next 25 years the H. W. Johns-Manville Company continued to develop primarily as a manufacturer and marketer of asbestos roofings, insulation, packings, and friction materials. After 1927, when the company passed from private to public control, the reorganized Johns-Manville Corporation embarked on an aggressive diversification program, entering much more broadly into the use of raw materials other than asbestos, including asphalt, cement, diatomite (the fossilized remains of microscopic marine plants), mineral and wood fibers, plastics, and rubber.

To give the reader an idea of the numerous end-product uses of these raw materials, a few examples follow. Asbestos fibers were combined with Portland cement to make structural building boards and pipe; with plastics to make vinyl asbestos floor tiles; and with diatomite and magnesium carbonate to make high-temperature insulations. Asbestos fibers were spun into yarn which was woven into fireproof, rotproof textiles or felted into papers. Mineral fibers were formed into small nodules for blowing into walls as an insulation or were made into batts and blankets to produce insulations for home freezers, refrigerators, kitchen ranges, and air-conditioning ducts. Wood fibers were used to make building board, decorative ceiling panels, acoustical panels, and roof insulation.

Diatomite was used to make filter aids for clarifying materials such as sugar, beverages, dry-cleaning fluids, oils, and chemicals; as a filler for paints, varnishes, soaps, and polishes; and as high-temperature insulations for industrial furnaces and kilns.

As a result of developing many new end uses for its raw materials, the Johns-Manville Corporation in the years 1927–57 developed a complex marketing operation. In entering into and developing each market, the corporation tailored its marketing and promotional methods to the individual market, employing those channels of distribution and those promotional tools which were required to distribute and sell products effectively. Planning and management was decentralized. Of nine divisions, established, six divisions handled manufacturing operations in the United States. They were: the Building Products, Industrial Insulations, Packings

Exhibit 1

JOHNS-MANVILLE CORPORATION

Products, Markets, and Channels of Distribution of the Building Products Division

Products	Markets	Channels of Distribution
Asphalt shingles and roofing Roof coating and putties Asbestos roof shingles Asbestos siding shingles Asbestos cement sheets Insulating board sheathing Decorative insulating board Hardboard Acoustical ceilings Mineral wool insulation Asphalt tile flooring Vinyl asbestos flooring	For building, repairing, or remodeling homes, farm buildings, and other forms of light construction.	Wholesalers ↓ Building materials dealers Large home builders Home improvement contractors
Built-up roofing Corrugated asbestos cement sheets Transitop-panels Asphalt tile flooring Vinyl asbestos flooring	Commercial, institutional, and industrial building.	Direct to industry or Wholesalers ↓ Approved contractors General contractors
Acoustical ceiling Sound conditioning Movable partitions	Commercial, institutional, and industrial building	Direct sales and contract sales (Johns-Manville maintained a contract sales function which handled all aspects of the use of certain Johns-Manville products in special large installation.)

Source: Building Products Division.

Exhibit 2

JOHNS-MANVILLE CORPORATION
Products, Markets, and Channels of Distribution of the Industrial Insulations Division

Products	Markets	Channels of Distribution
Thermoflex high-temperature refractory fiber felt (includes foil-encased blankets, insulated shrouds, components, etc.) Min-K high-temperature molded missile and rocket insulation	Aviation	Direct sales to aviation industry
Fibrocel medium-temperature pipe and block insulation 85% magnesia high-temperature pipe and block insulation Spintex glass fiber duct insulation Aerolag glass fiber pipe insulation Aerotube foamed plastic pipe and tube insulation Colorlith laboratory table top material	Commercial construction (public buildings, schools, institutions, office buildings, colleges, etc.)	1. Direct sales 2. Through distributors 3. J-M contract units
Thermobestos high-temperature calcium silicate pipe and block insulation 85% magnesia high-temperature pipe and block insulation Insulating firebrick Blazecrete and firecrete refractory cements Insulating cements H. T. Banroc high-temperature block insulation Zerolite low-temperature insulation Asbestos papers	Process industries (chemical, petrochemical, petroleum, paper, etc.)	1. Direct Sales 2. Through distributors 3. J-M contract units
Rock Cork low-temperature pipe and block insulation Asbestocite asbestos-cement sheet material	Cold storage (freezers, cold-storage room, etc.)	1. Direct sales 2. Through distributors 3. J-M contract units
Insulating firebrick Superex high-temperature block insulation	Metal fabrication (heat-treating ovens, etc.)	1. Direct sales 2. Through distributors 3. J-M contract units
Marinite asbestos-diatomaceous silica insulating sheet material Reeferite asbestos-cement board material 85% magnesia high-temperature pipe and block insulation Thermobestos high-temperature calcium silicate pipe and block insulation Insulating firebrick Blazecrete and firecrete refractory cements	Marine	1. Direct sales 2. Through distributors 3. J-M contract units

Exhibit 2—Continued

Products	Markets	Channels of Distribution
Quinterra purified asbestos electrical insulation Quinorgo purified asbestos electrical insulation Quinterrabord purified asbestos electrical insulation Quinorgobord purified asbestos electrical insulation Ohmstone asbestos-cement electrical board material	Electrical manufacturing	1. Direct sales 2. Through distributors 3. J-M contract units
Thermobestos high-temperature calcium silicate pipe and block insulation 85% magnesia high-temperature pipe and block insulation Superex high-temperature pipe and block insulation H. T. Banroc high-temperature block insulation Insulating firebrick Blazecrete and firecrete refractory cements	Power generation (public utilities, steam generating plants, etc.)	1. Direct sales 2. Through distributors 3. J-M contract units
Insulating firebrick Superex high-temperature block insulation H. T. Banroc high-temperature insulating block Blazecrete and firecrete refractory cements Thermobestos high-temperature calcium silicate pipe and block insulation	Primary metals	1. Direct sales 2. Through distributors 3. J-M contract units
Spintex glass fiber insulation Cerafelt refractory fiber felt	Equipment (manufacturers of home appliances, oil-burner fireboxes, etc.)	Direct sales only

Source: Industrial Insulation Division.

and Friction Materials, Pipe, Celite, and Dutch Brand divisions. The products sold, the markets served, and the channels of distribution employed by each of the divisions are outlined in Exhibits 1 through 6. The combined sales of the company in 1956 were $310,390,000.

Promotional Strategy

Because of the nature of their products and markets, the above six operating divisions of Johns-Manville had always placed primary emphasis upon working to and through the trade—particularly upon the element of personal selling. Overall the divisions maintained sales offices in 62 United States cities and a sales force of about 1,000 men, who were sup-

Exhibit 3

JOHNS-MANVILLE CORPORATION

Products, Markets, and Channels of Distribution of the Packings,
and Frictions Material Division

Products	Markets	Channels of Distribution
Packings and Textile Sales Department: Molded packings used in hydraulic and pneumatic mechanisms Oil and grease seals designed to protect bearings Mechanical packings used in pumps and on reciprocating and rotating rods and shafts	Original equipment, manufacturers, industrial purchases (of maintenance packings), and governmental agencies	Large buyers sold direct Smaller accounts sold through distributors
Friction Materials Sales Department: Four-Star brake lining sets PB Power-Bilt brake lining sets Wireklad brake lining Fleet-Tested lining sets Four-Star brake blocks	Original equipment, manufacturers brake and clutch, rebuilders, large bus fleets, and automobile dealers and repair shops	Large accounts sold direct Smaller accounts sold through warehouse distributors and wholesale distributors

Source: Packings and Frictions Material Division.

Exhibit 4

JOHNS-MANVILLE CORPORATION

Products, Markets, and Channels of Distribution of the Pipe
Division

Products	Markets	Channels of Distribution
Transite Pipe for water and sewer mains Ring-Tite Pipe Couplings Transhield Pipe Line Wrap	U.S. Government Bureaus, municipal and local governments, and pipeline companies and builders	Direct sale
Electrical Conduit Pipe Transite House Pipe for venting and waste disposal	Plumbing, heating, and air-conditioning contractors, industrial equipment contractors, electrical contractors, telephone companies, and irrigation equipment contractors	Distributors

Source: Pipe Division.

Exhibit 5

JOHNS-MANVILLE CORPORATION

Products, Markets, and Channels of Distribution of the Celite
Division

Products	Markets	Channels of Distribution
Filter aids	Manufacturers of chemicals, foods, and dry-cleaning solvents, and handlers of water (swimming pools, processors, secondary oil recovery, etc.)	Large accounts sold direct Smaller accounts sold through distributors
Mineral fillers	Manufacturers of paint, paper, insecticides, fertilizer, polishes, detergents, and waxes	
Synthetic calcium silicates	Manufacturers of insecticides, fertilizer, animal-feed supplements, salt, spices, and dry-food products, paint, paper, and detergents	
Cement additives	Manufacturers of Redi-mixed cement and of concrete block and pipe	

Source: Celite Division.

Exhibit 6

JOHNS-MANVILLE CORPORATION

Products, Markets, and Channels of Distribution of the Dutch
Brand Division

Products	Markets	Channels of Distribution
Friction tape Plastic tape Paper tape Rubber tape Sponge rubber Sand blast stencil Tile and tub sealer Rubber cement	Electrical industry Automotive industry General industry	Direct to original equipment manufacturers; automobile parts wholesalers, hardware wholesalers, and mill and industrial supply houses

Source: Dutch Brand Division.

ported by a variety of sales promotional tools. These tools are briefly described below.

The Building Products Division emphasized sales aids for building material dealers, contractors, and builders, and used extensive advertising schedules in trade media to inform all factors in the market of Johns-Manville building materials. *The Industrial Insulations Division* provided its salesmen with technical literature for prospects, sales aids for distributors, ran advertisements in trade papers and technical journals, and participated in key trade shows. *The Packings and Friction Division* placed considerable emphasis on sales aids (such as signs, decals, and point-of-purchase pieces) for dealers, distributed technical literature, and employed advertising in trade papers and technical journals.

The Pipe Division relied on technical literature, key trade shows, motion pictures (showing actual installation of pipe to prospects), and advertising in trade papers and technical journals. *The Celite Division* used selling aids and emphasized trade shows and advertising in trade papers and technical journals. *The Dutch Brand Division* extensively used selling aids for jobbers (such as mats, decals, photographs, and direct-mail material), literature for end-use customers, and advertising in trade papers.

Overall the divisions spent approximately $1,250,000 annually on selling aids for distributors, dealers, and direct prospects, and approximately $1 million annually on advertisements in about 200 trade and technical publications. Selected examples of division advertising are given in Exhibits 7 and 8.

In addition to working to and through the trade, Johns-Manville for some years had been a consistent user of consumer media. During World War II, when the executives found the corporation's products being allocated rather than sold, they decided that it would be desirable to increase the amount of consumer advertising in order to maintain the Johns-Manville name before the public. Hence the corporation bought a five-minute radio news show, five days a week, first on CBS and then on Mutual, with Elmer Davis and later Bill Henry as news commentators. This program was continued for 12 years, until the 1952–53 program season.

At that time management decided to drop the news program for two reasons. First, it was believed that television had taken the audience which Johns-Manville wanted to reach away from radio. Second, the corporation's sales organization was keenly interested in the possibilities of a television program because of its impact upon potential customers, dealers, and distributors and because competitors were employing television.

Since Johns-Manville could spend between $1\frac{1}{2}\%$ and 2% of sales on promotion, it was not feasible for the corporation to buy a nation-wide network television show on a weekly basis. However, after considerable negotiation, Johns-Manville was able to purchase "Meet the Press," a show featuring prominent public figures who were questioned by newsmen, in cosponsorship with Pan American Airlines. Because the budget would not allow the purchase of a full network, however, the telecasting of "Meet the Press" was restricted to about 43 major markets.

In the spring of 1957, Mr. Johnson and other members of management decided that television should be dropped for two reasons. First, Johns-Manville had exposed its message sufficiently to the type of audience which watched "Meet the Press" and, second, the corporation, if it was to continue an over-all corporate advertising program, needed to cover the national market.

Exhibit 7

JOHNS-MANVILLE CORPORATION

Example of Advertising of the Industrial Insulations Division

In soaking pits, Johns-Manville Sil-O-Cel C-22 Insulating Brick provide outstanding performance as back-up insulation.

Specify
Johns-Manville SIL-O-CEL C-22 Insulating Brick

the diatomaceous silica brick that retains its high cold crushing strength of 700 psi throughout normal service range

Because of its exceptional strength Sil-O-Cel C-22 Insulating Brick has gained wide acceptance as an all-purpose insulating brick. It is especially recommended for soaking pits, open hearth bottoms, slab heating furnaces, hot blast stoves, coke ovens and other high temperature equipment.

Millions of microscopic cells provide Sil-O-Cel C-22 brick with excellent heat resistance up to 2000F. It has a thermal conductivity of only 1.88 Btu in/sq ft/F/hr at 1000F mean temperature. In addition, with a density of 38 lb/cu ft, it is light and easy to handle.

For direct exposure or back-up to 1600F, use Sil-O-Cel 16L Insulating

Brick. This newest member of the J-M diatomaceous silica insulating brick family has *less than 0.1% reversible thermal expansion at 1600F.* Conductivity is 1.07 Btu in/sq ft/F/hr at 1000F mean temperature with a density of 33-35 lb/cu ft. Cold crushing strength is 350 psi. Sil-O-Cel 16L serves equally well as back-up insulation or exposed refractory lining.

For back-up at higher temperatures, specify Sil-O-Cel* Super Insulating Brick with an unusually high temperature limit of 2500F.

Write today for further information on Sil-O-Cel Insulating Brick and Insulating Fire Brick. Ask for Brochure IN-115A. Address Johns-Manville, Box 60, New

York 16, N.Y. In Canada, 565 Lakeshore Road East, Port Credit, Ontario.

 Johns-Manville *first-in* **INSULATION**
MATERIALS · ENGINEERING · APPLICATION

This advertisement appears in
Iron Age—April 7, 1955
Steel—April 18, 1955
Blast Furnace & Steel Plant—May, 1955
Metal Progress—May, 1955
Iron & Steel Engineer—April, 1955
Open Hearth Proceedings (Rescale)—August, 1955
Industrial Heating (Rescale)—May, 1955

TT-3101

Exhibit 8

JOHNS-MANVILLE CORPORATION
Example of Advertising of the Pipe Division

So strong you can step
on it, so lightweight you
can carry the longest length!

Save time by the hour
...concrete by the cubic foot

Transite Air Duct being installed in
Ridgewood Homes, Inc., Worth, Ill.
Clifford J. Wood, Builder: Brainerd
Heating and Sheet Metal Co., Heat-
ing Contractor.

Taped joints are this easy to make,
right at the job site.

Transite is ideal for loop or radial
systems.

...with
easy-to-install Transite air duct!

Transite® offers you unmatched dollar savings for perimeter heating and cooling systems! Here's why:

First, Transite is light in weight. This means it is easy to truck, stack, and carry on the job. Easy to assemble, too . . . permanent, efficient joints are quickly made with easily applied Ductite® Tape.

NO ENCASEMENT NEEDED

More important, Transite saves substantially in both time and concrete. Transite needs no concrete encasement . . . can be laid directly on the prepared bottom. Transite won't "float". . . needs no special supports or anchoring. Just position ducts and pour concrete . . . Transite won't crush, dent, or deform.

AVAILABLE IN LONG LENGTHS

Installation is still faster and easier because of Transite's long, 10-foot lengths . . . fewer joints to be made to complete the installation. And fittings can be made right on the job . . . simply cut the pipe to shapes desired and tape sections together.

MANY HOME OWNER ADVANTAGES

Transite offers home owners long, trouble-free service. Made of asbestos and cement, it is fully corrosion-resistant inside and out, it won't flake or flap down to impede air flow . . . will never rot or give off odor. For free booklet, TR144A, write to Johns-Manville, Box 14, N.Y. 16, N.Y. In Canada, 565 Lakeshore Road East, Port Credit, Ont.

Johns-Manville TRANSITE AIR DUCT

TT-5488

This advertisement appears in
American Artisan—December, 1956
Heating, Air Conditioning, Contractor—December, 1956

Future Use of Consumer Media

In considering what should be done next, Mr. Johnson and other members of management were particularly interested in two problem areas which had arisen in the early 1950's.

First, they were concerned with the problem of selling Johns-Manville's products against specialized competitors who were capable of maintaining larger promotional budgets in given product areas. (The traceable advertising expenditures of selected competitors of Johns-Manville are given in Exhibit 9.)

Second, Johns-Manville executives recognized that the corporation over the years had developed the reputation of being primarily a producer and marketer of asbestos roofing, insulation, and building materials and that its competitive position would be stronger if it was known for what it actually was, a highly diversified supplier of products made of asbestos and other raw materials. To verify its view of what the public thought about Johns-Manville, management had its advertising agency, J. Walter Thompson, undertake a study of "Public Attitudes toward the Johns-Manville Corporation." Among other questions, the agency asked members of its *consumer panel* to indicate those products which they thought Johns-Manville sold. The results were as follows:

Product	% Stating that the Product Was Sold by Johns-Manville
Roof shingles	87.2
Siding shingles	85.4
Home insulation	84.3
Asbestos products	77.2
Industry insulations	73.6
Wallboard	49.2
Acoustical tile	36.9
Brake lining	33.7
Water and sewer pipe	25.4
Floor tile	23.3
Gaskets	20.1
Adhesives	14.0
Tapes	11.5

Because of the problems of selling against specialized competitors and of the reputation of being primarily a marketer of asbestos products, Mr. Johnson felt that a portion of the corporation's total promotional budget could be effectively employed in an expanded advertising program in consumer media. The principal idea of such a program would be to make Johns-Manville or "JM products" the "common denominator" for the over 400 Johns-Manville brands. "The Johns-Manville name is the umbrella or family trade name," Mr. Johnson said, "that ties all our brands together. It is essential to have individual brands for each product because each material has to be called something or has to be given a number. However, it is not possible to be completely effective in advertising each

Exhibit 9

JOHNS-MANVILLE CORPORATION

Total Traceable Consumer Advertising Expenditures of Selected Competitors of Johns-Manville Corporation, 1956

COMPANY	SELECTED COMPETITIVE PRODUCTS	TOTAL COMPANY EXPENDITURES			
		Magazines	Network Television	Sunday Supplements	Total
Allied Chemical & Dye Corp.	Barrett roofing and shingles	$ 879,854	. . . . . .	. . . . . .	$ 879,854
Aluminum Co. of America.	Industrial pipes, roofing, siding	1,749,727	$2,285,215	$ 2,142	4,037,084
Armstrong Cork Co.	Acoustical materials, floors, walls	2,144,276	1,890,933	435,285	4,470,494
Bird & Son.	Roofing, siding, floors, walls	. . . . . .	. . . . . .	221,460	221,460
Celotex Corp.	Asphalt shingles, insulations, wallboard, sound materials	347,413	. . . . . .	. . . . . .	347,413
Congoleum-Nairn, Inc.	Floors, walls	380,771	103,425	126,360	610,556
General Tire & Rubber Co.	Bolta wall and floor tile	1,080,188	186,168	68,200	2,062,556
Johns-Manville Corp.	Products as given in Exhibits 1–6	842,809	736,635	. . . . . .	1,579,144
Kaiser Aluminum & Chem. Corp.	Roofing, pipe, siding	916,249	994,841	. . . . . .	1,911,090
Masonite Corp.	Walls, ceiling panels, siding	457,360	. . . . . .	. . . . . .	457,360
National Gypsum Co.	Roofing, siding, wallboard	869,731	. . . . . .	. . . . . .	869,731
Owens-Corning Fiberglas Corp.	Home insulation and building materials	675,791	. . . . . .	2,678	678,469
Reynolds Metals Co.	Acoustical products, roofing, siding, building materials	623,079	2,085,629	186,087	3,393,745
U.S. Gypsum Co.	Insulation, wallboard, roofing, siding	141,207	. . . . . .	. . . . . .	141,207
U.S. Plywood Corp.	Industrial and home panels	811,640	. . . . . .	. . . . . .	811,640

of the separate brands because there are too many to support completely and economically in separate programs. Thus it seems desirable to support the family trade name in some type of consumer media, thereby reaching all buying factors, helping to sell selected major products, and to develop an awareness of Johns-Manville as a highly diversified source of products."

Exhibit 10

JOHNS-MANVILLE CORPORATION

Recommended Media, Schedule, and Featured Product for
September–December 1957, Advertising Program

Media	Featured Product	Insertion Schedule
The Saturday Evening Post	Terraflex Floor Tile	Sept. 14
Business Week	Transite Pipe	Sept. 14
Life	Fibretex Acoustical Panels	Sept. 23
The Saturday Evening Post	Industrial Insulations	Sept. 28
This Week	Home Insulation	Sept. 29
Time	Transite Pipe	Sept. 30
Sunset	Fibretex Acoustical Panels	Sept. issue
*Star Weekly**	Colorbestos Sidewalls	Oct. 12
The Saturday Evening Post	Colorbestos Sidewalls	Oct. 12
Life	Transite Pipe	Oct. 14
Time	Industrial Insulations	Oct. 14
The Saturday Evening Post	Brake Lining	Oct. 26
This Week	Terraflex Floor Tile	Oct. 27
Better Homes & Gardens	Home Insulation	Oct. issue
Sunset	Seal-O-Matic Shingles	Oct. issue
*La Presse**	Colorbestos Shingles	Nov. 2
Life	Seal-O-Matic Shingles	Nov. 4
Time (Canadian)	Industrial Insulation	Nov. 11
Business Week	Industrial Insulation	Nov. 16
This Week	Decorative Insulating Board	Nov. 1
The Saturday Evening Post	Transite Pipe	Nov. 23
*MacLean's**	Fibretex Acoustical Panels	Nov. 23
Better Homes & Gardens	Colorbestos Sidewalls	Nov. issue
Sunset	Decorative Insulating Board	Nov. issue
Time	Brake Lining	Dec. 2
Better Homes & Gardens	Transite Pipe	Dec. issue

* Canadian publications.
Source: Company records.

In considering what kind of over-all advertising program might be employed, management and the advertising agency agreed that national consumer magazines should be the medium employed, because magazines would cover the national market, color could be used, and the schedule of use could be adjusted to the size of the budget. It was also felt that salesmen, distributors, and dealers would be much more enthusiastic about print media than television, because printed advertisements could be used more effectively as a merchandising tool than television commercials.

Exhibit 11

JOHNS-MANVILLE CORPORATION

Advertisement Proposed for Campaign in Consumer Media

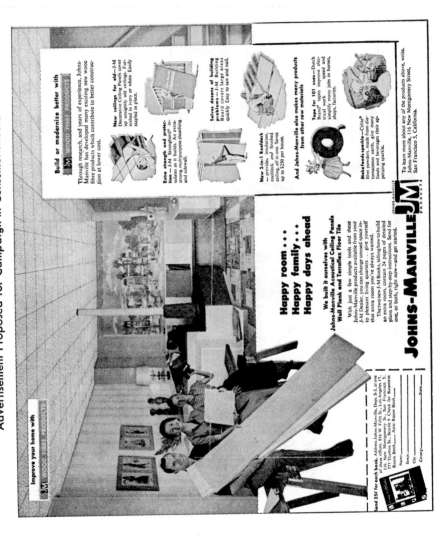

Exhibit 12

JOHNS-MANVILLE CORPORATION

Advertisement Proposed for Campaign in Consumer Media

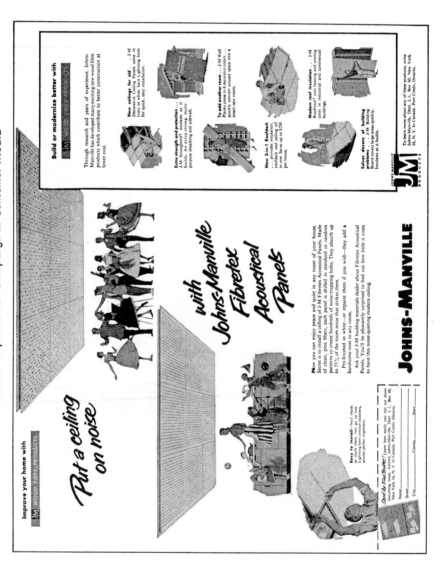

As a preliminary basis for exploring the over-all corporate advertising program, the advertising agency suggested that a series of advertisements might be built around the idea "here are the Johns-Manville products that go into a home" or "here are the Johns-Manville products that go into an industrial plant." Consideration was also given to the possibilities of advertisements which focused on the most important product in each product line. Finally, discussion focused upon the possibilities of a type of advertisement which featured a specific product on one page and mentioned seven other Johns-Manville products on one-half page adjacent to the full page.

To provide a more specific basis for making a decision, management asked the agency to prepare a detailed program for the period September–December 1957 based upon the latter approach.

The schedule, media, and featured products recommended are given in Exhibit 10. Examples of the kinds of advertisements which might be employed in the proposed campaign are given in Exhibits 11 and 12.

If used, most advertisements were to include a coupon, offering readers literature regarding the featured product or the product field, e.g., a booklet on home insulation. In addition, Mr. Johnson thought that if the campaign was undertaken, it would be desirable to make up a merchandising portfolio for Johns-Manville salesman to use with distributors and dealers.

The cost of the 26 advertisements proposed for the period September–December 1957 was approximately $900,000. If the campaign was continued in 1958, the cost would be approximately $1,300,000.

In May 1957, Mr. Johnson and other members of management were faced with these questions: Should the corporation undertake a major advertising program in mass-consumer publications? If so, should the specific program developed by the advertising agency be used? If not, what kind of program should be undertaken?

~~~

CASE 3: GREAT RIVER PAPER CORPORATION [1]

QUESTIONS TO CONSIDER: *(1) What corporation image is management seeking? (2) Whom does management wish to influence? (3) What patronage motives might be of significance in Great River's marketing operation? (4) Has the advertising agency come up with a good statement of objectives? (5) Should the company conduct an institutional campaign? If so, what type of campaign? (6) What alternative uses might management make of the monies proposed for institutional advertising?*

---

[1] Fictitious name. Written by Martin V. Marshall.

In November 1955, Mr. William Walters, vice president of sales of the Great River Paper Corporation, Savannah, Georgia, was in the process of making a final decision regarding the institutional advertising program of the company for 1956. Specifically, he was concerned with the objective of the company's institutional campaign in general business media.

Company Background

The Great River Paper Corporation was founded in 1911 as a manufacturer of magazine publication papers. It prospered until the early 1930's when sales and profits decreased significantly. At that time management decided to undertake what came to be known as the Corporate Diversification Program, which took the company into the manufacture and marketing of what were essentially five categories of paper: (1) bonds and related grades, (2) coated grades, (3) uncoated grades, (4) uncoated groundwood papers, and (5) corrugated boxboard and boxboard liner.

Bonds and related groups consisted of bond papers for letterheads and general printing papers, register bond paper for business and accounting forms, ledger paper, mimeograph papers, duplicator papers, and opaque paper. These papers were sold either to paper merchants, who in turn sold to printers and other customers, or to paper converters or other large users, who used the paper to make business and accounting forms. In 1954 Great River held 9.9% share of industry sales of bonds and related groups.

Coated paper grades consisted of papers with special pigmented (conversion) coatings which were used for covers for catalogues, pamphlets, booklets, magazines, advertising pieces, and so forth; machine coated papers which were used for the cover and body of magazines; and label papers for labels. These papers were sold either to paper merchants, who in turn sold to printers, or to magazine publishers. Most of these papers were made in two grades, one for letterpress printing, the other for offset lithography. In 1954 Great River held 8.1% share of industry sales of coated grades.

Uncoated grades consisted of offset printing papers, supercalendered papers for magazines, rough-finish papers for book publishers, envelope stock, and tablet papers. These papers were sold to paper merchants, magazine and book publishers, and converters (envelope and tablet manufacturers). In 1954 Great River held 6.8% share of industry sales of uncoated grades.

Uncoated groundwood grades consisted primarily of printing and offset papers and some converting grades. These were sold to paper merchants and converters. In 1954 Great River held 9.8% share of industry sales of uncoated groundwood grades.

By 1955 Great River was one of the ten largest of approximately 20 principal competitors manufacturing products competitive with Great

River's lines. Total Great River sales in 1954 were $135 million, about equally divided between *white* papers (bonds, coated and uncoated grades, and uncoated groundwood grades) and *brown* papers (boxboard and boxboard liners). Since the beginning of its Corporate Diversification Program, the company had been profitable, profits in 1954 being 5.5% of sales after taxes.

The Company's Channels of Distribution

In 1955 the Great River company sold *white papers* through three channels of distribution. (1) On a tonnage basis, 54% of total sales were through paper merchants. This paper was either shipped directly to the merchant's warehouse for reshipment in smaller quantities to his customers, or was shipped directly to a merchant's customers if the order constituted a carload sale. (2) Sixteen per cent of total volume was sold direct to paper converters or large users who usually purchased carload lots. (3) Thirty per cent of total volume was sold direct to two types of publication accounts: publishers of magazines and books. Magazine accounts were usually sold on a contract of a year or longer with set prices for at least 90-day periods during the year. Book publishing account orders were shipped direct to the printer from the mill and billed either direct or through a merchant for each shipment.

A summary of traceable sales of white papers in tons by end-use for Great River versus the industry for the year 1954 follows:

	Great River White Paper Sales	% of Total Great River White Paper Sales	Total Industry White Paper Sales	% of Total Industry White Paper Sales	Great River % of Industry
Commercial printing......	109,704	39.4%	1,614,396	32.9%	6.8%
Magazines...............	103,586	37.2	1,749,459	35.7	5.9
Book publishers..........	16,975	6.1	268,394	5.5	6.3
Converting..............	41,588	14.9	1,190,369	24.2	3.5
Second and job lots........	5,352	1.9	84,126	1.7	6.4
All others...............	1,293	0.5	....	...	...
Total..............	278,498	100%	4,906,744	100%	5.7%

All paperboard products were sold direct, usually on the basis of a long-term contract.

The Company's Sales Organization

The sales organization of the Great River Paper Corporation was headed by the vice president of sales who maintained his principal office in Savannah, Georgia, and a second office in New York. He was assisted by three sales managers who were located in the Savannah, New York, and Chicago sales offices. There were four salesmen in the Savannah office, all of whom sold the complete line of white papers manufactured by

the company. They called on users of paper, printers, and paper merchants. There were seven salesmen in the Chicago office. Six sold the
company's entire white paper line, and one specialized in printing grades
of paper. There were ten salesmen in the New York office. Seven sold the
company's entire white paper line, two specialized in book publishing
grades, and one specialized in printing grades. In addition, three other
salesmen reported to the sales manager in New York. Two salesmen were
located in Boston, where one sold all Great River white paper lines and
the other called on firms specializing in promotional materials. The third
salesman was located in Philadelphia and sold the entire Great River white
paper line.

The brown papers were sold by a small, separate sales force.

The Company's Sales Promotional Activities

During the period 1935–55, Great River executives believed that a
sound sales promotional and advertising program was essential to the accomplishment of their Corporate Diversification Program. The company's sales promotional activities could be separated into roughly three
periods: 1935–39, 1940–46, and 1946–55.

1935–39. Sales promotional efforts during this period were restricted
to the use of sales aids for company and merchant salesmen: sample books,
e.g., a book showing all grades of bonds manufactured by the Great River
company; and demonstration portfolios, e.g., a portfolio showing bristols
as covers for various types of advertising pamphlets. Expenditures for
sales aids during this period ranged from $20 thousand to $40 thousand
annually.

1940–46. In 1940 company executives believed that they had made
sufficient progress on their Corporate Diversification Program so that
they could profitably spend a larger sum of money on promotion. In that
year they began to publish a house organ, *Great River Printing News,*
which was sent to approximately 15,000 individuals interested in the
graphic arts: printers, advertising agencies, advertisers, and so forth. In
addition, they began to use trade papers. Expenditures during this period
were approximately $20,000 annually for sales aids, $50,000 for advertisements in trade papers, and $15,000 for the *Great River Printing News.*

1945–55. At the end of World War II, Great River executives believed
that they should (1) increase expenditures for promotion, and (2) begin
a Corporate Advertising Program—an institutional advertising program.
The increased expenditures for promotion for the years 1945–55 are summarized in Exhibit 1. With regard to the Corporate Advertising Program,
Mr. Walters said:

> At the end of the war, we felt that we were about at this stage in the accom-
> plishment of our Corporate Diversification Program: We now had diversifica-
> tion—we were in the printing business, book publishing, magazine-publication,
> and boxboard markets; we had pretty strong representation among paper mer-

Exhibit 1

GREAT RIVER PAPER CORPORATION

Sales Promotional and Advertising Expenditures of the Great River Paper Corporation, 1945–55

Year	White Paper Division						Brown Paper Div.	Pulp	Misc.	Dept. Exp.	Total
	Trade Papers	National Media	House Organ	Promot. Portfolio	Direct Mail*	Sample Books					
1945	$61,938	....	$18,917	$12,627	$ 7,080	....	....	....	....	$ 19,478	$120,040
1946	60,972	$ 28,368	38,325	39,494	15,312	....	$ 1,577	$10,172	$9,464	23,667	227,351
1947	69,556	35,730	28,759	87,050	33,380	....	8,634	11,789	7,455	25,764	308,117
1948	60,000	72,000	53,695	96,920	23,491	$13,424	4,839	12,972	8,406	31,000	376,747
1949	21,222	54,329	53,700	97,410	26,055	36,394	5,867	....	9,285	40,000	344,262
1950	42,925	....	32,075	84,398	23,118	46,031	5,381	8,185	1,650	50,841	294,604
1951	32,000	49,898	49,694	65,438	24,833	32,163	14,251	8,738	3,668	50,250	330,933
1952	32,037	229,690	35,203	120,613	28,023	53,969	15,026	8,845	1,924	60,771	586,101
1953	50,853	175,333	43,394	128,172	28,600	84,670	13,236	9,251	....	75,000	608,409
1954	52,000	153,000	42,000	148,575	36,000	57,175	29,135	9,625	1,500	100,000	619,010
1955†	52,500	172,500	47,000	154,000	36,000	84,500	35,000	9,600	766	95,000	732,866

* Expenditures for the mailing of promotional portfolios, reprints of advertisements, and other sales material to the trade.
† Budget figures for 1955.

Source: Company records.

chants; and we had some recognition among specifiers and users of paper. But we did not feel that we yet had enough acceptance for Great River, "A Quality Paper for Every Need."

Hence, it made sense to us to undertake an advertising campaign, the purpose of which was to build strong attitudes toward the Great River company and trade-mark among every kind of audience that might have some effect on the buying of paper.

We began this program with $28,000 expenditure in *Business Week* in 1946 and have continued the program ever since, with the exception of 1950, which was a year of recession in the white paper industry.

The Corporate Advertising Program in 1956

During 1955 Mr. Walters had given more than ordinary attention to the planning of the company promotional program for 1956, because the company's director of advertising was retiring at the end of the year and Mr. Walters wanted this executive's successor to have the benefit of an intensive review of past and future promotional strategy. Although Mr. Walters had raised many questions regarding the company's promotional strategy during the year, in November he was primarily concerned with the question of the objectives of the Corporate Advertising Program.

At the time, Mr. Walters had various information before him bearing upon the question. This information is given below.

Agency Recommendations. The following is a digest of the written recommendations of the company's advertising agency regarding the Corporate Diversification Program for 1956.

Objectives. Why should the Great River Paper Corporation undertake a national, broad-base program of corporate advertising? What are its principal reasons for doing so, and in what order might these reasons most logically be stated?

Anyone, knowing Great River and being required to answer these questions, could do so. But his answers would be based primarily upon a personal interpretation of corporate advertising to him. To avoid personal opinion of this sort, we shall answer the questions against a background of facts.

In November 1953, McGraw-Hill Publishing Company conducted a survey among a cross section of national industrial advertisers, in order to ascertain the major objectives of their corporate advertising and the relative importance of each. Contributing to the survey were 863 companies which gave the following objectives of their corporate advertising and of the order that we shall use in defining the objectives of Great River corporate advertising.

1. To establish, maintain, and increase profits
2. To keep the corporate name before buyers
3. To publicize the company's facilities and services
4. To aid salesmen and distributors
5. To create public interest in the corporation
6. To emphasize company experience and skill
7. To establish product quality to overcome price competition
8. To establish position in industry
9. To address distributors
10. To suggest other media of advertising

Within the framework of these ten basic objectives can be included virtually any complementary objective, major or minor, that has not been included here, for corporate advertising, by its very nature, provides the background for underscoring its user's aspirations and accomplishments.

Alternative Approaches. The style and technique of corporate advertising are virtually limitless, ranging from the pure editorial, all-type advertisements in one color to the two-page, multi-illustrated advertisements in full color. The themes are lot less limitless, ranging from the institutional story told in many words of self-adulation to the impressionistic story told in the fewest words possible.

It is not our purpose to recommend a single, specific approach, except to return in 1956 to the use of full color, because full color will enhance the advertising, attract more readers, and allow better reproduction. Instead, we wish to explore various possibilities.

The agency suggests six possibilities.

First, the company could return to the trade-mark series of 1952–53. Here the name "Great River Papers" would be dramatically emphasized, e.g., a card section at a college football game spelling out "Great River Papers," and the copy would point out the quality, characteristics, and versatility of Great River papers for virtually any and every printing need and use, as well as the experience, know-how, progress, and growth of the Great River Paper Corporation.

Second, the company could take a completely new approach to the trade-mark series. The trade-mark could be sculptured, cut, woven, etc., in marble, wood, silver, etc., in three dimensions and then photographed in appropriate surroundings. As the series progresses, a fascinating collection of trade-marks could be accumulated for exhibits at conventions and by merchants. Copy could point out that fine craftsmanship requires fine paper; that Great River papers are unsurpassed; and that Great River experience, know-how, and research provide fine paper for every printing need.

Third, the company might profit from an American industries series, i.e., promote other American industries and businesses. Here we envision advertisements composed of imaginative paintings symbolic of different industries and copy indicating that Great River is a manufacturer for every American industry; without paper, industry would grind to a halt; and Great River papers help keep America growing.

Fourth, the company could feature an industrial research series. Here we envision dramatic paintings of the products of research that have yet to scratch the surface of their future potentialities: the solar battery, the man-made satellite, automation, the transistor, etc. Copy would emphasize that research is big business. Because of research, our standard of living increases. Without paper, research couldn't be done.

Fifth, the company could run a reader-benefit series. The purpose of this series would be to make graphic, with the use of human-interest paintings, how paper in general and Great River papers in particular touch and effect the lives of everyone. Copy would emphasize that Great River papers are a part of everyday living: a child can thank Great River for education; a purchasing agent can thank Great River for making his work easier, etc.

Sixth, the company could use the corporation story series: the history, growth, and significance of Great River. Here we'd like to tell Great River's story with a series of dramatically rugged paintings of the women and men who, from the woods to the shipping of the finished products, are responsible for the making of Great River papers.

One of the six possible alternatives, in our opinion the American industry series offers the highest potential, i.e., the highest promise of attaining the ten basic objectives of Great River corporate advertising. It is important, unselfish, and refreshing. Against the background of all American industry, the significance and leadership of Great River can be told with restraint. It can create the climate most favorable to the effectiveness of corporate advertising: reader interest, believability, and an effective acceptance of advertised facts.

Our second choice is the industrial research series, and our third choice is the reader-benefit series.

Media. In 1956, we recommend the continued use of *Time* and *U.S. News and World Report* on the basis of 13 insertions, because (1) by advertising 13 times, you are represented in every fourth issue of these publications and thus enjoy the continuity so important to the effectiveness of corporate advertising; and (2) by advertising 13 times, you enjoy a 13-time rate.

If the budget permits, we should like to see *Fortune* added to the schedule for 12 insertions, because *Fortune* has become an important, well-read magazine among top-management men.

There are, of course, other publications that could be given serious consideration: *Newsweek, Business Week, Nation's Business, Forbes, Barron's,* and the *Wall Street Journal.*

Alternative media schedules follow.

SCHEDULE No. 1

			Cost per Page	
Time.....................	Full-page, two-color	13 times	$11,525	$149,825
U.S. News & World Report....	Full-page, two-color	13 times	4,360	56,680
Fortune...................	Full-page, two-color	12 times	4,010	48,120
			Total.........	$254,625

SCHEDULE No. 2

Time.....................	Full-page, B & W	13 times	$ 9,295	$120,835
U.S. News & World Report....	Full-page, B & W	13 times	3,775	49,075
Fortune...................	Full-page, B & W	12 times	3,320	39,840
			Total.........	$209,750

Mr. Walters' Views on the Corporate Advertising Program. Having been for many years a marketing executive and member of the company's Advertising Committee, Mr. Walters believed that he knew the general views of various members of top management regarding the Corporate Advertising Program. He said,

All of us agree that it was wise to undertake the Corporate Advertising Program, but there are several different views regarding the specifics of it.

First, there is a disagreement concerning how much we spend on it. The program is budgeted at $172,000 for 1955, and the agency is proposing an expenditure of $255,000 in 1956. We can only spend so much in total for all promotion. How much is this program worth to the corporation?

Unfortunately, we don't have quantitative information to use in evaluating the program. Its effect cannot be measured in sales increases per se. Nor do we have readership figures for our advertisements. We do know that all of us can cite situations in which we think that our relationships with businessmen, merchants, and printers have been helped by the corporate advertising. We know that we are now known as a big factor in the business and printing paper fields by many persons, and yet there is some evidence that some people aren't convinced. For example, we know that many business people don't think of us when they specify bonds for letterheads. They think of Company A. Yet we sell nearly as much bond for letterheads as Company A.

Second, there is disagreement regarding the approach we should take in our corporate advertising. Here are a few examples of what we have done in the past [see Exhibits 2 and 3].

Exhibit 2

GREAT RIVER PAPER CORPORATION

Advertisement in 1949 Issue of *Fortune*

Illustration:	Man and woman looking at huge deposit and withdrawal slips painted on a red wall.
Headline:	What shall it be?
Copy:	The steady rise in personal savings—they are now up to an annual rate in excess of 15 billions—has the economists asking questions: Is it a buyers' strike? Is it fear of depression? Is it preparation for a spending spree?
	Whatever the answer, the purchasing power exists to make retail sales potentially enormous this year.
	Paper, as usual, will be a major factor in the successful tapping of this great reservoir of accoumulated savings and its use in the form of advertisements, booklets, catalogues, folders, letters, displays, and packages will determine the winner of the paper battle between deposit and withdrawal slips.
	Great River Papers of the Great River, Madison, and Newark lines—by the makers of a Quality Paper for Every Need—are completely impartial in the world of selling. Intelligently used, they can sell savings accounts as persuasively as they can sell anything worth saving for. Specify and use them for good printing, better impressions, and "the best buy in paper today."

Source: Company records.

One group of our executives would like to continue to emphasize our name, for example, the trade-mark series. They would like to associate it with our progress in research—we have just completed a new, million-dollar research building. Another group would like to develop a specific campaign aimed at a given kind of business, for example, the letterhead business, as Company A has done. Another group believes that our national media program should be exclusively product advertising. And another group looks upon the program in a broader sense: They feel that our corporate program should be addressed to eight audiences: the general public; stockholders; employees, particularly union members; businessmen who specify paper; printers; merchants; advertising agencies; and graphic arts specialists.

Another Executive's Views. The following expresses another executive's views:

It is extremely difficult to generalize about how or why given brands or even grades of paper are purchased or the value of an institutional advertising program.

In the magazine field, we have developed special papers at considerable expense to meet the needs of several large publishers. As long as we maintain acceptable quality and a competitive price, the only other factor affecting sales is to maintain a good personal relationship. Actually there is really no problem, because we have asked our principal accounts to purchase at least 50% of their

Exhibit 3

GREAT RIVER PAPER CORPORATION

Advertisement in 1954 Issue of *Time* (Trade-mark Series)

Illustration: Navajo Indians weaving a huge rug with "Great River Paper" in center, in four colors.

Headline: Planning a new catalogue?

Copy: Whatever products your catalogue will be designed to sell, it will be, itself a product of *paper*. So start right there. Choose a paper that will do justice to the reproductions of the products it must sell, and thus increase your chances of making people buy. For the best by letterpress, insist on Newark Enamel, the aristocrat of glossy coated. For tops by offset, specify River-rite Offset. These are only two of many Great River Papers which include covers in a wide range of colors.

Great River Papers mean business, as your printer or lithographer, backed by America's leading paper merchants everywhere, will tell you.

Great River Printing News, a colorful quarterly now in its fourteenth year, shows Great River Papers at work. Called "the most stimulating paper demonstrator ever produced," each issue is chock-full of ideas. If you are an advertiser or a creater or a producer of advertising of any sort, a complimentary copy will be mailed to you in exchange for your request on your business letterhead.

Source: Company records.

requirements elsewhere, whereas they would like to obtain more tonnage from us.

In the book field, when we sell direct, quality, price, and direct selling are important. When we sell through merchants, business is obtained primarily on the basis of the friendship between the merchant and his book account. If he provides a good quality paper at a competitive price, and provides good service, he will retain his accounts. And it is difficult for him to take business away from a competitive merchant.

The printing field is more complicated. As a rule, printers maintain several sources of supply. In some cases, they tend to give most of their business to one paper merchant through sheer habit, so long as the merchant stocks acceptable grades and brands of papers. In other cases, they switch merchants, grades, and brands continuously, for a variety of reasons. For one thing, prices do vary. For another, printers are always finding fault with papers, principally because there are many things that can go wrong on a printing job and more often than not the printer will blame the paper—often rightly so.

I might mention here that herein lies one of the real problems of selling printing papers. On the one hand, if a printer finds a given mill brand works well for him, it is almost impossible to get him to change brands. On the other hand, if we try to sell a printer on one of our grades, he may use it, but a dozen things can go wrong so that it is difficult for him to determine the specific virtues of any given paper.

In this field we find it worthwhile for our own salesmen to do quite a good deal of work, not only in selling a printer on our papers but in watching him to see to it that he uses our papers properly.

Undoubtedly the paper merchant is the important factor in the printing paper market. If he maintains complete stocks, competitive prices, excellent service, and good personal relationships, he will develop an excellent business for us over a period of time.

Cracking the business paper market is extremely tough. A lot of our people feel that businessmen will specify a mill brand bond for letterheads, particularly Company A's, and that, accordingly, we should seek to establish a brand preference of our own Great River and River-rite trade-marks among businessmen. My own view is that businessmen pretty much depend upon their printers to come up with a good letterhead—paper and printing—and don't know and don't care about the mill brand used. Hence, the printer probably determines the mill brand used, and he, in turn, probably buys pretty much on a basis of habit.

By and large, white papers are all pretty well standardized, both in quality and price. Since we do push our merchants more than competitors do, however, they tend to be more aggressive on price in contrast to other merchants. All things considered, though, sales at the merchant level depend primarily on their own sales, promotional, and service efforts.

Merchants pretty much stick to one or two mills as sources of supply, since they have established relationships with suppliers which extend 20, 50, 70 years. They seldom change suppliers. As long as they have good paper supplied them, at a cost which will allow them to be competitive price-wise in their markets, plus some sales, promotional, and advertising aid, they are satisfied. If they are satisfied with the basic marketing program of a mill, they'll stick. It takes a major disagreement to cause a merchant to change suppliers.

~~~

CASE 4: DETERMINATION OF THE USE OF INSTITUTIONAL ADVERTISING IN OTHER INSTANCES

Reconsider the following cases with respect to whether some type of institutional advertising might be effectively employed.

Section IV

THE BUILDING OF ADVERTISING PROGRAMS

An Introductory Note

In the previous section, stress has been laid upon appraising the opportunity, if any, to employ advertising effectively in the marketing mix for the longer term. Inevitably, consideration of advertising as a selling tool for the longer term raises questions about and involves discussion of specific sales promotional programs, including specific advertising programs. For example, analysis of the Emery Air Freight Service case invited consideration of detailed problems of advertising copy and media. But the previous section was designed not to deal with the problems of planning and implementing sales promotional and advertising programs but rather to allow the reader to develop skill in analyzing and acting upon advertising as a strategic selling tool in the marketing mix. Accordingly, this section builds upon that skill; but the stress is shifted to consideration of a number of problems that usually occur in the building of advertising programs.

Because a decision regarding any part of an advertising program is interrelated with decisions regarding the advertising program as a whole and of the over-all sales promotional program of which it is a part, cases were chosen for this section which allow analyses to be made in the light of these pertinent interrelationships. For example, Carpet Institute, Inc. (F), a case in this section, concerns issues of copy and media in the light of the information given in Carpet Institute, Inc. (A–E), in Section II. One chapter of declaratory material is given to present an over-all view of the major considerations governing the building of advertising programs.

Chapter 10

∿∿∿∿∿∿∿∿∿∿∿∿∿∿∿∿∿∿∿∿∿∿∿∿∿∿∿∿∿∿∿∿

BACKGROUND MATERIAL ON
THE BUILDING OF
ADVERTISING PROGRAMS

The task of building an advertising program calls for consideration of countless problems. Although advertising specialists usually
handle the details of many of these problems, particularly those of advertising copy and media, members of management should have an understanding of them in order to work effectively with specialists and in order properly to direct and evaluate their efforts. For our purposes there
are six problem areas relating to the building of advertising programs that
are of significance to management: (1) the determination of advertising
objectives, (2) the choice of advertising messages (that is, advertising
copy), (3) the selection and use of media, (4) the co-ordination of advertising with the other tools of sales promotion, (5) the evaluation of advertising, and (6) the control of the advertising budget. These problem
areas are discussed below.

Determination of Advertising Objectives

At the outset it should be recognized that the most important problem
area involved in the building of advertising programs is the determination
of advertising objectives, and that it is management which has chief responsibility for establishing these objectives.

If good objectives are developed and clearly stated at the beginning of
the building process, then all those who are concerned with the planning
of advertising programs can attack the other problem areas with relative
ease and good purpose. Copy specialists can utilize their talents to solve a
specific problem, not simply to prepare interesting advertisements; media
experts can use their knowledge effectively; the sales force can co-ordi-

nate its sales presentations with the theme of the advertising; and so on.
Too often, advertising objectives are not clear-cut, are too general, or
are nonexistent. Under these circumstances, everyone concerned with the
building process lacks good direction and consequently finds it difficult, if
not impossible, to use his knowledge and skills effectively. Probably the
most important reason for the often-expressed dissatisfaction with the
work of specialists stems from managements' failure to give specialists
clear-cut, sound objectives for advertising.

As is evident from analysis of cases in previous sections, the specific
objectives sought in advertising programs of various businesses are
infinite in number. It may be useful, however, to list several objectives
which are commonly employed by business.

A. Commonly employed objectives for programs of consumer advertising:
  1. To inform prospects of the existence of a new product (or service).
  2. To inform prospects and users of the differentiating characteristics
     of an established brand.
  3. To correct misconceptions or poor attitudes toward a brand.
  4. To increase the frequency of use of a product.
  5. To suggest new uses for a product.
  6. To inform prospects and uses of improvements which have been
     made in an established product.
  7. To remind users to use a product.
  8. To educate customers in how to use a product.
  9. To build patronage motives, such as the service organization behind
     a product.
  10. To present special offers, such as premiums, price deals, or contests.
  11. To inform prospects of the retailers selling a brand.
  12. To enhance the image of the brand by identifying it with ideas,
      persons, or objects having positive associations.
  13. To solicit inquiries.
  14. To obtain sales, particularly mail-order sales.
  15. To build a corporate image.
B. Commonly employed objectives for programs of advertising directed
   to the trade:
  1. To inform the trade of the existence of a new product.
  2. To present reasons why the trade should stock and sell a brand.
  3. To keep the trade informed of marketing and promotional programs
     for a brand which are directed to consumers.
  4. To present special offers to the trade, such as trade deals.
  5. To build patronage motives, such as the availability of special train-
     ing programs for retailers' salespeople.
  6. To solicit middlemen and retailers.
  7. To give an explanation to the trade of company practices and ac-
     tivities.
C. Commonly employed objectives for programs of industrial advertising:
  1. To inform prospects of a new product (or service).
  2. To present detailed technical information about a new product.
  3. To build desired product image.
  4. To inform prospects of the differentiating characteristics of an es-
     tablished product.
  5. To suggest new uses for a product.

6. To inform prospects and users of improvements in a product.
7. To build patronage motives, such as technical service provided by the manufacturer.
8. To build corporate image.
9. To solicit inquiries from prospects for the use of salesmen or sales representatives.
10. To solicit inquiries for literature.

The lists of objectives given above are not all-inclusive, and the objectives, as stated, are fairly general. In any given situation, the reader should try to be much more explicit in his definition of objectives. To illustrate, in the Baumritter Corporation case (see pages 222–43), which, it will be recalled, described the marketing mix of a furniture manufacturer, a few of the objectives to which advertising might have been directed may be defined as follows:

1. To illustrate for prospects the pieces in the "Ethan Allen" line, in order that prospects could see for themselves the *design* of the furniture.
2. To educate prospects regarding the values of a co-ordinated line, that is, the values of being able to buy pieces of furniture for many rooms in a house which had been designed so that all pieces were harmonious.
3. To educate prospects regarding the values of buying open-stock furniture, that is, if a consumer bought a piece of Ethan Allen furniture today, he could also buy another co-ordinated piece five or ten years from today.
4. To build the reputation of the brand for "good quality at a reasonable price."
5. To list exclusive Baumritter dealers.
6. To describe the decorating counsel provided by Baumritter dealers.
7. To solicit inquiries from consumers.

The Baumritter company did not seek to attain all of these objectives, primarily because of a limited promotional budget, but the main point illustrated by the list is that in any given situation fairly specific objectives can be developed. Which objective or objectives to seek among many possible ones turns on value judgments of which objectives are most important, which are most likely to lend themselves to effective presentation in advertising, and whether sufficient funds are available to accomplish the objectives.

As was indicated in Chapter 6, analysis of market forces and marketing elements bearing on the marketing mix leads to a reasonably clear-cut picture of the selling job to be done. Responsibility for accomplishing various parts or stages of the selling job may then be assigned to the various selling tools. In the Baumritter company situation, for example, company sales representatives were assigned the major burden of getting the Baumritter "story" across to dealers so that they in turn would display and promote Baumritter furniture effectively to consumers. Advertising was employed primarily to elicit trade effort, only secondarily to inform consumers of the characteristics of Baumritter furniture. Given this specific objective for advertising, specialists could effectively employ their talents in devising Baumritter advertising.

Management must assume chief responsibility for the determination of advertising objectives, because of its control of the marketing mix and because the purposes to which advertising are put are dictated by the marketing mix that management chooses to employ. Further, the considerations which ultimately lead to the final determination of the objectives of an advertising program naturally evolve out of analysis of market forces and marketing elements bearing on the mix, an analysis that has to be done primarily by management, not advertising specialists. Too frequently management tries to shift responsibility for the determination of advertising objectives to specialists, with unsatisfactory results. Specialists are not privy to all of the considerations governing the establishment of advertising objectives; they can counsel with management, but they cannot make decisions for management. To illustrate, the advertising objectives to seek are always determined in large part by the size of the fund which management can and is willing to appropriate to sales promotion. Only management can make this decision.

One other aspect involved in the determination of advertising objectives should be emphasized, namely, that after management has defined the ideal objectives which it wishes to seek, it must reconsider them in the light of the realities which develop when advertising specialists attempt to implement them. In many instances, objectives must be modified because specialists cannot develop effective advertisements; for example, the original objectives may be too abstract to be effectively communicated to prospects. In other instances, objectives must be redefined because the costs of attaining them are more than the company can afford. In still other instances the kind of media required to obtain a given objective may not be available; for example, manufacturers frequently may desire to employ spot television announcements in order to demonstrate products, but find that suitable times for such announcements cannot be purchased. Accordingly, as the building process proceeds and management and specialists analyze the detailed problems involved, the reader should appreciate that newly found considerations may call for changes in the objectives which were initially established.

Advertising Copy

Advertising copy is discussed next rather than advertising media, because decisions regarding the advertising messages to be employed in an advertising program are usually considered to be somewhat more important than decisions regarding the media in which they are presented. It should be recognized, however, that analyses and decisions regarding copy and media are undertaken more or less simultaneously, and that often the media decision must be made first in order to determine the specific type of advertising message to employ. For example, if demonstration of the product is desired, it may be necessary to commit the advertising program to the use of television before it is worthwhile to have specialists develop specific advertisements. Another reason for discussing advertising copy next is that, in one sense, the end product of all analyses and decisions regarding the use of advertising in the sales promotional program is *the advertisement*. The effectiveness of advertising as a selling tool is determined in large part by the ability of the advertisement to communicate a message to prospects which will inform or influence them to favor the product or service being advertised.

The chief problem confronting management with respect to advertising copy is that there are many conflicting views as to what is an effective or ineffective advertisement and as to what is involved in the task of communicating messages to people in advertisements and in various types of advertising media. Accordingly, management must have some basis for approving or disapproving the alternative advertisements presented to it by advertising specialists. Several fundamental considerations governing management's decision making on advertising copy are given below.

An Over-all View. Over the years advertising practitioners have developed a useful body of working generalizations regarding the creation of advertisements. These generalizations are helpful to advertising specialists when they develop alternative advertisements for management's approval. An understanding of these generalizations by management facilitates mutual appraisal of alternatives. But useful working generalizations do not provide the basis for management to predict the ability of a particular advertisement to solve its particular advertising problem. This conclusion must be based upon empirical reasoning, value judgments, the use of measurement techniques, or a combination of all three.

It should be recognized that in most instances management operates with incomplete knowledge of consumer buying behavior and consequently must expect a good deal of uncertainty in its own thinking and that of its advertising specialists with respect to the probable effectiveness of any advertisement. It cannot expect advertising specialists to guarantee that a particular advertisement will solve a particular advertising problem. A wise management takes a realistic view regarding the degree of uncertainty involved in its advertising operation and tries over time through analyses of operating experience, experiments, and special projects to reduce the degree of uncertainty.

The Number of Objectives. In preparing an advertisement or a series of advertisements, there is a natural desire to accomplish as many objectives as possible. There is the ever-present desire to include *one more appeal* in a particular advertisement or in a campaign. But the weight of empirical evidence suggests strongly that the most effective advertisements and advertising campaigns are those which focus upon a single objective and which emphasize a single idea or piece of information. Most manufacturers have employed this approach; for example, for years "Lux" soap has proclaimed itself as the soap used by Hollywood movie stars, "Maxwell House" coffee has emphasized that "it is good to the last drop," and "Scotties" facial tissue has emphasized its "wet-strength" properties. Further, the evidence indicates that even a single objective is difficult to obtain in a short period of time; a great deal of repetition of a single key appeal is characteristic of most advertising programs. Consequently, in selecting problems to be solved and in evaluating alternative advertisements, management must have particular care for the number of objectives it seeks to accomplish. A decision regarding this issue essentially involves a value judgment of the probable effectiveness of a given schedule of given advertisements in given media.

Types of Advertisements and Advertising. Perusal of the literature of advertising and study of advertisements by the reader will indicate that there are many useful classifications of types of advertisements and advertising which can be of help to management when it appraises potential advertisements. Some of these classifications will be considered in the cases of Chapter 12, which concerns the preparation of advertisements, and some of the literature dealing with advertising copy is listed in selected references in Chapter 12. Suffice it to state here that although the preparation of specific advertisements is essentially the province of advertising specialists, members of management who make decisions regarding advertising should have some understanding of the creative aspects of advertising. They should have some knowledge of the principal theories and ideas of advertising specialists regarding what is involved in the communication process and of the nomenclature they used in their work.

Although members of management cannot always be expected to have a knowledge of the creative aspects of advertising comparable to that of specialists, they should be familiar with the means by which specialists and management can evaluate the effectiveness of various types of advertisements.

The Evaluation of Advertisements. Everyone working in the field of advertising has appreciated that there is usually a good deal of uncertainty regarding the probable or actual effectiveness of an advertisement or a series of advertisements and that it is desirable, insofar as possible, to seek to reduce the degree of uncertainty by utilizing certain tools of so-called copy research. Generally the tools of copy research have been referred to as "premeasurement" or "pretesting" and "post-measurement" or "post-testing" methods. In other words, tests are conducted to determine the probable effectiveness of an advertisement before it is published and studies are made after publication to determine whether the advertisement was in fact effective. The principal aspects of testing are discussed below.

Determination of What Is to Be Tested. When advertisements are to be tested, the advertiser must decide what he seeks to test. Is it sales effect or something short of sales?

Let us go back briefly to the definitions and classifications of advertising set forth in the Chapter 1. There we pointed out that a majority of the advertising of manufacturers does not seek a direct sales response and therefore it may be expected that measurement of an advertisement which has an immediate objective other than sales may not be measurable in sales or profit contribution. For example, the advertisement published by Columbia for its stereophonic high-fidelity equipment (see page 7) was not designed to obtain a sale but was designed to develop favorable attitudes toward the Columbia brand which might eventually affect the shopping and buying behavior of consumers. On the other hand, mail-order advertising seeks immediate sales response; hence, the sales and profit contributions may be determined.

Therefore, in testing indirect-action advertisements, it should be noted that the testing techniques commonly employed *do not measure directly* the effect of an advertisement upon buying behavior and thus upon sales. Rather they are usually used to obtain a measurement of whether or not an advertisement communicates the message which the advertiser desires to communicate and, if so, to what extent. What happens to the prospect's buying behavior after he understands the advertiser's message is a subject requiring consideration of all elements which may affect his buying behavior.

The Purposes of Pre- and Post-Measurements. The purposes of pre- and post-measurements have already been touched upon. Premeasurement techniques are employed to provide evidence which will help management make a better prediction of the ability of alternative advertisements to solve a problem before they are published; post-measurement techniques are made in order to appraise attainment after they are published, and to provide further a basis for improving the effectiveness of the advertising operation in the future. Over-all, measurements of the ability of advertisements to communicate messages are desired by management in order that it may establish guiding principles by which to operate. This desire for guides is reflected in the widespread efforts of advertisers and advertising practitioners to build "check lists" by which to develop and appraise advertisements before publication. The advertiser wishes to be sure that his advertisement will be seen or heard and that it will leave a deep impression or will bring a desired response. Ever since advertisers started to dissect advertisements to determine what made them effective, formulae to guide the creation of advertisements have been sought. The efforts to build check lists have been aided in recent decades by the fact that managements generally have been more aware of the need for objective evidence regarding the value of different types of advertisements and have been willing to appropriate funds required to make measurements.

It should be emphasized again that check lists can be useful guides in building individual advertisements, but that they do not provide an automatic formula for creating advertisements of known effectiveness.

The Techniques of Pre- and Post-Measurement. The most widely used measuring techniques are briefly noted below. When appropriate, they are discussed in detail in the cases of this section. No attempt will be made here to appraise the relative merits of the various methods.

In *pretesting*, advertisers generally make use of three techniques: (1) consumer juries, (2) inquiry tests, and (3) local area tests. Only the consumer-jury method may truly be considered a pretest. Inquiry and local area tests involve post-measurements in a restricted area or restricted media to determine the advertisements to be employed in larger operations.

1. The consumer-jury method essentially involves the exposure of alternative advertisements to a sample or "jury" of prospects and the securing of their opinions or reactions to the advertisements. The method may make use of a captive panel, that is, a group of prospects gathered in one place, or a sample of prospects who are independently visited by interviewers or contacted by mail. The method may seek a simple or complex response from the jury member, based upon unaided or aided recall of the advertisements just seen or heard by him. It can be used to test any type of advertisements but is usually employed to pretest print, radio, and television advertisements. The consumer-jury method has been widely used by advertisers because it affords a quick, economical check on the subjective judgment of management and its specialists.[1]

2. Inquiry tests consist of analysis of inquiries from alternative advertisements which have been published independently or on a split-run basis. From the viewpoint of most advertisers, the principal weakness of inquiry tests lies in the fact that they measure the ability of an advertisement to obtain inquiries, not the ability of an advertisement to communicate messages of an indirect-action character. In order to elicit an inquiry, the advertisement must also hold out an offer to the audience: a sample of the product, a useful booklet, a small premium, etc. Thus, inquiry tests tend also to indicate the drawing power of the offer rather than the strength of the advertiser's indirect-action appeals. In mail-order selling inquiry tests of course are quite useful.[2]

3. Local area tests are occasionally used to pretest alternative advertisements because the advertiser desires to try to measure the effect of advertisements on sales or he wishes to obtain a measurement which reflects the ability of advertisements to communicate effectively under normal

---

[1] For a more detailed description of the consumer-jury method, see D. B. Lucas and S. H. Britt, *Advertising Psychology and Research* (New York: McGraw-Hill Book Co., Inc., 1950), chap. xv, pp. 412–36. For an example of a consumer-jury test, see J. S. Cross, R. G. Eldridge, and R. Barbarosa, "The Consumer Jury Method of Measuring Advertising Effectiveness—A Case Study," *Journal of Marketing*, April 1952, pp. 435–39.

[2] For a more detailed description of this method, see Lucas and Britt, *op. cit.*, chap. xix, pp. 524–62. For an example of the use of inquiries, see the Pitney-Bowes, Inc., case in this section (page 920).

operating conditions. When attempting to measure sales effect, the advertiser publishes different advertisements in different local markets that are similar in characteristics and then obtains sales data, either from retailers or consumers, to provide him with data for measurement. There are numerous problems involved in measuring sales effect; suffice to say here that measurements of sales effect are seldom obtained for indirect-action advertising because of the time-lag problem and because the many variables involved are difficult to control.

In *post-testing* advertisements, advertisers have experimented with a great variety of techniques, particularly in recent years. These techniques may be classified usefully in terms of purpose, as follows: (1) measurements of direct response, (2) measurements of whether the advertisement is seen or heard, and (3) measurements of the extent to which communication is obtained.

1. The measurements of direct response of prospects have already been indicated. By maintaining detailed records of inquiries obtained by advertisements, advertisers seek over time to build better guides as to what are effective or ineffective advertisements for them in the light of the conditions under which they operate. By significantly varying the advertisements published in different local areas and through examination of purchase data obtained from retailers or consumers, the advertiser seeks over time to discover significant variations in sales results which he can attribute to differences in the advertisements.

2. Measurements of whether an advertisement is seen or heard include so-called "readership" and "listenership" studies that basically give the advertiser quantitative data regarding the portion of a given audience who saw or heard the advertisements to which the total audience was potentially exposed. These measurements may also seek to obtain quantitative data regarding the parts of an advertisement which were seen or heard.

The best known of the regular readership studies is the Starch Advertisement Readership Service, carried on by Daniel Starch and Staff. This service consists of reports on the readership of all advertisements of one-half page or larger in a selected list of magazines and business publications. The reports give for each advertisement the percentage of readers of the publication who "noted" the advertisement; who associate it with the brand or advertiser—the so-called "seen-associated" rating; and who "read most" of the advertisement.[3]

3. Measurement of the extent to which communication is obtained include recall, attitude, prestige, and brand-product-idea association tests. As distinguished from readership and listenership tests, these tests attempt to obtain a measurement of the extent to which prospects retain advertis-

---

[3] A more complete description of the Starch Advertisement Readership Service is given in the appendix to Pan American Coffee Bureau (D), a case in this section (page 655).

Exhibit 1

A CLASSIFICATION OF TYPES OF ADVERTISING MEDIA

1. *Newspapers*
   a) Daily newspapers (morning and evening)
   b) Sunday newspapers
   c) Weekly newspapers
   d) Religious newspapers
   e) Foreign language newspapers
   f) Newspaper-distributed magazines, such as Sunday supplements (e.g., *This Week, Parade, American Weekly*)

2. *Consumer Magazines*
   a) Mass-audience magazines (e.g., *Life, Look, Readers Digest, The Saturday Evening Post*)
   b) General-audience magazines (e.g., *The New Yorker, Time*)
   c) Women's service magazines (e.g., *Good Housekeeping*)
   d) Women's specialized magazines (e.g., *Harper's Bazaar, True Story*)
   e) Special-interest magazine (e.g., *Model Trains*)
   f) Special-audience magazines (e.g., *Modern Bride*)

3. *Farm Publications*
   a) National
   b) Regional

4. *Business Papers*
   a) General-audience publications (e.g., *Business Week*)
   b) Vertical publications i.e., publications dealing with interests of a particular industry (e.g., *Iron Age*)
   c) Horizontal publications, i.e., publications dealing with interests of a particular functional group (e.g., *Factory Management*)

5. *Radio (Daytime and Nighttime)*
   a) Local stations—programs and spot announcements
   b) Regional networks—programs and spot announcements
   c) National networks—programs and spot announcements

6. *Television (Daytime and Nighttime)*
   a) Sponsored programs (local or network)
   b) Participation in programs (local or network)
   c) Spot announcements (local)

7. *Direct Mail*
   a) Under name of manufacturer
   b) Under name of dealer

8. *Outdoor Advertising*
   a) Twenty-four-sheet posters
   b) Painted posters
   c) Electric spectaculars

9. *Transportation Advertising*
   a) Car cards (in interior of buses, subways, etc.)
   b) Traveling displays (on exterior of cabs, buses, etc.)

10. *Point-of-Purchase Display*
    a) Advertising on the package
    b) Window display
    c) Floor display
    d) Shelf display
    e) Merchandise tags
    f) Booklets for customers
    g) Banners and streamers

11. *Miscellaneous Media*
    a) Motion-picture advertising
    b) Match folders
    c) Novelty giveaways
    d) House organs (when edited for customers)
    e) Classified section of telephone directory

ing messages and have views which may have been induced by an advertisement.

The leading standard service in this area of measurement is the "Impact" reporting service of Gallup & Robinson, Inc., which regularly reports on advertisements published in *Life*, *The Saturday Evening Post*, and *McCall's*. Impact is defined as the depth of impression which an advertisement makes on readers' minds as evidenced by (*a*) registration of the name of the product or advertiser, and (*b*) registration of the advertising message. Evidence of the registration of the advertising message is obtained in the form of verbatim playback of ideas and impressions regarding the advertisements on which readers were able to prove product or advertiser registration.[4]

Advertising Media

The many types of media from which advertisers may choose are indicated in Exhibit 1, which is an arbitrary classification of types of

Exhibit 2

EXPENDITURES IN ADVERTISING MEDIA FOR SELECTED YEARS 1935–57

(In Millions of Dollars)

Medium	1935	1940	1945	1950	1955	1957
Newspapers........	$ 762.1	$ 815.4	$ 921.4	$2,075.6	$3,087.8	$ 3,283.3
Magazines.........	136.3	197.7	364.5	514.9	729.4	814.3
Television.........	....	....	....	170.8	1,025.3	1,026.7
Radio.............	112.6	215.6	423.9	605.4	544.9	622.5
Farm publications...	3.5	6.8	11.8	21.2	33.8	33.7
Business papers.....	51.0	76.0	204.1	251.1	446.2	567.6
Outdoor...........	31.1	44.7	71.7	142.5	192.4	206.1
Direct mail........	281.6	333.7	334.4	803.2	1,298.9	1,470.9
Miscellaneous*.....	311.8	397.7	586.9	1,125.3	1,835.7	2,021.3
Total.........	$1,690.0	$2,087.6	$2,874.5	$5,710.0	$9,194.4	$10,310.6

* This classification includes expenditures for the cost of advertising departments, weekly newspapers, transportation advertising, and point-of-purchase advertising.

Source: "Advertisers' Guide to Marketing for 1959," *Printers' Ink*, Section II, October 31, 1958, pp. 154–55. These data were compiled by the Research Division of McCann-Erickson, Inc., under the direction of Robert J. Coen.

media. Some idea of the relative importance of major media can be gained from Exhibit 2, which presents expenditures for major advertising media for selected years, 1935–57.

Problems of Media Selection and Use. The selection and use of advertising media present problems which are seldom solved altogether satisfactorily by management or media specialists for reasons that are indicated later. In using media, the objective of management is to place its

---

[4] A more complete description of the Gallup & Robinson Impact method is given in Pan American Coffee Bureau (H), a case in this section (page 872).

advertising messages in the media which will reach the maximum number of prospects with the greatest effectiveness at the lowest cost. To achieve this objective, analyses must be made (1) of the match between the prospects whom the advertiser desires to reach and the prospects delivered in the audience of a medium, that is, markets determine media; (2) of the relative ability of different types of media to communicate effectively the advertising messages the advertiser desires to use; and (3) of the actual costs of reaching prospects as contrasted to the costs of buying a medium's audience which provides simply the opportunity to reach prospects.

Matching Prospects and Media Audiences. As emphasized several times previously, the marketer's first job is to identify and define the buyers and potential buyers of his product in order that he may give good direction to all phases of his promotional effort. It was also pointed out that marketers usually can only partially define the characteristics of prospects. This problem has been seen in many of the cases so far in this book, an excellent example being found in the Carpet Institute, Inc., cases. Accordingly, in selecting advertising media, the advertiser's appraisal of media is often hampered by the fact that he does not know precisely whom he desires to reach with his advertising and cannot define the social, economic, geographical, and other relevant characteristics of prospects.

The problem is complicated further by the fact that advertising media make available to advertisers information on their audiences which is designed to meet the needs of *all potential advertisers*, not the needs of the individual advertiser. Thus, the classifications of audience characteristics used by media usually do not coincide with the classification of prospect-characteristics which have been developed by the advertiser.

We cannot here describe the audiences delivered by various media or the strengths and weaknesses of information about media audiences which the advertiser has to consider in each instance when he selects and uses media. Those who select media should build a good understanding of magazines, newspapers, business papers, radio and television stations and networks, outdoor advertising, transportation advertising, direct mail, point-of-purchase display advertising, and any other media of possible use to them, and of the sources and quality of information available regarding their audiences. Although advertising media have been quite aggressive in recent years in developing more and better information about their audiences, the reader must be forewarned that he will usually be disappointed in the quantity and quality of audience information that is relevant to the analysis of a specific media problem.

The various kinds of audience information which are made available to advertisers can be classified as follows, however. (1) *Circulation data:* the number of copies distributed of print media; the number of listeners or viewers of radio and television; the number of persons passing a location for an outdoor poster; and so on. (2) *Total audience data:* the number of readers of print media based upon studies of readers per copy; the number of viewers of a television program; and so on. (3) *Audience characteristic data:* the social, economic, geographical, and other characteristics of a medium's circulation or total audience. (4) *Special study data:* such as the income and expenditure patterns of a medium's audience, the shopping habits of the audience, the audience's ownership and usage of products, etc. (5) *Cumulative audience data:* the accumulated audience of a medium over a period of weeks or months.

The principal sources of media-audience information, as of April 1959, are indicated in Exhibit 3.

Ratings of Media. Having determined that certain media reach desired prospects, the question of which medium or media to employ has to be answered by management's value judgment, because definite ratings of media for constant application are impossible. There are no definite ratings of the ability of various types of media to communicate effectively various types of advertising messages, that is, there is no definite evidence which would allow the management of the Baumritter company, for example, to rate the ability of various types of media to communicate advertising messages about furniture. There are so many variables which have a bearing upon the ability of a particular medium to communicate various types of advertising messages that it is impossible to build clear and irrefutable arguments regarding the exact contribution which any medium can or has made to the effectiveness of a sales promotional program.

In evaluating the relative ability of various media to do a particular task, management or its media specialists must consider *countless variables*, such as, to list only a few: (1) the character of the advertising messages to be used; (2) their compatibility with the editorial matter, advertisements, and audience of a medium; (3) the technical requirements imposed by the message upon a medium, for example, most magazines require several weeks lead time for submission of advertisements, which does not allow messages to be based upon the most current events; (4) the availability of preferred space or time; (5) the promotional possibilities afforded by use of a medium; (6) the degree to which it is used by competitors; and (7) the manner in which a medium is received and used by prospects. Which of these variables to consider and what relative weight to give each when making a final decision regarding media can be determined by management and its specialists only if they are skillful in making good use of the evidence which is available and are willing to take the time that is required for thorough analysis.

In trying to appraise the qualities of media, advertisers have had to rely primarily upon their own experience with media over time, inasmuch as media and media associations have not, until very recent years, devoted much attention to the development of helpful, objective evidence. Advertisers have, with respect to building knowledge about the potentialities of various media, essentially studied the audience data available to them in

Exhibit 3

PRINCIPAL SOURCES OF MEDIA—AUDIENCE INFORMATION

Medium	Source	Type of Information
Newspapers	Audit Bureau of Circulations, Inc. (A.B.C.), 123 North Wacker Drive, Chicago, Illinois.	Semiannual publishers' sworn statements and annual audited statements of paid circulation.
	Standard Rate and Data Service— Newspaper Section, published by Standard Rate and Data Service, Inc. (SRDS), 1740 Ridge Avenue, Evanston, Illinois.	Net paid circulation by zones of circulation. Information is essentially condensation of publishers' A.B.C. statements.
	Individual publishers.	A.B.C. statements; special analyses of circulation records; and special consumer and reader research studies. The quantity and quality of data supplied by individual publishers varies substantially.
	Bureau of Advertising, American Newspaper Publishers Association (ANPA), 570 Lexington Avenue, New York City.	Data on the markets covered by newspapers and special studies upon request of advertiser.
Magazines	Audit Bureau of Circulations, Inc.	Semiannual publishers' sworn statements and annual audited statements of paid circulation.
	SRDS—Consumer Magazine and Farm Publication Section.	Total circulation.
	Individual publishers.	A.B.C. statements; special analyses of circulation records; and special consumer and reader research studies. Of particular note are numerous studies of the number of readers of selected magazines which have been made since 1937, sponsored by Life, Look, Good Housekeeping, Better Homes & Gardens, The Saturday Evening Post.
	"The Starch Consumer Magazine Report," published semiannually by Daniel Starch, Boston Post Road and Beach Avenue, Mamaroneck, New York.	Data on the audiences of selected magazines, giving information on socio-economic-geographical characteristics, product ownership, and purchase intentions.
	Magazine Audience Bureau, 271 Madison Avenue, New York City.	Data on the audiences reached by magazines.
Business, trade and professional papers	Audit Bureau of Circulations, Inc.	Semiannual publishers' sworn statements and annual audited statements of paid circulation.
	Business Publications Audit of Circulation, Inc. (B.P.A.C.), 420 Lexington Avenue, New York City.	Audited publishers' statements for both paid and "free" circulation publications.
	SRDS—Business Publication Section.	Total circulation; circulation by 12 territorial classifications, if available from the publisher; and cir-

Exhibit 3—Continued

Medium	Source	Type of Information
Business, trade and professional papers (cont.)	Individual publishers.	culation among various classifications of readers, if available. A.B.C. and B.P.A.C. audited statements; special analyses of circulations; and sometimes special reader studies.
Radio	Nielsen Radio Index, A. C. Nielsen Co., 2101 Howard Street, Chicago 45, Illinois.	Five types of reports: (1) biweekly measurements of the audiences of network programs, based upon data obtained from Audimeters* in 1,200 U.S. homes; (2) bimonthly measurements of automobile-radio audiences, based upon data obtained from diary entries and Recordimeters;† (3) bimonthly measurements of weekly and four-week cumulative audiences of radio stations in 75 metropolitan areas, based upon data obtained from Audimeters and diary entries; (4) every eight weeks, measurements of total audiences by three-hour broadcast segments of radio stations in 75 metropolitan areas; (5) special analyses.
	The Pulse, Inc., 730 Fifth Avenue, New York City.	Two types of reports: (1) monthly measurements of audiences of network programs in 26 metropolitan areas by ¼-hour segments, based upon aided recall personal interviews in the home; (2) occasional measurements of audiences of local programs in 200 metropolitan areas by ¼-hour segments.
	Trendex, Inc., 535 Fifth Avenue, New York City.	Special studies based upon telephone-coincidental method.
	C. E. Hooper, Inc., 579 Fifth Avenue, New York City.	Monthly measurements of sets in use and share of audience of programs and stations by ¼-hour segments in 60 cities and similar measurements periodically in 115 other cities, based upon telephone coincidental method.
	Individual stations and networks.	Occasionally have information obtained from special studies.
Television	Nielsen TV Index, A. C. Nielsen Co.	Five types of reports: (1) biweekly measurements of audiences of network programs, based upon

* A mechanical device which records minute-by-minute tuning of radio and television receivers in homes.
† A simplified Audimeter.

Exhibit 3—Continued

Medium	Source	Type of Information
Television (cont.)	Nielsen TV Index (cont.)	Audimeters in 1,050 television homes, giving total television audience in number and as a per cent of total television homes and per cent and number of homes reached by each network show; (2) every two months, a complete report, summarizing bi-weekly reports with additional information: program viewing by regions of the U.S., by county size, by age of housewife, by size of family, and minute by minute; (3) monthly measurement of shares of total television audience obtained in 23 metropolitan areas where all networks have affiliates; (4) every few months a National Audience Composition report, stratifying audience by age and sex; (5) Special analyses.
	The Pulse, Inc.	Three types of reports: (1) monthly measurements of audiences of network programs in 22 metropolitan areas by ¼-hour segments, based upon aided recall personal interviews in the home; (2) monthly measurements of audiences of syndicated programs in same markets by ¼-hour segments; (3) occasional measurements of spot television in over 150 cities.
	Trendex, Inc.	Two types of reports: (1) monthly measurements of audiences of network programs in 20 cities, based upon telephone-coincidental method, and giving sets in use, share of audience by program, audience composition and sponsor identification; (2) monthly measurements of audiences of local stations in approximately 50 cities, giving same information as above.
	American Research Bureau, Inc., 400 Park Avenue, New York City.	Three types of reports: (1) twice monthly measurements of audiences of network programs, based upon diary method, diaries being maintained by about 300 homes in each of about 150 cities; (2) twice monthly measurements of audiences of stations in about 100 cities, monthly measurements in 16 cities, and varying reporting periods for other cities.

Exhibit 3—Continued

Medium	Source	Type of Information
Television (cont.)	Individual networks and stations.	Occasionally have information based upon special studies.
Transportation advertising	SRDS—*Transportation Advertising Section.* National Association of Transportation Advertising, Inc., 30 Rockefeller Plaza, New York City.	Data regarding average number of monthly riders. Continuing studies of the audiences of transportation advertising (in association with Advertising Research Foundation).
Outdoor advertising	Traffic Audit Bureau, Inc., 60 East 42nd Street, New York City.	Circulation data for outdoor advertising companies.

conjunction with evidence regarding response to advertising copy. As a result, changes in media and copy have been made until advertisers find combinations which appear to be effective. They have continuously watched for evidence of declining effectiveness and have continuously experimented with various types and combinations of types of media. Further, almost every significant change in the advertiser's basic advertising strategy has caused change to be made in media usage.

Despite the general lack of objective evidence regarding the abilities of various media, the reader should not ignore the desirability of continuously examining the rather substantial quantity of information which now streams forth from media, media associations, and other advertising organizations regarding the "effectiveness of a medium." Some of this information consists merely of "success" stories. Much of it describes, often in useful detail, the experiences of individual advertisers with various media. Such information provides one source of new ideas regarding media usage. Occasionally, the information reports the results of well-conceived and executed media studies. Because of the countless variables of concern when rating media, those who select and use media must continuously appraise the value of any information which gives additional understanding of the effect of any variable upon media usage.

Cost Comparisons among Media. Cost comparisons among media require careful judgment, because significant considerations are involved which cannot be reflected in a simple comparison of cost figures derived from existing sources of cost information.

When comparing costs, advertisers ideally seek to determine for each medium the cost of reaching a given number of prospects (the number 1,000 is typically used and is often referred to as the cost-per-thousand calculation or concept). This cost, however, can be determined only, if at all, by an analysis of highly tenuous data. Such an analysis calls for an estimate (1) of the total audience of a medium, and (2) of the portion of that total audience who are real prospects. Earlier in this chapter some of the problems associated with the determination of the size of audience of media were indicated, the principal consideration advanced there being that only in a few instances can advertisers be reasonably sure of the approximate size of the total audience offered by a medium. Usually they must work with something less: audited circulation figures, general estimates of the size of television audiences, and so on. Further, either because of their own lack of knowledge of the characteristics of prospects or because of a lack of knowledge of the characteristics of the medium's audience, advertisers seldom can adequately determine the number of their prospects offered in the audience of a medium.

In practice advertisers generally use several types of cost data for comparative purposes when selecting media: (1) the cost per thousand of actual circulation, if known; (2) the cost per thousand of best estimate of audience size; (3) and the cost per thousand "useful circulation" or "useful audience," which is the advertiser's estimate of the portion of the medium's circulation or audience that is probably useful to him. An advertiser of ladies' shoes, for example, might define the useful audience of *Life* magazine as being only female readers of *Life* sixteen years and older.

Any cost comparisons between media, particularly between different types of media such as, say, magazines and television, must also take into account the abilities of the media to communicate various types of advertising effectively. Many of the countless variables discussed under "Ratings of Media" above must enter into cost comparisons. The cost per impression, that is, the cost to get a person to see, read, or listen to an advertisement, is of particular importance. Sizes of advertisements, length of radio or television commercials, intensity of readership or viewership, loyalty of the audience to a medium, and the total amount of advertising in a medium are only a few of many variables to be pondered in cost comparisons. It is here that intimate knowledge of the media under discussion assumes particular importance for those who select media.

The selection and use of media are also affected by two other important considerations: (1) the size of space or the amount of time employed, and (2) the frequency of insertion. Ideally the advertiser desires to use sufficient space or time with sufficient frequency so that he obtains the attention of desired prospects. Just what size of space or amount of time and just what frequency of insertion is required to obtain attention are difficult questions to answer. For example, what is the value of a one-half page advertisement versus a full-page advertisement in *Life?* What is the value of 20 one-half page advertisements versus ten full-page advertisements in *Look?* In general the advertiser must appraise the many variables involved in establishing an advertising schedule for each medium that he employs, giving particular attention to whether the space or time used on a given schedule will be effective. Often advertisers are forced to employ fewer media in order to obtain effective schedules, because of budget limitations.

Co-ordination of Advertising with the Other Tools of Sales Promotion

Many sales promotional programs involve use of personal selling and quick-action stimuli in conjunction with advertising. In planning advertising programs in such instances, management must relate advertising to these other selling tools in order to obtain proper scheduling and co-ordination of the total promotional effort and in order to obtain the maximum effectiveness of each selling tool.

Relating Advertising and Personal Selling. In relating advertising and personal selling, there are many pertinent considerations, only a few of which will be noted here. Many advertising programs call for the use of space or time advertising together with extensive point-of-purchase advertising. Thus, special attention must be directed to the ability of the sales force to co-ordinate distribution and use of point-of-purchase advertising materials with the publication schedule of advertising. Most advertising programs usually provide the basis for special personal selling effort, such as getting dealers to tie in with the program by featuring the product advertised and by employing the same copy themes in their own advertising and selling. Hence, in order to make advertising programs more effective, special provision should be made to inform and guide the sales force in order that they may induce desired dealer support. Often the principal purpose of an advertising program is to elicit inquiries; accordingly, plans must be laid for effective handling and follow-up of inquiries received.

Scheduling and co-ordination of advertising and personal selling are brought into clear focus in campaigns to launch new products. Cases in Chapter 11 deal with such campaigns. Therein the whole gamut of activities involved in scheduling and co-ordinating advertising and personal selling from the time that a product is developed in the research laboratory until it is finally established in the market place will be indicated.

Quick-Action Stimuli. In the selling of many products, particularly in the selling of so-called "consumer packaged goods," it has become a common practice for manufacturers to employ, in conjunction with their indirect-action advertising, various quick-action stimuli, such as special-price sales, coupons, premium offers, contests, and combination deals. These and other stimuli have been used especially when advertisers are introducing new products and desire to induce sampling by consumers, or when advertisers are selling in a highly competitive market and seek to differentiate their products through promotional devices as well as product characteristics.

When quick-action stimuli are employed, the prime objective of advertising for a given time period may be to give *news* about the offer. Consequently, there is a special need for exact scheduling and timing of advertising and the quick-action stimuli and for assessing the power of advertising to induce desired consumer action. Special-price deals, for example, particularly if they involve so-called special-pack merchandise, move through channels of distribution effectively only if they are properly presented to the trade so that the trade schedules its display simultaneously with advertising. Special-price deals, it should be noted, are essentially a form of tactical price competition. The objectives of advertising are affected accordingly.

Although manufacturers have employed quick-action stimuli with increasing frequency since the 1920's, they have been reluctant to disclose the results of their operations so that relatively little of value has been published about the use of such stimuli and the problems of effectively implementing them by advertising. Several of these quick-action stimuli are considered in cases of this section.

The Evaluation of Advertising

Of basic interest to management is advertising's over-all contribution to the sales and profits of the business. As a practical matter, this contribution does not lend itself to easy evaluation or measurement, inasmuch as advertising is only one of many variables in the marketing mix which affects sales. Consequently, as has been pointed out previously, management evaluates the potential or actual contribution of advertising to its marketing operation primarily by *value* judgments based upon a thorough analysis of information regarding the market forces and marketing elements bearing on sales. These value judgments necessarily are relatively uncertain because definitive knowledge of all of the variables affecting demand is unavailable.

In order to obtain better evidence upon which to base evaluation of advertising, management seeks not so much to measure advertising's over-all contribution to sales but rather attempts more often to analyze and measure various parts of the advertising program on the premise that if the various parts appear to be effective, then the whole advertising program probably will be contributing effectively to sales and profits.

Various approaches are employed to obtain better evidence. As indicated earlier in this chapter, it is desirable to seek post-measurements of advertising in order to determine whether advertisements have been seen or heard. Clearly, if advertisements are not seen or heard or are low in communication ability relative to advertisements for comparable products, then the advertising probably is ineffective and change is called for. Evidence that advertising is seen or heard is not enough, however; the advertiser needs also to know the degree to which prospects retain messages and have been induced to develop favorable attitudes toward the product advertised. Studies of prospect attitudes regarding brands, if designed well, can also provide much evidence that will aid management in its evaluation of specific advertising programs. Such studies essentially involve before and after research or research over time which measures changes in prospect attitudes that can be attributed to advertising.

Although advertising may build favorable attitudes toward a brand among prospects, buying action may not occur. Consequently, advertisers seek to trace the effect of advertising even further, obtaining if they can evidence regarding consumer buying activity which throws light on the effectiveness of advertising. Studies have been made, for example, of the purchases of consumers, some of whom were known to have been exposed to given advertisers, others not. Comparison of purchase data in such studies often reveal significant differences in brand patterns which appear to be attributable to advertising. Advertisers also make frequent use of purchase data obtained from continuous consumer panels in order to relate changes in consumer purchases to changes in their own and competitors' advertising.

Advertisers frequently seek to evaluate alternative types and amounts of advertising by experimentation in so-called test markets. Under this procedure, advertising is published in test markets and results are contrasted with other markets—so-called control markets—which have had the regular advertising program. The measurements made to determine results may be measurements of changes in sales, changes in consumer attitudes, changes in dealer display, and so on, depending upon the objectives sought by the advertiser. Although experimentation in test markets provides an excellent means for testing alternative advertising approaches to see if they are effective in actual operations, the measurements made are actually measurements of the effectiveness of the sales promotional program as a whole rather than measurements of the effectiveness of advertising itself.

Sound evaluation of advertising calls for a good understanding of what is involved in marketing, promotion, and advertising, and a good understanding of the strengths and weaknesses of the various techniques of marketing research. Many of the cases in this section raise questions about the evaluation of advertising. The reader should not analyze the cases with the idea in mind that he may simply recommend that research be undertaken to solve problems or another questions. In many instances the questions which the advertiser would like to answer are unanswerable, given the research techniques currently available. In other instances the questions may be answerable but only at a research cost exceeding the cost of advertising. Recommendations regarding research must be governed accordingly. The basic questions are: What should be evaluated? What kind of information is needed to make these evaluations? Will the information be worth the cost?

The Advertising Budget

Managements follow various procedures in establishing the size of the advertising expenditure. Generally, whatever the specific procedure, the budgetary process involves two steps: (1) the determination of a tentative working budget, which will give general guidance to specialists as they analyze the problem areas of advertising programs; and (2) the determination of the final budget, which interrelates everyone's thinking about all aspects of the advertising program.

Tentative Considerations. Managements often establish a tentative advertising budget by simply applying the percentage of past sales spent on advertising to estimated sales for the budget period. Such an approach quickly gives a total dollar figure which can be used as the basis for discussion. Or they may apply a fixed amount per unit to be sold, inasmuch as many manufacturers develop accounting data on a per unit basis. This approach, too, will quickly give a total dollar figure. Often consideration will be given to the expenditures of competitors, and the tentative budget may be set to equal or exceed the advertising expenditures of individual competitors.

More often, however, managements will employ somewhat more complicated methods in establishing criteria for the determination of both the tentative and final advertising budgets by utilizing budgetary control systems (or what are also called profit planning systems).

Budgetary Control. In order to appraise better the effectiveness of past expenditures and to determine the advertising budget more effectively, many managements have sought to break down their total operations into smaller parts in order to establish the profitability of products, customers or types of customers, channels of distribution and geographical markets, and to employ a system of budgetary control which will help to measure attainment. In other words, managements have found it unwise merely to appropriate advertising funds with a check only on final sales and profit results, because that result, even though favorable, may represent a combination of losses for some products or markets and profits in others. Accordingly, they have developed systems of budgetary control which allow more penetrating analysis.

Systems of budgetary control as applied to advertising require the setting of good standards and the effective tracing of sales and selling expense. Standards commonly employed are product, customer, or market quotas; buying power indexes; and share of market. Each can be established only by good use of statistical techniques. The tracing of sales may or may not be a simple task, depending upon the distribution operation of the individual manufacturer and upon the type of standard selected to measure attainment. Reliable tracing of selling expenses is usually difficult and not too accurate, because cost accounting procedures as applied to marketing operations present difficult problems which have as yet not been solved.

To illustrate, let us briefly describe the budgetary control system employed by a manufacturer of an industrial product. This product was purchased by three classes of customers. Industry association data were available which indicated the total consumption of the product by each of the three classes, that is, the total market. This was the standard used by the manufacturer against which to measure attainment. Sales to each of the three classes were directly traceable to customers through sales invoices; hence, the manufacturer's measure of attainment was his share of the total market in each of the three classes. Personal selling expense was also traceable through salesmen's records, which indicated time spent with each class of customer. Although the manufacturer had reservations regarding the accuracy of the time reporting procedure employed, he felt that it generally reflected approximate personal selling costs for each class of customer. Advertising expenses were traced fairly accurately because all advertising monies were spent in trade papers and the circulation of these papers could be traced to each of the three classes of customers. Thus, the manufacturer could establish the approximate profitability of his marketing operation as it served three classes of customers.

It should be noted that this manufacturer used his budgetary control system to determine his total advertising budget and to allocate it among his three prime markets. In late 1958 he concluded that the 1959 advertising budget should be increased in order to gain an increased share of business among one class of customers whose total consumption of the product had been increasing at a rapid rate for the three previous years.

The foregoing illustration describes a budgetary control system which was developed in an ideal situation: total market figures were available, and sales and selling expense could be traced fairly accurately. The reader should appreciate that in most instances manufacturers face much more complex situations when they attempt to develop useful systems. Generally, total market data are not easily obtainable and the determination of other types of meaningful standards is difficult, particularly for sellers of consumer goods. The establishment of market research to enable sellers to have a record of their own and competitors' sales at retail is one of the important developments in recent years which has significantly affected the budgetary procedures of managements. Such evidence may come from special surveys of sales of retail stores or purchases of consumers or from regular services, such as those offered by the A. C. Nielsen Company and Market Research Corporation of America.

The reader should also appreciate that the tracing of selling expense is usually difficult, particularly the tracing of advertising expense. For example, the advertiser who employs network television usually cannot definitely allocate the cost of such advertising to markets or classes of consumers because he does not have good evidence regarding the actual number or classes of consumers who have viewed his programs.

While hopeful progress can be reported in the development of techniques for budgetary control, high attainment cannot as yet be claimed. Cost accounting as applied to marketing and promotion is far less accurate than that applied to production. Large parts of total marketing costs must be allocated, usually on the basis of crude approximation. Likewise, in the setting of standards, it can be said that the art is still in an immature stage. Since World War II, however, much progress has been made in the development of statistical techniques which promise to be rewarding when properly applied to problems of marketing and promotional control.

Final Budget Considerations. The final determination of the advertising budget is usually based upon management's consideration of all of the thinking done by itself and its specialists regarding the problem areas of advertising programs. Final budget sessions provide the basis for interrelating all thinking about advertising objectives, copy, media, measures of effectiveness, and so on.

Generally, the size of the advertising expenditure is guided primarily by management's desire to obtain certain objectives. It employs the so-called *task approach*, that is, how much will it cost to support an advertising program that promises to attain stated objectives? This cost is then related to other budgetary considerations: the total budget for all sales promotion, the total budget for marketing, and the total budget for the business. The final dollar figure to be spent on advertising must be in accord with the over-all financial condition of the business.

In the final budget session, management is often faced with the dilemma that the total cost of an appropriate advertising program seems unfeasible in the light of all demands made upon the company's total budget. At this point judgment of the highest order is required. In many instances management reduces the advertising budget without modifying the advertising objectives to be accomplished. Such action usually results in unsatisfactory attainment. The establishment of the size of the advertising expenditure is the critical decision made by management, and it must be made with a good understanding of what can and cannot be accomplished with a given expenditure. Because of its intangible nature, advertising always provokes considerable differences of opinion among members of management, which are seen most clearly in budget sessions.

Chapter 11

~~~~~~~~~~~~~~~~~~~~~~~~~~~~~~~~~~~~

CASES INVOLVING PROBLEM
AREAS ENCOUNTERED IN THE
BUILDING OF ADVERTISING
PROGRAMS

This chapter consists of a selection of cases which deal with various problem areas that are encountered in the building of advertising and promotional programs. Generally, in analyzing these cases, attention should be given to the problem areas indicated in Chapter 10, namely: (1) the objectives of advertising; (2) advertising copy, including the means of evaluating copy; (3) advertising media; (4) the co-ordination of advertising with the other elements of the promotional program; (5) the measurement of the effectiveness of advertising; and (6) the determination of the size of the advertising expenditure. Because each of the cases in this chapter focuses upon particular problem areas, questions are given at the beginning of each case to direct attention to the areas which might be considered.

~~~

CASE I: B. F. GOODRICH COMPANY[1]

NOTE: *The major problem areas encountered in the building of advertising and promotional programs are clearly seen in instances where new products are being introduced to the market. This and next three cases*

[1] Written by Neil H. Borden.

473

*describe the development and introductory marketing of four new prod-
ucts; they provide the basis particularly for analyzing the problems of co-
ordinating advertising with other promotional and marketing activities.
This case describes the development and introductory marketing of the
first tubeless tire.* QUESTIONS TO CONSIDER: *(1) Was the product adequately
tested? (2) Did product testing provide good evidence regarding what
might be effective selling appeals? (3) Was there any way in which Goodrich could have found out about the "safety" feature earlier? (4) Was
the marketing and promotional program tested adequately? (5) Did Goodrich depend too much on publicity, too little on advertising, to develop
a market for the tubeless tire? (6) Over-all, did Goodrich proceed too fast
or too slow in its introduction of the tubeless tire?*

In September 1954 formal announcement was made in the business
press that tubeless tires would be original equipment on 1955 automobiles.
This adoption of tubeless tires by the auto manufacturers was looked
upon as forecasting the not-distant demise of the traditional outer casing
equipped with inner tube. The move brought a tremendous spurt forward
in the sales and use of a product which, up to this time, was still a *new*
product on the market, although as new products go it had made relatively rapid strides in gaining public acceptance. In spite of its relatively
quick adoption, however, the tubeless tire illustrates well the difficulties
met by industry not only in the perfection of a product idea but in getting
consumer and trade adoption of the idea. The story of the tire illustrates,
also, the importance of good management techniques in bringing success
in the launching of a new product.

History of Product Idea and Its Development

The idea of a tubeless automobile tire was not new. Tire executives
reported that such a tire had been a goal of tire manufacture since the
opening of the automotive era, for inner tubes were looked upon as the
cause of most flat tires and tire difficulties. It was inner tubes that blew
out, went flat, held in the heat which caused tire temperatures to rise, got
chafed and pinched by the casing. Much research had been devoted to
the problem of producing a tubeless tire, but no marketable product had
been turned out.

Early in World War II the United States Army asked the B. F. Goodrich Company and other rubber companies to develop a truck tire that
would enable a vehicle to return to its home base safely in combat service without the tires becoming flat, even though the tires were riddled
with bullets. The company accepted the challenge and assigned a young
research or project engineer, Frank Herzegh, to take charge of the company's development of such a tire. These tires were intended for operation with tubes, but as a by-product of his work on combat tires, Herzegh
developed a combined bead-locking and air-sealing device which made
it possible to operate combat tires without tubes. The combat tire was
suitable for operation without a tube because it embodied a thick rubber

lining which not only stiffened the sidewalls of the tire but also held the air in the tire.

Tubeless tires had been made previously, but they were unsuccessful in service. One of the main difficulties was that air could slowly pass through natural rubber. Accordingly, the previous tires made of natural rubber permitted the air to leak through the wall of the tire. Then air pockets would form between the tire carcass and the tread; the tread would soon separate from the carcass, making the tire unusable. Butyl, a man-made rubber developed just before World War II, is highly impervious to air, having 10 to 12 times greater resistance to the loss of air than crude rubber tubes. Herzegh recognized this quality of Butyl as the answer to the problem of providing a liner which would retard the diffusion of air into the casing. He then undertook exhaustive work and experiments to develop a satisfactory way to build and maintain a liner of Butyl rubber in a tire. In addition, he had to lick the difficult problem of designing a tire that would be sealed to the wheel rim without allowing leakage of air.

The advertisement in Exhibit 1, appearing in *The Saturday Evening Post* of October 31, 1942, announced the B. F. Goodrich invention of a tubeless tire which would eliminate the use of inner tubes in heavy vehicle tires. It dealt primarily with the rubber-saving aspects of the tubeless tire and the fact that by doing away with the tube the cause of many tire failures would be eliminated.

The war ended before any of these tires were put in service, but the tire was tested in combat maneuvers in the United States and proved equal to the exacting demands made by the military services.

Having developed a satisfactory tubeless truck tire for combat service, Mr. Herzegh, then busy on other war assignments, requested permission to work in his spare time on the development of a tubeless passenger tire. Since the combat tire was not suitable for passenger car service, he had to begin his engineering research anew to develop a light, easily applied tire suitable for high speeds on passenger cars. A man of innate curiosity, high imagination, enthusiasm and skill, Mr. Herzegh worked nights on the problem in his workshop at home.[2]

During this early work, Herzegh made up many tubeless passenger car tires, with various modifications. At about the end of the war he had arrived at a design which was satisfactory and which had proven successful in tests. In this tire Herzegh, in order to make an airtight seal to the rim, adopted a series of ridges on the casing where it came in contact with the wheel rim. As the air was applied, these ridges pushed against the rim and gave a positive seal against loss of air. Even under abnormal, high-speed driving conditions with air pressure low and car swerving, the tires clung snugly to rim and wheel.

---

[2] For an article on Mr. Herzegh and his tire research, see *Life*, February 14, 1949.

Exhibit 1
B. F. GOODRICH COMPANY

TUBELESS TIRE INVENTED BY B.F.Goodrich

**Sensational rubber-saving development promises
big after-war savings for commercial users**

A Great *typical example of B. F. Goodrich development in truck tires*

CLIMAXING a 50-year dream of tire engineers, The B. F. Goodrich Company announces an invention which eliminates the use of inner tubes in heavy vehicle tires.

Tested and Proved

The new B. F. Goodrich tubeless tire has been tested and proved both in the laboratory and on the highway and is now undergoing further impartial tests. While the amount of rubber saved by this new invention varies depending upon the size of the tire, the saving is approximately 7% to 17% of the rubber content of the casing, tube and flap combined.

The Silvertown that doesn't need a tube has been made possible by a simple change in truck tire design plus a mechanical device the details of which are being kept secret in the interest of national defense. The tire is inflated just like any ordinary tire and tube—but instead of the air going into a tube, it goes directly into the tire and *stays there.*

If put into use during the war, the tubeless tire will be a major step in the conservation of America's precious rubber stockpile. That's good news to all of us. And it's good news to every truck and bus operator to know that after the war inner tubes may become a thing of the past!

Remember, the inner tube is the source of much tire trouble. Do away with the tube and you have eliminated the cause of many, many failures! And repairs can be made quickly because there is no tube to consider. Just think what this would mean in terms of lower costs, fewer delays, and simplified repairs! It's too early to make promises—but here is a hint of more good news to come later. In War or Peace, you can always look to B. F. Goodrich for leadership.

In war or peace
B.F.Goodrich
FIRST IN RUBBER

At this time Herzegh was ready to recommend the tubeless tire to his superiors for consideration as a commercial product. It was evident to all the technical people that putting tubeless tires into production as a commercial proposition would involve considerable expense. Before funds for this costly research were forthcoming, consultation with sales executives was required in order to appraise the marketing promise of the tubeless tire and to determine whether the research project had sufficient promise to justify the necessary outlay.

Reportedly, the young engineer, Herzegh, was the only one at the meeting who radiated enthusiasm for the idea. The engineers and sales-people present failed to see that the new product presented benefits and claims that would make the American public want tubeless tires in pref-erence to the very satisfactory tire-and-tube combination of the time. The discussion served, however, to crystallize to some degree the advan-tages that should be sought to make the product promising marketwise.

At the meeting a modest sum for further development was author-ized. The research engineering group was admonished that to be success-ful the new tire would need unusual advantages that could be felt, seen, and demonstrated to the consuming public.

In 1946, nearly a year after this first meeting, Herzegh came up with a new tire to show the sales heads. Undaunted by the cool reception to his first model, he and his associates had worked skillfully and assiduously, trying and changing their ideas, to develop a product which would incor-porate advantages such as the sales department had specified.

Tests made with the new version convinced the engineers that the new tubeless tire had definite riding advantages; it gave an easier, smoother, better ride than the regular tire-and-tube combination. While the easier riding qualities could not be measured, they could be felt by those testing and comparing the tire with regular tires. The easier riding was attribut-able to the absence of an inner tube which in contact with sidewalls of the casing gave them rigidity. Moreover, a puncture sealant, which was quite reliable in use, had been developed and was presented as a special feature of this tire.

At a meeting of sales heads and engineers, the sales department's re-sponse to the new tire was enthusiastic. This version seemed to offer ob-servable, provable benefits. If the tire did what the engineers said, not only would it make possible the promise of easier car riding but also it would actually seal punctures and thus eliminate the annoyance of punctured tires and the hazards connected therewith. All present wanted to see the tests, to ride in cars equipped with the tires, and to stick ice picks into the tires to assure themselves that they would not go flat.

At this second meeting adequate sums were appropriated without hesi-tation to provide for the building of enough of the tires to carry on the extensive road testing on the fleets of test cars which the company main-tained in Texas and in other sections of the country and on the cars of executives and field organization. The following news release was issued to the press and radio after the testing program was under way:

Akron, Ohio, May 12, 1947. . . . Tubeless tires—goal of tire manufacturers since the opening of the automotive era—have been developed by The B. F. Goodrich Company, Akron, Ohio, and are now undergoing all known tire tests, it was announced here today.

The new tire, perfected after more than three years of engineering, combines the safety features of puncture-sealing inner tubes with improved riding qualities, high bruise resistance, and remarkable ability to retain air pressure, according to James J. Newman, vice president. The tubeless tire embodies rayon cord construction.

In addition to a high-speed road testing program in the southwest, tubeless tires are in service on a taxicab fleet in a middle western city, on state police cars, and a number of privately owned passenger cars.

The tubeless tire will be offered only for a limited sale at this time, the company stated. Applications have been filed with the United States Patent Office.

The better part of a year was spent on the testing program and in further improvement of the tire prior to marketing. Intensive study was devoted to learning the many things about the application, mounting and demounting, repairing and recapping that would be needed in teaching the thousands of people engaged in servicing American automobiles. In the meantime careful plans were laid for producing and marketing the new tire.

Already considerable expenditure for equipment to manufacture the tire had been risked in order to get the tires needed for the test. Existing tire-making machines were modified to produce the new tire. Because the tubeless tire was a special new product, its manufacture was carried on in the Akron plant, smallest of the company's five tire plants, where production was carefully hovered over by the engineering group that had developed the tire. Plans were laid, however, to start production in the Tuscaloosa, Alabama, plant once the marketing program was under way.

Decision to Test Market the Tire

In the fall of 1947 management decided to enter on a test marketing program for the tubeless tire on a regional basis. This was a radical departure from the usual method followed in the tire industry. To the best of management's knowledge, a tire had never before been introduced on such a test marketing basis. Over the years there had been gradual developments in tires, from cotton to rayon cord, from small tires to balloon tires, from high pressure to lower pressure. New treads were constantly introduced. The practice of tire companies generally in putting out a new tire, such as the low-pressure balloon tire, or a new tread, had been to maintain as great secrecy as possible regarding the new development. When once a new tire had been subjected to the rigorous product testing normally carried on, molds were made and enough tires were produced to stock dealers nationally before publicity on the new tire broke.

The tubeless tire was such a revolutionary development, however, that the management decided a market test in one sales district was advisable before spending millions of dollars trying to market on a nation-wide basis. The sales department and the business research department discussed objectives of the test and laid plans for the marketing research measurements to be made. The objectives for the test were as follows:

1. To learn possible product defects under conditions of actual consumer use. Even though the tire had already passed extensive tests on taxi and police fleets and on company-driven cars, management wanted to be sure that the tire would give complete satisfaction when used by a wide cross section of typical motorists.

2. To study carefully consumer reception of the new tire prior to national marketing.

3. To get an indication of consumer sales response in order to lay a basis for establishing budgets for sales, production, and capital expenditure. Was it a product of wide appeal or a product with appeal to a limited group?

4. To measure the effectiveness of advertising appeals used in an effort to find the most effective advertising approach.

5. To carry on price experimentation in order to check hypotheses regarding selling prices and price policies.

6. To learn the difficulties that might be experienced in training dealers and stores to maintain and service the tire properly.

7. To limit the sales repercussions of any possible major product defects and to permit corrections before nation-wide sales efforts were undertaken.

8. Over-all, to determine the effectiveness of marketing methods employed so that adjustments might be made to increase the effectiveness of marketing programs to be used later in other sales districts.

Area Chosen for the Market Test

The Cincinnati sales district was chosen for the test. In this district, which covered half of Ohio, most of West Virginia, Kentucky, and a portion of Indiana, were city streets, hills, mountains, winding roads, and rough roads; in short, practically every type and kind of driving could be found in this area that would be encountered in the rest of the United States. In addition, Cincinnati was only 200 miles from Akron. Management could easily supervise operations and keep in close touch with the market test.

Although the entire Cincinnati district was made the testing ground, the metropolitan Cincinnati district was the segment selected for close scrutiny and detailed observations and measurements. In this localized area special arrangements were made to:

1. Measure the degree of improvement in public knowledge and attitudes toward the tire as the marketing program progressed.

2. Measure actual exposure of newspaper readers to the advertising and the effect of this exposure upon knowledge of the tire and, if possible, their purchase of the tire.

3. Measure week-by-week unit sales of tubeless tires.

4. Determine the attitudes of motorists who had purchased and used the tubeless tire.

Baseline Survey

Stocks of the new tire adequate to stock dealers in the Cincinnati sales district were being built up for shipment before the opening of the selling program which was set for February 2, 1948. Early in January, before the selling program broke, however, the business research department carried out a "baseline" survey in Cincinnati in which it sought to determine the extent of consumer knowledge of the tubeless tire which might have come from the limited publicity that had been conducted up to this time and to measure consumer attitudes towards the tubeless tire idea. The survey was to serve as a baseline against which the results of a survey to be taken several months later might be compared, thereby to learn what progress the company had made in its marketing program toward building a consumer knowledge of the tire and gaining acceptance for it. Some 500 interviews were made in Cincinnati and its environs.

Some of the more important findings from this survey were as follows:

1. Few people, only 2%, could identify the tubeless tire when asked if they knew of any new tire development to be put upon the market and what it was.

2. To the statement "One tire manufacturer has developed a new tire that needs no tube at all. Have you heard of such a tire?" 43% responded that they had heard of such a tire.

3. When asked to name one other new special feature of the tubeless tire, however, only about 5% of the respondents could name the puncture-sealing feature.

4. Approximately 17% gave a correct answer as to whether a special rim would be needed for the new tubeless tire or whether it could be put on rims now on the respondent's car.

5. Seventeen per cent claimed to know the name of the company that was making the tubeless tire, but of this 17%, only 5.6% correctly named B. F. Goodrich; 6.2% named Goodyear; 2.2% named Firestone; while 3% named other companies.

6. To the question "We would like to know whether the tubeless tire appeals to you" the following responses were given: it does appeal, 49%; it does not appeal, 24%; undecided, 16%; must know more about it, 11%.

7. "As a matter of fact, this tubeless tire needs no inner tube and it can be put on rims you now have on your car. If you needed new tires, do you think you would probably get tubeless tires or would you buy the regular tires?" Would buy tubeless tires, 26.3%; would buy regular tires, 21.5%; it depends (on price, proof of worth, etc.), 43.7%; don't know, 8.5%.

8. "The list price of a standard tire of the regular type is $14.95 for the casing, plus $2.75 for the tube. The price of the tubeless tire is $21.95. Considering the price and features of the tubeless tire, would you probably buy the regular or the tubeless tire?" Regular, 29.9%; tubeless tire, 50.6%; don't know, 19.5%.

The recorded comments on the questionnaires gave the company additional information that was helpful in program formulation. They indicated that many people were intrigued by the idea of a tubeless tire. Common questions were "How would you ever hold it on a wheel?"; "No tire can be built that can hold air without a tube!"; "I would be afraid to ride on a tire like that." All in all, there was evidence from the survey that the respondents wanted to know more about the new tire—how it held air, how it could be held on the rim or wheel, and whether it was as safe or safer than the present tube-and-tire combination. Such information was an aid in drawing up the advertising and publicity for the program.

Beginning of the Selling Program

The product was presented to the dealers of the Cincinnati sales district on January 19 and 20. At this meeting the story of the development of the new product was dramatically unfolded. Its riding qualities and puncture-sealing feature were demonstrated for the dealers.

The sales department also presented a movie showing how the tire was to be serviced. At this meeting and later dealer meetings the sales department went exhaustively into proper treatment of rims, application of tires, and all questions involving servicing. The new tire was found easier to apply with the drop center rim used on passenger cars than the average tire-and-tube combination. But the management felt that in the introduction of a radically new tire it was wise to take extra precautions to make sure that the proper service was rendered, because failures in the new tire would be likely to produce a more adverse reaction than similar failures in the accepted standard tires.

At the meeting the dealers placed their orders. Shipments were made, accompanied by point-of-purchase material, to be available in advance of the February 2 opening.

Publicity

In the introductory program and for over a year subsequent, the B. F. Goodrich management placed great reliance on publicity to spread knowledge and understanding of the tire. Its revolutionary character and the striking demonstrations that had been developed to show its puncture-sealing and riding qualities were appraised as being so newsworthy as to be of real interest to press and radio. Accordingly, in opening its selling program on February 2 in Cincinnati, the management held a press and radio luncheon attended by local dignitaries, automotive leaders, and

B. F. Goodrich dealers. Mr. Joseph A. Hoban, vice president in charge of tire sales, and Mr. Herzegh, the development engineer, spoke. Then the spike-board demonstration was made in downtown streets before city officials. In this demonstration automobiles were driven over boards with rows of long spikes protruding without loss of air from the tires.

On following days the management representatives went to other leading cities in the sales district for similar luncheons and demonstrations.

In the Cincinnati sales territory, newspapers and radio stations gave prominence to the story about the tubeless tire and a number mentioned the new tire as being available at B. F. Goodrich dealers. At this time a large fleet of Cincinnati taxicabs which for several months had been operating on tubeless tires carried banners saying that they were equipped with B. F. Goodrich Tubeless Tires. In turn, the news wire services picked up the story of the tire and its qualities and sent it nation-wide where it got an amazing coverage.

In order to intensify the prestige to be had from this national publicity the company ran full-page advertisements in the *New York Times* and the *Wall Street Journal* on February 8 and 9, respectively, under the headline "Tubeless Tire that Seals Punctures Invented by B. F. Goodrich." A dominating photograph showed a tire rolling into spikes driven through a board. Full copy explained tire construction from a cross section illustration. This illustration and copy told how the concentric rings in the casing hugged the rim and kept the air from leaking out. They explained also how the patented blowout protective sealant in the crown of the tire closed punctures. Copy played up the benefits of no punctures, greater safety, and improved riding comfort.

Not until March 4, more than a month after the Cincinnati opening, did the company publish its first advertisement on the tire in Cincinnati newspapers. In the meantime the demand on dealers for the tire, stimulated by the extensive news and radio publicity and the taxicab banners, was so great that the company had difficulty keeping dealers adequately stocked with the tires.

Advertising

In the Cincinnati district test no special additional appropriation was made for the tubeless tire. The advertising program of the management normally provided an appropriation for local co-operative advertising over the dealer's name. The management used the appropriation that ordinarily would have been employed for the regular line of B. F. Goodrich tires and devoted it to the tubeless tire. As the year went on, an increase in the size of expenditures occurred in the district because the advertisements were larger in size than they normally would have been. Large space was used—a few full pages and the rest half pages—all of which was over the dealer's imprint.

To this local advertising the dealers contributed one half the space costs and were permitted to spend up to $1\frac{1}{2}\%$ of their purchases from B. F. Goodrich. Management stated that it had no problem in getting the dealers to use the allowance that was available to them; the problem rather was to hold the dealers down from requesting more than the allotted percentage of purchases. The advertisements were prepared and placed by Batten, Barton, Durstine & Osborn, Inc., the B. F. Goodrich Company's agency.

The advertisements ordinarily used a dominating illustration which usually was a closeup of the automobile tire in the spike-board test, with a headline such as "New B. F. Goodrich Tire Has No Tube—Seals Punctures." The character of the copy is indicated by the subheads:

> "No Inner Tube"
> "Seals Punctures"
> "Holds Air Better"
> "Gives Greater Safety"
> "Gives Greater Riding Comfort"
> "Proved"

Often the advertisements carried a cross section of the tire mounted on the rim with numbered arrows to indicate explanatory information in the copy.

As time wore on, the advertisements carried testimonial statements from users, extolling the qualities of the tire, thus supporting the company's statements.

The extent of space advertising in the district is indicated by the fact that during the first year somewhat over 20,000 lines of advertising were placed in newspapers.

Measurement of Advertising Effectiveness

Between March and June, six advertisements had been placed in the *Cincinnati Inquirer*. On each of these the business research department secured a readership report. These reports showed that the first full-page advertisement was seen by 41% of the men interviewed. Later half-page advertisements had a somewhat smaller readership record. The large spike test illustration was found to have high attention-gaining value.

In June a second survey was made among 510 Cincinnatians to see what progress had been made in gaining understanding and awareness of the tire since the survey made in early January. The following comparisons indicate the progress made:

1. To the query calling for unaided recall of the tubeless tire as a new tire development, 11% of those interviewed correctly named the tubeless tire, as against 2% in January.

2. Over 78% of those interviewed actually knew or claimed on aided recall to have heard about the tire, as against 45% of those interviewed in January.

3. Some 15% could name "puncture proof" as the additional feature of the tire, whereas only 5% could name this feature in January.

4. Knowledge that regular wheel rims were suitable for the new tire was claimed by 37%, as against only 17% in January.

5. B. F. Goodrich was correctly identified as the company manufacturing the tire by some 21%, as against only 6% in January. There was still a good deal of confusion between Goodyear and B. F. Goodrich in that 10% named the former company as the maker, but such confusion between these names was generally found in consumer surveys.

6. The responses regarding the appeal of the tubeless idea to interviewees were much as they had been in January.

Rough computations of the data of this survey when applied to the total of 142,000 motorists in Cincinnati and environs showed that definite awareness of the tubeless tire by about 12,000 motorists had been gained at an advertising cost to date of 42 cents for each motorist. An additional 47,000 who claimed to be aware of the tubeless tire when their recall was aided had been gained at an advertising cost of 11 cents a motorist. The cost of getting B. F. Goodrich correctly identified by 25,000 of the motorists was about 25 cents each. Of course, a considerable part of this awareness was ascribable to publicity and selling efforts.

An indication of the effect of the newspaper advertising upon readers was had by breaking down the ratio of response in the second attitude survey among those exposed and those not exposed to the *Inquirer* advertisements. Of 510 respondents, 249 were *Inquirer* readers, 261 were not. The awareness of the tire and its features was significantly greater among *Inquirer* readers than among those not exposed to the *Inquirer* and its advertisements. It must be recognized, of course, that all respondents had opportunity to be exposed to the very extensive publicity and to the taxicab banners that had played an important part in the introduction of the tire.

The business research department sought evidence of any direct selling power of the *Inquirer* advertisements by comparing the record of sales of the tires during the week following the appearance of the advertisements with the sales of the week preceding. From such a comparison management gained the feeling that the advertisements had an appreciable immediate sales effect.

Survey of Users

Shortly after the awareness survey had been made the business research department conducted a mail survey among 979 purchasers of the tubeless tire. Half the letters of inquiry went out on B. F. Goodrich letterheads; half on a blind letterhead of a research company. Fifty-nine per cent responded to the B. F. Goodrich letterhead; 49% to the blind letterhead.

Highlights of the findings of the mail questionnaire were as follows:

1. Eighty-two per cent said they liked the tubeless tire better than the conventional tire. Only 7% said they did not like it as well as the conventional tire.

2. Sixty-eight per cent said they would definitely recommend it to their friends, and another 17% said that they probably would recommend it.

3. Eighty-one per cent said they would repurchase the tubeless tire.

4. Important reasons given for wanting to repurchase the tire indicated that the freedom from puncture trouble and the safety and the riding qualities of the tire all ranked high with users.

5. Of the 85 respondents who said they would not buy again, the company got evidence of troubles with the new tire which would soon occupy the attention of management. Further evidence that the company still had a task of establishing quality control in manufacture was indicated by the fact that 36% of the users stated that they had had some trouble with the tire, although many of those so saying had not had so much difficulty as to stifle their willingness to recommend the tire to others.

The chief cause of difficulty was leakage of air from the tire.

The business research department telephoned purchasers who had not responded to the mail questionnaires and got answers to the questions in much the same ratios as were obtained in the returned questionnaires.

Pricing and Pricing Tests

When planning the market test the management made an important decision regarding pricing the tubeless tire. The issue was whether to promote the tire as a specialty at a premium price or whether to price it on a basis of costs and of margins which would put the tire more in line with regular mass-demand tires. Put another way, should the tire be priced on the basis of costs with a reasonable addition for the plus values of the new tire to consumers?

Traditionally, the tire industry had most of its demand in regular first-grade, standard tires. On this main line there was keen price competition among the producers. In addition to its basic line each tire company normally put out premium tires with special features. These tires were given relatively high list prices with a much wider percentage margin available to dealers than was to be had on standard tires. Dealers could use this wide margin for trade-in allowances, thereby inducing consumers to put premium tires on their cars in place of standard tires. The relationship of prices of standard tires to premium tires is indicated by the ratio of 100:150 to 200.

The management reasoned that the tubeless tire had substantial benefits over the conventional casing and inner tube combination for which consumers would pay a reasonable price differential above the combined price for tube and casing. On the other hand, any such differential in list prices as was normally set on premium tires would act as a deterrent to sales and might well make the new tire a product with narrow appeal.

Moreover, experience indicated that only a part of the dealers were successful in selling premium tires. The management hoped that the new tire might have wide appeal and that all dealers would participate in their sales.

Pricing Test

The question of price level on the tire was made part of the market test. Early in the Cincinnati district introduction the business research department was given the task of conducting a pricing test. On the basis of its judgment regarding sales response to several prices to be tried, the level of the price on the new tire relative to the standard tire was to be set. During the first 12 weeks the 600×16 tire was priced at $21.95 as compared with a price of $18.85 at the time for the conventional casing and inner tube, or a ratio of 100:116. During the next eight weeks the price on the new tire was raised to $23.75, a ratio of 100:126; during the following four weeks the price was raised to $24.95, which made the ratio with the standard tire and tube price, 100:132.

At this time the consumer could get protection from tire punctures in regular tires by using the B. F. Goodrich Company's Seal-O-Matic inner tube, an inner tube lined with sealant material. The list price of a standard casing with the Seal-O-Matic tube was $27.70. The price of this tube and a premium-quality tire was $46.30. Thus, all the prices used in the price experiment were appreciably lower than for a tire and the puncture-sealing inner tube combination.

On the basis of sales response to the several prices and costs of producing and marketing the tire, the business research department decided that $24.95 was the optimum price; in other words, on the basis of volume and margins the company and its retailers would derive more dollar profit from this price than from either lower or higher prices. The prices on other sizes of tubeless tires were set approximately in the same ratio with standard tires, that is, in the neighborhood of 100:130–135. The margin available to the dealer, if he followed these prices, was slightly wider than for standard tires—38% versus 35%.

As previously noted, the management gave prominent display of prices in its advertising, thereby calling attention to the fact that the new tubeless tire with its puncture-sealing feature and other benefits cost only about one-third more than the standard tire-and-tube combination and less than the standard tire and puncture-sealing tube.

Forecast of Future Tubeless Tire Sales

One of the objectives of the market test was to get data of consumer sales response which might serve as a guide for future production and sales planning. On the basis of sales in the district during the test, a member of the business research department concluded that the future sales promise of the tire was great. A very large market was developing very quickly. The fact that over 40% of sales were to Ford, Chevrolet, and Plymouth owners indicated that the appeal of the tire at the prices adopted was not alone to owners of high-price cars. The market researcher estimated on the basis of all Cincinnati data that in the first year after national distribution was completed, about 20% of the replacement tire sales of the company would be tubeless tires.

The Cincinnati market test produced evidence helpful to the management in ways other than those mentioned thus far. The dealer enthusiasm for the tire and the sales results attained indicated the wisdom of the company's placing promotional emphasis on the tubeless tire in its advertising and selling rather than on the company's premium tire and its Seal-O-Matic puncture-sealing inner tube, which had been receiving emphasis.

The test had also revealed that instruction of dealers' service personnel in large regional meetings was not sufficient. Individual demonstration in dealers' places of business was necessary to insure satisfactory service.

Lastly, and of great importance, the market testing period revealed the significant selling points of the tire and the nature of buyers' reactions; thus the advertising appeals and the method of presenting them could be pointed accordingly.

Start of Expansion to National Market and Product Troubles

With sales going well in the test market, plans were made for entry into the Indianapolis district in June 1948. Because of the rapid increase in sales in Cincinnati and the need for substantial stocks to fill the pipelines of the Indianapolis district, production of the tire was undertaken at the Tuscaloosa plant.

As in the Cincinnati district the plan of putting on demonstrations of the tire before public officials was followed in Indianapolis. In every city a large amount of publicity was obtained.

Sales activities had not proceeded far in Indianapolis when the management was confronted with the appearance of consumer troubles arising from imperfections that showed up in many of the tires in the heat of summer weather. Consumer complaints regarding tires tend to peak in the hot months when, in addition to higher air temperature, there is more driving, especially high-speed driving, and increased driving over rough roads.

Early investigation showed that the problem stemmed from the move to Tuscaloosa and mass-production methods. The first tires made in the Akron plant under the careful supervision of the engineering staff stood up. When moving to Tuscaloosa, precautions were taken to maintain quality. Only tire makers with long experience were assigned to produce the new tires. The factory set up rigid inspection and thought that it had good quality control. But, as so often happens when a new product is moved from a pilot operation into mass production, unforeseen product shortcomings appeared.

As the summer grew warm and a rash of complaints on the new tire developed, the management went into high gear to meet the situation. The tubeless tire had had tremendous publicity. The dealer organization had adopted the product with enthusiasm. Sales in the Cincinnati district had been surprisingly good. If the product went sour at this point, the reputation of the company would be gravely injured among dealers and consumers. The management felt that it had to guard against such injury at all costs.

Management stopped the manufacture of tubeless tires in the Tuscaloosa plant and set up production in the Akron plant under the careful supervision of the technical group as had been practiced before.

The sales department took up all dealer stocks that were defective and replaced these with stocks produced in the Akron plant that were known to be good. The new tires produced to quality standards in Akron were marked so that dealers would know they were satisfactory. This move of replacing questionable tires with tires marked as good was looked upon later as an important turning point in dispelling doubts of the dealers and in restoring confidence in the tire.

While the above steps were in progress, the service department, the development department, and the sales and engineering forces were busy investigating the product complaints, determining the causes of troubles and satisfying consumers. On many a day a plane would leave Akron in the morning and members of the sales, engineering, and service departments would spend the next several days talking with users of the new products and finding out what difficulties, if any, had developed. Tires giving trouble were replaced.

Many of the defective tires were taken to Akron and were there cut up and carefully studied to get at causes. Much of the consumer trouble came from leakage of air which might stem from any of a number of troubles. One cause was defective bead construction, the defects of which were not caught by inspectors. It was the opinion of some executives that the trouble stemmed in part from using experienced tire makers in the Tuscaloosa plant. Although trained to turn out the new tire, they were inclined to go back to old methods which were deeply set by habit.

Sometimes the difficulties came from poor servicing and mounting of tires, a problem which the service department finally ironed out. Other difficulties arose from puncture sealant that was defective. In some instances the sealant did not seal; in others it tended to run to the center, giving a thump or shimmy to the wheel.

By year's end, after some six months of intensive work, the management had found the causes of the difficulties and how to overcome them. In order to be sure of the product, however, production was kept under careful supervision in the Akron plant. In consequence, production was limited and expansion was retarded.

Management was under no pressure from unused productive capacity to speed up opening of new territories. In fact, all production of tubeless tires was carried on in Akron until 1950 when, after build up of a substantial manufacturing know-how and under the pressure from expansion of sales, production was moved to other plants.

Expansion Territorially

By late fall of 1948, with quality control firmly established in manufacture and with production capacity increased, the management decided to start territorial expansion again and elected to open up the Jacksonville sales district as a starter in February 1949. Several reasons dictated entry into this territory:

1. The management decided to subject the tire further to the rigors of hot-weather driving such as might be found in Florida when it was winter in the North.

2. By exercising showmanship there was opportunity to get a great deal of publicity about the tire and to expose it to an influential group of consumers.

The Florida district was opened with the same publicity techniques that had been followed in Cincinnati and Indianapolis. After the dealers of the district had been indoctrinated, a series of demonstrations and a dinner meeting were put on in Miami, attended by President Collyer and Vice President Hoban, by automotive leaders, public officials, and important guests who were in Florida at the height of the winter season. Skillful showmanship was employed to impress observers with the benefits of the tire. Cars were driven over broken glass. The spike-board test was put on. Then came the dramatic swerve test in which cars driven at high speeds were swerved from side to side to demonstrate the holding ability of the tire. Pretty diving girls put ice picks into the tires under water. Seminole Indians from nearby reservations shot arrows into the tires, all without loss of air. Mr. Collyer and Mr. Hoban told the story of the development of the tire.

Even though press and radio had carried extensive news stories nationally about the tire a year before, these new demonstrations in Florida got a tremendous national news coverage. The revolutionary product development, together with the striking demonstrations, served to keep the news alive.

Further Publicity

Not only did the management get a large quantity of newspaper and radio news stories but leading magazines ran feature articles on the tire.

—*Life* had a story on Herzegh in its issue of February 14, 1949, just in advance of the Florida opening.
—In April of 1949, *Popular Science* ran a three-page story on the tire.
—*Reader's Digest*, in its May issue, ran a digest of the *Popular Science* article.
—In the early summer, *Mechanics Illustrated* carried a story.
—The *Wall Street Journal* in June carried a story regarding the successful market reception of the tire.

Still further publicity was had through movie newsreels, which showed films of the demonstrations that had been put on with such showmanship in Miami.

That the public throughout the country was becoming increasingly aware of the tire, although it was on sale only in three sales districts, was shown by surveys conducted by Elmo Roper, Inc., among a sample representative of the whole country. The first of these surveys was made in May 1948; the second in May 1949. To the question "Do you happen to know of any new auto tire put on the market since the War?" the following percentages gave responses of awareness of the tubeless development:

> May 1948......................1.6%
> May 1949......................9.5%

Further Territorial Expansion before the Korean War Outbreak

After the Florida district had been opened, the sales department moved next to the Minneapolis district. This jump clear across the country to the north was dictated by a desire to get established in the far northern states to learn what problems might develop in the tire under conditions of intense cold. Butyl inner tubes had given trouble in cold weather after their introduction. The management also wanted to know what would happen to the sealant inside the tire in intensely cold weather. Both hot and cold tests had been made in the tire during the developmental period, but the management felt the need of testing the tire under actual consumer use to determine possible difficulties not revealed by usual product tests.

In the Minneapolis district a new advertising approach was tested. Up to this time large-size advertisements similar to those employed in the Cincinnati district had been used in Indianapolis and Florida. In Minneapolis the management decided to see whether the same lineage devoted to a large number of small-space reader advertisements would prove more effective than the page and half-page advertisements that had been employed up to this time. In short, the hypothesis to be tested was whether an expenditure for frequent small-reader advertisements would generate more sales response than would the same expenditure in fewer large advertisements with dominating illustrations.

For this test they took four cities in the Minneapolis district in which the reader-type advertisements would be used and matched these cities as well as they could for similarity of characteristics with four cities where the usual large advertisements would be run.

On the basis of sales data the test was inconclusive. Sales in cities running the small advertisements were not appreciably different from those in which the large advertisements were run. As is so often the case in such tests of advertising as measured by sales, the inability to control and keep uniform many variables affecting sales results, such as the degree and aggressiveness of dealers' personal selling effort and the quality of point of purchase display, made appraisal of advertising effect uncertain.

The Minneapolis district proved to be an excellent sales territory for the new tire. What had previously been considered a price-minded market became a good market for the puncture-sealing tubeless tire at its higher price. In this area of wide open spaces characterized by many gravel roads with proclivity for puncturing tires, the new puncture-sealing feature won converts.

Subsequent to the Minneapolis expansion, starting in August of 1949, the sales department stepped up its entry into other territories as indicated in the following schedule:

Pittsburgh Sales District...August 1949	Denver	Sales District	February 1950
Cleveland " " ...November 1949	Los Angeles " "		February 1950
Detroit " " ...January 1950	Salt Lake City " "		February 1950
Omaha " " ...January 1950	San Francisco " "		March 1950
St. Louis " " ...January 1950	Seattle " "		March 1950

With the outbreak of the Korean War in March of 1950, further expansion was halted. Restrictions on rubber prevented any increase in production of tubeless tires. A production schedule based on previous production records permitted the territories opened up to carry on their selling. In January of 1951, six southern districts were permitted to handle the tire, but stocks were inadequate and no promotion was undertaken. Some 10 of 30 districts were still without the tire.

In opening up the territories listed above, much the same patterns of publicity, sales effort, and promotion were followed that had been developed in Cincinnati. In the fall of 1950, with the rapid opening of territories, single magazine advertisements on the tubeless tire were run in *The Saturday Evening Post* and *Life* in August. In October, on the network television program, "Celebrity Time," the first TV commercials on the new tire were given, demonstrating the spike-board test.

Discovery of Safety from Blowouts

During the latter part of 1948, management became aware of a major consumer benefit in the new tire of which it had no knowledge previously —namely, safety from blowouts, one of the chief hazards of driving, particularly high-speed driving. The company had come into the Cincinnati and Indianapolis districts preoccupied with the smooth riding and puncture-sealing benefits.

After introduction of the tire the service department kept a careful record of all consumer complaints and difficulties. During and after the summer months when complaints had become more numerous, analyses were made of all reported tire weaknesses and failures. From these analyses the service department people discovered that among all the difficulties reported tire blowouts did not appear.

A study by the technical people indicated the reason for this fact. Blowouts in the traditional tire-and-tube combination developed from a break of cords in the body of the tire, usually from injury in hitting a chuck hole, a curbing, or some object. In the ordinary tire-and-tube combination the tube worked into the break and eventually became chafed to a point where it let go, blowing through the side wall or tread of the tire. Studies showed that when a tubeless tire was bruised and the Butyl liner which was a part of the carcass developed a break or crack, there occurred what might be described as a "slowout" rather than a blowout. Instead of a sudden release of air, the tire would go down in a slow, safe flat. Before any use could be made of a claim of safety from blowouts, however, the matter had to be fully investigated by the technical people. They devoted approximately a year to laboratory and field tests investigating the reasons for the freedom from blowouts and established with certainty the propriety of the company featuring such a claim.

After the research had been made, the company invited the American Automobile Association to supervise a test and to certify the blowout protection. Subsequently, when the claim of safety from blowout was incorporated into the advertising, a statement made by the AAA certifying the blowout safety of the tubeless tire was featured for some time in magazine, newspaper, radio, and, later, television advertisements.

Entry into National Blanket Advertising

Although at the start of 1951 production was still restricted and some ten sales districts were still without the tire, the management decided, starting with February, to devote its national advertising to the tubeless tire. Thereafter practically all of the company's passenger car tire advertising, up to the time that this case was gathered, was devoted to the tubeless tire, not only the magazine and television advertising but also the local advertising carried on co-operatively with dealers. This policy was followed even though tubeless tire sales made up a small part of car tire sales at the time the national campaign was started. The new tire was the leader of the line. In it were the most significant consumer benefits in tires produced by B. F. Goodrich research; hence it was selected as the most interesting attention-gaining idea on which to build reputation and sales for all the car tire lines.

Development of the Safety Tread

During the period when Korean War restrictions were placed upon tire manufacture, the development department perfected another tire feature that the management decided to incorporate into the tubeless tire—namely, a tread unusually effective in reducing the dangers of skidding on wet or ice- and snow-covered roads. The improved traction of the new tread was secured by crosscutting the tread to provide 10,000 tiny grip blocks, which, when the driver applied the brakes, clung tightly to the road. Instead of sliding across a wet road these blocks would wipe the road dry and resist skidding.

In early 1952, with restrictions on tire manufacture no longer in force, the company was ready to go to national distribution with a tubeless tire for which it could claim not only better riding and puncture sealing qualities but also protection of car owners against blowouts and dangerous skidding. The tire was named the *Life-Saver*.

National Distribution and Advertising of Life-Saver Tires

The company filled the pipelines with Life-Saver tires throughout the nation and entered on a program of national advertising of this tire in April 1952. Thereafter, and even as this case is being written, practically all the company's tire advertising was devoted to the Life-Saver.

In the development of its advertising copy on the tubeless tire the advertising department and its agency from the start made use of various copy testing techniques in an attempt to increase the effectiveness of its advertisements—first readership reports and then Gallup-Robinson Impact records.

Demonstration of the product was the keynote of both publication and television advertising. Guided by readership analysis and the "playbacks" of the Gallup-Robinson reports, the advertising department sought to determine the type of illustration and copy that carried desired information to consumers and registered with them.

Just as demonstrations of the new tire in the introductory period had proved effective, large-size illustrations dramatically demonstrating the product which were used in publication advertisements were indicated to be effective in the copy research studies.

On the "Burns & Allen" television program the commercials gave an actual demonstration of the performance of the new tire. People saw the puff of dust and heard the bang when the tire with inner tube blew out and the rim hit the road. They heard the slow escape of air when the new tubeless tire had a slowout. They saw the tire roll over spikes without going flat. They saw the Life-Saver stop an automobile a car length sooner than other tires on wet roads.

Research reports showed the need of featuring price of the new tire in advertisements. Surveys showed that people were interested in the tire but assumed the price was high. Accordingly, the company adopted the unusual practice of advertising the price of the tubeless tire in its national advertisements.

Research studies also showed the importance of telling people where to get the new tire, so in all national publication advertising and TV commercials the practice was adopted of asking the consumer to look for the address of the nearest B. F. Goodrich dealer in the yellow pages of the telephone directory.

The volume of advertising on the tubeless tire in the period 1948–54, inclusive, is indicated in the following estimates, based on data from *Media Records* and *Publishers' Information Bureau:*

Year	Newspaper Dealer Co-operative (in Lines)	Magazines and Newspapers	Television	Radio
1948	20,000	Full page—*N. Y. T.* Full page—*W. S. J.*	. . . .	. . . .
1949	31,000	. . . .	. . . .	. . . .
1950	159,000	Full page—*Life* Full page—*S. E. Post*	One show in October devoted to report of users	. . . .
1951	159,000	$400,000	Appreciable part of expenditures of $762,000	. . . .
1952	739,000	$505,000	$864,000	. . . .
1953	191,000	$530,000	$849,000	$35,000
1954	849,000	$585,000	$994,000 network	. . . .

Development of the Safetyliner Tire

From the very outset of the tubeless tire marketing, the B. F. Goodrich Company made these tires available to the automotive industry in order that car manufacturers might test and keep themselves abreast of the tubeless development. Working with car manufacturers and incorporating some of their suggestions, the company put on the market in the Houston district a tubeless tire without the puncture sealant.

The management was anxious to get consumer experience of a tire without the sealant, which added appreciably to manufacturing costs. There was a feeling that if the tubeless tire was to be adopted as part of original equipment by automotive manufacturers, it was necessary to get the price of the tire down to that of the conventional tire and tube.

The tire without sealant had most of the features of the Life-Saver. It was tubeless, gave an easier ride, insured slowouts instead of blowouts, and lacked only the permanent puncture-sealing feature and the special crosscut tread. Because of the Butyl liner it gave temporary puncture-sealing resistance; that is, if a nail were picked up, the chances were that the driver could get to a nearby service station or possibly to his home, but the tire would go flat if the nail were pulled out. In turn, elimination of the sealant element gave a somewhat lighter tire, a feature that had appeal to automotive engineers trying to reduce the unsprung weight of cars. In addition, it gave a tire that was particularly fitted for long, high-speed driving because it did not heat up as much as other tires. Texas was chosen as an especially good testing ground for such a tire because of the long-distance, high-speed driving that occurred there in its warm climate. It was announced and advertised as "A Tire for Texans." From the Houston district the tire was introduced into Dallas, Oklahoma City, Kansas City, Denver, Omaha, and Minneapolis districts, all high-speed, long-distance areas.

From the start the product gave excellent service. Complaints were few. Sales were not large because the price was too near that of the Life-Saver tire with its puncture-sealing appeal. The Safetyliner was priced relative to the conventional tire and tube at 100:125. Costs at the time were thought to justify this price. The Life-Saver, with a ratio of 100:135, cost the consumer so little more that he generally chose it over the non-sealant tire.

After the above districts had been covered, the company was in a position to move fast. It was no longer held back by production limitations. Named the Safetyliner, the tire was introduced in other sales districts. No great sales volume was obtained on the tire. Advertising and sales effort were devoted primarily to the Life-Saver. The management was more interested in proving the suitability of the Safetyliner than in making high replacement sales. Realizing the need of a good story to induce the auto manufacturers to accept the tire, the management wanted to build a success story, and did so.

In May 1954 the B. F. Goodrich Company reduced the price of the Safetyliner to the conventional tube-and-tire level. With this reduction in price came announcement of adoption of tubeless tires as original equipment on 1955 models. Automobile manufacturers had had the tire, had tested it, and knew its value from their own tests as well as from reports regarding consumers' experience.

In October 1954 the B. F. Goodrich Company announced a new Safetyliner tubeless tire available nationally at the price of the conventional inner tube and tire. In this new tire the structural features of the original Safetyliner were combined with an entirely new tread design which provided unusual traction and skid resistance and quiet operation.

Competitive Activity

The B. F. Goodrich Company's announcement of the tubeless tire late in 1947 evidently caught the tire industry by surprise, for no competitive tubeless tire was placed on the market until 1951, three years after the B. F. Goodrich introduction of the tire in Cincinnati.

Reportedly, many executives in the rubber industry looked upon the B. F. Goodrich tire as a promotional stunt without real threat to the conventional tire. Two of the leading companies were known to have so informed their dealers. A survey by one of the large tire companies in 1948 contained this statement:

The new B. F. Goodrich tubeless tire is only an advertising promotion. Don't let your dealers be concerned. If it is ever a success we will build it.

Another large manufacturer bulletined its entire sales and dealer organization as follows:

The activity of a large manufacturer in announcing for sale tubeless tires has caused questions by quite a number of our dealers and organization. This is to advise you that we do not believe the tubeless tire would be better than a tire-and-tube combination, and we regard this product as more of an advertising novelty than a permanent new product innovation.

While the competing tire companies may have played down the tubeless development in their own dealer organizations, subsequent events indicate that they probably put their development staffs to work to produce a tubeless tire, for by 1954 all the leading tire companies had placed tubeless tires on the market.

During the various stages of development of the tubeless tire the B. F. Goodrich Company had made application for various patents, and on February 26, 1952, the company announced that the United States Patent Office had granted patents covering many features, including the Butyl liner and the rim seal ridges.

Upon receiving its patents the management faced the issue of whether to license other manufacturers to build tubeless tires. The decision on this question was in the affirmative, and all tire manufacturers were informed of their opportunity to license. As of the end of 1954 no licenses had been applied for.

In 1951 the Firestone Tire & Rubber Company announced its "blowout safe, puncture-sealing, tubeless tire." The Firestone tire provided a sealant and along with it an inner diaphragm to provide a slow letdown of the tire in case of blowout. The Firestone tire made use of rim-sealing ridges similar to those employed in the B. F. Goodrich tire. The new tire was a premium-priced tire. In 1953 Firestone brought out a lower-priced tubeless tire without the diaphragm. Both of the Firestone tubeless tires received heavy advertising in newspapers and national magazines on their introduction. Later they received advertising as well on the Firestone Company's radio and television programs.

No further tubeless tires by competing companies were announced and placed on the market until 1954, when there appeared in quick succession:

Kelly-Springfield—January 1954
The U.S. Rubber Company—May 1954
Goodyear Tire & Rubber Company—August 1954
General Tire Company—August 1954

The decision of the automobile manufacturers to make tubeless tires standard equipment occurred early in 1954, and the leading tire companies shared in this original equipment business.

In May 1953 the B. F. Goodrich Company filed suit in the U.S. District Court in Cleveland, charging Firestone with infringing its patents in the manufacture and sale of tubeless tires. Subsequently, B. F. Goodrich also brought suit against the U.S. Rubber Company.

Sales and Profitability of Tubeless Tires

Sales of the tubeless tire in the early months of the Cincinnati market were so excellent that they led to the business research department's optimistic forecast that some 20% of the company's replacement sales would be tubeless tires in the year after national distribution was attained. But the plans for expanding to the national market were greatly retarded by the dropping of production at Tuscaloosa and the rundown of product difficulties. Subsequently, restrictions on production in 1950–51 during the Korean War again prevented expansion nationally, and the increase in sales that had been planned.

Once restrictions on production were removed and the improved Life-Saver was marketed nationally in 1952, the company experienced an increase in sales far beyond anything it had ever experienced before with a specialty tire. By the end of 1951, sales of tubeless tires, substantially all of which were the BFG self-sealing tire, represented 1% of the industry's sales of replacement tires. By 1954, over 20% of B. F. Goodrich brand sales of replacement tires were tubeless. By the time the tire was adopted as standard equipment by automobile manufacturers in 1954 the B. F. Goodrich Company had manufactured and marketed in the neighborhood of 3½ million tubeless tires, which it was estimated had been driven 60 billion miles.

With the adoption of tubeless tires as standard equipment for 1955 automobiles, the sales and production picture quickly changed. A large percentage of the production of the industry's car tires was put on tubeless tires. Executives in the industry estimated that probably two thirds of 1955 car tire production would be tubeless and that this percentage would rise to 75 or 80% in 1956.

Profitwise the tubeless tire gave a good account of itself as new products go. A substantial loss was incurred on 1948 operations, in large part because of the expenses attending the running down of product difficulties and the replacement of defective stocks.

Losses were incurred during the early part of 1949 when replacement of tires was still under way, but by the end of 1949, with regained confidence and mounting sales, the tubeless operation produced enough profit to break even. Sales in 1950 and 1951 were held back by the Korean situation, but the operation was profitable.

With the launching of the Life-Saver in 1952 and the rapid sales increases that occurred, profits were reported very satisfactory.

~~~

CASE 2: JULES MONTENIER, INC.[1]

NOTE: *This case describes the first four years of introductory marketing activity for "Stopette Spray" deodorant. Probably it is desirable to analyze the various steps taken in promotion on a year-to-year basis.* QUESTIONS TO CONSIDER: *(1) Was the company wise to proceed in its introduction of the product without product testing? (2) Was it wise to begin the introductory promotion in Chicago rather than in a smaller community? (3) Was it wise to begin with department stores rather than to begin with widespread distribution? (4) After the Chicago "success," did the company proceed soundly? (5) Was good use made of co-operative advertising allowances? (6) Of other promotional devices? (7) Did the company move from a "push" to a "pull" strategy quickly enough? (8) As of the end of the case, what do you see as the principal problems facing Montenier's management? For example, what are the principal problems faced with respect to (a) advertising copy, and (b) the size of the advertising budget?*

Jules Montenier, Inc., was organized in Chicago in June 1947 to distribute "Stopette Spray," a new spray-type personal deodorant which was manufactured in the Chicago plant of the Hubbard Chemical Company. Dr. Jules B. Montenier, the president, was one of the country's leading cosmetic research chemists who had developed "Arrid" deodorant, "Lustre-Creme" shampoo, "5-Day Deodorant Pads," and a number of the "Dana" brand cosmetics. He and Mr. William A. Wright, sales vice president, who had considerable experience working with wholesale and retail buyers and in newspapers, publicity, public relations, investment banking, and organizational work, were determined to make Stopette Spray the No. 1 deodorant in the United States by the end of 1951.

Their initial marketing plan was to introduce Stopette Spray to the market immediately, even though the company had no significant advertising and sales promotional fund; to obtain wide distribution as quickly as possible; and, once sales income was received, to use earnings to promote aggressively further sales of Stopette Spray.

Deodorants and Their Use

A deodorant is a chemical compound which masks or destroys offensive odors temporarily. An antiperspirant deodorant will destroy an offensive odor and prevent the formation of further odor by closing the pores of the skin in desired places. The human body contains approximately $3\frac{1}{2}$ million sweat glands located in the deeper layers of the skin. Through minute pores of the skin, these glands exude perspiration, 98% water and 2% salts, such as sodium chloride. Working in harmony with these sweat glands are the apocrine glands and the sebaceous glands, the latter of which secrete "sebum," a fatty, oily matter to lubricate the skin surface. In addition, the skin pores eliminate other organic matters which are the reject of dead body cells. This oily, fatty combination of waste matter

---

[1] Written by Martin V. Marshall.

becomes decomposed and gives off offensive odor. As a result of years of research, antiperspirant deodorants have been developed which not only destroy odors but also close temporarily the pores of the skin from one to seven days in the desired places by astringent action, thereby checking the perspiration and odor.

Most deodorants are made from salts of the metal aluminum, which salts are colorless, nontoxic, and possess an excellent astringent action. Certain aluminum salts, such as aluminum chloride and aluminum sulfo-carbolate, also possess antiseptic properties. Aluminum chloride, the most efficient deodorant, owes its action to the fact that it is a very acid salt, and the more acid the salt, the better the astringent action. If used alone in a cosmetic preparation, the high acidity of the salts of aluminum chloride acts as a strong irritant to the skin of many persons and is destructive to fabrics and colors, particularly if a hot iron is pressed against the fabric. To prevent these effects, the chloride salts generally are modified or buffed by a modifying chemical. Aluminum sulphate is another good astringent salt, and while it is less destructive to cotton fabrics than the chloride, it has a more destructive action on some silk fabrics.

In establishing the formula for Stopette Spray, Dr. Montenier utilized the efficient, strong properties of aluminum chloride and aluminum sulphate, modified by other chemicals, to make a deodorant particularly safe for contact with skin and clothing. Some of his processes were patented; some were kept secret.

The Deodorant Market

Jules Montenier, Inc., executives believed that a large market existed for deodorants. For instance, a Crowell-Collier Publishing Company survey indicated that at least 90% of the women readers of *Woman's Home Companion* used some type of deodorant. A *Milwaukee Journal* survey indicated that about 80% of the women in 12 major market areas and about 21% of the men in ten major market areas used deodorants.

In 1947 there were a number of brands of deodorants on the market, either of the powder or cream type. Mr. Wright estimated total annual sales to be approximately $27 million to $28 million. He had concluded from market research data that Arrid, a cream deodorant, was the leader in the field, with an estimated 25% of the total market. Although Dr. Montenier and Mr. Wright believed that most of the deodorants available were good products, they felt that a spray-type deodorant in a completely new type of container, a thermoplastic bottle, would be preferred over the older types of deodorants which required application by hand and the consequent bother of washing. Moreover, cream deodorants in the course of time tended to dry out. To use Stopette Spray the user merely squeezed the bottle to eject, through a special built-in atomizer head, a misty spray, which enveloped the intended skin area and dried instantly. The thermoplastic bottle would not break, spill, or leak if the bottle top was firmly replaced, and it could be carried safely in pocket, purse, or traveling case. In one 2¼-ounce bottle there was sufficient liquid for hundreds of sprays, enough for about a year's use.

The retail sale of deodorants was seasonal because consumers usually thought deodorants were needed most during the warm or hot months. Consequently, in July 1947, in order to take advantage of the remaining favorable selling season, Montenier executives decided to introduce Stopette Spray to the market at once, without testing. Moreover, the finances of the company were not sufficient to delay entry until a year later. The company had about $55,000 available to launch the enterprise. The costs of maintaining the company organization for the year would drain resources, unless sales income were developed.

Mr. Wright realized that he had an exceedingly difficult marketing job in 1947, because the toiletries field in general was in a noticeable slump; and in order to support production and marketing costs, the retail price for Stopette Spray would have to be high relative to competitive products. The range of deodorant prices was from 25 cents to about $1.00 for packages which would last customers from six months to a year, depending on the size. On the basis of estimated production and marketing costs, Mr. Wright believed that at the start the retail price for Stopette Spray (2¼-ounce bottle) would be at least $1.75 plus the 20% luxury tax. If sufficient volume were obtained and some production and marketing corners were cut, however, the product could be fair-traded at $1.25 plus tax. In anticipation of obtaining a satisfactory volume, the price was set at $1.25 plus tax. A margin of 40% was allowed retail outlets which were sold as direct accounts.

The Introduction of Stopette Spray

For a summary of the advertising and sales promotional activities of the Montenier company for the period 1947–50, see Exhibit 1. Items of this program are discussed below.

In July 1947 Mr. Wright, as the company's sole sales representative, called on the cosmetic buyers of the Chicago department stores. Some of the buyers' comments were: "It's too late in the season. We're not buying anything now." "It's new and revolutionary, but it won't sell." "It's priced too high. Why don't you sell it for a dollar or less?" "The public wants a cream deodorant, not a liquid." "Your package needs color." "The order book is closed until September." "Business is too slow."

Finally the cosmetic buyer of Mandel Brothers, a leading department store in Chicago, gave Mr. Wright an initial order and agreed to place advertisements in Chicago newspapers which were to be paid for by the Montenier company. Following this initial sale, two other leading stores, Marshall Field & Company and Carson, Pirie & Scott, gave orders to Jules Montenier, Inc. All three stores introduced the product on the same day, and in the first day all three stores sold their initial orders in three hours.

Mandel Brothers sold 1,200 bottles in three days, an unusual sales volume for a deodorant in such a short period.

Mr. Wright had called earlier on the beauty editors of the Chicago newspapers to tell them of the unique characteristics of Stopette Spray Deodorant. Just previous to the offering of the product by the three department stores, four leading feature articles concerning Stopette Spray appeared in the women's pages of the four leading dailies.

On August 21, 1947, Mr. Wright sent out a direct-mail piece, playing up the success of the Chicago introduction of the product, to 3,000 department-store buyers and merchandise managers, to 1,500 women's page editors, 200 buying syndicate representatives, 75 consumer and business paper editors, all newspaper-column syndicate editors, all radio and newspaper wire services, all radio commentators, and all leaders of women's clubs. The direct-mail piece consisted of a covering letter, reprints of the four newspaper feature stories, a broadside, and a sample bottle of Stopette Spray. The covering letter follows:

JULES MONTENIER, INC.

417 North State Street
Chicago 10, Illinois
Superior 9133
August 21, 1947

Dear Mr. Jones:

I thought you would be interested in reading the enclosed broadside which aims to give credit where credit is due, to the Chicago department stores and newspapers, for the successful introduction of STOPETTE SPRAY DEODORANT to the consuming public.

Without such help, I feel that any product in the toiletries field, no matter how good, would lie dormant. When a product is truly fine in quality, such superb backing by department stores and newspapers cannot fail to make it known to the public, and secure in acceptance.

Very sincerely yours,

JULES MONTENIER, INC.

/s/
William A. Wright
Sales Manager

WAW:VO

The broadside was a fourfold piece, 17 inches by 22 inches, the first fold reading "Here's How——." On the second fold, the broadside read: "New Stopette Spray—Complete sellout in three days of more than 1,000 bottles of Stopette Spray at Mandel Bros. as a result of *one single ad!*" The inside of the broadside had a full 17 inches by 22 inches of space, and is shown in Exhibit 2. Mr. Wright made the layout and wrote the copy for the broadside and for all other broadsides during 1947.

Immediately after sending out the direct-mail piece, Mr. Wright em-

Exhibit 1

JULES MONTENIER, INC.

Summary of Advertising and Sales Promotional Activities, 1947–50

Year	Sales Goal (Bottles)	Actual Sales (Bottles)	Plan	Advertising and Sales Promotional Activities	Expenditure
1947 (last 6 months)	500,000	518,000	(1) To introduce Stopette Spray to the market through the trade by use of direct mail, publicity, and cooperative newspaper advertisements. Concentration on department and women's specialty stores. (2) Considerable emphasis upon personal selling.	(1) Direct mail and publicity: July 17 – Feature story appeared in Chicago Herald American, telling of Stopette Spray. July 18 – Feature story – Chicago Daily News. July 21 – Feature story – Chicago Sun July 23 – Feature story – Chicago Daily Tribune July 23 – Mandel Bros. store advertised Stopette Spray in Daily Tribune and sold 1,200 bottles in first day. Aug. 21 – Direct-mail piece telling of success of Stopette Spray at Mandel Bros. sent to all department and women's specialty store cosmetic buyers and to publicity people. Oct. 17 – Direct-mail letter telling buyers of the success of Stopette Spray after 8 weeks in the market. Oct. 24 – Direct-mail piece entitled "Let's Look at the Record." Oct.–Dec. – Additional mailings about every 7 days playing up any news of Stopette Spray which Mr. Wright thought might be of interest to the trade. December – Direct-mail letter to beauty-shop suppliers, offering an exclusive distributorship in their territory for Stopette Spray. 1947 Total expenditure (2) Cooperative newspaper and radio advertising.	$ 10,000 5,000 $ 15,000
1948	2,000,000	2,187,336	(1) To continue emphasizing department and women's specialty stores as retail outlets while widening distribution through attention to beauty-shop suppliers, independent druggists, and drug chains. (2) To launch a consumer advertising program when there was (1) evidence of repeat purchases and (2) sufficient funds available to support such a campaign.	(1) Direct mail – Continued use of mass mailings and periodic follow-up mailings to department stores, women's specialty stores, beauty-shop suppliers, independent druggists, and chain druggists. (2) Cooperative newspaper advertising appearing under store names, with 100% payment by Jules Montenier, Inc. (3) Trade papers – one beauty-shop paper and 6 pharmaceutical journals. (4) Rotogravure and newspaper advertising in selected markets under the Montenier company name. (5) Magazines – Cosmopolitan and The New Yorker. (6) National radio spots. (7) Point-of-sale material. (8) PM's. (9) Miscellaneous sales promotion 1948 Total expenditure	$ 10,000 14,000 6,000 15,000 10,000 8,000 12,000 26,000 2,500 $103,500

Year	Budget	Actual	Objectives	Expenditures	Amount
1949	5,000,000	5,077,953	(1) To concentrate promotional efforts on present distribution channels and outlets. (2) To increase the expenditures in consumer advertising with the objective of moving rapidly to establish Stopette Spray as one of the 2 or 3 leading deodorants by 1950.	(1) Direct mail.	$ 4,000
				(2) Cooperative newspaper advertising, with 100% payment by Montenier.	73,000
				(3) Trade papers – Beauty Fashions, Cosmetics and Toiletries, Modern Beauty Shop, American Hairdresser, Post Exchange and Ship's Service Stores, McKesson & Robbins Moneymaker, Southern Pharmaceutical Journal, Pacific Drug Review, Northwestern Druggist, Central Pharmaceutical Journal, Southeastern Drug Journal, Apothecary.	13,000
				(4) Rotogravure and newspaper advertising – New York News, Newark News, Philadelphia Inquirer, Pittsburgh Press, New York Times, Boston Globe, Washington Star, Baltimore Sun, Buffalo Courier-Express, Providence Journal, Cleveland Plain Dealer, Columbus Dispatch, Akron Beacon-Journal, Toledo Blade, Indianapolis Star, Louisville Courier-Journal, Youngstown Vindicator, Detroit News, Atlanta Journal, Nashville Tennessean, New Orleans Times-Picayune, St. Paul Pioneer News, Cincinnati Enquirer, Minneapolis Tribune, Milwaukee Journal, Springfield (Mass.) Republican, Des Moines Register, St. Louis Post-Dispatch, Denver Post, Salt Lake City Deseret, San Antonio Express, Chicago Tribune, Los Angeles Times, Houston Chronicle.	47,000
				(5) Magazines – Life, Look, Cosmopolitan, Charm, Glamour, Mademoiselle, McCall's, Today's Woman, The New Yorker.	118,000
				(6) Television – Spots and women's participation programs	10,000
				(7) Point-of-sale material	30,000
				(8) PM's	67,000
				(9) Miscellaneous sales promotion	4,400
				1949 Total expenditure	$366,400
1950	10,000,000	8,563,875 (as of 9/1/50)	To establish a strong consumer brand preference for Stopette Spray Deodorant and to make the product one of the top two deodorant brands by the end of 1950.	(1) Direct mail.	$ 8,000
				(2) Cooperative newspaper advertising, with 100% payment by Montenier.	125,000
				(3) Trade papers (same as in 1949)	16,000
				(4) Rotogravure and newspapers (same as in 1949)	138,000
				(5) Magazines (same as in 1949)	175,000
				(6) Television program – "What's My Line?"	322,000
				(7) Point-of-sale material	88,000
				(8) PM's	unknown
				(9) Miscellaneous sales promotion	18,000
				1950 Total expenditure	$882,000

ployed and trained three additional sales representatives. In addition, in August he exhibited Stopette Spray at the Philadelphia Cosmetic Show. In Mr. Wright's opinion the product received outstanding attention at the show. In September, he exhibited it at the Chicago Toiletries Show with similar success in getting attention. Shortly thereafter, more salesmen were added. Eventually the company had a total of nine salesmen. No salesman covered less than three states or more than seven. On the basis of his estimates of national deodorant sales and figures of population and income, Mr. Wright developed a sales quota for each state and, from those figures, a quota for each sales territory. The company's national sales goal for the last six months of 1947 was set at 500,000 bottles of Stopette Spray Deodorant.

In 1947 and 1948 salesmen were paid 8% commission on sales; in 1949, 7½%; and in 1950, 5% on the first third of quota, 7% on the second third, and 10% on the last third. In 1950 the range of salesmen's commissions was from $10,000 minimum to $30,000 maximum, with better than half of the salesmen receiving over $19,000 per year.

For the remainder of 1947 Mr. Wright established a system of continuous bulletins and mailings, including personalized letters to buyers, merchandise managers, news editors, and salesmen. He picked up anything that he could find in the company's current marketing experience that would make a good story and prepared a direct-mail piece telling the trade of the story. Mr. Wright believed that no mailing should be sent out to the same list until at least seven days had elapsed. Typically these direct-mail pieces consisted of a covering letter and a broadside.

The following letter of October 17, 1947, which was addressed to cosmetic buyers in department and specialty stores, is an example of the type of follow-up direct mail being used during this period:

JULES MONTENIER, INC.

417 North State Street
Chicago 10, Illinois
Superior 9133
October 17, 1947

Dear Mr. Jones:

Will you help me to arrive at a decision?

At the outset of our efforts to introduce STOPETTE SPRAY DEODORANT to the consumer public, we decided on a policy of distribution to the finest department stores and women's specialty stores.

Proffered advice in the beginning stated that not only were we introducing an antiperspirant deodorant too late in the season (I thought people needed it all year round), but that a deodorant is an item suitable only for mass distribution through every available outlet. We formulated our policy on the theory that fine stores could and would do the necessary job of distribution in securing sizable consumer volume.

Since the initial introduction of STOPETTE SPRAY eight weeks ago, our belief and decision have been vindicated. Not only have initial orders from stores been extremely large in quantity but reorder after reorder during these past weeks have been equally heavy. At this writing, our production facilities are taxed to the utmost in a vain attempt to keep apace with incoming orders and reorders.

Obviously, all this is very gratifying to us, but I am thinking now of the near future—the months of November, December, January, February—and need your advice as to what course of action you feel I should follow to stimulate your sales and increase your everyday number of men and women customers.

My questions are these:

1. Will department stores continue to advertise and promote STOPETTE SPRAY DEODORANT? Will you?
2. Do you think department-store buyers and merchandise managers agree with *Women's Wear Daily* in its statement that STOPETTE'S "novelty action and appearance appealed to buyers as having good Christmas sales potentialities, particularly as a stocking gift." What do you think?
3. What can I do to help you sell more STOPETTE SPRAY, and thus maintain during the coming months the splendid momentum we have gained in such a few short weeks?

Can we, for example, arrange to send a bottle of STOPETTE SPRAY to each of your salesgirls in conjunction with a store promotion? Can we tie in with a store advertising promotion by sending bottles of STOPETTE SPRAY to each of a list of organized men's clubs, women's clubs, university fraternities and sororities, or other group organizations in your locality? Can we tie in with a store fall fashion promotion or radio program, or with a local sporting event affecting and affected by the store?

All over the nation department stores are still breaking out with advertisements announcing the introduction of STOPETTE SPRAY as the newest, most revolutionary idea to hit the cosmetic market, and the ads are paying off, as witness a few of the orders over the past few weeks:

Woodward & Lathrop, Washington, D.C.	10 Gross
J. L. Hudson Co., Detroit, Mich.	5 "
Gimble Bros., Philadelphia, Pennsylvania	5 "
Ed. Schuster & Co., Milwaukee, Wisc.	5 "
The White House, San Francisco, Calif.	5 "
J. W. Robinson Co., Los Angeles, Calif.	4 "
The Dayton Co., Minneapolis, Minn.	5 "
Wm. Filene's Sons Co., Boston, Mass.	5 "
Joseph Horne Co., Pittsburgh, Pa.	5 "
Burdine's, Miami, Fla.	4 "
O'Connor, Moffat & Co., San Francisco, Calif.	4 "
Jordan Marsh, Boston, Mass.	5 "
Kaufmann's, Pittsburgh, Pa.	5 "

To my mind this is evidence of enthusiastic consumer acceptance, but I believe it would be unsound business to assume this will continue unaided. Only by intelligent planning and sound promotional ideas can we keep STOPETTE SPRAY bouncing along in your store. This is where you can help me, if you will.

Will you write me at your earliest opportunity?

With best personal regards.

Very sincerely yours,
JULES MONTENIER, INC.

/s/
William A. Wright
Sales Manager

Exhibit 3 shows an example of one of the many broadsides used by the company during this introductory period.

The total expenditure by the company for direct mail during the last six months of 1947 was $10,000.

In addition, during the introductory period, a co-operative promotional program was offered in the form of a contract to retail outlets, providing for the selection of one of three promotional alternatives, if desired.

Under alternative (1) a store would permit Jules Montenier, Inc., to give PM's[2] 10% of the *retail* price of Stopette Spray to each retail sales-clerk upon presentation to the Montenier company of a bonus card, signed by the retail salesclerk and countersigned by the store owner or buyer. Retail salesclerks were furnished with a bonus card which could be folded into an envelope addressed to the Montenier company. The bonus card provided 40 spaces for bonus stickers. The bonus stickers were small black-and-white stickers that came with each package of Stopette Spray Deodorant. The retail clerk removed a sticker from the package at the time of the sale and placed it in one of the spaces on the bonus card. Upon securing ten or more stickers the retail salesclerk could send the bonus card to the Montenier company and a bonus check was immediately sent in return.

Under alternative (2), in place of an offering of PM's, a retail store could take advantage of a co-operative allowance for newspaper or radio advertising. All advertising was to be invoiced to Jules Montenier, Inc., on the basis of local rates and was to be accompanied by tear sheets. All invoices submitted to the company were paid, with the proviso that the co-operative newspaper allowances should not exceed 10% of the full *net* purchase price of the retail store's direct purchases from Jules Montenier, Inc. Suggested newspaper cuts and radio commercials were furnished to the retailer.

Under alternative (3), both PM's and allowances for co-operative newspaper and radio advertising could be used, but the combined PM and advertising allowance could not exceed 10% of the full *retail* price of the retail store's direct purchases from the company. A PM of an amount agreed upon by the Montenier company and the retail store was paid to retail salesclerks in the same manner as in alternative (1), except that the bonus card had to be completed with no less than 20 bonus stickers, and, necessarily, the PM was less than under alternative (1). All advertising was invoiced to the company as in alternative (2).

All three promotional alternatives required the retailer's use of counter or window display material during the time the arrangement was in effect. Upon a 30-day written notice either party could cancel the signed agreement with regard to any of these alternatives.

---

[2] The term "PM" stands for "premium merchandise," for the sales of which special commissions are given to retail salesclerks in order to stimulate special selling efforts. "PM" is sometimes referred to as "push money."

Exhibit 3

JULES MONTENIER, INC.

Nieman-Marcus Broadside

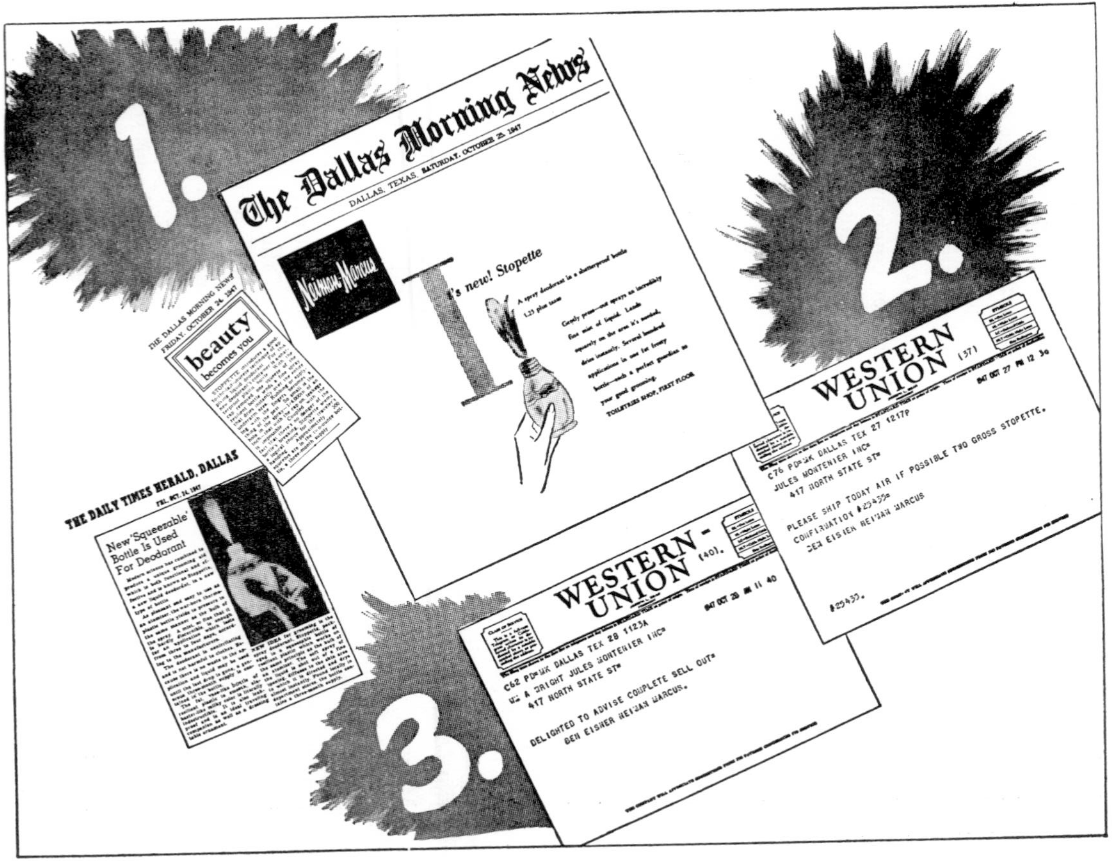

The total expenditure by the company for the last six months of 1947 under these alternatives was $5,000.

In December 1947 Mr. Wright obtained one order of two gross of Stopette Spray from a Chicago beauty-shop supply house, which, two days later, ordered an additional ten gross. Following up on this entry into a new retail channel, Mr. Wright sent a mailing to a selected list of beauty-shop suppliers in key centers, offering exclusive wholesale distributorships for Stopette Spray Deodorant.

Stopette Spray Advertising and Promotion—1948

In late 1947 Mr. Wright began planning the 1948 Stopette Spray campaign. He decided to continue to emphasize promotion of the product through department and women's specialty stores, but also to give increased attention to securing distribution and promotion of the product through drugstores and beauty shops. He established a national sales goal of two million bottles for the year and an advertising and promotional budget of about $100,000.

During January, February, and March 1948, Mr. Wright visited the principal retail stores in major cities throughout the United States, giving particular attention to those cities where Stopette Spray had not yet obtained distribution in the important department and women's specialty stores. This sales trip was preceded by a special mass mailing which offered each store display material, sales ideas, and 100% payment on a series of 200- or 300- line newspaper advertisements. Mr. Wright believed that this offer was an attractive incentive to induce desired retail outlets to promote Stopette Spray for the first time.

Initial experience had indicated that Stopette Spray was a new, salable deodorant which, once introduced into a market with some newspaper advertising and store display, gained wide acceptance and repeat purchases by the stores. Telling this success story to cosmetic buyers, first by direct mail and then by a personal sales call, was the principal objective of Mr. Wright's three-month sales trip. The merchandising appeal of Stopette Spray, coupled with a promise of advertising and point-of-sale aid by the Montenier company, generally created considerable interest among cosmetic buyers.

Mr. Wright improvised special advertising to meet special conditions in several cities. In Milwaukee, for example, there was a general slump in the toiletry business; the floor space allotted to toiletry departments had been reduced, and buyers were found to be eager to obtain new products and promotional aid. Mr. Wright induced Gimbel Brothers, Edward Schuster & Company, and The Boston Store to allow their names to be placed jointly under a series of 400-line advertisements which the Montenier company paid for. Mr. Wright believed that this joint-name advertising was unusually successful. After the introductory series of advertisements, the three Milwaukee stores continued to promote Stopette Spray individually. The Montenier company paid for the newspaper space. Subsequently this form of joint-store advertising in newspapers was used in Pittsburgh, Philadelphia, San Francisco, and Fort Worth.

As a result of the success of the joint-name co-operative advertising and because of his dissatisfaction with the amount of co-operative advertising under alternative (2), Mr. Wright followed a policy during the remainder of 1948 of paying 100% of the cost of co-operative advertising appearing under retailers' names. Specific authorization was given a retailer for such co-operative advertising, usually for from 6 to 12 advertisements of 100, 200, and 300 lines to appear during a stated period of time, say, three months. The cost of this space could not exceed stated space rates agreed upon by the retailer and the Montenier company.

In March 1948 another mass mailing was sent out to all department and women's specialty store buyers, a modified list of beauty-shop suppliers, 20,000 independent drugstores, all buying headquarters of chain drug companies, and a selected list of men's stores.

For each month from February to August, at least one mailing per month was sent to each name on selected lists. Often the same broadside was used several times with the same list. One example follows:

JULES MONTENIER, INC.

                                        417 North State Street
                                        Chicago 16, Illinois
                                        Superior 9133
                                        July 16, 1948

Dear Mr. Jones:

The Telephone Order Board (40 telephone girls) of Famous-Barr Company (The May Department Stores Company) of St. Louis, Missouri, *sold 1,271 bottles of STOPETTE SPRAY DEODORANT during the month of May,* and received from Jules Montenier, Inc., a PM of 8% of retail (10 cents on each bottle sold), a total of $127.10.

Telephone board operators are *telephone salesgirls* who produce real additional value.

Besides extensive advertising in newspapers throughout the entire nation to back up co-operative store efforts, Jules Montenier, Inc., has gone farther with continuous direct advertising via leading national magazines. One example is the enclosed proof of our advertising appearing regularly in *Cosmopolitan* magazine.

With best personal regards.

                                        Very sincerely yours,
                                        JULES MONTENIER, INC.

                                        /s/
                                        William A. Wright
                                        Sales Manager

WAW:DM
Encl. 2

By the middle of 1948, Jules Montenier, Inc., having obtained fairly wide distribution through the leading department and women's specialty stores, gave increased emphasis to securing distribution through other types of retail outlets. The following letter indicates the type of direct mail used to extend further distribution through beauty-shop supply jobbers:

JULES MONTENIER, INC.

417 North State Street
Chicago 10, Illinois
Superior 9133
June 22, 1948

Dear Mr. Jones:

At the suggestion of Mr. A. C. Bailey of Bailey's Beauticians Supply Company, Chicago, Illinois, I am writing to you to acquaint you with the tremendous possibilities to you concerning our product, STOPETTE SPRAY DEODORANT, a second full-page advertisement on which appears in the July issue of *Modern Beauty Shop* magazine (as enclosed).

Since January 1st of this year, Mr. Bailey has purchased from Jules Montenier, Inc., a total of 137 gross of STOPETTE SPRAY, accomplishing easily a most outstanding job of sales of our most unusual product to beauty shops throughout his territory.

So that you may have the complete story, I am sending to you under separate cover a full-size bottle of STOPETTE SPRAY for your consideration.

On May 5th, I wrote also to a small number of other selected beauty-shop supply distributors. As a result, White Cross Supply Company of Dayton, Ohio, wired me to rush four gross and has since reordered the same quantity.

As another result, Geo. P. Haldy Company of Cedar Rapids, Iowa, ordered on May 15th a trial order of one gross, together with counter cards and salesman's catalogue sheets. This beauty-shop supplier received the merchandise on May 20th. On May 22nd, Haldy's wrote me to please rush *three additional gross* in the four-color carton displays, and stated "we have hardly had a chance to start this item but believe it will be one of the best sellers we have had for sometime." On May 27th, Haldy's wired me to rush an additional *five gross* in open stock and two-dozen display cartons. Reorders are still coming in in similar quantities.

Here are further examples.

Frank's Beauty Supply Company of Amarillo, Texas, telephoned me to order *five gross.* Schwartz Brothers of Youngstown, Ohio, also *telephoned* to order *five gross.* There are quite a few more one to three gross orders, as a result of my letter, from jobbers who will be the *exclusive distributors* of STOPETTE SPRAY to beauty shops in their territories.

I approach you to be our *exclusive distributor* to beauty shops in your area because, in line with our firm policy, *there will be but one beauty-shop supply distributor in any individual area.* Consequently, our beauty-shop jobbers are to be very limited in number.

I want you to be the *exclusive distributor* of STOPETTE SPRAY DEODORANT in your area, but, unless I hear from you soon, I must necessarily offer exclusive distributorship to another beauty jobber in your territory.

We are expending thousands of dollars advertising every week in daily newspapers throughout the nation, as well as additional thousands of dollars by advertising in national consumer magazines—*Cosmopolitan,* the *New Yorker, Vogue, Harper's Bazaar,* and others.

STOPETTE SPRAY is a liquid-cream, antiperspirant deodorant retailing at $1.25. Our terms are 1% 10 days, 30 net, F.O.B. Chicago and San Francisco. Discounts to beauty supply jobbers are 33⅓% and 33⅓%.

Gross Retail	Less 33⅓%	Less 33⅓%	Your Profit per Gross	Shipping Wgt. per Gross
$180.00	$120.00	$80.00	$40.00	38 lbs.

Minimum shipping quantity is 12 dozen bottles, individually packaged or in the four-color unit display No. 1.

May I hear from you on this?

Very sincerely yours,

JULES MONTENIER, INC.

/s/
William A. Wright
Sales Manager

WAW:DM

Similar mailings were used to independent druggists and drug-chain headquarters.

The Montenier company also used space in trade publications in the drug and beauty-shop fields during 1948. Advertisements in these trade papers occasionally featured special offers. For example, included in the full-page advertisements in *Modern Beauty Shop* was a coupon offer to the reader to secure a full-size, $1.25 bottle of Stopette for a charge of 25 cents for handling and mailing. These coupons were followed up by sending the name of the respondent to the beauty-shop supplier with the suggestion that his salesman call upon this potential customer. By October 1950 Jules Montenier, Inc., was selling Stopette Spray Deodorant through approximately 200 beauty-shop supply jobbers. The number of beauty shops selling Stopette Spray was not known.

As Mr. Wright sensed that there was a good deal of confusion among buyers and salesclerks with regard to various types of deodorants and their use, in mid-1948 he helped Dr. Montenier prepare a 12-page booklet entitled *Here Are the Facts about Deodorants, Anti-perspirant Deodorants and Their Effects on Your Skin and Clothing*. This booklet was primarily factual and covered such areas as: What is a deodorant? What are the properties of various aluminum salts? How has the cosmetic chemist produced the harmless, efficient, antiperspirant deodorant? What are your skin glands and how do they function? And so forth. Subsequently, 500,-000 booklets were distributed to buyers, salesclerks, and other interested people. Mr. Wright believed that this booklet was particularly well received and had served to educate salespeople more effectively in the real uses and merits of personal deodorants.

In the booklet special emphasis was placed on the necessity of using deodorants during the entire year rather than only during the warm or hot months, when the average consumer believed a personal deodorant was most needed. From the beginning, in his sales planning, Mr. Wright

Exhibit 4

JULES MONTENIER, INC.

Newspaper Mat for Retailers

NEWEST OF ALL!

Stopette

SPRAY

UNDERARM
DEODORANT

Sprays underarm odor away

Squeeze the new unbreakable thermo-plastic bottle to create magnificent misty spray ...that Sprays underarm odor away and checks perspiration effectively.

No messy fingertips—no waste. This new patented lotion, made of "kindest-to-your-skin" ingredients, is harmless to clothing.

Economical, too—a year's supply in each bottle!

$1.25 plus tax

SQUEEZE THE BOTTLE...
IT SPRAYS!

2¼-oz. $1.25   1-oz. 60c

STORE NAME

AD-MAT No. 107—2 cols. x 100 lines—14"

had desired to reduce the seasonal factor in deodorant sales; therefore, whenever possible, attention was given to this objective. (Note the mention of this objective in the letter of October 17, 1947.) Mr. Wright felt that retail salespeople, both buyers and clerks, could do the most effective job in reducing the seasonal factor because they explained deodorants to the consumer and thereby exercised considerable influence.

Until March 1948 Montenier executives had delayed adopting national consumer magazines because they desired to assure themselves, first, of repeat sales of Stopette Spray, and, second, of sufficient volume of sales to support the high costs of such advertising. In the light of sales success by March 1948, the company planned consumer magazines advertisements to appear from March to October 1948. The advertisements, which appeared in *Cosmopolitan* and *The New Yorker,* were placed with the objective of securing consumer brand preference for Stopette Spray Deodorant. The company spent $10,000 in these publications during 1948, which permitted a staggered schedule of black-and-white advertisements of one column or less and allowed for the appearance of an advertisement in one of the two publications each month.

A broadside mailed by the Montenier company in late 1948 summarized for retailers the principal advertising activities being carried on by the company and the promotional aids available to retailers. A summary of the advertising and of the promotional aids as given in the broadside follows:

1. National monthly advertising in two consumer magazines.
2. National weekly advertising in daily newspapers with an estimated 50 million readers.
3. A two-color, 24-bottle counter display carton.
4. A window display card, 20 inches by 30 inches.
5. A counter card, 9 inches by 12 inches.
6. A lucite display, featuring a hand holding a bottle of Stopette with a simulated spray.
7. A fact booklet for salesclerks.
8. A statement insert, 3¼ inches by 6¼ inches.
9. Six newspaper mats in six different sizes. (See Exhibit 4 for an example.) of one of the suggested advertisements.)
10. A co-operative newspaper authorization.
11. Ten cents per bonus sticker for retail salesclerks.

Exhibit 5 shows some of the point-of-purchase display material, mentioned above, available to retail outlets. Pictured are the 20-inch by 30-inch window display card; the two-color, 24-bottle counter display carton; and the lucite hand display.

Advertising and Promotion—1949

On January 25, 1949 Mr. Wright issued a special confidential bulletin to company sales representatives outlining the company's 1949 marketing plan. Pertinent portions of this bulletin follow:

Exhibit 5

JULES MONTENIER, INC.

Point-of-Purchase Display Material

1. The fair-trade retail of the 2¼ ounce bottle of STOPETTE SPRAY DEODORANT will remain at $1.25.

2. PM's (Promotional Money) to salesgirls are to be set up on a flat rate on the sticker plan as follows:

Item Price	PM Allowance
$0.60	$0.05
1.25	0.10

3. Beginning in April issues (end of March appearance), STOPETTE SPRAY will be advertised continuously in large (full-column) advertisements in *Life*, *Look*, *Cosmopolitan*, *Charm*, *Glamour*, *Mademoiselle*, *McCall's*, *Today's Woman*, and the *New Yorker*.

4. STOPETTE SPRAY DEODORANT will be trade advertised continuously in *Beauty Fashions, Cosmetics and Toiletries, Modern Beauty Shop, American Hairdresser, Post Exchange and Ship's Service Stores, McKesson & Robbins Moneymaker, Southern Pharmaceutical Journal, Pacific Drug Review, Northwestern Druggist, Central Pharmaceutical Journal, Southeastern Drug Journal,* and *Apothecary.*

5. All department-store buyers and all direct retail-store accounts of Jules Montenier, Inc., will receive a mailing in February advising them of all details of the 1949 promotion on STOPETTE SPRAY DEODOR-ANT. Enclosed in that mailing will be the blanket advertising authorization of STOPETTE SPRAY DEODORANT as enclosed. In brief, any retail-store account (your efforts in this should be directed primarily to setting up such advertising schedules *only* with department stores) is authorized to place eight 200-line advertisements on STOP-ETTE SPRAY DEODORANT, the first four of which must appear in a newspaper before July 1st, and the second four before September 15th (but not necessarily after July 1st.)

    Jules Montenier, Inc., will pay 100% of the advertising rate cost at the store advertisement rate of each of the *first four advertisements,* and 50% of each of the *second four advertisements.*

    Our two provisos are that (1) *each* advertisement must be backed with a minimum purchase of six dozen bottles of STOPETTE SPRAY DEODORANT, and (2) the store advertising rate must be in the cost range of 1 cent and 60 cents per line (14 cents to $8.40 per inch).

6. There will be no other co-operative advertising allowance available on STOPETTE SPRAY DEODORANT.

7. The regular *24-bottle, two-color* counter display carton (A-20) will continue to be available to all Jules Montenier accounts whether wholesale or retail.

8. The *12-bottle, two-color* counter display carton (A-30) will be available *only* to the following: wholesale druggists, beauty supply companies, and chain drug stores (only when necessary to secure greater, or total counter display in all stores).

9. The *new, six-bottle, two-color* counter display carton (A-40) will be ready for shipment on February 1st, and will be available *only* to the following: wholesale druggists and beauty supply companies.

10. Jobber salesmen's bonus[3] will apply only to *wholesale* salesmen, and only on sales of the 12-bottle counter carton (A-30).

11. Based on the compilation of quarterly volume from all territories in 1948, your territory should produce *11%* of your 1949 net dollar business during January, February, and March; *30%* during April, May, and June; *38%* during July, August, and September; and *21%* during October, November, and December.

12. Lucite hand displays for counter use are available *only* to department stores and *the better* drugstores in your territory. A *memo charge* of $5.00 will be sent to *each* store for *each* lucite display. Payment . . . will not be [required] if the store continues to make use of the display.

13. Statement inserts (imprinted or unimprinted) on STOPETTE SPRAY DEODORANT . . . are available in any stated quantity for *depart-*

---

[3] The bonus consisted of 50 cents paid to wholesale druggist salesmen for each special deal sold and delivered during the period July 1 to September 15, 1949. The special deal consisted of a two-color counter display carton and the sale of 12 one-ounce bottles and four 2¼-ounce bottles of Stopette Spray. In addition, a free 2¼-ounce bottle was included in the deal.

ment stores. There is no required minimum purchase of merchandise. . . .

Mr. Wright established a sales quota of five million bottles for 1949 and an advertising budget of about $366,000. If possible, he desired to keep his advertising budget under 15% of sales.

A direct-mail piece, dated May 9, 1949, announced the introduction of a new one-ounce bottle of Stopette Spray Deodorant retailing at the fair-trade price of 60 cents. The one-ounce bottle was brought out to meet the competition of other deodorants in this price range and to meet the pricing needs of certain retail outlets, particularly limited-price variety syndicates. Mr. Wright arranged with Mr. H. A. Johnson, a merchandise executive of the F. W. Woolworth Company, to secure initial distribution of the one-ounce bottle in various Woolworth territories. Within three weeks, 500 Woolworth stores were selling the one-ounce bottle of Stopette Spray. The successful marketing of the one-ounce bottle in these Woolworth stores was made the subject of a broadside, which was distributed to Woolworth store managers to lead them to order Stopette Spray from Woolworth warehouses. The same broadside was sent out each of the next three months with the addition of new sales figures.

In May 1949 the Good Housekeeping Seal of Approval was given to Stopette Spray Deodorant.

Advertising and Promotion—1950

The strategy of the advertising and promotional plan for 1950 was essentially the same as that of the 1949 plan, except that less emphasis was placed in 1950 upon securing new or additional retail outlets. Mr. Wright believed that almost complete retail distribution for this type of product had been obtained in 1949. More emphasis was given in 1950 to establishing a strong consumer brand preference nationally for Stopette Spray and to acquiring greater sales volume through established outlets. (See Exhibit 6 for a summary of Jules Montenier, Inc., distribution.)

Exhibit 6

JULES MONTENIER, INC.
Summary of Distribution

Type of Outlet	Number of Outlets	% of Total Sales
Department and women's specialty stores.............................	1,500	28.3%
Wholesale druggists..............	30,000 drugstores ⎱	
Independent drugstores...........	3,600 ⎰	59.5
Chain drug companies............	425	
Variety syndicates................	100	7.0
Military exchanges...............	100	1.0
Beauty-shop jobbers..............	200	3.2
Miscellaneous....................	500	1.0
		100.0%

The sales goal for 1950 was fixed at ten million bottles, and the advertising budget was increased to $882,000. Included in this budget was an appropriation of $322,000 for a television program, "What's My Line?" This half-hour television program consisted of a panel of well-known persons who, on the basis of questions asked, attempted to guess the occupations of individuals selected from the audience.

By October 1950 Mr. Wright believed that Stopette Spray had become the No. 2 brand in the highly competitive deodorant field, second only to Arrid. After examining a number of sources of market information, including the A. C. Nielsen Company's Food-Drug Index and various figures released by *Seventeen, Red Book, Cosmopolitan, Glamour,* and *Chain Store Age,* he estimated that Arrid had approximately 16% of the total deodorant market and Stopette Spray a little over 10%. (See Exhibit 7 for figures on the brand preferences of the readers of *Seventeen* maga-

Exhibit 7

JULES MONTENIER, INC.

Survey of Brand of Deodorant Used by *Seventeen* Magazine's
Consumer Panel

Brand Used	1947	1948	1949
Arrid	15.6%	14.2%	12.6%
Veto	14.6	14.9	12.2
Fresh	14.0	13.9	11.0
Mum	15.4	14.1	10.9
Tussy	8.8	8.2	9.7
Stopette		1.6	6.9
Ever-dry	3.5	4.7	5.0
Odo-ro-no	5.4	6.1	4.3
Five-Day Pads	2.4	3.4	3.3
Avon	1.7	2.8	3.0
Helena Rubenstein	2.6	3.7	2.9
Dorothy Gray	1.4	1.6	2.8
Yodora	2.8	2.1	2.6
Etiquette	2.0	2.3	2.3
Sprite (spray)			1.6
Quest	1.3	1.3	1.5
Dew (spray)			1.4
Heed (spray)			1.2
Non-Spi	1.4	1.1	1.1
Miscellaneous	15.2	15.7	13.5

Source: Seventeen Magazine Consumer Panel 1950 Beauty and Personal Care Survey, *Seventeen* Magazine, New York, August 1949, p. 11.

zine for 1947, 1948, and 1949.) In view of the rapid gains by the Montenier company in three and one-half years, Mr. Wright fully expected to see Stopette Spray become the No. 1 brand in the deodorant field in 1951.

~ ~ ~

CASE 3: BRISTOL-MYERS COMPANY[1]

NOTE: *This case provides the basis for an interesting comparison with Jules Montenier in that it describes the introduction of another new deodorant, "Ban," by a large, well-established manufacturer rather than by a small, new marketer.* QUESTIONS TO CONSIDER: *(1) Did Bristol-Myers use a sound approach in developing and testing its new deodorant? (2) Did Bristol-Myers face risks not faced by Jules Montenier, Inc.? (3) Was it desirable to test advertising copy? (4) Was the national distribution program for the product well conceived? (5) As of 1958 what do you see as the principal promotional problems facing management with respect to Ban?*

Early in 1958 the newly formed Product Planning Committee of the Bristol-Myers Company met to review the history of several of the company's successful products. In this review the committee was interested in formulating some generalizations about developing and introducing new products which might be useful in guiding the committee's actions on future products.

The Product Planning Committee

The committee had emerged from a reorganization of the company's marketing operations, the objective of which had been to improve the company's planning and development of new products. Under the new arrangement the responsibility for new products was centered in the Product Planning Committee in which group the product group supervisor for new products assumed the responsibility for co-ordinating the efforts of all the departments in the company during the development of new products. Formerly, one of the advertising product managers usually had been assigned the responsibility of guiding a product through research and in co-ordinating the efforts of various departments to bring the product to the stage of market launching. (See Exhibit 1 for old and new organization charts.)

Before 1958 the screening of ideas for new products had been accomplished by an informal group which met at irregular intervals at the discretion of the director of product planning, whose responsibility was primarily that of directing technical research. The group consisted of a large number of management personnel from several eschelons throughout the company; executives from the corporate level on down through supervisory personnel participated. The group members went to the meetings prepared to present their ideas relating to the kinds of new products the company ought to be considering. After some discussion of the ideas expressed, the group voted informally. The outcome of this vote had shaped the new research projects of the product planning department. Most of the ideas introduced at these meetings had originated

---

[1] Written by Salvatore F. Davita and Neil H. Borden.

Exhibit 1

BRISTOL-MYERS, INC.

Organization Charts

ORGANIZATION BEFORE 1958

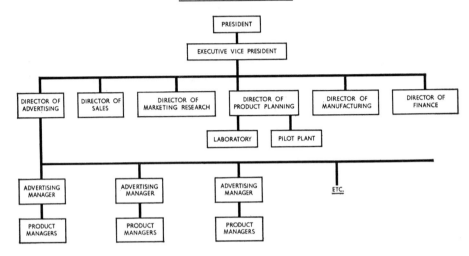

ORGANIZATION 1958

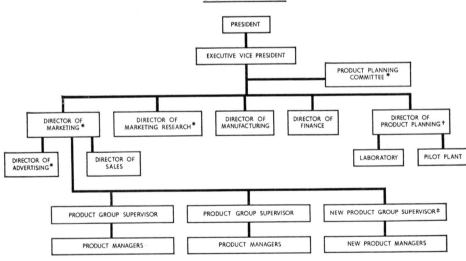

* Members of Product Planning Committee.

† Concerned only with technical development of new products.

‡ Concerned only with introduction of new products. After a new product was introduced, the responsible product manager was transferred to one of the other product groups.

from all parts of the company. Some ideas had come to the company from outside sources through letters from consumers, customers, or other groups.

This method of screening ideas for new products had worked well while the company was small. However, as the company grew, particularly in the period between 1953 and 1957 (see Exhibit 2), this method

Exhibit 2

BRISTOL-MYERS, INC.

Net Sales and Net Income Figures for the Period 1946–57

Year	Net Sales	Net Income (after Taxes)
1946	$ 47,828,189	$7,190,633
1947	44,654,979	3,942,810
1948	45,307,793	4,324,677
1949	42,777,942	2,714,611
1950	52,266,448	4,404,568
1951	61,616,962	5,288,961
1952	56,610,504	2,589,499
1953	55,464,572	2,540,598
1954	62,376,248	3,603,769
1955	75,746,827	4,865,752
1956	89,403,544	5,586,168
1957	106,847,430	6,404,076

Source: Company records.

became increasingly cumbersome and ineffective. The number of people involved became large; communications between departments broke down; and the task of screening ideas for new products was not getting the attention it deserved. Consequently, along with other organizational changes which were made to adapt the organizational structure to the increasing size of the operation, the Product Planning Committee was formed. The management believed this small committee and the centering of new product planning in a product group supervisor for new products would overcome the difficulties which had developed under the former method. All concerned with new product development enthusiastically accepted the arrangement as an effective approach to product planning.

Company Background

Bristol-Myers was one of the leading manufacturers and distributors of proprietary drug products, toiletries, ethical drugs, brushes, and collapsible metal tubes for use in the drug business. A list of Bristol-Myers' products is contained in Exhibit 3. The company operated eight manufacturing plants in the United States and at least one in each of ten foreign countries.

The first product the committee selected to review was "Ban," the company's lotion deodorant. After its introduction in 1955 Ban had captured and maintained a larger share of the deodorant market than was held by any other competing deodorant. It had become one of the company's outstanding products.

Exhibit 3

BRISTOL-MYERS, INC.

List of Bristol-Myers Products

Bristol-Myers

Ipana toothpaste
Bufferin—a tablet for relief of pain
Sal Hepatica—a saline laxative
Vitalis—a hair preparation
Mum—a deodorant
Mum Mist—a spray deodorant
Ban—a lotion deodorant
Theraderm—a dandruff remedy
Trig—a men's deodorant
Trushay—a hand lotion

Grove Laboratories

Minit Rub—a counter-irritant
Ammen's Medicated Powder—an antiseptic powder
Bromo Quinine—a cold tablet
4-Way Cold Tablet—a cold remedy
Pazo Ointment—an antiseptic ointment
Fitch Dandruff Remover Shampoo

Bristol Labs

Antibiotics
Tetrex
Centrine
Bristamin
Neurocentrine
Flo-Cillin
Alminate
Mytinic

Luzier Products

Luzier's cosmetics

Kimball Fibre Glass

Kimball fibre glass reinforced plastics

Development of the Product

The development of Ban started in 1948 when the product planning group saw the need for a new kind of deodorant. The group had become aware that the application of either of the two major kinds of deodorants, creams or sprays, was a messy operation.[2] While the application of the creams required the user to get her hands messy with the cream, the drip from the application of the spray usually soiled underclothing. The group, therefore, was principally interested in developing a new type of deodorant which would overcome the difficulties of the creams and

---

[2] Bristol-Myers' Mum cream deodorant was one of the two leading cream deodorants.

sprays. The idea was turned over to the laboratory for experimentation.

The laboratory set out to develop a deodorant in the form of a lotion. After several months of laboratory work a formula for a lotion was found, and it seemed to be more effective in its action than "Mum." It was not only a deodorant but also an uncommonly fine antiperspirant.[3] In the laboratory tests the lotion appeared soothing to normal skin, smooth in texture, and pleasing in scent and color. The management decided to carry out a market test to learn how consumers would view the lotion.

The new product, under the name of "Mum Lotion," was taken to Dallas, Texas, in 1949. The market research department selected this site because it wanted to test the product under the trying conditions of a warm climate. Mum Lotion, in a plain glass bottle, was introduced to the consumer through the drug channels alongside the other Bristol-Meyers' products. The product was advertised extensively in the local newspapers around the theme "Three pink drops and odor stops." However, even before the product got into the hands of the consumer, it had become evident that further work on the formula was needed. The lotion broke down into two separate liquids under the high temperatures. In addition, one of the two liquids thickened to the point of becoming a pasty substance. The original consistency could be restored by shaking and was not impaired by the heat. Nevertheless, it was believed that consumers would not react well to having to shake the bottle vigorously to make the lotion usable. After four months of discouraging sales, Mum Lotion was withdrawn from the Dallas market. The laboratory sought to overcome the product's shortcomings.

By 1950 the lotion was ready once again for testing. However, the management was not satisfied that the lotion when packaged in an ordinary bottle offered enough advantage to consumers over creams and sprays to warrant launching it on the market. The management feared that some of the lotion might drip onto clothing when being applied and felt that a better method of application would have to be devised. Accordingly, further market tests were postponed and the company's package designers were put to work to develop a new package which would make application easy and avoid the drip hazard.

Early in 1951 the package designers came upon the idea they needed. A small manufacturer on the West Coast approached Bristol-Myers with a new bottle applicator which utilized the principle of the ball-point pen. The bottle contained a large marble in its top which was free to revolve in any direction. The ball picked up a film of liquid on the underside and carried it to the outside when the user rolled the marble applicator. Upon trial in the laboratory the proposed bottle proved unsatisfactory for use

---

[3] A deodorant acts to mask the characteristic odor resulting from contamination of apricine sweat and ordinary surface bacterial flora by killing the bacteria and hence the odor. An antiperspirant acts to prevent the flow of apricine sweat by mildly inflaming the skin, which in turn closes or partly closes the sweat glands.

with the lotion; nevertheless, the idea was purchased from the manufacturer, and a vigorous program was undertaken to develop a suitable ball applicator.

After extensive laboratory work an applicator was designed which appeared to work well and was capable of being mass produced. This bottle was equipped with a specially designed neck to accommodate a friction polyethylene neck ring in which the revolving marble was mounted. The marble was made of red plastic material, and the cap was a hard white plastic. The applicator idea was so enthusiastically received by the management that preparations for market tests were begun while the applicator was still being developed.

In June 1952 the new product, "Mum Rolette," was taken to six markets: Philadelphia, Baltimore, Washington, D.C., Cleveland, Columbus, and Dayton. The major criterion for selecting the test cities centered around the speed with which distribution might be achieved. Since most of the drugstores in these cities were operated by chains, these cities were selected. Drugstores were the principal channel of distribution for deodorants at that time. From these tests, the market research department wanted to learn what degree of acceptance the new product would secure at the retailer and consumer levels and to test at what price the new product should be marketed.

The company undertook local advertising campaigns to introduce the product. The advertising copy emphasized that Mum Rolette was a new kind of deodorant. Television and newspaper media were used. The television advertising was limited to daytime one-minute spot announcements. In addition, dealers were given a variety of display materials to help introduce the product to the consumer.

Each bottle of Mum Rolette included a card requesting information about the customer's attitude toward the product. In return for this information, the company offered to send the consumer a small gift. Through this card technique the company expected to learn whether or not the customer liked the product, what qualities about the product she liked best, and whether she intended to purchase another bottle. In addition, this card technique provided the company with the names and addresses of Rolette users who could be contacted later for further consumer interviewing.

In addition to testing acceptance of the product the company sought to test consumer acceptance at various price levels. The company had estimated that the high cost of producing a bottle of Rolette would necessitate a retail price higher than that of the giant-size deodorants on the market.[4] The research department had estimated that if a reasonable sales volume were achieved, a 79 cents retail price would permit relatively

---

[4] Average retail prices of deodorants: 25 cents for the regular size, 45 cents for the large size, and 65 cents for the giant size.

small promotional expenditures and a desired profit margin. Since the research group felt that a large promotional expenditure would be necessary, a test was designed to see how acceptable the product would be at a higher price. The price selected was 98 cents. Accordingly, Mum Rolette was introduced in three of the cities at 79 cents and in the remaining three at 98 cents.

As the test got under way, once again the product ran into trouble. Some of the marbles were sticking and failing to revolve freely. Consumers complained to the retailers, and some consumers returned the defective bottles for replacements. Amidst all the complaints, the company found one attitude prevalent in all six markets: the customer usually wanted another bottle in spite of the annoying experience the defective bottle had caused. Customers appeared to hold their complaints to the bottle applicator; they applauded the lotion.

After four months of testing, it was clear to the company that the consumers wanted the new deodorant in its novel package. The company had succeeded in capturing a larger share of the deodorant market in these test areas than they had expected, and this was accomplished in spite of the defective applicators. In addition, the results of the store audits indicated that consumers responded in almost as large numbers to the 98-cent price as to the 79-cent price for the deodorant. On the basis of these encouraging findings the company felt sure that this deodorant, at 98 cents, was going to be a successful new product.

While the market test was still underway, the laboratory engineers were working feverishly toward solving the problem of the sticking marbles. The problem had been identified as having been caused by the unequal expansion of the marble and the neck when exposed to changes in temperature. After studying more than 450 different combinations of glass, plastics, and metals, the laboratory adopted the combination that worked best of all. The applicator consisted of a one-ounce cylindrical glass bottle, fitted with a polyethylene neck ring and with a clear hard polystyrene marble and cap. The marble had to be a sphere with small tolerances to insure against jamming or evaporation; its diameter was not to vary more than 3 one thousandths of an inch. The clear cap was adopted to permit the consumer to see the marble inside.

In the fall of 1953, after the market tests were completed, but while the ball-point package was still under development, the company undertook to sample its own consumer panel to observe the attitude of a different group of people. The company had operated a consumer panel for many years. It consisted of ten cells of 600 people each, a total of 6,000 people. Each cell was considered to be representative of the population at large. Among the characteristics which were used to construct the cells were: size of family, occupation of the head of the household, income, education, type of dwelling, and geographic location. The company replaced panel members who dropped out of the panel from a list of people who had indicated an interest in expressing their opinion relative to products submitted for test.

Cards containing data about each panel member were maintained by the market research department. In addition to data about the characteristics of the panel member, the cards included data which indicated the kinds of products the panel members used and the brands they normally purchased. From these data the company frequently constructed special panel groups of persons who used certain brands or types of products with which Bristol-Myers wished a comparative test of a new Bristol-Myers product.

In submitting Mum Rolette to its consumer panel the company constructed two special panel groups by selecting the panel members who used spray deodorants and those panel members who used cream deodorants. These panel members then were given a package of the new Mum Rolette and were asked to use it and compare it to the deodorant they normally used. In addition, the panel members were given a card to fill out and return to the company after both deodorants were consumed. They were asked to indicate their preference and the reasons for their preference. The results of this test indicated that seven out of every nine cream deodorant users and nine out of every 11 spray deodorant users preferred the new Mum Rolette. The respondents praised the ease and the neatness with which the lotion could be applied. The respondents also praised the effectiveness of the lotion.

To insure that the encouraging results achieved in the test panel were not the product of a bias factor, the company engaged an independent panel to repeat the test. The results of this test were about the same as those obtained from the Bristol-Myers' panel, and they strengthened the management's confidence in the product. In addition, the company used the independent panel for measuring what the management called the "fatigue factor" of the product; the fatigue factor was indicated by the number of repeat purchases the customer might be expected to make before turning to another brand. The results of this part of the panel test indicated that those customers who preferred the Rolette had a low fatigue factor. To supplement this test, the company went back to interview some of the customers of the 1952 Rolette market test. Each of these customers was asked, by telephone, to recall if she had purchased more than one bottle, and if so, how many. The evidence accumulated here was particularly encouraging in spite of the fact that the marbles in many of the bottles sold in the test markets had failed to turn freely.

All the evidence accumulated by spring 1954 indicated that the consumer liked and would buy the new roll-on deodorant. The Bristol-Myers management, on the basis of this evidence, decided to take the steps necessary to introduce the product to the national market.

At this point in the development of Ban, executives estimated the company had invested approximately three quarters of a million dollars in the product, in research, and in the various market tests. An accurate figure was not readily attainable because an over-all budget had not been prepared and the accounting records would not easily provide the answer.

Selecting the Name, the Label, and the Package

The first question which had to be answered in going national was what name to give the new deodorant. A limiting criterion was set by the size of the bottle, which had been fixed as a one-ounce cylindrical bottle. Hence the name had to be sufficiently short to fit on the label, yet large or striking enough to be readily recognized. After screening a long list of inactive names which Bristol-Myers had registered over many years, the name "Ban" was selected. Ban was thought to be particularly appropriate for the deodorant since it suggested that the lotion banished odor. The advertising department thought this three-letter word would lend itself well to advertising and promotion.

At the same time the advertising department adopted the exclamation point as an image symbol of the new roll-on package. It was used on the label, in all the advertising, and on all the point of sale material. Also, black-and-gold colors were adopted for the label on the hypothesis that these colors would appeal to men as well as women.

In addition, the advertising department decided to use a boot, that is, a cardboard frame, to hold the bottle. This was adopted in order to provide more space on the package for advertising and also to make the package stand out on the retail shelf. To increase the visibility of the package still further the boot was made a bright pink. It was thought also that pink would give the package more feminine appeal than it would have otherwise. It was also believed that the sharp contrast between the black and pink helped to differentiate the package from the other packages on the shelf.

Developing the Advertising

In developing the advertising copy for introducing Ban, two schools of thought emerged. One group felt that the advertising should focus on the roll-on feature of the bottle, while the other group felt that it was important to focus the advertising on the idea of a totally new kind of deodorant. In order to resolve the difference of opinion, the company decided to test the effectiveness of the two approaches.

Three months before the product as "Ban" was to be subjected to a market test, the company ran both types of copy with a hidden offer in two markets, Toledo, Ohio, and Madison, Wisconsin. One copy focused on the convenience of application and the uniqueness of the ball-point container, and the second copy emphasized that Ban was a totally new kind of deodorant. In both cases, the copy indicated that Ban was not yet available in stores and, buried deeply in small print, the company offered to send a bottle of Ban to a customer for the price of one dime. The response to these advertisements was to provide a measure of the effectiveness of the two copy approaches.

When all the responses were in, it was evident that the approaches had been equally effective. The company had received 703 dimes from one approach and 701 dimes from the other approach. The advertising department, therefore, prepared a new copy which emphasized in headlines the idea of "a new kind of deodorant" and "Ban rolls on" (see Exhibit 4).

Market Testing

While the advertising was being tested early in 1954, the sales department, the market research department, and the advertising agency were working together to prepare for the introduction of Ban in the test markets. The objectives of this test were to measure consumer acceptance by determining the share of the market that might be achieved. The cities selected for testing were Toledo, Ohio; Madison, Wisconsin; Jacksonville, Florida; and Johnstown, Pennsylvania. These cities were selected because the company had good sales coverage in these cities and because each city had its own newspapers and television stations. Also, Toledo was selected as a representative industrial city, Jacksonville as a representative southern city, and Madison as a representative city of the midwest area. Johnstown was selected because Nielson figures were available for it. The test was designed to extend over a four-month period between May and September. In this period the management hoped to capture 5% of the deodorant market.

The sales department worked out a closely co-ordinated campaign to insure quick and adequate coverage in the four test areas. Task sales forces involving both home office and regular sales personnel were organized, and together the areas were covered in five days during the last week in May. The advertising manager and the agency's account executive participated in this sales campaign in order to get a firsthand understanding of the kind of acceptance the product was meeting at the retailer level.

At the end of the sales effort, the task forces met to compare notes on their observations on initial dealer acceptance. The group noted that dealers seemed to be fascinated by the marble and usually worked it while the sales solicitation was going on. All were in agreement that the retailers were enthusiastic about the product. In light of the advertising that company expected to undertake and the encouraging response from the dealers, the management felt sure the product would be a success.

By June 15, when local advertising broke, the stores had been stocked by the task forces. The company sold and shipped directly to all stores which were classified as key accounts. Smaller accounts were serviced through wholesalers or rack operators even though the company salesmen obtained the order. The company relied mostly on TV spot advertising, having used one-minute and 20-second spot announcements during the day. In addition newspaper advertising was used.

Exhibit 4

BRISTOL-MYERS, INC.

Example of New Copy Approach for Ban

In order to measure how well the product was selling, store panels were set up in each market. The panels consisted of about 20 drugstores each and a few food stores. The stores were asked to submit to a biweekly audit of all the deodorants they sold during the two-week period. An independent firm was engaged to conduct this audit. On the basis of these data the company was able to estimate the share of the market it was achieving. By the end of the four-month period, these data indicated the company had captured 8% of the dollar volume of the deodorant market, 3% more than was the company's goal. On the basis of this evidence, management was anxious to proceed with the introduction of Ban nationally.

Before committing itself to national distribution, the management wanted to see how successful the product would be if no aggressive personal sales effort was made to get the product stocked. Accordingly, another market test was conducted in September. In this test, regular salesmen sold the product while on their normal calls. To test the product under difficulties, two of the three cities selected were drawn from the 1952 test areas in which the marbles had failed to turn. The feeling of the management groups was that if Ban was well received in these two cities in which the applicator was faulty, the product clearly was ready for national distribution.

In the September 1954 test, Ban was introduced in Cleveland, Columbus, and Pittsburgh. The advertising employed in the June test markets was used, and measurement of stores sales of deodorants was undertaken. By the end of the second month, the data resulting from the store audits indicated a close similarity to the results achieved in the June tests. Again, the company had succeeded in capturing a larger share of the deodorant market than it had set as a goal. Now, the time had come for the company to decide how and when to expand the distribution.

National Introduction

Late in November the decision was made to rush Ban to the national market with simultaneous introduction in all parts of the country. The management put pressure on all the departments of the company to get Ban into the stores by February 15, 1955, to be ready for a March 15 introductory advertising campaign. Ban was given first priority in production and in sales force efforts. The advertising agency, meanwhile, was told to prepare the advertising program, and the sales department was advised to prepare its plans.

During January, starting five weeks after the decision for national distribution had been made, the sales department held four field sales meetings, of one and one-half days each, in New York, Chicago, New Orleans, and Los Angeles. Every company salesman attended one of these meetings at which some of the company's top management and the company's top sales executives served to generate a great deal of enthusiasm for the product.

The salesmen were briefed about the product and were given an historical account of the research and the testing that had gone into Ban. The salesmen were told how good an acceptance the product had received in the market tests; how retailers had shown enthusiasm for the ball-point package; and how consumers had written to the company to get additional bottles of Mum Rolette after it had been taken off the market. In short, they were told that Ban was going to be a great success.

To help the salesmen in closing sales, the company distributed a summary of the points the salesmen might use in his solicitation. In addition, he was given a schedule of the planned advertising together with sample copies of print advertisements to show retailers. He was also given sample display and point-of-purchase material. Lastly, he was told that several dozen cartons of sample bottles of Ban had been shipped to his home and included in these were a dozen empties for use in demonstrating how the ball-point applicator worked.

Salesmen were also briefed on a special introductory offer to the retailer. One bottle was offered free with every 11 ordered or two free with every 22 bottles ordered. These offers increased the store's gross margin from the normal 40% to 41.8% or 44.9%, respectively, and were good on all orders received through June 15, 1955. On the purchase of "2 free with 22" the company also offered to engage in a co-operative advertising program with the dealer whereby the company would pay the cost of advertising up to 25% of the dealer's net purchases of Ban, provided the dealer used company mats and ran the advertising between February 15 and July 15.

Finally, salesmen were given schedules against which they would have to work, namely, shipments to the stores to begin on February 15 and national advertising to break on March 14.

By the time the advertising broke, the company had obtained a 73% effective distribution for Ban according to Nielson reports, that is, Ban was in the drugstores which sold 73% of all deodorants. By April 15 this figure had increased to 89%. This distribution was considered to be an excellent achievement for two months' work in view of the fact that salesmen normally visited their accounts on the average of once every three months and their smaller accounts once each year.

The advertising broke simultaneously across the country. Ban was advertised in every major newspaper, in a number of the popular magazines, and on television and radio. The company spent over one million dollars on advertising Ban in 1955.

In all the advertising, the company presented the idea that Ban was a new kind of deodorant in a new roll-on bottle. The copy focused on the idea that Ban was applied more easily than other deodorants and was more effective; it was pointed out that of the people sampled, seven out of ten preferred Ban.

The magazine advertising for Ban consisted of full-page, black-and-white advertisements in *Life, Ladies' Home Journal, McCall's,* and *Woman's Home Companion.* After the first six months, *Life* and *Woman's Home Companion* were dropped while the *Ladies' Home Journal* and *McCall's* were continued. Advertisements were essentially unchanged throughout the advertising campaign.

The newspaper advertising at the beginning of the campaign consisted of full-page advertisements in Sunday supplements in addition to smaller advertisements in the daily editions. The size of the smaller advertisements varied between 51 lines and 304 lines (see Exhibit 5).

Exhibit 5

BRISTOL-MYERS, INC.

Examples of Ban Newspaper Advertisements

The most effective Ban advertising, in the opinion of Bristol-Myers executives, was that done by Arthur Godfrey over network TV and radio on his daytime show. One executive said "Arthur took this product to his bosom and sold as only he can—and soon he had them (audience) chomping at the bit to go out and buy Ban." Ban was advertised on the Godfrey show one day each week for a period of one and one-half years. In addition, Ban also assumed sponsorship of the "Alfred Hitchcock Presents" show in October 1955.

In addition to paid advertising, Ban in 1955 received a great deal of free publicity as the result of an intensive effort by company and agency personnel. The new type applicator was news, and it was picked up and talked about in a number of the women's magazines and in the women's pages of local newspapers. Many of the beauty and trade magazines carried long stories on Ban. One executive summed this up in this way: "We got the breaks on every major news service and we were incorporated into countless radio and television shows, and we got pictures and stories into many of the leading magazines and supplements. From a publicity standpoint we were on the map."

Since its introduction, Ban's sales have consistently continued to climb, and in 1959 Bristol-Myers executives expected Ban's sales to climb to new heights. In its first eight months on the market in 1955, Ban moved into the number-three position in drugstore sales, and in seventeen months Ban became the top-selling deodorant in dollar volume in food and drug outlets combined. By the close of 1958 Ban's share of the deodorant market was 65% greater than that of the number-two brand, having captured 16% of the total market in which 45 brands competed on a national scale. By all standards, Ban had been and still was a very successful product.

~~~

CASE 4: S. C. JOHNSON & SON, INC. (A)[1]

QUESTIONS TO CONSIDER: (1) How does S. C. Johnson's approach to new-product development compare to that of Bristol-Myers? (2) Was there a good sales potential for the proposed space deodorant? (3) Was the product adequately tested? (4) Was it desirable to give as much attention to pricing, packaging, brand name, and scents as was given? (5) Was it a sound decision to introduce the product ahead of schedule without completion of market tests? (6) Was the introductory promotional program well conceived? (7) In your opinion, was good advertising copy employed in the introductory advertising program (see Exhibit 2)? Were appropriate media employed? (8) What recommendations would you make regarding the promotion of "Glade" in 1958?

In January 1957, as a part of the company's product diversification program, S. C. Johnson & Son, Inc., marketed two new space deodorants under the brand name "Glade." The new space deodorants, one an aerosol type and the other a wick type, were designed for household use in destroying malodors through a unique chemical action. By the end of 1957 Johnson executives estimated that the two Glade products had achieved slightly more than the budgeted 10% market share, but they were not fully satisfied with the progress of the products. This case reviews the development and testing of Glade and the first year of experience in marketing and promoting the product.

---

[1] Written by David W. Nylen and Martin V. Marshall.

Company Background

In 1886 Samuel Curtis Johnson founded a firm in Racine, Wisconsin, to manufacture and market parquet flooring, and, in response to consumer demands, he developed a paste wax for care of the wooden flooring. In 1906 the firm took the name S. C. Johnson & Son, Inc., and began to diversify its product line with additional wax-based products, the flooring line being discontinued in 1917. During the 1920's various wax-based auto and floor care products were developed, and in the 1930's the company developed one of its best selling products, "Glo-Coat," a self-polishing floor wax. During World War II the company produced numerous wax products for the armed forces, an activity that continued after the end of the war.

Through the constant addition of new products to the line, the company enjoyed steady growth: by 1954 the company had 1,350 employees in the United States; 650 in foreign subsidiaries; district offices and warehouses in 21 states; and plants in six countries. The company's headquarters in Racine was the site of Johnson's highly modern factory, office, and research buildings.

By 1957 the company's product line included about 30 branded consumer products plus commercial maintenance and industrial products. Consumer products includes waxes and cleaners for floors, furniture, and automobiles, and a group of insecticides. Well-known brands included "Glo-Coat," "Stride," "Jubilee," "Pride," "Raid," and "Carnu." Johnson's commercial and institutional maintenance products line included agricultural waxes, special lubricants, and coolants for the metalworking industry, and commercial finishes for furniture manufacturers. The company also sold such allied products as floor polishers and heavy-duty floor machines.

Johnson consumer products were distributed by a sales force of about 350 men to jobbers, wholesalers, and chains. The salesmen handled the full line of 37 products, but a separate sales force sold the automotive and polisher-scrubber line to nongrocery outlets. Johnson divided the United States into eight sales regions, each one of which was subdivided into numerous districts (a very large metropolitan area) and zones (other areas). The salesmen, most of whom were young men, did sales work with chain-store buyers, wholesalers, and jobbers, and also performed selling, service, and display work in the individual stores. A sales priority, which determined the relative sales attention that a given product was to receive, was established by the sales manager working with the advertising-merchandise director. New products were usually given the greatest sales priority. Industrial and commercial products were sold by a separate sales force.

Johnson had consistently advertised its consumer products, considerable emphasis being placed on network television advertising. During the

1956–57 season Johnson sponsored 50% each of "Red Skelton," a half-hour evening comedy show, and "Robert Montgomery Presents," a one-hour evening dramatic show. In 1957–58 "Steve Allen," a one-hour evening variety show was substituted for "Robert Montgomery Presents." Any Johnson product could participate on the Johnson television programs; the advertised product was charged by the company according to the time used. In addition to television many of the Johnson consumer products were advertised in print media and spot radio and television broadcasts. Exhibit 1 shows Johnson's traceable advertising expenditures for 1957.

Exhibit 1

S. C. JOHNSON AND SON, INC. (A)

Traceable Advertising Expenditures, 1957

Product	Expenditures
Industrial wax	$ 4,705
Off insect repellent	17,635
Beautiflor	107,550
Blem	1,100
Floor polisher and scrubber	73,672
Glade wick deodorant	105,509
Glo-Coat	420,375
Jubilee wax	63,800
Paste wax	67,242
Pride wax	126,035
Johnson's products	1,500,163
Stride wax	55,220
Wax products	1,244,065
Waxes and polishes	1,153,103
Raid insect spray	93,070
Carnu	73,640
J-Wax	143,870
Total	$5,251,354

Source: National Advertising Investments, 1957.

Johnson's Diversification Program

Before 1952 it had been a company policy to limit the product line to wax-based products, but Johnson's marketing research department indicated that the wax business was a declining market for two reasons. First, the advent of plastics had led to superior surfaces that required less wax, and, secondly, an increasing desire of women for greater leisure had led them to wax surfaces less often. Executives of the company decided that if the company were to grow, new products outside of the wax field would have to be developed.

In establishing the policy for selecting possible new products, executives decided that a new product had to take advantage of Johnson's principal asset, marketing know-how. That is, the product had to "fit" the existing Johnson marketing operation. Second, executives believed that any new product should have a "demonstrable product plus" in order to insure consumer acceptance. It was only after a product met these two criteria that it was analyzed for potential profitability as compared to necessary investment.

The development of new products centered in a new products division which was established in 1955 with Mr. Samuel C. Johnson as its first director. The new products division, which had four members in 1957, reported directly to the executive vice president, in order to give the department stature and independence. Its primary function was one of co-ordinating the exploration, screening, development, and test marketing phases of new products.

When a new product idea was suggested, the idea was first screened by a panel of four or five interested people who without extensive investigation evaluated the product in terms of fit, demonstrable product plus, and the investment-profit ratio that might be expected. If the new product passed the screening, the idea was passed to a "sponsor" group, which was a temporary problem-solving group of three to seven numbers, usually including the person who conceived the new product idea, a man from the laboratory who would be doing the technical work on the product, the marketing man who would be responsible for selling the product, financial and production department representatives, and, in all cases, a member of the new products department. The sponsor group was responsible for such problems as developing the product name, product and marketing testing, the advertising program, and the sales schedule. After test marketing and preparation for full-scale introduction, the product was turned over to one of Johnson's regular product managers.

Development of Glade Space Deodorant

During the Korean War a Johnson executive read that a consultant under government contract had sought and found a compound for use in hospital planes that would destroy gangrenous (organic sulphur containing) odors and yet would not mask other odors such as smoke or gas that would indicate danger in an airplane. Johnson researchers took the idea and developed a compound suitable for household use that actually chemically joined with odors, thus destroying them.

Investigation of the market for space deodorants then on the market revealed that there were essentially three types: (1) the aerosol type, (2) the spray type that masked odors with a heavier odor, and (3) the wick type that temporarily desensitized the user's sense of smell. Executives believed that a product that would actually destroy odors would have a "demonstrable plus." The product, which was distributed in grocery outlets, fit the Johnson marketing know-how. It was estimated that the new Johnson space deodorant could be placed in 80% of all outlets handling space deodorants.

In order to obtain a better estimate of the market, the company purchased back-audits on the space deodorant market from A. C. Neilsen. With these data Johnson market researchers were able to estimate the market at about $20 million a year. Executives estimated that Johnson could get 15% to 20% of this market. The data indicated that aerosol deodorants had over half the market on a dollar basis; wick type had about one third of the market; and spray deodorants had the remainder. Because aerosol products retailed at a considerably higher price than wick-type products, the unit volume of the aerosol category was well under 50%. The data also indicated that the total space deodorant market was growing rapidly, sprays were declining in share, wicks were steady or possibly declining, and aerosols were expanding rapidly. It was estimated that the total market would increase between 30% and 80% in the following five years. There was one dominant brand in the aerosol field, Colgate's "Florient," and one dominant brand in the wick field, "Air Wick." The numerous other firms in the space deodorant market were small and held minor market shares.

Johnson executives estimated that the company could expect to gain 10% of the market the first year, and over the long run, 20% of the market. They estimated a gross profit of 60% of sales, or $2.4 million gross profit in three years. Capital expenditures were estimated at $33,000 for the cost of development, $1,100,000 for test marketing and introductory expenses, and $52,000 for other expenses. Total expenses were expected to be $1.2 million as against three-year profits of $2.4 million.

In December 1954, after two years of research, Johnson chemists had developed the chemical to neutralize malodors, tested it for toxicity, and found that it could be packaged as an aerosol. Although the product was relatively simple to develop, executives believed that it would take at least a year for competition to match the product.

In early 1955 the company decided to proceed with the new product and began an extensive testing program. Numerous technical tests were performed by the Johnson research staff and by independent research laboratories. By these tests it was determined that the product was not toxic, that it had an adequate shelf life, that a noncorrosive container could be developed to contain the material, and that the product was effective in use. The highly complicated tests to confirm the effectiveness of the new product were necessary not only in terms of satisfying customers but in terms of justifying advertising claims. Test results, which had indicated that the product effectively destroyed odors, were confirmed by independent laboratory tests.

When Johnson officials first tested the new odor-destroying compound, they considered producing the product without any added scent. For two reasons they later decided to add a scent to the product. First, it was found that the odor-destroying compound itself had a slightly objectionable odor (similar to musty hay) that needed to be masked. Second, in consumer tests of the scented versus the unscented compound, housewives believed that the scented product seemed to work better than the unscented product.

It was then necessary to determine what scent or scents to use and what level of scent to use. Numerous consumer and laboratory tests were used to narrow down the choice of scents, the level of scent, and the concentration of active ingredient. The alternatives were narrowed down to four scents, and a final consumer test was conducted for Johnson by an independent market research firm. The final consumer test was conducted in March 1956 in five cities, comparing the four Johnson product alternatives and a principal competitive brand. In the test, housewives who regularly used a space deodorant were chosen to participate in the test. Each participant was asked in advance of the test to complete a questionnaire that requested background information on the family and information on the housewife's use of space deodorant. The housewife was then given two containers, each containing a different space deodorant, which were labeled only as "A," "B," "C," "D," or "E," and asked to use and compare the two products for two to three weeks. The participants were asked to use the two test products in different rooms, switching the rooms in which each product was used halfway through the test.

At the end of the test period, participants were asked to complete a questionnaire, the principal question concerning which product the participant preferred and why. Results from the consumer test indicated that two Johnson scents, evergreen and blossom, scored highest in preference tests and would satisfy almost all of the market. Johnson executives decided to market the product in these two scents. Among all participants, the Johnson products over-all were preferred to the competitive product. However, while the Johnson product was highly preferred by higher-income participants, the competitive brand with its strong floral scent was preferred by lower-income participants. Johnson executives noted that test participants tended to express their preference for the products in terms of the scents rather than in terms of effectiveness in removing odors.

Company executives had been undecided whether or not to introduce a wick-type deodorant as a companion to the aerosol product. Although the wicked segment of the market was not growing, it did represent about one third of the total dollar market and nearly one half of the total units sold. Executives also believed that it would be an advantage to Johnson salesmen to be able to offer a full line to stores rather than a line aimed at only a segment of the market. They also believed that offering consumers a choice of either type of product would keep them loyal to a Johnson product, whereas offering only an aerosol product would force some consumers to purchase from a competitive company.

Despite the desire to market a companion wick-type product, Johnson researchers found that the new odor-destroying compound could not be effectively distributed by a wick-type product. Therefore any such product would have to contain the nose desensitizing features common to competitive products, thus giving the Johnson product no demonstrable product plus. Working to overcome this problem, a Johnson design group devised a unique package in which the wick stood above the neck of the bottle and was covered when not in use by a deep plastic cap. Thus the wick did not have to be fished from the bottle as in competitive products. In addition, the bottle was spillproof. Executives decided that as a companion product, the package features gave the product a demonstrable plus and therefore decided to market the wick deodorant in two scents as a companion to the aerosol product.

The pricing of the new product was decided upon without elaborate research. The competitive retail price for the aerosol product in early 1956 was 79 cents, which allowed about a 28% markup for the retailer. Because of the cost of manufacturing the new product, Johnson could not profitably set a price lower than the competitive price and they did not believe that the new product's advantages were sufficient to support a price higher than competition. It was therefore decided to market the product at the current competitive price.

By January 1956 the following timetable had been developed for the new product:

March 12	Final selection of name
April 9	Complete package design
April 23	Order containers
May 7–21	Order raw materials
June 1	Complete sales plans
June 18	Fill orders for test markets
July 2	Start test market
August 6	Fill orders for national sales
September 3	Begin national sales

Possible names for the new product were suggested by the company's advertising agency, by the sponsor group, by other people in the company, and by examination of names unused from previous new products. The suggested names were forwarded to the legal department which checked to be certain that the name was unregistered and could be used. This greatly reduced the list of names, the remaining candidates then being given to the company advertising agency for consumer testing to eliminate confusing names or names that had unpleasant connotations.

The list of names for the new product was narrowed to four: "Glade," "Bel Air," "Bon Air," and "Glen." These names were then tested with a sample of housewives in order to gain further information on consumer reaction to the names. In the test the housewife was first given the name to be tested and asked what the name made her think of. The interviewer continued, becoming more specific, and concluded by telling the housewife that the name was being considered for an air freshner and asked the consumer if she thought that she would be interested in the product. The name finally chosen by this process was "Glade."

Meanwhile, personnel from Johnson's advertising agency, Benton and Bowles, Inc., were brought to Racine and given a review of the new product. It was quickly concluded that advertising should concentrate on Glade's "plus," the unique property of actually destroying odors. The agency devised the slogan "makes indoor air seem fresh as all outdoors," and began work on visual devices that would demonstrate Glade's advantages.

Design of the Glade package label was conducted by an experienced independent label designer working closely with Johnson personnel. Numerous designs were drawn trying to denote the idea—makes indoor air seem fresh as all outdoors. Executives desired all Glade containers to have a basic family resemblance, but wanted each scent to be distinctive. The final choice was selected subjectively by Johnson personnel and the label designer.

Package designs were completed on the scheduled date. The wick-type package was finalized in the form previously mentioned. Designers were limited in the Glade aerosol package to one basic container type, but they did devise an unusual, large, round plastic cap that allowed the cans to be stacked one atop the other on store shelves, thus giving desirable label display.

In mid-April 1956, because the company was slightly behind its production schedule (trade-mark difficulties were experienced, and suppliers were having trouble in producing the plastic caps), it was decided to postpone test marketing until October 1 and to go national in September 1957. By the end of July 1956 executives found that the proposed October 1 test marketing date and the September 1 national sales date conflicted with over-all company marketing plans. The test market date was therefore changed to September 1, 1956, and the national sales introduction to January 1957. At the same time it was decided to pack the product in cases of 24, containing 12 of each scent since consumer tests had indicated about equal preference for each odor.

In July 1956, three months before the scheduled Glade test marketing, Johnson executives learned through their sales force that Colgate's Florient was being test marketed in three new scents.

Glade Test Market

Test marketing of Glade commenced in September 1956 in the Johnson northeast sales region, including all of New England and northern New York state, an area containing 10% of the total United States population. Because of several aggressive local brands, the northeast region was an area of intense competition in air fresheners. Executives believed that if Glade were successful in this region it could be expected to succeed in all areas. The purposes of the test were to determine how well the sales force could introduce the product, what share of market could be gained, and what consumer repeat business would be attained.

A sales meeting attended by the 25 salesmen from the northeast region was held in Boston to explain the new product and the introductory test campaign. The northeast sales manager had previously spent a week in Racine familiarizing himself with Glade and the marketing program.

Both newspaper and television advertisements were scheduled for the test market. Two newspaper advertisements told the background story of the source of the product discovery, illustrated the Air Force problem, and told how the product was adapted to consumer use. The second newspaper advertisement carried a coupon that entitled the purchaser to 25 cents off on a can of Glade if the coupon were presented to the grocer. The Johnson advertising agency arranged to have Glade television commercials inserted by television stations in the northeast region in place of other Johnson commercials on the regular Johnson programs, "Robert Montgomery" and "Red Skelton." The television advertisements attempted to illustrate the odor-destroying properties of Glade and utilized the theme—makes indoor air seem fresh as all outdoors.

Evaluation of the test market was to be made from a store audit project, from shipment figures, and from reports from the sales force. The Benton & Bowles research staff established an audit in a sample of stores in Syracuse, Springfield, Binghamton, and Boston in order to measure distribution and sales progress in the test market. In the co-operating panel of stores, Benton & Bowles market research personnel recorded each month the shelf and storeroom inventory, receipts, transfers, and returns for all brands of air fresheners. From these data, unit sales and distribution figures were derived. Information from the sales force primarily concerned trade acceptance and trade attitudes toward the product.

Glade National Marketing

In late September, after one month of test marketing, Johnson executives received reports that Florient was about to be introduced nationally in three new scents, and they feared that if Glade were not introduced first, distribution channels would be clogged, thus hampering trade acceptance of the product. Early reports from the test market indicated that initial acceptance of Glade by the trade was surpassing expectations, although it was too early to determine anything about consumer acceptance. Results from the store audits were not yet available. It was decided to start national marketing at once. Shipments to the trade began in October, and Glade appeared in stores nationally by mid-December 1956.

A sales meeting was called in Racine in mid-October for regional, district, and zone sales managers solely for the purpose of explaining Glade and its introduction. The sales managers were told the source of the new product, the selling points, and the marketing program planned. Several demonstrations were presented to show the effectiveness of the product. After the presentation the sales managers were to return to their regions and present the story to the sales force.

Johnson provided salesmen with a sales aid conceived by the research department that the department personnel believed gave a convincing demonstration of the effectiveness of the product. In demonstrating to a buyer, the salesmen dipped a glass rod in a bottle of ammonia. The buyer was asked to smell the pungent odor, after which the salesmen sprayed the rod with Glade which removed the odor. The buyer was then asked to smell the rod again, thereby demonstrating the effectiveness of the Glade.

Both a consumer and a trade sales promotion were conducted during the introductory period. On the initial order, the retailer was given one case of Glade free with each ten cases purchased. The retailer was encouraged to match the premium with extra advertising, although this was not required. The principal purpose of the trade premium was to encourage retailers to stock the product. Johnson executives realized that a free-goods offer to retailers was considerably less popular than a price rebate because the dealer had to sell the extra case before he realized the profit on the free goods whereas a cash discount was realized sooner. However, it was considerably less expensive for Johnson to pay in merchandise rather than cash.

The consumer promotion was a 25 cents refund offer. Introductory shipments of Glade contained a cardboard collar around each can informing consumers that they would receive a 25 cents refund if they mailed a Glade Aerosol label to the S. C. Johnson company. The purpose of the promotion was twofold: to encourage consumers to try the new product and to induce retailers to stock the product because the promotion would increase the product's movement. The mail-in offer was chosen because executives knew by previous experience that this type of promotion was inexpensive, returns being about 5% of sales. No consumer promotion was offered for the wick product.

National advertising for Glade commenced in January 1957 and was concentrated primarily on the Johnson network television programs. In the first six months, 15 one-minute Glade television commercials were run, eight appearing on "Robert Montgomery Presents" and seven on "Red Skelton." Television commercials emphasized Glade's unique ability actually to destroy odors through chemical action and utilized the theme—makes indoor air seem fresh as all outdoors. Exhibit 2 shows one of the story boards used in the preparation of 1957–58 television advertisements.

In addition to the television advertising a full-page, four-color insertion, that included a 25 cents off coupon, was placed in 93 Sunday supplements during January. In February a two-page spread (shown in Exhibit 3) was run in the *Reader's Digest* telling the story of the discovery of the odor-destroying compound and its use by the Air Force. Most of the advertising was concentrated on the aerosol product rather than the wick product, because the aerosol market was the fastest-growing segment. A small introductory campaign was used for Glade Wick and included two ⅔ page and one ⅓ page black-and-white advertisements in *True Story*, all run between January and June 1957. Executives believed

Exhibit 2

S. C. JOHNSON & SON, INC. (A)

A Story Board Used in the Preparation of 1957–58 Television Advertising

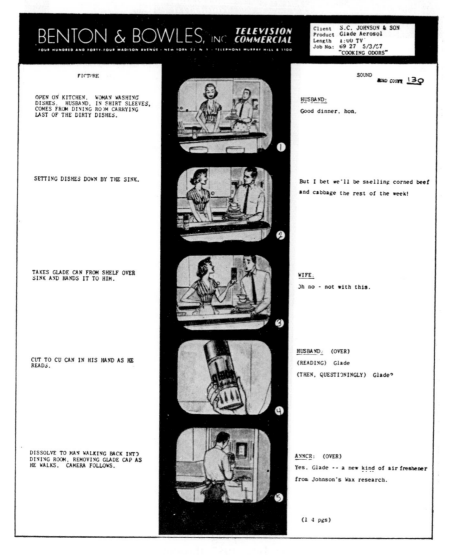

that because both products had the same name, the wick product would benefit from the aerosol promotion.

At the beginning of the summer of 1957 all Glade advertising was discontinued for the summer season because summer was the seasonal low point for air-freshener sales and because commercial time was needed for the auto care and insecticide products which were at their seasonal high point in the summer. In September the advertising for Glade started again

Exhibit 2—Continued

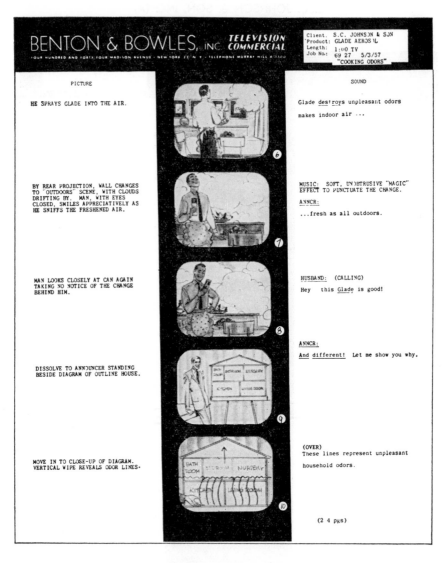

on Johnson's network television programs "Red Skelton" and "Steve Allen." For the fiscal year July 1957 through June 1958, Glade was scheduled for 23 one-minute television participations. The advertisements continued the same copy themes that had been used in the introductory season, and almost all emphasis was placed on the aerosol product.

Evaluation of Glade's Progress in 1957

At the close of 1957, Johnson executives were evaluating the progress of the new product. The latest market-data report for October–November

Exhibit 2—Continued

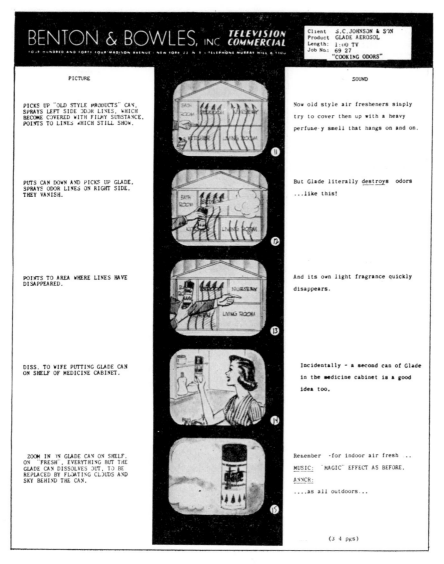

1957 showed that Glade (both aerosol and wick) had gained a 10.6% share of the total market for air fresheners and that Glade was distributed in stores that did 54% of the air-freshener business. Distribution and market share for Glade Aerosol was considerably better than that for Glade Wick. Neither product had shown any significant difference in sale by scent.

Although the Glade market share was slightly above the 10% budgeted for the end of 1957, Johnson executives were not completely satisfied with the progress of the product. In particular the executives were dis-

Exhibit 2—Continued

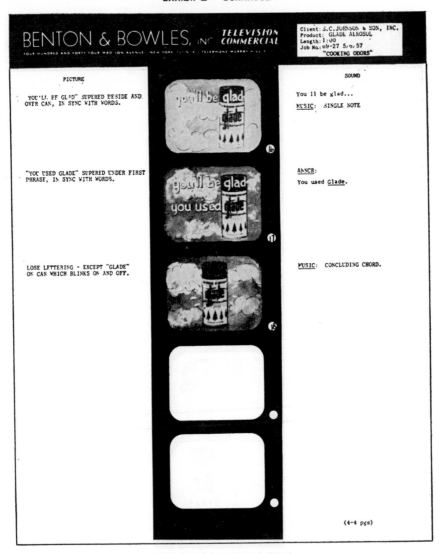

satisfied with the per cent of distribution achieved, although they considered that the Johnson sales force had given the product satisfactory effort. Some Johnson executives stated the belief that it had been an error to halt advertising efforts during the first summer. Because the product was new to consumers, the advertising early in the year did not carry over the summer, and consequently sales share dropped severely during the summer. As a consequence, Glade, in effect, had to start over again in September.

Exhibit 3

S. C. JOHNSON & SON, INC. (A)

Two-Page Advertisement which Appeared in the February 1957 Issue of *Reader's Digest*

Research on the odor problem in hospital planes leads to a remarkable new product for killing odors in the home!

New Air Freshener

Literally Destroys Indoor Odors

When the Air Force began to fly wounded soldiers out of field hospitals in Korea, an old problem arose. There wasn't enough air circulation in the crowded planes to carry away the overpowering "hospital smells". And air deodorants of the types generally used in the home just didn't do an acceptable job.

A group of the country's leading civilian chemists was asked to collaborate with the Air Research and Development Command on the problem of killing these hospital odors without affecting "alarm odors," like leaking gasoline or hot wiring. Many materials were tested for their odor-controlling properties. Finally, the chemists found certain organic compounds which purported to control the major malodors in hospital planes, yet did not eliminate the important "alarm odors". The potential household applica-

tions of this research were quickly recognized by S. C. Johnson & Son, makers of Johnson's Wax and other household products.

New studies were launched which established that ordinary room deodorants do not actually eliminate odors at all. Of the two common types, one merely covers up offensive odors with a heavy scent . . . usually a lingering, strong-smelling perfume that often becomes unpleasant itself. The other type simply dulls the sense of smell temporarily. For a time, it is difficult to smell not only the bad odor, but anything else as well.

S. C. Johnson chemists, however, made an important new discovery . . . one of the chemical compounds they were testing literally *neutralized* offensive odors, instead of just covering them up with a heavy, sickly

sweet perfume. But the question still remained, would this dramatic compound prove effective against the kind of odors found in the average home . . . . particularly in so-called "problem areas" like the kitchen and bathroom? Was it safe for home use?

Only after extensive investigation were the Johnson chemists satisfied that they had actually found the answer. Laboratory tests with special infrared ray equipment proved that this remarkable compound effectively removed the major types of household odors. And the total evidence seemed conclusive . . . offensive odors were eliminated by a harmless chemical reaction that literally destroyed them.

Then, as a scientific double-check, an independent laboratory conducted still another series of tests. The Johnson findings were confirmed. Here indeed was a product which effectively *neutralized* offensive odors instead of just covering them up with a heavy and overpowering perfume.

The final laboratory step was then taken. The formula was successfully adapted to aerosol form to permit

easy and complete dispersal throughout any room. It is now being marketed via grocery, drug and hardware stores under the trade name "Glade".

Time and again, Glade's remarkable elimination of the most common household odors has been demonstrated in home use. Furthermore, the product's own light fragrance quickly disappears, leaving the air smelling clean and fresh. And just as extraordinary is the fact that Glade apparently has the capacity to attack bad odors more readily than pleasant ones.

Naturally, the manufacturers of Glade are proud of their new product. As one of the company's chemists recently remarked, "Most of us react to a bad smell as something to get away from fast. Now we can get the smell away fast instead. We're happy that the women who've tested Glade for us in their own homes seem to agree . . . the problem of unpleasant indoor odors has finally been licked."

AEROSOL

GLADE
Air Freshener

BY THE MAKERS OF
Johnson's Wax

MAKES INDOOR AIR FRESH AS ALL OUTDOORS!

"Johnson's" and "Glade" are trademarks of S. C. Johnson & Son, Inc.

CASE 5: GENERALIZATIONS REGARDING THE BUILDING OF PROMOTIONAL PROGRAMS FOR NEW PRODUCTS

In the light of your analyses of the B. F. Goodrich, Jules Montenier, Bristol-Myers, and S. C. Johnson (A) cases, develop a list of useful generalizations regarding the building of promotional programs for new products. Give special attention to (1) product testing, (2) branding, (3) market testing, (4) testing of advertising, (5) publicity, and (6) the co-ordination of advertising with other marketing activities.

~~~

CASE 6: DOW CHEMICAL COMPANY (A)[1]

NOTE: *The next four cases concern the steps taken by Dow management to devise a new advertising strategy for "Saran Wrap," a household wrapping material. They will allow a detailed analysis to be made of the problems encountered in the determination of advertising objectives. Case (A) describes the introductory marketing of Saran Wrap and the situation facing management as of mid-1955.* QUESTIONS TO CONSIDER IN CASE (A): *(1) Dow's management is not satisfied with the sales of Saran Wrap through mid-1955. As a member of management, how would you evaluate Saran Wrap's progress through mid-1955? (2) Assume that management desires profit of 30% of sales before taxes. What is the profit picture for Saran Wrap as of mid-1955? (3) In the light of the information given in the case, what in your judgment are the principal problems facing management with respect to Saran Wrap? (4) What steps do you think Dow's management should take to devise a new advertising strategy for Saran Wrap? (5) Tentatively, do you think Saran Wrap advertising should be directed to heavy, light, former, or nonusers? (6) What would you like to learn from the two consumer studies which were in process?*

In mid-1955 the top management of the Dow Chemical Company, Midland, Michigan, decided to devise a new advertising strategy for "Saran Wrap," a transparent, moistureproof, self-clinging plastic household wrapping material which Dow had been marketing for about two and one-half years. This decision was made by management as the result of examining the operating statement for the product for the fiscal year ending May 30, 1955, which indicated that total sales were too low relative to promotional expenditures and that profits were not satisfactory.

Although the operating statement for Saran Wrap was not available for publication, for the purpose of case discussion, the following assumptions may be made:

---

[1] Written by Martin V. Marshall.

```
Net sales income per case........................$6.60*
Net cost of goods per case........................ 3.60
Gross margin per case............................$3.00
Brokerage fee per case............................ 0.33
Margin available for promotion and profit per case.....$2.67
```

* These data are based upon estimates obtained from the plastics trade, not upon figures supplied by the Dow Chemical Company.

Saran Wrap was packaged in two sizes: regular and Queen. The regular size contained 25 feet of 12-inch film which sold at retail on the average for about 34 cents; the Queen size contained 25 feet of 18-inch film which sold at retail on the average for about 47 cents. Actual case sales (a case being 24 packages of the regular size or the equivalent) for the years 1953–55 are given in Exhibit 1.

Exhibit 1

DOW CHEMICAL COMPANY (A)

Sales of Saran Wrap in Cases, 1953–55

Month	1953	1954	1955
January	4,000	114,000	176,000
February	7,000	146,000	132,000
March	8,000	120,000	130,000
April	6,500	90,000	130,500
May	6,000	80,000	130,000
June	7,500	84,000	134,000 est.
July	8,000	109,000	150,000 est.
August	8,000	120,000	162,500 est.
September	20,000	144,000	140,000 est.
October	25,000	154,000	124,000 est.
November	24,500	172,000	162,000 est.
December	36,000	164,000	154,000 est.
Total	160,500	1,497,000	1,725,000 est.

Source: Company records.

As a first step toward devising a new promotional strategy for Saran Wrap, Dow executives reviewed the marketing and promotion of the product. Pertinent information on the company, the development of the product, and the marketing and promotion of Saran Wrap follows.

Background Information on the Dow Chemical Company

In 1955 the Dow Chemical Company was a highly diversified manufacturer of organic and inorganic chemicals, plastics, and magnesium, with sales in excess of $429 million annually. Some of the company's principal chemical products were agricultural chemicals, ammonia, calcium chloride, carbon tetrachloride, caustic soda, germicides, fungicides, ethyl chloride, fine chemicals, hydrochloric acid, methylene chloride, phenol, bisphenol, and glycols. Principal plastic products were polystyrene which was sold under the trade names "Styron" and "Styrofoam"; copolymers of vinyl and vinylidene chloride sold under the trade name "Saran" and the trade name of licensees; and ethyl cellulose sold under the trade name "Ethocel." Until the advent of Saran Wrap, the company had never marketed a product directly to consumers through food distribution channels.

The Development and Initial Marketing of Saran Wrap

"Saran" plastic film was developed by Dow in 1941 for the U.S. Army as a material for the packaging of machine guns, carburetors, and other types of intricate assemblies that had to be kept moisture-free. The original film was a heavy-duty, oily, somewhat smelly plastic. Subsequently, Dow's product-research group developed a transparent, odorless Saran film possessing a strong surface charge of static electricity which made the film cling to itself. Within a few years after World War II, this film was well established as an industrial food packaging material, being used particularly in the packaging of cut meats, cheese, baked goods, and other items where moisture retention was necessary or a significant advantage.

Meanwhile, Dow's product-research group and others in the company belived that the product had real advantages to offer to housewives as a household wrap. Its moisture and vaporproofness meant that it would keep food fresh over a longer period of time; its capacity to preserve flavor meant that various odoriferous foods (such as onions) could be stored without odor migration; its transparency allowed identification without uncovering or unwrapping a container; and its self-clinging qualities provided a simply made and almost airtight seal.

As a matter of policy, however, the company had never marketed products to consumers directly through food channels and therefore initiated a search for a firm in the food distribution field which might be interested in taking over the saran film as a consumer product. Several firms were interested, but agreement could not be reached on a bulk price. Finally a decision was made to allow a group of Flint, Michigan, businessmen, who formed the Saran-Wrap Corporation, to take over national distribution rights in late 1949. The corporation, selling the product as "Saran-Seal Wrap," undertook several market tests, began to promote the product through local newspaper and radio, and attempted to gain broad distribution. In early 1952, when it became apparent to all concerned that the Saran-Wrap Corporation would not be successful, Dow management bought and dissolved the corporation.

Reconsideration of the Consumer Market

Having dissolved the Saran-Wrap Corporation, Dow's management was offered recommendations by two groups of executives. One group took the position that the consumer version of the product should be abandoned because the industrial applications of saran film were increasing rapidly, the company was not experienced in consumer marketing, and the household wrap market was highly competitive. At the time, 30 competitors were marketing household wraps; two, Scott Paper Company in the wax paper field and Reynolds Metals Company in the aluminum foil field, being dominant in their respective product fields. The other group of executives believed that Dow should continue to market the consumer product because it was an excellent product, possessing unusual properties of value to housewives, and because it could produce profits for the company. Further, it was their opinion that Saran-Seal Wrap had not been successfully established in the market because it had not been effectively promoted. Although excellent distribution had been obtained in several markets, they believed that consumers had not purchased Saran-Seal Wrap because they did not know what it was or what it would do. Thus, they felt the product would be successful if promoted properly and if sufficient funds were allocated to promotion.

In December 1952 Dow's management decided to undertake the test marketing of the consumer product, under the trade name "Saran Wrap."

Test Marketing

In order to determine the possibilities of developing the consumer market for Saran Wrap, Dow executives decided to gain information and experience by test marketing for one year. Four Ohio market areas, Columbus, Cincinnati, Dayton, and Toledo, were selected, in order to experiment in markets having varying sizes of population, varying balances between urban and rural population, varying educational and income levels; and at the same time, to test various combinations of advertising media. Since the defunct Saran-Wrap Corporation had developed a nucleus of food brokers, distribution in test markets was restricted to food brokers. Plans were made to measure factory sales, store sales, and how consumers learned of Saran Wrap.

After five months of marketing experience in the four Ohio markets, by April 1953 Dow executives thought that there was sufficient evidence to justify the following conclusions:

1. That food brokers were an efficient system of distribution.
2. That a large promotional effort was necessary to get a housewife to buy her first roll of Saran Wrap.
3. That television was by a wide margin the most effective medium to inform consumers of what Saran Wrap was and what it would do—62.0% of consumers surveyed in the four markets first heard of Saran Wrap in television advertising.
4. That the primary appeals were transparency, cling, and the fact that Saran Wrap kept foods fresher, longer.
5. That the product did not compete directly with established household wrapping materials but added to total sales of the category.
6. That consumer repurchase averaged 1.5 units a year.

At the time Dow executives gave considerable attention to estimating probable national sales, promotional expenditures, and profits. Dow's marketing research department, after undertaking a number of surveys and gathering considerable consumer-purchase data, came to the conclusion that the Ohio test market indicated annual national sales of 38,600,000 units provided that the same intensity and duration of promotional effort was given to the national market as had been given to the four Ohio markets.

Although the advertising schedules employed in each of the test markets differed slightly, the schedules employed in Columbus and Cincinnati are indicative of the promotional effort placed behind Saran Wrap in all test markets. These schedules follow. In Columbus: 9,450 lines of newspaper advertising; ten announcements on daytime television each week for 13 weeks; and five announcements on daytime radio each week for 13 weeks. In Cincinnati: 11,800 lines of newspaper advertising; six announcements on daytime television each week for 13 weeks; and eight announcements on daytime radio each week for 13 weeks.

Decision to Go National

After considering the experience gained in test marketing, Dow executives decided that they would not introduce Saran Wrap nationally on a traditional market-by-market approach, but would introduce the product nationally in 65 major markets simultaneously. This decision was based upon two considerations: first, the marketing research department stated that 65% of the purchasers of household wraps could be reached if distribution was obtained in about 20,000 grocery stores in Class A and B markets; and, second, since television had been selected as the principal medium, television could be purchased most economically on a network basis, thereby affording advertising coverage of about 65 major markets.

Introduction of Saran Wrap nationally began in August 1953 when Dow began working with its 55 food brokers to obtain intensive distribution of the product. (Within seven months, by March 1954, distribution had been gained in 70% of the food outlets in the 65 prime markets, and within two years, by mid-1955, distribution had been gained in those food outlets which did 90% of the total United States food business. Thus, in mid-1955, Dow executives were not concerned with distribution or the product's in-stock situation; for some months Saran Wrap had maintained distribution and in-stock positions which was as good or better than those of any other household wrapping material.)

In devising its initial promotional strategy for Saran Wrap, Dow executives decided that they would rely almost exclusively upon advertising to inform consumers of the product's qualities and usages and to induce initial purchases. Advertising copy emphasized how Saran Wrap worked and its use as a food wrap. Initial purchases were not to be induced through the use of introductory deals, combination offers, premiums, or any other sampling device. Special seasonal promotions were to be used, however, in order to obtain in-store point-of-purchase display.

During the national introductory period starting in August 1953, Dow executives had to gain experience quickly in the selection and use of consumer advertising media. For the fall 1953 television season, they purchased commercial time on a participation basis[2] on three television programs: "Today," an early morning news and variety show starring Dave Garroway; "The Kate Smith Hour," an afternoon variety show starring Kate Smith; and "Show of Shows," a Saturday evening program starring Sid Caesar and Imogene Coca. In addition, commercial time on 15 local television shows was purchased in seven markets in which one of the network shows was not available. In order to establish package-color identification, four-color advertisements were run in *This Week*, a Sunday supplement distributed in 33 markets. Local support was also given through a schedule of advertisements appearing in 35 newspapers in 22 markets. Total promotional costs for the period September 1953–May 1954 were approximately $2,700,000.

Beginning in May 1954, Dow began to change its media strategy. A decision was made to turn from participation television programs to the development of the company's own television program. The company purchased "Medic," a highly dramatic Monday evening program which concerned the activities of the medical profession and evoked considerable public interest. This program was purchased for the full year and was televised 39 times, i.e., it was televised three weeks out of four. A shift was also made from relying exclusively on *This Week* to the use of women's services magazines, including *Ladies' Home Journal*, *Woman's Home Companion*, *Good Housekeeping*, *McCall's*, *Family Circle*, and *Woman's Day*, and the general medium *Time*. The company's advertising schedule and budget for the periods May–December 1954 and January–December 1955 are given below:

Medium	May–Dec. 1954		Jan.–Dec. 1955	
	No. Ads	Cost	No. Ads	Cost
Today.........................	77	$ 278,536	....	....
Saturday Night Review...........	7	300,415	....	....
Kate Smith.....................	5	68,043	....	....
Medic:				
U.S..........................	12	716,300	16	$ 713,059
Canada......................	9	17,806	21	37,341
Total Network Television....	110	$1,381,100	37	$ 750,399
Local television..................	479	29,064	8	800
Consumer publications...........	26	262,210	13	133,885
Trade publications...............	15	24,043	8	7,537
Newspapers.....................	56	35,982	....	....
Preparation.....................	....	104,084	....	78,416
Promotion*.....................	....	196,203	....	77,810
Total.....................		$2,032,686		$1,048,847 est.

* The promotional expenditures listed above were for point-of-purchase materials and related items which the company used in three special in-store promotions each year: during the Christmas–New Year's Holiday season, the pre-Easter season, and the summer season.

[2] Commercial time bought on a participation basis meant that Dow purchased a segment of a program and thus had relatively little opportunity to be identified by viewers as the sponsor of the program.

Dow Reconsiders Saran Wrap

As the result of reviewing the marketing and promotion of Saran Wrap, Dow executives began to consider a number of areas, which are discussed briefly below.

Packaging. Ever since Saran Wrap had been marketed, Dow executives had been well aware that the package had caused users difficulties, the principal one being that users "lost" the edge of the film because the edge, newly cut, often slipped back into the package and adhered or clung to the roll. Four different packages had been used to eliminate this and other difficulties. Dow had recently tested a fifth package designed by Raymond Loewy and Associates, and the test results indicated that the new package would be a substantially better package and would eliminate many consumer complaints. Thus, at the time, packaging appeared no longer to be an area of major concern.

Media. Tentatively, Dow executives were of the opinion that changes should be made in media. They felt that "Medic" had done an excellent job for Saran Wrap but that the program's audience had now been saturated. Further, since "Medic's" audience was fairly stable, i.e., its audience of approximately 12 million families was quite loyal to the program, the company had to turn to other media if it wished to expose Saran Wrap to a new audience. Also, Dow executives felt that there was a need to use media which had a greater appeal to women, more turnover of audience, and which would allow greater frequency of advertising. Commercial time available on "Medic" was already being used for Dow products other than Saran Wrap, and the company's advertising agency had been asked to prepare new media plans for Dow's consideration which were based upon the use of print media as the prime medium.

Promotional Budget. With respect to the promotional budget for Saran Wrap, there were two budgets being considered. Both proposals provided that promotional expenditures would continue at the rate of $1,000,000 a year for the remainder of 1955. One proposal provided a budget of $2,700,000 for the period January 1, 1956, to May 30, 1957, and was based on seeking annual sales of 60 million units. The other provided for a promotional expenditure of $1,722,000 for the same 18-month period and was based on maintaining Saran Wrap sales at the existing level, i.e., at an annual rate of about 41 million units.

In considering what the sales goal and promotional budget should be, the Dow executives who were responsible for Saran Wrap prepared a special presentation for top management consisting of four charts.

Chart No. 1 reviewed promotional expenditures and sales as follows:

Time Period	Promotional Expenditure	Sales/Unit	Prom. Exp. per Unit
11/15/53–9/15/54..........	$2,136,273	20,800,000	$0.1025
9/16/54–12/31/54..........	1,242,344	15,600,000	0.0800
1/1/55–3/1/55.............	422,215	7,000,000	0.0580

Chart No. 2 was as follows:

—Existing sales based upon a national average for the period October 1954–January 1955 are 4.87 cases per 1,000 families per month.

—Existing sales per 1,000 families per month based upon the period October 1954–January 1955 in selected markets are: New England, 7.05; New York City, 5.96; Birmingham, 2.17; New Orleans, 4.88; Chicago, 7.28; Los Angeles, 4.43; Phoenix, 2.56; Columbus (Ohio), 7.12; Cincinnati and Dayton, 4.82; and Toledo, 4.13.

—Sales per 1,000 families per month at an annual rate of sales of 60 million units: 6.67 cases.

Chart No. 3 compared the consumer purchase patterns experienced in the four Ohio test markets with the existing consumer purchase patterns in the Chicago market, as follows:

Type of Consumer	Ohio Test Markets	Chicago Market
Heavy user (1 unit or more a month)...................	10%	10.6%
Light user (less than 1 unit a month)....................	35	6.4
Former user....................	10	24.1
Subtotal....................	55%	41.1%
Nonuser (never used)..........	45	58.9
Total....................	100%	100.0%

Chart No. 4 estimated the penetration of Saran Wrap on a national basis as of June 1, 1955, as follows:

Type of Consumer	No. of Families	% of Total Families	No. of Units Used per Year
Heavy user..............	4,750,000	10%	33,000,000
Light user..............	7,100,000	15	18,000,000
Former user.............	4,750,000	10	....
Nonuser.................	28,500,000	65	....
Totals.............	45,100,000	100%	51,000,000

Research. In addition to numerous research projects which Dow had undertaken in connection with the four Ohio test markets and various types of packages, the company purchased Nielsen Drug-Food Index data which kept executives well informed regarding Saran Wrap's distribution, in-stock and out-of-stock situation, retail prices, share of the total household wrap market, and so on. In order to get additional information that might help them devise a new promotional strategy, Dow executives had hired two consulting firms. The Institute of Motivational Research, Inc., headed by Dr. Ernest Dichter, was asked to determine whether there were any psychological "blocks" inhibiting consumer buying of Saran Wrap. This study was to be completed by August 1955 at a cost of $16,-

500. Nowland and Company was asked to study Saran Wrap's sales situation, particularly with respect to what was limiting sales. This study was to be completed by October 1955 at a cost of $34,500.

~~~

CASE 7: DOW CHEMICAL COMPANY (B) [1]

QUESTIONS TO CONSIDER: *(1) What conclusions do you draw from the progress report? (2) What factors appear to be retarding the sales growth of Saran Wrap? (3) Does the progress report provide you with new ideas regarding what might be an effective new advertising strategy for Saran Wrap? (4) Tentatively, do you think that a good opportunity exists to increase sales to 60 million units yearly? (5) Tentatively, what should be the objectives of Saran Wrap advertising? What kind of advertising copy should Dow employ? What changes should be made in media strategy?*

While in the process of devising a new promotional strategy for "Saran Wrap," Dow executives received in mid-1955 a preliminary report from The Institute for Motivational Research, Inc., entitled "Progress Report Outline on Saran Wrap." This report follows:

PROGRESS REPORT OUTLINE ON SARAN WRAP

This outline summarizes our tentative findings to date. It is based on an analysis of our first wave of 31 depth interviews, representing users, past users, and non-users of Saran Wrap and other types of wraps and food coverings. These interviews were conducted in 6 states distributed in the East, Far West, Southwest, and South.

Since we are developing plans to validate these findings by further research, it is possible that few if any of these provisional conclusions will remain in our final report. We hope, however, that the present report will convey a sufficient idea of the direction in which we are moving.

INTRODUCTION

Saran Wrap is different from most other wrapping materials people have been accustomed to. Here lies possibly one of its major problems. It violates many of the wrapping stereotypes: Good wrapping is thick, BUT Saran Wrap is thin. Protective wrapping is opaque, BUT Saran Wrap is visually penetrable. Most wrapping materials are hard, BUT Saran Wrap is soft. Most wrapping materials are not "magnetic," BUT Saran Wrap clings. Furthermore, the effort to impose some kind of structure, some shape to objects during the wrapping process is unsatisfied. For Saran Wrap takes the shape of the objects it is supposed to protect. A feeling ensues of having a sloppy wrapping on one's hands.

The user feels something like this: "I'm trying to make a package and this Saran Wrap won't cooperate with me; it makes the kind of package it wants; it doesn't go where I wish, but where it wishes."

Added to this new wrapping experience is the feeling that the material is silky and soft, sheeny and luxurious. To use it makes one feel guilty, maybe

---

[1] Written by Martin V. Marshall.

even sinful. "It's just too nice." To manipulate it for everyday purposes is just a bit too hard for the average person to accept. The average user simply isn't accustomed to such a wrapping experience.

And so, apart from conscious manual difficulties (to which we will refer again below), the user reacts with psychological misgivings at a deeper, subconscious level. To be sure, these reactions are irrational and not at all related to the objective situation. They must, however, be recognized for their motivational force upon the reactions to Saran Wrap. Thus, Saran Wrap's major advertising problem may well be in selling its "differentness," rather than its "betterness."

Our tentative major recommendation, therefore, that our analysis to date leads us to suggest, is that the public needs to be appraised of this new type of wrapping as a new type of food protection. Since it is NEW, a major goal of advertising and promotion is to avoid dangerous comparisons between Saran Wrap and any of the older, well-known wrapping materials. The public, in other words, needs a new conception of wrapping. As this new conception becomes implanted, the receptive foundation for the acceptance of Saran Wrap will have been laid. In order to change these older stereotypes we have to know where they come from. It is the purpose of the following pages to delineate these sources.

I. The Psychology of Food Protection

1. Women who leave food uncovered are considered lazy, sloppy in other respects, unthrifty, poor housekeepers, and even poor marital risks. The following quotation, though stated colorfully, finds a strong echo in most of our interviewing:

"When you see a woman put food in her icebox and leave it uncovered you can be sure that she leaves dirty dishes in the sink and crumbs on the tablecloth. Sounds like I might be talking about my ex-wife. Ha, ha, ha. No kidding, it's a bad sign when you look in a woman's icebox and see containers of food, uncovered, overnight, it's ruined. It loses its flavor and takes on the flavor of the icebox. Besides it dries out. . . . I do think when a woman leaves food, uncovered, in the icebox it indicates something undesirable in her make-up. One thing, it sure as the dickens indicates that she is not thrifty . . . A fellow had sure better find out something about a girl before he marries her. He'd sure better look in her icebox first. Ha, ha, ha."

A practical application of this popular inclination is to channel Saran Wrap into this wave. Such slogans as, "Saran Wrap Fights Food B. O.," and "Saran Wrap Fights Food Waste," could be designed to ride on the back of this well entrenched attitude. To instill in the public mind the association between the use of Saran Wrap and housekeeping proficiency would tap a positive feeling force for the product.

2. Why do people cover food? Why are they concerned with food protection? Four reasons stand out: A. Appearance: Uncovered food appears unappetizing. B. Disturbs eating enjoyment. C. Freshness. To prevent drying preserve flavor. D. Sanitation: 1. To disbar bacteria and dirt; 2. To delay or prevent deterioration.

These reasons stem from deep emotional involvements regarding food protection, and can be further summed up as follows: (a) *Life and Death Concern:* To ward off hidden, powerful enemies of health—germs, moisture, and other unseen enemies that attack my food. The user seeks an ally in food protection. (b) *Mummification:* To maintain food exactly as when put away—unchanged. To keep it as appetizing as before—"embalmed."

Implication of these hidden fears is that people seek a means, an ally, in protecting their food from pollution by powerful enemies. For *their* food will soon be *they, their own persons.* Therefore, a useful angle for Saran Wrap to follow is to abjure half-way measures—"99 and 99/100% sure is not enough; be 100% sure." In some such ways, the deep emotional desire for 100% sealing and protection might be tapped for Saran Wrap.

II. SARAN WRAP IS DIFFERENT

1. *Moldability:* The moldability of Saran Wrap may tend to prevent the "ordering" desire in the wrapping act. The desire to have neat, tidy-looking packages may not be fully satisfied.

It may therefore be necessary to instill a new concept about it. "Saran Wrap is a *new* kind of *protective* wrapping." "Saran Wrap adapts to your food." "Saran Wrap is a loving care wrap."

2. *Transparency:* Rationally considered, many people like the transparency of Saran Wrap. But, subconsciously, transparency creates the illusion of thinness, which, of course, adds to the actual perceived quality of thinness. What you can "see through" gives the impression of leaking, and suggests the notion that Saran Wrap is vulnerable, too easily penetrated, pierced. Added to this, as we saw above, uncovered food is unappetizing to look at, for people desire their food to be hidden, away from sight when it is covered. Instead the food appears naked to the eye, for Saran Wrap, being "nude" enables an obscene penetration of it to be made.

Hence, people get the impression that Saran is vulnerable. And related to this, on the other hand, since its unclothed nudity lacks "body," it is itself incapable of covering a "body." In other words, the impression is given that Saran Wrap lacks protective power. The following quotation, for instance, puts these ideas in the housewife's words:

"I just bought it once. I bought it for my daughter's birthday party to wrap up the candies. I used the rest of it for the cheese. For meat, it seems to me it's not strong enough. I don't really know because I didn't try. I just didn't. There was a certain funny feeling to it. It was kind of soft, it didn't give me the feeling of any body to it. I like to feel that wrapping has body, otherwise I don't get the feeling that it properly protects the food."

The public needs to be educated to the strength of this new kind of wrapping material, similarly as the public at one time needed to be persuaded—educated—about the strength of aluminum, though thin, as compared to iron and steel. But the educational task regarding Saran Wrap is not so much to persuade people of its technological improvements, but of its emotional value for those who use it. For example, advertising might approach the problem in this way: "You might be a little startled at first when you wrap your food in Saran Wrap because it doesn't look as if you have done anything. But you have really done a lot more than you normally do."

Most people have come to accept the view that the thicker something is the better it protects. Yet we are asked to believe that Saran Wrap, a very thin material, not only protects but protects better than most other wrapping materials. This appeal is not conducive to the believability in the ads of the product.

Hence the approach should be changed from the present stress on transparency alone to include also the protective fortitude of Saran Wrap. For example, the slogan, "Soft as Silk, Strong as Steel," might be effectively introduced. The product ought to be shown in action—in ads and TV commercials—in a variety of stressful situations, yet capable of preserving its enclosures unchanged, unharmed by the stresses. People must be taught to overcome their resistance to thin materials for protective covering. Again, advertising might say, "only a fraction of an inch thick but as protective as a steel wall—nothing gets in or out."

3. *Cling:* The clinging quality of Saran Wrap is desirable, insofar as it creates an air-tight package. But, psychologically, both the term "cling" and the actual clinging behavior of Saran Wrap sets off associations about the product which are summed up by such terms as: fickle, tricky, stubborn, capricious, sticky, "clinging-vine," uncooperative.

These reactions result in a feeling of *wasting time* in dealing with it. More important, the user feels he is wasting money when the product uncontrollably sticks to itself. Undesired extravagance in time and money are consequently counteracted by sales resistance.

A possible way to overcome this difficulty is to desist from using the term, "cling," and change to some such term as "automatic sealing," which later would, in turn, reinforce the belief in its protective alliance in active partnership with the housewife or general user.[2] Again it might not be wrong from a sales standpoint to admit that it is a little hard to cope with the cling quality, but to insist that the advantages of protection and transparency and all the other good qualities of Saran Wrap are worth the little extra effort.

4. *Saran Wrap's "Reluctance" Causes Counter-Reactions:* First, the user struggles, then he cajoles, then he loses patience, and finally he severs relations with the product. Being unable to do with it whatever he wishes—to make it unroll easily, to re-roll it evenly, or to apply it without sticking either to itself or to the user—the user is hurt psychologically because of his lack of control over it. He comes to feel Saran Wrap doesn't play ball with him, that it isn't fair. He is therefore annoyed by its performance, uses it infrequently or never buys it again. Because the cling quality is oversold in ads, he tends to quarrel with them, the product, and the advertiser. Basically he gets mad at himself for having "swallowed a line." However, he blames not himself but the product, the ad and the advertiser.

One respondent put it this way:

"Frankly, I've never discussed any kind of food wrapping with my friends, until very recently. Actually, when I bought this roll of Saran Wrap I was so annoyed that it did not cling as the advertisements said it would that I felt a need to ask other users what they thought of it. I found that most of my friends bought a roll because they were curious to see how true the claims that were made for the product actually were. Whether they will continue to use it I do not know."

A practical suggestion might be to include a "directions-for-use" slip in each carton, pointing out the best way to handle the product. Another approach especially on TV might be to present one woman showing another woman how to use it.

5. *The Wax Paper Habit:* People rationally favor the wonderful qualities of Saran Wrap—its transparency, cling, re-usability, air-tight seal-in. But they bring their old habits and expectations of the Wax Paper Era to the Saran Wrap Era. These traditional habits and expectations need re-conditioning. Difficulties will almost certainly be encountered, for instance, if one will expect to rip off a piece of Saran Wrap as speedily as a piece of wax paper. These difficulties should not be dodged. They should be recognized and counteracted. With this end in mind, slogans and demonstrations of slogans such as the following are suggested: "A little extra care will pay off." "Food care deserves the best con-

---

[2] We understand that Dow engineers are presently overcoming some of these clinging difficulties. Until such time that technological difficulties disappear, it would be well to be cognizant of them and to counteract them accordingly.

sideration." "Half-way measures in food protection are not good enough."

Take the consumer through the paces: Another useful idea in overcoming consumer resistance in this kind of product is to show him step-by-step how the product is best taken out of the box, unrolled, rerolled, used, re-used, and so on. Everybody is from Missouri nowadays, especially in a highly competitive market. To fail to educate the user, the prospective user, and the past-user in the most efficient way for using the product is to invite a boomerang effect such as expressed by the following doubting Thomas: "I sometimes wonder how much practice the TV demonstrator has had so that her Saran unrolls so easily. Or is that a specially prepared roll?"

The housewife is apt to be made to feel inferior to the woman on TV; for her role as a housewife is endangered by her not being able to do in *her* kitchen what someone else does in hers. It would be helpful therefore to demonstrate, in easy steps the best way to handle the product for proper use. In this way the user feels he is being educated to control the product and will derive satisfaction in performing his lesson to perfection. The believability of Saran Wrap ads are thus likely to increase, doubting the ads and disdaining the product to go down, and sales to go up.

6. *I like Saran Wrap's Seal-in Quality:* Among those who use Saran Wrap regularly there is a tendency to use it primarily for long-time protection. For food that is to be eaten in a day or two, wax paper tends to get priority over other types of materials. But for longer periods of non-use, Saran Wrap wins first place. This infrequent usage though commendable from one point of view is damaging in another, that is, damaging to sales. For it means fewer re-purchases. Hence a re-education campaign might stress the *food-saving, protection giving* qualities of Saran Wrap even for short-term wrappings. "It saves food to seal for short periods. Seal and Save with Saran." Demonstrations illustrating the relative merits of different wrappings compared to Saran Wrap in protective function for even short time intervals would also be desirable.

III. THE PERSONALITY OF SARAN WRAP

1. *Saran Wrap Is Feminine:* The product is referred to by such terms as pretty, silky, dainty, pliable, glistening, soft, glamorous, clinging, moist, beautiful, nice.

But, being feminine, Saran Wrap is "coy," it has "moods" (it wrinkles, wads up, tears unexpectedly, sticks together, is unmanageable). This "feminine prerogative" causes consumer resistance.

These resistances might be counteracted by admitting to the "spirited" aspects of this queenly product, yet stressing the all significant virtues of protection, air-tight seal, and beauty. Emphasizing Saran Wrap's tensile strength and stability would also add a touch of the masculine without ruining its inescapably feminine appearance and sensuous appeal.

2. *Saran Wrap Brings Out the Beauty in Its Contacts:* Like a beautiful woman in a house, Saran Wrap makes things it comes into contact with appear more glamorous than they are otherwise. It makes food look appetizing. It gives it a good appearance. These functions of Saran Wrap give the person who uses it a sense of feeling beautiful himself. It was he (or she) who did it. It is to him or her that the credit goes. To look at appetizing food or at anything that elicits a heightened aesthetic appreciation enlivens the beholder as well as the beholden. The *live* quality of Saran Wrap, in other words, is contagious. It would be well then to stress the beautifying and appetizing function of this product. "Saran Wrap beautifies and appetizes."

3. *Personality of Dow:* Although most of our respondents have never heard of the Dow Chemical Company, or if they have heard of it, that it is the manu-

facturer of Saran Wrap—they all conceive of the company behind the product as "modern, progressive, scientific, large." Among those who do know about Dow, some wonder how a chemical firm can know about the problems of the housewife in the kitchen. Hence they would probably like to see a more feminine interest on the part of the company. If a "Betty Crocker" type of association were emphasized by the company, it would most probably act as an effective agent to promote Saran Wrap. In other words, this product, having feminine associations in the minds of users, needs to be bolstered by a more feminine-associated organization.

IV. ECONOMY

The fact that Saran Wrap is a little more expensive than other similar products is, needless to say, an active deterrent to sales. But it need not be the *deciding* "NO" at the point of purchase. Several damaging conceptions exist in people's minds about the kind of people who would use this product. These factors are probably even more deterring from a sales viewpoint than the few cents extra that this product sells for. Psychological expensiveness, in other words, is often the stronger deterrent than monetary expensiveness.

For example, it is commonly held that Saran Wrap is a "showy" product. To use it, therefore, for daily purposes, is eschewed, for it gives the average user a feeling of over self-indulgence in a luxury. The user soon classifies Saran Wrap as "one of the items that he can easily do without." The luxury-associations of the product create in him the *guilt of wastefulness*. As a result, he is apt to regard those who use it as "meticulous" or "showy" people.

Several suggestions may be made to help overcome these areas of resistance:

1. Play down the extravagance associations of Saran Wrap. Refer to it as a "simplified food locker" or "food safe" for everyday use. Create the notion about it as an "everyday luxury."

2. Create an atmosphere of "moral permission" concerning the destruction of Saran Wrap. Make it OK to throw the stuff out without trying to find ways to "re-use it because advertisements say you can." A slogan here might be: "Always keep your Saran Wrap Handy."

3. Play up "everyday, everybody" conceptions. Not only showy people, not only the young, adventurous, or nouveau riche, use it—but *everybody uses it everywhere all the time.*

4. To overcome the resistance of the relatively high price per carton, it might be useful to suggest all the different things that can be wrapped with a single roll of Saran Wrap: Mom's cakes and left overs, Dad's hats, shoes and shirts while on a trip, Jimmy's flora and fauna specimens, etc. This type of appeal would mutually reinforce the "food safe" idea suggested above—both contending, in effect, that Saran Wrap costs less in the long run!

V. MARKETING PROBLEMS

We have not undertaken to conduct a market survey in the usual sense of the term. However, in the course of our interviewing we made a special point to get whatever information we could which would in any way affect the sales of Saran Wrap.

Tentatively, we can now say several things about the name, Saran Wrap, which we feel could be useful. First, the term, "Saran," is more often than not reacted to unfavorably by our respondents. It is felt to be a "foreign-sounding" word or one which sounds like a drug or chemical. Second, the term, "Wrap" suggests comparisons with other similar products, a danger which should be avoided as much as possible. The product in question is a new type of wrapping or sealing material and should itself suggest by its very name its *new* direction. Third, the term "Wrap" is too narrow a term for it tends to restrict the imagination regarding all the possible uses to which it can be put.

We suggest, therefore, that, if possible, the name "Saran Wrap" be changed. Such ideas as "air-tight protection" or "vacuum seal" would be wise to consider in choosing a different name.

As for enlarging the market, we have found that many new uses can be found for Saran Wrap, too detailed to record here. Since this is so, it would appear best to de-emphasize the kitchen uses for the housewife, as is now being stressed. Instead, why not make the kitchen only one of its many diversified applications?

To bring in the notion of its use "For Mom," "For Dad," "For Baby," etc., rather than for the different articles as is now presented on the carton, would excite a more personalized interest from the prospective and current user. To offer a booklet describing its various uses might also be helpful.

We have already made several recommendations . . . regarding changes in packaging. Since the Dow company is presently examining this matter in detail it is not necessary to extend this discussion to any length.

It is well to stress, however, this point: that since Saran Wrap is a new type of product on the market, it needs to be presented to the public as such. This is in keeping with the major recommendation of this report. Hence, it would be helpful if the carton had a little window, perhaps made of Saran Wrap, which would permit a sensuous bridge to the product inside. People could thereby both see it and touch it at the same time. This innovation—the signature of the product on the box—would remove the *barrier* fortification that the carton ominously presents now.

We have also found that many people feel there is insufficient material on the roll. They still have the notion that because it is packaged like wax paper and has some of the same uses as wax paper it should also have the same amount per roll as wax paper. The transparency of Saran Wrap probably reinforces the illusion of thinness, that is, of a sparse, seedy-looking roll. The brown color of the tube, moreover, is not aesthetically appealing and not at all in keeping with the beauty of the product. Therefore, our visual aides department is presently investigating means to give an illusion of depth in these tests: a) to change the coloring of the tube; b) change the color of the material (we are using differently tinted cellophane); c) interlard the roll with thin, differently color tissue paper.

VI. ADVERTISING PROBLEMS

One of the areas we have yet to investigate fully is the advertising effectiveness of the different media used for Saran Wrap. But we have already some data that suggest the need for certain changes.

The Feeling of Betrayal: Many people have developed a negative disposition toward Saran Wrap because they feel they have been let down. They had expected so much from advertisements regarding its miraculous qualities, yet they run into one difficulty after another in using it. The "re-use" claim, for instance, creates a negative climate of opinion rather than, as a rational approach might anticipate, a positive feeling for the product.

The reason for this negativity stems from difficulties encountered in re-using the product: Washing and drying problems; tearing, sticking or wadding up; and so on. It is not easy to re-use the product, yet advertising claims that one can re-use it. The claim that one can re-use it gets extended in the user's mind to "one *ought* to re-use it," resulting in a reaction such as this: "If I try and fail, it is either because I am stupid, or because I've been fooled." Most people naturally hook on to the second alternative. Result: Spasmodic or one-time users.

The re-use claim also elicit other negative counter-claims such as: "Why should I? There's enough to do besides washing Saran Wrap," or "To re-use a wrapping is unsanitary since you can never really get it clean again."

A practical way to overcome these resistances might include consideration of stopping the "reuse campaign." In its stead, a strong selling point might be to stress the endurance and durability of Saran Wrap, such as *"It Lasts As Long As You Need It."*

Other "let-down" antipathies result from unrolling difficulties, unclean tearing, and not always clinging, as when wet. When these difficulties occur a subconscious hostility arises toward Saran Wrap as if the product possessed an animate personality. The user comes to feel negatively disposed in some such way as: "It destroys itself by needlessly tearing or ripping; it is therefore self-dissipating; I hate it; it makes me feel guilty for having had the bad sense to buy it in the first place." Quite likely these reactions would not arise if certain unexpressed expectations had not built up about the miracle qualities of Saran Wrap.

Saran Wrap is indeed a chemical miracle, but the user is apt all too easily to extend his expectations beyond the rightful limits of the product's claims. In all fairness, however, the public is not entirely at fault here, for advertising to date has led it willy nilly into this self-defeating *cul de sac*.

The Commercials on the Medic Program. The commercials tend to be well presented—"they don't talk down to the audience,"—a fact well appreciated by respondents. But their seriousness does not provide a sufficient contrast with the seriousness of Medic. Hence, they are not so likely to stamp in their message as they might be if they were made, for example, comical. We are planning intensive analysis of consumer reactions to your present ad appeals in the next phases of our research.

Word-of-Mouth Advertising. It is our impression that word-of-mouth advertising provides the greatest single introduction for Saran Wrap. Not only are people more readily induced to buy the product under these conditions, but they probably like it better and use it more frequently and without quarreling with it when it becomes "moody."

We would recommend, therefore, that Saran Wrap advertising should try to duplicate the word-of-mouth introduction—"Mrs. Jones telling Mrs. Brown." Moreover, if Mrs. Jones could be shown demonstrating to Mrs. Brown the best way to use the product, it would create a greater familiarity with the product and the way to handle it.

TV commercials might well use the kitchen as an advertising medium to advantage. For example, a party is in progress. One woman wanders into the kitchen and sees the hostess at work, wrapping: "Oh, I see you are using Saran Wrap. How do you find it?" "Oh, wonderful! Mrs. Brown just introduced it to me last week and I think its wonderful. She told me about it, so I bought some. I have three rolls right here and I'm almost through with them. I certainly intend to keep on using it."

Featuring the Dow Insignia. Efforts should also be made to feature the Dow sign more prominently, or perhaps a special sign for Saran Wrap, so that the sign could more easily become associated with the product. Such reinforcements on memory and the imagination cannot help inducing greater familiarity in the product. They lend to it a mythical or ritualistic aura of importance, even of friendship.

In conclusion, we believe there are psychological resistances to the purchase of Saran Wrap. When these negative motivational factors are adequately tapped, it will be possible to institute means for coping with them. In this report we have presented those areas which we have already investigated and we have made recommendations wherever we considered it necessary. Our report, however, is tentative, and is subject to change in minor or even major ways, depending upon our further research and validation procedures.

FURTHER STEPS

Below is presented a summary of research procedures that we are planning to carry out to confirm and extend our findings. This, we expect, will be ready by July 15 for a final verbal report, and by August 15 for a final report.

1. *Second Wave Depth Interviews:* These interviews represent a continuation of our initial wave of interviews. They focalize on those points which we have found to be most fruitful and are directed to potential and actual Saran Wrap consumers.

2. *Projective Interviews:* The projective interviews are designed to test our major hypotheses and to validate and quantify our tentative findings. For example, one of our tests will concern the different attitudes, if any, between the types of covering to be used for partially consumed foods (left-overs) as compared to fresh foods. A picture showing different foods, some covered, some uncovered, will be presented to the subject. He will be given a list of different food coverings, and asked to pick the covering that he feels would best suit his needs. In this manner, we will get at not only a series of simple answers to simple questions, but also, by probing at a deeper level, we can expect to unearth basic, though inconspicuous, feelings toward Saran Wrap.

And the projective test will concern the desire for structurization in the wrapping process as opposed to the amorphous package. We may wrap square or other geometric-shaped items having rigid forms, and we will present them side by side with amorphous shapes. Subjects will then be asked to talk freely about their feelings about each type of package. This would be a Thematic Apperception Test (TAT) insofar as the situation is rather unstructured from the viewpoint of the subject, allowing him to range freely in his imagination. In this manner he *projects* his feelings, without his being aware that he is being probed.

Still another test may be something as follows, in which the subject is told: "You go into a kitchen where you will find a package of Saran Wrap. What kind of woman would you say runs that kitchen?" In this way we will test our findings about the image of the Saran Wrap user, as well as uncover further vital data.

3. *Experimentation:* Consumer Responses to Trail Packages of Saran Wrap. Respondents will be given a carton of Saran Wrap, and nonuser depth interviews will be made a week later, presumably after they've have a chance to use the product.

4. *Field Testing:* Field testing will be conducted in supermarkets to explore the dynamics of the actual Saran Wrap buying situation. a) Point of purchase observation; b) Reactions to display materials; c) Open-ended questioning.

5. *Pyschometric Ad Tests:* Ad tests are to be conducted with current advertising material to test the effectiveness of current appeals and to explore new avenues for copy approach. Along these lines, further research will also be conducted to determine the impact of "Medic" in conjunction with the commercials.

6. *Panel Families:* Saran Wrap commercials will be tested for effectiveness and appeal among our "panel families." We will be especially interested to

observe children during play, in which Saran Wrap will be an object of play. Children are usually less inhibited than adults, so that they may use the product in a less concealed fashion in expressing their pleasure with it. Thus, new uses may be discovered.

7. *Package Testing:* Package testing will be conducted to test reactions to the label, inserts, brand symbols, and possible innovations in packaging.

8. *Candid Camera:* Candid photos will be made of people in actual wrapping situations—both during the use of Saran Wrap, and other products. We hope thereby to validate and extend our findings.

After careful analysis of all the data, blue print for action and specific suggestions for advertising, merchandising and selling approaches will be developed.

~~~

CASE 8: DOW CHEMICAL COMPANY (C)[1]

QUESTIONS TO CONSIDER: *(1) What conclusions do you draw from the Nowland report regarding the relative opportunity to increase sales among heavy, light, former, and nonusers? (2) What factors appear to be retarding sales of Saran Wrap? (3) Do you agree with the conclusions in the Nowland report? (4) Would you accept the recommendations in the report? (5) Should Saran Wrap be promoted as a kitchen or a household wrap? (6) At this stage in your analysis, do you think an opportunity exists to increase sales to 60 million units yearly? (7) Tentatively, what should be the objectives of Saran Wrap advertising? What kind of advertising copy should Dow employ? What changes should be made in media strategy?*

In October 1955 Dow executives received a report from Nowland and Company, professional, consultants, entitled "Factors Influencing the Purchase of Saran Wrap." The report consisted of 73 pages subdivided into five sections: Introduction, Character of the Market, Analysis in Relation to Promotion of Saran Wrap, Summary and Conclusions, and Recommendations. A summary of the report follows.

Plan and Method of the Study

The objective of the study was to isolate and examine factors which operated to inhibit or to facilitate the sale of Saran Wrap, particularly with reference to the consumer as such in her day-to-day use of the product.

To achieve this objective, three areas of information were probed: (1) the nature and scope of the sources of knowledge and attitudes which consumers have with respect to the properties and the uses of Saran Wrap; (2) the nature of the experiences which consumers have had with Saran Wrap and which may have influenced its use and acceptance; and (3) the relationship between the personal and background characteristics of the

---

[1] Written by Martin V. Marshall.

consumer as they influence the use and acceptance of the product.

Information from consumers was gathered by means of a series of depth interviews with 407 subjects, distributed among nine markets as follows: Springfield, Mass., 46; Columbus, Ohio, 44; Bronx County, N.Y., 46; Peoria, Illinois, 45; Atlanta, Georgia, 43; Indianapolis, Indiana, 45; Richmond County, N.Y., 47; Oakland, California, 45; and Oklahoma City, Oklahoma, 46.

Interviews were conducted in a relatively unstructured and conversational manner, each lasting about an hour. The interviewer, a Nowland staff member with psychological training, was given an interviewing guide consisting of the information which was to be derived from the interviews, but the phrasing and ordering of questions was left largely to his discretion.

The Character of the Market for Saran Wrap

The Nowland study segmented its sample of 407 into four consumer groups, as follows:

a) 112 heavy users: persons who claimed to use more than one roll a month.
b) 71 light users: persons who claimed to use less than a roll a month.
c) 52 former users: persons who had tried but discontinued the use of Saran Wrap.
d) 146 nonusers: persons who had heard of Saran Wrap but never tried it.

Two per cent of the persons interviewed had never heard of Saran Wrap, and 5% were still using their first roll.

Heavy Users. The heavy user was found to be a Saran Wrap enthusiast, replacing other wrapping materials to a great extent with it; 74% of heavy users virtually used nothing but Saran Wrap for wrapping purposes. In sharp contrast, more than 40% of the light users used competitive wrapping materials for the same wrapping purposes. Exhibit 1 contrasts the heavy user with the light user in terms of the extent to which other materials are replaced.

Heavy users, more than any other group, were found to be susceptible to new ideas, as more likely to try out suggested new uses for Saran Wrap. Also, the heavy user on her own initiative tried the product on as many things as she could think of. The varied assortment of uses to which Saran Wrap could be put was illustrated in the comment of a lower-income Bronx housewife who said:

> Saran Wrap is handy stuff. My daughter uses it to carry sandwiches in her pocketbook so she doesn't have to carry an extra bag for her sandwiches. The odors do not escape. We have used it to carry diapers when traveling, and my daughter uses it to wrap soap that she takes to work. I wrap peeled eggs in it for my husband's lunch and my sons carry candy in it when they go to the movies. . . . After I started using it I found more uses for it.

The heavy user was also found to be a person who did a considerable amount of kitchen wrapping, who was interested in the kitchen, and who loved "to work and fuss" in the kitchen. Exhibit 2 indicates that heavy users were likely to be more "kitchen oriented" than other users or non-users. The Nowland report went on to state:

The heavy user, more than any other group, is the type of housewife who says, "I love cooking and fussing"; "cooking is my hobby"; or "That's my favorite, I'd rather cook than do anything." This is the type of person for whom cooking is a rewarding experience and not a necessary chore in running her house. Rather, the kitchen is a place for her to achieve status and recognition from her family. The kitchen is one place in the home where this

Exhibit 1

DOW CHEMICAL COMPANY (C)

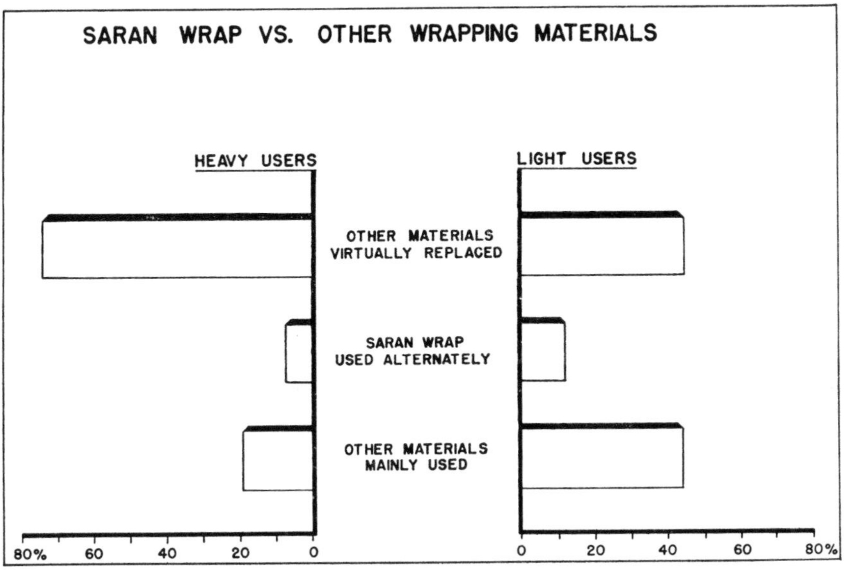

kind of woman has an opportunity to express her creativity and to be rewarded for it by husband and family. The kitchen-oriented housewife is the person who most readily sees in Saran Wrap something more than just another kitchen wrap. Her interest in using Saran Wrap goes beyond an appreciation of its functional advantages that can make her kitchen tasks easier. Her desire to use Saran Wrap stems from her interest in doing more than just preparing a meal or keeping her kitchen neat and straightened up. She is as much interested in *how* things are done as in seeing them done. She is as much interested in what she works with as she is in turning out a fine meal. Her interest in Saran Wrap may be likened to the interest of a skilled artisan who not only takes pride and pleasure in turning out a masterful piece of work, but also derives great satisfaction in having the finest tools with which to work.

Light Users. With respect to the light user, Nowland reported as follows:

The factor distinguishing the light from the heavy user is a sense of discrimination and a colder, more rational attitude toward Saran Wrap. Compared with the heavy user she is less apt to replace other materials with Saran Wrap; she is more selective in using it for particular items and as a consequence uses less of it. She is a person who recognizes Saran Wrap's distinct characteristics and appreciates them in the uses *for which in her view they are most applicable.* These are uses for which she believes Saran Wrap can uniquely do the job. In uses where Saran Wrap's superiority is not worth the higher cost, she rejects it. In [Exhibit 3] the extent to which Saran Wrap is used exclusively for different items (such as are usually wrapped in the kitchen) is shown for light

Exhibit 2

DOW CHEMICAL COMPANY (C)

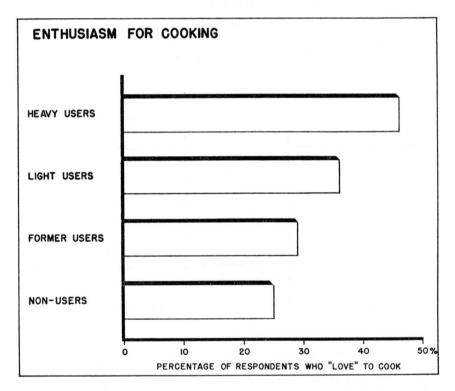

users and for heavy users. Those items for which the two groups show the greatest disparity are listed at the bottom, while the items of least disparity are at the top. The greatest differences occur for those items where the special qualities of Saran Wrap appear to the housewife to be *least* at issue; there is no difference at all when these qualities serve a well-recognized and much appreciated purpose. Thus, for covering bowls, for which Saran Wrap is clearly ideally suited, there is no difference between heavy and light users. The longest bar in [Exhibit 3] indicates that three-fourths of the light users cover their bowls with Saran Wrap, and this is their greatest use, and the heavy user does not exceed this to any appreciable extent. The light user will keep her fruits and vegetables in a plastic bag, or unwrapped in the refrigerator drawer: she is apt to say or imply that wrapping them in Saran Wrap offers no advantages. The heavy users, however, wrap such produce in Saran Wrap twice as much as do light users.

The lack of interest of the light user in the exceptional characteristics of Saran Wrap, as such, as well as her indifference toward using it unless she conceives it to be beneficial, is apparent in the reasons she gives for not using it. The major reasons she gives for not using Saran Wrap on those items which

Exhibit 3

DOW CHEMICAL COMPANY (C)

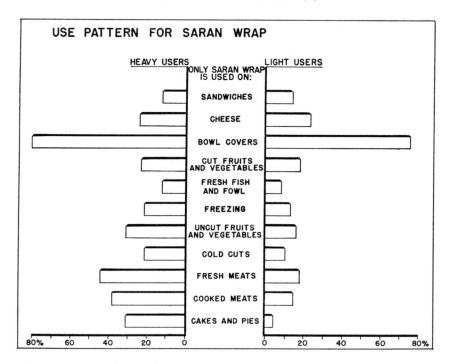

she wraps in some other materials are: "I never thought of using it," "the other materials are satisfactory," and "Saran Wrap would not be as good as other materials."

That Saran Wrap means less to the light user is seen in the responses of a Springfield housewife with three children. She bought Saran Wrap about a month after she saw it advertised on television. Her friend had mentioned Saran Wrap to her but she did not buy it until she saw if again in the A & P. She bought it to cover bowls of "leftovers" as suggested by the television commercial and said she has "neither the intention or the occasion to use it differently." As for her preference for Saran Wrap over wax paper, she said, "Saran Wrap keeps foods fresher but that's not too important . . . I don't keep leftovers that long that wax paper won't do the job . . . the expense doesn't justify its qualities . . . I just usually grab what's in the closet, Saran Wrap or wax paper. It doesn't make too much difference."

When asked how important the qualities of Saran Wrap were, she said about cling: "I don't know. It makes it harder to handle than wax paper, but it makes up for that in keeping things fresher, *if that's important.*"

About transparency she said: "That's the advantage it has over wax paper. *It makes it more attractive but I can do without it.*"

Such responses clearly show some confusion on the part of the housewife. True, price is always a consideration, and "leftovers" might be of little real concern to her. But she seems unconcerned about freshness, and therefore about the reasons for keeping food fresh; and she confuses transparency with attractiveness, and therefore probably has no real insight into what these apparently very obvious qualities mean.

Former Users. Nowland reported on former users as follows:

The former user is the person who reacts most strongly to the cost and handling disadvantage Saran Wrap has in comparison with other kitchen wrapping materials. Because of her lack of kitchen orientation she does not have that enthusiasm for using Saran Wrap which would make her accept any concern she might have about price, and the slight amount of extra care needed in handling Saran Wrap, as incidental to the gratifications she gets from using it. Nor is she, like the light user, willing to pay extra both in time and money for the functional advantages to be gained from using Saran Wrap. In other words, handling and dispensing difficulties are obvious annoyances to fasten onto, and being the sort of woman she is, she displaces her own impatience and annoyance somewhat irrationally upon the Saran Wrap, exaggerating the difficulties. There is no evidence that former users are in a physiological sense less dexterous than other women, so that handling should not be a real problem for them for such reasons. The fact is that her own impatience leads her to exaggerate the part played by cost (she isn't any less well off than others), and also the difficulties of handling and dispensing.

There are some, of course, amongst the former users who have ceased buying Saran Wrap for good enough reasons: the husband of one housewife, for example, was out of work, and she had to cut expenses at every corner possible. She will use it again when she can afford it.

Cooking interest, the major key to kitchen orientation, has been found in this study to be a very important factor in determining the seriousness of one's concern over the cost and the potential handling difficulties of Saran Wrap. Not only are the former users, as a group, not as enthusiastic over cooking as are the heavy users, but they have largely no interest in cooking, or actually dislike it.

Since she is basically uninterested in the kitchen, the former user tends to displace her negativism onto anything which is associated with it. Thus Saran Wrap, seen by her as a kitchen wrapping material, is subject to her irrational impatience, which causes her to exaggerate, (not consciously, of course) its cost and handling disadvantages. Instead of being willing to take some care in handling Saran Wrap, the need for care becomes an obstacle and an irritant which causes her to abandon it for simpler and less costly things, like wax paper. Thus, she is quite unlike the heavy user, who dismisses a query about handling difficulties with a remark such as: "No, it's no bother, I take my time with it," and who wants to talk about how "nice" Saran Wrap is to use. The former user would rather dwell upon those aspects of the product that annoy her and says instead:

"If I could afford it if I liked it well enough . . . I used it over the top of the melon—it kept it fresh, but I'm always in a hurry. It stuck to itself like it had electricity or something. It was satisfactory but the only thing was that it was difficult and as far as saving time goes, you just don't fool around with things if they're too hard to handle. Plastic bags handle very easily. I like them."

The reaction of the former user toward Saran Wrap may be summed up as follows: Here is a kitchen product that has certain advantages and disadvantages. The heavy and light users can see the advantages for the psychological gratifications it gives a kitchen-oriented person, and its functional advantages. The former user is a different sort of person. She takes the disadvantages of the product and uses them as an object upon which to displace her essential distaste for the kitchen.

Nonusers. The most striking characteristic of the nonuser, according to the Nowland study, was the small amount of kitchen wrapping that she did, as indicated in Exhibit 4. This was explained in part but not wholly

Exhibit 4

DOW CHEMICAL COMPANY (C)

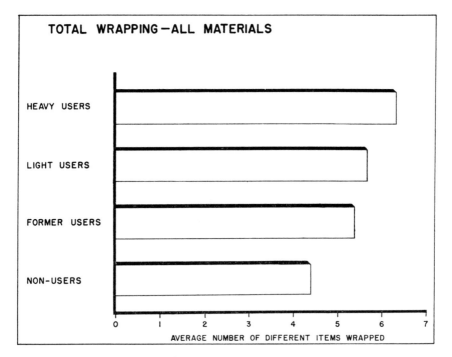

in that nonusers tended to have somewhat smaller families and therefore had somewhat less need to wrap. The Nowland report then went on as follows:

That this does not completely explain the lack of wrapping needs of this group, however, is suggested by one Peoria housewife with four children who, when asked if she knew of Saran Wrap's qualities, said:
"Yes, I suppose they are very good. Nevertheless, we don't wrap that much. We have been using Cut-Rite ever since I can remember. It's habit, I guess. I have no problems (with wax paper) and we have no leftovers and if we saved leftovers it would probably be of use. The dog gets our leftovers."
The nonuser has never tried Saran Wrap because she sees no real need to try it. She explains that she doesn't use it because other materials are good enough,

or that she doesn't do much wrapping or that she forgets to buy it. But such reasons are clearly closely tied to a lack of interest in the kitchen. Twice as many of this group than of any other state that they hate to cook.

This failure to use Saran Wrap does not derive from any ignorance of Saran Wrap's qualities in the abstract. Virtually all nonusers know of it as a wrapping material, and three-quarters know something of its cling, air-tightness and moisture-proofness. About a third of those who know of these qualities, however, do not attach any importance to them.

Some further insight as to why nonusers have not been moved to try Saran Wrap is found in their image of it. When asked what they thought Saran Wrap's main use was, a quarter of this group spontaneously answered "like wax paper." All of the respondents, of course, referred either to kitchen use (mostly bowl covers) or for "storing foods."

With such a strong image of Saran Wrap as a competitor of wax paper and with relatively little interest in the kitchen it is hardly surprising that nonusers are not interested in trying the product.

The situation for the nonuser, therefore, is characterized by the more dominant part played by wax paper in wrapping situations. She confuses wax paper and Saran Wrap. Like the light user and the former user she is little interested in the kitchen, but in this case she thinks of Saran Wrap as just another wax paper, and she has no compelling motive to change this image of it.

In addition to studying the character of the market for Saran Wrap in terms of the characteristics of types of users and nonusers, Nowland also studied two other areas: the cost and handling of the product and psychological resistances to the product. Nowland's findings regarding these two areas are given below:

THE COST AND HANDLING OF THE PRODUCT

The effect of merchandising Saran Wrap as a kitchen wrapping material has been to give the customer a point of reference against which she may react to its cost and handling-dispensing difficulties. The extent to which consumers will pay more and take some care in handling then becomes a function of their desire to use a better and more higher priced kitchen wrap with specific functional advantages.

Because of the price differential between Saran Wrap and wax paper the relatively high cost of Saran Wrap is latent in the mind of all who use it. That this is also true for even the heavy users is indicated in [Exhibit 5] which shows that although some concern with cost is equally prevalent for all groups, there are obvious differences between the groups. If the bars representing slight concern and severe concern were added together, there would be little difference among the three groups. This serves to indicate that all Saran Wrap users are concerned with the cost of the product in some degree. When we consider the right side of the chart, however, which indicates the extent to which Saran Wrap is severely limited by virtue of the cost, the difference in concern among the three groups is clearly demonstrated.

Most of the heavy users limit their use because of cost only slightly, but they do limit it. Heavy users, for example, may not use Saran Wrap on sandwiches or some other item where using it is perceived by them to be least essential because, they say, it is too expensive for that and wax paper can do the job just as well.

The point to be emphasized here is that *even among heavy users promotional stress on the uses which are easily served by less expensive materials can instill sharp awareness of the price difference between Saran Wrap and other materials even though for other purposes the consumer may not even consider it.* The only difference between the heavy user and the light and former users, in this respect, is that her greater interest in the product itself holds back price consciousness until the extremes of nonessential uses are reached.

One device which has been employed by Dow and Company, in at least an incidental way, in the hope of minimizing the cost disadvantage of Saran Wrap, is to advertise the product as being reusable. In fact, about a third of consumers do reuse the product. Among those who do, there is a small group who look upon Saran Wrap not as a disposable item but as a nondisposable wrap-

Exhibit 5

DOW CHEMICAL COMPANY (C)

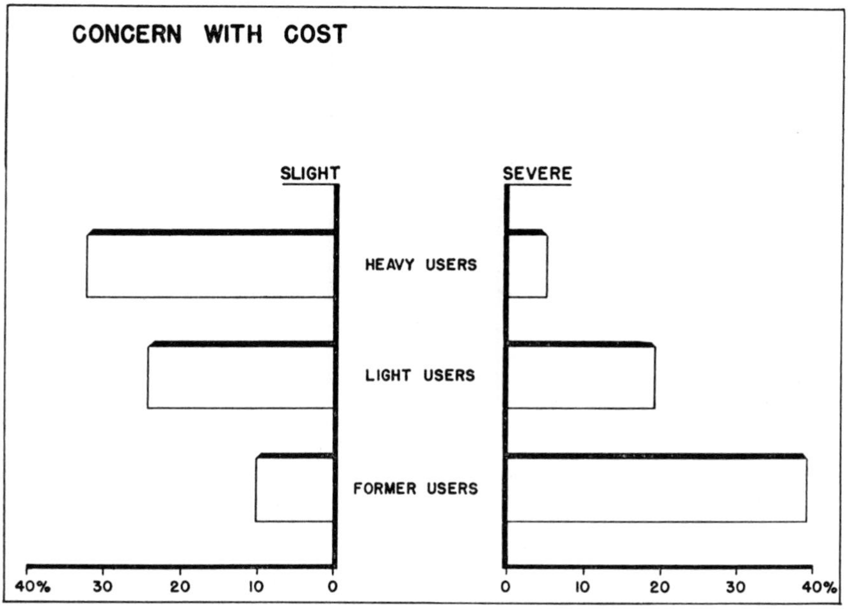

ping material. This tendency to reuse appears to have a compulsive character and is clearly evident in about 4% of the consumers in the sample who had at some time used the product. One extremely discriminating yet heavy user of Saran Wrap who uses it extensively both in the kitchen and outside, explained that when she wraps sandwiches for the adult members of the family she wraps them in Saran Wrap because the adults bring the Saran Wrap back home so that it can be reused. Because the children forget to bring back the wrapper she uses wax paper to wrap sandwiches for school.

The total effect of the higher cost of Saran Wrap can be summarized as follows:

Among those respondents who have had any direct experience with Saran Wrap; i.e., heavy users, light users and former users: 47% were not at all concerned with cost; 26% were somewhat concerned but did not limit their use of Saran Wrap; 25% were concerned to the extent of slightly limiting their use of Saran Wrap; 8% severely limited their use of Saran Wrap; and 8% have discontinued using Saran Wrap because of cost considerations.

Only 6% of nonusers knew the cost of Saran Wrap was more than that of wax paper.

The extent to which handling and dispensing problems restrict the use of Saran Wrap is presented in [Exhibit 6]. Unlike [Exhibit 5], on which the total

Exhibit 6

DOW CHEMICAL COMPANY (C)

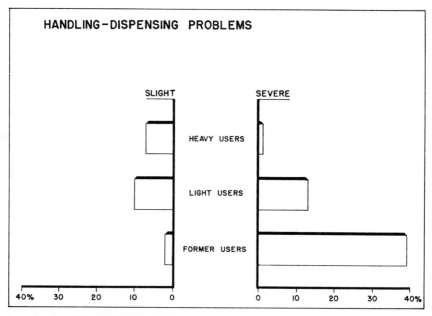

length of the bars are about the same size for each group, in [Exhibit 6], the impatience of the former user becomes quite dramatic. However, the total effect of the handling-dispensing problem can be summarized as in the case of cost as follows:

Again among those respondents who have had some experience with Saran Wrap: 69% were not at all concerned with handling-dispensing; 11% were somewhat concerned but did not limit their use of Saran Wrap; 7% were concerned to the extent of slightly limiting their use of Saran Wrap; 6% severely limited their use of Saran Wrap; and 7% have discontinued using Saran Wrap because of handling-dispensing consideration.

Only 10% of nonusers were aware of handling-dispensing difficulties. However, their reasons for not trying Saran Wrap were the same as those of other nonusers.

For the group with the greatest interest in using Saran Wrap, the heavy user, there is virtually no severely restricting concern over handling-dispensing problems. For the light user the handling-dispensing problem is somewhat greater, and it is greatest for the former users who have little or no interest in Saran Wrap. *The important point here is that the housewife's appreciation of the versatility of Saran Wrap determines the difficulty she thinks she has with the handling-dispensing problem.* Those who use Saran Wrap most, complain least about it; those who use it least, have the most severe criticisms to make.

What is cause here, and what effect is, of course, the problem. Have the handling-dispensing difficulties led to impatience with the Saran Wrap, or has impatience and inadequacy in the kitchen led to an exaggeration of these handling-dispensing matters, out of all proportion to their tangible or real amount? What the competent housewife regards as a minor difficulty, the less adequate homemaker exaggerates into what psychologically can be termed a *displacement* of her own impatient personality. In this way she vents her feelings upon the Saran Wrap. She is intrinsically impatient and displaces this at little provocation upon the Saran Wrap, which, realistically regarded requires some care in handling and dispensing, and thus offers a ready target for her feelings of impatience. Our own conclusion is that there is a good deal of *displacement* of this kind. This means that the many complaints about handling-dispensing that have come to Dow's attention are at least partly symptomatic of something else. This something else is, of course, the housewife's use of wax paper and kitchen wrapping as her standard of evaluation, and consequently her judgment and dismissal of Saran Wrap for the wrong reasons.

PSYCHOLOGICAL RESISTANCES TO THE PRODUCT

Other factors influencing the attitude of some few housewives about Saran Wrap are perhaps more specifically irrational in nature, one example of which is the reluctance some women have in using it on fresh meat. This is quite apart from such rational considerations as that at room or refrigerator temperatures meat requires air, so that it will not discolor or slime. The trouble is an unusual squeamishness and distaste on the woman's part. Probably the most clear-cut example of this kind of resistance was the case of one former user who, when asked what kinds of things she would not care to wrap in Saran Wrap remarked:

". . . liver—fish. I don't know, it just seems like it isn't meant for that . . . Well, I can't give you a real reason. I just never tried . . . No, I'm sure it's clean. They wouldn't let it be sold if it wasn't. It's just because liver is so wet and everything. Maybe I just don't like to see it wrapped in Saran Wrap because it's so transparent. It looks so naked like there's no skin on it. Besides, if we don't eat liver or fish right away, I freeze it and then I put it in foil."

Statements of this kind can be made with strong feelings of repugnance and distaste. It would be very remarkable indeed if some women did not react in such a way to the nakedness of liver, and the more sophisticated the woman, the more likelihood there would be for such repugnance. But this is certainly not likely to make many women resist Saran Wrap altogether: the woman who feels a bit squeamish about wrapping liver in Saran Wrap could well be an enthusiastic user for more congenial purposes.

That is, we find little or no evidence of a *general* resistance to using Saran Wrap for any so-called *unconscious* reasons, i.e., because of the association of Saran Wrap with nakedness, sensuality, sex, or anything of the kind. Some few women can be found who react to Saran Wrap in this way; and no doubt Saran Wrap as a material has certain sensual features *per se;* but there is simply no evidence that these women are numerous, or that any unconscious factors of the material have entered into the purchase situation. Such factors, if present, have not acted as a resistance to initial purchases, nor as a deterrent to continued usage, nor as a cause for either giving up or buying Saran Wrap.

Analysis in Relation to the Promotion of Saran Wrap

In this section of its report, the Nowland company pointed out that, as a wrapping material, Saran Wrap appealed adequately only to a relatively small segment of women—the heavy user, who liked the product because she liked the kitchen. The report continued as follows:

In her case the satisfaction she derives from using Saran Wrap makes it a staple in her kitchen: she is likely to find permanent and increasing use of the product. But this use is severely *kitchen oriented*, as is the heavy user herself: its use is in the kitchen, for wrapping fruits, etc., and covering bowls, etc., for the refrigerator. This is true, also, for the uses to which light users put Saran Wrap.

THE MOTIVES SATISFIED BY SARAN WRAP

The basic motives which are gratified by current users of Saran Wrap are two: the heavy user finds her satisfactions as a cook, etc., in her kitchen, and Saran Wrap's benefits for her there make an immediate and lasting appeal. Not only does it do a good job for her, but she can scarcely conceive now that she could do without it. She is interested in the kitchen; in a real sense she expresses her needs there and enjoys the rewards of good cooking, etc., and Saran Wrap fits into this enjoyment like a hand fitting into a glove. The other motive, or set of motives, lies behind the way the *light* user employs Saran Wrap for "special" purposes only. She has no real interest in the kitchen, but knows a good thing when she sees it, and she is sufficiently gratified by the functional advantages of Saran Wrap (notably for covering bowls, odorous foods, etc.) to make use of it for such special purposes. She satisfies her rational impulses this way by being efficient: not a good cook, but a sensible housewife.

ATTITUDES TOWARD SARAN WRAP

The heavy users are of course enthusiastic about Saran Wrap. They do not confuse it with wax paper, and find a natural place for both products in their kitchens. Undoubtedly the Dow Chemical Company has its most enthusiastic and loyal customers in this group. Their motivation, as we saw above, expresses itself in pride and satisfaction in the kitchen, and this makes such women ready purchasers of Saran Wrap.

The fact that *light* users grasp the advantages of Saran Wrap for "specific" purposes only appears to be building up a *resistive, self-defeating* attitude about Saran Wrap. The firmer she grasps a few special usages for Saran Wrap, the less is she prepared to use the product for what seems to her to be inappropriate usages. These women are not kitchen oriented, and therefore Saran Wrap is not a "natural" for them to use. But the very uniqueness of Saran Wrap for covering a bowl makes it seem so appropriate that she quite unwittingly resists using it for other or wider purposes for which such uniqueness is not apparent to her. There is something of the "high-quality" factor here, but it is an inhibitory effect due to Saran Wrap's very uniqueness, and not due to a high-quality, high-cost conception. The image of its uniqueness, so to speak, refuses to let her use Saran Wrap where these advantages are not apparent.

The *former* user, as we saw earlier, has a distinctly negative attitude toward her kitchen, which she displaces upon Saran Wrap by focusing upon its cost and handling difficulties. She has not stopped buying Saran Wrap because she has forgotten about it, or because it didn't impress her very much: she resists her kitchen and therefore anything associated with it as well, more especially, of course, if she can fasten upon what seems to her to be legitimate reasons for being critical and for expressing her dissatisfactions.

The *nonuser* brings to light a seriously limiting attitude, namely, the way she thinks of Saran Wrap as just another kitchen wrap, like wax paper. To the extent that any user, heavy or other, supposes that Saran Wrap is just like wax paper, the more is she likely to limit her use. So long as Saran Wrap is perceived as an expensive and difficult to handle substitute for less expensive wax paper, its sale is bound to be militated against. The nonusers bring this point sharply into focus. It is true that they are not basically kitchen-oriented: but they could be *light* users if the confusion with wax paper could be dispelled.

SUMMARY

Two groups of motives are at issue, then, which for brevity we might call *cookery-motive* (kitchen orientation) and efficiency-motive (the more rational drives of the lighter users). Four attitudes are distinguishable—that of great enthusiasm for Saran Wrap (of the heavy users), that of *resistance* due to the uniqueness of Saran Wrap (of the light users), that of a distinct *negativism* (of the former users), and the *mistaken attitude* that Saran Wrap is just another, more expensive sort of wax paper.

EFFECT OF DOW'S PROMOTION AT THIS TIME

Saran Wrap is perceived by most of the market as "another or better wax paper." This perception, created in part inadvertently by Dow's promotion efforts, has had advantages as well as disadvantages especially in the initial phases of launching the product. At the present time, however, disadvantages outweigh its advantages.

The factors most responsible for creating this wrong perception is the customer's mind are the following: In promotion the language used is "kitchen wrapping language" which does not express the unique values of Saran Wrap in a concrete way, and implies a wax paper type of wrap. The Saran Wrap advertising has presented the consumer with a mixture of uses for Saran Wrap, some of which she believes are appropriate, and some of which infringe on her sense of appropriate usage. She knows full well, for example, that some kinds of sandwiches become sodden if wrapped in Saran Wrap, and any implication to the contrary is self-defeating in that it builds up the negative picture in her mind of just another more expensive wax paper. Emphasis on abstract qualities (cling, transparency, etc.) has not gotten across to the individual housewife *why* she should use the product in terms of concrete benefits to her. She does not grasp the logical implications of these characteristics, and therefore she does not relate them to herself and her own needs and problems. Promotion of characteristics of lesser importance to the customer (neatness, transparency, ability to reuse, attractiveness) had made the customer believe she understands how Saran Wrap differs from wax paper and why it costs more. She perceives Saran Wrap as a better wax paper which clings to itself.

If promotional efforts continue along present lines without modification, in all probability there will be little change in the present unsatisfactory ratio between the cost of promotion and the volume of sales.

DESIRABLE CHANGES IN PROMOTION

Within its present promotional framework, some increases could be made in the use of Saran Wrap as a kitchen wrap by appealing increasingly to the *cookery-motive* of the women who are so oriented. The very colorful ads of food products (e.g., General Mills, Campbells, etc.) indicates that the motive here is a strong one, and pays good dividends. But steps can also be taken to make these enthusiastic users more *insightful* about Saran Wrap so that they will extend the range of uses for it in the kitchen and outside it. The matter is better attended to, however, in discussing what to do for light users.

The light user, as we have seen, is willing to pay a premium price for uses for which Saran Wrap is obviously functionally superior. For covering bowls, cheese, etc., she is willing, even eager, to use Saran Wrap. Not so however, when it comes to wrapping such things as whole vegetables, etc. Little is served by appealing to any cooking-motive, for she is not that interested in the kitchen. However, give her a good reason for using Saran Wrap, and she will use it. After all, half the battle is won in her case—she buys some rolls of Saran Wrap. To make her buy more requires that she grasp more suitable uses for Saran Wrap. Only in this way can we hope to break the strength of the *resistive* attitude to which attention has been drawn. This might be covered from two angles: a search might be made for *other motives*, upon which promotion might be pin-pointed, or, special steps could be taken to *educate* these light users (and therefore all women, heavy, former, and nonusers as well) about what Saran Wrap can do, and why it is better to use it than anything else.

As for other motives: the kitchen doesn't appeal to the light user, but the nursery might, or the desire to *dress well* might. Many uses for Saran Wrap are apparent for the nursery, and the same applies where a woman is careful about her home and her clothes. The important point here, as for the cookery-motive, is for Dow through its promotion policies to appeal to motives, as well as to this or that specific use of Saran Wrap. Promotion means appealing to kitchen-oriented women in the case of heavy users, and this means bringing Saran Wrap into their lives as staple aids to their every day satisfactions. Promotion to the nursery-motivated woman has to fasten on the total context of bringing up a baby, likewise, and not only on specific *uses* for Saran Wrap in the nursery. This of course is obvious to Dow, but is stressed here in order to make our next remarks clear. One doesn't appeal to the motives underlying a woman's satisfaction in and need to be a meticulous housekeeper, only by describing to her the virtues of Saran Wrap in isolation. Rather she is given such tips as protecting gloves and woolens, or simplifying their storage in a "good housekeeping" framework, possibly as a spring-cleaning motif, for example. Similarly all promotion must make use of topical interests, e.g., at present many women are sending parcels overseas to friends and servicemen, and advantage should be taken of such interests. At Christmas, similarly, there are special uses to which Saran can be put appropriately.

As for the matter of *education:* all women can be educated as to what are appropriate uses for Saran Wrap, and why. There have been hints in early studies, as in our own work above, that the promotion of the clinging and transparency qualities of Saran Wrap has been very effective, in fact too much so. There are other qualities, of simplification, preservation, esthetic, etc., and no doubt these too could be impressed on users' minds by concentrated promotion. However, what has been missing in the past has been any concerted effort to given women the *reasons* for using Saran Wrap. We have found women confused in this respect. The reasons have to be "spelled out" in great detail, because they are not at all as obvious to many women as copywriters may suppose. They simply cannot be taken for granted. The housewife cannot be expected to perceive the relationship between the abstract ability to cling and the fact that wrapping silverware in Saran Wrap will keep the silver from tarnishing. This is not necessarily because some women are stupid, but because what they carry away with them from TV shows *is what is spelled out*, not what is logically implied. It is indeed a mistake to promote the *attributes* as such of Saran Wrap, (cling, transparency, simplification, etc.): the correct approach, psychologically, is to appeal to a motive, show *appropriate* uses, and give a *reason* for these usages. *The transparency, cling, simplification, etc., attributes will then speak for themselves. This point and its implications, we consider to be of key importance.*

Summary

The Dow Chemical Company has, in our view, correctly launched its promotion by appealing to the kitchen-oriented woman and has gained its staunchest and most enthusiastic customers on this account. These are permanent users of Saran Wrap—for them it is a staple product.

It would be more in keeping with modern psychology, however, to promote *appropriate functional uses* of Saran Wrap, and to spell out in detail the *reasons* for these in the functional sense, rather than to place the emphasis (as seems to have happened, perhaps unwittingly, in the past) on the physical attributes of Saran Wrap (its cling, transparency, electrostatic charge, etc.). It is not enough to show what Saran Wrap is, but also *why* it is the proper wrap for the purpose in hand.

By stressing the *kitchen-motif* (as Campbell's, General Mills, etc., are doing so successfully), or by building upon additional motifs, such as that of the nursery or the homemaker, the sales position of Saran Wrap as a staple can be strengthened, and reasons for confusing it with wax paper progressively eliminated. By stressing the *reasons* for using it, rather than overdoing its remarkable *qualities* as such (of cling, transparency, etc.), much can be done to break into the light user's resistances, the former user's prejudices, and the nonuser's ignorance.

Saran Wrap as a Household Staple

The one key idea to get across is that Saran Wrap is a very useful material, that you cannot do without in the home. There are innumerable uses about the home for Saran Wrap, e.g., as an inner wrap for parcels, as a decorative wrap for Christmas parcels (it's cheaper than other fancy wraps), as a cover for valuable books, pictures, etc. *The notion to instill is that you need Saran Wrap in the house at all times because it is handy stuff.* This does not mean that Dow has to play down the importance of Saran Wrap in the kitchen, but to play up its use in the house as a *handy* wrapping material with unique advantages.

The key here is to present a home situation, where a problem arises, and which is solved by Saran Wrap. A woman, sending a parcel overseas, or packing a small but valuable gift, can be shown how essential Saran Wrap is as a protective inner lining underneath paper covers. Without the inner wrap the parcel breaks; the paper softens in rain; the goods inside spoil or roll loose, etc. Saran Wrap keeps what's inside intact, whatever happens, and is an added protection on all accounts. Dow's Marketing Research Department can point to very many household problems of this kind.

There is an excellent opportunity to foster the promotion of Saran Wrap as a household wrapping material on firmly conceived psychological principles. These, it cannot be too strongly stated, consist of appealing to existing motives of women. The woman in her home with all her prides, interest, satisfactions, problems etc., is the target. The appeal is by demonstrating Saran Wrap in *concrete, appropriate uses* giving the reasons for every use in detail. The *attributes* of the product are not made the center of the promotion: appropriate uses *are*.

Conclusions

As a result of interpreting its field interviews, the Nowland company concluded that more Saran Wrap had not been sold because the product was incorrectly perceived by a large section of the market to be another variety of wax paper, not a better kitchen wrap, but a better wax paper. This conception of Saran Wrap had developed because Dow presented the product as a higher-priced, general-purpose kitchen wrap with several excellent features, and this presentation had been translated by consumers into their own daily experience as simply meaning that Saran Wrap was "a better wax paper which clings and is transparent."

With respect to future policy, Nowland said:

You have been successful in the case of the heavy user because Saran Wrap makes a natural appeal to kitchen-oriented women. But you are not likely to increase your sales volume substantially until and unless you promote Saran Wrap on the basis of a radically different promotion policy and different promotion tactics. It is reasonable to suppose that you had the right policy to introduce Saran Wrap; but it is evident that to continue in the future along these same policy lines will not increase sales substantially beyond present levels.

The key to future action is this basic truth about the markets: that even though consumers perceive Saran Wrap inadequately, most of them use it *correctly*. Their inadequate perception is your problem and the chief limitation on the customer's present usage and on sales; their appropriate usage is the basis of your present success and therefore should be the basis of your future policy.

Since the concept of "appropriate usage" is so important, an expanded definition of this concept is warranted:

DEFINITION OF CONCEPT OF APPROPRIATE USAGE

Appropriate usage means:
1. Uses which preserve
2. Unique uses for Saran Wrap
3. Uses relevant to customer's interests in the home
4. Uses which the individual believes to be important to him
5. Uses which do not accentuate the user's cost consciousness
6. Uses that do not imply changing the consumer's way of living (e.g., sandwiches two days in advance)
7. Should not be uses confined to only one area of the house (the kitchen)
8. Does not have to be uses with very wide appeal

   (This point deserves some explanation since the heart of your promotion up to the present time has been the assumption that you must hit those uses which are most universal in their appeal. This assumption is valid for introducing the product, but no longer valid at this time for these reasons:

   a) The only time a person is induced by TV to buy Saran Wrap is when a particular use is tied in with a special interest of the person. The findings show that this is the main job and the only job now done by TV. The only way you can now add *new* customers is by appealing to motives you have not yet appealed to effectively even though these may be less universal.

   b) This is the only way you can create enthusiastic users among non-kitchen-oriented people and there is no other way of creating enthusiastic users.

   c) The best way of communicating the chief use of Saran Wrap—to preserve and protect—is by getting the customer to use Saran Wrap for several different uses.

   d) The only way to get users to consume a minimum rate of Saran Wrap and get them to regard it as handy to have around the house, is by getting them to use it for several different applications even though each is minor, because there may not be other major applications comparable to bowl covers, although as an inner wrap for parcels Saran Wrap has wide applicability.

Two key concepts should dominate consideration of your long-range strategic policies:

1. It is crucial to change the consumer's concept of Saran Wrap as just a better wax paper to the concept of it as *a special use, household product, with unique ability to protect and preserve, both inside the kitchen and outside it in the home.*

2. Long-range success depends upon Saran Wrap's acceptance by the market as a *household staple.* There is evidence in our findings that the market is receptive for such a staple. You have been promoting Saran Wrap as a general purpose kitchen wrap, and continuation of this policy will not achieve your objectives. Saran Wrap's becoming a staple depends upon consumers using more than two or three rolls a year: sufficient frequency of purchase is important, to keep the customer aware of the product, and on the shopping list. The way to achieve this requisite rate of consumption is by successfully promoting *several* different but appropriate uses, where you now have only one (bowl covers). The key to successful promotion of appropriate uses is effectiveness in finding out the right *why* for each such use. This requires continuing research.

The objective of making Saran Wrap as a staple depends upon the market's use of it for *a number* of specific uses: you should not be afraid of promoting Saran Wrap as a special use product because this concept, and not general use promotion, is the true key to increasing volume.

Recommendations

The concluding section of the Nowland report offered 16 recommendations, which are given below:

1. Promote Saran Wrap as a special purpose household staple, explaining what a handy thing it is to have around the house.
2. Be very, very explicit to the housewife in spelling out the benefits she will derive from such uses, stressing the major benefit common to all uses: namely, the ability of Saran Wrap to preserve that which it is protecting. Do not assume that the housewife will make the logical step between an abstract attribute of Saran Wrap and the concrete benefit to her of such use.
3. Make the concept of "appropriate usage" the cornerstone of new promotional policy.
3a. Avoid recommending uses which violate the housewife's sense of appropriate usage.
4. In addition to promoting uses which appeal universally to all segments of the market (bowl covers and inner wrapping of parcels) also promote uses and motives which may appeal to any narrow segment, but appeal strongly to these (e.g., protecting paint brushes). The chief consideration should not be the size of the segment appealed to, but the appropriateness of the use in question.
5. Promote nonkitchen uses heavily.
6. Tie such nonkitchen uses in with appeals to nonkitchen motive such as love of good clothes and appearance, love of decorating, etc.
7. Do further research to learn the reasons that are most effective to po-

tential buyers and meaningful to customers. (Recommended: Very detailed analysis of Dichter-Nowland interviews by Dow, Agency, Nowland).

8. No change of name is indicated. There is probably not enough benefit to be gained from changing the name to warrant the expense of so doing.

9. Do not change the roll put up of Saran Wrap, but alleviate as many handling-dispensing problems as possible without major expenditures. Such improvements will help sales somewhat over the long run but not substantially.

10. Avoid appeals in terms of Saran Wrap's attributes (cling, transparency, etc.).

11. Users' association of Saran Wrap with extravagance is still a problem.
    a) Relate the cost of Saran Wrap to the value of the object saved.
    b) Avoid expensive context of presentation (protecting expensive foods).
    c) Avoid uses which accentuate the housewife's cost consciousness (sandwiches, lunches, etc.).
    d) Use nonkitchen uses to combat cost consciousness because these are not associated with the comparison with wax paper.
    e) Attempt to bring the retail price down to below 30 cents. Such price reduction will help to reduce present restriction in usage, but not sufficiently to warrant profit margins radically reduced on existing volume.

12. It is more important to lower the price, than to increase the length of the roll. It is desirable, though not crucial, to increase the length of roll over the course of time to about 25%–40%, though not at the expense of profit margins. Increase in volume would not be sufficient to warrant major profit per roll sacrifices.

13. In-store display is an absolute necessity to the successful promotion of Saran Wrap.

14. Do not conceive commercials for the primary purpose of achieving believability. Believability is not the problem! Relevancy to consumer's interests and uses is.

15. Evaluate present advertising media in the light of the necessity for hard, personal selling and the criteria.

16. Avoid subsidiary appeals in promoting Saran Wrap such as the following: a) Transparency, b) Neatness, c) Reuse, [and] d) Attractiveness.

~~~

CASE 9: DOW CHEMICAL COMPANY (D)[1]

QUESTIONS TO CONSIDER: (1) Do you think that Dow's management was wise in its decision to seek sales at the rate of 41 million rather than 60 million units yearly? Or would you recommend reconsideration of this decision in the light of your analysis of the situation? (2) Do you think that the objectives established for advertising were sound? Or would you recommend reconsideration? (3) How should Dow go about restudying the media to be used for advertising Saran Wrap? (4) Given the $1.7 million promotional budget allocated to Saran Wrap by Dow's management,

---

[1] Written by Martin V. Marshall.

outline the promotional program that you would recommend for the period January 1956–May 1957.

After receiving and studying the reports of The Institute for Motivation Research, Inc., and Nowland and Company, Dow executives came to these conclusions: (1) for the short run, the company should seek to maintain existing sales volume with a reduced promotional budget, thereby obtaining satisfactory profits; and (2) for the longer run, the company should seek to find promotional means whereby existing customers would be induced to use more Saran Wrap and prospects would be induced to try and to continue to use the product.

In the light of these conclusions, Dow executives took several steps. First, they allocated Saran Wrap a total promotional budget of $1.7 million for the period January 1956–May 1957, the latter month being the end of Dow's 1956–57 fiscal year. Second, they definitely decided to cease sponsorship of "Medic" effective January 1, 1956, and to restudy the whole media problem. And, third, they decided to give special attention to the determination of the kind of advertising strategy and advertising messages which would most likely be effective in increasing the sales of Saran Wrap.

Determination of Advertising Strategy

As a first step in defining advertising strategy, Dow executives decided that the principal objective of the advertising of the product would be "to make Saran Wrap a specialty staple by stimulating the imagination of large segments of the consuming public to think in terms of appropriate uses of Saran Wrap." As a second step, from the findings of The Institute of Motivation Research and Nowland reports, Dow executives concluded that there were three general uses which were particularly applicable to Saran Wrap: (1) when the item to be wrapped required extra protection; (2) when the item was worth extra protection; and (3) when a wrapping was needed to enhance the beauty of the item. As a third step, these general uses were expanded into 11 areas of appropriate uses, and a list of 180 specific, different uses. These 11 areas together with the specific benefits which could be presented to consumers for each are summarized in Exhibit 1.

As executives considered the appropriate-use approach, they became concerned with the problem of the frequency of advertising which would be required to effectively educate consumers regarding the 11 areas of appropriate uses. It was obvious to them that the $1.7 million promotional budget could not buy enough advertisements to support a campaign for each area, and the question was raised as to whether it would be advisable to focus advertising on one or several areas.

As an alternative, it was suggested that instead of trying to educate consumers regarding a number of specific uses for Saran Wrap, the advertising of the product might focus on the three areas of use: when the item

Exhibit 1

DOW CHEMICAL COMPANY (D)

Summary of Appropriate Uses and Consumer Benefits

AREA OF APPROPRIATE USES	SPECIFIC CONSUMER BENEFITS PRESENTED

Freezing
A. Home Freezers or Lockers
  1. Meats of all kinds.
  2. Poultry.
  3. Fish—sea food.
  4. Foods prepared in large quantity to freeze:
    a) Casseroles.
    b) Chili.
    c) Soups.
    d) Stews.
    e) Cakes.
    f) Pies.
    g) Bread and rolls.
	A. Convenience
	  1. Holds moisture when foods are thawed with no mess to clean up.
	  2. Easy to see at a glance the foods the homemaker wishes to use.
	  3. Saran Wrap is easy to use because:
	    a) It takes the contour of the shape of the object to be wrapped.
	    b) You can exclude more air because of the clinging qualities.
	    c) It clings to object while tape is being applied.
	B. Economy
	  1. Keeps the food flavor fresh, and foods do not become dried out, and fats retain brightness.
	C. Convenience and Economy
	  1. Saran Wrap allows you to prepare more than one of a given item such as chili, soups, cakes, etc., and freeze thus having ready for use at a later date.

B. Freezing Compartment of Refrigerator
  1. Leftover roasts, poultry, sea food.
  2. Leftover ice cream, pastry, and cakes.
  3. Small quantities of fresh meats for short periods of storage.
	The same points apply for this category as for home freezers. A convenience and economy use: stress the idea that Saran Wrap helps small families to relieve the monotony of meal planning.

Travel Uses
A. Protecting the contents of a traveling bag from:
  1. Contamination.
  2. Spillables.
  3. Damp objects.
  4. Delicate garments from snagging.
	C. Convenience and Economy
	  1. Clean clothes cannot be soiled by shoes, soiled clothing, liquid cosmetics, powder, etc.
	  2. Damp articles such as shaving brushes, tooth brushes, and washcloths cannot soil other articles in the traveling bag.
	  3. Delicate garments such as hose and blouses will be kept from snagging on shoe heels or other sharp objects.

Monetary Valuables
A. Wrapping of silver and jewelry
	A. Convenience
	  1. Keeps bright and shiny between uses.
	  2. Eliminates need for cleaning, thus saving time and work.
	  3. No need to worry about appearances before using—particularly timesaving in case of unexpected guests or sudden use.

Exhibit 1—Continued

Area of Appropriate Uses	Specific Consumer Benefits Presented
	B. Economy 1. Saran Wrap protects the investment of silver or jewelry considered choice, special, and expensive. 2. Protects from scratches during long periods of storage.
B. Wrapping Woolens 1. Electric blankets. 2. Sweaters. 3. Scarves. 4. Woolen baby garments.	A. Convenience 1. Saves time and work. B. Economy 1. Eliminates danger of damage by moths. 2. Keeps articles clean and free from dust. 3. Protects investments and eliminates need for costly repairs. 4. Protects baby garments for future use or sentimental reasons.
C. Wrapping Heirlooms 1. Linens. 2. Books. 3. Ornaments. 4. Jewelry.	B. Economy 1. Protects individually from dust, soil, marring, and moisture. C. Convenience and Economy 1. Facilitates handling without soiling and with ready identification without unwrapping.
D. Wrapping Choice Linens 1. Table linens. 2. Bed linens. 3. Bathroom linens. 4. Baby clothes for reuse.	A. Convenience 1. Saran Wrap keeps them clean and ready to use at a moment's notice for unexpected guests. 2. Reduces laundry, saving time and work. 3. Sachet and fragrance will be maintained.
E. Sporting Equipment 1. Fishing reels.	B. Economy 1. Protects from dust, moisture, and other soil. C. Convenience and Economy 1. Facilitates handling without soiling and with ready identification without wrapping.
Food A. Preparation 1. Moisture retention and order control.	C. Convenience and Economy 1. Foods requiring moisture such as salads can be prepared ahead of time and can be served fresh and crisp. 2. Foods in which moisture must be kept out of such as hors d'oeuvres, flaky pastries, and desserts can be prepared ahead of time, preserving flavor and freshness. 3. Prevents transferring of odors such as onions, cheese, and melons in preparation storage.

Exhibit 1—Continued

Area of Appropriate Uses	Specific Consumer Benefits Presented

B. Preservation
  1. Moisture retention and odor control.
	C. Convenience and Economy
	  1. When Saran Wrap is used for leftovers, roasts, or bowl covers, flavor is retained over prolonged periods.
	  2. Leftover dishes will not dry out, keeping leftovers appetizing to your family.
	  3. More flexibility in use of leftovers because of long protection.
	  4. Leftovers are not contaminated nor do they contaminate other foods in the refrigerator.

C. Protection and Appearance	A. Convenience 1. Foods taken outside of the home can be protected in transit and appearance of dishes can be enhanced by Saran Wrap—examples: picnics, church suppers, PTA.

Do-It-Yourself
  A. Home Repair
  B. Hobbies
	B. Economy
	  1. Protects individually from dust, soiling, marring, drying out of models, photography supplies, ceramics (clays and paints), artists paints and brushes.
	  2. Keeps flats of new plants from drying out thus giving seedlings a chance to grow.
	C. Convenience and Economy
	  1. Saran Wrap will not allow wet paint brushes, partially used cans of paint, putty, or wet plaster of Paris to dry out between uses.
	  2. For handling without soiling and permits ready identification without unwrapping.

Source: Company records.

to be wrapped was worth special protection, required extra protection, or where beauty and appearance was desired. Thus, Saran Wrap advertising could focus on three objectives rather than many. The thought was that the consumer could, once she understood a use concept, vicariously visualize many uses for Saran Wrap. Discussion of this alternative led to the written description and elaboration, as follows:

All promotional effort is to be aimed at increasing the use of the *light user*. Effort expended in this area will also increase use by heavy users, former users, and nonusers. This concept postulates some familiarity with Saran Wrap on the part of our audience. The product is not to be promoted as *new*.
Advertising will:

1. Emphasize uniqueness of Saran Wrap; avoid inadvertent comparison with other wrapping material. Example: wrapping sandwiches in Saran Wrap.
2. Define appropriate use concept:
   a) *When the product is worth protection.* Examples: freezing area—expensive large roasts; travel area—ladies blouses; monetary or sentimental area—silver service; food area—one half of a cantaloupe; do-it-yourself area—lens for camera.
   b) *When extra protection is required.* Examples: freezing area—steaks; travel area—sheer lingerie; monetary or sentimental area—a wedding handkerchief; food area—raw onions; do-it-yourself area—unused portion of a can of paint.
   c) *When the benefit of Saran Wrap protection is obvious or believable and not too far from standard home practice.* Examples: freezing area—making three pies at one time and freezing two; travel area—protecting shoes by wrapping in Saran Wrap; monetary or sentimental area—mothproofing woolens by wrapping in Saran Wrap; food area—preparing barbecue foods ahead of time; do-it-yourself area—wrapping wet paint brushes.
   d) *When it is desirable to enhance beauty of product wrapped for appearance or neatness.* Examples: monetary and sentimental value—heirloom linen; food area—cake to be taken outside of the home.
3. Develop new vocabulary. Example: contour wrapping.
4. Demonstrate use and explain why in terms of benefits to item wrapped and users, not properties. Example: a melon will not dry out when protected by Saran Wrap.
5. Admit difficulty of handling but emphasize that benefits are worth the extra effort. Example: the effort of wrapping silver is more than worth the time spent in polishing silver.
6. Wherever it fits, emphasize strength and toughness of Saran Wrap.
7. Employ uses which do not accentuate cost consciousness.

~~~

CASE 10: RADIO CORPORATION OF AMERICA[1]

QUESTION TO CONSIDER: *In the light of the information given in the case, what steps would you recommend that RCA executives take in order to develop a promotional program which promises to increase the sales of color television sets?*

In late 1957 executives of Radio Corporation of America (RCA), the world's largest manufacturer of electronic equipment with sales of over $1.1 billion, were attempting to devise a sales promotional strategy to increase the sales of RCA Victor color television sets. As a preparatory step the executives were reviewing RCA's three years of experience in marketing color television sets, including a review of a special promotional test of five weeks which had been undertaken in May and June 1957 in Milwaukee, Wisconsin.

---

[1] Written by David W. Nylen and Martin V. Marshall.

A Review of RCA Experience in Marketing Color Television Sets

RCA developed the first color television set in the industry in 1940, and in 1941, RCA, with the co-operation of its subsidiary, the National Broadcasting Company (NBC), made the first experimental color telecast. World War II halted development of color television, but with the end of the war numerous electronics firms, including RCA, resumed work to develop a commercial color television set. By 1950 RCA and the Columbia Broadcasting System (CBS) had developed dissimilar color receiving tubes and color television transmission systems. The CBS system was noncompatible, that is, black-and-white television sets then in existence could not receive this type of color telecast in black and white without installation of an adapter. The RCA system was compatible, that is, existing black-and-white television sets could receive the RCA type of color telecast in black and white without modification of the sets. Under neither the CBS nor the RCA system could existing black-and-white television sets receive color telecasts in color.

In October 1950, after lengthy hearings and tests, the Federal Communications Commission (FCC) ruled that the CBS system would be adopted for color telecasting by United States television stations. During the next year very few television sets were marketed and very little color telecasting was done. In November 1951 the National Production Authority, acting under powers granted for the Korean emergency, prohibited further production of home color television sets. In March 1953 the United States House of Representatives Committee on Interstate and Foreign Commerce held hearings to determine the present status and future possibilities of color television, concluding with the recommendation that the FCC reverse its ruling and accept the RCA system as the basis for color telecasting in the United States. In December 1953 the FCC approved the use of the RCA system.

In the spring of 1954, RCA, which had obligated itself during the various hearings to market color television sets and to provide color telecasting, began to market color television receivers. RCA's first model was a 12-inch receiver which sold at retail for $1,000. Other companies, including Raytheon, Magnavox, Emerson, Westinghouse, Motorola, CBS-Columbia, and DuMont, produced a limited number of color television receivers but did not aggressively market them. In 1956, after 27 months on the market, RCA introduced an improved 21-inch receiver series of 11 models retailing from $495 to $850, and in 1957 the "Mark" series, five improved 21-inch models, retailing from $550 to $895.

RCA color television sets were marketed through RCA's well-established independent distributor and dealer organization that handled other RCA products such as black-and-white television. By 1957 RCA color television sets were sold through 84 distributors to about 9,000 dealers.

RCA had advertised color television consistently since 1955, about 25%

of the company's total television-set budget being devoted to color. Traceable advertising expenditures for RCA Victor television sets were $1.9 million in 1955; $1.5 million in 1956; and $1.3 million in 1957.[2] Advertising was directed at the mass market through use of such magazines as *Life, Look,* and *The Saturday Evening Post.* Advertisements were designed to overcome consumer concern over such problems as the compatibility of color television and the ease of tuning color sets. For the period 1954–57 the trade estimated industry sales as follows: 1954, 5,000 sets; 1955, 35,000; 1956, 120,000; and 1957, 160,000. RCA accounted for almost all of these sales. Meanwhile, in the period since the end of World War II, more than 40 million black-and-white television sets had been sold, thereby fairly well saturating the market.

Problems in Marketing Color TV

In considering their more than three years' experience in marketing color television sets, RCA executives were aware of several problems which had limited the growth of color set sales. These problems are discussed below.

Lack of Consumer Familiarity. RCA executives believed that the lack of consumer familiarity with color telecasts was the foremost factor retarding sales of color television receivers. According to a survey conducted for RCA in 1957, only 25% of the American people had ever seen color telecasts, and it was believed that only one half of these people had seen color telecasts under favorable conditions. Further, there was evidence that many consumers were skeptical about the quality of color telecast, and about the ease of operation of a color receiver.

RCA executives felt that one key to increasing sales was to expose consumers to color television in order that they would develop an appreciation of what color television offered them as compared to black-and-white television and in order that skepticism regarding the quality of color telecasts would be dispelled. Concerning the quality of color television in 1957, *Fortune* magazine stated, "The color picture itself, although not to be compared with good color photography or fine-color printing, is nevertheless a sensationally different TV picture, and few people who have seen color TV on a properly adjusted set are not enthusiastic about it."[3]

Color Programming. RCA executives stated that another obstacle to greater sales of color television receivers had been the limited amount of color telecasting. On the one hand, some consumers were resisting purchase of a color set until there were many color programs; on the other hand, sponsors were hesitant to underwrite the additional cost of a color program when color-set circulation was low. NBC made no additional charge to sponsors for time if color were used, but RCA executives esti-

---

[2] National Advertising Investments 1955, 1956, 1957.

[3] William B. Harris, "RCA Organizes for Profit," *Fortune,* August 1957, p. 115.

mated that a sponsor's production costs were 10% to 25% higher for color than for black-and-white telecasts. In part this increase was the result of the sponsors' desire to produce more elaborate programs in order to take advantage of color. RCA executives stated that advertisers did not dispute the great effectiveness of color television with people who had color receivers.

Since 1954, NBC, a division of RCA, had been the leading network color telecaster. In 1957 NBC regularly scheduled color telecasts one hour each weekday; one hour each night, Monday through Saturday; and two hours each Sunday night, plus several color "specials," such as the World's Series. Among the NBC programs regularly broadcast in color were "Steve Allen," "Dinah Shore," "Kraft Theatre," and "Perry Como." NBC scheduled 667 color hours in 1957 as compared with 485 hours in 1956. In contrast to NBC, CBS was telecasting less than 1½ hours in color each week for a total of 45 hours for the year 1957 as compared to 80 hours in 1956. The third active television network, American Broadcasting Company, had broadcast no color, although the company was reportedly planning color facilities for future use.

In order to transmit network color programs, local television stations had to have color equipment. By late 1957 about 65% of all stations were able to transmit color. In addition, by late 1957, 37 stations were broadcasting local color programs.

Lack of Industry Marketing Efforts. In 1957, as in previous years, RCA was the only company aggressively marketing color television sets. Other companies, including Admiral, Emerson, Hoffman, Magnavox, Montgomery Ward, Motorola, Sears Roebuck, Sylvania, and Westinghouse, had color sets available in 1957, but were not actively marketing them. Almost all of these sets utilized the RCA color picture tube.

RCA executives said that they would welcome greater marketing efforts by competitors because the influence on consumers of combined marketing efforts of several firms would greatly speed the introductory marketing phase that had to precede large volume sales. RCA offered to sell to competitors the components necessary for color-receiver manufacture, but competitors, apparently judging that there were no immediate profits in color, were allowing RCA to develop the color market by itself. Competitors maintained token production and research on color, however, so that they could enter the market quickly when it became profitable.

Dealer Disinterest. Another problem that arose from lack of industry-wide marketing efforts was the dealer attitude that color television sets were difficult to sell. Dealer disinterest was the result of numerous public pronouncements made by executives of black-and-white television-set manufacturers questioning the quality and value of color television. In addition, salesmen of black-and-white sets tended to speak unenthusiastically of color to dealers. For every enthusiastic RCA color television salesman calling on a dealer, there were several unenthusiastic salesmen from other companies. This resulted in both dealer and consumer attitudes that sets were priced too high, difficult to operate, expensive to maintain, and gave poor color rendition. The long-term effect was that dealers had developed the attitude that color television sets were difficult to sell. Thus, in spite of 20% to 30% margins which resulted in high unit dollar margins, dealers, for some years, gave relatively little attention to selling color receivers.

In order to counter dealer disinterest, RCA had attempted to show dealers that retail personal selling and demonstration would sell color receivers and result in high profits. Some dealers accepted this idea, but many resisted it, because personal selling and demonstration was a type of selling which dealers did not like. RCA executives believed, however, that some progress had been made by late 1957 in getting dealers to recognize the opportunities in selling color.

Servicing of Color TV. Since the introduction of color television, RCA had worked continuously to provide adequate service for color receivers, utilizing its own service centers for RCA products which had been maintained for many years in 150 large cities. All of these centers could, in 1957, service color television receivers. In addition, RCA held service clinics to train employees of independent servicing organizations. Between 1954 and 1957 RCA had held over 1,500 service clinics which were attended by over 100,000 servicemen.

RCA executives stated that color television receivers required about as much servicing as had black-and-white sets in a comparable stage of development. However, service contracts for color television sets, if desired by purchasers, represented a substantial addition to the price. A 90-day service contract, which most new owners purchased, cost $40. A full-year service contract on a new color set cost $99.95 for the first year and $119 for the second year.

Price. Color television receivers, which started in price at $495, represented a substantial investment for most consumers. Comparable size (21-inch) black-and-white table model television sets listed from $150 to $300 to over $795, depending on the cabinet. There had been considerable industry debate concerning RCA's pricing policy, some contending that the price was too high for volume sales, others contending that the price was too low for profit making.

RCA executives reported that the possibility of a reduction in the price of color receivers was dependent upon cost reductions that might be obtained through either mass production or development of a simplified color tube. They stated that mass-production savings would not be great; it was estimated that production of a million sets a year would result in savings of less than $100 a set. Both RCA and other firms were actively attempting to develop simplified color receiving tubes, because the color tube and its associated components represented the largest cost item in a receiver. DuMont's "Lawrence" tube and Philco's "Apple" tube were two prototypes of simplified tubes. RCA had constructed numerous types of experimental tubes, but, like other companies, had found no satisfactory substitute for the three-gun tube being used. RCA executives predicted that no substantial development in new tubes would take place for at least three years and probably not even in five years, that is, by 1963.

Although it was recognized that lower prices would broaden the color-set market (RCA price-cut promotions on discontinued television lines had been highly successful), the realities of tube cost and mass-production savings indicated that there was no immediate prospect for a price decrease on color television receivers. RCA executives very firmly believed that there was a substantial market for color television at 1957 price levels.

Research conducted by RCA in 1957 indicated that persons who made up the most promising potential market for color television sets were in high-income groups, were experimentally minded, and in the middle-age groups.

Milwaukee Promotional Test

In reviewing their experience in marketing color television, RCA executives also considered the results of a test conducted in Milwaukee, Wisconsin, during May–June 1957. The test was conducted in order to determine, in the light of the foregoing problems experienced in marketing color, what sales and promotional techniques could be used effectively in selling color television. RCA executives hoped that the results of the test would assist them in developing a city-by-city color television promotion for the approaching 1957–58 selling season.

Milwaukee was selected as the test city because the area RCA distributor was particularly co-operative, the local NBC television station was particularly co-operative and had local color facilities, the market was good-sized, and its economy was representatively balanced. The five-week test was conducted at the beginning of the seasonal low point for color television sales, the peak sales months being September through February.

The sales test, which was run entirely through the local RCA distributor, had as its theme "Milwaukee Color Carnival." In order to participate, and RCA dealer was required to purchase five RCA color sets, to identify his store with Color Carnival promotional material, and to allocate an advertising budget, the size of which was established in proportion to his store's sales volume. RCA offered its usual co-operative advertising allowance of 50% of the dealer's advertising media cost. In most instances, dealers agreed to give home or in-store demonstrations of color television. As an incentive to dealers, RCA agreed to pay through the distributor the cost ($10) of any home demonstration that did not result in a sale. In addition the RCA distributor paid the cost of telephone solicitors who worked from the dealer's store with the dealer's customer list to develop and screen demonstration prospects. Fifty-six of the 67 Milwaukee RCA dealers participated in the Color Carnival.

In addition to the advertising of participating dealers, the RCA Milwaukee distributor ran advertisements promoting the Color Carnival. Dealer and distributor advertising appeared in all major local media (newspapers, radio, television, billboards, car cards, and direct mail), the advertising copy encouraging consumers to ask dealers for a color television demonstration. A heavy program of publicity featuring the local appearance of NBC entertainment stars was conducted. During the test period, several noncompetitive products conducted tie-in promotions. Dealers were supplied with elaborate display material relating to the Color Carnival theme.

In addition to the two salesmen regularly employed by the RCA distributor, RCA itself supplied eight experienced RCA salesmen who performed a wide variety of services on the dealer level for the distributor during the test. These salesmen were also useful to RCA management in reporting firsthand the reactions and results of the promotion on the local level.

With an assist from RCA in the form of extra advertising money, the local NBC television station carried the regular NBC network color programming plus 30 hours a week of local color programs. Over 200 total hours of color were broadcast in Milwaukee during May 1957.

The various promotional techniques used in the Color Carnival were evaluated when possible in terms of sales or in terms of inquiries. The source of inquiries and sales resulting from home or in-store demonstration, telephone solicitation, and direct mail were identified and recorded by dealers at the time of the inquiry and sale. Inquiries attributable to other media such as newspapers, radio, and television could also be determined since, in most cases, dealers used only one medium in addition to direct mail and telephone solicitation. All inquiries not directly attributable to direct mail or telephone solicitation were attributed to the dealers' third advertising medium.

Results of the Milwaukee Test

Although the Milwaukee test was conducted at a typically low sales season, sales in Milwaukee during the test increased from an average of 12 color sets a week to 106 color sets a week. The greatest sales volume was not in the $495 sets but in the higher-priced sets.

In evaluating the results of specific promotional techniques, RCA executives stated that the only completely effective technique was demonstration used in conjunction with a telephone solicitation. This technique called for the telephone solicitor to screen prospects eliminating those persons obviously not able to afford a color set. When prospects were adequately screened, two out of three demonstrations resulted in a sale. At an average cost of $10 for each home demonstration, this method of selling averaged $15 per actual sale plus a prorated share of the cost of a telephone solicitor at $20 a day. In-store demonstrations were also rated as highly effective. During the test period, nine in-store demonstration sales were made for every ten home demonstration sales. No average cost per sale figure for in-store demonstration was available. Despite the sales success of the demonstration technique, many dealers found this method of promotion disagreeable because it involved too much night work and personal selling.

The direct-mail campaign soliciting demonstration prospects was judged unsatisfactory on the basis of 100 replies to 20,000 mailings costing 7 cents each. Newspaper advertisements gave the least satisfactory results. Newspaper advertisement inquiries that resulted in home or in-store demonstrations created sales at a cost of about $100 per set sold plus the cost of demonstration. Radio and television spots created sales at a cost of about $25 each plus the cost of the demonstrations. Sales results could not be directly attributed to display material.

At the conclusion of the Milwaukee test, RCA conducted a survey among 30 of the 56 dealers who had participated in the promotion. To the question, "What phase of the Milwaukee promotion helped you the most?" the replies were:

Newspaper ads	10
Radio spots	10
Television spots	3
Salesmen's contest	2
Home demonstration	1
Telephone solicitation	1
Nothing	3
Radio and newspaper together	6

In appraising the answers to this question, which were almost directly contrary to their own beliefs as to the effectiveness of various techniques, RCA executives stated that the results reflected the fact that dealers disliked demonstrating because it required night work and personal selling, both of which were contrary to the way dealers usually did business. Dealers preferred to set up displays on the selling floor with the hope that customer traffic would create sales.

RCA reported that sales were highest at the beginning of the promotion and tended to diminish during the term of the promotion. They also found that after the promotion, Milwaukee color television sales returned to a level that was only average when compared to sales in other areas of the United States. In the follow-up survey of 30 dealers, the question was also asked: "Have you continued the color promotion since the end of the five-week period?" The replies were:

Have not continued promotion at all	17
Have continued somewhat	10
Have continued wholeheartedly	3

When asked "Why have you or have you not continued the promotion?" the replies were:

Off season, too costly, service problems. 17
Just using newspaper because want traffic in
  store. 10
Good results. 3

Reasons for Continued Marketing of Color TV

Despite the fact that they had experienced numerous problems in marketing color television sets, RCA executives were determined to continue actively marketing color television receivers. They stated that the company expected to derive benefits from color television both in their television broadcasting business and their receiver manufacturing business.

The television broadcast business, executives stated, could derive increased revenues through (1) greater set circulation, (2) doing a better job for sponsors, and (3) attracting new sponsors. Since black-and-white set circulation was already 85%, there was little room for improvement in that area. The greatest improvement that television could present to attract new sponsors and do a better job for existing sponsors was the introduction of color.

In the television receiver manufacturing industry, unit prices and margins had dropped sharply by 1957 due to excess industry capacity. RCA executives estimated that the industry needed volume of six million sets a year in order to operate at a profit. For the years immediately following 1957, RCA predicted sales of about a million sets a year to newly formed families and sales of one million sets a year as second sets. The remaining four million set sales a year would have to come from the replacement market, but with average set life estimated at ten years (the life of two average black-and-white picture tubes), RCA executives estimated that it would be 1960 before large-scale replacements took place. RCA executives believed that the successful marketing of color television sets would solve the industry's problem by speeding obsolescence of black-and-white sets, raising unit prices, and raising margins.

~~~

CASE II: PAN-AMERICAN COFFEE BUREAU (A)[1]

NOTE: *The next three cases concern the steps taken by executives of the Pan-American Coffee Bureau to devise an advertising program which would help to increase the consumption of coffee. These cases differ from the Dow cases in that they involve not only the determination of advertis-*

---

[1] Written by Joseph W. Newman.

*ing objectives but also the consideration of specific advertisements which
might be used to obtain those objectives.* QUESTIONS TO CONSIDER: *(1)
What conclusions do you draw from the "digest of findings and recommendations"? (2) What, in your opinion, should be the specific objectives of the Bureau's advertising? (3) Assume that you are responsible for
working with the Bureau's advertising agency. What suggestions would
you give to the agency regarding advertising copy?*

Early in 1955, executives of the Pan-American Coffee Bureau, New
York City, were considering the possibility of undertaking additional
consumer research in order to learn more about how coffee consumption
might be increased. Before 1955 the Bureau's research had consisted of
quantitative surveys of coffee use and preference and of economic
studies of the total demand for coffee. Believing that research of this
type was needed as a basis for planning more effective promotional efforts
to increase coffee consumption, Bureau executives called in Dr. Ernest
Dichter, head of The Institute for Motivational Research, Inc., to talk
about a motivational study. They discussed research which would seek
to learn what coffee meant to people, believing that once such an understanding had been gained, objectives and ideas for future advertising
and public relations approaches would become clearer.

Background of Bureau

Established in 1936 as a nonprofit organization, the Bureau was supported by an assessment on each 132-pound bag of green coffee shipped
to the United States and Canada by the 11 Latin American member
countries: Brazil, Colombia, Costa Rica, Cuba, Dominican Republic, Ecua-
dor, El Salvador, Guatemala, Honduras, Mexico, and Venezuela. Its primary objectives were to promote increased use of coffee in the United
States and Canada and to maintain good relationships between producers
and consumers. (The Bureau did not buy, sell, or trade in coffee.)

The Bureau, managed by Mr. Charles G. Lindsay, had four specialized
departments: advertising, consumer services, public relations, and research.

The advertising department was charged with the responsibility of developing advertising themes which would broaden the total market for
coffee and which would create a background against which the advertising of individual coffee brands might be more effective. Working with
an advertising agency, the advertising department prepared advertisements for its programs addressed to both consumers and the trade. It also
developed display pieces, posters, television and radio advertising, and
other promotional items. Some of this material was offered to the coffee
trade for use in support of special projects such as the annual holiday
safety program sponsored by the Bureau.

To stimulate interest in new and better ways of using and brewing
coffee, the consumer services department supplied newspapers, magazines, and radio and television stations with articles, pictures, scripts, and
a monthly "Coffee Newsletter" which contained tested recipes, food

photographs, and news items. It also made available educational material for classroom use such as booklets and filmstrips on the production and history of coffee, coffee uses (for home economics students), and coffee's importance in inter-American trade (for social science studies). The public relations department disseminated a wide range of information on coffee—its economics, culture, production, and importance—through news releases, feature articles, photographs, radio and television scripts, motion pictures, filmstrips, booklets, and speeches.

The research department had two principal functions: first, to collect, maintain, and publish statistics on coffee production and to analyze various aspects of the national and world coffee markets; and, second, to conduct studies of consumer use of coffee. Consumer and market research efforts, described by Dr. James E. Wood, director of research, included the following:

1. A survey of coffee consumption in the United States, conducted by an advertising agency in 1939: A number of direct questions were asked of a sample of nearly 5,000 housewives to find out such things as who drank coffee, how much they drank, when and where they drank it, how they made coffee, how often they bought it, and whether they regarded coffee as good or harmful. While this study has been superseded, it is cited as an example of early research. Among its findings: about 80% of all adults drank coffee, the average daily consumption was three cups, 88% of the housewives said their husbands liked the coffee they made, and 40% of the women used less than two level tablespoons of coffee per cup, the amount considered by the Bureau as necessary for a good cup of coffee.

2. Annual surveys of amount of coffee drinking in winter, conducted by The Psychological Corporation of New York starting in 1950: This information was obtained in personal interviews in which people were asked how many cups of coffee they drank on the preceding day.

3. Starting early in 1954, the Bureau received weekly, monthly, quarterly, and annual reports on purchases of coffee, both regular and instant, by families in the national panel of the Market Research Corporation of America, New York City. The Bureau converted these figures into their green coffee equivalent in which terms total demand was expressed.

4. Two studies of the number of cups extracted from a pound of coffee had been made for the Bureau by Nation Family Opinion, Inc., of Toledo, Ohio, one in 1953 and the other in 1955. For them, housewives reported the amount of coffee used for a specified meal and the number of cups made from that amount.

Need for Research in 1955

The need for research which would add to understanding the nature of demand for coffee and how it might be increased was felt even more

keenly in 1955. Per capita consumption of coffee in the United States
had been declining from 16.3 roasted pounds in 1946 to 12.3 roasted
pounds in 1954. This was a period when people were receiving more purchasing power than ever before and when the per capita consumption of
certain other beverages—notably fruit juices, soft drinks, tea, and wine—
was rising. Data collected on coffee brewing practices in American households showed that the extraction rate for regular coffee had risen from
approximately 46 cups per pound in 1949 to 62 in 1954.

The outlook was for more coffee being offered on the market several
years hence as the price increases of 1953 had prompted new plantings of
trees which would start producing when five years old. Increases in coffee
supply in the past always had been accompanied by substantially more
than proportionate decreases in price.

The Bureau hoped to learn of sales appeals for coffee which could be
used more effectively by companies selling coffee at retail than the "more
cups per pound" claims a number of them had been making for their
brands. It was feared that these claims might lead to the making of weaker
coffee and further reductions in per capita consumption. The Bureau in
its advertising had been urging the use of two level tablespoons of coffee
per cup, believing that many people drank less coffee than they might because they made it too weak for maximum enjoyment.

Executives wanted to know how effective the Bureau's advertising had
been and whether its "coffee-break" theme used since 1950 should be continued or modified in some way.

As of early 1955, the Bureau's consumer advertising program consisted
largely of running full-page, black-and-white advertisements once a
month in both *Life* and *The Saturday Evening Post*. The advertisements
promoted the "coffee break" by calling attention to coffee's role as a stimulant. Large photographs were used to portray "stress-and-strain" situations. Typical was the advertisement run in February 1955, which showed
a somewhat weary-looking secretary drinking coffee at her desk (see Exhibit 1). It suggested hot coffee as a "Wonderful way to break the tempo
of work and ease the strain of concentration. Nothing else offers such a
friendly lift." The advertisement also stressed "Enjoy coffee often—and
make it right. Use 2 level tablespoons (or 1 Standard Coffee Measure)
for every cup." Examples of other advertisements in this campaign appear in Exhibits 2 and 3.

The Motivational Study

In early conferences, executives of the Bureau and The Institute for
Motivational Research, Inc., prepared a number of questions to serve as a
preliminary definition of the research assignment. Later, the following
motivational research areas were identified as most likely to yield the desired information:

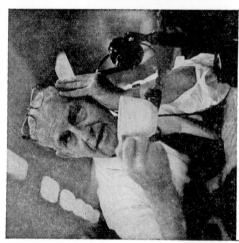

1. What is coffee's "cultural label"? What should be coffee's cultural status in the future?
2. What are the attitudes toward coffee by age, income, and social groups?
3. What are the personality patterns of the coffee drinker?
4. Under what circumstances is coffee bought and used? Is it bought and consumed in a certain "coffee mood"? Is coffee purchasing really an established part of a living pattern or does it yield to impulsive purchases?
5. How can noncoffee drinkers be converted into coffee drinkers? How rigid are people about their coffee habits? Is it possible to increase consumption among coffee drinkers?
6. Does coffee evoke specific childhood associations? If so, how do they influence teen-age and adult coffee habits?
7. Do people have definite pictures of coffee which include specific good and bad qualities?
8. How important is price? Is coffee really expensive or only psychologically so? What is the correct psychological price of coffee?
9. Is there an ideal coffee? Does this vary by region, economic, social, and cultural background?
10. How do employees view the "coffee break"? Employers? Is there a conflict? If so, how can it be reconciled?
11. Is there a new attitude toward coffee because of new nutritional concepts?

In describing the planning of the research, Mr. Ernest Angel, a psychologist who served as director of the coffee study, said:

> You know certain things from your training in the social sciences, from doing other research (the Institute had done five studies for individual coffee companies), and from talking with people. For instance, we knew that strength of coffee was likely to be an important area to investigate—some people drink coffee "straight" like some people do whiskey. Also, we knew that the utility versus pleasure and social aspects probably were important. Some people drink coffee as a "must" to get started; others do it for pleasure. They like the aroma, variety, etc. We also knew that coffee had some connection with maturity and that it was an issue between parents and children, doctors and patients, teachers and pupils. While we knew some of these things, we did not know the detailed implications, why certain things were true, or what should be done about them in writing advertising copy.

Two waves of depth interviews were conducted to develop points such as those indicated above and to learn of others of importance. Concepts arrived at by this process then were tested by the use of projective questions, coffee taste tests, and tests of reactions to advertisements which had been run by the Pan-American Coffee Bureau.

The Depth Interviews. In the depth interview, the basic research technique used, a trained interviewer encouraged the respondent to talk freely about his associations and feelings related to coffee. Direct questions seldom were asked. Instead, the interviewer attempted by skillful probing to learn of what was important to the respondent and to investigate the emotional factors which often determined apparently rational behavior.

For the first wave of 36 depth interviews, for example, the interviewers were given instructions which included a brief description of the general objectives and a list of broad areas for investigation. They were told that it would be most helpful if they could just get people to talk freely for an hour or so on all of their feelings about coffee. At the start, interviewers were to encourage maximum free association to get everything that came into people's minds when they thought of coffee. Then the respondents would be encouraged to be more specific by talking about their last few cups of coffee—how they felt from the moment they thought of coffee through the drinking of it and how they felt afterwards. Interviewers were instructed to probe in detail for all sensory impressions such as smell, taste, and appearance.

Research areas which were suggested for probing after free association had been exhausted included kinds of coffee, coffee drinking occasions, what the respondent considered to be the best cup of coffee he had tasted, childhood impressions of coffee, attitudes toward children drinking coffee, frequency of coffee drinking, and feelings about coffee and health.

The interviewers also were given instructions about choosing respondents so that the sample would include men and women, "dark strong" and "light weak" coffee drinkers, and "heavy" (six–eight cups a day) and "light" (two–three cups per day) coffee drinkers.

Persons with some training in the social sciences were preferred as interviewers because they were more likely to be able to make the respondent feel free to talk, skillfully probe to get at the roots of feelings, and avoid leading questions. Among those regarded as top interviewers were a number with some training in clinical psychology and a few young psychoanalysts. Interviewers were instructed to take as nearly verbatim notes as possible. If they wished to report any observations or interpretations, they were asked to do so only after they had completed their verbatim notes as to what was said. Occasionally interviews were recorded on tape. Frequently, new interviewers had to be trained to learn to distinguish between their own feelings and what others said. It was common for them at first to unconsciously project their own feelings into interview write-ups.

In reading the write-ups of the interviews, the study director searched for new ideas, noted patterns of response, and developed concepts. By this process, it became clearer what areas should be explored further, and a guide was prepared for the second wave which included 93 depth interviews.

Spontaneity of response was encouraged in the second wave of interviews as it had been in the first, but the interviewer also was to be sure to cover in detail areas suggested by the guide. The first area, for example, was that of the coffee stereotype, and questions which illustrated how the topic might be developed included the following. What comes to mind when you hear the word "coffee"? What pictures come into your mind?

What associations do you have with coffee? Why do you think people drink coffee? What does coffee do for them? Why do women drink coffee? Men? What are the major functions that coffee fulfills? How important do you think coffee is in American life?

The second wave of interviews were apportioned by geographical region and by several groups of respondents: parents of children five to ten years of age; people 50 years of age and older; newlyweds; teachers; pediatricians; employers who did and employers who did not have a coffee break for their employees; employees who worked at plants or offices which did and which did not have coffee breaks. A separate guide was used for interviews with unmarried college students.

Half of the interview reports in the second wave were read by the study director and half by an assistant. Both looked for ideas which suggested theories to be tested in further field work. Their qualitative analyses were supplemented by statistical tabulations of responses by broad content groupings.

The repetitive nature of the responses was evidence that the depth interviews had served to identify most of the ways people thought and felt about coffee and its use. The remainder of the field work, therefore, was devoted to three different tests of the importance of these factors.

The First Test.   One test employed a questionnaire with a variety of direct and projective questions devised so that the results could easily be quantified. Information about the respondent (name, address, sex, age, marital status, number and ages of children, ethnic origin, occupation, income) was recorded on the cover sheet.

Part I of the questionnaire included questions dealing with the frequency, amount, time, and place of coffee drinking; what people usually took in their coffee; whether coffee was regarded as a necessity, a regular-use item, or a luxury as compared with other foods for which the same information was obtained; and how well the respondent thought he liked coffee as compared with other people.

In Part II, the respondent was asked to tell about his own coffee history. While he was to be encouraged to talk in his own way, the interviewer was instructed to look for changes in coffee consumption, and when and why they occurred. A form was provided so that coffee consumption in cups per day could be plotted against age as the respondent talked. The dots could be joined to give a coffee-use profile. Space was provided for detailed explanations of the occasions for starting to drink coffee and for changes in coffee consumption. The respondent also was questioned about what strength of coffee he used when he started drinking it; his parents' attitude toward his early coffee drinking; and his opinion as to whether coffee was habit forming, whether it was a good or bad habit, and why.

The next part sought the respondent's feelings about coffee by asking his ideas as to what kind of a personality would drink coffee in different strengths and amounts and with varying amounts of cream and sugar. For this purpose, the respondent was told that four women were having lunch together: a clergyman's wife, a nursery school teacher, a lady senator, and a department-store buyer. After lunch each woman ordered her coffee exactly the way she wanted it. The respondent was asked what each woman would order. For example, the clergyman's wife would order (a) strong coffee, (b) average coffee, or (c) weak coffee. She would use (a) lots of cream, (b) a little cream, or (c) no cream, etc.

The respondent also was asked to compare the usual cup of coffee with the best she could imagine; and the usual cup with the cup she got in her favorite restaurant. She also was asked about her knowledge of various kinds of coffee (coffee as served in various foreign countries, etc.); causes of bad coffee; her image of coffeegrowers; and her knowledge of coffeegrowing and the Pan-American Coffee Bureau.

Part III consisted of multiple-choice questions about the respondent's reasons for drinking coffee and for not drinking it more often.

The questionnaire was used in interviews with about 200 people.

Coffee Taste Tests. Taste tests were conducted with 128 respondents living in four different regions of the country to learn of the acceptability of coffee of different strengths and to determine whether it might be possible to increase consumption by getting people to drink coffee in different forms on different occasions.

Respondents were chosen so that half were women, half men, and half were "coffee-sophisticated" (exposed to a variety of different coffees before), and half were "coffee-naive." They were invited in groups of four to interviewers' homes where the tests were conducted in a relaxed, informal atmosphere, but in a way to avoid one respondent influencing another.

Comparisons were made of different strengths of conventional American coffee and of a different or "exotic" coffee. Each test group tasted two of the alternatives, the respondents being asked which they liked the better and why. Two brands of coffee were used for all of the tests, one representing conventional coffee and the other the different or exotic coffee. Strengths of coffee were according to Coffee Brewing Institute specifications. Comparisons were made of the following in the series of tests:

1. Conventional American coffee: standard strength versus strong. (The strong coffee was rejected by more than three fourths of the respondents.)
2. Conventional American coffee: standard strength versus weak. (The weak coffee was rejected.)
3. Conventional American coffee of standard strength versus "different" coffee of strong coffee strength. (The different coffee was preferred by more than two thirds of the respondents.)
4. Same as No. 3 except that the different coffee was introduced with a prestige-promoting remark: "This is the coffee the coffee people them-

selves consider best." (The number favoring the stronger coffee was increased slightly by the prestige introduction.)

While the numbers involved in the tests were not large, results were strongly consistent. They were interpreted as confirmation of people's readiness to accept change when it was offered as "variety," while they would reject it if offered only as the same thing but stronger.

The Advertisement Tests. The advertisement tests, administered to 217 respondents, provided a further check on earlier findings by obtaining reactions to 11 Coffee Bureau advertisements which had appeared in *Life* and *The Saturday Evening Post* from 1952 to 1955. Only three of the advertisements were used in each interview. The interviewer started by asking for general impressions of coffee advertising and detailed comments on any advertisements the respondent remembered.

The respondent then was shown the first of the three advertisements. She was asked to look over the advertisement, return it to the interviewer, and tell about everything that ran through her mind when she looked at the advertisement: her recollections, associations, impressions, images, or questions. This was repeated for the other two advertisements. This information was to be obtained by encouraging maximum spontaneous association as was done in the depth interviews. The purpose was to get comments which would reveal the respondent's reactions and explain why she liked or disliked an advertisement or parts of it. The interviewer was instructed to probe for these explanations and to guard against the respondent assuming a role of advertisement expert. Whether the respondent considered one advertisement to be a "good" advertisement and another "poor" was viewed as largely irrelevant.

In the next stage of the interview, the respondent was given each advertisement once more. As she looked at it, the interviewer probed in detail for associations to each part of the advertisement: the illustration, heading, color, slogans, and each section of the copy. The interview concluded by asking the respondent what she would do to improve the advertisement.

While over-all reaction to many of the advertisements was favorable, a number of feelings were expressed which indicated how improvement might be made. For example, 80% of the respondents expressed dissatisfaction with the way coffee was portrayed in the advertisements (dull and cold rather than hot); 20% objected to being told how to make coffee (two level tablespoons per cup) and preferred to be free to make coffee in their own way; generally people accepted the message of the advertisement much more readily if they did not feel that they were being "sold"; and many pointed out that the spirit of the coffee break was negated when the advertisement showed people having coffee at the actual place of work (beside a machine or at a drawing board).

Reactions to one of the advertisements are given in more detail here for illustrative purposes. The advertisements showed a father, mother, and daughter seated in the front seat of a car stopped for a coffee break. The parents were drinking coffee, the daughter nothing. Everyone liked the idea of the family being out together, but they commented adversely on several things as is shown in the sample comments which follow:

> *Comment No. 1:* Well, I like it, but I'm disappointed that the child didn't have anything. You would think she would have ice cream or a coke, but she doesn't have anything in her hand. As for the rest, I like the family scene. It seems a typical family.
>
> *Comment No. 2:* I have a feeling that someone ought to tell the group to get out of the car and then they could relax even more. It's good to have the family group, but the little girl ought not to be left out of things.
>
> *Comment No. 3:* In a sense the advertisement is not realistic. What about the little girl? She seems as though she doesn't belong in the picture. Everybody's enjoying a drink, but not she. I would give that poor child something to drink, or take her out of the car to relax even more. You can't really relax all stuffed in the front seat.

A Digest of Findings and Recommendations

Findings and recommendations growing out of the research were presented in a 150-page report. Its main theme was that coffee had become a utilitarian staple in this country and that for consumption to be increased coffee must be rediscovered as an exciting beverage of pleasure, one more appropriate to life in contemporary America. This point was summarized as follows:

> Something has happened to coffee. Because of its universal acceptance and the fact that most people like coffee, we have at the same time been lulled into a complacency about it. Many of the coffee advertisers, because of their great emphasis on convenience, economy, brewing techniques, have helped accelerate the change from coffee as an exciting, luxurious beverage to a commonplace utilitarian staple. Thus, when we are asked how we can increase coffee consumption, our answer is: By helping people to rediscover coffee in all its many facets. The very reason for the existence of coffee is that it is not a utilitarian product. By making it one, the coffee roaster is barricading its road to progress. . . . We feel that every one of the specific questions, such as how to get people to drink more coffee, to take more coffee breaks, to start drinking coffee at an earlier age, etc., are all in one way or another dependent upon this revitalization of coffee which we have set forth as the most immediate task.

Several specific objectives were cited. One was to change coffee from a sinful and escapist beverage to a positive, life-accepting product. While many people liked coffee, they also were afraid of drinking too much of it or of giving it to young people. A second objective was to introduce greater variety into coffee flavors, to make coffee not just an adjunct on a restaurant's menu but to give it the status of a full-fledged course by listing four or five varieties of coffee. A third recommendation was that people be left free to decide how to make and drink their coffee. Interviews showed that people were proud of their individual tastes and that some resented being told in an authoritarian manner how to make coffee.

A summary of findings which led to the above conclusions is presented below:

I. The First Change: From "Escapism" to "Coping"

Strong remnants of puritanical attitudes are still alive in the American consumer, and they influence his feelings towards coffee. He enjoys coffee but is at the same time convinced that coffee has many drawbacks. Thus, he is caught in a coffee conflict. Contributing to this conflict is a punishing attitude toward pleasure, especially sensory pleasure. Any feeling of "sinning" usually is followed by an expectation and fear of "punishment," although the "sinner" may not always be aware of this.

Of 125 coffee drinkers, 67% expressed concern about their coffee habit (55% worried about drinking too much coffee, 12% about the habit-forming and dependence aspect). In another test, 55% of 129 respondents expressed their belief in coffee's ill effects on health and sleep. Lingering feelings of "sin" and "punishment" in coffee drinking were spontaneously expressed again and again in the depth interviews.

Three principal aspects of coffee's "sinfulness" emerged from the research:

1. Coffee was seen by some as a drug-provoking addiction. The words "habit" and "dependence" appeared frequently in responses. Coffee often was compared to liquor. The two principal notions that supported the coffee-drug-liquor identification were that heavy coffee drinkers are nervous, neurotic people, and that coffee drinking promotes loss of control over one's appetite.

2. Coffee was felt to be a dangerous drink tending to overstimulate the heart and other organs of the body in an artificial and detrimental way.

3. Coffee was accused of aiding in laziness. Many respondents said that coffee provided an excuse to get away from the requirements of modern life. The words "excuse," "postponement," and "procrastination" frequently were connected with coffee, sometimes revealing apology or guilt, sometimes amounting to accusation.

The conflict which coffee represents was indicated by the fact that in each of the three areas itemized above coffee also had on its side powerful factors pointing in the opposite direction. For example, many felt that coffee, unlike liquor, aided in better control. In responding to the following incomplete sentence: "A doctor receives a call at 3:00 A.M., and first gets himself a cup of hot coffee. The coffee will _____," 65% agreed that it will "wake him up and give him control." People also felt that coffee relaxed while it stimulated; that it served to bring back one's natural resources. If coffee is used by some as an "excuse" for dodging work, it is used by many as a reward for hard or long work, punctuating successful work completion.

In summary, one of the major tasks for the coffee industry is to help in changing coffee from a sinful and escapist beverage to a positive and life-accepting one. The modern consumer has gone partly in this direction. He is, however, still caught in conflict. He likes coffee and yet is afraid of drinking too much of it or of giving it to young people.

How to change sin to morality is a big task, and we cannot state exactly what the creative translation will look like. We have attempted, however, to indicate a number of steps we feel should be taken. Among these: make coffee a helper in coping with life and coexistence with stress; purify coffee morally by showing it as a natural product; dramatize its help in independence and self-control; associate it with well-known, realistic "copers" in life; present the coffee bean as nature's magic treasure chest; reassure about the universal acceptance of coffee by pointing out that all the world loves coffee and by citing what poets and writers have said about it.

II. BRIDGE THE SOCIAL LAG

In the last few years, people have become aware of several cultural changes with which coffee has not kept pace: (1) A desire for more gracious living. People are tired of patterns of living and working that entail continuous tension, haste, and push. They feel that they have to learn to relax and desire to develop ways of living more pleasurably and graciously. (2) Americans are moving away from earlier restrictions imposed on enjoying sensory pleasures. Recent examples of this trend are two-tone cars, more color in men's clothing, and a growing receptivity for more refined and new types of food. (3) A new kind of individualism which has as its goal the expression of one's personality by more individualized consumption and appreciation and enjoyment of differences and variety.

Coffee has lagged behind these trends. It has become too utilitarian; it is related more to nutritional rather than emotional health; and coffee drinking has become routinized. Such phrases as "I must have it . . . ," and "I can't do without it . . ." recurred frequently in the interviews. People were aware of coffee's role as a remedy and aid in emergencies (a help in cases of shock, cramps, and overdose of sleeping pills; it makes aspirin act faster; stimulates regularity, etc.). Many also mentioned coffee as an eye-opener in the morning "to make them feel alive . . . human." Men appeared to be more luxury minded about coffee than did women in answering this incomplete sentence: "I drink coffee primarily _____." Forty-four per cent of the men as contrasted with 16% of the women mentioned drinking coffee primarily as a part of a good meal. Forty-four per cent of the women as opposed to 26% of the men mentioned drinking coffee primarily to get started in the morning. This finding suggests appealing to the woman as a coffee consumer and not as a coffee maker for men. If she sees coffee as part of a good meal herself, she would be more inclined to pay more attention to it.

Coffee has become "frozen" psychologically. People feel that most brands do not reflect varieties of flavor, and that shopping for coffee is not rewarded by discovery. The advertiser has contributed to this result by stressing economy and convenience.

At the same time, taste tests indicated that people are willing to accept change in coffee when it is offered as variety. Three fourths of the respondents rejected a "strong" conventional American coffee when comparing it with the same type of coffee in standard strength. However, 69% preferred a different or "exotic" coffee of stronger than standard strength when it was compared against average coffee of standard strength.

The depth interviews showed that coffee could be made to heighten the pleasure of life. Respondents frequently expressed a desire for more gracious living and saw coffee as a symbol of a better, more leisurely life. Coffee was credited with making a variety of pleasures more pleasurable: cigarettes, music, a picnic, etc. There were 129 spontaneous references in the depth interviews to the pleasure, leisure, and luxury roles of coffee. These referred to taste, flavor, aroma, its social role in helping conversation, and coffee as a symbol of leisure. It is significant that these references were almost equal in number to the 140 spontaneous references to the utilitarian functions.

A high percentage of respondents had heard of and tried varied types of coffees such as demitasse, Cafe Royale, and Turkish coffee. This is an indication of a trend toward taste individualism and experimentation with new sensory pleasures. Many respondents made coffee in different ways for different times of the day. They told of numerous ways of serving, preparing, blending, and roasting coffee, and were eager to learn more about more and different coffees.

Coffee is widely regarded as a beverage without nutritional value other than that of the cream or sugar put in it. From a nutritional health point of view, it is tolerated as a necessity of modern life. However, a large majority of consumers also realize and appreciate coffee's contribution to their emotional health. Our modern pace of living not only exhausts many people physically but also fills them with bitterness and anger at the world and themselves. For such moods, from grouchy and morose to aggressive, coffee is a great "healer" that makes life appear worth living again.

The findings indicate that the coffee break is assuming a much more important role in our culture than that of a rest or relaxation period. It gratifies deep and often deeply hidden emotional needs in workers as well as their bosses. Almost everybody has some smouldering resentment against duties, work, the boss, the drudgery of necessary routine. The coffee break offers a harmless, socially acceptable outlet for such resentment; it provides the housewife with an excuse to get away from her "drudgery" for a while without feeling guilty about it; it permits the worker to indulge in a legitimate breach of discipline and to get "something for nothing"; and it serves every kind of "rebellion" against rut and routine, even the routine of marriage and family life. The most positive reactions to coffee breaks by employees referred to the intention of the employer rather than to the break itself. Allowance of some time off for coffee seems to be almost taken for granted. But the warmest spontaneous comments related to the way the break was provided, to any little actions that show the employer going out of his way to make his employees happy. Employees are sensitive to management's feelings about the coffee break and resent it if they notice that the break is considered a "necessary evil."

In summary, this section has pointed to the need to change coffee from utility to pleasure of life, to stress its sensory pleasures, and to make it more of a food for emotional health. Variety should be introduced in many ways. The coffee break should be proof of creative considerateness by the employer and a legitimate breach of discipline and a reward for hard work. Coffee consumption should be increased by encouraging a "fill 'er up" psychology dramatizing the completion of the second cup: "it is the second cup that counts."

III. Change from Authoritative to Permissive Approach

Once a person, usually in adolescence, obtains permission from parental authority to drink coffee, he is proud to retain his individual rights to coffee. The authoritative origin of coffee drinking and the reaction against it appeared in the interviews in a number of ways. The most important finding was the rejection by the overwhelming majority of respondents of any conception of someone's "right" way to make coffee. The feeling expressed seemed to be composed of the following main elements:

A. There was a widespread expression of diversity in the way coffee affects people and the ways in which people prefer coffee. The underlying assumption reflected by most respondents is their personal need to discover just the right amount of coffee, just the right strength, just the correct brewing method, just the right flavor, and just the right number of cups per day or per meal for themselves personally. This is accompanied by a recognition that other people, even other members of the family, may have varying preferences.

B. Many respondents expressed great pride in their individual art of coffee brewing and serving. Their "coffee freedom" was seen as a precious expression of individuality.

C. Most respondents reported some change in their brewing method or taste preference or quantity of coffee they liked over the past years. More important, they indicated their receptivity to trying new and different kinds of coffee flavors or brewing methods when they were offered these varied taste experiences by friends or by restaurants.
D. People tend to reject any prescription of rigid rules as to strength or brewing methods as being correct for all coffee drinkers. Our evidence indicates rejection of any advertising tone or slogan that sounds like "coffee authoritarianism." This was reflected in negative reactions to the injunction to "use two tablespoons full."

Most people still tend to think of coffee as masculine. A new trend was indicated in the interviews, however, by the existence of a small number of men who prefer light coffee and a larger number of women who have come to prefer strong or black coffee. To some degree they seem defensive about their preferences when they do not conform to the expected cultural stereotype of their sex and feel the need to justify them. Coffee advertising could resolve some of these conflicts by promoting recognition of the idea that coffee taste preference is an individual matter, cutting across the sexes rather than being sex-related. This should reduce the danger of people turning to tea because they can't get coffee on their own terms.

Almost all parents express sharp rejection of any outside suggestion relating to children drinking coffee. While they are willing to open the door to coffee drinking at varying age levels, they desire to retain control over this expression of their children's growing up. In the most strongly voiced rejections, respondents referred to coffee as something parents whom they did not respect might give to their children instead of milk.

Mothers frequently were receptive to coffee as a milk vehicle and reported results occasionally achieved in getting children to drink milk more readily when it was flavored with just a drop of coffee. Nearly 30% of the respondents first tasted coffee as children when they got a little coffee with a lot of milk. Coffee frequently is used with children as a special treat or as a reward for "being good," particularly when the latter takes the form of an approved kind of mature or adult behavior.

The role of coffee as a symbol of initiation into maturity for children was reflected in two ways. A child on his own initiative might drink coffee in a friend's home or in a restaurant, expressing rebellion against his parents and his desire to be treated as a grownup. Another example is when parents for the first time offer to a child a cup of coffee which contains more coffee than milk rather than more milk than coffee. This is recognized as an expression of the child's movement to maturity and adulthood.

Recommendations based on the findings in this section include changing from an authoritative to a permissive approach in all communications about coffee with the public. Do not order people; instead, invite them to try and experiment and discover for themselves. Respect people's individual feelings about coffee; give them permission to brew and drink coffee as they like. Let more parents know about other parents' success with coffee as a milk vehicle and use good-humored approaches to help them introduce coffee to children as part of growing up. Provide moral permission for women, as well as men, to prefer strong coffee and for men to like weak coffee.

IV. The Image or Personality of Coffee

Coffee's image in the minds of consumers is reflected in their talking about coffee in the depth interviews. Some of coffee's characteristics follow:

A. Coffee is intimate. When speaking of people meeting over a cup of coffee, respondents use such words as "close," "closer together," "feeling warmer toward people." Closeness and warmth are conducive to a feeling of good fellowship.

B. Coffee removes barriers and promotes understanding between people. It stimulates talk and makes it easier to be silent, too. Coffee talk is described as relaxed talk through which you get to know people. Business talks tend to lose their competitive coldness when carried on around the coffee table.

C. It appears from our study that coffee, even more than food, is for many people a measure of interest in homemaking, in receiving friends in a warm, appreciative fashion, and in their ability to give. Good and strong coffee expresses abundance and generosity, while poor and weak coffee is identified with poverty, skimping, and stinginess.

D. Whenever people talk about coffee they mention its strong, masculine character. As a parallel, weak, poor coffee is considered a symbol of poverty and skimping.

E. Our responses strongly suggest that many people are eager to enjoy pleasures of the senses and have a desire to develop a sense of flavor and taste discrimination if properly aided and stimulated. Thus, coffee has a good chance to become an outlet for those who do not get sufficient sensory gratification from their daily food due to American mass food production and preservation (canned, iced, artificial flavoring, etc.).

F. Our findings indicate strongly that aroma is still more prevailing in the experience of coffee than flavor. Childhood experiences, which often color a person's feelings toward coffee over a lifetime, are particularly marked by impressions of odor; they often connect with nostalgic feelings about childhood pleasures and childhood security. Hence, coffee for many stands as a symbol of "Paradise Lost," a paradise that can be revived by similar sensory experiences of odor and aroma.

G. Coffee is a symbol of grownup relaxation.

Advertising copy and art should follow this image of coffee. Coffee should be shown in social surroundings with the elements of intimacy and closeness. Wide open spaces as background would be wrong. Even cowboys when drinking coffee pick a protected spot, an oasis of intimacy.

V. Other Findings

The interview and test responses indicated that the American housewife represented the best potential market for increased use of coffee. Her job is one of monotony and drudgery and few rewards. It calls for an excuse for interruptions and relaxation. Coffee can supply this and also be an inviting reward for her dull and lonely work. Coffee can provide her with a sense of security by heightening her alertness and sense of mastery of the situation. While most housewives look forward to relaxing over a cup of coffee with a neighbor, there are many times when this is not possible. It is at these times that coffee, as a symbol of sociability, can provide comfort and relaxation by serving as a substitute for a companion.

The report recommended that the housewives be encouraged to experiment with different blends, roasts, and methods of preparing coffee with the primary goal being to extend her pleasures in having and drinking coffee. Increased use of coffee by the housewife likely will be reflected in the general consumption of her family. As a coffee drinker, she will be more careful to keep a supply on hand, and will be more inclined to offer it to her family and guests and to think in terms of using coffee in new ways.

Respondents repeatedly commented that coffee tastes better at home than in a restaurant. Most restaurant situations, often accompanied by serving of mass-produced coffee, tend to deny coffee as a symbol of closeness, hospitality, and relaxation. When special emphasis is placed on the type or quality of coffee, however, it meets with favorable feelings of luxury. Coffee is seen by many people as an index of a restaurant's quality, a finding that could be of considerable significance for coffee advertising to the trade.

The report also presented findings (not summarized here) on consumer attitudes toward price, the Pan-American Coffee Bureau and the Latin American coffeegrowing countries, and uses of coffee in addition to its major role as a hot beverage.

~ ~ ~

CASE 12: PAN-AMERICAN COFFEE BUREAU (B)[1]

QUESTIONS TO CONSIDER: (1) *Do you think that the new advertising approach employed in late 1955 (see Exhibit 1) was sound? (2) Would you use the information given in Exhibit 3 as the basis for developing the Bureau's new advertising campaign? (3) How would you go about selecting the advertisements to be employed in the new advertising campaign?*

Some of the principal findings of the motivation study described in Case (A) had been made known earlier in interim discussions between representatives of the research firm and the Bureau. They were reflected in the final consumer advertisements of 1955, time permitting the making of certain modifications within the general character of the year's campaign. The later advertisements used photographs of people happily enjoying coffee, thereby departing somewhat from the "stress-and-strain" note characteristic of the earlier advertisements. They also refrained from telling people to make coffee in one "right" way.

Instead of showing black coffee in ordinary cups, the advertisements for October featured attractive cups of coffee with a dash of whipped cream on top. The copy talked about "good, full-bodied delicious coffee —made just the way you like it best." It suggested that the "next time you serve coffee, why not try it this different way? Top it off with a swirl of whipped cream—the way they do in old Vienna!" (see Exhibit 1).

The copy of some advertisements stressed that it was socially acceptable for a woman to drink coffee black or for a man to drink it with cream or sugar. This was done by talking about the "figure-conscious girl who drinks hers black," "the businessman, cream, two sugars," "the driver, black with apple pie," "the motherly-type, light, one sugar" (see Exhibit 2).

The main import of the research findings, however, was to come in the 1956 advertising campaign for which the report was used as the basis for

---

[1] Written by Joseph W. Newman.

Exhibit 1

PAN-AMERICAN COFFEE BUREAU (B)

Good neighbors enjoy a "Coffee-break"

Beds are made, dishes done, Dad's off to work and the youngsters have gone to school. What better time for a pleasant, relaxing "Coffee-break" with the neighbor next door? Good, full-bodied, delicious coffee — made just the way *you* like it best. Even the aroma perks you up! Fact is, there's nothing better than a cup of coffee — unless it's a second cup! And next time you serve coffee, why not try it this *different* way? Top it off with a swirl of whipped cream — the way they do in old Vienna! Delicious! Get *extra* pleasure from your "Coffee-break." PAN-AMERICAN COFFEE BUREAU, 120 Wall Street, New York 5, N.Y.

There is nothing so satisfying as a cup of good coffee

creative planning. In this connection, the creative man on the account at the Bureau's advertising agency, Robert W. Orr & Associates, Inc., studied the report and summarized its recommendations in chart form to guide his thinking (see Exhibit 3).

In an attempt to come up with a creative translation which would be the core of the 1956 campaign, some 20 different advertisements were prepared in rough form. All but six of these advertisements were elimi-

Exhibit 2

PAN-AMERICAN COFFEE BUREAU (B)

Bus stop "Coffee-break"

A few minutes ago, a bus stopped at Wayside, U. S. A. A group of strangers got off to stretch and have a snack. Now, they're getting acquainted, American-style — over a good, hot cup of coffee. The figure-conscious girl (who drinks hers black) is telling the businessman (cream, two sugars) about college. The driver (black, with apple pie) is reassuring the motherly-type (light, one sugar) that the bus is on time. When the driver kids the waitress about the coffee, the motherly-type will tell him her recipe for good coffee (two level tablespoons of coffee to each cup). The driver will listen courteously and agree. His wife's been making it that way for years. PAN-AMERICAN COFFEE BUREAU, 120 Wall St., New York 5, N. Y.

There is nothing so satisfying as a cup of good coffee

nated from consideration in discussions between agency and client personnel. The next step was to decide which, if any, of the six advertisements (see Exhibits 4–9) should be used as the keynote for the new campaign.

~~~

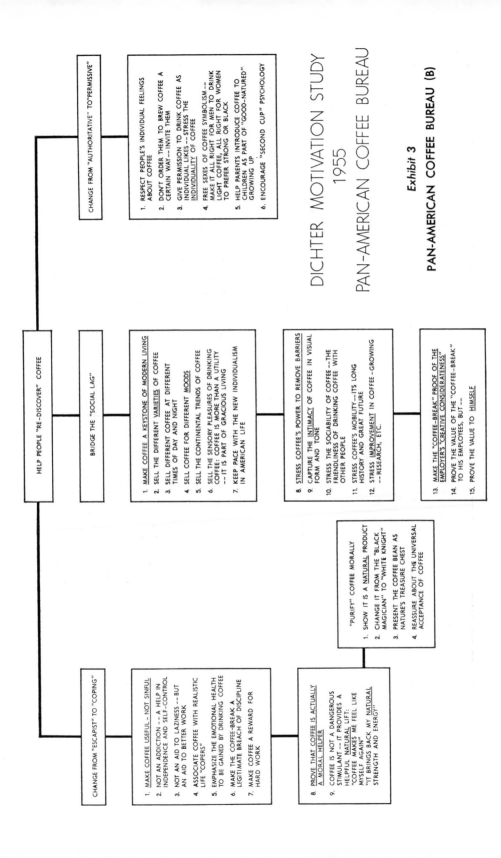

HELP PEOPLE "RE-DISCOVER" COFFEE

CHANGE FROM "AUTHORITATIVE" TO "PERMISSIVE"

1. RESPECT PEOPLE'S INDIVIDUAL FEELINGS ABOUT COFFEE
2. DON'T ORDER THEM TO BREW COFFEE A CERTAIN WAY—INVITE THEM
3. GIVE PERMISSION TO DRINK COFFEE AS INDIVIDUAL LIKES—STRESS THE INDIVIDUALITY OF COFFEE
4. FREE SEXES OF COFFEE SYMBOLISM—MAKE IT ALL RIGHT FOR MEN TO DRINK LIGHT COFFEE, ALL RIGHT FOR WOMEN TO PREFER STRONG OR BLACK
5. HELP PARENTS INTRODUCE COFFEE TO CHILDREN AS PART OF "GOOD-NATURED" GROWING UP
6. ENCOURAGE "SECOND CUP" PSYCHOLOGY

BRIDGE THE "SOCIAL LAG"

1. MAKE COFFEE A KEYSTONE OF MODERN LIVING
2. SELL THE DIFFERENT VARIETIES OF COFFEE
3. SELL DIFFERENT COFFEE AT DIFFERENT TIMES OF DAY AND NIGHT
4. SELL COFFEE FOR DIFFERENT MOODS
5. SELL THE CONTINENTAL TRENDS OF COFFEE
6. SELL THE SENSORY PLEASURES OF DRINKING COFFEE: COFFEE IS MORE THAN A UTILITY --IT IS PART OF GRACIOUS LIVING
7. KEEP PACE WITH THE NEW INDIVIDUALISM IN AMERICAN LIFE

8. STRESS COFFEE'S POWER TO REMOVE BARRIERS
9. CAPTURE THE INTIMACY OF COFFEE IN VISUAL FORM AND TONE
10. STRESS THE SOCIABILITY OF COFFEE—THE FRIENDLINESS OF DRINKING COFFEE WITH OTHER PEOPLE
11. STRESS COFFEE'S MOBILITY—ITS LONG HISTORY AND GREAT FUTURE
12. STRESS IMPROVEMENT IN COFFEE-GROWING --RESEARCH, ETC.

13. MAKE THE "COFFEE-BREAK" PROOF OF THE EMPLOYER'S "CREATIVE CONSIDERATENESS"
14. PROVE THE VALUE OF THE "COFFEE-BREAK" TO HIS EMPLOYEES, BUT --
15. PROVE THE VALUE TO HIMSELF

CHANGE FROM "ESCAPIST" TO "COPING"

1. MAKE COFFEE USEFUL - NOT SINFUL
2. NOT AN ADDICTION -- A HELP IN INDEPENDENCE AND SELF-CONTROL
3. NOT AN AID TO LAZINESS -- BUT AN AID TO BETTER WORK
4. ASSOCIATE COFFEE WITH REALISTIC LIFE "COPERS"
5. EMPHASIZE THE EMOTIONAL HEALTH TO BE GAINED BY DRINKING COFFEE
6. MAKE THE COFFEE-BREAK A LEGITIMATE BREACH OF DISCIPLINE
7. MAKE COFFEE A REWARD FOR HARD WORK

8. PROVE THAT COFFEE IS ACTUALLY A MORAL HELPER
9. COFFEE IS NOT A DANGEROUS STIMULANT -- IT PROVIDES A HELPFUL NATURAL LIFT: "COFFEE MAKES ME FEEL LIKE MYSELF AGAIN" "IT BRINGS BACK MY NATURAL STRENGTH AND ENERGY"

"PURIFY" COFFEE MORALLY

1. SHOW IT IS A NATURAL PRODUCT
2. CHANGE IT FROM THE "BLACK MAGICIAN" TO "WHITE KNIGHT"
3. PRESENT THE COFFEE BEAN AS NATURE'S TREASURE CHEST
4. REASSURE ABOUT THE UNIVERSAL ACCEPTANCE OF COFFEE

DICHTER MOTIVATION STUDY
1955
PAN-AMERICAN COFFEE BUREAU

Exhibit 3

PAN-AMERICAN COFFEE BUREAU (B)

Exhibit 4

PAN-AMERICAN COFFEE BUREAU (B)

There's only one thing better than a cup of Coffee

... and that's a second cup!

What a delicious pick-me-up in that first cup of coffee! What deep-down satisfaction in the second cup. It's a special pleasure to take time to drink it. And later, mid-morning or mid-afternoon, with your "coffee-break" you really relax so that you think better, work better, feel better. There's nothing like good hot coffee with its always refreshing aroma. Nothing else has coffee's own rich flavor. Incidentally, in the evening, have you thought of serving coffee with a little heavy cream floating on the top? It's a touch of elegance that most folks really enjoy. Try it sometime soon.

PAN-AMERICAN COFFEE BUREAU, 120 Wall St., N.Y. 5, N.Y.

**There's nothing so satisfying
as a cup of good coffee**

Exhibit 5

PAN-AMERICAN COFFEE BUREAU (B)

THAT'S COFFEE FOR YOU!

Your lift into today — your joyous wake-me-up — your friendly exhilaration — that's coffee for you! That's coffee whose very aroma is exciting, whose marvelous fragrance is itself a pleasure. And what compares to that deep-down richness of taste? Drink a cup of coffee — do it right now — and discover again how really satisfying it is. PAN-AMERICAN COFFEE BUREAU, 120 Wall St., New York 5, N.Y.

Exhibit 7

PAN-AMERICAN COFFEE BUREAU (B)

Exhibit 6

PAN-AMERICAN COFFEE BUREAU (B)

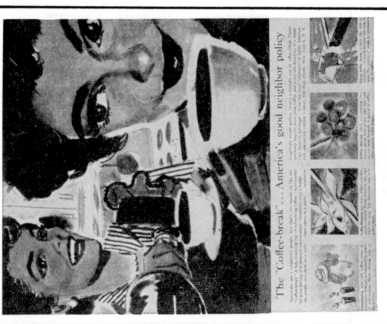

Exhibit 9

PAN-AMERICAN COFFEE BUREAU (B)

Exhibit 8

PAN-AMERICAN COFFEE BUREAU (B)

CASE 13: PAN-AMERICAN COFFEE BUREAU (C)[1]

QUESTIONS TO CONSIDER: (1) *Was a good procedure used to test the six advertisements shown in Case (B)? (2) What alternative procedures might have been employed? (3) Would you agree with the conclusion that advertisement No. 6 was the most effective advertisement? (4) In the light of the information gained from the testing procedure utilized, what recommendations would you make regarding advertising copy for the Bureau's new advertising campaign?*

The Pan-American Coffee Bureau and its advertising agency, Robert Orr & Associates, Inc., worked to develop a consumer advertising campaign for 1956 which would effectively implement the strategy suggested by the study of the meanings of coffee made by The Institute for Motivational Research, Inc. In order to learn more about the relative effectiveness of the six advertisements shown in Case (B), the Bureau employed The Institute for Motivational Research, Inc., to investigate the reactions to them of American coffee drinkers, particularly women. The Institute was asked to determine which of the themes, advertisements, or combinations of advertisements would serve best to further the over-all plan of stimulating a "rediscovery of coffee." In addition, information was to be obtained on how well each of the advertisements succeeded in accomplishing its more specific goals.

The Testing Procedure

The advertisements were tested in interviews with 81 respondents representing each of the four main geographical regions as well as various age, economic, marital status, and coffee consumption categories. Two thirds of the respondents were women. In order that the individual advertisements might be given detailed attention, only three of them were used in any one interview. Two groupings of three advertisements were made on the basis of a content analysis which showed that the six advertisements included three pairs with roughly the same basic theme as follows:

Ads	Theme
1 and 2	Breakfast lift
3 and 4	Neighborliness (good neighbor policy, coffeegrowing)
5 and 6	Coffee is many beverages

The interviews were planned so as to get about an even distribution of the two groups of advertisements (1–3–5 and 2–4–6), and interviewers were instructed to change the sequence of presentation from respondent to respondent.

---

[1] Written by Josheph W. Newman.

The advertisements were shown one at a time in the interviews. The procedure involved three principal phases of questioning with each advertisement. The purpose of the first phase was to get initial over-all impressions. The respondent was shown one advertisement for no more than half a minute, when the advertisement was taken away. During this time he was encouraged to talk freely about his first thoughts and feelings, relating "everything that comes to mind—no matter how unimportant or unrelated it seems to you." The second phase was addressed to getting a more thorough reaction to the copy of the same advertisement which again was given to the respondent who was asked to read the copy aloud. The interviewer was instructed to encourage the respondent to "feel free to say anything and everything, as it occurs to you, even if in the middle of a sentence of reading. Tell me every feeling, reaction, idea that comes to your mind . . ." The interviewer was instructed to probe to try to get at reasons underlying the attitudes expressed. In the third phase, the respondent's attention again was directed to the entire advertisement (picture and copy) and the interviewer was asked to probe deeper for associations and feelings in regard to the advertisement in its entirety.

After the above procedure had been followed for each advertisement, all three of the advertisements were spread out before the respondent who was asked to tell which he liked the best, which he liked the least, and, for both answers, why? After the free flow of reactions was obtained, the respondent was asked: "Which of the advertisements make your mouth water for a cup of coffee?" He then was asked further questions relating to advertisement influence: "How were your feelings or ideas regarding coffee changed or at all influenced by the advertisements?" "Did you discover anything of special interest to you from these advertisements— anything new that you hadn't known before?" In conclusion, he was asked for his reactions to any coffee advertisements he had seen in the past.

Criteria for Viewing Reactions

The reactions of respondents were gauged against two sets of criteria as follows:

1. *General Advertisement Testing Criteria*
   a) To what degree and how frequently did the advertisement permit and evoke reader identification and/or ego-involvement?
   b) To what degree did it produce stimulation of the senses? (Aroma, flavor, taste, appearance.)
   c) To what degree did it arouse desire for immediate use or rehearsal for future use ("the most significant of all reactions").
2. *Specific Criteria: "Goals of Presentation"*
   In addition to the general criteria, specific criteria were arrived at for each advertisement from a content analysis. They were the reactions which the advertisement was intended to evoke in line with the strategy developed from the Institute's study, "A Motivational Research Study of the Role of Coffee in 1955."

Interview reports were analyzed qualitatively to measure the reactions against the criteria. In addition, several quantitative measurements were employed. One, which was used in comparing the three advertisements within each group, included the number of respondents who named each advertisement when asked the question: "Which of the advertisements make your mouth water for a cup of coffee?" Measurements also were made of the frequency of spontaneous expressions of "ego-involvement," "identification," "sensory stimulation," and "desire for immediate use." They facilitated comparisons among all six of the advertisements.

The headline for each advertisement in the test and the number by which the advertisement was identified in Case (B) appear below:

Number	*Headline*
1	There's only one thing better than a cup of Coffee . . .
2	That's Coffee for You
3	The "Coffee-break" . . . America's good neighbor policy
4	"Here I am planting a Coffee tree in Latin America!"
5	"Imagine! Coffee in this exciting new way!" (Coffee Boston)
6	Get all the "breaks" of coffee!

Results of the Inquiry

The results of the research were presented in a 97-page report. In order to indicate its nature, a reasonably complete version of the section on advertisement No. 6 is given in the Appendix to this case. In addition to the main report, a summary was prepared of the analysis and comments and it appears below:

Summary.

1. *Most Effective Advertisement: "Get all the 'breaks' of the coffee!" (No. 6)*

   The one advertisement which proved by far most effective among the six advertisements submitted was "Get all the 'breaks'. . ." We found that it stimulated the senses and whetted the immediate appetite of most respondents most of all; it provided ample opportunity for identification for both women and men without stirring up negative feelings or associations. And it went furthest in prompting what we call the "rediscovery of coffee" as a multifold, helpful and pleasurable beverage, capable of adjusting to any mood or occasion, from the daily morning lift to a festive end of the day.

   Recommendation: Addition of some pictorial human touches to achieve more change and vividness.

2. *Second in Mouth-Watering Appeal: Coffee Boston (No. 5)*

   Ranking second mainly on the basis of strong stimulation of the senses is the Coffee Boston advertisement. It produced a spontaneous desire for immediate use in about half as many respondents as did advertisement No. 6. However, the impression of rich and heavy food, to which the cake greatly contributed, evoked many negative reactions, such as fear of gaining weight, etc. Men, especially, tended to associate the picture with "being a sissy," and to exclude themselves.

   Recommendation: Modification of the cake (change in color and/or removing from focus). Heightening of coffee aroma.

3. *The Breakfast Scene (No. 1) Is Second in Emotional Appeal*

The husband-wife breakfast scene provided an outlet for widespread ego-involvement: Men and women alike liked to identify with and find satisfaction in the breakfast-with-love combination. However, some elements in the picture were apt to confuse or disappoint respondents.

Recommendation: Respondents' wish for more realism should be fulfilled: Morning situation calls for less rigid and complete clothing, and less of a "front." Modify the "big smiles." Integrate coffee better into the situation (pouring!).

4. *"Coffee Klatsch" Appeal Suffers from "Policy" (No. 3)*

The appeal of advertisement No. 3 (two housewives) proved a strong second in ego-involvement—despite some intensive negative reactions, touched off by the attempt to combine "neighborliness" with "good neighborhood *policy*." The widely held negative attitudes spread to the coffeegrowing strip, some data in which nourished suspicion.

Recommendation: Attempt to mix neighborly feelings with "policy" and business should be dropped. Coffeegrowing information, if freed from suspicion-arousing connections, can find a willing audience by providing a tie-in between coffee cultivation and coffee pleasure.

5. *& 6. Lowest in All Categories: "Lift" and "Planting" (Nos. 2 and 4)*

These two advertisements scored lowest in all categories and evoked predominantly negative reactions or indifference.

"Lift" (No. 2): The idea of a pictorial symbolization of the coffee lift was not rejected as such, but only the too energetic feeling tone of the lift as suggested by the picture.

Recommendation: The basic theme and idea of symbolization could be saved, if the "elevation" would be one of *relaxation*, release, and delight, instead of one of weird jet propulsion. Expression and posture of the girl would have to change accordingly. Coffee cup and its content would have to convey sensory pleasure and to prevent "pot" associations.

"Planting" (No. 4): Since the basic idea, as well as its presentation, prevented identification and aroused strong negative feelings in a majority of respondents, no specific recommendations are being made.

Over-all Recommendation: Advertisement No. 6 ("Get all the 'breaks' of coffee!") seems indicated as the key advertisement whose six subthemes can then be developed in more detail, in advertisements along the lines of the breakfast scene (No. 1), the Coffee Boston advertisement (No. 5), and the positive elements of the two housewives (No. 3).

Appendix

EXCERPTS FROM REPORT, "AN INQUIRY INTO THE RELATIVE EFFECTIVENESS OF SIX PAN-AMERICAN COFFEE BUREAU ADS"[1]

In the following pages we shall discuss, on the basis of our findings, to what degree and in what way our respondents reacted to each of the six ads; what feelings, associations, or ideas tended to serve, or to counteract the particular intentions of each ad, as well as the over-all goal of "rediscovery of coffee."

Both types of reactions will be discussed under the headings, "Bridges" and "Barriers," respectively, followed by practical applications after each chapter. A comparative quantitative analysis is contained in the last chapter.

I. AD NO. 6: "GET ALL THE 'BREAKS' OF COFFEE!"

ADVERTISER'S INTENTIONS AND GOALS OF PRESENTATION

Rediscovery:
1. Coffee is many beverages, fits many occasions
2. From utility to pleasure (capture of aroma)

Secondary Goals:
3. Coffee as a helper
4. Neighborliness
5. Housewife's market
6. Invitational, not authoritarian, approach

SUMMARY

According to all qualitative and quantitative results, reactions to this ad showed clearly that it has to a high degree fulfilled its specific intentions, and, at the same time, it has come closest to the general goal of stimulating a "rediscovery" of coffee in readers' minds.

BRIDGES

"That's me!"

None of the other five ads evoked such a strong sense of identification or ego-involvement without which the entire message of the ad could not be conveyed so successfully.

In the following responses the identification is largely based on the fact that the ad was able to "capture the aroma" of coffee, and to touch upon feelings as well as realistic situations which most readers recognized as their own:

". . . all things you could really do with coffee."
The mugs with the hot steaming coffee give such a sense of a *cold morning* and the *pleasant warm feeling of hot coffee* . . . and I like the advice that it gives . . . the extra spoon for the pot is what makes it a real cup of coffee . . . you see with this ad, *I can identify myself . . . find myself . . .*

---

[1] Reproduced here is a reasonably complete version of the section on advertisement No. 6.

(Reads the afternoon break copy) This is true, too . . . this is me . . . it tells my thoughts and ideas . . . it expresses some of the things I feel, such as the lift I get from coffee when fatigued . . .

Oh, this one made me want some coffee. The cups here look like they are just *steaming hot and it looks good and strong*. And this cup here at the top (upper left) *is just the size I drink out of*, so it made me want some. These are all things you could really do with coffee practical.

1. *Rediscovery*

For a great many readers, the ad led toward a real "rediscovery of coffee" as a beverage whose role and potential role in their lives is more important, richer, more manifold and more rewarding than they were conscious of.

". . . all the wonderful occasions."

This really has the feeling of ritual or ceremony—and the wonderful occasions when you have coffee—it justifies your drinking it a 100 times a day if you want to . . . after dinner . . . with your neighbor . . . all the pleasant hours spent over coffee cups . . . It shows you all the different kinds of coffee—and I love different and interesting types of coffee . . . it gives me a sense of well-being—of socialness, of conviviality.

I could really sit right down and have a pot, this is lovely! Gives me a feeling of well-being all day long, very pleasant and satisfying.

. . . it makes you hungry. Makes you wish you could afford to buy more, and had more time to sit around and drink it. Sure looks good. Would probably appeal to ladies more . . . I can see myself telling the fellows to drop by for a cup of coffee . . . But the ad makes you wish you had some, or could get some, anytime.

"Coffee Boston" paved the way to discovery of coffee's "festive" potentials:

Guest coffee—makes you feel this is a very festive way to serve it with the cream on top. The silver service, the tray, looks very inviting; they present a very charming and different way of serving the guests you are entertaining.

. . . I think I will try it the next time I have company. That's the only time I serve sweet cream—when we are entertaining guests.

2. *Capture of Aroma (from Utility to Pleasure)*

Strong sensory stimulation was one of the main keys to open up this ad for the reader and the reader for the ad:

The feeling of the steam rising from the cup gives you the feeling—a reaction to your senses—you can almost feel it touching your lips and mouth. Appeals to the sensory feelings more than the others.

The colors on this ad are very pleasant and what I remember most at such a quick glance was the steam coming forth from each cup of coffee. That particularly impressed me because I abhor cold coffee. I love coffee that is hot—hot to the taste and hot to the touch.

The coffee and the food that goes with it and the coffee pot is all there. The coffee is in the cup—or in all the cups I should say, and it looks ready to be had because of the smoking that is the smoke coming out of the cups —not smoke, but you know what I mean.

"I want coffee right now!"

In some of the following responses one can watch how the ad, by its "capture of the aroma" and its "coffee realism" produces a momentary craving for coffee which becomes strong enough to be expressed in words:

> This ad is so pleasant and relaxing that you want to have a cup of coffee *right now*. There is nothing like a cup of coffee when you are finished shopping. When your feet hurt and you are exhausted from fighting the crowds in the stores, a cup of hot coffee is about the most welcome thing you can have.

> The steaming hot cup of coffee looks so real and so inviting that I would love to have a steaming hot cup of coffee *right now*. When you look at the ad even for a couple of seconds, it makes you want to stop whatever you are doing and enjoy a good cup of coffee.

> This makes your mouth water for coffee. I could go for several cups of coffee *right now*.

> I get a feeling that if I were to see this as I was going through the papers early in the morning at my desk, I would become very impatient for a 10 o'clock "coffee break". . .

3. *Coffee as a Helper*

In the following two respondents, a woman and a man, the ad evoked an awareness of another aspect of "rediscovery" of coffee's useful role as an "emotional food," as a helper of man in coping with the tasks and problems of living:

> I think for a person who is not too well-organized in her housework (and who likes coffee) this might give her ideas on how to work out a schedule so you have time to relax during the day.

> I will say that it is relaxing and does me a lot of good. I think of the times when I have had very exacting problems and I have been at it hot and heavy—sometimes a solution evades me. I stopped, went out, had a cup of coffee. When I came back I found it easier to solve my problem. It may have been the rest but I like to feel that the cup of coffee did it just because I like coffee so much.

4. *Neighborliness*

> It just makes me think of having a few friends in probably and talking with them over some nice hot coffee. Coffee drinking is such a nice *sociable* thing. I really can't separate the idea of friends dropping in or invited over without the idea of the pot brewing on the stove. As soon as I hear the doorbell, and friends drop in, I find myself saying to myself, go put the pot on. If I ever am so busy or distracted that I don't mention the coffee as soon as they get through the door practically, my friends ask, "Ethel, what's wrong, are you sick?"

> (Mid Morning Break) This is nice, too . . . it makes you think of the social sense of coffee . . . and coffee, as far as I am concerned is something social. I like to have coffee with someone . . . just the way I do a cigarette or a cocktail—there's something social about coffee.

"Coffee is a companion when I'm alone . . ."

I have very pleasant associations. It takes the place for me of a companion when I am alone and helps me to relax whatever tensions I may have at anytime. I looked at this ad and felt the need for a cup of coffee. I felt very stimulated.

I find that even taking a coffee break alone with just a paper and a cigarette gives the day a different look.

5. *Coffee as a Helper—Neighborliness—Housewife's Market*

The following response combines the effects of three important appeals and also demonstrates strikingly the degree to which a typical housewife was invited and stimulated by the ad to identify with its pictorial and verbal propositions:

> . . . "the wake-up coffee." Yes, that's me. The first thing in the morning when I wake up—that's what I want—a nice hot cup of coffee. I'm not really awake until that coffee is down. "Mid-morning break." I don't call up a neighbor, but I sit and drink coffee with my daughter-in-law all morning long. She lives upstairs and at about 10:30 she's either down at my house or I'm upstairs and we sit and drink coffee for the rest of the morning. Sometimes we do this at another time of the day, too—that is sometimes twice a day—not only in the morning. I think I get through with the housecleaning as fast as I do because I am thinking about and looking forward to that break with my daughter-in-law. "Afternoon break . . ." If I'm downtown shopping, I nearly always stop and have a cup of coffee. It seems to pick me up, nothing else does. You know how tired you get when you're out shopping. You know there's another couple of stores you feel you just have to do before you go home, but your energy is gone and the thought of going through another revolving door and jostling with the crowd is just too much. But somehow after the coffee break, the thought doesn't seem quite so menacing anymore, and somehow I do manage to go on for another store or two . . .

6. *Invitational, Not Authoritarian Approach*

On earlier occasions, respondents have frequently expressed resentment at what they felt was undue pressure and an authoritarian approach of the advertiser. This ad, although it addresses the consumer on three occasions with certain suggestions ("Add another tablespoon . . ." "Why not serve coffee a new way . . . ?") evoked similar resentment in only about 5% of the people, while a number of others showed acceptance of the way in which these suggestions were expressed:

> (The respondent read the luncheon caption) Now this doesn't high-pressure me—doesn't offend me—it's a suggestion—friendly and nice—have two cups of coffee—and the second cup often does taste better than the first.

> . . . I like the specific suggestions—which are not commands—but pleasant ideas to make you think of coffee all through the day.

BARRIERS

There were very few negative feelings aroused by this ad.

1. *"Too much to look at . . ."*

The lack of a "central area" was felt in one way or another by about 2% of our respondents. But even some of these were made to feel like having coffee.

2. *"Another tablespoon" stirs up price resentment*

Price resentment still was found smouldering beneath the surface in a number of people. In two respondents, it was stirred up by the suggestion to add another tablespoon.

> And I don't like my coffee too strong. "Just add another tablespoon to the pot" just sounds like a coffee company's propaganda to me, to get some more coffee in there.

3. *Details of Pictorial Presentation*

   a) "It has black coffee and that's not for me . . ."

   > (Wake-up coffee): I'm wondering whether they mean instantaneous coffee—I guess not. The thing that stands out there is the Father on the cup. I have several of those mugs at home. And the toaster standing there makes sort of a nice ensemble. But it still has black coffee and that's not for me. I'd rather like to see the creamer pitcher and sugar bowl standing nearby.

   b) *Food in picture arouses negative feelings*

   > I get the same reaction as when you see artificial food in a restaurant window. You know what I mean, it's something I don't like.

   > I don't like the picture of the turkey . . . I don't like food on the table with coffee at dinner . . . it's rather repelling . . . (Respondent read the last caption.) This is very interesting . . . I wonder what kind of coffee to use . . . just regular coffee do you think? It gives you a sense of giving yourself a break with a coffee break . . . I like the look of the warm, steaming cups of coffee . . . the only thing that rather offends me is the turkey, as I said, and the stale white bread in the sandwich.

   c) *Mother begrudges father*

   > I see father likes the big cup; I wonder what mother does. I suppose there are still some families where father gets a big cup.

   d) *Dripolator and carafe*

   > One thing strikes me as backwards in these two pictures. The dripolator is on the table for company, and the nicer carafe is on the table for what appears to be a lunch for someone all by themselves.

PRACTICAL APPLICATIONS

1. Perhaps a few human touches could be added to the pictures, so as to break the pattern in an optimal way. It may be suggestions of human presence, adjusted to time of day and occasion; a hand and dressed-up sleeve at dinner, a handbag, etc.
2. Color of coffee itself could be varied (cream pitcher and sugar bowl suggested).
3. Sandwich less "stale" and "artificial," perhaps by changing the bread and red color in it.
4. On dinner table—suggestions: Replace turkey by almost finished plate; white and festive table cloth, for a change; demitasse.
5. Wake-up coffee: "mother" feels she deserves a cup, too—perhaps smaller.
6. Perhaps carafe and dripolator should be exchanged between pictures 3 and 6.
7. Mid-morning: Wall clock is felt to suggest office, not kitchen or living room. Remedy: smaller table clock.

8. "Add another tablespoon" was interpreted by some as referring to instant coffee. If it is the intention to avoid this impression, without change in copy, a pictorial suggestion is indicated.
9. Top headline: Dr. Dichter suggests that the "all" be emphasized.

~ ~ ~

CASE 14: MARCUS TYLER & ASSOCIATES, INC. (A)[1]

QUESTION TO CONSIDER: *How should Mr. Smallwood test advertisements for the New England Brewing Company?*

In December 1956, Mr. Edwin Smallwood, account executive in charge of the account of the New England Brewing Company for Marcus Tyler & Associates, Inc., a Boston advertising agency, was concerned with the testing of several alternative copy themes for "New England" ale, one of which was to be the copy theme for an advertising campaign to be run in the period May–August 1957.

Background of the Account

For many years before World War II, according to Mr. Smallwood, the New England Brewing Company had been a moderately successful marketer of a heavy ale, which had been sold principally through taverns in draught form. After the war the company had experienced severe declines in sales, partially because the New England market had rapidly changed from an ale market to a beer market and partially because the company's management had not been aggressive promoters. In 1949 new management assumed control of the company and, in the next few years, attempted to revitalize the company through the marketing of bottled and canned ale, the introduction of a new, light beer, and the use of an aggressive sales promotion program. For a number of reasons the moves of the new management failed to increase sales or return a profit so that the company was sold to a group of local businessmen in early 1955.

Under the third management group, a number of changes were made. Despite the decreasing size of the total ale market, it was decided that the company should concentrate on the ale market because funds were not available to compete in the beer market, where sizable funds were required to compete against the large regional and national brewers. In line with this policy decision, the company's ale packages were redesigned, so that they were, in the opinion of management, attractive and "modern." The new packages were introduced to the market in mid-1955, the introduction being supported by a heavy schedule of newspaper advertising which emphasized "New England Ale—The Modern Ale."

Subsequently, the company's sales increased, primarily, it was believed,

---

[1] All names fictitious. Written by Martin V. Marshall.

as the result of a series of special consumer price deals. Approximately every other month from June 1955 until October 1956, the company offered some form of price inducement to consumers. Although these deals increased sales, they did not do so at a profit. Hence, in the latter part of 1956, the company's management decided to shift marketing emphasis from price promotion to some type of strong brand advertising, on the premise "that if we can't build a strong brand pull for our ale, then we might as well go out of business." In order to obtain new thinking, the company's management selected a new advertising agency, Marcus Tyler & Associates, Inc. The Tyler agency was to assume responsibility for the account on April 1, 1957.

Agency Thinking on Copy Themes

As a first step in handling the new account, Mr. Smallwood spent a good deal of time in the field talking with ale consumers, "package" store owners and clerks, tavern owners and bartenders, and malt beverage distributors. In addition, he examined several published studies of malt beverage consumption, including the beer study sponsored by the *Chicago Tribune*. As a result of this work, Mr. Smallwood came to several conclusions regarding copy themes for New England Ale.

First, he did not believe that the agency could determine why consumers purchased ale without undertaking extensive consumer research, and that such research was currently beyond the means of the New England Brewing Company. Second, he did not feel that his discussions with the trade and consumers had allowed him to develop any firm convictions regarding what might be weak or strong selling appeals for New England Ale. Finally, he thought that those brewers who had been successful in the building of strong brands for their ales had done so as the result of "pounding away month after month on a single theme with imaginative variation."

As a second step in handling the account, Mr. Smallwood had the agency's copy department develop a number of layouts suitable for use in newspapers, which was one medium the agency proposed to use in the summer campaign. These layouts included only headlines and illustrations. Then company and agency executives analyzed the layouts and selected five as being "potentially promising." A description of these layouts follows:

Layout No. 1 consisted of a large illustration of a well-known sports personality and the headline: "I Like New England Ale, because It's *Smooth* and *Hearty*." (It was proposed that this approach would require the use of four or five well-known New Englanders during the campaign with minor variations in testimonials.)

Layout No. 2 placed emphasis on the fact that New England Ale was brewed for the taste of New Englanders. A large illustration showed a map of New England with the state of Vermont emphasized. The headline read: "In Vermont, in All New England, It's Hearty New England Ale—Brewed for New Englanders." (It was proposed that this approach feature numerous New England states, cities, and towns.)

Layout No. 3 consisted of a large illustration of a middle-aged man in work clothes relaxing in an easy chair in his home and the headline: "Really Hits the Spot at the End of the Day . . . Yes Sir . . . Good Old New England Ale!" (It was proposed that this approach depict many "ordinary individuals relaxing with a bottle of New England Ale in everyday settings.")

Layout No. 4 sought to associate New England Ale with modernity. The illustration consisted of a glistening bottle of New England Ale against a background which showed a hi-fi set. The headline read: "For the 1 Man in 20 Who Wants the Best—Smooth, Hearty, New England Ale." (It was proposed that this approach feature many articles having a connotation of modernity, such as contemporary furniture, sports cars, power boats, and barbecue pits.)

Layout No. 5 consisted of an illustration of a man pausing in his work on a kitchen cabinet and the headline: "New England Ale—the Ale that Satisfies." (It was proposed in this approach to illustrate men in a number of do-it-yourself jobs, pausing in their work to enjoy New England Ale.)

As a third step, Mr. Smallwood proposed to test the five layouts through the use of some form of consumer jury test.

Testing Alternatives

Because of the limited promotional funds available to the company, Mr. Smallwood could not spend much money on testing. Consequently, he was seeking to test the layouts through the use of some form of consumer jury test which would, on the one hand, be inexpensive and, on the other hand, reliable.

Mr. Smallwood had obtained a list of 216 ale drinkers from 32 packaged liquor stores in the Greater Boston area. He proposed to use this list as the basis for selecting a consumer jury. In undertaking a test, he believed that there were three alternatives.

First, he could arrange for groups of ten to twenty of the men on his list to meet in the agency's office at night and there be asked to rank the layouts on some basis. He believed that he could obtain the co-operation of a reasonable number of men for a payment of $5.00 or $10 for their time. Second, he thought that it would be possible to conduct a test by mail. The five layouts could be printed on a single sheet of paper and sent to a list of ale drinkers along with an instruction sheet and a rank list. This alternative would allow the use of ale drinkers throughout New England. Mr. Smallwood believed he could use the mail approach at a cost of about 50 cents a name. He did not know what rate of return he might expect, but he understood that some advertisers had obtained returns in excess of 10%. Finally, he could use the services of a local marketing research organization which was willing to undertake in-home interviews in the Greater Boston area for $5.00 a call.

Tentatively, Mr. Smallwood believed that he would employ the order of rank method, i.e., the respondents would be asked to decide which layout was best, next best, and so on. He was not yet sure of how to define "best." He had drawn up a list of questions which might be asked respondents, one of which had to be chosen for use in the test. Mr. Smallwood's list of questions follows:

1. Which one of these advertisements would most likely lead you to buy "New England Ale?"
2. Which one of these advertisements do you like best?
3. Which one of these advertisements do you think would most likely lead people to buy "New England Ale"?
4. Which one of these advertisements do you find most interesting?
5. Which one of these advertisements would you most likely read?

If Mr. Smallwood used either the captive jury or in-home interviews, he thought that he might employ the paired comparison method rather than the order-of-rank method, i.e., each respondent would be asked to state a preference for each layout relative to every other layout. This method would require the respondent to make ten choices rather than four choices on each question.

If this method of testing produced significant results, Mr. Smallwood proposed to recommend a single copy theme to the executives of the New England Brewing Company, which would be used in newspapers, radio announcements, and television announcements.

~~~

CASE 15: BELL AND HOWELL COMPANY[1]

QUESTIONS TO CONSIDER: *(1) Were good procedures employed to test the effectiveness of Bell and Howell's 1955 advertising campaign? (2) What alternative approaches might have been used? (3) What recommendations would you make to management with respect to future advertisements?*

In the fall of 1955 executives of Bell and Howell Company, a 50-year-old Chicago manufacturer of quality amateur motion-picture equipment, were considering which of two alternative advertising approaches to employ in the company's 1956 advertising campaign. The 1955 advertisements had featured, for the first time, an editorial-style format, while advertisements before 1955 had featured a product-oriented format. In their deliberations, the executives considered the findings of a research

---

[1] Written by David W. Nylen.

study conducted by their advertising agency, McCann-Erickson, Inc., on the effectiveness of the 1955 advertising campaign.

Bell and Howell Marketing Program

Bell and Howell Company was founded in 1907 by Messrs. Bell and Howell to produce high-quality motion-picture equipment. In the 1920's the company started manufacturing a line of 16 millimeter home movie cameras and projectors, and in the 1930's a line of 8 millimeter home movie equipment. These two lines gradually became the company's principal products.

Before World War II the company's high-quality and high-priced products were manufactured on an individual, craft basis. However, with the rapid postwar growth of the market for amateur camera equipment, Bell and Howell established mass-production facilities in order to share in the market growth. The greater part of the market growth was not in high-priced camera equipment for the serious amateur, the market in which Bell and Howell had specialized, but in the low-priced, casual hobbiest market. In 1954 in order to supply the low-priced market, Bell and Howell introduced an 8 millimeter movie camera retailing for $49.95 and an 8 millimeter motion-picture projector for $99.95. The new movie camera featured a simplified lens aperture setting device, the "sun dial," which eliminated the use of the f-stop system of setting the correct lens opening.

In addition to the new low-priced line, Bell and Howell in 1955 sold 8 millimeter cameras retailing for $90 to $200 and 8 millimeter projectors to $200. Bell and Howell's 16 millimeter movie cameras, which found a market with the more serious amateurs, started in retail price at $180 and went to several thousand dollars, depending upon the accessories included. Sixteen millimeter projectors started at $200 retail. In addition to cameras and projectors, Bell and Howell sold a line of photographic accessories.

In January 1954 Bell and Howell acquired Three Dimension Company, the world's largest manufacturer of slide projectors, which were sold under the TDC brand name. Three Dimension Company also produced tape recorders. The acquisition of new product lines gave Bell and Howell sales of over $40 million in 1954.

Bell and Howell products were distributed nationally through camera specialty stores by a direct sales force in 1955 of 30 men. There was also a limited amount of distribution through department stores, and the company was adding distribution through retail drugstores for the lower-priced lines.

Kodak and Bell and Howell were the largest factors in the movie equipment market with additional competition from Keystone, Revere, DeJur, and Bolex, a Swiss import. Principal competition to Bell and Howell in the slide projector market came from Argus and Kodak. With a few exceptions, the marketing program of competition was similar to Bell and

Howell's. Some camera equipment manufacturers used wholesalers to distribute their equipment to camera specialty shops. Kodak had extended distribution of its low-priced lines to drugstores more aggressively than had other camera manufacturers.

Bell and Howell Advertising

Bell and Howell had advertised in national consumer magazines for many years. The advertisements illustrated specific Bell and Howell products, with copy emphasizing the high quality of the equipment. Executives of Bell and Howell believed that the advertisements had assisted in establishing Bell and Howell's reputation as a manufacturer of highest quality motion-picture equipment.

In 1954 when Bell and Howell introduced its new low-priced line—an 8 millimeter camera for $49.95 and an 8 millimeter projector for $99.95— consumer advertising featured these products. The advertisements for the new line contained a large illustration of the movie camera, and the advertising copy described product features, the ease of operation, and the low price. These advertisements appeared 13 times in *Life* and six times in *Parents* as half pages, two-thirds pages, and full pages in black and white. The sizes of advertisements and dates of insertions were varied so as to give the greatest advertising emphasis prior to the periods of greatest sales volume—Christmas and spring.

In addition to advertising of the new low-priced line, Bell and Howell continued in 1954 to advertise the more expensive 16 millimeter products in *Holiday, National Geographic, Time,* and *Newsweek.* These magazines were chosen because of the high income of their readers. The advertisements were less than full page in size, featured a specific product, and emphasized the high quality of the product.

Bell and Howell also advertised extensively in nonconsumer magazines. The company used camera fan magazines such as *Modern Photography* and *Popular Photography;* dealer trade magazines such as *Photo Dealer;* educational magazines such as *The Instructor;* and business magazines such as *Sales Management.* Bell and Howell did not grant cooperative advertising allowances to dealers, although one competitor, Keystone, did grant an allowance. It was estimated by Bell and Howell that Kodak received the greatest dealer advertising support; Keystone was second; and Bell and Howell was a close third.

Bell and Howell's New Advertising Approach

In late 1954 executives of Bell and Howell and their advertising agency, McCann-Erickson, Inc., decided to use a new approach in the 1955 consumer advertising campaign. The executives were concerned that advertisements such as were used in 1954 featuring a low-priced product would destroy the quality image of Bell and Howell and the company's products. In the 1955 consumer advertisements, rather than featuring a specific product, the advertisements had an editorial format that stressed the benefits to be derived from owning a camera. Each advertisement had a large, human interest, family illustration with copy explaining that ownership of a movie camera permitted recording such scenes. The copy included information on a specific camera which was also illustrated. Two additional smaller illustrations and copy blocks were included, one featuring a movie projector and the other one featuring a slide projector.

The advertising agency, in a presentation explaining the new advertising concept, stated, "This [new] advertising is different in its attempt to sell specific products and yet do so within a broader integrated concept;

Exhibit 1
BELL AND HOWELL COMPANY
1955 Consumer Advertising Media Schedule

Publication	Date	Size of Insertion
Life	January 17	Page
Parents	February	Page
Life	February 14	Page
Sports Illustrated	February 14	Page
Life	March 14	Page
Parents	April	Page
Life	April 11	Page
Sports Illustrated	April 18	Page
Life	May 9	Page
Sports Illustrated	May 23	Page
Parents	June	Page
Holiday	June	Page
Esquire	June	Page
Life	June 27	Page
Holiday	July	Page
Sports Illustrated	July 4	Page
Life	July 18	Page
Parents	August	Page
Sports Illustrated	September 12	Page
Life	September 19	Page
Parents	October	Page
Holiday	October	Page
Sports Illustrated	October 10	⅓ page
Life	October 17	½ page
Sports Illustrated	October 31	⅓ page
Holiday	November	Page
Time	November 7	2-page spread
Sports Illustrated	November 14	⅓ page
Life	November 14	½ page
Life	November 21	2-page spread
Life	November 28	⅓ page
Parents	December	Page
Holiday	December	2-page spread
Esquire	December	2-page spread
Life	December 5	Page

namely, through communicating an image of authority, vitality, and quality about Bell and Howell and its products."

The new advertisements were pretested by showing consumers the contemplated advertisements and asking a series of depth questions designed to determine what ideas consumers retained from the advertisement and how convincing and believable the advertisements were. Results of the test convinced the executives that the new advertisements conveyed with believability the intended ideas of Bell and Howell's authority, vitality, and quality, and therefore it was decided to use the new approach.

The media schedule used in 1955 was similar to the 1954 schedule. *Life* and *Parents* were used for the advertisements for low-priced equipment; and *Sports Illustrated, Holiday, Esquire,* and *Time* were used for higher-priced equipment. The complete 1955 consumer advertising media schedule is shown in Exhibit 1.

Testing the Shorter-Term Effectiveness of 1955 Campaign

In August 1955, after the new advertising campaign had run for about seven months, Bell and Howell executives became increasingly concerned about the short-term effectiveness of the new campaign. While executives were convinced from the pretest that over the long term the new campaign would convey the image of authority, vitality, and quality desired for Bell and Howell, they were concerned that in the shorter term the advertisements were not securing registration of the company name, association of products with that name, or association of specific selling ideas with the product and the brand name. At the company's request, McCann-Erickson conducted a research study to determine to what extent the 1955 campaign sacrificed short-term effectiveness in the interest of long-term objectives.

Because the long-term objective of the 1955 campaign was qualitative and therefore difficult to measure accurately, the research concentrated on measuring the short-term effectiveness of two advertisements: (1) in terms of registration of the advertiser's name and the products being advertised, and (2) in terms of impact, the ability of consumers to recall specific selling ideas. Two advertisements, "A" and "B," were tested. Advertisement "A," which is shown in Exhibit 2, was especially designed for the test to represent straight product selling. Advertisement "B," which is shown in Exhibit 3, was one of the advertisements used in the 1955 campaign. Both advertisements contained illustrations and copy concerning the same three products with the same degree of emphasis.

Method Used for Advertising Study

The McCann-Erickson research report contained the following description of the research method used in the study:

Two groups of respondents were obtained. Each group was matched with the other with regard to important criteria, such as camera equipment buying intent, socioeconomic status, age and education. A total of 309 interviews were completed.

Each group was given the same folder of nine page black and white advertisements. (An assortment of advertisements from several different product fields.) A tenth advertisement was included in each folder. For one group, Bell

Exhibit 2

BELL AND HOWELL COMPANY

Advertisement "A"

Exclusive Sun Dial makes movies as easy as snapshots!

BELL & HOWELL 220 WILSHIRE—$49.95! Perfect home movies with the ease and low cost of snapshots is the promise the 220 makes to thrifty, active families. Set Sun Dial to suit lighting conditions, sight and shoot. The 220 is the *only* 8mm cam-

era with wide-angle lens as standard equipment. All metal case protects tooled precision of Bell & Howell craftsmen. This top quality costs a low $49.95, and the results you get are priceless! Send today for your *free copy* of "Tips on Making Home Movies."

DO-IT-YOURSELF SOUND MOVIES are easy as tape recording with the Filmosound 202 projector. You just add your own sound *right on film* while picture is projected. Clutch stops motion for "stills." Switch reverses film direction. Wide use of the 202 in homes, schools and industry is proof of Bell & Howell leadership

HONORARY ACADEMY AWARD 1954 To Bell & Howell for 47 Years of Pioneering Contributions to the Motion Picture Industry

COLOR SLIDE FAN? TDC's Headliner 300 is America's most outstanding slide projector value. Why? Performance and price! Powerful 300-watt lamp is blower-cooled. With Selectron changer that selects, changes and refiles slides, only $49.00

Bell & Howell 7100 McCormick Road · Chicago 45, Illinois

Exhibit 3

BELL AND HOWELL COMPANY

Advertisement "B"

BELL & HOWELL WAS THERE

IT TOOK A MOVIE CAMERA to catch Curtis Van's "look-at-me" action on his first two-wheeler bike. You can be an expert at preserving family events like this *in color* with your Bell & Howell 220 Wilshire. Simply set Sun Dial to suit lighting conditions, sight and shoot. Easy as snapshots. The 220 is the only 8mm camera with wide-angle lens as standard equipment. Just $49.95, and the results are priceless! *Free, "Tips on Making Home Movies."* Write Bell & Howell, Dept. L-4, Chicago 45, Illinois.

HONORARY ACADEMY AWARD 1954 To Bell & Howell for 47 Years of Pioneering Contributions to the Motion Picture Industry.

BRING 'EM HOME ALIVE! You can "stroll" through the zoo at your leisure with TDC's Headliner 300, America's most outstanding slide projector value. Blower-cooled 300-watt lamp. With Selectron changer that selects, changes and refiles, only $49.99

FORMULA FOR LAB SAFETY: Add sound to sight with Bell & Howell's Filmosound 202 projector. In scene from school-made movie, student shows caution in acid test. Instructor later describes action *right on the film.* Business leaders use the 202 to reach customers, teach employees. Write for name of your nearest dealer.

experience leads to **Bell & Howell**

and Howell Company advertisement "A" was included and for the other group, Bell and Howell Company advertisement "B" was included.

All respondents were given one of the two folders of ten advertisements. They were asked to look through the folder as though it were a magazine. They were told to take as much time as they liked, and the interviewer encouraged the respondent to at least look at each page.

The folders were then taken away from the respondents, and with the folders closed, a number of questions were asked. Tabulations of these questions determined:

Which of the two ways of advertising (ad "A" or ad "B") produced more recall and identification of Bell and Howell Company.

Which of the two ways of advertising produced more recall of specific products advertised.

Which of the two ways of advertising produced more recall of specific parts of the advertisements, particularly any selling points.

In addition, all respondents who recalled seeing the Bell and Howell Company advertisements were asked to discuss whatever ideas about Bell and Howell Company that came to their mind as a result of seeing the advertisement they just saw.

Following the Registration and Impact Study part of the interview, each respondent was then shown the Bell and Howell Company advertisement again. In addition, he was also shown the Bell and Howell Company advertisement not included in his particular folder.

The respondents were requested to look at both advertisements together. They were then asked to discuss the advertisements, with the discussion being guided by the interviewer to elicit attitude with regard to the relative ability of the advertisements to convince the respondent to buy the products advertised.

This part of the interview was used to evaluate the information from the Registration and Impact Study . . . to help understand why the two groups reacted as they did.

Findings of the Advertising Study

Advertisements "A" and "B" were about equally successful in name registration, although advertisement "A" did a better job in this respect with nonprospective camera buyers than did advertisement "B." Advertisement "A" produced greater recall of the three products being advertised, although in both advertisements there was a sharp drop off in the number of people who could recall that a movie projector and a slide projector were advertised. Only a third of the respondents could recall the movie projector, and less than one half of this number could recall the slide projector. The advertising agency attributed the drop off in recall for the slide projector to the fact that prospects for movie cameras were not usually prospects for slide projectors; therefore any advertisement featuring movie cameras tended to screen out slide projector prospects.

The research also revealed that the movie camera prospect and the slide projector prospect had a different attitude toward photography as a hobby. The movie camera or movie projector prospect was found unsophisticated with regard to photographic technique and equipment. He was found to desire simplicity of equipment operation. The slide projector prospect, on the other hand, was found greatly interested in photographic technique and equipment specifications.

As would be expected, advertisement "A" was more successful than advertisement "B" in communicating features of the 8 millimeter camera. Advertisement "B," on the other hand, generated more ideas about picture taking in general. Advertisement "A" also generated greater recall than advertisement "B" of product points on the movie projector and slide projector, although there were very few comments on any features of these two products.

The research showed a wide difference in recall between prospective camera buyers and nonprospective buyers. The prospect was found more interested in camera or projector product features and details than the nonprospect who was more interested in the general benefits of picture taking itself. The tabulations showed little difference in recall between men and women, although advertisement "B" with a family interest illustration was of slightly greater interest to women than to men.

As executives of Bell and Howell reviewed the company's previous consumer advertising programs and results of the McCann-Erickson research study, they attempted to decide whether the company should continue the editorial type consumer advertisements (such as Exhibit 3) or return to product-oriented advertisements (such as Exhibit 2), which were used in years before 1955.

~~~

CASE 16: PAN-AMERICAN COFFEE BUREAU (D)[1]

QUESTIONS TO CONSIDER: (1) What does the Starch Readership Service measure? (2) What conclusions do you draw from the Starch Ratings of the Bureau advertisements? (3) As the result of considering the Starch Ratings, what changes, if any, would you suggest making in the Bureau's advertising?

In the summer of 1957, executives of the Pan-American Coffee Bureau and the Bureau's advertising agency, Fuller & Smith & Ross, began to plan an advertising campaign for the first half of 1958 which would be effective in increasing coffee consumption in the United States. In this connection the marketing situation and past promotional efforts were reviewed.

The Bureau carried on a variety of research and promotional activities through its specialized departments: advertising, consumer services, public relations, and research. It had an annual budget of about $1,500,000, of which approximately half was spent for consumer advertising.

In its consumer advertising run from 1950 to 1956, the Bureau had promoted the "coffee break." In 1955, for example, the campaign had consisted largely of full-page, black-and-white advertisements once a month in both Life and The Saturday Evening Post; "stress-and-strain" situations were portrayed in large photographs. In addition to calling attention to coffee's role as a stimulant, the advertisements emphasized "Enjoy coffee often—and make it right. Use 2 level tablespoons (or 1 standard coffee measure for every cup)."

---

[1] Written by Joseph W. Newman.

In an effort to provide a basis for preparing more effective advertising, the Bureau in 1955 employed The Institute for Motivational Research, Inc., to conduct research. A new consumer advertising campaign subsequently was prepared on the basis of the findings and recommendation as set forth in the report, "A Motivational Research Study on the Role of Coffee in 1955," and on the basis of later field testing by the Institute of the relative effectiveness of six advertisements prepared in the process of developing an effective creative translation of the advertising strategy.

The change in advertising approach and how it was effected is illustrated in the first three advertisements which appeared in color in *The Saturday Evening Post* and the *Ladies' Home Journal* starting in March 1956. Emphasis was shifted gradually from the "coffee break" to the new theme of helping people rediscover coffee. The headline of the first advertisement was "Good time for a 'coffee-break'!" (See Exhibit 1.) The headline of the second advertisement was "Get *all* the 'breaks' of coffee!"[2] (See Exhibit 2.) Both advertisements included six pictures to show coffee served attractively in different ways at different times of the day and used the slogan, "There is nothing so satisfying as a cup of *good* coffee." The reader was invited to try given brewing directions.

In the third advertisement, "coffee-break" was dropped from the headline which read "It's a *good* day with coffee" (see Exhibit 3). The copy under the first of six illustrations read: "Good morning! Start the day with the wake-up aroma of good, hot coffee—then enjoy the coffee itself (*extra*-strong, the way folks like it for breakfast)." This copy appeared under the second photograph: "Good neighbor. It's the friendly thing to do, having a mid-morning 'Coffee-break' with your neighbor. (Your husband's probably having coffee at work.)" The last picture featured a special coffee and the copy read "Good idea! Treat guests to simple Caffè Cappuccino: add steaming milk to strong coffee (half and half). Dust cinnamon over the top. Superb."

The findings of the motivational study also were used in the development of a promotional campaign for iced coffee which many people in the industry felt could not be sold successfully. Coffee consumption in the three months of June, July, and August had been 16% below the average for the other three quarters of the year, and Dr. James E. Wood, director of research for the Coffee Bureau, estimated that this slump cost the coffee industry about $100,000,000 in sales annually.

To start the campaign for iced coffee, a three-page, gatefold advertisement was run in the June 2, 1956 issue of *The Saturday Evening Post* (see Exhibit 4). Using colored photographs, the advertisement featured six different ways of serving iced coffee; (1) "Coffee Float—drop a generous amount of your favorite ice cream into good iced coffee"; (2) "Iced Coffee Mocha—add a teaspoon of chocolate syrup or cocoa per cup";

---

[2] This advertisement essentially was the one which won the field test, modified to incorporate suggestions growing out of the research.

Exhibit 1

PAN-AMERICAN COFFEE BUREAU (D)

Good time for a "Coffee-break"!

First pleasure of the day is the exhilarating, familiar aroma of brewing coffee—then comes the coffee itself! It's made a bit stronger as a "wake-me-up."

Mid-morning "Coffee-break"—a helpful break in housekeeping routine—and the chance for a neighborly chat. Doesn't time pass pleasantly over coffee?

Lunch on left-overs can be delicious — especially with good, fresh coffee! There's only one thing better than a cup of coffee—and that's a second cup!

Shopping can be tiring—until you perk up with a mid-afternoon "Coffee-break" — maybe with a snack. See how quickly you feel like yourself again.

Dinner coffee at your favorite restaurant can be a special taste adventure. Ask for spicy Café Brûlot or Caffè Espresso with a twist of lemon peel!

Why not make your coffee as the experts do? Drip, percolator, or vacuum methods, use 1 Standard Coffee Measure to each 6 ounces of clear, cold water.

©1956

There is nothing so satisfying as a cup of good coffee
PAN-AMERICAN COFFEE BUREAU, 120 Wall Street, New York 5, N. Y.

(3) "Spiced Iced Coffee—pour 3 cups of hot, double-strength coffee over 2 cinnamon sticks, 4 cloves and 4 allspice berries"; (4) "Iced Coffee Junior —sweeten the youngster's milk a little and color it with the cold coffee— you're the best judge of the amount"; (5) "Coffee Julep—add a dash of

Exhibit 2

PAN-AMERICAN COFFEE BUREAU (D)

Get all the "breaks" of Coffee!

Wake-up coffee. Nothing else starts a day so right! Especially when you use 1 Standard Coffee Measure to each 6 oz. of clear, cold water, like the experts.

Mid-morning break. All's quiet on the home front. Why not call in a neighbor for a friendly cup? (Your husband's enjoying a "Coffee-break" at work.)

Luncheon coffee. Even the simplest bill of fare looks good with a fresh, steaming cup of coffee alongside. (The second cup tastes even better than the first!)

Afternoon break. It's much more fun to shop these days—but still pretty tiring. Doesn't that cup of coffee taste good? It seems to bring your strength back.

Dinner coffee. Nothing finishes a meal in such fine style as coffee. It tastes wonderful – and makes an occasion out of every meal you put before the family.

Guest coffee. Some evening, try coffee a new way! Coffee Boston, for instance. Just float a layer of cream on top; sip your coffee through it. Delicious!
© 1955

There is nothing so satisfying as a cup of good coffee
PAN-AMERICAN COFFEE BUREAU, 120 Wall Street, New York 5, N.Y.

mint flavor and serve in silver or aluminum cups, well-frosted"; and (6) "Iced Coffee Viennese—topped with a snowy swirl of whipped cream." The advertisement also featured "three ways to make delicious iced coffee every time!" because it was felt that improperly made and served iced coffee had been a major barrier to increased consumption in the past. A similar single-page version of this advertisement appeared in *Look* magazine late in June.

The Bureau's director of consumer services prepared a 48-page booklet, *Fun with Coffee,* which represented a collection of "the world's finest coffee recipes—100 different ways to enjoy America's favorite beverage." The iced coffee advertisements described above contained a coupon which readers could use to send with 25 cents for a copy of the recipe booklet.

Various point-of-sale material was prepared for us in food stores including a colorful "Cool off with Coffee" mobile with glasses of iced coffee hanging from it, and pads of recipes for making iced coffee.

Various steps were taken to inform the trade of the motivational study and to invite roasters to make use of the findings in advertising their own brands of coffee. The research and the Bureau's advertising and promotion plans were among the topics emphasized at regional seminars for coffee roasters and others of the industry held early in 1956 in New York, Chicago, New Orleans, and San Francisco. Several articles relating to the promotion of iced coffee appeared in the February 1956 issue of *Coffee and Tea Industries,* a trade publication. The summer slump in coffee consumption was discussed by Dr. Wood in one article and in another, Mr. Edward E. Van Horn, the Bureau's director of advertising, described the 1956 advertising and promotion plans for iced coffee. In a third article, entitled "The Conflict of Iced Coffee," Dr. Ernest Dichter, president of The Institute for Motivational Research, Inc., wrote about consumer attitudes and how they might be turned into promotional assets for iced coffee.

In addition to printing the complete report of findings of the motivational study, the Bureau prepared a 12-page summary of it for distribution within the coffee industry. Entitled "New Horizons for Coffee Promotion," the summary was organized around these recommendations for promotion "to help people rediscover coffee in all of its many aspects:

1. Feature coffee as a beverage to heighten the pleasures of life; give it the variety required by modern living.
2. Dramatize coffee's role of helping people to meet with everyday problems.
3. Promote the 'coffee-break' in all of its implications.
4. Remove consumer doubts about coffee drinking.
5. Change from a dictatorial to an invitational approach in recommending coffee brewing methods.
6. Approach the teen-age market with care and consideration."

In addition to the advertisements described earlier, three others were run in 1956 and two more in early 1957 in both *The Saturday Evening Post* and *Ladies' Home Journal* (see Exhibits 5–9). One of the 1957 advertisements, bearing the headline "How to make a good cup of coffee!" also was run in the April 1957 issue of *Seventeen.*

Exhibit 3

PAN-AMERICAN COFFEE BUREAU (D)

It's a good day with Coffee!

Good morning! Start the day with the wake-up aroma of good, hot coffee—then enjoy the coffee itself (*extra*-strong, the way folks like it for breakfast).

Good neighbor. It's the friendly thing to do — having a mid-morning "Coffee-break" with your neighbor. (Your husband's probably having coffee at work.)

Good eating. Good coffee makes even the simplest lunch taste better. Coffee seems to go just right with *everything* — and every time, too.

Good feeling. What a relief to be off your feet a few minutes during the mid-afternoon. Your "Coffee-break" perks you up so pleasantly!

Good evening. Perfect finish to supper — *coffee* made the way the experts do: 1 Standard Coffee Measure to each 6 ounces of clear, cold water. Delicious!

Good idea! Treat guests to simple Caffè Cappuccino: add steaming milk to strong coffee (half and half). Dust cinnamon over the top. Superb!

© 1956

There is nothing so satisfying as a cup of good coffee

PAN-AMERICAN COFFEE BUREAU, 120 Wall Street, New York 5, N. Y.

Exhibit 4

PAN-AMERICAN COFFEE BUREAU (D)

HOW TO COOL OFF WITH ICED COFFEE

An analysis of the Starch readership ratings received by the 1956 and early 1957 advertisements was prepared by the agency's research department (see Exhibit 10). A description of the Starch Readership Service is given in the Appendix to this case.

Per capita consumption of coffee in the United States had been off sub-

Exhibit 5

PAN-AMERICAN COFFEE BUREAU (D)

How to cool off with coffee!
Wonderful new ways to serve iced coffee—save this page!

Coffee Float – drop a generous amount of your favorite ice cream into good iced coffee—coffee ice cream, of course, or vanilla, chocolate, mint or maple walnut.

Iced Coffee Mocha – so easy when you add a teaspoon of chocolate syrup or cocoa per cup—at the last minute or when making your good, full-strength iced coffee.

Iced Coffee Junior –makes youngsters feel "grown up" and tastes good! Just sweeten milk a little, color it with cold coffee—you're the best judge of the amount.

Three
*ways to make delicious
Iced Coffee every time!*

Quick way. Make coffee double strength, use half the amount of water—pour over regular ice cubes. Extra-strength coffee compensates for dilution from melting ice.

Pre-cooled way. Make coffee full strength— use 1 Standard Coffee Measure (2 level tablespoons) of coffee for each cup. Cool in a non-metal container, tightly covered, for no more than 3 hours. Pour over ice cubes.

Coffee Cube way. Freeze freshly brewed, regular strength coffee into coffee cubes in your refrigerator trays. Pour freshly brewed coffee over the coffee ice cubes.

Coffee Julep – coolest looking, coolest tasting midsummer drink! Add a dash of mint flavor to iced coffee; serve in silver or aluminum tumblers, well frosted.

Iced Coffee Viennese – topped with a snowy swirl of whipped cream, your iced coffee is Continental! A delightful way to win praise from guests and family!

Instant Note – mix *twice* the usual amount of instant coffee with a little water (hot or cold according to brand) in each glass. Add ice cubes—fill with cold water.

FUN WITH COFFEE

Send for this exciting, helpful, new booklet
Dozens of ways to enjoy America's favorite beverage

A collection of the world's finest coffee recipes—glamorous serving suggestions—proper-brewing methods—all tested and approved—and the whole remarkable story of how your good friend, Coffee, reaches your table! 32 colorful pages.

Fill in this coupon, enclose 25¢, mail to:

PAN-AMERICAN COFFEE BUREAU
P.O. Box 33,
Old Chelsea Station,
New York 11, N. Y.

Enclosed please find 25¢ for my copy of FUN WITH COFFEE. Send to:

Name...............................

Street..............................

City................Zone....State........

G

---

stantially since 1946, and industry promotional efforts had been unable to produce any appreciable change in the situation. Data collected on coffee brewing practices in American households showed a marked trend toward weaker coffee. The extraction rate for regular coffee had risen from approximately 46 cups per pound in 1949 to about 64 pounds in 1957. Dr. Wood estimated that coffee sales would run $500,000,000 higher if housewives brewed coffee the way they did in 1949.

Information recently supplied by the Coffee Brewing Institute was

Exhibit 6

PAN-AMERICAN COFFEE BUREAU (D)

For safety's sake <u>STOP</u> for a "Coffee-break"

Self-starter for your trip, breakfast coffee! For "wake up" strength, the experts use 1 Standard Coffee Measure to each 6 ounces of clear, cold water per cup.

On the road, stop for a "Coffee-break" every 100 miles, or every few hours. It's the delicious way to keep alert. With Iced Coffee, you cool off, too!

Picnic high light — even the simplest sandwich tastes better with coffee! Hot or Iced, coffee travels well — stays fresh for hours — always has superb flavor.

Send for this exciting, helpful, new booklet

FUN WITH COFFEE

Dozens of ways to enjoy America's favorite beverage

A collection of the world's finest coffee recipes — glamorous serving suggestions — proper brewing methods — all tested and approved — and some unusual facts about your good friend, Coffee! Thirty-two colorful pages — full of useful information.

Enclosed please find 25¢ for my copy of FUN WITH COFFEE. Send to:

Name_____

Street_____

City_____ Zone____ State_____

                                                 G

Coffee Float — just the thing for a roadside snack — well-brewed Iced Coffee, topped with your favorite ice cream. It's perfect for an afternoon "Coffee-break."

Reward at the end of the drive — a good, full-bodied cup of coffee! It's the very pleasant way to relax in peace and quiet, especially after a hearty meal.

Fill in this coupon, enclose 25¢, mail to:
PAN-AMERICAN COFFEE BUREAU,
P. O. Box 33, Old Chelsea Station, New York 11, N. Y.

There is nothing so satisfying as a good cup of coffee

regarded as new evidence that a more direct approach might work. The Institute was a nonprofit corporation formed in 1952 by the Pan-American Coffee Bureau and the National Coffee Association to carry out research and educational activities that would bring about improvement of coffee as a beverage. Its work on the problem of how to describe or measure the quality of coffee beverage had shown that a measurement of the concentration of material extracted by water, called the soluble solids,

Exhibit 7

PAN-AMERICAN COFFEE BUREAU (D)

Spiced Coffee Eggnog Punch — easy-to-make glamour that will delight holiday guests! Ingredients: 2 cups double-strength coffee (use twice as much coffee with usual amount of water), 1 tablespoon broken stick cinnamon, 6 whole cloves, 6 allspice berries, 2 quarts dairy-bottled eggnog, 1 tablespoon vanilla, 1 cup whipping cream, 1 quart of vanilla or coffee ice cream. Combine coffee and spices in sauce pan. Simmer 15 minutes, strain and chill. Combine eggnog, vanilla and spiced coffee in large mixing bowl. Chill well. Whip cream and fold in. Pour over ice cream in punch bowl. Sprinkle with nutmeg. Makes 18 delicious cups.

Try these "Happy Holiday" Coffees !

Send for this exciting, helpful, new booklet FUN WITH COFFEE
Dozens of ways to enjoy America's favorite beverage—a collection of the world's finest coffee recipes—glamorous serving suggestions—proper-brewing methods—all tested and approved. 32 colorful pages. Fill in this coupon, enclose 25c. Enclosed please find 25c for my copy of FUN WITH COFFEE. Send to:

Name_____

Street_____

City_____Zone____State_____

Viennese Velvet — push scoop of vanilla ice cream down into glass. Add another scoop. Slowly, carefully, fill with hot double-strength coffee. Top with swirl of whipped cream — add a dash of nutmeg.

Petit Café — serve French "small coffee" with canapés before holiday feasting. Use 1½ Standard Measures (3 level tablespoons) for each 6 ozs. of cold water. Serve with twist of lemon peel, no cream.

Fill in this coupon, enclose 25¢, mail to:
PAN-AMERICAN COFFEE BUREAU,
P O. Box 33, Old Chelsea Station, New York 11, N.Y.

There is nothing so satisfying as a good cup of coffee

provided a useful index of quality if the brewing formula used also was known.[3]

The Institute had been exploring the relationship between the per cent

---

[3] The Coffee Brewing Institute in November 1957 published a booklet, *The Soluble Solids in Beverage Coffee as an Index to Cup Quality* written by Dr. Ernest E. Lockhart.

Exhibit 8

PAN-AMERICAN COFFEE BUREAU (D)

How to make a good cup of Coffee!

Drip Maker

Rinse with very hot water. Never use less than ¾ capacity of drip pot. For each cup of coffee, bring to boil 6 fluid oz. fresh cold water (¾ measuring cup) in kettle or other pot. Put 1 Standard Measure (2 level tablespoons) of "drip" grind coffee, per cup, into filter section. Slowly pour vigorously boiling water into upper section. After dripping, remove upper section and stir. To keep hot, place over very low heat or on an asbestos pad over lowered flame. Do not boil. Serve as soon as possible. Because coffee is at its best only when fresh, do not re-heat it.

Vacuum Maker

Rinse with very hot water. For each cup of coffee, bring to boil in lower bowl 6 fluid oz. fresh cold water (¾ measuring cup). Never use less than ¾ capacity of maker. Use 1 Standard Measure (2 level tablespoons) of "drip" or "fine" grind coffee, per cup. Remove boiling water from heat. Fit upper bowl with filter over lower — twist tight. Place on reduced heat. When most of the water has risen into upper bowl, stir. In 1 to 3 minutes, depending on grind used and strength desired, remove from heat. Serve at once. (Rinse filter thoroughly and store in cold water.)

Percolator

Rinse with very hot water. Never use less than ¾ capacity of maker. For each cup of coffee, bring to boil in percolator 6 fluid oz. fresh cold water (¾ measuring cup). Put 1 Standard Measure (2 level tablespoons) of "regular" grind coffee, per cup, into basket. When water boils, lower heat, put basket into percolator, cover. Percolate very slowly for 6 to 8 minutes. To keep hot, place over very low heat or on an asbestos pad over the lowered flame — do not boil. Serve as soon as possible. And because coffee is at its delicious best only when fresh, do not re-heat it.

SEND FOR this exciting, helpful, new booklet — dozens of ways to enjoy America's favorite beverage

A collection of the world's finest coffee recipes — glamorous serving suggestions — proper brewing methods — all tested and approved. (Brewing directions as formulated by The Coffee Brewing Institute, Inc.) 32 colorful pages. Send name and address and 25¢ to:

PAN-AMERICAN COFFEE BUREAU
P. O. Box 33, Old Chelsea Station, New York 11, N.Y.

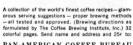

There is nothing so satisfying as a good cup of coffee

of the solids extracted from the coffee bean (a maximum of about 30% could be extracted), the dilution or per cent of soluble solids in the beverage, and the brewing formula in terms of gallons per pound. The results had led Dr. Ernest E. Lockhart, the Institute's scientific director, to believe that there was an optimum rate of extraction of solids from the coffee bean which actually was exceeded in most coffee making, producing bitter, unacceptable coffee. He expressed the opinion that this bitterness

Exhibit 9

PAN-AMERICAN COFFEE BUREAU (D)

"Do-it-yourself" is easier–with a "Coffee-break"

Keep some baby oil or soft soap on your hands, especially the nails and cuticles, for easy wash-up after painting. For a restful, zestful "lift" on the job, give yourself an occasional "Coffee-break"!

Upholstering is a two-fisted job. Hold fabric or webbing taut with one hand, hammer tacks in with the other—a magnetic hammer picks up the tacks for you. A good, full-bodied cup of coffee makes work easier.

Less chance of the big ones getting away if your equipment is in top order beforehand. For tops in coffee every time, too: use 1 Standard Measure (2 level tablespoons) for each 6-oz. cup of cold water.

What's the pleasantest way to avoid "Gardener's back"?—a "Coffee-break"! Planting hint: don't skimp on stakes — tie up all the young plants you want to grow strong, straight and healthy.

Smart carpenters when working in hardwoods, use soap on screws or saws. And they cool off with good Iced Coffee. Hint: Freeze coffee cubes in refrigerator trays and use with regular strength coffee. It won't dilute.

Now with the job well done, you owe yourself a rest and a reward – a "special recipe" coffee! For the colorful 32-page booklet, "Fun With Coffee," send 25¢ and your name and address to the Coffee Bureau.

There is nothing so satisfying as a good cup of coffee

PAN-AMERICAN COFFEE BUREAU, P.O. BOX 33, OLD CHELSEA STATION, NEW YORK 11, N.Y.

commonly had been passed off as strength by the consumer who had to dilute the coffee in order to lessen the intensity of the unpleasant effect.

Dr. Lockhart believed that people would prefer coffee made at an optimum rate of extraction which should be used regardless of the strength of coffee preferred. If a person desired a coffee weaker than that produced at the optimum rate of extraction, he should add water after the brewing had been completed, not before.

Dr. Lockhart believed it unlikely that people's coffee preferences actually had changed to the extent represented by the rise since 1950 from 46 to 64 in cups per pound. Instead, he attributed the increase to the effects of war shortages in coffee, economic pressures, and the competitive "more cups per pound" advertising claims by coffee roasters who apparently believed that it was impossible to overextract coffee.

In order to lead people to use stronger coffee, Dr. Lockhart said, it

Exhibit 10

PAN-AMERICAN COFFEE BUREAU (D)

Starch Ratings

Ladies' Home Journal

DATE	HEADLINE	SIZE AND COLOR	% WOMEN READERS			READERS PER DOLLAR		
			Noted	Seen-Assoc.	Read Most	Noted	Seen-Assoc.	Read Most
4/56..........	Good Time	JrP4C	30	26	8	88	77	24
5/56..........	Get all	JrP4C	28	26	6	83	77	18
6/56..........	It's a good	JrP4C	38	33	6	112	97	18
7/56..........	How to	P4C	48	44	16	113	103	38
9/56..........	For safety's	P4C	40	38	13	94	89	31
11/56........	Eggnog	P4C	39	32	10	92	75	23
	Average—3 ads	JrP4C	32	28	7	94	88	24
	Average—3 ads	P4C	42	38	13	100	89	31
	Average—6 ads					97	86	25
PACB vs. all food ads (1956—6 issues—177 ads).............						−10	−15	+0
1/57..........	How to make	P4C	42	30	10	103	73	24
4/57..........	Do it yourself	P4C	27	25	9	60	56	20
	Average—2 ads	P4C	34	27	9	81	64	22
PACB vs. all food ads (1957—2 issues—57 ads)..............						−27	−38	−4

PACB versus All Ads in Issue

Ladies' Home Journal
Women Readers

DATE	PACB READERS PER DOLLAR			ALL ADS IN ISSUE READERS PER DOLLAR			PACB % BETTER		
	Noted	Seen-Assoc.	Read Most	Noted	Seen-Assoc.	Read Most	Noted	Seen-Assoc.	Read Most
4/56........	88	77	24	92	84	17	−4%	−8%	+41%
5/56........	83	77	18	89	82	15	−7	−6	+20
6/56........	112	97	18	102	96	13	+10	+1	+38
7/56........	113	103	38	99	99	16	+14	+4	+137
9/56........	94	89	31	100	89	17	−6	+0	+82
11/56.......	92	75	23	83	75	14	+11	+0	+64
1/57........	103	73	24	103	86	20	+0	−15	+20
4/57........	60	56	20	95	85	16	−37	−34	+25

Exhibit 10—Continued

Starch Ratings

The Saturday Evening Post
Men Readers

DATE	HEADLINE	SIZE AND COLOR	% MEN READERS			READERS PER DOLLAR		
			Noted	Seen-Assoc.	Read Most	Noted	Seen-Assoc.	Read Most
3/3/56......	Good Time	JrP4C	8	5	1	15	9	2
3/31........	Get all	JrP4C	12	8	2	23	15	4
4/28........	It's a good	JrP4C	9	8	1	17	15	2
6/2........	*Gatefold:*							
	How to	PBW	20	......	9	44	......	20
	Wonderful	PBW						
	New ways	P4C	25	19	3	22	17	3
8/4........	How to	P4C	23	17	3	34	25	4
10/6.......	For safety's	P4C	25	16	1	37	24	1
12/15......	Eggnog	P4C	20	7	1	29	10	1
	Average—8 ads†					28	14	5
PACB vs. all food ads (1956—7 issues—49 ads).....						−10	−42	+150
Average—12 PBWB ads in 1954-55................			30	21	6	64	45	14
Average—15 P4C ads in 1952-54................			28	19	4	57	40	7
2/9/57......	How to make	2C4C	29	19	*	40	26	*
3/16/57.....	Do it yourself	P4C	18	11	2	25	15	3
Average—2 ads..............						32	20	1
PACB vs. all food ads (1957—2 issues—13 ads).....						−11	−31	−50

* No persons reported upon.
† Gatefold averaged as two ads—PBW and 2-page spread.

would not suffice merely to tell them to make their coffee stronger as the Bureau had done in its advertising in past years. Instead, the emphasis had to be placed on making coffee in such a way that the optimum rate of extraction would not be exceeded. The advertising of an optimum brewing formula, he said, could not be expected to lead to the use of stronger coffee if it turned out that people actually preferred coffee at a strength of 64 cups per pound even when it was properly made.

Evidence of consumer preference for coffee made to certain specifications had been obtained in tests conducted by the Brewing Committee of the National Coffee Association and, more recently, by the Midwest Research Institute. In the latter study, it was concluded that the most acceptable cup of coffee would be prepared if the soluble solids ranged between 1.15% and 1.35% and the extraction between 18% and 22%. To obtain beverage meeting these requirements, the brewing formula would have to be between 1.83 and 2.53 gallons per pound.

Thus far, the Institute had concerned itself with working out objective measures of coffee quality. While it planned eventually to run tests to determine consumer acceptance of coffee of varying qualities, it had as

Exhibit 10—Continued

Starch Ratings

The Saturday Evening Post
Women Readers

DATE	HEADLINE	SIZE AND COLOR	% WOMEN READERS			READERS PER DOLLAR		
			Noted	Seen-Assoc.	Read Most	Noted	Seen-Assoc.	Read Most
3/3/56......	Good Time	JrP4C	39	31	6	78	62	12
3/31........	Get all	JrP4C	39	33	13	78	66	26
4/28........	It's a good	JrP4C	42	37	6	84	74	12
6/2.........	*Gatefold:*							
	How to	PBW	30	......	17	71	......	40
	Wonderful	PBW						
	New ways	P4C	40	38	10	38	36	9
8/4.........	How to	P4C	62	52	22	98	82	35
10/6........	For safety's	P4C	44	32	10	70	51	16
12/15.......	Eggnog	P4C	47	29	12	74	46	19
	Average—8 ads*					74	52	21
PACB vs. all food ads								
(1956—7 issues—49 ads).....						−5	−24	+91
Average—12 PBWB ads								
in 1954–55................			36	28	11	83	65	25
Average—15 P4C ads								
in 1952–54................			39	32	9	83	67	19
2/9/57......	How to make	2C4C	57	40	6	85	59	9
3/16/57.....	Do it yourself	P4C	38	29	8	56	43	12
Average—2 ads..............					7	70	51	10
PACB vs. all food ads								
(1957—2 issues—13 ads).....						−10	−26	+0

* Gatefold averaged as two ads—PBW and 2-page spread.

yet not done so. In the opinion of Institute officials, however, the results of the test mentioned above had been supported by the judgment of many coffee and restaurant men who had watched the brewing demonstrations sponsored by the Coffee Brewing Institute throughout the country, and who had compared the flavor of coffee prepared according to recommended procedures against watered or overextracted brews.

Dr. Lockhart explained that the Institute's work had been with standard blends of coffee which accounted for 90% of the coffee consumed. He did not regard the information he presented as an argument against efforts to get people to try new varieties of coffee.

Information compiled by the Bureau's research department showed that 75% of the total annual coffee consumption took place in households, 13% in public eating places, 9.5% at work or while on the job, 2% in institutions, and about one half of 1% of the coffee went into industrial uses. A number of studies showed that coffee was used in about 96% of American homes, but that three quarters of them consumed less coffee than the 25% of the homes classified as "heavy consumers." This was interpreted by Dr. Wood to mean that there is a great potential for en-

Exhibit 10—Continued

PACB versus All Ads in Issue

The Saturday Evening Post

DATE	PACB READERS PER DOLLAR			ALL ADS IN ISSUE READERS PER DOLLAR			PACB % BETTER		
	Noted	Seen-Assoc.	Read Most	Noted	Seen-Assoc.	Read Most	Noted	Seen-Assoc.	Read Most
Men Readers									
3/3/56......	15	9	2	38	32	5	−61%	−72%	−60%
3/31........	23	15	4	40	36	4	−43	−58	+0
4/28........	17	15	2	37	33	4	−54	−55	−50
6/2, front pg.	44	......	20	39	31	3	+13	....	+567
2-pg. spread..	22	17	3				−44	−45	+0
8/4.........	34	25	4	50	42	7	−32	−40	−43
10/6........	37	24	1	39	31	3	−5	−23	−67
12/15......	29	10	1	42	33	4	−31	−70	−75
2/9/57......	40	26	*	37	29	4	+8	−10	−0
3/16/57.....	25	15	3	38	32	6	−34	−53	−50
Women Readers									
3/3/56......	78	62	12	42	33	5	+86%	+88%	+140%
3/31........	78	66	26	42	31	3	+86	+113	+767
4/28........	84	74	12	39	31	3	+115	+139	+300
6/2, front pg.	71	......	40	41	35	4	+73	....	+900
2-pg. spread..	38	36	9				−7	+3	+125
8/4.........	98	82	35	48	42	5	+104	+95	+600
10/6........	70	51	16	36	30	5	+94	+70	+220
12/15......	74	46	19	49	35	5	+51	+31	+280
2/9/57......	85	59	9	39	30	4	+118	+97	+125
3/16/57.....	56	43	12	37	29	4	+51	+48	+200

* No persons reported upon.

Starch Ratings

Seventeen

DATE	HEADLINE	SIZE AND COLOR	% WOMEN READERS			READERS PER DOLLAR		
			Noted	Seen-Assoc.	Read Most	Noted	Seen-Assoc.	Read Most
4/57........	How to make	P4C	19	15	6	29	23	9
PACB vs. all food ads (1957—1 issue—7 ads)...............						−44	−42	−18

PACB versus All Ads in Issue

DATE	PACB READERS PER DOLLAR			ALL ADS IN ISSUE READERS PER DOLLAR			PACB % BETTER		
	Noted	Seen-Assoc.	Read Most	Noted	Seen-Assoc.	Read Most	Noted	Seen-Assoc.	Read Most
4/57........	29	23	9	71	57	20	−59	−60	−55

larging the market among the people who already use coffee but who use relatively little of it. Households in cities of 50,000 population and over were found to be heavier users of coffee than those in the smaller cities, towns, and rural areas.

The heaviest purchasers of coffee were in households where the age of the housewife was between 35 and 54. Households where the housewife was under 35 years old accounted for only 14% of the heavy purchasers. Thirty-eight per cent of all married women in the country were under 35 years of age. "The figures indicate that people in the middle-age brackets tend to drink more coffee," Dr. Wood explained, "but that as they move out of those brackets they tend to drink less. At the same time, the older people remain relatively more important consumers of coffee than the younger ones. This description of the distribution of coffee consumption by age groups is certainly not meant to suggest a "law" that will necessarily apply to the future. Indeed, if an increasing proportion of the younger people should become habituated to a weak brew and stay with it into middle age, the incidence of coffee use among the different age groups would in a few years be quite different from what it is today. Putting aside that consideration, we should note carefully that the light consumption of coffee among the younger people, together with the increase that is taking place in the youth population, emphasizes the growing importance of promoting coffee drinking among the younger adults and the teenagers."

The top one fourth of the households in income accounted for one third of the heavy coffee purchasers. The low-income households had one third of the light coffee purchasers and only 18% of the heavy. In general, the households headed by skilled workers and laborers were better purchasers of coffee than were those of professional and executive men and farmers.

Appendix

DESCRIPTION OF STARCH READERSHIP SERVICE

The following description of the Starch Readership Service is taken from a publication of the Starch organization entitled, *Brief Description of the Scope, Method, and Technique of the Starch Advertisement Readership Service.*

Introduction

The Starch Readership Service measures the reading of advertisements in magazines and newspapers, using a standard technique developed by Daniel Starch and staff during 24 years of continuous experience in readership studies.

More than 500,000 advertisements have been studied since the beginning of the service. Annually, the Starch program covers 30,000 advertisements in 1,000 issues of consumer and farm magazines, business publications and newspapers. Over 240,000 personal interviews are made each year in order to carry out this program.

Purpose

The Starch Readership Service provides a continuous source of readership data that answers the following questions: 1. to what extent is my advertisement seen and read; 2. are my present advertisements better read than past advertisements; 3. are my advertisements better read than those of my competitors; 4. is the reading of my current campaign increasing or decreasing; 5. how can I tell my ad story so that it will be better read against broad averages?

Starch Readership data can be used to determine: (1) relative effectiveness of size and color, page position, season of the year, etc., (2) relative effect of internal characteristics (headline, illustration, format, etc.), (3) best scoring ads.

Examine the ad for layout. Is it simple or complicated? How important is the illustration? Is the eye led through the copy and into the signatures? How have copy blocks been handled? Where is the headline in relation to the illustration?

Study ads for theme and method of treatment. How do display ads compare with editorial type ads? With comic strip ads? Is the direct or indirect approach best suited to your type of product?

This treatment can be extended to parts of the ad. Is the illustration predominant? Does it show the product as it is bought, or used? Are copy blocks or headlines overlying a part of the illustration? Is the illustration general in appeal, or does it point specifically to the product advertised?

The use of Starch Readership Reports as briefly illustrated above will provide a useful analysis of the performance of your advertising, as well as a practical means of improving its effectiveness in the future.

Use of Reports

The readership data contained in Starch reports are actually "working tools" with which an advertiser or agency can build better ads. These "working tools" must be accumulated before performance of the campaign can be determined. If the data on a single ad is merely compared to the results of another ad, the data can only serve the function of a "score sheet." Figures for individual ads should not be used for sharp comparison, but should be regarded as broad indicators subject to modification with the addition of more data. The Starch Readership Service is designed to provide continuous surveys on a large number of ads.

In order to realize the greatest potential use of the readership data, the following "points" must be kept in mind: (1) Average figures for several insertions rather than use figures for single ads, (2) Look for recurring factors so as to establish trends and principles, and (3) Season judgment with common sense.

There are many ways in which readership data can be meaningful. The method to be used depends upon your needs and desires. Outlined below are several ways in which the data can be compared:

1. Comparison of your ads (your competitor's) against previous ads.
2. Comparison of your current campaign (your competitor's) against old campaign.
3. Comparison of your campaign (your competitor's) against product group averages.
4. Comparison of your campaign averages (your competitor's).

Over-all Findings

Advertisements differ enormously in readership. Two advertisements may be of equal size and color, for the same type product, appear in the same publication, in fact in the same issue, and one may attract two or three times as many readers as the other—and as much as seven or eight times as many thorough readers.

Readership provides data on two factors causing this difference.

a. Product Interest—People are more interested in some products than in others.
b. Communicative power of an ad is indicated by the extent to which the readership of a particular ad or campaign rises above or falls below the general interest level or the product group.

It is important to reach as many people as you can for three reasons:

a. The more readers you attract, the more prospects, on the average, you reach.
b. Many persons who are not presently prospects may be prospects in the future or may become prospects by reading your advertisement.
c. The more observers an advertisement attracts, the more thorough readers, on the average, it attracts.

Current Issue Report

The final report consists of a summary sheet showing the over-all percentages, readers per dollar, cost ratios and ranks for all ads, grouped by product categories. The summary sheet is attached to a labeled copy of the issue in which each ad is marked to show the percentage results for the ad-as-a-whole and for each component part checked for readership. All ads one-half page or larger are included in these studies. Smaller ads may be included on advance notice.

Readers per Dollar indicates the number of primary readers attracted by the ad for each dollar invested in space cost.

"Readers per Dollar"—Magazine (Primary) Readers Multiplied by per cent *"Noted," "Seen-Associated" or "Read Most"* Divided by Space Cost

"Cost Ratios" express the relationship between "Readers per Dollar" and the corresponding *median* average "Readers per Dollar" for all half-page or larger advertisements. A "Noted" "Cost Ratio" of 175, would mean that from a standpoint of having stopped the reader, the ad did 75 per cent better than par for all ads in the issue.

Ranks shows the numerical order of the "Readers per Dollar" for all ads listed from the highest (Rank 1) to the lowest.

In addition to these figures for each ad-as-a-whole, percentages are computed to show seeing and reading of the various component parts of each advertisement.

Tabulating and Computing

Readership results are placed on IBM cards and tabulated by IBM machines.

Results are expressed for the three degrees of reading: "Noted," "Seen-Associated" and "Read Most"—in terms of Percentages, Readers per Dollar, Cost Ratios and Ranks.

Percentages reflect the actual percentage of readers who indicated they saw or read a given ad. For example, of 150 men and 150 women interviewed on a certain issue of *The Saturday Evening Post* the readership of a Campbell Soup ad might be:

MEN			WOMEN		
Noted	*Seen-Assoc.*	*Read Most*	*Noted*	*Seen-Assoc.*	*Read Most*
22%	21%	1%	61%	57%	10%

Before interviewing, each ad to be studied is "coded" uniformly in the interviewer's copy in accordance with a bulletin prepared in the home office. The bulletin lists code numbers for the component parts of the ad. Thus, the readership of the various parts of all ads is reported uniformly.

The sample is not a panel. No respondent is asked to read the issue prior to the interview. The first step is to determine if the respondent had possession of the issue and qualifies as a reader because he had previously opened and read some part of the issue prior to the interview.

Having fulfilled these requirements, the respondent is then questioned on his observation and reading of specific ads. The interviewer goes through the issue with the respondent page by page inquiring about each ad under study. The starting point is randomized in order to equalize the fatigue element in long interviews.

The respondent is asked, "Did you see or read any part of this advertisement?" If yes, he is asked to indicate exactly what was seen or read. These questions determine which component parts of each ad the respondent saw or read. Component part readership is obtained: (1) to assure the respondent actually had read the advertisement, and (2) to determine what parts were seen and read.

All data resulting from the interviews are recorded on standardized questionnaires. After the interviewing is completed, approximately one week is allowed for all interviewers' sheets to reach the home office where they are tabulated. Checking, tabulating and printing requires about three weeks.

Interviewing begins a reasonable length of time after the issue is placed on sale, to permit respondents time to obtain and read their copy. Interviewing on weekly and bi-weekly consumer magazines begins three days after the on-sale date and continues for seven days (two weeks in the case of bi-weeklies). On monthly consumer magazines, interviewing begins two weeks after on-sale date and continues for three weeks. Interviewing periods were established as a result of tests to determine the optimum time period for obtaining typical readers.

Interviewing

A permanent staff of more than 175 interviewers is carefully trained and supervised in order to obtain the most accurate data on readership. All inter-viewers are personally selected and trained by one of nine regional supervisors. New interviewers are required to pass personality and performance tests which are evaluated at the home office. Before the new interviewer is permitted to interview on her own, she conducts training interviews under the personal supervision of the supervisor.

The work of each interviewer is continuously spot checked in two ways. The first check is conducted by mail and personal reinterviews to determine honesty and adherence to procedural instructions. The second is made by com-paring work of each interviewer with that of all interviewers to determine if there is understanding and proper application of the recognition method.

Each interviewer is assigned a specific number of interviews to be obtained on each publication assigned to her. To minimize bias, the quota for each inter-viewer is small. Thus, a Starch study reflects the work of 30 to 40 interviewers.

The Sample

The Starch Readership Studies use a national sample of 20 to 30 areas for each study. Each sample parallels circulation by geographic area, urban and suburban areas.

Interviewers must find, within a particular area, an assigned number of readers who are 18 years of age and over, of various occupations, sizes of family, marital and economic status. It is intended that the results obtained will be representative of the readers of the magazine studied.

Most interviews are conducted in homes, with the balance taken in the respondent's place of business.

The size of the sample varies by publication. At the level of 100 to 200 interviews for one sex, major fluctuations in readership tend to level off. Starch studies are based on 100 to 200 interviews per sex, depending upon the publication.

Scope

Starch surveys employ the "recognition" method. With the magazine open, the respondent tells to what extent he or she has read each ad. Three principal degrees of reading are measured for each advertisement:

"*Noted*"—is the per cent of readers who remembered that they had seen the advertisement in the particular issue.

"*Seen-Associated*"—is the per cent of readers who have seen or read any part of the ad which clearly indicates the product or advertiser.

"*Read Most*"—is the per cent of readers who read 50 per cent or more of the written material in the ad.

In addition, data are collected on the observation and reading of the component parts of each ad—headline, subheads, pictures, logotype, copy blocks, and so forth.

~ ~ ~

CASE 17: C. W. BARR COMPANY[1]

NOTE: *The last several cases have focused upon the determination of advertising objectives, advertising copy, and methods of evaluating advertisements. This and the next several cases will bring into consideration other problem areas: advertising media and the advertising budget.* QUESTIONS TO CONSIDER: *(1) What conclusions do you draw from the marketing experience of the company to date regarding the potential sales volume for the "Jet" lantern? Regarding the Manhasset hardware store experience? Regarding the Easton department-store experience? Regarding Mr. Perry's New York sales trip? (2) Outline the promotional and advertising program you would recommend for use after March 1952? How much should be spent on promotion? For what selling tools?*

In March 1952, Mr. Raymond Perry, assistant to the president of the C. W. Barr Company, was re-evaluating his experiences in the sale and promotion of the "Jet" lantern and was planning his future course of action. The Jet was only one of the many lanterns in the Barr line. Mr. Perry, who had joined the company in June 1951, had been given, among other projects, the job of promoting this product in a special segment of the company's market. Not satisfied with the progress made thus far, he desired to lay out a campaign which would give a profitable volume of sales.

Background Information

The Barr company, founded in 1840 by Theodore F. Barr, had had a father-to-son management throughout its long history. Through years of peace, prosperity, war, and depression, the company had attempted to live up to its policy of "making the world's best lantern" and to maintain the leadership which its lanterns enjoyed all over the world.

The company had been ever alert to the changing requirements in portable lighting. Improvements in lighting power, burning reliability, safety, economy, and appearance had been sought and incorporated into all its products throughout the years.

The management of the company was proud of its record of accomplishments and the many "firsts" which it had pioneered. The old showboats that glided down the Mississippi River were lit by Barr lanterns. The "forty-niners" on their way to California carried Barr lanterns with them. Wood-burning locomotives, opening up the great West, had Barr lanterns shining in front. The first automobile headlight was an adaptation

---

[1] Fictitious name. Written by Charles G. Ellington, Jr.

which Barr made for that new industry. In its early history the company had much to do with popularizing the kerosene lantern; after being in business for over 110 years, the Barr name was still setting standards for the trade. In early 1952 the Barr company and one other company were the only two kerosene lantern manufacturers remaining in the United States.

Kerosene lanterns and motor-electrical accessories comprised the two main groups of the company's products. Lanterns accounted for the majority of sales, but the electrical line was becoming increasingly important to the management because of the downward trend in the kerosene lantern market. Approximately 400 different items were manufactured by the company, of which less than 50 were in the lantern line.

Included among the electrical accessories were such products as fog lights, light switches, searchlights, directional signals, dome lights, flares, headlights, and tractor lights. These items had been designed and laboratory tested to meet the requirements of all states, as well as specifications set by various engineering groups.

The Barr company, however, had never become a very important member of the electrical-lighting industry, always being overshadowed by the large firms that dominated the field. The management believed furthermore that it could never become a leading producer in the electrical-equipment industry because its small volume would not enable the company to get its costs down to a competitive level. In the lantern industry, on the other hand, members of Barr's management believed that because of their long experience and know-how they had a distinct advantage. Moreover, kerosene lanterns were sold generally throughout the country. In the rural areas, even on electrified farms, lanterns were a common source of portable light. Railroads and trucking firms used a great many lanterns in their day-to-day operations. Many contractors and highway departments found it necessary to mark excavations and equipment with kerosene lanterns. Exhibit 1 shows the net sales of the company from 1937 through 1951.

The modern-day tubular kerosene lantern evolved from crude hand lamps that used candles and sperm oil. The tubular lantern had a transparent case enclosing a kerosene burner fed by a wick for lighting. This wick gave a steady light, because burning was governed by a well-controlled volume of air, which was fed through bent tubes. The burner acted as a carburetor to which the tubes conveyed a properly directed flow of air. When mixed with air in a proper ratio, the kerosene vapor from the wick gave a good light without smoke.

Basically, two types of lanterns were manufactured by the company: the cold-blast lantern and the hot-blast lantern. The cold-blast lantern was constructed so that only fresh, cold air entered the tubes, while the spent air was diverted and expelled. The hot-blast lantern, on the other hand, because of its construction at the top, permitted a portion of the spent air to circulate through the tubes. A cold-blast lantern produced about double the light of a hot-blast lantern.

All Barr lanterns were protected by international patents. They were made of cold-rolled steel plates, electrically sprayed with metallically ray-baked enamel. The largest lantern in the Barr company catalogue was 16 inches high, held 32 ounces of kerosene, and could burn for 45 hours on that fuel supply. The lantern, which would light up to the point of 10 candle power, had a wick which was 7/8 of an inch long. Its rising cone burner locked on the top so that the oil could not spill.

Exhibit 1

C. W. BARR COMPANY

Net Sales, 1937–51

Year	Domestic Lantern Sales	Domestic Motor Sales	Total Export Sales*	Total Net Sales
1937	$1,182,000	$ 259,000	$ 440,000	$1,881,000
1938	875,000	316,000	329,000	1,520,000
1939	876,000	259,000	695,000	1,830,000
1940	956,000	311,000	686,000	1,953,000
1941	1,526,000	425,000	935,000	2,886,000
1942	1,693,000	432,000	664,000	2,789,000
1943	1,708,000	592,000	846,000	3,146,000
1944	1,691,000	1,100,000	958,000	3,749,000
1945	1,496,000	1,567,000	994,000	4,057,000
1946	1,409,000	1,888,000	1,447,000	4,744,000
1947	1,555,000	2,183,000	2,013,000	5,751,000
1948	1,165,000	1,191,000	3,211,000	5,567,000
1949	1,100,000	558,000	1,126,000	2,784,000
1950	1,464,000	688,000	820,000	2,972,000
1951	1,747,000	1,013,000	819,000	3,579,000

* The sales manager estimated that lanterns usually accounted for 90% of export sales.
Source: Company records.

The company's factory and general offices, occupying a total of 115,-000 square feet of floor space, were located in a brick and concrete four-story building in Easton, Pennsylvania. The manufacturing departments included a press department, an assembly department, a buffing and polishing department, a plating department, and a paint shop.

In the manufacture of the kerosene lanterns and electrical equipment, the operations included blanking, drawing, forming, perforating, trimming, rolling, subassembly work, and finished-product assembly. The company had punch presses, toggle drawing presses, welders, buffing and polishing machines, spray dipping and electrostatic painting equipment, and manual and conveyorized oven equipment.

Most of the operations in the manufacture of the lanterns were of a stamping nature; the materials used were steel, brass, aluminum, glass, cotton wicking, and corrugated cartons for packing. The company personnel, 302 in number, included 62 punch-press operators, 19 solderers, 52 assemblers, 6 maintenance workers, 78 miscellaneous hands (which included painters, buffers, and truckers), 49 office-clerical personnel, 23 foremen, and 13 executives.

Mr. Frank J. Barr, the 34-year-old great-grandson of the founder, had been active in company operations since 1936 and had been president of the firm since 1950. His brother, Mr. John F. Barr, age 30, had been with the company since 1940; he was vice president in charge of electrical-equipment sales to manufacturers of end products, such as automobile manufacturers. The other officers had been with the company a considerable period of time and, except for the treasurer, were all over 55 years of age.

Distribution Policies

The company's lantern products were distributed in the traditional manner of manufacturer to wholesaler to retailer. The management estimated that 90% of the lanterns were sold to hardware wholesalers and mill supply houses; the remaining 10% took miscellaneous paths to the consumer. For example, the city of New York purchased its lanterns directly from the Barr company. Usually the hardware wholesaler or jobber sold only to retail hardware stores, whereas the mill supply houses sold to contractors, highway departments, municipalities, industrial plants, and similar types of customers.

Wholesalers and mill supply houses used by the C. W. Barr Company were located in the principal jobbing centers of the United States and had nonexclusive arrangements with the company. The sales manager estimated that there were some 2,000 mill supply houses in the country and approximately 600 hardware wholesalers. Out of these 2,600 firms, the Barr company did business with about 1,200, which were secured on a selective basis. In the kerosene lantern trade the typical wholesale markup was 33%. The hardware retailer secured between 40% and 50% markup on his selling price.

The Barr company employed six salesmen to call on its 1,200 accounts. Three of these men were full-time employees, the others being manufacturers' agents who were paid on a commission basis. All salesmen sold the full line of lantern equipment, and all sales were made on a uniform basis. For example, a wholesaler who purchased one dozen lanterns during a year secured the same discount as a wholesaler buying 50 dozen lanterns during that period of time.

Distribution channels for the electrical-accessories line were substantially different from those for lanterns. The company's sales manager said that in the lantern trade it was easy to tell who wholesalers were, for the distribution channels were sharply defined. With electrical products such was not the case. Although the company's policy was to follow a traditional distribution pattern of selling only to wholesale motor-parts distributors and to original-equipment manufacturers in the automotive trades, it was difficult to know exactly who was a wholesaler and who was not. In that field the wholesale-retail relationships were not clearly drawn.

Selling agents throughout the United States were utilized in an effort to reach motor-parts wholesalers; approximately 14 of them handled the entire Barr line of electrical-motor equipment.

The company's treasurer explained that in its advertising for both lanterns and automotive-lighting equipment, the Barr company used the following media: (1) space advertising in trade journals aimed at hardware

Exhibit 2

C. W. BARR COMPANY

Typical Lantern Advertisement from a Highway Maintenance Trade Paper

BARR

NITE-BEAM
LANTERN

STRAIGHT-LINE, PENCIL BEAM IS VISIBLE FROM ALL ANGLES, NEARBY OR AT REALLY GREAT DISTANCES.

Its exclusive fresnel globe is moulded with optically perfect prisms, designed to concentrate the light rays into a parallel, vertical beam of greatest possible intensity assuring a safety and warning light of greatest visibility. The NITE-BEAM is the best burning lantern of its kind.

THE NITE-BEAM is strongly made, finished in Contractors' Yellow; Ruby Fresnel Globe with Peep-hole. Also accommodates Barr Little Soldier and Little Soldier Globes. Burns a generous 100 hours. 8″ high, 6¾″ diameter at nontip base.

Write for circular.

Exclusive trip-lock releases chimney for easy lighting, etc.

Self-locking.

C. W. BARR COMPANY ★ EASTON, PENNSYLVANIA

jobbers and at manufacturers and users of trucks; and (2) product catalogues and price lists. Although he believed that expenditures in the second category were not, strictly speaking, advertising expenses, they were treated as such on his accounting records. He estimated that approximately 75% of advertising expenses were in the first category and 25% in the second. The treasurer stated that about 3% of the company's sales dollar was spent on advertising. Exhibit 2 shows a typical advertisement which appeared in a highway maintenance trade paper.

Jet Lantern

In 1935 the company began to manufacture a small, cold-blast lantern for the export market. This lantern called the "Jet" was 8½ inches high, much smaller than any other in the line. It held five ounces of kerosene and was painted a dull silver-gray. The management thought it was the smallest, practical lantern possible to manufacture. The Jet was an immediate success. It sold extremely well in China, Japan, India, and other Far Eastern countries. The Jet was not introduced to the domestic market in 1935 because the sales manager thought that if this cheaper lantern was available in hardware stores, customers might purchase it instead of a larger, more expensive lantern. The "factory cost" of the Jet was approximately 75 cents. Exhibit 3 gives net sales of Jet lanterns from 1946 to 1951.

In 1950, because the domestic market for lanterns appeared to be in a slump, the new president decided to introduce the Jet lantern to hardware

Exhibit 3

C. W. BARR COMPANY

Jet Lantern Net Sales, 1946–51

Year	Export Sales	Domestic Sales	Total Net Sales
1946	$309,000		$309,000
1947	666,000		666,000
1948	949,000		949,000
1949	264,000		264,000
1950	142,000	$ 79,000*	221,000
1951	105,000	115,000	220,000

* Jet introduced to domestic market in September 1950.
Source: Company records.

stores through the ordinary channels of distribution. Shortly after this decision he became extremely busy with other company problems.

In June 1951, Mr. Frank Barr hired Mr. Raymond Perry, a recent graduate of a large eastern university, to become his assistant. As assistant to the president, Mr. Perry was assigned several projects, among them an appraisal of the Jet lantern's sales possibilities. In studying the opportunities for this lantern, he decided that, because of its unique size and its pleasing appearance, the product might have some sales possibilities not only in hardware stores but in other types of outlets.

The Jet was of solid construction with a compactness that gave it an expensive look; from the time of its introduction to the domestic market the lantern was painted a bright, cherry red which made it extremely attractive. Although its appearance was much the same as an ordinary lantern, because of its small size the Jet looked much more like a unique, novelty item.

Late in June 1951, after spending some time thinking about the Jet, Mr. Perry decided that department stores offered the best outlet, since there was little chance of their aggravating the regular hardware jobbers. The young executive visualized the lantern as having many varied uses.

He thought that any household could use one for unexpected emergencies whenever the primary source of light failed; he believed it would be equally useful to gardeners, picknickers, hikers, campers, and anyone who was traveling or participating in sports. The lantern was not difficult to operate. The instructions which the company issued with the Jet were as follows:

TO FILL—Remove the fount cap. Pour in up to ½ pint of a good grade kerosene.

TO LIGHT—Depress lever at right of globe until it locks in notch. Be sure wick is set low. Wheel turned to left lowers wick. Ignite wick and slowly release lever to lower globe.

TO CLEAN GLOBE—Put bail (handle) in upright position, lift by ring on top of lantern, tilt the globe back. *If wick needs trimming, cut straight across.*

Lantern burns best with full supply of kerosene in fount;—it will burn dry to last drop. Be sure in advance that you have enough oil and the jet will never, never fail you.

In trying to establish a tentative budget for the Jet lantern promotion, Mr. Barr and his assistant had no historical data to guide them. Since the company had never singled out any one lantern for special promotion before and since there had been no experience in selling to other than the hardware trade, they had no idea what such a job would cost. They both decided that $10,000 would be adequate for the first year's trial; after that time, if the lantern should become popular, they believed that more concrete information would be available.

In the spring of 1951, one of the hardware stores on Long Island, New York, which carried the entire line of Barr lanterns, used the Jet for a special promotion. Exhibit 4 is a reprint of an article which appeared in the May issue of a hardware trade paper which described that event.

In order to test his conclusions about the Jet lantern as a good novelty item, Mr. Perry called upon the merchandise managers of two large department stores in Easton. He hoped to get their appraisal of the product's sales appeal and ideas which might be helpful to him in planning a department-store campaign. Both store executives agreed that a 40% markup on the selling price was necessary and thought that $1.98 would be a good retail price. At that time the product was listed for $2.09 in the hardware stores.

In July, executives of one of these Easton department stores decided to make the Jet a promotional item in its sporting goods department and ordered three dozen lanterns. A half-page advertisement was run in the local newspaper Thursday night to promote Jet sales on Friday, since the store was closed on Saturdays during the summer. A 90-second television spot announcement was also used over the local station; at the same time several counter display cards were prepared. On that Friday, 28 lanterns were sold in the sporting goods department, which was located in the

Exhibit 4

C. W. BARR COMPANY

Hurricanes Blow Business to Wright*

Manhasset, on the North Shore of Long Island, New York, is not much different from any other truly suburban community, except that a hurricane seems to hit it every four years, and the wind does a bang-up job in knocking out the electricity wires. This means that lights are out, sometimes for days. When darkness strikes, every lantern in the hardware stores for miles around is snapped up in a few hours.

Arthur Wright, president of the Wright Hardware Company, one of the most progressive dealers in the New York area, had on hand a good supply of lanterns when the last wind hit, but they all sold much too fast.

Shortly after this recent big storm, this wide awake hardwareman saw the show "Ladies in Retirement," put on by the local Little Club. In it the new, colorful Barr Jet lantern played a minor but interesting part. Arthur recognized this lantern from a color insert in a hardware trade paper and spoke to the writer about an idea he had during intermission. "That little lantern is downright cute. It should appeal to the ladies as well as the men. I realize that it is a grand lantern for picnics, for sportsmen, and general outdoor use, but I have an idea I can put it over as an emergency light as well."

"People in Manhasset should be alert to the need of good, portable light when the house lights go out—they'll remember only too well sitting by candlelight or with no light at all when a storm hits. Monday, I am placing an order for some with my jobber."

Wright was right. Dropping in at his store a few weeks later, we noted a large table (where garden material or gifts usually were featured) loaded with Barr Jet lanterns. Attractive display stands, supplied with every dozen by the manufacturer, C. W. Barr Company, Easton, Pennsylvania, were attractively used at the top level of each step of the pyramid of boxes. Each of these displays of blue, yellow, and red, with a semi-circular stage of gold foil, displayed a Jet lantern, each brilliantly catching the light.

On the display was a hand-lettered sign, "The Next Time You Need Them, They'll Be All Gone." Then in a smaller lettering, "Why wait until the lights of Manhasset go out again—buy a JET NOW." One of the clerks, and Wright has upward of 20 on a week end, stated, "They often buy two, and some come back for more. The kids go for them too, and the ladies are buying them as gifts and prizes. Sold one today as a shower gift—never knew a lantern had such feminine appeal."

Arthur Wright's idea of warning in advance about power failure has paid out in quantity sales, not just dozens, but actually hundreds upon hundreds.

What was planned at first as a three-week display on the basis of getting them while the lights are out, has stretched on for over two months and is still going strong.

Instead of cutting down the display area, Mr. Wright added standard

---

* *Source:* Reprinted from a hardware trade paper in May 1951.

Exhibit 4—Continued

lanterns such as the Barr Nite-Beam and Little Soldier. A window display was planned—but delayed and delayed. Finally, a handsome window packed full of Jet lanterns made its appearance months later. Imagine a window some 20 feet wide and 10 feet high lined full of fire engine red lanterns with clear glass globes, while more Jet lanterns are strung on wooden arms overhead. The effect was dramatic, and sales which have stretched out over months of promotion took an added zest. Every Jet was sold, and more ordered.

This story is interesting because it shows the results of a very smart idea by a progressive hardware merchant who had the courage to follow through the idea with practical merchandising. Arthur Wright has generally been successful in his efforts. Lanterns are basically a standard product, taken for granted by many dealers, stocked for sale when needed. Arthur Wright saw the glamour in the new little Jet and made a specialty sales promotion that is one of the outstanding success stories of its kind.

The writer has played down rather than exaggerated the story because Mr. Wright, like many other dealers, does not like to release his exact sales figures. However, we can drop the clue that his one store in a community of only 17,000 people most certainly purchased for their own use the equal that a substantial jobber might stock for his entire trade during a similar period. That means a lot of sales in any man's business. The promotion is still going on full blast and still the biggest specialty sales. Later, Wright plans to display them with garden and gift items.

---

basement of the store. On Monday morning the buyer in the sporting goods department reordered six dozen Jets from the Barr company.

Mr. Perry, who was in the store during part of the selling day, noticed that the traffic in the sporting goods department was poor. He further observed that almost all the lanterns were purchased by women. Apparently the attractiveness of the product pulled some women into the sporting goods department who might not otherwise have shopped there. Most of the customers to whom Mr. Perry spoke that day indicated that they were buying the lantern for emergency use only. Several customers asked the clerk where they could obtain kerosene for the lantern. Mr. Perry thought that a few more sales would have resulted if customers could have purchased fuel at the same time.

From this short test the young executive drew the following conclusions: (1) the Jet was a salable product; (2) it would be difficult for a department store to develop large sales volume on lanterns; (3) the product was a "traffic item," needing heavy display to attract attention and introduce purchase. Consequently, in his spare time throughout the remainder of the summer, Mr. Perry attempted to design counter displays for his product.

After this experience in the department-store field, Mr. Perry visited a

large, local toy shop to get some opinions from the manager. The owner
of the store liked the Jet and purchased half a dozen lanterns. He said
that if he could not sell them he would keep them in his own shop for use
during an emergency. From time to time during the next few months he
ordered a few lanterns.

In August the second Easton department store that Mr. Perry had contacted used the lantern as a promotional item. The buyer ordered six dozen
lanterns and placed them in the housewares department on the fourth
floor. A two-column-by-seven-inch advertisement was inserted on the
comic page of the local newspaper in preparation for Friday's selling;
and two small displays exhibiting the lanterns were used on the fourth
floor, one at the head of the elevators, the other at the point where the
Jets were being sold. On that Friday, 40 lanterns were sold and 14 mail
orders were secured from the newspaper advertisement. On the next
Monday morning the housewares buyer reordered six dozen Jet lanterns.
Both the buyer and Mr. Perry were disappointed in the mail response
which the newspaper advertisement secured; however, the housewares
buyer said he was still convinced it was a good item.

Mr. Perry was undecided as to how to promote and advertise the Jet.
In re-evaluating his experiences in both department stores, he came to the
conclusion that in general space advertising was not too helpful in the sale
of his product and that for it to do well, the customer had to see it. It was
his opinion that point-of-purchase display was extremely important if the
Jet lantern was to be a success.

Mr. Perry believed furthermore that it might become necessary for
him to provide fuel for the lantern if his product was to sell successfully
in department stores. In several instances since introducing the Jet he had
encountered resistance because kerosene was not easily obtainable for
department-store customers. Although kerosene was usually available at
gasoline stations and hardware stores, he reasoned that if he could sell a
small container of kerosene at the time of the initial purchase, more sales
might be made; the customer could then replenish his kerosene supply
from the ordinary outlets.

Mr. Perry, therefore, started to experiment with various types of containers for kerosene and to contact sources of supply. One of the large oil
companies in Easton offered to sell him "deodorized" kerosene. The fuel
could be packaged in 16-ounce cans, which the oil company had available.
The Barr company would have to buy at least two gross of the cans, at a
cost of 8 cents for each can. The cost of the kerosene would be approximately 4 cents for 16 ounces. Mr. Perry estimated that the cost of packing
the kerosene and having labels printed would be 20 cents a can. Sixteen
ounces would be about a 40 hours' fuel supply for the Jet. He had no idea
what pricing policy he should follow if he decided to offer the kerosene
to department stores.

In early September 1951, Mr. Perry went to New York City to call on some of the retail buying offices of department stores located there and to meet with the advertising agency which had handled the Barr lantern account for many years. The merchandise managers of the Easton department stores had suggested that he go to New York retailers as a means of getting distribution in the department-store field. Before he left he compiled a list of buying offices and stores in New York City, and then he called these organizations from his hotel for appointments. Among the contacts which he hoped to make were: Abraham & Straus, Bloomingdale's, Macy's, Gimbel's, Allied Stores, Inc., and Arkwright Merchandise, Inc. In most cases Mr. Perry contacted the housewares buyer by telephone, but he was able to secure only two appointments for the next day. The Easton stores which had sold the product gave him introductions to their New York buying offices. The Allied Stores representative was not interested in the Jet, but he did take a sample. The representative of Arkwright, a buying syndicate, promised to send a "merchandise flash" to its 325 stores.

Before he left his hotel room on the second morning, Mr. Perry had a call from the Allied representative telling him that one of the Allied stores on Long Island was interested in the product and urged him to go out there. When Mr. Perry visited the store, the merchandise manager expressed interest in the Jet lantern and requested a $100 advertising allowance to assist in the promotion of the item. Mr. Perry was undecided as to what to do about this request. Thinking the allowance might be highly desirable, he contacted the sales manager of the Barr company that afternoon but was told that the company had never granted any advertising allowances because allowances were deemed to be price cuts. Meanwhile, three Allied buyers who were in their New York offices saw the sample lantern sitting on a desk and ordered four dozen apiece.

The next day Mr. Perry met with the executive of the New York advertising agency and presented to him an advertising schedule which he had drawn up for the department-store campaign. The account executive agreed to prepare advertisements to meet the deadline dates imposed by the schedule. He persuaded Mr. Perry that it would be better to spend money on national advertising, for the prestige value, rather than to offer allowances to department stores. In setting up plans for the future, Mr. Perry emphasized to the agency executive that he wanted to be certain of getting the promotion geared up so that the Jet might be sold as a Christmas item. The previous year the Jet had been introduced too late for the Christmas buying season. The meeting concluded with an agreement to send a "giant postal card" as a first direct-mail piece to department-store housewares buyers and to do a small amount of national advertising in *The Saturday Evening Post, American Home*, and *Better Homes & Gardens* during the latter part of November and the month of December. The account executive's cost estimates for insertions in these magazines were as follows:

. . . *Saturday Evening Post* ($20 per line), 45 lines December 1 or November 24. Circulation, 4,129,334. Cost, $900.

Better Homes & Gardens ($16.66 per line), 45 lines in December. Circulation, 3,648,211. Cost, $740.70.

American Home ($12.80 per line), 45 lines December. Circulation, 2,897,-621. Cost, $576.

Total cost for the three magazines, $2,225.70. Total circulation, 10,675,-166 . . .

The postal card was to be completed by the agency within the next few weeks.

Direct-Mail Campaign

The first direct-mail piece which Mr. Perry sent out was the giant postal card suggested by the New York advertising agency. The account executive there told Mr. Perry that he had previously used that type of mailing successfully to industrial buyers. The card measured 10 inches by 8½ inches, was in two colors, and offered a free sample of the lantern on a detachable business reply card. The giant postal card is reproduced in Exhibit 5. Mr. Perry ordered 3,000 of these mailing pieces. The total cost to the Barr company was $468, which included about $100 for the artwork.

Although Mr. Perry originally planned to mail the card to 3,000 names, the pressure of time, shortage of help, and inability to gather what he thought was an adequate mailing list, resulted in his sending the giant postal card to only 458 housewares buyers in department stores between October 10 and November 14, 1951. Mr. Perry realized that the cards would be received entirely too late for Christmas buying, but the advertising agency was unable to produce the finished cards any sooner.

Within a week after this first mailing, Mr. Perry had received eight requests for free samples. These eight prospects later developed into sales to two different department stores. One store ordered two dozen lanterns; the other ordered four dozen lanterns.

On November 28, 1951, Mr. Perry followed up his first mailing with a letter, a two-color broadside, a reprint from the August issue of the hardware trade paper, two "stage-money" inserts, and a business reply card. Exhibit 6 reproduces the letter which was sent with this material. This mailing was directed to 475 housewares buyers in department stores, who comprised essentially the same mailing list that he had used previously. The second mailing cost Mr. Perry $71.55. He received requests for free samples from seven department stores, three of which purchased a total of 24 dozen lanterns.

On December 11, 1951, Mr. Perry sent a third mailing piece to 476 names on this basic list. This mailing included a letter, the same broadside as in the November 28 mailing, a business reply card, and a new nickel. Exhibit 7 reproduces the letter sent with the December 11 mailing. This

Exhibit 5

C. W. BARR COMPANY

Giant Postal Card Used as the First Direct-Mail Piece

BARR
LANTERNS

To See the Jet is Worth a 1,000 Pictures

10,000 words can't express the "sell-on-sight" quality of the BARR JET LANTERN—no picture can reproduce the glamor of this little red lantern with the big light. You must see it, as have other stores. To see it is to buy it—to display it is to sell it. The JET is one of those products so loaded with sell-appeal that no advertisement such as this can do it justice.

So Send the Post Card for Free Sample

We want you as buyer, at our expense, to examine firsthand its utility, good looks, and fair-sex appeal and to know why some dealers have sold gross after gross (names on request) to a quick-to-buy public.

If you prefer we will send a trial order of two dozen JET LANTERNS at a special discount of 40% *and* 5% off list of $25.00 per dozen F.O.B. Easton (shipping weight 17 lbs. per dozen). They won't keep long—and we know you'll want lots more for Christmas. Mats, counter display, display cards, stuffers, photos, etc., are available for promotion.

Every Home Should Own One or More Jet Lanterns

"Lights out" in blackouts,- - - - - - - - - - - - - - - - -
or from sudden darkness, create a need for a reliable, safe, and portable standby light indoors or out—in any weather.

The "Jet" won't drip on furnishings or clothing. If tipped over it goes out—but otherwise never unexpectedly and only until last drop of kerosene is burned.

NEW! TOP VALUE! IN-EXPENSIVE!

Only 8½" high. Fire Engine Red, Raybaked. Enamel Finish. Burns 12 hours.

BARR JET LANTERN

Backed by over a century and a decade of world leadership, in the manufacture of portable light.

Universal Appeal to All Ages—Both Sexes

For fun as well as utility— for picnics, travel, sport, camping and for general use after dark. MAKES FAST SELLING GIFTS, PRIZES.

BARR JET LANTERN
IS NATIONALLY
ADVERTISED

Saturday Evening Post
Better Homes & Gardens
American Home, Etc.

SEND AS FOLLOWS

C. W. Barr Co.
Sales Promotion Dept.
P.O. Box #1214
Easton, Pa.
Gentlemen:

‗‗‗‗

‗‗‗‗

‗‗‗‗

Buyer‗‗‗‗
Store‗‗‗‗
Address‗‗‗‗

‗‗‗‗

Exhibit 6

C. W. BARR COMPANY

Direct-Mail Letter of November 28, 1951

Dear Mr. Buyer of Housewares:
>   This is chicken feed, but you don't have to
>   scratch for REAL money with the RED JET!

Our national ads (*Saturday Evening Post, Better Homes & Gardens,* and *American Home*) will soon bring you customers, *and* we'll refer factory inquiries to you, too! Remember, you've a generous $1.30 margin in the advertised price of $2.49 on the All Year 'Round JET.

Look how Wright's Suburban Hardware Store sold nearly 70 *dozen Jets* in three months—then realize you have 600% more opportunities for big sales—just as Dallas, St. Louis, Kansas City, Providence, Boston, and Syracuse profitwise department stores are discovering.

Every one of the 44,000,000 families in the United States is a prospect for one or *more* Jets, for emergency standby light, for fun, or antique atmosphere—and the Jet is a fine gift that can be featured all the year so there's no warehousing after the Christmas rush.

NOW . . . make that date with the Jet . . . return this postal card and order enough JETS for a large display like Dallas' TITCHE-GOETTINGER and FAMOUS-BARR of St. Louis just did!
>   Cordially,
>   C. W. BARR COMPANY
>   /s/ R. PERRY
>   R. Perry

P.S. Not only are we advertised in *Better Homes & Gardens* for December—but page 53 has a wonderful Christmas idea for Red Lanterns.

⊦   NOTE: This mailing included the letter above, four-color broadside featuring window displays of the Jet, two stage-money bills, and a reprint from the August 1951 issue of a hardware trade paper featuring the Jet.

mailing cost the Barr company $64, which included printing costs and the 476 nickels. Twenty-eight replies were received which developed into nine orders and sold a total of 92 dozen lanterns.

Mr. Perry then built up the mailing list to a total of 773 names, to whom he sent out the final mailing on January 20, 1952. By mid-March, the company had received 14 more requests for free samples. Exhibit 8 shows the letter in this final mailing; a business reply card was included. Exhibit 9 shows the Jet department-store sales and expenses charged to the department-store campaign in 1951 and early 1952.

Exhibit 10 shows Jet lantern sales by dozens during the months of 1951 and early 1952.

Future Planning

As Mr. Perry looked ahead to the spring season, he set for himself the following goals: (1) to compile a bigger and better department-store mailing list and to send out a new series of direct-mail pieces; (2) to follow up closely on any favorable publicity that the Jet might receive;

Exhibit 7

C. W. BARR COMPANY
Direct-Mail Letter of December 11, 1951

Dear Buyer of Housewares:

$$\left\{ \begin{array}{c} \text{Five-cent} \\ \text{piece attached} \\ \text{here.} \end{array} \right\}$$

Relax, have a "Coke" on me and pause to think about the little red JET lantern.

In Reading, Pennsylvania (population 110,500), POMEROY'S sold 36 dozen JETS in five weeks, and their margin was 53.5%! Already Ralph C. Koppelman, POMEROY'S buyer, has ordered another 12 dozen to start 1952 off right, and says, "If anyone will display the JET like I did, he'll sell it just like I did!" Look carefully at the display Mr. Koppelman duplicated for only two days and start planning how you can display the JET in your department.

National advertising is working for you—inquiries, too. Sales helps are available for the asking.

JORDAN MARSH of Boston, POLSKY'S of Akron, HUTZLER'S in Baltimore, St. Louis' FAMOUS-BARR, J. L. HUDSON in Detroit, and dozens of other stores from Tampa to St. Paul are *selling* the refreshingly new Jet. Now . . . order 18, 12, or 10 dozen just as these stores are doing and get your 53.5% return on a large display.

Cordially,

/s/ R. PERRY

R. Perry

sm

P.S. It's late, but there's still time for a Christmas display, since we'll ship immediately, as we did today to T. A. Grisson, of Polsky's, who needed 24 dozen since he sold 8½ dozen in 3 hours Saturday!

---

(3) to follow up on the stores that had done well with the lantern and ask them how the Barr company could assist them further; (4) to make up a complete promotional package of stuffers, mats, and display material to present to the department-store buyers; and (5) to make a personal trip to large midwestern department stores for the purpose of promoting the Jet lantern.

In addition, Mr. Perry speculated as to how he might profitably sell the Jet lantern to the Red Cross and to Civil Defense units as a good source of portable light for disaster service. He thought that he might paint the lantern white to make it attractive to those groups. The young executive wondered about supermarkets and mail-order firms and whether they might possibly be good outlets for the product. A friend of his who was the local distributor for a national farm-machinery company suggested that he paint the lantern a bright yellow, which was that company's "color," and offer it to the company for use in its promotion programs.

Exhibit 8

C. W. BARR COMPANY
Direct-Mail Letter of January 20, 1952

WE STUCK OUR NECK WAY OUT . . . .

Last November when we introduced the high-powered little red JET LANTERNS, we boldly stated "if you display the JET big you'll sell 'em big . . . and repeat fast." We even offered you a trial order of only two dozen at:

\$25 per dozen less 40% less 5%	\$14.25
Nationally advertised retail price	2.49
Your MARKUP on each JET	1.30

Did we get it in the neck? No sir! Store after store displayed JETS— sold JETS and reordered again and again in gross lots. One store sold a gross in two days—another store displayed JETS in two departments, one, a main floor display—sold out in two days and had to reorder twice!

Now, this letter is still addressed only to the *original*, preferred list of buyers—you who have not taken advantage of the previous offer. WE ARE CONTINUING OUR SPECIAL OFFER AND GUARANTEEING SAME DAY SHIPMENT FOR THE NEXT 30 DAYS.

With spring in the offing—sports, picnics, gardening, trips—the demand for the JET, from young and old, will hit a peak. But give them more than a "peak"—give a big display. Like Bry's of Memphis who sold JETS in the Bar-B-Que section, you will be able to say "Sales results were good. We sold 120 lanterns in two days and have 40 mail orders waiting for delivery of the 60 placed on reorder with you. We plan to buy 144 and run the same ad in February."

Let's hear from you . . . and you won't "stick *your* neck out" either, we guarantee.

Cordially,
C. W. BARR COMPANY
/s/ R. Perry
R. PERRY

sm
January 20, 1952

During the latter part of January, Mr. Perry went to New York City again to talk with the advertising agency. By this time he was convinced that although the agency was doing its best, it did not have the organization necessary to do an adequate job for him, and that if he expected to improve the Jet's chances for success, he would have to get agency help elsewhere. Mr. Perry considered doing the job himself; but since his responsibilities were growing in other company affairs, he was able to devote only about 25% of his time to the Jet lantern department-store campaign.

After discussing the situation with the president, Mr. Perry was given a free hand to change agencies if he so desired. Accordingly, he decided to choose a local Easton agency so that he could work more closely with

Exhibit 9

C. W. BARR COMPANY
Department-Store Campaign
Jet Sales to Department Stores

Month	*Dollar Sales*
September 1951	$ 203
October 1951	514
November 1951	1,641
December 1951	2,813
January 1952	1,225
February 1952	313
Total Sales	$6,709

Expenses Charged to Department-Store Campaign

1951	$4,977	
1952	343	(January and February only)
	$5,320	Total Expenses

Note: Expenses are net advertising expenditures (newspaper and magazine space charges, etc., telephone and telegraph costs, promotional trips, display material. No salary is included.)

that organization. He decided to make the change in the next few weeks in order that the new group might make a merchandise plan for the next Christmas selling season.

After carefully screening several local advertising agencies, Mr. Perry chose the largest agency in the city. On February 20, 1952, he met with

Exhibit 10

C. W. BARR COMPANY
Number of Jet Lanterns Sold in 1951 and in
January and February of 1952

Year and Month	*Dozens of Jet Lanterns Sold*
1951:	
January	1,400
February	1,200
March	1,300
April	450
May	200
June	300
July	250
August	400
September*	800
October	950
November	1,400
December	950
1951 Total	9,600
1952:	
January	1,300
February	900

* Department-store campaign began in September 1951.

Source: Company records.

the account executive and his young assistant shortly thereafter to bring them up to date on the Jet lantern. Following are the conference notes which the account executive's assistant wrote after the meeting.

Present at Conference: Raymond Perry, Harvey Goodale, and Bob Jackson.

Product: Jet kerosene lantern.

Distribution: Barr company is well established in hardware channels. However, the Jet is not being sold aggressively through hardware jobbers. Less than half of present jobbers now carry it. Decision was made last October to sell Jet through department stores directly, no wholesalers.

Prices and Discounts and Profits: The Jet is set up to sell at $1.98 retail. It has sold successfully for as high as $2.49 retail. Cost to department stores is $25.00 per dozen, less 40% and 5%. Department store sets its own retail price. Ray Perry talks a higher retail price than $1.98 when attempting to sell stores— giving them the idea of a larger margin to play with. Gross profit to Barr is approximately $5.00 per dozen. They need to sell 3,000–3,500 dozen for one year to break even in a selling campaign to department stores.

Salesmen: No sales force other than Perry (part-time) is available for reaching department stores. Everything must be done by mail.

Sales Volume: November, December, and January, $5,800 (to department stores).

Sales Cost: $4,600 (same three months).

Previous Sales Record: Sold some 12,000 dozen in the domestic market since its introduction in September 1950, of which about 500 dozen were sold through department stores.

Previous Promotion to Consumers: One small advertisement in *The Saturday Evening Post, American Home,* and *Better Homes & Gardens* was purchased for merchandising value.

Previous Promotion to Prospective Department Store Outlets: One direct-mail piece and several letters.

Results of Promotion to Store Prospects: In the first place, mailings were very late and most of the buying had already been done. The elaborate post card was sent to 500 stores, and pulled only three replies. One of Perry's later letters, however, pulled 46 replies.

Results of Over-all Promotion to Department Stores: Some cities have flopped; some have been excellent.

Perry says that a clear pattern has developed in the stores which have made a success of the Jet. They give the Jet a mass display. The big problem connected with this is that the Jet is so low in price that it isn't worth very much floor space—it doesn't produce enough dollar volume. One suggestion was made: give the department store the merchandise on a consignment basis for display use only—in windows, on floors, on counters, etc.

Advertising Allowance: Almost without exception, each department store has asked for a newspaper advertising allowance. The most popular size seems to be around 3 columns × 8 or 10 inches. For some reason, Macy's in New York ordered only the minimum (two dozen). Didn't ask for an advertising allowance, and refused to accept goods on consignment for display purposes. The Allied Store Syndicate is doing very well with the Jet. One of the other syndicates is not doing well.

Advertising Appeals: Everything to date has been along the line of buy this lamp for emergency use." (A suggestion was made to broaden this appeal in order to add continuous value to the lamp. Talk about other uses. Show thumbnail sketches of them, etc.)

Of course, this is a good item at Christmas. And in the spring and summer it has been promoted as a camp item.

Immediate Problem: To produce a campaign and a plan which will get the Jet into as many department stores throughout the nation as we can, in time for Christmas consumer buying. As of right now, we have $4,000 until September with which to do this. Unfortunately, toy buying for Christmas is already well underway.

Long-Range Problems: How to keep department stores active in promotion of the Jet? How to expand and maintain distribution?

~~~

CASE 18: GRAHAM MANUFACTURING COMPANY[1]

QUESTIONS TO CONSIDER: *(1) Over-all, what type of selling strategy should the Graham company employ in 1958 and thereafter? (2) Should the company participate in any of the trade shows being considered by management? If so, how should the shows be used to stimulate sales? (3) Would you recommend hiring the Chicago public relations firm? (4) Should the company undertake advertising in trade papers? If so, for what purposes? What kind of advertising copy do you think should be employed in trade papers?*

In early 1958 the new general manager of Graham Manufacturing Corporation, Needham Heights, Massachusetts, a manufacturer of stored energy stud welding equipment, was considering what type of promotional strategy to employ in the future. Since its founding in 1947, the company had relied exclusively upon selling by executives, several salesmen, and selling agents to promote sales. For 1958 the company planned to commit itself to a promotional budget of $24,000, to be spent only if some type or types of promotion promised to be effective. In early 1958 the new general manager was considering three types of promotional activities: (1) participation in trade shows, (2) publicity, and (3) trade paper advertising.

Stored Energy Stud Welding

During World War II the necessity of finding a simple and rapid method of securing various materials to ships' bulkheads led to the development of the electrical stored energy welding method, which was neither resistance nor arc welding, but combined many of the best features of those methods so that studs could be welded to light, as well as to heavy gauge, metal sheets without fillets or distortion and without heating the metal so as to mar the plating or paint on the opposite surface. No flux, special material, or preparation was required except for a special stud which had a tip as an integral part. The welding of the studs to metal

---

[1] Written by Martin V. Marshall.

sheets was accomplished through energy supplied by one or more capacitors storing sufficient electrical energy to supply a current density of about 300,000 amperes per square inch of stud cross-sectional area. As the arc was made between the stud and the metal, a hammer blow completed the weld in about $\frac{1}{1000}$ of a second. A graphic representation of the stored energy welding process is shown in Exhibit 1.

The principal advantage of stored energy welding was the fact that studs could be welded to thin metal sheets without marring the opposite surface. Other welding methods applied heat in such a way that the op-

Exhibit 1

GRAHAM MANUFACTURING COMPANY

Graphic Representation of Stored Energy Welding Process

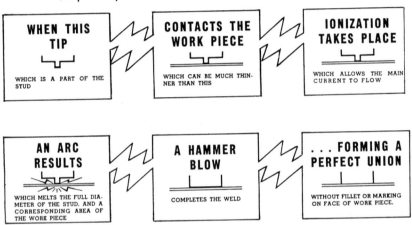

posite surface of thin sheets usually were marred. Stored energy welding was adaptable to any low carbon ferrous and most nonferrous metals: steel could be welded to steel, steel to lead-free brass, steel to stainless and plated steel, steel to copper, aluminum to aluminum, aluminum to die cast zinc, and so on.

Product Line

In 1958 the Graham company manufactured and marketed five types of stored energy welding equipment. Pictures of this equipment are shown in Exhibit 2.

The Model 6000D welder was a portable insulation-pin welder, designed primarily for use in welding pins (or nails) to heating and air-conditioning duct work—insulation materials were then impaled and secured on the pins by means of a special clip. The company also sold the special pins and clips which were required for this type of welding. The welder sold for $1,600, F.O.B. Needham Heights. The two largest selling sizes of pins sold for $5.05 and $6.10 a thousand; the clips for $5.90 a thousand.

Although generally used by heating and air-conditioning contractors, the Model 6000D welder was occasionally purchased as a bench welder for welding studs up to size No. 10 by other types of businesses, such as electrical contractors for installing junction boxes, restaurant equipment manufacturers for attaching stainless steel trim, and building contractors for the hanging of dropped and acoustical ceilings from steel supports above.

The Model 3000 welder was a single gun bench welder, designed primarily for use in manufacturing operations involving metalworking, such as the attachment of legs to electric frying pans, of trim to automobiles, and of name plates to electrical appliances. For operations allowing automation, automatic and multiple gun bench welders were available, Models 2000, x 8000, and 10000, with one to eight pneumatically operated guns and a capacity as high as 4,800 welds an hour. The Model 3000 welder cost $3,500 F.O.B. Needham Heights, and the Models 2000, x 8000, and 10000 welders, depending upon the number of guns, cost up to $15,000 F.O.B. Needham Heights. Studs for these welders were manufactured to the specifications of the user and cost from $2.00 to $150 a thousand, except for some common-sized studs which were carried in stock.

The company had patents on all phases of its process and did not have any direct competition.

In general, Graham equipment and suppliers were more expen-

Exhibit 2

Graham's Stored Energy Welding Equipment

MULTIPLE GUN BENCH WELDER
MODEL 2000

SINGLE GUN
BENCH WELDER
MODEL 3000

PORTABLE
INSUL-PIN WELDER
MODEL 6000-D

AUTOMATIC
BENCH WELDER
MODEL 8000

MULTIPLE GUN PRESS WELDER
MODEL 10000

sive than other methods of welding. Users usually had net savings, however, because the Graham process did not require grinding or polishing of marred metal.

Graham's Marketing Operation

The Graham company distributed its products through two company sales offices, which were located in New York and Chicago, and 26 sales agents, which were located in other key market areas. Eight of the agents were specialists in heating and air-conditioning equipment and sold only Model 6000D welders. The other 18 agents were specialists in welding equipment and carried all Graham welders, as well as four or five lines of noncompetitive arc and resistance welding equipment and supplies. Agents were paid a commission of 20% on welders and insulation pins and 10% on studs and clips. Each of the sales offices had one sales representative and one serviceman, and each cost about $15,000 a year to operate. The service expense was charged to customers at cost, and servicemen's salaries and expenses were not charged to sales office expense. Annual sales of the sales agents and the sales offices in 1957 ranged from a low of $149 (for a new sales agent) to a high of $107,000.

Sales Promotion Policy

Throughout its history the Graham company had developed sales primarily through sales calls on businesses which potentially looked as if they might be able to use stored energy stud welding. Many of the company's principal customers had been obtained as the result of the personal selling efforts of Mr. Harry Graham, the developer of the Graham stored energy welding process, who devoted much of his time to the development of key accounts. Sales agents usually promoted sales as they thought best in their territories. They were provided by the company with three selling aids: a four-page descriptive brochure on the Graham stud welding process; two-page brochures on each type of welder; and a sample stud board which displayed five types of studs for 14 different combinations of metals. For some years sales agents had devoted approximately one half of their selling efforts to the heating and air-conditioning contracting field and one half to the development of sales in other businesses.

In working with prospects, sales agents often had to have the company prepare sample studs for testing by the prospect. In 1957 approximately 150 samples had been prepared at a cost of $12,000, which was charged to selling expense.

In 1957 the company's gross sales were approximately as follows:

—Sales of Models 6000D welders, usually to heating and air-conditioning contractors: $250,000.
—Sales of pins and clips, usually for securing insulation: $230,000.
—Sales of Models 2000, 3000, and x 8000 bench welders, usually to electrical

appliance manufacturers and automobile fabricated parts subcontractors: $125,000.
—Sales of studs, usually made to specifications for use on Models 2000, 3000, and x 8000 welders: $260,000.

In late 1957 the general manager had hired one of the best sales agents as the company's sales manager with the expectation that he would gradually develop long-term plans for the sales operation.

Generally speaking, according to the company's new sales manager, sales agents developed business in other fields by "cold" calls on what appeared to be likely prospects. "About all that the agent has been able to do," he said, "is to present the Graham story to a firm and hope that the firm sees some application for the process in its operation. If he finds that a given type of business buys, for instance, a toy manufacturer, then he calls on other toy manufacturers. However, this is a costly process. One of our men, for example, sold equipment to a fireproof door manufacturer. He then called on other fireproof door manufacturers, but couldn't make any sales. Finally he discovered that the original buyer was using Graham equipment on escalator railings, not fireproof doors. It's very, very difficult to find out how Graham equipment is actually used even though we know who has purchased it."

"The stored energy welding process is so versatile," said the general manager, "that we don't know where to focus our selling effort. For instance, here is a list of manufacturers for whom we have recently prepared sample studs." The list included manufacturers of automobile radiators, strip light fixtures, vending machines, elevators, laundry machines, TV trays, voting machines, automobile shock absorbers, cameras, juke boxes, and automobile trailers. "Right now it appears that three markets might develop into major markets: business machine manufacturers, subcontracting sheet metal shops, and stainless steel fabricating plants. But we have no real evidence as to the potentials of these markets."

It was the opinion of the general manager that some means had to be developed to provide the company's sales representatives with good leads. Steps had already been taken to determine specifically where and how existing Graham equipment was being utilized. However, he did not feel that this information would throw much light on what types of businesses or applications to focus selling effort in the future. He thought that much new business would develop if industry knew of the potentialities of stored energy stud welding. Thus the company was primarily interested in finding an economical and effective method of getting information about the Graham process to product-design engineers in large companies, who were considered to be the key factor in determing the method of welding used and who could best visualize new applications of the process, and to the general management of smaller companies who made all product-design decisions.

Hence in early 1958, the general manager and the sales manager were

Exhibit 3. Floor Plan of the American Welding Society's 1958 Welding Show

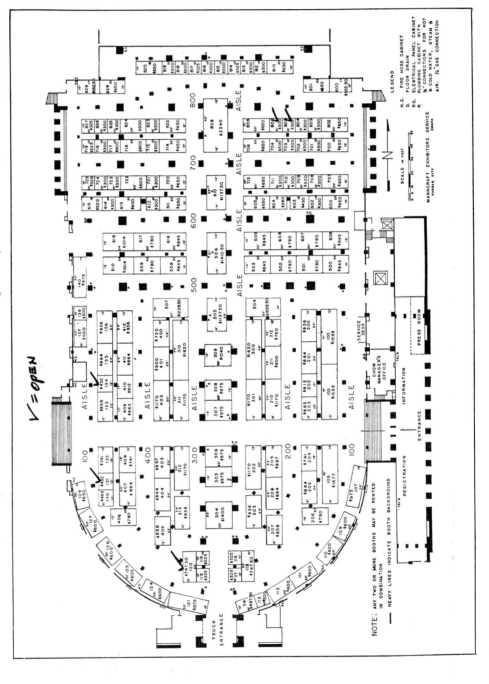

considering the use of trade shows, publicity, and trade paper advertising to educate product design engineers and general management about the Graham process.

Trade Shows

Consideration was being given three trade shows: The American Welding Society's "Welding Show," to be held in Kiel Auditorium, St. Louis,

Exhibit 4

GRAHAM MANUFACTURING COMPANY

Analysis of Attendance of Welding Show, Philadelphia, 1957

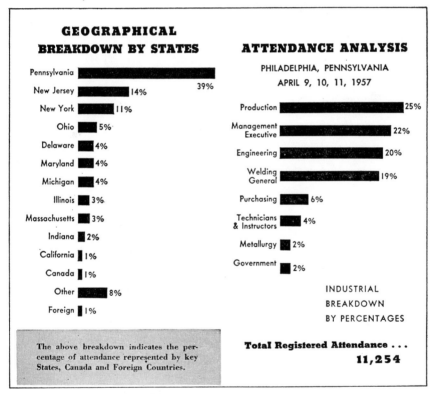

April 15–17, 1958; the American Society for Metals' "National Metals Exposition," to be held in the Cleveland Public Auditorium, Cleveland, October 8–12, 1958; and the American Society of Heating and Air-Conditioning Engineer's "International Heating and Air-Conditioning Exposition," to be held in Convention Hall, Philadelphia, January 26–29, 1959.

As of early 1958, 104 exhibitors had already signed up for the Welding Show and only five locations were still available, as indicated on the floor plan which is reproduced in Exhibit 3. Two of the locations were 12 feet by 12 feet and priced at $432; one was 10 feet by 23 feet and priced at $747.50; and two were 10 feet by 10 feet and priced at $300. An analysis of the attendance of the 1957 Welding Show is given in Exhibit 4.

Exhibit 5. Floor Plan of the 1958 National Metal Exposition

40th National Metal Exposition....

Cleveland Public Auditorium

OCTOBER 27-31, 1958

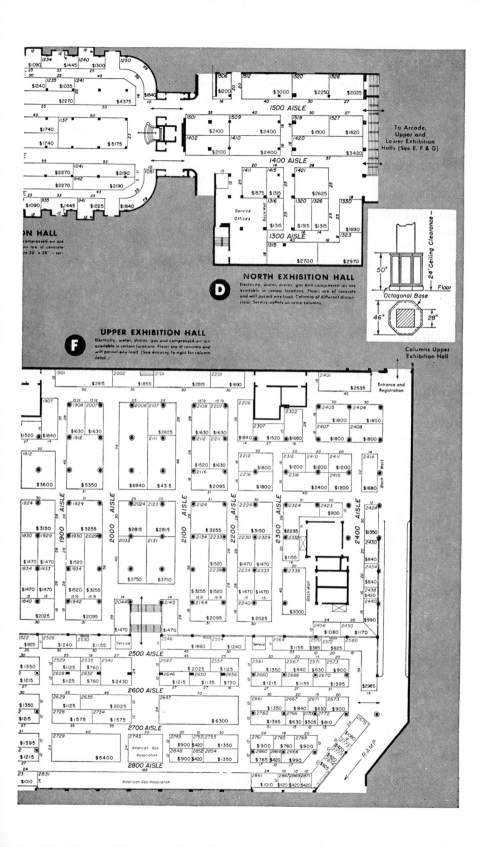

The floor plan for the National Metal Exposition is shown in Exhibit 5 with prices noted for each space. An analysis of attendance at the 1957 exposition was not available to Graham's management.

The floor plan of the International Heating and Air-Conditioning Exposition is shown in Exhibit 6 (cost of space being in the lighter type). An attendance analysis for the 1955 exposition is given in Exhibit 7.

Management had no evidence which indicated the potential value of participating in any of the trade shows. In addition to space costs, it was estimated that it would cost an additional $3,000 to $3,500 a show to ship and set up equipment and to man the company's booth. If the company participated in trade shows, it was planned that equipment would be demonstrated in a variety of ways, that photographs of successful applications would be shown, and that appropriate literature would be available for distribution to visitors. This literature would have to be developed, however, as the company's sales brochures were not considered adequate.

Publicity

In considering the possibilities of obtaining publicity, the company's sales manager had recently met with a Chicago public relations firm which specialized in obtaining technical and editorial publicity for manufacturers of specialized industrial products. This firm suggested that the Graham company might undertake a technical information program, which is described below:

First, a technical information program is a *program*—not a mere listing of things you do (or should do). It is a program which follows a *plan* and a schedule. It is a program which is *directed* by regular meetings involving (1) sales management, (2) engineering management, and (3) sales promotion management.

Second, it embraces all company activities intended to bring the *knowledge* and *understanding* of your markets (prospects, customers, and dealers) *up to those levels* and *along those avenues* which make it easier for the salesman to close.

A good technical information program does much of the salesman's missionary and educational work for him. It saves time for discussing the particular issue—not the general theory. It produces better informed prospects—and better armed representatives.

A technical information program courts and sorts inquiries. It helps you to be invited to call in the right places at the right time (where business likelihood really exists). A good technical information program persistently reaches a hundred prospects you'd *like* to call on for every one you *can* call on—and three or four additional sales-influencing factors for every prospect who might actually buy or specify (e.g., development engineers, research men, designers at the board, production management, purchasing agents, test engineers, chemists, metallurgists, and such).

Your technical information program, therefore, includes:
1. Your engineering application bulletins.
2. Your program of preparation of articles for trade, technical, and business magazines (and reprints thereof).
3. Your news and technical release program.

Exhibit 6

GRAHAM MANUFACTURING COMPANY

Floor Plan of the 1959 International Heating and Air-Conditioning Exposition

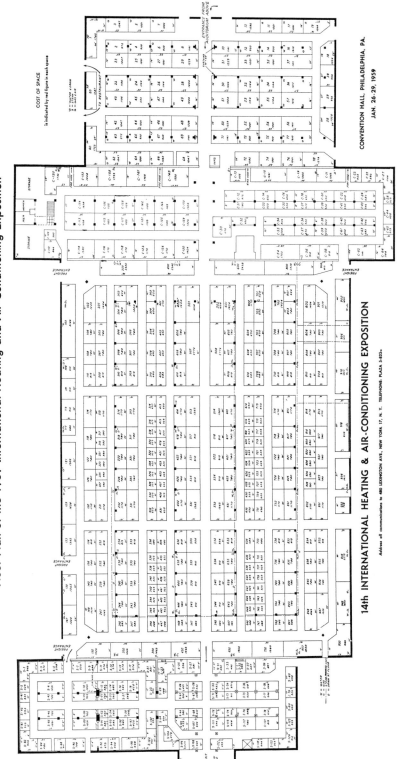

CONVENTION HALL, PHILADELPHIA, PA.

JAN. 26-29, 1959

14th INTERNATIONAL HEATING & AIR-CONDITIONING EXPOSITION

Address all communications to 480 LEXINGTON AVE., NEW YORK 17, N. Y. TELEPHONE: PLAZA 5-8734.

Exhibit 7

GRAHAM MANUFACTURING COMPANY

Breakdown of Registered Attendance at 12th International Heating & Ventilating Exposition—Philadelphia, 1955

OCCUPATIONAL ANALYSIS

EXECUTIVE

Board Chairmen	5
Presidents	1,411
Vice Presidents	695
Chief Engineers	255
Secretaries	139
Treasurers	76
Directors	613
Proprietors, Owners, Partners	23
Real Estate Owners, Agents, Managers	175
General Managers	737
Managers	304
Jobbers, Wholesalers, Distributors, Dealers	1,589
Manufacturers' Agents	817
Sales Managers and Sales Executives	1,076
Salesmen	2,385
Sales Engineers	84
Advertising Departments	27
Auditors and Accountants	40
Attorneys and Business Consultants	6
Comptrollers, Statisticians	245
Purchasing Agents	193
Administrative Workers	154
Exporters	8
Insurance Agents	7
Miscellaneous	8
	11,072

OPERATION

Managers: Production, Plant, Department	210
Superintendents	194
Chief Engineers	301
Plant and Operating Engineers	228
Maintenance Engineers (39), Departments (38)	77
Industrial Engineers	29
Inspectors	53
Supervisors	171
Foremen	228
Master Mechanics, Mechanics, Machinists	274
Tool and Die Makers, Miscellaneous Operators	15
Miscellaneous Department Heads–Workers	96
Production Depts. (35), Miscellaneous Depts. (20)	55
	1,931

TECHNICAL

Engineers, Heating (106), Power Plant (20)	126
Engineers, Heating, Ventilating and Air Conditioning	6
Engineers, Mechanical	156
Engineers, Consulting	577
Engineers, Electrical	50
Engineers, Civil	84
Engineers (Titles Not Given)	971
Research Directors (26), Research Engineers (44), Dev. and Test Engineers (59)	129
Research Managers (28), Departments (29)	57
Technical Directors	66
Technicians	89
Project Engineers	123
Chemical Engineers (26), Chemists (11)	45
Metallurgists (8)	58
Miscellaneous (15 Titles)	14
	2,556

CONSTRUCTION

Architects	92
Building Contractors	141
Contractors (10 Titles)	2,388
Designers, Design Engineers	267
Engineers, Construction	36
Estimators	198
Draftsmen	207
Superintendents	161
Foremen	212
Service Engineers	70
Service Managers (220), Servicemen (386)	606
Installers	104
Steamfitters	99
Plumbers	215
Sheet Metal Workers	53
Electricians	45
Mechanical Trades (5 Titles)	106
Miscellaneous	3
	5,003

NOT OTHERWISE CLASSIFIED

Professors, Instructors, Students	249
Educational Institutions Operating Staff	5
Publishers, Editors, Publishers' Staffs	52
Home Owners	9
Miscellaneous	238
Unclassified	10
Total	**563**
Total	**21,125**

INDUSTRIAL ANALYSIS

DISTRIBUTION CHANNELS

Contractors, General, Building	266
Insulation	38
Electrical	67
Plumbing	68
Plumbing and Heating	1,481
Plumbing, Heating, Ventilating and Air Conditioning	436
Heating	944
Heating and Ventilating	66
Heating and Air Conditioning	573
Heating, Ventilating, Air Conditioning, Plumbing and Refrigeration	84
Air Conditioning (223), Refrigeration (61)	284
Air Conditioning and Refrigeration	202
Sheet Metal	450
Miscellaneous	341
Sales and Service	469
Distributors	831
Distributors—Contractors	805
Jobbers	1,215
Wholesalers	1,178
Dealers	530
Dealer—Contractors	822
Sales Representatives	227
Importers and Exporters	71
	11,457

PUBLIC UTILITIES

Transportation: R.R., Motor, Air, Marine	89
Telephone and Telegraph	56
Electric and Gas (420), Water (12)	432
	577

REAL ESTATE MANAGEMENT AND OPERATION

Real Estate Management	86
Hotels	12
Institutions	74
Hospitals	42
Restaurants	14
Department Stores	75
Warehouses and Storage (9), Laundries (7)	16
	319

INDUSTRIAL USERS

Adhesives	12
Air Conditioning Equipment	182
Air Filters	74
Automotive (31), Aviation (26)	57
Boilers (388), Furnaces (231), Stokers (23)	642
Building Materials	164
Chemicals and Chemical Products	265
Coal and Coke	71
Electrical Products	37
Fans and Blowers, Ventilating Equipment (249), Diffusers (43)	357
Food	292
Heating Equipment, Unit, Water, Stoves	130
	325

INDUSTRIAL USERS (Continued)

Heating, Air Conditioning (412), Heating Ventilating (12), Heating, Ventilating, Air Conditioning (287), Air Conditioning and Refrigeration (445)	1,156
Humidifiers	15
Instruments, Temperature (206), Electrical and Etc. (189)	395
Leather	4
Machinery	225
Metals: Non-Ferrous	68
Metals: Iron and Steel and Metal Products	282
Mill–Hardware–Foundry Equipment	56
Oil Burners (211), Gas Burners (28), Oil and Gas Burners (22)	261
Paint, Varnish, Etc.	11
Paper	21
Petroleum	121
Pipe and Pipe Fittings (166), Valves (124), Heat Exchangers (103)	393
Plastics	39
Plumbing and Heating Supplies	101
Pumps (130), Compressors (16)	146
Radiators and Grilles	103
Railroad Equipment	32
Refractories–Abrasives–Glass	51
Refrigerating Equipment	84
Shipbuilding	18
Steam Specialties	135
Textiles	58
Tools (56), Welding Equipment (12)	68
Turbines and Engines	21
Miscellaneous Manufacturers	137
	6,508

OTHER USERS AND SPECIFIERS

Architects	191
Engineers—Consulting Plant (39), Mechanical (42), Electrical, Power Plant (39)	361
Engineers—Construction	127
Engineers, Heating, Ventilating, Air Conditioning and Refrigeration	214
Engineers, Design and Development	54
Designers, Graphic Arts, Etc.	21
Advertising, Printing, Publishers	269
Bankers, Brokers, Consultants	71
Insurance	37
Research and Development Laboratories	222
Lawyers (10), Auditors (1)	11
Associations	76
Home Owners	9
Miscellaneous	52
	1,715

MISCELLANEOUS

Government Departments—Federal (205), State (25), City (63), Foreign (7)	300
Colleges and Schools—Executives and Staff (5), Professors (37), Teachers and Instructors (16), Students (184)	242
Unclassified	7
	549
Total	**21,125**

NOTE: By actual count these visitors came to the Exposition 34,758 times.

4. Your papers before technical societies and trade associations.
5. Your technical literature and data sheets.
6. The information you prepare for your salesmen and representatives (both for their knowledge and reference and for them to give to the prospect).
7. Your case history file.
8. Your external periodical.
9. All that your sales and engineering people say about the construction and application of your products.
10. All that your customers and dealers say about your products.

An *advertising program* is one thing. *Sales work* is another. A *technical information* program is a third.

Any company which makes products for technical buyers who puts them to technical use should have all three—well formulated, well organized, and well prosecuted.

As the result of discussing the technical information program with the sales manager, the public relations firm recommended that a modest beginning might be made by preparing a series of technical application bulletins. For $300 a bulletin, the public relations firm would visit a company using Graham equipment and obtain a complete story on the company's use of that equipment, including application photographs. This material would then be written up as a "raw" report, including application information and photographs, and suggestions as to how to use the material for publicity releases, advertisements, and salesmen's kits. If the "raw" report was edited as a "finished, approved and accepted-for publication" article in appropriate trade papers, the fee was $500 a report. Graham's sales manager was shown numerous examples of the public relation firm's work and thought well of what he saw. A raw report often ran to seven or eight pages of double-spaced, detailed application information and sales promotional suggestions.

Graham's sales manager wondered whether the company's products offered much publicity potential as no new products had been introduced since 1952. On the other hand, he believed that news of new uses probably would receive some editorial comment since many trade paper representatives had been asking him if he wished to give them such news.

Trade Paper Advertising

In considering the use of trade paper advertising, management had considered the possibility of using advertisements in vertical media[2] circulating among members of the heating and air-conditioning, automobile trim, electrical appliance, vending machine, camera, strip light fixture, and business machine industries. This possibility was temporarily tabled, how-

---

[2] "Vertical media" are those which deal with the interests of a particular industry and which accordingly are subscribed to by companies or individuals within a particular industry, e.g., *The Coin Machine Journal*. "Horizontal media" make their appeal to the interests of functional groups and are subscribed to by the companies or individuals in numerous industries, e.g., *Sales Management*.

Exhibit 8

GRAHAM MANUFACTURING COMPANY

Analysis of the Circulation of the May 1957 Issue of Metal Progress

3. BUSINESS ANALYSIS OF TOTAL PAID SUBSCRIPTION CIRCULATION FOR THE MAY, 1957 ISSUE. (Not an average for 6 months)

NOTE—Total paid subscription circulation of this issue was 1.01% greater than average total paid subscription circulation for period. Breakdown of total to left by Title and Occupation

Classification by Business & Industry	Associa- tion Subs.	Total of figures to right	%	Subs. in Company Name	Corporate Officials & General Managers	Dept. & Mgrs & Supts.	Plant & Production Super- visors & Foremen	Other Person- nel	Engineering & Design Dept. Heads & Engrs.	Other Person- nel	Dept. Heads & Engrs.	Metallurgy & Chemical Metal- lurgists	Other Person- nel	Purchas- ing	Sales	All Other Employees	Awaiting Classi- fication by Title
1. Manufacturers of Assembled Metal Products, Equipment & Machinery	329	11,029	38.93	251	1,131	787	789	500	2,771	305	999	1,809	862	82	823	150	99
2. Commercial Processing Plants & Parts Manufacturers:																	
(a) Forging, Stamping, Welding, Machining, Heat Treating & Finishing Plants	16	1,331	4.62	15	527	141	94	91	83	17	61	117	52	8	118	16	7
(b) Plate & Structural Fabricators		101	0.34		25	16	5	5	9	5	4	11	3		10	7	1
(c) Foundries & Die Casting Plants	6	950	3.28	8	262	97	30	31	65	11	81	173	42	2	133	17	4
(d) Other Parts, not End Products	14	889	3.09	8	167	101	75	36	125	17	66	162	57	10	58	14	7
3. Railroads & other Transportation Service, Public Service Corporations; Mines; Manufacturers of nonmetal products	436	1,716	7.38	405	150	99	65	42	462	45	112	154	125	14	409	44	26
4. Producers of Metals (Ferrous & Nonferrous): Blast Furnaces, Steel Works, Rolling Mills, Smelters & Refiners	125	5,827	20.36	110	493	502	276	142	559	45	632	1,269	584	16	1,203	83	38
5. (a) Federal State Municipal & Foreign Government Departments, Offices & Personnel	225	1,238	5.02	217	29	58	50	123	225	48	107	332	136	4	8	119	7
(b) Commissioned Officers in Armed Services	1	132	0.46	1	1	5	2	2	8	1	3	6	5		1	99	1
6. Distributors, Dealers & Exporters of Machinery, Ferrous & Non-ferrous Metals, Hardware Products, Mill & Factory Supplies	1	958	3.29		394	21	4	3	17	5	10	19	7	15	433	6	5
7. Consulting & Contract-Engineers & Firms	52	1,042	3.74	45	307	28	24	12	247	18	93	155	91	4	32	26	12
8. Trade Associations, Chambers of Commerce, Libraries, Colleges & Vocational Schools including Professors & Instructors	375	979	4.63	375	58	24	8	10	161	20	270	59	159		8	179	23
9. Students	40	511	1.75	33	14	2	1	3	2	2	1			2	506	
10. Miscellaneous	135	175	0.60	19	3		1		3	1	3	2	1		3	100	4
11. Awaiting Classification by Industry	588	731	2.51	407	19								4		5	19	268
TOTAL PAID SUBSCRIPTION CIRCULATION FOR THE MAY, 1957 ISSUE	2,208	26,981	100.00	1,875	3,577	1,884	1,422	1,000	4,744	540	2,442	4,272	2,125	155	3,266	1,385	502
Percentage	7.55	92.45		6.43	12.26	6.44	4.83	3.42	16.22	1.84	8.36	14.63	7.38	0.53	11.19	4.73	1.74

4. GEOGRAPHIC ANALYSIS OF TOTAL PAID CIRCULATION FOR THE MAY, 1957 ISSUE. (Not an average for 6 months)

NOTE—Total paid circulation of this issue was 1.01% greater than average total paid circulation for period.

STATE	Subscriptions	%
Maine	37	
New Hampshire	38	
Vermont	11	
Massachusetts	1,026	
Rhode Island	131	
Connecticut	917	
NEW ENGLAND	2,160	7.40
New York	2,534	
New Jersey	1,195	
Pennsylvania	3,558	
MIDDLE ATLANTIC	7,287	24.96
Ohio	3,023	
Indiana	899	
Illinois	2,048	
Michigan	1,989	
Wisconsin	598	
EAST NORTH CENTRAL	8,557	29.31
Minnesota	201	
Iowa	214	
Missouri	417	
North Dakota	2	
South Dakota	5	
Nebraska	11	
Kansas	166	
WEST NORTH CENTRAL	1,016	3.48
Delaware	117	
Maryland	399	
District of Columbia	198	
Virginia	163	
West Virginia	55	
North Carolina	122	
South Carolina	113	
Georgia	145	
Florida	168	
SOUTH ATLANTIC	1,480	5.07
Kentucky	159	
Tennessee	247	
Alabama	174	
Mississippi	7	
EAST SOUTH CENTRAL	587	2.01
Arkansas	3	
Louisiana	74	
Oklahoma	127	
Texas	749	
WEST SOUTH CENTRAL	953	3.26
Montana	8	
Idaho	21	
Wyoming	3	
Colorado	225	
New Mexico	119	
Arizona	91	
Utah	115	
Nevada	27	
MOUNTAIN	609	2.09
Washington	426	
Oregon	163	
California	1,886	
PACIFIC	2,475	8.48
Single Copy Sales		
Miscellaneous		
Unclassified	5	
UNITED STATES	25,124	86.06
Alaska	4	
Hawaii	1	
U. S. Possessions & Other Areas	5	
U. S. TERRITORIES & OTHER AREAS	502	1.74
Canada	1,801	6.18
Foreign	2,232	7.66
Miscellaneous Excluding U. S.	22	0.08
Military or Civilian Personnel Overseas		
	25,134	86.08

Metal Progress

Issued Monthly

Rate Card No. 11

Issued April 27, 1956
Effective April 1, 1957

1. GENERAL ADVERTISING RATES

Application of Rates: Rates are based on the total space used in one year, not the number of insertions. Fractional page rates for ⅓ and ⅔ pages scale back to the full page editorial position rates. If there is any question as to the lowest applicable rates, please check with publisher.

Full Page Rates

a.

RUN OF BOOK RATES		EDITORIAL POSITION RATES	
1 Page	$508.00	1 Page	$600.00
3 Pages	494.00	3 Pages	582.00
6 Pages	480.00	6 Pages	564.00
9 Pages	466.00	9 Pages	546.00
12 Pages	452.00	12 Pages	528.00
18 Pages	438.00	18 Pages	510.00
24 Pages	424.00	24 Pages	492.00
36 Pages	410.00	36 Pages	474.00
48 Pages	396.00	48 Pages	456.00

b. Minimum unit—¼ page.

c. COLOR RATES
Standard colors (AAAA red, orange, blue, green, yellow)—$80.00 per page.
Special colors—$110.00 per page.

d. Metallic inks or special color combinations—rates on request.

e. Bleed, per page—$35.00.
Full page plate size 8⅜" x 11½", trims to 8¼" x 11¼". ⅔ page plate size 5¼" x 11½", trims to 5⅛" x 11¼". (No bleed charge for covers.)

f. Inserts—space rates apply.
Back-up charges on request.

g. Preferred Positions—rates on request.

h. Rate Protection: Advertiser is protected for minimum of 90 days in event of rate revision. Contract may be cancelled at the time revision becomes effective. Should cancellation be desired, it will be made without short rate adjustment on space already run, provided the contract rate has been earned up to the date of cancellation.

Fractional Page Rates

Fractional page rates are quoted for the convenience of advertisers using a series of ads of the same size. Fractional page rates for ⅓ and ⅔ pages scale back to the full page editorial position rates. If there is any question as to the lowest applicable rates, check with publisher.

Unit	1 time	3 times	6 times	9 times	12 times	18 times	24 times
*⅔ Page	$412.00	$400.00	$388.00	$376.00	$364.00	$352.00	$340.00
*½ Page (island)	386.00	375.00	364.00	358.50	353.00	342.00	331.00
½ Page (regular)	261.00	254.00	247.00	243.50	240.00	233.00	226.00
*⅓ Page	212.00	206.00	200.00	197.00	194.00	188.00	182.00
¼ Page	134.00	130.50	127.00	125.50	123.50	121.75	120.00

*Editorial Positions

2. SPECIAL CLASSIFICATIONS

a. Classified Advertising— not accepted. See *Metals Review* magazine.

b. Special mail order and book advertising rates. NONE.

3. COMMISSION AND DISCOUNT

a. Agency Commission, 15%.

b. Cash Discount, 2%, 10 days from date of invoice.

4. COPY AND CONTRACT REGULATIONS

a. Regulations covering acceptance of advertising. The publishers reserve the right to refuse libelous or unfair copy. The advertiser agrees to indemnify the publisher against any claims or expenses resulting from the unauthorized use of any name, photograph, sketch, or words protected by copyright or registered trademarks, labels, etc., in connection with his advertising.

b. Cancellations not accepted after closing dates.

c. Positions other than those known as preferred or editorial accepted as run-of-book. Editorial rate guarantees a position opposite or adjacent to editorial matter.

5. MECHANICAL REQUIREMENTS

Space can be used in any of the standard N. I. A. A. forms:

Bleed advertising plate	11½ in. deep x 8⅜ in. wide
Full advertising page	10 in. deep x 7 in. wide
Half page	10 in. deep x 3⅜ in. wide
or	4⅞ in. deep x 7 in. wide
Quarter page	4⅞ in. deep x 3⅜ in. wide

EDITORIAL POSITION ADS

Two-thirds page	10 in. deep x 4½ in. wide
Half page (island)	7½ in. deep x 4½ in. wide
Third page	4⅞ in. deep x 4½ in. wide
or	10 in. deep x 2⅛ in. wide

Exhibit 10

GRAHAM MANUFACTURING COMPANY

Analysis of the Circulation of the May 1957 Issue of Product Engineering

3. BUSINESS ANALYSIS OF TOTAL PAID SUBSCRIPTION CIRCULATION FOR THE MAY, 1957 ISSUE: (Not an average for 6 months)
NOTE—Total paid subscription circulation of this issue was 1.02% greater than average total paid circulation for period.

Breakdown of total to left by Title and Occupation

Classification by Business & Industry	Total of figures to right	%	Subs. in Company Name	Corporate Officials & General Managers	Dept. Mgrs. & Supts.	Super- visors & Foremen	Other Person- nel	Dept. Heads & Engrs.	Other Person- nel	Dept. Heads & Engrs.	Metal- lurgists	Other Person- nel	Purchas- ing	Sales	All Other Employees	Awaiting Classi- fication by Title
1. Manufacturers of Assembled Metal Products, Equipment & Machinery	26,165	71.58	4,253	3,258	1,641	420	180	14,182	1,560	30	13	9	77	251	157	134
2. Commercial Processing Plants & Parts Manufacturers:																
(a) Forging, Stamping, Welding, Machining, Heat Treating & Finishing Plants	611	1.67	144	201	69	4	2	162	13	2				10	1	3
(b) Plate & Structural Fabricators	154	0.42	30	27	26			58	6			2	2	2	1	3
(c) Foundries & Die Casting Plants	219	0.60	55	33	25	2	1	89	5	1		1		4		3
(d) Other Parts, not End Products	1,304	3.57	243	215	141	18	9	565	46	3	1			45	9	9
3. Railroads & other Transportation Services and Public Service Corporations (Subscriptions in Manufacturing Plants are included in Classification #1); Mines; Manufacturers of Nonmetal Products	1,721	4.71	509	188	177	22	12	666	50	14	2	2	6	36	16	23
4. Producers of Metals (Ferrous & Non-ferrous); Blast Furnaces, Steel Works, Rolling Mills, Smelters & Refiners	709	1.94	162	49	73	8	7	331	41	2	1		2	18	12	3
5. (a) Federal, State, Municipal & Foreign Government Departments & Offices & Personnel (Subscriptions in Government Manufacturing Plants & Shipyards are included in Classification #1)	853	2.33	343	5	49	9	22	361	22	3	1	1	2		24	11
(b) Commissioned Officers in U. S. Armed Services	44	0.12		44												
6. Distributors, Dealers & Exporters of Machinery, Ferrous & Nonferrous Metals, Hardware Products, Mill & Factory Supplies	203	0.56	49	80	4		1	32	4	1			4	23	1	4
7. Consulting & Contracting Engineers & Firms	3,021	8.26	474	1,067	43	28	29	1,080	249	1	2	3	3	12	14	16
8. Trade Associations, Chambers of Commerce, Libraries, Colleges & Vocational Schools, including Professors & Instructors	889	2.43	543	34	3	2	2	78	14				2	2	204	5
9. Students	36	0.10													36	
10. Miscellaneous	281	0.77	73	74	9	3	2	32	4	1		1	1	35	40	7
11. Awaiting Classification by Industry	344	0.94	109	30	18	2	3	42	7					2		131
TOTAL PAID SUBSCRIPTION CIRCULATION FOR THE MAY, 1957 ISSUE	36,554	100.00	6,987	5,305	2,278	518	270	17,678	2,021	56	19	18	98	440	515	351
PERCENTAGE		100.00	19.12	14.51	6.23	1.42	0.74	48.36	5.53	0.15	0.05	0.05	0.27	1.20	1.41	0.96

4. GEOGRAPHIC ANALYSIS OF TOTAL PAID CIRCULATION FOR THE MAY 1957 ISSUE:* (Not an average for 6 months)
NOTE—Total paid circulation of this issue was 1.02% greater than average total paid circulation for period.

STATE	Subscriptions	%
Maine	36	
New Hampshire	117	
Vermont	33	
Massachusetts	1,528	
Rhode Island	208	
Connecticut	1,159	
NEW ENGLAND	**3,081**	**8.43**
New York	4,679	
New Jersey	2,157	
Pennsylvania	2,036	
MIDDLE ATLANTIC	**8,872**	**24.27**
Ohio	2,676	
Indiana	888	
Illinois	2,489	
Michigan	2,526	
Wisconsin	928	
EAST NORTH CENTRAL	**9,507**	**26.01**
Minnesota	472	
Iowa	267	
Missouri	439	
North Dakota	7	
South Dakota	11	
Nebraska	73	
Kansas	168	
WEST NORTH CENTRAL	**1,437**	**3.93**
Delaware	117	
Maryland	530	
District of Columbia	146	
Virginia	249	
West Virginia	77	
North Carolina	143	
South Carolina	36	
Georgia	113	
Florida	175	
SOUTH ATLANTIC	**1,586**	**4.34**
Kentucky	124	
Tennessee	223	
Alabama	121	
Mississippi	22	
EAST SOUTH CENTRAL	**490**	**1.34**
Arkansas	22	
Louisiana	80	
Oklahoma	157	
Texas	596	
WEST SOUTH CENTRAL	**855**	**2.34**
Montana	7	
Idaho	44	
Wyoming	7	
Colorado	146	
New Mexico	121	
Arizona	121	
Utah	69	
Nevada	15	
MOUNTAIN	**530**	**1.45**
Washington	446	
Oregon	139	
California	5,183	
PACIFIC	**5,768**	**15.78**
Single Copy Sales	2	
Miscellaneous		
Unclassified	131	
UNITED STATES	**32,126**	**87.89**
Alaska	4	
Hawaii	29	
U. S. Possessions & Other Areas	22	
U.S. TERRITORIES & OTHER AREAS	**32,181**	**88.04**
Canada	1,415	3.87
Foreign	2,932	8.02
Miscellaneous Excluding U. S. Military or Civilian Personnel Overseas	26	0.07
GRAND TOTAL	**36,554**	**100.00**

*Paragraph 4:
Subscription figures are based on the percentage for each State determined by analysis for Nov., 1956 issue and these percentages are projected against the total for May, 1957 issue.

Exhibit 11

GRAHAM MANUFACTURING COMPANY
Advertising Rates of *Product Engineering*

GENERAL

All orders subject to terms and provisions of current rate card. Orders subject to changes upon notice from publisher. However, contracts may be canceled as time change becomes effective without incurring a short rate adjustment, provided contract rate has been earned up to date of cancellation.

The term "regular issue" refers to any issue other than the annual Design Digest Issue. (See listing following "Circulation" for rates, other details covering *Product Engineering's* Design Digest Issue [formerly Handbook Issue].)

RATES

	1 Time	*4 Times*	*7 Times*	*13 Times*
1 page	$781.00	$752.00	$741.00	$707.00
⅔ page	547.00	527.00	519.00	496.00
½ page*	417.00	402.00	396.00	381.00
⅓ page	288.00	278.00	274.00	264.00
¼ page*	219.00	211.00	207.00	201.00
⅙ page	156.00	150.00	148.00	141.00

	26 Times	*39 Times*	*52 Times*	*78 Times*
1 page	$678.00	$673.00	$667.00	$655.00
⅔ page	473.00	467.00	462.00	453.00
½ page*	364.00	358.00	352.00	345.00
⅓ page	253.00	246.00	244.00	238.00
¼ page*	193.00	188.00	186.00	182.00
⅙ page	136.00	135.00	133.00	131.00

* Not available in the Research and Development Edition.

DESIGN DIGEST ISSUE

Published in mid-September of each year, in addition to the regular weekly issues. Rates for advertising in this issue are based on the total space contracted for and used within a 12-month period.

COVERS

1st cover—not available for advertising.
Other covers—rates on request.

SPECIAL POSITIONS

Front covers not available for advertising. Rates for other covers will be quoted upon request. Facing ⅔ pages accepted only with editorial columns each page at total position premium of 70.00. Other special position rates on request.

INSERTS

Available in Design Edition. Available in Research and Development Edition under some circumstances. Standard inserts furnished complete by advertiser ready to bind—regular black-and-white rate. Please contact business manager for details, possible extra binding charges covering gatefold or other special inserts, backup charges, closing date, address of bindery, etc.

Exhibit 11—Continued

Special mechanical requirements apply to Research and Development Edition—details on request.

SPLIT RUN

Available for advertisements of ⅓ page or larger in regular issues only. Rates and details on request.

COLORS

AAAA standard yellow, orange, red, blue, or green in regular color forms:

1 color, if standard, per page extra...........................$ 90.00
If other than standard, per page, extra......................... 130.00
2 colors, both standard, or 1 standard and 1 matched, per page, extra 265.00
2 matched, colors, per page, extra............................. 310.00
4 process colors, per page, extra............................. 405.00
Rate for 4 process colors based on publisher's standard process inks and sequence. Details on request.

Rates on request for four process colors deviating in inks or sequence from publisher's standard, and for metallic inks or multipage black and two-color printing.

Minimum space for color, ¼ page—takes full-page color rate.

BLEED

1 page extra...$45.00
Additional consecutive pages, same issue, per page extra....... 40.00
Additional consecutive ⅔ page, same issue, per ⅔ page........ 40.00
2-page spreads (two facing full pages) no charge for gutter bleed if each plate does not exceed 7½ × 10″. Minimum bleed ⅔ page at full-page bleed rate. Under some circumstances. ⅓ page (vertical) may bleed. Details on request.

Source: Publisher's statement.

ever, because management thought that the use of vertical media would not be economical until the company had definitely defined its potential markets. Thus, in early 1958, management had narrowed its discussion to two horizontal media: *Metal Progress* and *Product Engineering*. (For information on other trade papers, see *Standard Rate and Data Service, Business Publication Section.*)

Metal Progress was published monthly and was aimed at "promotion of the engineering and sciences connected with the manufacturing, fabricating, treating, welding, and use of metals." Of its total paid circulation of 28,898, 26,759 subscriptions were included in the membership dues of the American Society of Metals, which published *Metal Progress*. The analysis of *Metal Progress'* circulation for the May 1957 issue is given in Exhibit 8; its advertising rates in Exhibit 9. *Product Engineering* was published weekly in two editions (26 research and development issues, 26 design issues) and was edited "for product-design and development engineers who design every kind of machinery, equipment and appliances and who specify all original equipment required in the design and manufacture of these products." Of its total circulation of 36,184, 34,609 were individually paid subscriptions. The analysis of *Product Engineering's* circulation is given in Exhibit 10; its advertising rates in Exhibit 11.

~~~

CASE 19: FOUKE FUR COMPANY[1]

QUESTIONS TO CONSIDER: (1) *What are the principal promotional problems facing the Fouke company?* (2) *What conclusions do you draw from the Chicago experiment?* (3) *What recommendations would you make to Fouke's management regarding its promotional programs for the 1958–59 and 1959–60 selling seasons?*

In February 1958 the management of the Fouke Fur Company of St. Louis, Missouri, was in the process of deciding what changes, if any, to make in its advertising and promotion of Alaska fur seals. The company was essentially a production operation, having specialized in the processing of fur seals since the early 1900's. As the result of its unique know-how in the processing and dyeing of fur seals, the company had for many years been the sole processor and selling agent for the United States government, which controlled the world's prime seal herd, the Great Alaska Seal or Pribilof herd; and for the governments of Canada, Japan, South Africa, and Uruguay, which either shared in the annual "kill" or "take" of the Pribilof herd or controlled secondary seal herds. Also, the company did similar work for private shippers. In total it handled well over 90% of the world's commercial supply of fur seals.

Under its contracts with the various governments the company received a fee for the processing function and a percentage of the selling price to use for advertising and promotion. The company had no direct control over selling price as all processed furs were sold by it at public auctions held annually in April and October.

As the result of the Pribilof herd increasing its size beyond the maximum propagation facilities of the Pribilof Islands in 1956–57, the Fish and Wildlife Service of the U.S. Department of Interior had decided to increase the annual take or kill of seals from 65,000 to about 90,000, which together with shipments from other herds would necessitate the company increasing its production schedules from about 90,000 to 115,000 or 120,000 skins a year. Consequently, Fouke's management was concerned with stabilizing the demand for garments made of Alaska and other fur seal so that the increased supply of skins would not result in depressed auction prices.

---

[1] Written by Martin V. Marshall.

The Marketing of Fur Seals

As has been stated, all processed seal skins were sold at public auction. Four types of buyers usually attended these auctions: (1) skin merchants who bought as much as $300,000 worth of furs for resale in small lots on credit to fur garment manufacturers and retailers who made their own garments; (2) skin brokers who purchased on account for a brokerage fee of about 3%; (3) large fur garment manufacturers; and (4) large retailers who maintained fur workshops, e.g., Marshall Field's. Skins were offered in graded cases of 70, 80, and 90 skins, depending upon size. The better grades sold in 1957 for as much as $125 a skin; scarred or poorer quality skins for as little as $50 a skin. Cases, when resold or sold as is, were split into bundles of approximately seven skins each, the number of skins required to make a fur garment of seal skins.

In 1958 there were approximately 100 fur garment manufacturers using fur seal in their operations, about 35 accounting for the majority of the fur industry's seal sales. Relatively few manufacturers specialized in fur seal, the majority devoting only 10% to 20% of their production to fur seal. Of those manufacturers specializing in fur seal, one accounted for about 20% of the prime grade seal skins marketed each year in the United States and another for about 10 to 15% of the scarred skins.

Furs were sold at retail by about 2,500 department stores, women's specialty shops, and independent furriers. In recent years it was believed that the retailing of furs had changed substantially. Formerly, manufacturers had wholesaled furs to retailers. Then, because of the highly competitive nature of the fur business, some marginal manufacturers in the post–World War II era began to put their furs into retail outlets on consignment, gradually forcing other manufacturers to follow the same policy. As the weakness of consignment selling appeared, namely, the return of large stocks of unsold garments at the end of the season, many manufacturers began to sell at retail in New York City either directly at their manufacturing locations or at newly established manufacturer-leased retail departments, thereby leading to a relative reduction in the wholesale function. Some members of the fur industry estimated that approximately 70% of the more expensive furs, such as seal and the better mink garments, were being sold direct to customers by garment makers in the New York market. Fouke's management had not been able to trace precisely the distribution or sales of seal garments, but, generally speaking, seal garments apparently were stocked and sold by most leading furriers in the northern part of the United States—north of a line through St. Louis. Distribution and sales apparently were quite limited in the southern, southwestern, and far western markets.

The Promotion of Alaska Fur Seals

In each of the ten years after World War II, the company employed approximately the same type of promotional program to stimulate the demand for fur seal, varying only the size of the promotional budget in accord with the auction price of skins. The promotional expenditure per skin ranged from a low of $2.22 in 1947 to a high of $3.16 in 1952. The total promotional budget ranged from a low of $120,951 in 1947 to a high of $200,809 in 1956. The company's promotional programs generally were aimed (1) at obtaining advertising and promotional effort by manufacturers and retailers, (2) at obtaining editorial comment in consumer publications, and (3) at motivating retailers to sell seal furs by providing dealers with selling aids. All promotional work was done by a New York advertising agency whose principal had been active in the fur industry for over 25 years.

The specific character of each of the company's promotional activities in 1957 are described below. The total promotional budget for the year was $156,996, plus an agency fee, allocated as follows:

Magazine advertising	$72,987
Trade paper advertising	11,280
Publicity materials	7,239
Reprints of editorials	4,482
Displays (enlarged photographs)	1,774
Style portfolios	26,686
Romance booklets (free copies)	1,797
Foreign promotion	27,396
Agency travel	3,355

Obtaining Advertising and Promotional Effort by Manufacturers and Retailers. To obtain advertising and promotional effort by retailers, the company offered a co-operative advertising plan whereby it would pay one half of the cost of a black-and-white advertisement and two thirds of the cost of a color advertisement in leading "class" magazines placed by either a retailer or manufacturer. Over the years a number of manufacturers and retailers had participated in the program. In 1957 the company's share of the cost of co-operative advertisements was $72,987. Generally, advertisements were run in three publications, *Harpers' Bazaar*, *Vogue*, and *Town and Country*, and occasionally in *The New Yorker* and *Social Spectator*. An example of a manufacturer's co-operative advertisement is given in Exhibit 1 and of a retailer's co-operative advertisement in Exhibit 2.

In addition, the company paid one half the cost of advertisements which manufacturers ran in *Women's Wear Daily*. In 1957 the company's share of the costs of these types of advertisements was $11,280.

When manufacturers participated in the company's co-operative advertising plan, they were encouraged to follow up the advertisement with retailers, either by personal selling effort or by mailing reprints of the advertisements. Fouke's management had not been able to measure the amount of follow-up promotion, but management knew from firsthand experience that some manufacturers had been very aggressive in using reprints of the co-operative advertisements.

Exhibit 1

FOUKE FUR COMPANY

Example of a Manufacturer's Co-operative Advertisement

Exhibit 2
FOUKE FUR COMPANY
Example of a Retailer's Co-operative Advertisement

FLOWING TIERS... BONWIT TELLER

An important
and impressive new treatment of Alaska fur seal ...
as if it were handled by a dressmaker with yards of satin.
The effect is unbelievably beautiful in black dyed or Matara*
processed brown Alaska fur seal 1650.00 plus 10% federal tax.

New York   White Plains   Chicago   Cleveland   Boston   Palm Beach

*Reg. Fouke Fur Co.

As advertised, full page, TOWN & COUNTRY, September, 1955

Obtaining Editorial Comment. Because of its location in New York City, the company's advertising agency was able to work frequently and closely with the editors of leading fashion publications regarding news about fur seal. By working through manufacturers and retailers or by mail releases, the agency was also able to offer news to editors of trade papers and newspapers. In 1956 the company, through a clipping service, listed 714 editorial comments regarding some aspect of fur seal, and in 1957, 821. Editorial comments varied in value, from a line or two of copy in fashion stories to feature stories on fur seal complete with pictures. Direct costs for publicity materials were $7,239 in 1957. Reprints of editorial comments, which were distributed by Fouke to manufacturers and retailers, cost $4,482.

Obtaining Retailer Effort. Over the years the company had not tried directly to influence retailers to undertake aggressive promotion of seal furs. About twice a year, however, a member of Fouke's management visited key retailers to discuss the current state of the fur market, to learn of retailing problems, and to maintain the favorable personal relationship which existed between the company and the trade.

Retailers were provided several selling aids, which are described below:

1. Each year the company's advertising agency prepared an "Alaska Fur Seal Style Portfolio" which illustrated and described one or two of the featured seal fur garments of every manufacturer who wished to have his garments included in the portfolio. In 1957 about 50 manufacturers participated and the portfolio illustrated over 100 seal garments. Two pages of the portfolio are shown in Exhibit 3. The portfolio cost $26,686 in 1957 and was sent to about 2,000 retailers. Manufacturers were provided enlargements of their illustrations in the portfolio, if they wanted them, for distribution to retailers as display pieces. In 1957 the company spent $1,774 for enlargements.

Fouke's management thought that the style portfolio had been well received and widely used by retailers. Its effectiveness was somewhat reduced, however, because by the time the agency obtained all the necessary illustrations and prepared the portfolio for distribution, it was well into the fur selling season; the portfolio usually was not distributed until October, whereas the "fur selling season" usually was September–December. In addition, management had been told by one large retailer that the style portfolio worked against the sale of fur seal. He said, "The retailer doesn't have to stock seal when he has your portfolio available. He can, if he has a customer who is interested in seal, simply use the portfolio like a mail-order catalogue. Without it, he might stock seal garments, and if he has a stock, there's pressure on him to sell seal."

2. Regularly the company provided retailers a 49-page booklet, entitled *The Romance of Alaska Sealskin,* for distribution to their customers,

Return to Elegance

Fouke-Dyed U.S. Gov't Alaska Fur Seal • Black • 'Matara'-processed • 'Kitovi'-processed

Magnificence...long or short

in the store, by mail, or at women's club meetings. Booklets were available in lots of 500 for $15 if the retailer desired his name to be imprinted on the booklets. If not imprinted, retailers were charged as follows: up to ten, free; 100 to 499, 5 cents each; and over 500, 3 cents each. Booklets were available free to students, schools, and so on. The company spent $1,797 for free-distribution booklets in 1957.

3. For fashion shows which a retailer might wish to present to women's groups, color fashion slides and a 16mm color movie film on the Pribilof seal herd were available at no charge, the retailer paying the shipping expense. In addition, the company had a sizable inventory of old-fashioned garments, including seal garments, which were available for fashion shows or window display at no charge. All of these promotional devices were in continuous use in 1957.

In addition to the promotional activities described above, the company had begun promotion of seal skins in foreign markets, spending about $25,000 for such promotion in 1957. Although management believed that foreign markets could eventually be developed so that they were major markets, it did not believe that those markets would materially help to absorb the significantly increased supplies of fur seal which would soon be available.

A Decision to Experiment

In anticipation of increasing supplies of fur seal, Fouke's management decided in the middle of 1956 to consider alternative promotional programs. Management thinking was as follows:

1. Mink, which had been the fashionable fur for some years, had become so widely used that many trade people believed it might well be replaced by a new fashion. Management knew from field trips that some retailers were interested in promoting another fur as *the* fashion. Hence it seemed that an opportunity might be present to increase the demand for fur seal substantially if a fashion trend toward seal started to develop or if it was developed by an aggressive and well-conceived promotion.

Management had mixed feelings regarding the possibility of seal becoming *the* fashion. On the one hand, seal was the most versatile of all furs: it could be handled like cloth; thus manufacturers had unlimited design opportunities when using seal skins. On the other hand, the prevailing fashion for some time had been short garments, such as stoles and jackets. Because of the natural size of a fur seal pelt, the skins could be more economically used to make long rather than short garments. In addition, some consumers looked upon seal "as something grandmother used to wear." Finally, seal was available only in four dark hues: a rich dark brown; a more neutral brown with overtones of bluish-grey; a dark grey with bluish overtones; and lustrous black. The first three colors were produced by different processes and were sold under the following trade-marks: "Safari," "Matara," and "Kitovi," respectively. Many of the better selling furs in recent years, however, had been quite light in color, as contrasted with the dark hues of fur seal.

The trade, too, had mixed feelings regarding the possibility of seal becoming the fashion. For example, a Chicago retailer said, "The market for seal is limited primarily because seal is and will continue to be a very expensive fur. Many women undoubtedly would like to own seal but they simply can't afford it. They must turn to those furs which they can afford to buy. On the other hand, mink is now fairly common and some women probably would be disposed to buying seal because it is not and will not be seen everywhere."

A Boston wholesale-retailer said, "Although mink is quite common because inexpensive garments of mink are readily available, women still dream of mink. And the woman who can afford expensive furs can find distinctive mink, which can be recognized for what it is—a very expensive, beautiful fur. From an objective viewpoint, both mink and seal are excellent furs. They have good durability—they will last 25 years if given proper care. Seal sales, in my opinion, will depend upon consumer attitudes which I can't predict. Seal was the fashion before the turn of the century, probably because of its durability. Then fox and later mink came in, and also the shorter garments such as capes, stoles, and jackets. Seal now affords a woman a selection of colors and design—many high-fashion seal garments are available. But I see no evidence that seal is increasing in popularity relative to expensive mink."

A New York City retailer said, "My clientele want the latest high fashion and they have turned to seal. However, they can afford to buy new furs frequently, perhaps every season, so that I doubt that my clientele's buying is indicative of the buying of women who look upon a fur coat or fur piece as a lifetime investment."

A Boston retailer who specialized in mink and seal took this view: "Mink is still the fashion because the mink people have been expert merchandisers. The minute any type or color of mink becomes popular, the mink people turn to new colors so that women can have something which is distinctive and different. Years ago the silver fox people and then the beaver people killed silver fox and beaver as fashionable furs because those furs became available in a wide range of prices. One woman would buy a scarf for $1,500, another for $800, and you couldn't tell the difference. Women insist on distinctiveness. Now seal has been distinctive for some years. I've been able to sell seal because it's expensive. Generally I've sold seal to women who already have a mink. But if seal begins to be available in lower-priced garments, I'm sure my customers will turn away from it. I ended this season with an overstock of seal garments because garments made of number two skins were being sold in the Boston market. I couldn't answer the question which women raised: 'Why are your seal coats $1,800 when I can buy the same kind of seal coat at _____ for $850?' "

2. Since sales of expensive furs apparently had been concentrated in New York, management thought that much of the potential in other markets was being neglected; thus an opportunity existed to stimulate demand in major markets, such as Chicago, Minneapolis, Cleveland, Pittsburgh, and so on. Management was of the opinion that its sales promotional programs in the past few years might have been weaker than desired because emphasis was on national promotion rather than local promotion.

While considering alternative strategies, the company's management was approached by a St. Louis advertising agency which suggested a promotional program aimed specifically at obtaining aggressive sales effort by retailers in key local markets. After considerable discussion, management decided to test the suggested program in one market. Chicago, the number two United States fur market, was selected.

The Chicago Experiment

During the 1956–57 selling season, the company undertook the following experimental program in Chicago.

Through special arrangements the company and its St. Louis advertising agency arranged to obtain 32 of the principal 1956–57 designs of 21 leading fur-garment manufacturers for a special fashion show which was presented to Chicago retailers and the women's editors of Chicago advertising media at the beginning of the selling season. Invitations were sent personally by the president of the company. After the garments were shown at a dinner meeting, Fouke management outlined its special Chicago promotional program, as follows:

1. Advertisements were to be run regularly in the Chicago newspapers by the Fouke company which would suggest seal as the year's fashionable fur. Exhibit 4 shows two of these advertisements, actual size.

2. Retailers were to be provided advance copies of newspaper advertisements and newspaper advertisement mats suitable for use under their own names.

3. Several advertisements were to be run in local "society" publications, similar to the newspaper advertisements.

4. Retailers were to be provided the company's regular dealer aids plus a lucite sign reading "Alaska Fur Seal."

5. During the season, agency representatives were to work frequently in the Chicago market (*a*) to obtain displays of Alaska fur seal in windows of establishments such as American Express Company, (*b*) to work closely with media people to obtain publicity regarding fur seal, and (c) to stimulate the interest of women's clubs in fashion shows which would be presented by retailers. Details on this latter program are given in Exhibit 5.

Exhibit 5

FOUKE FUR COMPANY

Dear Program Chairman:

We are pleased to offer our program for one of your meetings. The subject - the elegant "limited edition" fur - ALASKA FUR SEAL. This program is available to you at no cost through the courtesy of the Fouke Fur Company of St. Louis, processors of Alaska Fur Seal for the United States Government.

MOVIE: "Passage to the Pribilofs," a 20 minute 16mm film in color and sound, takes you by boat, to the fog-bound Pribilof Islands, home of the Alaska Fur Seal. Here we visit the great herd in its natural habitat. Later, we return to attend the famous Fur Seal Auction at the Fouke Fur Company in St. Louis.

SLIDES: The Fashion color slides represent some of the most elegant and regal Alaska Fur Seal Coats, Capes, and Stoles from French and American Couturier Collections. The slides and commentary are keyed with corresponding numbers.

EXHIBITS: Actual fur pelts of Alaska Fur Seal are available which show the important stages of processing - also the three colors: Black-dyed, Matara-processed and Kitovi-processed.

If you don't have the following readily available, you can make arrangements with local Movie Equipment Rental Service: a 16 millimeter sound projector, a movie screen, a 35 millimeter slide projector and a competent operator

Our reason for sending this copy as a working sheet to you in advance of your meeting, is to allow you time to become acquainted with the material and to allow for deletions or additions in the commentary.

Naturally, there is no charge -- all we ask is special care be given the film and slides. Immediately after your showing, please return by prepaid express to Fouke Fur Company, 1328 South Kingshighway, St. Louis 10, Missouri.

If you will send the postal card enclosed with the film and slides when the meeting is concluded, we will appreciate it.

Cordially,

FOUKE FUR COMPANY
1328 South Kingshighway
St. Louis 10, Missouri

6. At the end of the fashion show a special merchandising book was given to retailers which outlined the program and offered suggestions regarding how the retailer might effectively tie in with it.

Those attending the fashion show were quite enthusiastic about the program. Chicago media people quickly contacted the company for publicity material and later featured seal furs in numerous fashion articles and on television shows. A number of women's clubs requested the use of the Fouke fashion show program material.

The direct costs of the Chicago experiment were as follows:

Fashion show	$ 7,692
Merchandising book for retailers	1,513
Newspaper advertisements	3,082
Chicago magazine advertisements	351
Advertising production	1,135
Newspaper mat service	159
Advance copies of newspaper advertisements	518
Lucite signs	168
Direct-mail follow-up	437
Women's club materials	1,182
Publicity contact time and materials	2,430
Clipping service	74
Special reports	828
Window display work	868
Agency staff time	8,271
Agency and company officials' travel expense	3,116
Miscellaneous expenses	1,158
	$32,962

Evaluation of the Chicago Experiment

In order to evaluate the effect of the special promotional program in Chicago, management checked the sales of 112 retailers in the Greater Chicago area for 1956 and 1957. Unit sales of these retailers for the two years are given in Exhibit 6.

Consideration of Future Promotional Strategy

As management considered the 1958–59 selling season, it was convinced that it had to stimulate fur seal sales in prime markets outside New York City, that retailers were—because of their knowledge of the Chicago experiment—looking to Fouke for continued promotional effort at the local level, and that the fashion trend was beginning to swing away from mink. There was, however, no positive evidence that a fashion trend was setting in for fur seal, except in New York City where fur seal had become fashionable among many women during the 1957–58 season.

Specifically, management in February 1958 was attempting to answer four questions:

1. What conclusions should be drawn from the Chicago experiment?

2. Should the company accept, reject, or modify a proposal by the St. Louis advertising agency for an extension of the Chicago experiment?

The St. Louis advertising agency had proposed that the type of promotional approach used in Chicago be extended to 11 markets (Chicago, Milwaukee, Minneapolis, St. Paul, Pittsburgh, Kansas City, St. Louis, Cincinnati, Columbus, Des Moines, and Indianapolis) with some modifications. The modified promotional approach proposed that advertisements similar to the Chicago newspaper advertisements be run in newspapers in the first five cities listed above and that publicity, fashion show programs by women's clubs, and retailer effort be sought in all cities. The fashion

Exhibit 6

UNIT SALES OF FUR SEAL GARMENTS BASED ON SALES REPORTS OF 112 RETAILERS IN THE GREATER CHICAGO AREA, 1956–57

	No. of Retailers	% of Total	Trend	Unit Sales 1956	% of Total	1957	% of Total	Units Increased or (Decreased) 1957 over 1956	% Increased or (Decreased) 1957 over 1956
Sold 10 or more units in either 1956 or 1957	20	17.86%	Increase	232	35.42%	428	51.38%	196	84.5%
	8	7.14	Decrease	172	26.25	144	17.29	(28)	(16.28%)
	1	0.89	No change	12	1.83	12	1.44	....	....
	29	25.89%	Increase	416	63.50%	584	70.11%	168	40.38%
Sold 8 to 9 units in either 1956 or 1957	6	5.36%	Increase	19	2.91%	51	6.12%	32	168.4%
	6	5.36	Decrease	49	7.49	27	3.24	(22)	(44.9%)
	12	10.72%	Increase	68	10.40%	78	9.36%	10	(14.7%)
Subtotal..........	41	36.61%	Increase	484	73.90%	662	79.47%	178	36.78%
Sold 0 to 7 units in either 1956 or 1957	22	19.64%	Increase	32	4.88%	75	9.01%	43	134.4%
	21	18.75	Decrease	81	12.37	38	4.56	(43)	(53.1%)
	28	25.00	No change	58	8.85	58	6.96	....	....
	71	63.39%	No change	171	26.10%	171	20.53%	....	....
	48	42.86%	Increase	283	43.21%	554	66.51%	271	99.3%
	35	31.24	Decrease	302	46.10	209	25.09	(93)	(30.79%)
	29	25.90	No change	70	10.69	70	8.40	....	....
Grand Total........	112	100.00%	Increase	655	100.00%	833	100.00%	178	27.18%

Source: Company records.

show was to be dropped because it was too difficult administratively to arrange shows in 11 cities.

Along with this general proposal, the agency submitted the following budget:

Newspaper space (in five cities)...............	$ 7,135
Advertising production (eight new advertisements).............................	650
1,000 merchandising books..................	850
Direct mail to retailers......................	841
Programs for women's clubs.................	300
200 window cards...........................	200
Travel expenses............................	2,500
Transportation expenses....................	1,263
Miscellaneous expenses......................	3,000
Agency fee...............................	29,500
	$46,238
10% reserve..............................	4,623
	$50,861

3. Should a significant change be made in the company's existing promotional strategy?

4. How much should the company spend on promotion? Management was willing to spend as much as $3.00 per skin processed, provided the promotional program promised to be effective and auction prices remained fairly stable.

~~~

CASE 20: CARPET INSTITUTE, INC. (F) [1]

NOTE: *Before analyzing this case, the reader may find it useful to review the information given in Carpet Institute, Inc., Cases (A) through (E) in Chapter 5. QUESTIONS TO CONSIDER: (1) What copy and media plans would you recommend for the advertising campaign to be directed to consumers? For the advertising campaign to be directed to carpet retailers? For the advertising campaign to be directed to influence groups? (2) In the light of your recommendations, how would you spend the $20,000 which has been allocated for advertising research?*

After some months of consultation with executives of member companies and several advertising agencies in the spring of 1954, executives of Carpet Institute, Inc., the trade association of the carpet industry, decided to advertise to consumers in order to try to increase the per capita consumption of carpets and rugs in the United States. Having made this decision, Institute executives selected Morey, Humn & Johnstone, Inc., as the Institute's advertising agency. This firm had been one of several agencies which had consulted with Institute executives.

---

[1] Written by Martin V. Marshall.

Initial Planning

As a first step in building a consumer advertising campaign, Institute executives, together with agency executives, tentatively determined the general nature and scope of the Association's promotional program for 1955 as follows:

1. A number of the Institute's long-time promotional activities were to be continued. Sixty thousand dollars was to be spent on a public relations program, which essentially consisted of disseminating useful information to appropriate consumer and trade groups; $58,000 was to be spent on a retail sales training program; $15,000 on analyses of retail-store operations and surveys of retail-store operating results; and $21,000 on a school educational program.

2. Principal emphasis in the 1955 promotional program would be placed on the consumer advertising campaign. Tentatively, about $900,-000 to $1,000,000 was to be spent on the campaign. The public relations and school educational programs were to tie in closely with the theme used in consumer advertising.

3. The chief objective of the consumer advertising campaign was "to educate and re-educate the public to the *values* in carpet."

4. Influence groups, such as interior decorators, architects, and builders, were to be conditioned to specify carpet more frequently through a trade paper campaign.

5. Retailers were to be informed and stimulated to tie in with the advertising campaign through a merchandising-aids program. Tentatively, about $125,000 was estimated to be the amount necessary to provide proper merchandising materials and clinics.

Having determined the broad outline of the Association's promotional program for 1955, Institute and agency executives next directed their attention to two questions: What media should the Institute use? What copy theme should the Institute use? Since Institute executives thought that answers to these questions were interrelated, they and agency executives worked on both questions simultaneously. Information regarding media and copy considerations follows:

Initial Work on Determination of Media

In order to provide a basis for discussion of media, the agency prepared three advertising schedules. The first provided for the use of six types of print media. The second provided for the use of three types of print media and television. The third provided for the use of 17 trade papers to reach influence groups. Each of these schedules will be discussed below.

    Schedule in Print Media. The agency proposed the use of six groups of print media as follows:

Circulation	Publication	Cost per Page, 4 Col.	Insertions	Total Cost
	GROUP 1—SHELTER AND WOMEN'S SERVICE PUBLICATIONS			
5,174,072	Ladies' Home Journal	$ 20,000	4	$ 80,000
4,441,842	Woman's Home Companion	17,220	6	103,320
4,253,798	McCall's	18,360	6	110,160
3,775,677	Better Homes & Gardens	17,500	6	105,000
3,690,672	Woman's Day	14,500	4	58,000
3,410,404	Good Housekeeping	12,760	6	76,560
3,167,360	American Home	13,500	6	81,000
608,722	House Beautiful	5,000	4	20,000
573,799	Sunset	3,500	4	14,000
537,310	Living	3,900	6	23,400
487,625	Small Homes Guide	3,600	2	7,200
426,876	House & Garden	4,400	4	17,600
68,049	Town & Country	2,000	4	8,000
30,616,206		$136,240	Total Cost....	$704,240
	GROUP 2—MASS MARKET PUBLICATIONS			
5,400,557	Life	$30,600	4	$122,400
4,935,813	The Saturday Evening Post	23,310	4	93,240
10,336,370		$53,910	Total Cost....	$215,640
	GROUP 3—FARM PUBLICATIONS			
2,880,010	Farm Journal	$11,100	3	$ 33,300
1,224,906	Path Finder Town Journal	6,500	3	19,500
2,557,003	Country Gentlemen	9,640	3	28,920
1,273,090	Successful Farming	5,500	3	16,500
1,227,329	Progressive Farmer	6,000	3	18,000
9,162,338		$38,740	Total Cost....	$116,220
	GROUP 4—BRIDE AND YOUNG ADULT			
522,162	Mademoiselle	$ 4,100	4	$16,400
145,912	Modern Bride	3,350	4	13,400
120,364	Bride's Magazine	3,450	4	13,800
788,438		$10,900	Total Cost....	$43,600
	GROUP 5—BUSINESS PUBLICATIONS			
1,747,066	Time	$12,845	4	$51,380
233,279	Business Week	3,410	4	13,640
1,980,345		$16,255	Total Cost....	$65,020
	GROUP 6—SUNDAY NEWSPAPER SUPPLEMENTS			
10,572,922	This Week	$33,510	4	$134,040
9,458,563	American Weekly	29,200	4	116,800
20,031,485		$62,710	Total Cost....	$250,840

The use of the above schedule entailed a total space cost of $1,395,560. The agency estimated that the cost of preparing advertisements for this schedule would be about $200,000.

In selecting the six groups listed, the agency used the following line of reasoning. Although the agency believed that there was some duplication of circulation among the 13 magazines given in Group 1, agency executives thought the entire list was necessary to cover and achieve a high degree of penetration of prospective purchases of carpets and rugs. *Life* and *The Saturday Evening Post* were recommended because the two publications reached the mass market and could be used as powerful merchandising tools with retailers and influence groups. Five farm publications, listed in Group 3, were recommended because carpet manufacturers had ignored the farm market in their advertising program and because the farm market was not reached adequately through women's service magazines. *Bride's Magazine* and *Modern Bride* were selected in order to reach the new homemaker at the time when she was thinking of furnishing her new home. *Mademoiselle* was included in Group 5 because it reached the pre-bride age group. *Business Week* and *Time* were included to reach men who bought for their businesses and homes. And the Sunday supplements were included because they had a high degree of husband and wife readership.

Print Media and Television. As an alternative to the use of print media only, the agency presented the alternative of a modified schedule of print media plus television. The modified schedule of print media included the full schedule of business publications as given in Group 5 above and a reduced schedule of shelter and women's service and bride and young adult publications, as indicated below:

Circulation	Publication	Cost per Page, 4 Col.	Insertions	Total Cost
	GROUP 1A—REDUCED SCHEDULE OF SHELTER AND WOMEN'S SERVICE PUBLICATIONS			
5,174,072	*Ladies' Home Journal*	$ 20,000	2	$ 40,000
4,441,842	*Woman's Home Companion*	17,200	3	51,660
4,253,798	*McCall's*	18,360	3	55,080
3,775,677	*Better Homes & Gardens*	17,500	3	52,500
3,690,672	*Woman's Day*	14,500	2	29,000
3,410,404	*Good Housekeeping*	12,760	3	38,280
3,167,360	*American Home*	13,500	3	40,500
608,722	*House Beautiful*	5,000	2	10,000
573,799	*Sunset*	3,500	2	7,000
537,310	*Living*	3,900	3	11,700
487,625	*Small Homes Guide*	3,600	1	3,600
426,876	*House & Garden*	4,400	2	8,800
68,049	*Town & Country*	2,000	2	4,000
30,546,206		$136,220		$352,120

GROUP 4A—REDUCED SCHEDULE OF BRIDE AND YOUNG ADULT PUBLICATIONS

522,162	*Mademoiselle*	$ 4,100	2	$ 8,200
145,912	*Modern Bride*	3,350	2	6,700
120,364	*Bride's Magazine*	3,450	2	6,900
788,438		$10,900		$21,800

The use of the modified schedule of print media entailed a total space cost of $509,990, in contrast to a total space cost of $1,395,660 for the all-print media schedule. The agency estimated that the cost of preparing advertisements for the modified schedule would be $71,050.

In considering the potentialities of television for the Institute, Institute and agency executives examined three types of television: daytime programs, nighttime programs, and one-minute commercials. They decided not to consider daytime television because daytime television did not reach husbands and wives. They found that a one-minute commercial television campaign probably would be "costly and uncertain" because one-minute adjacencies were sold out for the 1954–55 winter television season. Consequently, they decided to investigate the use of nighttime television shows.

Upon investigating the availability of nighttime television shows, Morey, Humn & Johnstone executives concluded that there were three possibilities: CBS' (Columbia Broadcasting System) "Omnibus," ABC's (American Broadcasting Company) "Ray Bolger Show," and two CBS spectaculars.

Omnibus. Pertinent information concerning Omnibus was summarized in a letter dated April 26, 1954, written by Mr. Edward P. Shurick, manager of CBS' Network Sales Development, to Mr. John (Jack) R. Warwick, vice president of Morey, Humn & Johnstone, Inc. Excerpts from this letter follow:[2]

Dear Jack:

Thank you for the opportunity to discuss a mutual interest—the carpet industry—and its possible use of network television.

One can find no better vehicle than the Ford Foundation's OMNIBUS to tell the advantages and reasons for the use of carpeting.

OMNIBUS

OMNIBUS next fall (October 17), will begin its third consecutive season on CBS Television. It returns to the day and hour of two previous successful runs—late Sunday afternoon, from 5 to 6:30 P.M.

Time period advantage: While the other networks have catered to the children of the family, CBS Television has concentrated on the development of a family type audience on Sunday afternoons. Its two hours of adult programming—OMNIBUS preceded by ADVENTURE—have been largely responsible for accomplishing this objective.

---

[2] Reprinted by permission of Mr. Shurick.

Audience composition: The most recent data available is that of ARB for March 1954, that shows for OMNIBUS:

	% of Total Audience	Individuals per Set
Men	37%	.96
Women	45	1.16
Children	18	.46

The period of Sunday at 5 to 6:30 P.M. during the fall-winter months is also an ideal time to reach commercial business people. Experience has shown that it is almost as important that a program be scheduled at an hour convenient to members of the advertising group as well as the public. *5 P.M. on Sunday is clearly just that!*

The rating success of OMNIBUS is an established fact. Practically overnight the program skyrocketed into the mid-twenties rating-wise—and just completed the past October thru March season (26 weeks average) with a 22.7 Nielsen rating, reaching 4,761,000 homes per program.

OMNIBUS in the latest Nielsen (March 14 & 21, 1954) had a 22.4 rating. This is a higher rating than 60 other commercial shows in television and compares to nighttime on ABC Television as follows:

SUNDAY—
    George Jessel 8.3
MONDAY—
    Jamie 17.1
TUESDAY—
    Make Room for Daddy 24.7
WEDNESDAY—
    Inspector Mark Saber 14.1
THURSDAY—
    Where's Raymond 14.0
FRIDAY—
    Pride of the Family 13.0
    Adventures of Ozzie & Harriet ...... 29.8 (of the 70
        odd stations, only 18 are "live")

On a strictly "popularity" basis between networks, Trendex for April, 1954 shows the following nighttime comparisons:

	CBS Television	NBC Television	ABC Television	Du Mont
Sunday	20.3	15.6	9.0	8.4
Monday	27.7	13.0	9.7	3.8
Tuesday	16.3	18.2	12.5	11.2
Wednesday	25.5	22.6	8.3	. . .
Thursday	13.8	32.1	9.5	. . .
Friday	20.3	21.4	8.9	5.5
Saturday	26.1	16.0	5.8	. . .
Total—all evenings	20.2	19.0	9.2	7.5

This comparison is particularly valuable for Trendex ratings are taken only in multi-station markets where each network has an equal opportunity for its programs to be seen.

A very gratifying aspect of OMNIBUS is the proven fact that because of superior program content the advertiser enjoys unusual prestige advantages—

and past sponsors will quickly attest to the fact that OMNIBUS as well sells merchandise and services.

American Machine & Foundry Company—(excellent prospect for a sponsorship return next fall)—President Morehead Patterson had this to say about OMNIBUS:

"We have received a great deal of response from OMNIBUS viewers. In one case over 6,000 pieces of mail followed a booklet offer (see following).

"A large number have thanked us for our part in bringing the television show into their homes, and a great many more have written that they enjoy our commercial featuring films of our various products and would like to see more of them."

Howard A. Reid, AMF General Products Group Advertising and Sales Promotion Manager, announced that OMNIBUS produced an "amazingly high conversion to sales of the inquiries on the De Walt booklet."

Greyhound Corp.—offered a free tour folder in the last 23 seconds of its final commercial on OMNIBUS during the 1952–53 season. The program produced 15,000 requests from all parts of the country. According to H. A. Hohman, President of Beaumont & Hohman, Chicago (Greyhound's agency):

"The letters asking for the folder praised the whole show and reflected high sponsor impact on viewers.

"Our research proves that OMNIBUS is a very popular show, and that, contrary to some people who thought it was over-sophisticated, *it is reaching the average American audience.* It is exactly what I think should be done in television because it lets an advertiser do a job on television according to his budget while providing both entertainment and education. We think *it's excellent public relations* for Greyhound and all the people in the company are proud to be associated with such a program."

The agency found that among OMNIBUS viewers, 7 out of 10 identified Greyhound and the air suspension ride promoted in its commercials.

Details of plans for 1954–55 season ahead

1. The expected date for OMNIBUS to return to the air is Sunday, October 17.
2. Time—as in the past season—5 to 6:30 P.M.
3. Four advertisers will again share sponsorship.
4. Commercial time will be two minutes weekly—with a five minute "institutional" every fourth week which in the past was used for the purpose of telling a story about the particular advertiser's industry.
5. Program price per advertiser—$17,500 gross per week.
6. Station list: A careful analysis has just been completed to determine the most efficient line-up of stations next fall to carry OMNIBUS. The present plan calls for 63 stations—representing 90.2% of total US television homes. Time cost on present rates would be $18,337 weekly per advertiser.

Spectaculars.   Agency executives also discussed the possible use of spectaculars with CBS officials. In his letter of April 26, 1954, to Mr. Warwick, Mr. Shurick summarized the possibilities of the Carpet Institute developing a suitable spectacular on CBS, as follows:[3]

---

[3] Reprinted by permission of Mr. Shurick.

Hour-Long Spectaculars

Another type of program we discussed was the possibility of twice yearly SPECTACULARS—like those of Ford and General Foods.

As explained, the timing of such programs has to be very carefully worked out. The advertisers mentioned were able to synchronize their plans with those of regular clients occupying the time periods—but this is a very complicated and difficult process, and not something that can be worked out too far in advance.

However, for such a day as the Sunday preceding Thanksgiving, Christmas or Easter Sunday, it always is possible to present a SPECTACULAR.

Program Suggestion

A program might be created by CBS Television under the title of "Best Bets." CBS Television, because of its array of high rating stars and its type of family appeal programs, could possibly present, for example:

1. Jack Benny in his famous "one finger concerto" skit.
2. Red Skelton in his routine of the upside-down room.
3. Possibly one of Lucy's better skits, etc., etc.

Such a program might be brought in for about $100,000 plus station time costs. The present BASIC REQUIRED list of CBS Television affiliates (44 stations) costs *$49,270 per nighttime hour.*

Another idea might be ROUTE 9 with Edward R. Murrow. This program would be excellent for Thanksgiving. He would interview families in all parts of the country to show how Thanksgiving is celebrated throughout the United States. The "home" atmosphere of course would be ideal for integrating commercials in behalf of the carpet industry.

Program cost for ROUTE 9 would be in the area of $75,000.

As you [Mr. Warwick] mentioned, ideas for such SPECTACULARS are not difficult to come by, and CBS Television would be most willing to work with your client if such an approach is decided to be the most practical.

Ray Bolger Show. Pertinent information regarding the Ray Bolger Show was given in a letter dated April 20, 1954, written by Mr. Charles R. Abry, national sales manager of ABC (American Broadcasting Company) to Mr. Warwick.[4] The letter follows:

AMERICAN BROADCASTING COMPANY
7 West 66th Street, New York 23, N.Y.
Susquehanna 7–5000

A B C   April 20, 1954
TELEVISION NETWORK

Mr. Jack Warwick
Morey, Humn & Johnson
350 Fifth Avenue
New York 1, New York

Dear Jack:

Thanks very much for the time you gave me yesterday. I found it a very interesting meeting and I hope you will agree that the Ray Bolger program represents an outstanding opportunity for the Carpet Institute.

---

[4] Reprinted by permission of Mr. Abry.

To confirm what we discussed, the Bolger program will move to Friday night, 8:30 to 9:00 P.M., NYT, effective the first week of July. This means it will immediately follow OZZIE & HARRIET which currently has a 31 Nielsen in the 8:00 to 8:30 time, which in turn is preceded by the Erwins, sponsored by General Mills, with a Nielsen of about 27 or 28. With these shows back to back, we feel we have put together one of the best "family audience" blocks of programming in television.

The Ray Bolger program offers your client co-sponsorship of one of show business' outstanding personalities, one that combines such rare quality of entertainment, perfect taste and great prestige. The Bolger name itself is a magic merchandising tool, as few if any show personalities have had such universal appeal and success.

Sherwin-Williams has renewed for the year, July 1, 1954 to July 1, 1955. With the move to Friday, American Tobacco will not renew as they already have a successful program on that evening on another network. Thus, the alternate sponsorship proposed to you is available. Sherwin-Williams very definitely wants cross-reference with the co-sponsor.

As there are three minutes of commercial time permitted, the current formula will be continued, in that one client would get two minutes of commercial one week and one the next. Thus, your client would have the benefit of 52-week continuity. I myself liken it to the print media, in that one week you have a page in color and the next week in black and white.

I attach another copy of the cost estimate that I left with you yesterday. As outlined to you, the program is only available on a firm 52-week basis, July to July. For your information, the Ozzie & Harriet sponsors have both renewed on that same basis so you are assured of the lead-in program for the same length of time.

If there is any further information that I can furnish you, I hope you will call me. Thanks again for a very pleasant meeting.

Best regards.

Sincerely,

Charles R. Abry
National Sales Manager

The cost estimated for the Ray Bolger Show was $553,500 for time and $583,625 for talent for 52 weeks, a total of $1,137,125.

Summary of Television Costs. The agency presented institute executives with the following summary of television costs:

Program	Program Cost	Cost of Commercials	Total
Omnibus................	$ 931,762	$25,000	$ 954,762
Ray Bolger Show......	1,137,125	25,000	1,162,125
Spectaculars (2)........	800,000	10,000	810,000

Trade Publications. As noted earlier, Institute executives desired a schedule of advertising in trade papers so that various influence groups would be reached. The agency, after some study, presented the following schedule for the consideration of Institute executives:

Circulation	Publication	Group	Cost per Page, BW	Insertions	Total Cost
36,549	*Institutions*	1	$930.00	8	$ 7,440
20,036	*American Motel Magazine*	1	335.00	8	2,680
12,335	*Tourist Court Journal*	1	293.25	8	2,346
8,765	*Hotel Management*	1	400.00	8	3,200
6,252	*Hotel World Review*	1	250.00	8	2,000
46,377	*Architectural Forum*	2	785.00	8	6,280
45,151	*Forecast for Home Economists*	2	850.00	8	6,800
40,790	*What's New in Home Economics*	2	795.00	8	6,360
37,011	*Architectural Record*	2	710.00	8	5,680
19,590	*Interiors*	2	460.00	8	3,680
8,969	*Interior Design*	2	330.00	8	2,640
33,509	*Retailing Daily*	3	526.00	8	4,208
28,345	*Department Store Economist*	3	595.00	8	4,760
17,039	*Floor Covering Weekly*	3	525.00	8	4,200
12,157	*Floor Covering Profits* (rug profits)	3	355.00	8	2,840
9,800	*Home Furnishings Magazine*	3	412.00	8	3,296
9,743	*National Furniture Review*	3	330.00	8	2,640
				Total...	$71,050

Initial Work on Determination of Copy Theme

While Institute executives were considering media to be employed by the Institute, agency personnel began to develop ideas regarding the copy approaches which might be used in print media. At one point in the initial work on the Institute's 1955 advertising campaign, the agency presented the following ideas to Institute executives:

It was the opinion of the agency that the Carpet Institute had to stir three consumer groups into action: "(1) those people who will soon move into houses and will buy floor covering for the first time; (2) those who already have hard-surface floor covering or area rugs in their homes; and (3) those who have worn-out carpet on the floor and keep it at the bottom of their buying list."

To reach these three groups effectively, the agency believed that the Institute's 1955 copy plan should emphasize two approaches. First, Institute copy should stress carpet as a basic need. It should also stress all the consumer benefits of carpet: beauty, warmth, comfort, ease of cleaning, safety, and economy. This approach would be directed to the first two groups of consumers indicated in the preceding paragraph. Second, copy should, when directed to consumers in the third group above, emphasize the need, the urgent need, for new carpet.

As examples of how these approaches might be carried out, the agency submitted the following headlines to Institute executives:

1. Competitive campaign to counteract efforts of hard-surface floor manufacturers: "If your floors are hard and cold . . . you can *feel* what carpet does for you" and "If your floors are hard and noisy . . . you can *hear* the difference carpet makes."

2. Campaign to "replace that worn-out carpet": "Do you hate to have your friends drop in? . . . HOW PROUD YOU'LL BE WITH *NEW*

CARPET" and "But *Mother*—what will my friends think when they see our shabby carpet? . . . WITH *NEW* CARPET HOW PROUD SHE'LL BE."

3. Educational campaign using personalities: " 'When you furnish your home,' says Mary Margaret McBride, 'always start with carpet' " and " 'When I redecorated my home,' says Maggie McNellis, 'here's how I started with carpet.' "

4. Campaign that "economy plus need for carpet": "How the George Ryans gave their home the quiet, comfort, and beauty of carpet . . . Mr. Ryan is a school teacher earning $3,900 a year" and " 'I always wanted carpet,' says Mrs. Ralph Brooks, 'but I *thought* we couldn't afford it.' "

5. Trend-setting campaign: "Carpet keynotes the newest trend in home furnishings, 'The Soft, Friendly Look' " and "The latest trend in modern interiors, 'The Soft, Friendly Look' that only carpet gives."

6. Campaign to new homeowners: "Modern carpet gives your home that soft, friendly look."

7. Campaign to hard-surface floored homes: "Only carpet gives your home the soft, friendly look."

8. Campaign to old carpet homes: "*New* carpet gives your home that soft, friendly look."

A Decision regarding the Promotional Budget

While Institute and agency executives were considering the strengths and weaknesses of various media and copy, Mr. Paul Jones, president of the Institute, and members of the board of directors were determining the Association's promotional budget for 1955. It was very clear that the members of the Institute could not finance an advertising expenditure of $1.7 million, so that it was finally decided that about $900,000 would be allocated for advertising and that the total promotional budget would be about $1,250,000.

Subsequently, Mr. Jones established the Institute's promotional budget for 1955, as follows:

Public relations	$ 60,000
Retail sales training	58,000
Retail operating analyses and surveys	15,000
School educational program	21,000
Administration	36,000
Advertising and merchandising	1,063,000
Total	$1,253,000

The allocation for advertising and merchandising was broken down further, as follows:

Advertising to consumers	$ 744,000
Advertising to carpet retailers	38,000
Advertising to influence groups	75,000
Advertising contingency fund	58,000
Merchandising aids and clinics	126,000
Advertising research	20,000
Total	$1,063,000

Mr. Jones then asked the agency for further media recommendations in the light of this tentative budget.

~~~

CASE 21: CARPET INSTITUTE, INC. (G)[1]

QUESTIONS TO CONSIDER: *(1) Do you think that the Institute made good decisions in its selection of a copy theme and media for the 1955 consumer advertising program? (2) What conclusions do you draw from the Starch Ratings for the Institute's advertisements? (3) Are the Starch Ratings useful in evaluating the media which were employed?*

In the fall of 1954 executives of Carpet Institute, Inc., decided to use 14 consumer magazines as the media by which to reach consumers of carpets and rugs. Further, they decided to use "home means more—with carpet on the floor" as the central copy theme of their 1955 consumer advertising program. Since they desired to evaluate the effectiveness of the Institute's advertising, they decided to study reports of Starch Readership Service at the end of 1955. Hence in February 1956, when the Starch reports for December 1955 were available, Institute executives made a study of the readership of Institute advertisements appearing in *Life, The Saturday Evening Post, American Home, Woman's Home Companion, Woman's Day,* and *Ladies' Home Journal.*

The Institute's 1955 Advertising

In 1955 the Institute published six different black-and-white advertisements in 14 consumer magazines for a total of 77 insertions. These six advertisements, which were coded C1 through C6 by the Institute, are shown in Exhibits 1 through 6. The Institute's 1955 national consumer media schedule is given in Exhibit 7.

Starch Data Relating to Institute Advertisements

A summary of the readership scores of each of the six advertisements published by the Institute is given in Exhibit 8. Detailed breakdowns of the readership of each advertisement are given in Exhibits 9 through 14.

---

[1] Written by Donald H. Thain and Martin V. Marshall.

~~~

Exhibit 1

CARPET INSTITUTE, INC. (G)

HOME MEANS MORE...WITH CARPET ON THE FLOOR

Where there's happy family living, carpet's in the picture. Carpet fills any room with a special kind of warmth, comfort and beauty. Luxuriously soft, restfully quiet, carpet gives your home the warm, friendly glow that invites family "get-togethers." A romp on the floor with the kids... a relaxing hour of TV...a visit from admiring neighbors—carpet adds so much.

Yes, home means more with carpet on the floor—more beauty, more quiet, more comfort. And carpet means more convenience, too, for just a whisk of the vacuum keeps it beautifully fresh and full of life.

Lovely, long-wearing carpet costs far less than you think. And it's so easy to buy on convenient budget terms. Ask your dealer to show you the wonderful colors and textures of today's new rugs and carpets.

> **Buy carpets designed and made for the American way of life by these American manufacturers:**
>
> Artloom • Beattie • Bigelow • Downs • Firth
> Gulistan • Hardwick & Magee • Hightstown
> Holmes • Karastan • Lees • Magee • Masland
> Mohawk • Nye-Wait • Philadelphia Carpet
> Roxbury • Sanford • Alexander Smith
>
> **CARPET INSTITUTE, INC. 350 Fifth Ave., N.Y. 1, N.Y.**

HOME MEANS MORE—WITH CARPET ON THE FLOOR
MORE QUIET, MORE COMFORT, MORE BEAUTY, EASIER CARE

#C1

This advertisement appears in the following National publications: American Home, February; Better Homes & Gardens, January; Bride's Magazine, January 15; House Beautiful, February; House & Garden, January; Life, January; Living for Young Homemakers, February; McCall's Magazine, January; Parents' Magazine, February; Saturday Evening Post, January 18; Sunset, January; Women's Day, February; and Woman's Home Companion, February.

Exhibit 2

CARPET INSTITUTE, INC. (G)

SNUG AS A BUG...ON SOFT, WARM CARPET

Did any one, any time, any where, ever say "snug as a bug on a cold hard floor"? Of course not! *Snugness* goes with *rugness* — and where there's carpet, you find warmth, safety and cozy comfort, not only for baby but for all the family.

Carpet adds so much to family living. The quiet of carpet makes your home a restful haven. The beauty of carpet swells your heart with pride as

you welcome in friends and neighbors. And carpet is so easy to keep clean with a whisk of your vacuum—no tiresome scrubbing, waxing or polishing.

Lovely long-wearing carpet costs far less than you think. And it's so easy to buy on convenient budget terms. Why wait? Ask your dealer to show you the exciting colors and textures of today's new rugs and carpets.

Buy carpets designed and made for the
American way of life by these American manufacturers:

Artloom • Beattie • Bigelow • Downs • Firth
Gulistan • Hardwick & Magee • Hightstown • Holmes
Karastan • Leedom • Lees • Magee • Masland
Mohawk • Nye-Wait • Philadelphia Carpet
Roxbury • Sanford • Alexander Smith

CARPET INSTITUTE, INC. 350 Fifth Ave., N.Y. 1, N.Y.

HOME MEANS MORE — WITH CARPET ON THE FLOOR
MORE QUIET, MORE COMFORT, MORE BEAUTY, EASIER CARE

C2

This advertisement appears in the following National publications: American Home, April; Better Homes & Gardens, March; House & Gardens, March; House Beautiful, April; Living For Young Homemakers, April; Sunset, March; Parents' Magazine, April; McCall's, March; Woman's Home Companion, April; Ladies Home Journal, March; Woman's Day, April; Life, March 7; Saturday Evening Post, February 19.

Exhibit 3

CARPET INSTITUTE, INC. (G)

CARPET IS SO EASY TO CARE FOR

With soft beautiful carpet, you can sing "goodbye forever" to scrubbing and waxing hard floors. Carpet is so easy to "pick up" and keep clean. A whisk of your vacuum keeps it delightfully fresh and full of life...so lovely to look at, you feel that extra thrill of pride in your home.

But there's so much more in carpet than meets the eye. Carpet brings relaxing peace and quiet, soft friendly warmth, cozy comfort—an atmosphere of hominess and security that makes every member of your family feel "there's no place like home." Today, more than ever, your family will appreciate the quiet comfort and restfulness of carpet.

Lovely, long-wearing carpet costs far less than you think. And it's so easy to buy on convenient budget terms. So why not start enjoying it now? Ask your dealer to show you the wonderful colors and textures of today's new rugs and carpets.

> Buy carpets designed and made for the
> American way of life by these American manufacturers
>
> Artloom • Beattie • Bigelow • Downs • Firth
> Gulistan • Hardwick & Magee • Hightstown • Holmes
> Karastan • Leedom • Lees • Magee • Masland
> Mohawk • Nye-Wait • Philadelphia Carpet
> Roxbury • Sanford • Alexander Smith
>
> CARPET INSTITUTE, INC. 350 Fifth Ave., N. Y. 1, N. Y.

HOME MEANS MORE — WITH CARPET ON THE FLOOR
MORE QUIET, MORE COMFORT, MORE BEAUTY, EASIER CARE

#C-3

This advertisement appears in the following National publications: American Home, June; Better Homes & Gardens, May; Bride's Magazine, April 15; House Beautiful, June; House & Garden, May; Ladies' Home Journal, May; Life, May 2; Living For Young Homemakers, June; Parents' Magazine, June; Saturday Evening Post, April 16; Sunset Magazine, May; Woman's Day, June.

Exhibit 4

CARPET INSTITUTE, INC. (G)

The pony express route is quieter with carpet

As any mother knows, a cowboy leads a hard life.

Hard on the ears, hard on the clothes and, very often, hard on the cowboy.

Carpet on the floor goes a long way toward making life easier all around.

Carpet not only gives warmth and dignity to a room, it is a highly successful investment in comfort, quiet and safety for those you love.

Carpet prevents the slips and skids that often turn a sheriff's posse into just two small boys crying. Carpet <u>swallows</u> noise . . . makes home a quieter, more peaceful place to be.

And keeping carpet clean is easy. Just once around with the vacuum. No scrubbing, rinsing, waxing or polishing.

Carpet gives so much and costs so little — in time, in work and in money. When you move,

of course, your lovely, long-wearing carpet goes with you. You haven't invested time and money in floors you leave behind.

Yes, all in all, you can't do better than carpet for more pleasant living — with or without cowboys. And, at today's prices, you can probably afford to do two rooms for what you think one will cost.

When you visit your carpet store, ask about their budget plan. Do it soon.

HOME MEANS MORE—WITH CARPET ON THE FLOOR
MORE QUIET, MORE COMFORT, MORE BEAUTY, MORE SAFETY, EASIER CARE

Buy carpets designed and made for the American way of life by these American manufacturers Artloom • Beattie • Bigelow • Downs • Firth • Gulistan • Hardwick & Magee • Hightstown • Holmes Karastan • Leedom • Lees • Magee • Masland • Mohawk • Nye-Wait • Philadelphia Carpet • Roxbury • Sanford • Alexander Smith CARPET INSTITUTE, INC. 350 Fifth Ave., New York 1, N. Y.

#C-4

Exhibit 5

CARPET INSTITUTE, INC. (G)

Soft, beautiful carpet makes you so proud of your home

We really can't blame you two for being so proud.

Every young couple we know feels that way about their house when it's carpeted.

Because there is nothing that does as much to make a house beautiful, does as much to make it a home, as carpet.

For carpet is not only handsome in itself — soft and warm and welcoming — it sets a rich and flattering frame around your furniture.

And carpet has a day-to-day practicality that makes it wonderfully easy to live with. Carpet is quiet because it swallows the noises that make a house "restless". And it provides safe, sure footing for playing children — or you, when you're rushing to the phone or the door.

Carpet adds so much and costs so little — in time, in work and in money. A quick vacuuming keeps it lovely . . . no tedious scrubbing, rinsing, waxing, or polishing. And, when you move, your carpet goes along with you — you haven't invested time and money in floors you leave behind.

Yes, all this — for so little. At today's prices you can probably afford to do two rooms for what you think one will cost.

Drop in at your store this week. See the display of lovely colors, modern patterns, exciting new weaves and textures. With small monthly payments you can have beautiful, long-wearing carpet on your floors right now. You'll be so glad you did.

HOME MEANS MORE—WITH CARPET ON THE FLOOR
MORE QUIET, MORE COMFORT, MORE BEAUTY, MORE SAFETY, EASIER CARE

Buy carpets designed and made for the American way of life by these American manufacturers Artloom • Beattie • Bigelow • Downs • Firth • Gulistan • Hardwick & Magee • Hightstown • Holmes Karastan • Leedom • Lees • Magee • Masland • Mohawk • Nye-Wait • Philadelphia Carpet • Roxbury • Sanford • Alexander Smith CARPET INSTITUTE, INC., 350 Fifth Ave., New York 1, N. Y.

Exhibit 6

CARPET INSTITUTE, INC. (G)

Soft, warm carpet adds so much to Christmas

More than anything else you can buy for your home, carpet says warmth, comfort, a snug home.

For Christmas — and for the days after Christmas, the years after that, carpet goes on living with you and giving to you. Carpet quiets the hundreds of noises that go with family living. It provides safety for children at play or adults in a hurry.

Carpet gives so much and asks so little in care, in time and in money. It costs far less than you'd expect to pay — with budget terms, only pennies a day.

So, see the wonderful new styles and colors at your store now. Give carpet or have carpet this Christmas.

HOME MEANS MORE—WITH CARPET ON THE FLOOR
MORE QUIET, COMFORT, BEAUTY, SAFETY, EASIER CARE

Buy carpets designed and made for the American way of life by these American manufacturers Artloom • Beattie • Bigelow • Downs • Firth • Gulistan • Hardwick & Magee • Hightstown • Holmes Karastan • Leedom • Lees • Magee • Masland • Mohawk • Nye-Wait • Philadelphia Carpet • Roxbury • Sanford • Alexander Smith CARPET INSTITUTE, INC., 350 Fifth Ave., New York 1, N. Y.

#C-6

This advertisement appears in the following National publications: American Home, November; Better Homes & Gardens, November; House Beautiful, December; House & Garden, December; Ladies' Home Journal, November; Life, December 5; Living for Young Homemakers, November; McCall's Magazine, November; Parents' Magazine, December; Saturday Evening Post, December 3; Sunset Magazine, November; Woman's Day, November; Woman's Home Companion, December.

Exhibit 7

CARPET INSTITUTE, INC. (G)
1955 National Consumer Media Schedule

Publication	Circulation	Jan.	Feb.	Mar.	Apr.	May	June	July	Aug.	Sept.	Oct.	Nov.	Dec.	No. Ins.
American Home	3,053,795	#C1		#C2		#C3		#C4		#C5		#C6		6
Better Homes & Gardens	3,780,883	#C1		#C2		#C3		#C4		#C5		#C6		6
House & Gardens	470,757		#C1		#C2		#C3		#C4		#C5		#C6	6
House Beautiful	650,286		#C1		#C2		#C3		#C4		#C5		#C6	6
Living for Young Homemakers	518,783		#C1		#C2		#C3		#C4		#C5		#C6	6
Sunset	552,015	#C1		#C2		#C3		#C4		#C5		#C6		6
Bride's Magazine	111,288	#C1			#C2			#C3		#C4				4
Parents'	1,527,599		#C1		#C2		#C3		#C4		#C5			5
McCall's	4,555,927		#C1		#C2		#C3		#C4		#C5			5
Woman's Home Companion	4,381,137		#C1		#C2		#C3		#C4		#C5			5
Ladies' Home Journal	4,926,515		#C1		#C2		#C3		#C4		#C5			5
Woman's Day (National Ed.)	3,957,818		#C1		#C2		#C3		#C4		#C5			5
Life	5,401,325	#C1 1/10	#C2 2/19		#C3 4/16			#C4 7/25		#C5 9/12		#C6 11/7		6
The Saturday Evening Post	4,444,900	#C1 1/8		#C2 3/7		#C3 5/2			#C4 8/27		#C5 10/22	#C6 11/19		6
Total Circulation	38,333,028													
% of carpet sales by months (1953)		8.5	8.0	7.6	8.4	8.2	6.7	6.1	8.2	8.1	11.9	10.6	7.7	
% of total dollar budget		9.8	8.7	9.1	9.0	7.2	4.6	7.3	8.4	9.9	8.2	15.5	2.3	
% of total circulation		9.2	8.8	9.3	8.9	7.2	4.6	7.0	8.6	10.0	8.2	16.2	2.0	

Total Impressions—210,426,596

Source: Carpet Institute, Inc.

Exhibit 8

CARPET INSTITUTE, INC. (G)

Summary of Readership Scores—1955 Carpet Institute Consumer Advertising

| | MEN | | | | | | | | | WOMEN | | | | | | | | |
| | Per Cents | | | Readers/Dollar | | | Cost Ratios | | | Per Cents | | | Readers/Dollar | | | Cost Ratios | | |
	N	SA	RM	N	SA	RM	N	SA	RM	N	SA	RM	N	SA	RM	N	SA	RM
Ad C-1.........	19	7	3	44	17	8	96	43	88	32	20	6	101	65	17	121	90	166
Ad C-2.........	19	8	2	45	18	4	102	48	69	38	20	5	124	67	15	157	99	118
Ad C-3.........	13	5	2	33	13	5	76	36	73	25	16	4	91	59	15	127	96	157
Ad C-4.........	19	12	2	46	20	5	104	54	73	32	19	5	101	61	16	124	91	168
Ad C-5.........	12	7	2	26	18	5	87	68	116	18	12	3	59	41	9	84	69	121
Ad C-6.........	9	3	1	20	7	1	69	33	44	23	26	2	72	51	8	110	92	76
Average ad C-1 through C-6....	15	7	2	36	16	5	72	47	77	28	17	4	91	57	13	121	90	134

Key: N—Noted
     SA—Seen-Associated
     RM—Read Most

Source: Carpet Institute, Inc.

Exhibit 9

CARPET INSTITUTE, INC. (G)

Starch Readership Scores of Advertisement C-1

MAG.*	DATE	SIZE ADS.	PG.	SIZE AND COLOR	MEN												WOMEN												
					Per Cents			R/$			Cost Ratios			Ranks			Per Cents			R/$			Cost Ratios			Ranks		
					N	SA	RM	N	SA	RM	N	SA	RM	N	SA	RM	N	SA	RM	N	SA	RM	N	SA	RM	N	SA	RM
Life......	1/10	47	47	1PBW	14	5	2	36	13	5	71	30	56	35	45	30	36	26	7	102	73	20	152	122	154	14	15	17
SEP......	1/8	30	52		14	6	3	33	14	7	66	31	70	24	30	19	34	23	9	88	60	23	144	111	383	11	12	6
AH.......	2	47	3		28	11	5	64	25	11	152	68	138	14	36	17	39	20	5	128	66	16	151	99	114	6	25	20
WHC.....	2	54	73														28	21	4	105	79	15	88	75	100	40	48	22
WD......	2	55	75														21	12	3	80	46	11	69	41	79	47	53	29
Average		46			19	7	3	44	17	8	96	43	88				32	20	6	101	65	17	121	90	166			

* SEP—The Saturday Evening Post
  AH—American Home
  WHC—Woman's Home Companion
  WD—Woman's Day

Source: Carpet Institute, Inc.

Exhibit 10

CARPET INSTITUTE, INC. (G)

Starch Readership Scores of Advertisement C-2

| | | | | MEN | | | | | | | | | | | | WOMEN | | | | | | | | | | | | |
| | | | | Per Cents | | | R/$ | | | Cost Ratios | | | Ranks | | | Per Cents | | | R/$ | | | Cost Ratios | | | Ranks | | |
MAG.*	DATE	PG.	SIZE AND COLOR	N	SA	RM	N	SA	RM	N	SA	RM	N	SA	RM	N	SA	RM	N	SA	RM	N	SA	RM	N	SA	RM
Life.....	3/7	92	145PBW	13	5	1	34	13	3	89	45	60	49	77	61	33	14	4	93	40	11	186	108	157	13	45	31
SEP.....	2/19	72	121	15	9	1	36	21	2	69	47	29	47	61	64	46	28	5	120	73	13	235	166	144	2	13	18
AH.....	4	94	7	28	9	3	64	20	7	149	53	117	25	74	40	35	19	4	115	63	13	147	102	100	22	44	40
WHC.....	4	70	83													37	20	3	139	75	23	142	84	144	14	53	25
WD.....	4	59	9													46	26	6	176	99	11	132	78	61	8	44	42
LHJ.....	3	154	45													28	15	5	101	54	18	101	57	100	75	143	76
Average		90														38	20	5	124	67	15	157	99	118			

* SEP—The Saturday Evening Post
AH—American Home
WHC—Woman's Home Companion
WD—Woman's Day
LHJ—Ladies' Home Journal

Source: Carpet Institute, Inc.

Exhibit 11

CARPET INSTITUTE, INC. (G)

Starch Readership Scores of Advertisement C-3

MAG.*	DATE	SIZE ADS.	PG.	SIZE AND COLOR	MEN												WOMEN											
					Per Cents			R/$			Cost Ratios			Ranks			Per Cents			R/$			Cost Ratios			Ranks		
					N	SA	RM	N	SA	RM	N	SA	RM	N	SA	RM	N	SA	RM	N	SA	RM	N	SA	RM	N	SA	RM
Life	5/2	95	63	1PBW	12	5	3	37	15	9	86	43	150	54	79	30	26	16	5	87	54	17	174	123	170	21	35	19
SEP	4/16	129	194		11	5	0	26	12	0	60	33	0	109	125	129	27	18	7	70	47	18	175	152	360	26	42	10
AH	6	76	6		15	5	3	35	12	7	83	32	70	50	71	44	23	12	2	88	46	8	114	75	100	31	48	34
WD	6	39	67														25	16	4	109	70	17	77	52	65	32	38	27
LHJ	5	145	211														25	19	4	101	77	16	95	77	89	80	113	81
Average					13	5	2	33	13	5	76	36	73				25	16	4	91	59	15	127	96	157			

* SEP—The Saturday Evening Post
  AH—American Home
  WD—Woman's Day
  LHJ—Ladies' Home Journal

Source: Carpet Institute, Inc.

Exhibit 12

CARPET INSTITUTE, INC. (G)

Starch Readership Scores of Advertisement C-4

Mag.*	Date	Size Ads.	Pg.	Size and Color	Men												Women												
					Per Cents			R/$			Cost Ratios			Ranks			Per Cents			R/$			Cost Ratios			Ranks		
					N*	SA	RM	N	SA	RM	N	SA	RM	N	SA	RM	N	SA	RM	N	SA	RM	N	SA	RM	N	SA	RM
Life..........	7/25	50	4	1PBW	15	6	2	40	16	5	90	38	100	30	45	20	34	18	7	99	52	20	143	88	230	9	30	7
SEP..........	8/27	44	71		24	19	3	59	22	7	100	43	70	23	44	33	42	27	6	116	74	17	155	137	283	4	10	10
AH..........	8	79	101		19	10	1	40	21	2	121	81	50	25	49	49	25	15	1	85	51	3	120	94	43	31	41	59
WHC..........	7	44	49														35	20	8	125	71	29	125	81	242	14	33	12
LHJ..........	8	71	102														23	16	3	82	57	11	79	56	44	53	64	58
Average..........					19	12	2	46	20	5	104	54	73				32	19	5	101	61	16	124	91	168			

* SEP—The Saturday Evening Post
AH—American Home
WHC—Woman's Home Companion
WD—Woman's Day
LHJ—Ladies' Home Journal

Source: Carpet Institute, Inc.

Exhibit 13

CARPET INSTITUTE, INC. (G)

Starch Readership Sources of Advertisement C-5

MAG.*	DATE	SIZE ADS.	PG.	SIZE AND COLOR	MEN Per Cents N	SA	RM	R/$ N	SA	RM	Cost Ratios N	SA	RM	Ranks N	SA	RM	WOMEN Per Cents N	SA	RM	R/$ N	SA	RM	Cost Ratios N	SA	RM	Ranks N	SA	RM
Life........	9/12	116	183	1PBW	12	8	1	32	21	3	97	81	75	60	75	72	11	7	1	32	20	3	78	57	60	73	85	72
SEP........	10/22	81	85		14	8	3	34	20	7	87	59	140	51	65	28	21	14	4	58	39	11	149	122	275	24	33	15
AH.........	10	99	125		9	6	2	19	13	4	76	65	133	66	71	25	22	18	4	75	61	14	95	102	200	53	48	22
WD.........	10	59	69														16	7	1	62	27	4	50	24	24	54	58	52
WHC........	9	67	53														20	13	3	71	46	11	78	56	85	48	56	37
LHJ........	9	147	200														15	14	3	54	50	11	55	55	79	139	139	94
Average.....					12	7	2	26	18	5	87	68	116				18	12	32	59	41	9	84	69	121			

* SEP—The Saturday Evening Post
  AH—American Home
  WD—Woman's Day
  WHC—Woman's Home Companion
  LHJ—Ladies' Home Journal

Source: Carpet Institute, Inc.

Exhibit 14

CARPET INSTITUTE, INC. (G)

Starch Readership Scores of Advertisement C-6

MAG.*	DATE	SIZE ADS.	PG.	SIZE AND Color	MEN												WOMEN												
					Per Cents			R/$			Cost Ratios			Ranks			Per Cents			R/$			Cost Ratios			Ranks		
					N	SA	RM	N	SA	RM	N	SA	RM	N	SA	RM	N	SA	RM	N	SA	RM	N	SA	RM	N	SA	RM
Life.........	12/5	117	13	1PBW	8	5	0	20	13	0	71	67	0	82	94	0	23	18	2	62	49	5	172	153	100	28	30	52
SEP.........	12/3	107	16		9	1	0	22	2	0	65	7	0	89	107	0	18	12	0	46	31	0	110	94	0	44	58	0
AH..........	11	75	125		9	3	2	19	6	4	70	32	133	54	67	23	24	14	4	82	48	14	100	80	140	38	46	31
WD..........	11	62	11														29	22	3	112	85	12	101	79	86	29	43	34
LHJ.........	11	150	142														17	13	2	57	44	7	66	54	54	128	144	98
Average.					9	3	0	20	7	1	69	33	44				23	26	2	72	51	8	110	92	76			

* SEP—The Saturday Evening Post
AH—American Home
WHC—Woman's Home Companion
WD—Woman's Day
LHJ—Ladies' Home Journal

Source: Carpet Institute, Inc.

CASE 22: TILDEN PAPER COMPANY[1]

NOTE: *This is the first case in this chapter which focuses upon a special promotion.* QUESTIONS TO CONSIDER: *(1) What are the objectives of the promotion proposed by Mr. Webb? (2) What are the objectives of the promotion proposed by the advertising agency? How does it differ from Mr. Webb's? (3) Does the agency proposal adequately take into account problems of scheduling and co-ordinating promotional efforts? (4) As Mr. Beal, would you accept, reject, or modify either of the proposals? What would be primary considerations governing your decision?*

In August 1955, Mr. John Beal, sales manager of the Tilden Paper Company, Montreal, Quebec, was considering what action he should take with regard to a promotional program for the company's paper napkins. His assistant, Mr. Charles Webb, had submitted a memorandum suggesting a promotion on the company's White Swan napkins (see p. 740 ff). Two days later the company's agency submitted a more detailed memorandum (p. 742 ff) for a promotional program on napkins involving a larger expenditure than had been suggested by Mr. Webb.

Stocking of an enlarged napkin line by the trade had been achieved by the company in May 1955, without any intensified advertising and promotional effort. The sales force had gotten extensive distribution while selling the established White Swan paper products. The special napkin promotion was suggested as an addition to or deviation from the advertising strategy which had been followed in 1955. This strategy had been to advertise White Swan as a family of consumer paper products with advertising copy devoted almost solely to White Swan toilet tissue with "hitch-hiking" mention of napkins in the tissue advertisements.

Company Background

The Tilden Paper Company was a leading Canadian manufacturer of industrial and consumer paper products. Founded in 1850 as a small family-owned enterprise, the company had expanded until in 1955 it included manufacturing facilities spread over 100 acres, 2,200 factory employees, 6,000 square miles of timberland, and 2,000 woodsmen.

The company's consumer products, which were also sold to institutions and industrial concerns, were toilet tissue, towels, and napkins. In 1954 sales of these products were $4,800,000, $1,200,000, and $600,000, respectively. Of the napkin sales, with which we are concerned in this case, $400,000 were to industrial and institutional concerns, $200,000 to consumers.

In 1951 the company had purchased a new type crepe-tissue paper-making machine, which was brought into production in 1954. The pur-

---

[1] All names are fictitious except the White Swan brand name. Written by Donald H. Thain and Martin V. Marshall.

chase of this machine had more than doubled the company's toilet tissue and napkin production capacity. Therefore, in an effort to increase sales, executives had made several major changes in branding and product-line strategy as described below.

Before 1954 the consumer products division marketed its products under several trade-marks. Among these was "White Swan toilet tissue," which was the company's most popular single product and which accounted for the major share of its toilet tissue sales. After examining various market surveys, executives concluded that the White Swan trade-mark and brand name had the best consumer acceptance of any consumer paper product brand in eastern Canada[2] which was the company's principal area of distribution. In the light of these and other facts, executives decided to use the White Swan trade-mark as a family brand and to make certain additions to their product line.

In August 1954 the company introduced a White Swan family of brands which consisted of the regular grades of toilet tissue, towels, and napkins (see Exhibit 1 which is an advertisement showing the White Swan line of products). All packages were new, and the tissue and napkins were new products produced on the new paper-making machine.

In December 1954, regular quality napkins were introduced in colors.

In May 1955, two-ply toilet tissue and two- and three-ply napkins were introduced. These products were known in the trade as de luxe grades. The addition of these products completed the family of White Swan brands shown in Exhibit 2.

Commenting on the results of these moves, Mr. Beal said, "Since these changes have been in effect for only a few months, it is difficult to judge how much sales have increased. To date, sales look promising. The company does not subscribe to any regular market research service providing retail sales data. Factory sales of all the new items have been above our original expectations. When we introduced the de luxe napkin line, we extended distribution to drug, variety, and department stores. So far, our efforts to sell to these new outlets have been successful."

Executives suspected, however, that the share of market for all three product lines had decreased slightly since 1950 because of the gains of several competitors.

Pertinent information concerning the napkins is given below:

Napkin Type	Size	Quality	Number per Package	Usual Retail Price per Package
1. 3-ply de luxe dinner.....	17″ × 17″	High	40	$0.33
2. 2-ply de luxe luncheon...	13½″ × 13½″	Medium	60	0.22
3. 1-ply colored luncheon...	13½″ × 13½″	Regular	60	0.17
4. 1-ply white luncheon....	13½″ × 13½″	Regular	70	0.17

[2] Eastern Canada included Ontario and all provinces east of Ontario.

Exhibit 2
TILDEN PAPER COMPANY
White Swan Family Advertisement

5 col. × 200 lines = 1,000 lines

The three-ply de luxe dinner-sized napkins were manufactured by fusing together three layers of tissue. They were described in advertisements as having a "smooth, high quality, substantial feeling," and being "attractively embossed in a tasteful pattern." Executives stated that they were of the highest quality available and were stronger and better looking than competitive de luxe quality napkins.

The de luxe two-ply luncheon-sized napkins were of slightly lower quality than the dinner napkins. They were embossed with a different pattern. Executives stated that the editors of several prominent Canadian women's magazines had endorsed them as being completely acceptable for all types of use, including use by guests.

The one-ply white and colored napkins were of a discernibly lower quality. Executives believed that housewives thought of them as being acceptable for most uses except certain types of "very special" entertaining.

All White Swan toilet tissue and napkin paper stock was manufactured on the new crepe-tissue paper-making machine. This machine was of the most advanced type available, and the quality of the tissue it produced was unsurpassed. It had run at 60% of capacity for the first seven months of 1955. Two of Tilden's competitors operated similar machines.

With distribution in approximately 90% of the possible retail outlets, Tilden executives believed that the entire White Swan product line had more intensive distribution in Ontario than any of their competitors' lines.

In eastern Canada the division's products were sold through grocery, drug, variety, and department stores. Thirty salesmen sold direct to wholesalers and chains (any company with five or more retail outlets). Salesmen spent about 20% of their time on missionary sales work with independent retailers.

The company sold napkins to wholesalers and chains at the following prices:

White Swan Napkin Type	Number of Packages per Case	Price per Case to Wholesalers
3-ply de luxe dinner............	24	$6.24
2-ply de luxe luncheon..........	24	4.14
1-ply colored luncheon..........	24	3.23
1-ply white luncheon...........	24	3.23

Approximately 11% of Tilden's selling price consisted of sales tax and freight. Therefore, the actual net price per case to the company was about 89% of the invoice prices stated above.

Up to August 1955 the advertising of the consumer products division, which totaled $480,000 in 1954, had been concentrated on White Swan toilet tissue. The only advertising devoted to napkins was a small amount of so-called "hitchhiking" in some tissue advertisements, for example, see Exhibit 1.

The advertisement shown in Exhibit 2 represented the company's first departure from the policy of devoting advertisements almost exclusively to White Swan toilet tissue. This advertisement was scheduled for insertion in eastern Canadian newspapers in the fall of 1955.

Explaining the difference between the marketing of toilet tissue and napkins, Mr. Beal said, "The market for tissue has been well developed and is highly competitive. Over the years, tissue has been advertised extensively by ourselves and several competitors. The napkin market, on the other hand, is comparatively undeveloped. Neither we nor our competitors have ever aggressively advertised and promoted napkins."

Information regarding the napkin market in Canada was summarized as follows in the report on a 1952 market study made for the company:

1. Eight of ten Canadian housewives use paper napkins, and six of the eight keep them on hand regularly.
2. Regular stocking is highest in the big cities and upper-income groups, lowest in Quebec.
3. Six out of ten buyers do not know the brands they buy. The remainder are widely split among the ten top brands which vary in importance between regions.
4. The most important source of purchase is the chain grocery store, followed by the independent grocer and the variety store. The relative importance of these and other retail outlets varies considerably between regions and between brands.

In August 1955 there were approximately nine competitors selling napkins in the Ontario market. Three of these competitors sold de luxe quality brands, four sold medium quality brands, and five sold regular quality brands.

The Promotion

On August 24, 1955, Mr. Webb submitted to Mr. Beal the following proposal as a basis for initiating planning action for the special promotion:

MEMORANDUM

DE LUXE NAPKIN PROMOTION

Current Situation

The budgeted sales of de luxe napkins are 5,376 cases of two-ply and 1,344 cases of three-ply for a total of 6,720 cases in 1955. The total budgeted contribution to overhead and profit expected from these grades is $12,338. With current prices, the budgeted sales volume will yield a contribution of $10,658 which is actually $1,680 short of the budgeted contribution.

Recommendation

It is recommended that we promote de luxe napkins to the extent of an investment of $30,000 to $36,000 to increase the volume and the profit on these lines and to obtain a substantial share of the potential market for these grades before our competitors are able to capture this potential for themselves. It is further recommended that the promotion be designed to emphasize and sell the whole family of White Swan napkins, including single-ply, white, and colored. The purpose of such a promotion would be to introduce de luxe grades of White Swan napkins to the consumer and to force distribution of all napkin grades.

Analysis

There are only two ways in which the sales department may improve on its present profit position of the de luxe grades. One method would be to raise prices and thus increase the unit contribution. The second method would be to increase volume. Since prices are determined by competitive conditions, an increase in volume would appear to be the most logical way in which to improve our profit position.

Assuming that total fixed overhead costs will remain unchanged, an increase in volume to 33,600 cases, combined two- and three-ply napkins would provide a total contribution of $53,290. This contribution would provide a $40,951 margin over budgeted overhead. This higher volume would also mean approximately six days' additional utilization of our new crepe-tissue machine which is currently operating at 63% of capacity.

Recognizing that promotion would be necessary to attain this volume, a $30,000 to $36,000 investment in advertising and sale promotion would still mean a $6,600 to $12,600 net increase in profit. This would represent a 20% to 40% initial return on the investment. To the extent that volume is maintained at a higher level than would have been the case without the promotion, the return would be much greater.

Granting the above, the problem then becomes one of determining the feasibility and probability of obtaining this volume of 33,600 cases, or 300 tons. Canadian napkin consumption in 1954 was in excess of 6,000 tons so that if we assumed no increase in consumption, the projected volume would represent a 5% increase in our relative market position. However, Canadian consumption is only 40% of the United States per capita rate. Therefore, it seems reasonable to assume that most, if not all, of the increased volume resulting from a promotion would be new business both for ourselves and for the industry.

Since the Canadian per capita consumption rate for napkins is so low compared with that of the United States, and there is a very high untapped market potential, there is a strong possibility that we could sell as many as 42,000 cases of napkins in a seven-week promotional period in the Ontario market alone. This possible sales estimate is based on the following reasoning; we are currently selling through 120 wholesalers who employ an average of five salesmen each. This makes a total of 600 wholesaler salesmen selling our product in Ontario. Assuming that we could get 20 working days from each salesman in the seven-week promotional period, we would have a total of 12,000 salesman working days on the promotion; assuming a minimum of the two cases sold per working day would result in a total of 24,000 cases sold through wholesalers alone. In addition to these outlets, there are the chain and independent stores that are large enough to buy direct. Of the 8,869 retail grocery stores in Ontario, 1,241—600 chain stores and 641 independent stores—have sales of over $100,000 annually. Assuming that each chain took five 5-case deals and each independent took one 5-case deal, total sales through all outlets would be 42,205 cases, or $189,152, divided as follows:

PROMOTION SALES ESTIMATE

	SALES	
	Cases	Dollars
Wholesalers:		
24,000 cases divided as follows:		
3-ply dinner at $6.24 per case..........	6,000	$ 37,440
2-ply luncheon at $4.14 per case.........	6,000	24,840
1-ply colored at $3.23 per case..........	6,000	19,380
1-ply white at $3.23 per case...........	6,000	19,380
Chains:		
600 × five 5-case deals at $24.20 = ...	15,000	72,600
Independent:		
641 × one 5-case deals at $24.20 = ...	3,205	15,512
Total.........................	42,205	$189,152

This is almost 30% more than the conservative sales estimate of 33,600 cases on which the budgetary calculations in this proposal are based.

On August 26, 1955, the advertising agency submitted a detailed plan for the promotion. The text read as follows:

PROPOSED WHITE SWAN NAPKIN PROMOTION FOR ONTARIO

A. GENERAL

With the sale and distribution of regular White Swan tissue progressing satisfactorily, we believe that increased napkin sales would provide the most profitable means of increasing crepe-paper tonnage.

In examining eastern Canada White Swan napkin sales for the 12 months ending June 30, 1955, we find that total sales amounted to 66,574 cases. Of this, Ontario (Toronto, Ottawa, Hamilton, and London Districts) accounted for 62% of this total and Quebec (Montreal, and Quebec City Districts) for 23%.

Over the past 18 months, White Swan napkin sales have increased 43% over-all—62% in Ontario and 55% in Quebec. The table below outlines this information in detail:

TOTAL WHITE SWAN NAPKINS SALES
(Cases of 24 Packages)

Sales Areas	12 Mos. End. Dec. 31, 1953	12 Mos. End. June 30, 1955	% Volume Increases	% of Province	% of Eastern
All Eastern........	46,486	66,574	43	....	100
Ontario:	25,633	41,490	62	100	62
Ottawa.........	6,383	8,293	30	20	12
Toronto........	13,903	27,034	94	65	41
Hamilton.......	2,693	3,188	30	8	5
London........	2,654	2,975	12	7	4
Quebec:	9,716	15,053	55	100	23
Montreal.......	8,233	13,452	63	89	20
Quebec City....	1,483	1,601	9	11	2

In considering sales areas for promotional purposes, we should select those areas which would produce the greatest return for the effort and dollars expended. The above sales figures indicate the larger franchise for White Swan napkins lies in Ontario.

Furthermore, the activities of competition should be considered when planning sales promotion. Our largest competitor has been most active in launching his new brand of two-ply luncheon and dinner napkins in western Canada. This effort encompasses almost all phases of sales promotion including household sampling, "team" sales operation, point-of-sale display, undoubtedly dealer allowances, and backed up by radio, television, and extensive newspaper campaigns. After their introductory promotion has been completed in the West, it would seem logical that they would "advance eastward."

Therefore, it is essential that in order to ensure the progress of White Swan napkins and, at the same time, introduce new de luxe napkins, a hard-hitting sales and advertising campaign be entered into immediately. Such a campaign is outlined as follows:

B. Objectives of Promotion

The main objectives of this promotion are to build the White Swan napkin franchise in Ontario and secure the maximum tonnage volume possible. These objectives should be accomplished by: (1) rapid promotional distribution in the stores which would provide maximum consumer movement; (2) erection of mass point-of-sale displays in the stores which would provide maximum consumer movement; (3) pressuring consumer movement to the fullest extent possible without destroying established pricing structure; (4) use of trade incentives.

C. Elements of the Promotion Plan

In order to accomplish the stated objectives, the following are the essential basic elements of the promotion plan: (1) consumer sampling via mail; (2) consumer couponing via mail; (3) local advertising; (4) special independent grocer deal; (5) special grocery chain-store deal; (6) point-of-sale display; (7) grocery jobber program.

1. Sampling

It is suggested later in this document that the de luxe napkins be featured by the sales force. This proposition is even more important when considering consumer promotion. The two- and three-ply de luxe White Swan napkins are new items to the housewife. It is felt that the three-ply dinner size would provide the most interest. Therefore, we propose primarily to feature the three-ply napkin in consumer promotion.

But just to talk about the three-ply napkin in advertisements is not enough as far as this promotion is concerned. We must get a sample of the three-ply into the hands of the housewife. To accomplish this, we suggest a "To the Householder" mailing.

Such a mailing would go to all households in the city limits of all towns and cities concerned in the campaign. The present estimate is about 700,000.

Mailings to all towns and cities would not be forwarded at the same time. As each locale has been covered by a sales team or teams, the mailing would then be released for that locale only.

Our last experience with sampling was favorable. It will be recalled that there was a 22% increase in toilet tissue sales in the Toronto area following an introductory sampling campaign about five years ago.

2. *Couponing*

Assume that the housewife now has a three-ply napkin sample in hand. Can we leave it to our advertising and displays alone to make her buy? If we provide her with a single napkin and a coupon which would give her a special introductory price on White Swan napkins, we believe that our chances of moving napkins will be multiplied many times. We estimate 25% coupon redemption. Without a coupon and with a sample only we might only expect 1% or 2% of the housewives to go out looking for our napkin.

It is our proposal to make the coupon part of the sampling mailer.

The coupon's retail value would be 5 cents and be good on:

> 1 box   —3-ply dinner napkins
> or
> 2 boxes—2-ply luncheon napkins
> or
> 3 boxes—1-ply napkin (white or colored)

From the consumer standpoint, the special promotion price in independent stores with coupon would be:

3-ply dinner napkin	28 cents per box instead of 33 cents
2-ply luncheon napkin	19½ cents per box instead of 22 cents
1-ply luncheon napkin	15⅓ cents per box instead of 17 cents

This offer, we believe, would be attractive to the housewife and provide the impetus we require to build franchise, move tonnage, and make this program a success.

3. *Consumer Advertising*

In order to back up the consumer sampling and couponing as well as the sales force effort, it is proposed that a series of advertisements be run in each local newspaper. The first advertisement should break the *day after* the sales have been completed in a city or town. The initial advertisement would be used to introduce the new de luxe napkins and should be approximately 1,500 lines. Three or four days later a 1,200 line advertisement would run. This time the advertisement would remind the housewife to "use her coupon." Then, at intervals of a week, two 375 line advertisements would run. The first featuring "sell," the second, the coupon.

We believe that the above newspaper campaign plus the chains and co-operatives' use of the mats we would supply would be sufficient to provide the impetus required.

4. *Independent Grocer Deal*

Although the objective of the promotion is to promote White Swan napkins in general, it is felt that, in order to provide the salesforce with the maximum impact available, the new de luxe napkins should be featured. It is essential that the de luxe products gain maximum distribution so as to support the consumer promotion outlined later in this document.

The deal listed below is suggested as the basic deal for this promotion. If a store cannot handle this small deal, then that store should not participate in the promotion.

SUGGESTED WHITE SWAN NAPKIN DEAL

No. Cases and Size	Item	Wholesaler Cost	Retailer Cost	Retail Price	Markup
1—40/24	3-ply de luxe dinner	$ 6.24	$ 6.86	33 cents	15%
2—60/24	2-ply de luxe luncheon	8.28	9.10	22 cents	15
1—60/24	1-ply colored	3.23	3.55	17 cents	15
1—70/48	1-ply luncheon	6.45	7.09	17 cents	15
5 cases		$24.20	$26.60	Value 30.59	

In other words, the retailer would be getting:

5 cases, or 144 packages,
at $26.60 instead of $28.79.
This saving he passes on to the consumer.

The wholesaler would be billed at the regular price, but the goods would be sold to the retailer at a 10% wholesaler markup instead of the usual 18%. We do not feel that the wholesaler should get his full markup since we are delivering the goods as well as providing the wholesaler with a large future turnover.

Not only will the consumer receive a "break" on price at the independent level but such pricing will put the independent grocer almost on a par with the chains for this promotion.

Now, how do we clinch this deal with the independent grocer and at the same time secure space for display? By simply *buying* that space! Our salesman, who is selling the promotion, hands the dealer three silver dollars for each deal he buys. In other words, the retailers' markup is not 15%, as stated above, but over 26%. *If sold with enthusiasm, we believe the sales teams won't miss a sale!*

5. Special Chain-Store Deal

This promotion plan cannot be successful without the full co-operation of the chain stores. Therefore, it is felt that chain headquarters should be contacted by top management so as to insure such co-operation.

The proposition to the chain stores would be essentially this:

a) The chain would agree to purchase five (or more deals) for each store in their chain in Ontario at $24.20 per deal—or a minimum order of $121.00 (25 cases) per store. The purchase would be made on a one-time basis only.

b) The chain would agree to lay the merchandise down in their individual stores by a specified date so that *our men* could build displays and thus ensure participation in local promotional efforts.

c) The chain would agree to use the newspaper mats supplied them on the dates we would specify.

d) For such agreements, we will allow the chain $2.50 per 5-case deal as promotional allowance.

6. Point-of-Sale Display

It is suggested that two pieces of point-of-sale material be used:

a) A combination case wrapper and window banner.

b) A combination shelf-talker and price card.

These two items are inexpensive but effective for this type of campaign. Quantities estimated are:

```
Case wrappers......................12,000 sales force use
Window banners..................... 3,000 jobber use
                                    15,000 Total
```

```
Shelf-talkers...................... 5,000 sales force
Price cards........................ 2,000 jobber
                                     7,000
```

7. Wholesaler Program

It is not contemplated that the wholesaler would participate directly in the White Swan napkin promotion. Since the program must be operated on a timetable, wholesaler participation would be most difficult. Also, the White Swan sales force would be working 33 municipalities on a planned basis, and wholesaler activity in the same areas would probably lead to confusion and thus reduce the effectiveness of the program.

However, since it would be impossible for the White Swan sales teams to cover all retail outlets, provision should be made to ensure over-all coverage. Here is a job for the grocery wholesaler. But, because of the possible confusion mentioned above, the wholesaler coverage should begin *after* the White Swan napkin promotion program. We want to make sure that the wholesaler will:

a) Provide floor stocks to supply retailer demand and
b) Make the White Swan napkin promotion a "must" with his salesmen.

We feel that not only should the wholesaler himself be made interested in the program but, more importantly, his salesmen must be. One of our major competitors in Ontario is now giving the wholesaler one dollar for each three cases of products sold. We do not believe we should "me too" this offer. Our proposal is as follows:

a) For a period of 30 days beginning *after* the White Swan sales force has completed its promotion, the wholesaler would receive a special 5% "promotion allowance" on White Swan napkins.
b) To gain the support of the salesmen, we would offer a "bonus" of 25 cents per case on all White Swan napkins for a period of 30 days. Such "bonuses" would be offered by our salesmen at wholesaler sales meetings so as to be sure the wholesaler salesmen know the offer and are acquainted with the program just completed.
c) Point-of-sale display material would be made available to the wholesaler salesmen.

It is imperative that the wholesaler program be implemented *immediately* after the completion of the White Swan sales force promotional operation. By rapid implementing, necessary stocks would be on hand to replace merchandise moved by the consumer promotion. The first consumer sale is not the most important sale. The second and third sales are. If merchandise is not available in the stores when the housewife is ready to repurchase, she will be forced to switch to another brand. The wholesaler program outlined above should provide the necessary follow-up.

D. Implementation of the Promotion Plan

1. *Geographical Areas*

Although the promotion is planned for Ontario, it is felt that promotional effort should be tailored to produce maximum results. Therefore, we propose that advertising and sales effort be confined to the 33 towns and cities which are now on the White Swan newspaper advertising list. This list of cities is composed of the locales which hold the greatest potential for White Swan napkins. The households in these towns and cities represent 57% of all households, and 80% of all urban households in Ontario. Urban households should provide the maximum potential for napkins. (A list of these towns and cities appears in Exhibit 3.)

2. *Sales Force Organization and Operation*

In order to cover the 33 markets as rapidly and efficiently as possible, it is proposed to use all available man power in the following manner:

a) All the consumer products salesmen in the district would be grouped as a "task force."

b) It is suggested that the 16 salesmen task-force group be divided into eight two-man teams with one team member being appointed "team captain." Each team would operate as a unit and be under the immediate control of the sales manager in whose district it is working. The purpose of a two-man team is to provide sufficient man power to sell the program and build displays.

3. *Transportation*

In order to provide the means of transporting teams, merchandise, and point-of-sale display materials, it is suggested that each team be provided with a hired station wagon or panel truck.

4. *Operation*

Each team would be assigned a certain town or towns to cover on specific day(s). A team might operate in the following manner:

a) The evening prior to the next day's operation, the team would:
   (1) Load vehicle with as many retailer deals as possible.
   (2) Load vehicle with sufficient point-of-sale material for next day's operation.
   (3) Check route lists of next day's operation to be sure no time is lost. Each team will be supplied with names of stores that must be called on.
   (4) Submit reports on previous day's operation.

b) In covering the route-listed stores each day, each team would operate as follows:

   (1) In making a call, one member of the team would make the sales "pitch"—the other member would stand by. Independent grocer orders would be made to the credit of the wholesaler indicated by the buyer.
   (2) When it is apparent that the sale is to be closed, the "pitcher" would establish that a display is to be built immediately and determine

Exhibit 3

LIST OF THE CITIES TO BE COVERED AND THE NEWSPAPERS IN WHICH ADVERTISING IS TO APPEAR

City	Population* (000's)	Newspaper	Circulation (000's)	Line Rate
1. Barrie	13.5	Examiner	6.8	$0.07
2. Belleville	21.2	Ontario-Intelligencer	10.4	0.065
3. Brantford	39.4	Expositor	19.9	0.10
4. Brockville	13.0	Recorder-Times	7.5	0.06
5. Chatham	23.1	News	13.7	0.09
6. Cornwall	18.1	Standard Freeholder	12.3	0.08
7. Galt	21.0	Reporter	10.7	0.08
8. Guelph	29.7	Mercury	11.8	0.08
9. Hamilton	225.9	Spectator	87.0	0.24
10. Kingston	45.0	Whig-Standard	19.8	0.09
11. Kitchener-Waterloo	62.5	Record	31.0	0.13
12. Lindsay	10.5	Post	2.6	0.035
13. London	103.1	Free Press	94.4	0.29
14. Niagara Falls	25.3	Review	13.5	0.08
15. North Bay	19.4	Nugget	11.9	0.08
16. Orillia	13.0	Packet & Times	5.5	0.06
17. Oshawa	47.5	Times-Gazette	13.0	0.09
18. Ottawa	221.8	Citizen	56.6	0.20
		Journal	62.5	0.20
19. Owen Sound	17.5	Sun-Times	12.5	0.08
20. Pembroke	13.5	Standard-Observer	5.4	0.06
21. Peterborough	43.1	Examiner	17.7	0.09
22. St. Catherine's	41.2	Standard	22.5	0.10
23. St. Thomas	19.0	Times-Journal	10.9	0.08
24. Sarnia	42.2	Canadian-Observer	13.1	0.09
25. S. St. Marie	36.5	Star	23.2	0.12
26. Smith's Falls	8.8	....	....	......
27. Stratford	20.1	Beacon-Herald	9.9	0.08
28. Sudbury	47.5	Star	23.2	0.12
29. Toronto	685.3	Globe & Mail	236.6	0.65
		Star	391.7	0.75
		Telegram	233.4	0.60
30. Welland	16.8	Tribune	13.9	0.09
31. Windsor	127.8	Star	74.8	0.25
32. Woodstock	17.0	Sentinel-Review	9.0	0.08
33. Additional small cities				0.71
Total				$6.07

* Population of city zone only—does not include population of entire metropolitan trading areas.

from the customer where such display is to be erected. Then, his "assistant" would begin to bring in from the vehicle the merchandise display materials.

(3) While the sale is being written up by the "pitcher," his "assistant" would begin erecting the display which would be completed by both men. Such team work will speed up operations.

(4) In the case of chain stores where merchandise has already been laid down, the team will build displays using point-of-sale displays material from their vehicle. Delivery of merchandise to chains and co-operatives is not contemplated.

(5) As soon as operations in a particular town or city have been completed, the team captain would contact the local newspapers and give release on advertisements to be run.

(6) Also, the captain would instruct local Post Office to release mailing to local households.

E. Costs

The estimated costs for the White Swan napkin promotion program outlined above are as follows:

1. *Consumer Sample Mailing:*
   a) Print 700,000 mailers—3 colors..............$ 3,360
   b) Postage at 1½ cents each................... 10,500
   c) Sorting, bundling, and delivery to Post Office at
       $8.25 per thousand....................... 5,775
           Total.............................. $19,635

2. *Couponing:*
   a) Redemption—estimated at 25% of mailing
       175,000 at 5 cents each...................$ 8,750
   b) Dealer handling—at 2 cents each............ 3,500
           Total..............................   12,250

3. *Newspaper Advertising:*
   4 ads—line at total line rate of $6.07
       (see Appendix 1):
       1—1,500 line
       1—1,200 line
       2— 750 line
           3,450 at $6.07........................   20,942

4. *Special Independent Retailer Deal:*
   Approximately 800 deals at $3.00 each.........$ 2,400

5. *Special Chain-Store Deal:*
   Approximately 600 stores at $12.50............ 7,500
           Total.....................................   9,900

6. Point-of-sale materials.........................$ 2,000
7. Dealer mats................................... 200
8. Transportation............................... 1,500
                                          3,700

        Total.............................. $66,427

At the present time as part of our regular White Swan advertising, we have scheduled two advertisements (see Exhibit 2) featuring White Swan towels and napkins. If the napkin promotion for Ontario is carried out, we would recommend that these two advertisements be canceled. This would constitute a budget saving of about $11,750. Also, since the newspaper schedule suggested for the special napkin promotion is sufficient to keep the consumer brand conscious of all White Swan products, we would recommend canceling one White Swan tissue insertion now scheduled for the Ontario newspapers. This would mean a saving of $4,133, or a total saving of $15,883. By using these moneys the estimated net cost of the Ontario napkin campaign would be $66,427 minus the total saving of $15,883, or $50,544.

~~~

CASE 23: PUROLATOR PRODUCTS, INC.[1]

NOTE: *Assume that you are the executive responsible for the 1950 pro-motional program of Purolator Products, Inc., and that you have been given a budget for advertising of $650,000. (1) What conclusions do you draw from Exhibits 1–14 regarding the selling jobs to be done? (2) Out-line the advertising and related selling programs that you would employ, including the timing of activities and the means of attaining co-ordination among the various elements of your promotional program.*

In 1950 Purolator Products, Inc., and its advertising agency, the J. Wal-ter Thompson Company, faced the task of building an advertising and sales promotion plan to meet the aggressive competition which the com-pany had encountered in the postwar period.

Purolator Products, Inc., pioneered the oil filter business when it de-veloped the first automotive oil filter to be produced commercially in 1923.

The importance of reducing engine wear was recognized by techni-cians early in our motor age, but preventive measures were confined to an oil change every 500 miles. This practice obviously was wasteful of oil; yet abrasion still occurred within the 500 miles. Out of this situation grew the concept of trapping harmful foreign particles in their passage through the engine and removing them from the oil stream, permitting the lubri-cant to perform its real function over a longer period of time than was possible under the old practice. This was the principle of the oil filter. From the time of the founding of the business up to the late 1930's, Puro-lator was by far the leader in the field.

The Purolator company owed much of its growth and continued suc-cess[2] to a steady program of research for ways and means of improving its product. During World War II, Purolator's laboratories developed the new "micromic" filtering principle, using plastic-treated cellulose for the fil-ter element. The output of this new type of element went exclusively into the war effort. Wartime military use proved the principle of this new-type paper element, which screens out foreign material as small as $\frac{1}{39}$ millionths of an inch.

---

[1] Written by Neil H. Borden.

[2] Moody's *Manual of Investments* gave the following report of sales and net profits after taxes for Purolator Products, Inc., for several years prior to 1950 :

Year	Net Sales	Net Profit after Taxes	Earnings on Common Stock
1946	$ 8,502,407	$221,476	$0.59
1947	10,983,778	705,308	1.88
1948	10,095,499	471,952	1.26
1949	11,117,001	106,498	0.28

Due to the scope of Purolator's war effort, the company was late in reconverting to civilian trade. During the interim, "Fram" filters made great inroads into the market. At the end of 1949, surveys indicated that Fram held about 40% of the oil filter refill market compared to Purolator's 30%. In the original-equipment market, however, Purolator successfully maintained its top position, supplying filter equipment to leaders in the automobile, farm implement, industrial engine, and aviation industries.

An oil filter consisted of two parts—the housing and the replaceable filter element. The filter housing was built for indefinite usage, while the filter element became dirty and needed to be changed every 4,000 to 5,000 miles under normal driving conditions. The need for a new filter element could be recognized by a good mechanic or service-station man from the color and cleanliness of oil in the crankcase.

To service oil filters, a dealer required about 12 different refill sizes. Purolator made refills to fit competitive housings as well as its own.[3] A refill element cost from $1.50 to $3.00 (depending on the make of car). Changing a filter element required about ten minutes. No special equipment was necessary for making the change. When dealers sold a refill element for a car, the sale also involved sale of a quart of oil, for the filter had to be refilled with oil after an element change.

Most new cars were factory-equipped with oil filters. Purolator was original equipment on all four Chrysler-made cars, as well as Packard, Nash, and Kaiser-Frazer. The General Motors Company used AC filters (produced by a wholly owned subsidiary), and Ford used Fram and Purolator filters. For cars that were not equipped with oil filters, Purolator made complete kits—housing, elements, oil lines, and fittings. Such kits sold at retail prices ranging from about $11 to $14. Installation required about an hour of a mechanic's time.

The company's sales organization was headed by a vice president, under whom there were three divisions, each with a sales manager. Salesmen in the National Accounts Division, which accounted for about 30% of volume, sold to the motor-parts departments of automobile manufacturers and to the TBA[4] departments of oil companies. The motor-parts departments of automobile companies sold to their own selected automobile dealers. The TBA departments of oil companies sold to individual service stations handling their gasoline, oil, and other automotive products. It was the practice of the TBA departments of the oil companies to make up promotions of various TBA products for the service stations which bought from them. The service stations were provided with detailed plans and dealer helps for these promotional drives. TBA departments generally made up their schedules of promotion at least six months in advance of the date of their planned execution at the retail level.

---

[3] Competing manufacturers also sold refills for competitive housings.

[4] Tire, battery, and accessory departments.

The Jobber Division salesmen sold to some 4,500 to 5,000 automotive wholesalers, who in turn sold to garages and service stations. Under the Jobber Division sales manager were some six zone sales managers, who in turn directed sales supervisors, one for each state of their respective zones. The supervisors and the salesmen under them devoted their time primarily to calls on wholesalers.

The sales manager in the Original Equipment Division had a small staff which dealt with automobile, tractor, and other types of automotive manufacturers for original-installation sales on new equipment.

Exhibit 1

PUROLATOR PRODUCTS, INC.

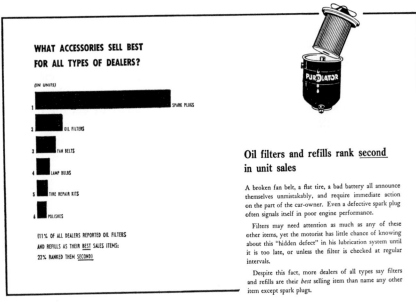

WHAT ACCESSORIES SELL BEST FOR ALL TYPES OF DEALERS?

(IN UNITS)

1 SPARK PLUGS

2 OIL FILTERS

3 FAN BELTS

4 LAMP BULBS

5 TIRE REPAIR KITS

6 POLISHES

(11% OF ALL DEALERS REPORTED OIL FILTERS AND REFILLS AS THEIR BEST SALES ITEMS: 22% RANKED THEM SECOND)

Oil filters and refills rank second in unit sales

A broken fan belt, a flat tire, a bad battery all announce themselves unmistakably, and require immediate action on the part of the car-owner. Even a defective spark plug often signals itself in poor engine performance.

Filters may need attention as much as any of these other items, yet the motorist has little chance of knowing about this "hidden defect" in his lubrication system until it is too late, or unless the filter is checked at regular intervals.

Despite this fact, more dealers of all types say filters and refills are their *best* selling item than name any other item except spark plugs.

In 1950 automotive industry sales (original equipment plus refills) were about $50 million annually at retail. The potential for refills alone, when figured at $1.50 per car for every 5,000 miles, was $115,500,000 per year.

Purolator filters were stocked by about 200,000 of the estimated 400,-000 automotive outlets which serviced the 40 million cars on the road in 1950. At that time new motor vehicles were coming on the road at the rate of approximately six million a year, 75% of which were filter-equipped. Older cars were being junked at the rate of two million or more a year. The new cars were priced higher than ever before in the history of large-scale automobile production. On the basis of these data, it was believed that these more costly new vehicles alone were adding to replacement of filter refills at the rate of some 10,800,000 units a year, excluding the market for complete filters on vehicles not equipped at the factory.

In 1949 the J. Walter Thompson Company was appointed to handle advertising for Purolator Products, Inc. One of the first steps taken was to recommend that a national survey be made at both the consumer and dealer levels. A well-known independent research agency was retained for nation-wide dealer interviews. The consumer survey was conducted through questionnaires sent to the 3,700 car owners of the J. Walter Thompson Consumer Purchase Panel. The results of this survey as shown in an agency report are reproduced in Exhibits 1 to 14, inclusive.

Exhibit 2
PUROLATOR PRODUCTS, INC.

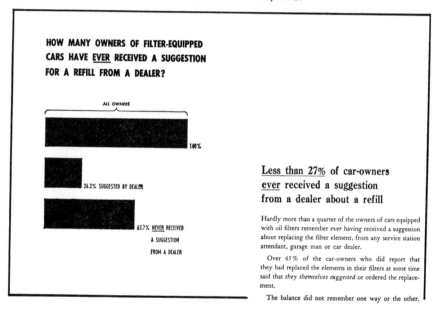

HOW MANY OWNERS OF FILTER-EQUIPPED CARS HAVE _EVER_ RECEIVED A SUGGESTION FOR A REFILL FROM A DEALER?

ALL OWNERS

100%

26.3% SUGGESTED BY DEALER

63.7% _NEVER_ RECEIVED A SUGGESTION FROM A DEALER

Less than 27% of car-owners ever received a suggestion from a dealer about a refill

Hardly more than a quarter of the owners of cars equipped with oil filters remember *ever* having received a suggestion about replacing the filter element, from any service station attendant, garage man or car dealer.

Over 65% of the car-owners who did report that they had replaced the elements in their filters at some time said that *they themselves suggested* or ordered the replacement.

The balance did not remember one way or the other.

The company and its agency decided to advertise to the consumer market through general magazines and to the farm market through the national farm journals. In order that students may have an idea of the costs of elements in a program, Exhibit 15 lists consumer and farm journals to be considered for use, their circulation, and their costs.

The agency media department found that some 16 trade and industrial publications were needed to give adequate coverage of wholesalers, service stations, garages, automobile dealers, implement dealers, fleet owners, automobile manufacturers, airplane manufacturers, tractor manufacturers, and others who were potential users or marketers of Purolator products. It may be assumed that a one-page insertion in all of these 16 publications involved an expenditure of about $7,000.

Costs of point-of-purchase material may be figured at prices assumed reasonable to the student in light of what he recommends. For instance,

Exhibit 3

PUROLATOR PRODUCTS, INC.

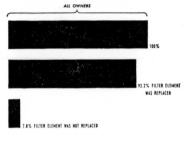

WHEN THE DEALER _DID_ SUGGEST A REFILL HOW MANY CAR OWNERS HAD THE ELEMENT REPLACED?

ALL OWNERS

100%

92.2% FILTER ELEMENT WAS REPLACED

7.8% FILTER ELEMENT WAS NOT REPLACED

IN MORE THAN 9 CASES OUT OF 10, WHEN A DEALER—SERVICE STATION, GARAGE OR CAR DEALER—DID SUGGEST A FILTER REFILL, THE CAR OWNER ORDERED THE ELEMENT REPLACED.

9 out of 10 car-owners bought a new element when it was suggested by a dealer

When a station attendant, garage man or car dealer *did* make a suggestion for replacing the filter element, the suggestion almost always resulted in a sale.

In 92.2% of the cases when such a suggestion was made, the car-owner reported that the element was replaced. Only 7.8% said they failed to order a new refill when it was suggested by a dealer.

Exhibit 4

PUROLATOR PRODUCTS, INC.

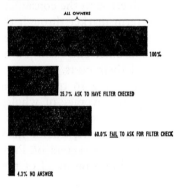

HOW MANY OWNERS OF FILTER-EQUIPPED CARS _ASK_ TO HAVE THE ELEMENT CHECKED?

ALL OWNERS

100%

35.7% ASK TO HAVE FILTER CHECKED

60.0% _FAIL_ TO ASK FOR FILTER CHECK

4.3% NO ANSWER

Only one-third of car-owners claim that they have the filter element checked regularly

Less than 36% of all owners whose cars are filter equipped say they make a practice of asking service men to check the oil filter. Among women, 38.5% say they do, and among men, 34.9% claim they ask to have the filter checked regularly.

Most frequently mentioned as the time when motorists request a check was "when the car is lubricated or the oil changed." Next in frequency was "every 5,000 miles."

Exhibit 5

PUROLATOR PRODUCTS, INC.

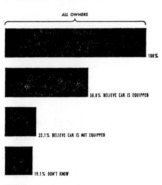

**HOW MANY OWNERS BELIEVE CAR
IS EQUIPPED WITH AN OIL FILTER?**

ALL OWNERS

100%

58.8% BELIEVE CAR IS EQUIPPED

22.1% BELIEVE CAR IS NOT EQUIPPED

19.1% DON'T KNOW

(IN THE CASE OF ONE LEADING MAKE, WHICH IS NOT FACTORY-EQUIPPED, 39.6%
BELIEVED IT WAS EQUIPPED. IN THE CASE OF ANOTHER LEADING MAKE, WHICH
IS FACTORY-EQUIPPED, 40.7% BELIEVED IT HAD NO FILTER, OR DID NOT KNOW.)

Owners reveal amazing ignorance about whether car is equipped with an oil filter

While 58.8% of car-owners "believed" their car was equipped with an oil filter, nearly 20% said they didn't know one way or the other.

More important, among owners of Car A, which is non-factory equipped with a filter, nearly 40% believed it did have a filter, which could only be true in the unlikely event that all of them had had a complete unit installed after buying the car.

And among owners of Car B, which *is* factory-equipped, over 40% believed the car was *not* equipped with a filter, or admitted they didn't know one way or the other. Among owners of Car C in the low-price group, which *is also* factory-equipped, over 25% thought there was no filter on the car, or did not know.

Exhibit 6

PUROLATOR PRODUCTS, INC.

**HOW MANY CAR-OWNERS HAVE <u>EVER</u>
HAD FILTER ELEMENT REPLACED?**

ALL OWNERS

100%

39.6% REMEMBER BUYING REFILL AT SOME TIME

50.3% NEVER HAD ELEMENT REPLACED

10.1% DON'T REMEMBER

**HOW MANY CAR-OWNERS HAVE EVER HAD
COMPLETE FILTER INSTALLATION SUGGESTED?**

OWNERS OF NON-EQUIPPED CARS

100%

74.4% NEVER HAD FILTER SUGGESTED

25.6% FILTER INSTALLATION HAS BEEN SUGGESTED

Less than 40% of owners remember ever buying a new refill

Among *all* car-owners, only 39.6% could ever remember buying an oil filter refill *at any time*, while 50.3% *never* had the element replaced, and 10.1% could not remember. Even among those who believed their car *was equipped with an oil filter*, only 67.4% said they remembered ever having the element replaced; another 25.3% said the element in the filter had *never* been replaced, and the balance of 7.3% did not remember one way or the other.

Experience shows it is a fair assumption that those who did buy a refill would remember it, while among those who claimed to have had the element replaced, some actually had not done so.

Among the owners of cars *not* equipped with filters, only 25.6% could remember ever having a filter installation suggested at any time.

Exhibit 7

PUROLATOR PRODUCTS, INC.

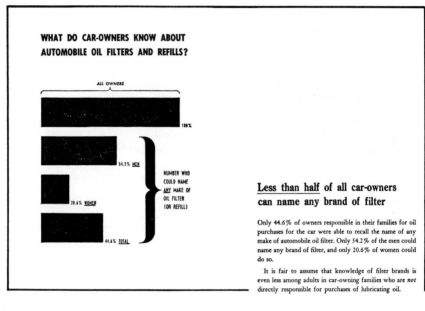

WHAT DO CAR-OWNERS KNOW ABOUT AUTOMOBILE OIL FILTERS AND REFILLS?

Less than half of all car-owners can name any brand of filter

Only 44.6% of owners responsible in their families for oil purchases for the car were able to recall the name of any make of automobile oil filter. Only 54.2% of the men could name any brand of filter, and only 20.6% of women could do so.

It is fair to assume that knowledge of filter brands is even less among adults in car-owning families who are *not* directly responsible for purchases of lubricating oil.

Exhibit 8

PUROLATOR PRODUCTS, INC.

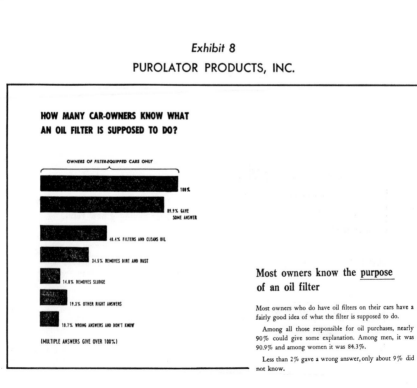

HOW MANY CAR-OWNERS KNOW WHAT AN OIL FILTER IS SUPPOSED TO DO?

Most owners know the purpose of an oil filter

Most owners who do have oil filters on their cars have a fairly good idea of what the filter is supposed to do.

Among all those responsible for oil purchases, nearly 90% could give some explanation. Among men, it was 90.9% and among women it was 84.3%.

Less than 2% gave a wrong answer, only about 9% did not know.

Exhibit 9

PUROLATOR PRODUCTS, INC.

**HOW MANY MILES DO CAR-OWNERS
THINK A FILTER REFILL LASTS?**

ALL OWNERS ·

100%

DON'T KNOW....................24.2% ✗

UNDER 5,000 MILES..............25.3% ⎫
                                     ⎬ ✓
5,000 MILES.....................20.6% ⎭

6,000 TO 9,000 MILES..................9.6% ⎫
                                          ⎬
10,000 MILES....................17.6% ⎭ ✗

OVER 10,000 MILES....................2.9%

✓ LESS THAN 46% HAVE A CORRECT IDEA OF WHEN A FILTER
  ELEMENT NEEDS TO BE REPLACED.

✗ NEARLY 25% HAVE NO IDEA—NEARLY 30% MORE HAVE
  A DANGEROUSLY WRONG IDEA.

More than half of all car-owners have a wrong idea about how long a refill lasts

Among owners of filter-equipped cars, 54.1% either had no idea, or a dangerously wrong idea, about the mileage of normal driving before the element should be replaced. Only 45.9% said 5,000 miles or less. Another 24.2% had no idea, and 29.9% thought the element could be safely used for upwards of 5,000 miles. Most of these owners set the figure at 10,000 miles or more.

Actually, to be on the safe side, the element should be replaced about every 4,000-5,000 miles of normal driving, and even oftener under dusty, or winter stop-and-go driving conditions.

Exhibit 10

PUROLATOR PRODUCTS, INC.

**HOW MANY CAR-OWNERS ACTUALLY
REPLACE FILTER ELEMENTS AS OFTEN
AS NECESSARY FOR SAFETY?**

CAR-OWNERS WHO HAVE HAD
FILTER ELEMENT REPLACED

100%

31.2% UNDER 5,000 MILES

47.6% OVER 5,000 MILES

21.2% DON'T KNOW

27.3% UNDER 6 MONTHS

34.8% OVER 6 MONTHS

37.9% DON'T KNOW

ACTUALLY, 5,000 MILES OR 6 MONTHS UNDER AVERAGE DRIVING
CONDITIONS ARE ABOVE THE SAFETY POINT FOR REPLACING FILTER
ELEMENTS. IT CAN FAIRLY BE ASSURED THAT CAR-OWNERS WHO
"DON'T KNOW" HAVE NOT HAD THEIR FILTERS CHECKED WITHIN
THE SAFE PERIODS OF 5,000 MILES OR 4 MONTHS.

Very few owners replace filter elements as often as needed

Among owners of filter-equipped cars who do recall having a refill installed, only 31.2% did so at under 5,000 miles, and only 27.3% did so before the end of five months.

On a mileage basis, 47.6% said the replacement had been made after more than 5,000 miles, and 21.2% did not know when it had been made. On a time basis, 34.8% said the replacement had been made after more than 6 months, and 37.9% didn't know.

In other words, considerably less than a third of car-owners have refills installed at proper intervals, *even when they have them installed at all.*

Among owners of filter equipped cars who do not recall ever having a refill installed, only 30.8% had driven *less* than 5,000 miles, 43.1% had driven *over* 5,000 miles, and 26.1% *did not know.*

Exhibit 11

PUROLATOR PRODUCTS, INC.

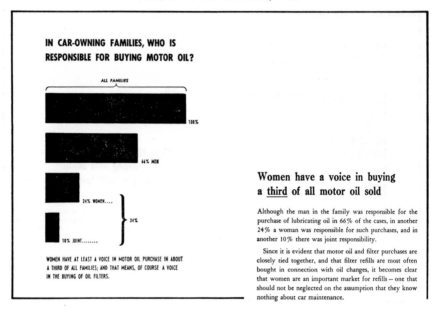

**IN CAR-OWNING FAMILIES, WHO IS
RESPONSIBLE FOR BUYING MOTOR OIL?**

ALL FAMILIES

100%

66% MEN

24% WOMEN....

34%

10% JOINT........

WOMEN HAVE AT LEAST A VOICE IN MOTOR OIL PURCHASE IN ABOUT
A THIRD OF ALL FAMILIES; AND THAT MEANS, OF COURSE A VOICE
IN THE BUYING OF OIL FILTERS.

Women have a voice in buying a <u>third</u> of all motor oil sold

Although the man in the family was responsible for the purchase of lubricating oil in 66% of the cases, in another 24% a woman was responsible for such purchases, and in another 10% there was joint responsibility.

Since it is evident that motor oil and filter purchases are closely tied together, and that filter refills are most often bought in connection with oil changes, it becomes clear that women are an important market for refills — one that should not be neglected on the assumption that they know nothing about car maintenance.

Exhibit 12

PUROLATOR PRODUCTS, INC.

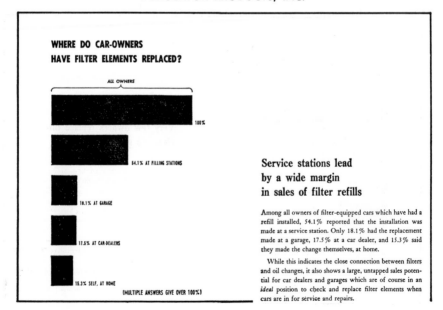

**WHERE DO CAR-OWNERS
HAVE FILTER ELEMENTS REPLACED?**

ALL OWNERS

100%

54.1% AT FILLING STATIONS

18.1% AT GARAGE

17.5% AT CAR-DEALERS

15.3% SELF, AT HOME

(MULTIPLE ANSWERS GIVE OVER 100%)

Service stations lead by a wide margin in sales of filter refills

Among all owners of filter-equipped cars which have had a refill installed, 54.1% reported that the installation was made at a service station. Only 18.1% had the replacement made at a garage, 17.5% at a car dealer, and 15.3% said they made the change themselves, at home.

While this indicates the close connection between filters and oil changes, it also shows a large, untapped sales potential for car dealers and garages which are of course in an *ideal* position to check and replace filter elements when cars are in for service and repairs.

Exhibit 13

PUROLATOR PRODUCTS, INC.

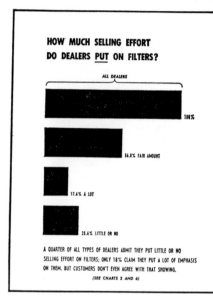

**HOW MUCH SELLING EFFORT
DO DEALERS PUT ON FILTERS?**

ALL DEALERS

100%

56.8% FAIR AMOUNT

17.6% A LOT

25.6% LITTLE OR NO

A QUARTER OF ALL TYPES OF DEALERS ADMIT THEY PUT LITTLE OR NO
SELLING EFFORT ON FILTERS; ONLY 18% CLAIM THEY PUT A LOT OF EMPHASIS
ON THEM. BUT CUSTOMERS DON'T EVEN AGREE WITH THAT SHOWING.
(SEE CHARTS 2 AND 6)

Less than 20% of dealers say they make any real effort to sell filters and elements.

On their own say-so, all types of dealers could be doing far more business in filters and refills than at present. Only 17.6% of dealers of all kinds claim they put "a lot" of sales effort into these items. Most dealers, 56.8%, say they put "a fair amount" of effort into them, and 25.6% admit they make "little or no" effort to sell filters and replacement elements.

Most of those who make little or no effort feel the car-owner will ask for a refill when he needs it. The experience of oil companies shows that drivers do not even keep track of the oil level, and would get into plenty of trouble if service station personnel were not trained to check oil.

Oil companies' experience also shows that, if their dealers were not so trained, many of them would wait for customers to ask for oil.

Exhibit 14

PUROLATOR PRODUCTS, INC.

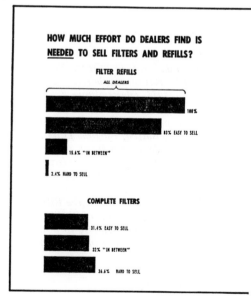

**HOW MUCH EFFORT DO DEALERS FIND IS
NEEDED TO SELL FILTERS AND REFILLS?**

FILTER REFILLS

ALL DEALERS

100%

82% EASY TO SELL

15.6% "IN BETWEEN"

2.4% HARD TO SELL

COMPLETE FILTERS

31.4% EASY TO SELL

32% "IN BETWEEN"

36.6% HARD TO SELL

More than 80% of all dealers find refills "easy to sell"

By an overwhelming majority, all types of dealers find filter refills "easy to sell." Almost 82% of those questioned placed them in that category, and only 2.4% of dealers find replacement elements "hard to sell." The balance of 15.6% said they found refills "in between" — neither hard nor easy. In other words, *four out of five* dealers regard refills as an easy sales item; almost none find them difficult to sell.

Complete filter installations, since they are more expensive and take more time to put in, obviously take more selling effort. Yet even here, 31.4% of dealers of all types find them "easy to sell." Another 32.0% say they are "in between" and only 36.6% report them actually "hard to sell."

Exhibit 15

PUROLATOR PRODUCTS, INC.

Space Costs for Selected Consumer Magazines of National Circulation, 1952

MAGAZINE	TOTAL CIRCULATION	PAGE		HALF-PAGE	
		Black and White	4-Color	Black and White	4-Color
American Magazine........	2,551,008	$ 6,725	$ 9,425	$ 3,875	$ 5,650
Collier's.................	3,150,444	9,125	12,875	4,570	7,100
Country Gentlemen........	2,330,344	7,300	10,000	3,925	5,775
Farm Journal............	2,886,191	7,400	10,100	3,800	5,700
Life....................	5,301,331	19,200	28,900	10,400	*
Look...................	3,260,927	10,415	15,290	5,645	8,835
Popular Mechanics........	1,171,904	1,800	2,750	900	*
Popular Science...........	1,152,786	1,790	2,750	895	*
The Saturday Evening Post..	3,994,969	13,710	20,360	7,335	11,735

* Not available.

Note: Assume production costs of advertisements at about 15% of space costs.

booklets in large lots may run in cost from about 5 cents for a small item to 50 cents or more for more elaborate booklets. Streamers will range from 5 cents each up, and window displays from 50 cents to several dollars. Counter displays may vary in accordance with their size and complexity, ranging from around 20 cents each to several dollars.

Direct-mail pieces may be figured as involving a minimum cost of 6 cents each.

~~~

CASE 24: NATIONAL CRANBERRY ASSOCIATION (A)[1]

NOTE: *At the end of 1958 the Association, marketers of "Ocean Spray" products, had an ending inventory of 345,000 barrels of cranberries, which was equal to about 65% of the Association's 1955 sales volume. Consequently, management was highly concerned with increasing sales. Case (A) concerns a proposal to undertake a special promotion, which was submitted by the Association's advertising agency, Batten, Barton, Durstine & Osborn, Inc. (BBDO). Case (B) concerns the development of a longer-term promotional strategy.* QUESTIONS REGARDING CASE (A): *(1) How do you account for the relatively low per capita consumption of cranberries? (2) Do you think the Association should make changes in its marketing mix, particularly pricing? (3) What are the essential elements of the BBDO proposal? (4) Would you recommend accepting, rejecting, or modifying the proposal? (5) Is the proposed advertising schedule adequate to obtain desired results? (6) Are there any alternatives which should be considered along with the BBDO proposal?*

[1] Written by Gerald A. Simon and Martin V. Marshall.

Cranberry Canners, Inc. (CCI), predecessor to the National Cranberry Association (NCA), was a cranberry grower co-operative processing and marketing organization formed in 1930 by the combination of three of the then largest cranberry sauce canning companies in the United States. This combination was initiated by Mr. Marcus L. Urann, head of the United Cape Cod Cranberry Company, who for many years before 1930 had been one of the leading figures in the cranberry industry.

Mr. Urann had organized the United Cape Cod Cranberry Company in 1907 and had pioneered the development and marketing of cranberries in sauce rather than a fresh state in the early 1920's. He had obtained rights to the trade-mark "Ocean Spray," later to become a well-known cranberry brand name, from a Canadian fish canning company and had spent relatively large promotional funds to build consumer preference for Ocean Spray products.

As president of CCI from 1930 to early 1955, Mr. Urann continued to be an aggressive promoter. His basic marketing objectives in the 1930's and 1940's were to widen distribution of CCI products, to establish Ocean Spray as a strong brand with the trade and consumers, and to emphasize canned rather than fresh cranberries. With respect to the latter objective, Mr. Urann tried to influence the second largest cranberry co-operative, American Cranberry Exchange, to merge with CCI and to can a greater portion of its cranberry crop. The Exchange, however, declined to merge and continued to market as much of its crop as possible as fresh fruit.

CCI continued to expand its canning capacity and sales of canned berries so that by 1945 the amount of berries required to permit economical plant operation exceeded the supply of cranberries. It was reported that under these conditions a considerable rivalry developed between CCI and the Exchange to obtain grower members and cranberry supplies. As a result of this revalry, there was an overexpansion of producing and processing facilities. In the period 1947–49, NCA (the association's name was changed in 1946) had sizable unsold inventories, ranging from 170,-000 to 370,000 barrels each year, and in the period 1953–55, unsold inventories, or pack carry-overs, were 244,000, 289,000, and 345,000 barrels, respectively. By 1956 NCA had a plant capacity of approximately 10,000,000 cases each year, whereas sales were 5,000,000 cases a year (10.5 cases = one barrel).

In view of increasingly grave financial and marketing problems facing the association, NCA's board of directors decided to bring in new top management, electing Mr. James E. Glover, a lawyer, as president.

Since the board members believed that organizational and financial problems should be given priority, Mr. Glover directed his primary attention to the solution of these problems. By the end of 1955 he had initiated policies and operations which the board members felt would gradually ameliorate the major organizational and financial problems of the association. Then, in late 1955 and early 1956, he turned his principal efforts to the solution of the marketing problems of the association.

NCA MARKETING OPERATION

NCA Products

The six principal products marketed by NCA in 1956 were: (1) fresh cranberries packed in one-pound window boxes or in cellophane or plastic bags; (2) whole cranberry sauce packed in small (seven-ounce) and medium (one-pound) cans for retail sale and in large-sized (two-pound, four-ounce) cans for the institutional market; (3) strained jellied cranberry sauce packed in the same can sizes as the whole berry sauce; (4) strained jellied dietetic cranberry sauce packed in seven-ounce and one-pound cans; (5) cranberry cocktail juice packed in pint and gallon bottles for the retail and institutional markets, respectively; and (6) frozen cranberry-orange relish packed in 11- and 20-ounce cans.

At various times NCA had attempted to market various other cranberry products, such as cranberry-orange marmalade, cranberry jam, cranberry jelly, and cranberry juice drinks. None of these products were produced on a commercial scale in 1956.

Brand Recognition

All NCA products were sold under the brand name Ocean Spray. Results of a brand awareness study of canned cranberry sauce, given in Exhibit 1, indicated that Ocean Spray was well known among consumers.

Channels of Distribution

All NCA products except fresh berries and frozen relish were sold through 96 food brokers who serviced 5,000 chain and wholesale accounts. These brokers employed 325 salesmen who called on retailers and 250 salesmen who contacted only chains and wholesalers. Fresh cranberries were sold through 80 fresh produce brokers, and frozen relish was sold through 40 frozen food distributors.

Brokers received commissions of 5% on their first $100,000 of sales and 3% thereafter. Brokerage fees averaged about $800,000 dollars annually.

NCA also employed five missionary salesmen who called on brokers. An additional two men were occupied in training brokers' retail salesmen to more effectively promote cranberries at the retail level.

Pricing

The objective of NCA pricing policy, Mr. Glover said, was "to price high enough to get the most that the market could afford to pay for the

Exhibit 1

NATIONAL CRANBERRY ASSOCIATION (A)

Canned Cranberry Sauce Brand Name, Company or Manufacturer That First
Comes to Mind to Women Respondents

		% OF TOTAL %	NORTHEAST		NORTH CENTRAL		SOUTH			WEST	
			New. Eng. %	Mid. Atl. %	E.N. Cent. %	W.N. Cent. %	So. Atl. %	E.S. Cent. %	W.S. Cent. %	Mountain %	Pacific %
Ocean Spray	1955	66.9	79.8	65.1	66.0	65.4	67.3	64.3	65.8	61.3	68.5
	1954	66.9	82.1	70.0	62.2	55.7	62.6	70.7	64.8	67.1	72.0
	1953	63.1	80.8	64.7	56.8	63.6	56.5	63.2	58.9	63.7	69.8
Brand A	1955	1.9	0.9	1.0	1.8	4.9	1.4	0.4	0.9	1.6	3.4
	1954	2.5	......	1.9	1.4	14.2	1.1	0.4	2.6	1.4	1.8
	1953	1.3	1.0	1.4	1.0	1.5	2.0	......	2.4	1.3	0.4
Brand B	1955	*	0.4	1.8	......	......	1.2	......	......	......	......
	1954	*	0.6	1.0	0.6	0.4	1.6	......	......	......	......
	1953	*	0.5	1.7	0.5	0.8	2.0	......	1.0	......	......
Brand C	1955	*	......	0.3	0.1	0.3	0.5	0.4	0.3	0.8	0.5
	1954	*	......	......	1.0	0.8	0.7	......	0.3	......	0.9
	1953	*	0.5	1.1	0.7	0.4	......	1.9	1.9	1.3	0.9
All others	1955	7.2	1.7	10.5	7.5	4.9	8.8	7.0	5.4	8.9	6.7
	1954	5.1	3.0	5.3	5.9	2.9	7.0	5.1	3.9	8.2	4.7
	1953	5.1	2.0	5.4	8.4	4.2	5.8	5.2	3.3	2.5	1.7
Don't know	1955	22.2	17.2	21.3	24.6	24.5	20.8	27.9	27.6	27.4	20.9
	1954	24.4	14.3	21.8	28.9	26.0	27.0	23.8	28.4	23.3	20.6
	1953	28.7	15.2	25.7	32.5	29.5	33.7	29.7	32.5	31.2	27.2
Base figures	1955	3,472	233	628	710	367	428	244	322	124	416
	1954	3,016	168	588	509	246	445	235	310	73	422
	1953	2,643	197	643	572	261	294	155	209	80	232

* Less than 1%.
Brands ranked according to 1955 totals.
This classification was not included in the 1946 to 1952 studies.
Source: National Cranberry Association records.

product and yet low enough to achieve high consumer sales and to avoid having to cut prices during the peak marketing season."

As a result of a favorable consumer demand situation, NCA had long followed the policy of "premium pricing" of its products. The only major branded competitor of NCA, the "Eatmore" brand of the American Cranberry Exchange, which had an estimated 5% of the total cranberry sauce market, was sold on price basis—$2.50 per case compared with the Ocean Spray price of $4.00 per case. Chain-store private brands which had been sold during peak marketing seasons at as low as $2.00 per case were thought to be a major factor in diverting potential business from Ocean Spray.

Trade and Consumer Acceptance

Among brokers, wholesalers, institutions, chain and independent retailers, which constituted the canned food trade, the standing of NCA was said to be excellent. Its products were considered to be as good or better than any other cranberry brands. The association was reportedly considered to be "businesslike in its methods and fair in matters of credit, terms, allowances, service, and policies."

According to Mr. Glover, the "strongest marketing asset of the association is the tremendous acceptance of the Ocean Spray brand among the consuming public." Trade executives reported that consumers sought Ocean Spray products by name more often than any other cranberry industry brand. Since the association had sold 75% or more of total processed cranberries for many years, its packages dominated retailers' shelves. Since it was in a better position than competitors to provide better stocks, make better deliveries, and meet other requirements of large users such as chains, it had achieved much wider distribution than any competitive cranberry marketer.

A market research survey made in 1945 reported that:

1. Practically all chains and retailers catering to the best trade stock Ocean Spray.
2. The largest and most representative wholesalers, surveyors, and specialized distributors not only handle Ocean Spray products but have a favorable attitude to the company.
3. Ocean Spray products have generally complete United States distribution. Despite wide variations in per capita sales in different areas, few regions might be called very weak or overlooked.
4. Ocean Spray products are best known and have widest distribution in most of the largest cities, indicating best response where company publicity has had widest circulation.
5. Many distributors and retailers reported progress in selling more cranberry products from year to year and on a more even spread of what was formerly highly seasonal business over all the months of the year.
6. No evidence was found of unsound merchandising or mere "price-cutting" success. On the contrary, the survey contacts generally indicated that Ocean Spray distribution is based on the best of canned food selling methods.

Advertising

According to Mr. Glover, the chief purpose of NCA advertising had been to publicize the Ocean Spray brand name and aid in moving the association's output. Since the demand for cranberry products exceeded the supply over the period 1943 to 1947, little advertising was done during that period.

Advertising was concentrated in the fall of each year; a relatively small percentage of the total budget was spent in the balance of the year to encourage year-round sales.

Annual advertising and promotional expenditures of NCA for the period 1951–55 are given in Exhibit 2.

A major portion of the advertising budget was placed in the period 1951–55 in national home and women's magazine and week-end paper supplements. Advertisements were fairly attractive, usually either one-half page or full page in size and, when surveyed by the Starch Readership Service, had consistently ranked high on value per dollar basis as compared with other advertisements in the same publications.

NCA executives reported that they "tested the interest in their advertisements from time to time by running coupon advertisements which

Exhibit 2

NATIONAL CRANBERRY ASSOCIATION (A)

Summary of Advertising and Promotional Expenditures, 1951–55

BUDGET CLASSIFICATION	FISCAL YEAR BEGINNING SEPTEMBER 1				
	1951	1952	1953	1954	1955
Newspapers..........	$ 59,129	$ 67,860	$ 77,887	$ 330,440	$157,880
Newspaper supplements	75,369	69,903	162,801	149,425	132,576
Magazines...........	112,926	188,763	100,507	225,094	179,189
Radio..............	7,648	92,442	277	129,263	40,868
Television..........	....	....	136,317	54,876	1,720
Co-operative advertising	200,033	255,838	269,066	229,278	239,679
Display material.......	31,175	25,361	26,038	30,717	105,863
Cookbooks..........	3,428	10,272	28,085	43,636	18,636
Publicity...........	4,076	8,361	11,576	18,419	14,821
Production..........	20,180	27,945	27,547	48,311	40,349
Total..........	$513,964	$746,745	$840,101	$1,259,459	$931,581

Source: National Cranberry Association records.

offered premiums such as plastic cranberry jelly figure cutters and silver cranberry spoons at a nominal charge." A heavy response to these offers running into thousands of requests indicated, executives believed, high reader interest in cranberry product advertising.

Approximately $200,000 a year was also spent on dealer co-operative advertising, primarily in local newspapers, with a view to building up sales in particular trading areas.

Mr. Glover stated that the motive and theme behind all NCA advertising was to increase total consumer demand for cranberries and to promote the Ocean Spray brand name. The principal copy themes had been:

1. Ocean Spray is a ready-to-serve cranberry sauce.
2. It can be used with turkey, chicken, and in other ways.
3. It is convenient.
4. It has health value.
5. It is economical.
6. It is a quality product.
7. New use recipes.

Reaction to the companies advertising in the trade and among its brokers was said to be good. The opinion that more of such advertising would
mean just that much more business was often stated. Trade personnel
were of almost unanimous opinion that advertising was an effective
method of expanding demand.

Sales Promotion

NCA's retail sales promotion activities had been limited mainly to special sales campaigns. Tests had proven to the NCA sales department that
generally any counter cards or dealer display pieces which were mailed
were not always used. Mr. Glover reported that "either such material
does not get by the broker because he just does not want to be bothered
or if he passes them to the wholesaler, they stop at that point. Even if they
do get by the wholesaler, he generally cannot take the time to push any
one item; the average dealer just does not take much interest in them. He
handles so many items in his store that he does not have the time to give
any one item attention unless it represents both an important part of his
aggregate volume and a product for which a representative is personally
there to suggest its importance and to help him with its display and sale."

Publicity

NCA had been quite successful in securing publicity in newspapers
and other media throughout the United States, including the most prominent publications. Such publicity appeared primarily in the home economics sections on the women's pages. The advertising manager previously in charge of this work for NCA wrote publicity articles and recipes,
suggesting the use of cranberry products. These were used by the home
economic editors of the various newspapers in preparing their columns.

Marketing Testing and New Products

From time to time NCA attempted to evaluate the potential of products by undertaking various marketing experiments.

"Cran," a concentrate with possibilities as a flavoring for both on- and
off-premise consumption of alcoholic beverages, was being promoted to
bartenders in New York City through the White Rock carbonated beverage distributor. In Providence a liquor distributor was calling on package stores on Cran's behalf. Other cranberry uses and marketing plans for
such items as sherbet base and edible pharmaceutical dyes were in various stages of early development.

A new method of stimulating off-season sales of sauce was test marketed by NCA in June 1955. A "Buy 2—Save 5¢" deal was personally
promoted to brokers in five markets by NCA executives. A 600-line advertisement which appeared in one newspaper in each of the five markets
was the only direct effort made to stimulate consumer demand for the
deal. However, broker salesmen attempted to get favorable display and
position for the deal by retailers.

NCA's total sales to the five brokers in June 1955 was seven times higher than the May–June monthly average of sales in 1954. In 77 stores which were checked in the five test markets, total Ocean Spray sales averaged four times higher than the estimated "normal" sales for the period. It was believed that the latter ratio was a conservative figure. Projecting the test results nationally a NCA executive estimated during the latter half of 1955 that with such a deal NCA could move 350,000 cases nationally during the "off-season." If accompanied by an intensive consumer advertising effort, it was estimated that 600,000 cases could be sold.

Market Research

According to Mr. Glover, marketing research efforts in the NCA had been practically nonexistent, the only data available being a set of sales figures by market areas which was compiled by the sales department and several pilot studies undertaken by the association's advertising agency.

Market Organization

The position of director of marketing had been created in late 1955 in order to obtain effective co-ordination of all phases of NCA marketing activity. Reporting to Mr. Lawrence E. Proesch, the director, were five departments: a canned sales department, consisting of a manager, five field men who contacted brokers, and three clerical assistants; a fresh fruit sales division, consisting of a manager, one field man, and a clerical assistant; a newly organized institutional sales department, consisting of two field men working principally in the New York area; the promotion and merchandising department, consisting of a manager who was responsible for the preparation, distribution, and supervision of use of retailer display and point-of-purchase materials; and a home economics department, consisting of a manager who was engaged in testing recipes, publishing recipe booklets, and preparing publicity material for the use of food editors and home economists.

Since the advertising director had resigned at the end of 1955, Mr. Glover had assumed her duties and was in the process of reorganizing the department. He was not convinced that an advertising director was required if NCA had a strong advertising agency and planned to defer a decision as to whether a new advertising director should be hired until he became familiar with the requirements of the job. Meanwhile, most of the routine work of the department was being done by the former director's secretary under Mr. Glover's supervision.

Compensation of Growers

Distribution of the net proceeds from operations was on the basis of a nation-wide "pool" of such proceeds. Thus, at the close of each season the net proceeds available for distribution were determined by deducting from total sales all manufacturing, marketing, administrative, and other expenses, advances on berries delivered, and any retained earnings. Total net proceeds were then divided by the number of barrels of cranberries received by the NCA and the resulting average or pool price was used to pay each grower on the basis of cranberries turned in by him. NCA operating statements, as presented in Exhibit 3, indicate the total proceeds available for distribution to growers in 1954 and 1955.

Exhibit 3

NATIONAL CRANBERRY ASSOCIATION (A)

Selected Operating Statement Items, 1954 and 1955
(Years Ending May 31)

	1955	1954
1. *Gross Sales:*		
Sauce	$18,678,384	$18,413,745
Fresh cranberries	3,073,705	87,008
Cocktail	675,690	588,548
Other	127,817	68,658
Total Gross Sales	$22,555,596	$19,157,959
2. *Expenses:*		
Administrative	$ 374,285	$ 241,296
Selling and delivery	1,449,195	922,574
Advertising	1,549,077	1,422,777
Grower relations*	86,248	61,704
Total Expenses	$ 3,458,805	$ 2,647,951
3. Net Proceeds from Year	$ 6,624,196	$ 8,364,275
4. *Application of Proceeds:*		
Payments on pools	$ 7,997,766	$ 7,328,368
Preferred and common stock dividends	192,551	162,437
Less: Undistributed proceeds at beginning of year	2,122,264	1,248,794
Undistributed proceeds at end of year	556,143	2,122,264
Total	$ 6,624,196	$ 8,364,275

* Includes cost of publishing *Cranberry News* house organ.
Note: Data on wholly owned Cranberry Credit Corporation not included.

Source: National Cranberry Association records.

NCA's Marketing Problems

Toward the latter part of 1955, Mr. Glover summarized his views on the association's marketing problems for the 1955 NCA annual report as follows:

We know that cranberries have a more competitive market than . . . they had . . . and selling campaigns must be adjusted for full effectiveness under today's conditions.

We know that crops will continue to be larger and that they are not going to stop at 1,000,000 barrels [see Exhibit 4]. Already we have had evidence of that. We know, too, that the gradual increase in demand for "Ocean Spray," no matter how steady, will be a long time in bringing cranberry sales up to 1,000,000 barrels. We do not expect or want our industry to have to rely on intermittent short crops or high wartime demands to help us balance supply and demand. We need new outlets that will require volume.

We are confident that we will hold on to the market we now have, and will increase it as much as we can, but we are not expecting any miraculous surges in the sales record of our standard products. We do look for increases that will

Exhibit 4

NATIONAL CRANBERRY ASSOCIATION (A)

NCA Barrels Handled, Total U.S. Crop, NCA Sales, NCA Carry-over Inventories, and NCA Earnings, September 1, 1946, to August 31, 1956

| Crop Year* | Barrels | | | | NCA Earnings per Barrel Produced† | Total U.S. Crop (Barrels) |
	Beginning Inventory +	NCA Barrels Handled −	Ending Inventory =	NCA Sales		
1946	N.A.	366,054	55,149	N.A.	$32.03	856,100
1947	55,149	404,786	170,838	289,097	13.06	792,200
1948	170,838	557,968	370,640	358,166	8.00	967,700
1949	370,640	286,398	262,371	394,667	7.11	840,800
1950	262,371	401,468	84,508	579,331	8.89	982,700
1951	84,508	491,700	73,112	503,096	13.04	910,300
1952	73,112	384,077	44,050	413,139	16.46	803,500
1953	44,050	689,679	244,060	489,669	14.16	1,203,300
1954	244,060	644,454	289,032	599,482	10.98	1,018,500
1955‡	289,032	585,193	345,000§	529,225§	....	1,035,400

* Crop year begins September 1 of year indicated.
† Barrels produced somewhat less than barrels handled due to natural effects of processing and handling.
‡ NCA estimate made in early 1956.
§ Assuming historic seasonal sales pattern.

Source: National Cranberry Association records.

grow with the population, with new recipes and with the expansion of our market. . . . But a large portion of NCA effort must be devoted towards discovering new outlets, not only in new products, but in new ways for other producers to use cranberries.

Cranberries have unique characteristics. . . . Their natural brilliance and flavor is in itself a commodity and can be used to enhance products of other manufacturers. This outlet, already being explored, could increase the demand for cranberries without the formidable expense of advertising and promotions necessary when introducing a new product or entering a virgin market.

This year we plan to make a strong bid for our share of trade with institutions and are already organizing an institutional sales department. Sales to hotels, restaurants, hospitals, schools, etc., could represent as much as 25% of our business. At present it is only 5%. Here is an encouraging potential that we hope to capture for cranberries.

Ocean Spray's fresh cranberry campaign for the new season should step up sales considerably over last year and we look forward to a more widespread demand for fresh cranberries every year.

. . . The problem of a surplus has long been with us, and it is time that we combined all our efforts to overcome it. Cranberries in freezers do not *make* money, they *take* money, and NCA's job of first importance is to keep our inventory at a workable minimum. . . .

In view of the large pack carry-over which NCA had had in the years since 1952, Mr. Glover believed that there was a basic inadequacy in the promotional programs employed by the association. In order to obtain new thinking regarding the promotional area, in late 1955 Mr. Glover discontinued using the services of a small, local advertising agency and hired a large New York agency, Batten, Barton, Durstine & Osborn, Inc. (BBDO), to service NCA's account in 1956.

In commenting upon NCA's marketing problems at this time, Mr. Glover said:

Our biggest problem is how to increase total consumer demand. Integral to this central problem are a lot of unknowns which are problems to us in our planning. For example, how expansible is the demand for cranberry products? In El Paso, Texas, we know that there is a heavy population who will buy cranberry sauce at 10 cents a can but won't touch it at 23 cents. How much can demand be increased? How do we find out what the market saturation point would be? What kind of promotional strategy do we use to saturate a market?

I can raise many important questions that we can't answer. Who buys cranberry sauce? Who likes it? What are the age groups? Who eats it, men or women? Why do they eat it? What do they like about it?

We just don't know the answers to these questions.

Our belief is that cranberry sauce appeals to the upper middle class. The heavy concentration of preference for cranberry sauce seems to be among people of Scandinavian and Anglo-Saxon extraction. It is least desired among Spanish or Italian people. We think this may be due to the fact that Scandinavians are familiar with the lingenberry which is very similar to the cranberry and which has been grown in their home country for many years.

Our highest per capita consumption lies in New England and New York. The nativity of the berry appeals to New Englanders, and New Yorkers have taken to it for similar reason. It appeals to the people in the Far West. I think they are more inclined to try something new than the more conservative groups in the central and southern parts of the country. Then there is no doubt that the quality of the brokers' sales organization and promotional efforts in a particular area have a great deal to do with how the product sells.

One of our biggest problems now is to increase the sales volume in all areas against a highly unfavorable price differential. We have had in the past few years relatively little cranberry sauce competition, maybe 300,000 to 400,000 cases a year. Last year competition altogether sold one and one half million cases. The reason for this volume was the deals that competitors offered the trade. They sold their sauce for $1.35 to $1.50 a dozen against our $2.00 a dozen. Safeway broke from buying our brand exclusively and bought other sauce as did American stores, Food Fair, Ralph's on the West Coast, and Kroger. The bulk of the chains got into these cheaper competitors' brands in various areas, and we are feeling the results. There are about six competitors involved. Their price structure is pretty much the same. They do no advertising, little promotional work, and give a very limited return to the grower—about $5.00 a barrel against our $10.00. This year, on 1955 berries, some of these companies haven't returned a cent yet to their brokers, whereas we have paid $5.50 already. This hasn't necessarily hampered us so much in our sales effort as it has hampered the entire cranberry sauce business. This price demoralization has the trade disturbed, and they haven't been purchasing cranberry sauce as they do in a healthy year.

There has been a strong tendency on the part of several chains to introduce their own private labels recently. This is only natural. These stores want to push their own brands. However, many of the chains and independents that are pushing their own brands and cheaper competitive sources are unhappy because it is staying on their shelves. There is no consumer demand for it, and so it doesn't move.

We have many other problems facing us. We don't know whether we are receiving the maximum worth from our point-of-sales and merchandising materials. We have not placed enough emphasis on big displays. One large display can move hundreds of cases of merchandise—there is no doubt about this.

Another unknown in our marketing program is that we have no factual analysis of the ability of our brokers. To my way of thinking there is a basic question here as to whether or not we should change from selling through brokers to going direct at least in some areas.

Our whole marketing organization is in a state of reorganization. I am convinced that we have adequate sales managers in the canned and fresh and institutional field, but we need to expand our efforts in the field. We should be making far more impact at the retail level.

Mr. Glover's most pressing problem in early 1956 was NCA's unsold inventory, which had amounted to 359,000 barrels as of January 1, 1956. Thus approximately 60 per cent of NCA's growers' 1955 cranberry crop was unsold; 47,000 barrels were in finished goods, and 312,000 barrels were in freezers and work in process. Meanwhile, NCA was paying interest on a short-term bank loan which had helped finance NCA's $5.50 per barrel advance to growers for the 1955 crop, and freezer storage charges were averaging 22 cents per barrel per month.

As the result of a sales incentive plan, retailers had stocked Ocean Spray heavily in December 1955. Consequently, sales to brokers in January–February 1956 totaled 12,000 barrels, which was 61% of sales made during the same two months of 1955. In 1954 there had been no sales incentive plan.

Mr. Glover wanted BBDO to help develop an effective promotional program by which the association's inventory could be reduced to 100,-000 barrels by September 1, 1956. After the agency had solved that problem, he wanted a sound long-range promotional program developed which would increase consumer use of cranberry products.

Proposed Promotional Plan to Reduce Pack Carry-over

By March 1956, BBDO and NCA personnel had developed a promotional plan designed to "move the carry-over." On March 2, 1956, BBDO representatives came to South Hanson, Massachusetts, to present the plan to the executive committee of the board of directors of the NCA for discussion and approval.

The presentation was made by the vice president in charge of the marketing department of BBDO, through the use of "flip-over" charts and a written script. The charts and script are as follows:

Chart 1

BBDO's PROPOSAL

TO THE

NATIONAL CRANBERRY ASSOCIATION

FOR

MOVING 1955 SURPLUS

During our previous meeting in 1956, we discussed . . .

Chart 2

PAST AND PRESENT

Conditions Related to Marketing

of

*FRESH BERRIES

*COCKTAIL JUICE

*RELISH

*CRANBERRY SAUCE

Each of these products has its own peculiar marketing problems so far as distribution to the trade and sales to the consumer are concerned. Because of this situation, each of these products will be treated separately by us relative to recommendations for advertising and sales promotion plans.

However, before specific plans are recommended for specific products, both NCA and BBDO have some basic decisions to make that involve:

Chart 3

THE

1955 SURPLUS

OF

CRANBERRIES

Ideally, this surplus should be sold through the trade to the consumer by September 1, 1956, at which time the "new crop season" starts. We were told that the carry-over into September 1955 exceeded 300,000 barrels. We were told that "1955 surplus" to be moved by September 1, 1956 was . . .

Chart 4

APPROXIMATELY

345,000 BARRELS

Translated into terms that will be more meaningful to some of us at BBDO, this means that NCA's present surplus is approximately equivalent to . . .

Chart 4—Continued

3½ MILLION CASES

OF

CRANBERRY SAUCE!

Therefore, the immediate objective is not to be taken lightly . . . that of "How to sell this surplus by September 1, 1956?" The size of the job that must be done is further emphasized when we consider that approximately 5,000,000 cases of cranberry sauce were sold by NCA during the entire year of 1955. In other words, we've got to try and sell two thirds of the 1955 sauce sales during the so-called off-season months in 1956. . . . April, May, June, July, and August.

Chart 5

> A TOUGH ASSIGNMENT?
>
> YES!!!
>
> AN INSURMOUNTABLE JOB?
>
> NOT NECESSARILY!!!

At least we should budget our proposed plan to meet this objective. We may not reach our total goal . . . but a carry-over of anything less than 300,-000 barrels into September 1956 will be better than what happened in September 1955.

Obviously . . . to accomplish this objective, or to even come close to it, we must resort to . . .

Chart 6

> BOLD SALES ACTION!
>
> DRASTIC SALES PROMOTION TECHNIQUES!
>
> SOMETHING DIFFERENT!
>
> SOMETHING TO BE TALKED ABOUT!
>
> A SALES PLAN WITH CALCULATED RISKS

For these reasons, we cannot afford the luxury of worrying about the 1956 crop . . . whether it will be greater than, or less than, previous years. We have adopted the attitude of "worrying about the '56 crop when it is harvested." Our proposed marketing plans that follow are built around the foregoing suppositions.

But first . . . let's go back and review some of the contributing factors relative to this surplus. Some are factors that NCA can control . . . others, NCA cannot control. All, however are . . .

Chart 7

> FACTORS . . . . .
>
> THAT . . . . .
>
> AFFECT . .
>
> SALES . .

We are sure that all of us at BBDO and NCA believe in the philosophy that "*it is no sin to make a profit.*" However, we're equally sure that few, if any, of us have been able to find the formula in business that allows us the privilege to *"have our cake and eat it, too."* Perhaps these illustrations are "too corny" . . . but we believe there is a definite application that can be made to the problem at hand . . . surplus cranberries.

We recognize the desire . . . and the need . . . for NCA grower-members to realize as high a "per barrel return" to them as is possible to attain for each year's crop.

None of us like . . . or want . . . to work for little or no return for our efforts.

Chart 8

```
?? CONFLICT ??

* * *

MAXIMUM RETURN TO

NCA GROWER-MEMBERS

VERSUS

INCREASED CARRY-OVER SURPLUS
```

However, it seems apparent to us that there is a definite conflict at hand between *maximum return to grower-members of NCA and the increased surplus that has been carried into 1956.*

The biggest market, at present, for absorbing most of this surplus lies in the CANNED CRANBERRY SAUCE area . . . *not* in fresh berries, cocktail juice, or relish. Therefore, our discussion from now on will refer specifically to the relationship between the canned sauce product and the surplus.

There is no short cut to successful sales movement of merchandise in any field. We have yet to find a magic formula that can be applied directly to a specific sales problem. Successful sales plans can only come from a practical, realistic appraisal of current problems. Hence, with a practical look at our present surplus, we think it only natural to assume that we *cannot* "get the job done" by continuing to pursue some of NCA's past sales policies and marketing practices.

Chart 9

```
SOMETHING

DIFFERENT

MUST BE

TRIED!!
```

We must honestly believe that a "change" is in order and that what has been done in the past can be improved upon for the future . . . in order to move a sizable amount of the present surplus. We refer to "changes" as they apply to our . . .

Chart 10

APPRAISAL OF . . . .

RECOGNITION OF . . .

AND APPROACH TO . . .

1. NCA's PRICING POLICY

2. COMPETITIVE PRICING CONDITIONS

3. PRESENT NCA BROKERS

4. SALES PROMOTION

5. ADVERTISING PHILOSOPHY

6. OVER-ALL NCA SALES POLICY

Now, let's discuss each of these six subjects in some detail.

Chart 11

NCA's PRICING POLICY

Obviously your pricing policy is directly related to your grower-member's "return per barrel." We believe the following data is a fair approximation of your present pricing schedule of canned sauce . . . at least for our present discussion purposes.

Chart 11—Continued

NCA	Per Case 24/300	Per Barrel
Selling price	$4.00	$40.00
Manufacturing and selling costs	2.65	26.50
	$1.35	$13.50
Present advertising and promotion costs	0.20	2.00
Gross Income	$1.15	$11.50

We must assume that the above "gross income" figure is considered to be a "satisfactory" return to NCA, under ordinary circumstances. However, it appears that we are *not* operating under normal or ordinary circumstances with our present problem. Adherence to this pricing policy format, in general, has left NCA with a larger surplus than ordinarily is carried over from one season to the next . . . and it is reasonable to assume that . . .

Chart 12

NCA

Is Losing Its Share

OF THE

Total Canned Sauce

Market

At least, that is what available data and known marketing conditions lead us to believe.

Therefore, we must adopt a doubtful attitude towards this rather fixed pricing policy so far as using it to move the surplus carry-over. In other words . . . now is the time for NCA and BBDO to admit that this. . . .

Chart 13

Past Pricing Policy

Has Not Been Adequate

To Maintain Proper Balance

BETWEEN

Production and Sales

Accordingly, let's look at other major factors affecting sales to see if we can isolate some "reasons why" this apparent imbalance occurs. Let's look at . . .

Chart 14

Competitive

Pricing

Conditions

While NCA was selling *Ocean Spray* canned sauce at a basic price of $4.00 per case ($2.00 per dozen) during the past two years, competitive products were being offered at these approximate prices:

	1954	1955
Ocean Spray	$2.00 doz.	$2.00 doz.
Competitive	1.60 doz.	1.50 doz.
Private label	1.50 doz.	1.35 doz.

As a major factor in the canned sauce market, NCA has obviously had to be the leader, if there was to be one, in any price stabilization for the industry. However, the results of the above price differential should be apparent to all of us. It certainly has had to be a major contributing factor in your loss of "share of market." With retailers taking normal markups on these price schedules . . . the consumer has been able to buy a competitive product for 25 per cent less than she can buy *Ocean Spray*. It can be even more of a difference . . . if the retailer decided, as he often does, to make a "football item" out of the cheaper, competitive brand names of canned sauce.

Under normal operating conditions today, the large food chains are looking for reasons to discontinue a so-called "second line." However, strange as it may seem, we find that this price differential has caused these same food chains to tell NCA that they "must add a second line of canned cranberry sauce" . . . to the *Ocean Spray* brand that is already stocked. Your competition has furnished these food chains with all the incentive they need . . . to stock a competitive brand . . . a price differential that is sufficient to be reflected in competitive retail shelf pricing at the local level.

We sum up this part of our discussion by asking ourselves a question, in view of the surplus that is staring at all of us:

Chart 15

How long can NCA

afford to

"Eat High on the Hog"

and

"Carry the Torch for the Industry"

relative to

maintaining a stablizing

effect on pricing policy?

Again, we repeat a previous statement. We think there is a serious conflict between present grower-member's "return per barrel" and the current realities of the market place where our product is sold to the ultimate user . . . the consumer.

Now, let's take a look at another major factor affecting NCA's sales . . .

Chart 16

Present

NCA Brokers

Due to the more complex distribution problems and the more intense competition facing you today . . . NCA must demand and receive more assistance from its brokers. In order to receive more assistance from your present brokers, however, the "demanding" must appear in the form of "leadership from NCA."

We must take the initiative . . . we must show them how to accomplish our objectives in their territories . . . we must provide the over-all plan . . . we must provide the brokers and their sales organizations the vehicle by which our plan is translated into "sales action" . . . at the wholesale and retail level.

With this in mind, we must next ask ourselves:

Chart 16a

> "How Much Do We Know
>
> ABOUT
>
> Present NCA Brokers?"

Accordingly, let's apply a yardstick against each of NCA's present brokers.

1. Is the top executive of the individual broker organizations promotion minded?
2. Does he have a sales staff that can be readily adapted to "new situations"?
3. Is this broker presently overburdened with other products?
4. Is he complacent . . . or is he hungry?
5. Does he provide *full* and *complete* territory coverage . . . or does his conversational coverage exceed his real sales coverage?
6. Are his salesmen on good terms with . . . and do they have ready access to *all* existing potential *Ocean Spray* outlets in his territory?
7. Has this broker's organization shown aggressive action . . . with good sales results on previous *Ocean Spray* promotions?
8. Does the broker have a good historical sales record for canned cranberry sauce?
9. Would you trust this broker to sit in on NCA meetings involving sales and advertising policies?

Satisfactory answers to these questions, and perhaps others, will guide us in selecting specific markets for putting our recommendations to work for us in the field . . . in an attempt to move some of the surplus carry-over. Neither NCA nor BBDO have the time, money, or effort to waste on potentially ineffective brokers.

Our analysis of your 1954 and 1955 "sales incentive plans" as related to actual sales results indicates that they have been successful . . . but *only* successful in the sense of "short-term" gains. Historically, this is no different from similar experiences in other fields of packaged goods. In the long run, your last two sales incentive plans have only increased your surplus carry-over problems . . . rather than to have solved them. Harsh words . . . YES! But we think we can reasonably explain such a statement.

Chart 17

> 1954
>
> Sales Incentive Plan

In 1954, you had an incentive plan built around a sliding scale reduction in price for the July–December period . . . aimed at making it more profitable for the retailer to buy in July, and progressively less profitable month by month until he was back to the "base price" of $4.00 per case of 24/300's at the end of the year. For example:

July purchases.........................	Less 18¢ case
August purchases.......................	Less 15¢ case
September purchases....................	Less 12¢ case
October purchases......................	Less 9¢ case
November purchases.....................	Less 6¢ case
December purchases.....................	Less 3¢ case

Chart 18

1955

SALES INCENTIVE PLAN

In 1955 you had an incentive plan built around a sliding scale price reduction for the July–December period . . . aimed at making it more profitable for the retailer if he purchased more merchandise in this 1955 period than he did during the same period in 1954. For example:

10% increase 1955 over 1954...............	Less 6%
5% increase 1955 over 1954...............	Less 5%
1955 purchases equal to 1954...............	Less 4%

Analyses of these incentive plans, on a customer-by-customer and broker-by-broker basis, indicates that the average account merely "bought earlier" than usual in 1954 . . . in order to take advantage of the price reduction . . . and the average account "loaded up" in December of 1955 . . . in order to qualify for the added discount earned by having a larger percentage increase in purchases, 1955 over 1954.

Chart 19

ANALYSIS OF

1954 AND 1955 SALES

OF 94 BROKERS

Our analysis of your broker's sales reveals many interesting results . . . some positive for NCA . . . others completely negative for NCA. For example, we can classify your present brokers into specific groups . . . based on past sales performance related to the 1954 and 1955 incentive plans. For identification purposes, let's call them:

1. "POSITIVE" result group (43)
2. "NEGATIVE" result group (11)

3. "Confusing" result group (31)

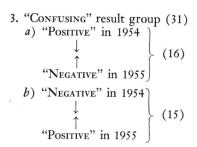

Note: Analysis of nine brokers omitted here due to lack of data at this time.

In other words, we've analyzed brokers' sales on the basis of "what actually happened" versus "NCA's objectives for the 1954 and 1955 incentive plans." To do this, we used sales figures of . . .

CANNED SAUCE 300's ONLY

Because the 1954 incentive plan was devised to "sell" more sauce in July and August, due to favorable discount schedule, it is fair to assume that the January–August share of total 1954 sauce business should have been "greater than" same period share of previous year, 1953. Likewise, because the 1955 incentive plan was devised to "sell" more sauce in November and December, due to favorable discount schedule, it is fair to assume that the January–August share of total 1955 sauce business should have been "less than" same period share of previous year, 1954.

Theoretically, let's assume that . . .

Chart 20

BROKER X

sold 30 per cent of his total 1953 sauce during January–August period. It should then be logical to assume that his January–August period volume share of total 1954 volume should exceed the 30 per cent figure of 1953 . . . due to design of the 1954 incentive plan. Likewise, due to design of 1955 incentive plan, the 1955 percentage share of January–August period should be less that 1954 . . . but not necessarily have any correlation with the 1953 30 per cent figure. Actually, we have every reason to believe that if Broker X had conformed to your 1954 and 1955 incentive plans . . . in a programmed manner, we might expect his January–August share of total sauce volume for these three years to resemble something like this:

Chart 20—Continued

(THEORETICAL PERCENTAGE FIGURES)

1953	1954	1955
(1) 30%	40%	32%

It certainly should *not* resemble this:

(THEORETICAL PERCENTAGE FIGURES)

1953	1954	1955
(2) 30%	22%	41%

Accordingly, based on these logical assumptions, we have grouped your brokers into the three previously mentioned groups . . . *positive, negative,* and *confusing.* Now let's take a look at these groups and see what we may expect from them, as groups or individual brokers, when we think of any plan . . . to move our present surplus.

Chart 21

	1953	1954	1955
CANNED SAUCE 300's ONLY "KEY ACCOUNTS" (100 Cases or More per Year)			
"Positive" Brokers (43):			
Total case volume...................	2,420,180	2,558,930	2,747,537
% of total year NCA sales volume.......	68%	69%	69%
% increase over previous year..........	. . .	5%	7% (14%)
Jan.–Aug. share of total................	31%	40%	33%
"Negative" Brokers (11):			
Total case volume...................	152,234	157,402	177,560
% of total year volume................	4%	4%	4%
% increase over previous year..........	. . .	3%	13% (17%)
Jan.–Aug. share of total................	43%	36%	46%
"Confusing" Brokers (A-16):			
Total case volume...................	673,804	650,878	693,810
% of total year volume................	19%	18%	18%
% increase over previous year..........	. . .	−3%	7% (37%)
Jan.–Aug. share of total................	32%	37%	40%
"Confusing" Brokers (B-15):			
Total case volume...................	327,521	330,193	368,556
% of total year volume................	9%	9%	9%
% increase over previous year..........	. . .	1%	12% (13%)
Jan.–Aug. share of total................	39%	33%	29%
All Brokers (85):			
Total case volume...................	3,573,739	3,697,403	3,987,463
% increase over previous year..........	. . .	3%	8% (12%)
Jan.–Aug. share of total................	32%	39%	34%

To sum up our view of this analysis, we believe it points to what many of us have probably known for a long time . . . that brokers, in general, are not "creative" sales organizations. They need prodding, pushing . . . and a real leadership program thrust upon them for maximum performance. It's our firm belief that the 1954 and 1955 incentive plans have merely played into their normal routine method of selling . . . rather than stimulating them to sell more canned cranberry sauce . . . so that more is moved through to the consumer. We'll have additional comments about how this might be correct later on in this discussion.

Another interesting result of our intensive digging into your sales figures, on a broker-by-broker and customer-by-customer approach, shows that far too

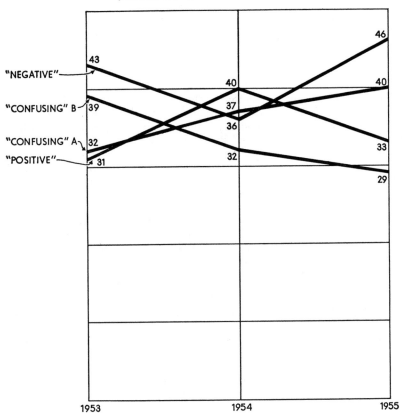

Chart 22

JANUARY–AUGUST SHARE OF TOTAL

many of your present brokers have fallen into the habit of "selling against last year's sales figures." We think the following illustrates this point:

Chart 23

SALE ANALYSIS RESULTS (IN CASES) ILLUSTRATING LACK OF "CREATIVE SELLING"		
1953	*1954*	*1955*
Broker "A".......26,338	28,100	28,100
Broker "B"....... 6,932	6,932	6,987
Broker "C"....... 6,498	6,494	6,435

This certainly shows a definite *lack of creative selling* with these three brokers. It should be quite obvious that brokers of this type will do NCA little good when it comes to moving your surplus . . . *unless* drastic, aggressive action is taken by you via a sales plan that is daring . . . and complete in every detail. In other words, we've got to pick our brokers with great care so far as the plan we will eventually propose is concerned.

Previously, we raised a question: "How much do we know about present NCA brokers?" We can partially answer that question . . . just from our analysis work. We believe the answer to be:

"From our detailed sales analysis, we know enough about past performance of the brokers to clearly indicate that NCA must provide the impetus to move our surplus product . . . clear through to the consumer."

And now to a short discussion on the subject of:

SALES PROMOTION MATERIAL

The special consumer promotion of "buy 2 cans . . . save 5¢" has apparently been successful, judging from the results of tests made in Columbus, Knoxville, and Chattanooga. We honestly believe this type of promotion will help to provide the "consumer interest" in our proposed plan. We strongly recommend this same type of promotion be used as the basis for moving the surplus.

If this is done, we feel that we should limit our sales promotion material to this deal only. Specially designed shelf talkers, stack cards, etc., should be prepared and a method of distribution set up with the brokers that will insure a better than average use of the material.

For the particular objective under discussion, that of moving surplus, we see no reason to dilute the promotion at the retail level by having regular promotion material in the store at that time. Further reasons for our attitude towards sales promotional material will appear a little later on.

What about our

ADVERTISING PHILOSOPHY?

The incentive plans of the past two years have, in reality, been "dealer loading" propositions. Your consumer advertising has been rather static. We can find but few cases where additional consumer advertising dollars were spent in specific markets where heavy dealer purchase occurred *as the result of* the dealer incentive plan. In order to assist the dealer in moving his stock off the shelves via in-store promotion, we must show him more concentrated consumer advertising impact. We believe this to be particularly true in view of our previous discussion under the heading of "competitive pricing conditions."

In order to arouse the dealer's interest towards more concentrated in-store Ocean Spray promotion, you've got to give him an incentive . . . something other than a reduced price . . . or early buying incentives. The one thing that can *force him* to promote a product is via *concentrated* consumer advertising at the local level. If properly done, this will cause more consumer sales . . . with a resulting market for our surplus.

If you want to make a dent in your surplus, the *consumer must buy* your product. Having the dealer buy it will *not* be enough. Hence, we are going to recommend a plan that will emphasize consumer advertising at the local level . . . in concentrated doses.

We also propose to use your present co-operative advertising allowance program with the retailers inasmuch as it is available from now until August. It's one more part of the over-all package.

So much for the discussion leading up to our recommendation. We feel that the foregoing is sufficient justification for us to make this broad over-all recommendation relative to moving the surplus and the . . .

OVER-ALL NCA SALES POLICY

With few exceptions, every broker has one or more accounts that have purchased over 1,000 cases of canned sauce per year during 1953, 1954, and 1955. As a result of this, each broker generally has one or more "key markets" in his territory . . . markets that usually account for a large proportion of this total yearly volume.

As an example, let's look at the results of this type analysis related to specific brokers' territories.

Chart 24

	1955 "Key Accounts"			
Territory	Total Cases 300's Sauce	Over 100 Case Accounts	Over 1,000 Case Accounts	Cities with 1,000 Case Accounts
Peoria................	9,048	8	2	2
El Paso...............	10,994	10	5	2
Birmingham...........	26,922	29	6	2
Denver...............	31,296	11	6	2
Oklahoma City.........	34,192	24	10	2
Grand Rapids..........	38,308	17	9	5
Total	150,760	99	38	15

For the past three years, the above "key accounts" have purchased 35 per cent, 34 per cent, and 38 per cent of their total yearly canned sauce stock . . . during the January–August period.

One barrel of cranberries is the equivalent of ten cases of canned sauce. Approximately 1,000 cases of sauce (100 barrels) is considered to be a "carload." The above brokers, as all brokers in general, sold approximately 35 per cent of their yearly volume during the January–August periods in each of the past three years. With the above group, this gives us a base of approximately 53,000 cases . . . or 53 carloads . . . that they could normally be expected to be sold during an average January–August period.

With the type of plan that we recommend using, NCA brokers will be budgeted a minimum of 1,000 carloads of surplus canned sauce . . . 1,000,000 cases . . . to be sold during April, May, June, July, and August of 1956. This is 25 per cent of your total canned sauce sales through brokers in 1955. Accordingly, by following a formula with variations dependent upon past performance, we would eventually pinpoint specific major cities and trading areas, where your major accounts are located . . . where an extra special promotion on canned sauce could be digested by retailer and consumer alike.

We propose a sales budget of 1,000 carloads of canned sauce surplus for this specific promotion in specific trading areas . . . providing . . . enough money is spent in each local market to make the promotion successful . . . on a "per carload basis." Stepped up advertising and promotion expenditures on a "per carload basis" would proportionately increase the number of carloads sold because you would be adding markets and/or saturating present markets.

Our definition of a "per carload basis" approach for promotion and advertising expenditures relates back to our previous discussion on NCA's pricing policy. At that time, we used a "gross income" figure of $1.15 per case ($11.50 per barrel) which allowed for an advertising and promotional expenditure of 20 cents per case ($2.00 per barrel). With 1,000 cases per car, this means that you would normally spend at the rate of $200 per car . . . advertising-wise.

However, we have a reservoir of $1.15 per case ($11.50 per barrel) in the gross income figure . . . which, in our estimation, must be used in some degree to "push" the sale of surplus. This is where it is difficult for us to see how you can "have your cake and eat it too." Hence, let's look at the potential investment per car that *could* be made . . . in an effort to concentrate heavily in these major markets.

Chart 25

"Gross Income" versus "Advertising per Car"			
Gross Income		Advertising Expenditure (per)	
Case	Barrel	Case	Car
$1.15	$11.50	20¢	$200
1.05	10.50	30	300
1.00	10.00	35	350
0.90	9.00	45	450
0.80	8.00	55	550
0.70	7.00	65	650
0.60	6.00	75	750
0.50	5.00	85	850

While NCA management must ultimately make the decision, relative to expenditures for a plan like this, we feel that proper impact for all concerned . . . broker, retailer, and consumer . . . could be obtained at somewhere near the rate of $500 per car. This is about 2½ times greater than presently being used. Also, anything more than that spent for selling the surplus would put the grower-member return below an $8.00 per barrel figure. This is not realistic nor practical from an economics viewpoint. However, we are certain that the grower-members *must* be willing to settle for something less than $11.50 per barrel . . . *if* they intend to sell much of the surplus.

What will "$500 per car" buy in the way of advertising? Let's use Denver and Grand Rapids as examples . . . as these two territories are good "test" possibilities if and when this plan is tried in the field. Using our previously discussed sales budget approach . . . the Denver territory would be an 8- to 11-carload market and Grand Rapids a 10- to 14-car market. Considering past performance variations, per our analysis, we arrive at 10 cars for Denver and 12 for Grand Rapids.

This means that we have $5,000 to spend in the Denver territory . . . based on $500 per carload for advertising. These sales budgets or quotas would be assigned to the brokers on the basis of "NCA is doing this . . . but you are expected to do that." We think this can be accomplished without too much trouble because . . .

Chart 26

"BBDO recommends that this special surplus advertising and promotion money be spent in each of these local markets in a period not to exceed ten days . . . from one Thursday through the following Saturday in order to catch two shopping week ends."

"Operation Carload"

A

Two-Week-End Promotion

Thurs., Fri., Sat.
Sun., Mon., Tues., Wed., Thurs., Fri., Sat.

With enough advance notice and planning, we can reasonably expect a food store to give us a two-week-end feature and promotion *if* our advertising is concentrated in this period of time. Accordingly, we would buy media on a saturation basis. It would be merchandised as "Operation Carload . . . the Cranberry Blitz" . . . or would be identified in some similar manner to indicate heavy concentration of NCA's advertising and promotional efforts. Advertisements would mention specific food outlets in local markets . . . on basis of tying in with Ocean Spray promotion.

Here is what our media department recommends as a schedule for Denver and Grand Rapids, on the above basis:

Chart 27

$500 PER CARLOAD
DENVER-PUEBLO MARKET

Denver

31,817 cases × 25% = 7,954 = 8 cars
31,817 cases × 35% = 11,136 = 11 cars
Sales analysis variation = 10 cars
10 cars × $500 =
$5,000

From a media standpoint, we feel it is necessary to combine the Denver area with the Pueblo area. The nature of distribution of Denver newspapers and the effective broadcasting range of Denver radio makes this market combination the most effective method of advertising in these two areas. The Denver-Pueblo area encompasses all of Colorado, the southwest quarter of Wyoming, the western tip of Nebraska, and the northwest corner of Kansas. The Denver area has a 13 carload potential, and the Pueblo area has a three-carload potential. Based on $500 per carload, $8,000 will be available for the ten-day saturation plan of advertising. The *Denver Post* will supply the major newspaper support, and station KCA the radion support. The following cities will receive a newspaper schedule:

City and Newspaper and Edition	Circ.	Schedule (Lines)	Line Rate	Total Cost
COLORADO:				
Denver Post (E)	248,890	4,000	$0.605	$2,722.50
Pueblo Chieftain Star-Journal (M & E)	38,104	2,000	0.18	360.00
Grand Junction Sentinel (E)	15,173	2,000	0.11	220.00
Greeley Tribune (E)	11,241	2,000	0.09	180.00
Ft. Collins Coloradean (E)	7,072	2,000	0.07	140.00
Boulder Camera (E)	8,115	2,000	0.07	140.00
Sterling Journal Advocate (E)	6,200	2,000	0.07	140.00
Colo. Springs Gazette Telegraph (E)	25,530	2,000	0.18	360.00
Trinidad Chronicle News (E)	4,622	2,000	0.07	140.00
Alamosa San Luis Valley Courier (E)	2,936	2,000	0.06	120.00
Durango Herald News (E)	3,380	2,000	0.06	120.00
Canon City Record (E)	3,893	2,000	0.05	100.00
WYOMING:				
Casper Tribune-Herald Star (M & E)	19,382	2,000	0.15	300.00
Cheyenne, Wyo., Eagle State Tribune (M & E)	20,669	2,000	0.16	320.00
Laramie Bul. Republican Boomerang (M & E)	5,642	2,000	0.09	180.00
NEBRASKA:				
Scottsbluff Star Herald (M)	13,793	2,000	0.09	180.00
Total	434,642			$5,772.50

Proposed Schedule	4,000 Lines	2,000 Lines
1st week: Thursday........	1,000 li., 2 clr.	600 li., B & W
Friday..........	600 li., B & W	400 li., B & W
Saturday........	....	....
Sunday..........	....	....
2d week: Monday........	....	....
Tuesday........	400 li., B & W	....
Wednesday......	400 li., B & W	....
Thursday........	1,000 li., 2 clr.	600 li., B & W
Friday..........	600 li., B & W	400 li., B & W
Saturday........	....	....

Spot radio will be used in Denver only. Although radio is available in Pueblo, as well as the other "outside" cities, Denver radio is strong enough to cover the Denver-Pueblo area. (Actual scheduling will depend upon available abilities and budget.) The following is an estimate for cost purposes only.

City	Radio Station	Cost per Min.	No. of Spots during Test Period	Total Cost
Denver......	KCA	$36.00	60	$2,160.00

In summary:

Newspaper..................$5,722.50
Radio...................... 2,160.00
Grand Total.............$7,882.50

Chart 27—Continued

GRAND RAPIDS MARKET
41,043 cases × 25% = 10,621 = 10 cars
41,043 cases × 35% = 14,365 = 14 cars
Sales analysis variation = 12 cars
12 cars × $500 =
$6,000

The Grand Rapids market encompasses the northern and western half of Michigan. This area represents a 12-carload potential, and at the rate of $500 per carload, $6,000 is available for use in the ten-day saturation advertising period. The *Grand Rapids Press* will supply the major newspaper support. Newspaper and spot radio schedules will be used in the following markets:

City and Newspaper and Edition	Circ.	Schedule (Lines)	Line Rate	Total Cost
Grand Rapids Press (E)....	112,331	4,000 B & W	$0.29	$1,320
Holland Sentinel (E)......	11,748	2,000 B & W	0.10	200
Muskegon Chronicle (E)....	43,937	2,000 B & W	0.18	360
Lansing State Journal (E)...	62,678	2,000 B & W	0.25	500
Kalamazoo Gazette (E).....	47,273	2,000 B & W	0.18	360
Total.............	277,967			$2,740

Proposed Schedule	4,000 Lines	2,000 Lines
1st week: Thursday.............	1,000 li., 2 clr.	600 li., B & W
Friday................	600 li., B & W	400 li., B & W
Saturday..............	....	....
Sunday................	....	....
2d week: Monday...............	....	....
Tuesday..............	400 li., B & W	....
Wednesday............	400 li., B & W	....
Thursday.............	1,000 li., 2 clr.	600 li., B & W
Friday................	600 li., B & W	400 li., B & W
Saturday..............	....	....

City	Radio Station	Cost per Min.	No. of Spots during Test Period	Total Cost
Grand Rapids........	WOOD	$13.75	60	$ 825
Holland............	WHTC	5.00	60	300
Muskegon..........	WKBZ	8.00	60	480
Lansing............	WILS	10.00	60	600
Kalamazoo.........	WKZO	16.00	60	960
Total.........				$3,165

In summary:

Newspapers.....................$2,740
Radio.......................... 3,165
Grand Total...............$5,905

We recommend that the "buy 2 cans—save 5¢" promotion be the major consumer deal . . . with 14 two-packs to the case as a retailer incentive. In addition, we recommend a "free goods" offer to the retailer in multiple units of 25-case orders . . . "buy 24 cases, get 1 case free." And, of course, your regular co-operative advertising contract would apply so as to encourage tie-ins in various omnibus advertisements run by the food chains.

SUMMARY

This, then, is our recommendation for moving some of the surplus. It's radical . . . it's different. It's based on the premise that the surplus is now costing NCA money just for the sake of maintaining it as surplus. It then resolves itself to:

Chart 28

```
HOW MUCH DOES
      NCA
WANT TO SPEND
      TO
MOVE SOME SURPLUS?
```

We think the above plan can be made to move 100,000 barrels . . . or 1,000,-000 cases of canned sauce. However, it will require bold action on the part of NCA . . . with some calculated risks.

We are not much interested in the 47 reasons why something like this won't work. Instead, we're looking for the one good reason why it *will work*. Marketing is often defined as something that moves people to move merchandise. We honestly think this plan will do just that!

~~~

CASE 25: NATIONAL CRANBERRY ASSOCIATION (B)[1]

QUESTIONS TO CONSIDER: (*1*) *Do you agree with Mr. Glover's conclusions regarding the major weaknesses of the Association's past promotional programs?* (*2*) *What marketing objectives do you think the Association should seek in the longer term?* (*3*) *Would you recommend accepting, rejecting, or modifying the BBDO proposed advertising program? What are the objectives of the program? Is there a basis for building effective advertisements? Is the media plan sound?* (*4*) *How much should be spent on advertising?* (*5*) *Would you recommend undertaking marketing-research studies or market tests? If so, for what purpose?*

In March 1956 the board of directors of the National Cranberry Association (NCA), a growers' co-operative, approved a special sales promotional campaign designed to reduce the association's inventory of cranberries of 345,000 barrels to 100,000 barrels by September 1, 1956. This campaign consisted of a consumer deal, "Buy 2—Save 5¢," making use of a special two-can cardboard multipack of 16-ounce jellied sauce, which was promoted by a short newspaper and radio campaign in selected major United States markets. A maximum of $500,000 was allocated by the board for the campaign.

By the end of May, the campaign was activated on a national basis. At that time, Mr. James Glover, president of NCA, turned his primary attention to the formulation of a long-range marketing strategy which would significantly increase the sales of the association's cranberry products. He began by reviewing the association's past marketing activities.

Mr. Glover's Review of NCA's Past Marketing Activities

In the decade following World War II, Mr. Glover stated, cranberry crops had increased greatly because of improved growing techniques. As the industry's largest co-operative marketers, NCA executives in the postwar period had been under continuous pressure to increase sales of "Ocean Spray" cranberry products in proportion to the increases in NCA members' cranberry crops. Although sales had increased significantly, sales had not kept pace with production so that NCA's year-end inventories grew in size, culminating in a record surplus of 359,000 barrels as of January 1, 1956.

---

[1] Written by Gerald A. Simon and Martin V. Marshall.

After examining NCA promotional activities for the period 1946–55, Mr. Glover concluded that there had been two major weaknesses: NCA had not tried to increase sales on the basis of a well-conceived, long-range promotional program, and NCA had not been entirely consistent in either the objective or the method of its promotional activity. "First," Mr. Glover said, "we apparently tried to work on the consumer. Then we switched objectives, emphasizing promotions which would increase trade activity. Then we went back to the consumer again. In our use of media, we shifted emphasis from magazines to television to billboards to newspapers, and we advertised only in the fall. Apparently we never stopped to ask ourselves, why? Why have we shifted emphasis? Why have we shifted media?" (NCA's traceable national advertising expenditures and case sales for the calendar years 1946 and 1950–55 are given in Exhibit 1. NCA's operating statements for the fiscal years ending May 31, 1955 and 1956 are given in Exhibit 2. NCA's processed case sales for the crop years ending August 31, 1950 through 1954 are given in Exhibit 3.)

Mr. Glover observed that national consumer advertising of canned sauce for the current crop year (September 1955 through August 1956) had been scheduled only for October, November, and December of 1955. (The "Buy 2—Save 5¢" deal promotion had not been decided upon until April 1956.) During these three months posters appeared in the New York subways and a total of 28 insertions were included in the following magazines and Sunday newspaper supplements: *Ladies' Home Journal, Good Housekeeping, Better Homes & Gardens, Parents' Magazine, American Girl, Girl Scout Leader, This Week,* and *American Weekly.* Most of the insertions were either two-color quarter pages or four-color half pages. Two-color half pages and black-and-white quarter pages were also used.

Mr. Glover also observed that NCA's advertising copy in the past had always emphasized cranberry sauce as an accompaniment to chicken and turkey. He was not sure that this copy theme should have been pushed continuously in the past or that it should be in the future. "Even in our current campaign," he said, "we are using the slogans 'Great with Chicken' and 'Serve with Chicken or Turkey.' But has this theme been overworked?"

He noted that total annual consumption of chicken in the United States increased by 48% between 1947 and 1954, while per capita consumption rose 33% (from 17.9 pounds to 23.8 pounds). Annual turkey consumption increased by 75% during the same period, while per capita consumption of turkey increased by 40% (from 3.5 pounds to 4.9 pounds).[2] Meanwhile, population increased by 15%. Mr. Glover believed that part of the increase in turkey consumption could be explained by an increase in nonholiday turkey sales. Production of broilers and of turkeys in 1956

---

[2] *Agricultural Statistics,* 1955, United States Department of Agriculture.

Exhibit 1

NATIONAL CRANBERRY ASSOCIATION (B)

National Consumer Advertising Expenditures and NCA Case Sales, Calendar Years 1946, 1950–55 (Canada Excluded)

Calendar Year	Company and Product	Magazines General	Magazines Farm	Magazines Total	Outdoor*	Network TV	Newspapers and Supplements	Total	NCA Process Case Sales (000)	Advertising Dollars per Case
1946	Cranberry Canners, Inc.:	(37,725)		(37,725)				(37,725)	N.A.	
	Ocean Spray Sauce	37,725		37,725				37,725		
1950	NCA:	(60,888)		(60,888)			(118,527)	(179,415)	4,898	$0.037
	Sauce	60,888		60,888			92,434	153,322		
	Cranberry Juice Cocktail						26,093	26,093		
1951	NCA:	(138,711)		(138,711)			(165,377)	(304,088)	4,277	0.071
	Sauce	132,086		132,086			154,824	286,910		
	Sauce and Swanson Canned Poultry	6,625		6,625			6,438	13,063		
	Cranberry Juice Cocktail						3,053	3,053		
	Miscellaneous						1,062	1,062		
1952	NCA:	(170,065)		(170,065)			(164,233)	(334,298)	4,557	0.073
	Sauce	170,065		170,065			129,563	299,628		
	Sauce and Swanson Canned Poultry						34,670	34,670		
1953	NCA:	(172,637)		(172,637)		(10,810)	(472,895)	(656,342)	4,665	0.141
1954	NCA:	(178,396)		(178,396)			(403,299)	(581,695)	5,084	0.114
	Sauce	178,396		178,396			271,636	450,032		
	Cranberries (fresh)						69,641	69,641		
	Cocktail						45,607	45,607		
	Cranberry-Orange Relish						16,415	16,415		
1955	NCA:	(157,945)	(8,000)	(165,945)	(20,471)*		(351,644)	(538,060)	5,195	.104
	Sauce	130,352	8,000	138,352			160,270	298,622		
	Cranberries (fresh)						97,830	97,830		
	Cocktail	27,593		27,593			78,420	106,013		
	Cranberry-Orange Relish						15,124	15,124		

* Outdoor records available for 1955 only; product breakdown not indicated.
Source: *National Advertising Investments*, 1946, 1950–55; *Expenditures of National Advertisers in Newspapers*, 1950–54; *Printers' Ink*, May 25, 1956; and National Cranberry Association records.

Exhibit 2

NATIONAL CRANBERRY ASSOCIATION (B)

Selected Operating Statement Items, 1955 and 1956

(Years Ending May 31)

	1956	1955
1. *Gross Sales:*		
Sauce	$18,600,264	$18,678,384
Fresh cranberries	2,490,672	3,073,705
Cocktail	871,231	675,690
Other	113,711	127,817
Total Gross Sales	$22,075,878	$22,555,596
2. *Expenses:*		
Administrative	$ 544,728	$ 374,285
Selling and delivery	1,577,987	1,449,195
Advertising	1,276,699	1,549,077
Grower relations	*	86,248
Total Expenses	$ 3,399,414	$ 3,458,805
3. Net Proceeds from Year	$ 5,479,339	$ 6,624,196
4. *Application of Proceeds:*		
Payments on 1953 pool†		$ 3,498,883
Payments on 1954 pool†	$ 2,577,331	4,498,883
Advances on 1955 pool†	3,238,547	....
Preferred and common stock dividends	222,095	192,551
Less: Undistributed proceeds at beginning of year	523,206‡	2,122,264
Undistributed proceeds at end of year	....	556,143‡
Advances on account of future earnings	(35,428)	....
Total Application of Proceeds	$ 5,479,339	$ 6,624,196

* Grower Relations Department discontinued. Continuing expenses, including monthly house organ, listed under Administrative expense.

† Growers' pools based on crop harvested in autumn of years indicated.

‡ $523,206—$556,143—($32,937) accounting changes.

Note: Data on a wholly owned Cranberry Credit Corporation not included. All of NCA's grower-members owned stock.

Source: National Cranberry Association records.

Exhibit 3

NATIONAL CRANBERRY ASSOCIATION (B)

Processed Case Sales for Crop Years 1950–54

(1,000 Cases)

1950	4,658
1951	4,516
1952	4,681
1953	5,412
1954	4,633

Source: National Cranberry Association records.

was expected to set new records, exceeding 1955 by perhaps 20% and 15%, respectively.[3]

NCA had concentrated advertising on its canned sauce products—jellied and whole sauce. Mr. Glover raised the question of whether the

[3] *The Poultry & Egg Situation,* July 18, 1956, Agricultural Marketing Service, United States Department of Agriculture.

association should continue to emphasize canned sauces when other products offered good promotional opportunities.

Mr. Glover also noted that sales results had been poor in some markets where large sums had been spent on advertising and had been good in other markets where relatively small sums were spent. Hence he had raised two additional questions: How effective is brand advertising? How effective is NCA's method of distribution?

Finally, Mr. Glover and other NCA executives believed that the growth of the private brands of large grocery chains was another important factor affecting NCA's attempt to increase sales. Most of the private-label cranberry merchandise sold by food chains was purchased from growers who were not members of NCA or other co-operatives. In the long run, however, there was the possibility that the growth of private brands would lead chains to solicit co-operative members as a source of supply.

Mr. Glover's Views regarding Long-Range Strategy

In working with marketing department and advertising agency personnel, Mr. Glover gradually formed views regarding the development of a long-range marketing strategy. He said,

Looking way ahead I think we should have a sales target of eight to ten million cases annually by 1966. To achieve this target we'll have to revise our brokerage system personnel-wise. And we'll have to gear our advertising program to the task.

More immediately, however, our greatest emphasis will have to be placed on increasing sales of our existing products. In addition we'll also have to add new products to our consumer line. Probably we should stick to established and new consumer products for the next few years because a greater proportional increase in consumer product sales can be obtained with far less effort than if we try to emphasize the institutional field.

We should seek increased consumer impact with our advertising. We should narrow down our fringe efforts and concentrate most of our advertising in media which we feel are most effective in reaching consumers and which are effective for our products. This means we are going to shift away from subway advertisements, media directed at home economics departments of high schools, and the like. We should concentrate on women's magazines with proven readership. We should hammer away at "Mrs. Consumer." It is our theory that the woman is the one who buys the product, and we must reach her. In addition, we probably should advertise year-round rather than during just a few months of the year.

In the near future we hope to put on the market two or three new products which have already been developed. The industry has long been searching for an improved whole sauce product and we have succeeded in developing one. We also have an excellent cranberry base for ice cream and sherbet and a juice concentrate which gives long-range promise for flavoring in vitamins and as a mask for medicines. It can be used for either supporting or altering the flavors of food products and as a natural food dye.

We are thinking about continuing a promotion campaign on "Cran," a product that NCA has had for years but which has been left dormant. Cranberry juice makes a good mixing agent for alcoholic beverages, principally gin and vodka, and we have given it the name "drink glorifier." Cran is already on the market, whereas our other new products are not. We think it is going to be a very profitable item, and with some good merchandising in the next five or ten years, we should build it to a sizable volume.

Our other new items, like the sherbet base, will not be products for retail distribution. The sherbet will be sold to ice cream manufacturers, and the concentrate mix will be sold to bakery houses. All of these items are being developed on an institutional level.

The cranberry industry is a sleeping giant. I feel that we have never scratched the surface of the institutional field. We have never even approached the saturation point as far as the potential consumer demand for regular cranberry sauce products.

A Promotional Proposal for the Period September 1956–August 1957

During the spring of 1956, NCA's advertising agency, Batten, Barton, Durstine & Osborn, Inc. (BBDO), had developed an advertising proposal for canned sauce products for the year September 1956 through August 1957, as the result of conferences with Mr. Glover and members of NCA's marketing department. This proposal was presented to NCA's board of directors in July 1956. Since the first advertisement was tentatively scheduled for publication in Sunday, September 16, newspaper supplements, Mr. Glover needed to have a final decision no later than August 1.

In presenting the canned sauce advertising program for 1956–57, BBDO representatives first summarized a cranberry usage study which had been made through the use of BBDO's National Panel of Consumer Opinion in October 1955. (BBDO had made their study in preparation for taking over the NCA account.) Usage was defined as the incidence of serving any brand of canned sauce at least once per year per family unit.

BBDO Cranberry Usage Study. The usage study indicated that slightly more consumers in urban areas served canned sauce than did consumers in rural areas. Regionally, usage was most common in the Northeast (94% of the families) and least common in the North Central (87%). In the latter area BBDO representatives thought that usage of canned sauce might be relatively low because of high usage of fresh cranberries. With regard to usage by annual family income, it was found that usage increased only slightly as income increased, from 86% for families earning under $3,000 to 94% for families earning over $7,000. One conclusion possible from these data was that a fairly broad market for canned cranberry sauce existed whether regarded from the viewpoint of geographical location or of income group.

The usage study also indicated that nine out of ten housewives served canned cranberry sauce at some time in the year. On the other hand, the BBDO usage study indicated that less than four out of ten housewives served canned sauce other than on holidays, i.e., Thanksgiving, Christmas, and Easter. Taking into account additional evidence which showed that year-round usage was greatest in the 35 to 54 age group, the BBDO

Exhibit 4

SALES TREND VERSUS POPULATION
1951–55

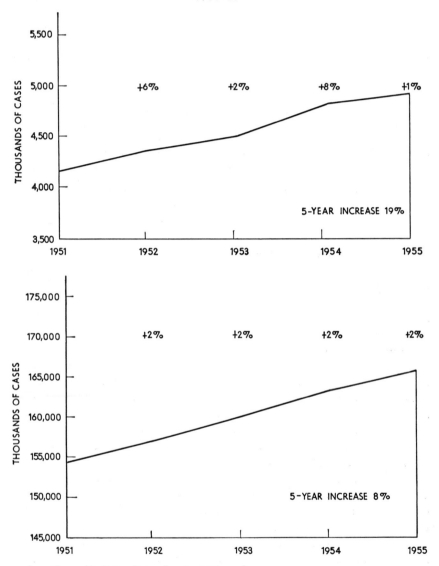

Source: Prepared by Batten, Barton, Durstine & Osborne, Inc.

study concluded that there was a need to cultivate a "younger market."

Referring to earlier brand awareness studies made in 1953, 1954, and 1955, BBDO representatives indicated that there had been a consistently high degree of Ocean Spray brand awareness among consumers: Ocean Spray ranked somewhat behind Gillette (razor blades) and still more behind Campbell (canned soup), both of which ranked quite high. Among canned sauce users, 83% were reported to prefer the Ocean Spray brand.

NCA Sales. Graphs illustrating the growth of NCA canned sauce sales and of the market for canned sauce between 1951 and 1955 were shown to the NCA board of directors. The graphs are given in Exhibits 4 and 5.

Exhibit 5
GROWTH OF CANNED SAUCE VERSUS POPULATION AND FOOD SALES
Index 1951 = 100

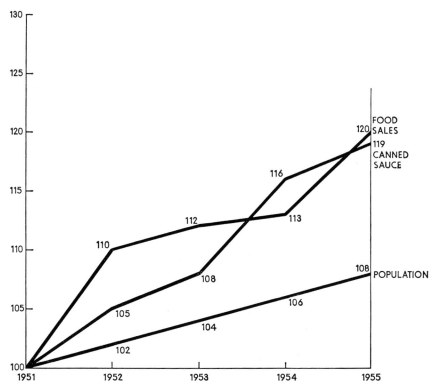

Source: Prepared by Batten, Barton, Durstine & Osborne, Inc.

Having depicted the growth of the market for Ocean Spray canned sauce, BBDO representatives showed the annual increase in sales during the January–August period. As a proportion of annual sales, January–August sales rose steadily from 12% in 1946, to a peak of 45% in 1954, and then dropped back to 36% in 1955. It was possible to conclude from such evidence, BBDO representatives thought, that year-round advertising might be profitably begun as a means of increasing long-run demand and eliminating the likelihood of future surpluses.

BBDO and NCA knew that NCA sales performance had been poorer in rural areas than in urban areas. In order to assess the opportunities for developing sales in rural areas, a comparison of 1955 "urban" and "rural" sales was made based upon an index of 100 for the United States. The sales performance index for urban areas ranged from 229 in Boston, to 122 in New York, to 102 in San Francisco, and to as low as 80 in Dallas. Rural area sales performance indexes ranged from 77 in Cedar Rapids, Michigan, to 58 in Sioux Falls, Iowa, to 30 in Duluth, Minnesota, and to as low as 22 in Lexington, Kentucky.[4]

Taking into account information describing the market for canned sauce given above and the lagging sales performance of "rural" areas, it was possible to conclude that one objective of NCA's marketing strategy should be to increase sales in markets with lower than expected consumption.

From an analysis of the relative sales performance of NCA cranberry sauce and cocktail products for the preceding five years, it was possible to come to some conclusions regarding general marketing strategy. BBDO's analysis of product sales follows:

NCA SAUCE AND COCKTAIL SALES AS PERCENTAGES OF TOTAL SALES, 1951–55

	1951	1952	1953	1954*	1955
Cocktail juice....	2.9%	3.8%	3.8%	5.0%	5.3%
Whole sauce.......	16.4	19.6	19.2	18.5	18.7
Jellied sauce.....	(80.7)	(76.6)	(77.0)	(76.5)	(76.0)
16-ounce.........	70.3%	65.4%	64.7%	62.3%	60.4%
7-ounce..........	10.4	11.2	12.3	14.2	15.6
Total...........	100.0%	100.0%	00.0% 1	100.0%	100.0%

* Introduced 48/7 ounce whole sauce in September 1954.

Tentative Marketing Objectives. NCA's marketing objectives, as tentatively developed by association and agency personnel, were summarized by the BBDO representatives as follows:

a) Build up seasonal usage.
b) Increase frequency of use.
c) Combat private label competition.
d) Develop lagging areas.

To obtain these objectives, BBDO representatives proposed the following media plan.

---

[4] BBDO built a United States index of 100 by equating 1955 food-store sales in dollars as 70 and number of families as 30. Thus a sales expectation figure could be developed for individual markets. Individual market indices were the result of dividing each market's percentage sales expectation by 1955 sales as a percentage of total 1955 United States sales. Hence Boston's index of 229 indicated a rate of sales 129 per cent greater than "might be expected," and Lexington, Kentucky's index of 22 indicated a rate of sales 78 per cent less than "might be expected."

Proposed Media Plan. Advertising would begin with September 1956 insertions and run through August 1957, with advertisements timed to appear during the autumn holiday season, plus Lent in February, Easter in April, Father's Day in June, and in August for light and cool summer dining. BBDO proposed 48 insertions, including in approximate equal number, four-color bleed pages, four-color full pages, four-color half pages, and black-and-white quarter pages. The following publications were recommended: *Ladies' Home Journal, Better Homes & Gardens, Woman's Home Companion, McCall's, American Home, Life, This Week,* and *Parade.*

PROPOSED ADVERTISING AND PROMOTIONAL BUDGET

	Current Year, Sept. 1, 1955, Aug. 31, 1956 (Add 000)	Plan 1, 1956–57, Sept. 1–Aug. 31 (Add 000)	Plan 2, 1956–57, Sept. 1–Aug. 31 (Add 000)
Media:			
Cranberry Sauce:			
U.S.	$ 205	$ 603	$ 940
Canada	15	30	43
Trade	....	17	17
Production	30	25	25
Surplus	500	....	....
Total	$ 750	$ 675	$1,025
Cranberry cocktail juice	115	100	100
Fresh cranberries	160	75	85
Reserve fund	....	150	125
Total	$1,025	$1,010	$1,335
Promotion:			
Incentive plan	$ 815	$ 475	$ 500
Promotional material	390	190	215
Co-operative advertising allowance	250	325	350
Kitchen, film, publicity, festival conventions, etc.	100	100	100
Total	$1,555	$1,090	$1,165
Grand Total	$2,580	$2,100	$2,500

After proposing the media schedule above, BBDO representatives recommended a $2,500,000 promotional budget for NCA, including $940,000 as the cost of media. BBDO also suggested an alternative $2,100,000 promotional plan. The second alternative essentially envisaged a pruning of the proposed media expenditure, as indicated below.

The reasons for relying on magazines were then stated. "(*a*) afford excellent color reproduction, (*b*) support promotions, (*c*) urban media, (*d*) leave 'ideas' with consumer, (*e*) audience selectively, and, (*f*) editorial atmosphere."

To emphasize the attempt to stimulate year-round sauce usage, 1955 seasonal sales were compared to the proposed seasonal expenditure of advertising dollars.

	Jan.–Aug.	Sept.–Dec.
Sales (in cases)	36%	64%
Recommended advertising dollars (1956–57)	62	38

Then, in order to indicate the increased year-round impact of consumer advertising, BBDO showed that total circulation under Plan 1 would be 44% greater than was true in 1955–56 and 99% greater under Plan 2. However, to allow for the fact that planned individual space insertions during 1956–57 would be larger than during 1955–56, BBDO converted circulation figures to the equivalent of full-page insertions. The circulation increase under Plan 1 was then 212% and under Plan 2, 373%.

As a measure of the proposed plan's attempt to increase sales in low per capita consumption areas, BBDO's presentation stressed that the percentage of total advertising circulation in the south and west would be somewhat greater than the percentage of total recent sales in those areas.

Possible Test Projects. BBDO's presentation concluded with a listing of possible future test projects, as follows:

Price increase on *whole* sauce
Larger package size
Television
Productivity of advertising investment in January to August period
Frozen berries
Frozen cranberry-orange relish
Cran
Develop other new products

NCA Consideration of BBDO Proposal. At the time NCA's board of directors was considering the BBDO proposal, sales reports indicated that NCA's inventory was likely to be reduced to manageable proportions by September 1, 1956, which was the beginning of the new crop and advertising year. June and early July store audits conducted by BBDO in several markets indicated that the "Buy 2—Save 5¢" deal was moving off dealer shelves. It was a little early, however, in the opinion of NCA executives, to assess the total amount of consumer demand for the deal, and thus, the final success of the short-run program to clear the way for sale of the new crop. In addition, the situation was further complicated because NCA's marketing director had designed a discount plan intended to encourage August retailer commitments for September shipment of canned sauce. Only as the results of this discount plan became evident would the size of the September 1 inventory be known.

Despite the lack of knowledge regarding the success of the short-term promotional plan, it was necessary for Mr. Glover to make immediate decisions regarding the 1956–57 national advertising program. He had already decided upon certain elements of his 1956–57 promotional plan.

Decisions Already Made. An expenditure of $65,000 for promotion of fresh cranberries was to be made as follows:

> BBDO publicity program..................$25,000
> Co-operative support of Sucaryl campaign
>   which advertises cranberries............ 20,000
> Point of purchase....................... 20,000
>   Total............................$65,000

Another $10,000 to $20,000 of the total budget was to be split between a co-operative advertising and promotion program with a West Coast apple growers' co-operative, some outdoor advertising in the Middle West, and a "service man" to work with certain brokers' retail salesmen on an experimental basis.

The budget for miscellaneous items, such as display material and cranberry cookbook distribution, was to be slightly less than 1955–56 expenditures. The co-operative advertising allowance of 5 cents a case for canned sauce was to be continued in 1956–57.

A final decision regarding the promotional budget for Cran, frozen cranberry-orange relish, and fresh frozen cranberries was to be delayed until October 1956, because Mr. Glover did not want to undertake promotions which might threaten dealer supplies of Ocean Spray canned sauce. By October the size of the 1956 cranberry crop and the success of the "Buy 2—Save 5¢" and discount promotions would be known.

If cranberry supplies were sufficiently large in October, Mr. Glover planned to recommend to the board test campaigns for fresh frozen cranberries and frozen cranberry-orange relish. The tests would start in December and would involve a 13-week promotion of fresh frozen cranberries in Pittsfield, Massachusetts, and a 26-week promotion of the relish in Rochester, Minnesota, and Madison, Wisconsin. The tests would cost approximately $40,000.

Additional Considerations. With regard to the current distribution of canned sauce, Mr. Glover was interested in preserving the dominant share of market which Ocean Spray had gained over competitive brands, including private label brands of the chains. NCA packed canned sauce under private labels at $1.70 per dozen 16-ounce cans, allowing no co-operative advertising allowance, as compared to the regular $2.00 Ocean Spray price, to customers requesting this service. Private label sales, however, amounted to less than 5% of total sales.

Although BBDO's 1956–57 advertising plan was not essentially concerned with the promotion of bottled cranberry cocktail, Mr. Glover was growing concerned with the low level of sales of the product. It was the psychological time, he and other executives agreed, to spend some money to do something "big." Ideally, they would have desired to embark upon a door-to-door consumer sampling program, costing $100,000 or more. Once consumers had an opportunity to try the cranberry cocktail drink, it was believed that advertising would be more effective. The cost of large-scale sampling, however, was too large to consider for 1956–57.

One departure from NCA's earlier practice was BBDO's suggestion to advertise in *Life*, a "dual-audience" magazine. Previously, NCA consumer magazine advertising had been concentrated in publications with a predominantly feminine readership. Mr. Glover wondered what the probably effect on demand for canned sauce and a dealer and broker salesman behavior would be if he accepted BBDO's *Life* recommendation. He was also interested in evaluating the other recommended departures from NCA practice, such as concentrating effort upon a younger group and in areas where canned sauce usage was relatively low. Although not a formal part of the BBDO presentation, he understood that 1956–57 copy would stress not only the ease of using sauce as it came out of the can but would also stress its use in appropriate seasonal food settings generally, not always with chicken or turkey.

If NCA was to advertise year-round, association executives believed special attention should be given to brokers to make certain that their salesmen followed through at the retail level and that dealer use of co-operative allowances should be controlled by new dealer co-operative advertising contracts as follows:

> Fourth quarter, 1956.................... 30%
> First quarter, 1957....................... 10
> Second quarter, 1957...................... 30
> Third quarter, 1957....................... 30
> One year, October to September........100%

In general, Mr. Glover had to decide whether BBDO's advertising proposal for 1956–57 fitted into the association's long-range plans and whether it appeared likely to succeed in the light of both the evidence presented and NCA's own experience. He knew that the promotional program selected needed to be justified to the board of directors in terms of its likely effect on the immediate and long-range return to NCA's grower-members.

~~~

CASE 26: THE SPEIDEL CORPORATION[1]

QUESTIONS TO CONSIDER: (1) *What has been Speidel's media strategy?* (2) *Has management followed good procedures in selecting media in the past?* (3) *How should Speidel go about solving its media problem as of June 1953?*

---
[1] Written by Raymond Armstrong and Martin V. Marshall.

In June 1953 executives of the Speidel Corporation of Providence, Rhode Island, met with their advertising agency to decide what the company's advertising program would be in 1953–54. Of particular importance at this meeting was the question, "Where does Speidel go from here in the television field?" Since 1949 the Speidel company had spent the major part of its advertising appropriation on network television advertising. Since 1949 sales had increased 35%, but executives did not believe they could determine how much of this gain could be attributed to television and how much to the widening of the company's line.

The contract for the company's existing show, "What's My Name?" (NBC-TV, 7:00–7:30 P.M., alternating Monday nights) was due to expire on June 30, 1953. Since the company had decided not to renew the contract, "What's My Name?" had been sold by its owner to a new sponsor for the fall season.

At the meeting several alternatives were considered; namely, (1) to start a new TV show, that is, one which had never been previously telecast; (2) to buy an established network TV show; and (3) to buy more than one TV show and use some form of cosponsorship to spread the cost. ("What's My Name?" had been cosponsored on alternate Monday nights by the Crosley Corporation.)

Product Line

The major source of sales for the Speidel company was a line of metal expansion watch bands and identification bracelets. These bands were highly stylized. Designs were changed frequently because consumer tastes changed from year to year. For this reason, executives sought to hold inventories to a minimum, and designers were constantly at work creating new models to offer consumers.

The trade considered Speidel bands to be a medium-priced line. Retail prices ranged from $6.50 to $14.50 for ladies' bands, and $8.95 to $17.95 for men's. In June 1953 the company sold ten different men's and ten women's styles of watch bands, each style available in white, yellow, and pink gold, and each style made in five different lengths. Each style had a special name which was associated with the band in all advertising, for example: "Catalina," "Raindrop," "Cortez," and "Golden Knight."

Since the company was spending over $1,000,000 each year on advertising, executives felt that a high-quality product was essential to protect the company's advertising investment and to bear out claims made by the company in its advertising copy. To determine what retail jewelers thought about the Speidel line, the management had engaged a market research firm to make a survey in 1950. From this survey of 600 retail jewelers, the company found that The Speidel Corporation was considered superior to competitors in the design and quality of its product, in the use of advertising and promotional material, and in packaging.

Background of the Market

Speidel introduced the metal expansion watch band in 1940, and in that same year the company licensed its competitors, giving them permission to imitate the expansion-type band.[2] The principal competitors were: Jacques Kreisler, Brunner-Ritter, Jacoby-Bender, Flexlet, Gemex, Bretton, and Forstner. In the period 1940–45, the watch-band industry grew slowly. Speidel's advertising manager described the growth of the watch-band industry as follows:

> In 1946 expansion watch bands were still relatively unknown to the general public and represented less than 1% of the retail jeweler's sales. They were unpublicized, except for Speidel's advertising efforts in 1944 and 1945, and without manufacturers' identification. In addition, they had the drawback of being an accessory and were distributed and sold through one of the poorest traffic outlets, the retail jeweler.
>
> By 1953 our aggressive national advertising had increased sales of all expansion watch bands to the point where they represented 8% to 10% of the retailers' volume and were considered the fastest turnover items in jewelry stores.

The advertising manager estimated manufacturers' sales of expansion watch bands in 1953 to be over 15,000,000 units. The Speidel Corporation was responsible for 40% of all United States watch-band dollar volume; and executives were looking forward to an even larger share of the market.

Distribution Channels

According to Speidel executives, sales of expansion watch bands were closely related to the level of sales of wrist watches. Also, sales were related to the retail outlets through which watches were sold. For this reason Speidel had limited its distribution to retail jewelry stores and jewelry departments of leading department stores. No Speidel bands were sold by drug or hardware stores, and the management considered this policy an important element in maintaining the goodwill of retail jewelers.

Another factor which made drug and hardware stores undesirable as retail outlets for the Speidel line was the inability of these stores to merchandise and sell the line properly. Executives felt that drugstores would be unable to carry a sufficient inventory of styles and sizes. Furthermore, they did not believe that the persuasive selling effort needed on the part of the retail clerk could be expected from the typical drug clerk. Finally, they felt that consumers would prefer to buy a gift item from a jewelry store rather than from a drugstore. (A survey of retail jewelers in 1951 by *Jewelers' Circular-Keystone*, a leading trade publication, showed that 58% of expansion watch bands were sold as gift items.)

The Speidel Corporation did not sell direct to retail jewelers. Sales were

---

[2] The Speidel Corporation had a special reason for licensing competitors which has no bearing on this case.

made by a force of six salesmen to about 250 jewelry wholesalers, who were described by the company's vice president as being "the blue bloods of the wholesale trade." These 250 wholesalers sold to about 18,000 retail jewelers[3] through their own salesmen. Most wholesalers carried five or six lines of watch bands and sold at least two brands to each retailer. Consequently, Speidel bands were sold to retailers on a competitive basis and, once inside the store, were sold to consumers against competition from at least one other brand.

Advertising History

The Speidel Corporation began its consumer advertising program in the fall of 1944 with small advertisements in *Redbook* and *Click* and two-column advertisements in three different issues of *Liberty*. Then followed a period of moving from one medium to another. For four years the company followed a policy of advertising in national consumer magazines. The company then experimented for two years with a national radio program. Finally, executives decided to allocate their entire consumer advertising budget to network television. (Exhibit 1 gives a summary of Speidel's consumer advertising effort from 1944 until June 1953.)

In the period 1944–53, the company was very active in promotional activity at the retail level. While executives did not believe in the use of co-operative advertising, they felt it was important for the company to give the retailer every possible aid in selling Speidel merchandise. Toward this end they had developed a comprehensive dealer display and dealer advertising program. Twice a year advertisements were run in the major trade magazines announcing the availability of the latest merchandise and trade material.

Transition from Radio to Television

After four years of brand advertising in national consumer magazines, company executives felt that the magazine audience had been saturated with Speidel advertising. As a result of this conclusion, they believed that it would be worthwhile to experiment with radio. They felt that radio offered an opportunity to reach a new segment of the market. Further they were interested to determine if radio commercials would lead to direct buying action. In May 1948, therefore, the company purchased "Stop the Music," a network radio "giveaway" show, as an experiment. As the executives observed the results of the show during 1948 and 1949, they decided that they were pleased with their experience on network radio.

Having found radio a successful new medium for the company, executives began to consider another new medium, television. As television

---

[3] The company's advertising agency estimated that there were 21,269 retail jewelry stores in the United States as of June 1953.

Exhibit 1

THE SPEIDEL CORPORATION
Summary of Consumer Advertising, 1944–53

Fiscal Year Beginning July	Type of Media	Media	Total Expenditures
1944	Consumer magazines	*Click, Liberty, Redbook*	$ 47,962
1945	Consumer magazines	*American, Cosmopolitan, Glamour, Good Housekeeping, Harper's Bazaar, Liberty, Modern Screen, Redbook, Screenland, Silver Screen, This Week, True, True Story, Vogue*	139,000
1946	Consumer magazines	*Colliers, Cosmopolitan, Esquire, Good Housekeeping, Ladies' Home Journal, Life, McCall's, The New York Times Magazine, Parents' Magazine, The Saturday Evening Post, Vogue, Woman's Home Companion*	291,000
1947	Consumer magazines	*Colliers, Cosmopolitan, Esquire, Good Housekeeping, Ladies' Home Journal, Parents' Magazine, Pic, The Saturday Evening Post, This Week*	371,000
1948	Consumer magazines	5 four-color pages in *Life* 3 four-color pages in *Ladies' Home Journal*	745,000
	Radio	NBC's "Stop the Music," starting in May 1949	
1949	Radio	NBC's "Stop the Music"	1,118,000
	Television	CBS's "Ed Wynn Show" for 13 weeks	
1950	Radio	NBC's "Stop the Music" until August 1950	1,000,000
	Television	NBC's "Jack Carter Show" for 6 weeks NBC's "What's My Name," starting in September 1950	
1951	Television	NBC's "What's My Name"	1,530,000
1952	Television	NBC's "What's My Name"	1,750,000

Source: Company Records.

grew in importance during 1949, they were extremely receptive to the possibilities of television advertising for watch bands. They felt that television would provide tremendous impact through the visual selling of this type of style merchandise. In the fall of 1949, they bought 13 weeks of the "Ed Wynn Show" (CBS-TV, 9:00–9:30 P.M., Thursday). The weekly charge for the "Ed Wynn Show" was $26,000 for talent and production and $5,300 for time.

It was not long, however, before the company began to shop around television circles for another program for this reason: executives felt that Speidel's sales message should be aimed at young adults because they were more style conscious than their elders and were more influential in the style shift to expansion bands. It was soon decided that Ed Wynn's reputation had been established with an older group, hence the search for a new show.

In the spring of 1950, Speidel sponsored six weeks of the 7:00–8:00 P.M. section of NBC-TV's "Saturday Night Review." This enabled the company to get wide coverage in a large number of TV homes, and in Jack Carter, the star and master of ceremonies of the show, they felt they had achieved the light-vein type of humor that would appeal to the audience the company was trying to reach. Weekly talent and production costs were $9,000, and time charges were approximately $8,400 for Speidel's share of the show. This show did not obtain the high Hooper ratings[4] that Speidel executives expected. Therefore, when it went off the air in the summer of 1950, company executives decided not to renew its contract for the fall. Instead, they decided to try a newcomer: a young ventriloquist named Paul Winchell had built a variety quiz show around his act and was looking for a sponsor. The company's advertising manager liked the idea of a variety quiz show with Winchell as the star, and in September 1950 Speidel went on television with "What's My Name" (NBC-TV, Mondays, 8:00–8:30 P.M.).

As the number of television stations and the number of TV sets in use increased, however, costs also increased. By the spring of 1953, costs for "What's My Name" were approximately $23,000 for talent and $30,000 for time on 64 stations. When executives found that television costs were becoming excessive for the company, they searched for a method of keeping a national TV show with a minimum of expense. They decided that they would be unable, within the limits of the budget they had set up, to present "What's My Name" weekly on a half-hour time basis. Since they also felt that a 15-minute program lacked the impact that was necessary for their product advertising, they were reluctant to reduce the time of the show.

In addition, the company was faced with another aspect of advertising

---

[4] C. D. Hooper, Inc., provided data on consumer listening to network television programs. The Hooper rating was a percentage of total homes found listening to a specific program.

impact, namely, the problem of program continuity. Executives believed that the television audience liked to watch the same show week after week, and they felt that any attempt to present a show on an every-other-week basis would result not only in a loss of valuable time commitments but also in a loss of audience. Finally it was decided that the best way to resolve these difficulties was to find a cosponsor who would take the show on alternate weeks. In January 1952 Speidel began using this method of alternate sponsorship with the Crosley Corporation on the "What's My Name" show. Crosley advertised a line of major electrical appliances, refrigerators, TV sets, and radios.

As soon as the company began cosponsorship with Crosley, both sponsors agreed to a system of "cross-plugging" as a method of getting maximum benefits out of network TV for both firms. By cross-plugging, Speidel received one commercial out of three and a 15-second closing plug on the nights that Crosley sponsored the show. Speidel reciprocated for Crosley when Speidel sponsored the show. This cross-plugging system was also used by Lucky Strike and Johnson's Wax on the "Robert Montgomery Show," the Toni Company and Pillsbury Mills on "Arthur Godfrey and His Friends," and by Anson and the B. T. Babbitt Company on "The Kate Smith Evening Hour."

Speidel's Policy Regarding TV

According to the advertising manager, it was Speidel's policy to use television for direct selling. Executives felt that two years of advertising on network radio between 1947 and 1949 had achieved brand name identification for Speidel watch bands. Television was expected to sell directly to consumers as well as to enlarge distribution.

Both Speidel and its advertising agency (Sullivan, Stauffer, Colwell, & Bayles, Inc.) agreed that a strong sales personality in an announcer could do more to put over a commercial than the best copy. Two of the personalities used by the Speidel company were Jinx Falkenburg and Donald Woods.[5] "Jinx was used for the sentimental approach," said the sales manager, "and Woods for the hard to sell." Both announcers were allowed to change the copy to fit their own personalities. Each sold only one item in a commercial.

The following commercial is an example of what Speidel called "the sentimental approach":

Jinx Falkenburg: Hi! I'm Jinx Falkenburg. I'd like to show you something I'm just crazy about! It's the fashion rage among young people everywhere, especially those away from home. It's Speidel's new photo-identification bracelet. See! A stunning identification bracelet for men! But that's not all. Underneath the name plate is a place to put your loved one's picture to always keep you close to the one you love.

---

[5] Both Jinx Falkenburg and Donald Woods had appeared in movies and were considered to be relatively well known to the public.

Can't you just imagine how pleased any man will be to receive this Speidel Photo-Ident from *you?* But be sure to get a genuine Speidel, because there's nothing to match it. So comfortable, so beautiful.

And look, here's a Speidel Photo-Ident for women. Here's where you put your loved one's picture. A Speidel Photo-Ident.

A thrilling gift for him.

A warm sentimental gift for her. Your jeweler will be glad to show it to you.

Executives believed they had sufficient evidence to establish the effectiveness of TV selling. Sales had increased steadily, and many of Speidel's 18,000 retail outlets had reported instances of sales that resulted from TV advertising. They informed the company that customers often came into the store looking for a specific style of Speidel band that had been advertised on television. If the jeweler didn't have the item in stock, they frequently left a deposit and purchased on the basis of what they had seen on TV.

In March 1953 a new item called the photo-identification bracelet (previously mentioned) was advertised in two commercials on the show, "What's My Name." By June, $2 million in retail sales had been made on this one item alone through the use of TV advertising. The advertising manager said that he had personally received 158 phone calls from retailers asking for the item within a week after the first March commercial.

Another example of the results achieved through television advertising was related by the sales manager. He said:

The head of a department store was watching TV one Saturday evening and was impressed with the display of the Speidel line on the Ed Wynn program. Monday morning, the program still in mind, he went down to his own jewelry department to see whether their Speidel display matched the one he had seen on television. It didn't.

The department store executive immediately went to work, got together with the head of his jewelry department and planned a separate Speidel counter on which the watch bands would be displayed to better advantage. During the subsequent three pre-Christmas weeks sales volume in watch bands increased 700% over the previous year and made the jewelry department the top department in that store.

Decision to Change Shows

Early in 1953, as has been indicated, executives had decided to drop the "What's My Name" show when its contract expired in June 1953. Although they considered it a successful show, they felt that it was not advisable for any sponsor to stay with one show over a long period of time. According to the advertising manager, the decision to switch to a new program was based on three factors. They follow:

1. When a show's contract expired, talent costs were established on the basis of demand. If several sponsors were bidding for a show, it normally went to the highest bidder. In 1953 Procter and Gamble bid against Speidel for the "What's My Name" show. Speidel executives felt that the show was not worth the price Procter and Gamble bid.

2. Executives found that the Winchell-Mahoney program drew an audience composed 60% of teen-agers, that is, the majority of the audience was somewhat under the age group of most Speidel customers. The show's fairly constant high rating (an average Nielsen of 34) throughout 1952–53, however, largely compensated for the slight discrepancy between audience desired and audience reached.

3. It was the company's policy not to saturate a market with advertising. They felt that any program or personality would reach a point of diminishing returns at which time it became desirable for the sponsor to reach a new audience, or else a composite of old and new audience with a fresh program format.

The sales manager described it this way:

One of the problems of our product is that we could easily exhaust our audience after a period of years. Assume that we sell five or six million watch bands a year. Figure then, that our TV program reaches an audience of 25 million. The answer is simple arithmetic.

The solution, on the other hand, is a matter of periodic changes in programs sponsored and, axiomatically, diversification of our line.

Selection of a New Show

Executives had approved an advertising budget for the 1953–54 fiscal year (July through June) of $2.5 million. Although this budget was large enough for the company to buy a top TV program of its own on a year-round basis, they were considering several alternatives.

They had the possibility of buying a show which was already being televised, had an established audience, and was available for purchase. Some of the network shows which were available are shown in Exhibit 2.

A second alternative they considered was to bring out an entirely new show as Speidel had done with the "What's My Name?" show in 1950. (Some new shows which were available are shown in Exhibit 3.) Executives felt that one of the major advantages of this alternative was that the cost for a new show with a relatively unknown name would probably be far less than that for an established show. Furthermore, because of the lower talent costs involved in a new show, it might be possible for them to sponsor two television shows and thus get additional coverage in the cities which had more than one TV station. Another factor favoring a new show was that it could be put on as a fill-in for the summer on a trial basis. A major disadvantage was the sometimes slow and difficult process of educating the audience to an unknown performer and a new show.

Encountered in the selection of a new program, and very much in executives' minds, were the related problems of time buying, station clearance, program hour, market coverage, and the various methods of cosponsorship. As an aid to resolving these problems, they decided to look at some current statistics on television.

The various data they considered follow:

1. An analysis of television coverage by Speidel sales territory which is attached as Exhibit 4.

Exhibit 2

THE SPEIDEL CORPORATION

Established Network Television Shows Available for Sponsorship in June 1953

Title	Time	Type	Appeal	Length	Net Price	Explanation
1. Colonel Flack.	Evening	Situation comedy	Adult	30 min.	$12,500	Allan Mowbray as the colonel
2. Hogan's Daughter.	Evening	Situation comedy	Family	30 min.	14,000	Sheilah Bond as the dizzy girl
3. Mr. Glencannon.	Evening	Comedy drama	Adult	30 min.	16,500	*The Saturday Evening Post* stories
4. Author Meets the Critics.	Evening	Panel	Adult	30 min.	2,807	Panel sessions
5. Captain Video.	Afternoon	Drama	Juvenile	30 min.	2,125	Science fiction
6. Jimmy Hughes, Rookie Cop.	Evening	Detective	Adult	30 min.	7,110	Conrad Janis as Jimmy
7. Twenty Questions.	Evening	Panel	Family	30 min.	8,662	Well-known parlor game
8. Treasure Hunt.	Evening	Audience participation	Adult	30 min.	2,276	Art appraisal
9. Kate Smith.	Afternoon	Variety	Women	60 min.	3,250 for 15 min.	Kate sings and talks
10. Hawkins Falls.	Morning	Serial drama	Women	15 min.	9,500	Small community life
11. Kukla, Fran and Ollie.	Sun. aft.	Variety	Family	30 min.	10,000	Burr Tillstrom puppets
12. Gabby Hayes.	Afternoon	Western	Juvenile	15 min.	1,560	Gabby conducts a variety show

Source: Company records.

Exhibit 3

THE SPEIDEL CORPORATION

New Television Shows Available for Sponsorship in June 1953

Title	Time	Type	Appeal	Length	Net Price	Explanation
1. Ray Bolger Show	Evening	Comedy variety	Family	30 min.	N.A.	Bolger dances and acts on film
2. Exposed	Evening	Mystery	Adult	30 min.	$17,500	Barry Sullivan plays a detective
3. George Jessel's Banquet Table	Evening	Variety	Family	30 min.	15,000	Jessel in storyteller role
4. Justice	Evening	Drama	Adult	30 min.	15,500	Legal-aid cases
5. The Last Word	Evening	Audience participation	Family	30 min.	6,500	New giveaway show
6. Passport to Adventure	Evening	Mystery	Adult	30 min.	19,000	Caesar Romero
7. White-Collar Girl	Evening	Drama	Adult	30 min.	22,500	Larraine Day

Source: Company records.

Exhibit 4

THE SPEIDEL CORPORATION

Distribution of Total Homes, TV Homes, and Retail Jewelry-Store Sales—a
Summary by Speidel Sales Territories

Territory	No. of Homes, 1/1/53*	No. of TV Homes, 5/1/53†	% TV Homes to Total	Retail Jewelry-Store Sales, 1952 (000)‡	Per Cent Distribution of United States Totals		
					Total Homes	TV Homes	Retail Jewelry-Store Sales
I.	4,046,400	2,737,110	68	$ 146,764	8.9	11.6	9.8
II.	15,317,400	11,024,920	72	522,912	33.5	46.8	35.0
III.	6,531,000	1,883,370	29	186,798	14.3	8.0	12.5
IV.	8,126,900	3,594,370	44	245,409	17.8	15.2	16.4
V.	5,509,900	1,268,750	23	179,009	12.1	5.4	12.0
VI.	6,107,400	3,073,720	50	213,520	13.4	13.0	14.3
	45,639,000	23,582,240	52	$1,494,412	100.0	100.0	100.0

* Total homes, January 1, 1953, a *Sales Management* estimate.
† TV homes, May 1, 1953, CBS estimate.
‡ Retail jewelry-store sales, 1952—*Sales Management* estimate.
Source: Sullivan, Stauffer, Colwell & Bayles, Inc.

2. A report showing the coverage of the "What's My Name" show in metropolitan markets versus nonmetropolitan markets. This report is shown in Exhibit 5.

Exhibit 5

THE SPEIDEL CORPORATION

Coverage of "What's My Name?" in Metropolitan and Nonmetropolitan Markets

Table A: Relative Number of Jewelry Stores and Jewelry Sales Metropolitan Markets versus Nonmetropolitan Markets

	Stores		Sales	
Total United States.........21,269	100%	$1,224,878	100%
Metropolitan markets........11,517	54.2%	864,377	70.6%
Nonmetropolitan markets..... 9,752	45.8%	360,501	29.4%

Table B: Metropolitan Markets Covered by "What's My Name?"

	Stores		Sales	
Metropolitan markets........11,517	100%	$864,377	100%
TV market................10,074	87.5%	735,403	85.1%
Non-TV markets........... 1,443	12.5%	128,974	14.9%

Table C: "What's My Name?" Coverage of All United States Stores and Sales

	Stores		Sales	
Total United States.........21,269	100%	$1,224,878	100%
Covered by TV............10,074	47.4%	735,403	60.0%
Not covered by TV.........11,195	52.6%	489,475	40.0%

Note: This does not take into account areas outside of metropolitan markets which may be within coverage areas of stations originating in these markets.

Source: Sullivan, Stauffer, Colwell & Bayles, Inc.

3. A chart showing total United States homes using TV by hours of day in 1953. This chart is reproduced in Exhibit 6.
4. An analysis of TV audience composition by hours of day (see Exhibit 7).

Exhibit 6

THE SPEIDEL CORPORATION

Total United States Homes Using TV by Hours of Day (1952)

Hour	Homes	Hour	Homes
7:00– 8:00 A.M.....	631,000	3:00– 4:00 P.M.....	5,029,000
8:00– 9:00 A.M.....	1,534,000	4:00– 5:00 P.M.....	5,782,000
9:00–10:00 A.M.....	1,782,000	5:00– 6:00 P.M.....	7,329,000
10:00–11:00 A.M.....	3,202,000	6:00– 7:00 P.M.....	8,705,000
11:00–12:00 A.M.....	3,789,000	7:00– 8:00 P.M.....	11,028,000
12:00– 1:00 P.M.....	4,849,000	8:00– 9:00 P.M.....	14,343,000
1:00– 2:00 P.M.....	4,375,000	9:00–10:00 P.M.....	14,591,000
2:00– 3:00 P.M.....	4,510,000	10:00–11:00 P.M.....	13,148,000
		11:00–12:00 P.M.....	8,727,000

Source: Sponsor Magazine, July 1953.

Exhibit 7

THE SPEIDEL CORPORATION
TV Audience Composition by Time of Day

Monday–Friday	Men	Women	Children under 16	Viewers per Set
6:00– 9:00 A.M.	33%	52%	15%	1.9
9:00–12:00 A.M.	10	63	27	1.6
12:00– 3:00 P.M.	13	56	31	1.9
3:00– 6:00 P.M.	14	36	50	2.1
6:00 P.M.–midnight	36	44	20	2.8

Source: Sponsor Magazine, July 1953.

After examining these data and the information on those shows available to them, executives had tentatively narrowed their choice down to four program possibilities. They were:

1. *"Make Room for Daddy,"* starring Danny Thomas, a well-known movie actor. This show was a family situation comedy available from ABC-TV, 9:00–9:30 P.M., Tuesday. The talent cost was $21,850, and time charges amounted to approximately $27,000 for the full network with 97 stations cleared. Competing shows at that hour were:

> "Fireside Theater," NBC-TV............ARB rating, 23.8[6]
> "The Music Show," Du Mont-TV.......ARB rating, 3.0
> "City Hospital," CBS-TV..............ARB rating, 12.9

2. *"What's My Line?,"* a panel quiz show, available on a cosponsor basis over CBS-TV, 10:30–11:00 P.M., Sunday. Talent cost for this show was $8,500, and time charges were approximately $28,000. The show had a 41.0 ARB rating for percentage of sets reached in the coverage area. There were no competing network shows at that hour.

3. *"My Little Margie,"* a situation comedy show available over CBS-TV from 10:00–10:30 P.M., Thursday. The talent cost for this show was $23,000. Time charges were approximately $23,000. The show had a 33.9 ARB rating for percentage of sets reached in the coverage area. Competing shows at that hour were:

> "The Big Idea," Du Mont-TV............ARB rating, 2.5
> "Martin Kane, Private Eye," NBC-TV....ARB rating, 23.7

4. *"Name That Tune,"* a new show starring Red Benson, an orchestra leader unknown to the general public. This was a musical variety quiz

---

[6] American Research Bureau Television Audience Rating for July 1953. "This rating is based only on the sample in areas where the program can be seen. For example, if a program was telecast in New York, Philadelphia, and Los Angeles, the rating would reflect its standing in those three areas only. The rating reflects total audience for each period covered, not average coincidental audience. When viewing for five minutes or more is reported, credit for the quarter hour is given. For hour length programs, ratings are shown for each half hour."

show that could be inserted in Speidel's established time spot, 8:00–8:30 P.M., Monday, NBC-TV. The talent cost for this new show was $10,000 a show, and time charges amounted to approximately $30,000 for 64 stations. Competing shows at that hour were:

> "Burns and Allen," CBS-TV . . . . ARB rating, 25.7
> "Inspector Mark Saber," ABC-TV . . . . ARB rating, 8.9

~~~

CASE 27: THE AMERICAN OIL COMPANY[1]

QUESTION TO CONSIDER: *What advertising schedule would you recommend for use in Memphis, Tennessee, for a period of time commencing August 1, 1958?*

In January 1957 the American Oil Company, a wholly owned subsidiary of Standard Oil Company of Indiana and a marketer of gasoline in Texas and 18 states east of the Mississippi River under the "Amoco" brand name, absorbed the Pan Am Southern Corporation, which was also a subsidiary of Standard Oil of Indiana. Pam Am Southern marketed gasoline under the "Pan Am" brand name in six southern states. Subsequent to the acquisition, Amoco executives decided to convert the 4,628 Pan Am service stations from "Pan Am" gasoline to "Amoco" gasoline. This conversion would place Amoco's entire gasoline marketing effort in the eastern and southern United States under one brand, Amoco.

Decision to Change Pan Am to Amoco

The American Oil Company carried on gasoline marketing operations in 19 states and the District of Columbia, serving over 15,000 gasoline stations, not including the newly acquired Pan Am operation. In its six-state territory of Louisiana, Kentucky, Alabama, Arkansas, Mississippi, and Tennessee, Pan Am's 4,628 dealers (service stations with the name Pan Am) had about 7% of the gasoline market. Pan Am gasoline was sold both through dealer-operated stations and through distributors who owned their stations. The 250 Pan Am independent distributors did about 80% of Pan Am's business.

The decision to change the Pan Am stations to Amoco gasoline involved altering the service-station signs and gasoline pumps and also involved introducing a new type of gasoline. While both the regular and premium Pan Am gasoline contained lead, the Amoco premium gasoline was unleaded. For several years the American Oil Company had actively promoted the superior qualities of its unleaded gasoline, which sold for one

---

[1] Written by David W. Nylen and Martin V. Marshall.

cent more a gallon than competitive premium gasolines. Executives considered the unleaded Amoco gasoline promotion highly successful.

New Orleans Test

Rather than convert all Pan Am stations to Amoco at one time, American Oil executives decided to run a test conversion in New Orleans where Pan Am had been established for 35 years. From the test, executives hoped to learn whether consumers would accept unleaded Amoco gasoline and what promotional techniques were effective in introducing the product. In addition, American Oil executives believed that if the test was successful, the experience could be used to gain the enthusiasm of the other Pan Am dealers for the change to Amoco which was scheduled for August 1958.

New Orleans was selected as the test city for the following reasons: (1) it was the largest city in the Pan Am market; (2) it was located midway between two Amoco markets—Houston, Texas, and Pensacola, Florida; (3) the city of New Orleans had dealer-operated rather than distributor-operated stations, which made sales measurement easier; (4) a small area adjoining New Orleans which was distributor operated could also be converted as a check on that type of operation; (5) New Orleans had good media coverage; and (6) New Orleans was the headquarters of the Pan Am territory, therefore executives could be on hand to observe the test.

The New Orleans conversion was scheduled for March 1, 1958, with advertising introducing the unleaded Amoco gasoline scheduled to break the day before and continue through June 1958. The advertising schedule used in the initial month was very heavy, in order to startle consumers and attract attention. Because it was important that the New Orleans test be a successful example, a large promotional budget was made available for the test. Over the four-month period of the test, $70,000 was spent on radio and television time and newspaper space. This four-month expenditure amounted to about 1.75 cents a gallon of gasoline each month at the average sales of one million gallons a month in New Orleans. A separate and ample budget was made available for station decoration and point-of-sale material. Pan Am's already large outdoor advertising campaign was converted to advertising the Amoco introduction.

The advertising schedule used in New Orleans was as follows:

Newspapers. Eighteen full-page, three-color advertisements were run in all New Orleans newspapers in March. Six different advertisements were used to announce the Pan Am change-over to the Amoco name and Amoco unleaded gas. After March, 1,500-line and 1,800-line, black-and-white newspaper advertisements were run, with seven insertions in April, six insertions in May, and eight insertions in June. Total space costs were $31,000. Exhibits 1 and 2 show newspaper advertisements used in the introductory program.

Exhibit 1

AMERICAN OIL COMPANY

Example of Full-Page, Three-Color Newspaper Advertisement Used

in New Orleans

New in Greater New Orleans! Amoco-Gas *guarantees*

MORE GAS PER GALLON!

Available at all Pan-Am stations

You get more gas because only Amoco is all gas*!*

TIME: *Today.* **PLACE:** *Your Pan-Am station in Greater New Orleans*

PRODUCT: *Amoco-Gas, the original special motor fuel*

GUARANTEE: *More gas per gallon*

It's a fact! Amoco-Gas and only Amoco-Gas is all gas! It's untainted by lead...untinted by color...undiluted by additives.

That's why crystal clear Amoco-Gas guarantees you more gas per gallon. That's why Amoco-Gas gives you more mileage, unexcelled economy, smoothest performance, highest natural octane, most natural power, and greater engine protection. There's no lead in

clear Amoco-Gas to foul plugs, pistons and valves. There's no lead to hasten muffler wear. There's no color to stain carburetors.

Here's your chance to discover what millions of motorists from Maine to Florida now enjoy. Amoco-Gas saves you money in gasoline, saves you money in repairs. Premium Amoco-Gas gives you more motoring pleasure, more gas per gallon! Try your first tankful today!

The demand for Amoco-Gas far exceeds present supply. So, in this area, you can get it only in Greater New Orleans. Don't wait. Try your first tankful today. We hope to make Amoco-Gas available in other areas in the near future.

Drive in today for your free introductory gift!

HERE'S PROOF:

All other "gasolines" are only part gas

Here are the artificial combustion and octane elements you pay for in leaded "gasolines"

Only premium Amoco is all gas

Untainted by lead... *Untinted by color...* *Undiluted by additives*

CRYSTAL CLEAR

Exhibit 2

AMERICAN OIL COMPANY

Example of 1,500-Line, Black-and-White Newspaper Advertisement Used in New Orleans after March 1958

Only lead-free Amoco-Gas guarantees you

MORE GAS PER GALLON

You get more gas because only Amoco is all gas!

Now--your Pan-Am Dealer offers you a bonus, truly revolutionary in Greater New Orleans.

Your bonus is Amoco-Gas, the world's only gas that's all gas. Untainted by lead. Untinted by color. Undiluted by additives.

That's why crystal clear Amoco-Gas guarantees you: more gas per gallon! Every other "gasoline" but Amoco-Gas is only part gasoline...tainted by lead.. tinted by color...diluted by additives.

Today, at the service station with the welcoming Amoco-Gas sign, you get more gas per gallon. You get more for your money more natural power, highest natural octane, greater mileage, smoothest engine performance and—guaranteed engine protection. Since Amoco-Gas is untainted by lead, there's no lead to foul plugs, pistons or valves or to hasten muffler wear

AMERICAN OIL COMPANY

Here's your chance to enjoy the bonus that millions of motorists from Maine to Florida have been enjoying. Full gasoline, full power, full thrift. Amoco-Gas gives you more gas per gallon! Try your first tankful today!

The demand for Amoco-Gas far exceeds present supply So, in this area, you can get it only in Greater New Orleans. Don't wait. Try your first tankful today. We hope to make Amoco-Gas available in other areas in the near future.

Available at all
Pan-Am Stations

HERE'S PROOF:

All other "gasolines" are only part gas

Here are the artificial combustion and octane elements you pay for in leaded "gasolines"

Only premium Amoco is all gas

CRYSTAL CLEAR

Untainted by lead...
Untinted by color..
Undiluted by additives

Radio. A saturation radio campaign was used with 525 one-minute spot announcements in March and 936 spot announcements in the period April–June. A variety of commercials were used based upon an Amoco jingle. Total radio time costs in New Orleans were $15,000.

Television. Two New Orleans television stations were used, and 63 one-minute spot announcements were run in March and 104 additional spot announcements in the next three months. Total time cost was $23,-000.

Outdoor. Thirty-six posters, 30-sheet size, in the New Orleans area were devoted to the Amoco introduction from March to June. Thirty-five railway express trucks also carried signs similar to the billboard posters announcing the new product. Exhibit 3 shows two of the introductory posters.

Exhibit 3

AMERICAN OIL COMPANY

Two of the Outdoor Advertisements Used in Introductory Campaign
in New Orleans

Point of sale. A large variety of point-of-sale material was given to service-station operators. The material consisted of pole signs, one sheet A-board posterettes with a spinning arrow afixed to the top, pump stickers, large and small window signs, large cardboard arrows attached to heavy roping to be strung from the pole sign to the light stanchion, island banners, and 600-foot pennant strings. The copy on the signs and posters concentrated on the introduction of the new product and the superior qualities of Amoco.

Special events. Five public-address systems were used on a rotating basis in stations, making periodic announcements about the new product and broadcasting the Amoco jingle. Five clowns, working in conjunction with the public-address systems, passed out free gifts of Amoco key chains, mechanical pencils, and book matches.

Amoco executives evaluated the success of the change-over by comparing sales and the premium ratio before and after the change. The premium ratio was the percentage of total sales represented by premium-grade gasoline. An increase in the premium ratio was considered desirable since it represented increased sales of higher-margined gasoline. In addition, in the New Orleans test, executives believed that an increasing premium ratio would indicate that the New Orleans promotional program was effective because the promotion was concentrated on Amoco unleaded gas, the premium grade.

In March 1958, the first month of the conversion, despite stormy weather which usually reduced gasoline sales, New Orleans Amoco sales were 27.6% above Pan Am sales of March the previous year, and the premium ratio increased from 42.2% in March 1957 to 49.3% in March 1958. When the rural areas surrounding New Orleans, which had also been converted to Amoco, were included in the comparison, the sales increase was 21.9% over the same month a year earlier and the premium ratio increased from 26.3% to 44.2%. The sales figures for the months following March continued to show approximately similar gains over the same month a year earlier.

Expansion of Change-over to Remainder of Pan Am Territory

The change-over of the remainder of the Pan Am territory to Amoco was scheduled to take place on August 1, 1958, and a meeting with distributors to explain the change and the accompanying promotion was scheduled for May 1958. Amoco executives had decided upon a total budget for the change-over promotion of $270,000 for newspaper space and radio and television time. This represented about 25% less money in proportion to average sales than was spent in the New Orleans test. As in New Orleans, a separate budget was established for point-of-sale and station decoration material. This budget, which allowed about $40 each for the large stations, was a slightly lower amount per station than was spent in New Orleans but was adequate to supply each station with a ten-foot pole sign, several one-sheet posters, window streamers, and 600 feet of red, white, and blue pennants. Outdoor advertising and Railway Express posters were a part of Pan Am's regular advertising program and could be used for the Amoco introduction as in New Orleans.

The six-state Pan Am territory, excluding New Orleans which had already been converted, included 54 markets that sold over 100,000 gallons a year, ranging from 129,000 gallons for the smallest to 16,000,000 gallons for the largest. For planning the promotional program, the markets were divided into "A," "B," and "C" markets as follows:

7 "A" markets with sales over 5,000,000 gal./year.
18 "B" markets with sales from 1,000,000 gal./year to 5,000,000 gal./year.
29 "C" markets with sales from 100,000 gal./year to 1,000,000 gal./year.

The budget of $270,000 was apportioned to each market in proportion to the average gallonage of that market. Executives of Amoco and the Amoco advertising agency, The Joseph Katz Company, hoped to use radio, television, and newspaper advertising in all markets, except the "C" markets where weekly newspapers and some radio stations were available. The executives were undecided as to how to cut down the program used in New Orleans in order that it would fit the reduced budget. They considered either shortening the length of the campaign or decreasing the intensity of the advertising.

One of the Pan Am "A" markets to be converted to Amoco was Memphis, Tennessee. The average annual sales in Memphis were 8,000,000 gallons. Memphis stations were served by an Amoco-owned bulk processing plant and were dealer operated. The pro rata share of the budget available for Memphis was $25,610 for newspaper space and radio and television time charges. Art and production charges would be negligible since the material developed for the New Orleans test would be reused. Point-of-purchase material and outdoor advertising were available under a different budget. Exhibits 4, 5, and 6 give cost data on newspapers, radio, and television in the Memphis market.

Exhibit 4

AMERICAN OIL COMPANY
Memphis, Tennessee, Newspaper Data

Commercial Appeal—morning and Sunday
Press-Scimitar—evening except Sunday
  (A Scripps-Howard Newspaper)

Line Rate:
  Press-Scimitar and *Commercial Appeal* combination............$1.00
  Press-Scimitar (evening).................................... 0.65
  Commercial Appeal (morning)............................ 0.81
  Commercial Appeal (Sunday) 0.85

Bulk Linage Discounts:
  Less than 1,000 lines.....No discount
  1,000– 4,999 lines...........13%
  5,000– 9,999 lines...........14
  10,000–24,999 lines...........15
  25,000–49,999 lines...........16
  50,000–99,999 lines...........17
  100,000 lines or more..........18

Full-Page ROP Discounts:
   1 full-page unit...............13%
   5 full-page units..............15
  10 full-page units..............16
  20 full-page units..............17
  30 full-page units..............18
  40 full-page units..............19
  50 full-page units..............20

	Comb.	CA	P-S	CA
Extra Costs for Color:	*(M&E)*	*(M)*	*(E)*	*(S)*
Black and 1 color...................	$375	$200	$175	$275
Black and 2 colors.................	500	275	225	375
Black and 3 colors.................	650	350	300	450

CIRCULATION (NET PAID—ABC 9/30/57)

	Total	City Zone	Retail Trade Zone	Other
Morning.............	201,143	94,553	44,585	62,005
Evening.............	146,169	90,836	27,390	27,943
Morning and evening...	347,312	185,389	71,975	89,947
Sunday.............	247,850	112,537	56,664	78,649

Notes: Where color is used, discounts apply to space only, not to color premiums.
Minimum size for color advertisements 1,000 lines.

Source: Standard Rate & Data Service, April 15, 1958.

Exhibit 5

AMERICAN OIL COMPANY

Memphis, Tennessee, Radio Data

Power (Watts)		Time of Operation	Time Class	One-Minute Time Charges in Dollars						
				One Time	13 Times	26 Times	52 Times	104 Times	156 Times
KWEM	1,000	Sunrise to sunset	All	$12.00	....	$11.40	$10.80	$10.20	$ 9.60
WDIA	50,000 day								
	5,000 night	4:00 A.M.–12:00 M	All	24.00	....	22.80	21.70	20.60	19.60
WHBQ	5,000 day								
	1,000 night	5:00 A.M.–12:00 M	All	18.00	....	17.10	16.20	15.30	14.40
WHER	1,000	6:00 A.M. to sunset	All	5.60	$ 5.30	5.00	4.70	4.40	4.10
WHHM	250	6:00 A.M.–12:00 M	All	12.00	11.40	10.80	10.20	9.60	9.00
WLOK	5,000	4:00 A.M. to sunset	All	7.50	7.25	7.00	6.75	6.50	6.25
WMC	5,000	Sunday, 7:00 P.M.–12:00 M	Daytime	....	13.50	11.50	10.50	9.00	....
(NBC)		Weekdays, 5:00 A.M.–12:00 M	Evening	....	9.00	8.00	7.00	6.00	....
WMPS	10,000 day	24 hrs. daily	6:00 A.M.–7:00 P.M.	....	....	....	23.00	22.80	21.60
	5,000 night		7:00 P.M.–6:00 A.M.	....	....	....	13.30	12.60	11.90
WREC	5,000	Sunday, 7:00 A.M.–12:05 A.M.	6:00 A.M.–10:30 P.M.	25.00	23.75	22.50	21.25	20.00	18.75
(CBS)		Weekdays, 5:00 A.M.–12:05 A.M.	10:30 P.M.–6:00 A.M.	17.00	16.15	15.30	14.45	13.60	12.75

Note: Considerable additional data as to special features available and charges for time periods of other than one minute are contained in SRDS.

Source: Standard Rate & Data Service, April 1, 1958.

Exhibit 6

AMERICAN OIL COMPANY
Memphis, Tennessee, Television Data

WHBQ-TV, ABC Television Network
Facilities—Video 316,000 watts, audio 160,000 watts, channel 13.
Antenna height: 1,013 feet above average terrain.
Operating schedule: 10:30 A.M. to midnight Monday through
Friday; noon to midnight Saturday and Sunday.

BASIC RATES, ONE-MINUTE SPOT ANNOUNCEMENTS

Class	1 Time	26 Times	52 Times	104 Times
(AA) 7:00 P.M.–9:30 P.M. daily...........	$200	$190	$180	$170
(A) 6:30 P.M.–7:00 P.M. and 9:30 P.M.– 10:30 daily....................	175	166	158	149
(B) 5:00 P.M.–6:30 P.M. daily and noon to 6:30 P.M. Sun...............	105	100	95	89
(C) Sign-on to 5:00 P.M. Mon.–Sat. and 11:00 P.M. to sign-off daily........	56	53	50	48

WMCT-TV, Basic NBC Network
Facilities—Video 100,000 watts, audio 60,000 watts, channel 5.
Antenna height: 1,013 feet above average terrain.
Operating schedule: 7:00 A.M.–12:00 midnight Monday through
Saturday; 10:00 A.M.–to 12:00 midnight Sunday.

BASIC RATES, ONE-MINUTE SPOT ANNOUNCEMENTS

Class	1 Time	26 Times	52 Times	104 Times
(AA) 7:00 P.M.–10:00 P.M. daily.........	$200	$195	$190	$180
(A) 6:30 P.M.–7:00 P.M. and 10:00 P.M. to 10:30 P.M..................	150	143	135	128
(B) 5:30 P.M.–6:30 P.M. Mon.–Sat.; 10:30 P.M.–11:00 P.M. daily; noon to 6:30 P.M. Sun...........	105	100	95	89
(C) All other times..................	70	67	63	60

WREC-TV, Basic CBS Network
Facilities—Video 100,000 watts, audio 60,000 watts, channel 3.
Antenna height: 1,002 feet above average terrain.
Operating schedule: 7:00 A.M. to 12:00 midnight Monday
through Friday; 8:00 A.M. to 12:00 midnight Saturday;
9:00 A.M. to 12:00 midnight Sunday.

Exhibit 6—Continued

BASIC RATES, ONE-MINUTE SPOT ANNOUNCEMENTS

Class	1 Time	26 Times	52 Times	104 Times
(AA) 7:00 P.M.–10:00 P.M. Mon.–Sat.; 6:30–10:00 P.M. Sun.............	$200	$195	$190	$180
(A) 6:30 P.M.–7:00 P.M. and 10:00 P.M.– 10:30 P.M. Mon.–Sat.; 10:00 P.M.– 10:30 P.M. Sat...................	175	166	158	149
(B) 5:30 P.M.–6:30 P.M. and 10:30 P.M.– 11:00 P.M. Mon.–Sat.............	105	100	95	89
(C) 8:00 A.M.–5:30 P.M. and 11:00 P.M. to sign-off Mon.–Fri. Sign-on to 5:30 P.M. and 11:00 P.M. to sign- off Sat. 5:00 P.M. to 5:30 P.M. and 11:00 P.M. to sign-off Sun.........	70	67	63	60
(D) Sign-on to 8:00 A.M. Mon.–Fri.; Sign- on 5:00 P.M. Sun................	45	43	41	38

Source: Standard Rate & Data Service, April 10, 1958.

~~~

CASE 28: PAN-AMERICAN COFFEE BUREAU (E)[1]

NOTE: *This second series of Pan-American Coffee Bureau cases concerns the planning of the Bureau's advertising program for the first half of 1958.* QUESTION TO CONSIDER: *How would you go about selecting the three advertisements to be tested for the new campaign?*

The Pan-American Coffee Bureau, through its director of advertising, Mr. Edward E. Van Horn, instructed its advertising agency, Fuller & Smith & Ross,[2] to create a campaign for the first half of 1958 which would help arrest the trend to the brewing of weaker coffee. The advertisements, for which $250,000 had been budgeted, were to run largely in consumer magazines. The decision to make a more direct attack on the problem of getting people to brew stronger coffee was made after a review of marketing data, past promotional efforts, and new information supplied by the Coffee Brewing Institute on what constituted an optimum brewing formula. Per capita consumption of coffee in the United States had been off substantially since 1946, and data on coffee brewing practices in American households showed that the average extraction rate for regular coffee had risen from approximately 46 cups per pound in 1949 to 64 cups per pound in 1957.

Work done by the Coffee Brewing Institute and others had led Dr.

---

[1] Written by Joseph W. Newman.

[2] Robert W. Orr & Associates, Inc., which had served the Bureau for several years, was absorbed by Fuller & Smith & Ross in 1957 after Mr. Orr's death.

Ernest E. Lockhart, the Institute's scientific director, to believe that there was an optimum rate of extraction of solids from the coffee beans which actually was exceeded in most coffee making, producing bitter, unacceptable coffee. In his opinion, this bitterness commonly had been passed off as strength by the consumer who had to dilute the coffee in order to lessen the intensity of the unpleasant effect. He believed that people would prefer stronger coffee, as they had before 1950, if it were properly made. The hope of starting a trend toward stronger coffee, he said, lay in getting people to make coffee in such a way that the optimum rate of extraction would not be exceeded. Bureau executives decided to try to do this.

A platform to guide the creative work on the advertisements was outlined by Mr. Richard Russell, account executive, as follows:

1. Establish a reasonable doubt in the consumer's mind that his or her coffee is not being brewed properly.
2. Show how coffee should be brewed.
3. Offer a reward of self-benefit if the coffee is brewed properly.

Batches of rough advertisements were prepared by the agency in July and August 1957, during which time there were 15 meetings of agency and client personnel. At these sessions, the advertisements were screened. The discussions gave rise to new ideas which were incorporated in still other advertisements. Each of the advertisements included a recipe for proper coffee brewing, based on Coffee Brewing Institute specifications.

At a final screening meeting, attended by both client and agency executives, 17 rough advertisements were inspected. From this number, several advertisements (preferably no more than three) were to be selected for consumer testing.

A listing of the rough advertisements (see Exhibits 1–17) appears below:

Exhibit 1

PAN-AMERICAN COFFEE BUREAU (E)

REALLY GOOD COFFEE!
and here's how to make it ➔

REALLY GOOD COFFEE

You can now make the best cup of coffee in the world, right in your own home, using your own favorite brand! Start with your own coffee maker, spotlessly clean — and clear, cold water. Measure carefully.

FULL-STRENGTH: per cup, 1 standard measure (2 level measuring tablespoons) and 6 ounces of water

MEDIUM: per cup, 1 standard measure and 7 ounces of water

WEAK: per cup, 1 standard measure and 8 ounces of water

Never boil coffee — and never use more water than recommended above. You'll happily discover all over again how good coffee can be!

NOTE: if you use "instant", vary the strength to suit your taste.

PAN-AMERICAN COFFEE BUREAU, 120 Wall Street, New York 5, N. Y.

Exhibit 2

PAN-AMERICAN COFFEE BUREAU (E)

"If you could only make coffee..."

But honey you can. It's easy with this simple recipe. Keep in mind the old, old maxim: "many a good marriage is made in the pot." Follow the directions for full-strength coffee. Measure c-a-r-e-f-u-l-l-y. Give him a man's coffee. That's all there is to it. Pan-American Coffee Bureau, 120 Wall St., New York 5, N. Y.

GOOD COFFEE EVERY TIME

You can now make the best cup of coffee in the world, right in your own home, using your own favorite brand! Start with your own coffee maker, spotlessly clean — and clear, cold water. Measure carefully:

FULL-STRENGTH: per cup, 1 standard measure (2 level measuring tablespoons) and 6 ounces of water.

MEDIUM: per cup, 1 standard measure and 7 ounces of water.

WEAK: per cup, 1 standard measure and 8 ounces of water.

Never boil coffee—and never use more water than recommended above. You'll happily discover all over again how _good_ coffee can be!

NOTE: if you use "instant", vary the strength to suit your taste.

Exhibit 3

PAN-AMERICAN COFFEE BUREAU (E)

Exhibit 4

PAN-AMERICAN COFFEE BUREAU (E)

Exhibit 5
PAN-AMERICAN COFFEE BUREAU (E)

Exhibit 6

PAN-AMERICAN COFFEE BUREAU (E)

Exhibit 7

PAN-AMERICAN COFFEE BUREAU (E)

Exhibit 8
PAN-AMERICAN COFFEE BUREAU (E)

Exhibit 9

PAN-AMERICAN COFFEE BUREAU (E)

I like my steak thick...
and my coffee full-strength

I make his coffee full-strength
...he thinks I'm a genius!

Exhibit 10

PAN-AMERICAN COFFEE BUREAU (E)

Exhibit 11
PAN-AMERICAN COFFEE BUREAU (E)

Exhibit 12
PAN-AMERICAN COFFEE BUREAU (E)

America-on-the-go
goes for full-strength coffee

Exhibit 13

PAN-AMERICAN COFFEE BUREAU (E)

Exhibit 14
PAN-AMERICAN COFFEE BUREAU (E)

Try this simple coffee experiment

...and remember ... add one for the pot

Exhibit 15
PAN-AMERICAN COFFEE BUREAU (E)

"I like my steak thick – and my coffee full strength"

Exhibit 16
PAN-AMERICAN COFFEE BUREAU (E)

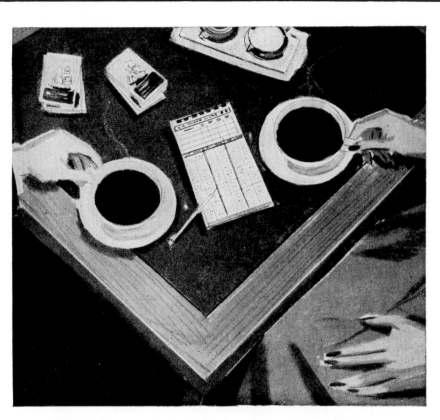

Perfect end to a Perfect Party

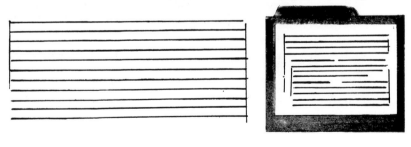

Exhibit 17
PAN-AMERICAN COFFEE BUREAU (E)

Exhibit	Headline of Advertisement
1.	Really good coffee! and here's how to make it
2.	"If you could only make coffee . . ."
3.	Half-hostess, ME?
4.	Have we lost the knack of making good coffee?
5.	Was coffee better in the "good old days?"
6.	Does your husband like someone else's coffee better than yours?
7.	Krisis in the kitchen
8.	Is your husband's disposition worth two cents?
9.	I like my steak thick . . . and my coffee full strength . . . I make his coffee full strength . . . he thinks I'm a genius (two advertisements to appear on facing pages)
10.	The secret of good coffee is you!
11.	Don't be a coffee miser
12.	America-on-the-go goes for full-strength coffee
13.	Try this simple coffee experiment (string on finger in illustration)
14.	Try this simple coffee experiment (illustration of woman drinking coffee)
15.	"I like my steak thick—and my coffee full strength."
16.	Perfect end to a perfect party
17.	Can your coffee pass the guest-test?

~ ~ ~

CASE 29: PAN-AMERICAN COFFEE BUREAU (F)[1]

QUESTIONS TO CONSIDER: (1) *What did the advertising agency seek to measure in its test?* (2) *What alternative methods of testing might have been employed?* (3) *What was learned from the test?* (4) *What approach do you think should be employed in the Bureau's advertising for the first half of 1958?*

After the rough layouts shown in Case (E) had been prepared and discussed in a series of client-agency meetings, three advertisements representing different approaches were selected for consumer testing to determine which one promised to be most effective in getting the stronger coffee story across (see Exhibits 1–3 in Case E). The test was conducted by the agency's research department which employed a set of criteria the agency had developed over a period of years.

The research approach and findings were described in a 90-page report prepared by Mr. Lawrence E. Dorne, research associate. His description of the method and scope of the study and his summary of findings appear below:

Research Method and Scope

Attitudes and reactions toward these advertisements were gathered from male and female heads of households where coffee was brewed from

---

[1] Written by Joseph W. Newman.

the ground bean. Only one person in a household was interviewed. In total, 408 interviews were conducted, as follows:

	Total	Coffee Cup	Cartoon	Black-and-White Close-up
Male........	154	51	50	53
Female.......	254	87	85	82
Total........	408	138	135	135

Due to regional differences in coffee extraction rates, the number interviewed on each advertisement was distributed evenly among the following four cities, each chosen to represent the extraction rate prevalent in its region:

City	Extraction Rate (Cups per Pound)
Boston..................................	55.71
Atlanta.................................	60.06
Minneapolis–St. Paul......................	69.62
San Francisco–Oakland.....................	72.32

In each city used, at least three interviewers were deployed in areas selected to produce an adequate representation of the city's middle economic levels. Each interviewer was instructed to conduct an equal number of interviews in her designated areas on each of the advertisements tested. Interviewing was done in person in the respondent's home. (See Exhibit 1 for classification data on respondents.)

Exhibit 1

PAN-AMERICAN COFFEE BUREAU (F)

Classification Data

NUMBER WHO DRINK COFFEE (PER HOUSEHOLD)	ADVERTISEMENT SHOWN			
	Total	Coffee Cup	Cartoon	Black-and-White Close-up
One.....................	15%	16%	14%	16%
Two.....................	60	62	59	58
Three...................	17	14	20	16
Four....................	5	5	6	5
Five....................	1	1	1	3
Six.....................	1	....	....	2
No report................	1	2	....	....

Among all the coffee users contacted, use of instant and ground coffee was as follows: instant users only, 27%; ground coffee users only, 35%; both, 38%. Only the latter two groups were interviewed on this copy pretest.

Exhibit 1—Continued

POUNDS OF GROUND COFFEE CONSUMED PER WEEK (PER HOUSEHOLD)	ADVERTISEMENT SHOWN			
	Total	Coffee Cup	Cartoon	Black-and-White Close-up
Less than ½ pound.........	8%	9%	7%	8%
½ pound to less than 1 pound..	21	21	21	21
1 pound to less than 1½ pounds...................	46	47	43	50
1½ pounds to less than 2 pounds...................	7	7	7	7
2 pounds to less than 2½ pounds...................	13	12	16	11
2½ pounds and over........	4	3	5	3
No report.................	1	1	1	....
*Base for percentages.......	408	138	135	135

* Total respondents shown advertisement.

Reported Consumption Rates Related to Other Characteristics Respondent

CHARACTERISTICS	CONSUMPTION RATE (POUNDS OF GROUND COFFEE PER USER PER WEEK)			
	High (1 Pound and Over)	Medium (½ Pound to Less than 1 Pound)	Low (Less than ½ Pound)	Not Reported
All respondents...............	15%	50%	34%	1%
By sex:				
Male...................	14	54	31	1
Female.................	15	47	37	1
By city:				
Boston.................	14	51	35	....
Atlanta................	12	48	40	....
Minneapolis............	14	53	32	1
San Francisco...........	20	46	31	3
By ad shown:				
Coffee cup..............	13	51	34	2
Cartoon................	16	50	33	1
Black-and-white close-up...	15	49	36	....

Note: Totals reading across are 100%.

During the interview, a single advertisement was shown the man or woman in order to gain an absolute evaluation of the potential impact of the advertisement when free from extraneous influences. Once a qualified respondent was contacted, he or she was asked to read a single advertisement thoroughly. The interviewer then removed the advertisement from sight and questioned him or her concerning the following points:

What was remembered from the advertisement and what it *meant* to the respondent.

Exhibit 2

PAN-AMERICAN COFFEE BUREAU (F)

American Research Associates   September, 1957
230 Park Avenue   P. O. S–6925
New York 17, New York

COFFEE-MAKING AD QUESTIONNAIRE

"I'm making a survey about coffee."
1. Is coffee served in your home?
      Yes ( ) Ask (*a*).   No ( ) End interview. *Do not count toward quota.*
   a) In your home, is coffee made from:
      Instant coffee only? ( ) End interview. *Do not count toward quota.*
          Ground coffee only?   ( )
          Both instant and ground? ( ) Continue with interview.
"Here is an advertisement about coffee. Would you please read this ad thoroughly so
we can talk about it for a moment."
   (Hand ad to respondent and allow as much time as he or she will take to read it
   thoroughly. Rotate your ads so the first respondent sees Ad "A," the second,
   Ad "B," and so forth. Check sex of respondent and which ad shown.)
          Sex of respondent: Male ( )   Female ( )
          Ad shown respondent: Ad A ( )   Ad B ( )   Ad C ( )
   (Remove ad from sight before asking Question 2.)
2. Would you please tell me everything that you can remember *reading* in this ad?
   Anything else?
   a) What does this mean to you personally? Anything else?
3. What did the illustration(s) show? Do you remember anything else about the
   picture(s)?
   a) What did the illustration(s) tell you about coffee or coffee making? Anything
      else? What does this mean to you?
   (After this point, ad may be shown to respondent again if desired.)
4. (Show attitude scale.) Here is a card numbered from zero to ten. We are using this
   card to find out how *interesting* this ad is to you. The *more* interesting it is, the
   higher the number you should select. If it is of *low* interest, you should give me a
   low number. Now, using the scale, please tell me how interesting you found this ad.
   (Circle number chosen.)
          0   1   2   3   4   5   6   7   8   9   10
   a) Why did you select this score rather than one higher or lower?
5. Using the scale again, tell me how *important* to you is the information contained
   in this ad. (Circle number chosen.)
          0   1   2   3   4   5   6   7   8   9   10
   a) Why did you select this score rather than one higher or lower?
6. Was there anything in the ad that you found hard to believe?
          Yes ( ) Ask (*a*).   No ( ) Go to Question 7.
   a) Please tell me about it. Anything else?
7. Was there anything in the ad that you found hard to understand?
          Yes ( ) Ask (*a*).   No ( ) Go to Question 8.
   a) Please tell me about that. Anything else?
8. Was there any question the ad raised but failed to answer, or any information you
   think it should have included but didn't?
          Yes ( ) Ask (*a*).   No ( ) Go to Question 9.
   a) Please tell me about that. Anything else?
9. Is there anything about this ad that bothers you, or makes you feel uncomfortable?
          Yes ( ) Ask (*a*).   No ( ) Go to Question 10.
   a) Please tell me about that. Anything else?
10. Is there anything about this ad that makes you feel pleased about coffee or coffee
    making?
          Yes ( ) Ask (*a*).   No ( ) Go to Question 11.
    a) Please tell me about that. Anything else?
    (Ask respondent to read recipe again)

Exhibit 2—Continued

11. This ad uses the words "full-strength, medium, and weak" to describe three different kinds of coffee. How do you feel about describing coffee in these ways? Please tell me if there is anything you *dislike* about these descriptions.

12. If you came across this ad in a magazine, do you think you would cut out the recipe and save it?

     Yes ( ) Go to Question 13. No ( ) Ask (*a*).
 a) Why not?

13. On the average, about how many *pounds* of *ground coffee* is bought or used per week in your household?_____pounds

14. How many people in your household drink coffee?_____people

Name of Respondent_____

Street Address_____City and State_____

Date_____Interviewer_____

Time interview completed_____A.M. P.M. (Circle time applicable.)

THANK YOU VERY MUCH

What the illustration showed; what it communicated about coffee making.

How interesting the respondent found the advertisement to be (scored in terms of an attitude rating scale). How important its message was considered.

Anything found hard to believe about the advertisement.

Anything hard to understand.

Any more information which the advertisement should have supplied.

A series of questions to pinpoint the respondent's emotional reaction to the advertisement in terms of positive or negative feelings aroused by it.

Whether he or she would cut out the recipe to save if they came across it in a magazine.

As is indicated in the above questioning procedure, this type of test is designed to evaluate the communicative power of the advertisement *when it is read, not* its initial stopping power. However, the extent to which the advertisements studied possess this important characteristic can be evaluated by other methods familiar to Fuller & Smith & Ross. (See Exhibit 2 for a copy of the questionnaire.)

Analysis and reporting of findings. By analysis of the information secured by field interviewers, a comparative evaluation has been made of the scores or ratings received by each advertisement on the various performance measures applied. These findings are reported in detail in the pages following.

Summary of Findings

Over-all rating of the advertisements. Of the three advertisements tested, the coffee cup promises the greatest over-all communicative effectiveness. The cartoon shows slightly less potential, while the black-and-white close-up is in third place.

Specific strengths and weaknesses. In all these advertisements, the strongest element was the coffee recipe. The recipe was found to carry heavy impact regardless of the strength of the rest of the advertisement. It was remembered in extensive detail even from those advertisements where there was a considerable amount of other copy competing for the reader's attention. But because the recipe did overshadow the other parts of the advertisement, some of the test measures applied, such as importance, did not indicate significant performance differences among the three advertisements.

Wherever further information was sought about any part of the advertisement, the question was generally directed toward the recipe. While this indicates that the recipe has high intrinsic interest, it also poses a problem. Quite a few readers asked for clarification of various recipe details. Since the recipe is so strong overall, and since it is the only copy element in the best-performing advertisement, it is vital that all effort be bent to make the recipe as clear as possible.

Each of the illustrations showed some points of strength and some points of weakness. The coffee cup illustration left readers with a pleased feeling about coffee making. It was mainly responsible for the high interest, believability, and understandability scores which that advertisement received. But some unfavorable comments were received about the color of the coffee in the cup.

The cartoon illustrations were recalled in considerable detail by those who read that advertisement. But that advertisement was lower in interest, believability, and understandability (among women) than was the coffee cup. The black-and-white close-up, together with its accompanying copy, was found least effective on a majority of the measures applied.

Summary of Test Scores

	ADVERTISEMENT SHOWN		
TEST MEASURE	Coffee Cup	Cartoon	Black-and-White Close-up
Average number of *copy points recalled* by each reader............	2.45	2.19	2.10
Percentage of readers reporting *favorable reaction to copy*..........	39	33	30
Percentage who felt *pleased about coffee making* after reading ad.....	50	39	34
Percentage whom the ad *did not make feel uncomfortable*..............	87	87	92
Average number of *illustration points recalled* by each reader...........	1.26	1.59	1.15
Percentage who *associated some further meaning* to the pictures......	68	75	37
Interest score.....................	62	55	43
Importance score..................	51	54	47
Believability (percentage who found nothing hard to believe).........	88	80	84
Understandability (percentage who found nothing hard to understand)..	92	89	91
Informativeness (percentage who asked no further question about the subject)....................	79	84	83
Recipe (percentage who report they would save the recipe)...........	25	33	29

A description and interpretation of these test measures appears in the pages following:

Copy recall. The amount and variety of the information recalled (or inferred) from reading the copy is one of the clearest indices of an advertisement's impact. While details of the recipe were heavily recalled among readers of all three advertisements, this was particularly true for the coffee cup, where the recipe had no copy competition. Other copy recall concerned specific features of the individual advertisements.

Copy meaning (including attitude toward the copy recalled). Perhaps because of the light technique used, the cartoon advertisement drew the fewest unfavorable reactions toward the *content* of the copy. But the coffee cup drew the greatest number of favorable responses. Since readers concentrated their attention on the recipe, the differences on this measure were not extensive.

What in the advertisement pleased readers. To probe more deeply into readers' reactions, all were asked whether *anything* about the advertisement they read made them feel pleased about coffee or coffee making. Among women, the coffee cup performed by far the best, while the black-and-white close-up did least well. Among men, the advertisements scored about equally, although the scores were generally lower than for women. These reader reactions appeared to be directed mainly toward the illustration rather than the copy.

What in the advertisement made readers feel uncomfortable. There were no extensive differences in the size of the groups reporting a negative reaction to anything in the advertisement they were shown. Those unfavorable reactions which did occur were occasioned mostly by the illustration or the situation it depicted.

Recall of the illustration and what the illustration meant to readers. Because of the extensive detail in the cartoon illustration, more detail was recalled about it than about either of the others. It also stimulated a greater number of associated meanings. The coffee cup did relatively well on these measures, while the black-and-white close-up performed noticeably less well.

Interest scores. The coffee cup proved by far the most interesting advertisement of the three, with the cartoon next. In general, the degree of interest these advertisements evoked was a direct reaction to the illustration used. It is worth noting that readers were considerably more interested in the coffee cup than in the cartoon, *despite* the fact that they recalled more detail about the latter.

Importance scores. Since readers' evaluation for importance was based primarily on their reaction to the recipe, scores for that measure did not vary greatly among the three advertisements tested. However, the cartoon and the coffee cup were ahead by a slight margin.

Believability. The straightforward coffee cup advertisement was easily the most believable. However, some details in the recipe were questioned. Because some readers found the party situation exaggerated, the cartoon was least believable.

Understandability. Except among women, differences in understandability were not significant. Among women the coffee cup was noticeably superior to the cartoon. Most of the things found hard to understand concerned some detail of the coffee recipe.

Informativeness. Informativeness scores represent the percentage of readers who had no further question about the advertisement. For these advertisements, most of the questions raised concerned the recipe. Since the coffee cup had no other copy to deflect attention from the recipe, that advertisement drew the greatest number of further questions and had the lowest "informativeness" score. In such a situation, a low score may be considered advantageous, since numerous questions provide merely another indication of a strong degree of interest rather than denoting an actual lack of informativeness. A study of the questions raised about the individual advertisements will be found particularly revealing.

Saving the recipe. As an additional index of the advertisements' over-all impact, readers were asked whether they would cut out the recipe and save it if they saw it printed in a magazine. Data from such a question may not be taken as a prediction of expected action, but they are useful for comparative purposes. Perhaps because of the word "secret" repeated on the recipe tab in the cartoon advertisement, more readers would clip that recipe than either of the others.

Evaluation of "full-strength, medium, and weak" as descriptive words for coffee. To find out whether there would be reader resistance to any of the words used to describe various coffee strengths, readers were asked for their reactions to the words "full-strength, medium, and weak." As a result, it appears that using "weak" will not create a serious problem. Further, it may be considered advisable to replace "full-strength" with "strong."

A reading of the detailed findings, with their accompanying tables, will point up a number of specific strengths and weaknesses in the three advertisements tested, which may be utilized to good advantage in finalizing the campaign selected.

Each section of the detailed report contained discussions of the findings and tabulations upon which they were based. In order to further illustrate the nature of the report, the first section on "Copy Recall" is reproduced in its entirety and selected summary statements from other sections are included in Exhibit 3.

A reading of the detailed findings, with their accompanying tables, will point up a number of specific strengths and weaknesses in the three advertisements tested, which may be utilized to good advantage in finalizing the campaign selected.

Each section of the detailed report contained discussions of the findings and tabulations upon which they were based. In order to further illustrate the nature of the report, the first section on "Copy Recall" is reproduced in its entirety and selected summary statements from other sections are included in Exhibit 3.

Exhibit 3

COPY RECALL

Although the coffee cup advertisement contained considerably less copy than the other advertisements tested, it was the best recalled of the three. Each advertisement was somewhat better remembered by women than by men.

AVERAGE NUMBER OF COPY POINTS RECALLED

	Coffee Cup	Cartoon	Black-and-White Close-up
All respondents...............	2.45	2.19	2.10
Male........................	2.13	1.94	2.06
Female.....................	2.64	2.34	2.11

Because it had no competition for reader attention in the coffee cup advertisement, the recipe was remembered most thoroughly by those shown that advertisement. But, in all the advertisements tested, several details of the recipe were found to have high retention value.

In particular, the instruction never to boil coffee attracted attention among a high proportion of readers. To some, this was a new and unfamiliar aspect of coffee making. To others, "never boiling" posed a variety of problems (which will be covered more thoroughly later).

Another part of the recipe which readers found especially memorable was the separate directions given for making coffee in three different strengths. In this connection, quite a few recalled that the recipe told them how much coffee to use, or how much water to use. Less precisely, some made general mention that the advertisement they saw contained a recipe for making coffee.

Still other details of the recipe found to have high retention value included using cold water, making certain that the pot was clean, and measuring the ingredients carefully.

Details from the Individual Advertisements.

Coffee Cup: A third of the readers of the coffee cup advertisement remembered in one form or another the headline claim about making good coffee.

Cartoon: One in five remembered the "Half-hostess, ME?" headline from the cartoon advertisement. An even greater number (37 per cent) recalled that the coffee at the party was too weak. Still others supplied the sequel: The half-hostess tried and succeeded with Mary's recipe for making coffee.

Black-and-White Close-up: This advertisement achieved good recipe recall, but surprisingly little detail was remembered from the headline or the body copy. In short, none of the copy elements of this advertisement except the recipe contributed appreciably to its over-all impact.

Details of what was recalled from the copy in each advertisement are available for study in the pages following.

Exhibit 3—Continued

COPY RECALL: COFFEE CUP

What Was Recalled	Total	Male	Female
Do not boil coffee....................	37%	27%	44%
Make coffee in three strengths.......	30	37	25
How to make good coffee...........	25	25	25
Use cold water....................	25	18	29
Use clean pot.....................	22	10	30
How much coffee to use...........	20	12	24
Ad gave recipe...................	17	8	22
How much water to use............	12	6	16
Measure carefully.................	9	8	9
Use instant to suit taste...........	7	6	8
Best coffee in the world............	7	8	6
"Really good coffee"..............	7	12	3
Use favorite brand................	6	4	7
Follow directions for good coffee.....	5	6	5
Pan American Coffee Bureau........	5	10	2
Vary to suit taste.................	4	4	5
Use clear water....................	2	2	2
Use any kind of coffee maker........	1	2	1
"Really good coffee and here's how to make it"......................	1	2	1
Don't use too much water..........	1	2	....
Strong coffee recipe...............	1	2	....
No report........................	1	2	....
*Total mentions...................	245	213	264
†Base for percentages..............	138	51	87

* Exceeds number shown advertisement because respondents recalled more than one copy point.

† Total respondents shown advertisement.

Exhibit 3—Continued

COPY RECALL: CARTOON

What Was Recalled	Total	Male	Female
Ad gave recipe	17%	14%	19%
Make coffee in three strengths	14	8	18
Do not boil coffee	12	8	15
How much coffee to use	12	12	13
Use clean pot	12	6	17
Use cold water	10	8	11
How much water to use	8	8	7
Measure carefully	6	6	6
How to make coffee	5	8	4
Best coffee in the world	5	6	5
"Mary's secret recipe"	5	2	7
Follow directions for good coffee	3	4	2
Use instant to suit taste	3	4	2
Strong coffee recipe	2	4	1
Use any kind of coffee maker	1	2	....
Use clear water	1	....	1
Recipe calls for too much coffee—too strong	1	....	1
Use favorite brand	1	....	1
Coffee was too weak	37	32	40
Half-hostess	21	26	19
She tried new recipe	12	10	13
Party was success until they tasted coffee	9	8	9
Woman had party	6	....	9
Now everyone wants a second cup	6	4	7
Pan American Coffee Bureau	3	6	1
No report	7	8	6
*Total mentions	219	194	234
†Base for percentages	135	50	85

* Exceeds number shown advertisement because respondents recalled more than one copy point.

† Total respondents shown advertisement.

Exhibit 3—Continued

COPY RECALL: BLACK-AND-WHITE CLOSE–UP

What Was Recalled	Total	Male	Female
Make coffee in three strengths.......	23%	28%	20%
How to make coffee...............	23	36	15
Ad gave recipe...................	22	22	22
Measure carefully.................	20	13	24
Do not boil coffee.................	16	11	20
How much coffee to use...........	16	13	17
Use cold water...................	13	6	18
Use clean pot....................	10	13	7
Use instant to suit taste............	8	6	10
How much water to use............	7	2	11
Follow the directions for good coffee..	7	6	7
Use favorite brand................	4	....	6
Best coffee in the world...........	2	2	2
Good coffee every time...........	1	....	1
Don't use too much water..........	1	2	....
Give him a man's coffee...........	7	15	2
"Many a good marriage is made in the pot"......................	7	2	10
If you could only make coffee.......	7	13	2
Easy with simple recipe...........	7	4	9
You can (make good coffee)........	3	6	1
Pan American Coffee Bureau........	4	4	5
No report........................	2	2	2
* Total mentions..................	210	206	211
†Base for percentages..............	135	53	82

* Exceeds number shown advertisement because respondents recalled more than one copy point.

† Total respondents shown advertisement.

Exhibit 3—Continued

COPY RECALL: COFFEE CUP

What Was Recalled	Total	Male	Female
Do not boil coffee.	37%	27%	44%
Make coffee in three strengths.	30	37	25
How to make good coffee.	25	25	25
Use cold water.	25	18	29
Use clean pot.	22	10	30
How much coffee to use.	20	12	24
Ad gave recipe.	17	8	22
How much water to use.	12	6	16
Measure carefully.	9	8	9
Use instant to suit taste.	7	6	8
Best coffee in the world.	7	8	6
"Really good coffee".	7	12	3
Use favorite brand.	6	4	7
Follow directions for good coffee.	5	6	5
Pan American Coffee Bureau.	5	10	2
Vary to suit taste.	4	4	5
Use clear water.	2	2	2
Use any kind of coffee maker.	1	2	1
"Really good coffee and here's how to make it".	1	2	1
Don't use too much water.	1	2	....
Strong coffee recipe.	1	2	....
No report.	1	2	....
*Total mentions.	245	213	264
†Base for percentages.	138	51	87

* Exceeds number shown advertisement because respondents recalled more than one copy point.

† Total respondents shown advertisement.

COPY MEANING

Immediately after telling what he (or she) recalled reading, each person was asked to describe what this meant to him personally. In addition to being tabulated in detail, these replies were analyzed as to whether they indicated a favorable or unfavorable attitude toward the copy the reader had remembered.

In this tabulation, the coffee cup advertisement has a slight edge in the percentage of favorable responses received; but this advantage is not maintained throughout the remainder of the table. Perhaps because of the lightness introduced by the cartoon technique, resistance to the cartoon advertisement was somewhat below that encountered by the other two. On this measure of over-all attitudes, therefore, none of the advertisements performs consistently better or poorer than the others. In all probability this is because readers tended to concentrate their attention on the recipe, to the relative exclusion of other elements in the advertisement.

A review of the detailed comments made about each advertisement provides clear evidence of the strong impact of the coffee recipe, regardless of

Exhibit 3—Continued

whether it is introduced by any lead-in copy device. Most readers stressed some aspect of the recipe or their reaction to it.

Among all the advertisements, readers emphasized that using the recipe would mean better coffee for them, or admitted that they should try to make better coffee. These impressions were reported most frequently by readers of the coffee cup advertisement, least frequently by readers of the black-and-white close-up.

Still others mentioned that the recipe sounded good and they thought that they would try it. Some actually identified the recipe as being the same as the one they regularly used.

Some readers of the coffee cup advertisement cited also its general attractiveness and its relative lack of detailed copy.

Readers who reacted unfavorably to the advertisements did so most commonly because they preferred their own recipe, or believed the recipe did not apply to them because they already knew how to make coffee.

WHAT IN THE ADVERTISEMENTS PLEASED READERS

All readers were asked whether there was anything about the advertisement that made them feel pleased about coffee or coffee making. In contributing to a positive, pleased feeling, the coffee cup advertisement again was found superior overall, with the black-and-white close-up least effective.

All three advertisements were about on a par among men. Among women, however, the coffee cup performed by far the best, while the black-and-white close-up did poorly. All scores were higher among women than among men.

For reasons unknown, persons living in low coffee consumption households gave the advertisements much higher scores on this measure than did those from high-consumption households.

What Made Readers Pleased about Individual Advertisements

Coffee Cup: The appearance, taste, and appetite appeal of the cup of coffee contributed most strongly to a pleased feeling on the part of those who read that advertisement.

Cartoon: Because of the recipe, this advertisement induced a feeling of housewifely competence in those of its women readers who identified the hostess' good coffee as similar to their own. This reaction, together with the social approval directed toward good coffee, left the reader with a pleased feeling.

Black-and-White Close-up: The recipe in this advertisement was pleasing to its readers in much the same way as was the recipe in the cartoon advertisement.

WHAT IN THE ADVERTISEMENTS MADE READERS FEEL UNCOMFORTABLE

All respondents were asked whether there was anything about the advertisement that bothered them, or made them feel uncomfortable. Scores for this measure represent the percentage of readers who were not bothered by anything in the advertisement they read.

On this basis, differences among the three advertisements are not extensive. In each one, most of the unfavorable reactions were caused by the illustration

Exhibit 3—Continued

or the situation it depicted; practically nobody mentioned any unpleasantness occasioned by the recipe.

What in Individual Advertisements Bothered Readers

Coffee Cup: Nearly everyone who was bothered by the coffee cup advertisement found some fault with the illustration. This indicates a need for close attention to such details as color reproduction and photographic or near-photographic realism in the cup of coffee.

Cartoon: Most of the problems on the cartoon advertisement were reported by readers who felt uncomfortable because they identified themselves strongly with the unfortunate hostess it described.

Black-and-White Close-up: Reactions of discomfort toward this advertisement were occasioned mainly by the situation shown in the illustration. A few remarked that this "did not look like a coffee advertisement."

WHAT THE ILLUSTRATIONS SHOWED

Because of the numerous details involved in the cartoon illustrations, more details were recalled about that illustration than about the other two. Except for a slight amount of confusion registered among those who saw the black-and-white close-up, all three of the illustrations were adequately recalled.

MEANING OF THE ILLUSTRATION

Each respondent was asked what the illustration he recalled meant to him in terms of coffee or coffee making. Since the advertisement had already been read before the illustration was asked about, the responses to this question cover considerably more ground than if only the illustration had been seen. However, the intention of the question was to discover how much of the remainder of the advertisement readers would clearly associate with the illustration.

While this was a difficult question for some, the cartoon illustration was most successful in eliciting further meanings. The coffee cup illustration did noticeably better among women than among men. The black-and-white illustration received considerably fewer responses than did either of the others, indicating again the relative weakness of that illustration.

Meanings Associated with Individual Illustrations

Coffee Cup: Inferred characteristics of the coffee shown in this illustration, plus references to the recipe, make up the bulk of readers' associations with the coffee cup illustration. Both favorable characteristics (good, hot) and unfavorable characteristics (brewed too long) were mentioned by various readers. However, favorable mentions were considerably more frequent.

Cartoon: Among the larger group who associated detailed meanings with this illustration, the strongest single association was the need for making stronger coffee. Frequent reference was also made to the importance of using a good recipe, the fact that people want and like good coffee, that good coffee helps a party, and that one should measure ingredients carefully.

Exhibit 3—Continued

Black-and-White Close-up: Among the relatively few who associated meaningful information with the black-and-white illustration, a general reference to the recipe and the confused inference "they like good coffee" were the most frequent references.

INTEREST SCORES

Interest scores represent an average of the individual interest ratings readers gave for the advertisement they were shown. The reader rated the advertisement for interestingness on a ten-point attitude scale where the lowest possible rating was zero, the highest ten. For easy comparison with other types of data, the average of these scores was then multiplied by ten.

On this basis, the coffee cup clearly carries the greatest over-all interest. The cartoon took second place; the black-and-white close-up third. All of the advertisements, and particularly the women's party cartoon, were more interesting to women than to men. Except for the cartoon, interest in the advertisements tended to increase as the reported ground coffee consumption rate in the household increased.

Reasons for Interest Ratings of Individual Advertisements

Coffee Cup: The strength of the illustration was the principal reason for the high interest rating given this advertisement. But the colors detracted somewhat from its over-all impact.

Cartoon: Women, especially, were interested in the colors used in the cartoons. Men's lack of interest in these "women's" pictures caused them to focus attention on the recipe.

Black-and-White Close-up: Here, again, reader interest scores were usually determined by reactions to the illustration. Those interested in the advertisement applauded the illustration, while those not interested either actively disliked the illustration or thought it did not look like a coffee advertisement.

IMPORTANCE SCORES

Importance scores were calculated in the same manner as interest scores. However, the respondent was asked how *important* to him was the information contained in the advertisement he read.

Overall, the importance scores were neither particularly high nor particularly low. The coffee cup and the cartoon achieved about equal importance with their readers, with the black-and white close-up scoring somewhat lower.

Reasons for Importance Ratings

Regardless of the advertisement a person read, the chief factor responsible for a high importance rating was the coffee recipe. Some readers also volunteered that they liked good coffee or (women) liked new recipes.

Low ratings were also the result of a reaction to the recipe, rather than a reaction to the other contents of the advertisement. Some women preferred their own recipe, or insisted that this was nothing new because they already know how to make coffee. Men remarked that they were not interested in coffee-making information, or that their wives usually made the coffee.

Exhibit 3—Continued

BELIEVABILITY OF THE ADVERTISEMENTS

All readers were asked whether there was anything in the advertisement they found hard to believe. Performance scores for believability represent the percentage who found nothing hard to believe in the advertisement they were shown.

On this basis, the straightforward coffee cup advertisement had the highest believability. The cartoon advertisement was least believable because quite a few readers found the party situation somewhat exaggerated.

What Was Hard to Believe in Individual Advertisements

Coffee Cup: The major source of unbelievability among readers of this advertisement was the instruction never to boil coffee. This point should perhaps be expanded for greater clarity in the final recipe used. Others thought that the coffee made by this recipe would be too strong (despite the three strengths described).

Cartoon: While some did find recipe points in this advertisement hard to believe, the major problem was in the party situation. Readers remarked that people wouldn't laugh at a hostess that way, or wouldn't complain about coffee, or that the success of a party doesn't depend on coffee.

Black-and-White Close-up: The situation in this advertisement was unbelievable to quite a few readers. Some remarked that marriage does not depend on good coffee; others that it was hard to believe that the woman did not know how to make coffee.

UNDERSTANDABILITY OF THE ADVERTISEMENTS

All respondents were asked whether there was anything they found hard to understand in the advertisement they had read. Scores for understandability represent the percentage who found nothing hard to understand about that advertisement.

On this basis, differences among the advertisements were not great. However, among women the coffee cup was noticeably superior to the cartoon.

What Was Hard to Understand about Individual Advertisements

Coffee Cup: Some readers of this advertisement raised again the point about never boiling coffee. Others thought that measuring by cups would be less confusing than measuring by ounces.

Cartoon: Of those who found something hard to understand about the cartoon advertisement, the greatest number raised some question about the recipe. However, some did not understand the headline phrase "Half-hostess" and a few found the arrangement of pictures confusing.

Black-and-White Close-up: While recipe mentions were the most frequent source of poor understanding here, two people questioned the phrase "Many a good marriage is made in the pot."

INFORMATIVENESS OF THE ADVERTISEMENTS

All respondents were asked whether there was any question that the advertisement they read failed to answer, or any other information they thought it should have included. Whether it is desirable to have many questions asked

Exhibit 3—Continued

about an advertisement may vary with the nature of the questions asked. Normally it is thought that an advertisement which raises few questions has communicated adequately and effectively. Thus the scores quoted are the percentages who raised no further question about the advertisement they read. On the other hand, numerous questions may indicate high reader interest in the advertisement. In the case of this recipe, they also point up areas of possible improvement.

Since the coffee cup advertisement had no other copy to deflect attention from the recipe, it drew the greatest number of further questions about the recipe. This is additional evidence for the strong inherent interest in the recipe itself. On the other two advertisements also, most of the additional questions concerned the recipe.

READERS WHO WOULD SAVE THE RECIPE

All respondents were asked whether they would cut out the recipe and save it if they saw it printed in a magazine. While replies to such a question do not afford any prediction of expected action, they do give an additional basis on which to compare the advertisements. Among both men and women, the cartoon performed somewhat better than the other two advertisements.

Readers who would not clip the recipe gave a variety of reasons. Women frequently emphasized that they preferred their own recipe. Men averred that they never make coffee, never clip recipes, or that they were just not that much interested in recipes. Several readers remarked that they already used this recipe, or did not need it for some other reason such as having an automatic coffee maker. A few thought the coffee would be too strong, despite the three strengths described in the recipe.

Since readers did not report why they *would* clip the recipe, the reasons for the better performance of the cartoon recipe are not contained in these findings. But since this recipe differed from the others only in using the word "secret" on the recipe tab, this strong word may well be responsible for its added impact.

PERFORMANCE OF WORDS DESCRIBING VARIOUS COFFEE STRENGTHS

To pinpoint any adverse reaction to the use of the word "weak" in describing coffee, respondents were asked whether there was anything they disliked about seeing coffee described as "full-strength, medium, and weak." Although none of the words was strongly criticized, "full-strength" rather than "weak" was found to cause the most difficulty. From the results of this question, it would not appear that using "weak" will create a serious problem. And using "strong" rather than "full-strength" might be reconsidered.

Reader Objections to the Words Denoting Various Coffee Strengths

Full-Strength: The great majority of those who objected to the phrase "full-strength" would have preferred that the recipe use the word "strong" instead.

Medium: Objections to this word did not form any clear pattern. The greatest single objection was that it would be adequate to describe one or two strengths instead of three.

Exhibit 3—Continued

Weak: Some who objected to the word "weak" suggested the word "mild" instead. Others reacted negatively to "weak coffee" on the ground that it suggested dishwater, mud, or just poor coffee.

~~~

CASE 30: PAN-AMERICAN COFFEE BUREAU (G)[1]

NOTE: *Given a budget of $250,000, outline the schedule of advertising which you think the Bureau should employ in the first half of 1958.*

Executives of the Pan-American Coffee Bureau had decided that the bureau's consumer advertising campaign for the first half of 1958 should be aimed at arresting the trend to the brewing of weaker coffee which had been under way since 1949. A major objective was to lead people to adopt a method of making coffee by which the optimum rate of extraction of solids from the coffee bean would not be exceeded. The importance of controlling the brewing process within certain limits had been emphasized in information recently supplied by the Coffee Brewing Institute which was engaged in research on the quality of coffee beverage. Overextraction, believed to be typical of contemporary American coffee making, produced bitterness which incorrectly was regarded as strength by the consumer who had to dilute the coffee in order to lessen the intensity of the unpleasant effect. The new campaign was prepared on the assumption that people would like coffee better if it were made at an optimum rate of extraction and that many of them then would prefer coffee stronger than that which they were now using.

In the process of selecting a keynote advertisement, three advertisements were submitted to a consumer test conducted by the research department of the bureau's advertising agency, Fuller & Smith & Ross. The winner of the test was a poster-type advertisement in four colors. It featured a large cup of coffee and gave special emphasis to a recipe for brewing coffee properly (see Exhibit 1). The agency developed several variations of the winning advertisement for use in a campaign; however, they were regarded by Mr. Edward E. Van Horn, the bureau's director of advertising, as markedly inferior to the basic advertisement. Inasmuch as the latter seemed particularly well suited for the job at hand, a decision was made to use it without variations.

This decision gave rise to the question of whether a poster-type advertisement should be repeated in the same publication. It had been the bureau's practice in the past to run several variations of the key advertise-

---

[1] Written by Joseph W. Newman.

Exhibit 1

PAN-AMERICAN COFFEE BUREAU (G)

REALLY GOOD COFFEE! *and here's how to make it*

The secret of REALLY GOOD COFFEE

Does your coffee have all the full, rich taste and wonderful aroma that it should? You can make excellent coffee, using your favorite brand. Start with a clean coffee maker, fresh coffee, fresh cold water. Use proper grind for your coffee maker. Measure and time carefully.

Per cup, one Standard Coffee Measure (2 measuring tbs.) to ¾ measuring cup (6 ozs.) of water. Time: Percolate gently no more than 8 mins. Vacuum, stir — hold in upper bowl no more than 3 mins. Drip — pour in boiling water — should go through coffee in 4-6 mins. Stir before serving.

Always use at least ¾ capacity of your coffee maker. Serve at once.

CAUTION: Brewing too long makes coffee bitter. If you want weaker coffee, dilute with water after brewing according to above recipe.

Once you learn the secret of good coffee, you'll find people saying, "Another cup, please!" After all, there is nothing as satisfying as a good cup of coffee!

NOTE: If you use "instant," vary the strength to suit your taste.

"FUN WITH COFFEE"—32 pages of coffee recipes and cooking hints—only 10¢.

PAN-AMERICAN COFFEE BUREAU, Box 33, Old Chelsea Sta., N. Y. 11, N. Y.

ment of a campaign in the same magazine for greater impact. But these advertisements had not been of the poster type.

Other questions which needed to be answered before the campaign could be put into effect included these: What publications should be used? What size of space should be used in each? What schedule of insertions should be followed?

The bureau had decided that the campaign based on the one advertisement should run in consumer magazines and/or newspaper magazine supplements; that the list of publications should offer national coverage; that the campaign should begin in January and end in May 1958; and that total space cost should be approximately $250,000. While the bureau wanted its advertising to reach both men and women, it preferred that somewhat greater emphasis be given to circulation among women.

The following market data were being examined in connection with the making of the media decisions:

Coffee was consumed in 96% of American homes.

The extraction rate (cups per pound) varied by both geographic region and age of housewife. The figures indicated that people living in the West and in the north central states made weaker coffee than those living in the Northeast and the South, and that younger housewives made weaker coffee than did older housewives (see Exhibit 2).

Per capita consumption of coffee varied by geographic region, being somewhat higher in the West than in the East (see Exhibit 3).

The heaviest purchasers of coffee were in households where the age of the housewife was between 35 and 54. Households in which the housewife was under 35 accounted for only 14% of the heavy purchasers.

While coffee consumption was relatively light among younger people, they were becoming a larger segment of the total population.

The top one fourth of the households in income accounted for one third of the heavy coffee purchasers. The low-income households had one third of the light coffee purchasers and only 18% of the heavy.

In general, the households headed by skilled workers and laborers bought more coffee than the households headed by professional and executive men and farmers.

Exhibit 2
PAN-AMERICAN COFFEE BUREAU (G)
Extraction Rates by Geographic Region and Age of Housewife—1957

REGION		AGE OF HOUSEWIFE				
	All Ages	Under 25	25–34	35–44	45–54	55 and Over
REGULAR COFFEE (IN CUPS PER POUND)						
Total U.S.	63.90	75.89	69.18	63.85	60.24	57.07
Northeast	55.71	62.74	58.72	58.68	51.80	51.27
South	60.06	73.28	62.90	61.60	56.20	52.43
North Central	69.62	81.16	77.65	65.76	66.25	64.72
West	72.32	88.58	78.96	72.57	68.58	60.00
INSTANT COFFEE (IN CUPS PER OUNCE)						
Total U.S.	13.35	14.52	13.59	13.57	13.04	12.95
Northeast	12.97	13.80	13.58	13.87	12.43	12.25
South	12.35	14.08	12.53	12.45	12.25	11.48
North Central	14.68	15.16	14.75	14.63	14.72	14.55
West	14.66	18.36	14.80	14.19	13.97	14.95

Source: National Family Opinion Survey, 1957.

Exhibit 3

PAN-AMERICAN COFFEE BUREAU (G)

Per Capita Consumption of Coffee and Number of Families by Geographic Regions

Region	Cups per Drinker per Day	Families (000)
1. *East:*		
New England...................	3.24	2,880.0
Middle Atlantic.................	3.53	11,507.0
Total........................		14,387.0
2. *South:*		
South Atlantic..................	3.40	4,744.5
East South Central..............	3.23	3,139.6
West South Central.............	3.62	4,605.8
Total........................		12,489.9
3. *North Central:*		
East North Central..............	4.01	10,231.2
West North Central.............	4.18	4,568.8
Total........................		14,800.0
4. *West:*		
Pacific........................	4.29	5,997.3
Mountain......................	....	1,808.3
Total........................		7,805.6
Total United States...........		49,482.5

Exhibit 4

PAN-AMERICAN COFFEE BUREAU (G)

Color Space Costs and Circulation for Each of Ten Magazines

American Home

Space Cost:
One page............four colors......................$16,100.00
One-half page........four colors...................... 8,800.00

Circulation by Region:
East:
New England...........................   257,658
Middle Atlantic........................   808,436
Total............................... 1,066,094

South:
South Atlantic.........................   252,332
East South Central.....................   136,257
West South Central.....................   209,105
Total...............................   597,694

North Central:
East North Central.....................   747,229
West North Central.....................   264,616
Total............................... 1,011,845

West:
Pacific................................   323,250
Mountain...............................   87,296
Total...............................   410,546
Grand Total........................ 3,086,179

Exhibit 4—Continued

Better Homes & Gardens

Space Cost:
One page............four colors......................$ 5,325.00
One-half page........two colors or horizontal—four colors. 3,195.00

Circulation by Region:
East:

New England............................	265,391
Middle Atlantic.........................	972,820
Total................................	1,238,211

South:

South Atlantic...........................	300,272
East South Central.......................	153,187
West South Central......................	277,671
Total................................	731,130

North Central:

East North Central......................	1,247,807
West North Central.....................	521,210
Total................................	1,769,017

West:

Pacific................................	518,220
Mountain.............................	163,201
Total................................	681,421
Grand Total........................	4,419,779

Good Housekeeping

Space Cost:
One page............four colors......................$19,700.00
Two columns.........four colors...................... 13,440.00
One-half page
horizontal..........four colors...................... 13,440.00

Circulation by Region:
East:

New England............................	266,986
Middle Atlantic.........................	929,360
Total................................	1,196,346

South:

South Atlantic...........................	290,650
East South Central.......................	155,266
West South Central......................	269,940
Total................................	715,856

North Central:

East North Central......................	816,674
West North Central.....................	335,156
Total................................	1,151,830

West:

Pacific................................	443,356
Mountain.............................	135,794
Total................................	579,150
Grand Total........................	3,643,182

Exhibit 4—Continued

Ladies' Home Journal
Standard Units

Space Cost:
  One page............four colors.....................$26,950.00
  One-half page........four colors..................... 15,300.00
  One-half page
    horizontal..........four colors..................... 15,750.00

Junior Units

  One page............four colors..................... 21,575.00
  One-half page vertical..four colors................... 14,425.00

Circulation by Region:
  East:
    New England...........................   391,383
    Middle Atlantic........................ 1,277,283
      Total............................. 1,668,666

  South:
    South Atlantic.........................   413,951
    East South Central.....................   211,798
    West South Central.....................   394,811
      Total............................. 1,020,560

  North Central:
    East North Central..................... 1,141,743
    West North Central.....................   493,051
      Total............................. 1,634,794

  West:
    Pacific................................   703,254
    Mountain...............................   231,387
      Total.............................   934,641
      Grand Total....................... 5,258,661

Life Magazine

Space Cost:
  One page............four colors.....................$39,500.00

Circulation by Region:
  East:
    New England...........................   490,634
    Middle Atlantic........................ 1,665,871
      Total............................. 2,156,505

  South:
    South Atlantic.........................   440,337
    East South Central.....................   185,664
    West South Central.....................   368,281
      Total.............................   994,282

  North Central:
    East North Central..................... 1,165,545
    West North Central.....................   394,835
      Total............................. 1,560,380

  West:
    Pacific................................   720,576
    Mountain...............................   198,562
      Total.............................   919,138
      Grand Total....................... 5,630,305

Exhibit 4—Continued

McCall's Magazine
Standard Units

Space Cost:
One page...........four-color......................$24,220.00
One-half page vertical..four-color...................... 13,250.00
One-half page
  horizontal..........four-color...................... 13,750.00
One-quarter page......four-color...................... 7,025.00

Circulation by Region:
East:
New England........................... 286,505
Middle Atlantic........................ 1,016,891

Total............................. 1,303,396

South:
South Atlantic......................... 423,065
East South Central..................... 213,882
West South Central..................... 393,169

Total............................. 1,030,116

North Central:
East North Central..................... 1,058,406
West North Central..................... 488,700

Total............................. 1,547,106

West:
Pacific................................ 601,422
Mountain............................... 192,624

Total............................. 794,046

Grand Total........................ 4,674,664

The Saturday Evening Post
Standard Units

Space Cost:
One page.............four colors......................$31,620.00
One-half page
  horizontal..........four colors...................... 18,815.00
One-half page vertical..four colors...................... 18,225.00

Junior Units
One page.............four colors...................... 25,300.00
One-page vertical......four colors...................... 16,910.00

Circulation by Region:
East:
New England........................... 388,385
Middle Atlantic........................ 1,091,118

Total............................. 1,479,503

South:
South Atlantic......................... 376,413
East South Central..................... 161,096
West South Central..................... 358,055

Total............................. 895,564

North Central:
East North Central..................... 1,023,648
West North Central..................... 493,336

Total............................. 1,516,984

West:
Pacific................................ 714,355
Mountain............................... 268,147

Total............................. 982,502

Grand Total........................ 4,874,553

Exhibit 4—Continued

American Weekly

Space Cost:*

One page............four colors.......................	$36,365.00
Seven tenths of page....four colors.......................	27,810.00
Three fifths of page....four colors.......................	24,760.00
One-half page........four colors.......................	21,660.00

Circulation by Region:

East:

New England...........................	665,925
Middle Atlantic.........................	2,459,534
Total...............................	3,125,459

South:

South Atlantic..........................	722,996
East South Central.......................	152,233
West South Central......................	757,250
Total...............................	1,632,479

North Central:

East North Central......................	2,451,071
West North Central.....................	577,341
Total...............................	3,028,412

West:

Pacific................................	1,760,921
Mountain.............................	229,408
Total...............................	1,990,329
Grand Total........................	9,776,679

* National Edition.

Parade Magazine

Space Cost:

One page............four colors.......................	$28,355.00
Seven tenths of page....four colors.......................	21,365.00
Three fifths of page....four colors.......................	19,050.00
One-half page........four colors.......................	16,725.0C

Circulation by Region:

East:

New England...........................	363,278
Middle Atlantic.........................	1,755,674
Total...............................	2,118,952

South:

South Atlantic..........................	662,656
East South Central.......................	202,152
West South Central......................	517,334
Total...............................	1,382,142

North Central:

East North Central......................	2,183,484
West North Central.....................	624,198
Total...............................	2,807,682

West:

Pacific................................	1,345,596
Mountain.............................	295,544
Total...............................	1,641,140
Grand Total........................	7,949,916

Exhibit 4—Continued

This Week Magazine
Colorgravure

Space Cost:
One page............four colors......................$43,140.00
Seven tenths of page....four colors..................... 32,510.00
Three fifths of page....four colors..................... 28,980.00
One-half page........four colors..................... 25,410.00

Circulation by Region:
East:
New England......................... 549,005
Middle Atlantic......................... 2,609,436
Total............................... 3,158,441
South:
South Atlantic......................... 871,437
East South Central...................... 548,947
West South Central..................... 835,017
Total............................... 2,255,401
North Central:
East North Central..................... 3,013,563
West North Central..................... 1,519,921
Total............................... 4,533,484
West:
Pacific............................... 1,433,478
Mountain............................ 692,819
Total............................... 2,126,297
Grand Total....................... 12,073,623

To provide a basis for further thinking about a desirable media program, the following information was prepared: (1) space costs and circulations for ten consumer magazines and newspaper magazine supplements; and (2) estimates of the total number of homes which would be reached by each of five tentative combinations of publications, allowing for duplication (see Exhibit 5).

Exhibit 5

PAN-AMERICAN COFFEE BUREAU (H)

Estimated Total Homes Reached by Each of Five Combinations of Publications, Allowing for Duplication

Publication and Circulation at Time of Duplication Study	New Homes Added	Duplicated Homes	Total Homes Reached
COMBINATION A			
Life, 5,500,000......................	5,500,000		5,500,000
Ladies' Home Journal, 4,900,000.........	3,900,000	1,000,000	9,400,000
The Saturday Evening Post, 4,500,000.....	2,600,000	1,900,000	12,000,000
COMBINATION B			
Life, 5,500,000......................	5,500,000		5,500,000
Ladies' Home Journal, 4,900,000.........	3,900,000	1,000,000	9,400,000
The Saturday Evening Post, 4,500,000.....	2,600,000	1,900,000	12,000,000
McCall's, 4,500,000....................	2,100,000	2,400,000	14,100,000

Exhibit 5—Continued

Publication and Circulation at Time of Duplication Study	New Homes Added	Duplicated Homes	Total Homes Reached
COMBINATION C			
ESTIMATED UNDUPLICATED HOMES REACHED			
Ladies' Home Journal, 4,900,000........	4,900,000		4,900,000
McCall's, 4,500,000.................	3,200,000	1,300,000	8,100,000
Better Homes & Gardens, 4,100,000.....	2,500,000	1,600,000	10,600,000
American Home, 3,000,000.............	1,300,000	1,700,000	11,900,000
COMBINATION D			
ESTIMATED UNDUPLICATED HOMES REACHED			
This Week, 11,700,000................	11,700,000		11,700,000
Parade, 7,200,000....................	6,200,000	1,000,000	17,900,000
Ladies' Home Journal, 4,900,000........	2,800,000	2,100,000	20,700,000
The Saturday Evening Post, 4,500,000.....	1,800,000	2,700,000	22,500,000

Publication and Circulation at Time of Duplication Study	New Homes Added	Duplicated Homes	Total Homes Reached
COMBINATION E			
This Week, 11,700,000................	11,700,000		11,700,000
American Weekly, 10,100,000..........	5,800,000	4,300,000	17,500,000
Parade, 7,200,000....................	5,000,000	2,200,000	22,500,000
Life, 5,500,000......................	2,500,000	3,000,000	25,000,000
Ladies' Home Journal, 4,900,000........	1,900,000	3,000,000	26,900,000
The Saturday Evening Post, 4,500,000.....	1,400,000	3,100,000	28,300,000
McCall's, 4,500,000.................	1,300,000	3,200,000	29,600,000
Better Homes & Gardens, 4,100,000......	1,100,000	3,000,000	30,700,000
American Home, 3,000,000.............	1,000,000	2,000,000	31,700,000

~~~

CASE 31: PAN-AMERICAN COFFEE BUREAU (H)[1]

QUESTIONS TO CONSIDER: (1) What does the Gallup & Robinson "impact" service measure? (2) How does it differ from the information provided in Starch Ratings? (3) Should the Bureau purchase the "impact" service? If so, what would you expect to learn from the information provided by Gallup & Robinson?

Mr. Edward E. Van Horn, director of advertising of the Pan-American Coffee Bureau, was considering whether the Bureau should become a member of the impact service for measuring the effectiveness of print-media advertising offered by Gallup & Robinson, Inc., of Princeton, New

---

[1] Written by Joseph W. Newman.

Jersey. A proposal that the Bureau subscribe had been made by Mr. Glenn Mohrman, Gallup & Robinson general service executive. In his presentation to Mr. Van Horn, Mr. Mohrman described the firm's services (see Exhibit 1 for summary) and gave name registration scores for a number

Exhibit 1

Summary of Gallup & Robinson Impact Techniques & Services*
Print Media

This is a description of the methods used in measuring the Impact of print advertising and the services Gallup & Robinson offers its member companies.

First, some general observations on the development of IMPACT: For the past 20 years print advertising evaluation has proceeded in good part from readership research—the techniques developed by Dr. Gallup in the middle 20's. Readership, of course, has been useful in studying audience response to advertising and has led creative people to make some important changes.

Dr. Gallup and many others, however, have long been bothered by the limitations of readership or "reading and noting" studies—the principal one being that reading and noting does not necessarily reflect *depth of impression* and *idea penetration*. The purpose of product advertising, of course, is to put selling ideas into people's heads. It is easy to demonstrate that reading and noting can be high but penetration of a selling message or of a name low.

We believe that an evaluation technique centering around *name registration, idea penetration* and *conviction* is the next great step beyond readership. This is the heart of the IMPACT system which, in addition to reporting quantitatively on the percentage of readers who register on the name of an advertiser, reports qualitatively their verbatim "playback" of the advertiser's message.

This new Impact reporting service began in the fall of 1949 on the advertising in *Life, The Saturday Evening Post* and McCall's. Since then the research has attracted the support of a large and distinguished group of advertisers.

Out of our experience with these member companies have developed some extraordinary case studies of stepped-up audiences and increased idea registration when IMPACT findings have been exploited.

In the mass magazine medium, to get our measures of effectiveness we talk to the audience on a nationwide basis, obtaining IMPACT scores on each ad one page or larger in our test issues and analyzing people's verbatim testimony on each ad.

To date we have checked thousands of ads in every product group and every school of advertising thought.

Perhaps the basic idea behind IMPACT can be expressed in this way:

If a reader is exposed to an advertisement in a *normal reading situation* where he has free play to accept or reject, flip the page or linger—then the effectiveness of that ad can be gauged by his ability to play back the advertiser's message with the magazine closed at a later date.

Although execution of this simple idea presented formidable research problems, a successful test was developed, based on the following key steps:

With the magazine closed—during the first week the magazine is out:

1. To qualify the respondent definitely as a reader of the current issue of the magazine.

---

* Prepared by Gallup & Robinson, Inc.

Exhibit 1—Continued

2. To determine which of all ads, listed on cards, the reader can remember and describe accurately.
3. To take down verbatim the reader's "playback" of the advertiser's message on these ads.

Thus determined, the IMPACT of an ad is the ability of a qualified reader of the magazine to remember that ad, describe it accurately and "playback" the sales or institutional message with the magazine closed. This is admittedly a rigorous test. And for that reason it is also revealing. Some ads rate as low as 1%, but others go to 40% and 50%. When the high IMPACT ads are compared with the low IMPACT ads, the difference in ad characteristics—both ideas and execution—prove very meaningful.

In almost any given product or institutional field we have seen IMPACT principles pay off dramatically to increase the efficiency of advertising dollars. Some advertisers, exploiting the research information, regularly communicate their product arguments to many times more people for the money they spend than other advertisers.

Gallup & Robinson tests ads in many different magazines and in newspapers. However, in order to build up data systematically for comparative analysis, and to provide a reporting and consulting service where the costs are shared by many participating companies, we conduct regular tests in *Life*, *Post* and *McCall's*.

Each week we make one study in rotation in *The Saturday Evening Post*, *Life* and *McCall's*. Over the course of a year this gives us a sampling of about half the ads in *Post* and *Life* and all ads in *McCall's*. Some member companies gear their insertion schedules to ours and get 100% coverage.

In general, the IMPACT service to member companies consists of the following, although we can and do fit the program to the advertiser's needs:

1. An IMPACT report prepared for each ad published by the member company in the magazines we study. These reports are submitted approximately three weeks after a magazine appears on the newsstand, and they include two principal measures of the ad's effectiveness:

   a) *Proved Name Registration Score.* The percentage of qualified readers who, with the magazine closed, remembered the ad and could prove recall by describing it accurately the first week out. This score is reported for both men and women readers. Also included in these reports for comparative purposes, are the average performance of all ads in the same product field, as well as the average performance of all ads in the magazine.

   b) *Verbatim Playback* of the sales or institutional message in the ad; also the respondent's description of what the ad looked like. In our questioning we ask the respondent to recall the message of the advertiser from several points of view. This testimony is given word for word in our report. We do not undertake to quantify this material in each individual report for the reason that only the advertiser himself can judge whether he is getting the kind of idea circulation which he wants.

      Incidentally, copywriters find this playback a valuable source book for copy ideas. It puts them in direct contact with the audience.

2. We also provide reports such as those just described for all the client's competitor's ads as well.

Exhibit 1—Continued

3. Every four months we come to the member company's offices to put on an Impact Advertising Clinic. In these clinics we cover:
   a) Analysis of the advertising of the member company and that of its competitors.
   b) Presentation of results of our continuing studies into the fundamentals of audience response to advertising.
   c) Reports on high and low IMPACT ads in other product groups in order to learn what advertising techniques are succeeding in registering ideas and company signature.
   d) Evaluation of new developments in advertising.

Following are a few of the many topics on which studies have been completed:

—News in Advertising; Effective Forms of News
—Irrelevance: Multi-Step Principle
—Hard to Make Illustrations Work Hard
—Impact of B & W vs. 4 Color vs. 2 Color ads
—Impact of One Page vs. Two Page Ads
—Brag & Boast vs. Consumer Benefit Headlines
—How to Write Effective Headlines
—Impact of Ads in Editorial-picture Format
—Realism in Illustration
—What Makes "Hard Sell" from the Consumer's Point of View
—Addiness—The Route of Mechanical Devices vs. Ideas
—Effective Use of Celebrities and Testimonials
—Demonstration in Advertising; Effective Forms of Demonstration
—How to Use Repetition Effectively
—Seasonal Influences
—Use of Coined Words
—Optimum Number of Ideas
—Price in Advertising
—Theme or Idea Testing

This is one of the unique features of the Gallup & Robinson IMPACT service—namely, the formulation of basic advertising concepts through a detailed analysis of all the observations in magazine advertising we have made to date.

We maintain a study group here in Princeton to distill out the meaning of our research data. Since we are studying thousands of ads in all product groups and from all schools of thought, we have an unusual opportunity to sift out those elements that predict and control audience behavior. The Ad Clinics bring the advertiser and agency the fruits of this continuous study.

4. We are flexible in the sense that we can provide member companies additional coverage in other magazines and in newspapers. We can pretest two or more versions of a given ad and we can talk to any audience that the advertiser desires particularly to reach. This work is done at cost for our member companies, and is contracted for separately.

Pretesting is done by means of an experimental magazine made up in our offices. It contains the test ad and a number of "control" ads which

Exhibit 1—Continued

have already been observed in the post-test situation. We leave the magazine with a cross-section of magazine readers, returning the following day for an IMPACT interview.

As you would expect, the technique yields more playback than the regular IMPACT test, and this is advantageous in diagnosing the ad's performance as a communicator. The ads in the pretest magazine and in the post-test perform *relatively* in about the same way and we can predict within a reasonable margin of error what the ad will do under normal reading conditions.

The pretest vehicle lends itself to split-runs where we make up sets of magazines exactly alike in every respect except for two or more versions of the test ad. More and more, member companies are making use of this service to reduce their risks in space.

Gallup & Robinson Special Research extends to tests of themes and illustrations, tests of understandability and comprehension, and other problems in copy research not covered by the IMPACT method.

Newspaper Impact tests are contracted for on an individual basis. All interviewing is completed within 24 hours after the test issue is delivered. Typically in newspaper research we ask a number of specific copy questions on the test ads in addition to the normal Impact questions, in order to assess understandability and comprehension and more detailed impressions. Split runs in newspapers also are frequently made.

As for the size of the sample we use for our regular IMPACT work, we obtain 400 cases on each magazine survey, 200 men and 200 women. Respondents are selected systematically in 18 metropolitan areas nationwide. We maintain a geographic distribution in our sample comparable to that of the magazine concerned.

One further word about our IMPACT Clinics. What seems to be happening is that the research is more and more reducing the mystery in advertising, and is sending a steady flow of practical information to sales and advertising people, which keeps them thinking in terms of good and effective advertising. In many member companies, our clinics are attended by the president, division heads, principal sales officers, promotion managers, and advertising managers, together with the agency people.

This Gallup & Robinson IMPACT service reporting on the advertiser's own ads in the books we check regularly and on other products or institutional ads in which they may be interested, three Ad Clinics per year, informal consultation, and the other services described, is open to any advertiser who wishes to join.

The budget for the basic IMPACT service is determined by the volume of advertising a member company carries in the books we test, by the type and amount of "competitive" advertising we report and by the cost of consultation and service anticipated on the account.

We also measure the IMPACT of television commercials and serve many TV advertisers. The television research program, however, should be covered separately as it differs considerably from the print media procedure and services.

of Coffee Bureau magazine advertisements which had been checked in past years.

Exhibit 2

PAN-AMERICAN COFFEE BUREAU (H)

"Bless your Daddy's heart—
He's making Coffee!"

'M-m-m! Nothing Smells as Good as Coffee!'

What better way to end a busy day than with the magic promise of coffee's rich aroma? As Mom tucks her tiny tornado off to dreamland, that aroma tells her she'll soon feel like her young self again!

'M-m-m! Nothing Tastes as Good as Coffee!'

And that taste! So delicious and satisfying! So perky with the promise of pick-me-up and cheer! That's why Mom—and you—and millions—have made coffee America's best-loved beverage!

'M-M-M...
Nothing Satisfies Like Coffee!'

DON'T SPOIL YOUR COFFEE BY TRYING TO "STRETCH" IT! For real satisfaction, take 1 Standard Coffee Measure (2 level measuring tablespoons) to each ¾ measuring cup (6 ounces) of cool, fresh water. Brew in spotlessly clean coffee maker and serve soon as possible. Never boil or reheat! For attractive plastic Standard Coffee Measure and complete instructions for all approved brewing methods, mail 10¢ to Pan-American Coffee Bureau, Dept. L-5, 120 Wall Street, New York 5, New York.

AMERICAN COFFEE BUREAU • Brazil • Colombia • Costa Rica • Cuba • Dominican Republic • El Salvador • Guatemala • Honduras • Mexico • Venezuela

"Impact" was defined by Gallup & Robinson as the depth of impression which an advertisement made on readers' minds as evidenced by (1) registration of the name of the product and/or advertiser, and (2) registration of the selling message. Information on these points was obtained in personal interviews with readers of *Life*, *The Saturday Evening Post*, and *McCall's*, the magazines regularly covered by the service.

Exhibit 3
PAN-AMERICAN COFFEE BUREAU (H)

March 31, 1956   81

"May keep the Marytay over here for another day."

"No doubt will. That Mrs. West is all 'or not getting seasick."

"Gives us another whole day, likely."

"For what?"

Crunch was silent for a moment. Then e said, "Think if we could locate that reasure cave tomorrow, it would—well, would do any good? Straighten those eople out?"

Des understood. He understood his ipper's meaning and his sympathetic irit, which often made him take part— urgent and sometimes dangerous art—in the tribulations of those who ad chartered him and his boat. Des w he said, "Unh-uh." He paused. "A llion bucks in doubloons wouldn't ake old Pete stop being a worm. And a illion wouldn't make a gent out of that exas gorilla."

"I hate to see—well, see George fly vay. See Wonder and her mother leave. e old Pete trek off to Lord knows here, beat. He sure takes a shellacking om that crowd."

"Bums," Des murmured.

"Not bums." Crunch thought of his ng years of experience with people well ough heeled to go deep-sea fishing. rouble is, people don't realize folks th money are still just folks. No better, worse. No different. Got problems, e the rest."

"Why," Des whispered hotly, "didn't te grab a marlin billy and at least lay en George's scalp, when he came up irking and cut off his fish?"

"Did he smirk? I thought so. Well, for- t it. Just an idea."

here was silence for a time, but Des 1 not lie back in his bed. "You men- ned we might be able to locate that t."

"The place where it was hidden. Yeah." p! Seeing it break up without discover- t if that Endibbie left a pile someplace if the whole routine is just screwy!" Crunch said, drowsily, "M'm'm'm." 'Have anything special in mind?'

'Tide's coming in now. Be going out— , around six-seven o'clock in the morn- . Be windy. Nobody be outside at it time."

"You mean—tonight?" Des flopped :k and sat up. "Man! You have a gle to cross, and gear to carry and— ht!"

'Only time when we could do it with- t a brigade of interested spectators."

'But night? Crocs, likely. 'Gators. akes."

'You know there aren't any crocs or tors in these Bahamas, Des. No poison- s snakes I ever heard of. Only boa con- ctors." Crunch chuckled softly. "And y're little ones."

Des lay still for a while. Then his an- sr came. He stood up in the murk. et dressing," he whispered.

They took a long time crossing the anda and moving down the rear stairs, e din in the bar helped to cover the it sounds they could not avoid.

n the street they halted. The sound of t sent them into a hibiscus bush till the guid native passed by. Then they ved forward until they saw, in the dis- ce, a glimmer of a bicycle lamp. They again, and a constablé whizzed by.

By such means they reached the water nt near the dock. Boats were tied up o and three deep and boats lay every- ere in the harbor. Some were dark, sers brilliantly lighted, where people racted by the story of treasure were nding a gay evening or a restless one— ndering, now that they had reached ndem Key, what had sent them off so

impulsively on such a wild-goose chase. There were people on the dock, talking, laughing, listening to an occasional num- ber played by a few of the Calypso musicians.

Crunch took his mate's arm and pointed to the boat silhouettes. "We wade in here, swim around yonder; then back and in."

Half an hour later two figures locked up the Poseidon again and dropped with silent care into the water. Strapped to their backs were various pieces of equip- ment which, in the starry dark, looked

like knapsacks. The packs made swim- ming difficult, but they took their time and, before long, both men—mere shapes in the night—waded out on shore again.

The wind blew evenly and they were cold. The island thoroughfare, however, was emptier of traffic and they did not have to hide so often. They hurried, when they could, toward the isthmus. Gradu- ally they grew warmer.

The journey through the jungle was, as Des said later, "The kind of thing crazy people do, and have nightmares about for the rest of their lives."

They followed the isthmus to the south bulge of the key and waded around it on the east side until they could no longer see a light from the harbor or the village. Then they broke into the black tangle of trees, brush and undergrowth, going without a trail, twice climbing trees to look at the stars for direction. They had flashlights, but used them sparingly.

When they reached the pond, they were exhausted, sweat-soaked, scratched in a thousand places and their clothing was tattered. They sat on the sandy rim of the lake, resting, (Continued on Page 84)

Get all the "breaks" of Coffee!

Wake-up coffee. Nothing else starts a day so right! Especially when you use 1 Standard Coffee Measure to each 6 oz. of clear, cold water, like the experts.

Mid-morning break. All's quiet on the home front. Why not call in a neighbor for a friendly cup? (Your husband's enjoying a "Coffee-break" at work.)

Luncheon coffee. Even the simplest bill of fare looks good with a fresh, steam- ing cup of coffee alongside. (The second cup tastes even better than the first!)

Afternoon break. It's much more fun to shop these days—but still pretty tiring. Doesn't that cup of coffee taste good? It seems to bring your strength back.

Dinner coffee. Nothing finishes a meal in such fine style as coffee. It tastes wonderful—and makes an occasion out of every meal you put before the family.

Guest coffee. Some evening, try coffee a new way! Coffee Boston, for instance. Just float a layer of cream on top; sip your coffee through it. Delicious!

There is nothing so satisfying as a cup of good coffee
PAN-AMERICAN COFFEE BUREAU, 120 Wall Street, New York 5, N.Y.

The name registration score of an advertisement was an index of the proportion of qualified readers who, with the magazine closed, could re- call the advertisement and prove it by describing the advertisement accu- rately. The index made allowances for (1) cost, with single-page, four-

Exhibit 4

PAN-AMERICAN COFFEE BUREAU (H)

NEW ways to take an ICED "Coffee-break"

Iced Coffee Secret. Cream double-strength Iced Coffee with Carnation Evaporated Milk. Brings out richer coffee flavor — lighter in calories, too. It's the ideal mid-summer refresher with a snack, a sandwich, a tidbit.

Iced Coffee Float. Scoop some of your favorite flavor ice cream—coffee, vanilla, chocolate or other —into Iced Coffee. Just taste how delicious it is with a generous wedge of cake so easily made with Betty Crocker Cake Mix.

Iced Coffee Mocha. Stir into Iced Coffee 2 tblsps. chocolate syrup and 2 tblsps. cream. Top with whipped cream if you like. A superb complete lunch when you serve it with a bacon sandwich made with Wilson Pan-Size Bacon — exactly sandwich size.

Iced Coffee Julep. Add a couple of drops of mint flavoring to Iced Coffee. Top festively with sprig of fresh mint. So cooling, especially with party-popular brownies, date bars and macaroons—quickly made with Betty Crocker Cookie Mixes.

3 ways to make good Iced Coffee.

1. Quick Method
Make extra-strength coffee by using ½ measuring cup (4 fluid ounces) of water for each Standard Measure (2 level tblsps.) of coffee — pour hot over ice cubes.

2. Pre-Cooled
Make coffee: 1 Standard Measure (2 level tblsps.) to each 6-oz. cup of water. Cool in covered non-metal container. For freshest taste, serve within three hours. Pour over ice cubes.

3. Instant
Mix twice the usual amount of instant coffee with a little water (hot or cold, according to brand)—add ice cubes, fill glass with water.

HINT: In refrigerator trays, freeze regular strength coffee into cubes — pour fresh coffee over them. Delicious — and no dilution!

Good restaurants serve good Iced Coffee—enjoy it often!

Why Iced Coffee Makes Friends So Fast
Today's Iced Coffee is so versatile that there's a kind to delight *every* taste! And every kind is cooling and refreshing! You may choose to serve guests an exotic Continental variety—in your finest glassware. Or you may want the relaxing lift that only a regular Iced "Coffee-break" gives. Try America's favorite beverage, coffee, *iced*. The new and different ways to enjoy it make Iced Coffee fun for everyone!

SEND FOR THESE COFFEE RECIPES NOW!
ONLY 10¢ for this exciting, helpful booklet, 32 colorful pages packed with information on best brewing methods, wonderful and new coffee recipes, serving suggestions and easy gourmet cooking hints. Write the Coffee Bureau for *Fun With Coffee* today!

Pan-American Coffee Bureau Dept. O, P.O. Box 33, Old Chelsea Station, New York 11, N.Y.

© 1957, Pan-American Coffee Bureau

color cost the common denominator, and (2) the amount of advertising in the magazine. This was done so that the scores could be used in comparing the performances of advertisements regardless of their size and color combinations or thickness of the magazine. The Gallup & Robinson organization pointed out that the scores provided a relative index of advertising impact, but that they could not be used to judge the relative effectiveness of various media.

Evidence of the registration of the sales message was obtained in the form of verbatim playback of ideas and impressions regarding the advertisements on which readers were able to prove name registration. The magazine was closed during the interviewing by which the playbacks were obtained.

Among the Coffee Bureau advertisements included in Mr. Mohrman's presentation were several from the 1950 consumer advertising campaign. A typical example was a full-page advertisement in four colors which ran in *Life* of May 22, 1950 (see Exhibit 2). Its score among women was 3. Among the more recent advertisements was one in four colors which occupied two-thirds of a page in the *Saturday Evening Post* of March 31, 1956 (see Exhibit 3). Its score among women was 15.

Mr. Mohrman also presented a sample Magazine Impact Report on the Bureau's full-page advertisement in four colors for iced coffee which had run in *McCall's* of June 1957. (See Exhibit 4 for the advertisement and Exhibit 5 for the report.) The report included the advertisement's score

Exhibit 5

PAN-AMERICAN COFFEE BUREAU (H)

Gallup & Robinson Magazine Impact Report on Pan-American Coffee Bureau Ad for Iced Coffee Which Appeared in *McCall's*, June 1957

COMPARATIVE PROVED NAME REGISTRATION (WOMEN)
Pan-American Coffee Bureau ad. 14
Product Group Average (Food—Institutional) 14
Average, This Issue. 16

REGISTRATION OF SALES MESSAGE (WOMEN)

It showed five or six pictures of different ways of making coffee. It had iced coffee and coffee mocha. Each one was in a different style glass or cup. The ad said coffee pickups for summertime. I learned that iced coffee picks you up when it's hot. I don't remember what went through my mind when I looked at the ad. The advertiser increased my interest in the product because it showed some clever ideas for fixing coffee.

The ad was colored and one page. It showed iced coffee which I can't stand. My coffee has got to be hot. They put milk with coffee in one. There were about four different glasses of different ways to fix cold coffee. It said make coffee appealing and cold in the hot weather. I learned that you can make up different concoctions of ice coffee. I can't stand cold coffee. Ice tea yes, but not coffee. It did not increase my interest because I just don't like it.

It was an ice coffee ad. Several glasses were shown, some with whipped cream, one with a mint spray, one with just the glasses filled with ice cubes and coffee. It said use ice cream for a coffee float or whipped cream and cocoa for mocha or mint flavoring. You can also send in ten cents for a booklet of coffee recipes. I learned that coffee can be fixed in numerous ways to make it more tempting and provide a variety. When I looked at this ad it reminded me that it's coffee time. It interested me because we love ice coffee. We drink too much

Exhibit 5—Continued

of it but we'd like a variety but I seldom think of it. I shall try to remember to use these recipes.

There were about a half dozen glasses of cold coffee fixed in that many ways. There was one where chocolate was added and cream to another and ice cream to another. I didn't get to all of them. They were all cool coffee drinks to give people in hot weather. That's all I remember. I read a few of the directions for making the coffee coolers. I don't remember any more than I have told you. I was reminded that coffee could be made cold which is one thing I never have. I think about ice tea but for some reason never about ice coffee. I don't think I would like it. I drink my coffee black and all those added ingredients would be sickening.

This must have been the ad that showed so many ways for making iced coffee. Well, at least a half dozen. The ad did make the coffee look so refreshing and yet, I have not tasted any. I even liked the different ways for preparing iced coffee. It said that there were so many ways. Maybe I would try it again some hot day. I've always used coffee. We like it hot.

It showed some new idea in flavoring iced coffee. There were four glasses, one mint, one with chocolate flavor, and one with ice cream. It said three ways to make it hot over ice, precooled and using instant. I learned that you do not store it in metal. Freeze coffee and pour regular strength coffee over the cubes of coffee. As I looked at the ad it reminded me that our coffee time is here. The ad did increase my interest. I like ice coffee especially with ice cream of many different flavors.

It had six big glasses of iced coffee. One had ice cream, one had whipped cream, one had mint, one was plain and there was another one. It was a full page in color. Very yummy looking. I don't remember what the ad said. It gave recipes for each float under each picture. I got good recipes from the ad. I'm already using most of them. It made me good and thirsty. It made me want a glass. The ad did not interest me because I guess I'm one of these rut characters.

It had all the summer ideas for cool summer coffee and desserts. It said something about iced coffee breaks. I learned that coffee can be used in various desserts and drinks. I like iced tea better than iced coffee. The product did not interest me because I like iced tea.

The ad showed glasses of iced tea. It had one with ice cream. Well, it told how to make it. You have to make it stronger. Well, I don't like it. I don't like cold coffee of any kind. Well, it looked delicious but as I said we don't go for it in our family. Hot coffee, yes.

It was a full page color ad with four different ways to prepare iced coffee. The first was plain coffee, the second was coffee float, the third, mocha coffee, and the fourth might have been spiced coffee. Each had directions. The ad said how refreshing and appetizing iced coffee is in hot weather. I learned that you use double strength coffee to ice and to sweeten with Carnation Brand Milk. When I looked at the ad it reminded me how long it has been since I've had a coffee float. The advertiser did increase my interest in the product because it was an appealing ad.

Exhibit 5—Continued

It showed a page of ways to make different kinds of iced coffee. Yes, it told how to make each one. I couldn't tell you, but I'm going to cut it out and save it as soon as my aunt gives me the book. It had no background but it showed the color of the coffee. There was a lot of it. It gave the recipe how to make the different iced coffees. I learned how to make fancy ice coffee. I'd like to get the recipes to keep. The advertiser increased my interest in the product because it looked good and cold and it told how to make iced coffee in different ways. As soon as my aunt is done with the book I'm going to cut it out and keep it. It looked good that's why I noticed it.

It was a full page ad in color with different ways for using coffee in iced drinks. It showed different ways of using coffee. I learned that appetizing cool drinks could be made from it. I would like to try them. I was interested in the ad because I guess I like to try new things. New drinks, new ideas and mixes.

DEFINITIONS

Sample
On *Life* and *The Saturday Evening Post* consists of approximately 200 men and 200 women each issue; on *McCall's,* approximately 200 women.

Respondents are representative readers of this magazine, eighteen years of age and over, in urban areas nationwide.

Sample includes "qualified readers" only. To qualify, respondent must, with the magazine closed, recall details of one or more editorial features read. All interviewing on *The Saturday Evening Post* and *Life* is completed within one week after newsstand release date; on *McCall's* approximately ten days.

Impact
is defined as the Depth of Impression which an advertisement makes on readers' minds, as evidenced by (1) Registration of the name of the product and/or advertiser, and (2) Registration of the selling message.

Comparative Proved Name Registration
is an index of the proportion of qualified respondents who, with the magazine closed, can recall an ad and can

prove it by describing the ad accurately. Respondents who say they have seen this ad before are excluded. This comparative index makes allowance for (1) Cost, with single page four color cost the common denominator, and (2) Amount of advertising in the magazine.

Thus, Comparative Proved Name Registration scores permit direct comparison of the performance of ads, regardless of their size and color combinations or thickness of the magazine.

Registration of Sales Message
gives verbatim playback of ideas and impressions regarding ads on which readers were able to prove name registration. Interviewing takes place with the magazine closed.

Product-Group Average
is the average performance of all advertisers in this product-group observed during the past 24 months.

Average This Issue
is the average performance of all ads single page or larger in this particular issue of this magazine.

among women as 14; the average score among women for all institutional food advertisements which appeared during the past 24 months in issues of the magazines regularly tested was 14; and the average score among women for all advertisements of a single page or larger run in that issue was 16. In addition, it included a number of verbatim playbacks of ideas and impressions regarding the advertisement.

Mr. Mohrman gave the schedule of regular impact tests to be made in 1958 in *Life, The Saturday Evening Post,* and *McCall's* (see Exhibit 6)

Exhibit 6
PAN-AMERICAN COFFEE BUREAU (H)
Gallup & Robinson's Schedule of Impact Tests for 1958

Magazine	Date of Issue	Magazine	Date of Issue
Life	January 27	*McCall's*	July
		Life	14
McCall's	February		August
Life	3	*Life*	11
Post	8		
Life	24	*McCall's*	September
		Life	1
McCall's	March	*Post*	13
Post	1	*Life*	22
Life	10	*Post*	27
Life	17		
Post	22	*McCall's*	October
Life	31	*Post*	4
		Life	13
McCall's	April	*Post*	18
Post	5	*Life*	27
Post	19		
Life	28	*McCall's*	November
		Life	3
McCall's	May	*Post*	8
Life	5	*Life*	17
Post	10	*Life*	24
Life	12	*Post*	29
Post	17		
Life	26	*McCall's*	December
		Life	1
McCall's	June	*Post*	6
Life	2	*Post*	13
Post	7		
Post	14		
Life	23		

and announced plans for several tests to be made in *This Week,* a newspaper magazine supplement.

The Coffee Bureau recently had approved a media schedule for the first half of 1958 which called for one full-page advertisement in four colors in *Life,* one junior page advertisement in four colors in *The Saturday Evening Post* and *McCall's,* and one three fifths of a page advertisement in four colors and one fifth of a page advertisement in two colors in *This Week* (see Exhibit 7). All issues of *McCall's* were on the Gallup &

Exhibit 7

PAN-AMERICAN COFFEE BUREAU (H)

PAN-AMERICAN COFFEE BUREAU
STRONGER COFFEE MEDIA PLAN
January – May 1958

Publication-Circulation	JANUARY	FEBRUARY	MARCH	APRIL	MAY	COSTS
This Week (11,972,920)	⅔ Pg 4c Jan 19	⅕ Pg 2c Feb 23				$37,230
Independents (1,051,040)						4,050.70
Life (5,851,168)		Pg 4c Feb 17				39,500
Ladies Home Journal (5,320,300)	OUT JAN 28 ←	Jr Pg 4c				21,575
American Weekly (10,307,458)			⅔ Pg 4c MARCH 16	⅕ Pg 2c APRIL 6		33,000
Mc Calls (4,830,102)		OUT FEB 20 ←	Jr Pg 4c			19,250
Parade (7,555,328)				⅔ Pg 4c April 13	⅕ Pg 2c May 4	24,760
Sat. Eve. Post (4,950,061)	Jr Pg 4c Jan 25					25,300
Better Homes-Gardens (4,302,019)			OUT MARCH 20 ←	Pg 4c		23,765
American Home (3,150,764)				OUT APRIL 22 ←	Pg 4c	16,100
TOTAL CIRCULATION 59,291,160						
Circulation by months	23,294,321	23,705,230	14,609,477	21,013,550	7,555,328	

Estimated Production   11,800

GRAND TOTAL $256,330.70

Robinson schedule. The issues which the Bureau planned to use of the other three publications were not those on the regular Gallup-Robinson schedule, so changes in insertion dates would have to be made if these advertisements were to be measured. Mr. Mohrman explained that the Gallup & Robinson service was offered on a yearly contract basis, the charge for which ranged from $7,500 to $30,000 depending upon the size of the client's product group, the size of his advertising schedule, and the volume of advertising run by his competition. He offered the service to the Bureau for $8,400 for one year.

Mr. Van Horn explained that while the Bureau planned to run magazine advertising in the first half of 1958, its media usage for the second half of the year had not been determined. A sizable increase in the Bureau's budget was probably effective July 1, 1958, which would permit consideration of other media which had not been used in the past because of budget limitations. It was possible, therefore, that national magazines might not be used in the second half of the year. In view of this consideration, he asked whether a special arrangement could be made to accommodate the Bureau's situation.

At a later meeting, Mr. Mohrman proposed a charge of $4,200 for six months' service plus $1,000 should the Bureau decide to drop the service at the end of the six-month period. Should the Bureau elect to continue the service beyond that time, it could do so at the same rate, $700 a month. Should the Bureau decide to drop the service sometime after the first six months, it would pay an additional $1,000, but the total charges would not exceed the yearly contract price of $8,400.

~ ~ ~

CASE 32: SOHIO[1]

QUESTION TO CONSIDER: *How should Mr. Kolb evaluate the effectiveness of the two television programs?*

In March 1956, Mr. Samuel H. Elliott, vice president of sales of the Sohio oil company, Cleveland, Ohio, was unexpectedly offered rights to cosponsor the telecasts of the 1956 games of the Cleveland Indians baseball club and the Cleveland Browns professional football team. Since the acquisition of these rights involved a supplementary advertising appropriation of approximately $200,000, Mr. Elliott and other members of top management, as well as the company's advertising director, Mr. Frank A. Kolb, engaged in considerable discussion of the value of each of the rights offered and finally decided to purchase both rights for reasons which will be given later. Immediately thereafter, Mr. Kolb began to confer daily with the Cleveland representatives of the company's advertising agency, McCann-Erickson, Inc., in order to develop detailed plans for the use of

---

[1] Written by Martin V. Marshall.

the two programs, particularly for the televising of the games of the Cleveland Indians since the Indians were to open their 1956 season against the Chicago White Sox in Chicago on April 17. In addition to developing plans for the use of these programs, Mr. Kolb was also particularly interested in devising a means by which he and Mr. Elliott could evaluate the effectiveness of the programs in selling company products.

Before the rights obtained by the Sohio oil company are described, general background information concerning the company, its marketing mix, and its promotional activities will be given.

General Company Background

In 1955 Sohio had total sales of $317,138,000, of which approximately 50% was motor gasoline. The other 50% of sales volume was obtained through sales of automotive oils, greases, antifreeze, batteries, battery rentals and recharges, tires and tubes, automobile accessories, automobile lubrication services, aviation gasoline, jet fuels, asphalt, heavy fuels and coke, waxes, liquefied petroleum gas, naphthas and solvents, agricultural sprays, oil-burner services, and distillates, such as kerosene.

These products were sold through a number of channels of distribution. In general, motor gasoline was sold to three markets: motorists, farmers, and other consumers (truck and bus companies, contractors, local governments, etc.). In selling to motorists, i.e., the so-called retail market, the company used three channels: company-owned-and-operated service stations, company-owned stations which were leased to independent operators, and independent operators who owned their own stations. The farm and other consuming markets were reached both by direct selling and the use of jobbers.

Other retail products, such as motor oils, TBA[2] products, and antifreeze, were generally sold through the company's retail channels indicated above. Since the question of how to evaluate the effectiveness of the sports programs does not call for a detailed description of the channels used to sell all other products, suffice to say here that all other products were generally sold direct.

Sohio was unique among large American oil companies in two respects: it operated exclusively in one state, Ohio; and it had a larger share of the market in which it operated than any other oil company—31.6%. (The market shares of Sohio's principal competitors in the Ohio market in 1955 were approximately as follows: Sunoco, 10%; Gulf, 8%; Pure, 7.5%; Shell, 7%; Ashland and Sinclair, 4.5% each; Texaco, 4%; Ohio, 3.8%; Socony and Cities Service, 3.5% each; Amoco, 2%; Atlantic, 1.8%; and Pennzoil, 0.5%.)

As a result of operating exclusively in the state of Ohio, the company had, over the years, enjoyed a number of competitive advantages,

---

[2] Tires, batteries, and automobile accessories.

but of an intangible nature so that it was difficult to evaluate them. As the Sohio oil company, operating exclusively in Ohio, the company had promoted itself and had become known as an Ohio company doing things for Ohioans. Having secured a total sales volume in one state equal to the total United States sales volume of some other well-known oil companies, Sohio enjoyed the benefits of size as well as the benefits of being close to

Exhibit 1

THE SOHIO OIL COMPANY
Geographical Organization of Divisions

the market place. In general, all Sohio sales personnel knew intimately every detail of the markets in which they were operating, e.g., key field personnel responsible for selecting new station locations had often lived in the part of Ohio concerned for 20, 30, or 40 years and had studied every important change in the development of an area, often on a weekly basis.

In order to obtain the full benefits of the company's unique market situation, Sohio's management had placed as much responsibility for sales management as possible in the hands of the managers of the company's 13 field divisions. (See Exhibit 1 for the geographical organization of divisions.) In general, divisional managers had authority to make all sales management decisions except for those involving pricing, large capital investments, and advertising. Advertising decision making was centralized in the Cleveland home office because most advertising decisions affected all operations of the company as well as the operations of divisions.

The fact that Sohio had 13 divisions was of particular significance to Mr. Kolb for two reasons. First, Sohio's market position varied among divisions; e.g., Sohio's market share of gasoline by divisions ranged from a low of about 28% to a high of about 34%. Second, numerous types of market information and sales analyses which he might wish to utilize were generally summarized by divisions.

Sohio's Marketing Mix

In order to evaluate any given advertising or promotional effort, including the two new television programs, Mr. Kolb realized that he had to consider the other elements involved in Sohio's marketing mix which affected sales performance. The following description, as given by an individual who had recently studied all aspects of the Sohio marketing operation, gives highlights of some of the principal elements of Sohio's marketing mix for retail products. He said,

What is Sohio's marketing mix?
Sohio's marketing mix is difficult to describe briefly, because so many variables are involved. In general, if one is to be successful in the oil business, he must have a good product available at convenient locations at the right price. In order for this general formula to be successful, and profitable, considerable attention must be given to a number of factors.

First, I think we should be clear that consumer buying behavior is complex: Mr. and Mrs. Motorist want convenience of purchase. They won't go more than several blocks out of their way to purchase gasoline or other oil products, if that far. Therefore, Sohio management must pay considerable attention to location of service stations, so that Sohio products are conveniently available to consumers. Although it is difficult to say that Sohio has X degree of advantage over competitors insofar as station numbers and locations go, I think it is safe to say that in the short run Sohio has excellent station locations vis-à-vis competitors and that the situation will not change so much during 1956 that it will significantly affect the problem of evaluating this year's advertising effort.

However, within the short run, station operation could, conceivably, affect the evaluation of advertising. Not only does the consumer desire convenience of purchase but he expects good service: quick service in the filling of his gas tank, wiping of the windshield, and so on. Although Sohio divisional managers, retail sales managers, and service station managers and operators constantly seek to maintain and improve standards of service, there is no doubt that there are variations in service and these variations could affect sales.

Further, you have this situation with regard to consumer buying: in general, because of the importance of the automobile in his life, the consumer wants to buy a "well-known" brand of oil products. Therefore, to an extent, the product of any large oil company may be generally acceptable to the consumer. However, at any one time, he may have a preference or greater acceptance of any one brand because he has had good experience with the brand he is using or because he has been particularly affected by the advertising of a given company.

Further, there is no doubt that many consumers are quite price conscious; they will tend to buy on a basis of price. Here Sohio has, for many years, followed a policy of being competitive on prices; the company has been the price leader in Ohio. I think it would be safe to say that in 1956 the company will not lose sales because of unsound pricing. In a few isolated areas Sohio may lose some sales to competitors because of intense price competition, but I don't think this would affect the general effectiveness of any Sohio advertising effort.

Let me summarize this facet of Sohio's marketing mix by simply saying that Sohio management has recognized the close correlation between number of stations and sales, and that the expansion in number of Sohio and competitive outlets in 1956 is unlikely to affect Sohio sales significantly from a competitive viewpoint.

Obviously, as a second important facet of the marketing mix, Sohio has to provide motorists with the best possible products for the operation of their automobiles or the company will lose competitive position. Consequently, company executives have devoted much attention to the study of existing product quality and to the development of improved products. On the basis of current technical and market studies, Sohio offers motorists excellent products and is at no significant disadvantage competitively. Rather, the situation is that Sohio enjoys several significant product advantages because of two products, "Boron" gasoline and "Premex" motor oil, the company's premium brands.

Boron was developed and marketed in late 1954 as a replacement for the company's existing premium grade of gasoline, "Sohio Supreme," and has been very successful, e.g., sales of Boron increased over 40% in 1955. Market studies show that Boron has been well received by motorists, and various road tests show that the use of Boron results in significant improvements in engine operation and condition, e.g., valves last twice as long, there is 45% less piston ring wear, and the product resists changes in engine heat and pressure which cause faulty burning and pre-ignition.

Premex is Sohio's premium motor oil, which was first marketed in July 1955. It has proved, through road tests, to be an excellent product. It reduces oil consumption by as much as 46%; increases gasoline mileage substantially, by as much as 18 miles to the tankful of gas, as the result of less engine friction; eliminates valve train wear; and doubles the efficiency of oil filters, thus reducing abrasive wear. Sales of Premex in the latter part of 1955 indicate that it has been well received by motorists, and sales should increase substantially in 1956.

Although the Boron story will not be so fresh in 1956 as it was in 1955—about 80% of all Ohio motorists have tried Boron—Boron plus Premex should maintain Sohio's lead in product quality, at least through 1956.

Consumer buying behavior, pricing, and product quality are only a few of the variables in the mix. Advertising and promotional programs are also important variables.

Sohio Promotional Activity

Since the end of World War II, Sohio had been one of the largest advertisers of any type in the Ohio market and consistently was the largest advertiser in Ohio media among oil companies. Media space and time expenditures for the years 1946 through 1955 varied from a low of $795,000 in 1948 to a high of $1,880,000 in 1954. On the promotional side, the company had used practically every type of promotional device, including point-of-purchase material, contests, direct mail, and giveaways. Expenditures for promotional effort usually had been about $1,000,000 a year.

During the previous decade, Sohio had allocated its advertising budget among media as follows:

Year	Television	Newspapers	Outdoor	Radio	Magazines	Total
1946	....	$346,000	$129,000	$372,000	$14,000	$ 862,000
1947	....	379,000	152,000	317,000	14,000	916,000
1948	$ 8,000	388,000	141,000	246,000	12,000	795,000
1949	10,000	421,000	183,000	332,000	15,000	961,000
1950	55,000	507,000	175,000	269,000	17,000	1,023,000
1951	134,000	560,000	212,000	290,000	22,000	1,218,000
1952	301,000	587,000	235,000	242,000	25,000	1,390,000
1953	378,000	505,000	258,000	244,000	25,000	1,410,000
1954	688,000	599,000	289,000	251,000	53,000	1,880,000
1955	801,000	610,000	266,000	114,000	49,000	1,840,000

In 1956 Sohio had allocated its advertising budget among media as follows:

Year	Television	Newspapers	Outdoor	Radio	Magazines	Total
1956	$1,082,500*	$493,000	$352,000	$123,000	$50,000	$2,100,500

* Includes supplementary television budget of $200,000.

The 1956 advertising budget was to be spent as follows:

—$420,000 for the "Sohio Reporter," a ten-minute news TV telecast, which appear live at 11:00 P.M., five times a week on eight TV stations, located in the Cleveland, Cincinnati, Columbus, Lima, Toledo, Youngstown, Dayton, and Zanesville divisions. (This program had consistently obtained high A.R.B. ratings[3] during 1955.)

—$312,500 for spot television coverage. Essentially this coverage consisted of about four to six 20-second commercials each week on Class AA time in each of the eight divisions listed above, plus a Steubenville TV station.

—$250,000 for the televising of the Cleveland Indians games.[4]

[3] Ratings published by American Research Bureau, Inc., based on a probability sample representing all television homes and using the diary method.

[4] In addition to a supplementary budget of $200,000, $150,000 was taken from other media budgets to cover the cost of these programs.

—$100,000 for the televising of the Cleveland Browns games.[5]
—$493,000 for a newspaper program which would give the company adequate coverage of all divisions in the state, particularly of markets not covered by television.
—$352,000 for outdoor advertising: $324,500 for a No. 100 showing[6] of 24-sheet posters in key urban areas and on main state traffic arteries and $27,500 for taxi posters in a few selected urban areas.
—$123,000 for radio: $98,000 for a "Sohio Reporter" newscast at 7:45 P.M. in all divisions except Portsmouth and at 6:15 P.M. in Portsmouth, and $25,000 for radio spots in the Canton division.
—$50,000 for trade papers and a magazine (Life).

In 1955 Sohio's principal competitors spent approximately the following amounts on major media, exclusive of magazines, in the state of Ohio:

Competitor	Television	Newspaper	Radio	Outdoor	Total
Sunoco		$ 370,000	$110,000	$ 90,000	$ 570,000
Pure	$ 60,000	120,000	50,000	50,000	280,000
Gulf	180,000	190,000	10,000	150,000	530,000
Shell	90,000	240,000	70,000	150,000	550,000
Ohio	90,000	30,000	10,000	70,000	200,000
Texaco	140,000	80,000	100,000	40,000	360,000
Cities Service		60,000	40,000	5,000	105,000
Socony		110,000		15,000	125,000
Sinclair	10,000	50,000	40,000		100,000
Total	$570,000	$1,250,000	$430,000	$570,000	$2,820,000

During the previous decade, Sohio had allocated its media budget among products, services, or subjects as follows:

Year	Gasoline	Motor Oil	Guaranteed Starting Program	Institutional	All Other Products
1946	$ 91,000	$267,000	$150,000	$249,000	$104,000
1947	144,000	194,000	127,000	246,000	151,000
1948	56,000	233,000	110,000	202,000	203,000
1949	229,000	227,000	102,000	168,000	235,000
1950	548,000	128,000	132,000	80,000	135,000
1951	328,000	610,000	124,000	54,000	102,000
1952	381,000	478,000	178,000	95,000	258,000
1953	479,000	389,000	165,000	166,000	211,000
1954	887,000	365,000	68,000	363,000	197,000
1955	1,403,000	229,000	22,000	48,000	138,000

As can be seen from the above data, in 1955 a substantially greater sum of money was spent to support gasoline sales than in previous years, e.g., $1,403,000, or 76.3% of the total advertising budget in 1955, versus $887,-

---

[5] Ibid.

[6] A No. 100 showing of 24-sheet poster panels provides thorough coverage of a market.

000, or 47.2% of the total budget in 1954. Advertising plans for 1956 called for approximately the same allocation of budget among products, services, and subjects as had existed in 1955.

Particulars concerning the New Television Rights

Sohio's sales management had often considered the possibility of televising the games of the Cleveland Indians and Browns because such telecasts offered the company an opportunity to reach a large number of males, the principal buyers of oil products, at an economical cost. In the past neither of the rights had been available to the company under favorable conditions. In March 1956, however, the sponsor of the Indians games offered to give rights of cosponsorship of a television schedule (i.e., one half of each game) which consisted exclusively of Saturday and Sunday games, 60 in number, at home and away, including a number of doubleheaders that offered the additional opportunity to sponsor an in-between games show.

Although the company's advertising program and budget were already established for 1956, Messrs. Elliott and Kolb were quite interested in the offer. They believed that the Indians telecast would be a highly effective advertising medium for the company. Further, they believed that the telecast would introduce "something distinctly new and different" in the company's advertising, which was desirable because they did not know how long the Boron story would continue to be effective and fresh. However, the Indians telecast had one disadvantage: it appeared only on a Cleveland TV station and thus gave Sohio coverage of the Cleveland and Akron divisions and parts of the Toledo, Youngstown, Mansfield, and Canton divisions, or 45% of the television homes in Ohio.

Within a few days of the offer of the television rights to the Indian games, however, rights to televise games of the Cleveland Browns became available, except for rights on the Cleveland TV station. The Browns' rights called for the televising of a schedule of 13 games on TV stations located in Columbus, Cincinnati, Lima, Zanesville, and Dayton, and seven games in Youngstown. Further, if the Detroit Lions football club gave permission, there was the possibility of televising four Browns games in Toledo, a city in northwest Ohio which fell within the orbit of the Lions.

Since the two programs gave most divisions some additional advertising and since the two programs allowed the company to be sponsoring sports telecasts through the remainder of 1956, Sohio management purchased both rights in late March.

In early April neither Mr. Kolb nor agency representatives had as yet had time to work out all details regarding usage of the Cleveland Indians telecasts. However, several decisions had been made: during each game Sohio had nine 50-second periods of commercial time available. In order to guard against overcommercialization, Mr. Kolb had decided to use only three of the nine periods for commercials. In addition, he expected that occasional use would be made of "superimpositions."[7] Further, it had been decided that the commercials would be done by Mr. Warren Guthrie, who was the Sohio TV reporter. Mr. Guthrie was a speech instructor at Western Reserve University who had shown a flair for newscasting. As the result of his news reporting for the company, he had become known to the public as "Mr. Sohio." Sohio executives believed that Mr. Guthrie was accepted by the public more as an official spokesman for the company than as a commercial announcer, and hence would be quite effective.

Although audience ratings of Indians telecasts had been high in 1955, Mr. Kolb did not know what to expect in 1956. In 1955 the Indians had been in the thick of the American League pennant race until the last few games of the season. As the result of "pennant fever," there had been great popular interest in the Indians telecasts. In 1956 the Indians were generally rated by sports writers as strong pennant contenders, but they were not picked by many sports writers to win the American League championship.

No detailed plans had been made for the handling of the Cleveland Browns telecasts because Mr. Kolb expected that experience gained in handling the Indians telecasts would help greatly in planning the use of the fall football program. Since the Browns program would be sent out over a network, not only in but beyond Ohio, it appeared that filmed commercials, cut in during the proper break by local stations, would be required.

In developing a method of evaluating the effectiveness of these programs, Mr. Kolb could obtain almost any kind of sales information that he desired. Sohio's sales staff had readily available almost any kind of sales data in almost any combination: sales by products, by type of channel. by time periods, by individual markets, by divisions, and so on.

Although the company's sales research department was currently busy with numerous sales and market studies, the director of the department was quite willing to undertake any special consumer study desired by Mr. Kolb, provided that the study was well defined.

Mr. Kolb also had available the research resources of the company's advertising agency. In the past the agency had made a number of special advertising studies: special audience ratings of the company's media; penetration studies, state-wide and by special markets; and attitude studies regarding Sohio advertising messages and products. In addition, Advertising Research Bureau ratings were available.

~ ~ ~

---

[7] A superimposition consists of showing a trade-mark, package, or advertising message in television over live action at a moment when the action has subsided, such as between the innings of a baseball game.

CASE 33: LUCKY TIGER MANUFACTURING COMPANY[1]

QUESTIONS TO CONSIDER: *(1) What is your appraisal of the testing procedures used by the Lucky Tiger company? (2) How should Mr. Harris experiment in the future?*

The Lucky Tiger Manufacturing Company of Kansas City, Missouri, established in 1919, manufactured and distributed a line of hairdressing products (see Exhibit 1). Two of the products, a hair tonic and a hair

Exhibit 1

LUCKY TIGER MANUFACTURING COMPANY PRICE LIST

Effective—January 1, 1958

Trade Discount, 16 2/3%

Terms: 2%, 10 days—E.O.M.

Product	Size	Whole List per Dozen	Suggested Retail	Case Pack	Case Weight
Lucky Tiger hair tonic.......	4 oz., Med.	$ 4.80	$0.59	1 doz.	7½
	4 oz., Med.	4.80	0.59	3 doz.	23
	9 oz., Lge.	8.80	1.09	1 doz.	15
Lucky Tiger Dandruff Treatment*....................	4 oz., Med.	6.00	0.75	1 doz.	7¾
	4 oz., Med.	6.00	0.75	3 doz.	23¼
	9 oz., Lge.	10.00	1.25	1 doz.	15
Lucky Tiger Butch hair wax..	Jar, 3½ oz.	4.50	0.59	1 doz.	6
	Stick	4.50	0.59	2 doz.	4
Lucky Tiger Liquid Butch hair wax....................	4 oz.	5.50	0.69	1 doz.	7½
Lucky Tiger Magic Dandruff* Remover Shampoo.........	4 oz., Med.	4.80	0.59	1 doz.	8
Lucky Tiger Rose hairdressing.....................	4 oz., Med.	1.80	0.23	1 doz.	7½
	2½ oz., Sm.	1.20	0.15	1 doz.	5½
Lucky Tiger Brilliantine......	4 oz., Med.	1.80	0.23	1 doz.	7½
	2½ oz., Sm.	1.20	0.15	1 doz.	5½

* Not subject to 10% Federal Excise Tax.

wax, accounted for nearly all of the company's sales volume which in 1957 amounted to about $1,000,000.

The Company's Product Line

The hair tonic had been the main item in the line for many years. Certain improvements were made in the formula in 1956. Upon completion of the laboratory work, the new formula was submitted to a consumer test in which 200 people in Kansas City compared the new formula against either the old one or one of several competing preparations by using them over a six-week period. The preparations were put up in identical, unlabeled bottles for test purposes. The results convinced the Lucky Tiger management that the new formula was clearly superior to the old and was

---

[1] Written by Joseph W. Newman.

at least as satisfactory as its principal competitors in the qualities of hair grooming and perfume.

An antiseptic, alcohol base product, "Lucky Tiger" hair tonic, was directly competitive with "Vitalis." Hair preparations of somewhat different types also competed aggressively for the same market. Prominent among them were "Vaseline" hair tonic, "Wildroot Cream Oil," and "Brylcream."

"Lucky Tiger Butch" hair wax for crew haircuts was rivaling the hair tonic in sales importance in 1957 after having been added to the line only two years earlier. It was offered in both jar and stick form. In October 1957 the company introduced "Lucky Tiger Liquid Butch" hair wax, an alcohol base preparation which featured ease of even distribution over the hair.

The other hair preparations in the line ("Lucky Tiger Rose" hairdressing, "Lucky Tiger Brilliantine" and "Lucky Tiger Magic Dandruff Remover Shampoo") were of relatively minor sales importance.

Distribution

While the company had national distribution for its hair tonic and hair wax, its sales were concentrated in the Southeast, Ohio Valley, Southwest, and West Coast. The leading metropolitan area in sales of Lucky Tiger products was Los Angeles. Nielsen drugstore audits indicated that Lucky Tiger had at least one size of one of its items (not counting hair wax) in from 92% to 96% of the drugstores in the Southwest, Pacific Coast, West Central, and Southeast. The figure was about 87% for the mid-Atlantic states and about 63% for New England and the New York area. Lucky Tiger products also were well represented in barbershops, although this segment of the business was not a profitable one because of keen price competition among suppliers and the size of barber dealer discounts. The company had only spotty distribution in grocery stores, which were reached through wholesalers, rack jobbers, and chains. Distribution figures for the company's hair wax were substantially below those for its hair tonic.

The company had a sales force of eight men, each of whom was responsible for a given geographical area. The salesmen attempted to call on all major accounts once every 90 days. In addition to calling on direct accounts, jobbers, and wholesalers, the salesmen were asked to make three detailing calls a day on retail stores. It was customary for either Mr. Stephen Harris, the president, or Mr. L. Chandler Smith, the executive vice president, to spend a certain amount of time during the year with each salesman, accompanying him on selected calls.

Sales Promotion

Early in 1958 the top executives were reconsidering the questions of how much the company should spend on a sales promotional program and what kind of a program would best enable it to increase its market position.

Lucky Tiger faced several major competitors with much larger promotional budgets. Vitalis, for example, was one of the products of Bristol-Myers Company, one of the nation's largest advertisers. Measured media expenditures indicated that the brand was spending about $2,000,000 in network television in 1957, $500,000 in general consumer magazines, and $394,000 in network television.[2] Advertising expenditures for the Vaseline hair line of Chesebrough-Pond's, Inc., were estimated to be in excess of $2,000,000, the bulk of this going for the alternate week sponsorship of the Bob Cummings Show on network television. Some magazine advertising was being used for "Valcream."[3] Measured media expenditures showed that the Wildroot Company, Inc., in 1957 was spending about $1,700,000 for network television advertising of "Wildroot Cream Oil." This figure was for gross time charges only and did not include production and talent costs.[4]

Lucky Tiger had never been a large advertiser, although its expenditures had increased somewhat over the last several years. The company had tried several different approaches. A limited amount of consumer magazine advertising was undertaken in the early 1950's. During this time, the company ran one full-page advertisement in *Esquire* and two full-page advertisements in *Popular Mechanics*. Designed to attract attention and to stimulate word-of-mouth advertising, the advertisements contained coupons by which readers could send in for a free colored photograph of "The Lucky Tiger Girl." (See Exhibit 2.) Many coupons were returned (39,000 in response to the *Esquire* advertisement and 54,000 in response to the *Popular Mechanics* advertisements), but the company could find no evidence that the advertising resulted in sales of Lucky Tiger hair tonic.

In 1955 the company tried spot radio announcements for its hair tonic, sharing with "Barbasol" shaving cream a schedule of 26 spots a week for 52 weeks in 15 markets. The number of spots per week alternated between six and 20 by six-week periods. In one such period Lucky Tiger had six spots a week while Barbasol had 20. In the next six-week period Lucky Tiger had 20 while Barbasol had six. The cost of a year's schedule to Lucky Tiger ranged from $8,000 to $20,000, depending on the size of the market.

The company put its advertising emphasis on spot television announcements in 1956, starting on a small scale and branching out on a market-to-market basis. In view of the costs involved, Mr. Harris believed that a small advertiser like Lucky Tiger could afford to use television only if it could

---

[2] *Advertising Age*, August 25, 1958, p. 73. This source described Vitalis as "a front runner in some areas, but more often last in the close three-way battle between Vaseline, Wildroot and Vitalis; its share of market is between 15 and 20%."

[3] *Ibid.*

[4] *National Advertising Investments*, Vol. IX, No. 2, 1957, compiled and published by Leading National Advertisers, Inc. The measurements of expenditures were made by Publishers Information Bureau which checked three media: Sunday magazine sections of newspapers, magazines, and network television.

avoid ineffective commercials. To this end the company developed a means of pretesting its commercials before undertaking the expense of producing and filming them.

The procedure was to let the first public viewing of the commercial serve as a test to gauge the commercial's effectiveness and to indicate whether improvements were needed. This was done by means of what was referred to as the "telephone gimmick." In the commercial an announcement was made that the company would give a free jar of Lucky Tiger

Exhibit 2

LUCKY TIGER MANUFACTURING COMPANY

hair tonic (or wax) to the first 100 persons who, in the next half hour, called the telephone number superimposed on the television screen. Actually a telephone answering service received calls for an hour, and sometimes for an hour and a half, after the commercial. All calls received were honored, each person being sent a card which he could exchange at a retail store for a 59 cents bottle of the product advertised. The company guaranteed to redeem the card from the retailer for 59 cents plus 2 cents for handling provided that it was used in accordance with the offer and providing that the retailer mailed it within 30 days to the Nielsen Coupon Clearing House in Chicago.

It was the company's practice to vary a commercial during testing until it was felt that the peak number of telephone calls had been reached. Then the commercial would be filmed with no changes—using the same actors, the same announcers, and the same backdrops. This procedure helped to keep production costs down. "The commercial may not look as much like a finished product as it would have if new props and fancier backdrops were substituted," said Mr. Harris, "but we are pretty sure the TV commercial as we have filmed it works."

While no direct evidence was available as to the sales effectiveness of a given television spot announcement, it was Mr. Harris' impression, gained from observing sales figures in selected markets in which spot television schedules were run, that there was a reasonably reliable relationship between the number of telephone calls and the sales results of the advertising.

The "telephone gimmick" was used for the first several showings of a spot announcement in a new market in order to check its acceptance there. "By this means," Mr. Harris explained, "we can estimate how the market probably will react to the product, particularly if we are using television spots there for the first time. The telephone gimmick gives us statistics we can work with after the first two or three times we are on the air.

"In 1956, we went into Denver with a commercial we had tested in Kansas City," Mr. Harris said. "We used a major chain as an inventory control test of sales of the product and the telephone gimmick as a guide to the effectiveness of the commercial. We found that the commercial produced more phone calls in Denver than it had in Kansas City. We stayed with our spot for a 26-week period and achieved the number-one position in the market for our product.

"There also have been instances where the reverse happened," Mr. Harris said. "But by using the telephone gimmick, we knew we were not getting across, so we pulled out of the market. In these cases, we may go back later with a different show and time.

"In order to be successful, the telephone-reaction technique must be used in co-operation with existing major factors in the market," Mr. Harris continued. "In our case, co-operation with chain stores, for instance, gives us sufficiently widespread outlets to provide a comprehensive cross section of the market. And this is most effectively accomplished where a close-range, personal management level relationship exists."

In 1957 the company spent about $120,000 for advertising, the bulk of which went for spot announcement television. A breakdown of the total follows:

Television time.		$ 54,322
Hair wax.	$45,104	
Hair tonic.	9,218	
Television films for Waterloo, Ia., test.		4,750
Telephone answering service plus cost of Nielsen Coupon Clearing		
House.		5,000
Cost of free samples.		5,000
Newspaper space—Denver test.		5,178
Magazine ad—Esquire, (9–57).		12,000
Space.	$ 8,400	
Other.	3,600	
Co-operative advertising allowances.		26,000
Trade publications.		7,500
		$119,750

The $7,500 total for trade advertising included both space and production costs. The company ran three or four advertisements during the year in two publications for retail druggists: *Profitunities,* published by McKesson & Robbins, Inc., and *DSC Buying Guide.* The company also advertised once a month in two barber publications: *Master Barber* and *Barber's Journal.*

In the co-operative advertising program, the company offered to pay retailers amounts up to 10% of their net quarterly purchases of merchandise for newspaper, shopping news, radio, or television advertising run on Lucky Tiger products. The company made available to the retailers newspaper mats, radio copy, and television films.

The major emphasis in 1957 was placed on Lucky Tiger's Butch hair wax which was the subject of 264 one-minute spot announcements on 36 television stations in 28 cities (see Exhibits 3 and 4). The commercials were scheduled from mid-March through September, although most of

Exhibit 3

LUCKY TIGER MANUFACTURING COMPANY

Date	Show	Time for Film	Show Rating	Film Number*

SCHEDULE FOR SHOWINGS OF BUTCH HAIR WAX COMMERCIAL FILMS
SHREVEPORT, LA., KTBS-TV ($100)†

Date	Show	Time for Film	Show Rating	Film Number*
Mar. 25, Mon.....	Between Dragnet and This Is Your Life	9:30	36.4	57.1
Apr. 1, Mon.....	"	9:30	36.4	57.1
Apr. 8, Mon.....	"	9:30	36.4	57.1
Apr. 15, Mon.....	"	9:30	36.4	57.1
Apr. 22, Mon.....	"	9:30	36.4	57.1
Apr. 29, Mon.....	"	9:30	36.4	57.2
May 6, Mon.....	"	9:30	36.4	57.2
May 13, Mon.....	"	9:30	36.4	57.2

DETROIT, MICH., WXYZ-TV ($150)

Date	Show	Time for Film	Show Rating	Film Number*
Mar. 10, Sun......	Cunningham's Jumbo Theatre	3:30–4:30		57.2
Mar. 17, Sun......	"	3:30–4:30		57.2
Mar. 24, Sun......	"	3:30–4:30		57.2
Mar. 31, Sun......	"	3:30–4:30		57.2
Apr. 7, Sun......	"	3:30–4:30		57.2
Apr. 14, Sun......	"	3:30–4:30		57.1
Apr. 21, Sun......	"	3:30–4:30		57.1
Apr. 28, Sun......	"	3:30–4:30		57.1
May 5, Sun......	"	3:30–4:30		57.1
May 12, Sun......	"	3:30–4:30		57.1
May 19, Sun......	"	3:30–4:30		57.2
May 26, Sun......	"	3:30–4:30		57.2
June 2, Sun......	"	3:30–4:30		57.2

* Film 57–1 invited viewers to telephone in to receive a free sample: film 57–2 did not. Both films were one minute in length.

† Figures in parentheses are approximate cost per showing of the one-minute film.

Exhibit 3—Continued

Date	Show	Time for Film	Show Rating	Film Number*
HOUSTON, TEXAS, KPRC-TV ($225)				
Mar. 20, Wed.....	Science Fiction Theatre	10:00–10:30	22.7	57.1
Mar. 27, Wed.....	"	10:00–10:30	22.7	57.1
ATLANTA, GA., WSB-TV ($100)				
Mar. 16, Sat......	Between Hit Parade and MGM Movie	11:00	22.5 avg.	57.1
Mar. 23, Sat......	"	11:00	22.5	57.1
Mar. 30, Sat......	"	11:00	22.5	57.1
Apr. 6, Sat......	"	11:00	22.5	57.1
Apr. 13, Sat......	"	11:00	22.5	57.1
ATLANTA, GA., WLW-A ($50)				
Mar. 25, Mon.....	World News	11:00–11:10	11.4	57.1
Mar. 26, Tues.....	"	11:00–11:10	7.0	57.1
Mar. 27, Wed.....	"	10:45–11:00	14.3	57.1
Mar. 29, Fri......	"	11:00–11:10	10.1	57.1
Mar. 31, Sun......	Movietime USA	2:30– 4:00	11.9	57.1
Apr. 1, Mon.....	World News	11:00–11:10	11.4	57.2
Apr. 3, Wed.....	"	10:45–11:00	14.3	57.2
Apr. 4, Thurs....	"	11:00–11:10	7.0	57.2
Apr. 5, Fri......	"	11:00–11:10	10.1	57.2
Apr. 7, Sun......	Movietime USA	2:30– 4:00	11.9	57.2
Apr. 8, Mon.....	World News	11:00–11:10	11.4	57.2
Apr. 10, Wed.....	"	10:45–11:00	14.3	57.2
Apr. 11, Thurs....	"	11:00–11:10	7.0	57.2
Apr. 12, Fri......	"	11:00–11:10	10.1	57.2
Apr. 14, Sun......	Movietime USA	2:30– 4:00	11.9	57.2
Mar. 19, Tues.....	Biff Baker	6:30– 7:00	18.2	57.1
Mar. 26, Tues.....	"	6:30– 7:00	18.2	57.1
Apr. 2, Tues.....	"	6:30– 7:00	18.2	57.1
Apr. 9, Tues.....	"	6:30– 7:00	18.2	57.1
ATLANTA, GA., WAGA-TV ($250)				
Mar. 27, Wed.....	Man Called X (within)	7:00– 7:30	20.6	57.1
Apr. 3, Wed.....	"	7:00– 7:30	20.6	57.1
Apr. 10, Wed.....	"	7:00– 7:30	20.6	57.1
MEMPHIS, TENN., WHBQ-TV ($55)				
Mar. 16, Sat......	Between Sky King and Teen Town	5:00	17.0	57.1
Mar. 23, Sat......	"	5:00	17.0	57.1
Mar. 30, Sat......	"	5:00	17.0	57.1
Apr. 6, Sat......	"	5:00	17.0	57.1
Apr. 13, Sat......	"	5:00	17.0	57.2
Apr. 20, Sat.	"	5:00	17.0	57.2
Apr. 27, Sat.....	"	5:00	17.0	57.2
May 4, Sat......	"	5:00	17.0	57.2

* Film 57–1 invited viewers to telephone in to receive a free sample: film 57–2 did not. Both films were one minute in length.

Exhibit 3—Continued

Date	Show	Time for Film	Show Rating	Film Number*
MEMPHIS, TENN., WREC-TV ($105)				
Mar. 26, Tues.....	Range Rider (within)	6:00–6:30	16.2	57.1
Apr. 2, Tues.....	"	6:00–6:30	16.2	57.1
Apr. 9, Tues.....	"	6:00–6:30	16.2	57.1
Apr. 16, Tues.....	"	6:00–6-30	16.2	57.1
SAN DIEGO, CALIF., KFMB-TV ($200)				
Mar. 19, Tues.....	This Day (within)	7:30–8:00	31.6	57.1
Mar. 26, Tues.....	"	7:30–8:00	31.6	57.1
Apr. 2, Tues.....	"	7:30–8:00	31.6	57.1
Apr. 9, Tues.....				
Apr. 17, Wed.....	Between This Day and Last of the Mohicans	6:30	20.2 avg.	57.1
Apr. 24, Wed.....	"	6:30	20.2	57.1
DALLAS, TEX., WFAA-TV ($105)				
Mar. 20, Wed.....	Mr. District Attorney	10:00–10:30	New	57.1
Mar. 27, Wed.....	"	10:00–10–30	New	57.1
Apr. 3, Wed.....	"	10:00–10:30	New	57.1
Apr. 10, Wed.....	"	10:00–10:30	New	57.1
Apr. 15, Mon.....	Final News	10:30		57.1
Apr. 22, Mon.....	"	10:30		57.1
Apr. 29, Mon.....	"	10:30		57.2
May 3, Mon.....	"	10:30		57.2
DALLAS, TEX., WBAT-TV ($290)				
May 2, Tues.....	Cisco Kid (within)	6:00–6:30		57.1
May 9, Tues.....	"	6:00–6:30		57.1
May 16, Tues.....	"	6:00–6:30		57.2
May 23, Tues.....	"	6:00–6:30		57.2
May 30, Tues.....	"	6:00–6:30		57.2
ALBUQUERQUE, N.M., KOAT-TV ($105)				
Mar. 25, Mon.....	Between I Led Three Lives and Live Wrestling	8:30	19.7	57.1
Apr. 1, Mon.....	"	8:30	19.7	57.1
Apr. 8, Mon.....	"	8:30	19.7	57.1
Apr. 15, Mon.....	"	8:30	19.7	57.2
Apr. 22, Mon.....	"	8:30	19.7	57.2
Apr. 29, Mon.....	"	8:30	19.7	57.2

* Film 57–1 invited viewers to telephone in to receive a free sample: film 57–2 did not. Both films were one minute in length.

Exhibit 3—Continued

Date	Show	Time for Film	Show Rating	Film Number*
	LOS ANGELES, CALIF., KTTV ($450)			
Mar. 17, Sun......	Jalopy Derby	2–5	9.5 avg.	57.2
Mar. 19, Tues.....	MGM Movies	10:15–11:35	14.0 avg.	57.2
Mar. 24, Sun......	Jalopy Derby	2–5	9.5 avg.	57.1
Mar. 26, Tues.....	MGM Movies	10:15–11:35	14.0 avg.	57.1
Mar. 31, Sun......	Jalopy Derby	2–5	9.5 avg.	57.1
Apr. 2, Tues.....	MGM Movies	10:15–11:35	14.0 avg.	57.1
Apr. 7, Sun......	Jalopy Derby	2–5	9.5 avg.	57.2
Apr. 9, Tues.....	MGM Movies	10:15–11:35	14.0 avg.	57.2
Apr. 14, Sun......	Jalopy Derby	2–5	9.5 avg.	57.2
	CHARLOTTE, N.C., WBTV ($200)			
Apr. 5, Fri......	Patti Page Show	6:50– 7:05	41.5	57.1
Apr. 12, Fri......	"	6:50– 7:05	41.5	57.1
Apr. 19, Fri......	"	6:50– 7:05	41.5	57.1
Apr. 26, Fri......	"	6:50– 7:05	41.5	57.1
May 3, Fri......	"	10:00–10:15		57.1
May 10, Fri......	"	10:00–10:15		57.1
May 17, Fri......	"	10:00–10:15		57.1
	NASHVILLE, TENN., WSM-TV ($86)			
Apr. 20, Sat......	Between Coke Dance Party and Roy Rogers	5:30	23.8 avg.	57.1
Apr. 24, Wed.....	Between Annie Oakley and Xavier Cugat	6:30	18.6 avg.	57.1
Apr. 27, Sat......	Between Coke Dance Party and Roy Rogers	5:30	23.8 avg.	57.1
May 1, Wed.....	Between Annie Oakley and Xavier Cugat	6:30	18.6 avg.	57.1
May 4, Sat......	Between Coke Dance Party and Roy Rogers	5:30	23.8 avg.	57.1
May 8, Wed.....	Between Annie Oakley and Xavier Cugat	6:30	18.6 avg.	57.1
May 11, Sat......	Between Coke Dance Party and Roy Rogers	5:30	23.8 avg.	57.2
May 15, Wed.....	Between Annie Oakley and Xavier Cugat	6:30	18.6 avg.	57.2
May 18, Sat......	Between Coke Dance Party and Roy Rogers	5:30	23.8 avg.	57.2
May 22, Wed.....	Between Annie Oakley and Xavier Cugat	6:30	18.6 avg.	57.2
May 25, Sat......	Between Coke Dance Party and Roy Rogers	5:30	23.8 avg.	57.2

* Film 57–1 invited viewers to telephone in to receive a free sample: film 57–2 did not. Both films were one minute in length.

Exhibit 3—Continued

Date	Show	Time for Film	Show Rating	Film Number*
FRESNO, CALIF., KMJ-TV ($115)				
Apr. 21, Sun......	Between Annie Oakley and Big Time Movie	6:00	22.8 avg.	57.1
Apr. 24, Wed.....	Between This Is Your Life and Man Called X	10:30	19.1	57.1
Apr. 28, Sun......	Between Annie Oakley and Big Time Movie	6:00	22.8	57.1
May 1, Wed.....	Between This Is Your Life and Man Called X	10:30	19.1	57.1
May 5, Sun......	Between Annie Oakley and Big Time Movie	6:00	22.8	57.1
May 12, Wed.....	Between Annie Oakley and Big Time Movie	6:00	22.8	57.1
DAYTON, O., WLW-D ($40)				
Apr. 22, Mon.....	Tonight in Sports	11:25–11:30	12.7 avg.	57.1
Apr. 24, Wed.....	"	11:25–11:30	12.7	57.1
Apr. 29, Mon.....	"	11:25–11:30	12.7	57.1
May 1, Wed.....	"	11:25–11:30	12.7	57.1
May 6, Mon.....	"	11:25–11:30	12.7	57.1
May 8, Wed.....	"	11:25–11:30	12.7	57.1
May 13, Mon.....	"	11:25–11:30	12.7	57.1
May 15, Wed.....	Candid Camera	11:15–11:30	12.7	57.2
May 20, Mon.....	"	11:15–11:30	12.7	57.2
May 22, Wed.....	"	11:15–11:30	12.7	57.2
May 27, Mon.....	"	11:15–11:30	12.7	57.2
May 29, Wed.....	"	11:15–11:30	12.7	57.2
WICHITA, KAN., KARD-TV ($125)				
Apr. 21, Sun......	Between Loretta Young and Whirlybirds	9:30	34.0 avg.	57.1
Apr. 27, Sat......	Between Hit Parade and News	10:00	34.4	57.1
Apr. 28, Sun......	Between Loretta Young and Whirlybirds	9:30	34.0	57.1
May 4, Sat......	Between Hit Parade and News	10:00	34.4	57.1
May 5, Sun......	Between Loretta Young and Whirlybirds	9:30	34.0	57.1
May 11, Sat......	Between Hit Parade and News	10:00	34.4	57.1
May 12, Sun......	Between Loretta Young and Whirlybirds	9:30	34.0	57.1
May 18, Sat......	Between Hit Parade and Waterfront	9:00	34.4	57.1
May 19, Sun......	Between Loretta Young and Whirlybirds	9:30	34.0	57.1
May 26, Sun......	Between Loretta Young and Whirlybirds	9:30	34.0	57.1

* Film 57–1 invited viewers to telephone in to receive a free sample: film 57–2 did not. Both films were one minute in length.

Exhibit 3—Continued

Date	Show	Time for Film	Show Rating	Film Number*

Madison, Wis., WMTV ($46)

Date	Show	Time for Film	Show Rating	Film Number*
Apr. 2, Tues.....	(3 spots between 2:00 and 11:15 P.M.)			57–1
Apr. 10, Wed.....	(3 spots between 2:00 and 11:15 P.M.)			57–1
Apr. 18, Thurs....	(2 spots between 6:00 and 11:15 P.M.)			57–1
Apr. 28, Sun......	(2 spots between 6:00 and 11:15 P.M.)			57–1

Little Rock, Ark., KATV ($90)

Date	Show	Time for Film	Show Rating	Film Number*
May 2, Thurs....	Between Broken Arrow and Telephone Time	9:00	19.7 avg.	57.1
May 4, Sat......	Between Ozark Jubilee and Wire Service	9:00	20.1	57.1
May 9, Thurs....	Between Broken Arrow and Telephone Time	9:00	19.7	57.1
May 11, Sat......	Between Ozark Jubilee and Wire Service	9:00	20.1	57.1
May 16, Thurs....	Between Broken Arrow and Telephone Time	9:00	12.7	57.1
May 18, Sat......	Between Lawrence Welk and Ozark Jubilee	8:00	32.9	57.1
May 23, Thurs....	Between Broken Arrow and Telephone Time	9:00	2.7	57.1
May 25, Sat......	Between Lawrence Welk and Ozark Jubilee	8:00	32.9	57.1

Colorado Springs, Col., KKTV ($50)

Date	Show	Time for Film	Show Rating	Film Number*
Apr. 20, Sat......	Between Lawrence Welk and Weather	10:05	32.1 avg.	57–1
Apr. 27, Sat......	"	10:05	32.1	57–1
May 4, Sat......	"	10:05	32.1	57–1
May 11, Sat......	"	10:05	32.1	57–1
May 18, Sat......	Between Late Show and Weather	10:05	32.1	57–1
May 25, Sat......	"	10:05	32.1	57–1
June 1, Sat......	"	10:05	32.1	57–2
June 8, Sat......	"	10:05	32.1	57–2
June 15, Sat......	"	10:05	32.1	57–2
June 22, Sat......	"	10:05	32.1	57–2

* Film 57–1 invited viewers to telephone in to receive a free sample: film 57–2 did not. Both films were one minute in length.

Exhibit 3—Continued

Date	Show	Time for Film	Show Rating	Film Number*
	Kansas City, Mo., KCMO-TV			
	Approximate Cost of Saturday plus Sunday Showings: ($350)			
Apr. 20, Sat......	Million Dollar Movie	10:00–12:00	47.3	57–1
Apr. 21, Sun......	"	2:00– 4:00	Combined	57–1
Apr. 27, Sat......	"	10:00–12:00	Combined	57–1
Apr. 28, Sun......	"	2:00– 4:00	Combined	57–1
May 4, Sat......	"	10:00–12:00	Combined	57–1
May 5, Sun......	"	2:00– 4:00	Combined	57–1
May 11, Sat......	"	10:00–12:00	Combined	57–1
May 12, Sun......	"	2:00– 4:00	Combined	57–1
May 18, Sat......	"	10:00–12:00	Combined	57–1
May 19, Sun......	"	2:00– 4:00	Combined	57–1
May 25, Sat......	"	10:00–12:00	Combined	57–1
May 26, Sun......	"	2:00– 4:00	Combined	57–1
	Chicago, Ill., WBBM-TV ($900)			
May 25, Sat......	Four Star Playhouse	9:30–10:00	27.7	57–1
June 8, Sat......	"	9:30–10:00	27.7	57–1
June 22, Sat......	"	9:30–10:00	27.7	57–1
	Chicago, Ill., WBKB-TV ($135)			
June 1, Sat......	Recordland Bandstand	1:30–3:30	New	57–1
June 15, Sat......	"	1:30–3:30	New	57–1
June 29, Sat......	"	1:30–3:30	New	57–1
July 6, Sat......	"	1:30–3:30	New	57–2
July 13, Sat......	"	1:30–3:30	New	57–2
	Omaha, Neb., KMTV ($65)			
June 1, Sat......	Between Masquerade Party and Father Knows Best	9:30	32.8 avg.	57–1
June 8, Sat......	"	9:30	32.8	57–1
June 15, Sat......	"	9:30	32.8	57–1
	Omaha, Neb., WOW-TV ($135)			
May 25, Sat......	Between Warm-up Time and Game of the Week	1:00	New	57–1
June 1, Sat......	"	1:00	New	57–1
June 8, Sat......	"	1:00	New	57–1
June 15, Sat......	"	1:00	New	57–1
June 22, Sat......	"	1:00	New	57–1
June 29, Sat......	"	1:00	New	57–1

* Film 57–1 invited viewers to telephone in to receive a free sample: film 57–2 did not. Both films were one minute in length.

Exhibit 3—Continued

Date	Show	Time for Film	Show Rating	Film Number*
	DENVER, COLO., KLZ-TV ($75)			
May 23, Thurs....	Dick Lewis Show	10:30–10:45	9.1	57–1
May 30, Thurs....	"	10:30–10:45	9.1	57–1
June 6, Thurs....	"	10:30–10:45	9.1	57–1
June 13, Thurs....	"	10:30–10:45	9.1	57–2
June 20, Thurs....	"	10:30–10:45	9.1	57–2
June 27, Thurs....	"	10:30–10:45	9.1	57–2
	DENVER, COLO., KOA-TV ($120)			
May 26, Sun......	Academy Theatre	9:00–11:00	13.0	57–1
June 2, Sun......	"	9:00–11:00	13.0	57–1
June 9, Sun......	"	9:00–11:00	13.0	57–1
June 16, Sun......	"	9:00–11:00	13.0	57–2
June 23, Sun......	"	9:00–11:00	13.0	57–2
June 30, Sun......	"	9:00–11:00	13.0	57–2
	WASHINGTON, D.C., WMAL-TV ($120)			
May 29, Wed.....	Town & Country Time	6:30–7:00	7.1	57–2
June 1, Sat......	Championship Bowling	6:00–7:00	8.8	57–2
June 2, Sun......	Three Musketeers	6:30–7:00	New	57–1
June 5, Wed....	Town & Country Time	6:00–7:00	7.1	57–2
June 8, Sat......	Championship Bowling	6:30–7:00	8.8	57–2
June 9, Sun......	Three Musketeers	6:00–7:00	New	57–1
June 12, Wed.....	Town & Country Time	6:30–7:00	7.1	57–2
June 15, Sat......	Championship Bowling	6:00–7:00	8.8	57–2
June 16, Sun......	Three Musketeers	6:30–7:00	New	57–1
	WASHINGTON, D.C., WTOP-TV ($150)			
June 1, Sat......	Stories of the Century	6:30–7:00	16.1	57–1
June 8, Sat......	"	6:30–7:00	16.1	57–1
June 15, Sat......	"	6:30–7:00	16.1	57–1
	CLEVELAND, O., WJW-TV ($120)			
June 2, Sun......	Nite Owl Theatre	11:20–concl.	19.8	57–1
June 4, Tues.....	"	11:20–concl.	Wkly.	57–1
June 6, Thurs....	"	11:20–concl.	Wkly.	57–1
June 16, Sun......	"	11:20–concl.	Wkly.	57–1
June 18, Tues.....	"	11:20–concl.	Wkly.	57–1
June 20, Thurs....	"	11:20–concl.	Wkly.	57–2
June 30, Sun......	"	11:20–concl.	Wkly.	57–2
July 2, Tues.....	"	11:20–concl.	Wkly.	57–2
July 4, Thurs....	"	11:20–concl.	Wkly.	57–2
June 12, Wed.....	News Parade	6:15–6:30		57–1
June 14, Fri......	"	6:15–6:30		57–1
June 26, Wed....	"	6:15–6:30		57–2
June 28, Fri......	"	6:15–6:30		57–2

* Film 57–1 invited viewers to telephone in to receive a free sample: film 57–2 did not. Both films were one minute in length.

Exhibit 3—Continued

Date	Show	Time for Film	Show Rating	Film Number*
SALT LAKE CITY, UTAH, KUTV ($135)				
May 18, Sat......	Frontier	10:00–10:30	26.7	57–2
May 25, Sat......	"	10:00–10:30	26.7	57–2
June 1, Sat......	"	10:00–10:30	26.7	57–2
EVANSVILLE, IND., WEHT-TV ($60)				
May 19, Sun......	My Little Margie	8:30–9:00		57–1
May 26, Sun......	"	8:30–9:00		57–1
June 2, Sun......	"	8:30–9:00		57–1
June 9, Sun......	"	8:30–9:00		57–1
PORTLAND, ORE., KPTV ($60)				
July 5, Fri......	Between Outdoor By Line and Famous Fights	5:45 P.M.		57–1
July 12, Fri......	"	5:45		57–1
July 19, Fri......	"	5:45		57–1
July 26, Fri......	"	5:45		57–1
Aug. 2, Fri......	"	5:45		57–1
Aug. 9, Fri......	"	5:45		57–1
Aug. 16, Fri......	"	5:45		57–1
Aug. 23, Fri......	"	5:45		57–2
Aug. 30, Fri......	"	5:45		57–2
Sept. 6, Fri......	"	5:45		57–2
Sept. 13, Fri......	"	5:45		57–2
Sept. 20, Fri......	"	5:45		57–2
Sept. 27, Fri......	"	5:45		57–2
COLUMBUS, O., WTVN-TV ($200)				
July 15, Mon.....	Between State Trooper and News	10:00 P.M.	30.2	57–1
July 22, Mon.....	"	10:00		57–1
July 29, Mon.....	"	10:00		57–1
Aug. 5, Mon.....	"	10:00		57–1
MINNEAPOLIS, MINN., KSTP-TV ($150)				
July 4, Thurs....	You Should Know	6:15–6:30 P.M.	21.5	57–1
July 11, Thurs....	"	6:15–6:30		57–1
July 18, Thurs....	"	6:15–6:30		57–1
July 25, Thurs....	"	6:15–6:30		57–1
Aug. 1, Thurs....	"	6:15–6:30		57–1
Aug. 8, Thurs....	"	6:15–6:30		57–2
Aug. 15, Thurs....	"	6:15–6:30		57–2
Aug. 22, Thurs....	"	6:15–6:30		57–2
Aug. 29, Thurs....	"	6:15–6:30		57–2

* Film 57–1 invited viewers to telephone in to receive a free sample: film 57–2 did not. Both films were one minute in length.

Exhibit 3—Continued

Date	Show	Time for Film	Show Rating	Film Number

SCHEDULE FOR SHOWINGS OF HAIR TONIC COMMERCIAL FILMS
COLUMBIA, S.C., WNOK-TV ($40)

Date	Show	Time for Film	Show Rating	Film Number
July 19, Fri......	Between Ray Milland and Zane Gray	7:30	Tonic	57-A
July 26, Fri......	"	7:30	Tonic	57-A
Aug. 2, Fri......	"	7:30	Tonic	57-A
Aug. 9, Fri......	"	7:30	Tonic	57-B
Aug. 16, Fri......	"	7:30	Tonic	57-B
Aug. 23, Fri......	"	7:30	Tonic	57-B
Aug. 30, Fri......	"	7:30	Tonic	57-B

CHARLOTTE, N.C., WSOC-TV ($225)

Date	Show	Time for Film	Show Rating	Film Number
July 17, Wed.....	Highway Patrol	9:30–10:00 P.M.	Tonic	57-A
July 31, Wed.....	"	9:30–10:00	Tonic	57-A
Aug. 14, Wed.....	"	9:30–10:00	Tonic	57-A
Aug. 28, Wed.....	"	9:30–10:00	Tonic	57-A

GREENVILLE, S.C., WFBC-TV ($62.50)

Date	Show	Time for Film	Show Rating	Film Number
July 19, Fri......	Movierama	10:30–11:00 P.M.	Tonic	57-A
July 26, Fri......	"	10:30–11:00	Tonic	57-A
Aug. 2, Fri......	"	10:30–11:00	Tonic	57-A
Aug. 9, Fri......	"	10:30–11:00	Tonic	57-A
Aug. 16, Fri......	"	10:30–11:00	Tonic	57-B
Aug. 23, Fri......	"	10:30–11:00	Tonic	57-B
Aug. 30, Fri......	"	10:30–11:00	Tonic	57-B

WATERLOO, IA., KWWL-TV ($65)
This Schedule Ran for 13 Weeks from July 1 through September 28, 1957

Date	Show	Time for Film	Show Rating	Film Number
Monday through Saturday.......	Between network program and News	10:00 P.M.		
Monday, Wednesday, and Friday.	News, weather, and sports	6:00–6:30 P.M.		

(During the week of July 1–6, commercials for Butch hair wax were shown. The telephone gimmick was used at 10:00 P.M. on July 2 and 4 at 6:20 P.M. on July 3. All other Butch wax spots were without the telephone gimmick. The remaining 12 weeks of the schedule were devoted to Lucky Tiger hair tonic.)

them appeared in April and May, the first two major months of the hair wax season. In order to reach men the company instructed its advertising agency to try to buy times between 7:00 P.M. and 10:30 P.M.

In selecting markets for advertising schedules, the company limited the number so that its relatively small sales force would be able to give them the necessary time. Several prospective markets were identified for each salesman on the basis of size and opportunity for obtaining adequate merchandising support from wholesalers, chains, and independent retail-

Exhibit 4

LUCKY TIGER MANUFACTURING COMPANY
Summary of Television Advertising by Cities

City	No. of TV Stations Used	No. of 1-Minute Commercials	Approximate Cost of Time
BUTCH HAIR WAX			
Albuquerque, N.M.	1	6	$ 630
Atlanta, Ga.	3	27	2,200
Charlotte, N.C.	1	8	1,600
Chicago, Ill.	2	8	3,370
Colorado Springs, Colo.	1	10	500
Cleveland, Ohio	1	13	1,560
Columbus, Ohio	1	4	240
Dallas, Texas	2	13	2,290
Dayton, Ohio	1	12	480
Denver, Colo.	2	12	1,170
Detroit, Mich.	1	13	1,950
Evansville, Ind.	1	4	240
Fresno, Calif.	1	6	690
Houston, Texas	1	2	450
Kansas City, Mo.	1	12	2,100
Little Rock, Ark.	1	8	720
Los Angeles, Calif.	1	9	4,050
Madison, Wis.	1	4	184
Memphis, Tenn.	2	12	860
Minneapolis, Minn.	1	9	1,350
Nashville, Tenn.	1	11	940
Omaha, Neb.	2	9	1,005
Portland, Ore.	1	13	780
Salt Lake City, Utah	1	3	405
San Diego, Calif.	1	6	630
Shreveport, La.	1	8	800
Washington, D.C.	2	12	1,530
Wichita, Kas.	1	10	1,250
	36	264	$35,104
HAIR TONIC			
Charlotte, N.C.	1	4	$ 900
Columbia, S.C.	1	7	280
Greenville, S.C.	1	7	438
Waterloo, Ia. (Test)*	1	117	7,600
	4	135	$ 9,218

* Nine of these commercials during the first week of the test were devoted to hair wax, the remainder to hair tonic.

ers. Final selections then were made after the advertising agency had determined the time costs and availabilities.

In July 1957 the company launched two market tests by which it hoped to learn more about the relative effectiveness of newspapers and television as media for its advertising. Both tests involved advertisements for Lucky Tiger hair tonic.

Exhibit 5

LUCKY TIGER MANUFACTURING COMPANY

Newspapers were used in Denver over a 13-week period starting Sunday, July 7. The schedule included 21 advertisements totaling 7,500 lines which appeared in both sports page and run-of-paper locations. Six 300-line advertisements were run in Sunday editions of the *Rocky Mountain News*. Four 600-line advertisements and 11 300-line advertisements were run in the *Denver Post*, ten of them appearing on Sunday and the others on Tuesday and Friday. Half of the advertisements featured "good grooming" (see Exhibit 5), while the other half employed a "blood cir-

Exhibit 6

LUCKY TIGER MANUFACTURING COMPANY

New Improved LUCKY TIGER *Speeds* Scalp Circulation!

SPEEDS CIRCULATION

POOR CIRCULATION

New, improved Lucky Tiger (left) now contains *special penetrating ingredients*. Laboratory tests have shown these ingredients in new, improved Lucky Tiger actually speed up circulation of vital hair-feeding blood. This means when you use new Lucky Tiger you have stronger, healthier hair. Lucky Tiger helps you keep your hair and scalp healthier!

But, old-fashioned hair tonic (right) does not stimulate the flow of vital blood that feeds the hair roots. Result? Hair becomes progressively undernourished and weaker. It eventually gets lifeless and dull and tends to die. Unless the blood circulates freely in the scalp zone, the condition of your hair automatically goes from bad to worse.

COVERS HAIR and SCALP in 9 SECONDS for BETTER GROOMING

The *special penetrating ingredients* and the non-greasy grooming agents in new, improved Lucky Tiger completely cover your scalp and hair in *only 9 seconds!* And this faster, better *coverage* grooms your hair perfectly and keeps it that way *all day long* with only one application! Just shake it on—look your best always!

Try new Lucky Tiger now!

LUCKY TIGER
hair tonic

Free!

Now, while they last — send in the coupon for your free package which contains enough new Lucky Tiger for a full application! Try it once, and you will always want to use new Lucky Tiger Hair Tonic!

LUCKY TIGER · 2901 FAIRMOUNT · KANSAS CITY, MO.

Please send me my FREE foil package containing enough Lucky Tiger for a full application.

(PLEASE PRINT)

NAME_____

ADDRESS_____

CITY_____

STATE_____

c

culation" theme (see Exhibit 6). Some of the advertisements contained coupons by which readers might send in for free samples. Total cost of newspaper space was $5,178.

In the test, sales were observed in a selected panel of 15 retail stores.

Sales were measured for seven weeks before the test started, 13 weeks during the test, and eight weeks after it had ended. The results were very disappointing to company executives who tentatively eliminated the possibility of mass promoting their products through newspapers. While some sales increase was noted, it was far from enough to justify the advertising cost. The advertisements also pulled a few requests for free samples.

On July 1, 1957 the company launched a test of spot television in Waterloo, Iowa, using a schedule of nine full-minute spots a week for a period of 13 weeks over KWWL-TV. The station's reception area was eastern Iowa, including Waterloo, Cedar Rapids, and Dubuque. While Waterloo was selected for the test primarily because it was one of the cities in which the A. C. Nielsen Company audited retail sales, it was regarded by company executives as being a reasonably representative market for Lucky Tiger products. The city's population was about 73,500. In the 12 months ending in July 1957, hair tonic sales per 1,000 population were an estimated $274 in Waterloo compared with $197 in the west central region and $177 for the total United States.

Two commercial films were shown, one featuring "hair grooming" and the other using a "blood circulation" theme. A fourth of the showings included the telephone gimmick by which people were invited to call in to receive free samples of hair tonic. The times at which the films were shown were 10:00 P.M., Monday through Saturday, and between 6:00 and 6:30 P.M. on Monday, Wednesday, and Friday. Total cost of television time was $7,600. In addition the films cost $4,750 to produce. The cost of the Nielsen store audit in the Waterloo area was about $180 a month.

The Nielsen panel included 13 key retail drugstores out of the 28 in the market. According to the panel data, Lucky Tiger hair tonic and Lucky Tiger's Butch wax each had less than 1% of the Waterloo hair tonic market in the two months before the test began. At the end of the first two months of the 13-week test, Lucky Tiger hair tonic was in second place among the brands on dollar sales with 10.6% of the market, while Lucky Tiger's Butch wax had 4.3% of the dollar sales. The shares of total unit sales were 11.5% and 4.9%, respectively (see Exhibits 7, 8, and 9). The company executives regarded the Waterloo test as a helpful step in determining what a reasonable advertising schedule would be. Hence, they had deliberately run a much heavier schedule there than sales results would warrant even if the campaign had succeeded in winning 100% of the hair tonic market for Lucky Tiger.

In the Waterloo test the telephone answering service was used in Waterloo and Cedar Rapids to receive calls in response to the 30 spot announcements which used the telephone gimmick. Free sample coupon cards were sent out to all of the 2,750 people who called in. A total of 950 of these coupons were redeemed in the succeeding four months, a slightly lower percentage than the company had experienced in other mar-

Exhibit 7

LUCKY TIGER MANUFACTURING COMPANY
Unit Sales and Shares of Hair Tonic Market in Waterloo, Ia.

Brand	Units Sold			
Vam....................	286	310	293	222
Brylcream...............	1,010	743	1,019	1,001
Valcream...............	89	50	84	87
Vaseline................	687	643	568	553
Vitalis..................	647	586	579	565
Wildroot...............	456	498	525	447
Butch hair wax..........	28	248	141	115
Lucky Tiger.............	34	588	280	116
All other...............	1,433	1,443	1,438	2,216
Total...............	4,670	5,109	4,927	5,322
	May June 1957	July Aug.	Sept. Oct.	Nov. Dec.

Brand	Per Cent of Units Sold			
Vam....................	6.1	6.1	5.9	4.2
Brylcream...............	21.6	14.5	20.7	18.8
Valcream...............	1.9	1.0	1.7	1.6
Vaseline................	14.7	12.6	11.5	10.4
Vitalis..................	13.9	11.5	11.7	10.6
Wildroot...............	9.8	9.7	10.7	8.4
Butch hair wax..........	0.6	4.9	2.9	2.2
Lucky Tiger.............	0.7	11.5	5.7	2.2
All other...............	30.7	28.2	29.2	41.6
Total...............	100.0	100.0	100.0	100.0
	May June 1957	July Aug.	Sept. Oct.	Nov. Dec.

kets. The blood circulation commercial pulled about four times as many telephone calls as did the hair grooming film. The blood circulation advertisement had outpulled the hair grooming advertisement 1.6 to 1 in the Denver newspaper test.

In making plans for 1958, the president again was faced with the questions of how much should be spent on advertising and how and where it should be spent. On the basis of past experience he believed that an expenditure of $125,000 was justified for a sales volume of about $1,000,000. In his opinion an increase in sales volume to $2,000,000 would reduce per unit costs sufficiently so that the company could afford to spend $400,000 for its advertising program. On the average the company had received 31⅓ cents after trade discounts from the 59 cents suggested retail selling

Exhibit 8

LUCKY TIGER MANUFACTURING COMPANY

Dollar Sales and Shares of Hair Tonic Market in Waterloo, Ia.

Brand	Sales in Dollars			
Vam...................	150	166	157	129
Brylcream..............	706	477	700	690
Valcream..............	38	27	43	39
Vaseline...............	365	338	335	319
Vitalis.................	470	335	313	343
Wildroot..............	276	322	338	309
Butch hair wax...........	16	147	85	71
Lucky Tiger.............	30	362	192	92
All other...............	1,247	1,231	1,149	1,756
Total...............	3,298	3,405	3,312	3,748
	May June 1957	July Aug.	Sept. Oct.	Nov. Dec.

Brand	Per Cent of Units Sold			
Vam...................	4.5	4.8	4.8	3.4
Brylcream..............	21.4	14.0	21.1	18.4
Valcream..............	1.2	0.8	1.5	1.0
Vaseline...............	11.0	10.0	10.1	8.6
Vitalis.................	14.3	9.8	9.4	9.1
Wildroot..............	8.3	9.5	10.2	8.3
Butch hair wax..........	0.5	4.3	2.6	1.8
Lucky Tiger.............	0.9	10.6	5.8	2.5
All other...............	37.9	36.2	34.7	46.9
Total...............	100.0	100.0	100.0	100.0
	May June 1957	July Aug.	Sept. Oct.	Nov. Dec.

price for the most popular size of its hair tonic and hair wax. Cost of materials was about 10 cents; personal selling expenses, 3 cents; and manufacturing overhead, 7 cents per bottle. This left about 11 cents for advertising, general administrative expenses, and profit.

Mr. Harris was considering devoting a substantial part of the 1958 advertising budget to further market testing in order to arrive, through experimentation, at a more efficient advertising program. His tentative plans included spot television tests in three markets in addition to Waterloo: Muncie, Ind.; Harrisburg, Pa.; and Roanoke, Va. These cities were regularly served by the Nielsen retail-store audit, and the company already had purchased bench-mark data consisting of sales and market

Exhibit 9

LUCKY TIGER MANUFACTURING COMPANY
Retail Store Inventories of Hair Tonics, Waterloo, Ia.

Brand	Units in Stock			
Vam...................	374	258	833	705
Brylcream..............	635	1,961	1,579	1,821
Valcream..............	117	554	395	331
Vaseline...............	2,751	2,438	1,544	1,203
Vitalis.................	895	912	863	716
Wildroot..............	1,247	1,066	1,877	1,707
Butch hair wax..........	46	41	159	241
Lucky Tiger............	110	111	285	201
All other..............	4,010	3,885	4,139	4,426
Total..............	10,185	11,226	11,674	11,351
	May 1, 1957	July 1	Sept. 1	Nov. 1

Brand	Per Cent of Units in Stock			
Vam...................	3.7	2.3	7.1	6.2
Brylcream..............	6.2	17.5	13.5	16.1
Valcream..............	1.1	4.9	3.4	2.9
Vaseline...............	27.0	21.7	13.2	10.6
Vitalis.................	8.8	8.1	7.4	6.3
Wildroot..............	12.2	9.5	16.1	15.0
Butch hair wax..........	0.5	0.4	1.4	2.1
Lucky Tiger............	1.1	1.0	2.4	1.8
All other..............	39.4	34.6	35.5	39.0
Total..............	100.0	100.0	100.0	100.0
	May 1, 1957	July 1	Sept. 1	Nov. 1

shares for a two-month period for each of these markets. The store auditing service cost an average of about $120 a month for each of the three markets. While schedules were yet to be determined, preliminary thinking had been in terms of test periods of 13 weeks during which three spots a week would be run in one market; two a week in another; and one spot a day for six days a week would be run in a third market.

A decision would have to be made as to how many of the spot announcements should include the telephone gimmick. Experience had shown that an average of about 150 telephone calls would be received in a half-hour period after a telephone gimmick commercial, although the number had run as high as 375. About 35% of the free sample coupon cards actually had been redeemed in the past. The regular 59 cents bottle, used as the free sample, was about a nine-week supply. The company paid full trade margins on the merchandise claimed by coupons (33⅓ cent for independent retailers, 40 to 42% to direct buyers). In addition it paid a 2-cent handling charge to the retailer and a 1-cent handling charge to the Nielsen Coupon Clearing House for each coupon card redeemed.

Company executives had decided that no consumer advertising would be run during the first three months of 1958. One reason was a desire to concentrate on hair wax advertising during the peak selling season which began in April. From then on, however, they wished to give promotional attention to the new liquid hair wax in addition to the hair tonic and the regular hair wax.

~~~

CASE 34: GENERAL MILLS, INC.[1]

NOTE: *Lay out the measurement program that you would recommend to General Mill's marketing research department. (1) Indicate the several measurement and copy research methods you would adopt to determine the advertising effectiveness of the Betty Crocker column. Point out the character of the measurements you would be making in each method. (2) Indicate the techniques you would employ to assure the validity of your measurements, including the queries you would make regarding the* Chicago Tribune *consumer panel operation. (3) Indicate the probable validity that you might expect from the various measurement methods you have recommended and comment upon the degree or reliance which you would place on those measurements.*

In January 1949 General Mills, Inc., began an experimental campaign of intensive newspaper advertising in the *Chicago Tribune.* The campaign was financed from the company's experimental advertising budget, which was set up specifically for the purpose of seeking new and effective methods to advertise and promote General Mills products.

The test started on January 7, 1949 and was planned to run through June 1950. The program called for a 400-line Betty Crocker editorial-type food column to run Monday through Friday of each week. In short, 104,000 lines a year were scheduled, where, at the minimum rate of the *Tribune,* cost approximately $140,000 a year, or about $200,000 for the life of the test.

Reportedly, General Mills, which has in recent years spent only a minor part of its large advertising expenditure in newspapers, was induced to make this test of a high-frequency, large-linage campaign by the American Association of Newspaper Representatives and the *Tribune.*

When soliciting the advertising, the *Tribune* was said to have stressed the availability of its consumer panel to help check results. This con-

---

[1] Written by Neil H. Borden.

Exhibit 1

GENERAL MILLS, INC.

Advertisement, "From Betty Crocker's Kitchen," Appearing in the *Chicago Tribune*,
May 10, 1950

FROM
  BETTY CROCKER'S
    KITCHEN   Minneapolis, May 9, 1950

We call this cake "Star of the Strawberry Season" and you can now see it in color in our magazine ads for Softasilk Cake Flour. The cake is our easy-to-make chiffon—the recipe is on the Softasilk box. And you'll find the icing tangy with the wonderful flavor of fresh strawberries. Note that it calls for only 3 ingredients.

FRESH
STRAWBERRY   (cut of cake)
ICING

Blend until fluffy and good spreading consistency.
  6 tbsp. soft butter or shortening
  3 cups sifted confectionery sugar
  3 tbsp. crushed strawberries
    (with juice)
Add additional crushed berries if
  icing appears too thick

Across America 1,500,000 cakes are made each week with our cake flour, Softasilk. Many homemakers have learned to use Softasilk Cake Flour when they want an especially high, light moist cake. Choose Softasilk Cake Flour next time you shop.

"ARE YOU SURE THAT CHICKEN'S TENDER?"

When you set out to buy a chicken for broiling, how often do you ask the butcher to make sure you get a really tender one? Watch for these things. 1. Chicken should weigh between 1½ and 2½ pounds. 2. Test the tip of breast bone; it should be soft and flexible. 3. Watch for a smooth, thin-skinned bird with only a small amount of fat under the skin over the back.

To cook: Place in shallow pan 6 inches from source of heat in pre-heated broiler. Broil 20 minutes; then turn skin-side-up and broil 10 to 15 minutes longer. Brush with fat often.

This is a glamorous, delicious eating pie—rich, creamy, chocolate filling on tender, flaky pastry made with our Betty Crocker pie mix, Crustquick.

CHOCOLATE MARVEL PIE

Make 9 inch Crustquick pie shell following package directions. Cool. Melt and blend together over hot water: one package semi-sweet chocolate pieces (6 or 7 oz.), 2 tbsp. sugar, 3 tbsp. milk. Cool. Add 4 egg yolks, 1 at a time, beating well after each addition, and 1 tsp. vanilla. Beat until stiff 4 egg whites. Fold into chocolate mixture. Pour into cooled baked pie shell. Chill several hours. Garnish with whipped cream.

Not long ago we ran a test. We had each of 198 homemakers make a pie with Crustquick—also the same kind of pie by their old method.

Exhibit 1—Continued

More of the women preferred the Crustquick pastry. They liked it because it was flakier and easier to handle. You can use Crustquick for any kind of pie, so do try it soon.

. . . .

VISITORS LEARN BAKING SECRETS

Inez was talking to a group of visitors in our kitchen when one woman asked, "Why do your recipes always call for sifted flour?" Inez replied, "That's a good question—and I'll answer it by showing you!"

First she dipped out a cup of flour straight from an open Gold Medal Flour sack and set the cupful aside. Then she sifted some flour onto a square of waxed paper, spooned this flour lightly into a second measuring cup, and leveled off the top with a spatula.

Next she took the first cupful of unsifted flour, sifted and measured it—and found there was ¼ cup flour left over. All the women were amazed! They had no idea that sifting flour made that much difference.

GOOD FOR EVERYTHING YOU BAKE

Gold Medal is our all-purpose flour that we mill so carefully to meet every baking need in your kitchen. It's a dependable flour—never varies in quality from sack to sack. Ask for Gold Medal "Kitchen-Tested" Enriched Flour the next time you shop.

. . . .

More than 4,600 people visited our kitchen last year, many of them from other countries.

Betty Crocker of General Mills

. . . .

Look for Betty Crocker's column every day, in this paper, Monday through Friday.

tinuous purchase consumer panel was started in March 1948 to get data on consumer purchases of foods, soaps, drugs, and toiletries. Approximately 600 families representing a cross section of families in the Chicago market kept diaries of purchases in the above classifications. The *Tribune* has issued grocery product reports every other month since the service was started.

The company planned the campaign with the thought of making use of the unique reputation and the wide following of Betty Crocker among housewives. In the column entitled "From Betty Crocker's Kitchen," Betty Crocker talks about General Mills products in a chatty way, giving recipes, household hints, and the kind of homemaking advice for which she has become known. (See Exhibit 1 for an example of one of Betty Crocker's columns, and see Exhibit 2 for one week's summary of the copy appeals used in the columns.) The company has followed the practice of giving primary support to four General Mills product items, especially Gold Medal Flour, but all the company's products have been brought into discussion over a period of time.[2]

In view of the fact that this newspaper project was set up as an experiment, the General Mills management was desirous of getting as good a check on its effectiveness as possible. The company's large and capable market research department was given the task of setting up a program

Exhibit 2

GENERAL MILLS, INC.

Copy Appeals Used in Advertisements "From Betty Crocker's Kitchen," May 3 through May 9, 1950

Day	Appeals	Product Advertised
Wednesday, May 3	1. Recipe for rich rhubarb pie 2. Husband loses appetite 3. So popovers always pop	Crustquick Vegetable Noodle Soup Gold Medal Flour
Thursday, May 4	1. Recipe for party-style pea soup 2. Men like it: creole sandwich pies 3. Chocolate devil's food cake	Split Pea Soup Bisquick Softasilk
Friday, May 5	1. Recipe for jelly roll 2. Unexpected guests 3. Soup wins blindfold test	Gold Medal Flour Crustquick Vegetable Noodle Soup
Monday, May 8	1. Recipe for frosted orange roll 2. Are your pie shells wallflowers? 3. When Dad makes lunch	Gold Medal Flour Crustquick Split Pea Soup
Tuesday, May 9	1. How to make pastry cookies 2. Twelve-year-old makes cake 3. School children collect Betty Crocker silverware coupons	Crustquick Devil's Food Cake Mix

for measurement of the effectiveness of the advertising in the *Tribune*. Among other things the market research department was charged with the task of carrying on copy research to determine how best to handle the column, what to feature, and how to present it. Beyond this the management hoped to find an answer as to whether such a program of newspaper usage should be extended to other areas.

~~~

---

[2] General Mills manufactured the following consumer products that were nationally advertised. (1) Breakfast cereals: Wheaties, Kix, and Cheerios. Also, these three cereals were combined in small-size packages in the Betty Crocker Cereal Tray. (2) Family flours: Gold Medal Flour and Softasilk Cake Flour. (3) Flour mixes: Bisquick, Pyequick, Crustquick, and four Betty Crocker cake mixes. (4) Soups: Betty Crocker Vegetable Noodle Soup Ingredients and Betty Crocker Split Pea Soup Ingredients. (5) General Mills Tru-Heat Iron.

CASE 35: PITNEY-BOWES, INC.[1]

QUESTIONS TO CONSIDER: *(1) Are inquiries a good basis for evaluating the effectiveness of Pitney-Bowes's print-media advertising? (2) In the light of the data given regarding print-media advertisements, what conclusions do you draw regarding the effectiveness of copy and media? (3) What additional information would you like to obtain in order to evaluate copy and media? (4) In the light of available information, would you recommend that any changes be made in Pitney-Bowes's advertising? If so, what changes?*

In December 1958 Mr. Frederick Bowes, Jr., vice president for public relations, and Mr. Richard K. Jewett, supervisor of advertising administration, reviewed the advertising activities of Pitney-Bowes, Inc. Pitney-Bowes was a leading manufacturer and marketer of office equipment. Messrs. Bowes and Jewett noted several questions which were of concern to them with respect to improving the effectiveness of the company's advertising in the future. They were particularly interested in improving, if possible, the effectiveness of Pitney-Bowes's print-media advertising. They felt that print-media advertising had been effective in attaining the objective established for it by management, namely, to create salesworthy impressions on the public before it was called upon by Pitney-Bowes salesmen. But they were not altogether satisfied that they had definite solutions to the usual problems which always confront any advertiser who employs print media, namely, the problems of selecting and properly evaluating advertising copy and media.

Background Information on the Company and Its Products

Pitney-Bowes, Inc., Stamford, Connecticut, was organized in April 1920 as the Pitney-Bowes Postage Meter Company to produce and market the first practicable postage meter machine for privately but legally printing postage. The company was a merger of Arthur H. Pitney's American Postage Meter Company of Chicago, which had been recently formed to develop a postage meter, and Walter H. Bowes' Universal Stamping Machine Company of Stamford, Connecticut, which had been for several years a prime supplier of canceling and postmarking equipment to the U.S. Post Office. Pitney-Bowes' first postage meter machine consisted essentially of a small, single-denomination, detachable, tamper-proof postage meter which could be set by post office personnel for the amount of postage designated by the user and then could be inserted in a high-speed postage meter mailing machine that stamped and sealed letter mail of banks and business firms. The meter itself was approved for use by the Postmaster General, and legislation permitting its use was passed by Congress in 1920. Stipulations were made that Pitney-Bowes (and any

---

[1] Written by Martin V. Marshall.

other manufacturers) retain title to the postage meters and be responsible for their location and proper operation. Thus, Pitney-Bowes did not sell but rented postage meters, while selling outright the machines which operated them and sealed envelopes.

Subsequently, Pitney-Bowes made many major improvements in the postage meter and the machines and equipment that could be used with meters. Some of the major improvements were as follows. The first Pitney-Bowes postage meter could be set for only one postage denomination. In 1929 a multi-denomination meter was developed, providing for five denominations from one to 25 cents. In 1933 an omni-denomination meter was introduced, allowing settings from one cent to $99.99. In 1928 the company arranged for postage meter users to include an advertising message on the postage imprint. In addition, the speed and ease of use of the postage meter was continuously improved by the development of various types of power-driven machines; and the use of meters was greatly broadened by the development of small, compact, desk-model meters which could be used by small businesses or offices at relatively low cost.

By 1958, United States metered mail, mostly imprinted on Pitney-Bowes meters, represented nearly one half of all United States mail and provided more than $1 billion a year in United States postal revenue.

In 1958 Pitney-Bowes offered 12 different models of postage meters for quarterly rentals ranging from $16.50 to $36.00. (In 1958 there were about 220,000 users of one or more postage meters, the total number of meters in use being about 250,000.) The company also had available, among other machines, 14 postage meter machines for the use and housing of the meters, priced from $135 to $3,750; four mail envelope inserting machines, priced from $6,060 to $7,065; and seven special attachments and cabinets, priced from $60 to $760.

Throughout the period 1920–58, Pitney-Bowes continued to manufacture and improve canceling machines and special mail-handling equipment for the U.S. Post Office, including a coin-operating public mailing machine. In addition, the company developed many other products for the handling of mail and paper, including cigarette tax stamping machines, folding machines, "Tickometer" machines which counted and imprinted pieces of paper, package imprinting machines, mail openers, scales, and mail tables. In total, in 1958 Pitney-Bowes quoted prices on 145 items.

Since its founding, Pitney-Bowes had had a steady increase in sales and profits. Selected operating data taken from the company's annual reports for the years 1948–57 are given in Exhibit 1. The expenditures for research and development should be noted, as they reflect management's emphasis upon new product development and the improvement of existing products. The large majority of sales income was generated by the postage meter machine line.

In 1958 the company had no active competitors in the postage meter business. In the past it had as many as eight competitors concurrently,

Exhibit 1

PITNEY-BOWES, INC.

Selected Operating Data for the Years 1948–57

Year	Gross Income	Profit before Taxes	Profit after Taxes	Research and Development Expense	Advertising Expense
1948.........	$16,011,895	$2,565,525	$1,547,025	$ 348,727	$ 364,849
1949........	18,466,654	2,887,062	1,717,062	360,002	457,800
1950.........	21,695,658	3,712,281	1,956,251	489,157	470,339
1951.........	26,120,559	4,536,408	1,542,588	459,395	467,424
1952.........	30,606,023	5,066,148	1,608,148	522,133	571,827
1953.........	32,811,928	4,712,096	1,809,096	1,031,964	731,415
1954.........	34,986,108	6,078,647	2,953,467	756,428	697,879
1955.........	39,259,213	7,595,122	3,566,122	1,070,575	922,821
1956.........	43,548,165	8,639,219	4,109,219	1,203,508	1,013,782
1957.........	45,906,583	8,577,147	4,137,147	1,778,554	1,093,090

Source: Company annual reports.

most of them dropping their postage meter line in the post–World War II period in order to emphasize development of other types of office equipment. Trade reports indicated, however, that several companies were planning to get into the postage meter business in the near future.[2]

The "Selling" of Postage Meters

Over the years Pitney-Bowes had found that postage meters were rented for many reasons: to handle large volume mailings efficiently; to obtain the use of postmark advertising on mailings; to eliminate the drudgery of licking and stamping envelopes; to stop stamp losses and simplify postage bookkeeping; to speed mail through the post office (metered mail requires no postmarking and canceling and often is placed on earlier transportation); to get a date on parcel post packages (ordinary parcel post carries no mailing date unless sent special delivery); to obtain prestige (small organizations often believed that they gained in prestige if they used the metered stamp employed by most large organizations); and so on. Thus, nearly every office which mailed letters and other materials was considered to be a potential user of postage meters, almost regardless of the size of the business or volume of mailings. In 1958 the number of such offices was estimated to be in excess of four million.

Many persons in an organization might affect the decision to use metered mail: general management, those responsible for the mailing

---

[2] Subsequently, early in 1959, Pitney-Bowes signed an antitrust consent decree which, while categorically denying any violation of the Sherman Act (Section II), allowed qualified companies which were approved by the U.S. Post Office Department to use Pitney-Bowes's existing patents, drawings, methods, and so on. At the time, Pitney-Bowes's management welcomed this development and was cited by the Justice Department's Anti-Trust Division as having a "constructive attitude."

operation, secretaries, mail girls and boys, advertising personnel, financial personnel, and so on.

In order to give direction to personal selling and advertising, the company had tried to identify and define active prospects through marketing research studies, analysis of the existing users of postage meters, and analysis of those users who did and did not renew their rental agreements. The evidence obtained from the latter-type analysis had been most helpful in identifying and defining the characteristics of active prospects, but the company relied primarily upon personal selling and advertising to obtain leads to good prospects. Accordingly, one of the objectives of the company's advertising was to obtain inquiries from active prospects for the use of the sales force.

The Sales Force

The Pitney-Bowes sales force was composed of about 600 salesmen and branch managers who operated out of about 100 sales and service branch offices. Each salesman was assigned responsibility for a sales territory, the territories varying in size from a single office building in New York City to a geographical area of several counties. Sales targets or quotas were established for each territory on the basis of the examination of past territory sales, an index of office equipment sales supplied by the Office Equipment Manufacturers' Institute, an index of social security payments of organizations, and other factors. Salesmen made many sales visits each day, usually making from six to eight contacts per day, some with existing customers but chiefly with prospects.

Salesmen obtained leads to prospects primarily from three sources: from knowledge of potential prospects which they gained as the result of operating in sales territories over time; from inquiries that were developed by direct-mail advertising; and from inquiries that were developed by the company's general advertising. Inquiries were also obtained from publicity, business shows, annual reports, and listings in the classified sections of telephone directories.

Inquiries Obtained from Direct-Mail Advertising

Direct-mail advertising was used in two ways to obtain inquiries. First, two to four direct-mail pieces were sent each year to existing users of postage meters for the purposes of promoting other Pitney-Bowes products. Second, two to four direct-mail letters were sent each year to prospects for postage meters who were selected by the salesmen from a master mailing list administered and used by the home office advertising department, with duplicate portions of the list administered in each branch office.

Salesmen were expected to develop and maintain good prospect mailing lists for their sales territories; and they had an incentive for doing so, since, in addition to their compensation for machine *sales*, they received a commission for meter *rentals* based upon an initial rental, not upon obtaining meter renewal rentals.

Salesmen's prospect mailing lists averaged 800 to 900 names a man, and each salesman had an actual "quota" of names to which he was entitled and which he was responsible for maintaining. A salesman could delete and add names to his list in any way he wished. The Pitney-Bowes adver-

Exhibit 2

PITNEY-BOWES, INC.

Direct-Mail Letter Sent to Prospects

PITNEY-BOWES, INC.
STAMFORD, CONNECTICUT

ORIGINATOR OF THE POSTAGE METER AND METERED MAIL WORLD'S LEADING MANUFACTURER OF MAILING MACHINES

November 1957

Is the Enclosed Mailing Label Correct?

It Will Bring You a Timely FREE Booklet

of New and Useful Mailing Tips

We have ready to mail to you -- without obligation -- the new, revised edition of a valuable booklet to help speed delivery of your mail and cut your mailing and postage costs. But first, to make sure we have your address correct, will you please check the mailing label enclosed?

Called "29 Timely Mailing Tips," this practical handbook -- now in its second printing -- tells what you can do to help the Post Office give you better service. A single suggestion, for instance, may help you get your mail delivered a whole day earlier. Another tip may enable you to avoid the greatest cause of undeliverable parcel post packages.

The booklet also brings you up-to-date on postal changes that can help you get more for your postage money. There's the Certified Mail service, for instance ...and the ruling that eliminates the "may be opened for postal inspection" notice on packages. You'll discover some odd and interesting facts, too. Did you know, for example, that First Class mail is sometimes less expensive than Fourth Class mail (parcel post)?

The final tip may be as important as any. For it tells how even the smallest office now can use Metered Mail to speed letters and packages to and through the Post Office. You'll see how the postage meter prints postage...ends the costly drudgery of licking and sticking stamps...gives your mail added prestige plus the advantage of Postmark Advertising.

The Post Office, today, is faced with an ever-increasing volume of mail -- and there's the strong possibility of increased postal rates next Spring. So the money-saving, time-saving tips in this booklet should be especially helpful to you at this time. To get your copy, simply check the correctness of your name and address on the enclosed label, and return it in the postage-paid envelope. We'll mail the booklet to you promptly -- with our compliments.

Very truly yours,

E. M. Davis
Vice President

EMD/TPB
Enc.

tising department helped him to revise his list periodically by purchasing new names from Dun & Bradstreet, testing the names, and then offering "proven" names to him.

The direct-mail pieces sent to existing or potential users usually consisted simply of a one-page letter, such as the letter shown in Exhibit 2, which held out an offer of a booklet on some aspect of mailing. Some of the booklets used in recent years were: *So You Have No Mailing Problems?*, which gave a basic explanation of metered mail; *What Every Boss Should Know about Secretaries*, which gave a humorous documentation of the "evils" of stamp licking and the need for metered mail; *Some Eye-Opening Facts I Found Out about Parcel Post*, which outlined helpful hints on handling parcel post and pointed out the advantages of using metered mail for parcel post; and *29 Timely Mailing Tips*, which offered news and information on the handling of regular mail and ways to cut postage costs.

Before undertaking a mass mailing, which would be sent to all names on the prospect list (over 450,000 in 1958), the advertising department tested proposed letters with a sample, usually of 10,000 names for each letter, seeking to determine the effect upon returns of variables such as the basic selling point or appeal made, style and salutation of headline, possible use of illustration, reply method, date or day of mailing and its receipt, and so on.

The results of the tests allowed the department to predict closely the number of leads to be obtained in a general mailing. The aim was to reveal enough sales points in the letter to qualify the ensuing leads, but not enough to cut down the percentage return to too low a volume. The objectives was to provide each salesman with one to two leads per working day. If a large number of leads was predicted, the general mailing was conducted over a longer period of time in order to allow salesmen adequate time for their follow-up function. Messrs. Bowes and Jewett believed that responses obtained from mass mailings were good, ranging from 3% to 6% for mailings to prospects and 5% to 12% for mailings to users.

Inquiries from Print-Media Advertising

In the 1950's Pitney-Bowes began to increase its use of advertising in magazines and business papers, primarily to provide a broader and heavier coverage of the market. Use of these media had gotten too "thin" in terms of both size and frequency of insertion. It was also desired to use print media as a means of developing inquiries. Occasional use was also made of newspapers. Greater use of print media was dictated in part by the introduction in 1950 of a new model in the postage meter line, the "DM," a desk model developed particularly for very small businesses and professional people having small volumes of mailings. The promotion of this model required the company to reach an even broader group of people than it reached with it previous advertising, which had been aimed primarily at executives. Further, by stepping up its schedule of advertisements in print media, company executives hoped to reach more office women and men who handled mail, and other persons who affected executives' decisions to use postage meters.

In its print-media advertising, the company essentially tried to present reasons for the use of postage meters by employing illustrations and copy that emphasized user benefits (see Exhibits 4–18). A small schedule of advertising was maintained for other Pitney-Bowes products, such as the Tickometer. All print-media advertisements which were one-half page or larger included a buried reply device for requesting a handy postal-rate chart and product booklet. Advertisements were coded by means of using different street addresses, such as 1055 Pacific Street, 1056 Pacific Street, and so on. Although actually a coupon, the coded address did not appear as such, making response thereto a better piece of evidence of readership of the advertisement than would have been true if a traditional-type coupon had been used.

Use of Inquiries

The company's minimum inquiry goal was one lead per salesman for each of the 225 working days in the year. (In 1958 it was estimated that the total number of inquiries from advertising alone would be 220,000, some 80% from direct-mail advertising and some 20% from print-media advertising and other sources.)

When a booklet request was received in Stamford, a typist prepared a mailing label and three carbon copies: a white slip for the salesman, a pink slip for the salesman's manager, and a yellow slip for the advertising department. The booklet was immediately mailed to the prospect, and the white and pink slips were sent to the salesman and his manager, respectively. Salesmen were continuously encouraged to follow up leads within 48 to 72 hours, preferably by a personal call and otherwise by a telephone call or letter indicating when he could call on the prospect. Branch managers were responsible for the effectiveness of salesmen's follow-up activities.

Other Promotional Devices

Salesmen were provided with numerous types of sales literature for customers, much of which was in the form of booklets that had proven popular in the past in mass mailings but which included also materials prepared especially for distribution by salesmen. Titles of some of the sales literature were *How to Increase the Prestige of Your Mail, Still Doing It the Hard Way?, 12 Case Studies of Savings by the Tickometer, Your Employees' Time Is Too Valuable to Waste, The Pitney-Bowes Package Imprinting Machine, Can Your Mailing Scale Pass the Silver Dollar Test?, You Can Do BIG Things with This Little Space—Postmark Advertising,* and *5 Case Studies of Major Savings in Time and Money in the Imprinting of Folding Cartons and Other Containers.*

From time to time on special occasions, the company prepared and distributed literature helpful to customers and prospects, such as large charts giving the latest postal rates and postal information.

Advertising Planning

After top management had established sales goals for the total operation and its parts, the advertising department determined the program of advertising and the expenditure for advertising required to help the sales organization attain its sales quota. Direct-mail advertising could be planned fairly easily inasmuch as past experience indicated the number of mailings required to obtain the number of leads desired by the sales organization. Print advertising presented a more difficult problem in that it was used not primarily to stimulate inquiry but rather to develop interest in postage meter and other Pitney-Bowes machines among the business public. The size of the company's advertising effort is indicated in Exhibit 3, which gives advertising budgets for 1956–58.

Exhibit 3

PITNEY-BOWES, INC.

Summary of Selected Information regarding Advertising Budgets,
1956–58

	1956	1957	1958 (Estimated)
Print-media advertising space costs .	$443,118	$ 488,831	$ 637,000
Advertising production costs	46,432	52,130	66,000
Direct-mail advertising costs	217,886	258,631	289,000
Sales literature.	74,096	67,504	96,000
Customer literature.	11,973	11,787	40,000
Business shows.	32,919	32,019	34,000
Advertising department expense. . .	103,022	103,235	111,000
Total.	$929,446*	$1,014,137*	$1,273,000

* Totals do not check with advertising expenditures totals in Exhibit 2 because of exclusion of advertising expenditures for Canada.

Source: Company records.

Print-Media Advertising Copy

In recent years, the objectives of print-media advertising had been: (1) To inform the public of the principal benefits and conveniences of the postage meter. (2) To explain how metered mail cut postage costs and eliminated the evils of old-fashioned lick-and-stick mailing, even in the smallest offices. Pitney-Bowes executives felt that two many organizations still considered themselves too small for a postage meter; so that Pitney-Bowes advertising copy attempted to correct this impression, particularly with the use of the headline: "Now Every Office Can Have One!" (3) To obtain inquiries from prospects. The latter objectives was secondary to the first two objectives.

In obtaining these objectives, Messrs. Bowes and Jewett had to contend with several problems which occurred because of the character of the market for postage meters. As indicated earlier, organizations decided to use metered mail for many reasons other than the need to handle large volumes of mailings, and many persons in an organization often affected the decision to use metered mail. Thus, the exact size and the characteristics of "best" prospects were not definitely known. Further, it was known that the buying behavior of prospects was very complex and that, accordingly, sales presentations made by salesmen or advertising had to be discriminating. To illustrate this point, Mr. Bowes commented as follows:

> We know from selling experience, for instance, that many people inquire about metered mail because they have discovered sizable losses resulting from the pilferage of postage. But they inquire on some other basis. They are reluctant to talk about a pilferage problem because it reflects, say, upon their control procedures. Consequently, it is difficult for the salesman to help solve the prospect's problem when the prospect is reluctant or completely unwilling to discuss it. We know also that sales are often blocked because of the way in which businessmen present the possibilities of postage meters to other people in their organizations. For example, it is not unusual to have this experience: an executive decides that he will use metered mail. He calls in his secretary and says, "I've decided to help you out by using a postage meter. What do you think?" The secretary being unprepared and perhaps suspicious of the motives of her boss will say no, she's getting along just fine, she doesn't need any postage meter. And that's the end of the sale.

Since March 1954 Pitney-Bowes had employed two different copy approaches or advertising campaigns. One, which was used in the period March 1954–November 1957, consisted of nine different advertisements in four or two colors featuring the "DM" postage meter machine and—with one exception—using the headline, "Now *every* office can have one!" The advertisements of this campaign are given in Exhibits 4 through 12. The second, which was used after November 1957 to date, consisted of six different advertisements in four or two colors featuring an attractive red-headed "secretary" and using various "stopper" headlines. The advertisements of this campaign are given in Exhibits 13 through 18. The first campaign varied the interests of advertisements by varying the cartoon situations illustrated; the second by telling a continuing story about the trials and tribulations of the red-headed secretary in working with ordinary stamps. In addition to these campaigns, Pitney-Bowes ran other advertisements in print media for products other than postage meters.

Because those who were considered to be the "best" prospects could be effectively and economically reached through direct-mail advertising, print-media advertising had been aimed at the broader market, particularly to smaller organizations and professional people. Direct-mail advertising was considered to be economical, especially when the names on a

Exhibit 4

PITNEY-BOWES, INC.

Now every office can have one!

WANT TO get rid of the nuisance and delay in licking and sticking old-fashioned adhesive stamps? . . Wet nursing stamps in a tin box? . Stamp losses and borrowing? . Running out of denominations you need? . . . Running down to the postoffice and standing in line to buy stamps? . . Then you want a postage meter!

Today the smallest office can afford to have modern, efficient metered mail—with the little inexpensive DM, desk-model postage meter.

The DM prints the exact amount of postage needed for any class of mail, directly on the envelope—with a dated postmark that helps your mail go through the postoffice faster Prints your own small ad at the same time, if you like.

Anybody can use a postage meter, save time and postage Dial the amount of postage wanted, press the lever, and your letter is stamped. The DM has a moistener for sealing envelopes, and also handles parcel post.

The DM is set by the postoffice for as much postage as you want to buy. And your postage in the meter is safe from loss and misuse.

Now THERE'S a Pitney-Bowes postage meter, electric or hand-operated, for every office. large or small. Ask the nearest PB office to show you —or send coupon for the free illustrated booklet.

FREE: Handy chart of Postal Rates with parcel post map and zone finder.

PITNEY-BOWES
Postage Meter

Made by the world's leading manufacturer of mailing machines offices in 93 cities in the U S and Canada.

PITNEY-BOWES, Inc.
1051 Pacific Street, Stamford, Conn.

☐ Send free Postal Rate Chart
☐ Send booklet on DM Postage Meter

Name_____

Address_____

Exhibit 5

PITNEY-BOWES, INC.

Now every office can have one!

You don't have to send a lot of mail, or spend a lot for postage, to use a postage meter.

With the inexpensive little DM, desk model, you do away with the disadvantages of lick-and-stick mailing, enjoy the speed and ease of meter mailing, and the convenience of always having the right postage on hand. And most meter users save on postage, too!

The DM *prints* any stamp you need, for any kind of mail, directly on the envelope—with a dated postmark that helps your mail get through the postoffice faster, and make earlier trains and planes. Prints your own small ad, at the same time, if you like.

It has a moistener for sealing envelope flaps, and even handles parcel post.

Anybody can easily use a postage meter. Simply dial the value of postage you want, press the lever, and your letter is stamped.

The meter is set by the postoffice for the amount you need. Your postage is safe from loss and misuse—and is automatically accounted for.

Today there's a Pitney-Bowes postage meter, electric or hand-operated, for every office, large or small. Ask the nearest PB office for a demonstration — or send coupon for the free illustrated booklet.

FREE: *Handy desk or wall chart of Postal Rates with parcel post map and zone finder.*

PITNEY-BOWES
(PB) Postage Meter

Made by the world's leading makers of mailing machines . . . offices in 94 cities. In Canada: Pitney-Bowes of Canada, Ltd., Dept. 379, 1156 Bay Street, Toronto.

PITNEY-BOWES, INC.
1179 Pacific Street, Stamford, Conn.

☐ Send free Postal Rate Chart
☐ Send booklet on DM Postage Meter

Name _____

Address _____

Exhibit 6

PITNEY-BOWES, INC.

Now every office can have one!

SAY adieu to adhesive stamps. Scrap that old-fashioned stamp box. Spare yourself any more unsanitary lick-and-stick mailing.

Today, even the smallest office can have a postage meter and all the advantages of metered mail. One out of three users of the DM, this little desk model, spends less than $1 a day for postage.

Print your postage in any amount, for any kind of mail, directly on the envelope—as and when you need it. At the same time, your meter prints a dated postmark to help speed your mail through the postoffice—and, with it, your own small ad, if you like.

The DM has a moistener for sealing envelopes; and prints postage for parcel post on special gummed tape.

You always have the right stamp on hand. The postoffice sets the meter for as much postage as you want to buy at a time. And you make fewer trips to the postoffice.

Postage in the meter is always protected from loss, theft, misuse. And is *automatically* accounted for!

The DM saves time, and postage; is worth its cost in convenience alone! And anybody can easily use it.

THERE's a postage meter, electric or hand operated, for every office, large or small. Ask the nearest Pitney-Bowes office to show you. Or send the coupon for free illustrated booklet.

FREE: *Handy desk or wall chart of Postal Rates, with parcel post map and zone finder.*

PITNEY-BOWES
Postage Meter

Made by world's leading makers of mailing machines . . . offices in 94 cities. In Canada, Pitney-Bowes of Canada, Ltd., Dept. 308, 1156 Bay Street, Toronto.

You see more and more metered mail!

PITNEY-BOWES, INC.
1008 Pacific St., Stamford, Conn.

☐ *Send free Postal Rate Chart*
☐ *Send booklet on DM Postage Meter*

Name...

Address...

Exhibit 7

PITNEY-BOWES, INC.

Now every office can have one!

Even if you are a one-man office, or the female other half of one ... you can afford a postage meter. And get rid of lick-and-stick mailing forever!

The DM, desk model postage meter, is *made* particularly for the small office One user in three spends less than $1 a day for postage.

Anybody can easily use a DM. You *print* postage as you need it—in any amount, for any kind of mail. Insert the envelope, dial the amount of postage wanted, and press the lever—and your letter is stamped. Postmarked, too, so it can take less time in the postoffice, often catch earlier trains and planes. And with every meter stamp, you can print your own small ad, if you want one.

Postage for parcel post is printed on

special tape. And there's a moistener for sealing envelopes!

With a postage meter, you always have the right stamp on hand. Your postage is protected from loss, theft, damage, automatically accounted for.

There's a meter, hand or electric, for every office. Ask the nearest Pitney-Bowes office to show you—or send coupon for free booklet.

FREE: *Handy desk or wall chart of Postal Rates, with parcel post map and zone finder.*

PITNEY-BOWES Postage Meter

Made by world's leading makers of mailing machines. Offices in 94 cities. In Canada: Pitney-Bowes of Canada, Ltd., Dept. 312, 1156 Bay St., Toronto.

Learn all about meter mailing...

PITNEY-BOWES, INC.
1012 Pacific St., Stamford, Conn.

☐ *Send free Postal Rate Chart*
☐ *Send booklet on DM Postage Meter*

Name..

Address..

Exhibit 8

PITNEY-BOWES, INC.

"I'm tempted to get a postage meter!"

There's nothing like the annual Christmas card mailing stampede to convince a man (a) that getting out the mail is a slow, tedious, messy job, and (b) that the girls in his office are right in needling him for a postage meter!

Once upon a time, meters were used only by big firms. But not so today. Now there's a postage meter, with all the advantages of metered mail, for even the smallest office. It's the DM, little desk model meter. One out of three users spends an average of less than $1 a day for postage.

The DM postage meter ends unsanitary, unpleasant licking and sticking — makes the old-fashioned stamp box a genuine museum piece.

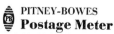

Anyone can easily use a DM postage meter, save time and postage. Dial the amount wanted, press the lever, and your letter is stamped. *And there's a moistener for sealing envelopes.*

The DM *prints*, directly on the envelope, the exact amount of postage for any class of mail, (on special gummed tape for parcel post), *with* a dated postmark that helps speed your mail through the postoffice, often catching earlier trains or planes. Prints your own small ad at the same time, if you like.

The postoffice sets the meter for as much postage as you want to buy. Your postage in the meter is safe from loss, damage or misuse—and automatically accounted for.

There's a postage meter, electric or hand-operated, for every office, large or small. Ask the nearest PB office to show you. Or send the coupon for free illustrated booklet.

FREE: *Handy desk or wall chart of Postal Rates, with parcel post map and zone finder.*

⬧ PITNEY-BOWES
🄿🄱 **Postage Meter**

Made by the leading maker of mailing machines. Offices in 96 cities. In Canada: Pitney-Bowes of Canada, Ltd., Dept. 333, 1156 Bay Street, Toronto.

Merry mailing to you... all year long!

PITNEY-BOWES, INC.
1033 Pacific Street, Stamford, Conn.

☐ *Send free Postal Rate Chart*
☐ *Send booklet on DM Postage Meter*

Name ....

Address ....

Exhibit 9

PITNEY-BOWES, INC.

Ah sure take a lickin' stickin' stamps!

Plumb wore out waitin' fer stamps!

Fraish out of stamps--
I'm gonna be late for our date!

This here critter even mails parcels!

Yippee! Mail out fast,
no lickum-stickum stamps!

Now <u>every</u> office can have one, pardner!

And out where the men are taller, stenographers scarcer, and the U.S. postoffices farther apart...a lot of people swear by the DM desk model postage meter—wouldn't go back to lick-and-stick mailing for anything!

This DM model is made specially for the small office. One user in three spends less than $1 a day for postage.

With the DM, you print postage as you need it—any amount for any kind of mail. Just insert the envelope, dial the amount of postage wanted, press the lever...and your letter is stamped. Postmarked, too, at the same time, so it takes less handling in the postoffice, often gets on its way earlier. And you can also print your own small ad with the meter stamp, if you like.

The DM has a moistener for sealing envelopes. And it will print postage

for parcel post, too—on special tape. Anybody can easily use the DM.

The postoffice sets the meter for as much postage as you want to buy. Your postage in the meter is protected from loss, theft, damage—and automatically accounted for on visible registers.

You save both time and postage with a postage meter. There's a model, electric or hand, for every office. Ask the nearest Pitney-Bowes office to show you. Or send coupon for free booklet.

FREE: *Handy desk or wall chart of Postal Rates, with parcel post map and zone finder.*

PITNEY-BOWES
Postage Meter

Made by the leading maker of mailing machines. Offices in 94 cities. In Canada: Pitney-Bowes of Canada, Ltd., Dept. 316, 1156 Bay Street, Toronto.

Like to put
my own brand
on my mail!

PITNEY-BOWES, INC.
1016 Pacific Street, Stamford, Conn.

☐ Send *free Postal Rate Chart*
☐ Send booklet on DM *Postage Meter*

Name..

Address ....

Exhibit 10

PITNEY-BOWES, INC.

Avoid those empty stamp box hassles!

Have this mail out in no time at all!

No more stamp licking --and sticking!

STAMPS

No waiting in line at the postoffice!

Makes mailing packages a pleasure, too!

Now every office can have one!

One what? A postage meter! No matter if your daily mail is only a handful...you can still have a postage meter — and all the advantages of metered mail! Such as:

• You can stop licking and sticking stamps, safeguarding stamps, running fresh out of stamps. (Hallelujah!)

• You can print postage as you need it, for any kind of mail. Easy! Insert envelope, dial amount of postage wanted, press lever — and your letter is stamped! *All meters have a moistener for sealing envelopes.*

• You can even print postage on special tape for parcel post!

• You can optionally print your own small ad on every envelope *with* the meter stamp.

• Your mail can often catch earlier trains and planes — because metered mail, already postmarked, needs less handling time in the postoffice.

• Your postage is safe from loss and misuse — automatically accounted for!

Can you afford it? Well, one in three users of the meter illustrated spends less than $1 a day on postage!

THERE'S a meter model, electric or hand, for every office — even the smallest. Ask the nearest Pitney-Bowes office to show you. Or send the coupon for free illustrated booklet.

FREE: *Handy desk or wall chart of Postal Rates, with parcel post map and zone finder.*

⚖ PITNEY-BOWES
Postage Meter

Made by the leading maker of mailing machines. Offices in 101 cities. In Canada: Pitney-Bowes of Canada, Ltd., Dept. 338, 1156 Bay Street, Toronto.

Meter mailing saves time and postage

PITNEY-BOWES, INC.
1038 Pacific Street, Stamford, Conn.

☐ Send free Postal Rate Chart
☐ Send booklet on DM Postage Meter

Name ....

Address ....

Exhibit 11

PITNEY-BOWES, INC.

Now every office can have one!

Today, even a one-girl office can have a postage meter and enjoy all the advantages of metered mail. Actually, one third of the users of the DM, desk model meter, average less than $1 a day for postage!

You're no longer stuck with stamps, stamp sticking, and running out of the right stamp. *You print postage as you need it,* for any kind of mail. Even a child can operate a DM. Insert the envelope, dial the amount of postage wanted, press lever—and your letter is meter stamped. There's a moistener for sealing envelopes. Makes mailing easy, saves postage.

The meter is set by the post office for as much postage as you want to buy at one time. Postage is protected from loss, damage and misuse; and accounted for on visible registers.

Metered mail, already dated and postmarked, takes less handling time in the postoffice and can often catch earlier trains and planes.

Extra feature: With every meter stamp, you can print your own small ad on the envelope, if you want one. Free advertising!

There's a postage meter model, hand or electric, for every office, small or big. Ask the nearest Pitney-Bowes office to show you. Or send coupon for free illustrated booklet.

FREE: *Handy desk or wall chart of Postal Rates, with parcel post map and zone finder.*

PITNEY-BOWES
Postage Meter

Made by the leading maker of mailing machines. Offices in 103 cities. In Canada: Pitney-Bowes of Canada, Ltd., Dept. 341, 1156 Bay Street, Toronto.

Prints our own ad with every meter stamp.

Pitney-Bowes, Inc.
1041 Pacific Street
Stamford, Conn.

☐ *Send free Postal Rate Chart*
☐ *Send booklet on DM Postage Meter*

Name ....

Address ....

Exhibit 12

PITNEY-BOWES, INC.

Exhibit 13

PITNEY-BOWES, INC.

Glamour job? Baloney!

"Your big break, they said. New small outfit, going places. You'll work with Mr. Big himself. Stimulating! Meet interesting people ... But nobody told me I'd get stuck with the mail every night ... Licking and sticking itsy bitsy stamps and envelope flaps. Utterly medieval! Tomorrow Mr. B gets a postage meter—or a new girl" ...

Get a postage meter—and you get rid of stamps and lick-and-stick mailing. Print postage as you need it, for any kind or class of mail. You always have the right stamp on hand. Mail fast and easy, save time and postage. And your *metered* mail needs less handling in the postoffice, often catches earlier trains and planes!

Today, *any* office can have a postage meter and the prestige of metered mail—with the little DM, desk model. One user in three spends less than $1 a day for postage! Electric models for larger mailers. Call the nearest PB office. Or write for free illustrated booklet.

PITNEY-BOWES
Postage Meter

Made by the leading manufacturer of mailing machines ... Offices in 107 cities. In Canada: Pitney-Bowes of Canada, Ltd., Dept. 355, 1156 Bay St., Toronto

A postage meter ...

seals as well as stamps envelopes; most models stamp and seal simultaneously.

● Protects postage from loss, damage, misuse. Does its own accounting. And saves trips to the postoffice.

● Provides *parcel* postage on special gummed tape, with a *dated* postmark.

● Prints your own postmark ad with the meter stamp, if you like.

● Requires no minimum mail volume; anyone can easily use a postage meter!

FREE: *Handy desk or wall chart of postal rates with parcel post map and zone finder.*

To: Pitney-Bowes
1055 Pacific St.
Stamford, Conn.

Send free □ *booklet,* □ *Postal Rate Chart to:*

Name

Address

Exhibit 14

PITNEY-BOWES, INC.

I've been framed!

*"I shudda quit when I found they didn't have a postage meter.
But they sweet-talked me into staying . . . made me think they'd
get one. But look! Still the same old lick and stick. Slow. Messy.
Bush league method. This time, I'm sure telling 'em: it's a
postage meter . . . or goodbye!"*

Get a postage meter—and you do away with licking and
sticking stamps and envelope flaps. You print your postage as
you need it, for any kind or class of mail, and always have the
right stamp on hand. Save mailing time and postage. And
your *metered* mail needs less handling time in the postoffice,
can often catch earlier mail trains and planes.

Now, even the smallest office can have a postage meter
and the prestige of metered mail—with the little, inexpensive
DM, the *desk model* meter. A third of DM users spend less
than $1 a day for postage. Electric models available.
Call or write for free illustrated booklet.

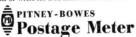

PITNEY-BOWES
Postage Meter

*Made by the leading manufacturer of mailing machines . . .
Offices in 107 cities. In Canada: Pitney-Bowes
of Canada, Ltd., Dept. 358, 1156 Bay St., Toronto*

A postage meter . . .

seals as well as stamps envelopes; most
models stamp and seal simultaneously.

● Protects postage from loss, damage,
misuse. Does its own accounting. And
saves trips to the postoffice.

● Provides *parcel* postage on special
gummed tape, with a *dated* postmark.

● Prints your own postmark ad with
the meter stamp, if you like.

● Requires no minimum mail volume;
anyone can easily use a postage meter!

FREE: *Handy desk or wall chart
of postal rates with parcel post map
and zone finder.*

To: Pitney-Bowes
1058 Pacific St.
Stamford, Conn.

Send free ☐ *booklet,* ☐ *Postal Rate Chart to:*

Name _____

Address _____

Exhibit 15
PITNEY-BOWES, INC.

"Most likely to succeed"

"Girl most likely to succeed, it says in my class yearbook. And look at me now. Stuck with all these darn bills to mail out—in the old messy way, licking and sticking stamps and envelope flaps. Phooey! Tomorrow I make another pitch for a postage meter . . . and they better listen!"

You can get rid of stamps, lick-and-stick mailing—with a postage meter. Print your postage as you need it, and always have the right stamp on hand for any kind or class of mail. Makes mailing faster and easier, saves time and postage. And metered mail needs less handling time in the postoffice, often catches earlier mail trains and planes.

With the inexpensive little DM, a desk model postage meter, even the smallest office can have the advantages and prestige of metered mail (one user in three spends less than $1 a day for postage). Electric models for larger mailers. Call the nearest Pitney-Bowes office. Or send for free illustrated booklet.

A postage meter...
stamps *and seals* envelopes; most models do both jobs simultaneously.
● Protects your postage from loss, damage, misuse. Does its own accounting. And saves trips to the postoffice.
● Provides *parcel* postage on special gummed tape, with a *dated* postmark.
● Prints your own postmark ad with the meter stamp, if you like.
● Requires no minimum mail volume; anyone can easily use a postage meter!

FREE: *Handy desk or wall chart of postal rates with parcel post map and zone finder.*

PITNEY-BOWES
Postage Meter

Made by the leading manufacturer of mailing machines . . . Offices in 107 cities. In Canada: Pitney-Bowes of Canada, Ltd., Dept. 361, 909 Yonge St., Toronto.

To: Pitney-Bowes
1061 Pacific St.,
Stamford, Conn.

Send free booklet □ postal rate chart □ to:
Name_____
Address_____

Exhibit 16

PITNEY-BOWES, INC.

Temper, temper!

"Fresh out of stamps again—and these bulletins have to go out tonight! Why won't they keep their big paws out of my stamp box? Now I gotta rush down to the postoffice, stand in line, lick and stick every blasted stamp—and keep my date cooling his heels. This is really IT—tomorrow we get a postage meter, or . . ."

With a postage meter you never run out of stamps. You *print* postage, as and when you need it, directly on the envelope with dated postmark—and with your own small ad, if you like.

Your metered mail can be handled faster in the postoffice, and in *your* office, too. Saves time, money, postage—and temper!

Today, any small office can afford a postage meter—thanks to the little DM (desk model shown below). One out of 3 users spends less than $1 a day in postage. Electric models for larger mailers. Call the nearest PB office, or send coupon for free illustrated booklet.

Postage rates are up! . . .

Letters now cost you 33⅓ per cent more—so postage control is more important than ever.

● A meter protects postage from loss, damage, misuse; does its own accounting.

● Postage can be "dialed" day or night, for any class of mail—even parcel post. And the meter moistens envelopes for sealing, too!

● A postage meter requires no minimum mail volume. And anyone can easily use one.

FREE: *Handy desk or wall chart of latest postal rates with parcel post map and zone finder.*

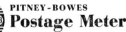

PITNEY-BOWES
PB Postage Meter

Made by the leading manufacturer of mailing machines . . .
Offices in 107 cities. In Canada: Pitney-Bowes
of Canada, Ltd., Dept. 364, 909 Yonge St., Toronto

To: Pitney-Bowes
1064 Pacific St.
Stamford, Conn.

Send free booklet ☐ Postal Rate Chart ☐ to:

Name_____

Address_____

Exhibit 17

PITNEY-BOWES, INC.

The day I flipped!

"It was a frantic Friday—noisy, boss on fire, both phones ringing. At 4:50 he hands me the new price lists; says, sorry, doll, they gotta go out tonight. Well, halfway through the licking and sticking, something snaps. I'd asked ten times for a postage meter—so now I'm drafting an ad: SITUATION WANTED—IN OFFICE HAVING POSTAGE METER."

Today, no one has to put up with slow, sloppy, tedious lick-and-stick mailing. The little DM (desk model) meter *prints* postage of any value directly on the envelope with a dated postmark—and your own small ad, if you like. Saves time, money, postage—and temper!

Now, even the smallest office can afford a meter—one DM user in three spends less than $1 a day for postage. Electric models for larger mailers. Call the nearest PB office for a demonstration. Or send coupon for a free illustrated booklet.

Postage rates are up! . . .

● Letters now cost you 33⅓ per cent more—so postage control is more important than ever.

● A meter protects postage from loss, misuse; does its own accounting.

● Postage is "dialed" for any class of mail—even parcels. And meters moisten envelope flaps for sealing!

● A postage meter requires no minimum mail volume. And anyone can easily use one—even the boss.

FREE: *Handy desk or wall chart of new postal rates with parcel post map and zone finder.*

PITNEY-BOWES
Postage Meter

*Made by the leading manufacturer of mailing machines . . .
Offices in 107 cities. In Canada: Pitney-Bowes
of Canada, Ltd., Dept. 365, 909 Yonge St., Toronto*

To: Pitney-Bowes
1065 Pacific St.
Stamford, Conn.

Send free ☐ *booklet* ☐ *Postal Rate Chart to:*

Name_____

Address_____

Exhibit 18

PITNEY-BOWES, INC.

No more lick-and-stick mailing!

"I've licked my last stamp, sopped my last envelope flap. They got me my postage meter! No more frantic 5 p.m. dashes to the postoffice for stamps, no more policing that silly old stamp box. We've gone modern, Man. We've got Metered Mail! Thank you, Boss!"

With a meter, you print postage as you need it, for any kind or class of mail—directly on the envelope, with a dated postmark, and your own small ad, if you like. You always have the right stamp on hand.

The meter seals as well as stamps your mail—most models do both simultaneously! Mailing is fast and easy. And metered mail requires less handling in the postoffice, often catches earlier mail trains and planes.

Today, even the smallest office can have a postage meter, now that there's a low-cost, desk model (the DM). One-third of its users spend less than $1.00 a day in postage! Electric models for larger mailers. Ask the nearest PB office for a demonstration. Or send coupon for free illustrated booklet.

Postage rates are up! . . .

● Letters now cost you 33⅓ per cent more—so postage control is more important than ever!

● A meter protects postage from loss, misuse; does its own accounting.

● Postage is "dialed" for any class of mail—even parcels. And meters moisten envelope flaps for sealing!

● A postage meter requires no minimum mail volume. And anyone can easily use one—even the boss.

FREE: *Handy desk or wall chart of new postal rates with parcel post map and zone finder.*

PITNEY-BOWES
PB Postage Meter

Made by the leading manufacturer of mailing machines... Offices in 107 cities. In Canada: Pitney-Bowes of Canada, Ltd., Dept. 367, 909 Yonge St., Toronto

PITNEY-BOWES, INC.
1067 Pacific St., Stamford, Conn.

Send free ☐ booklet ☐ Postal Rate Chart to:

Name_____

Address_____

mailing list were proven to be good prospects. Otherwise it was cheaper to reach the largest possible potential market through publication advertising.

Advertising Print Media

Over the years Pitney-Bowes had experimented with many types of print media and was continuing to do so when extra funds were available for experimentation. Its existing media strategy was generally as follows: business executives and owners could be reached best through news, management, and business papers; secretaries and other women handling mail (as well as small business and professional people) could be reached best through general-audience publications. Thus, in recent years, print-media advertising had been placed primarily in four business papers) *Business Week, Forbes, Fortune,* and *Nation's Business*) and three general-audience magazines *The Saturday Evening Post, The New Yorker,* and *Time*). The schedules of postage meter advertising in these media for the years 1955–58 are given in Exhibit 19. Circulation and space costs of these publications, as of December 1958, are given below:

PUBLICATION	PAID CIRCULATION	SPACE RATES (1 TIME)	
		1 Pg. 4-Color	1 Pg. 2-Color
Business Week..............	322,332	$ 5,100	$ 3,645
Forbes....................	260,448	4,089	3,168
Fortune...................	304,000	6,025 (6-ti.rate)	5,105
Nation's Business...........	774,235	5,675 (6-ti.rate)	5,235
The New Yorker...........	425,545	4,500	3,850
The Saturday Evening Post....	5,709,725	46,100	29,340
		28,005 (Jr. Unit)	22,395 (Jr. Unit)
Time....................	2,282,307	17,340	14,335

The Evaluation of Copy and Media

In order to develop conclusions which would help them plan future print-media campaigns, Messrs. Bowes and Jewett periodically examined the information available to them regarding the effectiveness of advertisements and media. Two types of information were available to them. First, they had a record of the number of inquiries which could be traced to a given advertisement in a given publication because of the address coding employed in each advertisement. Second, they had data on each advertisement from the readership studies of Daniel Starch and Associates.

A summary of data regarding inquiries obtained from print-media advertising is given in Exhibit 20 (it should be noted that the advertisement number used in Exhibit 20 is also the number of the exhibit in which the advertisement is shown.) A summary of Starch readership data is given in Exhibit 21. Information is not given on advertisement number 18 because it was not yet published. Publication was scheduled for early 1959.

Exhibit 19

PITNEY-BOWES, INC.

Postage Meter Publication Schedules, 1955–58

Magazine	Date	Number of 4-Color Full-Page Ads	Number of 2-Color Ads
Business Week................	1955	2	4
	1956	5	3
	1957	3	3
	1958	6	0
Forbes.....................	1955	0	4
	1956	0	4
	1957	0	4
	1958	3	1
Fortune....................	1955	2	4
	1956	2	4
	1957	4	3
	1958	6	1
Nation's Business............	1955	2	5
	1956	3	4
	1957	4	3
	1958	6	1
The New Yorker.............	1955	2	5
	1956	2	4
	1957	4	3
	1958	6	1
The Saturday Evening Post.....	1955	2	5
	1956	4	5
	1957	4	3
	1958	7	0
Time......................	1955	2	4
	1956	3	4
	1957	4	3
	1958	6	1

Source: Company records.

Exhibit 20

PITNEY-BOWES, INC.

Summary of Data regarding Inquiries Obtained from Print-Media Advertising

Ad. No.	Publi-cation*	Date of Pub.	No. of Inquiries	Cost per Inquiry	Ad. No.	Publi-cation*	Date of Pub.	No. of Inquiries	Cost per Inquiry
						F	6/57	50	84.80
						D	8/57	73	76.10
	NOW EVERY OFFICE CAN HAVE ONE! CAMPAIGN				11	B	8/57	272	18.94
						A	9/57	673	35.06
4	A	3/54	1,363*	17.10		E	9/57	132	32.20
		3/55	973(½p.)	20.60		C	10/57	358	43.99
	B	12/54	706	6.76		F	10/57	81	58.09
	C	12/54	1,234	10.41		D	11/57	93	59.73
	D	4/55	235	21.26	12	A	10/57	728	34.75
	E	7/55	330	11.83		B	11/57	392	13.15
	F	12/55	283	11.43		C	11/57	554	28.43
5	A	8/54	1,196	19.49		E	11/57	178	23.88
	B	4/55	478	10.78					
	C	4/55	745	18.22		RED-HEADED SECRETARY CAMPAIGN			
	F	5/55	109	31.28					
	D	8/55	140	35.68	13	A	3/58	549	46.08
6	A	9/55	740	27.08		B	3/58	136	46.63
	E	11/55	204	19.12		F	3/58	69	73.91
	B	12/55	449	11.48		C	4/58	284	61.66
	C	12/55	481	28.21		D	4/58	79	72.59
	F	12/55	175	19.49		E	4/58	54	83.33
	D	4/56	123	42.64		G	4/58	47	82.09
7	A	3/56	892	24.27	14	A	4/58	568	44.54
	B	4/56	476	10.83		B	5/58	138	38.64
	C	4/56	625	23.23		C	5/58	272	63.75
	F	5/56	98	43.27		F	5/58	52	98.08
	E	7/56	289	13.49		D	6/58	56	102.41
	D	8/56	87	60.29		E	6/58	127	35.43
8	A	12/56	583	37.13		G	6/58	61	63.25
		12/57	644	39.29	15	A	6/58	492	51.42
	B	12/56	245	21.03		B	7/58	96	57.55
		12/57	208	24.77		E	7/58	87	51.72
	C	12/56	360	40.33		F	7/58	62	86.26
		12/57	255	61.76		C	9/58	341	50.85
	D	12/57	55	101.00		D	9/58	48	119.48
	E	12/56	147	28.91	16	A	9/58	415	67.48
		12/57	149	28.52		B	9/58	148	37.33
	F	12/56	95	44.63		E	9/58	48	93.75
		12/57	42	112.02		F	8/59	65	78.46
9	A	9/56	655	33.05		C	10/58	264	65.68
	B	11/56	361	14.27		D	10/58	86	66.69
	C	11/56	374	38.82		G	10/58	69	55.91
	F	11/56	71	59.72	17	A	9/58	357	78.45
	E	12/56	154	27.60		B	10/58	110	50.23
	D	4/57	95	58.47		E	10/58	61	73.77
10	A	4/57	590	39.99		F	10/58	26	196.15
	E	5/57	76	55.92		C	11/58	307	56.48
	B	6/57	264	19.52		D	11/58	26	220.58
	C	6/57	290	54.31					

* Pitney-Bowes recorded inquiries for 18 months. Thus, the number of inquiries recorded for advertisements published before June 1957 are complete; for advertisements after June 1957, they are incomplete.

Exhibit 21

PITNEY-BOWES, INC.

Summary of Starch Readership Data

Ad. No.	Publication	Date of Publication	% Noted		% Seen-Assoc.		% Read Most	
			M	W	M	W	M	W
4	A	3/54	16	23	13	19	3	4
		3/55	20	16	16	13	3	3
	C	12/54	36	....	33	....	5	....
	F	12/55	41	....	35	....	10	....
5	A	8/54	29	30	27	33	6	5
	C	8/55	19	....	17	....	5	....
	F	5/55	27	....	24	....	9	....
6	A	9/55	14	10	12	9	3	1
	C	12/55	21	....	20	....	2	....
	F	12/55	30	....	28	....	7	....
7	A	3/56	12	15	9	12	2	1
	C	4/56	20	....	17	....	4	....
	F	5/56	22	....	21	....	8	....
8	A	12/56	26	31	19	20	1	1
		12/57	26	29	20	20	1	3
	C	12/56	35	....	29	....	2	....
		12/57	35	....	33	....	1	....
	F	12/56	37	....	37	....	12	....
		12/57	24	....	22	....	3	....
9	A	9/56	7	16	4	15	1	3
	C	11/56	13	....	13	....	3	....
	F	11/56	34	....	34	....	8	....
10	A	4/57	12	13	11	12	....	2
	C	6/57	15	....	15	....	3	....
	F	6/57	17	....	17	....	6	....
11	A	9/57	9	13	8	11	2	1
	C	10/57	18	....	16	....	1	....
	E	9/57	20	25	20	18	11	9
	F	10/57	25	....	25	....	7	....
12	A	10/57	12	14	12	12	2	3
	C	11/57	15	....	15	....	6	....
13	A	3/58	18	32	11	22	3	4
	C	4/58	17	....	13	....	4	....
	F	3/58	32	....	27	....	7	....
14	A	4/58	7	21	5	16	....	1
	C	5/58	29	....	27	....	7	....
	F	5/58	26	....	23	....	5	....
15	A	6/58	8	16	5	12	1	2
	C	9/58	18	....	17	....	3	....
	F	7/58	42	....	38	....	13	....

Exhibit 21—Continued

Ad. No.	Publication	Date of Publication	% Noted		% Seen-Assoc.		% Read Most	
			M	W	M	W	M	W
16	A	9/58	9	25	4	19	. . . .	3
	C	10/58	18	. . . .	16	. . . .	. . . .	. . . . . .
	E	9/58	34	31	22	30	11	9
	F	9/58	34	. . . .	30	. . . .	12	. . . . . .
17	Not available in December 1958							

~~~

CASE 36: CLUETT, PEABODY & COMPANY, INC.[1]

QUESTIONS TO CONSIDER: (1) *Does the company have a good basis for determining its sales potential?* (2) *What conclusions can you draw from the data given in Exhibit 8 regarding reasons for better-than-average or worse-than-average performance?* (3) *What additional information would you like to have in order to evaluate the relationship between sales performance and advertising expenditures?* (4) *In the light of the information given in Exhibit 9, would you consider the use of newspaper advertising in low performance areas?*

In the fall of 1958 Mr. R. A. Ziegler, advertising manager of Cluett, Peabody & Company, Inc., reviewed the advertising and sales activity of the company for the previous year. In the review he compared the sales potentials established for the company with actual sales as an aid in determining whether or not any changes should be made in the company's advertising and promotional program.

Background of Cluett, Peabody

Cluett, Peabody was the world's largest manufacturer of branded men's shirts. It manufactured and sold a complete line of dress shirts, casual wear (sport shirts and sweaters), boys' wear, ties, handkerchiefs, and underwear. These products were all nationally advertised in consumer magazines and bore the trade name, "Arrow." Domestic sales (*not including* Arrow International; Clupak, a stretchable paper licensing operation; J. Schoeneman Products, clothing manufacturers; the Bud Berman Sportswear Company; or the Sanforized Division) amounted to approximately $69 million in 1957, of which 80% was shirt sales.

There were several thousand brands of shirts on the market with Arrow accounting for approximately 22% of total United States shirt sales. Other leading manufacturers were the Manhattan Shirt Company, with about 7% of total shirt sales, and the Phillips-Jones Corporation, maker

---

[1] Written by David W. Nylen.

of "Van Heusen" shirts, with about 9% of total shirt sales. Both Manhattan and Van Heusen were also nationally advertised. In addition to these nationally advertised brands of shirts, a large number of private brands of shirts were distributed in certain markets, particularly through department stores in large cities.

Cluett, Peabody Advertising

The 1957 advertising campaign of Cluett, Peabody was typical of advertising campaigns employed by the company for many years. The

Exhibit 1

CLUETT, PEABODY & COMPANY, INC.

Advertising Budget for 1957

Acct. No.	Account	Per Cent
1.	Dealer Newspaper Mat Service	6.3%
2.	Direct Mail	2.0
3.	Point of Sale Advertising	12.1
4.	Itinerant Displays	3.0
5.	Trade Advertising (A & M)	
6.	Trade Advertising (Space)	
7.	Magazine Advertising (A & M)	8.4
8.	Magazine Advertising (Space)	42.6
9.	Newspaper Advertising (A & M)	
10.	Newspaper Advertising (Space)	
11.	Youth & College Advertising (A & M)	1.2
12.	Youth & College Advertising (Space)	3.3
13.	Sundries	2.1
14.	Administration	8.9
15.	Materials for Resale	1.4
16.	Public Relations	3.2
17.	Market Research	1.3
18.	Salesmen's Promotional Material	3.4
19.	Label & Package Development	0.2
20.	Youth & College Promotions	0.4
21.	Television	0.2
	Total	100.0%

budget for 1957 for magazine space for Arrow products was $1.5 million. In addition, substantial expenditures were made for other advertising functions, as indicated in Exhibit 1.

Exhibits 2 and 3 show typical magazine advertisements run in 1957 and 1958. Cluett, Peabody did not grant co-operative advertising allowances to dealers as did most of its competitors, but newspaper mats as shown in Exhibit 4 were supplied to dealers. Exhibit 5 shows the Arrow national advertising schedule for 1957.

Use of Sales Potentials

In appraising the company's advertising program, the advertising manager used sales potentials which had been established by the Arrow Mar-

Arrow's colorful **CARIBBEAN COLLECTION**
gives you Arrow fashion...Arrow comfort

Casual wear fashion at its most brilliant heights! Proof once
again that you're always smart to *insist on the Arrow label.*

It's your guarantee of fashion, comfort, value—in bountiful
measure. Arrow Sport Shirts are expertly tailored by the makers
of Arrow Shirts ... preferred five to one throughout America.
Dress right ... you can't afford not to.

SPORT SHIRTS—Short sleeves $5.00.

Look for the Arrow label and get these Arrow Sport Shirt extras

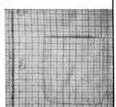

Unexcelled comfort (and smart appearance) with collar closed. Color-fast fabrics. "Sanforized" label means permanent fit.

Exclusive Arafold convertible collar. No neckband to show when worn open. Always neat ...always fashion-right.

So easy to iron. This Arafold collar has fold-line *built in*. Just iron it flat, then flip it over into position.

Patterns perfectly matched at pocket and collar. Everything is casual about an Arrow except the way we make it.

Exhibit 3
CLUETT, PEABODY & COMPANY, INC.
Typical 1957–58 Magazine Advertisement

Christmas favorites: Arrow "Dale" and "Par"

Shirts: Dale $5.00, Par, $4.00. All-silk ties, $2.50. (Other Arrow Shirts, $4 to $13.50)

His "just what I wanted" will really ring true when you give him a *Dale* or *Par*. It's no chance matter that these fine Arrow "whites" are the most-wanted and most-given shirts on Christmas morning. There's an extra touch of luxury to their "Sanforized" broadcloth, their punctilious tailoring, and their handsome Arrow collars. Both *Dale* and *Par* are available in French or button cuffs at your Arrow retailer's.

ARROW — first in fashion

Cluett, Peabody & Co., Inc.

Exhibit 4

CLUETT, PEABODY & COMPANY, INC.

1957 Newspaper Mats

ket Research Director for the company's 601 trading areas. Over the years, Cluett, Peabody's officers had experimented with several methods for establishing trading areas and creating market potentials for such areas.

In 1957 the company was using a system developed in its own research departments, based on the Hearst Trading Areas map. Exhibit 6 shows the northeast section of the United States as shown on the Hearst Trading Areas map. These trading areas had been developed by Hearst after years of extensive study and research. They were "irregular shaped units of territory based on the flow of retail trade, the boundary lines of which are fixed at the farthest point to which the influence of one principal trading

Exhibit 5

CLUETT, PEABODY & COMPANY, INC.

Arrow Advertising Schedule, 1957

Date	Publication	Space	Merchandise Featured
January 10	*Esquire*	Two-color page	Golden Arrow Shirts
January 11	*Scholastic, Jr.* and *Sr.*	Page, black and white	Boys' Wear—Glen L.C. Permanent Stay
February 1	*Sports Illustrated*	Page, four-color bleed	Casual Wear—Red, White and New
February 1	*Scholastic, Senior*	4th cover, black and white	Boys' Wear—Squire
February 7	*Life*	Inside cover page, four-color	White and Fancies—Valentine Shirts and Ties
February 17	*This Week* and supplements*	½ page, black and white	White Shirts—Permanent Stay
February 19	*The Saturday Evening Post*	Page, four-color	Fancy Feature—Town Trio Ensemble
February 22	*Scholastic, Jr.* and *Sr.*	⅔ page, black and white	Boys' Wear—Glen Link Cuff
February 26	*The Saturday Evening Post*	Page, four-color	Casual Wear—Game Room Casuals
March 5	*The Saturday Evening Post*	½ page, black and white	White Shirts—Dart-Dale
March 6	*Esquire*	Page, four-color	Fancy Feature—Sketchbook Prints Ensemble
March 7	*Life*	½ page, black and white	White Shirts—Link Cuff (Lane and Glen)
March 15	*Scholastic, Jr.* and *Sr.*	⅔ page, black and white	Boys' Wear—Glen Link Cuff
March 21	*Life*	Page, four-color	Fancy Feature—Travel Trio Ensemble
March 22	*Sports Illustrated*	Page, four-color bleed	Casual Wear—Coffee Tones
April 4	*Life*	½ page, black and white	White Shirts—Par F.C.
April 5	*Scholastic, Jr.* and *Sr.*	⅔ page, black and white	Boys' Wear—Bi-Way B.D.
April 10	*Esquire*	Two-color page	Golden Arrow Shirts
April 12	*Sports Illustrated*	⅔ page, black-and-white bleed	Casual Wear—Free-Way
April 14	*This Week* and 8 independents*	7/10 page, four-color	Fancy Feature—Batiste Oxford Ensemble
April 16	*The Saturday Evening Post*	½ page, black and white	White Shirts—Link Cuff (Lane and Glen)
April 18	*Life*	Page, four-color	Casual Wear—Trim-Way
April 26	*Scholastic, Junior*	Page, black and white	Boys' Wear—Glen L.C. Permanent Stay
April 26	*Scholastic, Senior*	Page, black and white	Boys' Wear—Squire
April 27	*This Week* and supplements*	⅖ page, black and white	White Shirts—Dacron-Cotton
May 2	*Life*	½ page, black and white	White Shirts—Dart-Dale
May 3	*Scholastic, Junior*	⅔ page, black and white	Boys' Wear—Glen Link Cuff
May 10	*Sports Illustrated*	Page, four-color bleed	Casual Wear—Vacation Mates

* See page 956 for reference.

Exhibit 5—Continued

Date	Publication	Space	Merchandise Featured
May 12.........	*This Week* and 8 independents*	⁷⁄₁₀ page, four-color	Fancy Feature—Sea Scape Colors Ensemble
May 14.........	*The Saturday Evening Post*	½ page, black and white	White Shirts—Par F.C.
May 17.........	*Scholastic, Jr.* and *Sr.*	⅔ page, black and white	Boys' Wear—Bi-Way S
May 30.........	*Life*	Page, four-color	Casual Wear—Checkaire
June 2.........	*This Week* and 8 independents*	⁷⁄₁₀ page, four-color	Fancy Feature—Ice Cream Tones Ensemble
June 4.........	*The Saturday Evening Post*	½ page, black and white	White Shirts—Bi-Way B.D. (Father's Day)
June 6.........	*Life*	½ page, black and white	White Shirts—Permanent Stay (Father's Day)
June 7.........	*Esquire*	Page, four-color	Casual Wear—Tartan Checks (Father's Day)
June 9.........	*This Week* and supplements*	⅖ page, black and white	White Shirts—Bi-Way (Father's Day)
August 8.........	*Esquire*	Four-color page	Fancy Feature Ensembles—Back to School (Cambridge Cloth—Checks and Stripes)
August 15.........	*Life*	Four-color page	Casual Wear—Back to School (Miniature Madras)
August 27.........	*The Saturday Evening Post*	Half-page, black and white	White Shirts—Glen, B.D.
September 10.........	*Esquire*	Four-color page	Fancy Feature Ensembles—Back to School (Cambridge Cloth—Solid Colors)
September 10.........	*The Saturday Evening Post*	Half-page, black and white	Casual Wear—Exact Sleeve Length Sport Shirts
September 13.........	*Scholastic, Jr.* and *Sr.*	Back cover, black and white	Boys' Wear—University Fashion Shirt (Cambridge Cloth)
September 15.........	*The New York Times*	Second cover, black and white	White Shirts—Dacron and Cotton
September 15.........	*This Week* and independents†	Half-page, black and white	White Shirts—Glen, Link Cuff
September 17.........	*Holiday*	Half-page, black and white	Casual Wear—Exact Sleeve Length Sport Shirts
September 20.........	*Scholastic, Jr.* and *Sr.*	Page, black and white	Boys' Wear—University Fashion—Glen (Cambridge Cloth)
September 22.........	*This Week* and independents†	⁷⁄₁₀ page, black and white	White Shirts—Dacron and Cotton
September 27.........	*Sports Illustrated*	Second cover, four-color page	Casual Wear—Nassau Cloth
October 1.........	*The Saturday Evening Post*	Four-color page	Fancy Feature Ensembles—Ripple Stripes
October 6.........	*This Week*	⁷⁄₁₀ page	Casual Wear Gabanaro
October 8.........	*The Saturday Evening Post*	Half-page, black and white	White Shirts—Dart

* See page 956 for reference.
† See page 956 for reference.

Exhibit 5—Continued

Date	Publication	Space	Merchandise Featured
October 9	*Time*	⅔ page, black and white	Casual Wear—Exact Sleeve Length Sport Shirts
October 10	*Esquire*	Four-color page	Golden Arrow
October 11	*Life*	Half-page, black and white	White Shirts—Dacron and Cotton
October 11	*Scholastic, Senior*	⅔ page, black and white	Casual Wear—Trimway Sport Shirt
October 13	*This Week* and independents†	⁷⁄₁₀ page, four-color	Casual Wear—Gabanaro Sport Shirt
October 18	*Sports Illustrated*	Four-color page	Casual Wear—Cavalier
October 24	*Life*	Page, black and white	White Shirts—Link Cuff (Glen)
October 25	*Sports Illustrated*	⅔ page, black and white	Casual Wear—Exact Sleeve Length Sport Shirts
October 27	*This Week* and independents†	⁷⁄₁₀ page, four-color	Fancy Feature Ensembles—Pebble Weave
October 31	*Life*	Page, black and white	White Shirts—Glen-Arden
November 1	*Scholastic, Jr. and Sr.*	⅔ page, black and white	Boys' Wear—Bi-Way
November 5	*The Saturday Evening Post*	Half-page, black and white	White Shirts—Par, French Cuff
November 7	*Esquire*	Half-page, black and white	Casual Wear—Exact Sleeve Length Sport Shirts
November 7	*Esquire*	Four-color page	Golden Arrow
November 17	*This Week* and independents†	⁷⁄₁₀ page, four-color	Fancy Feature Ensembles—Compatible Checks and Stripes
November 19	*The Saturday Evening Post*	Page, black and white	White Shirts—Permanent Stay
November 22	*Scholastic, Senior*	⅔ page, black and white	Casual Wear—Trimway Sport Shirt
November 27	*Life*	Page, black and white	White Shirts—Dart-Arden
December 1	*This Week* and independents†	Half-page, black and white	White Shirts—Dart
December 3	*The Saturday Evening Post*	Four-color page	White Shirts—Dale-Par
December 5	*Life*	Four-color page	Fancy Feature Ensembles—Yule Tones
December 6	*Scholastic, Junior*	⅔ page, black and white	Boys' Wear—Par
December 8	*Philadelphia Inquirer*	³⁄₅ page, four-color	Casual Wear—Gabanaro Sport Shirt
December 8	*This Week* and independents†	⁷⁄₁₀ page, four-color	Casual Wear—Gabanaro Sport Shirt
December 13	*Scholastic, Jr. and Sr.*	Page, black and white	Boys' Wear—Glen

* Atlanta, Ga., *Journal Constitution*; Buffalo, N.Y., *Courier Express*; Columbus, Ohio, *Dispatch*; Louisville, Kentucky, *Courier Journal*; St. Paul, Minn., *Dispatch* and *Pioneer Press*; Seattle, Wash., *Times*; New York, N.Y., *Times*; Chicago, Illinois, *Tribune*.

† Atlanta, Ga., *Journal Constitution*; Buffalo, N.Y., *Courier Express*; Columbus, Ohio, *Dispatch*; Louisville, Kentucky, *Courier Journal*; St. Paul, Minn., *Dispatch* and *Pioneer Press*; Seattle, Wash., *Times*; New York, N.Y., *Times*; Chicago, Illinois, *Tribune*; Philadelphia, Penn., *Philadelphia Inquirer* (Dec. 8).

Source: Company records.

Exhibit 6

CLUETT, PEABODY & COMPANY, INC.
Northeast United States Hearst Area
Reproduced by Permission

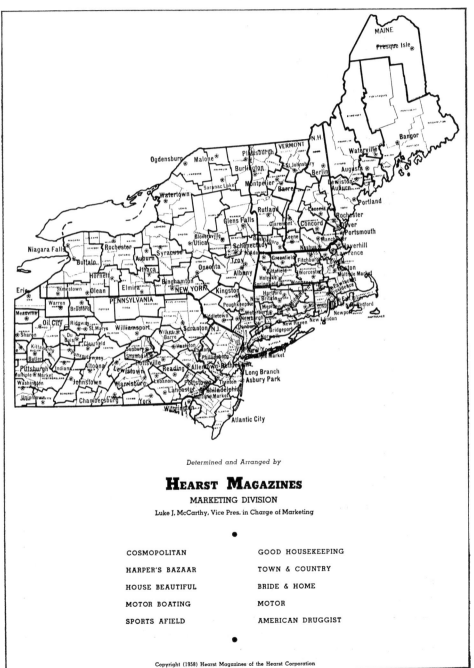

Determined and Arranged by

HEARST MAGAZINES
MARKETING DIVISION
Luke J. McCarthy, Vice Pres. in Charge of Marketing

•

COSMOPOLITAN	GOOD HOUSEKEEPING
HARPER'S BAZAAR	TOWN & COUNTRY
HOUSE BEAUTIFUL	BRIDE & HOME
MOTOR BOATING	MOTOR
SPORTS AFIELD	AMERICAN DRUGGIST

•

Exhibit 7

CLUETT, PEABODY & COMPANY, INC.

Hearst's Thirty-Three Factors Which Determine the Principal
Trading Centers and Their Consumer Areas

Physical Characteristics:
   1. Location of cities and towns
   2. Topography of each section
   3. Climate
   4. Natural resources

People and Homes:
   5. Population
   6. Native white population
   7. Age and sex characteristics
   8. Families
   9. Literacy
  10. Dwellings
  11. Home ownership
  12. Educational, resort, and residential advantages

Transportation, Communication, and Distribution Machinery:
  13. Transportation facilities (freight terminals, transfer points; rail, air, and auto roads)
  14. Telephone and radio sets
  15. Newspapers and extent of their individual circulations
  16. Public warehouses
  17. Wholesale outlets
  18. Retail stores
  19. Range of store deliveries
  20. Distribution of gas and electricity

Valuation of Products and Sources of Personal Income:
  21. Agricultural occupations
  22. Industrial establishments
  23. Mining enterprises
  24. Public service occupations

Volume of Business, Wealth, and Standards of Living:
  25. Volume of business, wholesale and retail
  26. Wealth
  27. Savings deposits
  28. Personal incomes
  29. Banking
  30. Car ownership
  31. Life insurance
  32. Wage earners
  33. Buying habits, customs, and trade tendencies

Source: Hearst Magazines, Inc., 1952.

center extends before consumer buying habits swing toward another dominant community. The borders of the areas follow county lines for convenience when possible, but not where consumer buying habits ignore such purely political boundaries."[2] The consumer trading areas were determined after studying 33 factors which the Hearst magazines' direc-

---

[2] *The Development of Consumer Trading Areas* by L. F. McCarthy, Director of Marketing, Hearst Magazines, Inc., 1936.

tors believed affected centers of community trading and their surrounding areas. These factors are listed in Exhibit 7.

The market research director of Cluett, Peabody had conducted extensive research before accepting the Hearst areas. He was convinced that the 601 areas formed a basis on which to establish marketing potentials for his company's products.

After adopting the 601 trading areas as a basis for sales planning, the market research director proceeded to construct a men's apparel buying potential for each area.

These potentials were based on the Hearst Buying Power Index:

The purpose of the Buying Power Index is to show the potential value of each market in terms of *percentage* of the U.S. total—also the relative value between one market and another.

The Buying Power Index is so broad in its foundation that it may be used without alteration for the average nationally advertised product and can be applied to any business selling to the consumer.

It has been established by a large array of basic factors; in fact, this Buying Power Index represents the *"par"* for each of the 601 Principal Trading Centers and Consumer Trading Areas. It assumes a *uniform* national distribution and expresses every sales quota *in percentage* to the total U.S. market.

This Buying Power Index not only takes into account all the data of the latest United States Census of Business and Population, but we have also analyzed, in its preparation, every additional available series of figures which would contribute toward establishing the soundest foundation for sales quota making.[3]

Twenty-one factors were used to determine the Buying Power Index. These included:

Population and families, personal income and federal tax collections, sales of Series "E" U.S. Savings Bonds, passenger car registrations, motor fuel purchased, life insurance sales, homes wired for electricity, radio sets, telephone home ownership, domestic gas consumers, consumer durable goods sales, manufacturing production, mineral production, agricultural income, wholesale-retail trade and outlets, business population, postal receipts, value of construction and bank deposits.

The 1952 Buying Power Index showed 601 Principal Trading Centers which accounted for 68.4% of the United States total buying power.

As used by Cluett, Peabody, the Buying Power Index represented the potential percentage of Arrow's United States sales in each area and for each major city within the area. A performance figure of 100 meant that average selling results had been achieved. For example, the Buying Power Index for the trading area of Bloomington, Indiana, was 0.0533 (0.0533% of total United States buying power). The actual Cluett sales for this same area were approximately 0.0560% of the total Cluett sales for 1957, or 105% of the potential.

---

[3] Hearst Magazines, Inc., 1952.

Exhibit 8

CLUETT, PEABODY & COMPANY, INC.
Market Analysis Report—1957–56*
First Twenty Cities

TRADING AREA		Pop. (000's)	HEARST B.P.I.	1957 Sales	1957 Perf.†	1956 Sales	1956 Perf.
1. New York MM	‡KC	10,830	9.4889	5,520,159	66	6,348,831	71
	§TA	14,075	11.5421	7,226,032	71	8,041,271	74
2. Chicago MM	KC	4,242	3.9761	2,499,665	71	2,753,829	74
	TA	3,688	4.7090	3,354,352	81	3,615,166	82
3. Los Angeles MM	KC	3,017	2.9648	1,997,628	76	2,106,833	76
	TA	5,432	4.0061	3,520,383	100	3,438,958	91
4. Philadelphia MM	KC	2,395	2.2380	1,804,435	91	2,022,517	96
	TA	3,863	2.8122	2,731,342	110	2,976,984	112
5. Detroit MM	KC	2,183	2.1130	1,506,899	81	1,766,454	89
	TA	3,433	2.6081	2,040,592	89	2,311,837	94
Total—1st 5 cities:	KC	22,667	20.7779	13,328,786	73	14,998,464	77
	TA	32,458	25.6775	18,872,701	83	20,384,216	84
6. San Francisco MM	KC	1,645	1.3048	1,958,417	147	1,927,860	136
	TA	3,184	2.2439	2,503,462	126	2,521,878	119
7. Boston MM	KC	1,366	1.3578	1,387,988	116	1,483,980	116
	TA	2,832	1.9309	1,800,328	106	1,903,820	105
8. St. Louis MM	KC	1,024	1.0196	749,209	83	796,258	83
	TA	2,299	1.4701	1,198,977	92	1,246,367	90
9. Pittsburgh MM	KC	812	.9748	1,240,333	144	1,225,735	134
	TA	2,167	1.4353	1,626,422	128	1,658,324	123
10. Cleveland MM	KC	1,189	1.2119	1,092,971	102	1,240,560	109
	TA	1,819	1.4338	1,369,168	108	1,514,340	112
Total—1st 10 cities:	KC	28,703	26.8467	6,428,916	83	6,674,393	86
	TA	44,759	34.1915	8,498,357	91	8,844,729	91
11. Washington, D.C.	KC	879	0.8306	877,626	120	926,011	118
	TA	1,883	1.1986	1,202,301	114	1,287,914	114
12. Minneapolis	KC	538	0.7297	732,698	114	701,379	102
St. Paul	KC	327	0.3438	308,742	102	333,203	103
Twin Cities	TA	1,621	1.1851	1,234,713	118	1,223,196	110
13. Baltimore	KC	998	0.9568	530,127	63	590,869	66
	TA	1,670	1.0764	631,474	66	704,599	70
14. Houston	KC	704	0.7155	377,452	60	502,789	75
	TA	1,366	0.9041	520,303	65	653,732	77
15. Kansas City, Kan.	KC	131	0.1323	68,579	59	68,964	55
Kansas City, Mo.	KC	492	0.6462	409,147	72	530,030	87
Kansas Cities	TA	1,165	0.8935	714,767	91	828,771	99
16. Covington	KC	66	0.0506	40,710	91	48,279	101
Cincinnati	KC	533	0.6139	548,738	101	584,405	101
Cincinnati-Covington	TA	1,312	0.8835	761,585	98	855,068	103
17. Milwaukee	KC	706	0.7186	601,683	95	688,306	102
	TA	1,240	0.8593	773,087	102	880,924	109
18. Dallas	KC	577	0.6908	401,216	66	374,436	58
	TA	933	0.8143	530,209	74	502,844	66

* Figures disguised.

† Performance as a percentage of potential.

‡ Key city in trading area.

§ Trading area.

Exhibit 8—Continued

TRADING AREA		Pop. (000's)	HEARST B.P.I.	1957		1956	
				Sales	Perf.†	Sales	Perf.
19. Buffalo	KC	588	0.4339	523,316	137	635,328	156
Niagara Falls	KC	98	0.0532	97,643	208	109,266	218
Buffalo–N. Falls	TA	1,320	0.8103	924,824	129	1,029,721	135
20. Seattle	KC	570	0.5995	595,817	113	669,005	119
	TA	916	0.6648	655,401	112	735,531	118
Total—1st 20 cities:	KC	35,910	34.3620	6,113,494	85	6,762,270	88
	TA	58,185	43.4814	7,948,664	92	8,702,300	93

* Figures disguised.
† Performance as a percentage of potential.
‡ Key city in trading area.
§ Trading area.

A complete analysis was made by Cluett, Peabody each year, comparing the sales for each of the 601 areas—by trading area and key city within the area—with its corresponding Buying Power Index. Cluett, Peabody's 1957 market analysis report included the following information for both the trading areas and key cities:

1. Trading area
2. Population
3. Buying Power Index
4. 1957 sales and performance
5. 1956 sales and performance

This analysis made possible quick comparisons between sales performance and potentials. The analysis was also broken down by salesmen's territory (approximately 150) and by Arrow's five regional offices. From these reports, strong and weak selling areas could be detected quickly, and the advertising manager could determine where increased sales and advertising effort was necessary. Exhibit 8 shows the 1957 market analysis report for the 20 largest trading areas.

Consideration of Supplementary Newspaper Advertising

After analyzing the 1957 sales potential and performance figures and comparing them with 1956 figures, Mr. Ziegler became concerned over the low performance in several of the large trading areas and key cities and by the decline of sales from 1956 levels in some large metropolitan areas. From previous analysis, Mr. Ziegler was aware that the large national consumer magazines in which Arrow advertising was concentrated did not give coverage in large metropolitan areas that was proportional to the large Arrow sales potential in the same areas. He believed that this coverage deficiency was a major factor in the poor sales performance in large trading areas.

In an effort to overcome this coverage deficiency and improve sales performance in these areas, Mr. Ziegler was considering the supplemen-

Exhibit 9

CLUETT, PEABODY & COMPANY, INC.

Comparison of Newspapers with *Life* for Five Metropolitan Areas

	STAGES		
	1	1, 2	1, 2, 3
ATLANTA, GEORGIA			
Newspaper circulation	452,630	943,172	1,155,439
Percentage family coverage	59.1%	63.7%	64.4%
Life circulation	102,573	166,760	174,850
Percentage family coverage	13.4%	11.3%	9.8%
Newspaper costs—full page	$2,649	$7,241	$9,877
Newspaper costs—1,000 lines	1,100	2,810	3,900
Newspapers—cost per M families:			
Full page	$5.85	$7.68	$8.54
1,000 lines	2.43	2.98	3.38
Life magazine—cost per M families:			
Total U.S. circulation and costs	$4.51	$4.51	$4.51
CHICAGO, ILLINOIS			
Newspaper circulation	851,102	1,263,522	1,465,148
Percentage family coverage	34.6%	43.0%	45.2%
Life circulation	309,818	359,596	386,153
Percentage family coverage	12.6%	12.2%	11.9%
Newspaper costs—full page	$4,375	$8,516	$11,079
Newspaper costs—1,000 lines	1,890	3,590	4,640
Newspapers—cost per M families:			
Full page	$5.14	$6.74	$7.56
1,000 lines	2.22	2.84	3.17
Life magazine—cost per M families:			
Total U.S. circulation and costs	$4.51	$4.51	$4.51
NEW YORK, NEW YORK			
Newspaper circulation	2,103,917		
Percentage family coverage	37.3%		
Life circulation	1,272,024		
Percentage family coverage	22.6%		
Newspaper costs—full page	$3,640		
Newspaper costs—1,000 lines	3,640		
Newspaper—cost per M families:			
Full page	$1.73		
1,000 lines	1.73		
Life magazine—cost per M families:			
Total U.S. circulation and costs	$4.51		
ST. LOUIS, MISSOURI			
Newspaper circulation	383,526	583,770	638,999
Percentage family coverage	45.7%	50.9%	51.4%
Life circulation	69,728	90,434	95,400
Percentage family coverage	8.3%	7.9%	7.7%
Newspaper costs—full page	$2,356	$4,735	$5,858
Newspaper costs—1,000 lines	950	1,920	2,370

Exhibit 9—Continued

	STAGES		
	1	1, 2	1, 2, 3
ST. LOUIS, MISSOURI (*Cont.*)			
Newspapers—cost per M families:			
Full page..............................	$6.14	$8.11	$9.17
1,000 lines............................	2.48	3.29	3.71
Life magazine—cost per M families:			
Total U.S. circulation and costs...............	$4.51	$4.51	$4.51
SAN FRANCISCO, CALIFORNIA			
Newspaper circulation.......................	204,911	699,299	793,804
Percentage family coverage...................	23.5%	38.5%	40.9%
Life circulation............................	130,676	257,339	269,216
Percentage family coverage...................	15.0%	14.2%	13.9%
Newspaper costs—full page..................	$2,128	$6,130	$7,703
Newspaper costs—1,000 lines.................	950	2,622	3,272
Newspapers—cost per M families:			
Full page..............................	$10.38	$8.77	$9.70
1,000 lines............................	4.64	3.75	4.12
Life magazine—cost per M families:			
Total U.S. circulation and costs...............	$4.51	$4.51	$4.51
TOTAL—FIVE METROPOLITAN AREAS			
Newspaper circulation.......................	3,996,086	5,593,680	6,157,307
Percentage family coverage...................	37.8%	43.0%	44.4%
Life circulation............................	1,884,819	2,146,153	2,197,643
Percentage family coverage...................	17.8%	16.5%	15.9%
Newspaper costs—full page..................	$15,148	$30,262	$38,157
Newspaper costs—1,000 lines.................	8,530	14,582	17,822
Newspapers—cost per M families:			
Full page..............................	$3.79	$5.41	$6.20
1,000 lines............................	2.13	2.61	2.89
Life magazine—cost—page, B & W.............	$26,275	$26,275	$26,275
Life magazine—cost per M families:			
Total U.S. circulation and costs...............	$4.51	$4.51	$4.51
Five area circulation and costs...............	$13.94	$2.24	$11.96

Source: Research Department, Bureau of Advertising.

tary use of newspaper advertising in certain low-performance metropolitan areas. As a preliminary step, Mr. Ziegler was studying an analysis, prepared for him by the Bureau of Advertising, comparing the coverage of newspapers with the coverage of *Life* magazine in five metropolitan areas—Atlanta, Chicago, New York, St. Louis, and San Francisco. Mr. Ziegler had selected these cities for analysis because they were the sites of Cluett, Peabody branch offices. If the preliminary analysis indicated that supplementary advertising in newspapers was desirable, he was considering an advertising test in the five cities, to be supervised by the branch offices in these cities. Since management had decided that the total advertising budget could not be increased, the additional cost of newspaper advertising would have to be offset by a reduction in some other expense category.

In the Bureau of Advertising analysis (shown in Exhibit 9) the leading newspaper in each of the five metropolitan areas was selected and a tabulation was made of the percentage of family coverage in all counties in which 10% or more of the families received this newspaper. One additional daily newspaper distributed in outlying counties of each area was taken in each of two successive stages. The percentage of family coverage in counties where over 10% received the outlying newspapers was then tabulated. In order to prevent one metropolitan area from extending into another, newspapers selected in stage 2 were not larger than those in stage 1, and those in stage 3 were not larger than those in stage 2. In the New York area, one newspaper gave such wide coverage that it was impractical to add the second and third stages. The analysis then compared this newspaper coverage with the coverage of *Life* in the same counties. Newspaper space rates were listed for a full page and for a 1,000-line advertisement in each stage. The pro rata cost of a full-page, black-and-white advertisement in *Life* was also listed.

~~~

CASE 37: SIMS FOOD COMPANY[1]

QUESTION TO CONSIDER: *What steps should the vice president take in order to devise a better method for establishing the advertising budget of the Sims Food Company?*

As a result of an unharmonious budget-making session in November 1955, the executive committee of the Sims Food Company[2] requested that the company's vice president of sales develop a new method of determining the promotional expenditure for use in 1956. The vice president of sales, among other things, discussed this problem with a consultant.

The Sims Food Company was organized in 1950 by a group of young businessmen who believed that they could profitably market a new salad dressing, "Zest." Through a unique combination of herbs, they had been able to create a salad dressing which received the praise of friends and test groups of consumers. By employing food brokers and giving high margins to brokers and retailers, the company had been able to obtain good distribution—approximately 60%—in food stores throughout the southern and southwestern states. Sales had increased rapidly, from

---

[1] Written by Martin V. Marshall.

[2] All names are fictitious.

$108,000 in the last six months of 1950 to $3,406,000 in 1954. Sales in 1955 were $3,101,000.

Since the company had about 30% of sales income available for promotional expenses and profit, it had spent relatively large sums on advertising, special aisle display pieces, and co-operative advertising. Throughout the period 1950–53, the company's executives were primarily interested in opening up new urban markets; therefore they spent all available promotional monies on a series of introductory campaigns in such markets. By the end of 1953, they decided that they should consolidate the position of Zest in existing markets before extending distribution nationally and that they should begin to take profits from the operation.

Consequently, the executive committee decided to spend 25% of 1954 estimated sales for promotion in 1954, or $750,000. Since actual sales exceeded estimated 1954 sales by about 13%, the committee decided to spend 25% of actual 1954 sales for promotion in 1955, or $850,000. When actual 1955 sales were less than actual 1954 sales, the committee became concerned and requested the vice president of sales to devise a new method of determining promotional expenditures. Meanwhile, the committee set the 1956 promotional budget at $750,000, on the assumption that 1956 sales would at least be slightly in excess of $3,000,000.

The vice president of sales had tentatively concluded that "the company had not progressed far enough so that we can budget advertising by any but the crudest means." He pointed out that the company knew little about its sales by markets, since the company's only sales statistics were sales to food brokers by months; and little about its share of market, since no data regarding consumer purchases were available to company executives.

Further, he said that the company had not yet adopted a consistent media policy so that it was difficult, if not impossible, to determine the relative effectiveness of various media. During the introductory period the company had used space advertising in newspapers. In 1953 it had used small-space advertising in newspapers, one-minute radio commercials, and 20-second television commercials, the latter in two markets. In 1954 a shift was made to 300-line advertisements in newspapers; and in 1955 a budget increase of $100,000 was spent for 20-second television commercials, the remainder of the budget being spent for 300-line advertisements. In 1955 another shift was made, from daily newspapers and television to Sunday supplements.

The Sims company had utilized one principal copy theme since 1950, namely, the "newness" and "differentness" of Zest. The vice president of sales said that the company's advertising agency had prepared numerous alternative copy approaches in the past but that these had always been turned down by the executive committee. He believed, however, that the committee would probably accept a new copy approach sometime during 1956.

The company's promotional expenditures for the period 1954–56 were as follows:

Item	1954	1955	1956*
Daily newspapers	$525,100	$523,000	$100,000
Television spots	......	102,800	......
Sunday supplements	......	......	500,000
Radio spots	17,000	12,200	15,000
Radio food program	25,300	26,700	......
Direct mail	3,300	3,000	4,000
Display material	38,000	41,600	35,000
Co-operative advertising	82,500	94,200	51,000
Overhead	36,800	43,600	45,000
Total	$728,000	$844,100	$750,000

* Budgeted.

Chapter 12

∿∿∿∿∿∿∿∿∿∿∿∿∿∿∿∿∿∿∿∿∿∿∿∿∿∿

CASES INVOLVING THE
PREPARATION OF
ADVERTISEMENTS

It is desirable that members of management have some understanding of the creative aspects of advertising. Accordingly, the cases in this chapter call for the preparation of advertisements in order that the reader may develop an understanding of some of the problems and processes faced by advertising specialists when they construct advertisements.

A Perspective

It has often been said that there are as many theories about advertising as there are persons exposed to it; this is, unfortunately, a fairly accurate description of the environment in which advertising decisions are made. All too frequently, businessmen and critics of advertising employ theories about advertising communication which are based upon little more than an emotional reaction to their own personal experience, not upon real study of what is, under any circumstances, a complex, difficult art. Even among those who have spent a lifetime studying the art of advertising communication, there is a wide range of views, each well supported and each extensively debated.

If the businessman is to deal effectively with advertising, he should understand the principal theories and the premises upon which they are based, and he should develop convictions regarding the theories that he is willing to use in given situations.

The work of preparing the assignments in this chapter will include the reading of selected literature in the field of advertising communication to give the reader a basis for formulating his own specific views and theories about the art. In order to generate initial thinking, some fairly traditional views are briefly described below.

967

A Traditional View Briefly Outlined

Although there are differences in approach in preparing advertisements for different media, in general most of the important considerations can be discussed in terms of preparing an advertisement for publication in print media. Thus, this brief discussion will focus exclusively upon the preparation of advertisements for print media. Selected readings will deal with the more specific considerations involved in the preparation of advertisements for other media.

1. *Advertisements should offer information.* Despite the fact that consumers and industrial buyers often are affected by so-called emotional buying motives, advertisers generally have sought to build their advertisements primarily on the basis of appealing to rational buying motives, that is, by offering information of value about their products and services. The need for giving information is clear in instances where new products are being marketed and where the market needs to be educated regarding the uses of and wants fulfilled by the new products, for example, the advertising of Masonite exterior siding (see page 347). Later, as products reach a more competitive stage in their evolution, there is need for informing prospects of the differentiating characteristics of the competing brands, for example, the advertising of Palm Beach clothing (see page 266).[1]

2. *Advertisements should stress buyer benefits.* Although advertisers generally seek to offer information of value in their advertisements, they do not do so simply by listing information or listing differentiating characteristics. Rather they try to translate product information into specific selling points which will appeal to the self-interests of prospects, that is, as buyer or user benefits to be obtained through use of the product being advertised. For example, the advertisement for "Stopette Spray" deodorant shown on page 513 took the key selling point for this new product, the spray method of application, and translated it into a buyer benefit, "no messy hands!"

In preparing advertisements, the reader should attempt to orient his thinking with that of prospects in order to visualize what will appeal to their self-interests and what will be significant buyer benefits to stress in advertisements.

3. *Advertisements should focus on one key appeal.* Today everyone lives in a busy, complex world, and is continuously exposed to a tremendous flood of messages: social, economic, political, technical, religious, educational, and advertising messages. As would be expected, advertisements do not ordinarily get concentrated attention from people. Conse-

---

[1] In recent years, there has been much criticism of the information approach. One of the principal critics has been Pierre Martineau, Director of Research and Marketing of the *Chicago Tribune*. His criticisms of the traditional approach are ably presented in *Motivation in Advertising* (New York: McGraw-Hill Book Co., Inc., 1957).

quently, it is difficult for the advertiser to build strong purchase-motivating ideas about his brand when attention to advertisements is casual, and when the reading, listening, or viewing of advertisements is done under a great variety of circumstances which conflict with the retention of ideas by people.

From advertising research, it is known that the readership of advertisements varies widely with the product interest of people. Women, for example, are more interested in food advertisements than men, and men are more interested in automobile advertisements than women. It is known that people cannot remember well what is said in advertisements, and that the attention to and retention of advertising by people varies substantially on the basis of what the advertiser shows in his illustration and what he says in his headline and copy.

In the light of the difficulties involved in gaining the attention of people and of communicating advertising messages to them, many advertisers have adopted the policy of building their advertisements—their advertising campaigns—around what have been variously entitled as "copy platforms," "central copy themes," "core ideas," and "the key selling appeal." This policy means that while many selling appeals or buyer benefits may be employed in the individual advertisements of an advertising campaign, the advertiser usually seeks to build his campaign around a *single* motivating idea by emphasizing that idea in one or a variety of ways in advertisement after advertisement. For example in recent years the Chrysler Corporation has pounded away at "The Forward Look," each successive advertisement in the campaign seeking to attract the attention of prospects through fresh treatment of "The Forward Look." Core ideas or central campaign themes are legion: "Dress right, you can't afford not to!"; "Got a cough? Got a cold? Switch from Hots to Kools!"; "You too can break the laxative habit—use Carter's Little Liver Pills"; "Wonder Bread Builds Strong Bodies 12 Ways"; and "Colgate Dental Cream Stops Tooth Decay Best."

4. *Advertisements should stick to one appeal—repetition.* Not only do advertisers generally emphasize a single idea in their advertising but they usually operate on the premise that a great deal of repetition is required. This view is reflected in the statement of a well-known advertising practitioner, James D. Woolf: ". . . H. L. Mencken once remarked that 'it is a terrific job to ram even the most elemental idea into the average man.' . . . It takes a long, long time to sell *homo sapiens* a new idea that conflicts with a cherished notion or an established habit . . . I hold to the conviction, based upon long experience, that when an advertiser has a promising idea that *he should stay with it.* For twenty years or more Lux Toilet Soap has clung tenaciously to one central copy theme, 'Nine out of ten movie stars use Lux.' Prudential Insurance Company has from time to time made changes in its advertising dress, but not once in a life-

time of years has it departed from its famous 'Rock of Gibraltar' central idea."[2]

5. *Advertisements should build a good brand reputation.* It should be noted that any product or brand has a reputation or "image" in the minds of users and prospects. This reputation or image is the sum total of all of the ideas that people have about a brand, whether gained from messages in advertisements, from discussions with retail sales personnel, from conversations with users of the brand, or from their own use of the brand. Accordingly, advertisers seek in their advertisements—however the advertisements are constructed—to leave an over-all impression about their brands which will help to build the reputations or images which they desire their brands to have in the minds of prospects.[3] Thus, in preparing advertisements, special attention should be given to what is often referred to as the "feeling tone" of an advertisement; that is, does the advertisement over-all leave a good impression in the mind regarding the brand? Do the headline, illustration, copy, and layout combined build a favorable over-all image of the brand?

The Elements of Print Advertisements

Almost all of the theories which concern the details of print-media advertising focus upon four key elements: (1) the headline, (2) the illustration, (3) the copy, and, these three elements taken together, (4) the layout.

The Headline. Usually the headline is looked upon as the principal attention-getter in a print advertisement; it is looked upon as the *hook* which will capture the attention of the reader as he looks through a publication and cause him to be drawn into reading the entire advertisement. The principal problem involved in developing headlines is to translate the key selling appeal—the key buyer benefit—into a good, attention-getting headline.

Headlines are classified by types in many ways. Four types will be mentioned here. (1) *News* headlines are used with great frequency in order to advertise new products, new features of existing products, special events (such as contests), and so on. The following are examples of news-type headlines: "The *newest* new cars are coming through with B. F. Goodrich tires with TYREX" and "BIG NEWS! Now you can have BEAUTYREST . . . SUPERSIZE." (2) *Information* headlines are not uncommon, that is, headlines which hold out a promise of information of value if the reader will look further into the advertisement. Some examples are: "You Save 2 Ways at Robert Hall's" and "You can afford your dream kitchen the Insured Savings and Loan Way." (3) *Novelty or curiosity* headlines are often used to obtain a fresh approach. Some examples

---

[2] *Advertising Age*, May 15, 1950.

[3] For a discussion of the implications of consumer attitudes toward brand, see Burleigh B. Gardner and Sidney J. Levy, "The Product and the Brand," *Harvard Business Review*, March–April 1955, p. 33.

are: "Drummed out of the Four Roses Society" and "a wife's warmest welcome is well chilled" (from a "Heublein" prepared-martini advertisement). (4) *Selective* headlines are occasionally used when the advertiser desires to attract the attention of a particular group of readers. For example, a "Mennen" baby powder advertisement was addressed to pregnant women: "To EVERY LADY-IN-WAITING."

With respect to headlines, advertising practitioners usually operate on these premises: (1) Any type of headline employed should be in tune with the self-interests of prospects, that is, it should be written so that it is likely to appeal to the interests of readers who are prospects. (2) The headline must be relevant to the basic idea of the advertisement. It would be inappropriate, for instance, to feature savings in the headline if the basic idea of an advertisement is to feature convenience of use. (3) The headline must get over its message in the flicker of an eye; thus, brevity is desirable. (4) The straightforward headline is usually preferred to the novelty, curiosity, or unusual headline unless the latter types of headlines are really pertinent and well done. (5) The headline should be specific rather than general in appeal. With regard to this last premise, advertisers recognize that although they would like to gain the attention of every possible prospect with each advertisement, it is much more effective and economical to be specific and thus gain the attention of some prospects than to be too general and thus fail to interest any prospects.

The Illustration. In many instances the illustration is as important as or more important than the headline in gaining attention, in being the hook in the advertisement. The kind and size of illustration used in a layout depends upon what the advertiser is seeking to accomplish with a given advertisement, upon the type of product or service being advertised, and upon what is most likely to induce reader interest, that is, a visual or verbal presentation of an idea. In making a decision regarding the use of illustration in an advertisement, the advertiser must be guided by a value judgment regarding how best to present the idea which he wishes the advertisement to contain.

In many instances it is easy to make a judgment that illustration will be an important element in the advertisement. For example, each year when the new model automobiles are introduced, it is clear that the advertisements prepared for their introduction must include large pictures of the model, because people are undoubtedly interested in automobile design. In other instances it may be difficult to use illustration effectively because the product does not lend itself readily to illustration. For example, advertisements for *Horizon*, a new magazine which was put on the market in 1958, gave little emphasis to illustration; the advertisements were devoted to copy which described the objectives of the new magazine and the articles which would be published in it. This information was of greater interest to prospects than illustration of the magazine itself.

Decisions regarding the size of illustration, the type of illustration, and the emphasis given to the illustration in the layout must be made in the light of the specific advertising objectives sought and the specific layout problems facing the creator of the advertisement. So far as possible, advertisers try to use illustration if appropriate, because "a picture is worth a thousand words" in communicating an idea. Illustrations typically attempt to include people because people are interested in people, and to include action because the action situation is usually more interesting than the static situation. For example, in an advertisement for an automatic washer, illustration would not show a woman looking at a new automatic washer but rather it would show the woman using her washer. Finally, as was indicated with respect to headlines, the advertiser attempts to make his illustration relevant to his principal selling approach.

The Copy. Copy is employed in an advertisement for two basic purposes: (1) to explain or amplify the headline, and (2) to introduce secondary selling points or buyer benefits not indicated in the headline or illustration. For example, an advertisement for an automobile may feature design in the headline and illustration, and then the copy will emphasize the mechanical features of the model.

Since the headline and/or illustration are developed to hook the attention of readers, the copy should immediately follow up the news, information, promise of information, or other basic idea given in the headline or illustration.

Generally, advertising practitioners try to make the reading of copy as easy and as inviting as possible by a variety of devices. Subheadlines are often used, to break up long copy and to provide additional hooks. Short sentences and short paragraphs are usually used. Words are employed that are familiar—concrete rather than abstract, active rather than passive. Clarity of thought is always sought.

Usually copy concludes with some type of *urge to action*, which may be a suggestion that the reader go see his dealer, send in for additional information, or write the item down on the shopping list.

The Layout. When using print media, the advertiser has only a limited amount of space to work with in any publication which he employs. Consequently, in using the space which is available, the advertiser seeks to lay out the three elements discussed above in as effective a manner as possible, in order (1) that the advertisement attracts attention; (2) that it provides ease of comprehension, that is, easy quick reading and understanding of the message; and (3) that it has a good "feeling tone," that is, a feeling tone consistent with the reputation or image which the advertiser wishes to establish for his brand.

To illustrate, consider the General Electric advertisement shown in Exhibit 1. Here the illustration is used as the principal attention-getter, and the headline, appropriately surrounded with white space, quickly gets over the news that "now, here is a toaster and oven in one." The copy, it should be noted, is broken down into four separate copy blocks, each with its own subheadline and each inviting readership because it is short. Over-

Exhibit 1

Now...a toaster **and** "oven" in one!

New General Electric Toast-R-Oven toasts "upstairs"... heats buns and other baked foods "downstairs"— right at your table!

Here's something shiny new in toasters—and new in "ovens," too.

The General Electric Toast-R-Oven does just about *all* your toasting and warming jobs—right at your table. "Upstairs," it makes perfect toast. "Downstairs," it heats rolls . . . muffins . . . frozen

waffles . . . toasted sandwiches . . . garlic bread . . . the list could go right off the page.

Your nearby General Electric dealer has the great new Toast-R-Oven now. See it soon. General Electric Company, Portable Appliance Department, Bridgeport 2, Connecticut.

Toasts any shade you want. Just set the control for your favorite shade—light, dark, or anywhere in between. Now press the button. Done! Toast pops up extra high—no digging, no burned fingertips. Bright chrome finish is a breeze to keep clean.

Makes toasted sandwiches, keeps up to six pieces of buttered toast warm at once, does *so* many jobs that used to mean using your range oven. Dial at left sets "oven" toasting time. Chart on "oven" drawer shows just-right settings. Drawer pulls out for easy cleaning.

For toast *alone*, nothing tops the General Electric truly *automatic* toaster.

It gives you toast the way you want it—every time. Features six-position light-to-dark control, extra high pop-up, snap-out crumb tray for easy cleaning. See it at your General Electric dealer's.

Progress Is Our Most Important Product

GENERAL ⊛ ELECTRIC

all, the layout is quickly comprehended and easily read. The feeling tone is in keeping with the reputation of General Electric as a manufacturer of quality products.

Selected References

The foregoing discussion indicated a few of the many considerations which are involved in the preparation of advertisements. In Exhibit 2 are selected references which should be read in connection with preparing the assignments in the cases which follow.

Exhibit 2

SELECTED REFERENCES REGARDING THE PREPARATION OF ADVERTISEMENTS

Unless Otherwise Noted, the References Are to Chapter Number

REFERENCE	GENERAL APPROACH	PRINT MEDIA				Direct Mail	RADIO	TELEVISION
		Headlines	Illustration	Copy	Layout			
Clark M. Agnew and Neil O'Brien, *Television Advertising* (New York: McGraw-Hill Book Co., Inc., 1958).	3–4, 13							5, 7
Clyde Bedell, *How to Write Advertising That Sells* (2nd ed.; New York: McGraw-Hill Book Co., Inc., 1952).		5		6–9, 14		11		
Earle A. Buckley, *How to Write Better Business Letters* (New York: McGraw-Hill Book Co., Inc., 1950).						1–5		
P. W. Burton, B. B. Kreer, and J. B. Gray, Jr., *Advertising Copywriting* (New York: Prentice-Hall, Inc., 1949).		7					16–17	18
John Caples, *Tested Advertising Methods* (New York: Harper & Bros., 1947).		2–5		8–10, 12				

Exhibit 2—Continued

| REFERENCE | GENERAL APPROACH | PRINT MEDIA | | | | | | RADIO | TELEVISION |
		Headlines	Illustration	Copy	Layout	Direct Mail			
Robert Collier, *The Robert Collier Letter Book* (6th ed.; New York: Prentice-Hall, Inc., 1950).						1–9			
E. DeLopatecki, *Advertising Layout and Typography* (New York: The Ronald Press Co., 1952).						1–5, 7			
S. Watson Dunn, *Advertising Copy and Communication* (New York: McGraw-Hill Book Co., Inc., 1956).	2–5	8	Pages 176–186	9–11	7		15	16
Melvin Hattwick, *How to Use Psychology for Better Advertising* (New York: Prentice-Hall, Inc., 1950).	3–8		10–11		9, 12			
Harry W. Hepner, *Modern Advertising* (New York: McGraw-Hill Book Co., Inc., 1956).	6, 17, 19	27	25	26	24, 31			
Otto Kleppner, *Advertising Procedure* (New York: Prentice-Hall, Inc., 1950).		4		6	10			

Exhibit 2—Continued

Reference	General Approach	Print Media				Direct Mail	Radio	Television
		Headlines	Illustration	Copy	Layout			
Darrell B. Lucas and Steuart H. Britt, *Advertising Psychology and Research* (New York: McGraw-Hill Book Co., Inc., 1950).	2-5, 7							
Pierre Martineau, *Motivation in Advertising* (New York: McGraw-Hill Book Co., Inc., 1957).	1-2, 9, 11							
C. H. Sandage and Vernon Fryburger, *Advertising: Theory and Practice* (5th ed.; New York: Richard D. Irwin, Inc., 1958).	12-14	16 to page 326	17	15	18, 19			
H. G. Wales, D. L. Gentry, and M. Wales, *Advertising: Copy, Layout and Typography* (New York: The Ronald Press Co., 1958).	3-4, 6-7	11		10, 12-13, 25	16-20	27	31	30
Charles L. Whittier, *Creative Advertising* (New York: Henry Holt & Co., Inc., 1955).	3-5, 10 to page 194	6	7	8	12-13		9, 10 (pp. 200-201)	9, 10 (pp. 201-10)
Mark Wiseman, *The Anatomy of Advertising* (New York: Harper & Bros., 1945), Vol. II.	1, 4	2-3						

CASE I: APPRAISAL OF SELECTED ADVERTISEMENTS FOR AIR CONDITIONERS[1]

The purpose of this assignment is to give you an opportunity to appraise critically several published advertisements before you construct advertisements yourself.

Exhibit 1

All new G-E <u>Thinline</u> Air Conditioner takes up ⅓ less space!

G-E Thinline is 16½ inches "thin"... no unsightly overhang!

Why swelter when you can switch from hot, humid misery to cool, cool comfort with a G-E Room Air Conditioner!

Here is a completely new concept in room air conditioners that offers top performance, yet actually takes up one-third less space than previous corresponding models.

It fits flush with your inside wall, yet has no unsightly overhang outside. And not only does it offer you amazing cooling capacity and dehumidification—its High

Power Factor Design *assures economy of operation!*

You have a choice of many different comfort-conditions just at the flick of a finger. Delightfully cooled, filtered air pours quietly into your room, makes your days and nights comfortable all summer long! See your G-E dealer today for a demonstration —he's listed in your classified phone book.

General Electric Company, Room Air Conditioner Department, Appliance Park, Louisville 1, Kentucky.

Most models available in Canada.

With a G-E Room Air Conditioner you choose your own weather with the flick of a finger. Knobs on top grille control 3 air directors, send cool, twice-filtered air to all parts of your room. Jet Air Freshener freshens your room in seconds.

Fits anywhere—in upper or lower sash. Can be mounted flush with inside wall as shown here or all-outside to allow windows to be closed. All inside installation is ideal for use in offices.

Look—it fits casement windows, too. The G-E *Thinline* can be installed in casement windows, without altering or defacing the windows. It can even be installed through any outside wall.

Progress Is Our Most Important Product

GENERAL ⊗ ELECTRIC

[1] Prepared by Martin V. Marshall.

Exhibit 2

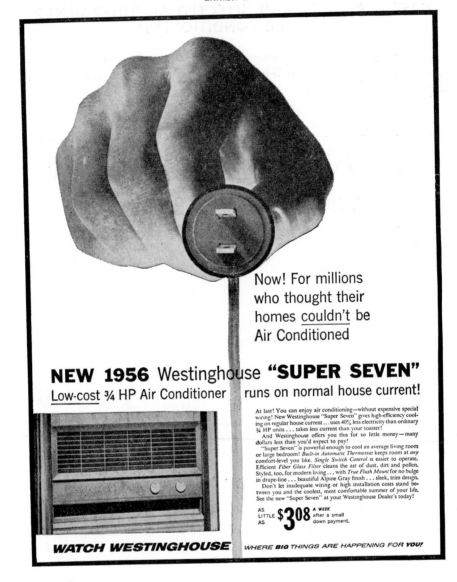

Now! For millions who thought their homes couldn't be Air Conditioned

NEW 1956 Westinghouse "SUPER SEVEN"
Low-cost ¾ HP Air Conditioner runs on normal house current!

At last! You can enjoy air conditioning—without expensive special wiring! New Westinghouse "Super Seven" gives high-efficiency cooling on regular house current... uses 40% less electricity than ordinary ¾ HP units... takes less current than your toaster!

And Westinghouse offers you this for so little money—many dollars less than you'd expect to pay!

"Super Seven" is powerful enough to cool an average living room or large bedroom! Built-in *Automatic Thermostat* keeps room at *any* comfort-level you like. *Single Switch Control* is easier to operate. Efficient *Fiber Glass Filter* cleans the air of dust, dirt and pollen. Styled, too, for modern living... with *True Flush Mount* for no bulge in drape-line... beautiful Alpine Gray finish... sleek, trim design. Don't let inadequate wiring or high installation costs stand between you and the coolest, most comfortable summer of your life. See the new "Super Seven" at your Westinghouse Dealer's today!

AS LITTLE AS **$3.08** A WEEK after a small down payment.

WATCH WESTINGHOUSE *WHERE BIG THINGS ARE HAPPENING FOR YOU!*

Assignment

In Exhibits 1 through 4 are advertisements for *room* air conditioners which were run by General Electric, Westinghouse, Fedders, and RCA Whirlpool, and in Exhibits 5 and 6 advertisements for *home* air conditioners run by Lennox and Vornado in the summer of 1956.

Write an appraisal of each of these six advertisements, treating the following questions:

Exhibit 3

"Are pickles worth more than people?"

asks FEDDERS WORLD'S LARGEST MAKER OF ROOM AIR CONDITIONERS

Don't laugh! Do you keep your pickles fresh and cool in a refrigerator costing hundreds of dollars more than a Fedders Air Conditioner—while you yourself swelter in humid, unhealthy summer heat?

Fedders Exclusive "Weather Wheel" design is the mark of America's best-made air conditioner. Choice of colors, models, and prices for every home and budget. Up to three years to pay!

You don't have to be a doctor to know how much a spell of hot, sticky sleep-destroying weather can take out of you. With a Fedders Air Conditioner in your home supplying clean, cool air you not only live more comfortably, but you give yourself the most modern health protection. Heat, excess humidity, and pollens never reach you.

With a Fedders you will have this protection year after year. Fedders units are the product of the world's most advanced air conditioning research laboratories. This year Fedders introduces the world's first full-size ¾ hp unit to run on normal house current *without special wiring*. Called the ¾ hp *Supreme*, this revolutionary air conditioner gives full cooling, yet uses 40% less electricity than other big ¾ hp units! (And gives 50% more cooling than ½ hp units.)

Drop in on your Fedders dealer today and ask him to show you the new Fedders line. You'll find his address in the yellow pages of your telephone directory.

Ask your dealer to show you
FEDDERS EXCLUSIVE NEW
SUPER 'F' COOLING SYSTEM

Integral Fin-Tube Design insures maximum cooling by bonding aluminum fins to copper refrigerating tubes through a unique Fedders manufacturing technique. This special feature is one of the reasons Fedders Air Conditioners give greater cooling power than other units.

Balanced Cooling. If too much or too little air is drawn in, an air conditioning system will not operate efficiently. The new '56 Fedders Air Conditioner develops maximum efficiency by maintaining the proper balance between air intake and refrigeration.

Silver-Bond Hermetic Seal. Heat-applied layer of silver at all joints seals in precise pressures . . . gives top refrigerating efficiency without corrosion or leakage. Silver-bond seals can't shake loose . . . can't wear out.

New Crescent Compressor Valve adjusts to compressor load automatically, provides optimum performance under any operating conditions. Made of imported steel to closer tolerances than those in the finest automobile engine. All compressor parts are guaranteed by Fedders for 5 years.

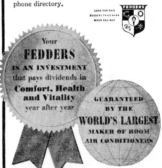

Your
FEDDERS
IS AN INVESTMENT
that pays dividends in
Comfort, Health
and Vitality
year after year

GUARANTEED
BY THE
WORLD'S LARGEST
MAKER OF ROOM
AIR CONDITIONERS

FEDDERS AIR CONDITIONERS

1. What is the advertiser trying to accomplish by the advertisement; that is, what does the advertiser want the reader to take away from the advertisement?
2. In trying to accomplish his objective, what appeal(s) does the advertiser use? Is it a good or poor selection?
3. Is an effective headline used?
4. Are effective illustrations used?
5. Is the copy effective?
6. Is the advertisement effective over-all? Is it as effective as competitive advertisements?

Exhibit 4

Which Wife is Yours?

Exhausted, wilting...breathing hot, humid dust- and pollen-laden air. Can't seem to get anything done—feels listless and bored. Obviously there's no air conditioning in this kitchen.

Peppy, enjoying her day...delightfully cool and breathing the cleanest, purest, freshest air possible, because her kitchen is air conditioned with a new Electronically-Advanced RCA WHIRLPOOL.

Stop tiring, irritating Summer heat—with a new
RCA WHIRLPOOL Electronic Filter Air Conditioner!

There's magic in the air for homemakers! New 1956 RCA WHIRLPOOL Electronic Filter Air Conditioners purify the air electronically—bring a new way of life right into your kitchen. You'll enjoy cool, refreshing air that's draft-free and dehumidified all Summer long. Enjoy "conditioned" air that's gently warmed for ideal ventilation in cold weather. And the ELECTRONIC FILTER means the cleanest, purest air ever *all year long*!

New compact RCA WHIRLPOOL Electronic Filter Air Conditioners fit modern kitchen decor. They make house cleaning far easier because everything stays cleaner, longer. They also provide new relief for hay fever sufferers. For truly modern, carefree homemaking, see the new RCA WHIRLPOOL Electronic Filter Air Conditioners at your dealer's now.

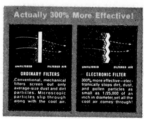

Actually 300% More Effective!

ORDINARY FILTERS
Conventional, mechanical filters screen out only average-size dust and dirt particles. Microscopic particles slip through along with the cool air.

ELECTRONIC FILTER
300% more effective—electronically stops dirt, dust, and pollen particles as small as 1/25,000 of an inch in diameter, yet all the cool air comes through!

Only an RCA WHIRLPOOL Gives You All These Advantages

- New Electronic Filter
- Automatic Thermostat for constant temperature control at your comfort level
- Air Velocity Control for infinite degrees of cooling
- Easiest operation—push-button controls concealed in "Climate Tuner" panel
- "Directionaire" Grille circulates draft-free air where you want it
- Whisper-quiet operation with "Hush-a-Bye" fans
- Decorator colors. Inconspicuous flush mounting
- "Heart-of-Cold" compressor with 5-year warranty

RCA Whirlpool
AIR CONDITIONERS
Use of trade-marks ® and RCA authorized by trade-mark owner, Radio Corporation of America

- AUTOMATIC WASHERS • DRYERS
- IRONERS • FOOD FREEZERS
- GAS AND ELECTRIC RANGES
Products of
WHIRLPOOL-SEEGER CORPORATION
ST. JOSEPH, MICHIGAN

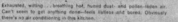

Exhibit 5

There's beauty in the **AIR** of a

Lennox
Beauty Conditioned
Home

Imagine living in a home where the very air is charged with beauty—beauty you can draw into yourself as a flower draws beauty from the sun...

Progressive builders are already creating such homes! *Lennox Beauty Conditioned Homes*—dedicated to beauty-minded women by builders seeking to make their homes ever more attractive . . . more enjoyable . . . more livable.

How you'd bloom in a Lennox Beauty Conditioned Home! No more blemished skin or problem hair from summer's humid heat. No premature wrinkling, lifeless hair from harshly heated *winter* air. Instead, the soft-as-a-petal skin and lustrous hair that are *naturally* yours—when you live in "Lennox-air"—air always at the right temperature and humidity to make you feel and look your best.

But Lennox beauty is more than skin deep! Live in this magic air and new health will put a sparkle in your eyes, new lightness in your step. For with Lennox All-Season Air Conditioning you sleep better, eat better—there's even less housework to tire you, because dust is almost completely eliminated.

Remember, too, that this same "Lennox-air"—so comfortable in winter, so invigorating in summer—is just as good for your family as it is for you. *It will give your children a start on good health and good looks that they'll bless you for as long as they live!*

All this is offered to you and your family by the prominent builders, listed on the opposite page, who are now creating Lennox Beauty Conditioned Homes. *If they think enough of your happiness to do this for you, think of all the other thoughtful features they must be offering in their homes!*

Don't you want to see *your* favorite builder about a Lennox Beauty Conditioned Home? *Don't you want to do it right away?*

More families buy

Sold through more than 5600 air conditioning experts

Lennox Industries Inc. Heating and Air Conditioning, founded 1895 Marshalltown and Des Moines Iowa Syracuse N. Y.
Columbus, Ohio, Ft. Worth, Texas, Los Angeles, Calif., Salt Lake City, Utah, Decatur, Ga. In Canada Toronto Montreal Calgary

©1956 Lennox Industries, Inc.

Exhibit 6

Vornado Revolutionizes Summer Cooling With

Complete Home Air Conditioning You Can Afford

Vornado engineers have long recognized the need for central air conditioning that would fit the average home, and the average budget. After years of research, they have developed a pre-packaged, pre-engineered central air conditioner that drastically lowers initial price, installation and operating costs. Vornado's "packaged" air conditioning is installed quickly...usually two men, in a single day, can complete the simple installation without muss or fuss. Operating costs are substantially lowered by Vornado's sensational twin-compressor unit and exclusive pre-packaged Vornadoduct. Yes, now for the first time . your family can enjoy the benefits of complete home air conditioning at a price within your budget!

AMAZING VORNADO CENTRAL AIR CONDITIONING FEATURES

Twin Compressors...Hermetically-Sealed System...the Finest Ever

Two powerful compressors provide super cooling economically. Normal summer days, one compressor maintains proper level of humidity and temperature, extremely hot days, both compressors operate for maximum cooling comfort.

Exclusive! Pre-Fabricated! Pre-Sized Fiberglas Vornadoduct

Pre-engineered for peak cooling efficiency! Pre-fabricated for quick, low-cost installation! Vornadoduct insures maximum, scientific delivery of cooling air to every room. It's flame resistant...will not sweat...feather quiet!

Designed for the Average Home and for the Average Budget!

Anyone can afford to install a Vornado in their home. Low operating cost KEEPS Vornado within your household budget! Performance has proved in thousands of homes that Vornado just cools BETTER for LESS...hundreds of dollars less!

Vornado JUST COOLS *BETTER!*

Product of THE O. A. SUTTON CORPORATION, INC., Wichita, Kansas • *Specialists in the manufacture of comfort cooling appliances*

CASE 2: B. THRESHER COMPANY[1]

In mid-November 1958 a buyer in the B. Thresher Company,[2] a Boston department store selling to a medium-priced clientele, made a special

---

[1] Written by Martin V. Marshall.

[2] All names are fictitious.

purchase of luxury-handle umbrellas. Since the buyer had purchased a large number of these umbrellas, he desired to conduct a special sale and to use sufficient space in the Boston newspapers to gain considerable attention.

There was a wide variety of styles in handles and materials. There were couturier[3] handles in gold-color metal, mock tortoise shell, lucite, and chrome plate. Some of these umbrellas with couturier handles had matching gold or silver-color tips. Other handles were horn, carved wood, simulated ivory, hooked, L-shaped, and straight. All umbrellas were covered with a good-quality 100% acetate rayon or nylon. There were plaids, checks, and solid colors in black, brown, navy, green, red, and wine. The nylon umbrellas came in solid colors only. The umbrella bar was on the street floor.

Ordinarily the umbrellas would have sold for prices ranging from $7.95 to $10. Because of the special purchase, the buyer decided to sell them for $5.00.

Assignment

1. Prepare an advertisement of approximately 1,100 lines for this sale to appear in the *Boston Herald* (a line is a unit for measuring space; it is one fourteenth of a column inch).

2. Write an analysis of no more than one page concerning the layout you have used in your advertisement.

~~~

CASE 3: W. W. FOX & COMPANY[1]

In mid-September 1958, a buyer in W. W. Fox & Company, a Boston department store selling to a medium-priced market, made a special purchase of unpainted furniture from his regular source of supply at a substantial saving. Since he had purchased 4,500 pieces of furniture, he desired to conduct a special sale and to use sufficient space in the Boston newspapers to gain considerable attention.

There were seven different pieces. All were built of knotty pine with early American burnished brass hardware. All were sanded to a smooth finish, which could be painted, stained, or varnished without additional preparation. The pieces consisted of:

1. Hutch-top server cupboard: has seven drawers, three shelves, and a two-section storage compartment; 37 inches wide, 72 inches high, and 16 inches deep; usually $59.98, priced at $42.98 for the sale.

---

[3] A term currently used to indicate high fashion.
[1] Fictitious name. Written by Martin V. Marshall.

2. Vanity table with mirror and bench: table is 35 inches wide, 30 inches high, and 18 inches deep; usually $17.98, priced at $12.98.
3. Four-drawer student's desk: 33 inches wide, 29½ inches high, and 18 inches deep; usually $21.98, priced at $16.98; desk chair extra for $4.98.
4. Four-section record cabinet: 15 inches wide, 28½ inches high, and 14½ inches deep; usually $11.98, priced at $8.98.
5. Sliding door cabinet: has two deep shelves and sliding doors; 36 inches wide, 26 inches high, and 14 inches deep; usually $23.98, priced at $18.98.
6. Mr. and Mrs. chest of drawers: has six full drawers and three small drawers; 46 inches wide, 33 inches high, and 14½ inches deep; usually $39.98, priced at $32.98.
7. Three-piece headboard ensemble: a headboard with built-in shelf for books and radio; 41½ inches wide, 36 inches high, and 9½ inches deep. Two matching chests with two drawers and a shelf each: 14¾ inches wide, 26½ inches high, and 11½ inches deep; usually $37.98, priced at $29.98.

The buyer wanted advertisements to appear in the Sunday newspapers, September 19. He would accept mail and telephone orders. The furniture was located in the housewares department, fifth floor, main store.

Assignment

1. Prepare an advertisement of approximately 1,200 lines for this sale to appear in the *Boston Sunday Herald* (a line is a unit for measuring space; it is one fourteenth of a column inch).
2. Write an analysis of no more than one page concerning the layout that you have used in your advertisement.

~~~

CASE 4: THE PROTECTO RAINWEAR COMPANY[1]

Having secured reasonable national distribution for a new men's raincoat, "The Protecto," by the end of 1953, the executives of The Protecto Rainwear Company, Portland, Maine, desired to increase the company's advertising effort. Consequently, they decided to use three one-quarter page advertisements in *Life* magazine during the spring of 1954. In view of the company's limited advertising funds, however, it was essential that these advertisements attract readership and induce sales.

"The Protecto" raincoat had been developed by company executives in 1952, because the president of the company believed that most vinyl film raincoats then available were of relatively poor quality, and did not stand up well under ordinary usage. "The Protecto," however, was made of a new, special vinyl film called "Alwayseal," which was made by the R. J. Goode Company of Boston. "Alwayseal" would not crack, stick, or peel. The seams of "The Protecto" were electronically welded so that they

---

[1] All names are fictitious. Written by Martin V. Marshall.

would not leak or pull apart. The raincoat had been put through a series of rigorous tests in the Protecto factory, had been tested by 100 students at Bates College during the winter of 1952–53, and had been tested by the laboratories of a number of leading department stores. All tests had indicated that the claims made for the new raincoat could be substantiated. In a survey of the 100 Bates College students, 89 said that they preferred "The Protecto" to any other vinyl film raincoat.

"The Protecto" was available in translucent gunmetal, cocoa, and forest green colors in small, medium, large, and extra-large in both regulars and longs at department and men's specialty stores. It was priced at $3.95 with snaps, $4.95 with buttons, and $5.95 with zipper. "The Protecto" was also available in sizes 4–12 for boys, with a hood and pouch in slicker yellow or gunmetal at $3.95.

Assignment

1. Prepare the first advertisement, one-quarter page in size, suitable for insertion in *Life* magazine.

2. Prepare two additional headlines suitable to include in the subsequent advertisements to be used in *Life*.

3. In not over one page, explain your visualization of the advertisement and of the core idea to be carried throughout the three advertisements in *Life*. Also, analyze your headlines, indicating their strengths and weaknesses.

~~~

CASE 5: MARCUS TYLER ADVERTISING AGENCY, INC. (B) [1]

In August 1956 Mr. Raymond L. White, an account executive of Marcus Tyler Advertising Agency, Inc., Boston, Massachusetts, was concerned with the preparation of an advertisement for the new "Dover E400," successor to the "Dover E250," a sports car manufactured by the Dover-Hood Motor Company, Limited, Leicester, England. The advertisement was to be published in *Esquire* magazine late in the fall of 1956. "The objective of the advertisement," Mr. White said, "is to top the growing part of the sports car market—those people who want a sports car for family, commuting, and pleasure driving. We have to convince them that the E400 is a satisfactory sports car for pleasure driving even though the E250 was not."

According to Mr. White the E250, since its introduction in 1946, had been popular among Americans as a competition sports car because it had excellent holding qualities at high speed, would do 110 miles per hour as

---

[1] All names are fictitious. Written by Martin V. Marshall.

a standard stock car, and was well engineered so that it had great durability. "Americans never accepted it as a pleasure car," he said, "for a number of reasons. The E250 was so tightly sprung that passengers had their teeth shaken to the roots on any kind of roughness. For the large man there was too little clearance between the steering wheel and the left door. The clutch and brake pedals were difficult to find and use. With the top up, the driver had no real idea of what was behind him. And there was inadequate room for baggage in the trunk because rear vision was poor. But all of these weaknesses have been corrected in the E400. It's a fine pleasure car and will compare favorably with our principal competitors in the low-priced foreign sports car field."

The Low-Priced Foreign Sports Car Field

According to Mr. White the Dover E400 would compete principally with five foreign sports cars: Porsche 1600, Jaguar XK140, Austin-Healey TR-3, and MG-A.

The Dover E400

The specifications of the Dover E400 were as follows:

Body: two-seater open sports steel body. Doors hinged at front with side windows of laminated glass. One-piece windshield with laminated glass. Over-all length: 123 inches. Wheelbase: 98 inches. Over-all width: 51 inches.

Seating: two bucket-type seats, adjustable fore and aft. Seats fold forward to give access to rear. Upholstered in leather in choice of five colors: black, brown, red, blue, and white. Interior body width: 47 inches.

Controls: buttons for carburetor choke, starter, windshield wipers, headlamps, parking and panel lamps, and high-beam warning lamp. Ignition lock.

Instruments: four-inch speedometer and four-inch tachometer positioned in front of driver. Separate instruments for fuel, water temperature, ammeter, and oil pressure below speedometer and tachometer. Ignition warning signal and direction indicator.

Luggage space: behind seats in rear compartment. Enclosed glove compartment in instrument panel with lock. Spare wheel housed in special compartment below rear compartment floor with lock.

Locks: dovetail, antirattle lock on each door.

Chassis: *Engine:* four cylinders. Bore—3.3 inches. Stroke—3.6 inches. Capacity—122 cubic inches. 105 B.H.P. at 5,000 r.p.m. Piston speed—2,850 feet per minute at 4,800 r.p.m. Compression ratio—8.5. Cylinder sleeves—replaceable, fitted in direct contact with cooling water. Pistons—aluminum alloy. Crankshaft—three bearings. Valves—overhead, push rod operated. Crankshaft—four bearings; drive by Duplex chain.

Cooling system: thermostatically controlled, 15 pints capacity. Circulation—pump. Drive D-H Belt Fan, 13-inch, four blades.

Fuel system: fourteen-gallon tank. Fuel pump—mechanical. Twin carburetors—D-H 9's.

Lubrication: pump submerged in sump, gauze filter. Oil Cleaner—Purolator bypass type, replaceable cartridge.

Ignition: coil, centrifugal and vacuum controlled automatic advance. Plugs—Champion, Type L-IOS. Dynamo—ventilated type.

Transmission: Dutch-Borg and Peck 9-inch diameter single dry plate. Hydraulically operated. Gearbox—four forward ratios. Silent helical gears. Gear change lever between bucket seats. Propellor shaft: all metal shaft, needle roller bearings.

Suspension: front-low periodicity independent suspension system with wishbone shackles top and bottom. Coil springs. Taper roller hub bearings. Rear—wide semielliptic springs with piston-type dampers.

Wheels: wire. Jacking: midpoint jacking.

Brakes: Lockheed hydraulic, front and rear 10 inch × 2¼ inch. Two leading shoe type on front wheels. Leading and trailing shoe type on rear wheels. Cast iron brake drums. Hydraulic.

Steering: high gear, cam and lever type. Optional right- or left-hand drive. Steering wheel—16-inch diameter, four spokes.

Battery: twelve volt, 51 amp./hour.

Frame: rigid structure, channel steel braced by a cruciform member.

"The E400," Mr. White said, "should really appeal to the pleasure driver. For $2,725, he'll get a sports car which will be on a par with the Austin-Healey and Jag for looks. And it'll be more comfortable, I think, than any other sports car. There's more leg room than in any car—you can shoot the seat back 18 inches in the E400. The brake and clutch pedals have been placed so that they are convenient, and the pedals are big— about the size you find on an American car. The windshield is three inches higher than the E250's, which makes it a lot bigger than those of other makes. And the tonneau cover is practically all glass. The rear-view mirror is mounted at the top of the windshield so that you have a real view of the rear.

"I think they've done a fine job on the interior's appeal, too. Instead of the walnut or mahogany finish you usually find in a foreign car, the E400 has a metal dash the same color as the body. The floor has a good grade of heavy carpet on it. And the hardware is all large chrome.

"It'll be a fine traffic car. The engine idles nicely and is really peppy. The E400 will hit 40 in 8 seconds and 60 in 10.5 seconds. Unlike most of the other sports cars, she'll snap-shift without strain—there's really smooth synchromesh action. And with the center of gravity lowered a little over an inch, the E400 has improved roadability.

"The doors are very easy to operate and it's less difficult to get into the E400 than other makes, because the door is four inches wider now— when it's opened there's plenty of room to slide in. The only lack of room is in the luggage compartment—you just can't get more than a couple of medium-sized suitcases in it."

The 1957 series of Dover E400's were available in five colors: black, off-white, red, green, and blue. Optional equipment included heater, radio, electrically operated overdrive, competition-type rear shock absorbers, competition-type front road springs, telescopic steering, and white sidewall tires.

Esquire Advertisement

According to Mr. White, the Dover-Hood company had originally intended to advertise the E400 only in a selected number of sports car publications and *The New Yorker*, for prestige. However, Mr. White had persuaded the American distributor to publish several advertisements aimed at a broader audience. Hence, in August Mr. White was concerned with the preparation of an advertisement which would appear in the December 1956 and March and April 1957 issues of *Esquire*. "Since Dover-Hood has produced a really fine pleasure sports car," he said, "I believe that an investment of $5,600 in *Esquire* will pay off."

Assignment

1. Prepare an advertisement of one-half page suitable for publication in *Esquire* magazine's December issue. Black and white or color may be used.

2. In no more than one page explain your treatment of the layout and copy.

~~~

CASE 6: WIGGINS AIR CONDITIONING COMPANY[1]

In February 1956 the advertising manager of the Wiggins Air Conditioning Company was planning an advertising campaign for trade papers and general business media which was to feature the company's line of self-contained air conditioners for small business premises. In this campaign he wished to reach the proprietors of small business establishments such as drugstores, tobacco shops, restaurants, banks, barber shops, beauty parlors, specialty shops, men's wear shops, etc. The objectives of the campaign were to convince the owners of such firms that (1) they could increase summer business and profits by installing air conditioning, and (2) a Wiggins self-contained air conditioner was the best brand to buy because of its superior features with respect to cooling; compactness; design; construction; engineering; and economy in original cost, operation, and maintenance.

Air conditioning was defined among the trade as the control of temperature by either heating or cooling the air, the control of humidity by either increasing or decreasing its moisture content, the purification of air by either washing or filtering it, and the control of air motion and ventilation.

Founded in 1921, the Wiggins company had pioneered in many developments in the air-conditioning field. The company manufactured and marketed a wide line of consumer and industrial air-conditioning equipment; its name was well known to the general public as a manufacturer

---

[1] All names are fictitious. Written by Donald H. Thain.

of residential air conditioners; and it enjoyed a good reputation among the trade.

Both residential and industrial air-conditioning fields were highly competitive. Among the Wiggins company's major competitors were Carrier, Chrysler Airtemp, Frigidaire, General Electric, Kelvinator, Universal, Westinghouse, Worthington, and York. These companies manufactured units which ranged in size and cost from small, standardized residential units which retailed for as low as $200 to large, custom engineered industrial air-conditioning installations which cost as high as $250,000.

The company's market research studies indicated that among all the different specialized markets for air-conditioning equipment, the market offered by small business establishments was potentially the most promising. As a result, in 1956, the company was increasing its sales promotional efforts on self-contained packaged unit air conditioners in the 2- to 15-ton[2] capacity range. These units were especially engineered to be appropriate to the varied needs of all types of small businesses.

Wiggins air-conditioning units for this market included all of the mechanical components for cleansing, cooling, dehumidifying, ventilating, and circulating air. Since they were designed specifically for installation in old buildings where heating facilities would exist, they did not include heating elements. Since the compressor motor was one of the quietest available and the cabinet was attractively designed and finished and the unit was entirely closed for safety, the unit could be placed in a location open to public view or contact. The mechanical parts were engineered to include the latest improvements of air-conditioning technology. The cooling unit was sturdy, dependable, and covered by a five-year warranty. The cabinet was fabricated from cold rolled steel and finished in a light gray baked enamel that withstood most types of abuse, including stains, burns, and scratches. The technical features included removable front panels for easy, fast, low-cost servicing; thermally and sound insulated cabinet; compact, quiet, lifetime guaranteed compressor; large cooling capacity; special thermostatic controls to prevent overheating of internal mechanisms; easy to operate thermostat controls for temperature regulation; high-quality, slow speed, vibrationless, spring-mounted air circulating fan; large capacity, airfin type cooling coil; safety cutout switches; large, heavy capacity, standardized cleaning filters; and efficient, water-cooled condenser. The unit occupied 10% less floor space than most competitive models. The size of the 2- to 15-ton capacity units were approximately 18 inches deep, 50 inches wide, and 70 inches high. They were suitable for every type of building construction.

During 1955, Wiggins salesmen had reported a large number of well-satisfied customers. They stated that the typical prospect in the small business operator classification viewed the installation of air conditioning

---

[2] A ton is an air-conditioning capacity measuring unit which means the cooling effect of melting a ton of ice over a 24-hour period.

on an investment cost versus business and profit increase basis, and they told of many buyers who reported, "Your air-conditioning unit is the best investment I ever made." For example: (1) a furniture store owner in St. Louis wrote, "Your 15-ton unit that I installed last summer at a total cost of $16,000, paid for itself in extra sales and profits in two months." (2) A barber shop operator in Chicago reported, "My business increased 350% after I installed one of your three-ton units which cost me $2,400." (3) A New Orleans restaurant manager reported that whereas patrons used to eat lightly during the city's hot, humid summers, when a five-ton unit was installed average checks increased by 40% because customers stayed longer and ate more. Moreover, his total summer business increased by 60% and waitresses were much less tired at the end of the day. Also, two new waitresses had left jobs in nonair-conditioned restaurants and came to work for the restaurant when they heard that it was air conditioned. (4) Many small retail stores such as drug and grocery stores reported 25% to 75% increases in summer business and substantial reductions in employee turnover. The files of the company's sales department contained many pictures of such units in use and the case histories of the various results in improved operations following the installation of air-conditioning units.

The installed price of units ranged from $2,500 for a two-ton unit to $17,000 for a 15-ton unit. Unit size and capacity requirements varied with the average outside temperature, layout and construction of the store's premises, and the type of traffic handled. Examples of requirements ranged from a five-man barber shop which needed a two-ton unit to a large and busy supermarket which required a 15-ton unit. Advertisements were to recommend that interested readers call or write local distributors who were qualified to study their air-conditioning requirements and recommend a unit of the correct type and capacity. The company sold to industrial customers through 870 distributors whose names were listed in the classified section of telephone books or who could be contacted through the company's home office in New York.

In order to achieve wide coverage of small business owners this campaign was to be placed in wide circulation general business media such as *Business Week*, and in a number of specialized trade journals such as *Progressive Grocer*, *Retail Druggist*, and *Restaurant Monthly* during the spring of 1956.

The space campaign was to be integrated with an intensive distributor promotion including showroom displays, direct mail, and co-operative newspaper and radio advertising.

Assignment

1. Prepare a one-page, black-and-white advertisement to appear in any one of the following general business media or specialized trade journals which were directed to the type of small business proprietor that the

Wiggins company wished to reach: *Business Week, American Restaurant, Progressive Grocer, Drug Topics,* or *Retailing Daily.*

Identify the publication you select. Since the page sizes of these publications vary, make your layout 7 inches × 10 inches, assuming that it would be resized if necessary. For mechanical requirements, circulation data, etc., see *Standard Rate & Data Service,* Business Publication Section.

2. In no more than one page, explain your treatment of the layout and copy.

~~~

CASE 7: WILLYS MOTORS, INC.[1]

In August 1955 Mr. Charles R. Mougey (pronounced Moojay), advertising manager of Willys Motors, Inc., was concerned with the preparation of advertisements for the 1956 Jeep advertising campaign to garage and service-station operators.

The company's current promotional plans called for separate industrial advertising campaigns to each of ten groups of Jeep users. For example, the company was going to advertise to farmers, ranchers, contractors and builders, lumbering and mining companies, etc., in appropriate trade journals through advertisements especially tailored to appeal to each of these different groups.

"We recognize garage and service-station owners as an important Jeep market," said Mr. Mougey, "because when we analyzed a sample of 41,-000 of our sales, we found that of the 100 more frequent occupations or uses for Jeeps, service-station use ranked fifth in importance after farming, ranching, pleasure, and mail carrying."

"Right now," continued Mr. Mougey, "I'm concerned with the problem of what kind of advertisements we should feature in our service-station owner campaign. We are in the process of crystallizing our ideas as to whether we should use general appeal or user testimonial-type copy. When we talk about general appeal-type advertising, we're thinking of advertisements which feature general statements about the Jeep features that would be of particular interest to all service-station operators, whereas, a testimonial-type advertisement would be built around the specific recommendation of an enthusiastic Jeep user.

"Since I am particularly interested in the possibility of testimonial-type advertising, I followed up on an unsolicited letter which I received from a service-station owner who is a real Jeep booster. I am going to ask our agency to prepare an advertisement based on this material." [The letters exchanged by Mr. Mougey and the service-station owner are shown in Exhibits 1, 2, and 3.]

[1] Written by Donald H. Thain.

"Of course," continued Mr. Mougey, "the letter I received from Mr. Cooley is a bit general. If we wish to, we can get more into what his specific likes about the Jeep are."

Additional service-station marketing information, contained in a market research report, submitted to Mr. Mougey in 1954, read as follows: "This market is recognized as one of the best for Jeeps and aggressive

Exhibit 1

WILLYS MOTORS, INC.
Letter from Mr. Cooley to Mr. Mougey

June 20, 1955

Dear Sirs:

I am enclosing pictures of my new Jeep which possibly you can use for your advertising. This is my third Jeep in the past ten years and I think it is impossible to have a successful service-station operation without one of these vehicles. I certainly feel that the Jeep is another right arm for me. We feel that this new Jeep is about the sharpest vehicle around these parts. I purchased it from Riverview Motors in Conklin, New York.

Thanks.

s/ Russ Cooley

Chenango St. at Nolan Rd.
Binghamton, New York

---

sales effort should produce appreciable additional volume. The latest available statistics show a total of 188,253 service stations in the United States of which 101,500 are in metropolitan areas. Conservatively, 20% or 30% of these should own vehicles of some type, and 50% of these vehicles should be Jeeps."

The 1955 price structure of the Model CJ5 Universal Jeep purchased by Mr. Cooley was as follows:

Jeep

List price	$1,476.25	
Federal tax	85.81	
Preparation and conditioning	25.00	$1,587.06

Accessories (Optional, but Usually Included)

Draw bar, oil bath air cleaner, oil filter, and directional signals	$ 59.83	
Heater and defroster	54.10	113.93
Total Factory Retail Price		$1,700.99

(Local taxes, transportation, and other optional equipment were in addition to the factory retail price.)

Exhibit 2

WILLYS MOTORS, INC.

Mr. Mougey's Reply to Mr. Cooley

WILLYS MOTORS, INC.
Toledo 1, Ohio
July 5, 1955

Mr. Russ Cooley
Atlantic Service Station
Chenango Street at Nolan Road
Binghamton, New York

Dear Mr. Cooley:

Thank you very much for your nice message of enthusiastic comments about your new "Jeep" and the interesting pictures of the vehicle which you sent along. It is always a pleasure to hear from proud "Jeep" owners, and your words of praise are just about the nicest we've ever read.

We would like to accept your kind offer to feature you and your statement, your station and your "Jeep" in our advertising. As you probably know, we are running a series of ads in *Super Service Station* and *Gasoline Retailer*. Reprints of several recent ads in the series are enclosed so that you can see how the stories are being handled.

The photos, which you sent me, are, of course, in color. These are good but, in order to get satisfactory reproduction in magazines, new black-and-white glossy (8-inch × 10-inch size) pictures should be taken.

Perhaps you can have a good local commercial photographer take the pictures for us. We would like to have the following:

1. General view of your station with your "Jeep" in front foreground.
2. A close-up of you and your new "Jeep."
3. A close-up photo of you.

The cost of the photos should be approximately $25 to $40 and you can have the bill sent directly to my attention and I will have it handled for payment. I would like to have the name of the Willys dealer from whom you bought your "Jeep." A set of the photographs can then be made available for both you and your dealer.

You will also find enclosed one of our standard release forms for your signature. Please return the form after you sign it. This gives us the right to use your statement and photograph in our advertising. Our check in the amount of one dollar ($1.00), made payable to you, is attached to the release. This, too, is a part of our standard procedure.

After the ad is prepared, we will submit copy for your comments and

Exhibit 2—Continued

---

suggestions. This will be done before it is released to the magazines.

We shall be happy to supply you with a quantity of reprints of the completed ad. You can hand them out or mail them to your customers to further advertise your station and your service.

Thank you again for your enthusiastic comments, your interest and cooperation.

Yours very truly,

s/ Charles R. Mougey

CHARLES R. MOUGEY
Advertising Manager

jm
enclosures

Exhibit 3

WILLYS MOTORS, INC.

Mr. Cooley's Reply to Mr. Mougey's Letter

Dear Sir:

I purchased my "Jeep" from Chester Smith who operates the "Riverview Motors" agency in Conklin, N.Y. I am enclosing the photos as you suggested and a bill for same. As I stated in my previous letter, I feel that the "Jeep" is my right arm and it is a traveling advertisement on wheels. I have received a lot of comments on the motto printed on the front of my Jeep, "Don't Fuss, Call Russ."

Thanks,

s/ Russ Cooley

The most important sales features of the Jeep were summarized by Mr. Mougey under five main headings:

1. *Powerful*
    —75 horsepower, four-cylinder, F-head type engine
    —low weight to horsepower ratio
    —four-wheel drive traction
2. *Ruggedness*
    —all steel body
    —strong K frame

　　　—airplane-type shock absorbers
　　　—extra heavy springs
　　　—weather resistant upholstery
　　　—easily cleaned surface
　3. *Economy*
　　　—low purchase price
　　　—low operating and maintenance cost
　　　—multipurpose operation, full use
　　　—long life
　　　—large payload
　4. *Safety*
　　　—low center of gravity
　　　—rugged construction
　　　—four-wheel brakes, large lining
　　　—extra engine compression braking power in four-wheel drive
　5. *Versatility*
　　　—it performs many different kinds of basic jobs—pulling, pushing, lifting, supplying power to other equipment
　　　—it goes anywhere, on or off the road in any weather
　　　—it shifts from four- to two-wheel drive and back as required by the job

Specialized optional equipment was also available for the Jeep. Of high appeal to service-station operators were a completely equipped, power-operated, folding, wrecking hoist that was available to purchasers for about $470 and a snowplowing unit that could be purchased for $300. Installation costs for each unit would be about $25 extra.

According to Mr. Mougey, a Jeep had many uses around a service station including service calls, snow removal, pushing and pulling vehicles, transporting materials, and serving as a wrecker.

Assignment:

1. Prepare a one-page advertisement (in two-color if you wish) to appear in *Gasoline Retailer* and *Super Service Station* trade papers. (For information as to the mechanical requirements of these publications, see *Standard Rate & Data Service*, Business Publication Section.)

2. Write an analysis of no more than one page concerning the copy approach you have selected for these advertisements.

3. Before developing this advertisement, spend a little time in talking with service-station operators concerning their use of a general station vehicle. Please do not generalize from the findings in any one station.

~ ~ ~

CASE 8: UNION TOOL COMPANY[1]

The Union Tool Company manufactured and marketed a line of hammers, hatchets, axes, files, wrenches, and mechanics' tool sets which en-

---

[1] All names are fictitious. Written by Donald H. Thain.

joyed high acceptance and reputation among carpenters, lumbermen, mechanics, and other users of such tools.

Union company executives placed great emphasis on research and experimentation for developing improvements in their products. "If there is a new improvement or innovation in our field," said Union's president, "we aim to be the leader in introducing it to the trade." In line with this desire to be first with new product improvements, the company had begun experimentation with a fiberglass reinforced plastic hammer handle in 1951. After three years of continuous testing under the most severe conditions company personnel were able to devise, executives were convinced that this new hammer handle was stronger than any yet made. The tests were mainly of two types: continuous hammering tests and stress tests.

The hammer made with the new handle, that was first manufactured in production lots in late 1954, was believed to be superior to any other ever offered to the market. The F. R. Plumb Company was believed to be the only other manufacturer of a similar type hammer.

Made of fiberglass reinforced bright green plastic, which was the strongest structural material known, it was, pound for pound, stronger than structural steel. The impact strength was so great that it would absorb the hardest shocks without fracture. It would not bend or split. It kept its shape permanently and would never warp or bend. The company had devised a special test for the hammer handle which tested it under impact strains that would be equal to the impact of an automobile crashing against a brick wall at a speed of 34 miles per hour. While it would flex in use, it would not deform. The hammer head and handle were normal in size, shape, and weight and had a proper over-all balance. Union hammers had long been tested for grip comfort, and the new handle had a grip piece that was shaped the same as that of the most popular Union hammer model. Extensive user tests confirmed the fact that hammer head, over-all weight, and grip design minimized fatigue and yet gave maximum results. The handle would not rust, corrode, shrink, or swell under any weather conditions. Head and handle were assembled with a Union company exclusive patented chemical weld. The handle was guaranteed to stay tight in the head.

The retail price of the hammer was $4.45. The retail prices of competitive steel-headed and wooden-handled hammers ranged from about $1.00 for a low-grade hammer to $4.00 for a high-quality carpenter-type model.

In addition to the regular trade and consumer advertising and sales promotion activities in introducing the new hammer, executives had decided to send a direct-mailing piece to a mailing list of 9,500 carpenters. There were approximately five different types of carpenters including cabinet makers, general mill workers, general construction men, interior trimmers, and wharf and bridge men. The number of carpenters in all classifications totaled about 50,000. The Union company mailing list was selected from the names of cabinet makers, interior trim, and general mill carpenters. These types of carpenters, generally speaking, did the interior finish in homes such as cabinets, closets, trim, repair work, and building construction. Company officers believed that these men came into contact with the public in their work more than any other types of carpenters.

Executives believed that the unqualified acceptance of the new hammer handle among carpenters was necessary to its success as a new product innovation. The purpose of the letter was to interest carpenters in trying the new hammer. To make it more attractive among carpenters, they were to be offered a 50 cents price reduction on presentation of the direct-mail letter at their usual supply outlet. By means of this direct-mail sales campaign, executives believed that they could get introductory sales among an important hammer-using influence group.

By means of a sales force of 160 men, the Union company sold through 490 hardware and mill supply wholesalers to retail hardware stores, mill supply houses, and other outlets for its profits. Department stores and chain variety store accounts were handled direct. The company had intensive national distribution for its production line.

Assignment

Prepare an appropriate letter for the mailing piece that the executives had in mind.

~~~

CASE 9: HARDWARE MUTUAL CASUALTY COMPANY[1]

In keeping with their usual practice, the executives of the Hardware Mutual Casualty Company planned to send a circular letter to prospective purchasers of automobile insurance. A business reply card was to be enclosed with each circular and also a slip of paper approximately the same size as the reply card on which statements were to be made of the financial condition of the Hardware Mutual Casualty Company and of the Hardware Mutual Fire Insurance Company as of December 31. The purpose of the entire letter was to secure an inquiry.

When an inquiry was received at the company's office, a letter was to be written to the prospect. At the same time the company planned to ask one of its salesmen to call on the prospect. In the company's opinion, if a prospect was interested enough to send in a reply card, that fact indicated that a large part of his sales resistance had been overcome.

The Hardware Mutual Casualty Company, organized in 1914 with its

---

[1] Written by Neil H. Borden.

home office at Stevens Point, Wisconsin, had become a nation-wide company operating in 46 states, ranking on a premium income basis as the fifth largest mutual automobile insurance company in the United States. The company wrote policies on the following lines of insurance: accident, automobile fire, theft and liability, plate glass, burglary, general liability including golf and sports liability, manufacturers' and contractors' liability, owners' liability, landlords' and tenants' liability, and elevator and teams' liability.

The company was affiliated with Hardware Mutual Fire Insurance Company, located in the same city. In addition it had close connections with several other mutual fire insurance companies. This affiliation had resulted in a combination considered to be one of the strongest in the United States. Because of these relationships the salesmen of the Hardware Mutual Casualty Company and also those of the fire insurance company had a complete line to sell, not only of casualty insurance but also of fire insurance. The company's salesmen were paid on a salary basis and reported either to the home office or to one of the company's 14 branch offices.

The company planned to use a four-page circular, $8\frac{1}{2} \times 11$ inches in size. It was designed so that the inside contained illustrations playing up the need for casualty insurance. The copy dealt entirely with the Hardware Mutual Casualty Insurance Company and attempted to sell the prospect the company's profit-sharing insurance. The following text appeared under the title "Profit Sharing Insurance—Saving 30% of Premiums—for the Past Ten Years."

Our policyholders share in our profits. Thirty per cent of the money paid to us by Automobile Insurance policyholders has been returned each year for the past ten years.

The premium you pay us is the same as you would pay to any of the leading stock insurance companies, but with our dividend, your cost is reduced.

This saving, each year, is paid to each policyholder, either in cash or as a credit on his renewal policy.

Surely this saving is worth considering.

Over $2,500,000 has been returned in dividends to policyholders, by this company.

A loss under the policy or failure to renew does not prevent a policyholder from receiving his dividend at the expiration of his policy.

In addition there were paragraphs telling of the company's financial strength, its nation-wide claim service, and the complete protection which the company's automobile insurance policies gave. The following statements are some of those which appeared under the headings:

Financial Strength

The Hardware Mutual Casualty Company enjoys the highest rating in Best's (Dun and Bradstreet of the insurance world) for prompt payment of claims and conservative management.

It is approved by every State Insurance Department in the United States with the exception of Nevada and New Mexico, where application for a license has not been filed. This is an accomplishment few insurance companies enjoy.

Hardware Mutual has policyholders in every state in the United States, including Alaska. Over 45,000 policyholders are now taking advantage of the financial stability, complete protection, and saving afforded by this company.

Further details of our financial strength will be found on the enclosed financial statement.

Nation-wide Claim Service

Hardware Mutual has an authorized attorney or adjuster located in every county and in every large city in the United States.

Over 2,600 capable attorneys and adjusters give Hardware Mutual automobile insurance policyholders "Immediate Claim Service" anywhere in the United States and Canada. Hardware Mutual has personal service for you in your locality. Troubles arising from automobile accidents are quickly and quietly settled. No worry—no fuss—no publicity—no useless lawsuits. Claims are paid justly and satisfactorily.

Complete Protection

Back of our Automobile Insurance Policies stand two companies: The Hardware Mutual Casualty Company and the Hardware Dealers Mutual Fire Insurance Company, both of Stevens Point, Wisconsin.

The inside of the folder also contained a list of the company's branch offices and the words "for full information and rates, mail enclosed card." On the outside front page of the folder it was planned to mimeograph a letter to the prospect. This letter was to be signed by a vice president of the company. This circular was not to be sent into the state of Massachusetts because the people there were required to carry automobile insurance and hence required a special type of letter. Approximately one million pieces were to be mailed.

Assignment

Prepare the letter to go on the first page of the circular and a reply card to accompany it.

~~~

CASE 10: HERMON W. STEVENS AGENCY, INC.[1]

On November 1, 1955 a casewriter was talking with Mr. Charles Bucklin, assistant vice president of the Hermon W. Stevens Agency, Inc., a Boston advertising agency, when Mr. Bucklin received a telephone call from an executive of the Salada Tea Company, one of the agency's ac-

---

[1] Written by Donald H. Thain.

counts. After completing his telephone conversation, Mr. Bucklin made the following remarks:

That was the advertising manager of the tea company. He asked me if I didn't think that we'd better get moving on a new iced tea television commercial for next summer. As you overheard, I said that I'd get Charlie Freeman, our art director, on this soon and that we would make a story-board presentation in about four weeks; that'll be early in December. It takes four to six months to plan and produce a television commercial. If we're going to have it

Exhibit 1

HERMON W. STEVENS AGENCY, INC.
Radio Commercial

Client: SALADA TEA COMPANY, INC.
Copy: *1-Minute Hot Tea Live* Copy to be Used with Jingle*

ET BAND #1	Jingle
LIVE	. . . and Salada tea time is always the occasion for a happy time! Whether you use famous Salada Tea Bags, or prefer Salada Packaged Tea, . . . your choice of Salada Tea means delightful refreshment every time, . . . and superior flavor every time! Join the millions who look forward with great pleasure to Salada Tea every day! They appreciate—and so will you—the special goodness of Salada Tea's flavor, so enjoy it soon! Then, whenever it's tea time, you'll agree. . . .
ET BAND #2	Jingle
LIVE	Salada Tea is America's quality tea!

* Not recorded, i.e., read by an announcer each time it is broadcast.

ready for the summer weather in May or June next year, we'll have to get rolling now.

Salada has been on television for several years now, and we have found that television is effective in reaching the homemakers who buy and serve tea. However, we couldn't use a regular network television show like Lipton Tea's Arthur Godfrey, for example, because Salada has only regional distribution. Our strategy is to use id's,[2] 20, and a few 60-second commercials in a spot campaign.

We made our first television commercials for Salada back in 1952. They were simple, straightforward photography. In those days, we could shoot two or three commercials in a day and the cost was low—not much over $200 each. Of course, the quality of television commercials has improved greatly. In fact the improvement since 1952 has been so great that, by today's standards, our first efforts look rather corny.

[2] Product identification commercials showing a still shot of the product. When the product identification shot was shown alone, with nothing else on the screen, the time was eight seconds, but if the id was shown with the station call letters superimposed on one corner, the time was ten seconds.

At first, we used funny situation pictures. For example, one showed a wrestler on the mat about to be pinned by his opponent. The action stops, he gets a cup of tea and is revived. Another showed a fellow pacing up and down outside a maternity ward. He's jumpy, nervous. He gets a cup of tea, is refreshed and relaxes. Another showed a woman who is droopy and all in after a shopping trip. She gets a cup of tea and is stimulated and revived, as if by magic.

We have also tried the quality appeal. Salada is made of the very best available orange pekoe and pekoe teas. It is grown high up in the mountains of Ceylon and other tropical countries where just the right climate, temperature, humidity, and weather conditions prevail. It is carefully planted to produce a

Exhibit 2

HERMON W. STEVENS AGENCY, INC.

Radio Commercial

Client: SALADA TEA COMPANY, INC.
Copy: *1-Minute Hot Tea Live Copy to be Used with Jingle*

ET BAND #3	Jingle
LIVE	. . . And there's real meaning to the phrase, "Enjoy Yourself, it's Salada Tea Time!" The conversation does sparkle—because there's an extra measure of pleasure . . . a heightened enjoyment—when your tea time features Salada Tea! Because—here is superior flavor, achieved through Salada's choice selection of fine teas, delicately blended, and brought to you, fresh and inviting, in those good-looking, easy-to-find packages with the big Salada lettering! Superior flavor—with Salada Tea—and remember. . . .
ET BAND #4	Jingle
LIVE	Salada Tea is America's quality tea!

delicious, refreshing pick-me-up. It's a hot or cold drink that fits well in any situation.

About five of the total of about 15 commercials we've produced have been for iced tea. In these commercials, the main appeal is the thirst-quenching coolness of a refreshing glass of iced tea that tastes so good. Believe me, there's nothing better when you're ready to wilt on a scorching hot, humid day.

In addition to television, Salada also does a lot of radio advertising. Most radio commercials are a combination of announcer and jingle. Just to give you an idea of types of copy used, here are some examples (see Exhibits 1 and 2).

The process of getting a television commercial from the idea stage to the finished product is complex and time consuming, but it's also very interesting. We start off by getting some ideas on paper. Charlie Freeman will draw up three or four roughs (see Exhibit 3). Then he and I and two or three others who work on the account get together to examine Charlie's visualizations, suggest changes or new ideas, and, in any way we can, contribute to the process of

---

[3] Semicomprehensive, i.e., more carefully finished than a rough but less carefully finished than a final comprehensive.

Exhibit 3

HERMON W. STEVENS AGENCY, INC.
Rough Story Board

creating several effective ideas for commercials. Next, Charlie draws two or three semicomps[3] that we will show to the client. To get to this stage usually takes two or three weeks, or a total of about three entire working days.

The next stage is to get the client's reaction. This means going through the same process of explaining the idea and discussing it with the client's personnel. They will criticize it, make new suggestions, and, through this process, contribute to its further improvement. Usually, it takes three or four such meetings, over the span of a month or two, to come up with an idea that we all agree is the best that our combined efforts can produce.

At this point, we will have the idea down on a comprehensive story board which shows the action with the script written underneath each frame (see Exhibit 4).

Then, Charlie Freeman and I go to New York to look at the work of various

Exhibit 3—Continued

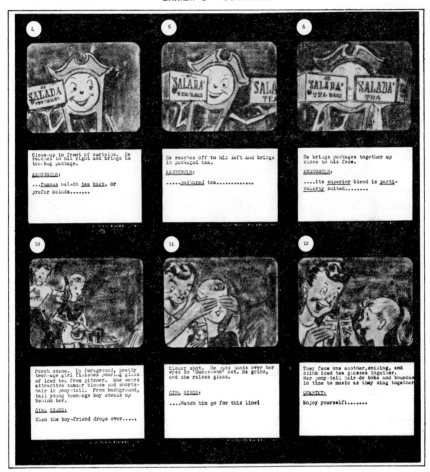

film producers and to decide which producer's studio could do the best job of getting the idea from the story board to film. Different studios specialize in different techniques. For example, we would use one studio for a straight photographic treatment, another for cartoon, another for a cartoon combined with photography, or another for a special musical background, and so on. We explain the thinking and ideas represented by the comprehensive story board and then the studio artists, photographers, and technicians go to work and transfer the idea to film. From the time that we turn over the final story board to where we see a work print of the film is about nine weeks. Either the account executive, or art director, or both check the studio's progress at various stages during this period for progressive approval of the work. The work print is the studio's idea of the best parts of the different shots put together for submission to us and the client, just prior to final editing and assembling. The final version is a

Exhibit 4

HERMON W. STEVENS AGENCY, INC.
Comprehensive Story Board

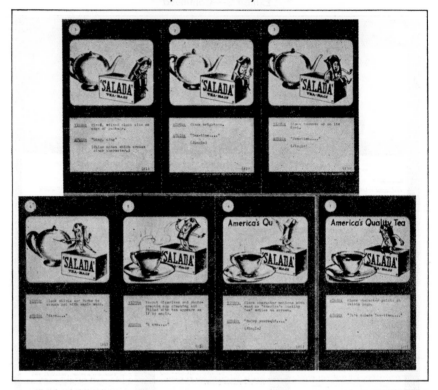

combination of what we all feel are the best parts from the best shots. To go from work print to final film takes another three weeks.

Last year, we produced a set of three commercials for iced tea—60- and 20-second lengths and id's—all from the same basic idea. Here's the story board for this set of commercials (see Exhibit 5), and here's how the idea of the commercial went.

In the first frame you see a tea package resting on a snowbank against the background of an icy pond. At this point, the jingle started (see script in Exhibit 5). The group that did this jingle was the "Satisfiers," who are now singing background on Perry Como's Saturday night television show. In the second frame a clock appears and does a skating routine which is concluded in farmes seven and eight with the words "Enjoy Yourself" being cut in the ice. Next, the clock skates off into the background, turns around, comes skating in quickly and stops, throwing up a spray of ice. From the spray of ice a glass appears on the snowbank. Then the words "Salada Tea," cut in blocks of ice, come in from the right. The letters combine, two at a time, to form ice cubes that come up off the ice into the glass. In frame 17 a package appears from the right and at the same time the glass starts to fill from the bottom. By frame 19 the trade-

Exhibit 5

HERMON W. STEVENS AGENCY, INC.
1955 Iced Tea Commercial Story Board

mark is enlarged. In frame 20, a piece of lemon appears on the edge of the glass and the words "America's Quality Tea" appear in frames 21 to 23 to finish the commercial.

This cost summary (see Exhibit 6) was compiled for the three iced tea commercials we made from this basic story board. The 20-second commercials were made by editing parts of the 60-second commercial with additions or deletions as necessary to fit the id or 20-second commercials.

Right now, I don't have any fixed ideas as to what treatment we should give the new iced tea commercial for next summer, nor the selling ideas that we should feature. We can use any type of treatment or talent providing that costs are kept within reason. A normal cost for high-quality production

Exhibit 5—Continued

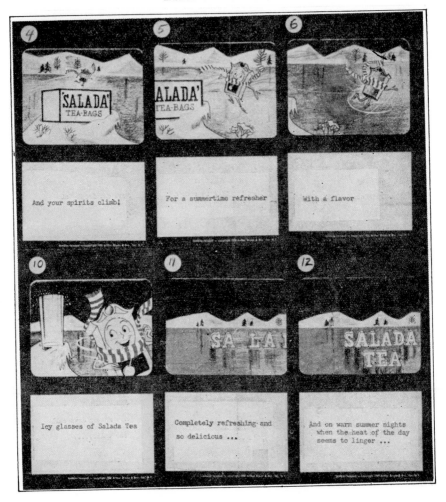

shouldn't run much over $15,000 for a set of three commercials—60 and 20 seconds, and id's—all based on the same idea.

The Tea Council of the USA, Inc., has undertaken extensive research on the problems of marketing tea. Here is some Tea Council information in which you might be interested. Following are excerpts from this material:

1. Annual per capita consumption of tea had risen from .80 to .92 pounds from 1944 to 1953.
2. 65% of all tea served was hot and 35% was iced.
3. Tea sales were 76% for home use and 24% for use outside the home in restaurants, institutions, etc.
4. 40% of people "never" drink tea. 40% of people drink tea "sometimes." 19% of people drink tea every day as a habit. The 19% of people who

Exhibit 5—Continued

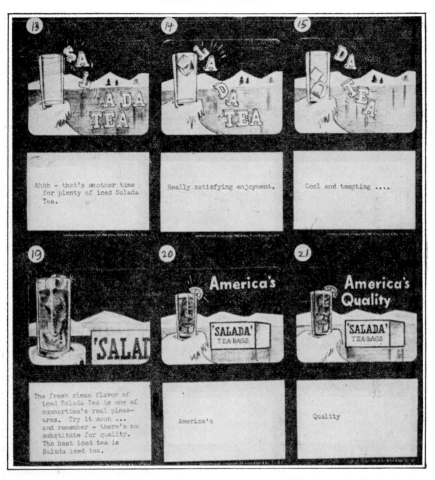

were in the habit of drinking tea accounted for 75% of total tea consumption.

5. As a result of a motivational research study done in 1953, the Tea Council concluded that the essence of what our advertising should be is as follows:
   (1) Tell people iced tea is the most refreshing drink and why.
   (2) Suggest they drink it at lunch, dinner, and between meals too.
   (3) Point out that iced tea is economical, saves money.
   (4) Show how to make it *Good Every Time* and how easy it is.

6. Some of the positive points uncovered by the same motivational research study in regard to attitude toward iced tea were as follows: "refreshing," "cool," "better than most drinks," "quenches thirst," "not filling—can drink all you want," "economical," "pick-up," "stimulating," "prepara-

Exhibit 5—Continued

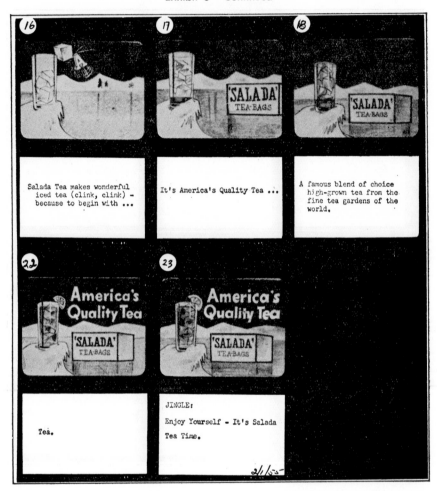

tion no bother—easy," "not sweet," "not carbonated," "good for digestion," "attractive color," "good to serve," "everybody likes it," etc.
7. Americans drink approximately one cup of tea for every three cups of
coffee.

Assignment

1. Create a story board including both audio and visual treatment for
a 60-second Salada iced tea commercial to be scheduled adjacent to general appeal television programs in the summer of 1956.

2. Write a one-page analysis of your treatment of this commercial.

Exhibit 6

HERMON W. STEVENS AGENCY, INC.
Salada Iced Tea Film Production
Income Statement

Billing to Salada......................		$16,259.10
Production Expense:		
Shamus Culhane Studios*............	$10,719.53	
Andy Love Productions†.............	850.00	
Talent and session payments‡........	1,724.62	
		$13,294.15
Out-of-Pocket Agency Expense:		
Travel and travel expense...........	495.01	
NU-VU story boards§..............	450.00	
Telephone and telegraph.............	40.32	
		$985.33

* Set and photography for film.
† Music and lyrics for background.
‡ Musical talent.
§ Free-lance studio story-board suggestions that were not used.

Comparison Producer Estimates and Actual Costs

	Producer Estimates	Actual Cost	Difference
Production Expense:			
Shamus Culhane Studios............	$10,650.00	$10,719.53	+$ 69.53
Andy Love Productions............	850.00	850.00	
Talent and session payments........	1,951.57	1,724.62	− 226.95
Total......................	$13,451.57	$13,294.15	−$157.42
Out-of-Pocket Agency Expense:			
Travel and travel expense..........	$ 600.00	$ 495.01	−$104.99
NU-VU story boards..............	529.43	450.00	− 79.43
Telephone and telegraph...........	50.00	40.32	− 9.68
Miscellaneous (clerical, unforeseen, etc.).....................	150.00	....	− 150.00
Total......................	$ 1,329.43	$ 985.33	−$344.10

~~~

CASE 11: S. C. JOHNSON & SON, INC. (B)[1]

In January 1956 Mr. Ralph Deihl, brand manager for "Stride," a new self-polishing, liquid floor wax manufactured by the S. C. Johnson & Son Company, Inc., Racine, Wisconsin, asked Mr. Daniel Welsh, account executive for Stride with Needham, Louis and Brorby, Inc., a Chicago advertising agency, to prepare a series of 60-second Stride television com-

[1] Written by Donald H. Thain.

mercials. These commercials were to follow a series of introductory commercials (one of which is shown in story-board form in Exhibit 1) and were to run on "Robert Montgomery Presents" (NBC, Monday nights, 9:30 P.M.) and "The Red Skelton Show" (CBS, Tuesday nights, 9:30 P.M.) in March and April, the peak selling season for floor polish.

Mr. Deihl stated that although he thought the existing television commercials were interesting and well done and had shown good results, he was afraid that they had been shown so many times to the same audiences that they were becoming repetitious. He therefore asked the agency to prepare a series of new commercials.

Because both the company and the agency had spent a considerable amount of time and money developing what they believed to be an effective copy platform, as described in the agency memorandum presented later in the case, Mr. Deihl wished to have the new commercials utilize the existing basic copy theme. He desired, of course, that the proposed series of commercials be entirely new and different from the existing commercials in both ideas and presentation.

The Product

Household floor polish products were divided into two general classifications depending on whether the basic polishing ingredient was a synthetically manufactured resin or a natural wax derived from the carnauba palm tree. "Glo-Coat," the company's largest selling self-polishing, liquid floor polish, was introduced in the 1930's and won immediate public favor, growing in popularity until, in 1955, it was the largest selling floor polish in the world. Although it was introduced as a wax base product, it was later changed to a resin base. The product was widely preferred because of its shiny, high gloss, scuff resistance, smooth appearance, ease of application, and self-polishing qualities. Johnson's "Solid Paste Wax" and "Liquid Beautiflor" were the company's principal natural wax base products. Both were in the medium quality and price range. They were preferred by many women because they produced a longer lasting and more mellow luster finish than any resin base polishes. However, surveys showed that women considered these natural wax products to have two main disadvantages: (1) they required buffing, either by hand or electric floor polisher, to bring up the shine; and (2) although the resulting finish was a deep luster that beautified and preserved a floor surface, it did not have the glossy, shiny, almost mirrorlike finish produced by most resin base polishes.

In February 1955 Johnson executives decided to manufacture and market a high-quality, self-polishing, liquid, floor-polishing product of the natural wax type to serve as a complementary brand to Glo-Coat, which was in the resin base product classification. After extensive research and testing of various product formulae, brand names, container types and sizes, package designs, and advertising appeals, plans were completed for the new product named "Stride," which was introduced to the market early in December 1955. The national introductory campaign consisted of extensive trade promotions and television and newspaper advertising.

Stride was a premium-priced product with more expensive ingredients and higher-quality characteristics than any other nationally distributed brand of self-polishing, liquid floor wax. According to one executive, it was the "Cadillac of the floor polishing field." Stride was priced as follows:

PRICES OF STRIDE AND GLO-COAT

	Pints	Quarts	½ Gal.	Gal.
List price of Stride.................	$0.89	$1.49	$2.59	$4.69
Usual price of Glo-Coat............	0.59	0.98	1.89	2.79

The advertising agency's basic thinking in regard to advertising strategy was presented to Johnson executives in the memorandum which follows:

MEMORANDUM

STRIDE ADVERTISING STRATEGY

September 1955

What do we want the initial Stride advertising to accomplish? With proper planning and proper media selection we believe it is logical to assign the following objectives to Stride advertising:

1. Stride advertising should have sufficient circulation and sufficient impact to help *obtain broad consumer sales—quickly*. Obviously the more people we get to try Stride, the more will level off into regular customers.
2. Stride advertising should move fast—shock a fast consumer reaction and help *consolidate early sales gains at the dealer and consumer level before* the *competition regains balance* and counterattacks through special trade programs or advertising counterclaims.
3. Stride advertising should *assist in getting deep traffic-store distribution fast*. It should be forceful enough to cause dealers to want to stock Stride —or at the least, make them aware that Johnson's Wax *means business* with this product.
4. Once a momentum is accomplished in advertising, an objective will be to *take consumers out of the market for other brands before March–April peak-season* deals move into stores.
5. And lastly—maybe most important for nothing can be accomplished without this—*Stride advertising should be different*. It must say that here is something new and different and good and definitely worth trying.

A man who is wise in advertising affairs said recently that the worst thing advertising has to face is the *sheer crush of advertising*. That this is true everyone who reads a newspaper, watches TV, listens to the radio, sees billboards, or subscribes to a magazine, can readily attest.

We also believe that this is so.

The problem today in advertising is not only to make yourself heard, but to crack a certain barrier of indifference that exists in the minds of people as a

Exhibit 1

S. C. JOHNSON & SON, INC. (B)

Story Board for Stride Television Commercial Entitled "Curly-top"

Smiling, curly-headed girl looks at us from right side of screen. She looks to lower left as a can enters from bottom by crawl,

ANNCR: (VO) She's smiling because,...

Title "Protects like paste wax".

Title: "Liquid wax"

Eyes follow can as it crawls from bottom to top.

ANNCR: (VO)...she has Stride on her floor,...

Titles go...spill pops on...gal scowls.

Title: "Self-polishing" follows.

ANNCR: (VO)...liquid wax,...

Dried spot pops on...girl scowls.

ANNCR: (VO)...Johnson's brand new, self-polishing,...

Cloth wipes away spot,...girl smiles.

ANNCR: (VO) Even dried up spills,...

8.

2.

7.

ANNCR: (VO)...wipe away without a trace.

ANNCR: (VO)...that protects like paste wax. With Stride on a floor,...

5.

6.

ANNCR: (VO)...spills...

Smiling girl moves to center screen.

12.

ANNCR: (VO) Good. Hmmm?

Dry mop buffs away...girl smiles.

11.

ANNCR: (VO)...buff away easily. No re-waxing.

Scar marks pop on...resigned look on girl's face.

10.

ANNCR: (VO)...Traffic marks...

Curls become shiny effect.

14.

ANNCR: (VO)...and try it yourself.

Sponge wipes away...girl smiles.

9.

PAUSE

Can dissolves in as face dissolves out. Curls remain.

13.

ANNCR: (VO) Remember Stride...

result of the *mass of advertising and conflicting things that they hear and see so frequently* in commercials and on the printed page.

We felt from the first that a major purpose of Stride advertising had to be the lifting of the product out of the ordinary. Practically each day sees a *new* product of one sort or another. There was a time not too long ago when just the word "new" in an advertisement was considered to be a fairly certain appeal to the buying curiosities of women. But like every other exception that falls *into overuse, its effectiveness is now much less.* When you consider that a well-organized supermarket contains 6,000 individual items, the importance of establishing an *identity* and *personality* for any new brand becomes apparent.

The worst thing that could happen in Stride advertising, we believe, is a restatement of product virtues in advertising patterns that have been used by other floor waxes and polishes, notably Glo-Coat, because advertising is salesmanship and draws effectiveness from new ideas well presented. What is needed is an entirely new form of advertising presentation to accomplish our objective of lifting Stride up out of the ordinary run of new product announcements. Stride advertising should *look different* and *sound different* for what people really buy are ideas . . . new ideas that pose a solution to old problems in new ways.

We, of course, are not interested in advertising tricks nor do we believe that anything good comes from a *conscious attempt* to look different. What we do believe is that if you approach an advertising problem objectively, uninfluenced by what has gone on in the business before, you almost invariably end up with a campaign that is notably different and sometimes even fresh and interesting enough to make a dent in the hard, hard wall of consumer indifference.

The over-all psychology of floor waxing unfolds through our studies as a five dimensional picture:

—*Women agree* what wax is—it's a protective covering.

—*They have* difficulty in naming different types.

—*Those who* wax, say they do so because it protects *things.*

—*Closer inspection* reveals that the thing they want to protect is themselves from more work. Ease of maintenance after a proper waxing is very important to them.

—*But "proper" waxing* is an unattainable idea. You have heard that most of the women questioned would prefer paste wax on their floors to any other preparation? They think it's the best, but too much work.

In specific research to determine what women think an ideal floor wax would be like, the basic wish for a preparation that would fulfill *these* functions is apparent in varying degree *in every major piece of research in the past five years:*

1. Resistance to water spotting.
2. Resistance to scuffing.
3. Rebuffability.
4. Long effective life on the floor judged in terms of maintenance advantages and less frequent rewaxing.

Let's take these four points as a tentative copy platform for Stride to see if the product fulfills them because these four points would represent an entirely new advertising direction.

1. Stride will not water spot even if spilled things are left for hours to dry on the floor.
2. Stride is a blend of the hardest, costliest, waxes known—as scuff resistant as it is possible for a wax to be.
3. If scuffs and mars do appear, they can be buffed out quickly and fairly easily. Damp mopping increases the luster. The shine can be brought back again and again.

4. Because water won't permanently spot it, damp mopping won't dull it, traffic won't *scratch* it, and buffing will restore it, Stride introduces an entirely new concept of ease in floor maintenance. The long life of Stride on the floor also is the economy of Stride.

The problem before us now is how to communicate in advertising all these product features so that the single impression retained by the reader is one of favor to the product and this single general impression is not diffused by too many ideas galloping off in opposite directions.

"Spill on it, Splash on it, Punish it"

Here's a simple phrase, in everybody's words, that covers the whole range of floor abuse. It says in eight words what this report just took two pages to say.

"Spill on it, Splash on it, Punish it!! Just an easy once-over restores the luster without rewaxing."

If brevity is the soul of wit, simplicity is the essence of advertising. With this headline—reading time three seconds—we pose to women their most severe floor care problems and offer them an entirely new and daringly simple solution. You may be interested in some of the background of this headline. We stated it in several ways in copy research, but this particular approach was selected by women because it presents problem and solution more or less in their own terms—once-over means different things to different women. The language of advertising gives way to the language of the people.

We have made in this headline extremely bold claims for Stride. To give such claims substance and believability, a strong validation is necessary—a quickly grasped reason why Stride performs as well as it does.

We know from research that paste wax is the criterion of wax quality and performance among housewives. They believe it is the best . . . an ideal that is unattainable only because using it requires more time and effort than they are willing to give.

Since the components and performance of Stride are so akin to paste wax, we believe we have exceptional validation of all our strong claims with this line:

"New from Johnson's Wax! A Self-Polishing Wax that protects like Paste Wax!" *Here is the ad* [see Exhibit 2] that will announce Stride to wax users on December 6. There are some things that ought to be said about this advertising. It's different mainly because all of the objective investigations into the product indicated that we have an advertising story of function of the product on the floor rather than the conventional shiny floor end result. To be perfectly candid, Stride has no major advantage over any quality wax or resin product in initial appearance on the floor. The differences come in performance of these two classes of polish while on the floor. As the little French boy cried when his father undertook to tell him about the difference between boys and girls, "Vive La difference!"

Note too, the dominance given to the striking new can and how the ad breathes new, new, new, in simple human terms. It interested all of us to learn from one piece of copy research that 92% of the women interviewed said that they knew of no other floor product like this, and 94% said they would either buy or try the product.

Other advertisements in the series also have an individuality of their own, *we think*.

Again, we are attempting to state the desirability of Stride in simple, human terms that everyone can understand and apply to his own situation, and to create a friendly projection of the personality of Johnson's Wax and its products.

The function of Stride television is much the same as that of the print ads. It is to put across in simple terms the *four basic Stride demonstrations* rather

Exhibit 2

S. C. JOHNSON & SON, INC. (B)
Stride Introductory Newspaper Advertisement

NEW STRIDE from JOHNSON'S WAX
A self-polishing floor wax that
...Protects like Paste Wax!

← NEW DRIPLESS SPOUT

JOHNSON'S WAX

new **Stride wax**
liquid self polishing
FOR ALL FLOORS
spill on it splash on it
protects like paste wax

SPILL ON IT, SPLASH ON IT, PUNISH IT
–JUST AN EASY ONCE-OVER RESTORES
THE LUSTER, WITHOUT RE-WAXING !

Johnson's Stride takes it like paste wax! Now from the Johnson's Wax Laboratories comes Stride— an entirely new kind of liquid self-polishing wax that actually protects like paste wax. It contains some of the hardest, longest lasting waxes known, imported from Brazil! Just spread Stride on—it dries to the same kind of rich luster paste wax gives. From then on, spills wipe away without a trace, *even if left for hours*. A little buffing erases scuff marks when they begin to show. Your usual damp mopping actually *brightens* the luster. So you wax less often—that's why Stride is the most economical floor wax you can use! There never was a self-polishing wax like Stride before. Try it! See the difference!

than a succession of shiny floors. This can most imaginatively be done with animation. Here is what we think is a pretty new look in floor wax commercials [see Exhibit 1].

MEDIA

. . . TV is by all odds the most popular advertising medium in history. In eight years set count has grown from 1,000,000 to 32.5 million. Four out of five households in metropolitan areas have one or more sets, and over 90% of the population is within signal range. In winter months, the average family spends six hours per day before the set. In the months of lowest viewing—July—it's still four hours. Robert Montgomery alone is viewed by over 8,000,000 families every Monday night.

Coincidentally with the commencement of newspaper advertising the full force of "Robert Montgomery Presents" will also be diverted to Stride. From November 28 through the show of March 5, every S. C. Johnson sponsored Montgomery show will contain a Stride commercial. One week Stride will be in newspapers across the country, the next week Robert Montgomery—one of the fabulous programs in a fabulous medium—will telecast a commercial via NBC into homes in 135 United States cities.

In March, Stride will move over to CBS-TV with the Skeleton Show and its 7,000,000 viewer families and Glo-Coat will return to Montgomery. Stride will be back on Montgomery in May and June.

In addition, Stride will take over the "Mickey Mouse Show" on ABC television in February, 1956. Thus Stride will be the first new floor wax in history to make use *of all three TV networks* on a program basis.

Assignment

1. Create a story board, including both audio and visual treatment, for a 60-second Stride commercial as requested by Mr. Deihl.

2. Write a one-page analysis of your treatment of this commerical.

Section V

ADVERTISING AGENCY RELATIONS

An Introductory Note

Advertising agencies play such an important part in conducting the advertising of most manufacturers that students of advertising should give considerable thought to the problems of proper selection and effective use of an agency. The declaratory and case material in this section deal with a few of the issues connected with the problems of agency selection and use.

Chapter 13

~~~~~~

BACKGROUND MATERIAL ON

ADVERTISING AGENCIES

An advertising agency is a firm specializing in advertising which provides counsel relative to the advertising and allied operations of its clients and actually prepares, buys space and time for, and places a large part of the advertising of its clients. It may also perform other services, such as conducting marketing research, preparing sales promotional materials, counseling on marketing management or on public relations, preparing and distributing public relations messages, and so on.

Historical Development of the Advertising Agency

Understanding of the modern advertising agency and its method of operation is helped by historical perspective.[1] Modern advertising is a recent development, its growth having come in less than a century—the period of industrial development of this nation since the Civil War. The advertising agency is a product of this development. In this period the annual national expenditure on advertising has grown from some $8 or $10[2] million to nearly $10.5 billion. As the function of advertising became increasingly important, it was natural that groups of specialists should evolve to handle this activity.

The first advertising agency in this country is said to have been started by Volney B. Palmer in 1841. The son of a newspaper publisher, he began by soliciting advertisements for his father. Later he became a

---

[1] For historical background, see Ralph M. Hower, *The History of an Advertising Agency* (2d ed.; Cambridge, Mass.: Harvard University Press, 1949); G. C. Rowell, *Forty Years an Advertising Agent* (New York: Franklin Publishing Co., 1926); Frank Presbrey, *The History and Development of Advertising* (Garden City, N.Y.: Doubleday, Doran & Co., Inc., 1929).

[2] During the Civil War, taxes were levied on periodical advertising and amounted in 1865 to $7,584,340.

selling agent for other newspapers. Shortly thereafter, others entered the business of selling space. In the early years, advertising agents operated in various ways in the selling of space in newspapers and periodicals. At first they were true agents of the publishers, selling space for a commission. Later they became merchants of space, that is, they sold space to advertisers and then bought space to fill orders. Thus they did not act as true agents for the publishers whose space they sold, although they retained the name of agent. Still later, about 1865, agents became space wholesalers for some newspapers, that is, they contracted for large blocks of space and sold them in smaller lots to advertisers, seeking a profit thereon, while continuing to act as selling agents for others. Shortly thereafter, these so-called agents began to contract annually for all the space in some publications. Even when agents contracted for space which they sold at higher prices to advertisers, the publishers continued to grant a commission on the space purchased.

In the 1860's and 1870's one of the great problems of the advertiser was buying space. Even the availability of newspapers was not easily determined. In the Centennial Exhibition of 1876, the Rowell agency's exhibit was a file of current newspapers from every town in the United States. Circulation figures were highly uncertain, as were advertising rates. Publishers were small and not well organized to sell or handle advertising. They needed the help of such a selling specialist as the agent. The stock in trade of these early agents became their "lists." An advertiser either bought an agent's list or had a number of agents bid on a list of papers which he himself had constructed. The more experienced the advertisers became, the more they tended to build their own lists.

In order to fill advertisers' desires, an agent, while acting as an independent wholesaler of space in certain papers, had to place orders for space in other papers in which he owned no space. He demanded a commission from the publisher on such orders; or, if necessary, he placed the order with the agent controlling the paper and sought a commission from the agent. Thus commissions were paid to agents both on the space sold on a wholesaling basis and on space bought for a specific client's needs from the publisher or the agent owning space rights in the publication.

Under these circumstances some agents fell into ill repute, because their methods of operation invited conflict among the interests of the publisher, agent, and advertiser. More and more agents found it advisable to offer counsel to advertisers to help them make their advertising effective. Yet as sellers of space they had a bias which operated against good counseling on lists of media to use. In counseling advertisers regarding media to use, they might alienate publishers by their recommendations; or, in competing on a price basis to meet the requirements of an advertiser's list, they might create friction with publishers by wrangling for special rates and favors.

About 1875 a change took place. Led by George P. Rowell, certain agencies began to announce a plan whereby they would not bid on advertisers' lists but would buy space solely in the advertisers' interests, disclosing to the advertiser the prices paid to publishers. Under this new arrangement the agent bought space at the lowest price obtainable in those publications listed by the advertiser. The agent, guided by his special knowledge, gave counsel on papers to include. For this service the agent, under Rowell's plan, was to receive the commission which the publishers allowed on space purchases. In a plan worked out by N. W. Ayer & Son, the advertiser was billed for the net rate—that is, the rate after all commissions, rebates, and special price concessions were deducted from the card rates. The advertiser then paid a commission to the agent on this cost of space for the services performed.

While some agents conducted their business with some advertisers on this new basis of working solely for the advertisers' interests, the old method of bidding on advertisers' lists persisted until about 1900. But the new method began to set the pattern for the industry. In time *general agents* or *advertising agents* evolved as those whose function was to *buy* space for clients. Not many agents accepted the net-cost-plus-commission plan established by Ayer. Instead, they followed the Rowell plan of obtaining their income from the commission which publishers and other media owners continued to grant to them. In time a stated commission was given to all who were granted *recognition*[3] by publishers as advertising agents. All these agents accepted the advertisers' interests as guiding the purchase of space.

Another group went in the opposite direction to become true selling agents for selected lists of publications. Such firms have become known as *special representatives* (also as *media representatives*) of the newspapers, magazines, radio or television stations, or other media owners for whom they sell. These representatives, who are paid on a commission basis by the media owners they represent, seek business from advertising agencies for the accounts of the agencies' clients.

A pertinent question is: Why do publishers continue to pay commissions to advertising agencies after these agencies cease to be space sellers and become space buyers? Such an arrangement has often been criticized as containing two major defects: their income is determined by the amount of money spent; and it is a source of possible bias toward the recommendation of the media most profitable to the agency because of low costs involved in preparing and placing advertisements in some media. For instance it is more troublesome and costly to prepare and place a campaign through newspapers than through large-circulation magazines.

---

[3] Recognition is given to agencies by individual media owners and by media associations. To obtain recognition, an agency must meet these requirements: be free from control of an advertiser or a media owner, not rebate any commission to clients, have adequate personnel to service accounts, and have financial capacity to meet obligations to media owners.

The answer to this question probably lies in the hesitation of business to depart from firmly imbedded practices. In the first half-century of their existence, agents were highly important in building advertising volume for publishers. The transition from space sellers to space buyers did not take place quickly but was a gradual evolution. The granting of a commission to the agent was firmly established by the time these agents had generally become buying representatives for advertisers. With the granting of commissions once established, no one publisher could withdraw his commission without probable loss of sales to other publishers. Nor could one class of media withdraw the commission without probable loss of revenue to another class of media which granted the commission. Moreover the plan has practically insured the use of advertising agencies by advertisers. Media owners have considered this practice of using agencies to be desirable, for agencies are believed to have made advertising more resultful. Increased effectiveness in turn has presumably led to expansion of the use of advertising. Agencies have also simplified and reduced the publisher's costs in the handling and preparation of advertising.

Although there have been occasional movements by advertising groups and individuals against continuation of this publisher commission to advertising agencies, such efforts have not advanced very far.

As a consequence of an attack on the commission method of payment in the late 1920's and early 1930's, several studies of the method were made and published.[4] Then, again, in the late 1950's, still another study was made under the sponsorship of the Association of National Advertisers.[5] All of these studies have essentially indicated that a huge industry has learned to operate under the commission method, and that any advantages advanced for its removal have not had enough weight to overcome the fears of the uncertainties and disadvantages that might result from upsetting the status quo.

As another consequence of the attack on the commission method of payment, the Justice Department in the mid-1950's charged several advertising associations[6] under the Sherman Act with unlawfully fixing and maintaining the commission rate at 15% of the gross rate. Subsequently,

---

[4] See James W. Young, *Advertising Agency Compensation* (Chicago: University of Chicago Press, 1933); A. E. Haase, *An Analysis of a Report Called Advertising Agency Compensation* (New York: Association of National Advertisers, Inc., 1933); and *Analysis and Criticism of a Study Entitled Advertising Agency Compensation in Theory, Law and Practice* (New York: American Association of Advertising Agencies, 1935).

[5] See Albert W. Frey and Kenneth R. Davis, *Advertising Agency Services; Working Relationships; Compensation Methods* (New York: Association of National Advertisers, 1958).

[6] They were Agricultural Publishers Association, American Association of Advertising Agencies, American Newspaper Publishers Association, Associated Business Publications, Periodical Publishers Association, and Publishers Association of New York City.

in early 1956, the American Association of Advertising accepted a consent decree which, among other stipulations, provided that the Association would not enter into, adhere to, promote, or follow any course of action which involved the fixing, establishing, or stablizing of agency commissions. However, the consent decrees related only to associations and did not affect individual arrangements between agencies and media; media have continued to pay commissions to agencies.

Development of Services to the Advertiser

From an early date advertising agencies began to counsel advertisers on media, copy, and other matters. When selling space, such advice was a help in getting orders. Later, when the idea of agencies acting in the interest of advertisers had evolved, the stage was set for a growth of agency services. With price competition on lists eliminated and with agency remuneration set largely by the publisher's commission, competition among agencies was in great degree placed on service to the advertiser.

Hower reports[7] that the N. W. Ayer & Son agency made its first analysis of a market in 1879 to determine a proper media list for the Nichols-Shepard Company, of Battle Creek, Michigan, manufacturers of threshing machines. Information regarding grain production was secured by telegraphic request from state officials. At the same time, circulations and rates of newspapers to reach the indicated threshing-machine market were assembled; and an advertising plan was devised. The Nichols-Shepard Company wished to buy the information. Ayer refused to sell it but would make it available to the company as a client, which the manufacturer became.

Hower also reports[8] that N. W. Ayer advertised in 1880 that the firm would give aid in the preparation of advertisements, and in 1884 it carried through the full planning and preparation of a campaign for "Police Plug" tobacco. Agents apparently resisted giving copy service; but, under the stress of competition, agency salesmen and principals spent much time in devising ideas and making copy suggestions. Agents often called in free-lance copy writers to give assistance. By 1890 the writing of advertising copy was becoming a well-recognized part of an agency's work; and by the turn of the century, separate copy departments had become common.

In the early period the printer and the engraver gave such help on layout and typography as was needed. The special artist and layout man did not come into being until about 1900 and was not generally found in agencies until several years later.

Since the turn of the century, with the advertising agency plan clearly crystallized and with agencies more and more accepting responsibility

---

[7] Hower, *op. cit.*, pp. 72–74.
[8] *Ibid.*, p. 79.

for offering full plans and for preparing, as well as placing, advertisements, the trend has been strong for agencies to offer more and more service and to become not just advertising counsel but marketing counsel as well. As the volume of advertising has become larger and the billings of agencies have grown, the size of their service departments has grown, particularly during the past three decades. The number of services offered and the competency in the services vary, of course, among agencies.

The American Association of Advertising Agencies thus describes advertising agency services:[9]

Agency service as defined by the American Association of Advertising Agencies, "consists of interpreting to the public, or to that part of it which it is desired to reach, the advantages of a product or service."

This interpretation is based upon:

1. A study of the client's product or service in order to determine the advantages and disadvantages inherent in the product itself, and in its relation to competition.
2. An analysis of the present and potential market for which the product or service is adapted:
   a) As to location
   b) As to extent of possible sale
   c) As to season
   d) As to trade and economic conditions
   e) As to nature and amount of competition
3. A knowledge of the factors of distribution and sales and their methods of operation.
4. A knowledge of all the available media and means which can profitably be used to carry the interpretation of the product or service to consumer, wholesaler, dealer, contractor, or other factor. This knowledge covers:
   a) Character
   b) Influence
   c) Circulation
       Quantity
       Quality
       location
   d) Physical Requirements
   e) Costs
       Acting on the study, analysis and knowledge as explained in the preceding paragraphs, recommendations are made and the following procedure ensues:
5. Formulation of a definite plan and presentation of this plan to the client.
6. Execution of this plan:
   a) Writing, designing, illustration of advertisements, or other appropriate forms of the message.
   b) Contracting for the space or other means of advertising.
   c) The proper incorporation of the message in mechanical form and forwarding it with proper instruction for the fulfillment of the contract.
   d) Checking and verifying of insertions, display or other means used.
   e) The auditing, billing and paying for the service, space and preparation.

[9] *The Structure of the Advertising Agency Business* (New York: American Association of Advertising Agencies, 1949), pp. 13–16.

7. Cooperation with the client's sales work, to insure the greatest effect from advertising.

These are the elements of agency service, whether all of the above functions are shared by a few persons or each function is carried on separately by a specialized department. Into this pattern fit account executives who contact the client, art directors, copy writers, space and time buyers, research workers, mechanical production and radio production people, and so on.

ADDITIONAL AGENCY SERVICES

In addition to advertising service there is a willingness among many agencies today to assist the client with his other dynamic activities of distribution. They do special work for the manufacturer in such fields as package designing, sales research, sales training, preparation of sales and service literature, designing of merchandising displays, public relations and publicity. But always the agency must justify such work by doing it more satisfactorily than can either the manufacturer himself or a competing expert.

Because of the trend toward the offering of more services, there has also been a trend in the 1950's toward the mergers of agencies. The addition of more services has added substantially to agency overhead; consequently, agencies have merged in order to be large enough to spread such overhead expense among a large number of accounts.

Sources of Agency Compensation

As has been indicated in the foregoing, the principal source of income of advertising agencies is the commission granted by advertising media. Nearly all major media allow such commission, usually 15% of the medium's published rate. Reportedly, about 75% of agency income (on the average) is derived from media commissions. The other 25% of income (on the average) is from clients for two types of services: (1) service charges added to the cost of materials and services purchased by agencies for the client—for instance, engraving plates, artists' fees, and television talent purchased for a client are billed at cost plus a fee, which is usually in the range of from 15% to 18% of costs; and (2) special fees for services performed which are not given as part of the service rendered under the publisher's commission—for instance, marketing research studies.

Two of the important questions usually involved in agency-client relationships are: which services are to be rendered for the commission; and which services are to be charged directly to the client. Policies vary among agencies and frequently within an agency according to the size of the account. Usually only the basic planning, creating, producing, and media-buying functions are performed without direct charge to the client on the majority of accounts. Other services, such as marketing counsel, marketing research, sales promotional work, and so on, are charged directly to the client on a fee or cost-plus basis, although such services are not infrequently rendered without charge, particularly to clients having large commissionable advertising expenditures. Generally, on small accounts for which there are small commissionable expenditures, agencies charge the client a service fee for handling the account and then credit any commissions received from media to the service fee. The service fee may be a percentage (either 15% or 17.65%)[10] of the cost of materials and services purchased for the client's account by the agency, which is added to that cost, or it may be a negotiated monthly or annual service fee or retainer, for example, $2,000 a month.

Agency Organization

The problem of effective organization of an agency, particularly a large agency, is not an easy one.[11] An advertising is a collection of advertising and marketing specialists—specialists in planning advertising and selling campaigns, in copy writing, in layout and typography, in production of printed advertisements, in production of radio and television shows, in market research, in media selection, and so on. To service a client well calls for the assignment of competent men to the account and good co-ordination of the work of the various types of specialists.

In agency operation the so-called "account executive" is usually a key man. As a rule he is made responsible for the account and is the chief contact man with the client. He interprets the advertiser's needs and views to the agency and in turn interprets the agency's views to the client. He plays an important part in the building of the plan and works with the various specialists to make sure that the advertisements produced are in accord with the plan and are suitable to the client. One of the most difficult organizational problems of an agency is to develop or obtain broad-gauge account executives fully versed in advertising and equally skillful in appreciating and in sympathetically handling the client's problems and views. It should be added, however, that some agencies purposely avoid having the account executive become too important in client relations, from fear that he may "walk off" with the account. In such cases contact is carried out through agency principals and a number of men who work on the account, such as the copy writer, the art department man, and so on.

Since an agency's account executives and specialists usually vary in ability and since the copy, art, production, and other specialists may have to be apportioned among accounts, the problem arises of maintaining a high level of attainment on all accounts. The largest agencies will have in excess of a hundred accounts and may work with clients from many branch offices. These accounts will vary from small to very large, although many large agencies will not take an account with billings under

---

[10] 17.65% of cost equals 15% of the final charge to the client.

[11] As a general reference on agency organization and operation see Roger Barton, *Advertising Agency Operation and Management* (New York: McGraw-Hill Book Co., Inc., 1955). For descriptions of the contemporary operations of large advertising agencies, see Martin Mayer, *Madison Avenue, U.S.A.* (New York: Harper & Bros., 1958).

$100,000 or even $500,000 unless it carries a promise of expansion. It is apparent that the problem of assuring good work on all accounts can, under these conditions, be a complex one. Naturally, each prospective client is likely to be interested in the agency's plan for handling his account.

In the small agency all hands may work on every account. Hence, every account has exposure to such skills and experience as exist in the agency.

Among large agencies various types of organization are found. Some agencies, despite the danger of spotty work, adopt the so-called "group plan." To each account executive, who may be responsible for several accounts, is assigned a copy writer, an art man, and possibly a production man. As a group these men handle the planning and creative work on the accounts assigned to them, calling on media, research, and other departments as needed. The aim in the group plan is to get teams well suited to particular accounts.

In an effort to avoid the danger of uneven work and to give all accounts the benefit of the thought of mature executives, the so-called "plans-board" method of operation is often followed. A plans board, composed of men of mature experience in copy, art, production, research, media, and other fields as needed, together with the account executive, either makes or approves the plan for an account and periodically reviews the plan and its execution. Often the board is a fixed group (except for the account executive) for all the agency's accounts. In other instances the board may have a few fixed members but otherwise have different composition from account to account and is, in essence, a modification of the group plan. As might be expected, the effectiveness of the plans-board method varies widely. Sometimes the board gives careful consideration to the accounts; in other instances, it is little more than window dressing.

Many variations of the two organization patterns described above will be found. The personalities and skills found in agencies, as well as the needs of accounts, have an important bearing on the organizational plan adopted.

Difference in Use of Agencies among Advertisers

Since advertising agencies render services in accordance with clients' needs or desires, wide variations exist in working arrangements between agency and client. Some clients call for many services, while others call for few services.

Some large advertisers elect to have advertising departments of their own heavily manned to study, plan, and direct their advertising. They carry on their own research, make independent study of media, analyze control and market research data, and often study copy effectiveness. Such advertisers usually exact a great deal of service from their agencies in the traditional areas of preparing, placing, and checking copy and often in other service areas, which may in part duplicate what the companies are doing themselves. These advertisers desire to arrive at judgments on the basis of their own analyses, which are checked against the recommendations of their agencies. Other large advertisers have relatively small advertising and research staffs and turn to their agencies to conduct needed services for them.

Since the character and size of advertising programs and the need for counsel on the several aspects of marketing vary, it is understandable that the facts of size and counseling needs bring wide differences in agency-client relationships. While some advertisers make their agencies serve practically as their advertising departments, other advertisers go so far as to insist on writing their own copy, and their agencies do little more than place advertisements and check publication.

For many years advertising agencies played a small part in the industrial-goods field, and the large majority of industrial publications did not give commissions. In the last 35 years this situation has changed materially. Numerous agencies have developed which specialize in industrial-goods accounts, and many agencies whose main interest is in consumer goods have established trade and industrial departments. In turn practically all industrial and trade papers now give commissions.

Since the space rates of business papers are low and commissions are correspondingly small, the fee arrangement, with commission credited against the fee, is a common practice.

Selection of an Advertising Agency

The selection of an advertising agency has much in common with the selection of professional counsel in other fields of business. First, management must determine what services it desires from an agency. Then the question is one of determining which agency among those available can and will do the best job for the advertiser. The considerations that may have to be weighed are many, and there are no hard and fast rules to follow in the selection of an agency.

Perhaps the most important area for management's concern when selecting an agency is that of its own part in the agency-client relationship. What specific services does it desire from an agency? How does it propose to work with an agency so that the agency will be able to service the account effectively? In general, study of agency-client relations indicates that the advertiser obtains exactly the quantity and quality of service that he requires of his agency; and that his ability to obtain good service depends primarily upon the degree to which he has made explicit the services that he requires and the degree to which he has structured his own organization and its method of operation so that it gives sound direction to the efforts of the agency. In selecting an agency, it is desirable that management give special attention to these questions and that it negotiate with prospective agencies on the basis of the specific agency-client relationship desired. Most ineffective agency-client relations are caused by a failure of management to make explicit from the beginning the relationship which it desires and expects to obtain in actual operation.

Management must give particular attention to the number of agency services which it desires. As has been indicated, some advertisers use their agencies simply to place advertising, others want agencies to serve as their advertising departments, and still others wish the agency to become an integral part of the marketing management group. The greater the number of services which the advertiser seeks, the more complex and difficult is the selection process.

In obtaining information about agencies and the services which they can supply, management must rely primarily upon its own sources of information. Although the names, locations, principal personnel, and clients of most agencies are to be found in *The Agency List of the Standard Advertising Register*[12] and *McKittrick's Agency List*,[13] specific information about the services provided by and the method of operation of agencies must be obtained through investigations carried on by management. In most instances advertisers who are seeking new agencies will prepare a questionnaire to guide their development of information. Often agencies are asked to fill out these questionnaires at length; in other instances management simply uses the questionnaire as a basis for obtaining desired information when talking with agency personnel.

Clearly, a decision regarding an agency will turn primarily upon management's evaluation of the experience and competency of the agency personnel who are most likely to work on the client's account. This evaluation necessarily is a subjective one, based upon an appraisal of the past experience of people and observation of how they conduct themselves in the negotiations.

---

[12] Published by the National Register Publishing Co., Inc., 147 West 42nd St., New York 36, New York.

[13] Published by McKittrick Directory of Advertisers, Inc., 108 Fulton St., New York 38, New York.

~~~~~~~~~~~~~~~~~~~~~~~~~~~~~~~~~~~

Chapter 14

CASES INVOLVING ADVERTISING AGENCY RELATIONS

~~~

CASE 1: CRITERIA FOR ADVERTISING AGENCY SELECTION

In selecting an advertising agency, it is desirable that management determine the services which it requires of an agency and establish criteria to guide its selection of an agency. Many of the cases in this book provide the bases for analyzing the services which management might desire of an agency. Accordingly, reconsider the cases listed below with the assumption in mind that the management concerned plans to select a new advertising agency. List the criteria in each instance which would guide your selection of a new agency.

~~~

CASE 2: ETNA COMPANY, INC.[1]

QUESTION TO CONSIDER: *Did Mr. Bellum follow a sound procedure in selecting an advertising agency?*

---
[1] Written by J. A. Wickert and Neil H. Borden.

The director of the Menex Division[2] of the Etna Company, Inc., began a search for a new advertising agency to handle the advertising of his division's product, "Menex." The Etna company was an affiliated company of one of the largest manufacturers of hospital and hygienic supplies in the country. It produced and sold a variety of products used by the medical profession, as well as ones used by the general public. The company's sales were in excess of $10 million.

The company was divided into four divisions. Each division was charged with the responsibility of one or more of the company's products and was headed by a man in a staff position. The division director was responsible for all matters concerning the net profit of his division. Mr. Roger Bellum was the director of the Menex Division.

Menex was the trade name of a product used in feminine hygiene. It was sold by 75 salesmen, who contacted drug wholesalers and did missionary work on all the company's products in drug, department, variety, and grocery stores. Menex was sold for approximately 50 cents and was retailed largely through drugstores, with some sales being made through department and variety stores. The sale of products of this nature by grocery stores was negligible.

There were five leading competing brands in this field, two of which had been well established over a period of time. Menex and the other two, however, were of a type relatively new to the market. These Menex-type products accounted for 15% of the market.

The sales expansion had been accelerated through the use of aggressive advertising programs by all three manufacturers of the Menex-type products. Despite the growing acceptance of these products, the management believed that much remained to be learned about the best way to advertise them. One of the company's biggest problems was caused by the erroneous belief among many women that these new products might be injurious to health.

The company's advertising agency had questioned 2,500 women in a nation-wide, door-to-door survey concerning use of Menex and competing products. The use of Menex-type products was extremely high among women in the nursing field. Use of these products, broken down by income groups, was reported as follows: high-income group, 30.4%; upper middle group, 28.4%; middle group, 22.7%; and low-income group, 18.5%. Extensive use of Menex-type products was reported by Negro women.

All five brands were aggressively advertised by their manufacturers. One company was spending approximately $1 million a year to promote its traditional-type product and $125,000 a year to promote its Menex-type product. Another manufacturer was spending approximately $560,000 a year to promote its Menex-type product. The Etna company was spending approximately $280,000 a year to promote its traditional-type

---

[2] All names are fictitious.

product and approximately $215,000 a year to promote Menex. All the companies advertised in women's magazines. One company also included farm magazines in its schedule; and another used women's magazines, farm magazines, and newspapers. Menex advertisements were usually one-column, black-and-white insertions.

The Etna company did not advertise to the trade; and, because dealers usually did not display products of this nature, it made small use of counter or window displays. The management had found that, because of the intimate nature of the product, salesclerks did little to influence the type or brand of product selected. Once a woman had selected a satisfactory type and brand, she tended to continue its use. For this reason, the director believed that his company should give special attention to young girls just entering the market. He reasoned that if these girls became enthusiastic users of the brand, repeat purchases would follow. Moreover, the young women might recommend Menex to friends.

The director began a search for a new advertising agency because he believed that a new organization might find a way to sell Menex better than had been found up to that time. He wanted the new agency to help him discover two things: (1) "What are our problems in making customers?" (2) "How can we solve them?" He believed that research contained the keys to these problems. Such research should not deal with such problems as the company's distributing organization or the relative standing of Menex in one market as contrasted with another, but rather it should center on problems of human reactions. He wanted to know who Menex customers were; why other women had not tried the brand; why when some women tried it they did not continue to use it; why some women would not try a new-type product for feminine hygiene; and how the company could make its product more acceptable to all women in the market.

After determining the nature of the job he wanted his agency to do, the director prepared a list of preliminary specifications. This list included the following items:

1. The agency must be a complete organization and contain all the regular departments—i.e., contact, copy, art, merchandising, research, media, and traffic.
2. The research department of the agency must be a complete department and should include several women on its staff.
3. The agency would preferably have a familiarity with products of a personal, feminine nature.
4. The agency must have a woman copy writer to prepare Menex copy.
5. The person proposed as the Menex account executive must be a man. (The former Menex account executive had been a woman.)

Mr. Bellum was not primarily interested in the qualifications of the man proposed as the account executive; rather, he wanted to find an agency with competent men in all departments. He felt certain that such an organization would naturally select a man capable enough to direct and co-ordinate the account.

The Etna company was located near Philadelphia. To facilitate communication between his office and the agency selected, the director restricted his considerations to agencies located in New York and Philadelphia, approximately 500 in number. After a study of the agency list of the *Standard Advertising Register*, he eliminated the smaller agencies and developed a list of 105 firms. After reviewing the products advertised by these agencies, he eliminated 70 of the agencies because they were not handling any drug accounts. A study of the accounts of the remaining 35 agencies disclosed that the drug products handled by many of them did not involve problems similar to those incurred in selling Menex. After such agencies had been eliminated, the director had a list of five agencies, all of which, he believed, had accounts that should have afforded pertinent experience. The five agencies under consideration will be designated as Agencies A, B, C, D, and E.[3]

Mr. Bellum personally visited the heads of the five agencies under consideration. He explained his position as director of the Menex Division of the Etna company and continued substantially as follows:

I am looking for an agency to handle my account. Annual expenditures for space will approximate $200,000. You are one of a select few agencies being considered. There is a lot of work to be done. We don't know well enough what our problems are. We don't know enough about how to sell Menex. We want an agency to help us find the answers.

Mr. Bellum did not ask for a presentation of copy and an elaboration on how the agency would handle the account, as was frequently done by advertisers seeking new agencies. Instead, he left each of the agencies a list of 17 questions and requested that they reduce their answers to writing and send them to him if they wished further consideration for the account. The questions are found in Exhibit 1.

Agency D was the first agency to reply to Mr. Bellum's request. The agency thanked him for his offer but declined further consideration because it was not in a position to handle the account.

In time, the four remaining agencies submitted their answers to Mr. Bellum's questions. Agencies A, B, and C all submitted typed answers bound in loose-leaf folders. These folders contained a foreword, the questions, and the agencies' answers. Agency E submitted a printed booklet which was entitled *Facts about Agency E*. The booklet contained a foreword, the questions, and the agency's answers, plus additional information concerning Agency E's operation. There were a list of clients who had been with the agency over 15 years, a list of those accounts served 10 to 15 years, a list served 5 to 10 years, and a list of those served

---

[3] Another agency which Mr. Bellum rated high was eliminated because it was handling an account which competed with Menex.

Exhibit 1

ETNA COMPANY, INC.

Questions Asked of the Five Agencies Considered for the Mendex Account

1. How many employees has your agency?
2. How many companies do you represent whose total billings through you are under $300,000? Over $300,000?
3. What accounts do you have that are closely allied in market, outlets, or sales appeal to Menex? How long have they been with you?
4. What experience have members of your agency had that is pertinent to the marketing, merchandising, and advertising of Menex?
5. What products do you advertise which are sold primarily to women?
6. Who in your agency would execute the following functions on Menex? What are their positions in the agency and qualifications in relation to our account?

   a) Contact   *e*) Research
   b) Copy   *f*) Media
   c) Art   *g*) Traffic
   d) Merchandising

7. Do you operate a professional department? Who heads it up, and what is his background?
8. What members of the Etna Company's affiliated companies are familiar with your agency or the individuals you would plan to have work on your accounts?
9. What publishing executives are familiar with the work of your agency?
10. What executives of those accounts mentioned in No. 3, above, may we contact concerning their experience with your agency?
11. Do you operate a true plans board? Would it be used on Menex; and if so, who would sit on it?
12. What is the policy of your agency with regard to planning, writing, and producing package inserts, broadsides, sales manuals, advertising booklets, mats, point-of-purchase displays, etc.?
13. Do you now do this work for any of the accounts mentioned in No. 3? Is this work done by your own organization or farmed out? Do you invite competitive bids on it?
14. Do you consider market, trade, product, and advertising appeals studies a part of your agency's service to the client?
15. To what extent is your agency departmentalized? Please list departments and outline how their work is co-ordinated in serving clients.
16. Who would be responsible on our account for basic policy, plans, and conception of the right appeal in our advertising?
17. What would be your procedure in handling Menex if appointed?

less than 5 years. There was also a list of new business obtained from old clients. The agency's drug staff, the junior board,[4] and the agency's marketing, merchandising, research, and copy-testing departments were listed; and their operations were discussed. The amount of Agency E's billing was graphically presented; and the agency's magazine, newspaper, and broadcasting activities were listed. A discussion of the various measurement tests employed by the agency—i.e., Starch readership data, the American Newspaper Publishers' Association continuing studies, Broadcast Measurement Bureau, and the Agency E County Panel[5] and Nation-Wide Panel[6]—was included. The booklet was illustrated with graphs and charts.

In addition to the booklet, Agency E submitted a folder presenting the people who would service the account should the agency become the Menex representative. This folder contained 7 × 10-inch photographs and short biographical descriptions of the president; the executive vice president in charge of account operations; the account supervisor; the account executive who would handle Menex; the vice president in charge of research, marketing, and merchandising; the merchandising executive; the vice president in charge of creative services; and the vice president in charge of the women's copy group.

During the time the four firms were preparing the answers to his questions, Mr. Bellum made further investigations of the agencies being considered. He studied the advertising of the various products handled by each agency. From this research he determined that while all four agencies used magazines, newspapers, and radio to some degree, each used some classes of media more than others. Agency E had large billings in all media but more in magazines and radio than in newspapers. Agency A had used radio and newspapers far more than magazines. Agency B and Agency C had large billings in all three media but more in magazines than in either newspapers or radio.

The director also contacted friends who were in companies which placed their advertising through the various agencies. During these talks he was able to ask specific questions which produced valuable information concerning the relationship between client and agency. In every case he found that the various clients of the four agencies were all satisfied with the agency-client relationship which existed.

The information obtained by these methods was supplemented by the answers supplied by the four agencies to Mr. Bellum's questions. After studying the agencies' replies, the director arranged a second interview with each agency. After talking with Agency A, Mr. Bellum eliminated

---

[4] The junior board consisted of approximately 200 young girls who worked for the agency. The board was used as a preliminary test group on various accounts.

[5] The County Panel was composed of 1,000 families in an eastern county and was a "cross section" of that county.

[6] The Nation-Wide Panel consisted of 3,000 families spread across the United States and provided a "cross section" of the entire country.

it from further consideration for three reasons: (1) He had found that
the agency placed a large share of its billing in radio and newspapers. Mr.
Bellum believed that Menex was a product which could be best advertised
in magazines. Radio would not take Menex advertising, and newspapers
went lower in the social strata than did magazines. Because there were
fewer Menex users in the lower-income strata in the higher groups, Mr.
Bellum felt that newspaper advertising would produce more waste circulation than would magazine advertising. (2) Another strong activity of
Agency A was its work in the use of premiums. Here again Mr. Bellum
could see no application to Menex. (3) Finally, his evaulation of the research department of the agency led him to conclude that it was not well
fitted to handle the special research demanded by his account.

Mr. Bellum's second meeting with Agency B consisted of a roundtable discussion among Mr. Bellum and various members of the agency's
organization. The president, chairman of the board, executive vice
president, research director, copy director, and media director were present. This meeting, coupled with his own investigations, convinced Mr.
Bellum that Agency B was competent for his account. It had a well-
manned research staff and emphasized adequate research for all its accounts. Moreover, it made extensive use of the various copy and media
research services and techniques. Finally, Mr. Bellum was convinced that
the agency's plans board was a working unit and not merely a "window
dressing." The board consisted of the president of the agency, executives
from each department, the account executive for the particular client
under consideration, and such other experts as were needed to assist in
aiding the client under discussion. It prepared plans for and reviewed all
campaigns of the agency. The board served to bring about a uniformity
in the quality of work produced by the agency by bringing to bear on
every account the thinking of key agencies personnel. Exhibit 2 contains the answers of Agencies B, C, and E to Mr. Bellum's Question 11
regarding their plans boards.

Despite all the features favoring Agency B, Mr. Bellum was hesitant
about selecting it because he felt from his conversations that many services which he desired would not be covered by the 15% commission allowed by media to agencies and would involve charges to his company.
He believed that the two remaining agencies might supply these services
as part of the work included in the 15% media compensation. The answers of the three agencies to Question 14 which he had asked (shown in
Exhibit 3) were partially responsible for this conclusion.

Agency E took the opportunity of Mr. Bellum's second interview to
stage a presentation of its agency. The presentation was made in the
agency's conference room and lasted two hours. It was conducted by the
director of Agency E's marketing department. After a few introductory
remarks, the director presented the vice president in charge of research
and marketing, Mr. Calhoun. Mr. Calhoun made a short speech in which

Exhibit 2

ETNA COMPANY, INC.

Answers to the Questions: "Do You Operate a True Plans Board? Would It Be Used on Menex; and, If So, Who Would Sit on It?"

Agency B

The plans board at Agency B plays an important part in our operations on all accounts. Any recommendations prepared for Menex will be prepared in the plans board, and our operations on the Menex account will be continually reviewed and studied by the plans board at regular intervals. The plans board at Agency B is a working body, not a reviewing body. Regular members of the plans board are as follows:

Chairman of the board
President
Executive vice-president
Treasurer
Vice president in charge of creative division

Vice president and research director
Vice president and radio director
Vice president and copy supervisor
Vice president and art director
Vice president and media director

Agency C

As in the case of merchandising, we do not have a specific group of people formally designed as "plans board." All of our key personnel (including principals) constitute Agency C's plans board.

It is our policy and practice to avoid the form of operation which can be compared to a group of individual agencies under one roof. The experience and abilities of any or all of our people are available, as needed to each client. This service is not "special" but characteristic of our routine procedure.

Primary responsibility, however, is definitely assigned to two individuals: one for contact, another for creative work.

Agency E

We do operate a plans board and it would be used on Menex. The board is set up to meet every Monday evening. Other meetings are called on "notice."

The fact that key people in the agency take time on their own to discuss our clients' problems is an indication of the tightening up and serious thought we endeavor to apply to our plans and recommendations. Our president is chairman of the plans board. Other members represent various functions with the agency. For example:

Executive vice president in charge of account services
Executive vice president in charge of creative work
Executive vice president in charge of marketing, research, and merchandising
Vice president in charge of radio
Vice president and account executive

The plans board is used at various times on all accounts. Plans are reviewed in the preliminary stage and criticized. Account executives are requested to appear before the board to discuss the advertising procedure which is being used.

It is a working group, and the constructive work it accomplishes in the interests of our accounts covers too many fields to enumerate here. It is, however, one of the most enthusiastic projects in the agency; and this, we believe, is the real reason for its success.

Exhibit 3

ETNA COMPANY, INC.

Answers to the Question: "Do you Consider Market, Trade Product and Advertising Appeals Studies a Part of Your Agency's Service to the Client?"

Agency B

Our policy can be briefly stated as follows: Research done for the purpose of increasing the effectiveness of advertising prepared by us is done for our own account. Research done in the interest of sales and marketing of a product is done for the client's account at cost. Any research done for the client's account is done only after the preparation and approval of a formal estimate. As indicated previously, we attach great importance to research and fact finding. Over the years we have proved it to be well worth its cost.

Agency C

We definitely consider such studies a part of our service to clients, but we make a distinction between research required for our own purposes and that required primarily for the advertiser's use.

In the case of studies which would not normally be required for the full and efficient performance of the agency's functions, we customarily bill the cost of research operations to the client.

Agency E

It is our job to make recommendations to the client. In this connection, we endeavor to back up our recommendations with factual evidence which in many cases requires marketing or field studies.

Out-of-pocket expenses for these jobs are charged back; but in each case, the cost is mutually agreed upon.

In studies of advertising appeals which may require copy testing, it is our policy to absorb these costs unless we conduct a study specifically requested by the client. The overhead of our departments such as copy testing, art, production, and so forth, is taken care of by the 15% agency commission.

To sum up:
   a) In cases where we use the facilities of our panel or field research or other collateral research which may involve out-of-pocket expense on the part of the agency, we charge this back at a mutually agreed-upon fee.
   b) In cases where we make studies on our own initiative to support our advertising recommendations and for the use of the various departments which we have set up in an effort to make our advertising more productive, there is no charge.

---

he related the operations of the agency's drug and food staff. A second agency officer discussed the agency's junior board operation. Mr. Phil Smith gave a speech regarding the agency's work in testing copy. Another officer presented some of the conclusions of the agency drawn from the *Continuing Studies of Newspaper Reading*. The use of Starch readership data was discussed by another officer. The heads of the creative services, media, library, and consumer surveys departments were presented; and each gave a short discussion of his group's activities. Each of these talks contained facts and examples of how Agency E worked on its various accounts.

Mr. Bellum was favorably impressed with the organization that had been demonstrated. He felt confident that the people who spoke could and would accomplish things if they were awarded the Menex account.

Mr. Bellum's second meeting with Agency C consisted of a roundtable discussion among Mr. Bellum and various members of the agency's organization. The president, the director of markets and media, the drug and cosmetics copy chief, the director of planning, and the head of the agency's medical department were present. Several features of this agency made it very desirable from Mr. Bellum's point of view. Of the three agencies still under consideration, it had the most experience with products which were allied in markets, outlets, and sales appeals to Menex. Among the products it handled, over a dozen were in the drug field, several of which were sold to women and had given the agency a background and experience that would be valuable in the advertising of Menex. In addition, it handled the advertising of ten products in the grocery and appliance fields which were sold primarily to women.

Agency E and Agency B had few personal, feminine products in comparison with Agency C. Of the 31 products used by women which were handled by Agency E, only 11 were drug products; and none of these was of the intimate nature of Menex. Agency B handled 20 products sold to women, but only three of these were drug products. This agency handled no products of a personal, feminine nature. Exhibit 4 contains the answers of Agencies B, C, and E to Question 4 which Mr. Bellum had asked regarding the experience which members of each agency had had that was pertinent to the marketing, merchandising, and advertising of Menex.

At the termination of the second round of interviews, Mr. Bellum collected all his notes on the three agencies. An analysis of these notes and of his impressions of the three firms led him to eliminate Agencies B and C. Agency C was eliminated because Mr. Bellum felt that its research department was not as strong as that of the other agencies under consideration. Only two or three people were engaged in full-time research work, and all but a few routine projects were farmed out. Agency B was eliminated because Mr. Bellum felt that the research work he believed so necessary would be done only at an additional charge above the standard agency commission. His investigations among clients indicated that such was the case of this agency in its workings with other firms. Mr. Bellum also knew that another Etna affiliate had eliminated this agency for the same reason.

Exhibit 4

ETNA COMPANY, INC.

Answers to the Questions: "What Experience Have Members of Your Agency Had That Is Pertinent to the Marketing, Merchandising, and Advertising of Menex?"

Agency B

This is a difficult question to answer, since practically all of our experience in marketing, merchandising, and advertising has some application to Menex. It has been our experience that fundamental advertising and marketing policies and strategy are no different in the drug field than in the food field, or in any other field. We have long believed in the importance of facts in approaching any marketing problem, and it has been our experience that, once enough is known about a problem and a product, where and how to advertise it becomes apparent. We have used the same fundamental approach in the sale of such different products as dog food, motor oil, men's and women's clothing, cigarettes, and automobiles. We believe in getting all the facts affecting the marketing and advertising of a product before undertaking to prepare advertising recommendations.

As you will see, the majority of our accounts have a special appeal to women; and we have consequently developed a creative staff that have specialized abilities in preparing advertising addressed to women.

Agency C

We believe that every key member of our organization in New York has had experience which can be valuable in the promotion of Menex. To outline all of their qualifications would require more detail than we believe you want in answer to this question.

For instance, one of our copy executives was for five years responsible for plans, appeals, and creative job for a product used in feminine hygiene; also sat in on the plans and copy for one of Menex's competitors. One of our research consultants has devoted the greater part of his life working on products created exclusively for women.

Additional information is given in the answer to Question 6 regarding the related experience of the copy executive who would be chiefly responsible for creative service to you.

Agency E

Agency E's people working on drug accounts naturally have a widespread knowledge of the sales, advertising, and merchandising techniques used in the drug field. In addition, our work in preparation and testing of retail ads for a large drug chain gives us a viewpoint which is rather unique in agency operation.

The chief purpose of our Drug Staff—an unselfish project on our part—is designed to bring our key executives into the field of retail drug selling. Sitting down with the important people in the drug field three or four times a year, we are in an excellent position to know what goes on, and as a result we feel our people are better informed. In this case we learn by exposure to the people who are responsible for the sale of our clients' drug products.

Exhibit 4—Continued

A list of people familiar with technique and preparation of retail drug advertising from the standpoint of account handling, copy writing, art, and merchandising, marketing, and research would be a large, comprehensive list and, to some extent, meaningless. We will attempt to high-spot some typical examples to show the type of people you would be working with if we were fortunate enough to work on your account.

James Garfield, while president of Agency E, is also chairman of the plans board and has taken an active interest in the packaged-goods field —both drug and grocery. He was selected by Proprietary Association as the agency member on their Advisory Committee on Advertising.

Fred Calhoun, vice president in charge of marketing, merchandising, and research, is naturally familiar with the day-to-day problems which we face on our drug accounts. He is responsible for the direction of the agency's Drug Staff.

Tom Lawless, formerly assistant advertising manager of a drug product. He had the experience of riding through the original introduction of this product. He is Mr. Calhoun's assistant in charge of merchandising.

Jack Finnegan is the drug member in the marketing and merchandising department. He is, in a sense, a drug specialist. Jack came to us from a chemical company with a background of selling, promoting, and advertising drug products for women.

Anton Baker, another member of our marketing and merchandising department, was for several years in charge of ethical advertising for a drug chain.

Phil Smith, vice president in charge of copy, has pioneered in the field of copy research and evaluation. He is the author of two outstanding books in his field.

Lester R. Jones, vice president and copy writer, has written copy on hospital products.

Alice Davis, vice president in charge of women's copy group. Her experience over a period of years has brought her in close contact with problems in the field of drug advertising.

The above people are connected with service departments. They do not include the account handlers and assistant account executives on our present drug accounts, several of whom are familiar with your problem. This additional list is available if you desire to see it.

Mr. Bellum felt that Agency E was, for his account, the best of the agencies he had investigated. He therefore asked Mr. Thomas A. Overman, president of the Etna company, to sit in on a report of the presentation which had been made to Bellum previously. As the second presentation neared its close, Mr. Eugene Davis, a vice president of Agency E, who was the account executive in charge of the Zip ginger-ale business, entered the conference room. He was introduced to Mr. Overman and

Mr. Bellum as the man who would be in charge of the Menex account if it were awarded to the agency. Mr. Overman asked Mr. Davis: "What accounts do you handle?" Mr. Davis replied: "I don't handle any, sir; they handle me!" Mr. Overman asked: "What is your drug experience?" Mr. Davis replied: "I am not a drug expert. I have worked on two drug products." No further questions were asked, and the balance of the presentation was given.

Mr. Overman and Mr. Bellum took three days to ponder their decision. They then informed Agency E (the Cadillac Advertising Agency) that it had been awarded the Menex account.

~~~

CASE 3: GOLDEN ROAST COFFEE COMPANY[1]

QUESTION TO CONSIDER: *As of the end of the case, what action should Mr. Forbes take in his investigation of advertising agencies?*

In October 1958 Mr. John S. Forbes,[2] vice president of sales of the Golden Roast Coffee Company, Philadelphia, decided that it was necessary to employ a new advertising agency.[3] He conferred with Mr. Luke Philips, the company's advertising manager, and together they agreed upon a list of specifications to guide them in their selection of a new agency. This list was as follows: "(1) Desirable but not absolutely necessary that the agency be a Philadelphia agency. Will consider a New York agency. (2) Must assign an account executive to our account who has had experience in food promotion. (3) The agency must be strong in the creation and production of television commercials. It must also have good contacts with individual television stations. (4) Must have own marketing research department which can handle our research requirements. (5) Our account must be of major importance to the agency."

As a first step in selecting a new agency, Messrs. Forbes and Philips examined the information which was available on 85 Philadelphia agencies in *The Agency List of the Standard Advertising Register* as well as information given in the last two annual surveys of advertising agencies published in *Advertising Age*. On a very general basis, according to Mr. Forbes, five agencies were selected as candidates for the Golden Roast account (they will be referred to as Agencies A, B, C, D, and E). The other agencies were eliminated because they were too large or too small or because they were primarily industrial advertising agencies.

---

[1] Written by Martin V. Marshall.

[2] All names are fictitious and facts have been changed to protect confidential information.

[3] The death of the major principal in the existing agency was given as the reason for changing agencies.

After discussion of alternative approaches to the five agencies, Messrs. Forbes and Philips decided to contact the agencies initially by mail. A letter was prepared and sent under the signature of Mr. Forbes to the presidents of the agencies. The letter is given in Exhibit 1.

Exhibit 1

GOLDEN ROAST COFFEE COMPANY
Letter Sent to Five Agency Presidents

October 9, 1958

Dear Mr. _____:

This company is in the process of selecting a new advertising agency. Yours is one of a few agencies which is tentatively being considered by us.

Our annual commissionable advertising expenditure is slightly in excess of $750,000. We are primarily interested in securing the services of an agency which is strong in the creation and production of television commercials, and which is in a position, because of the size of its spot television billings, to obtain the best possible time spots for our commercials, which are primarily id's and 30-second spot announcements. We are also especially interested in having an account executive with good food experience and an agency marketing research department which can help us tackle any research questions which come up.

Our present agency, the Whitedale agency, knows that we are looking for a new agency, and the new president, Mr. Ogden, has indicated a willingness to talk with any agency about us, if we give permission.

If your agency has an interest in our account, would you please call Mr. Luke Philips, our advertising manager, and arrange a time of mutual convenience for Mr. Philips and me to call upon you. Probably we would like to spend several hours with you, learning about your agency and discussing any questions that you have about us.

Mr. Philips can be reached at the following telephone number: XX5–0101, extension 12.

Very sincerely yours,

John S. Forbes
Vice President of Sales

Subsequently, Agency E informed Mr. Philips that it was unavailable for the Golden Roast account because it had just acquired a coffee and tea account. During late October, Messrs. Forbes and Phillips called on the other four agencies. A description of their visits, as recalled at a later date, is given below.

Agency A

Agency A was located in an old building in an older part of Philadelphia but had very modern and pleasant office furnishings. The agency had

33 accounts, of which 19 were consumer-goods accounts. The agency's total billings were in excess of $3 million. Individual client billings ranged from less than $25,000 to slightly more than $300,000.

After being greeted by Agency A's president, John Newhouse, Messrs. Forbes and Philips were taken to a conference room where they met William Evans, vice president of Agency A's Consumer Products Division; John Eldor, account executive; Mrs. Betty Williams, chief copy writer; Ed Hawley, head of the art department; and Miss Helen Yeager, manager of marketing research.

William Evans began the meeting by describing the development of Agency A. It had been founded in the mid-1920's as an industrial advertising agency. In the early 1950's, agency management had decided to diversify, and at that time had brought in Mr. Evans to head up the newly formed Consumer Products Division. Mr. Evans said that before joining Agency A, he had spent some ten years in selling and sales management in two food manufacturing companies and over 19 years in various phases of advertising agency work. Mr. Forbes felt that Mr. Evans had a good background in food distribution and promotion.

Since 1953 the new division had "grown handsomely," according to Mr. Evans, having in 1958, 19 accounts, of which five were food accounts that he thought would be of interest to Messrs. Forbes and Philips. He then described the accounts and indicated when the agency had acquired them. The accounts included a regional baker; a manufacturer of spaghetti, macaroni, and noodles; a local dairy; a manufacturer of Italian frozen foods; and a small meat packer.

These food accounts, Mr. Evans said, were handled by the account team present at the meeting. John Eldor acted as account executive for the accounts; a James Wellborn, who was not present, assisted him as associate account executive; Mrs. Williams specialized in food copy; Ed Hawley supervised all art and layout work for the accounts; and Miss Yeager handled the marketing research requirements of the accounts.

At this point Mr. Evans said that he would like to describe how Agency A would handle the Golden Roast account, if it were acquired by the agency. As a first step, he said, he and John Eldor would study Golden Roast's entire marketing operation and then prepare a complete marketing plan. Mr. Evans showed Messrs. Forbes and Philips several thick, mimeographed volumes, which he said were the marketing plans which had just been prepared for three of Agency A's clients. He also showed them a three-page check list of information usually desired by the agency from its clients. After quickly examining the check list, Mr. Forbes expressed the opinion that it was very thorough and complete.

Mr. Evans stated that the agency had already studied the Golden Roast account to a limited extent. He then turned to a flip chart and explained that the agency's marketing research department had just compiled data on several aspects of the coffee market. The first chart was a listing of special price promotions of all coffee brands for the period January–September 1958, as obtained from ten chain supermarkets in the Philadelphia area. Mr. Evans pointed out that the Golden Roast company apparently did not utilize special price promotions as a part of its promotional program. Next he showed a chart which indicated Golden Roast's market share in five large metropolitan markets, as obtained from newspaper studies. These data indicated that Golden Roast had had a decreasing share of market in each of the five markets for the years 1954–57. Mr. Evans said that he tentatively attributed this fact to the failure of the Golden Roast company to use special price promotions. Next Mr. Evans showed a chart which indicated the length of time that various Golden Roast television commercials had been used on Philadelphia television stations. He expressed the opinion that Golden Roast's television commercials had probably lost their effectiveness inasmuch as they had been used, on the average, for at least 18 months. He believed that the company could make its television effective only if it continuously used new, fresh television commercials.

Mr. Forbes was quite interested in Mr. Evans' views on special price promotions and asked several questions. Mr. Evans then discussed special price promotions at some length. He felt very strongly that any manufacturer of coffee, particularly a regional manufacturer, had to fight fire with fire, namely, that it had to use special price promotions if it were to compete with the major coffee brands. He discussed a number of special price promotions which had been used by various coffee companies and stated that consumer studies indicated that most people purchased on a basis of price rather than brand. He concluded his discussion of special price promotions with the comment that he would not wish to offer any final recommendations until he and John Eldor had had ample opportunity to study Golden Roast's entire marketing operation and competitive position.

Mr. Forbes then asked about Agency A's television operation. Mr. Eldor replied that the agency had only recently begun to do television work for its clients but that its billings in spot television would probably be well over $100,000 in 1958 and $300,000 in 1959. He said that television creative work was done by the best free-lance people available in New York City and that television production work was done by two of the best-known television production organizations in New York City. Mr. Eldor went on to explain how the agency worked with outside creative and production people. He arranged quickly for a projection machine to be brought into the conference room and he then showed a number of commercials which had recently been made for three different clients. Neither Mr. Forbes or Mr. Philips had any strong opinions about the quality of the commercials.

Mr. Evans stated that if the Golden Roast account was obtained, Agency A was prepared to establish its own television announcement creative group, because the agency's spot television billings would then be approximately $1 million and the agency could afford the overhead of such a group. He also stated that if the account was obtained, Mr. Eldor would be assigned exclusively to the account and would be relieved of other duties. Mr. Evans felt that Mr. Eldor could service the company's television requirements effectively because he had been gaining a great deal of experience as the agency's contact with New York television people.

Mr. Philips asked Mr. Evans about the agency's marketing research facilities. Mr. Evans said that Miss Williams was a very experienced marketing researcher, having had some 15 years' experience in the marketing research department of a large paper products company. Miss Williams stated that she had completed or was in the process of completing over 150 marketing research projects for Agency A's clients. Most of the projects were of the mail-questionnaire type; larger projects were farmed out to outside marketing research organizations. Miss Williams had one assistant.

At this point, Mr. Evans stated that the agency's guests probably were a little tired and perhaps hungry. He invited Messrs. Forbes and Philips to lunch, but they declined, indicating previous appointments. Mr. Forbes told Mr. Evans that he would get in touch with him shortly.

Agency B

Upon arriving at Agency B, Messrs. Forbes and Philips were taken into the president's office. The president, Mr. Robbins, indicated that he had set up a schedule for their visit, which consisted of three parts: (1) a discussion of the agency's operation, (2) a discussion of Golden Roast's advertising problems, and (3) a presentation of how Agency B handled several of its clients' accounts. He asked if the schedule met with their approval, which it did.

Subsequently, in a period of about an hour, Mr. Robbins brought in the agency's vice presidents of media, copy, marketing research, and client contact. Each man briefly described the size and operation of his department. At the end of the period, Messrs. Forbes and Philips were given a large brochure, which contained the agency's organization chart, pictures and biographies of agency personnel, and a list of the agency's clients and length of service.

After coffee, Mr. Robbins, the vice presidents, and a newcomer, Mr. Ed Atikin, an account executive, asked Mr. Forbes questions about Golden Roast's marketing and advertising. Mr. Forbes was much impressed with the nature of the questions and felt that all of the men present quickly grasped the principal problems confronting him. During a period of about two hours, Messrs. Forbes and Philips answered questions almost continuously.

Mr. Robbins and one of the vice presidents then took their guests to lunch. The luncheon conversation was general. The president of the agency commented that he knew the president of the Golden Roast company fairly well.

After lunch, Messrs. Forbes and Philips were taken into a conference room where Mr. Atikin and several other people were assembled. Mr. Atikin said that he wished to describe how Agency B had handled the XYZ Milk Company since 1955. He had selected the account because it was comparable to Golden Roast's in many respects.

Mr. Atikin then used a flip chart to describe marketing research which had been done when the agency first took over the XYZ account. Mr. Forbes felt that many of the problems described by Mr. Atikin were similar to his. Mr. Atikin then introduced Agency B's television production supervisor, who described how Agency B made commercials and then showed a dozen or so which had been made for the XYZ company. Mr. Atikin said that Agency B had billings of about $1.5 million in spot television. The session ended with a brief description by a media man of how he had managed to obtain good time spots for XYZ spot announcements through continuous contact with television station personnel.

Mr. Robbins asked if Messrs. Forbes or Philips had any questions. Several questions were raised about how the agency would handle the Golden Roast account, if it secured it. The president said that he would prefer to answer those questions after some thought and after another discussion with Messrs. Forbes and Philips. He suggested that the agency would like to visit the Golden Roast company, and a date was agreed upon.

Agency B had 42 accounts, most of which were manufacturers of consumer products with billings ranging from less than $50,000 to more than $500,000. Food accounts included the XYZ dairy, a cheese products company, a manufacturer of dog food, a manufacturer of canned meats, a soft-drink bottler, a wine company, a local candy retailer, and a brewery.

Agency C

Agency C was a smaller agency with five accounts: four food accounts and one patent medicine account. It had total billings of about $2.5 million, of which about $2 million was placed in spot television.

Upon arriving at Agency C, Messrs. Forbes and Philips were met by the three principals of the agency: William Jackson, the president; and William Young and Oscar Hughes, vice presidents. Mr. Jackson stated that the agency had been established in 1955 by the three principals because they wanted to be in business for themselves. Mr. Jackson had been a media representative since the early 1920's. Mr. Young had been with a number of advertising agencies, most recently as a vice president in charge of copy for a medium-sized New York agency. Mr. Hughes had held many jobs with various food manufacturing organizations, most recently as director of marketing research for a large food manufacturer.

Mr. Jackson stated that the three principals worked on all accounts together. As an example of their method of working with a client, he began to describe how they had handled a brewery account, which had been acquired in mid-1957. For the next hour, the three principals described in detail the problems facing the brewery and the changes which they had recommended in product, packaging, brand names, method of distribution, and promotion. Mr. Forbes was very much impressed by the details given him. He felt that Mr. Hughes especially had an exceptionally good grasp of the practical problems confronting the brewery.

After the discussion of the brewery account, the three principals escorted Messrs. Forbes and Philips around the agency's offices. Mr. Forbes was very much impressed by the agency television projection room, where, according to Mr. Hughes, the agency tested television commercials in the rough. Mr. Hughes said that the agency had a capable young artist who could develop commercials in rough and then photograph them on film so that they approximated the finished commercial. The agency then tested these rough commercials with panels of housewives and others to determine probable effectiveness. Several rough commercials were run off as well as a few finished commercials. Both Messrs. Forbes and Philips were of the opinion that the commercials were "different and imaginative."

Mr. Young stated that the agency did all of its own creative work on television commercials but had them produced by a well-known New York City production organization, one of the same firms which was used by Agency A.

Messrs. Forbes and Philips were introduced to everyone in all offices, including secretaries. Only a few moments were spent in these offices.

About this time, a secretary informed Mr. Jackson that one of the clients had dropped into his office, the president of the brewery. Mr. Jackson asked Messrs. Forbes and Philips to meet the president. After introducing them, Mr. Jackson said that he and Messrs. Young and Hughes had described the brewery account in detail. The brewery president remarked that the agency had done a fine job for his company. He then asked if he might see the new commercials which he understood had been delivered to the agency. A showing was arranged for him. He then asked Mr. Forbes if he had been told about the new campaign which the brewery was about to launch. When told that they had not discussed the campaign, the brewery president took about 15 minutes to explain how the agency had come up with a novelty approach to the advertising of beer which he thought was excellent. He invited Messrs. Forbes and Philips to view the commercials, which they did. Mr. Forbes liked the television commercials very much and thought that he had developed several ideas which might be used in his own advertising.

Mr. Jackson invited everyone to lunch and shortly thereafter took them by taxi to the Hotel Barclay where they had cocktails and a leisurely luncheon. Mr. Forbes noted that Mr. Jackson seemed to know almost all of the people who came into the dining room. Mr. Jackson stated that after 35 years in the media rep business, he knew practically everyone. He then proceeded to tell about his career, which among other things, included participation in the 1920 Olympic games, acting as business manager for one of the largest United States newspapers, and being president of advertising clubs in three different cities.

Mr. Forbes later said that Mr. Jackson was by far the most interesting person that he had met in any of the four agencies.

At the end of the luncheon, about 2:30, as Messrs. Jackson and Forbes walked from the dining room, Mr. Jackson said that he and his associates would like to discuss among themselves the possibilities of effectively taking on the Golden Roast account. He said that they did not want the agency to become too large. He asked Mr. Forbes if it would be all right if he called him in several days and discussed the situation further. Mr. Forbes said it would be all right.

Agency D

Agency D was the largest of the four agencies visited by Messrs. Forbes and Philips, having over 60 accounts and total billings in excess of $10 million.

Mr. C. L. Lyons, executive vice president, met Messrs. Forbes and Philips upon their arrival at the agency and took them to his office. He expressed pleasure that the Golden Roast company was considering Agency D for its account and asked Mr. Forbes how he would like to proceed. Mr. Forbes repeated the general information which he had given in his letter to the agency and then said that he and Mr. Philips would be interested in the specific ways in which Agency D would handle the Golden Roast account.

Mr. Lyons stated that Agency D had fairly formal methods for handling accounts. He then asked his secretary to bring in the "manuals," which were a number of large loose-leaf notebooks. Moving to a position between Messrs. Forbes and Philips, Mr. Lyons then went over the manuals in some detail. One manual described procedures for the contact man to use in general servicing of an account. Other manuals concerned copy, media, research, traffic, and cost accounting procedures employed by the agency.

After discussing the manuals for approximately an hour, Mr. Lyons changed the conversation to the subject of account executives. He said that he and the agency's president had considered various possibilities for some time and had come up with five possibilities. He gave Messrs. Forbes and Philips the résumés of five of Agency D's account executives (see Exhibit 2) and said that as yet he had no opinion as to whom would be the best account executive for Golden Roast. He felt that if Mr. Forbes became seriously interested in Agency D, probably he and Mr. Philips would like to talk with each of the five men on the list.

Mr. Lyons stated that Agency D would like to study Golden Roast's

Exhibit 2

GOLDEN ROAST COFFEE COMPANY
Résumés of Five Agency D Account Executives Summarized

Robinson T. Yates. Graduate, Swarthmore College, 1922. Salesman, lumber company, 1922–24. Retail copy writer, Philadelphia department store, 1924–27. Copy writer, Philadelphia agency, 1927–31. Copy writer, chief copy writer, head of copy department, Agency D, 1931–43. Since 1943, senior account executive. Worked on 18 different accounts in last 15 years, including one coffee account in 1945–48.

James D. Hardy. Graduate, Dartmouth College, 1948. Trainee, assistant account executive, New York advertising agency, 1948–53. Director of advertising of a manufacturer of wool products, 1953–55. Since 1955 assistant account executive and account executive with this agency. Worked on four different accounts in last three years, all consumer products.

Phillip C. Davman. Graduate, University of Pennsylvania's Wharton School, 1947. Salesman, paper company, 1947–50. Assistant sales manager of small building materials manufacturing company, 1950–51. Assistant account executive, Newark advertising agency, 1951–52. President, Davman Advertising Agency, Philadelphia, 1952–56. Account executive with Agency D since 1956. Worked exclusively on food-chain account, 1956–58.

Robert S. Turner, Jr. Graduate, Columbia University Journalism School, 1937. Reporter, Atlanta newspaper, 1937–41. Major, U.S. Army, 1941–45. Public relations counselor, Chicago firm, 1946–49. Head of Public Relations Division, Chicago advertising agency, 1949–50. Vice president of another Chicago advertising agency, 1950–53. Account executive with Agency D since 1954. Worked on seven accounts, primarily drug accounts.

Hugh Waters. Graduate, Bucknell University, 1950. With Agency D since graduation, in marketing research, media, copy, and traffic departments. Assistant account executive, 1955–58. Made account executive in July 1958 and placed in charge of beverage account.

marketing situation for about a week and then make a special presentation. He said that the agency was prepared to send a team of three people to the company during the week of November 7–11 and that the agency could make its special presentation by the last of November.

Mr. Forbes asked what would be the nature of the presentation. Mr. Lyons replied that it would be a fairly complete advertising program for 1959, including a copy and media plan. If Messrs. Forbes and Philips liked the plan, then Agency D would be prepared to take on the account. If they did not, there were no obligations and the Golden Roast company would be free to use any of the ideas which were obtained from the presentation.

Mr. Forbes said that he would think the matter over. Since Mr. Lyons did not seem to be interested in talking further, according to Mr. Forbes, he and Mr. Philips left Agency D after about two hours' discussion with Mr. Lyons.

In early November Messrs. Forbes and Philips discussed the agency selection problem at some length. Mr. Forbes felt that there was a need for proceeding fairly quickly in the selection of a new agency because he and Mr. Philips had to present their 1959 advertising program to the board of directors by mid-December. He did not, however, have any strong feelings about any of the four agencies visited in late October. He told Mr. Philips that he would soon have to respond to Mr. Lyons of Agency D, however, because Mr. Lyons desired to send his team into the company in the third week in November. He characterized Mr. Lyons as "a very persistent gentleman."

Mr. Philips was of the opinion that the company should make a much more extensive search for a new agency and proposed that a questionnaire, together with a covering letter, be sent to a list which he had developed of 15 additional Philadelphia agencies and ten New York agencies. Mr. Philips' questionnaire is given in Exhibit 3. Mr. Forbes had some reserva-

Exhibit 3

GOLDEN ROAST COFFEE COMPANY
Mr. Philips' Questionnaire

1. How many accounts do you have? What are your total billings—approximately? How many accounts do you have whose billings are in excess of $700,000 annually? What is the approximate size of your spot television billings?

2. If you had our account, who would be assigned to it as the account executive? Please give reasonably detailed background information on their experience.

3. What services does your agency provide other than normal agency services? Please give us a brief description of your services. How many people do you have in each department?

4. Does your agency create its television commercials? Does it produce them?

5. Do you have a marketing research department? If so, please give us brief information concerning the extent of its services.

6. Does your agency operate a plans board? If so, please give us a short description of how it operates.

tions about requesting information via mail. He felt that written answers to the questions proposed by Mr. Philips would not be too revealing. Mr. Philips felt, however, that agency answers would provide a basis for determining quickly who were and were not good potential candidates for the Golden Roast account. He did not feel that he and Mr. Forbes had learned too much from their visits to the four Philadelphia agencies.

~~~

CASE 4: WHITE & SHAW CO., INC.[1]

QUESTION TO CONSIDER: *How should Mr. Shaw compensate the Hansen-Lindberg-Hill agency?*

White & Shaw Co., Inc.,[2] Waltham, Massachusetts, was established in 1952 to manufacture modular metal and plastic office furniture which had been designed by a young Boston architect. The company grew steadily thereafter, and in mid-1958, company executives decided that the company should sell outside New England. A number of franchised dealers were established in key United States metropolitan markets in late 1958, and a beginning was made in developing a sales promotion program for use nationally. In late 1958, Mr. Shaw, sales manager of the company, saw the need for the help of an advertising agency and after talking with many Boston agencies, he decided to employ the firm of Hansen-Lindberg-Hill. In March 1959 Mr. Shaw was in the process of deciding how to compensate the agency.

Tentatively, the company was prepared to spend a total of $50,000 for all types of promotion in 1959. Preliminary discussions with various agencies in late 1958 and early 1959 had led Mr. Shaw to the conclusion that the company should spend its funds in selected business papers in order to begin to establish the name of the company as a source of well-designed office furniture. In addition, he thought that the company probably should develop selling aids and other promotional materials for the new dealers.

In his last discussion with the Hansen-Lindberg-Hill agency, Mr. Shaw had learned that the agency wished to handle the White & Shaw account on a fee basis; the agency desired a fee of $12,000 annually. Mr. Shaw asked for more details and received the following letter from Mr. Hill, who was to be the agency account executive for the company:

Mr. Alfred E. Shaw
Sales Manager
White & Shaw Co., Inc.
Waltham, Mass.

Dear Al:

The last time we talked, you requested additional information about the basis for our request for an annual fee of $12,000 to service your account. This

---

[1] Written by Martin V. Marshall.
[2] All names are fictitious.

fee was based upon our analysis of the costs of servicing your account for the period March 1959–February 1960. I will give you our analysis and an explanation of each item.

A. *Direct Expenses Chargeable to the White & Shaw Account*

1. One third of the annual salary of J. J. Hill: $5,000. (Because your firm is just beginning to get into national distribution, I will be spending a great deal of time with you, helping you to plan a marketing program as you requested. Therefore, I have allocated one third of my time to your business. As you can appreciate, you are primarily using my services as a marketing consultant rather than as an advertising agent.)

2. Travel and entertainment: $1,200. (In our discussions, you indicated that you would like me to spend a good deal of time traveling in the field, in order to help you work with dealers. Therefore, I have budgeted $100 a month for such travel, which may well be on the conservative side.)

3. Copy: $300 (I estimate that 20 hours of our copy writers' time will be spent on your account in 1959. The standard charge is $15 an hour for a copy writer's time. If we operate on a fee basis, we will absorb the copy expense, regardless of how much it totals.)

4. Art: $250. (Based upon an estimate of ten hours at $25 an hour. As above, we absorb the art expense if we operate on a fee basis.)

5. Media: $300. (We expect to prepare a complete media plan for you. This figure is based upon 20 hours of work at $15 an hour.)

6. Production: $200. (Based on ten hours at $20 an hour.)

7. Research: $1,500. (As we promised, if we get your account, we will make a study of the office furniture market for you at our own expense, which is estimated above.)

8. Publicity: $500. (As we also promised, our publicity group will work on your behalf to place good stories about White & Shaw in the trade and business paper press. They estimate their expenses at $500.)

9. Telephone and telegraph: $100.

10. Miscellaneous: $100. (For any contingencies which may develop.)

B. *Indirect Expenses*

As you realize, we must allocate our general overhead expenses to all accounts, which we do here at Hansen-Lindberg-Hill on the basis of allocating that portion of total overhead to each account which is represented by each account's direct expenses as a percentage of all direct expenses of the agency.

Overhead to be allocated to White & Shaw account: estimated at $2,000. (We estimate that your account will account for about 2% to 2½% of our total direct expenses in 1959.)

To recapitulate, our analysis of our profit and loss statement for your account for the first year is as follows:

A.	Net income	$12,000
B.	Direct expenses	9,450
C.	Gross profit	$ 2,550
D.	Allocated expenses	2,000
E.	Net Profit	$ 550

We would credit to your account all income received by us in media commissions, which, based upon your tentative budget of $35,000, would amount to $5,250. Therefore, your net fee to us would be $4,750.

If you would prefer to operate on another basis, we would consider servicing your account on an actual cost basis plus a commission, a method which we employ with many of our clients.

Under this method, we would bill you monthly for all time charges plus 15% and for all materials bought for your account plus 17.65%. Under this method, charges would be as follows:

1. Account executive: $50 a day for each day spent on your account + 15%.

2. Travel and entertainment: actual expenses only.

3. Copy: $12.50 to $20.00 an hour, depending upon the copy writer used on your account, + 15%.

4. Art: $25 an hour + 15%.

5. Media: $15 an hour + 15%.

6. Production: actual cost + 17.65%.

7. Research: actual cost + 15%.

8. Publicity: $25 an hour + 15% and actual cost of materials + 17.65%.

9. Telephone and telegraph: actual cost.

10. Miscellaneous: actual cost.

Under this method, we would give you an estimated cost for any work which we undertook on your behalf and would only undertake it after receiving your approval. Bills would be submitted monthly to you. All commissions received from media would be credited to your account.

We would prefer, of course, to operate on the basis of an annual retainer fee of $12,000, as such a fee would allow us to plan the work on your account in an orderly fashion. Under the actual cost plus commission approach, we would have to await your approval before planning our work.

I hope that you will make an early decision on this matter, because we would like to begin to help you as soon as possible.

Sincerely,

s/ Joe
Joseph V. Hill

Mr. Shaw did not know how to react to Mr. Hill's letter. He had not had experience with advertising agencies and therefore was unfamiliar with their methods of compensation. Originally, he had thought that the agency would service his account for the commissions it received from media. He now saw that some other arrangement would have to be made with the Hansen-Lindberg-Hill agency. He also wondered how the agency desired to be compensated for the preparation of dealer selling aids and other types of sales promotional materials.

INDEXES

GENERAL INDEX

ALPHABETICAL LIST OF CASES

This book has been set on the Linotype in 10 point Janson, leaded 2 points, and 9 point Janson, leaded 1 point. Chapter numbers are in 24 point Lydian Cursive; chapter titles are in 18 point Spartan Heavy italics. Section numbers are in 24 point Lydian Cursive with Bold italic roman numerals; section titles are in 18 point Lydian bold italics, with the accompanying text in 9 point Caledonia Bold, leaded 2 points.